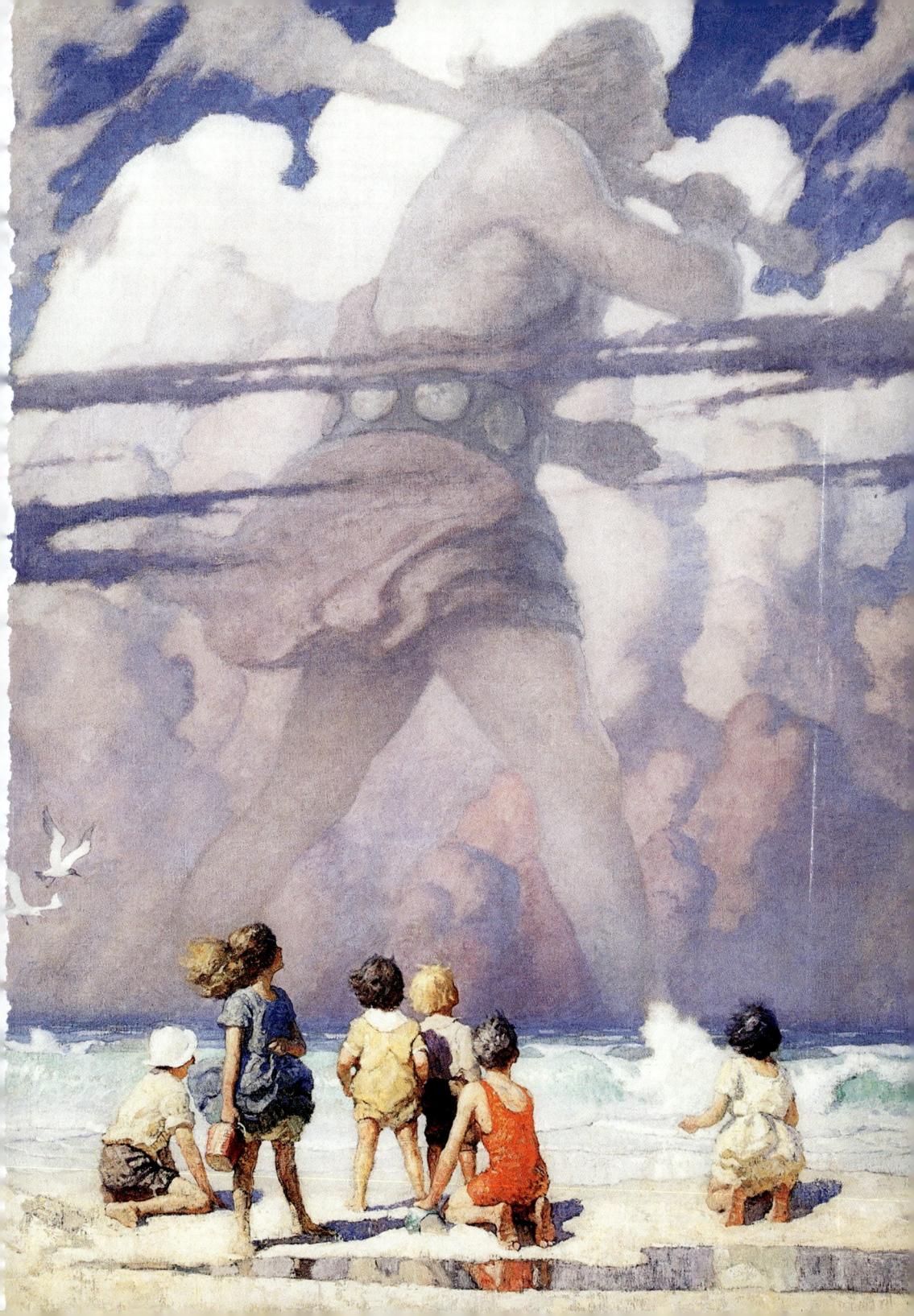

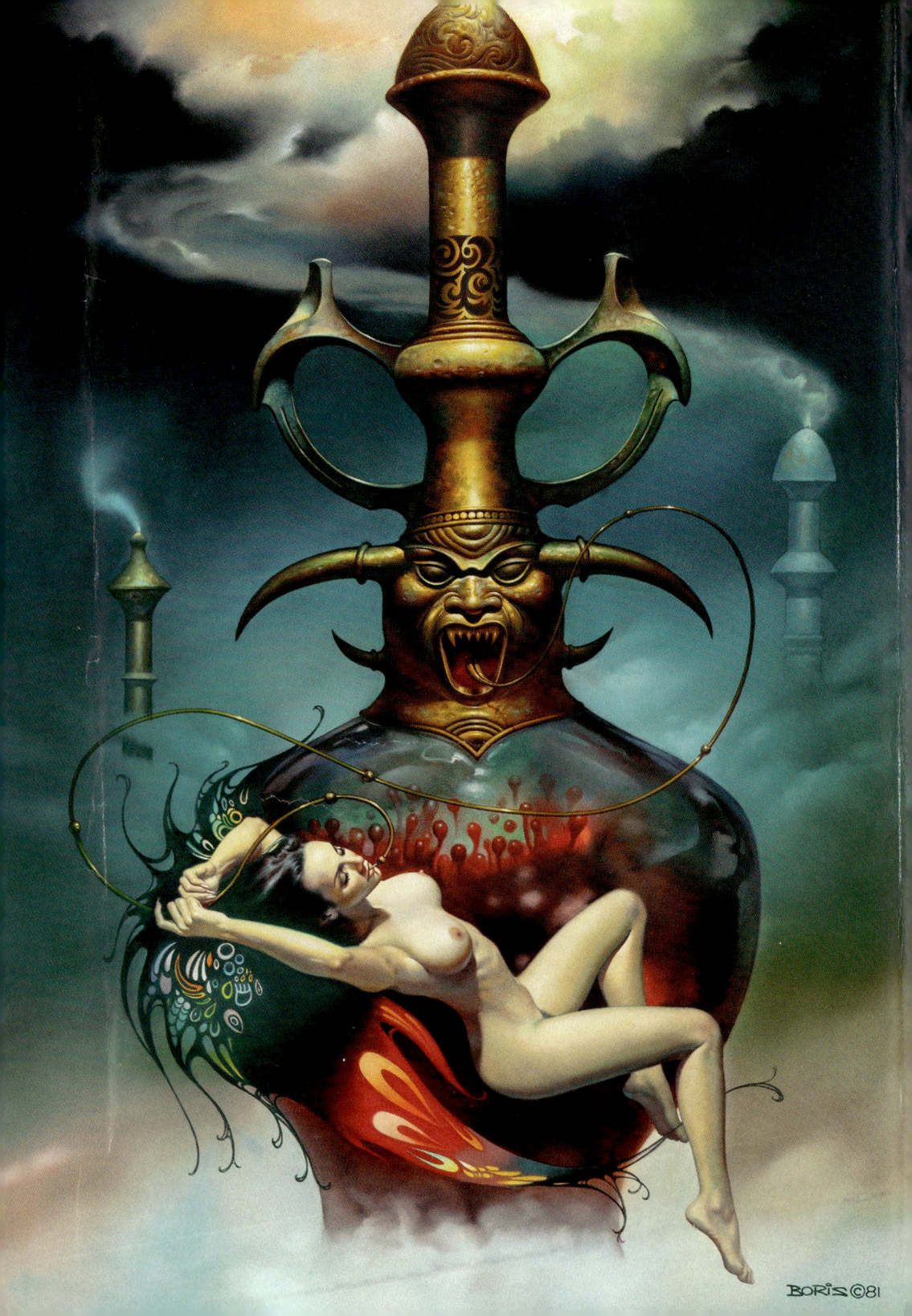

DIAN HANSON

Masterpieces of Fantasy Art

TASCHEN

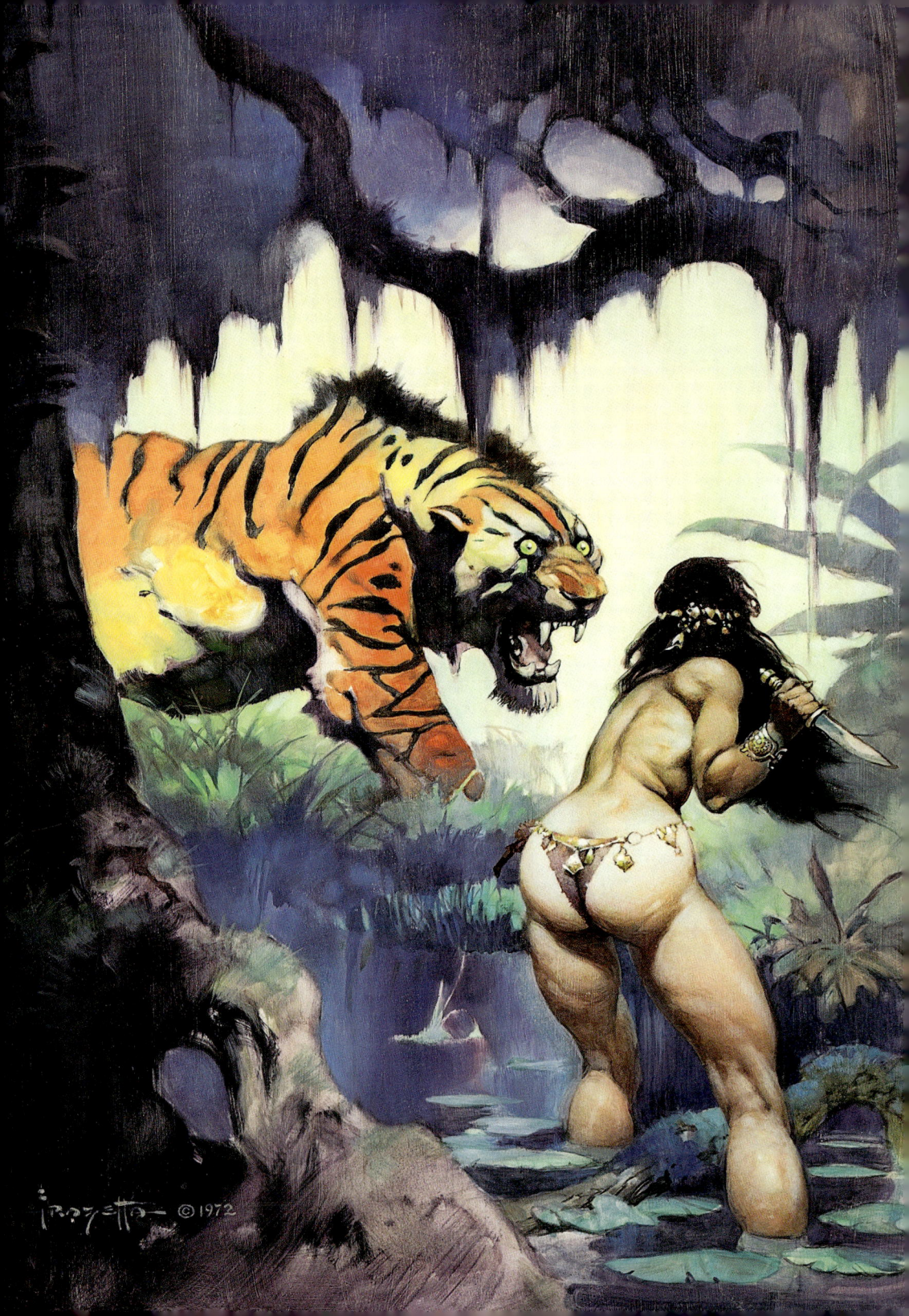

ALL TEXT BY DIAN HANSON UNLESS
OTHERWISE NOTED

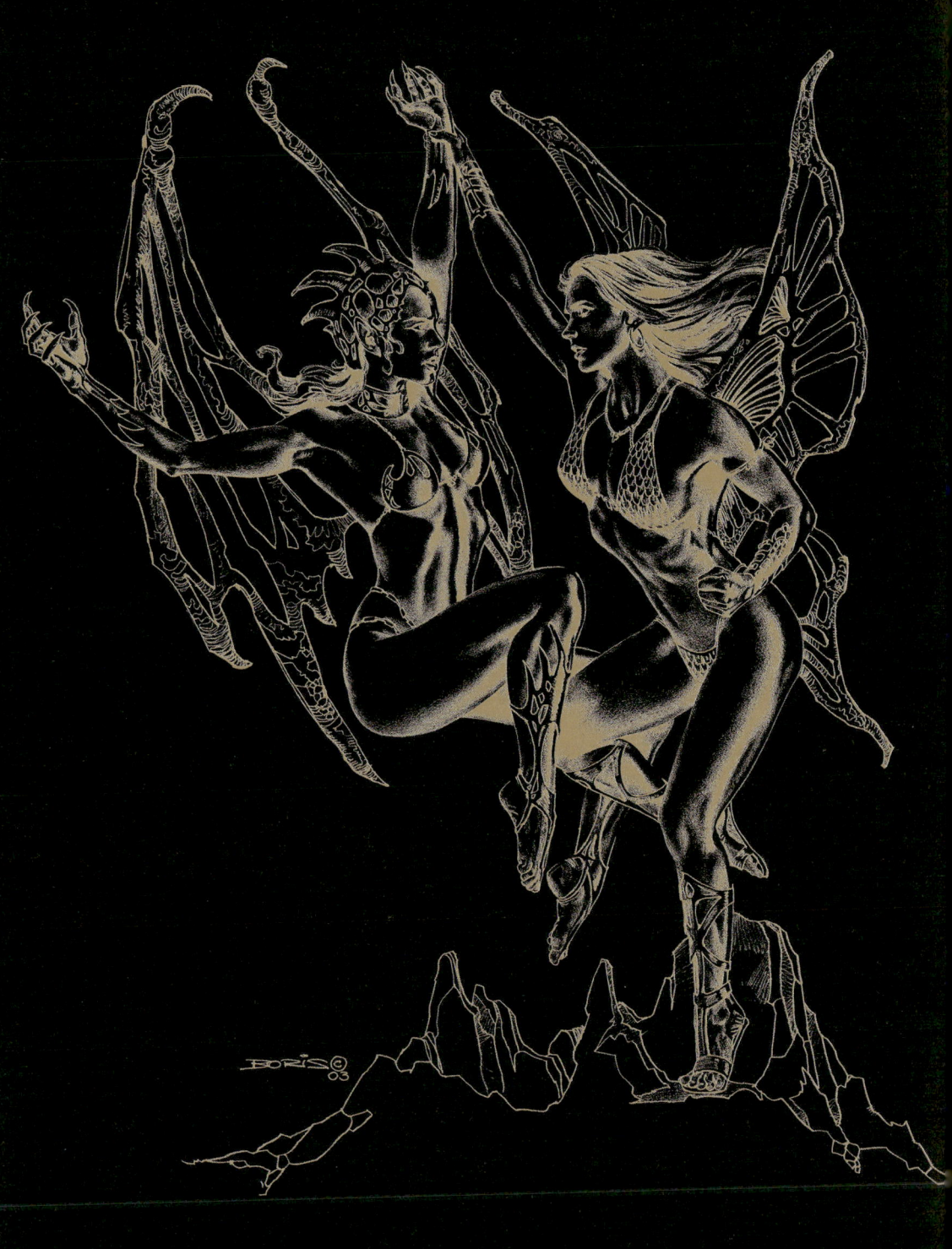

MY FANTASY LIFE

BY BORIS VALLEJO

I was born in Lima, Peru, and lived there the first 22 years of my life. When I was 16 years old, and still attending school, I started working part time as a professional artist. At the time I could never imagine that this would become my actual profession and identity throughout life. Art was simply a way to use my inborn talent to make some extra money with something that was fun; it didn't feel like real work. Although my parents had high respect for art and encouraged my own addiction to it, they fully expected that I would study medicine and become a neurosurgeon, since being a professional artist in Peru was the equivalent of starving. In my parents' minds, art was just a wonderful way to entertain myself along the way to developing my career as a future rich doctor.

In my early 20s, still going to medical school and working freelance doing drawings for advertising agencies, I developed a strong aversion to the requirements needed to head into a medical career. Around the same time one of the art directors at an advertising agency I worked with in my part-time job pulled me aside and said that, although I was doing great work as an artist, I would not really have a profitable career in my own country. He strongly suggested that I should move to the U.S.—New York, to be exact. A few weeks later I quit medical school to follow my true passion: art. Within a year, I had saved up enough money for a one-way ticket to New York City with $80 to spare. I got on that airplane and set the wheels in motion to claim my life as a true professional artist.

What made that move turn out to be the best move of my life was becoming acquainted with the work of fantasy artists such as J. Allen St. John and, most importantly, Frank Frazetta, whose art I had never seen in Peru. I loved the fact that the work was realistic, but also took me to a unique world created by their imaginations. Even more exciting to me, beyond these fantasy lands, was the way that Frazetta, in particular, portrayed human bodies. I was into bodybuilding as a young man, so the muscular, powerful look and exaggerated motion of the bodies that he painted was enormously appealing, while the stylization of the background scenery blew my mind.

From that point on, my journey into the world of fantasy art has been a long and winding road, full of seemingly magical adventures that have both knocked me around and given me immense satisfaction. Currently, the most exciting and influential part of my art world and my life is my wife, Julie. The fact that our children are also wonderful professional artists on their own is the icing on the cake. Having the privilege of taking this journey and playing my part in the world of fantasy art is a reward beyond my wildest dreams, which, I'll admit, can be pretty wild!

Page 1: The Giant, print by N. C. Wyeth.

Page 2: Hookah, Opium Dream, by Boris Vallejo, for the book *Mirage* from Ballantine Books, 1982. Oil on board, 1981, 73.6 x 50.8 cm (29 x 20 inches).

Page 4: Nobody did female flesh like Frank Frazetta, and no booty was better than Princess Duare's for Edgar Rice Burroughs's *Escape on Venus,* 1972. This painting, understandably, was used on several reprints of the novel. Oil on board, 40 x 50.8 cm (15.75 x 20 inches).

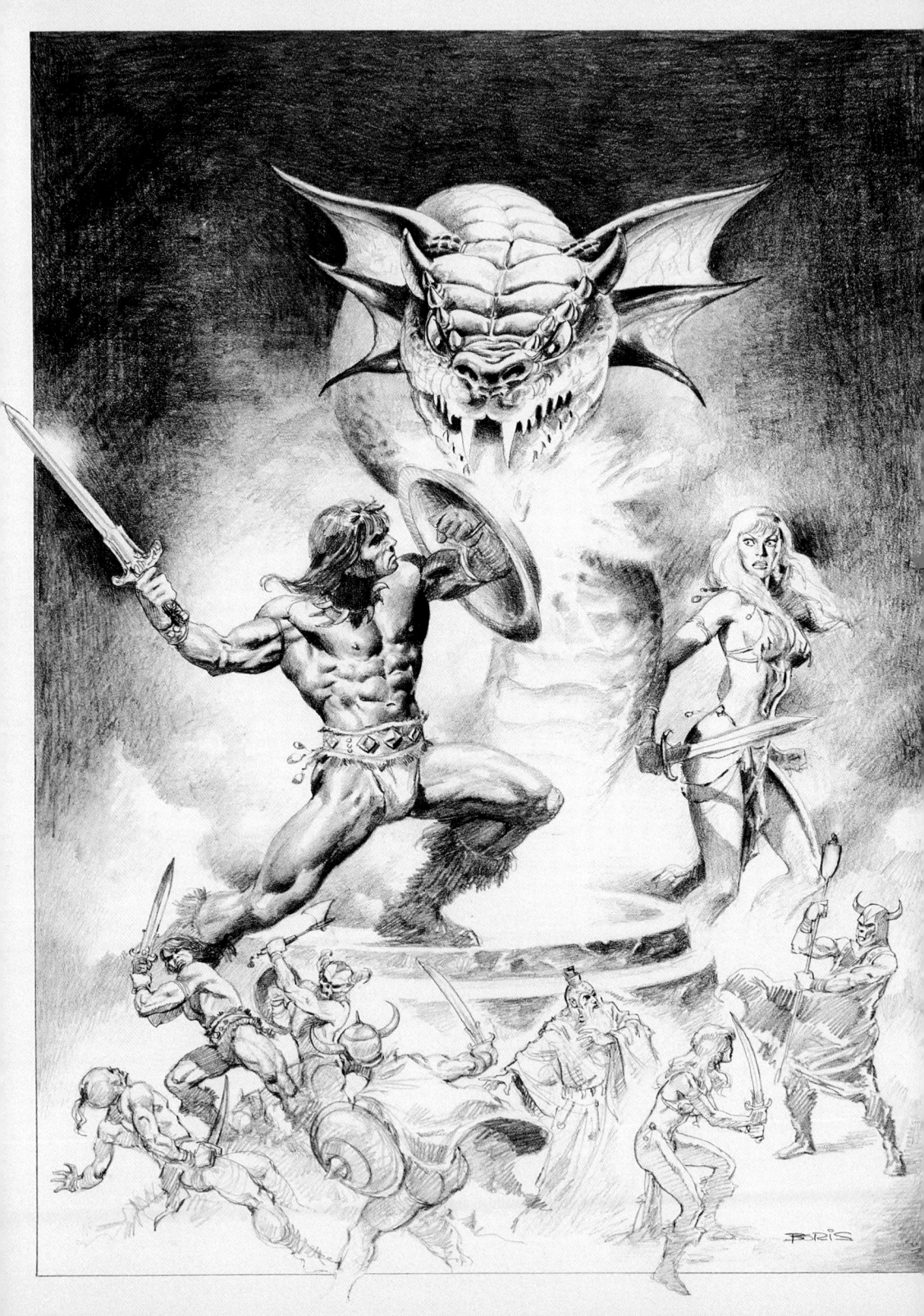

MEIN FANTASYLEBEN

VON BORIS VALLEJO

Ich wurde in Lima, Peru, geboren und verbrachte dort die ersten 22 Jahre meines Lebens. Schon als ich 16 Jahre alt war und noch zur Schule ging, begann ich, nebenher als professioneller Künstler zu arbeiten. Damals konnte ich mir nie vorstellen, dass dies einmal mein Leben lang mein eigentlicher Beruf werden und meine Persönlichkeit ausmachen würde. Kunst war schlicht eine Möglichkeit, mein angeborenes Talent zu nutzen, um mit etwas, das Spaß machte, ein bisschen Geld dazuzuverdienen; als richtige Arbeit empfand ich das nicht. Obwohl meine Eltern der Kunst großen Respekt entgegenbrachten und mich ermutigten, meinen eigenen künstlerischen Neigungen nachzugehen, erwarteten sie natürlich, dass ich Medizin studierte und Neurochirurg wurde, denn ein Leben als professioneller Künstler in Peru war gleichbedeutend mit dem eines Hungerleiders. In den Vorstellungen meiner Eltern war Kunst nur eine wunderbare Art der Zerstreuung auf dem Weg, auf dem ich meine Karriere als künftiger wohlhabender Arzt voranzubringen hatte.

Mit Anfang 20 – ich besuchte noch die medizinische Hochschule und fertigte als Freischaffender Zeichnungen für Werbeagenturen an – entwickelte ich eine starke Abneigung gegen die Anforderungen, die das Einschlagen einer Karriere als Mediziner mit sich brachte. Etwa zur gleichen Zeit nahm mich einer der Artdirektoren einer der Werbeagenturen, für die ich in meinem Teilzeitjob arbeitete, zur Seite und meinte, auch wenn ich als Künstler tolle Arbeit leiste, hätte ich in meinem Heimatland nicht unbedingt eine einträgliche Karriere zu erwarten. Er empfahl mir dringend, in die Vereinigten Staaten überzusiedeln – genauer gesagt: nach New York. Ein paar Wochen später ließ ich die medizinische Hochschule sausen, um meiner wahren Leidenschaft nachzugehen: der Kunst. Innerhalb eines Jahres hatte ich genug Geld für ein One-Way-Ticket nach New York City angespart und dazu noch 80 Dollar übrig. Ich stieg in den Flieger und brachte mein Leben als hauptberuflicher Künstler in Gang.

Dieser Schritt stellte sich als die beste Entscheidung meines Lebens heraus, denn nun wurde ich mit dem Werk von Fantasykünstlern wie J. Allen St. John und – am allerwichtigsten – dem von Frank Frazetta vertraut, dessen Kunst ich in Peru noch nie gesehen hatte. Ich liebte den Umstand, dass diese Werke realistisch waren, mich jedoch gleichzeitig in eine einzigartige Welt entführten, die ihren Fantasien entsprang. Abgesehen von diesen Fantasywelten – noch mehr begeisterte mich die Art und Weise, in der insbesondere Frazetta den menschlichen Körper darstellte. Als junger Mann stand ich auf Bodybuilding, und deshalb übten die muskulösen, kraftvoll wirkenden Körper mit ihren übersteigerten Bewegungen, die er malte, eine enorme Anziehung auf mich aus. Und die Stilisierungen der Hintergrundszenerien hauten mich um.

Von da an gestaltete sich meine Reise in die Welt der Fantasykunst als ein langer und kurvenreicher Weg, reich an magisch anmutenden Abenteuern, die mir sowohl zu schaffen machten als auch große Befriedigung einbrachten. Die aufregendste und einflussreichste Rolle in meiner Kunstwelt wie in meinem Leben spielt derzeit meine Frau Julie. Die Tatsache, dass auch unsere Kinder eigenständige und wunderbare professionelle Künstler sind, ist das Sahnehäubchen auf dem Kuchen. Das Privileg zu haben, diese Reise unternehmen und meine Rolle in der Welt der Fantasykunst spielen zu können, ist eine Auszeichnung, die ich mir in meinen kühnsten Träumen nicht vorgestellt habe. Und meine Träume können, wie ich gestehen muss, ziemlich kühn sein!

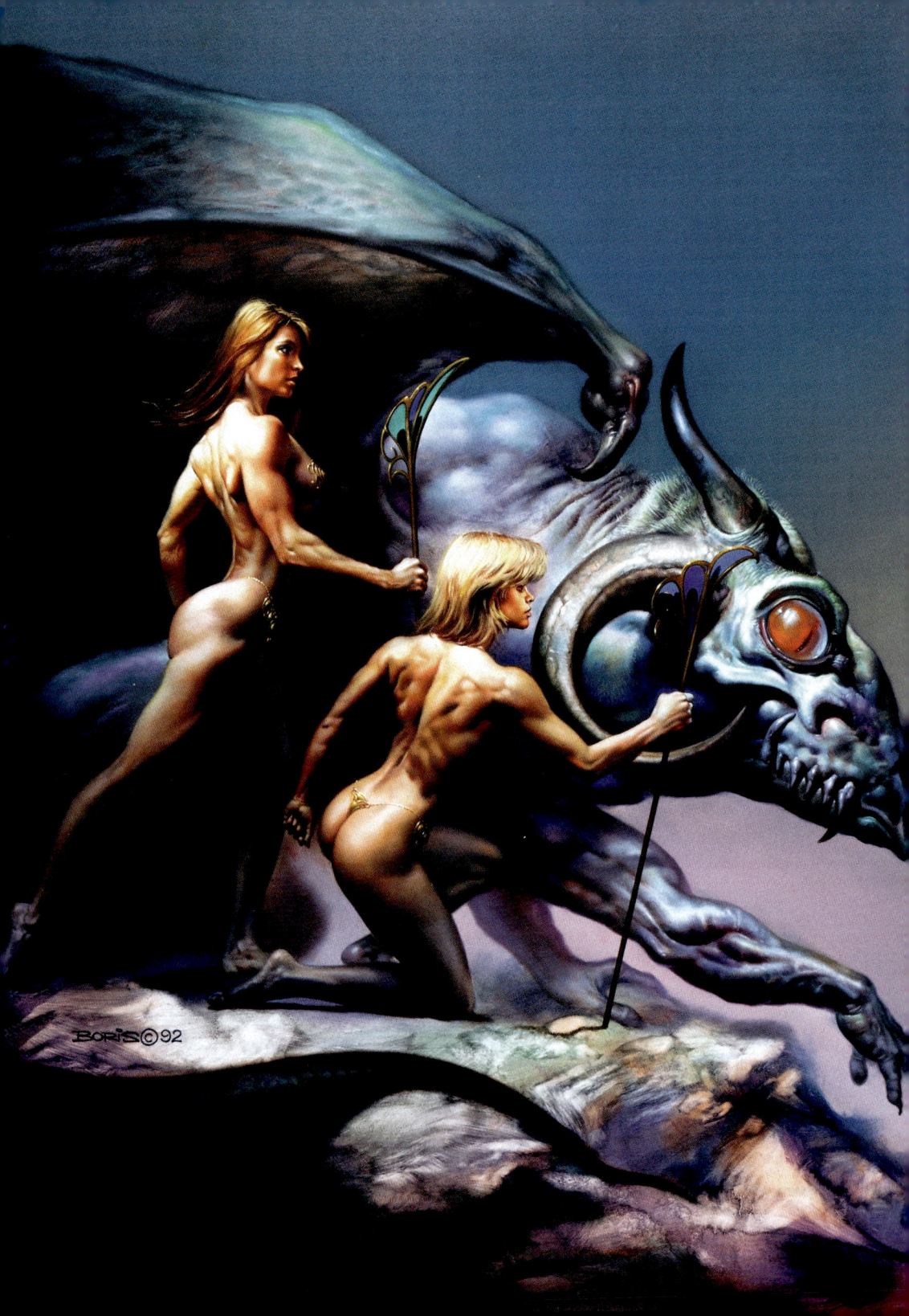

MA VIE FANTASY

PAR BORIS VALLEJO

Je suis né à Lima, au Pérou, où j'ai vécu les 22 premières années de ma vie. À 16 ans, encore lycéen, j'étais aussi artiste professionnel à temps partiel. À l'époque, je n'aurais jamais imaginé que cela deviendrait mon vrai métier et l'identité de toute une vie. L'art était simplement pour moi un moyen d'exploiter mon talent inné pour gagner un peu d'argent tout en m'amusant ; je n'avais pas l'impression de travailler. Mes parents avaient beaucoup de respect pour l'art et ont encouragé mon addiction, mais ils s'attendaient à ce que j'étudie la médecine pour devenir neurochirurgien, parce qu'au Pérou être artiste c'était mourir de faim. Dans l'esprit de mes parents, l'art était juste un merveilleux moyen de me divertir tout en préparant ma carrière de futur médecin riche.

Quand j'ai eu une vingtaine d'années, je fréquentais toujours l'école de médecine tout en dessinant en freelance pour des agences de pub, et j'ai développé une aversion profonde pour les exigences et contraintes d'une carrière médicale. À peu près au même moment, un directeur artistique d'une agence avec laquelle je collaborais m'a pris à part et m'a dit que, même si je faisais du super boulot, je ne pourrais jamais vraiment percer en tant qu'artiste dans mon pays. Il m'a fortement conseillé de partir pour les États-Unis, New York en particulier. Quelques semaines plus tard, je lâchais mes études pour suivre ma vraie vocation. En l'espace d'un an, j'ai économisé suffisamment pour me payer un aller simple pour New York, avec 80 $ à dépenser en rab. Je suis monté à bord de cet avion et j'ai mis en marche le moteur de ma nouvelle vie d'artiste à temps plein.

C'est la meilleure décision que j'ai prise de ma vie, parce que c'est là que j'ai découvert le travail d'artistes de fantasy comme J. Allen St. John et surtout Frank Frazetta, dont je n'avais jamais rien vu au Pérou. J'adorais que leurs œuvres soient réalistes mais m'embarquent aussi dans un monde unique né de leur imagination. Ce qui me fascinait le plus, au-delà de ces mondes fantasmés, c'était la façon dont Frazetta, en particulier, représentait le corps humain. J'étais branché bodybuilding quand j'étais jeune, alors ces silhouettes musculeuses et puissantes à la gestuelle excessive me plaisaient énormément et les décors stylisés me faisaient halluciner.

À partir de là, mon voyage dans le monde du fantasy art a suivi une longue route sinueuse, parsemée d'aventures magiques qui m'ont malmené mais apporté une satisfaction immense. Aujourd'hui l'élément le plus excitant et inspirant de mon univers artistique et de ma vie est mon épouse, Julie. Le fait que nos enfants soient devenus de remarquables artistes à leur tour, c'est la cerise sur le gâteau. Avoir eu le privilège de faire ce voyage et de jouer un rôle dans le monde du fantasy art est une récompense qui dépasse mes rêves les plus fous… ce qui, je l'admets, est difficile à concevoir !

Page 6: *Demon versus Nymph* preliminary study by the great Boris Vallejo. Ink on board, 2003, 52 x 40.6 cm (20.5 x 16 inches).

Page 8: *Conan the Barbarian* film poster preliminary sketch, pencil on board, circa 1981, 48.2 x 35.5 cm (19 x 14 inches).

Opposite: Jotun, a figure of German mythology, followed the Valkyries into battle as a source of power. Oil on board for the 1993 *Boris Vallejo and Julie Bell Fantasy Calendar*, 67.3 x 52 cm (26.5 x 20.5 inches).

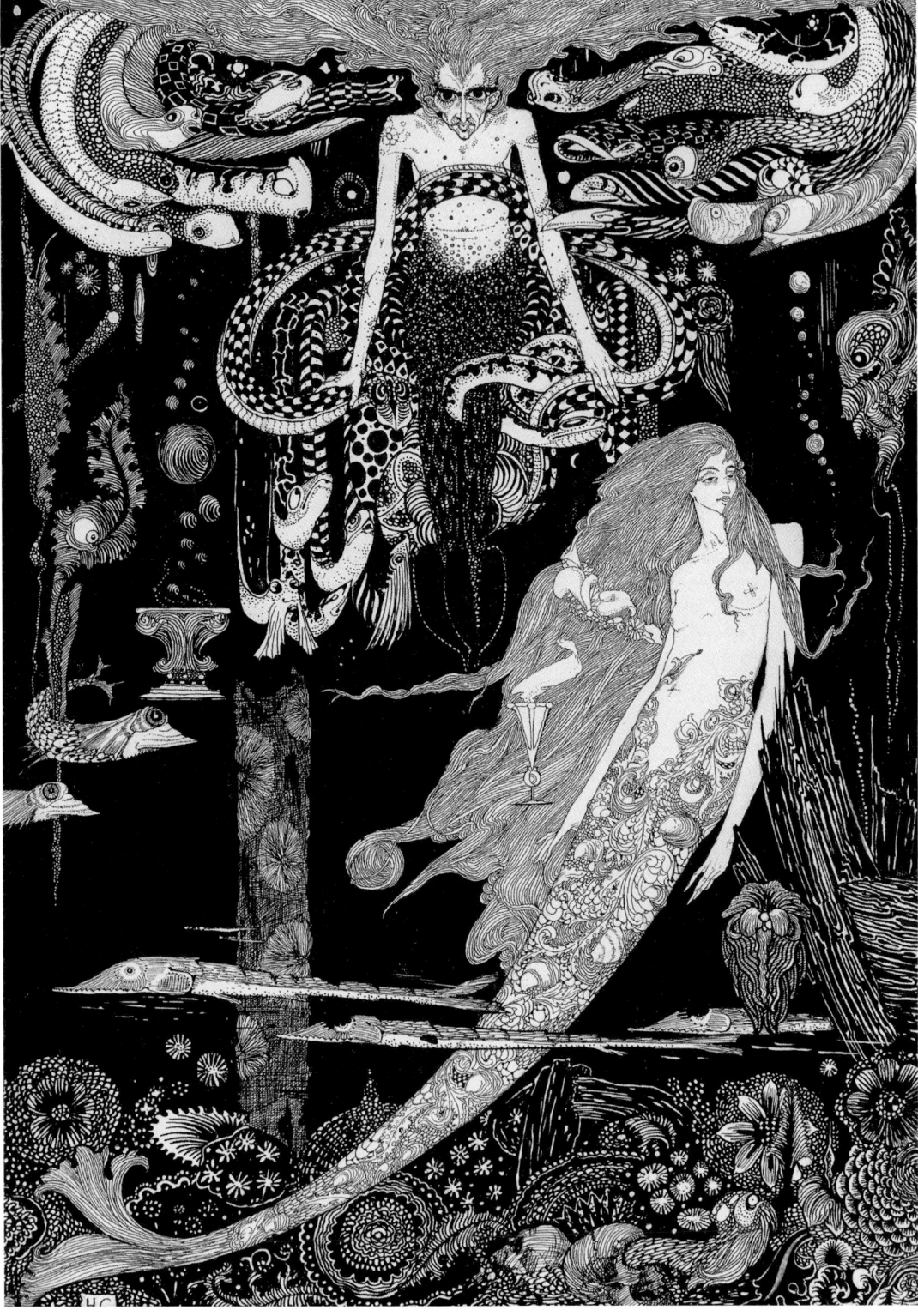

FANTASY: THEN, NOW, AND ALWAYS

BY DIAN HANSON

In 2011 the neuroaesthetics department at University College London, clearly suffering from too much time or money or probably both, recruited dozens of people with no particular interest in art and administered MRI scans to their brains while bombarding them with images by historic painters. The scans measured blood flow in the medial orbitofrontal cortex, a part of the brain associated with pleasure and desire, to see what effect fine art would have.

The conclusion was that certain types of art make us feel very good—not just good, but something akin to the intense pleasure of gazing upon a loved one—while other types leave us cold. In the subsequent press release a Professor Zeki said this was proof that "beautiful paintings make us feel much better." Better than what? And exactly what kind of beauty?

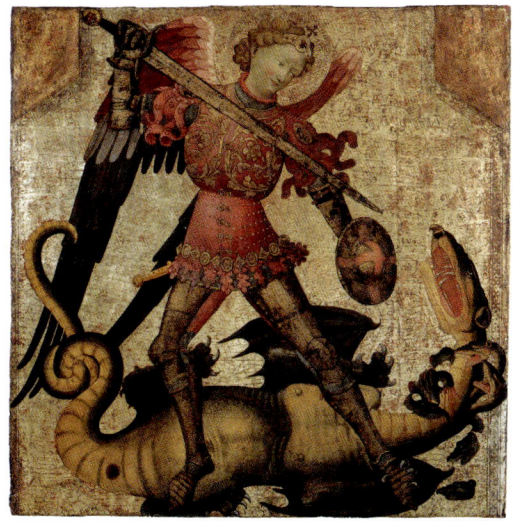

Well. Two of the three artists whose works produced the greatest response were Guido Reni and Jean-Auguste-Dominique Ingres, both distinguished by rich colors and heroic tableaux of muscular men, fleshy nude women, and mythical creatures. In short, fantasy art.

Of course in Reni's time (1575–1642) and Ingres's (1780–1867) there was no concept of fantasy art. Reni painted religious, mythical, and allegorical subjects. Ingres was a historical classicist. When they painted dragons or winged avengers they were not inventing new worlds, but illustrating a specific past many thought plausible. Fantasy is defined as "the activity of imagining things that are impossible or improbable," thus fantasy art could not exist until we gave up belief in dragons, witches, gorgons, griffins, and nymphs, all creatures with specific and immutable qualities in centuries past. When mankind abandoned mythology the door to

Opposite: Harry Clarke was an Irish member of the 19th-century Arts and Crafts movement, creating stained glass as well as book illustrations. *The Little Sea Maid* was done in ink and pencil on artist's card for the 1916 edition of *Fairy Tales by Hans Christian Andersen.* 31.7 x 38.7 cm (12.5 x 15.25 inches).

Above: Most don't realize that dragons had a place in Christian theology and were very popular in early Christian artworks. Here the Archangel Michael slays a dragon during a war in Heaven, by an unknown Spanish artist, circa 1405, oil and gilt on board.

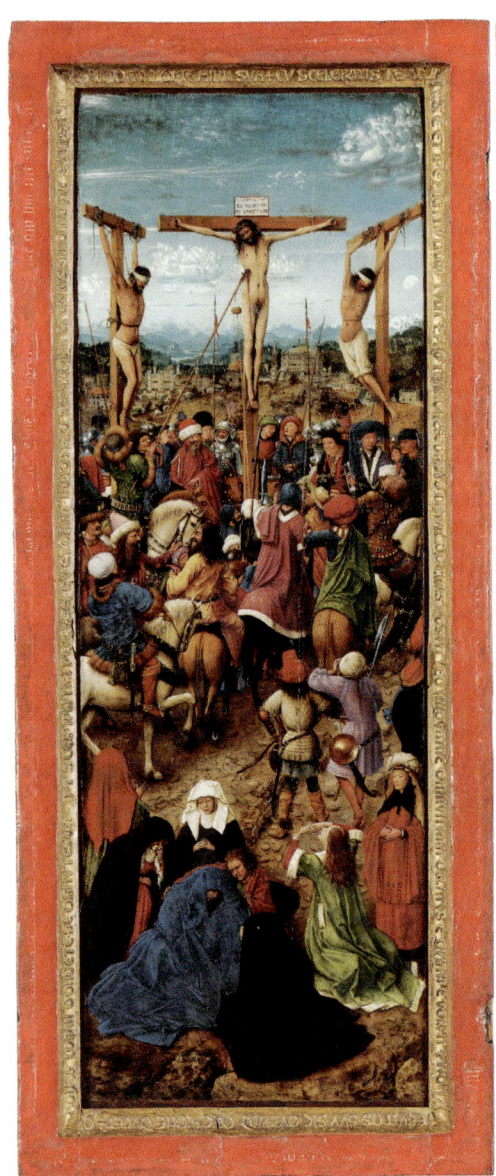

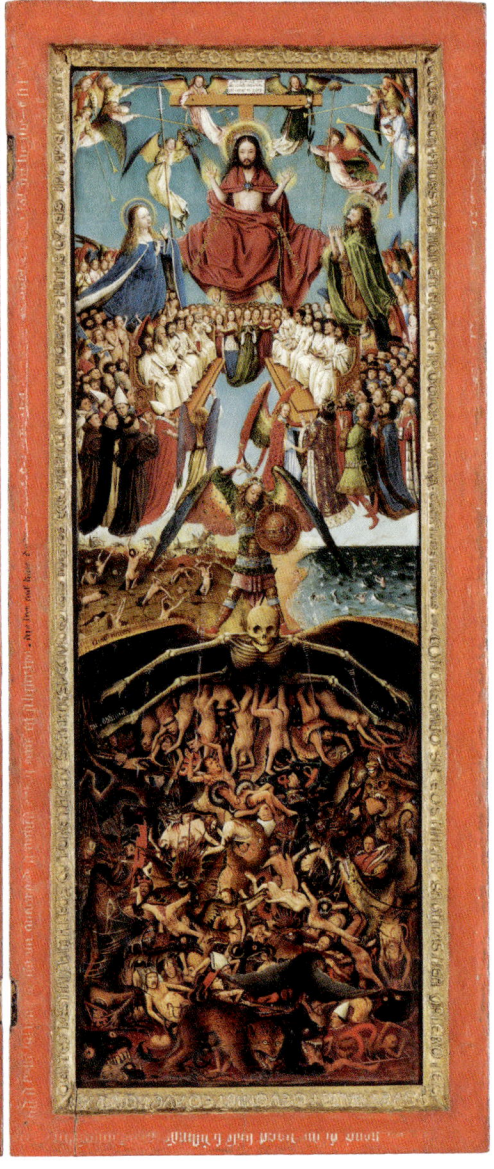

Above: Jan Van Eyck was court painter to Philip the Good, Duke of Burgundy, a great champion of the French arts. *The Crucifixion/Last Judgement* diptych is thought to have been a triptych originally, with a center panel now lost. The right panel portrays Heaven, and especially Hell, in the fantastic way popular at the time. Oil on canvas, transferred to wood, 1440–41, each panel 56.5 x 19.7 cm (22.25 x 7.75 inches).

Opposite: Guido Reni painted the Old Testament parable of the virtuous *Susannah and the Elders*, two scoundrels attempting to blackmail her into sex, circa 1620. He was known for his biblical and mythic paintings of fleshy women and heroic men. Oil on canvas, 150.5 x 116.6 cm (59.2 x 45.9 inches).

imagination opened. And as Professor Zeki confirmed, the results can be almost equal to love, if not respect.

Before the camera, people relied on artists to communicate the appearance of landscapes, architecture, objects, animals, plants, and individuals. An artist's talent was measured by how accurately he could depict these things, while his income depended on patronage by the church or wealthy portrait clients. Even painters like Hieronymus Bosch—often considered the first fantasy artist—and the above-referenced Reni and Ingres were attempting to represent reality, if in fanciful form. When photography arrived, representing reality became cheap and pedestrian, available to the middle and eventually even the working classes. As photographic quality improved through the late 19th century, painters found themselves running second to a mere machine and began to experiment with radical new art forms.

First came impressionism, arising in France around 1860, with rapid, obvious brushstrokes to capture a fleeting moment, followed by neo- and post-impressionism, Fauvism, cubism, and expressionism, concerned with portraying raw emotion, which ran high in the Weimar Republic, where it was most enduring, before fine art plunged on into complete abstraction. While each successive wave further separated art from photography, it also separated the average viewer from art appreciation. The mainstream still longed for something pretty on canvas; it was not a fan of Edvard Munch.

The sinuous nature-inspired cult of art nouveau, encompassing craft and architecture as well as art, was more pleasing to these viewers. It was realism on steroids, a sensually overgrown garden of

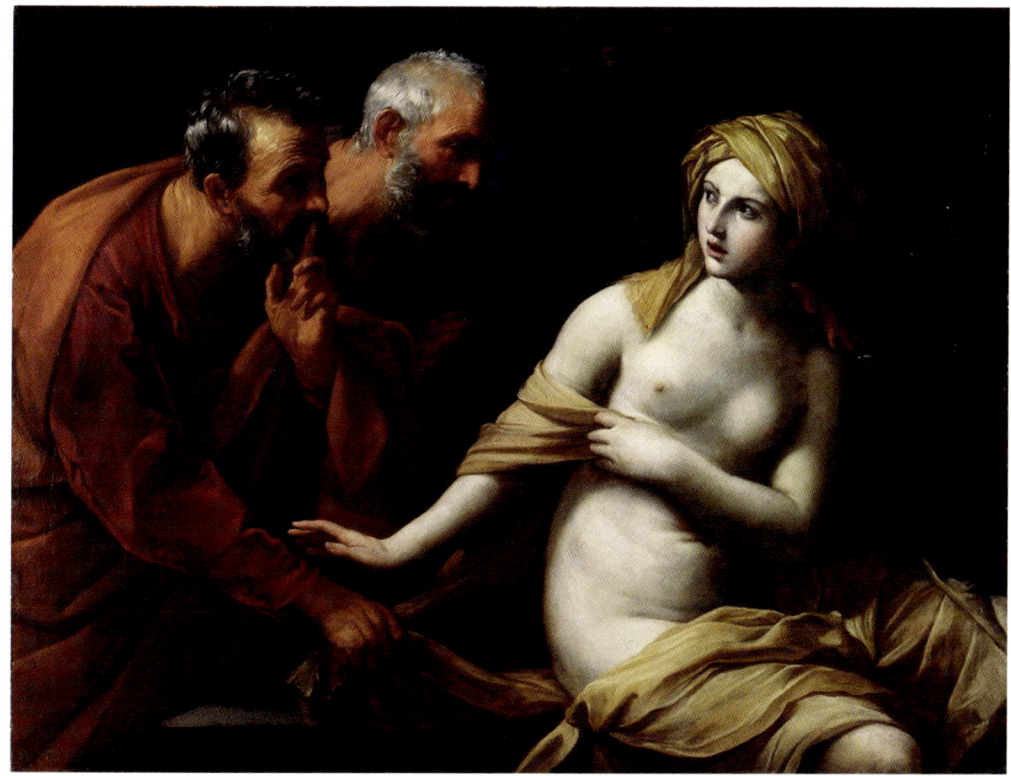

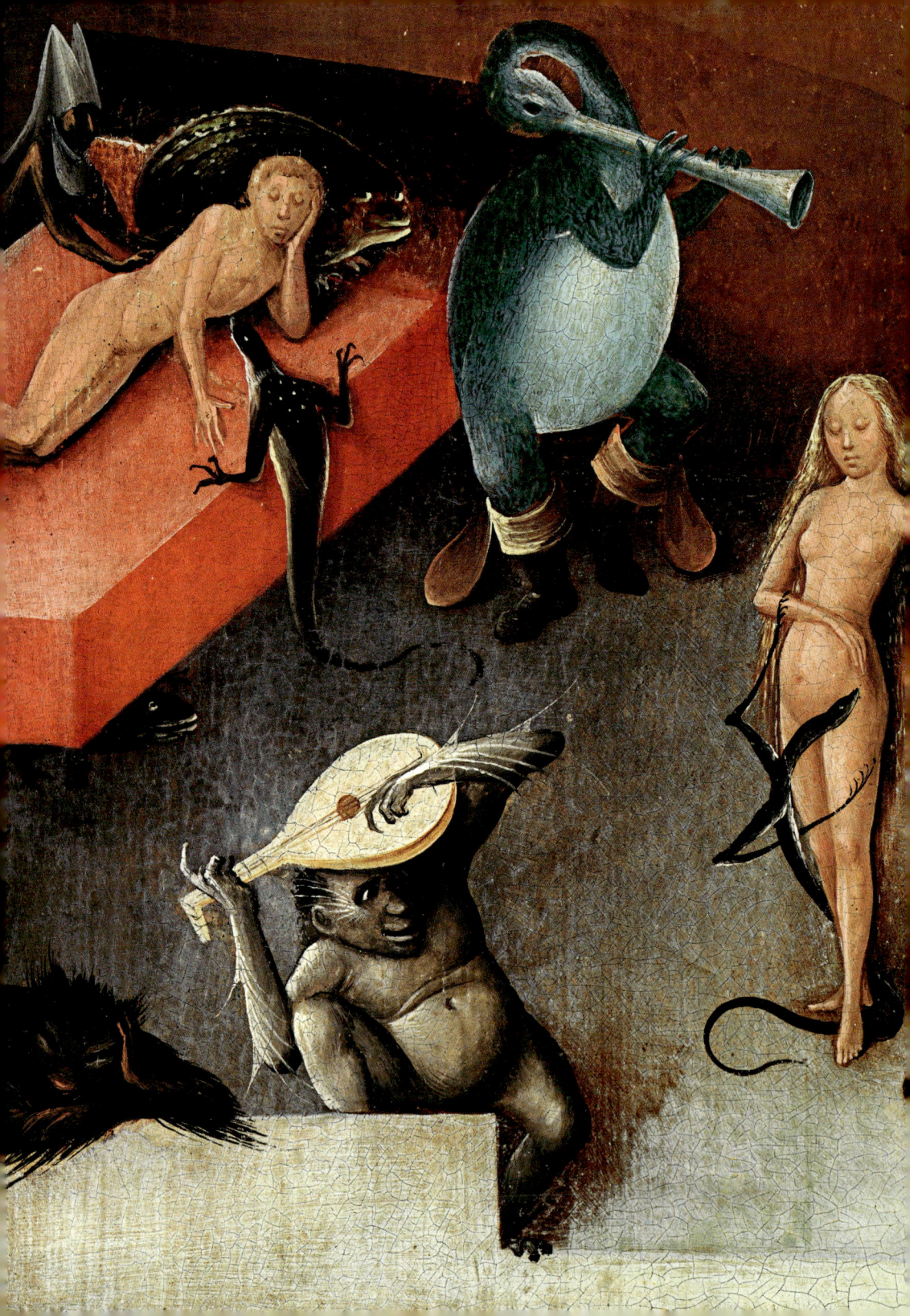

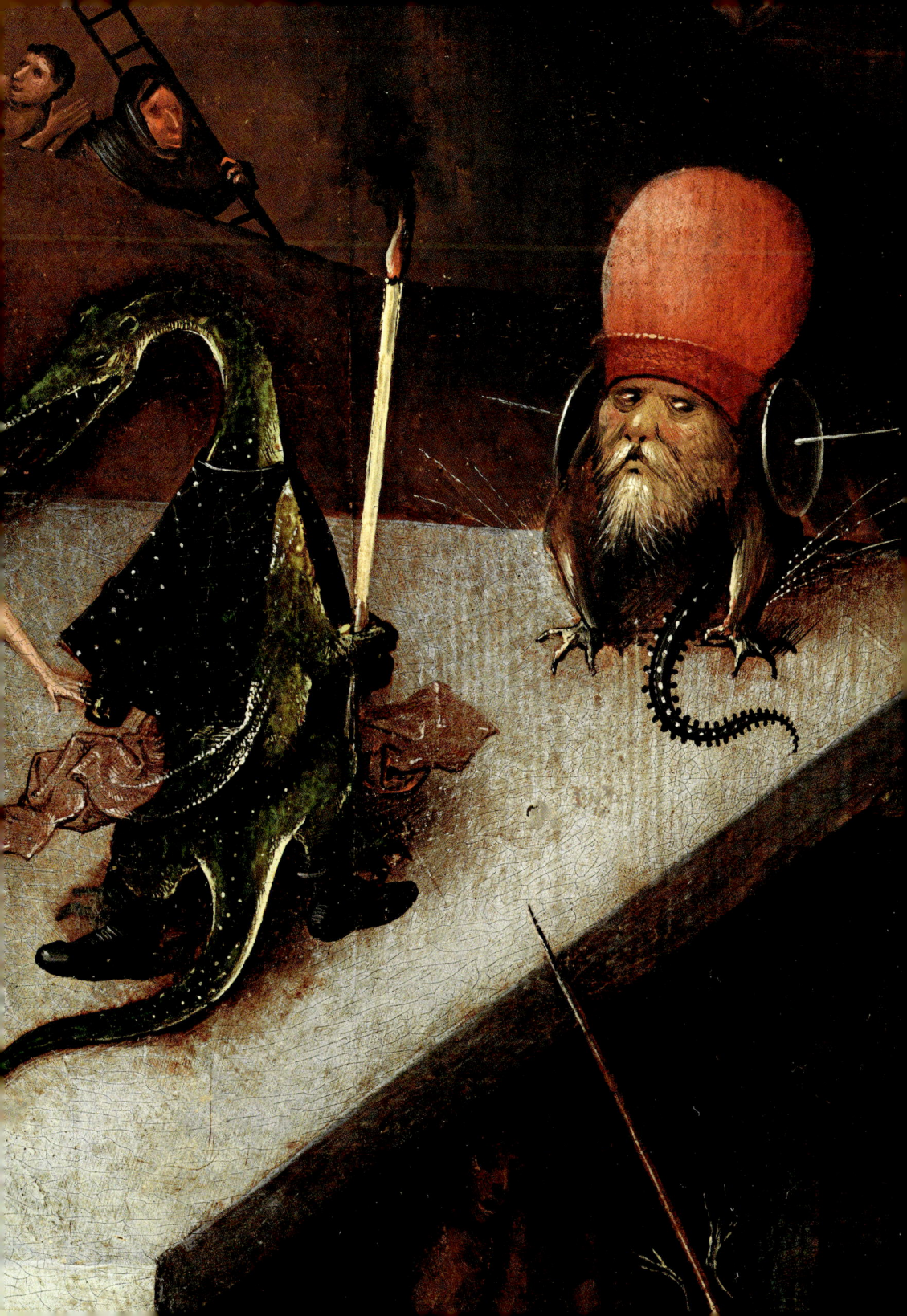

earthly delights, without the ironic horror of Bosch's infamous masterwork. Many fantasy artists cite art nouveau as an early inspiration, though surrealism is the most direct precursor of the genre. Like fantasy art, surrealism is grounded in recognizable people, places, and things, altered in an attempt to "resolve the previously contradictory conditions of dream and reality into an absolute reality, a super-reality," as André Breton defined it in 1924.

Unlike surrealism, however, fantasy art was born of commerce, and therein lies its struggle for acceptance by the art establishment, if not by its millions of fans worldwide. The art snob is offended that no special education is required to enjoy it: your orbitofrontal cortex lights up

Previous spread: The Dutch Artist Hieronymus Bosch is often cited as the first fantasy artist. His dark vision, here, a detail from the central panel of the triptych, The Last Judgment, showing Satan's minions torturing humans condemned to hell, were intended as biblical admonitions against sin. Oil on wooden board, circa 1482, 163.7 x 242 cm (64.4 x 95 inches).

Below: Roger Freeing Angelica by Ingres. The painting was inspired by a poem by Orlando Furiosa, featuring a knight on a mythical beast called a hippogriff rescuing a maiden being sacrificed to a sea monster. Oil on canvas, 1819, 198.8 x 146.8 cm (78.3 x 57.8 inches).

Opposite: Michelangelo was only 12 or 13 when he created *The Torment of St. Anthony* — his first painting — a genius artist's version of the monsters any 12-year-old boy might doodle in class. Oil and tempera on board, circa 1487, 47 x 35 cm (18.5 x 13.7 inches).

Following spread: Dragons grew bigger and fiercer through the centuries. This depiction of St. George, from the workshop of Italian Luca Signorelli, features what looks like a winged dog. Oil on board, circa 1500, 55 x 77.5 cm (21.6 x 30.5 inches).

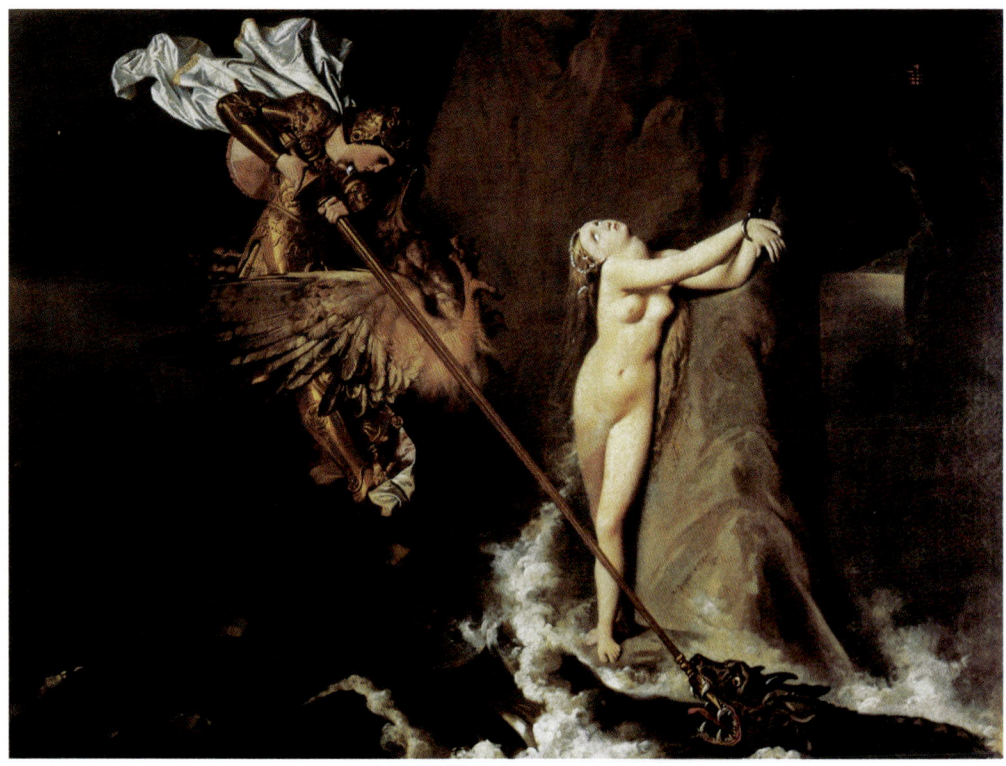

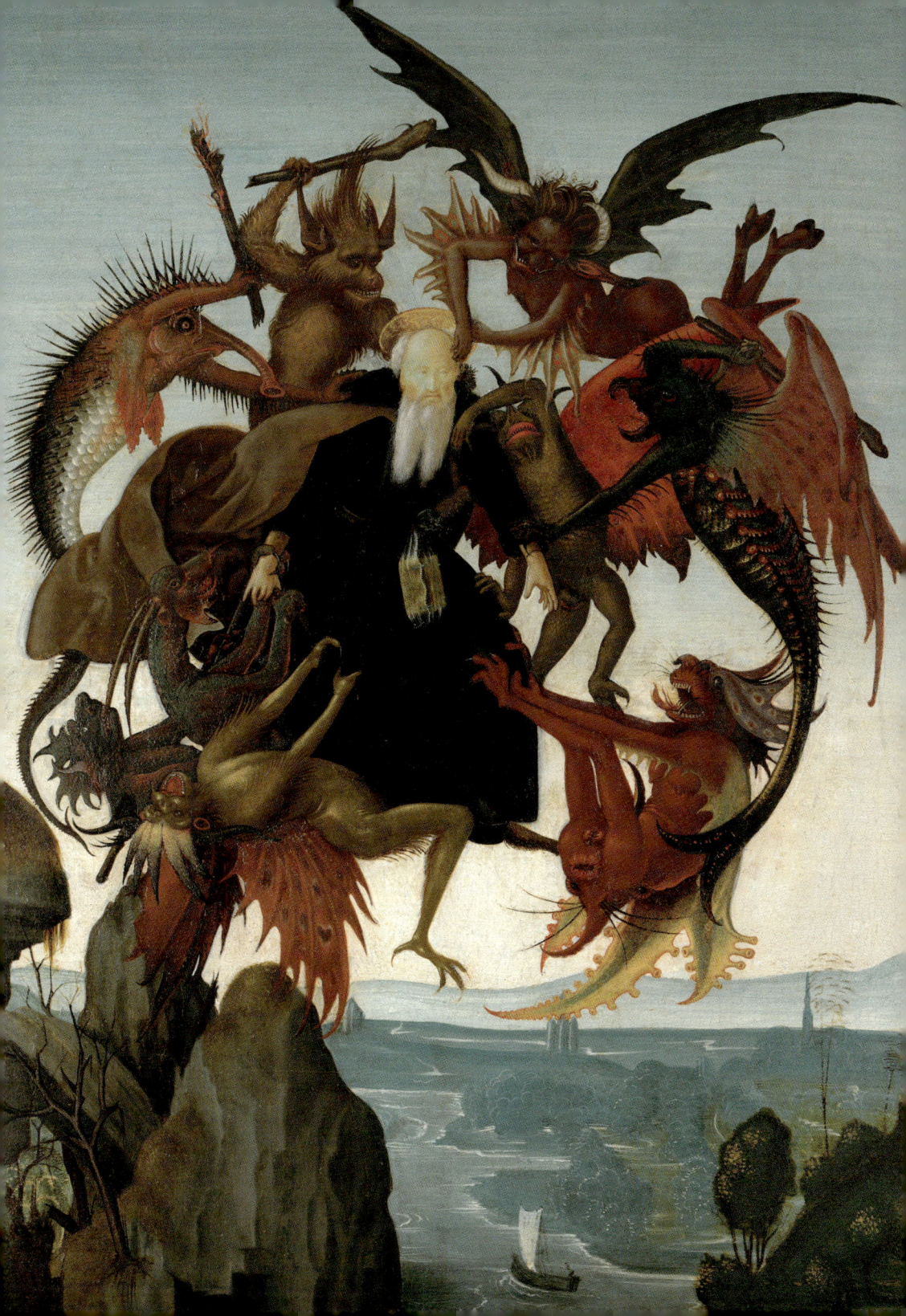

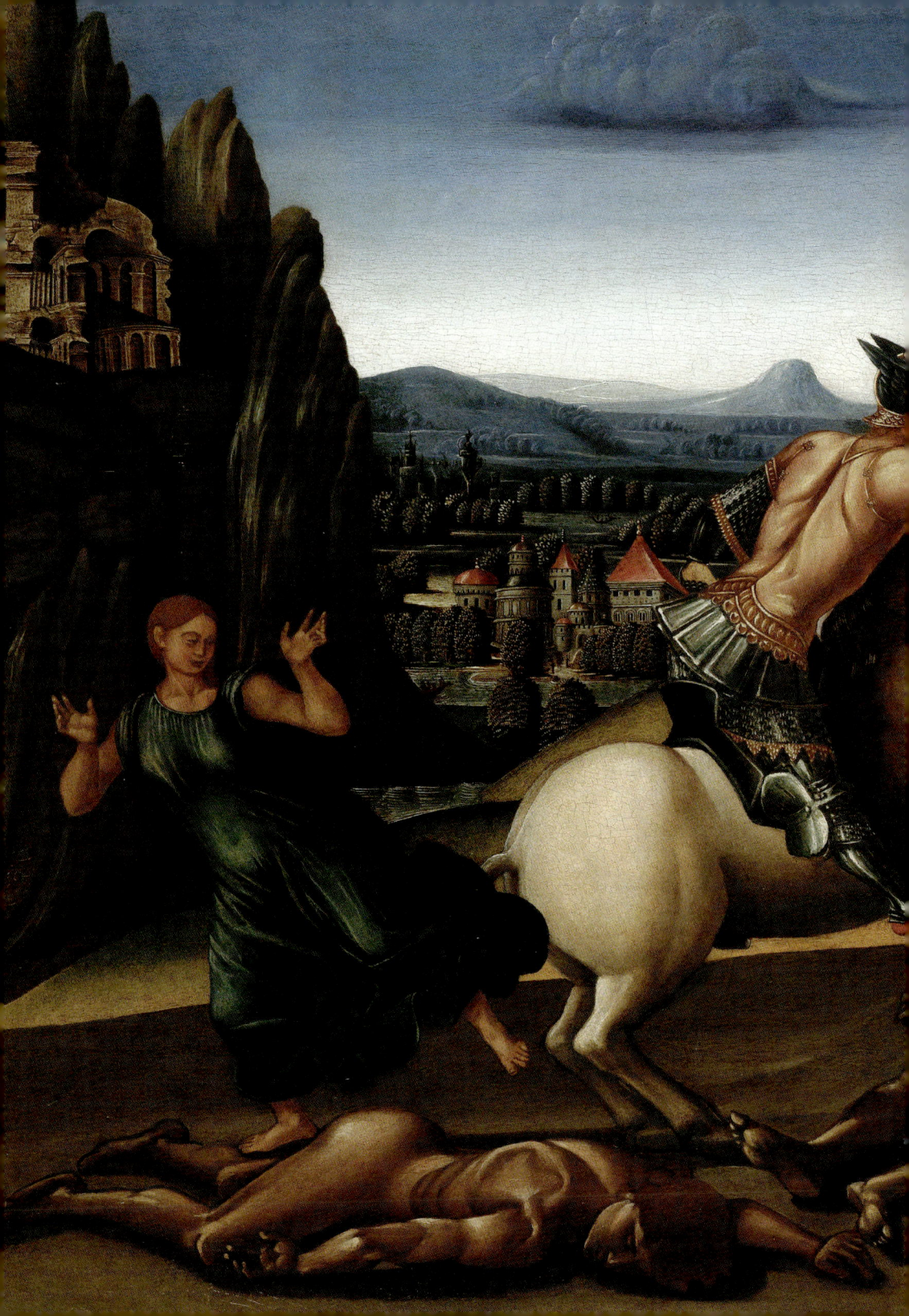

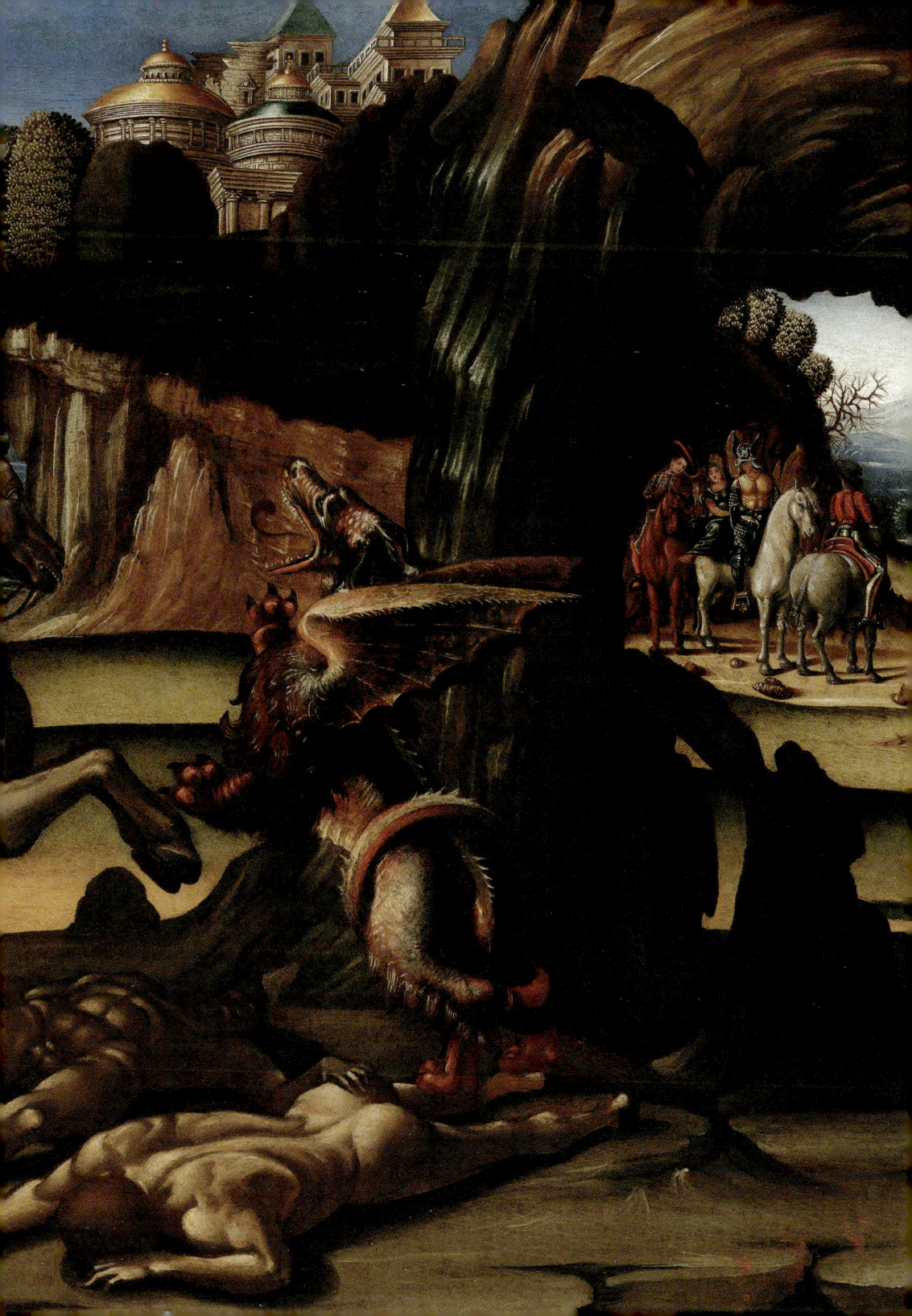

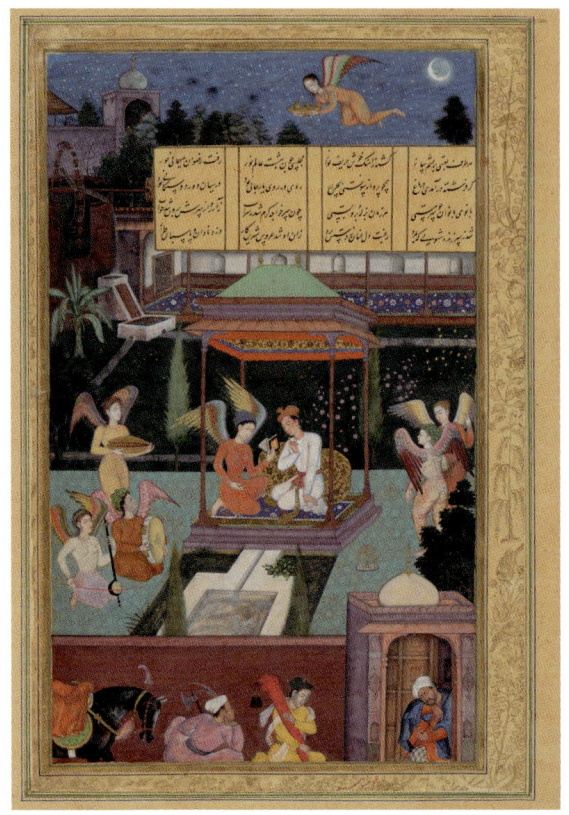

without prompting before you read the signature or the price tag. Even children love fantasy art; it was likely the first art you really enjoyed, discovered on a comic book, paperback, or record album cover. Whether Mœbius, Rodney Matthews, Boris Vallejo, or Rowena Morrill, you could almost feel the blood vessels expanding in your brain as your eyes crawled over the image, absorbing the rich colors, the alien landscape, the idealized human figures, the threatening beasts, the sure sense that might and right would prevail in the struggle depicted. Since fantasy art is largely created as work for hire, no matter how talented the artist, it has always been accessible, displayed prominently on the newsstand, to its advantage and curse. Is Salvador Dalí more talented than Frank Frazetta because one painted for the gallery and the other for EC Comics? Many would have it so, and yet your brain, and quite possibly every brain, lights up with something much like love on viewing a Frazetta maiden's fat dimpled buttocks, swoons in endorphin ecstasy for Druillet's bright primary colors and "feels much better" gazing upon a Hildebrandt dragon.

The uninitiated conflate fantasy with science fiction; though visually related they are very separate art forms, sci-fi being rooted in science — and thus conceivably possible, like the Starship Enterprise — while fantasy adheres to no rules, a crapshoot of imagination run wild. If ever in doubt about where a piece of art falls, invoke the rocket rule. Is there a spaceship? Then it's sci-fi. No rocket? Check for dragons, the official mascot of fantasy art.

Dragons arose separately in Western and Eastern mythology as the ultimate opponent, the natural match to the human hero. Early dragons were more snake-like, reflecting fear of a known creature. With time and artistic license they grew multiple heads, sprouted wings, gained a facility to spit fire, became, in general, larger and ever more fanciful, until they stabilized as instantly recognizable creatures of pure imagination. And then they were fit for fantasy art.

Above: An illustration from the Mughal emperor Akbar's private copy of the Indian poet Amir Khusrau Dihlavi's *The Story of the Princess of the Blue Pavilion: The Youth of Rum Is Entertained in a Garden by a Fairy and Her Maidens,* 1597. Fairies, like dragons, are common to many cultures.

Opposite: Mythology was a favorite theme of classical art; an excuse to paint subjects otherwise deemed socially unacceptable. Here we have another dog-beast, this time representing the sea monster slain by Perseus to save the Ethiopian princess Andromeda. Yes, we're to believe this paper-white blonde by Giuseppe Cesari, circa 1592, is Ethiopian. Oil on slate, 70.5 x 54.9 cm (27.7 x 21.6 inches).

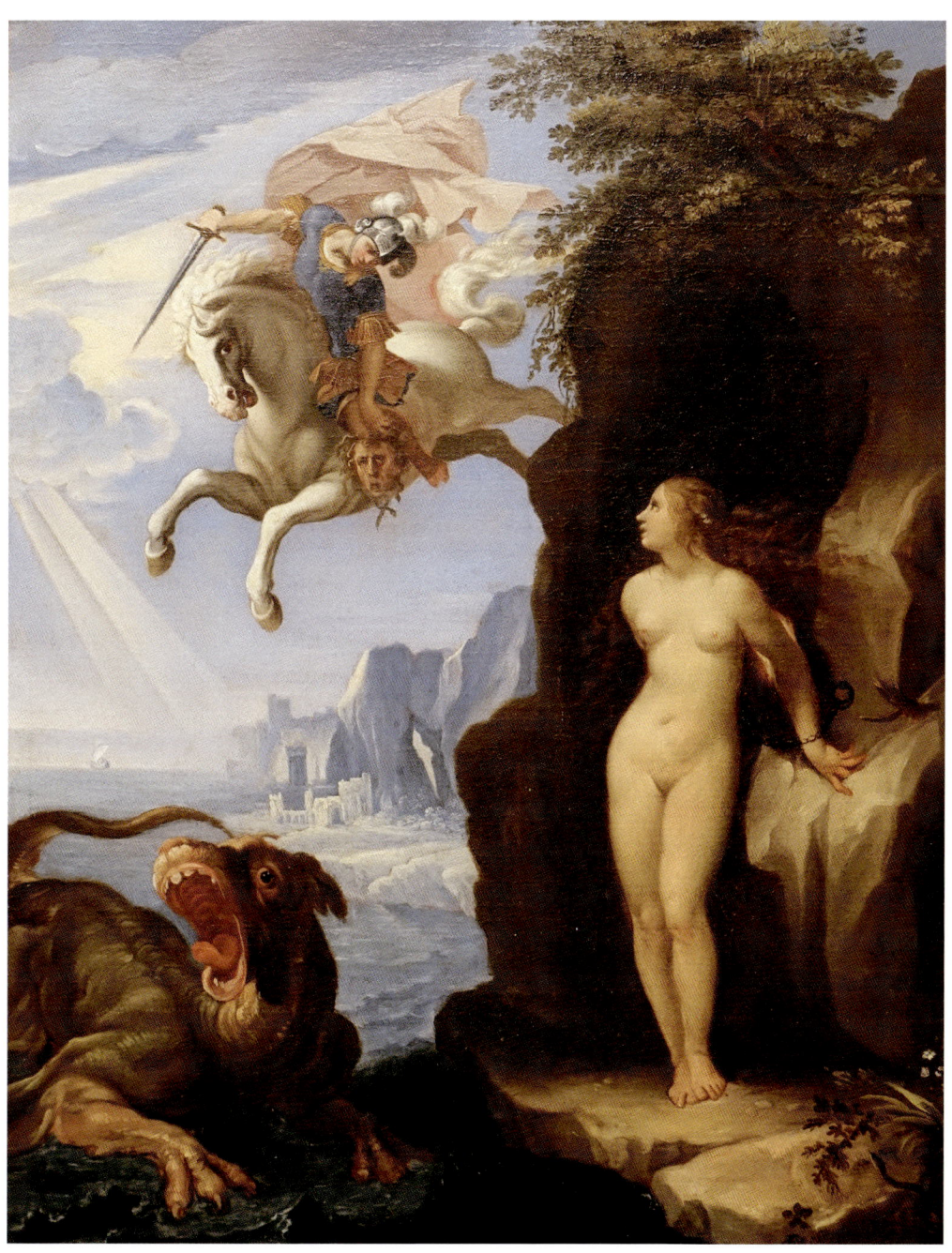

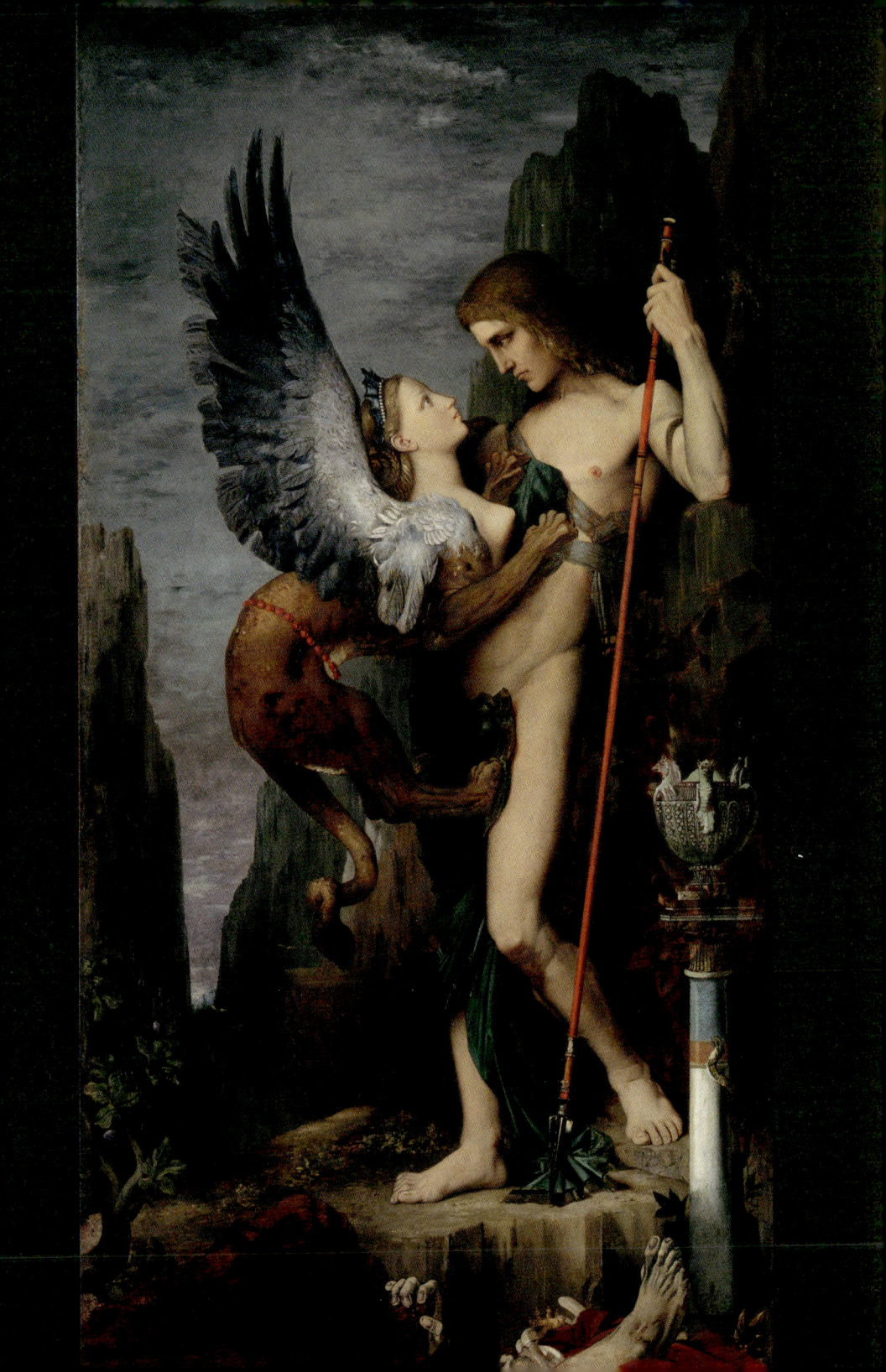

Hieronymus Bosch (c. 1450–1516) really didn't have a feel for dragons. His images of heaven, hell, and cultural mythology were far more imaginative than his contemporaries', but he was still just painting religious allegory, with heavy emphasis on the wages of sin, unleavened by heroic struggle. There was much nudity, though little eroticism; many threatening creatures, but no dragons.

The much later Maxfield Parrish (1870–1966) is a more obvious first fantasy artist. His landscapes are lush and dreamlike, populated by beautiful youths and nubile maidens. Castles feature occasionally and his 1901 oil *The Reluctant Dragon*, produced to illustrate Kenneth Grahame's story of the same name in the 1902 children's book *Dream Days*, is a fine example of the breed. Perhaps most significant, he was a commercial artist, illustrating magazines, children's books, calendars, and even toothpaste ads. His best-known painting is *Daybreak*, 1922, an ethereal garden inhabited by two languorous women, that became the best-selling art print of the 20th century. Just one year after its completion *Weird Tales*, the world's first sci-fi/fantasy fiction magazine, debuted. Conceived by journalist/editor J.C. Henneberger, an Edgar Allan Poe fan, *Weird Tales* followed the formula of other single-theme fiction titles of the period: several short stories, printed on cheap pulp paper, wrapped in a luridly painted cover. *WT*'s first cover was by Richard Ruh Epperly, a tepid landscape painter who nonetheless came up with a sinister octopus attacking a flapper. Cover quality improved dramatically over the next few years, in stride with the writing.

Because fantasy art has always been tied to fantasy fiction, certain writers were crucial in shaping the genre. Robert E. Howard introduced Conan the Cimmerian in the December 1932 issue of *Weird Tales* with the story "The Phoenix on the Sword" (cover art by J. Allen St. John), followed by "The Tower of the Elephant" (cover by Margaret Brundage) in the March 1933 issue, with 17 more Conan stories published before his suicide in 1936. The muscular hero inhabiting a savage primitive world hit a nerve with readers, the same one strummed when Edgar Rice Burroughs's "Tarzan of the Apes" debuted in *The All-Story Magazine* in March 1912 (cover by Clinton Pettee). Both characters were the strong, silent kick-ass type favored by a largely male, blue-collar pulp audience. For balance, Fritz Leiber created Fafhrd, a large barbarian, and the Gray Mouser, a small thief, as heroes with more human frailties, and better language skills, than Conan and Tarzan. They used wits to vanquish foes, but still inhabited a complex fantasy world every bit as compelling as Conan's Cimmeria. Leiber's first of many Fafhrd and the Gray Mouser stories appeared in the August 1939 issue of *Unknown*, alongside fiction by L. Ron Hubbard, future founder of the Church of Scientology and wielder of great power over Hollywood elites, if little over fantasy fiction fans.

H.P. Lovecraft's Cthulhu Mythos was also spawned and refined in the fantasy pulps, beginning with "The Call of Cthulhu" in *Weird Tales*, February 1928. His highly developed, heavily layered vision is still studied and dissected by fantasy fans, from the Outer Gods who rule a malevolent alternate universe loosely plucked from Greek mythology — with all goodness and beauty drained away — to the 180-plus Great Old Ones, earth-bound horrors, including Cthulhu, worshipped by debauched human cults. Lovecraft's was a frightening world where humans stood little chance, but it, too, offered a fantasy escape, a chance to experience a life far worse than anything the Depression could dish out. Other writers who got their start in the fantasy pulps, and thus

Opposite: Gustave Moreau won his place in the Paris Salon in 1864 with this interpretation of *Oedipus and the Sphinx*, and how could he not? From her fluffy wings and glossy coat to her assertive approach and perky breasts the Sphinx is one sexy beast, while the sheer size of the painting is overwhelming. Oil on canvas, 206.4 x 104.8 cm (81.3 x 41.3 inches).

influenced the art form, include Robert Bloch, Ray Bradbury, Arthur C. Clarke, Paul Ernst, Frank Herbert, C.L. Moore, and Clark Ashton Smith.

Weird Tales proved there was a market for fantasy fiction, but fantasy art remained an adjunct for some time, due largely to the pulp publishers' limited budgets. Pulp paper was cheap, but so absorbent it was no good for printing anything but text or simple line drawings. The coated paper used for the covers reproduced color well, but was too costly for interior use. And with publishing's time-honored contempt for the masses and their presumed lack of aesthetic taste, why did they need anything better? Other publishers took notice of *Weird Tales'* success, however, and competitors emerged, which drove innovation. Hugo Gernsback launched *Amazing Stories* in 1926, and in so doing drew the dividing line between fantasy and science fiction.

Gernsback was a wonderful whacko who would become known as the Father of Science Fiction, or, as he preferred, scientifiction. He was also a tech nerd, perhaps the first tech nerd, with a deep fascination for electricity and radio. His magazine *Electrical Experimenter*, released in 1913, succeeded by *Science and Invention* in 1920, reveled in improbable science, and included fiction early on. Both titles were printed on high-quality paper, with full-color covers celebrating the crackpot fringes of scientific research, including a graphic "End of the World" cover in 1925. It was thus a short step for Gernsback to come up with *Amazing Stories*, a magazine completely devoted to "scientifiction," followed by *Air Wonder Stories* and *Science Wonder Stories* in 1929, both of which were combined to become simply *Wonder Stories* in 1930.

Unlike the digest-sized *Weird Tales*, *Amazing Stories* and *Wonder Stories* were full 8.5-by-11.75-inch magazines. The fiction initially leaned toward reprints of H.G. Wells, Jules Verne, and Edgar Allan Poe, but the cover art by Frank R. Paul was new and superb, and helped establish him as the first great sci-fi artist.

But for those who loved the mythological origins of true fantasy art, Paul painted just

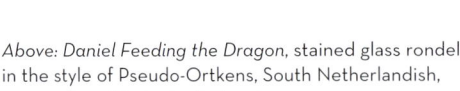

Above: Daniel Feeding the Dragon, stained glass rondel in the style of Pseudo-Ortkens, South Netherlandish, 1520, 21.6 cm (8.5 inches) diameter.

Opposite: Arminianism as a Five-Headed Monster referred to a branch of Protestantism based on the Dutch theologian Jacobus Arminian. Though closely related to other Protestant sects of the early 17th century some viewed it with alarm, thus the five heads representing avarice, deceit, sedition, opinion, and stupidity, while the hands hold envy and war, and the feet trample innocence, in the form of a child. Illustration circa 1620.

MASTERPIECES OF FANTASY ART

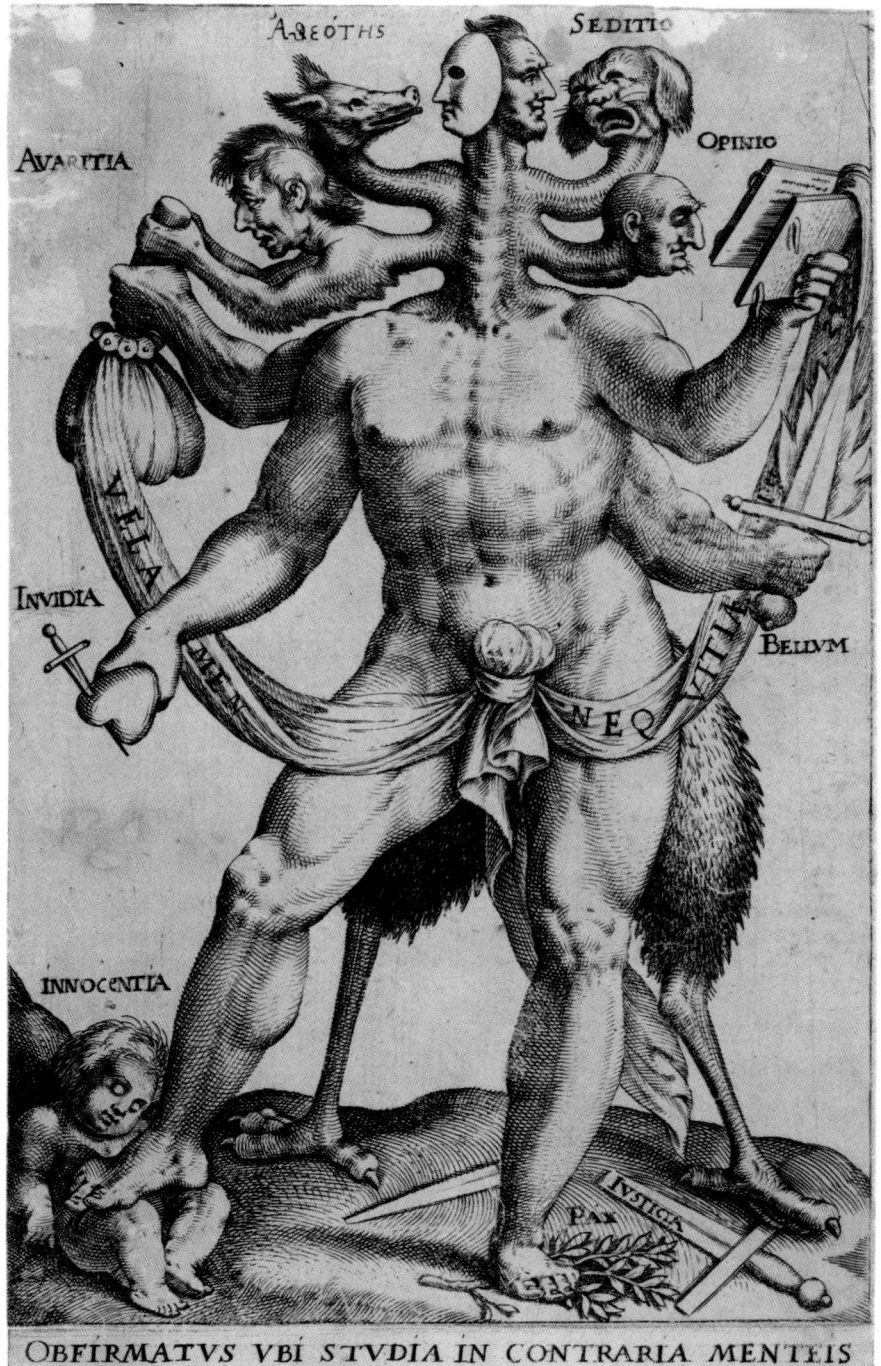

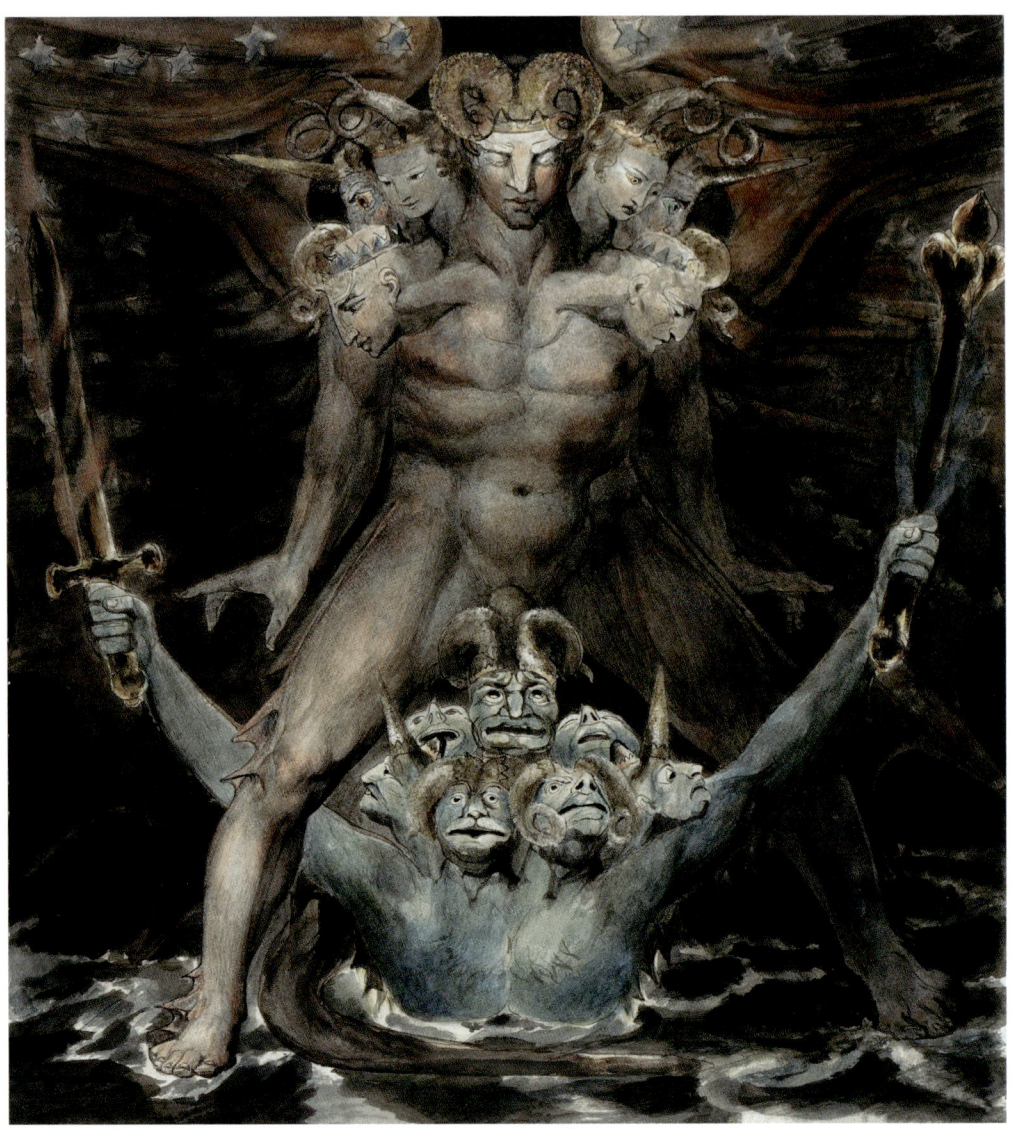

Above: William Blake, poet, painter, and visionary, was considered a madman in 18th-century England, and now a seminal figure of the Romantic Age. Between 1805 and 1810 he was commissioned to illustrate books of the Bible, which became *The Great Red Dragon* series of fantasy watercolors inspired by Revelations. Here, *The Great Red Dragon and the Beast from the Sea*, 40.1 x 35.6 cm (15.7 x 14 inches).

Opposite: James Allen St. John, who signed his works J. Allen St. John, was one of the earliest fantasy artists, best known for illustrating the earliest *Tarzan* novels of Edgar Rice Burroughs. During the Great Depression, at age 60, he produced covers for *Weird Tales* and *Amazing Stories*. This, titled *Ave Pan*, was one of his last, painted for *Fate* magazine, September 1950, when he was 85 years old. Casein on paper. Courtesy of Heritage Auctions.

MASTERPIECES OF FANTASY ART

a few too many spaceships, especially for the flight-themed *Air Wonder Stories*. It came back to the possible-versus-impossible argument: no matter how fanciful the spaceship, space travel is based on solid scientific principles, while dragons are not. Science fiction is mechanical, fantasy organic, the first concerned with the creations of man, the second with those of an alien god. Sci-fi also tends to take place in the future, while fantasy references worlds of the distant past. How else to explain so many tattered furry garments? The incidence of hi-tech bikinis notwithstanding.

With *Weird Tales* and *Amazing Stories* the fantasy pulp floodgates opened wide. *Astounding Stories of Super-Science* debuted in 1930, followed by *Strange Tales of Mystery and Terror* and *Miracle Science and Fantasy Stories* in 1931; *Terror Tales* in 1934; *Marvel Science Stories* in 1938; *Unknown*, *Strange Stories*, *Startling Stories*, *Mystery Tales*, *Fantastic Adventures*, and *Planet Stories* in 1939; and *Fantastic Novels* and *Astonishing Stories* in 1940. The deprivations of the Depression years made fantasy a welcome escape, and as the competition increased the magazines not only introduced talented new writers, but better-quality, more eye-catching cover art. By which I mean more women with fewer clothes.

Weird Tales, always the innovator, was the first to sexualize fantasy art. A wild proliferation of pulp titles in the early 1930s drove down sales, leading many publishers to cut cover prices from a quarter to a dime. With so many Americans out of work even that was a significant expense for a nonessential item, but sex has always been recession-proof: men will pay for pleasure even as they starve. Several publishers had experimented with "spicy" pulps in the 1920s, most featuring

bad fiction with poor-quality pin-up covers; then in 1932 Frank Armer and Harry Donenfeld, the main publishers of these pulps, joined forces to form Super Magazines, soon changed to Culture Publications. That same year artist Margaret Brundage entered the office of *Weird Tales* editor Farnsworth Wright. It's doubtful that publishers Armer and Donenfeld knew Wright, a mere editor, but there's a good chance his artistic choices inspired theirs. Culture Publications would launch *Spicy Detective Stories*, *Spicy Adventure Stories*, and *Spicy Mystery Stories*—its take on fantasy—in 1934, all pulps with mildly provocative fiction and spectacularly sexy covers painted by talented illustrators Harry Lemon Parkhurst and Hugh Joseph Ward. These pulps were an immediate success, selling out at 25 cents while others languished on the newsstands at 10 cents, and are credited with launching the first sexual revolution in American publishing.

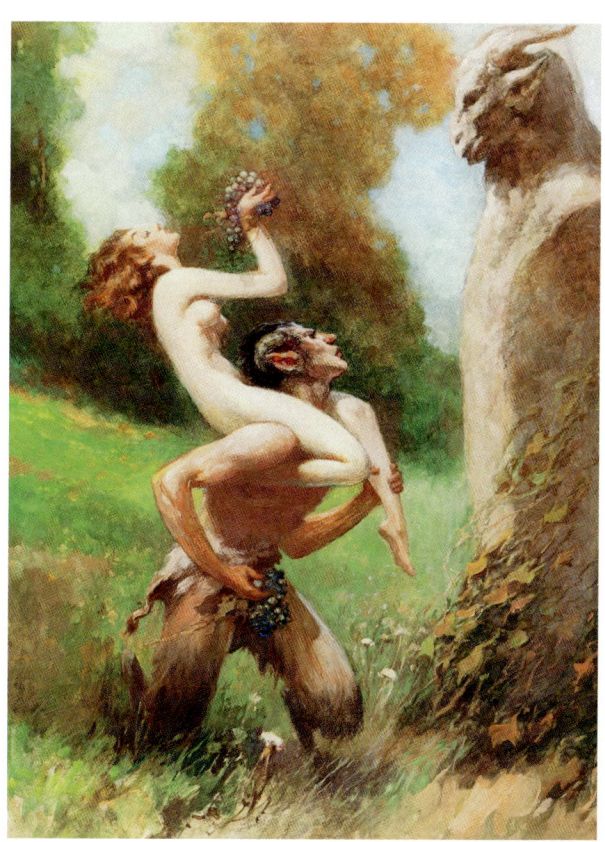

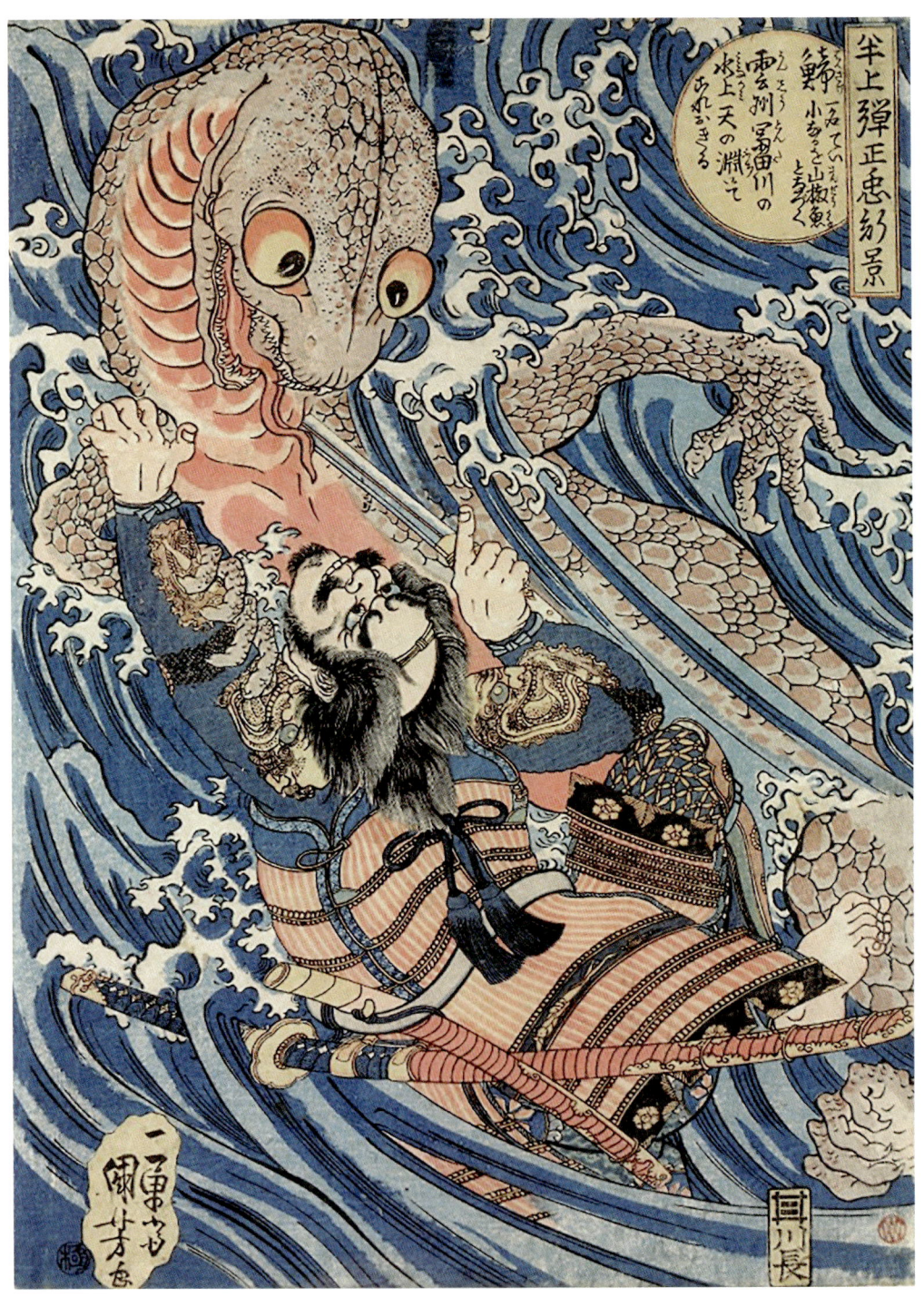

Weird Tales, however, went there first. Brundage's debut cover appeared on the September 1932 issue, the original pastel so spicy it was censored in print. Was she asked to portray a topless woman? History leaves no note, but from June 1933 through August 1936 she supplied every cover for *WT*, 39 in total, pushing out the supremely talented, but less lurid J. Allen St. John and firmly establishing the nude as a staple of fantasy art. In 1936 she was joined by Virgil Finlay, Hugh Rankin, and the elegant Hannes Bok, before New York mayor Fiorello La Guardia launched a crackdown on spicy newsstand titles in 1938. Though he primarily targeted Culture Publications' magazines, fantasy pulps, most notably *Weird Tales*, were swept up as well, and the sex was dialed back until after the war.

The sweep did not deter Martin Goodman, the man who would found Marvel Comics in 1939; he launched *Marvel Science Stories* in May 1938 with such salacious content that readers actually complained—while embracing the superb sexy covers by Norman Saunders. Goodman toned it down, a bit, and changed the name to *Marvel Tales*. In 1939 *Mystery Tales* and *Planet Stories*, in which Ray Bradbury got his start, took the same path, with a steady stream of Amazons, space vixens, and bondage covers by H.W. Scott, Allen Anderson, and Alexander Leydenfrost. All somehow slipped through La Guardia's dragnet.

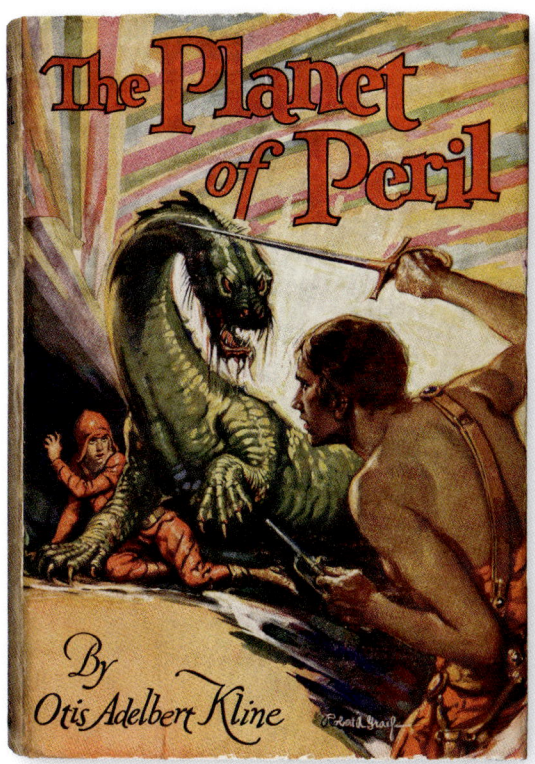

After World War II, which elevated pin-ups to an acceptable American art form, there was a general loosening of the La Guardia prohibitions. New artists, including Robert Gibson Jones, Lawrence Sterne Stevens, Ed Emshwiller, Frank Kelly Freas, Harold McCauley, and Chesley Bonestell, for whom the yearly Chesley Awards for science fiction and fantasy art are named, entered the field, along with new magazines including *Avon Fantasy Reader*, 1947; *A. Merritt's Fantasy Magazine*, 1949; *Out of This World Adventures*, 1950; *10 Story Fantasy*, 1951; and *Imaginative Tales*, 1954. Wartime paper rationing had killed off most of the old fantasy titles, however, leaving only *Weird Tales*, *Startling Stories*, *Thrilling Wonder Stories*, *Amazing Stories*, *Fantastic Adventures*, *Famous Fantastic Mysteries*, and *Planet Stories*. By the end of 1955 they had all ceased publication, with the exception of *Imaginative*

Opposite: Hanagami Danjo no lo Arakage Fighting a Giant Salamander, by Utagawa Kuniyoshi, portrays a legendary samurai battling a distinctly Japanese monster. Color wood block print, circa 1835.

Above: Otis Adelbert Kline's *Planet of Peril* was described by one reviewer as "an open imitation of Burroughs," who was setting the standard for fantasy fiction in 1929. The hardcover did feature a great illustration by fantasy pulp artist Robert Graef, however.

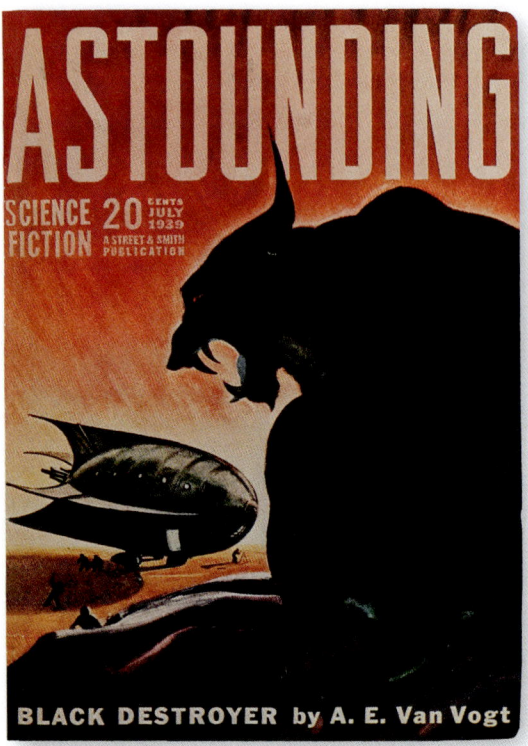

BLACK DESTROYER by A. E. Van Vogt

Tales, which succumbed in 1958, and *Amazing Stories*, which soldiered on under various publishers until 2005.

Pulp died because America lost its taste for short fiction. Television picked off the more visually inclined, while the reading audience opted for paperback long fiction. Those who bought fantasy pulps for the covers were more likely to embrace comic books, especially after EC Comics introduced its new line in 1950. *Weird Science* and *Weird Fantasy* went after the same audience as the fantasy pulps, but with illustrations on every page. Wally Wood became a regular cover artist in 1952, while Roy Krenkel, Al Williamson, and a young Frank Frazetta provided interior comics. EC's new line was very popular and sadly short-lived. Enjoying greater longevity were the cheap fantasy paperbacks that first appeared in the early 1960s.

Some fantasy authors always wrote long fiction and produced books. *The Hobbit, or There and Back Again*, by J.R.R. Tolkien, was published in 1937. The Father of Fantasy Fiction was himself influenced by the books of Scottish author George MacDonald, who said, "I write not for children, but for the childlike, whether they be five, or fifty, or seventy-five." Tolkien took this to heart, also writing to an adult audience, and painted the cover for *The Hobbit*, as well as creating interior illustrations in pen, pencil, paint, and crayon. While no equal to the caliber of his writing, these works guided the many fantasy artists who'd later illustrate his *Lord of the Rings* trilogy, released in 1954. These books, and *The Chronicles of Narnia* by C.S. Lewis, released in seven volumes between 1950 and 1956, contributed to a second wave of fantasy fandom, boosting writers, artists, and the demand for novel-length fiction.

Another powerful contributor to this next wave was Ace Books, a purveyor of cheap paperbacks, established in 1952. In 1953 Ace published its first sci-fi novel, A.E. van Vogt's *The World of Null-A*, combined with his *The Universe Maker*. Within two years, spurred by the success of Tolkien and Lewis, the company was publishing more sci-fi and fantasy than any other genre, providing steady work for cover artists. The remaining pulp alumni, notably Ed Emshwiller, Virgil Finlay, Frank Kelly Freas, and Roy Krenkel, vied for these jobs, with Krenkel landing the plum

Above: Astounding Science Fiction magazine began in the 1930s, but came into its own when John W. Campbell took over as editor in 1937. With the issue seen here, July 1939, he introduced the first stories by A. E. Van Vogt and Isaac Asimov, fronted with a striking cover by Graves Gladney.

Opposite: Tsukioka Yoshitoshi's The Wrestler Onogawa Kisaburo Blowing Smoke at a One-Eyed Monster is a color wood block print from the series One Hundred Ghost Tales from China and Japan, 1865, trading on the classic theme of a big muscular man besting a beast. 34.4 x 23.6 cm (13.5 x 9.3 inches).

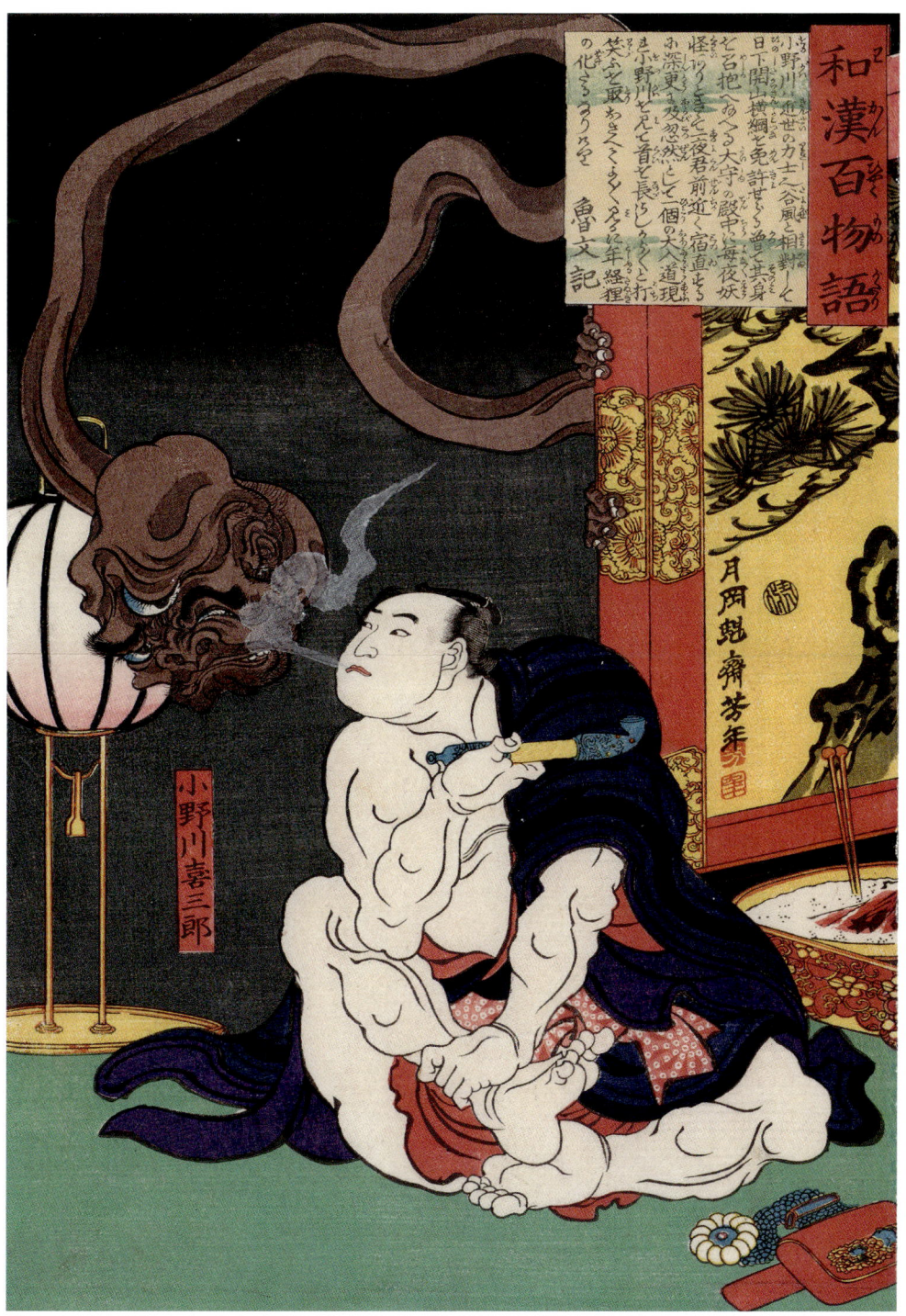

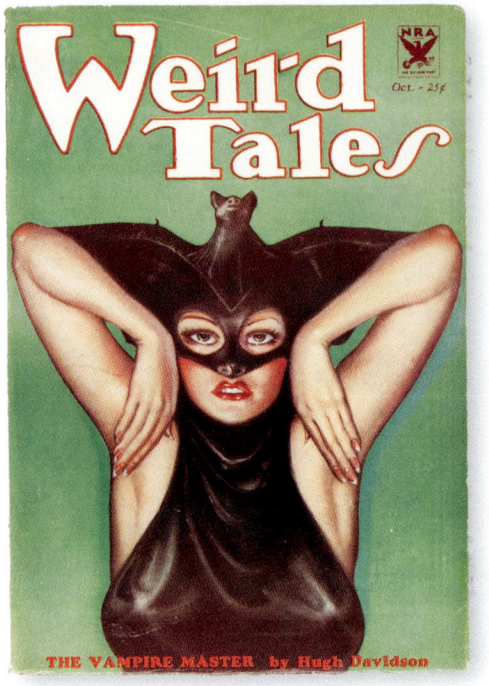

THE VAMPIRE MASTER by Hugh Davidson

assignment of Ace's Tarzan covers. In 1962 he recommended his friend Frank Frazetta for interior illustrations. With Edgar Rice Burroughs out of copyright, Tarzan was a popular choice for reprints, and soon rival fantasy publisher Canaveral Press seized upon his works and hired Frazetta to do the covers, replacing the more abstract Mahlon Blaine. By 1966, when Lancer Books, yet another paperback house, acquired the rights to Conan, Frazetta had grown so popular he was able to negotiate a cover contract that allowed him to retain all rights to his artwork, unheard of in the work-for-hire market of the 1960s when publishers routinely tossed out original art after use. Because of this clause Frazetta was inspired to paint some of the greatest works of his career, knowing they'd actually belong to him. The series sold in excess of 10 million copies, in large part due to these stunning covers, and a Frazetta archive was created that has been preserved to this day.

Meanwhile, EC's fantasy titles were shot down in 1954, when the American government accused comic books—especially EC comic books—of inciting juvenile delinquency. In response, a coalition of publishers created the Comics Code Authority to police their own product, outlawing the use of "horror," "terror," and "weird" on any comic cover. EC fought back, but without the Comics Code approval was unable to get distribution and had to drop its offending titles. Fans mourned, until, 10 years later, Warren Publishing launched *Creepy*, followed by *Eerie* and *Vampirella*, directly inspired by EC's horror comics, but in a full-sized magazine format exempt from Comics Code censorship.

Creepy's covers were big, bright, and glossy, perfect for rich color reproduction. The interiors were black and white only, but what glorious black and white, complex and highly detailed, originally by the old EC alumni: Wally Wood, Roy Krenkel, Al Williamson, and Frank Frazetta, who were soon joined by Richard Corben, Jeff Jones, Bernie Wrightson, Don Maitz, Ken Kelly, and many others. This younger group was nurtured by EC, but also by a shifting moral climate as the 1960s gave way to the '70s. Psychedelic art, attempting to mimic hallucinatory visions, emerged and cuddled up to fantasy, spawning a hybrid genre best expressed, initially, on record album covers.

Above: Brundage's most famous cover for *Weird Tales* is this October 1933 "bat woman" pastel, now lost. Because Brundage signed her cover illustrations "M. Brundage" readers thought she was a man. When it was revealed that she was a woman, reader complaints about her "immoral" covers increased.

Opposite: Norman Saunders holds the record for the greatest number of pulp cover illustrations: 867 in a career that spanned 32 years. This, for the April/May 1939 issue of *Marvel Science Stories*, was one of many that brought criticism on the fledgling Marvel company as catering to prurient interests. Oil on canvas, 47 x 71 cm (18.5 x 28 inches). Courtesy of Heritage Auctions. © 2020 Marvel.

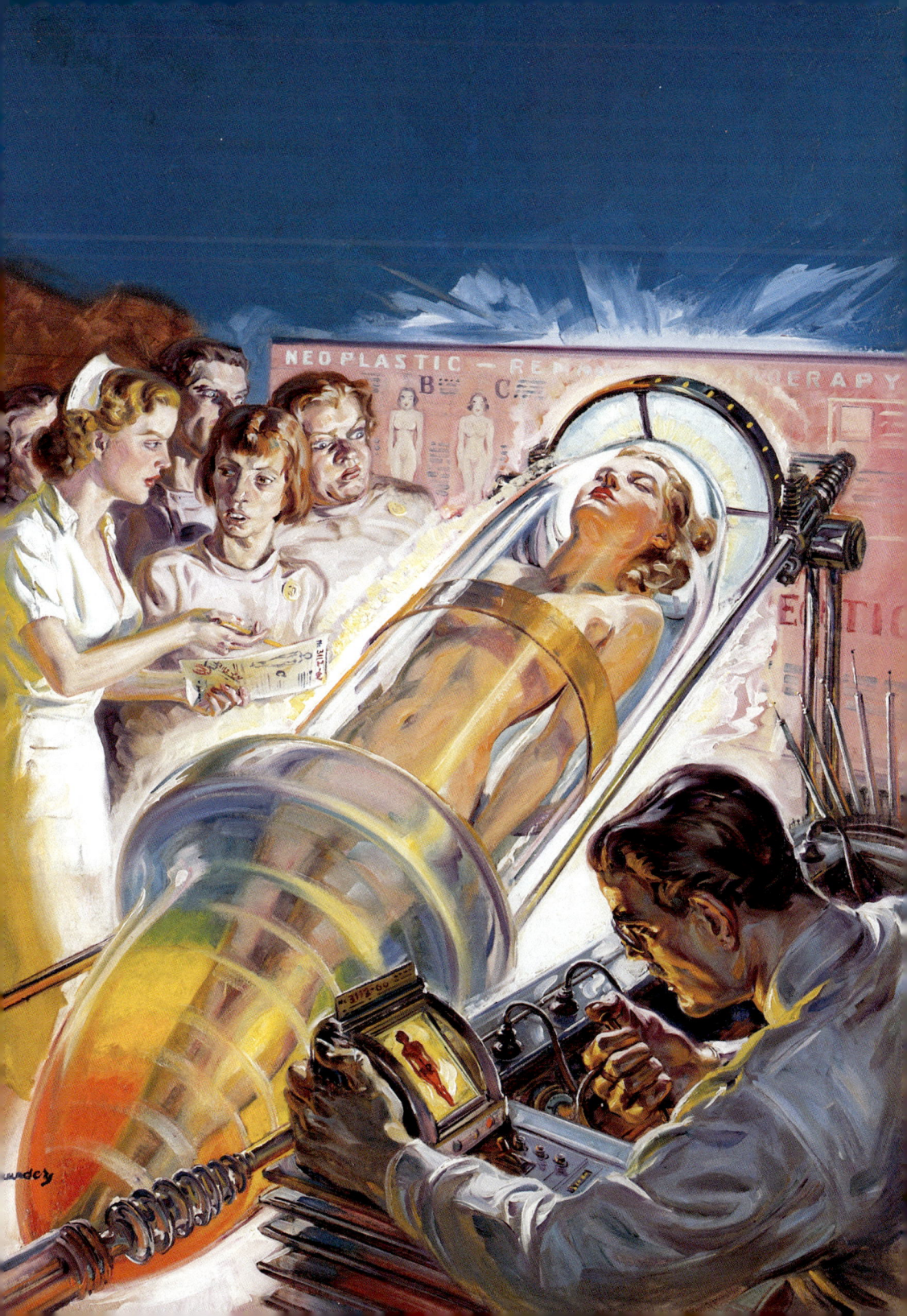

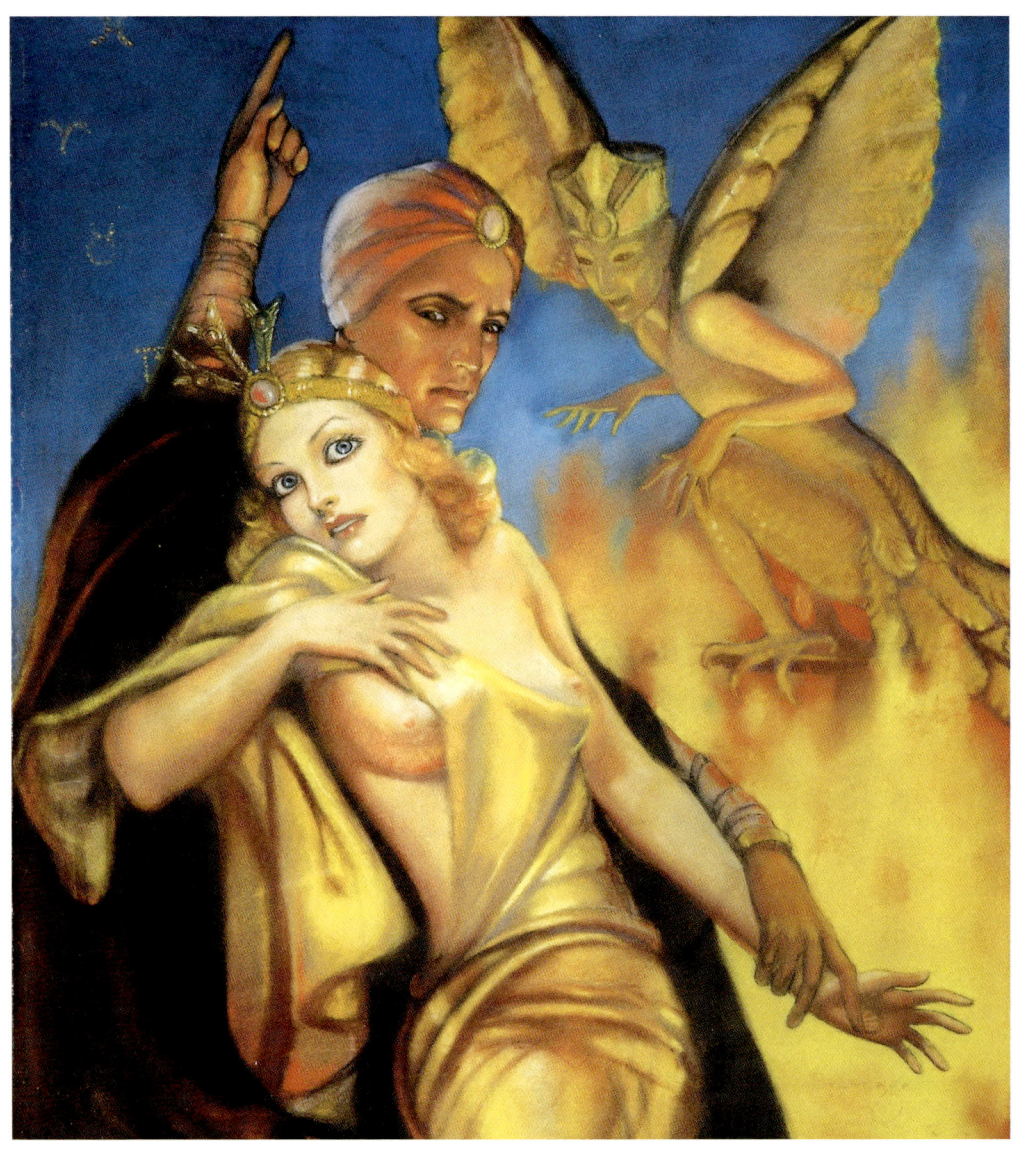

Australian Martin Sharp was one of the innovators of this style. Called a pop, rather than fantasy, artist, his covers for Cream's *Disraeli Gears* and *Wheels of Fire*, released, respectively, in 1967 and '68, paved the way for Roger Dean and Rodney Matthews's more frankly fantasy covers for Yes, Gentle Giant, Asia, Scorpions, Nazareth, Magnum, and Thin Lizzy. As with the pulp magazines and paperback novels, album cover art was basically seen as an advertising ploy, an alluring package to sell the contents, but record albums offered a much bigger canvas than a paperback novel. I remember how, as teenagers, my friends and I studied that art, and I remember buying albums based solely on the cover art; the Osibisa flying elephant cover by Dean coming to mind. It didn't take long for record companies to realize that the outside was as important as the inside and to commission ever more fantasy covers.

Then, in December 1974, came a magazine from France that marked yet another epic leap forward for fantasy art. *Métal Hurlant*, variously translated as screaming metal or howling metal, was conceived in Paris by two artists, Philippe Druillet and Jean Giraud, aka Mœbius; one editor/writer, Jean-Pierre Dionnet; and, most important for any group of artists, a business manager, Bernard Farkas. Collectively, they were known as Les Humanoïdes Associés. *Métal Hurlant* was a high-quality magazine in the world of scruffy Belgian/French comics, but more important it was fantastic, psychedelic, futuristic, witty, sexy, and indisputably French. Europe, at last, had a big dog in the fight for fantasy supremacy, and that dog chewed up all competition. Mœbius introduced inscrutable wordless Arzach, mounted on a mutant pterodactyl, cruising a blasted alien landscape, and Major Grubert, intrepid explorer of *The Airtight Garage*. Druillet's work, featuring Lone Sloane, was harder, more threatening, in brilliant primary tones in contrast to Mœbius's dreamy weed-fueled pastels. The magazine launched as a quarterly, but went monthly by the ninth issue, taking in other European artists, including Enki Bilal, Yves Chaland, Serge Clerc, Guido Crepax, Jean-Claude Gal, H.R. Giger, Gaetano Liberatore, Milo Manara, Masse, Chantal Montelier, Jean-Michel Nicollet, Joost Swarte, and Alain Voss, plus Chilean Alejandro Jodorowsky, and Americans Richard Corben and Bernie Wrightson. In 1976 the publisher of the American humor magazine *National Lampoon* came upon *MH* in Paris and licensed it for U.S. publication as *Heavy Metal*, which debuted in April 1977. *HM* initially contained the French content with text translations only, making for low production costs and immediate profit. With time, *Heavy Metal* became its own magazine, with contributions from an international mix of artists, including Chris Achilleos, Julie Bell, Simon Bisley, Charles Burns, Clyde Caldwell, Howard Cruse, Alex Ebel, Alex Horley, Jeff Jones, Michael Kaluta, Paul Kerchner, Rod Kierkegaard, Karl Kofoed, Walter Simonson, Lorenzo Sperlonga, Arthur Suydam, Stefano Tamburini, Boris Vallejo, Luis Royo, and many more.

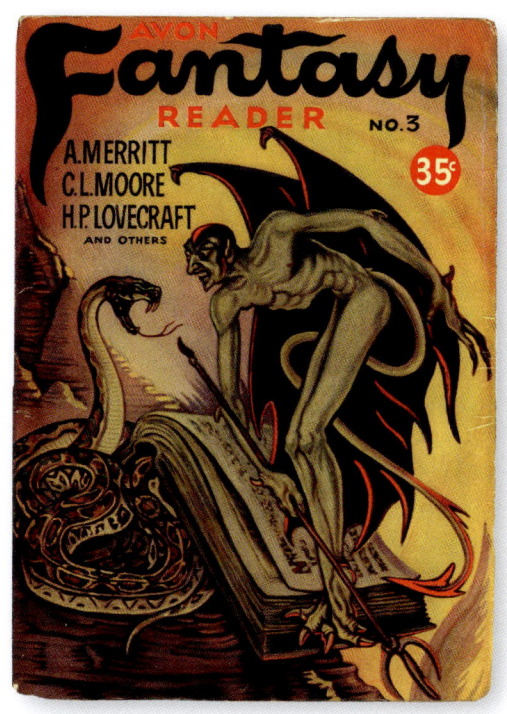

Though always popular with a core group of rabid fantasy comics fans, both magazines struggled with shifting tastes, management disputes and inevitable criticism for the increasingly sexualized content. Some fantasy art fans weren't interested in, say, the hypertrophied

Opposite: Margaret Brundage was *Weird Tales'* most prolific cover artist—and its most provocative. This, her first cover painting, for the September 1932 issue, had to be censored in printing, She went on to produce 65 more covers for the magazine. Pastel on paper, 44.5 x 50.8 cm (17.5 x 20 inches). Courtesy of Heritage Auctions.

Right: Avon Books entered the pulp magazine market in 1947 with *Avon Fantasy Reader,* a sort of *Reader's Digest* of previously published fantasy fiction. This Hannes Bok cover helped to sell No. 3, 1947.

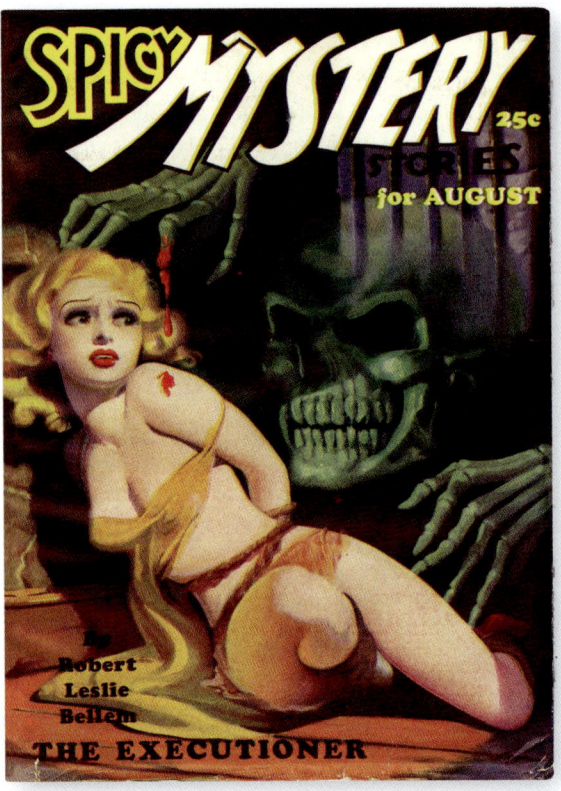

genitalia of Richard Corben's Den, or the hyper violence of Tamburini/Liberatore's RanXerox. For them, there was the gentler parallel development of *Lord of the Rings* culture, spearheaded by the Brothers Hildebrandt, John Howe, Alan Lee, and Ted Nasmith, and more significantly, in 1974, by the appearance of the role playing game Dungeons & Dragons, inspired by this Tolkien world.

D&D started small and simple —basically a dice game for experienced war gamers—and spawned, in 1977, the far more complex and tightly structured Advanced Dungeons & Dragons. Both games offered players the chance to function as diverse fantasy characters joined in adventure within an alien realm, directed by a dungeon master. D&D invited visual interpretation, first as crude line drawings in the original player's manual, moving to more sophisticated color covers and interior illustrations when Jim Roslof took over manual design in 1975 and hired Clyde Caldwell, Jeff Easley, Larry Elmore, Jim Holloway, Keith Parkinson, Harry Quinn, and Tim Truman as staff artists. With each new edition new artists were introduced, including Brom, Douglas Chaffee, Ralph Horsley, Todd Lockwood, Erik Olsen, rk post, Wayne Reynolds, and Eva Widermann.

Then, in 1993, the Seattle-based game developer Wizards of the Coast introduced Magic: The Gathering, the first fantasy card game. D&D, whose parent company was gobbled up by Wizards in 1997, was producing high-quality illustrated game manuals at that point, but with only a painting on the cover and very few full-page interiors, while 600 new Magic cards appeared each year, every one featuring an original piece of art with the artist's name prominently displayed, making it easy to build a fan following among its five million international players.

The Magic cards inspired other successful fantasy trading card games, including Dragon Ball Super Card Game, Yu-Gi-Oh!, and Final Fantasy Trading Card Game, all from Japan, where fantasy art, and artists, have flourished in the 21st century.

Above: The "Spicy" pulps, including *Spicy Adventure, Spicy Detective,* and *Spicy Mystery* were launched in 1934 as fiction magazines that hinted at sex, making them extremely popular. The covers hinted more than the stories, as here, by H.J. Ward.

Opposite: Weird Tales, launched in March 1923, was the first fantasy fiction magazine in the world, the place where many fantasy writers began. This, the December 1932 issue, featured the introduction of Robert E. Howard's Conan the Cimmerian, with the story "The Phoenix on the Sword." The cover illustration is by J. Allen St. John.

And then there's Hollywood. *Star Wars* premiered in 1977, the same year as Advanced Dungeons & Dragons, and proved conclusively that there was a market for sci-fi and fantasy films beyond the tacky B-movies of the 1950s and '60s. Ralph Bakshi's animated *Lord of the Rings* followed in 1978, an admittedly flawed film still eagerly embraced by fans of the books. Both films' posters were conceived by veteran Hollywood concept artist Thomas Jung, but Lucas hired the Brothers Hildebrandt to repaint Jung's *Star Wars* original, adding in the droids R2-D2 and C-3PO and Darth Vader's looming head for the British release.

Following *Star Wars'* overwhelming success, studios viewed fantasy artists with (slightly) more respect, though Ridley Scott had to fight 20th Century Fox to hire H.R. Giger as concept artist for *Alien* in 1978. The studio thought his work too grotesque for the screen, but Scott persevered, resulting in a creature at once elegant, terrifying, and artistically compelling. The film won Giger international acclaim—and an Academy Award for Best Visual Effects. Bakshi took notice and teamed with Frank Frazetta to create his next animated film, *Fire and Ice*, in 1983. Likewise, when Peter Jackson took on the *Lord of the Rings* trilogy in 1998 he hired fantasy artists John Howe and Alan Lee, and made his production crew faithfully follow their concept drawings to build and populate Middle Earth.

And then there's Alejandro Jodorowsky's *Dune*. Mœbius created 3,000 production drawings for the most famous fantasy film never made, with additional input from Giger and Chris Foss. While the script ballooned into what was estimated to be a 14-hour film, costing $20 million to make—a significant sum in 1974—studios backed away one after another, leaving only a magnificent and legendary book. The *Dune* book, containing all the concept art, was self-published by Jodorowsky in a print run of 10 and distributed to the studios he approached for financing. Eight copies disappeared; the final two belong to Mœbius's widow, Isabelle Giraud, and to Jodorowsky. The film, and the book, were the subject of the documentary *Jodorowsky's Dune*, released in 2013.

Besides concept collaborations, many fantasy artists were tapped for posters following *Star Wars*. The Hildebrandts went on to create posters for *Clash of the Titans* in 1981 and *The Secret of NIMH* in '82, while brother Tim painted the one-sheet for *The Deadly Spawn* in 1983. Jeff Jones was selected for *Dragonslayer* in 1981. Frank Frazetta created the *Conan the Barbarian* preview poster in 1982, after years of illustrating posters for Hollywood comedies including *What's New Pussycat?* (1965), *Hotel Paradiso* (1966), and *After*

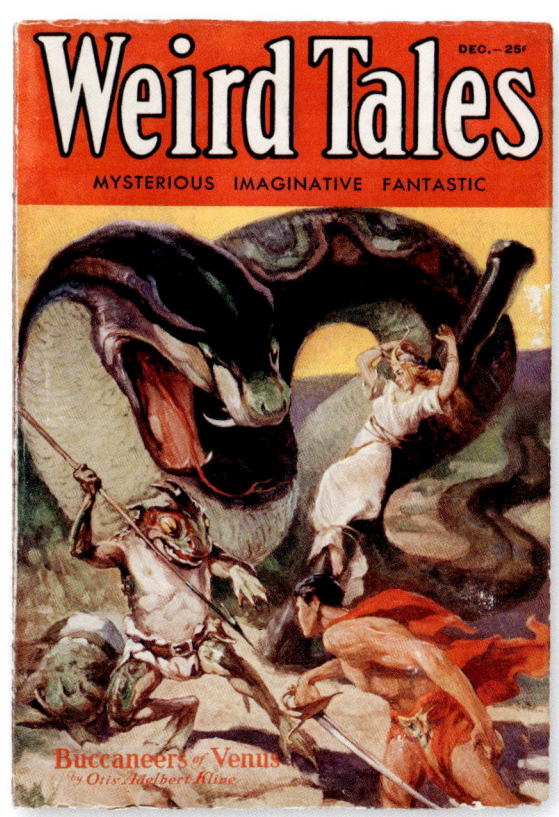

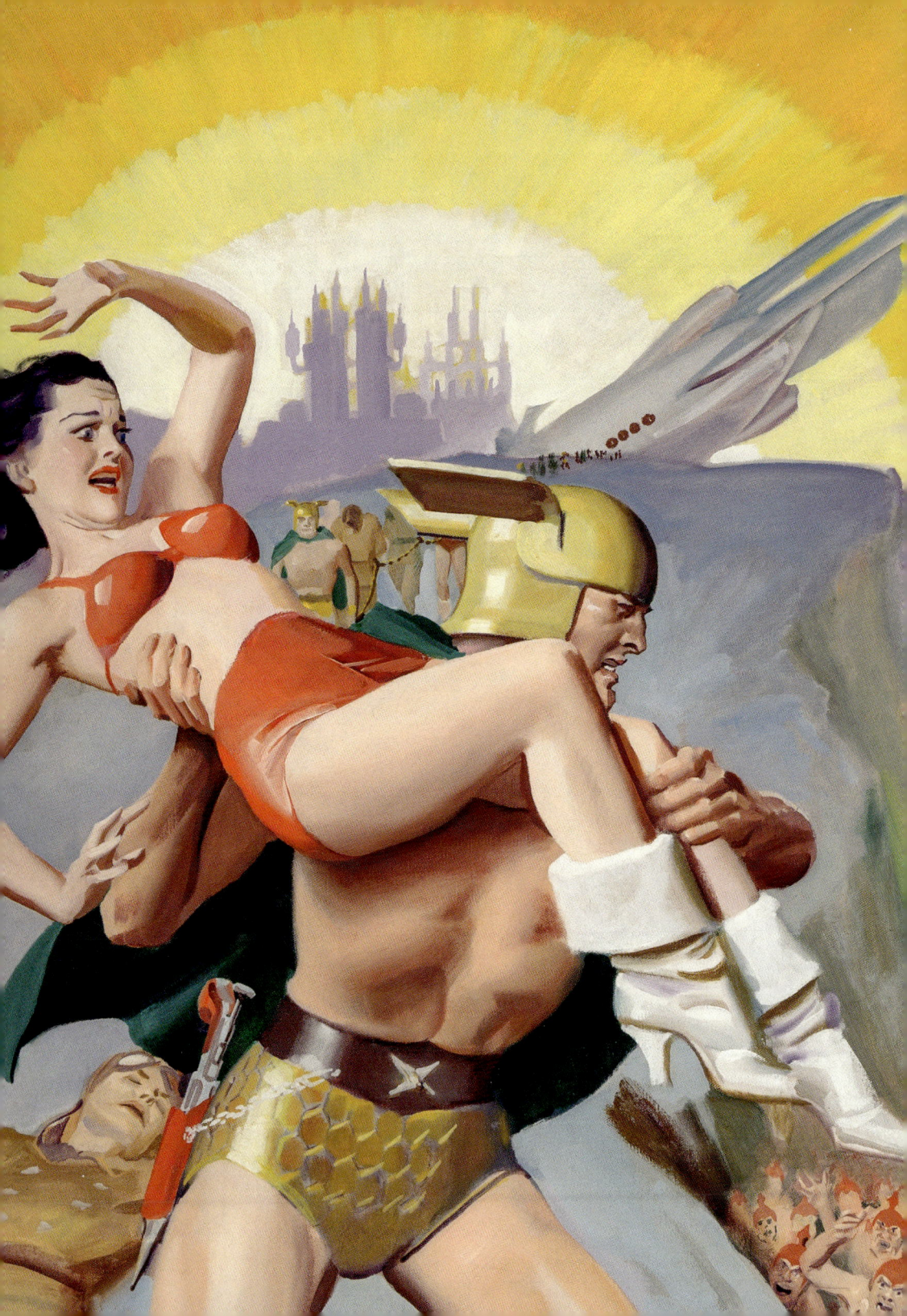

the Fox (1968). Mœbius made the poster for *Les Maîtres du Temps* (The Time Masters) in 1982. And long before all of these, in 1968, Philippe Druillet painted three posters for French director Jean Rollin's vampire films: *The Shiver of the Vampires*, *The Nude Vampire*, and *Requiem for a Vampire*. He was also responsible for a bizarre French poster for the American film *The Name of the Rose*, combining his signature sinister faces with a portrait of Sean Connery. The artist who quickly rose to the top of the fantasy film poster heap, however, was Boris Vallejo.

Vallejo hooked the poster assignment for *Barbarella* the same year *Star Wars* debuted and produced a series of posters for *The Empire Strikes Back* in collusion with Coca-Cola in 1980, followed in quick succession by *The Sword and the Sorcerer* and *Q* in 1982, *Deathstalker* in '83, *Barbarian Queen* in '85, and the cheesy *Naked Warriors* in 1988. In mockery of these heroic works he landed the commissions for *National Lampoon's Vacation* in 1983, and *European Vacation* in 1985. Many

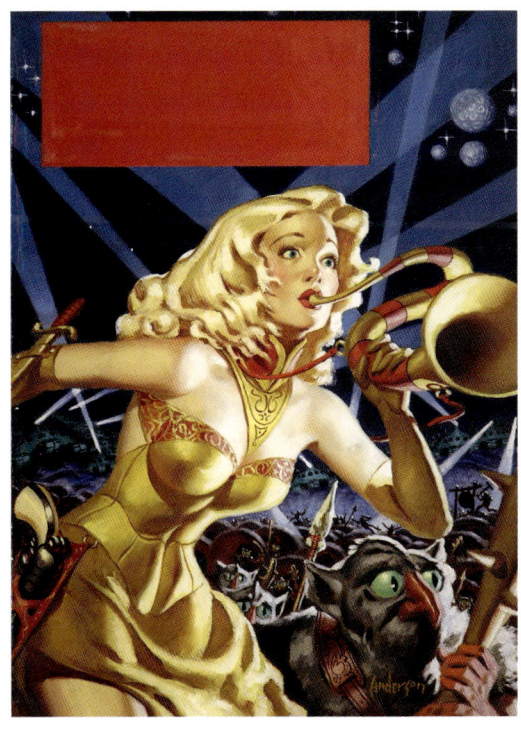

years later, in 2007, Boris's wife Julie Bell was commissioned to do a poster for *Aqua Teen Hunger Force Colon Movie* that referenced her husband's *NatLamp* work, adding mimicry to mockery.

With the advent of digital painting software fantasy art became a popular means of online expression in the 2000s. Amateur artists can be found on sites including Elfwood, DeviantArt, Epilogue, and QuantumMuse, while the surviving greats of the 1970s and '80s draw crowds at Comic-Con International, World Fantasy Convention, World Science Fiction Convention, Lucca Comics and Games, Dragon Con, and a score of smaller "cons" held in cities around the world. Most of these conventions blend fantasy with sci-fi, gaming and liberal doses of cosplay, as fans impersonate their fantasy idols. With fantasy magazines, paperbacks, and album covers mostly in the past, artists now count on collectors to buy prints and original works, finally moving the genre from illustration to fine art by process of elimination and a breakdown of old prejudices. With the rise of online auction houses, nontraditional collectors are tempted to buy what they want, rather than what a gallerist advises, letting the old medial orbitofrontal cortex do the choosing. And once you turn those pleasure centers loose, let's face it: most of us are going to go with those colorful, dynamic works of fantasy that make us all feel so much better.

Opposite: Loot for the Lords of Doom, by H.J. Ward, for the cover of *Spicy Adventure Stories*, August 1940. Oil on canvas, 30 x 21 inches.

Above: Allen Anderson was part of the second wave of pulp artists, arriving in the 1940s to provide covers for a diminishing number of fantasy titles. His style originally resembled his friend Norman Saunders's, but by 1953, when he created this cover for the May issue of *Planet Stories*, it was clearly his own. Oil on board, 35.5 x 50.8 cm (14 x 20 inches).

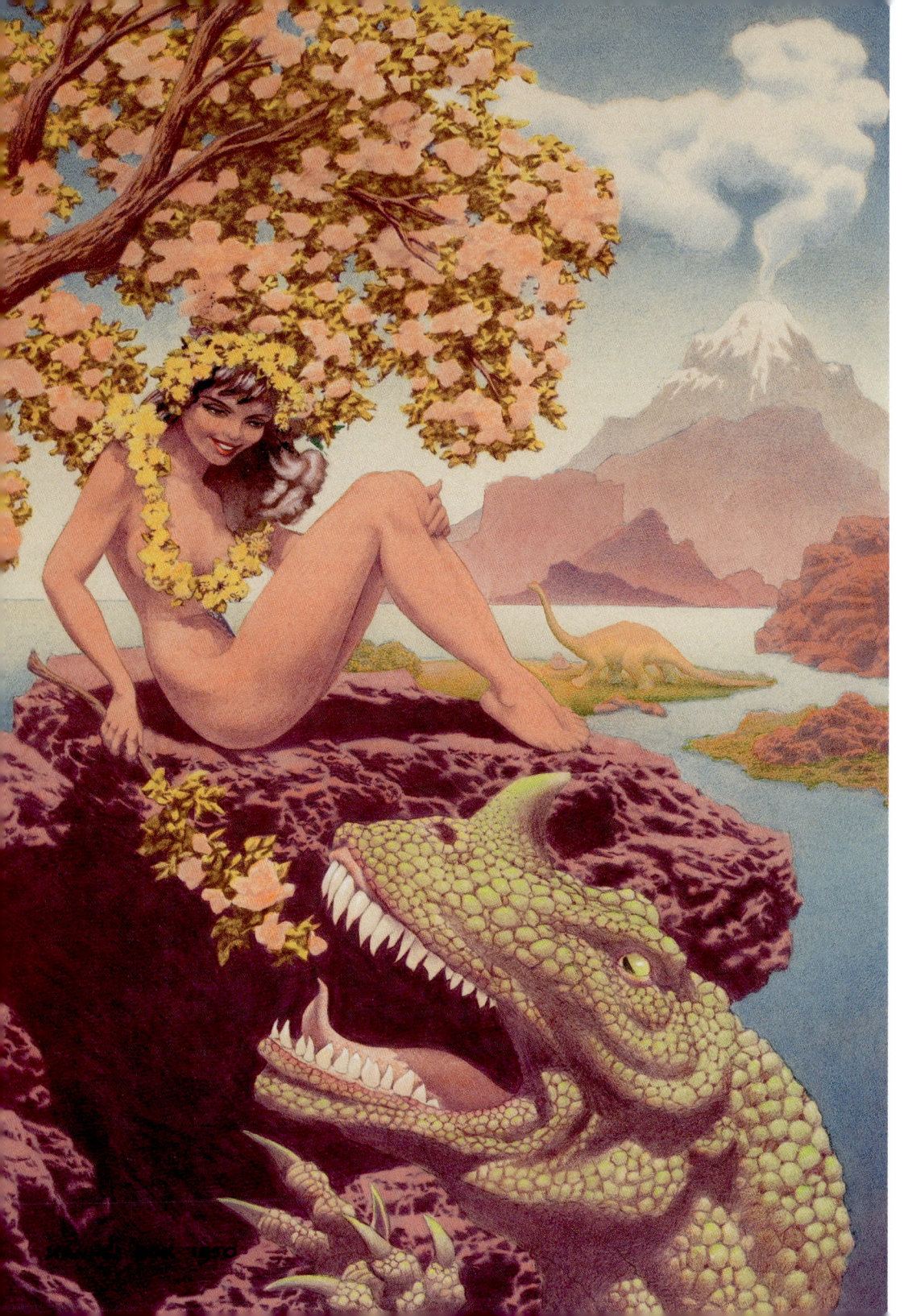

FANTASY: DAMALS, HEUTE UND IMMER

VON DIAN HANSON

2011 hatte die Abteilung für Neuroästhetik am University College London offenbar zu viel Zeit oder Geld oder vermutlich von beidem zu viel, denn sie rekrutierte Dutzende von Leuten ohne besonderes Interesse an Kunst und unterzog die Probanden MRT-Scans, während sie mit Bildern historischer Maler bombardiert wurden. Die Scans maßen die Durchblutung im mittleren Orbitofrontalkortex, jenem Teil des Gehirns, der Genuss und Verlangen zugeordnet ist, um festzustellen, welchen Effekt die Kunst haben würde.

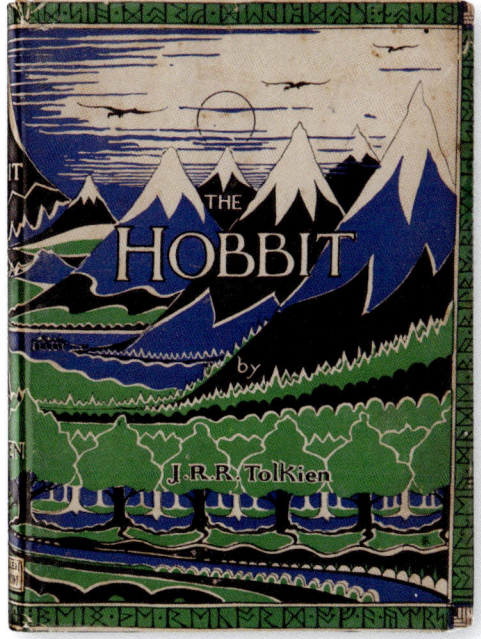

Das Ergebnis war, dass uns bestimmte Arten von Kunst ein großes Wohlgefühl vermitteln – nicht einfach nur ein angenehmes Gefühl, sondern eines, das unseren Empfindungen beim Anblick eines geliebten Menschen ähnlich ist. In der anschließenden Pressemitteilung meinte ein Professor Zeki, dies sei der Beweis dafür, „dass schöne Gemälde dafür sorgen, dass wir uns viel besser fühlen". Besser als was? Und welche Art von Schönheit ist gemeint?

Nun ja. Zwei der drei Künstler, deren Werke die besten Reaktionen hervorriefen, hießen Guido Reni und Jean-Auguste-Dominique Ingres, beides Künstler, deren Werk sich durch satte Farben und heroische Darstellungen muskulöser Männer, üppiger nackter Frauen und mythischer Geschöpfe auszeichnet. Kurz – Fantasykunst.

Den Begriff „Fantasykunst" gab es zu Renis (1575–1642) und Ingres' (1780–1867) Zeiten natürlich noch nicht. Reni malte religiöse, mythische und allegorische Motive. Ingres war ein historischer Klassizist. Wenn diese Künstler Drachen oder geflügelte Rächer malten, erfanden sie

Opposite: Hannes Bok, who got his start illustrating *Weird Tales* in 1939, grew increasingly reclusive and obsessed with astrology as the years passed. He had nearly stopped illustrating at the time he completed this cover for the October 1953 issue of *Science Stories* digest. He would die in poverty 11 years later at age 49. Mixed media on board, 28 x 41.2 cm (11 x 16.25 inches).

Above: The Hobbit, by J.R.R. Tolkien, was first published in 1937, and illustrated by the author. While many technically superior artists would interpret the novel in succeeding years, Tolkien's own illustrations set a tone all followed. Courtesy of Heritage Auctions.

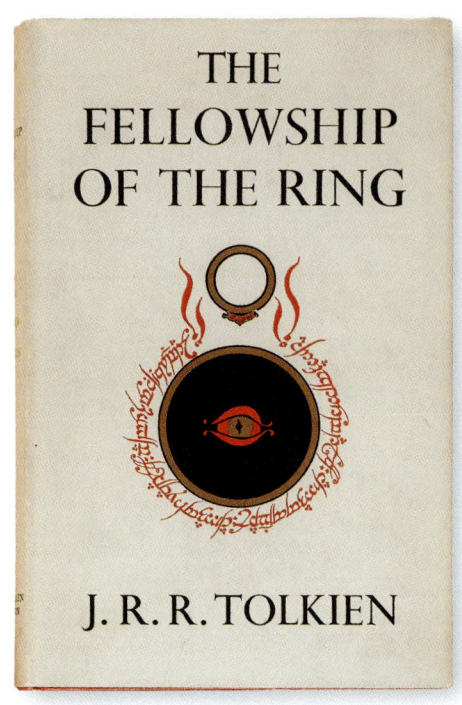

keine neuen Welten, sondern illustrierten eine bestimmte Vergangenheit, die vielen glaubwürdig erschien. Fantasy (Fantasie) wird definiert als „die Aktivität, sich Dinge vorzustellen, die unmöglich oder unwahrscheinlich sind", mit anderen Worten – Fantasykunst konnte es erst geben, nachdem wir den Glauben an Drachen, Hexen, Gorgonen, Greife und Nymphen aufgegeben hatten, allesamt Geschöpfe, denen in vergangenen Jahrhunderten bestimmte und unveränderliche Eigenheiten zugeschrieben wurden. Als der Mensch die Mythologie aufgab, öffnete sich die Tür zur Imagination. Und wie Professor Zeki versicherte, können die Ergebnisse fast mit Liebe, zumindest mit Respekt verglichen werden.

Seit es Kunst gibt, gibt es Kunstsnobismus. Ich stelle mir vor, wie das Neandertalerkerlchen an seiner Höhlenkunst vor sich hin arbeitet und der Cromagnonschnösel hereinschneit und beim Anblick seiner Punkte und Handabdrücke grinst. Sicher, 45.000 vor Christus mochte alle Welt Punkte und Handabdrücke, doch das, was die Massen mögen, wird stets als anspruchslos verachtet – 'tschuldigung, Neandertaler –, und die Cromagnons waren mit ihren figurativen Höhlenbildern von Bison, Elch und jagenden Menschen die vielversprechenden, angesagten Neulinge. Von jenem Tag an, an dem der arrogante Schnösel das Kerlchen tötete und fraß, beherrschte – bis zur Erfindung der Fotografie 1839 – Realismus die Welt der Kunst.

Bevor es Kameras gab, waren die Menschen zur Übermittlung des Erscheinungsbilds von Landschaften, Architektur, Objekten, Tieren, Pflanzen und Individuen auf Künstler angewiesen. Das Talent eines Künstlers wurde danach bemessen, wie akkurat er diese Dinge darstellen konnte, während seine Einkünfte von der Unterstützung durch die Kirche oder wohlhabende Porträtkunden abhängig waren. Selbst Maler wie – der oft als der erste Fantasykünstler gesehen – Hieronymus Bosch und die zuvor erwähnten Reni und Ingres bemühten sich, die Realität wiederzugeben, wenn auch in fantasievoller Form. Mit dem Aufkommen der Fotografie wurde die Darstellung der Wirklichkeit eine preiswerte und nüchterne Angelegenheit, die auch der Mittelklasse und schließlich sogar der Arbeiterklasse zur Verfügung stand. Als sich die fotografische Qualität im späten 19. Jahrhundert immer weiter verbesserte, fanden sich die Maler an zweiter Stelle hinter einer bloßen Maschine wieder und begannen, mit radikalen neuen Kunstformen zu experimentieren.

Zuerst kam der Impressionismus auf, der um 1860 in Frankreich entstand, mit seinen schnellen, augenfälligen Pinselstrichen, mit denen ein flüchtiger Moment eingefangen werden sollte, danach

Above: *The Fellowship of the Ring*, released in 1954, was the first of what would become Tolkien's *Lord of the Rings* trilogy, the most successful fantasy books of all time.

Opposite: *The Lion, the Witch and the Wardrobe* by C.S. Lewis, published in 1950, was the first of seven novels that formed *The Chronicles of Narnia*, second only to *The Lord of the Rings* trilogy in its influence on fantasy fiction.

MASTERPIECES OF FANTASY ART

folgten Neo- und Postimpressionismus, Fauvismus, Kubismus und der Expressionismus, dem es um die Darstellung unverfälschter Emotion ging und der in der Zeit der Weimarer Republik seinen Höhepunkt erreichte und sich lange hielt, bevor die Kunst in die völlige Abstraktion überging. Während jede neue Welle die Kunst immer weiter von der Fotografie abtrennte, separierte sie auch den durchschnittlichen Kunstbetrachter vom Genuss an der Kunst. Der Mainstream verlangte noch immer nach etwas Schönem auf der Leinwand; ein Fan von Edvard Munch war er nicht.

Besser gefiel diesen Betrachtern der gewundene, von der Natur inspirierte Kult des Jugendstils (der Art nouveau), der Handwerk mit Architektur wie auch mit Kunst verband. Es war ein gewissermaßen mit Steroiden aufgepäppelter Realismus, ein lustvoll zugewucherter Garten irdischer Wonnen, ohne den ironischen Horror von Boschs berüchtigtem Meisterwerk. Viele Fantasykünstler nennen den Jugendstil als eine frühe Inspiration, obgleich der Surrealismus der direkteste Vorläufer des Genres ist. Wie die Fantasykunst ist der Surrealismus in erkennbaren Menschen, Orten und Dingen verankert, die in einem Versuch, „die vormals widersprüchlichen Bedingungen von Traum und Wirklichkeit in einer absoluten Realität, einer Superrealität, aufzulösen", wie es André Breton 1924 definierte, verändert werden.

Anders als der Surrealismus entstand Fantasykunst aus kommerziellen Gründen, und deshalb muss sie, abgesehen von ihren Millionen Fans weltweit, um Akzeptanz beim Kunstestablishment kämpfen. Der Kunstsnob ist beleidigt, dass es keiner besonderen Bildung bedarf, um sich an ihr zu erfreuen: Ihr Orbitofrontalkortex leuchtet ohne Aufforderung auf, noch bevor Sie die Signatur oder das Preisschild lesen. Selbst Kinder lieben Fantasykunst; wahrscheinlich war dies die erste auf einem Comic, einem Taschenbuch oder einem Albumcover entdeckte Kunstform, die Sie wirklich mochten. Ob Mœbius, Rodney Matthews, Boris Vallejo oder Rowena Morrill – Sie konnten es

fast spüren, wie sich Ihre Blutgefäße im Gehirn erweiterten, als Ihre Augen über das Bild schweiften, die satten Farben, die fremdartige Landschaft, die idealisierten Menschenfiguren, die bedrohlichen Tiere wahrnahmen und Sie das sichere Gefühl überkam, dass Macht und Recht im dargestellten Kampf obsiegen würden. Da Fantasykunst, unabhängig davon, wie begabt der Künstler ist, hauptsächlich als Auftragsarbeit geschaffen wird, war sie immer zugänglich und, Fluch und Segen zugleich, prominent am Zeitungskiosk ausgestellt. Ist Salvador Dalí begabter als Frank Franzetta, nur weil der eine für Galerien, der andere für EC Comics malte? Viele sehen das so, doch beim Anblick eines der drallen Hinterteile von Franzettas Jungfern mit ihren Grübchen kommt Ihr Gehirn, möglicherweise jedes Gehirn in Schwung, reagiert mit verzückter Endorphinekstase auf Druillets leuchtende Primärfarben und „fühlt sich" beim Betrachten eines Hildebrandt-Drachen gleich „viel besser".

Die Nichteingeweihten können Fantasy und Science-Fiction nicht auseinanderhalten;

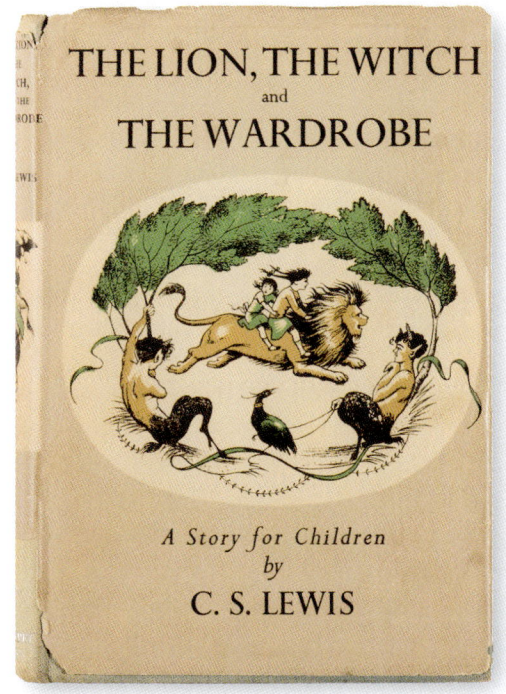

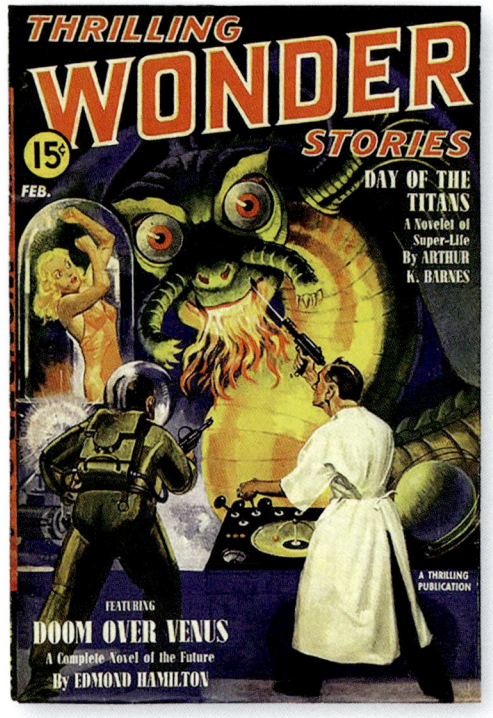

obgleich visuell einander ähnlich, so handelt es sich doch um zwei sehr eigenständige Kunstformen, Science-Fiction ist in Wissenschaft verankert – und daher, wie das Raumschiff Enterprise, denkbar und realisierbar –, während Fantasy mit ihren Zufallstreffern wild gewordener Imagination an keine Regeln gebunden ist. Sollten Sie mal nicht sicher sein, zu welchem Genre ein Kunstwerk gehört, halten Sie sich an die Raketenregel. Gibt es ein Raumschiff? Dann handelt es sich um Science-Fiction. Keine Rakete? Dann halten Sie mal Ausschau nach Drachen, den offiziellen Maskottchen der Fantasykunst.

Drachen kamen unabhängig voneinander in der westlichen wie in der östlichen Mythologie als der ultimative Gegenspieler, das natürliche Gegenstück des menschlichen Helden auf. Frühe Drachendarstellungen glichen eher Schlangen und spiegelten die Angst vor einer bekannten Kreatur wider. Mit der Zeit und künstlerischer Freiheit wuchsen ihnen mehrere Köpfe und Flügel, sie gewannen die Fähigkeit, Feuer zu spucken, und wurden, ganz allgemein, größer und immer abstruser, bis sie sich als auf Anhieb erkennbare Geschöpfe reiner Fantasie verstetigt hatten. Nun passten sie perfekt in die Fantasykunst.

Hieronymus Bosch (um 1450–1516) hatte überhaupt kein Gefühl für Drachen. Seine Bilder von Himmel, Hölle und kultureller Mythologie waren weit fantasievoller als die seiner Zeitgenossen, doch malte er immer noch bloß religiöse Allegorien mit deutlichem Akzent auf der Sünde Lohn, unbenommen von heroischem Kampf. Da war viel Nacktheit, doch wenig Erotik; zahlreiche bedrohliche Geschöpfe, aber keine Drachen.

Der viel später aktive Maxfield Parrish (1870–1966) ist ein offensichtlicherer erster Fantasykünstler. Seine Landschaften sind opulent und traumhaft und bevölkert von schönen Heranwachsenden und anziehenden Jungfrauen. Schlösser kommen gelegentlich vor, und sein Ölgemälde *The Reluctant Dragon* von 1901, als Illustration zu Kenneth Grahames gleichnamiger Geschichte für das 1902 erschienene Kinderbuch *Dream Days* entstanden, ist für das Genre ein gutes Beispiel. Das vielleicht Charakteristischste – er war ein kommerzieller Künstler, der Illustrationen für Zeitschriften, Kinderbücher, Kalender und sogar für Zahnpastaanzeigen lieferte. Sein bekanntestes Gemälde ist *Daybreak*, 1922, das Bild eines ätherischen Gartens, in dem sich zwei

Above: Hugo Gernsback's *Wonder Stories* was selling poorly by the mid-1930s, a victim of competition and the Great Depression. In 1936 he sold the title to the publisher of *Thrilling Detective* and *Thrilling Love Stories* and it became *Thrilling Wonder Stories*. This issue, February 1940, features a cover by Howard V. Brown.

Opposite: Kelly Freas began his fantasy/sci-fi illustration career with a cover for *Weird Tales* in 1950. This cover, titled *Ark of Mars*, was for *Planet Stories*, September 1953. Courtesy of Heritage Auctions.

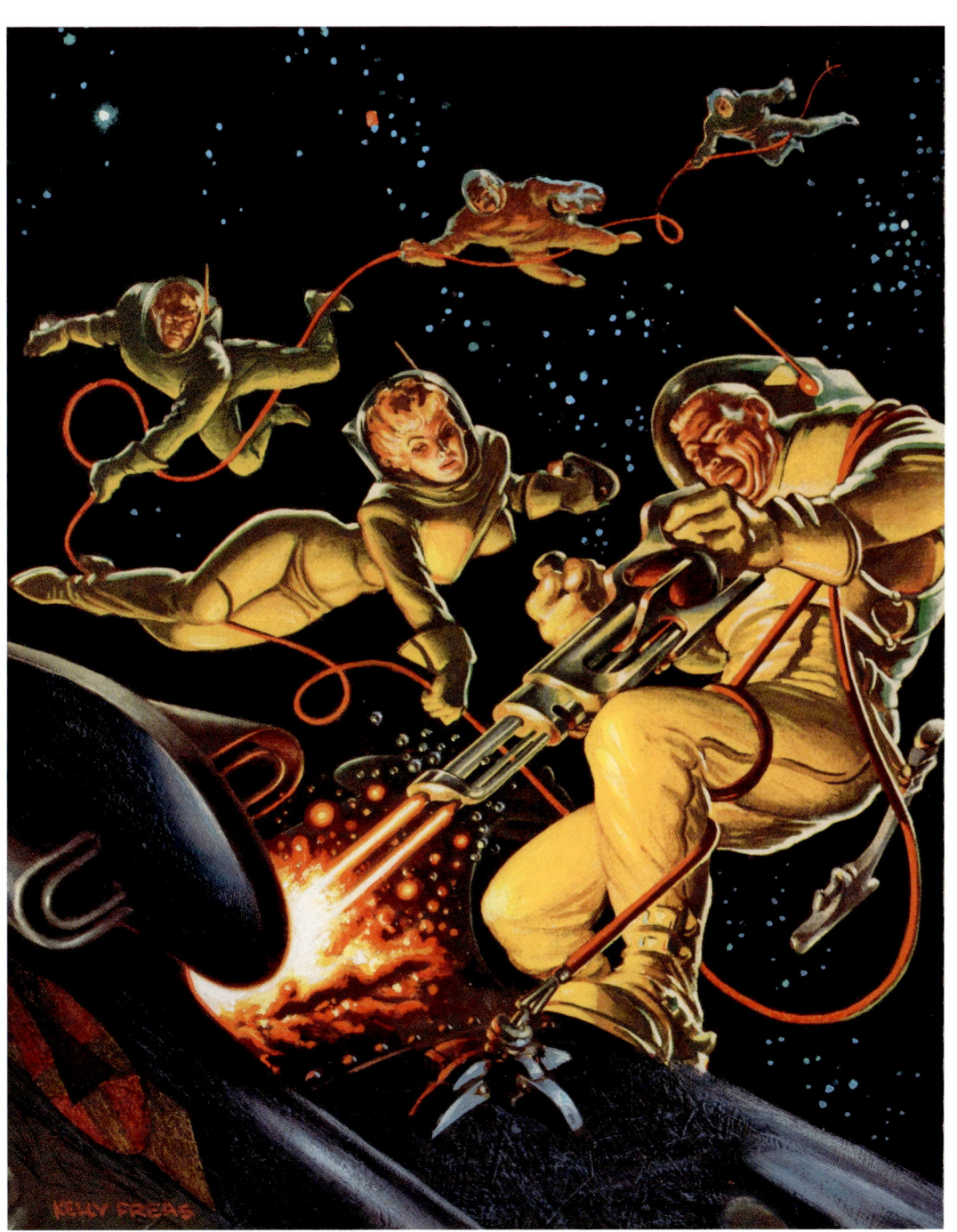

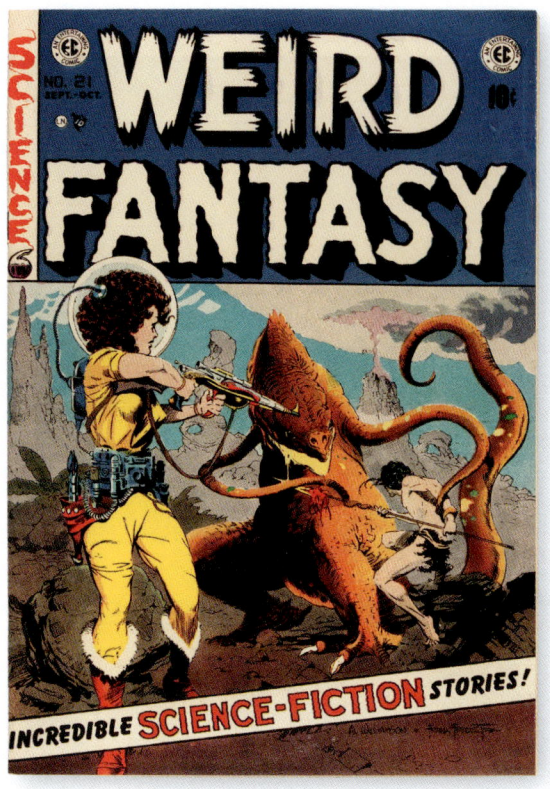

wohlig-träge Frauen aufhalten, und das sich zum meistverkauften Kunstdruck des 20. Jahrhunderts entwickelte. Nur ein Jahr nach seiner Fertigstellung debütierte *Weird Tales*, die erste Zeitschrift der Welt für Science-Fiction- und Fantasygeschichten. Konzipiert von J. C. Henneberger, einem Journalisten, Redakteur und Edgar-Allan-Poe-Fan, hielt sich *Weird Tales* an das Muster anderer, auf Geschichten eines bestimmten Themenkreises spezialisierter Titel: mehrere Kurzgeschichten, gedruckt auf billigem holzhaltigen Papier und mit einem grell gemalten Titelbild ausgestattet. Das erste Cover von *Weird Tales* stammte von Richard Ruh Epperly, einem mittelmäßigen Landschaftsmaler, der gleichwohl das Bild eines unheimlichen Kraken lieferte, der ein Flapper Girl attackierte. Die Qualität der Titelbilder verbesserte sich, zugleich mit den Texten, im Laufe der nächsten Jahre erheblich.

Da Fantasykunst stets in Zusammenhang mit Fantasyliteratur stand, waren bestimmte Autoren entscheidend für die Ausformung des Genres. Mit der Geschichte „The Phoenix of the Sword" (Titelbild von J. Allen St. John) stellte Robert E. Howard in der *Weird-Tales*-Ausgabe vom Dezember 1932 Conan den Cimmerier vor. Ihr folgte in der Ausgabe vom März 1933 „The Tower of the Elephant" (Titelbild von Margaret Brundage), und vor dem Selbstmord des Autors 1936 erschienen noch weitere 17 Conan-Geschichten. Der in einer barbarischen, primitiven Welt lebende Muskelheld traf den Nerv der Leser, denselben, der angeschlagen wurde, als Edgar Rice Burroughs im *The All-Story Magazine* vom März 1912 (Titelbild von Clinton Pettee) mit „Tarzan bei den Affen" debütierte. Beide Figuren entsprachen dem starken, stillen Wahnsinnskerl, der bei einem größtenteils männlichen Pulp-Publikum aus der Arbeiterklasse so beliebt ist. Zum Ausgleich schuf Fritz Leiber Fafhrd – einen großen Barbaren – und den Grauen Mausling – einen kleinen Dieb – als Helden mit mehr menschlichen Schwächen und besseren Sprachfähigkeiten als Conan und Tarzan. Sie nutzten ihren Verstand, um Feinde zu überwältigen, lebten aber gleichwohl in einer komplexen Fantasywelt, die mindestens genauso

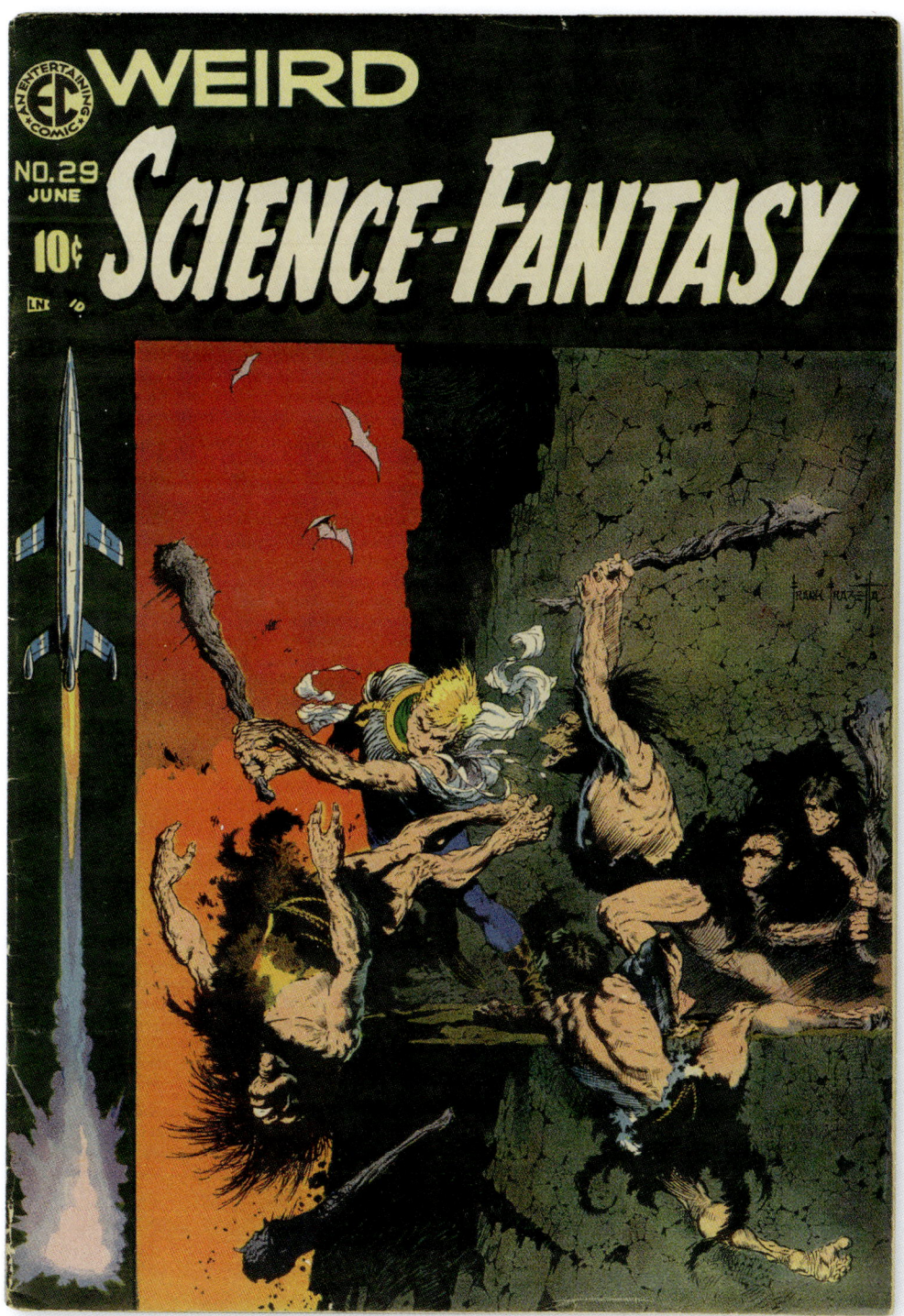

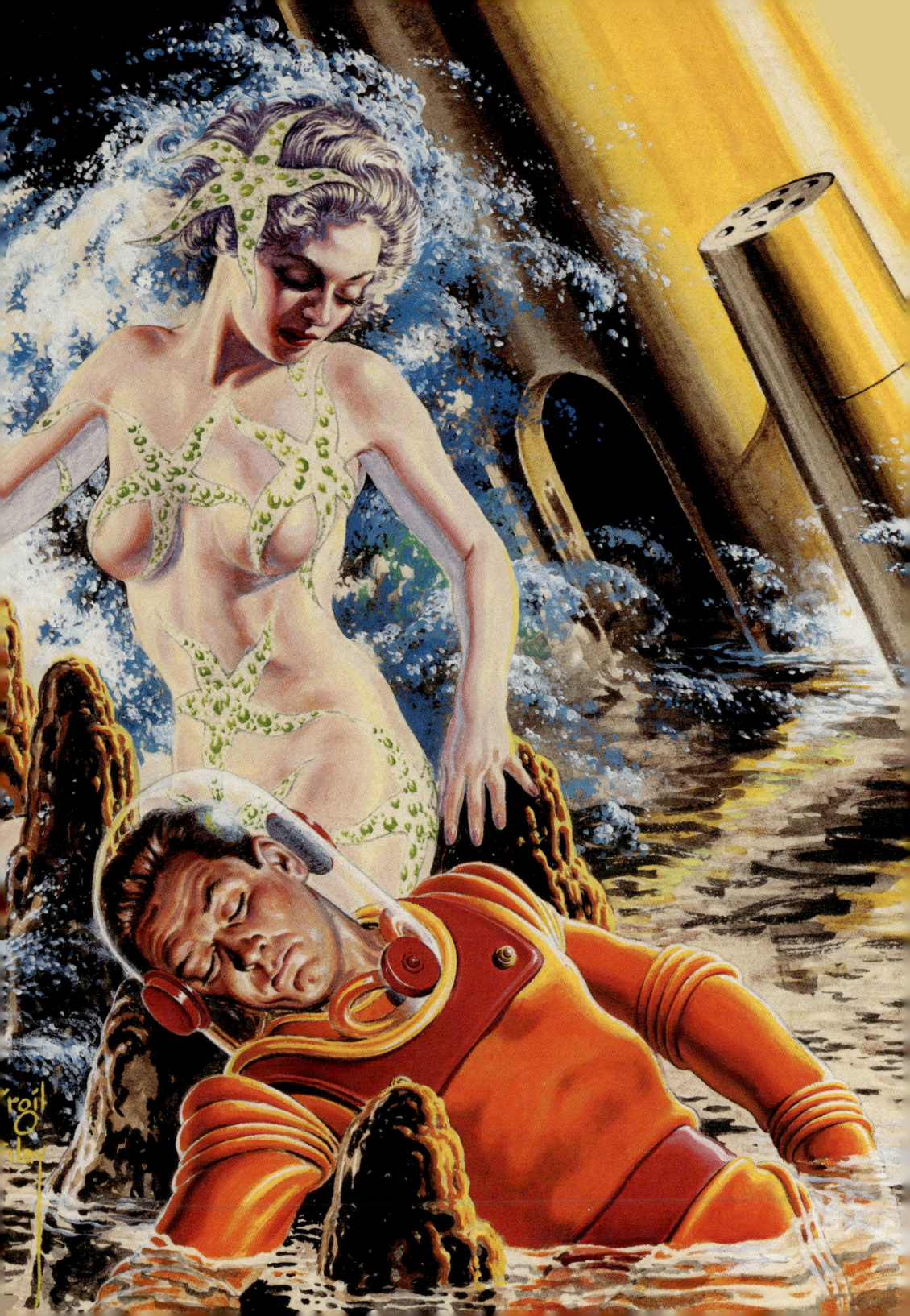

verlockend war wie Conans Cimmeria. Leibers erste von vielen Geschichten um Fafhrd und den Grauen Mausling erschien in der *Unknown*-Ausgabe vom August 1939 neben einem Erzähltext von L. Ron Hubbard, dem künftigen Gründer der Scientology-Kirche, der große Macht über Hollywoodeliten, allerdings wenig über Fantasyfans hat.

Auch H. P. Lovecrafts Cthulhu-Mythos wurde, angefangen mit „The Call of Cthulhu" in *Weird Tales*, Februar 1928, von Fantasy-Pulps hervorgebracht und kultiviert. Seine hoch entwickelte, vielschichtige Vision von den Äußeren Göttern, die ein grausames alternatives Universum beherrschen, das locker aus der griechischen Mythologie abgeleitet ist, der jedoch alle Tugend und Schönheit entzogen wurde, bis zu den 180plus Großen Alten, fantasielosen Schreckgestalten, einschließlich Cthulhu, dem mit verkommenen Menschenkulten gehuldigt wird, wird von Fantasyfans noch immer studiert und analysiert. Die Welt Lovecrafts, in der Menschen kaum Chancen hatten, war furchterregend, doch auch sie bot eine Fantasyfluchtmöglichkeit,

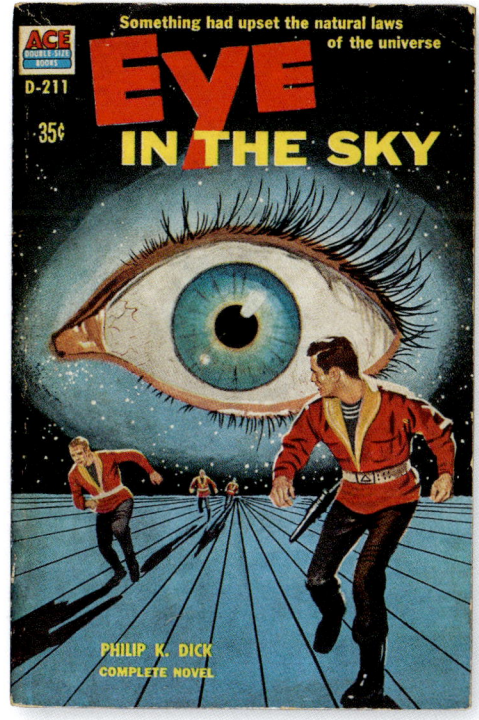

die Gelegenheit, ein Leben wahrzunehmen, das noch weitaus schlimmer war als alles, was die Depression zu bieten hatte. Zu den Autoren, die ihre ersten Texten in den Fantasy-Pulps veröffentlichten und so diese Kunstform beeinflussten, gehören auch Robert Bloch, Ray Bradbury, Arthur C. Clarke, Paul Ernst, Frank Herbert, C. L. Moore und Clark Ashton Smith.

Weird Tales bewies, dass es einen Markt für Fantasygeschichten gab, Fantasykunst jedoch blieb, vor allem aufgrund der begrenzten Budgets der Pulp-Verlage, eine geraume Zeit nur eine Beigabe. Das Papier für die Pulps war billig, doch so saugfähig, dass es sich, außer für Text oder einfache Strichzeichnungen, für den Druck kaum eignete. Das für die Titelseiten benutzte gestrichene Papier gab die Farben gut wieder, war für die Innenseiten allerdings zu kostspielig. Und in Anbetracht der den Massen von den Verlagen traditionell entgegengebrachten Geringschätzung und deren mutmaßlichen Mangels an ästhetischem Geschmack – wozu brauchten sie denn überhaupt Besseres? Anderen Verlagen blieb der Erfolg von *Weird Tales* jedoch nicht verborgen, und so kam Konkurrenz auf, die eine Erneuerung vorantrieb. Hugo Gernsback brachte 1926 *Amazing Stories* auf den Markt und zog damit die Trennlinie zwischen Fantasy und Science-Fiction.

Opposite: Fantasy magazine covers grew sexier in the 1950s as community standards loosened, particularly on art as opposed to photography. This stunning Virgil Finlay oil on board, titled *Viridi, Goddess of Nature*, was created for the cover of *Other Worlds Science Stories*, June 1956. 20.3 x 29.2 cm (8 x 11.5 inches). Courtesy of Heritage Auctions.

Above: Eye in the Sky is Philip K. Dick's ninth written, fourth published novel, released by Ace Books in 1957, at a time when the struggling author claimed he couldn't pay the fees on an overdue library book. The sales were helped immensely by this cover by Ed Valigursky.

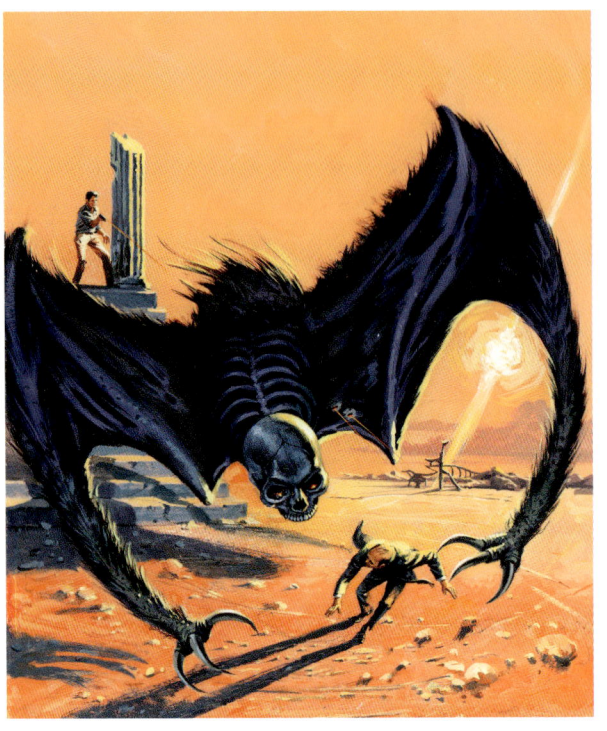

Gernsback war ein wunderbarer durchgeknallter Typ, der als Vater der Science-Fiction – oder der Scientifiction, wie er es selbst am liebsten bezeichnete – bekannt werden sollte. Zudem war er ein Tech-Nerd, vielleicht der erste seiner Art, mit einer ausgeprägten Begeisterung für Elektrizität und Radio. Seine 1913 zum ersten Mal publizierte Zeitschrift *Electrical Experimenter*, der 1920 *Science and Invention* folgte, schwelgte in unglaublicher Wissenschaft und bezog schon früh Erzählliteratur ein. Beide Titel waren auf Papier bester Qualität gedruckt, mit farbigen Titelbildern, die die verrückten Randbereiche wissenschaftlicher Forschung feierten und zu denen 1925 auch ein anschauliches „End of the World"-Cover gehörte. Für Gernsback war es also nur ein kleiner Schritt, die *Amazing Stories* herauszugeben, eine Zeitschrift, die sich ausschließlich der

„Scientifiction" widmete und der 1929 *Air Wonder Stories* und *Science Wonder Stories* folgten, die beide 1930 zu schlicht *Wonder Stories* zusammengelegt wurden.

Im Gegensatz zu den *Weird Tales*, die im Digest-Format daherkamen, hatten die *Amazing Stories* und die *Wonder Stories* das volle Zeitschriftenformat. Was die literarischen Texte anbelangt, so tendierten sie zu Nachdrucken von Texten von H. G. Wells, Jules Verne und Edgar Allan Poe, doch die Titelbilder von Frank R. Paul waren neu und vorzüglich und trugen dazu bei, dass er sich als der erste große Science-Fiction-Künstler etablieren konnte.

Doch für jene, die die mythologischen Ursprünge wahrer Fantasykunst liebten, malte Paul einfach ein wenig zu viele Raumschiffe, zumal für die thematisch auf Flug ausgerichteten *Air Wonder Stories*. Nun kam wieder die Diskussion „möglich gegen unmöglich" ins Spiel: Egal, wie fantasievoll ein Raumschiff gestaltet ist, Raumfahrt basiert auf soliden wissenschaftlichen Grundsätzen, während Drachen derlei fehlt. Science-Fiction ist mechanisch, Fantasy organisch, SF beschäftigt sich mit Schöpfungen der Menschen, Fantasy mit denen eines Alien-Gottes. Zudem spielen sich Science-Fiction-Geschichten in der Regel in der Zukunft ab, während sich Fantasy auf Welten

Above: An appropriately scary cover for *Creepy,* August 1969, by Vic Prezio. Oil on board, 52 x 43.8 cm (20.5 x 17.25 inches). Courtesy of Heritage Auctions.

Opposite: Roy Krenkel is best known for his interpretation of Edgar Rice Burroughs's stories for Ace Books in the 1960s, bringing renewed interest to the writer with a young audience. This painting was for the cover of the 1962 edition of *At the Earth's Core,* 25.4 x 35.5 cm (10 x 14 inches)

MASTERPIECES OF FANTASY ART

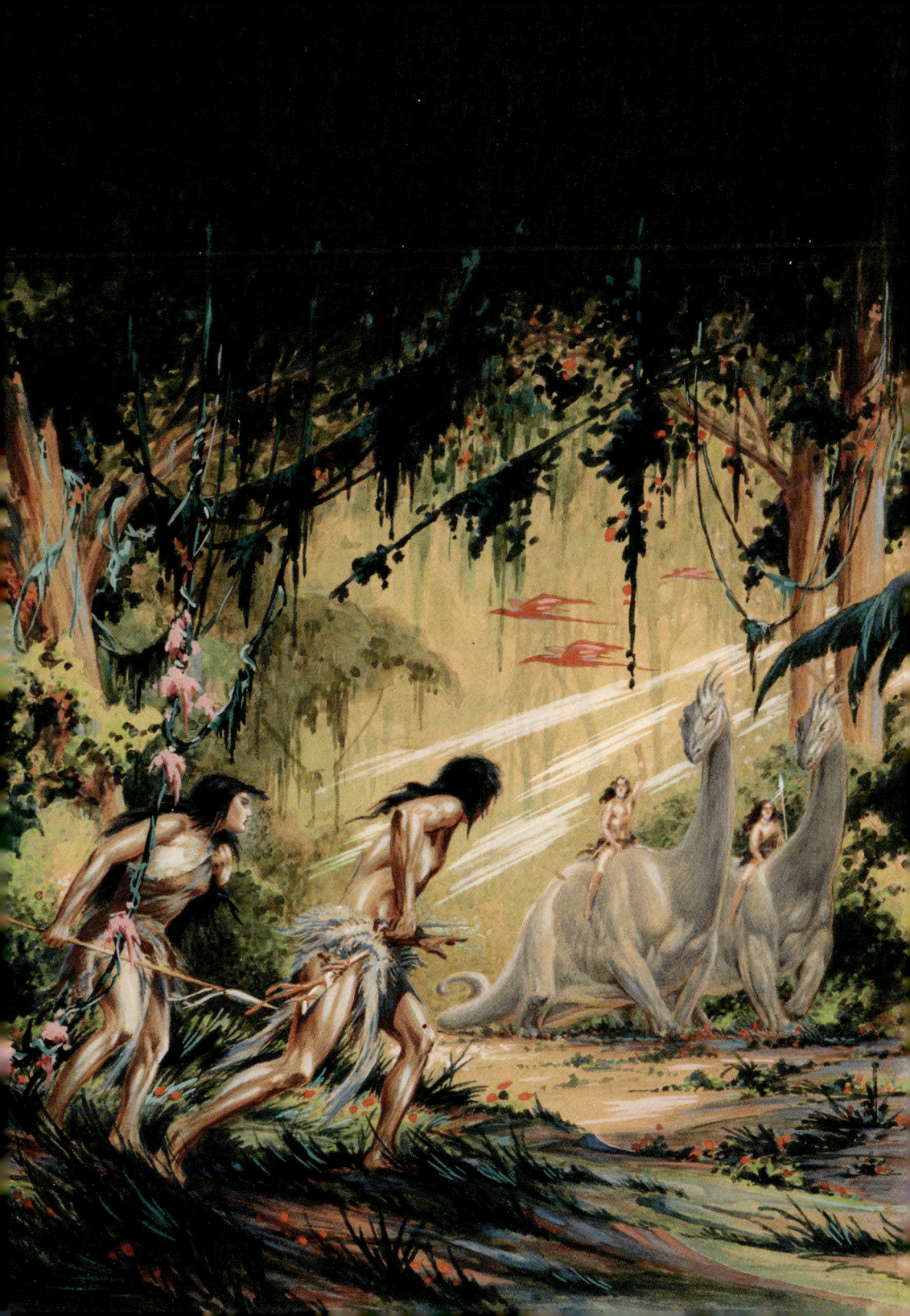

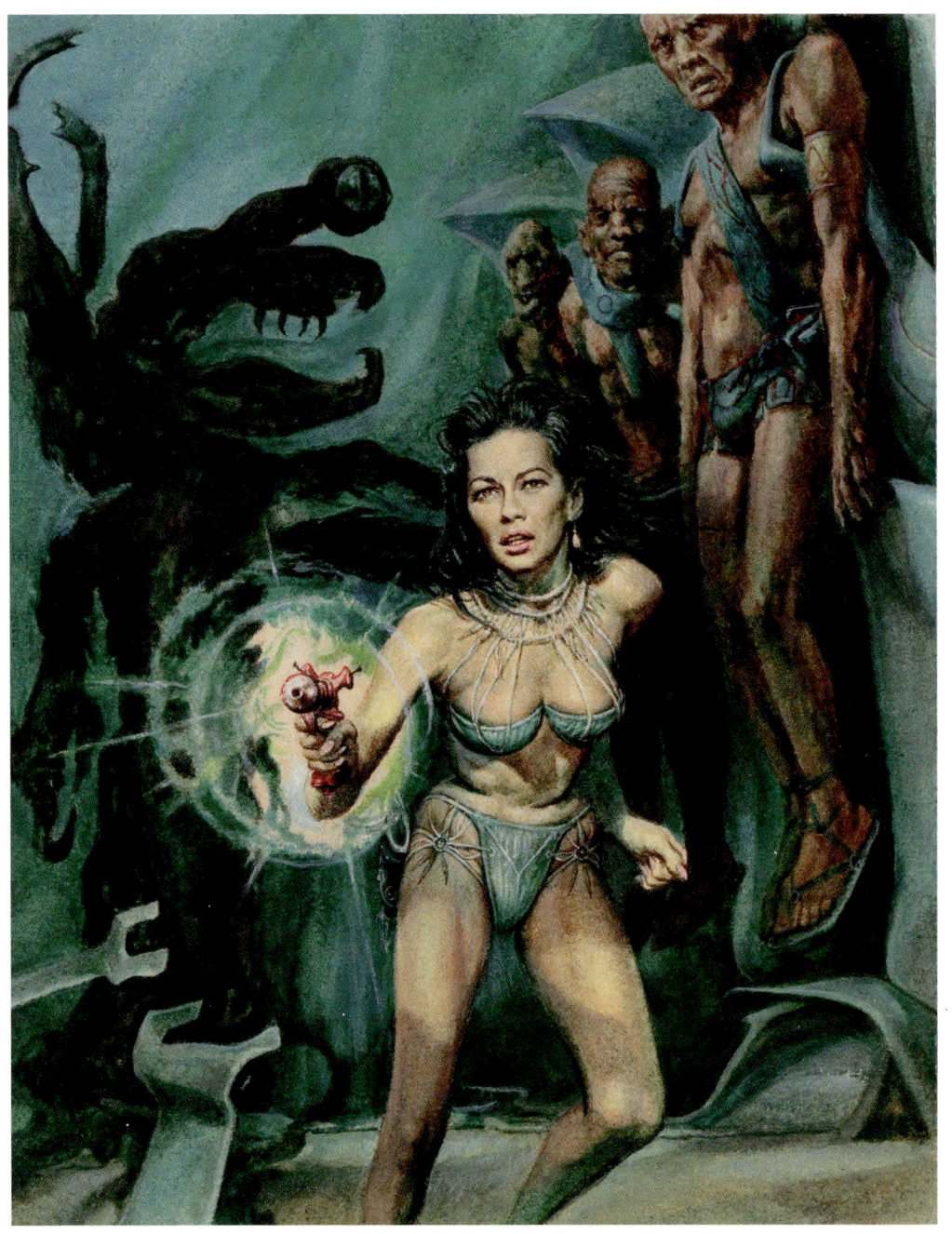

Above: Josh Kirby cover painting for the English edition of Edgar Rice Burroughs's *Escape From Venus*, 1966.

Mixed media on board, 15.2 x 12 cm (6 x 4.75 inches). Courtesy of Heritage Auctions.

MASTERPIECES OF FANTASY ART

einer fernen Vergangenheit bezieht. Wie sonst sind so viele zerfledderte Pelzgewänder zu erklären? Dass auch Hightechbikinis vorkommen, ist unbenommen.

Mit *Weird Tales* und *Amazing Stories* öffneten sich die Fantasy-Pulp-Schleusentore weit. *Astounding Stories of Super-Science* kamen 1930 erstmals auf den Markt, 1931 folgten *Strange Tales of Mystery and Terror* und *Miracle Science and Fantasy Stories*; *Terror Tales* 1934; *Marvel Science Stories* 1938; *Unknown, Strange Stories, Startling Stories, Mystery Tales, Fantastic Adventures* und *Planet Stories* erschienen 1939 und *Fantastic Novels* und *Astonishing Stories* 1940. Die Entbehrungen der Depressionsjahre machten Fantasy zu einer willkommenen Fluchtmöglichkeit, und mit zunehmender Konkurrenz stellten die Zeitschriften nicht nur talentierte neue Autoren vor, sondern bemühten sich auch um auffälligere Titelbilder besserer Qualität. Damit meine ich mehr Bilder von Frauen mit weniger Kleidung.

Weird Tales, seit jeher Wegbereiter, waren die Ersten, die Fantasykunst sexualisierten. Ein Wildwuchs an Pulp-Titeln sorgte in den frühen 1930er-Jahren dafür, dass die Verkaufszahlen sanken. Dies führte dazu, dass viele Verlage die Heftpreise von 25 auf 10 Cent heruntersetzten. Für die vielen arbeitslosen Amerikaner war sogar das noch eine nicht unerhebliche Ausgabe für etwas, das nicht lebensnotwendig war. Sex allerdings war schon immer konjunktursicher: Männer zahlen für dieses Vergnügen, selbst wenn sie hungern. Einige Verlage hatten in den 1920er-Jahren mit „pikanten" Pulps experimentiert, die meist mit schlechten Texten und Pin-up-Titelbildern von mäßiger Qualität aufwarteten. 1932 jedoch taten sich Frank Armer und Harry Donenfeld, die wichtigsten Verleger solcher Pulps, zusammen und gründeten Super Magazines, einen Verlag, der bald schon in Culture Publications umbenannt wurde. Im gleichen Jahr suchte die Künstlerin Margaret Brundage das Büro des *Weird-Tales*-Herausgebers Farnsworth Wright auf. Es ist fraglich, ob die Verleger Armer und Donenfeld Wright, der nur Redakteur war, überhaupt kannten, doch es ist gut möglich, dass ihre künstlerischen Entscheidungen von seinen inspiriert wurden. 1934 brachten Culture Publications *Spicy Detective Stories, Spicy Adventure Stories* und *Spicy Mystery Stories* – ihre Fantasyversion – heraus, alles Pulps mit verhalten provokativen Texten und eindrucksvoll sexy Titelbildern, die die talentierten Illustratoren Harry Lemon Parkhurst und Hugh Joseph Ward gemalt hatten. Diese Pulps hatten sofort Erfolg und waren für 25 Cent pro Exemplar schnell ausverkauft, während andere Hefte für 10 Cent an den Kiosken liegen blieben, und sie setzten die erste sexuelle Revolution im amerikanischen Verlagswesen in Gang.

Weird Tales jedenfalls machten den Anfang. Brundages Debütcover erschien auf der Ausgabe vom September 1932. Das Originalpastell war so pikant, dass es für den Druck zensiert wurde. Wurde sie darum gebeten, eine Frau oben ohne darzustellen? Die Geschichte hat uns dazu keinen Hinweis überlassen, aber von Juni 1933 bis August 1936 lieferte sie jedes Titelbild für die *Weird Tales*, 39 insgesamt, stach damit den hochbegabten, doch weniger reißerischen J. Allen St. John aus und etablierte die Nackte nachdrücklich als grundlegende Figur der Fantasykunst. 1936 kamen als Kollegen Virgil Finlay, Hugh Rankin und der elegante Hannes Bok hinzu, bis der New Yorker Bürgermeister Fiorello La Guardia 1938 schließlich gegen delikate Titelbilder von Zeitschriften an den Kiosken einschritt. Obgleich er es vor allem auf Zeitschriften von Culture Publications abgesehen hatte, waren auch Fantasy-Pulps, insbesondere die *Weird Tales*, ebenfalls betroffen, und in Sachen Sex war bis nach dem Krieg erst einmal wieder alles beim Alten. Martin Goodman, den Mann, der 1939 Marvel Comics gründete, schreckte die Razzia nicht ab; er brachte im Mai 1938 die *Marvel Science Stories* mit einem so schlüpfrigen Inhalt heraus, dass sich Leser sogar beschwerten – die prachtvollen sexy Cover von Norman Saunders hingegen akzeptierten sie. Goodman milderte alles ein bisschen ab und benannte die Publikation um in *Marvel Tales*. 1939 beschritten

Mystery Tales und die *Planet Stories*, in denen Ray Bradbury seinen ersten Text unterbringen konnte, mit beständigen Auftritten von Amazonen, Weltraumvixen und Bondage-Titelbildern von H. W. Scott, Allen Anderson und Alexander Leydenfrost den gleichen Weg. Dies alles schaffte es, durch La Guardias Netz zu gehen.

Nach dem Zweiten Weltkrieg, der Pin-ups zu einer akzeptablen amerikanischen Kunstform erhob, setzte sich eine generelle Lockerung der Verbote von La Guardia durch. Neue Künstler wie Robert Gibson Jones, Lawrence Sterne Stevens, Edmund Emshwiller, Frank Kelly Freas, Harold McCauley und Chesley Bonestell – nach dem die jährlich verliehenen Chesley-Preise für Science-Fiction- und Fantasy-Kunst benannt sind – traten auf den Plan. Zugleich kamen neue Zeitschriften auf den Markt, darunter *Avon Fantasy Reader*, 1947, *A. Merritt's Fantasy Magazine*, 1949, *Out of This World Adventures*, 1950, *10 Story Fantasy*, 1951, und *Imaginative Tales*, 1954. Die kriegsbedingten Rationierungen von Papier hatten allerdings den meisten der alten Fantasytitel ein Ende bereitet, nur *Weird Tales*, *Startling Stories*, *Thrilling Wonder Stories*, *Amazing Stories*, *Fantastic Adventures*, *Famous Fantastic Mysteries* und *Planet Stories* waren übrig geblieben. Gegen Ende des Jahres 1955 hatten sie alle ihr Erscheinen eingestellt, mit Ausnahme der *Imaginative Tales*, die 1958 aufgeben mussten, und der *Amazing Stories*, die sich bei verschiedenen Verlagen noch bis 2005 durchkämpften.

Pulp starb, weil Amerika seinen Geschmack an Kurzgeschichten verlor. Das Fernsehen griff die eher visuell Orientierten ab, während sich das Lesepublikum für Taschenbücher mit längeren literarischen Texten entschied. Diejenigen, die Fantasy-Pulps wegen der Titelbilder kauften, neigten nun eher zu Comics, insbesondere nachdem EC Comics 1950 seine „New Line" auf den

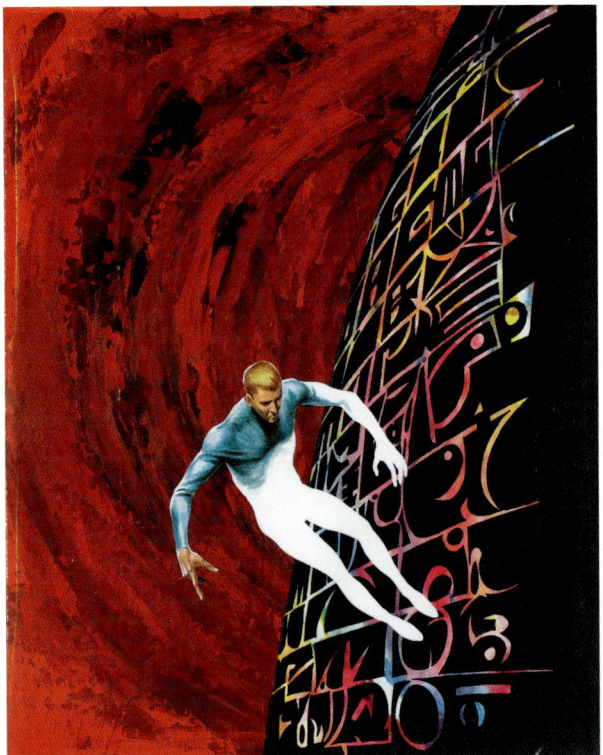

Markt gebracht hatte. *Weird Science* und *Weird Fantasy* hatten das gleiche Publikum im Blick wie die Fantasy-Pulps, doch mit Illustrationen auf jeder Seite. Wally Wood wurde 1952 regelmäßig die Gestaltung der Cover anvertraut, während Roy Krenkel, Al Williamson und ein junger Frank Franzetta die Innenseiten der Comics lieferten. ECs „New Line" war sehr populär, nur leider kurzlebig. Die billigen Fantasytaschenbücher, die erstmals in den frühen 1960er-Jahren erschienen, erfreuten sich dagegen einer größeren Lebensdauer.

Einige der Fantasyautoren schrieben schon immer längere Texte und produzierten Bücher. *The Hobbit, or There and Back Again* von J.R.R. Tolkien wurde 1937 veröffentlicht. Der Vater der Fantasyliteratur selbst war von den Büchern des schottischen Autors George MacDonald beeinflusst, der einmal meinte: „Ich schreibe nicht für Kinder, sondern

für die Kindlichen, ob sie nun fünf, fünfzig
oder fünfundsiebzig Jahre alt sind." Tolkien
nahm sich das zu Herzen und schrieb ebenfalls
für ein erwachsenes Publikum, malte das Cover
für *The Hobbit* und schuf auch mit Feder, Blei-
stift, Farbe und Buntstiften Illustrationen für die
Innenseiten. Diese Bilder reichten zwar nicht
an das Kaliber seiner Texte heran, doch dienten
sie den vielen Fantasykünstlern, die später
seine 1954 erschienene *Herr-der-Ringe*-Trilogie
illustrierten, als Richtschnur. Diese Bücher und
die zwischen 1950 und 1956 veröffentlichten
sieben Bände der *The Chronicles of Narnia* von
C.S. Lewis trugen zu einer zweiten Welle von
Fantasyfans bei, was Autoren und Künstler
beflügelte und die Nachfrage nach Texten von
Romanlänge verstärkte.

Ein weiterer einflussreicher Förderer dieser
neuen Welle war Ace Books, ein 1952 gegründe-
ter Lieferant von billigen Taschenbüchern. 1953
veröffentlichte Ace Books seinen ersten Science-
Fiction-Roman, A.E. van Vogts *The World of
Null-A*, zusammen mit dessen *The Universe Maker*. Innerhalb von zwei Jahren und angespornt
vom Erfolg von Tolkien und Lewis, publizierte
der Verlag mehr Science-Fiction und Fantasy als
Bücher irgendeines anderen Genres und hatte
damit regelmäßig Aufträge an Künstler für die

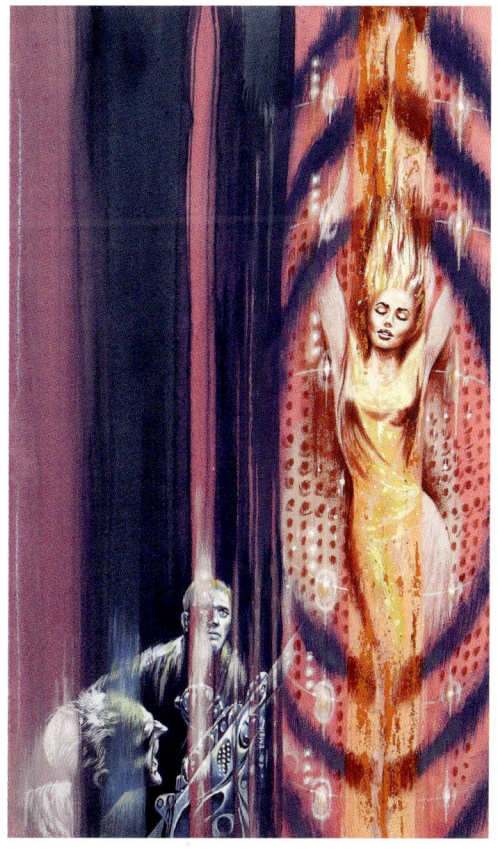

Gestaltung von Titelbildern zu vergeben. Die verbliebenen ehemaligen Pulp-Gestalter, vor allem Ed
Emshwiller, Virgil Finlay, Frank Kelly Freas und Roy Krenkel, wetteiferten um diese Aufträge. Einen
Volltreffer landete Krenkel, der einen Vertrag für die Tarzan-Cover von Ace Books bekam. 1962
empfahl er seinen Freund Frank Franzetta für Illustrationen von Innenseiten. Da Edgar Rice Burroughs keine Copyright-Ansprüche mehr hatte, war Tarzan eine beliebte Möglichkeit für Reprints,
und bald schon griff die Konkurrenz, der Fantasyverlag Canaveral Press, diese Werke auf, ersetzte
den eher abstrakten Mahlon Blaine und beauftragte Franzetta mit der Gestaltung der Cover. 1966,
als Lancer Books, ebenfalls ein Taschenbuchverlag, die Rechte an Conan erwarb, war Franzetta bereits so populär, dass er einen Vertrag für die Titelbilder aushandeln konnte, der ihm alle Rechte an
seinen Bildern beließ – beispiellos für den Markt für Auftragsarbeiten der 1960er-Jahre, als Verlage
die Originalwerke nach Gebrauch üblicherweise wegwarfen. Aufgrund dieser Klausel, da er nun
wusste, dass sie ihm gehören würden, war Franzetta so inspiriert, dass er einige der bedeutendsten

Opposite: Jack Gaughan, like Freas and Emshwiller, was a master of mid-century modern fantasy illustration, as here for the cover of Philip K. Dick's *Solar Lottery*, 1968. Acrylic on board, 48.2 x 39.3 cm (19 x 15.5 inches). Courtesy of Heritage Auctions.

Above: Edmund Emshwiller brought a modern sophistication to fantasy illustration in the 1960s, exemplified by this cover for Isaac Asimov's Lancer paperback novel *End of Eternity*, 1963. Gouache on board, 28 x 47 cm (11 x 18.5 inches).

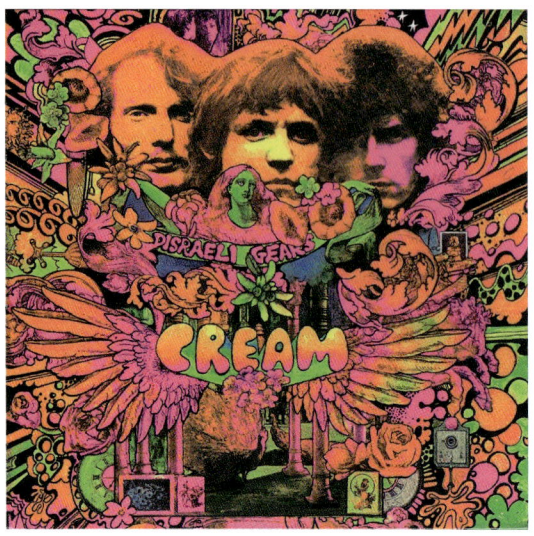

Werke seiner Karriere malte. Von dieser Buchreihe wurden mehr als zehn Millionen Exemplare verkauft, zu einem guten Teil dank dieser tollen Titelbilder. Zudem wurde ein Franzetta-Archiv eingerichtet, das bis zum heutigen Tag aufbewahrt wurde.

Unterdessen waren die Fantasytitel von EC 1954 abgeschossen worden, nachdem die amerikanische Regierung Comics – insbesondere die von EC – verantwortlich gemacht hatte, zu Jugendkriminalität anzustacheln. Als Reaktion darauf gründete ein Zusammenschluss von Verlegern die Comics Code Authority, die ihre eigenen Produkte überwachen sollte. Fortan war die Benutzung von Begriffen wie „Horror", „Terror" und „Weird" (sonderbar) auf allen Comictitelseiten geächtet. EC wehrte sich, doch ohne die Freigabe der Comics Code Authority wurde kein Titel von den Vertriebsfirmen akzeptiert, und so musste EC seine anstößigen Hefte einstellen. Die Fans trauerten, bis – zehn Jahre später – Warren Publishing *Creepy* und kurz darauf *Eerie* und *Vampirella* herausbrachte, die direkt von EC-Horrorcomics inspiriert waren, im vollen Zeitschriftenformat erschienen und sich damit der Zensur der Comics Code Authority nicht zu unterwerfen hatten.

Die Cover von *Creepy* waren groß, strahlend und glänzend, perfekt für Reproduktionen in satten Farben. Die Innenseiten waren zwar nur schwarz-weiß, aber was für ein herrliches Schwarz-Weiß, komplex und äußerst detailreich, gestaltet von den alten Ehemaligen von EC: Wally Wood, Roy Krenkel, Al Williamson und Frank Franzetta, zu denen sich bald Richard Corben, Jeff Jones, Bernie Wrightson, Don Maitz, Ken Kelly und viele andere gesellten. Diese jüngere Gruppe war bei EC groß geworden, aber auch, da die 1960er-Jahre langsam in die 1970er-Jahre übergingen, in einem sich verändernden moralischen Klima aufgewachsen. Psychedelische Kunst, die versuchte, halluzinatorische Visionen nachzuempfinden, kam auf, verband sich eng mit Fantasy und brachte ein hybrides Genre hervor, das anfangs seinen besten Ausdruck auf den Covers von Plattenalben fand.

Der Australier Martin Sharp war einer der Wegbereiter dieses Stils. Eher als Pop- denn als Fantasykünstler gesehen, bereiteten seine Cover für die Cream-Alben *Disraeli Gears* und *Wheels of Fire*, die 1967 bzw. 1968 herauskamen, den Weg für die offensichtlicheren Fantasycover, die Roger Dean und Rodney Matthews für Yes, Gentle Giant, Asia, Scorpions, Nazareth, Magnum und Thin Lizzy schufen. Wie bei den Pulp-Magazinen und den Taschenbuchromanen wurde die Coverkunst

Above: Australian Martin Sharp was a psychedelic renaissance man, not only producing some of the first pop art album covers, but co-writing songs for Cream, and illustrating the epic hippie magazine *OZ*. He claimed his cover for Cream's second studio album, *Disraeli Gears,* was meant to capture the band's "warm fluorescent sound."

Opposite: Barbara Remington had never read *Lord of the Rings* when she was contracted to create covers for Ballantine Books' first paperback editions in 1965. Tolkien was perplexed by what he took to be pumpkins in the trees and lions in this triptych. Mixed media on paper, 65.4 x 35.5 cm (25.75 x 14 inches). Courtesy of Heritage Auctions.

MASTERPIECES OF FANTASY ART

für Plattenalben im Grunde nur als Werbemasche gesehen, als verführerische Verpackung, mit der die Inhalte verkauft werden sollten. Schallplattenalben jedoch boten einen viel größeren Malgrund als die Titel eines Taschenbuchromans. Ich erinnere mich, wie meine Freunde und ich diese Kunst als Teenager studierten, und weiß noch, dass ich Alben auch nur wegen der Gestaltung der Cover gekauft habe; das Osibisa-Album mit dem fliegenden Elefanten auf dem von Dean gestalteten Cover fällt mir dabei ein. Es dauerte nicht lange, da begriffen die Plattenfirmen, dass das Äußere genauso wichtig wie das Innere war, und so gaben sie fortan immer mehr Fantasycover in Auftrag.

Dann, im Dezember 1974, kam eine Zeitschrift aus Frankreich heraus, die für die Fantasykunst einen weiteren gewaltigen Schritt nach vorn bedeutete. *Métal Hurlant*, unterschiedlich als kreischendes oder heulendes Metall übersetzt, wurde in Paris von zwei Künstlern konzipiert, Philippe Druillet und Jean Giraud aka Mœbius, einem Redakteur/Autor, Jean-Pierre Dionnet, und – besonders wichtig für jede Künstlergruppe – einem Manager für das Geschäftliche, Bernard Farkas. Gemeinsam waren sie als Les Humanoïdes Associés bekannt. In der Welt der schlampig gemachten belgisch-französischen Comics war *Métal Hurlant* ein hochwertiges Magazin. Noch wichtiger – es war fantastisch, psychedelisch, futuristisch, geistreich, sexy und unleugbar französisch. Europa hatte im Kampf um die Fantasyvormacht endlich einen großen Hund, und dieser Hund fraß die gesamte Konkurrenz auf. Mœbius führte den unergründlichen, wortlosen Arzach ein, der auf einem mutierenden Pterodactylus hockte und über eine öde fremdartige Landschaft rauschte, und Major Grubert, den unerschrockenen Erforscher der Hermetischen Garage. Druillets Werk, in dessen Mittelpunkt Lone Sloane stand, war härter, bedrohlicher und in prächtigen Primärfarben gehalten, im Gegensatz zu Mœbius' verträumten, unkrautartigen Pastellen. Die Zeitschrift erschien zuerst vierteljährlich, ab der neunten Ausgabe jedoch monatlich und bot damit auch anderen europäischen Künstlern eine Plattform, darunter Enki Bilal, Yves Chaland, Serge Clerc, Guido Crepax, Jean-Claude Gal, H. R. Giger, Gaetano Liberatore, Milo Manara, Masse, Chantal Montelier, Jean-Michel Nicollet, Joost Swarte und Alain Voss, sowie dem Chilenen Alejandro Jodorowsky und den Amerikanern Richard Corben und Bernie Wrightson. 1976 traf der Verleger des amerikanischen Humormagazins *National Lampoon* mit den Machern von *Métal Hurlant* in Paris zusammen und

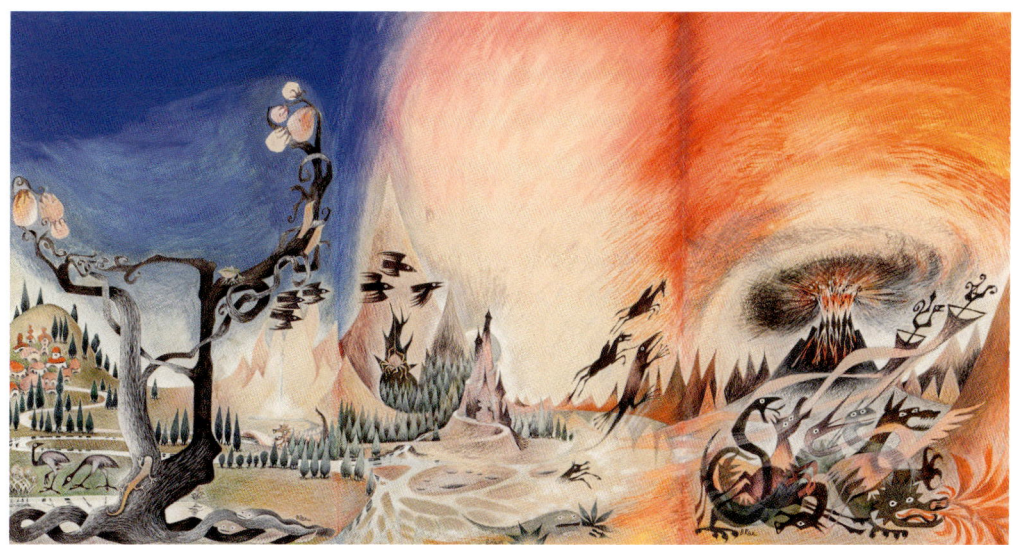

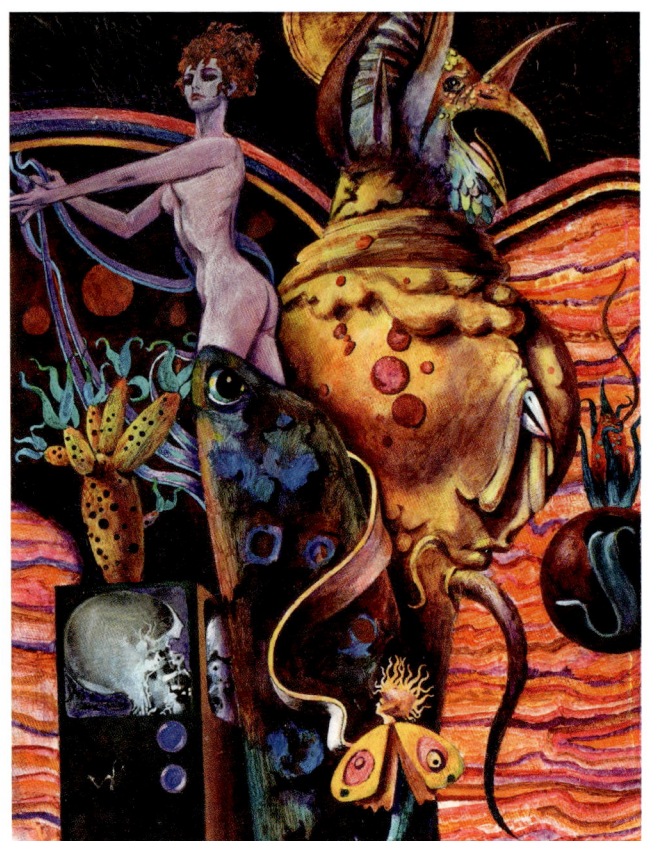

erwarb die Lizenz für eine US-Ausgabe mit dem Titel *Heavy Metal*, die im April 1977 erstmals erschien. Anfangs bot *Heavy Metal* nur die französischen Inhalte mit übersetzten Texten. Damit wurden die Produktionskosten niedrig gehalten und sofort ein Gewinn erwirtschaftet. Mit der Zeit jedoch entwickelte sich *Heavy Metal* zu einem eigenständigen Magazin mit Beiträgen von internationalen Künstlern wie Chris Achilleos, Julie Bell, Simon Bisley, Charles Burns, Clyde Caldwell, Howard Cruse, Alex Ebel, Alex Horley, Jeff Jones, Michael Kaluta, Paul Kerchner, Rod Kierkegaard, Karl Kofoed, Walter Simonson, Lorenzo Sperlonga, Arthur Suydam, Stefano Tamburini, Boris Vallejo, Luis Rojo und vielen anderen.

Obwohl sie bei einem harten Kern fanatischer Fantasycomicfans immer beliebt waren, hatten beide Zeitschriften mit einem Wandel des Geschmacks zu kämpfen, mit Managementstreitigkeiten und der unvermeidbaren Kritik am zunehmend sexualisierten Inhalt. Manche Fans der Fantasykunst waren an, sagen wir mal, den hypertrophischen Genitalien von Richard Corbens Den nicht interessiert oder an der extremen Gewalt von Tamburini/Liberatores RanXerox. Für dieses Publikum ergab sich die freundlichere parallele Entwicklung der *Herr-der-Ringe*-Kultur, eingeführt von den Gebrüdern Hildebrandt, John Howe, Alan Lee und Ted Nasmith und, maßgeblicher noch, im Jahr 1974 durch das Aufkommen des Rollenspiels *Dungeons & Dragons*, das von dieser Tolkien-Welt inspiriert war.

D&D begann klein und einfach – im Grunde als Würfelspiel für erfahrene Kriegsspieler – und brachte 1977 das sehr viel komplexere und straff strukturierte *Advanced Dungeons & Dragons* hervor. Beide Spiele boten Spielern die Möglichkeit, angeleitet von einem Verliesmeister (Spielleiter), in die Rollen verschiedener Fantasyfiguren zu schlüpfen, die in einem fremdartigen Reich gemeinsam Abenteuer bestehen. D&D reizte zu visueller Interpretation, zuerst in Form roher Strichzeichnungen im Originalspielerhandbuch. Später, als Jim Roslof 1975 die Gestaltung des Handbuchs übernahm und Clyde Caldwell, Jeff Easley, Larry Elmore, Jim Holloway, Keith Parkinson, Harry Quinn und Tim Truman als künstlerische Mitarbeiter engagierte, wurde es mit anspruchsvolleren farbigen Covers und Illustrationen der Innenseiten ausgestattet. Mit jeder neuen Ausgabe kamen auch neue Künstler hinzu, darunter Brom, Douglas Chaffee, Ralph Horsley, Todd Lockwood, Erik Olsen, rk post, Wayne Reynolds und Eva Widermann.

Schließlich, 1993, führte der in Seattle angesiedelte Spieleentwickler Wizards of the Coast *Magic: The Gathering* ein, das erste Fantasykartenspiel. D&D, dessen Mutterfirma 1997 von Wizards geschluckt wurde, produzierte zu diesem Zeitpunkt hochwertige illustrierte Spielehandbücher, doch mit nur einem Gemälde auf dem Cover und sehr wenigen ganzseitigen Abbildungen auf den Innenseiten, während für *Magic* jedes Jahr 600 neue Karten erschienen. Auf jeder dieser Karten war ein Originalkunstwerk abgebildet, und der Name des Künstlers wurde an prominenter Stelle genannt. Das machte es einfach, unter den fünf Millionen internationalen Spielern eine Fangemeinde aufzubauen.

Die *Magic*-Karten inspirierten zu anderen erfolgreichen Sammelkartenspielen, darunter das Dragon Bell Super Card Game, Yu-Gi-Oh! und das Final Fantasy Trading Card Game, die allesamt aus Japan stammten, wo im 21. Jahrhundert für Fantasykunst und -künstler eine Blütezeit einsetzte.

Und dann ist da noch Hollywood. *Star Wars* feierte seine Premiere 1977, im gleichen Jahr wie Advanced Dungeons & Dragons, und bewies eindeutig, dass es auch jenseits der kitschigen B-Movies der 1950er- und 1960er-Jahre einen Markt für Science-Fiction- und Fantasyfilme gab. 1978 folgte dann Ralph Bakshis Trickfilmversion von *Der Herr der Ringe*, ein zugegebenermaßen zwar mangelhafter Streifen, der von den Fans der Bücher jedoch begierig aufgenommen wurde. Die Plakate für beide Filme entwarf Thomas Jung, der Veteran unter den künstlerischen Gestaltern Hollywoods, doch George Lucas beauftragte die Gebrüder Hildebrandt damit, eine neue Version von Jungs *Star-Wars*-Original zu schaffen, die für den Start des Films in Großbritannien die Droiden R2D2 und C-3PO und einen angedeuteten Kopf Darth Vaders hinzufügten.

Nach dem überwältigenden Erfolg von *Star Wars* brachten die Studios Fantasykünstlern (langsam) mehr Respekt entgegen, obwohl Ridley Scott mit der 20th Century Fox zu kämpfen hatte, bis er 1978 H. R. Giger als künstlerischen Gestalter für *Alien* engagieren konnte. Die Verantwortlichen des Studios waren der Ansicht, dessen Werk sei für die Leinwand zu grotesk. Doch Scott blieb beharrlich, und es entstand ein Geschöpf, das elegant, furchterregend und künstlerisch überzeugend zugleich war. Mit dem Film gewann Giger internationalen Zuspruch – und einen Oscar für die besten visuellen

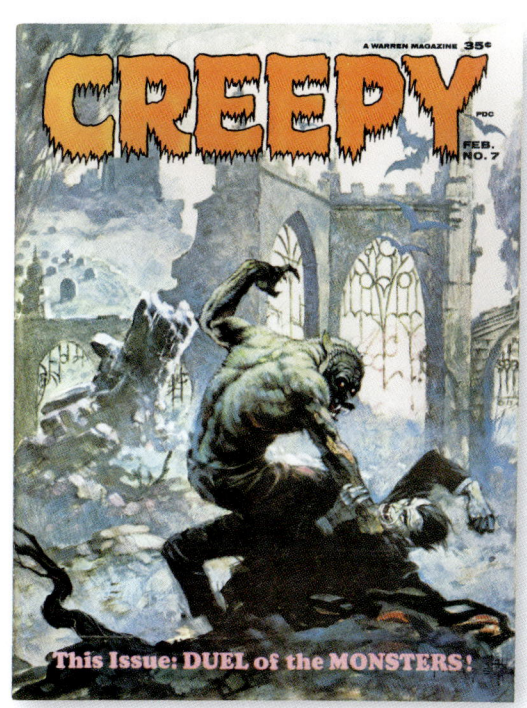

Effekte. Bakshi nahm davon Notiz und tat sich für seinen nächsten Trickfilm, *Fire and Ice*, 1983 mit Frank Frazetta zusammen. Desgleichen heuerte Peter Jackson für die *Herr-der-Ringe*-Trilogie 1998 die Fantasykünstler John Howe und Alan Lee an und sorgte dafür, dass sein Produktionsteam die Entwurfszeichnungen der Künstler für die Ausgestaltung und die Population von Mittelerde getreulich umsetzte.

Und dann ist da Alejandro Jodorowskys *Dune*. Mœbius schuf für diesen berühmtesten nie entstandenen Fantasyfilm 3.000 Produktionszeichnungen, dazu kamen noch Arbeiten von Giger und Chris Foss. Während das Drehbuch sich zu einer Vorlage für einen Film von geschätzten 14 Stunden auswuchs, der 15 Millionen Dollar kosten sollte – 1974 eine erhebliche Summe –, nahmen die Studios eines nach dem anderen Abstand von diesem Projekt. Übrig blieb nur ein prachtvolles und legendäres Buch. Das *Dune*-Buch, das sämtliche Kunstwerke enthält, hatte Jodorowsky auf eige-

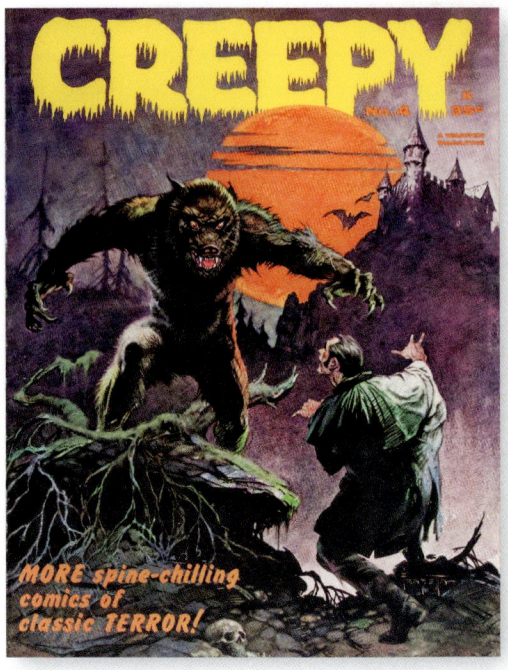

ne Kosten in einer Auflage von nur zehn Exemplaren drucken lassen, die er den Studios übergab, die er für die Finanzierung des Films ansprach. Acht Exemplare bleiben verschwunden; die letzten beiden gehören Mœbius' Witwe Isabelle Giraud und Jodorowsky. Der Film und das Buch waren Thema des 2013 erschienenen Dokumentarfilms *Jodorowskys Dune*.

Neben der Mitarbeit an Entwürfen wurden nach *Star Wars* viele Fantasykünstler für Plakate eingespannt. Die Hildebrandts setzten ihre Arbeit mit der Gestaltung von Plakaten für *Clash of the Titans*, 1981, und für *The Secret of NIMH*, 1982, fort, Bruder Tim malte zudem das Motiv für das Poster zu *The Deadly Spawn*, 1983. Jeff Jones wurde 1981 für *Dragonslayer* erwählt. Frank Frazetta schuf 1982 das Previewposter für *Conan der Barbar*, nachdem er früher bereits mehrere Jahre lang Plakate für Hollywoodkomödien gestaltet hatte, darunter *What's New Pussycat* (1965), *Hotel Paradiso* (1966) und *After the Fox* (1968). Mœbius gestaltete 1982 das Plakat für *Les Maîtres du Temps* (The Time Masters). Und lange vor all diesen Aufträgen malte Philippe Druillet 1968 drei Plakate für die Vampirfilme des französischen Regisseurs Jean Rollin: *Sexual-Terror der entfesselten Vampire*, *Die nackten Vampire* und *Die Folterkammer des Vampirs*. Er verantwortete auch ein bizarres französisches Poster für den amerikanischen Film *Der Name der Rose*, auf dem er die für ihn typischen finsteren Gesichter mit einem Porträt von Sean Connery kombinierte. Der Künstler,

Above: Creepy No. 4, 1965. This issue included the origins of Uncle Creepy and this great Frank Frazetta cover. Courtesy of Heritage Auctions.

Opposite: The Executioner, by Frank Frazetta, for the cover of *Creepy* No. 17, 1967. At the time Frazetta's contract allowed him to create the art and a writer would make a story to go with it. The story accompanying this cover was "Heritage of Horror." Oil on canvas-wrapped board, 1967, 48.8 x 39.3 cm (19.25 x 15.5 inches). Courtesy of Heritage Auctions.

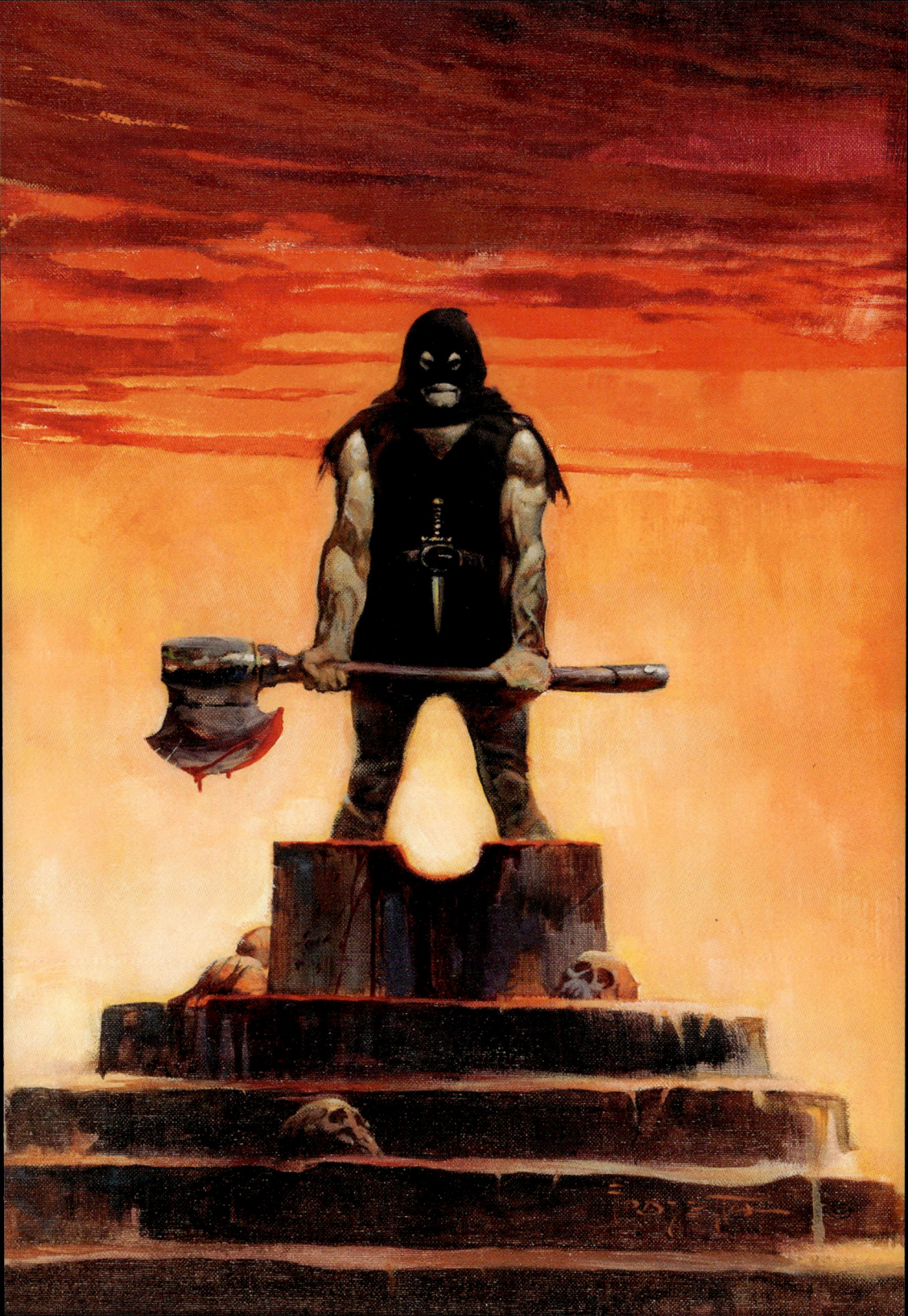

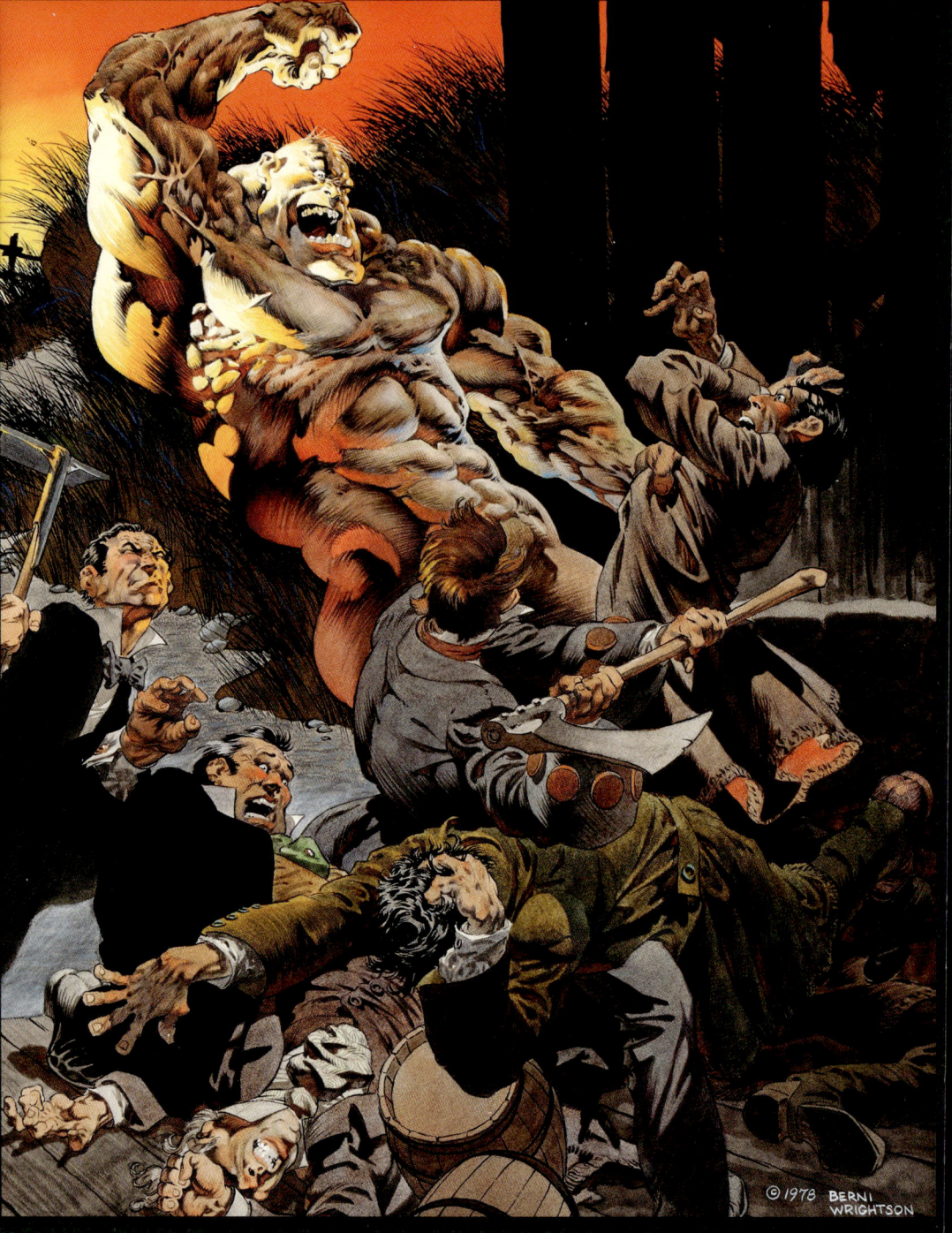

der rasch den Spitzenplatz unter den Künstlern einnahm, die all die Fantasyfilmposter gestalteten, hieß allerdings Boris Vallejo.

Im gleichen Jahr, in dem *Star Wars* debütierte, schnappte sich Vallejo den Posterauftrag für *Barbarella,* und 1980 produzierte er in Absprache mit Coca-Cola eine Serie von Plakaten für *The Empire Strikes Back,* denen sich in schneller Folge 1982 *The Sword and the Sorcerer* und *Q,* 1983 *Deathstalker,* 1985 *Barbarian Queen* und 1988 das Plakat für den geschmacklosen Streifen *Naked Warriors* anschlossen. Wie zur Verspottung dieser heroischen Bilder zog er 1983 den Posterauftrag für die Komödien *National Lampoon's Vacation* und 1985 den für *European Vacation* an Land. Viele Jahre später, 2007, wurde Boris' Frau Julie Bell mit dem Plakat für *Aqua Teen Hunger Force Colon Movie* beauftragt, das auf das ihres Mannes für *NatLamp* verwies und dem Spott noch Mimikry hinzufügte.

Mit dem Aufkommen digitaler Malsoftware wurde Fantasykunst in den 2000er-Jahren zu einer populären Onlineausdrucksmöglichkeit. Auf Webseiten wie Elfwood, DeviantArt, Epilogue und QuantumMuse sind Amateurkünstler zu finden, während die überlebenden Großen der 1970er- und 1980er-Jahre auf Kongressen wie der Comic-Con International, der World Fantasy Convention, der World Science Fiction Convention, der Lucca Comics and Games, der Dragon Con und einer Reihe kleinerer Tagungen in Städten auf der ganzen Welt die Massen anziehen. Die meisten dieser Kongresse bringen Fantasy mit Science-Fiction, Games und – da Fans gerne ihre Fantasyidole darstellen – großzügigen Parts an Kostümspielen zusammen. Da Fantasyzeitschriften, Taschenbücher und Albumcover hauptsächlich in der Vergangenheit eine Rolle spielten, zählen die Künstler heute auf Sammler, die Drucke und Originalwerke kaufen, und sorgen schließlich dafür, dass das Genre nach der Beseitigung und dem Zerbröseln alter Vorurteile mittlerweile nicht mehr nur als Illustration, sondern als ernst zu nehmende Kunst gesehen wird. Mit dem

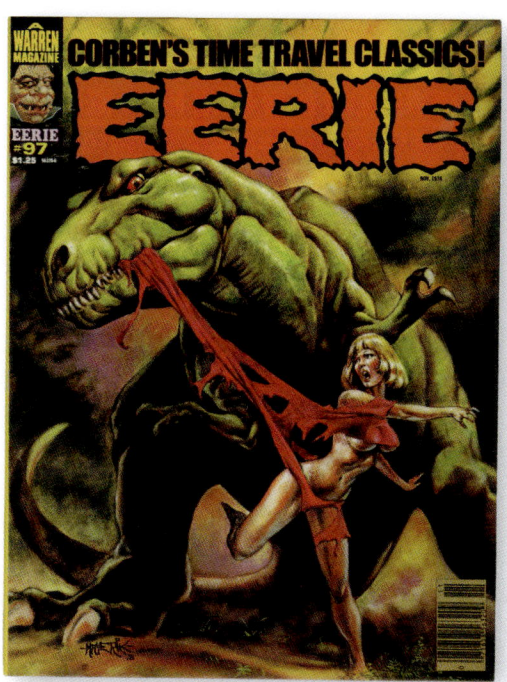

Aufkommen von Onlineauktionshäusern sind nichttraditionelle Sammler versucht, das zu kaufen, was sie wollen, statt das zu kaufen, was ein Galerist rät, und die Auswahl dem alten medialen Orbitofrontalkortex zu überlassen. Und wenn man diese Vergnügungszentren erst einmal losgelassen hat, seien wir ehrlich: Die meisten von uns werden sich für diese bunten, dynamischen Werke der Fantasie entscheiden, die uns alle so viel besser fühlen lassen.

Opposite: Bernie Wrightson, co-creator of Swamp Thing, is equally renowned for his horror and fantasy work at Warren Publishing. In 1978 he created the character Captain Sternn, an amoral spaceship captain with various sidekicks, one of whom was Hanover Fiste, seen here in a painting from Wrightson's oversized 1978 portfolio *Apparitions.* Colored ink on illustration board, 45.7 x 55.8 cm (18 x 22 inches).

Right: Warren Publishing's *Eerie Yearbook,* 1978, with cover by Val Mayerik.

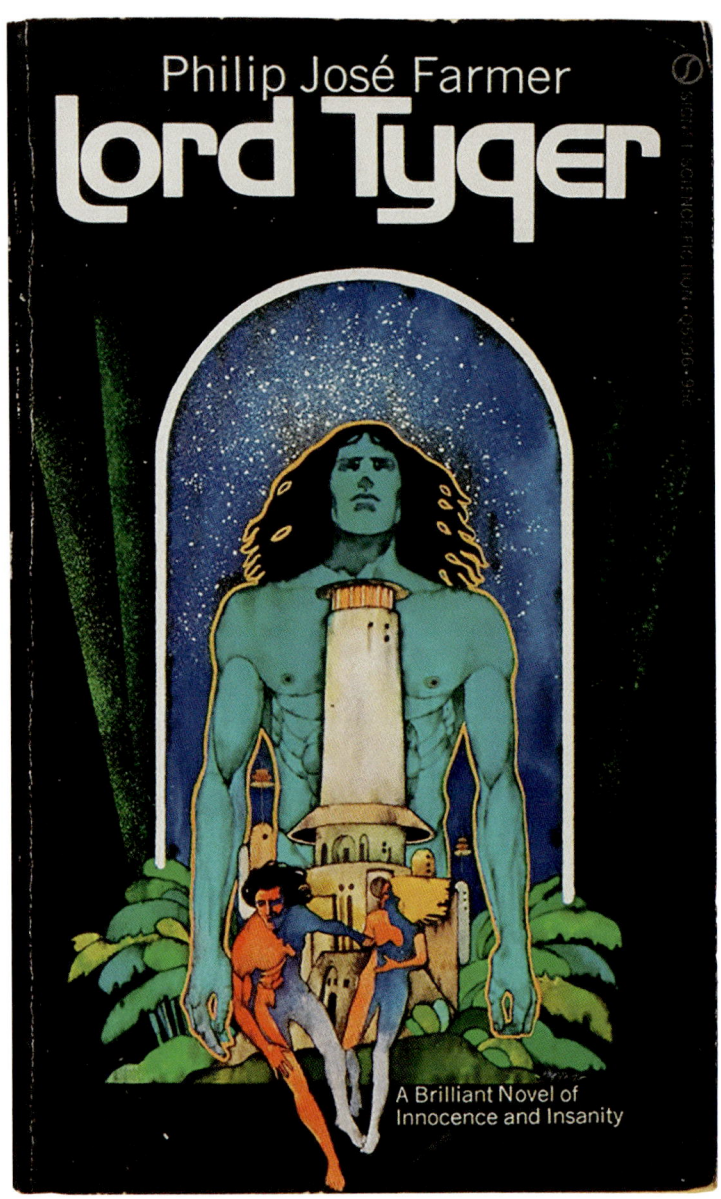

Philip José Farmer

Lord Tyger

A Brilliant Novel of
Innocence and Insanity

Above: Philip José Farmer's 1972 science fiction
classic *Lord Tyger*, a sort of homage to Tarzan, with
a cover by Bob Pepper.

Opposite: Josh Kirby was an English artist best known
for his fantasy film posters, including *Star Wars:
Return of the Jedi*, *The Beastmaster* and *Krull*. In the 1960s
and '70s he also illustrated a number of fantasy book
covers; this for the 1970 Ace Double *The Gates of Time/
Dwellers of the Deep*. Mixed media on board,
14.6 x 24.7 cm (5.75 x 9.75 inches).

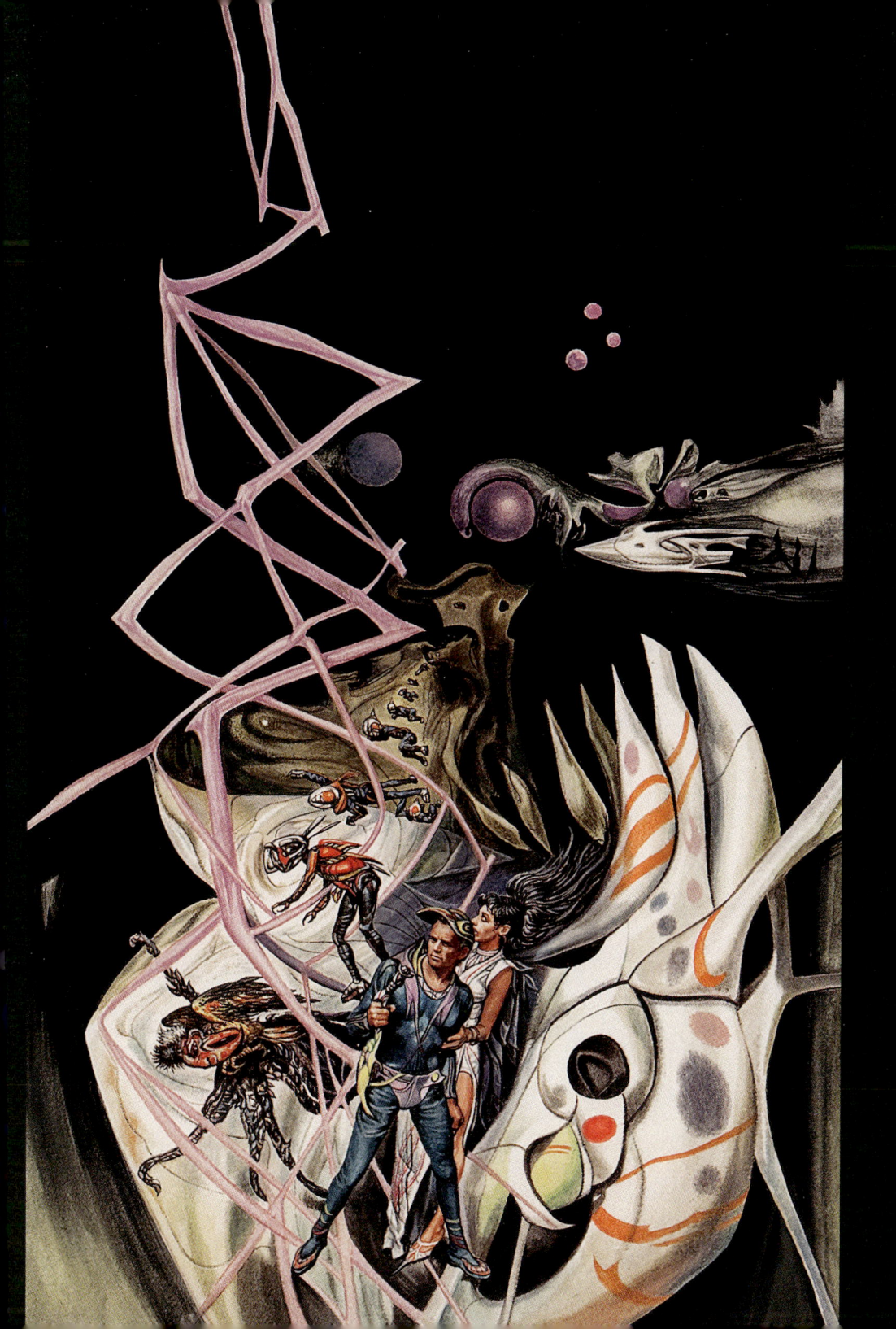

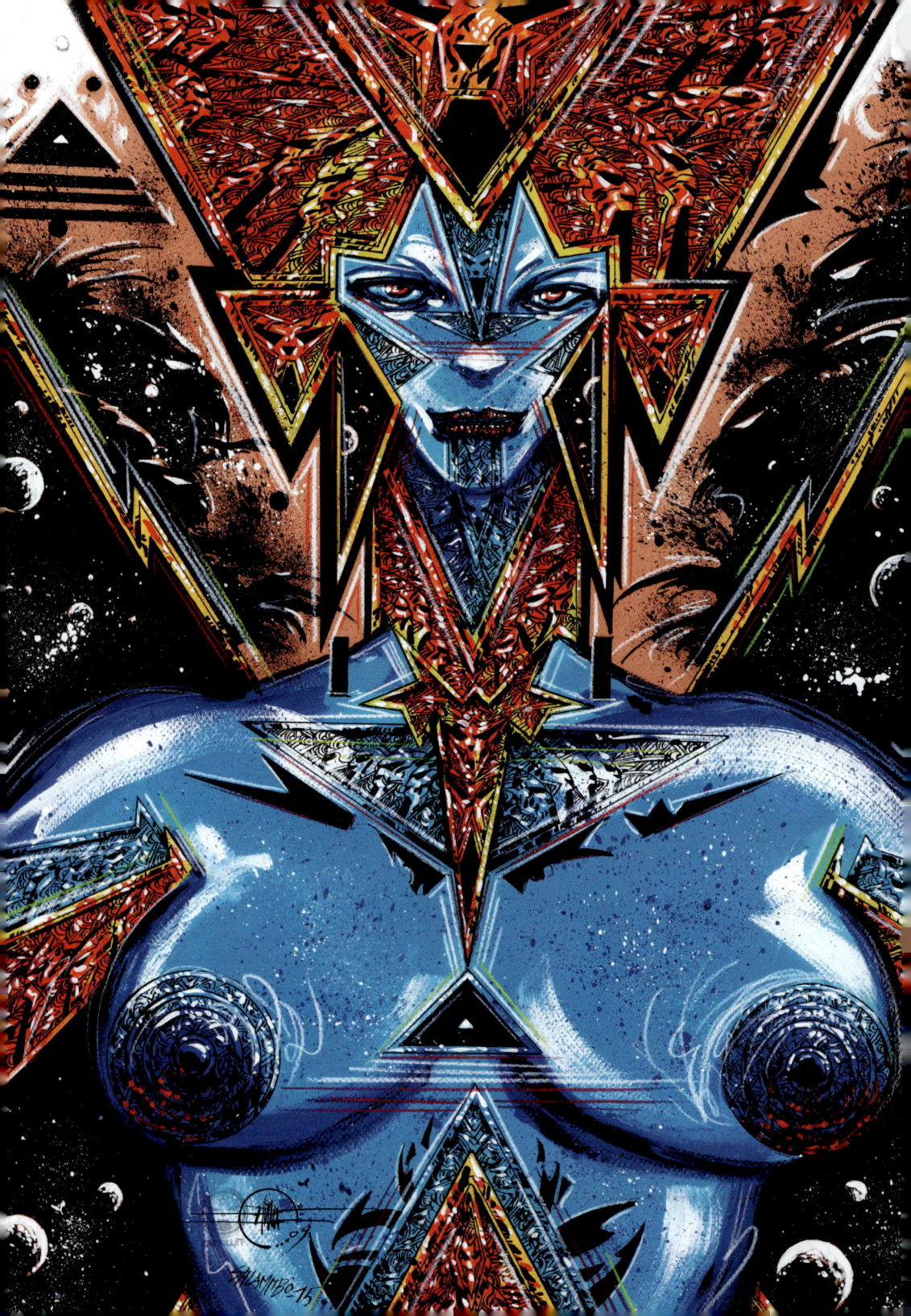

LA FANTASY AVANT, MAINTENANT ET TOUJOURS

PAR DIAN HANSON

En 2011, le département neuroesthétique de l'University College de Londres, souffrant à l'évidence d'un surcroît de temps, de fonds, ou probablement des deux, recruta des dizaines de personnes n'ayant pas de goût particulier pour l'art et soumit leur cerveau à des IRM tandis qu'ils étaient bombardés d'images représentant les œuvres de grands peintres. Les chercheurs mesurèrent ainsi le flux sanguin dans le cortex orbitofrontal médian, la zone du cerveau associée au plaisir et au désir, pour observer l'effet produit par le bel art.

Ils parvinrent à la conclusion que certains types d'art nous procurent, plus qu'un simple bien-être, un plaisir intense proche de celui que nous ressentons lorsque nous regardons l'être aimé – quand d'autres nous laissent froids. Pour un certain professeur Zeki cité dans le communiqué de presse de l'université, c'était la preuve que « grâce aux beaux tableaux, nous nous sentons beaucoup mieux ». Mieux que quoi ?

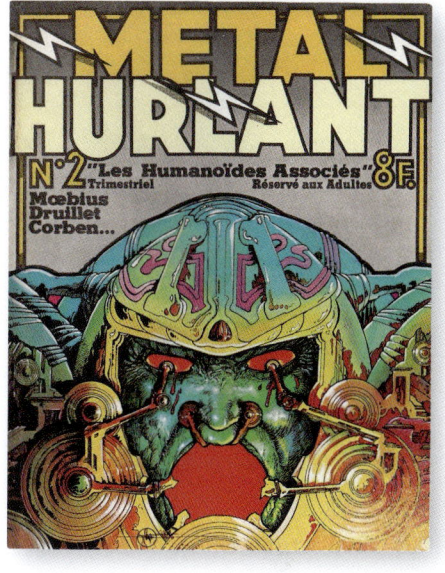

Et puis de quelle beauté parle-t-on ? Eh bien parmi les trois artistes dont les œuvres ont généré les réponses cérébrales les plus enthousiastes figurent Guido Reni et Jean-Auguste-Dominique Ingres, tous deux adeptes des couleurs riches et des représentations héroïques d'hommes musculeux, de femmes nues bien en chair et de créatures mythiques. Bref, du fantasy art.

À l'époque de Reni (1575–1642) et d'Ingres (1780–1867), bien sûr, le fantasy art n'existait pas. Reni a peint des scènes religieuses, mythologiques ou allégoriques. Ingres était un classiciste adepte des sujets historiques. Lorsqu'ils peignaient des dragons ou d'autres vengeurs ailés, ils n'inventaient pas de nouveaux mondes, ils illustraient un passé précis que beaucoup jugeaient plausible. Le terme fantasy, traduit tantôt par fantasme, tantôt par fantastique, imaginaire ou rêvé,

Opposite: Philippe Druillet was one of the original collaborators who formed Les Humanoïdes Associés to publish *Métal Hurlant* magazine in 1975. His harsh, intimidating visions contrasted nicely with the soft pastel fantasies of fellow Humanoïd Mœbius.

Above: Métal Hurlant (Howling Metal) debuted in France in 1975 and changed the direction of fantasy art, replacing the gentle Hobbits with drug-fueled, blatantly sexual fantasies more in touch with 1970s youth culture. Here, issue No. 2, with cover by Philippe Druillet, co-founder, along with artist Mœbius, writer Jean-Pierre Dionnet, and financier Bernard Farkas.

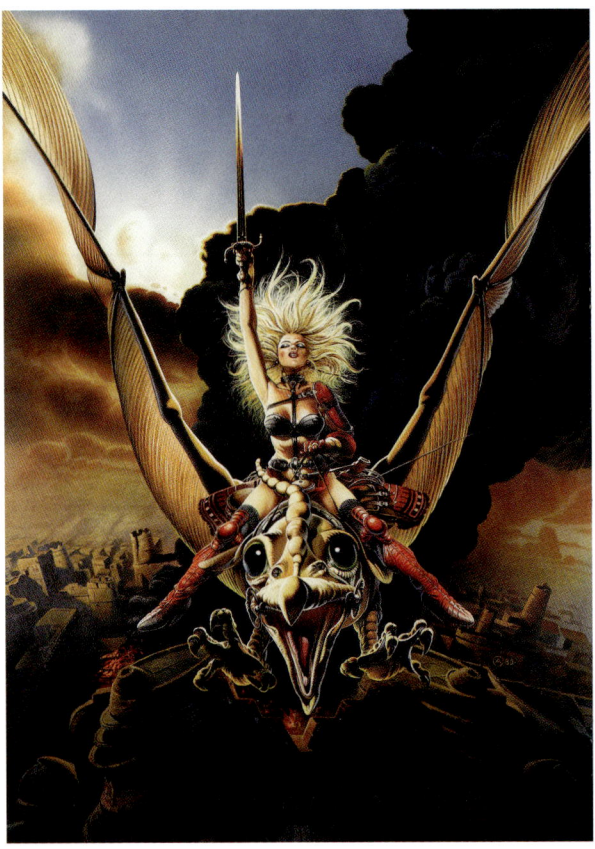

est ainsi défini, en anglais, comme « le fait d'imaginer des choses impossibles ou improbables ». Ce qu'on appelle le fantasy art ne pouvait donc pas exister tant que nous n'avions pas renoncé à croire aux dragons, sorcières, gorgones, griffons et nymphes, des créatures dotées de caractéristiques uniques et immuables au fil des siècles passés. Quand l'humanité a tourné le dos à la mythologie, les portes de l'imaginaire se sont ouvertes.

Et comme l'a si habilement démontré notre professeur Zeki, il en découle quelque chose comme de l'amour, sinon du respect.

Le snobisme esthétique existe depuis que l'art existe. J'imagine Moutard Néandertal qui s'échine sur sa fresque rupestre et Zigue Cro-Magnon qui débarque dans la grotte et toise avec mépris ses points et ses empreintes de main. Alors oui, en 45000 av. J.-C. tout le monde était dingue de points et d'empreintes de main, mais ce qu'aiment les masses est toujours considéré comme rase-mottes – désolée, les Néandertal – et les Cro-Magnon étaient les étoiles montantes, les petits gars qui arrivaient en ville avec leurs représentations figuratives de bisons, d'élans et de chasseurs humains. Le réalisme a régné sur l'art du jour où le suffisant Zigue a fumé Moutard jusqu'à l'invention de la photographie, en 1839.

Avant la photo, les gens s'en remettaient aux artistes pour se représenter les paysages, l'architecture, les objets, les animaux, les plantes et les individus. Le talent d'un artiste se mesurait à la précision avec laquelle il dessinait ces choses ; quant à ses émoluments, ils dépendaient de la générosité de l'Église et des riches clients qui lui commandaient des portraits. Même des maîtres comme Jérôme Bosch – souvent considéré comme le premier tenant du fantasy art – ou les susmentionnés Reni et Ingres cherchaient à représenter la réalité, fût-ce sous une forme fantasmée. Lorsqu'arrive la photographie, représenter la réalité devient un loisir abordable, bientôt banal, accessible à la

Above: Chris Achilleos, born Christos Achilléos in Cyprus, produced fantasy art for *Heavy Metal*, book covers, and the gaming industry. His most famous *Heavy Metal* cover is this 1981 rendition of Taarna, from the film *Heavy Metal*. 91.4 x 124.4 cm (36 x 49 inches).

Opposite: Boris Vallejo rose to become America's most prolific fantasy artist in the 1970s. He has illustrated more calendars, paperbacks, and fantasy film posters than any contemporary in his field and continues turning out astounding work in his later years. *The Ram*, a paperback cover illustration, was completed in 1979. Oil on board, 47 x 71 cm (18.5 x 28 inches).

MASTERPIECES OF FANTASY ART

classe moyenne, puis à la classe ouvrière. À mesure que la qualité des appareils s'améliore, à la fin du XIXᵉ siècle, les peintres passent en second plan derrière une bête machine et commencent à explorer des formes d'art radicalement nouvelles.

D'abord vient l'impressionnisme, qui émerge en France vers 1860 à coups de pinceau rapides, visibles, qui tentent de saisir le moment fugace, suivi du néo- et du postimpressionnisme, du fauvisme, du cubisme et de l'expressionnisme, qui veut représenter l'émotion brute et connaît son âge d'or pendant la république de Weimar, avant que les beaux arts plongent dans l'abstraction totale. Chacune de ces vagues successives éloigne un peu plus l'art de la photo, tout en éloignant aussi l'observateur lambda d'une juste appréciation de l'art. Le grand public réclame encore que les toiles soient jolies ; il n'est pas fan d'Edvard Munch.

L'Art nouveau et son culte des ondulations organiques, qui s'empare de l'artisanat et de l'architecture mais aussi de l'art, séduisent davantage. C'est un genre de réalisme sous stéroïdes, un jardin des délices foisonnant et sensuel, vierge de l'épouvantable ironie qui imprègne l'œuvre de Bosch. Beaucoup de hérauts du fantasy art citent l'Art nouveau parmi leurs premières inspirations, même si le précurseur le plus direct du genre est le surréalisme. Comme le fantasy art, le surréalisme

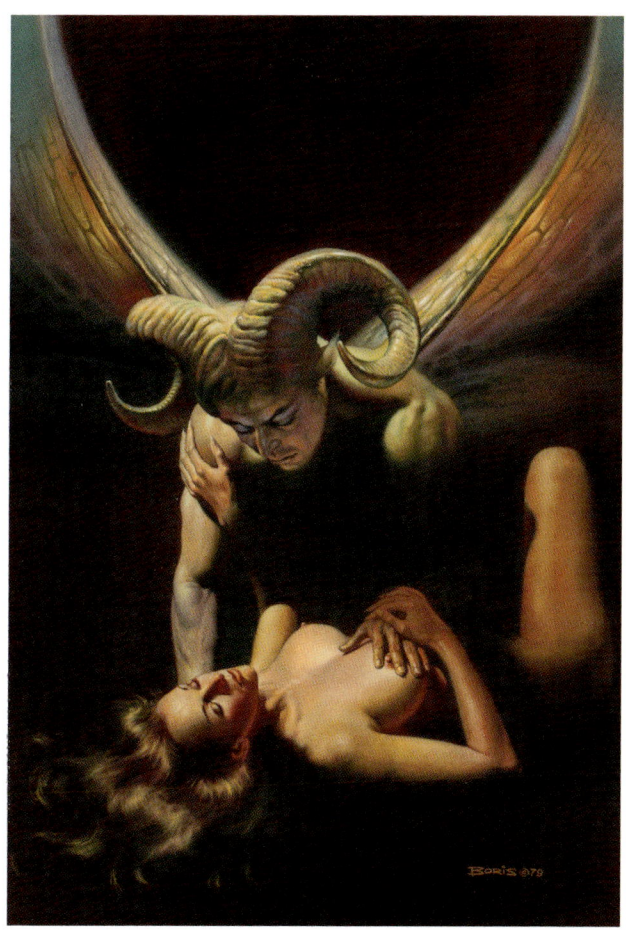

s'ancre dans des personnages, des lieux et des objets reconnaissables, qu'il altère pour tenter de résoudre « ces deux états, en apparence si contradictoires, que sont le rêve et la réalité, en une sorte de réalité absolue, de surréalité », selon la définition d'André Breton en 1924.

Contrairement au surréalisme, en revanche, le fantasy art est né du commerce, et c'est ce qui explique le combat que les tenants de ce genre ont dû mener pour être acceptés par l'establishment artistique, même s'ils avaient conquis des millions de fans dans le monde. Le snob trouve offensant qu'aucune formation ne soit requise pour l'apprécier : le cortex orbitofrontal s'éclaire spontanément avant que vous ayez lu la signature ou le prix sur l'étiquette. Même les enfants adorent le fantasy art ; c'est souvent la première forme d'art que vous avez vraiment appréciée, découverte en couverture d'un *comic book*, d'un livre de poche ou sur une pochette de disque. Qu'il s'agisse de Mœbius, de Rodney Matthews, de Boris Vallejo ou de Rowena

Morrill, vous sentiez presque vos vaisseaux sanguins se dilater dans votre cerveau tandis que vos yeux se promenaient sur l'image, absorbant les couleurs riches, le paysage étranger, les silhouettes humaines idéalisées, les bêtes menaçantes, la certitude que la puissance et le droit prévaudront. Puisque les œuvres du genre étaient réalisées sur commande, aussi talentueux et connu que soit l'artiste son travail était toujours accessible, largement exposé dans les kiosques à journaux – un avantage autant qu'une malédiction. Salvador Dalí est-il plus talentueux que Frank Frazetta parce que l'un peignait pour des galeries et l'autre pour EC Comics ? Beaucoup le pensent, pourtant votre cerveau s'éclaire probablement comme sous l'effet de l'amour lorsqu'il perçoit le fessier rebondi et les fossettes d'une donzelle de Frazetta ; il se pâme, étourdi par les endorphines, face aux couleurs primaires franches de Druillet et « se sent bien mieux » lorsqu'il contemple un dragon des Hildebrandt.

Les profanes confondent fantasy et science-fiction. Il s'agit pourtant, malgré leur parenté visuelle, de deux formes d'art très différentes : la science-fiction s'ancre dans la science, elle décrit une réalité concevable, comme l'Enterprise de *Star Trek*, alors que la fantasy ne se conforme à aucune règle, c'est l'imagination libérée de toute entrave. Si vous vous demandez où classer une œuvre d'art, recourez à la règle de la fusée. Il y a un vaisseau spatial ? Alors c'est de la science-fiction. Pas de fusée ? Cherchez le dragon, mascotte officielle du fantasy art.

Les dragons sont apparus séparément dans les mythologies occidentale et orientale comme l'adversaire ultime, l'homologue naturel du héros humain. Les premiers dragons évoquaient davantage le serpent, créature connue incarnant le mieux la peur. Avec le temps et la licence artistique, il leur a poussé plusieurs têtes, des ailes, ils ont appris à cracher du feu et sont devenus, de façon générale, toujours plus grands et majestueux, jusqu'à ce qu'ils acquièrent leur aspect

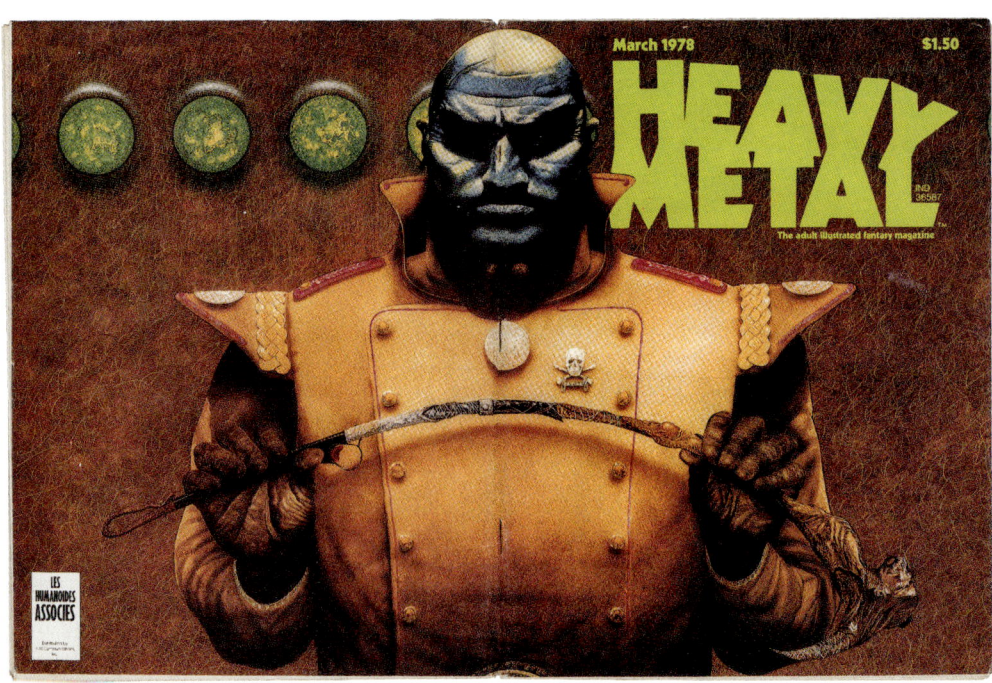

durable, immédiatement reconnaissable, celui d'un pur fruit de l'imagination. Ils étaient mûrs pour le fantasy art.

Jérôme Bosch (v. 1450–1516) n'était pas du tout intéressé par les dragons. Ses représentations du paradis, de l'enfer et de la mythologie culturelle transcendaient largement l'imagination de ses contemporains, mais il se contentait encore de peindre des allégories religieuses, en insistant lourdement sur le prix du péché, qu'aucun combat héroïque ne saurait racheter. Il y a beaucoup de nudité, bien que peu d'érotisme ; beaucoup de créatures menaçantes, mais pas de dragons.

Le bien plus tardif Maxfield Parrish (1870–1966) semble un pionnier plus évident du fantasy art. Ses paysages sont luxuriants et oniriques, peuplés de magnifiques jeunes gens et de vierges nubiles. On trouve aussi chez lui des châteaux et sa toile de 1901 *The Reluctant Dragon*, produite pour illustrer la nouvelle éponyme de Kenneth Grahame dans le recueil d'histoires pour enfants *Dream Days*, publié en 1902, en est un parfait exemple. Plus significatif peut-être, il a dessiné pour la publicité, la presse magazine, des livres pour enfants, des calendriers et même des réclames pour du dentifrice. Son tableau le plus connu, *Daybreak* (1922), qui représente un jardin céleste avec deux femmes

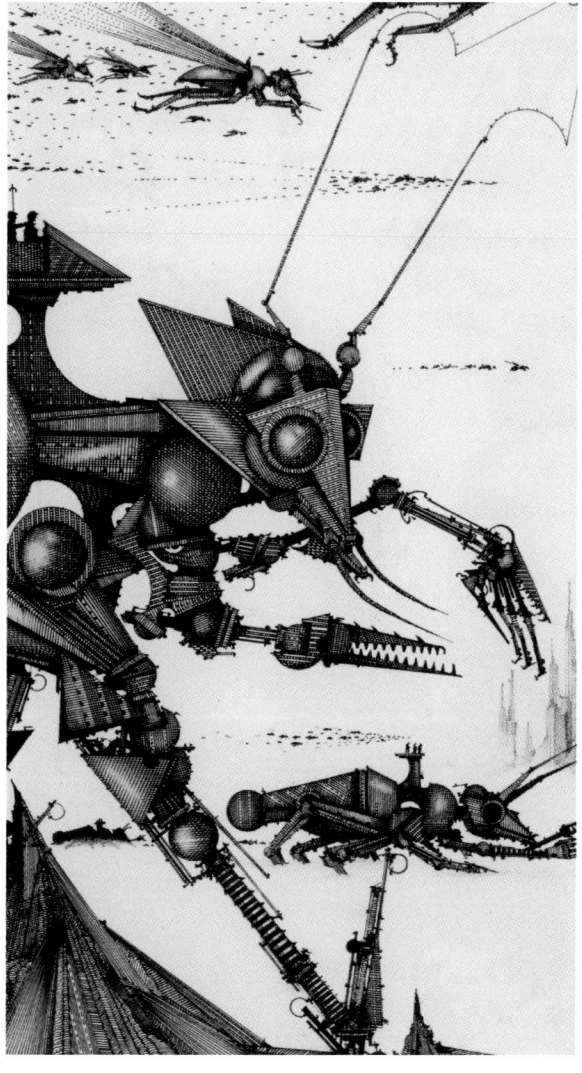

langoureuses, est devenu la reproduction d'œuvre d'art la plus vendue au XXe siècle. Un an plus tard sortait *Weird Tales*, le premier magazine de science-fiction et de fantasy au monde. Créé par le journaliste et éditeur J.C. Henneberger, grand admirateur d'Edgar Allan Poe, *Weird Tales*

Opposite: A great Jim Burns wraparound cover on the March 1978 issue of *Heavy Metal* magazine. The title was licensed in 1977 from *Métal Hurlant* for distribution in the U.S. and was originally an English translation of the French magazine. In 1979 the magazine was revamped to include more original American content.

Above: Ian Miller is a British fantasy artist who contributed extensively to the development of war gaming in the 1980s, as well as illustrating a number of Tolkien and H.P. Lovecraft stories. This 1979 piece was for a Bantam books trade edition of *The Martian Chronicles*. Pen on board, 8.9 x 15.8 cm (3.5 x 6.25 inches). Courtesy of Heritage Auctions.

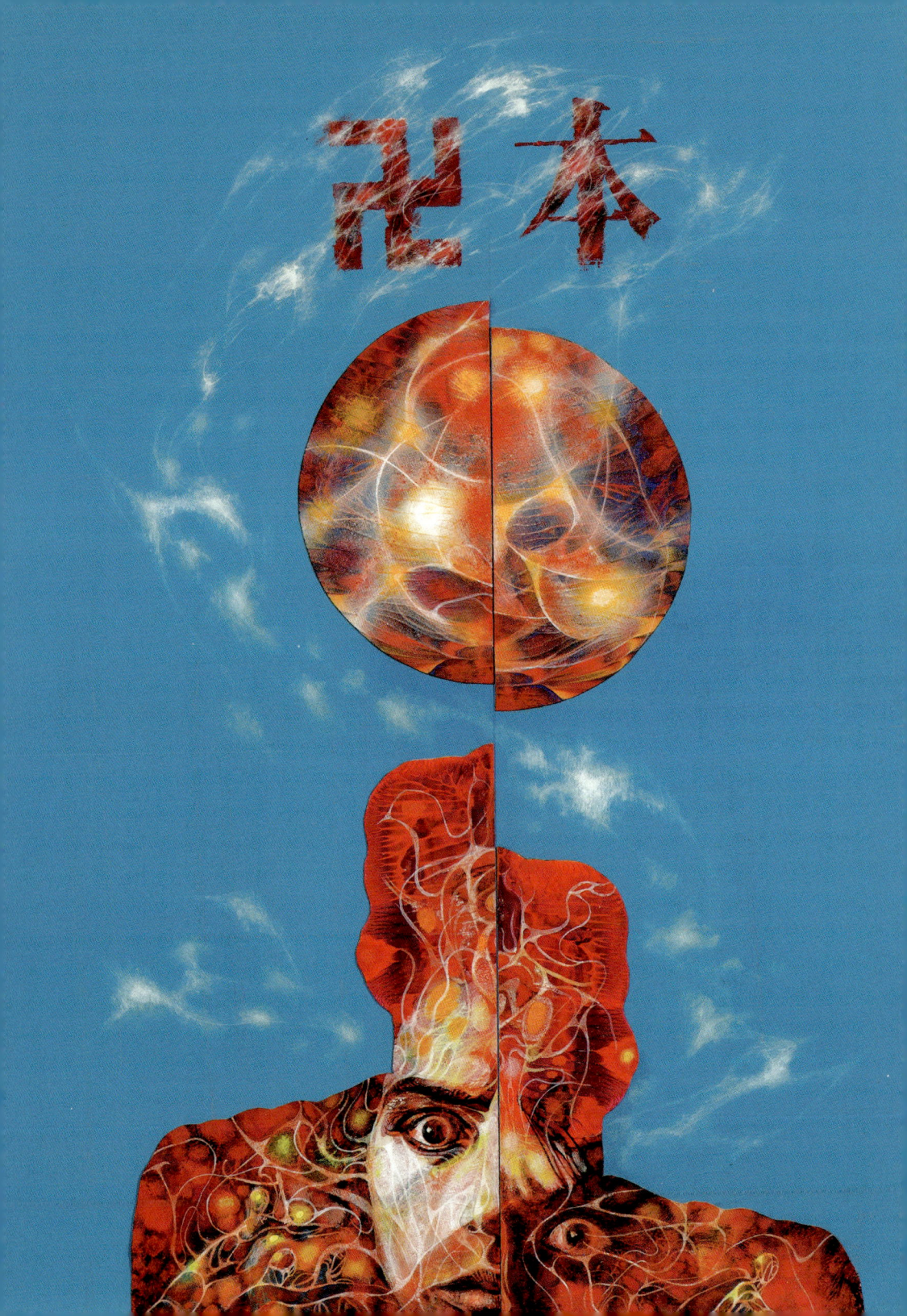

imitait la formule déjà éprouvée par d'autres titres de
fiction thématiques à l'époque : plusieurs nouvelles,
imprimées sur du papier bon marché (le fameux *pulp
paper*), emballées dans une couverture peinte aux
couleurs criardes. La première une de *WT* est signée
Richard Ruh Epperly, un peintre paysagiste falot
qui parvint tout de même à imaginer une horrible
pieuvre attaquant une garçonne apeurée. La qualité
des couvertures s'améliora de façon spectaculaire au
cours des quelques années suivantes, tout comme
celle des récits.

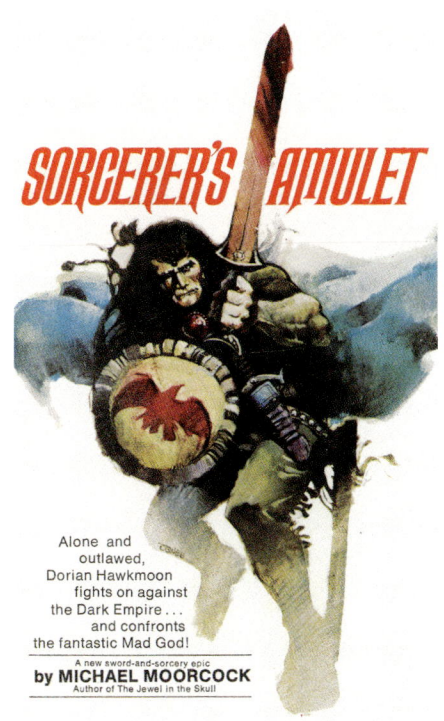

Parce que le fantasy art a toujours été lié aux
œuvres de fiction fantasy, certains écrivains jouèrent
un rôle crucial dans l'élaboration du genre. Robert E.
Howard présenta ainsi Conan le Cimmérien dans le
Weird Tales de décembre 1932 avec « Le Phoenix sur
le glaive » (« The Phoenix on the Sword », illustration
de couverture par J. Allen St. John), puis « La Tour
de l'éléphant » (« The Tower of the Elephant »,
couverture de Margaret Brundage) dans le numéro
de mars 1933. Dix-sept autres aventures de Conan
seront publiées jusqu'à son suicide, en 1936. Ce héros
tout en muscles qui évolue dans un univers primitif
et brutal toucha la corde sensible des lecteurs, celle
qu'avait déjà fait vibrer Edgar Rice Burroughs avec

son « Tarzan, seigneur de la jungle », apparu dans le *All-Story Magazine* de mars 1912 (couverture
de Clinton Pettee). Les deux personnages, des forces de la nature mutiques, étaient plébiscités
par un lectorat majoritairement masculin et en col bleu. Pour plus d'équilibre, Fritz Leiber créa
le grand barbare Fafhrd et le Souricier gris, un voleur à la petite semaine, des héros qu'il dota de
certaines fragilités humaines et d'aptitudes linguistiques plus développées que Conan et Tarzan.
Ils vainquent leurs ennemis à coups de traits d'esprit mais vivent dans un univers fantasmatique
complexe tout aussi captivant que la Cimmérie de Conan. La première histoire du long « Cycle
des épées » (« Fafhrd and the Gray Mouser ») parut dans *Unknown* en août 1939, aux côtés d'une
fiction signée L. Ron Hubbard, futur fondateur de l'Église de scientologie, qui exercera un grand
pouvoir sur les élites hollywoodiennes – à défaut de séduire les fans de fantasy.

Le mythe de Cthulhu élaboré par H.P. Lovecraft fut aussi développé et affiné dans les *pulps*
fantasy, à partir du *Weird Tales* de février 1928, qui publia l'histoire « L'Appel de Cthulhu ». Les
multiples strates de sa vision extraordinairement sophistiquée sont encore étudiées et disséquées
par les fans de fantasy, entre les Dieux Extérieurs qui règnent sur un univers alternatif malveillant

Opposite: Frontispiece for the 1988 edition of Philip K.
Dick's *Man in the High Castle*, mixed media with collage
on board by Richard M. Powers, fantasy surrealist.
1988, 74.9 x 57.1 cm (29.5 x 22.5 inches).

Above: Jeff Jones, later known as Jeffrey Catherine
Jones, was one of the most talented, and tormented,
fantasy artists, struggling with depression and body
dysmorphia throughout his life. This cover for *Sorcerer's
Amulet* by Michael Moorcock is from 1968.

librement inspiré de la mythologie grecque, asséchée de toute bonté et beauté et les quelque 180 Grands Anciens, d'atroces entités envoyées sur Terre parmi lesquelles se trouve Cthulhu, à laquelle des humains débauchés vouent divers cultes. L'univers créé par Lovecraft est effrayant et l'humain semble y avoir peu de chances de survie, mais il offre aussi une fuite dans l'imaginaire, l'occasion de faire l'expérience d'une vie bien pire que ce que la Dépression avait engendré dans ses heures les plus sombres. D'autres auteurs débutèrent dans les *pulps*, influant ainsi sur la définition formelle du fantasy art, notamment Robert Bloch, Ray Bradbury, Arthur C. Clarke, Paul Ernst, Frank Herbert, C.L. Moore et Clark Ashton Smith.

Weird Tales prouva qu'il existait un marché pour la fiction fantasy, mais le fantasy art conserva encore un temps le statut de second couteau, en grande partie à cause du budget limité des éditeurs de *pulps*. La pâte à papier était peu chère mais absorbait tant l'encre qu'il était impossible d'y imprimer autre chose que du texte ou de simples traits de dessin. Le papier couché employé pour les couvertures prenait bien la couleur mais coûtait trop cher pour être utilisé en pages intérieures.

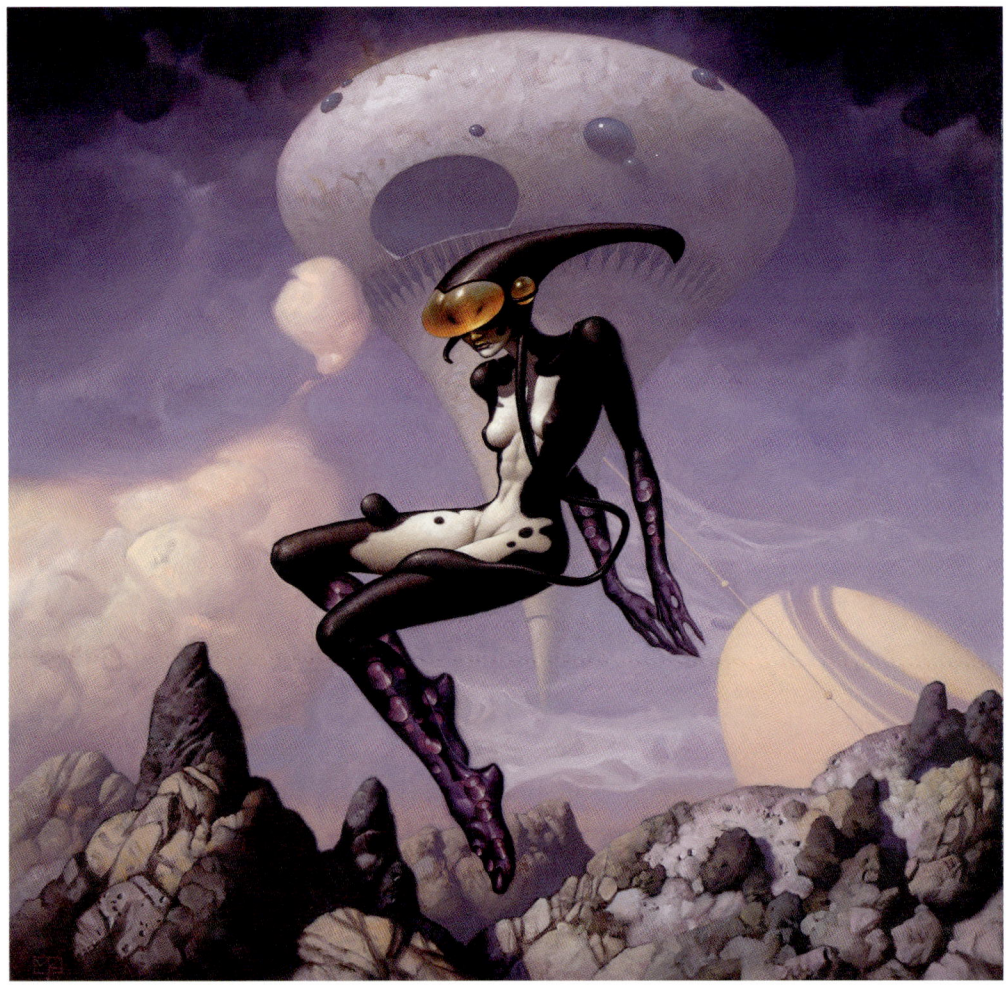

Et puis étant donné le mépris proverbial des éditeurs pour les masses et leur supposé manque de goût, il n'est pas étonnant qu'ils n'aient pas cherché à proposer mieux à leurs lecteurs. D'autres éditeurs prirent cependant note du succès de *Weird Tales* et une concurrence émergea, qui suscita l'innovation. Hugo Gernsback lança *Amazing Stories* en 1926 et, ce faisant, il traça la frontière entre fantasy et science-fiction.

Gernsback était un doux dingue plus tard surnommé le Père de la Science-Fiction – même s'il préférait le terme de *scientifiction*. Féru de technologie, surtout fasciné par l'électricité et la radio, il fut sans doute le premier geek. Son magazine *Electrical Experimenter*, sorti en 1913, suivi en 1920 de *Science and Invention*, regorgeait de science improbable et contint très tôt de la fiction. Les deux titres étaient tirés sur du papier de qualité supérieure, avec des couvertures en quadrichromie qui mettaient à l'honneur les marges les plus déjantées de la

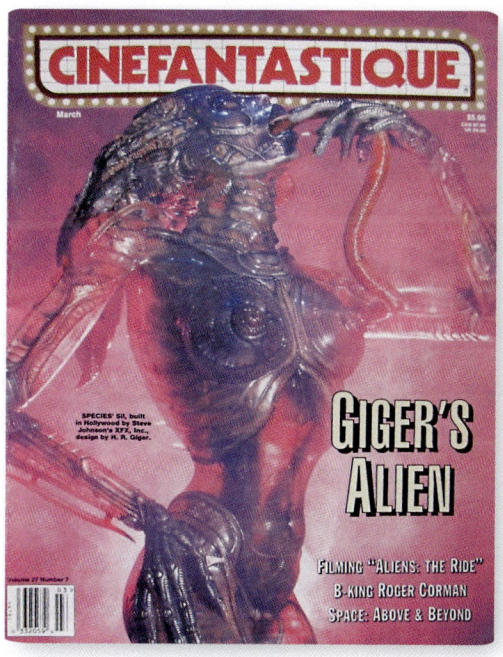

recherche scientifique, comme le graphique intitulé « Fin du Monde » qui fit la une en 1925. Inutile pour Gernsback d'aller bien loin pour concevoir *Amazing Stories*, un magazine complètement dédié à la *scientifiction*, puis *Air Wonder Stories* et *Science Wonder Stories* en 1929, combinés sous le titre *Wonder Stories* en 1930.

Contrairement à *Weird Tales*, publié au format digest, *Amazing Stories* et *Wonder Stories* étaient au format magazine standard (21,6 x 29,8cm). La partie fiction était au départ alimentée par des rééditions de H.G. Wells, Jules Verne et Edgar Allan Poe, mais les illustrations de couvertures de Frank R. Paul étaient inédites, splendides, et participèrent à faire de lui le premier grand artiste de science-fiction.

Les vrais amoureux des origines mythologiques du fantasy art jugent cependant que Paul abusait un peu trop des vaisseaux spatiaux, en particulier pour *Air Wonder Stories*. On en revient à l'argument « possible ou impossible » : aussi fantaisiste que soit le vaisseau, le voyage spatial n'en demeurait pas moins fondé sur des principes scientifiques solides, contrairement aux dragons. La science-fiction est mécanique, la fantasy organique, l'une s'intéresse aux créations humaines, l'autre à celles d'un dieu extraterrestre. La science-fiction s'inscrit en général dans l'avenir, alors que la fantasy fait référence aux civilisations d'un lointain passé. Comment expliquer autrement cette palanquée de guenilles en fourrure (nonobstant les anachroniques bikinis high-tech) ?

Weird Tales et *Amazing Stories* ouvrirent grand les vannes du *pulp* fantasy. *Astounding Stories of Super-Science* sortit en 1930, suivi de *Strange Tales of Mystery and Terror* et *Miracle Science and Fantasy*

Opposite: Xenon by Mark Zug. Oil on canvas, 2012, 60.9 x 60.9 cm (24 x 24 inches).

Above: The French film magazine *Cinefantastique*, March 1996, with a cover story about Giger's concept art for *Alien*.

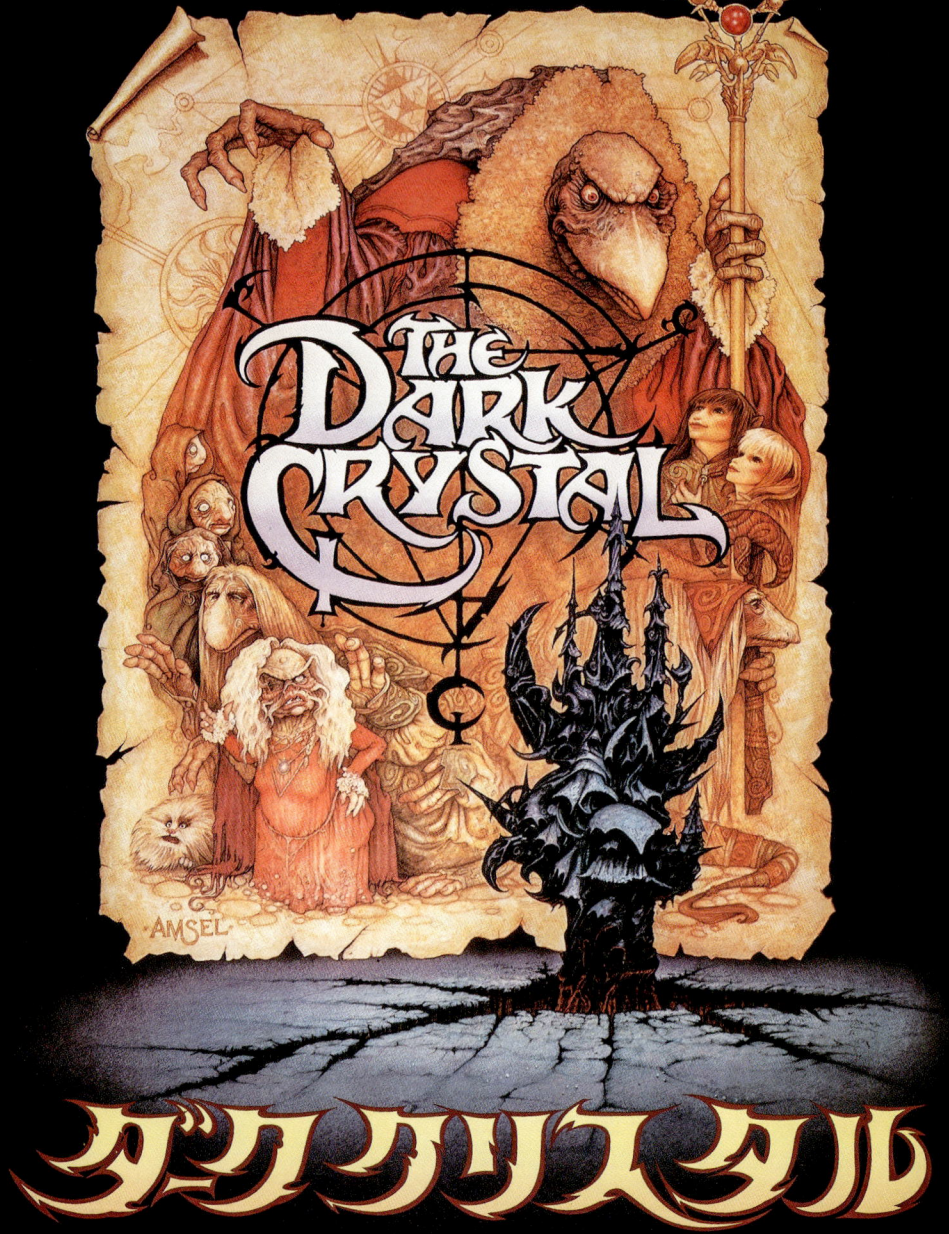

不思議な映像へ　ようこそ!!世界初の映像革命《ロボットロニクス》
3つの太陽が1つになるとき…クリスタルに奇跡が起きる

THE DARK CRYSTAL

AMSEL

ダーククリスタル

ロード・グレイド/ITCエンターテイメント提供　ジム・ヘンソン作品"THE DARK CRYSTAL"　監督ジム・ヘンソン/フランク・オズ　製作ジム・ヘンソン/ゲーリー・カーツ　脚本デビッド・オデール
ストーリー/ジム・ヘンソン　音楽トレバー・ジョーンズ　原案ブライアン・フロード　製作総指揮デビッド・レーザー　DOLBY STEREO　原作翻訳/角川文庫刊　ユニヴァーサル映画　CIC配給　映倫

Stories en 1931, *Terror Tales* en 1934, *Marvel Science Stories* en 1938, puis *Unknown*, *Strange Stories*, *Startling Stories*, *Mystery Tales*, *Fantastic Adventures* et *Planet Stories* en 1939 et *Fantastic Novels* et *Astonishing Stories* en 1940. Pendant les années de privations de la Dépression, la fantasy constituait une évasion bienvenue et la compétition croissante entre les magazines les poussa à publier de nouveaux talents, mais aussi des couvertures plus accrocheuses et de meilleure qualité… C'est-à-dire plus de femmes avec moins de vêtements.

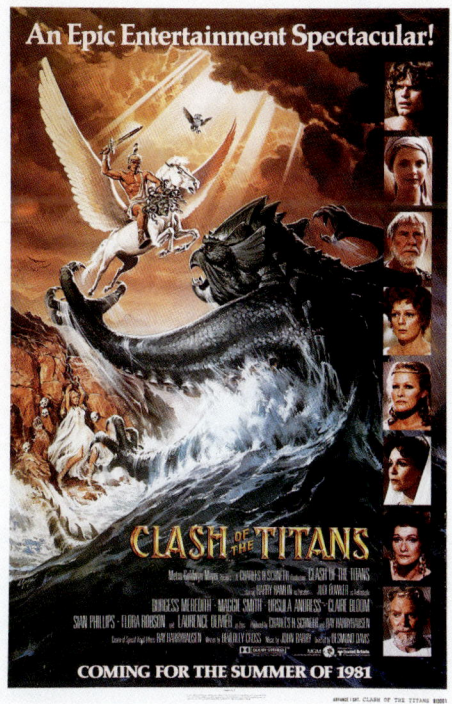

Weird Tales, toujours pionnier, fut le premier magazine à sexualiser le fantasy art. La prolifération incontrôlée de *pulps* au début des années 1930 fit chuter les ventes de chaque titre, ce qui poussa certains à baisser leur prix de 25 à 10 cents. Tant d'Américains étaient au chômage que même cette somme minime représentait une dépense importante pour un bien non vital, mais le sexe résiste à n'importe quelle récession : les hommes paieront toujours pour se faire plaisir, même le ventre vide. Plusieurs éditeurs s'étaient essayés aux *pulps* « osés » dans les années 1920, le plus souvent avec de la fiction bas de gamme et des couvertures à pin-up tout aussi médiocres. En 1932, Frank Armer et Harry Donenfeld, à la tête de la plupart de ces titres, joignirent leurs forces pour former Super Magazines, bientôt rebaptisé Culture Publications. La même année, l'artiste Margaret Brundage entrait dans le bureau du rédacteur en chef de *Weird Tales* Farnsworth Wright. Il semble peu probable que les huiles de l'édition Armer et Donenfeld aient connu Wright, simple rédacteur en chef, mais il y a de grandes chances qu'ils se soient inspirés de ses choix artistiques. Culture Publications sortira *Spicy Detective Stories*, *Spicy Adventure Stories* et *Spicy Mystery Stories* – dans la veine fantasy – en 1934, tous des *pulps* proposant de la fiction vaguement provocante avec en couverture les illustrations outrageusement sexy de deux artistes talentueux, Harry Lemon Parkhurst et Hugh Joseph Ward. Ces titres remportent un succès immédiat et s'arrachent à 25 cents alors que d'autres peinent à se vendre à 10 et on leur attribue souvent d'avoir déclenché la première révolution sexuelle dans l'édition américaine.

Weird Tales n'en demeure pas moins le premier à s'être aventuré dans cette voie. Brundage réalisa sa première couverture pour le numéro de septembre 1932 ; le pastel original était si corsé qu'il fut censuré à l'impression. Quelqu'un lui avait-il demandé de représenter une femme torse nu ? L'Histoire ne le dit pas, mais de juin 1933 à août 1936, elle illustra l'intégralité des couvertures de *WT*, 39 en tout. Elle poussa vers la sortie l'extrêmement talentueux mais bien moins

Opposite: The Dark Crystal movie poster (Japanese), with artwork by Richard Amsel, 1983, 72.3 x 51.4 cm (28.5 x 20.25 inches). Courtesy of Heritage Auctions.

Above: After the success of *Star Wars* in 1977, and the popularity of the *Star Wars* fantasy poster, Hollywood produced more fantasy films, with more fantasy art posters. This for *Clash of the Titans*, 1981, is by Dan Guzee.

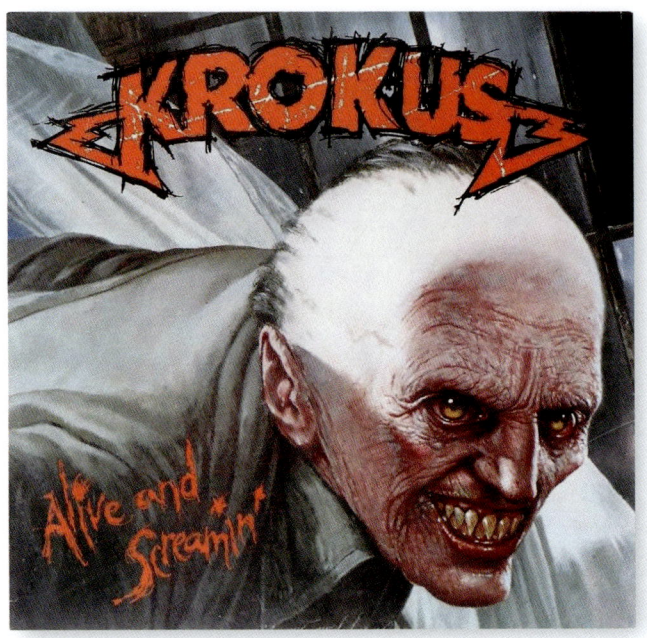

déluré J. Allen St. John et établit le nu comme un ingrédient fondamental du fantasy art. En 1936, elle fut rejointe par Virgil Finlay, Hugh Rankin et l'élégant Hannes Bok, avant que le maire de New York Fiorello La Guardia ne sévisse contre les titres trop érotiques vendus en kiosque, en 1938. Il visait au départ les magazines de Culture Publications, mais les *pulps* fantasy, et plus particulièrement *Weird Tales*, furent balayés aussi et le sexe fut remisé dans les fonds de tiroir jusqu'au lendemain de la guerre. Ce revers ne décourage pas Martin Goodman, l'homme qui fondera Marvel Comics en 1939 ; il commença par lancer *Marvel Science Stories* en mai 1938 avec un contenu tellement salace que les lecteurs s'en plaignent – alors qu'ils sont séduits par les superbes couvertures sexy de Norman Saunders. Goodman calme le jeu, un peu, et change son nom pour *Marvel Tales*. En 1939, *Mystery Tales* et *Planet Stories*, dans les pages duquel débute Ray Bradbury, ont emprunté le même chemin avec des apparitions régulières d'amazones, de *space vixens* et de couvertures bondage créées par H.W. Scott, Allen Anderson et Alexander Leydenfrost, qui sont tous passés entre les mailles du filet tendu par La Guardia.

Après la Seconde Guerre mondiale, qui éleva les pin-up au rang de forme d'art américain acceptable, les restrictions imposées par La Guardia se relâchent. De nouveaux artistes, parmi lesquels Robert Gibson Jones, Lawrence Sterne Stevens, Ed Emshwiller, Frank Kelly Freas, Harold Mc-Cauley et Chesley Bonestell (qui donnera son nom aux prix annuels récompensant les meilleurs artistes de science-fiction et de fantasy) entrent en scène, tout comme de nouveaux magazines : *Avon Fantasy Reader* en 1947, *A. Merritt's Fantasy Magazine* en 1949, *Out of This World Adventures* en 1950, *10 Story Fantasy* en 1951 et *Imaginative Tales* en 1954. Cependant le rationnement de papier avait asphyxié la plupart des vieux magazines de fantasy ; seuls avaient survécu *Weird Tales*, *Startling Stories*, *Thrilling Wonder Stories*, *Amazing Stories*, *Fantastic Adventures*, *Famous Fantastic Mysteries* et *Planet Stories*. Fin 1955, ils avaient tous mis la clé sous la porte à l'exception d'*Imaginative Tales*, qui ne succomba qu'en 1958, et d'*Amazing Stories*, qui se maintint vaillamment chez divers éditeurs jusqu'en 2005.

Above: Les Edwards is a British artist best known for his fantasy, sci-fi, and horror book covers, and for his illustrations for Games Workshops role-playing products. *The Croglin Vampire* was licensed by the Swiss band Krokus for its *Alive and Screaming* album in 1986.

Opposite: The Selenites, an interior illustration for the 1990 edition of H.G. Wells's *The First Men on the Moon* by Bob Eggleton. Acrylic on board, 1989, 39.3 x 57.7 cm (15.5 x 22.75 inches).

MASTERPIECES OF FANTASY ART

Le *pulp* est mort parce que l'Amérique s'est lassée des nouvelles. La télévision récupéra ceux dont l'intérêt était surtout visuel et les lecteurs se reportèrent sur les fictions longues en format poche. Ceux qui achetaient des *pulps* fantasy pour leurs couvertures se tournèrent plutôt vers la bande dessinée, en particulier après la sortie de la nouvelle collection d'EC Comics en 1950. *Weird Science* et *Weird Fantasy* cherchaient à séduire le même public que les *pulps* fantasy, mais avec des illustrations à chaque page. Wally Wood se chargea régulièrement des couvertures à partir de 1952, tandis que Roy Krenkel, Al Williamson et le jeune Frank Frazetta fournissaient les comics en pages intérieures. La nouvelle collection d'EC était très populaire, mais ne dura malheureusement pas longtemps. Les livres de poche fantasy bon marché, qui apparurent au début des années 1960, connurent une plus grande longévité.

Certains auteurs de fantasy ont toujours écrit de la fiction longue et publié des livres. *Le Hobbit (The Hobbit, or There and Back Again)* de J.R.R. Tolkien sortit en 1937. Le Père de la fantasy littéraire fut lui-même influencé par les livres de l'Écossais George MacDonald, qui déclara : « Je n'écris pas pour les enfants, mais pour les enfantins, qu'ils aient cinq, cinquante, ou soixante-quinze ans. » Tolkien prend le sujet à cœur ; il écrit aussi pour un lectorat adulte, il peint la couverture pour *Le Hobbit* et crée les illustrations intérieures au crayon, au stylo, à la craie grasse et à la peinture. Si elles ne sont pas du calibre de son écriture, ces œuvres ont guidé les nombreux artistes fantasy qui illustreront plus tard la trilogie du *Seigneur des Anneaux*, publiée en 1954. Ces livres, tout comme *Les Chroniques de Narnia* de C.S. Lewis, sorties en sept tomes entre 1950 et 1956, contribuent à former une seconde vague de fantasy grand public, qui stimule les auteurs, les artistes et la demande de fictions longues.

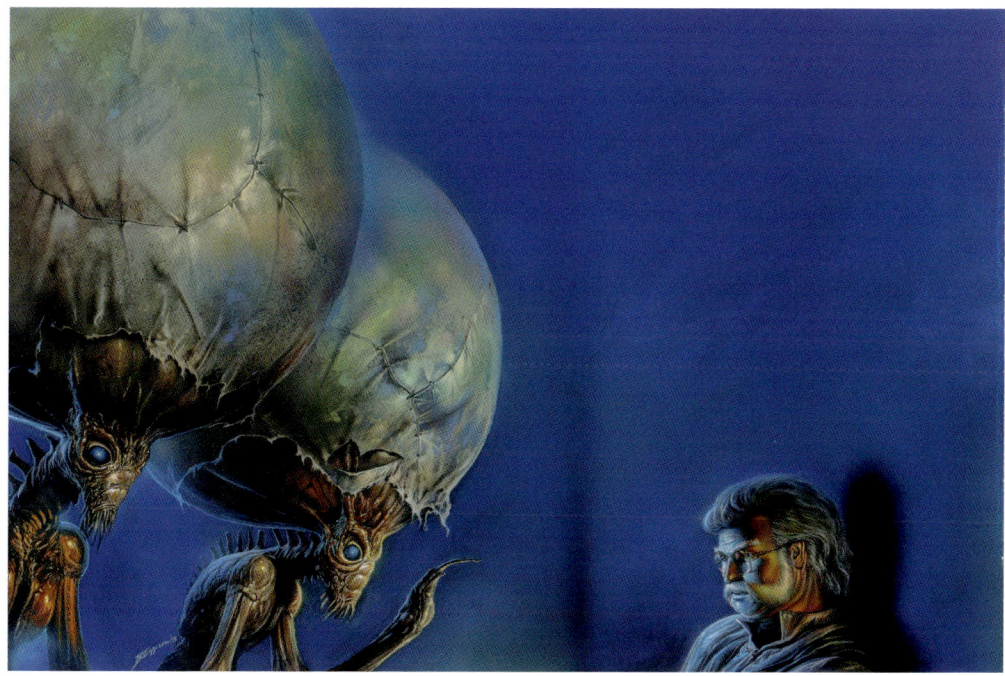

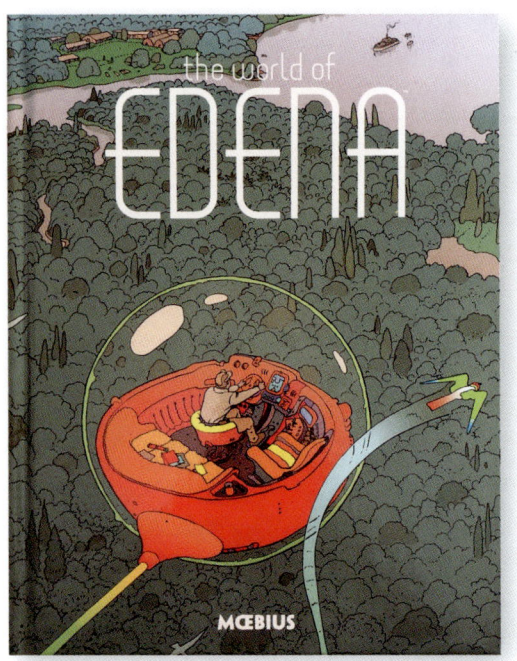

Autre acteur majeur de ce renouveau, le pourvoyeur de poches à bas prix Ace Books naît en 1952. En 1953, Ace publie son premier roman de science-fiction, *Le Monde des A-* (*The World of Null-A*, traduit en français par Boris Vian, NdT) de A.E. van Vogt, ainsi que son autre fiction *Créateur d'univers (The Universe Maker)*. Deux ans plus tard, sur l'impulsion du succès de Tolkien et Lewis, la maison publie plus de science-fiction et de fantasy que de tout autre genre, procurant des commandes régulières aux illustrateurs de couverture. Les vétérans des *pulps*, notamment Ed Emshwiller, Virgil Finlay, Frank Kelly Freas et Roy Krenkel rivalisent pour les décrocher et c'est Krenkel qui remporte la timbale chez Ace avec les couvertures de Tarzan. En 1962, il recommande son ami Frank Frazetta pour les pages intérieures. Edgar Rice Burroughs étant entré dans le domaine public, Tarzan est un candidat idéal à la réédition et le concurrent d'Ace dans le créneau fantasy, Canaveral Press, ne tarde pas à se saisir de ses œuvres et engage Frazetta pour réaliser les couvertures à la place du plus abstrait Mahlon Blaine. En 1966, quand Lancer Books, un autre éditeur de livres de poche, acquiert les droits pour Conan, Frazetta est devenu si populaire qu'il est en position de négocier un contrat pour la réalisation des couvertures qui lui permet de conserver la propriété intellectuelle de ses œuvres – une première sur ce marché du travail à la commande des années 1960, où les éditeurs jettent le plus souvent les œuvres originales au panier après impression. Grâce à cette clause, Frazetta se sent libre de peindre certaines des œuvres les plus réussies de sa carrière, parce qu'il sait qu'elles lui appartiennent. La série se vend à plus de 10 millions d'exemplaires, en grande partie grâce à ses couvertures saisissantes, et le fonds Frazetta, qui existe toujours, est créé pour archiver son travail.

Dans le même temps, les magazines fantasy d'EC mettent la clé sous la porte en 1954, quand le gouvernement américain accuse la bande dessinée en général, et les comics d'EC en particulier, d'inciter la jeunesse à la délinquance. Une coalition d'éditeurs riposte en créant la Comics Code Authority pour régenter sa propre production et décide de prohiber l'emploi des termes « horreur », « terreur » et « bizarre » *(weird)* en couverture de quelque *comic* que ce soit. EC se défend, mais privée de l'aval du Comics Code, la maison se retrouve sans distributeurs et doit abandonner

Above: First published in France as *Le monde d'Edena*, *The Edena Cycle* of graphic novels by Mœbius grew out of a commission from the French car company Citroën in 1983. The first English-language edition was published in 1988.

Opposite: Leo and Diane Dillon created fantasy novel covers and children's book illustrations together from the time of their marriage in 1957 until Leo's death in 2012, considering themselves to be one artist in two bodies. This unique piece titled *Space Adventure* was for a fantasy advent calendar, 1985. Mixed media on paper, 23.8 x 36.5 cm (9.375 x 14.375 inches). Courtesy of Heritage Auctions.

les titres incriminés. Leurs fans pleurent cette perte jusqu'à ce que, 10 ans plus tard, Warren Publishing lance *Creepy*, puis *Eerie* et *Vampirella*, directement inspirés des comics d'horreur EC mais en format magazine et libérés de la censure du Comics Code.

Les couvertures de *Creepy* sont grandes, hautes en couleur, sur papier glacé, parfaites pour des reproductions de qualité. Les pages intérieures sont en noir et blanc uniquement, mais c'est un noir et blanc magnifique, complexe, dense et détaillé, dans lequel excellent les vétérans d'EC – Wally Wood, Roy Krenkel, Al Williamson et Frank Frazetta, bientôt rejoints par Richard Corben, Jeff Jones, Bernie Wrightson, Don Maitz, Ken Kelly et bien d'autres. Ce groupe plus jeune surfe sur l'héritage d'EC mais aussi sur un climat moral qui bascule quand les années 1960 laissent la place aux années 1970. L'art psychédélique, qui tente de représenter les visions hallucinatoires, émerge puis s'acoquine avec la fantasy pour donner naissance à un genre hybride qui s'exprime surtout, au départ, sur les pochettes de disques.

L'Australien Martin Sharp en est un des pionniers. Qualifié d'artiste pop plutôt que fantasy, il signe pour les magazines *Disraeli Gears* et *Wheels of Fire* de Cream deux couvertures, respectivement en 1967 et 1968, qui ouvrent la voie aux compositions plus franchement fantasy de Roger Dean et Rodney Matthews pour les groupes Yes, Gentle Giant, Asia, Scorpions, Nazareth, Magnum et Thin

Lizzy. Comme les magazines *pulp* et les livres de poche, les pochettes d'album étaient globalement considérées comme des supports publicitaires, un emballage attractif pour mieux vendre le produit, mais les pochettes offraient un espace de jeu plus grand que les romans de gare. Je me souviens qu'adolescents, mes amis et moi étudiions ces illustrations et je me souviens avoir acheté des albums seulement parce que j'aimais leur pochette ; je revois en particulier un éléphant volant de Dean sur un album d'Osibisa. Les maisons de disques ont vite compris que l'extérieur comptait autant que l'intérieur et commandent toujours plus de pochettes fantasy aux artistes.

Ensuite, en décembre 1974, un magazine devenu mythique arrive de France qui propulse le fantasy art dans une nouvelle dimension : *Métal Hurlant* a été fondé à Paris par deux artistes,

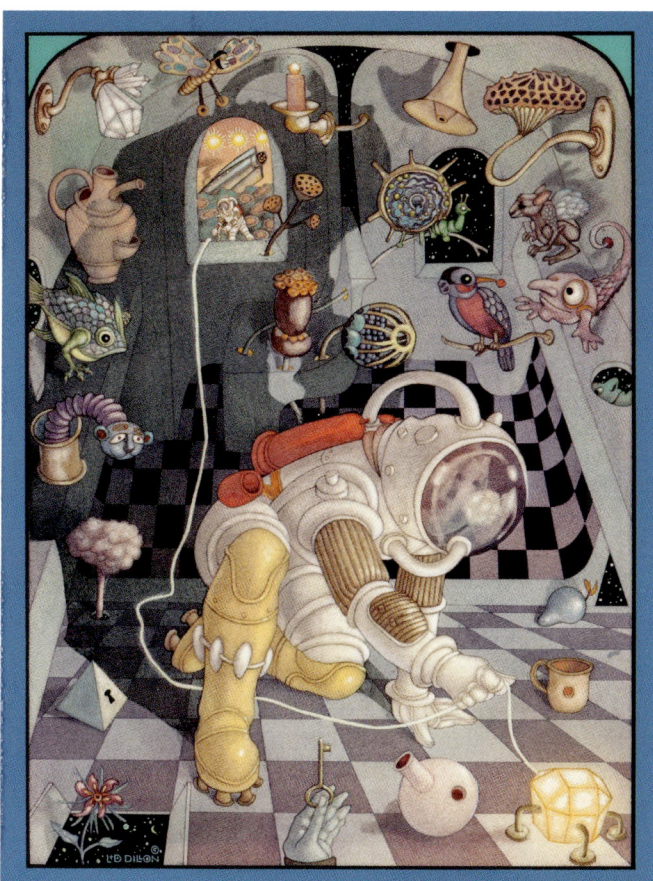

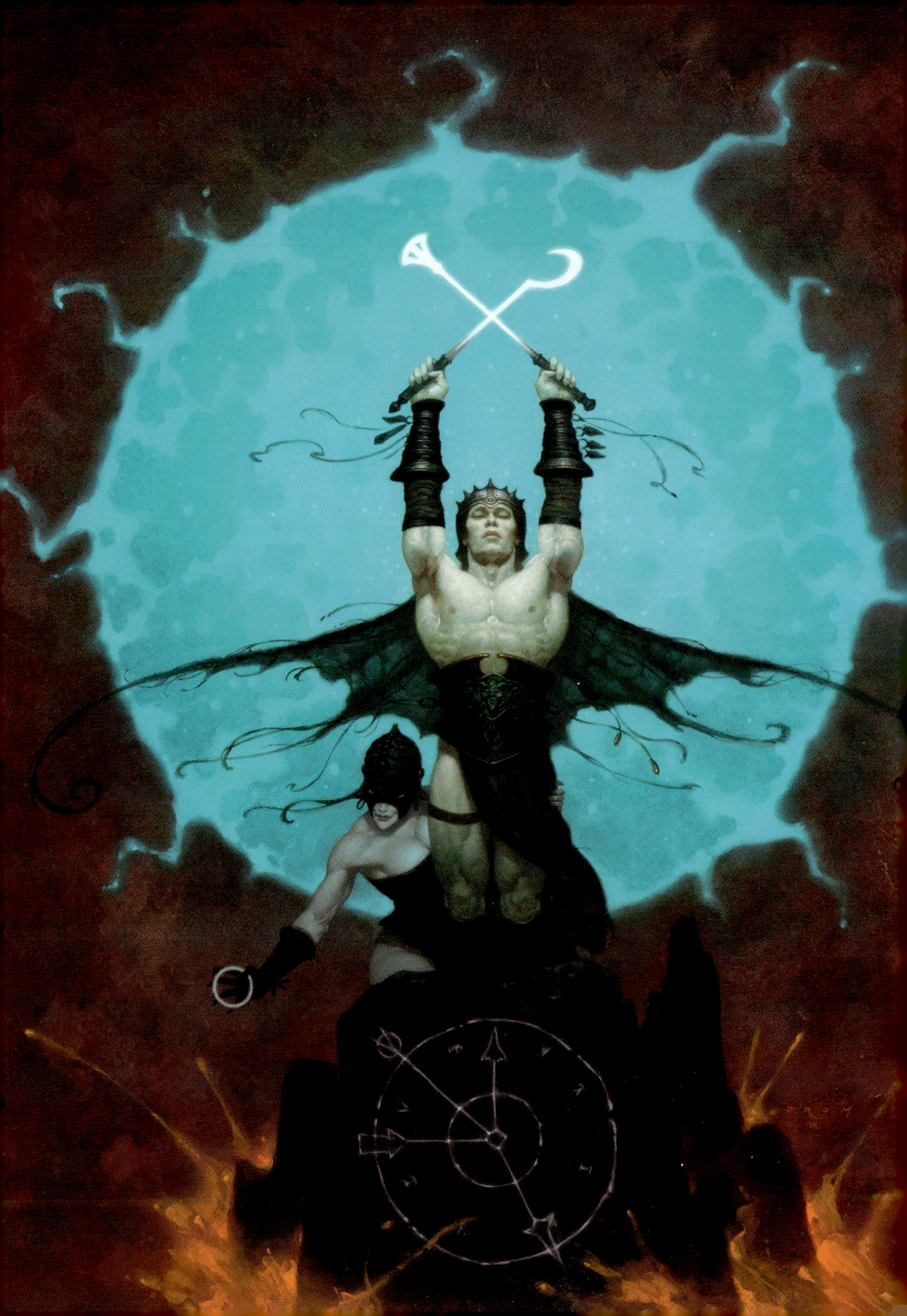

Philippe Druillet et Jean Giraud, alias Mœbius, un rédacteur/éditeur, Jean-Pierre Dionnet et, poste capital pour tout groupe d'artistes, un directeur commercial, en la personne de Bernard Farkas. Ensemble, ils forment Les Humanoïdes associés. *Métal Hurlant* est un magazine haut de gamme qui tranche dans l'univers débraillé de la bande dessinée franco-belge, mais surtout c'est un titre fantastique, psychédélique, futuriste, spirituel, sexy et diablement français. L'Europe lance enfin une bête de taille dans le combat pour la suprématie sur le monde de la fantasy et cette bête-là dévore tous ses adversaires. Mœbius invente l'insondable et mutique Arzach, qui chevauche un ptérodactyle mutant à travers des

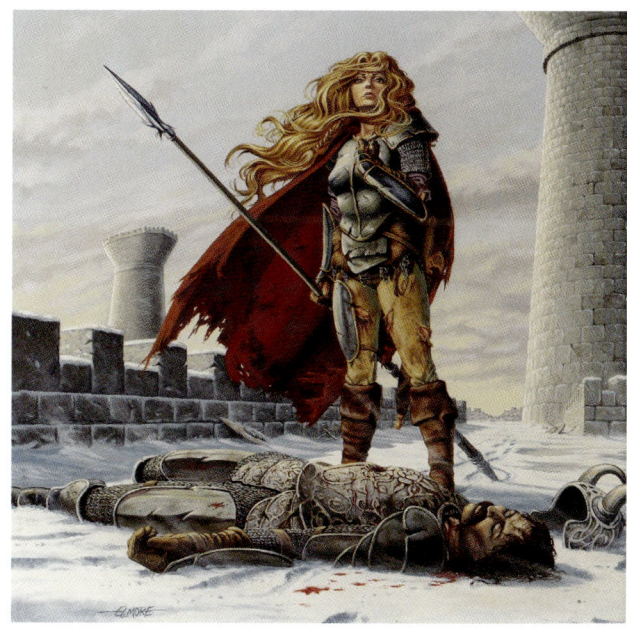

paysages extraterrestres dévastés, et le major Grubert, l'explorateur intrépide du Garage hermétique. Le Lone Sloane de Druillet est plus dur, plus menaçant, rendu dans des tons primaires lumineux qui contrastent avec les pastels estompés, oniriques, de Mœbius. Le magazine est au départ un trimestriel, mais devient mensuel au neuvième numéro et intègre d'autres artistes européens dans l'équipe, parmi lesquels Enki Bilal, Yves Chaland, Serge Clerc, Guido Crepax, Jean-Claude Gal, H.R. Giger, Gaetano Liberatore, Milo Manara, Masse, Chantal Montelier, Jean-Michel Nicollet, Joost Swarte et Alain Voss, ainsi que le Chilien Alejandro Jodorowsky et les Américains Richard Corben et Bernie Wrightson. En 1976 l'éditeur du magazine humoristique américain *National Lampoon* tombe sur *MH* à Paris et en achète les droits pour le marché états-unien ; *Heavy Metal* sort en avril 1977. Il ne contient à l'origine que le contenu français dont les textes ont été traduits, ce qui limite les coûts de production et optimise les profits immédiats. Avec le temps, *Heavy Metal* devient une entité propre, à laquelle contribuent des artistes venus du monde entier, notamment Chris Achilleos, Julie Bell, Simon Bisley, Charles Burns, Clyde Caldwell, Howard Cruse, Alex Ebel, Alex Horley, Jeff Jones, Michael Kaluta, Paul Kerchner, Rod Kierkegaard, Karl Kofoed, Walter Simonson, Lorenzo Sperlonga, Arthur Suydam, Stefano Tamburini, Boris Vallejo et Luis Royo.

Bien que toujours très appréciés d'un noyau dur de fans absolus de bande dessinée fantasy, les deux magazines peinent à suivre les goûts changeants du public, des conflits émergent sur leur gestion et ils font aussi face à des critiques pour leur contenu de plus en plus sexualisé. Certains

Opposite: Gerald Brom, known simply as Brom, was hired by TSR as a game illustrator in 1989, at age 24. *Maelstrom*, oil on board, 1998, 63.5 x 45.7 cm (25 x 18 inches).

Above: Larry Elmore was the first staff artist at TSR, producers of Dungeons & Dragons, joining in 1981. When

TSR undertook the *Dragonlance* series in 1984 he created the look of the saga, including this powerful painting, *The Death of Sturm.* Acrylic on board, 48.2 x 48.2 cm (19 x 19 inches). Courtesy of Heritage Auctions. © Wizards of the Coast LLC.

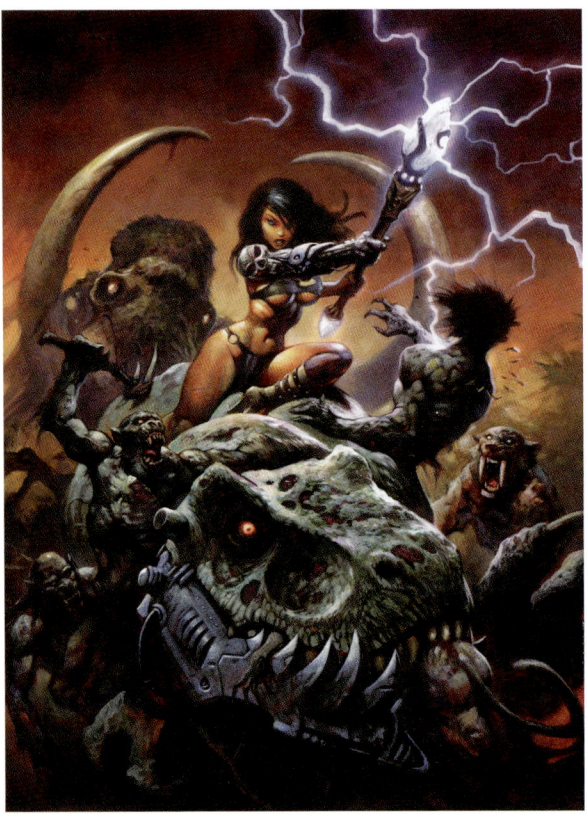

fans de fantasy ne s'intéressent par exemple ni au membre hypertrophié du Den de Richard Corben ni à la violence extrême du RanXerox de Tamburini et Liberatore. Pour eux, il y a la saga plus douce du *Seigneur des Anneaux*, dont le culte se développe à cette époque sous l'égide des frères Hildebrandt, de John Howe, Alan Lee et Ted Nasmith, et surtout la sortie en 1974 du jeu de rôle *Donjons & Dragons*, inspiré par l'univers de Tolkien.

D&D fait des débuts modestes – il s'agit au départ d'un simple jeu de dés pour experts en stratégie guerrière – mais publie en 1977 une version bien plus complexe et structurée, les *Règles avancées de Donjons & Dragons*. Les deux versions permettent aux joueurs d'incarner différents personnages de fantasy qui vivent diverses aventures dans un royaume imaginaire sur lequel règne un maître du donjon. D&D s'ouvre peu à peu à l'interprétation visuelle. Ses manuels, où l'action apparaissait à l'origine sous la forme de lignes rudimentaires tracées sur une grille, s'enrichissent de couvertures et d'illustrations intérieures en couleur sophistiquées quand Jim Roslof reprend leur conception en 1975 et qu'il engage Clyde Caldwell, Jeff Easley, Larry Elmore, Jim Holloway, Keith Parkinson, Harry Quinn et Tim Truman. À chaque nouvelle version, de nouveaux artistes sont sollicités, notamment Brom, Douglas Chaffee, Ralph Horsley, Todd Lockwood, Erik Olsen, rk post, Wayne Reynolds et Eva Widermann.

En 1993, le concepteur de jeux Wizards of the Coast, basé à Seattle, présente *Magic : The Gathering*, le premier jeu de cartes à jouer et collectionner de fantasy (récemment sacré jeu le plus complexe du monde). D&D, dont la maison mère a été avalée par Wizards en 1997, produit alors des manuels d'utilisation illustrés haut de gamme, mais la couleur se limite à une couverture peinte et quelques rares pleines pages, alors que 600 nouvelles cartes *Magic* sortent chaque année, chacune arborant une œuvre originale et le nom de son auteur, si bien qu'il est facile pour les artistes de se créer une communauté de fans parmi ses cinq millions de joueurs dans le monde.

Above: Savage Queen, by Alex Horley, was created for Horley's 2014 San Diego Comic-Con Exclusive Sketchbook. Mixed media on board.

Opposite: Cross Generation Entertainment, better known as CrossGen, was a comic book and entertainment company founded in 1998 and bought out by Disney in 2004. Joe Jusko produced this dynamic cover for the trade edition of their title *Sojourn* in 2000. Oil on board, 38 x 55.8 cm (15 x 22 inches).

MASTERPIECES OF FANTASY ART

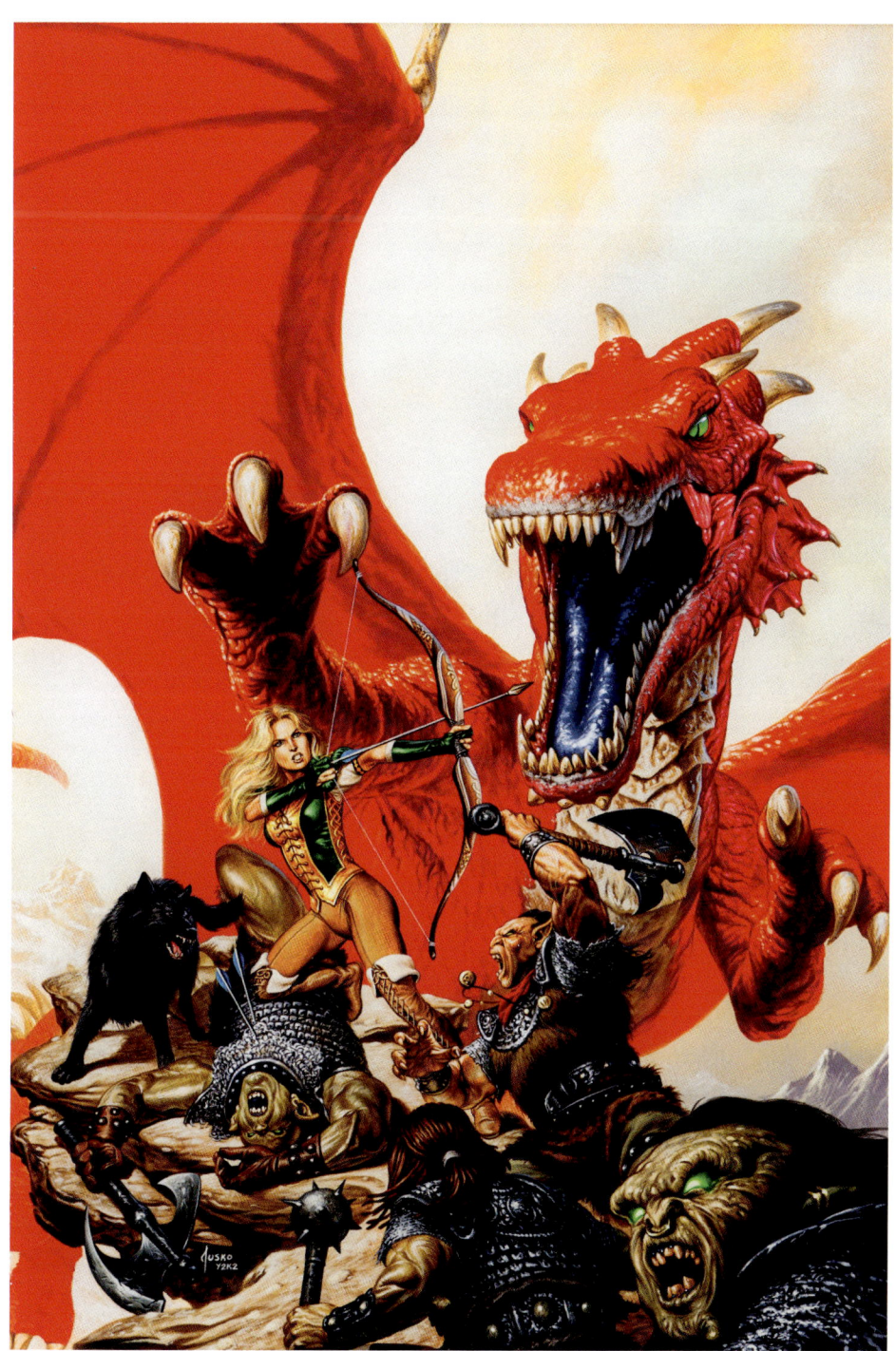

LA FANTASY AVANT, MAINTENANT ET TOUJOURS

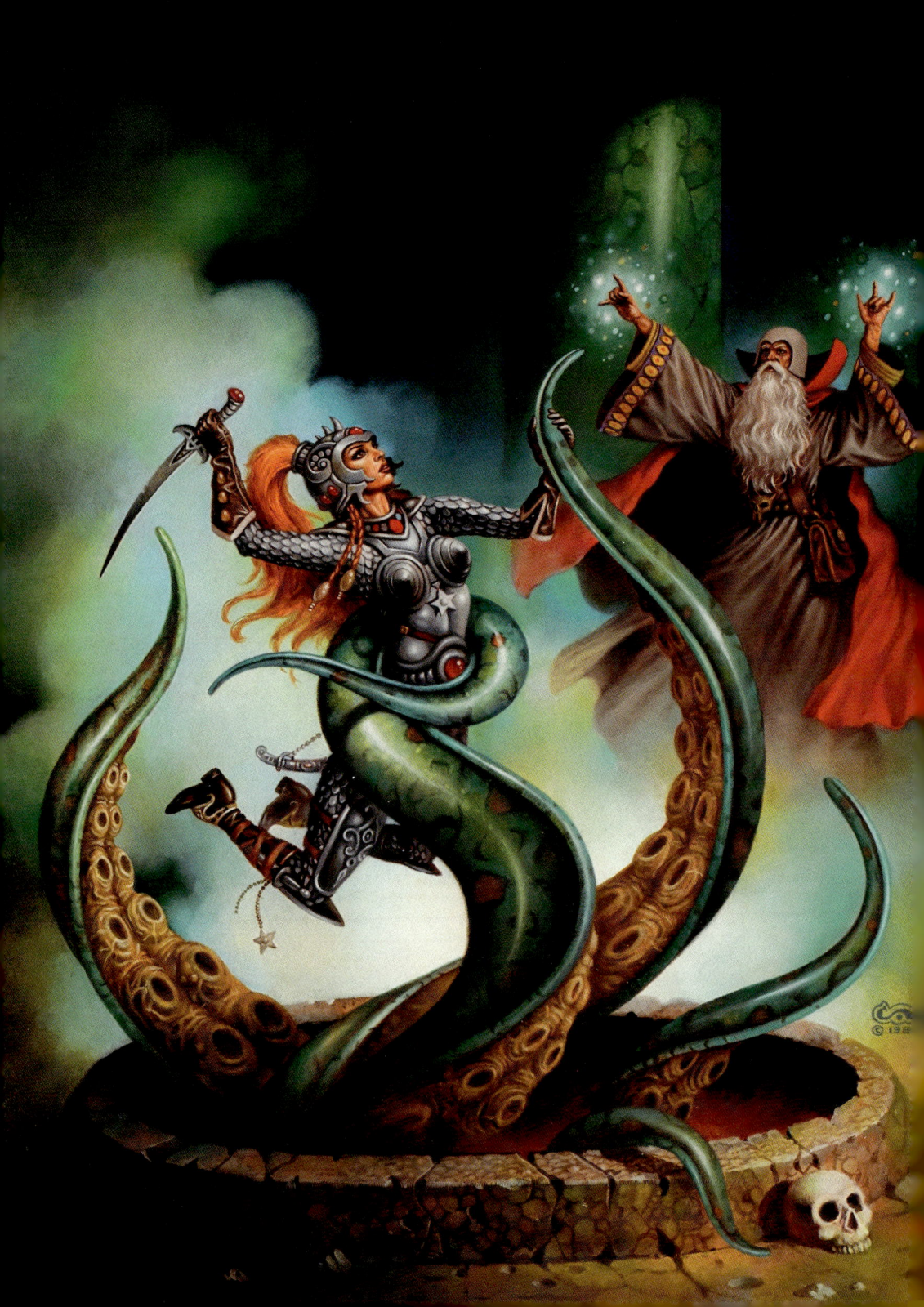

Les cartes *Magic* inspirent d'autres jeux fantasy de cartes à échanger, comme le *Super jeu de cartes Dragon Ball*, *Yu-Gi-Oh!* et celui de *Final Fantasy*, tous nés au Japon, où l'art et les artistes fantasy s'épanouissent au XXIᵉ siècle.

Et puis il y a Hollywood. Le premier volet de *Star Wars* sort en 1977, la même année que AD&D, et démontre de façon spectaculaire qu'il existe un marché pour les films de science-fiction et de fantasy, au-delà des séries B kitsch des années 1950 et 1960. L'année suivante, c'est au tour du *Seigneur des Anneaux* animé par Ralph Bakshi, très bien accueilli par les lecteurs passionnés de la saga malgré ses évidentes imperfections. Les affiches de ces deux films ont été conçues par Thomas Jung, un grand nom de l'illustration à Hollywood, mais Lucas demande aux frères Hildebrandt de repeindre l'original de Jung pour *Star Wars* et d'y ajouter les droïdes R2-D2 et C-3PO et le masque spectral de Dark Vador pour la sortie britannique du film.

Après le succès retentissant de *Star Wars*, les studios regardent les artistes de fantasy avec un œil neuf, sinon avec respect… Même si Ridley Scott doit se battre avec la 20th Century Fox pour engager H.R. Giger comme concept artist sur *Alien* en 1978. Le studio trouve son travail trop grotesque à l'écran, mais Scott persévère et impose cette créature à la fois élégante, terrifiante et artistiquement puissante. Le film vaut à Giger une reconnaissance internationale et l'Oscar des meilleurs effets visuels. Bakshi prend note de ce succès et s'associe à Frank Frazetta pour son film d'animation suivant, *Tygra, la glace et le feu* (*Fire and Ice*, 1983). De la même manière, quand Peter Jackson s'empare de la trilogie du *Seigneur des Anneaux* en 1998, il embauche les artistes fantasy John Howe et Alan Lee et demande à ses équipes de production de respecter scrupuleusement leurs dessins pour bâtir et peupler la Terre du Milieu.

Et puis il y a le *Dune* d'Alejandro Jodorowsky. Mœbius crée 3 000 croquis pour le plus célèbre film de fantasy jamais réalisé, un projet faramineux auquel participent aussi Giger et Chris Foss. Lorsque le script enfle jusqu'à prévoir 14 heures de film pour un budget de 15 millions de dollars – une somme conséquente en 1974 –, les studios se retirent les uns après les autres, pour ne laisser qu'un livre merveilleux, légendaire. Jodorowsky fait imprimer à compte d'auteur dix exemplaires du livre *Dune*, qui rassemble toutes les œuvres préparatoires, et les dépose dans les studios dont il sollicite un financement. Huit exemplaires ont disparu ; les deux autres appartiennent à la veuve de Mœbius, Isabelle Giraud, et à Jodorowsky. Le film et le livre font l'objet d'un documentaire, *Jodorowsky's Dune*, sorti en 2013.

En plus de leurs collaborations à l'étape de conceptualisation, nombre d'artistes fantasy sont sollicités pour des affiches de films après *Star Wars*. Les Hildebrandt signeront celles du *Choc des Titans* (*Clash of the Titans*, 1981) et de *Brisby et le Secret de NIMH* (*The Secret of NIMH*, 1982), et Tim peint seul le petit format pour *The Deadly Spawn* en 1983. Jeff Jones est choisi pour *Le Dragon du lac de feu (Dragonslayer)* en 1981. Frank Frazetta crée la première affiche de *Conan le Barbare* en 1982, après avoir illustré pendant des années des affiches de comédies hollywoodiennes, notamment *Quoi de neuf Pussycat ?* (*What's New Pussycat ?*, 1965), *Paradiso, hôtel du libre-échange* (*Hotel Paradiso*, 1966) et *Le renard s'évade à trois heures* (*Caccia alla volpe*, 1968). Mœbius réalise les affiches des *Maîtres du Temps* en 1982. Et bien avant, en 1968, Philippe Druillet a peint celles de trois films de vampires de Jean Rollin : *Le Frisson des vampires*, *La Vampire nue* et *Requiem pour un vampire*. Il

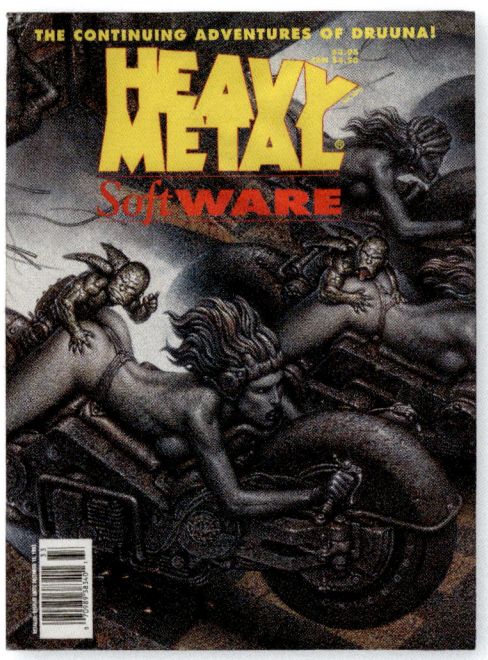

signe aussi l'étrange affiche française du film américain *Le Nom de la Rose* qui combine les visages sinistres dont il a le secret et un portrait de Sean Connery. Pourtant c'est un autre artiste qui domine bientôt la mêlée dans ce domaine : Boris Vallejo.

Vallejo décroche le contrat pour l'affiche de *Barbarella* l'année où *Star Wars* sort en salles et il produit une série de visuels pour *L'Empire contre-attaque* en collusion avec Coca-Cola en 1980, suivie de près par les affiches de *L'Épée sauvage (The Sword and the Sorcerer)* et *Épouvante sur New York (Q)* en 1982, *Deathstalker* en 1983, *Barbarian Queen* en 1985 et le si ringard *Naked Warriors* en 1988. Il accepte volontiers de tourner en dérision ces compositions héroïques pour *National Lampoon's Vacation* en 1983 et *European Vacation* en 1985. Des années plus tard, en 2007, l'épouse de Boris, Julie Bell, signera une affiche pour *Aqua Teen Hunger Force Colon Movie* en clin d'œil au travail de son mari pour *NatLamp*.

Avec l'avènement des logiciels de peinture numérique, le fantasy art est devenu un moyen d'expression populaire sur Internet dans les années 2000. Les artistes amateurs se retrouvent sur des sites dédiés comme Elfwood, DeviantArt, Epilogue et Quantum Muse, pendant que les dernières grandes figures des années 1970 et 1980 croquent la foule qui se presse au Comic-Con International, à la World Fantasy Convention, à la World Science Fiction Convention, au Lucca Comics and Games, au Dragon Con et dans d'autres « conventions » plus confidentielles dans le monde entier. La plupart de ces rendez-vous pour passionnés mélangent science-fiction et fantasy, univers du jeu vidéo et un peu de cosplay, quand les fans se déguisent en leurs idoles fantasy. Les magazines, jaquettes et pochettes fantasy faisant majoritairement partie du passé, les artistes comptent aujourd'hui sur les collectionneurs désireux d'acheter des tirages et des œuvres originales. C'est ainsi que le genre finit par sortir du créneau commercial, « illustratif », pour devenir, par voie d'élimination, un bel art libéré des anciens préjugés. Les enchères en ligne ont le vent en poupe et des collectionneurs d'un nouveau genre sont tentés d'acheter ce qui leur plaît plutôt que ce que leur conseille un galeriste… C'est ce bon vieux cortex orbitofrontal médian qui décide. Et une fois que vous avez lâché la bête, soyons francs : la plupart d'entre nous choisissent les œuvres les plus colorées et dynamiques, ce fantasy art qui nous fait tant de bien.

Above: Oscar Chichoni is an Argentinean fantasy illustrator, motion picture concept artist, and video game designer who combines flesh and machines in a style similar to H.R. Giger. This wraparound cover for *Heavy Metal* appeared on the 1993 Software special edition.

Opposite: Edward Binkley is a fantasy book cover illustrator and fine artist living in Madison, Wisconsin, where he also teaches at Madison College. This 2018 piece, titled *Rickshaw Pass*, is digital and colored pencil, 40.6 x 50.8 cm (16 x 20 inches).

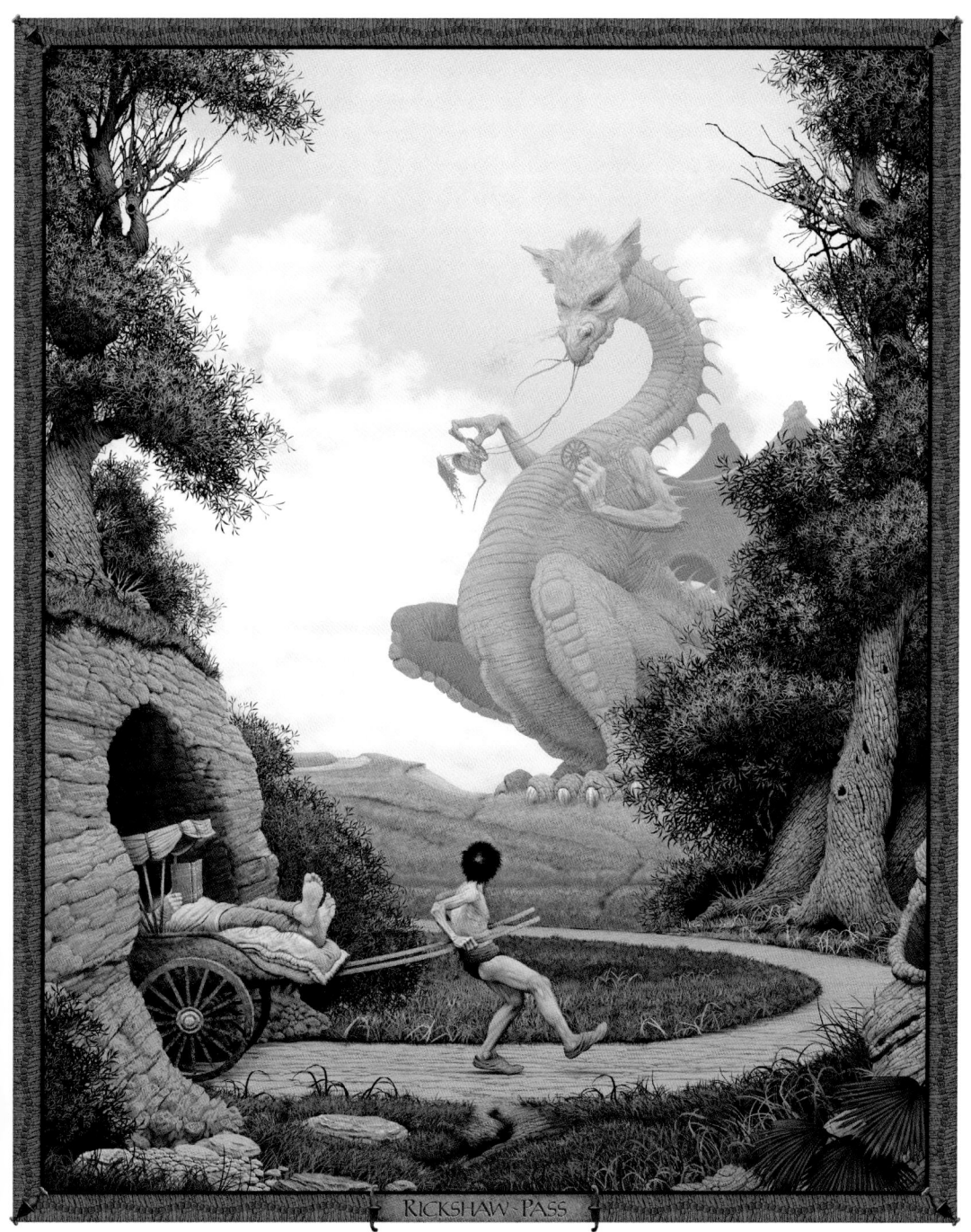

RICKSHAW·PASS

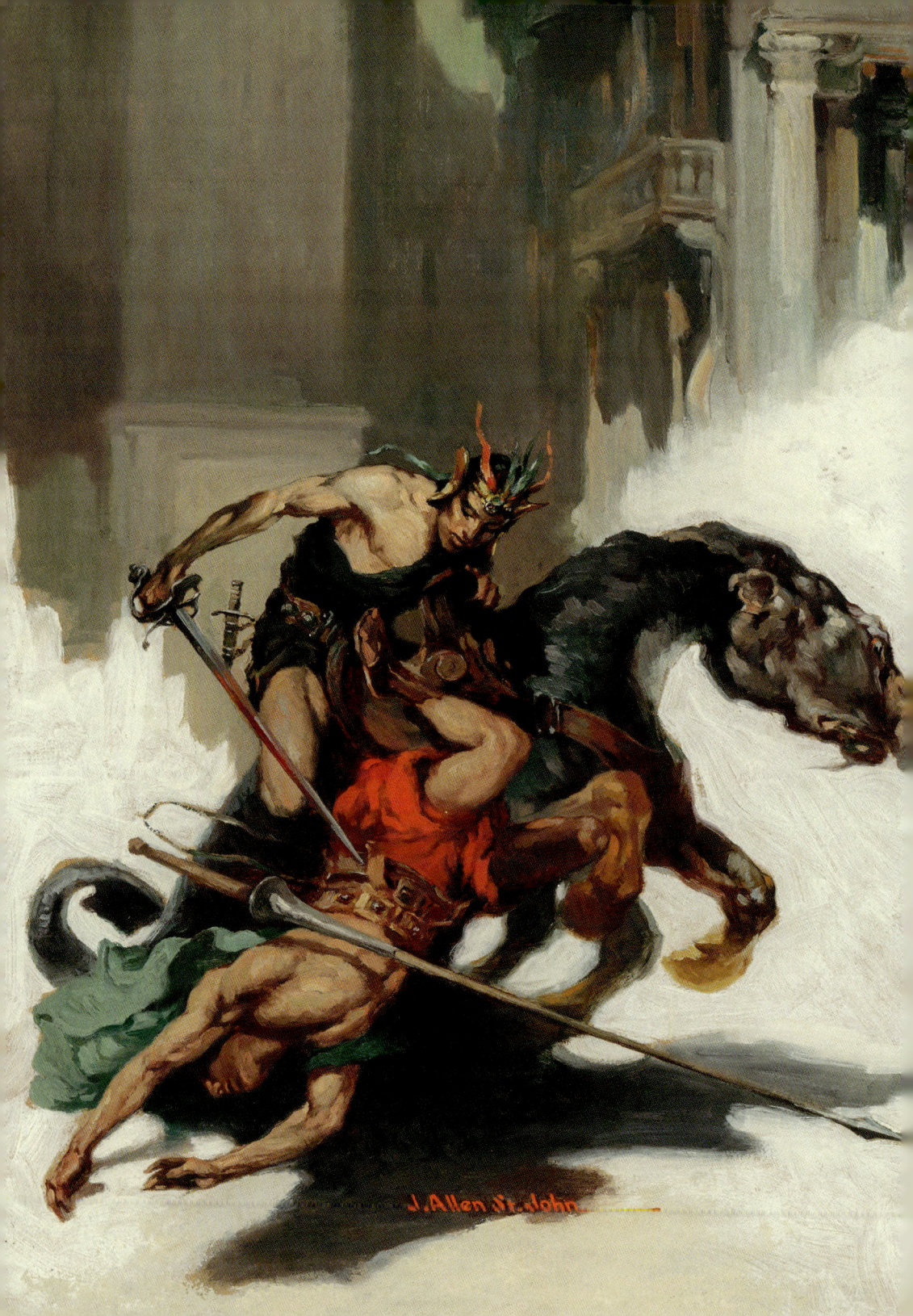

J. Allen St. John

FANTASY ART ORIGINS

BY DIAN HANSON

We often see Hieronymus Bosch or Maxfield Parrish cited as the first fantasy artists, but the immediate forerunners of fantasy art were a group of late 19th-century/early 20th-century children's book illustrators. Children's literature evolved away from grim moral tales to more fanciful entertainment in the mid-1800s. *Alice's Adventures in Wonderland* led the way in 1865, inspiring authors to rewrite traditionally gruesome folktales into lighter, more playful fairy tales. The period from 1880 to 1914, when WWI slowed all book printing, is now hailed as the Golden Age of Children's Literature, with the publication of *The Adventures of Pinocchio* in 1883 followed by L. Frank Baum's *The Wonderful Wizard of Oz* in 1900, Beatrix Potter's *Tale of Peter Rabbit* in 1902, Lord Dunsany's *The Gods of Pegana* in 1905, J. M. Barrie's *Peter Pan in Kensington Gardens* in 1906, Kenneth Grahame's *Wind in the Willows* in 1908, leading to the more robust *Tarzan of the Apes*, by Edgar Rice Burroughs,

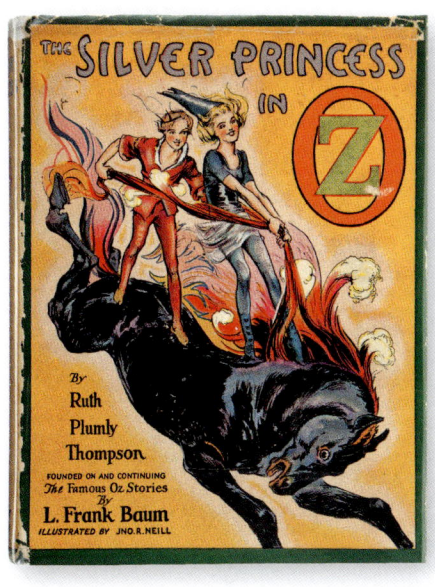

in 1912, and, from there, into more adult fantasy tales. Books for children generally used painted covers to increase shelf appeal, but *Peter Rabbit* was the first book to include illustration throughout the book, greatly enhancing its success. Publishers quickly leapt to produce illustrated editions of children's literature and a new category of artists emerged to meet the demand. The most successful maintained a childlike imagination that often colored all areas of their lives.

Walter Crane, one of the earliest, illustrated his first "toy" book of fairy tales — six-page books selling in England for sixpence — in 1865. In 1888 he collaborated with Oscar Wilde on his *Happy Prince and Other Stories*, and in 1891 he illustrated *The Story of the Glittering Plain*, William Morris's seminal fantasy novel. At the same time he was active in the early socialist movement and alienated American fans by attending anarchist meetings.

Henry Justice (H.J.) Ford's imaginative illustrations for Andrew Lang's Fairy Books (*The Blue Fairy Book*, *The Red Fairy Book*, etc.), published between 1889 and 1910, gave early shape to fantasy

Opposite: James Allen St. John, one of the earliest fantasy artists, is best known for illustrating the first *Tarzan* novels of Edgar Rice Burroughs. Here, the cover for *The Chessmen of Mars*, oil on board, 1922, 83.8 x 59 cm (33 x 23.25 inches). Courtesy of Heritage Auctions.

Above: John R. Neill illustrated magazines and children's books in the early 20th century. He is best known for illustrating L. Frank Baum's and Ruth Plumly Thompsons's *Land of Oz* stories, including *The Silver Princess*, a late work issued in 1938, when he was 61.

tropes such as dragons, griffins and invincible heroes, but Ford faced censure when, at age 61, he married a 26-year-old war widow.

William Wallace (W.W.) Denslow made his name collaborating with L. Frank Baum on *The Wonderful Wizard of Oz*, *Father Goose: His Book*, and *Dot and Tot of Merryland*. The two fell out over a royalty dispute, but Denslow still made enough off Baum to buy Bluck's Island, near Bermuda, where he retired to crown himself King Denslow I. There was no Queen Denslow; W.W. divorced all three of his wives.

John R. Neill took over illustrating L. Frank Baum's Oz books after Baum's split with Denslow, and became a noted Oz historian. On a darker note, he also illustrated the 1908 edition of *Little Black Sambo*.

Arthur Rackham's turn-of-the-20th-century illustrations for *Gulliver's Travels*, *Rip Van Winkle*, *Alice in Wonderland*, *Peter Pan*, and *Fairy Tales of the Brothers Grimm* were darkly sinister compared to contemporary children's fare, typically rendered in pen and ink and smoky ink washes to keep the fear factor in fairy tales. He was a devoted father to his only daughter, who was often depicted in these drawings.

Sidney Sime endured five years in the coal mines of northern England before he could afford art school. He was rescued, and his career established, by the author Edward Plunkett, 18th Baron of Dunsany, known simply as Lord Dunsany, who crafted the fantasy world of Pegana before fantasy fiction's invention. Sime illustrated *The Gods of Pegana* in 1905 and all of Dunsany's subsequent work until 1922.

Newell Convers (N.C.) Wyeth was the most successful of the American children's book illustrators; making enough off his paintings for *Treasure Island* in 1911 to purchase a house and

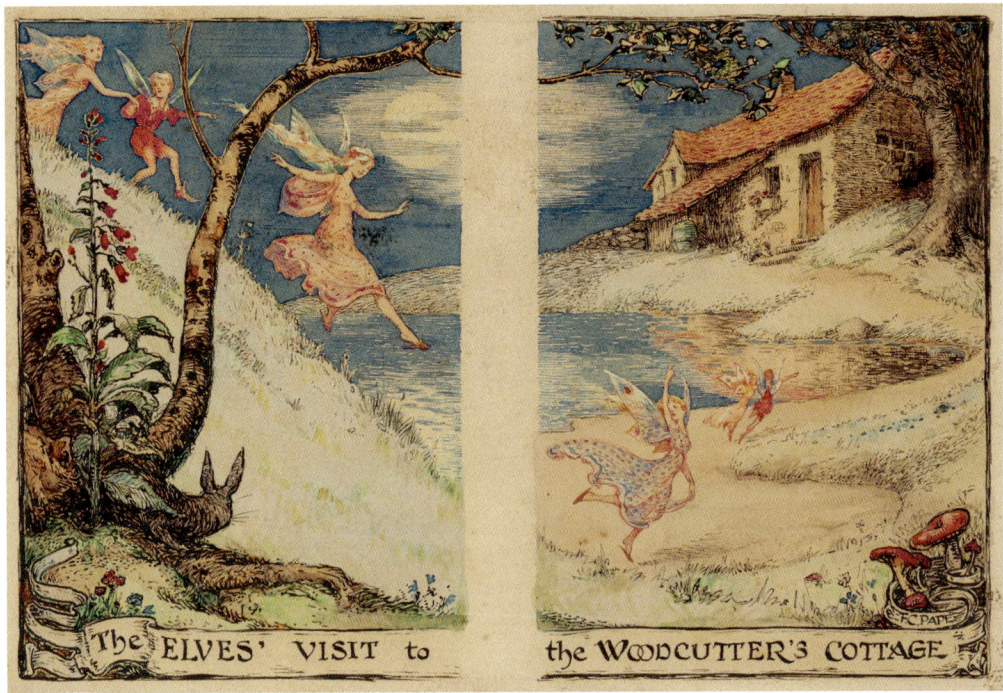

studio. Other classics of youth literature followed: between 1913 and 1921 he illustrated *Kidnapped*, *Robin Hood*, *The Last of the Mohicans*, *Robinson Crusoe*, and *Rip Van Winkle*. He claimed to despise the commercial projects that made him rich, and was moving entirely into fine art when he and a grandson were killed by a train in 1945.

William (Willy) Pogány grew up in an Austro-Hungarian farmhouse shared with the family's livestock. He worked his way through art school in Budapest and Paris, and found himself in London when Rackham's *Rip Van Winkle* came out in 1906. The book heightened the demand for fairy-tale illustration, and Pogány delivered with *The Welsh Fairy Book*, followed by *The Rime of the Ancient Mariner*, and *Tannhauser*, *Parsifal* and *Lohengrin*, making enough to immigrate to the U.S. in 1914. There he eventually found work in the film industry, which is more fantasy than any fairy tale.

Harry Clarke made a name for himself as a stained glass artist, working in the Art Nouveau style, but is also known for illus-

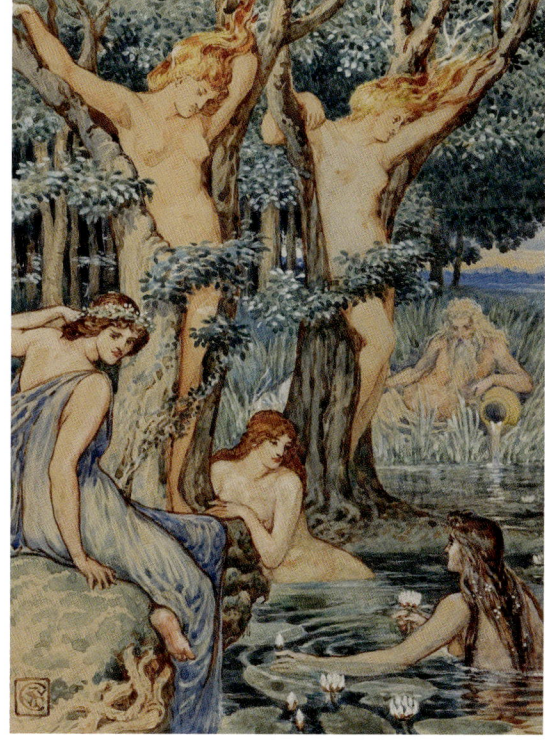

trating *Fairy Tales of Hans Christian Andersen* in 1916, followed by *Edgar Allan Poe's Tales of Mystery and Imagination* in 1919. Like Poe, he died young, of tuberculosis.

Both James (J.) Allen St. John and Clinton Pettee are best remembered for illustrating the works of Edgar Rice Burroughs, most notably Tarzan. St. John was already a successful artist and illustrator, aged 43, when tapped to provide illustrations for *The Return of Tarzan* in 1915, followed by covers for 32 subsequent Edgar Rice Burroughs novels. Pettee was a less accomplished pulp illustrator, but has the distinction of painting the first known image of Tarzan, for the October 1912 issue of *The All-Story Magazine*, now considered the most valuable pulp collectible, with issues going as high as $60,000. Whether through chance or the Tarzan connection both artists lived notably blameless lives.

Opposite: England led the world in children's book production in the late 19th and early 20th centuries, producing a number of talented fantasy illustrators who lay the foundation for fantasy art as we know it. Frank C. Papé was one of the most successful, with a smooth transition from children's books to adult fare after WWI. This, titled *The Elves Visit to the Woodcutter's Cottage*, is undated, circa 1910, ink and watercolor on paper, 26.6 x 17.7 cm (10.5 x 7 inches). Courtesy of Heritage Auctions.

Above: The first fantasy art was produced for children's books, as fantasy was linked to fairy tales and mythology. Walter Crane helped define what was known as the English "nursery motif" in the late 19th century. *Dryads and Naiads* is undated, watercolor on paper, 16.5 x 23.5 cm (6.5 x 9.25 inches). Courtesy of Heritage Auctions.

Following spread: Parrish's *Daybreak*, painted in 1922, is the most popular print of the 20th century, outselling DaVinci's *Last Supper*. The original painting sold for $7.6 million in 2006. Oil on board, 114 x 67.3 cm (45 x 26.5 inches).

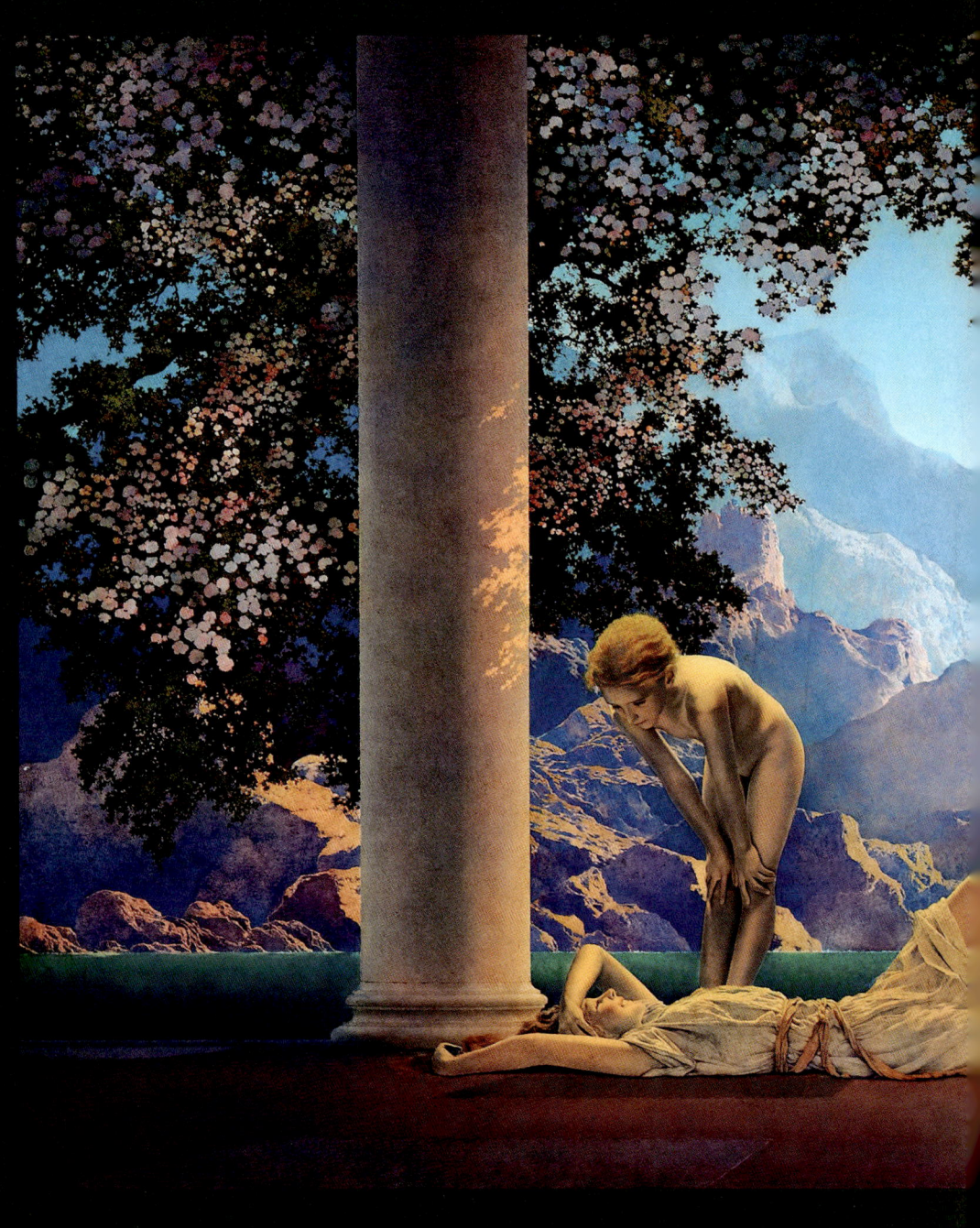

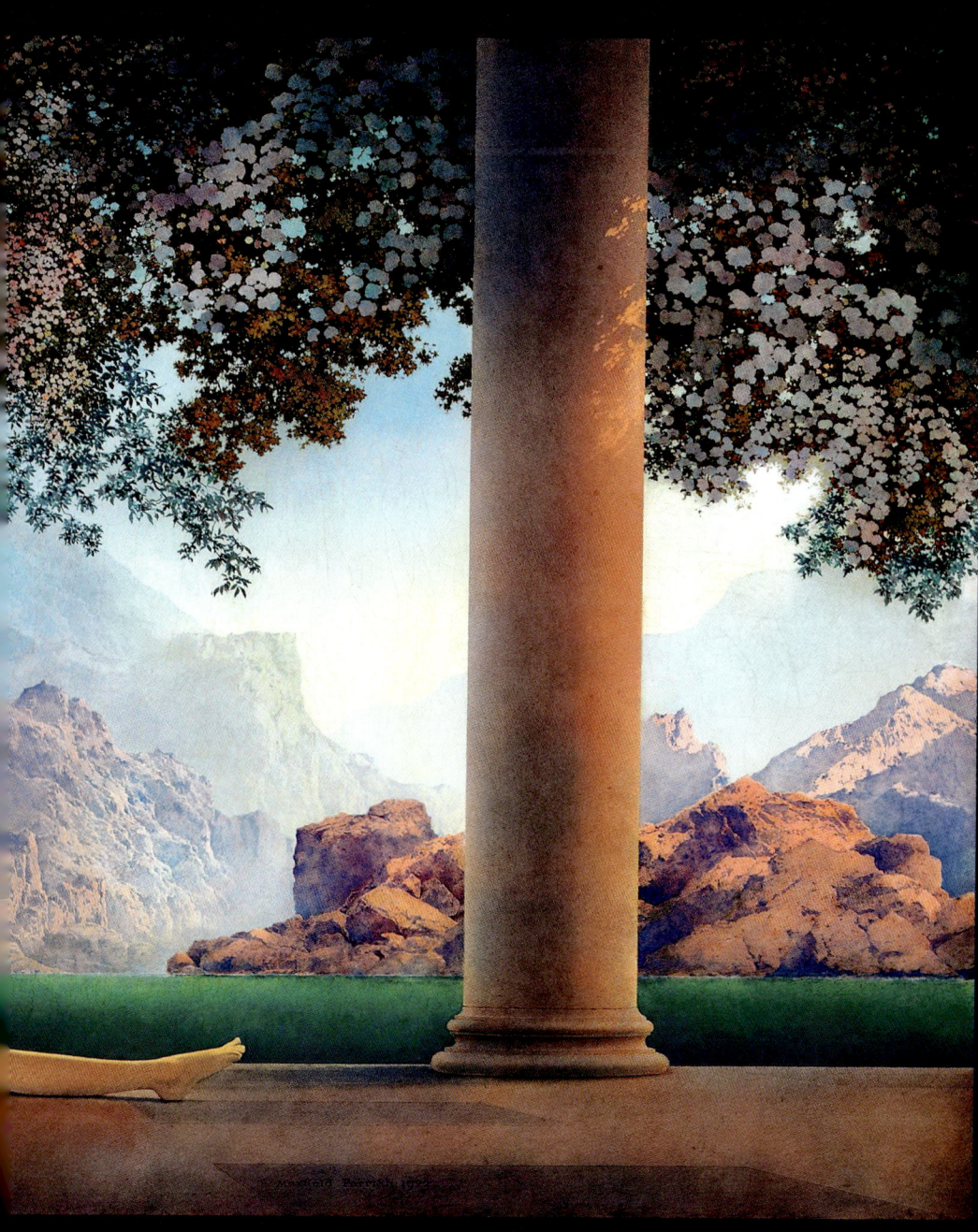

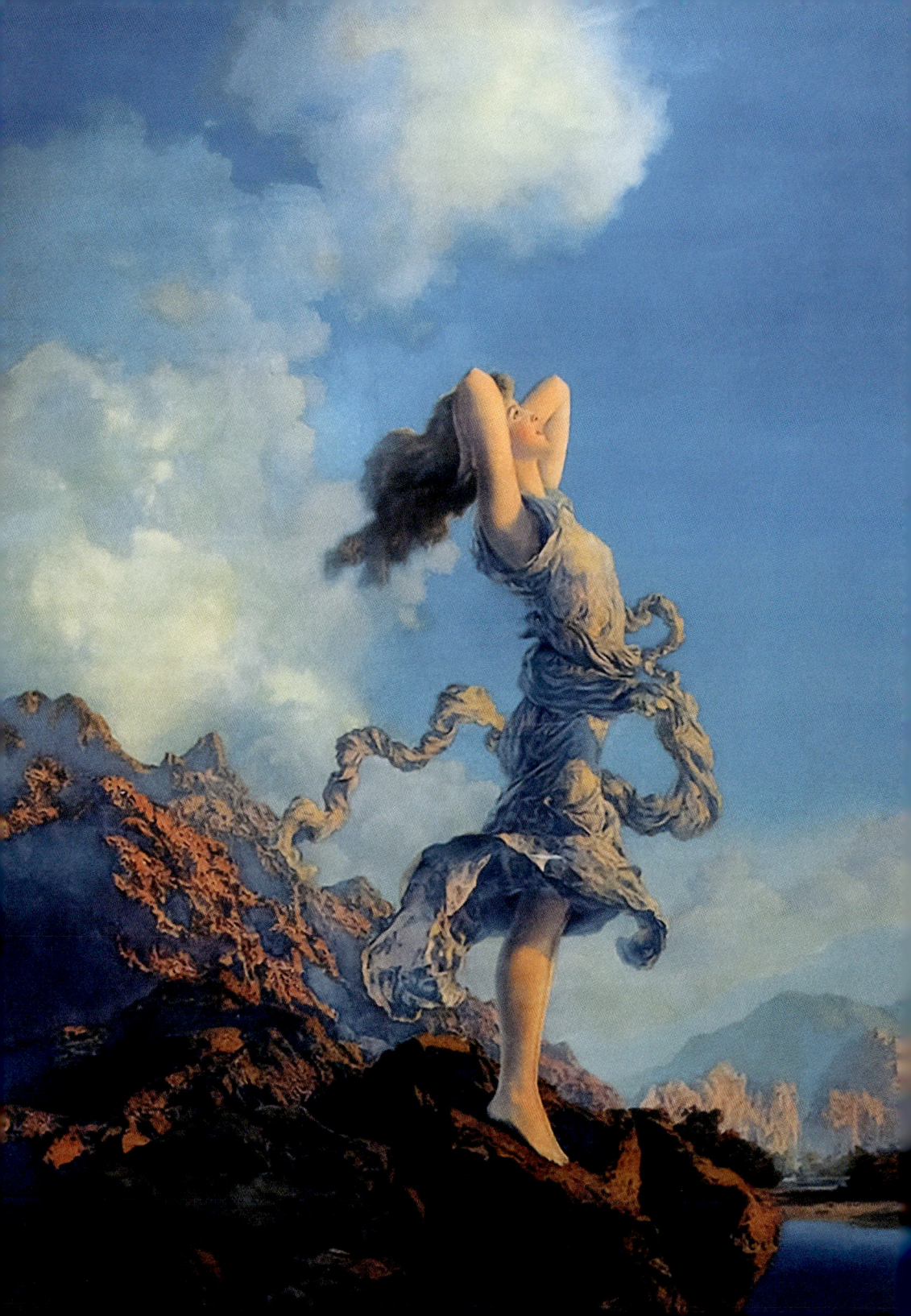

DIE URSPRÜNGE DER FANTASYKUNST

VON DIAN HANSON

Oft werden Hieronymus Bosch oder Maxfield Parrish als die ersten Fantasykünstler genannt, doch die unmittelbaren Vorläufer der Fantasykunst war eine Gruppe von Kinderbuchillustratoren des späten 19./frühen 20. Jahrhunderts. Um die Mitte des 19. Jahrhunderts entwickelte sich die Kinderliteratur weg von den verbissenen Moralgeschichten, hin zu einer fantasievolleren Unterhaltung.

Alice's Adventures in Wonderland wies 1865 die Richtung und inspirierte Autoren, traditionell grausame volkstümliche Erzählungen zu leichteren, eher spielerischen Märchen umzuschreiben. Der Zeitraum zwischen 1880 und 1914, als der Erste Weltkrieg die gesamte Buchproduktion drosselte, wird inzwischen als das Goldene Zeitalter der Kinderliteratur gefeiert: 1883 wurden *The Adventures of Pinocchio* veröffentlicht, dem folgten 1900 L. Frank Baums *The Wonderful Wizard of Oz*, 1902 Beatrix Potters *Tale of Peter Rabbit*, 1905 Lord Dunsanys *The Gods of Pegana*, 1906 J. M. Barries *Peter Pan in Kensington Gardens* und 1908 Kenneth Grahames *Wind in the Willows*. Dies führte 1912 schließlich zum robusteren *Tarzan of the Apes* von Edgar Rice Burroughs und von diesem aus zu Fantasygeschichten, die eher für Erwachsene gedacht waren.

Um von den Regalen aus attraktiver zu wirken, wiesen die Titelseiten der Bücher für Kinder in der Regel ein gemaltes Motiv auf, *Peter Rabbit* jedoch war das erste dieser Bücher, das auch auf den Innenseiten durchgängig illustriert war, was seinen Erfolg erheblich steigerte. Die Verleger gingen schnell dazu über, illustrierte Ausgaben von Kinderbüchern zu produzieren, und so bildete sich, um der Nachfrage zu entsprechen, eine neue Gruppe von Künstlern heraus. Die Erfolgreichsten unter ihnen wahrten eine kindliche Fantasie, die oft alle Bereiche ihres Lebens verschönerte.

Walter Crane, einer der Ersten, illustrierte sein erstes „Spielzeug"-Buch mit Märchen 1865 – es waren sechsseitige Publikationen, die in England für eine Sixpence-Münze verkauft wurden. 1888 arbeitete er mit Oscar Wilde für dessen *Happy Prince and Other Stories* zusammen, und 1891 illustrierte er William Morris' einflussreichen Fantasyroman *The Story of the Glittering Plain*. Gleichzeitig war er in der frühsozialistischen Bewegung aktiv und irritierte amerikanische Fans mit seiner Teilnahme an Anarchistentreffen.

Henry Justice (H. J.) Fords fantasievolle Illustrationen für Andrew Langs Märchenbücher (*The Blue Fairy Book*, *The Red Fairy Book* etc.), veröffentlicht zwischen 1889 und 1910, verliehen Fantasytropen wie Drachen, Greifen und unbesiegbaren Helden eine frühe Prägung, doch sah sich Ford heftiger Kritik ausgesetzt, als er im Alter von 61 Jahren eine 26 Jahre alte Kriegswitwe heiratete.

Opposite: Between 1918 and 1932 Maxfield Parrish produced yearly calendars for the Edison Mazda Lamp Division of General Electric. Each explored the concept of light, Parrish's artistic forte, and became some of his most popular works. Here is *Ecstasy*, painted for the 1930 calendar, 47 x 97.8 cm (18.5 x 38.5 inches).

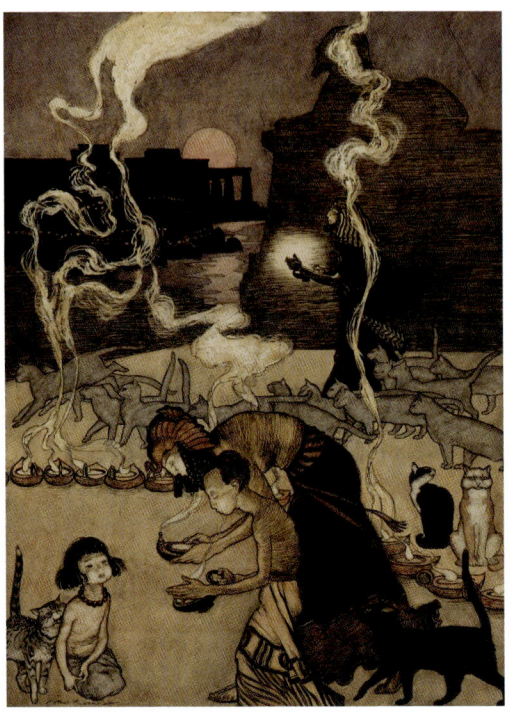

Am bekanntesten ist Maxfield Parrish für seine kommerziellen Drucke, doch war er auch ein Kinderbuchillustrator, und sein 1901 für die Geschichte *The Reluctant Dragon* geschaffenes Gemälde, das in dem 1902 veröffentlichten Buch *Dream Days* enthalten war, verfestigte das Bild des Drachens als einer Hauptfigur der Fantasyliteratur.

William Wallace (W. W.) Denslow machte sich durch seine Zusammenarbeit mit L. Frank Baum an *The Wonderful Wizard of Oz*, *Father Goose: His Book* und *Dot and Tot of Merryland* einen Namen. Ein Streit um Honorare brachte die beiden auseinander, doch auch ohne Baum verdiente Denslow noch genug, um sich Bluck's Island bei den Bermudas zu kaufen, wohin er sich zurückzog, um sich selbst als König Denslow I. zu krönen. Eine Königin Denslow gab es nicht; W. W. ließ sich von all seinen drei Frauen scheiden.

Nach Baums Trennung von Denslow übernahm John R. Neill die Illustrationen zu L. Frank Baums *Oz*-Büchern und wurde ein bekannter *Oz*-Historiker. Er illustrierte auch, in einem düstereren Ton, die 1908 erschienene Ausgabe von *Little Black Sambo*.

Arthur Rackhams um die Wende zum 20. Jahrhundert entstandenen Illustrationen zu *Gulliver's Travels*, *Rip Van Winkle*, *Alice in Wonderland*, *Peter Pan* und *Fairy Tales of the Brothers Grimm* waren, verglichen mit der zeitgenössischen Kost für Kinder, düster-unheimlich, normalerweise mit Feder und Tusche ausgeführt und in rauchigen Farben laviert, um den Gruselfaktor der Märchen zu wahren. Seiner einzigen Tochter, die in diesen Zeichnungen oft dargestellt wurde, war er ein hingebungsvoller Vater.

Sidney Sime stand fünf Jahre in den Kohleminen von Nordengland durch, bevor er sich die Kunstschule leisten konnte. Er war gerettet, und seine Karriere sicherte dann der Autor Edward Plunkett, 18. Baron von Dunsany, schlicht als Lord Dunsany bekannt, der die Fantasywelt von Pegana entwarf, noch bevor Fantasyliteratur überhaupt erfunden war. Sime illustrierte 1905 *The Gods of Pegana* und alle noch folgenden Werke Dunsanys bis 1922.

Above: Arthur Rackham was the premier illustrator of children's fairy tales and fantasy books in the early 20th century, the leader of the Golden Age of British Illustration, though his visions tended to be dark and often frightening. Here, *All Through Egypt Every Man Burns a Lamp,* from the book *The Land of Enchantment,* 1907. Ink and watercolor on paper, 28 x 43 cm (11 x 17 inches). Courtesy of Heritage Auctions.

Opposite: Edgar Church was an artist of modest talents who spent most of his career illustrating ads for phone books, as well as this 1910 science fiction illustration. He is best remembered today as the most famous collector of early comic books, amassing approximately 20,000 high-grade comics by his death at age 89 in 1978. Ink, chalk, and watercolor on paper, 33 x 48.2 cm (13 x 19 inches).

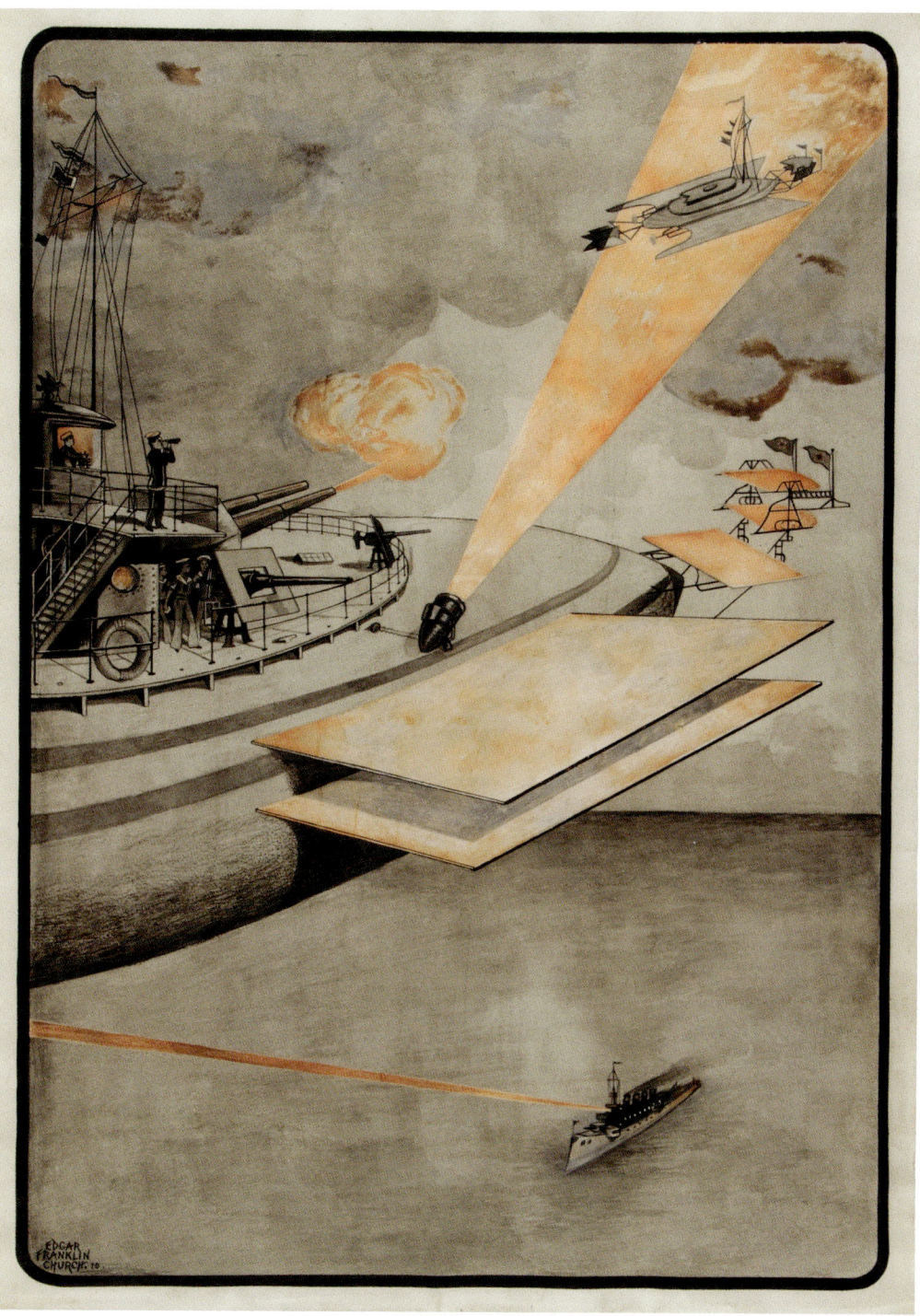

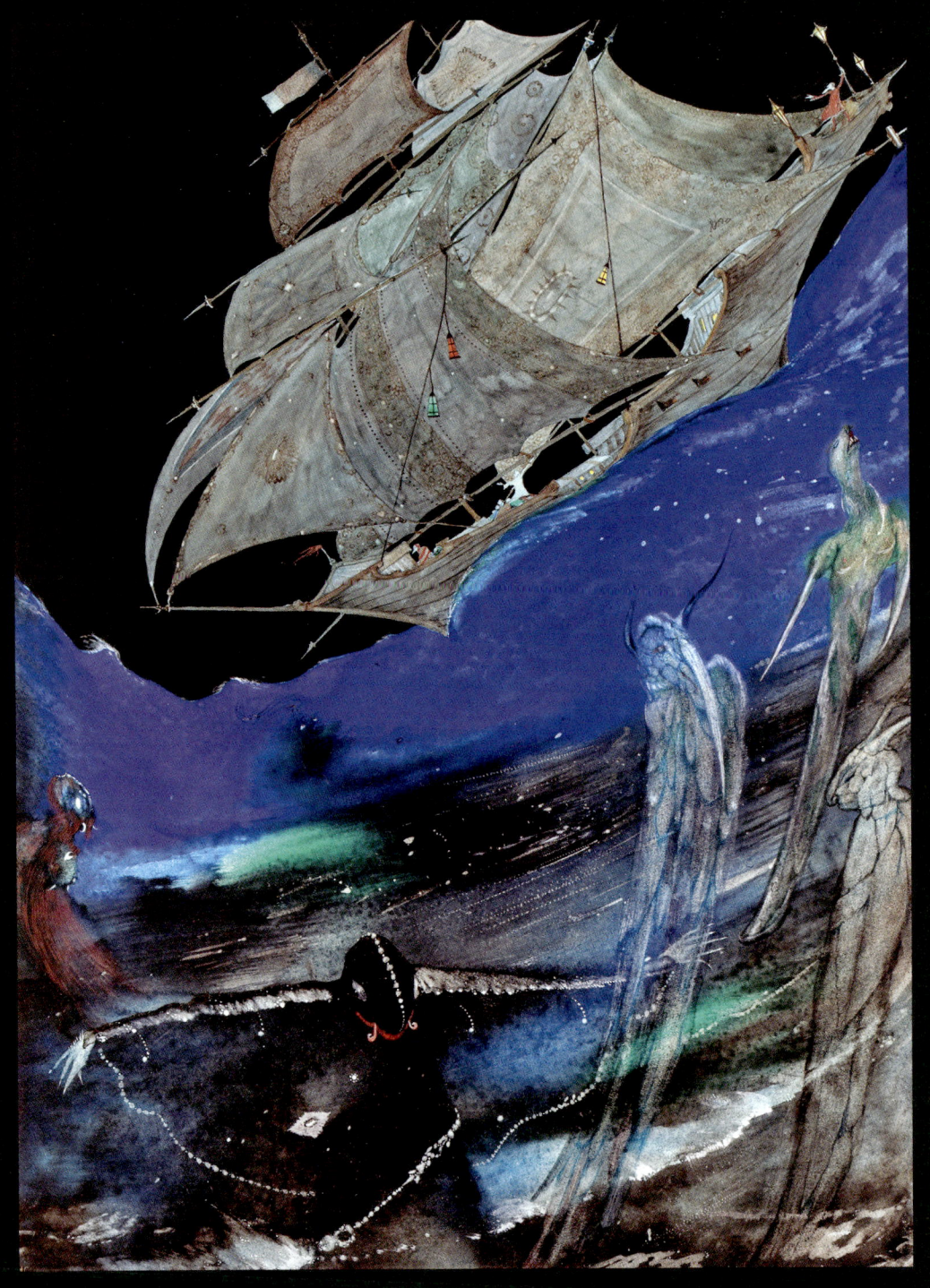

Newell Convers (N. C.) Wyeth war der erfolgreichste der amerikanischen Kinderbuchillustratoren. Mit seinen 1911 entstandenen Bildern für *Treasure Island* verdiente er genug, um sich ein Haus und ein Atelier kaufen zu können. Andere Klassiker der Jugendliteratur folgten: Zwischen 1913 und 1921 illustrierte er *Kidnapped*, *Robin Hood*, *The Last of the Mohicans*, *Robinson Crusoe* und *Rip Van Winkle*. Er behauptete, die kommerziellen Projekte, die ihn reich gemacht hatten, zu hassen, und wollte sich künftig nur noch der bildenden Kunst widmen, als er und ein Enkel 1945 bei einem Verkehrsunfall mit einem Zug ums Leben kamen.

William (Willy) Pogány wuchs in einem österreichisch-ungarischen Bauernhaus auf, das die Familie mit ihrem Vieh teilen musste. Er schlug sich durch, bis er Kunstschulen in Budapest und Paris besuchen konnte, und landete schließlich in London, als 1906 Rackhams *Rip Van Winkle* erschien. Das Buch steigerte die Nachfrage nach Illustrationen für Märchen, und Pogány lieferte – *The Welsh Fairy Book*, danach *The Rime of the Ancient Mariner*, *Tannhäuser*, *Parsifal* und *Lohengrin*. Nun hatte er genug verdient und konnte 1914 in die USA emigrieren. Dort fand er schließlich Arbeit in der Filmindustrie, die mehr an Fantasy zu bieten hat als jedes Märchen.

Harry Clarke machte sich als Glasmaler, der im Art-nouveau-Stil arbeitete, einen Namen, doch er ist auch bekannt für seine 1916 entstandenen Illustrationen der *Fairy Tales of Hans Christian Andersen*. Danach illustrierte er, 1919, *Edgar Allan Poes Tales of Mystery and Imagination*. Wie Poe starb er jung an Tuberkulose.

Sowohl James (J.) Allen St. John als auch Clinton Pettee sind vor allem für ihre Illustrationen der Werke von Edgar Rice Burroughs, besonders für Tarzan, in Erinnerung. Mit 43 Jahren war St. John bereits ein erfolgreicher Künstler und Illustrator, als er 1915 die Anfrage erhielt, Illustrationen für *The Return of Tarzan* zu liefern, ein Auftrag, dem Aufträge für die Cover von 32 weiteren Romanen von Edgar Rice Burroughs folgten. Pettee war ein weniger versierter Pulp-Illustrator, der jedoch hervorsticht, weil er für die Ausgabe vom Oktober 1912 der Zeitschrift *The All-Story* das erste bekannte Bild von Tarzan malte. Das Heft gehört mittlerweile zu den bei Sammlern begehrtesten Pulps und wird mit bis zu 60.000 Dollar gehandelt. Ob durch Glück oder dank der Tarzan-Connection, beide Künstler genossen ein bemerkenswert problemloses Leben.

Opposite: Irish artist Harry Clarke first illustrated Edgar Allan Poe's *Tales of Mystery and Imagination* with dark black and white drawings in 1919, to great acclaim. In 1923 a new edition was released, adding eight color plates to the original drawings. This painting illustrates *A Descent into the Maelstrom*. Mixed media on paper, 28 x 38 cm (11 x 15 inches). Courtesy of Heritage Auctions.

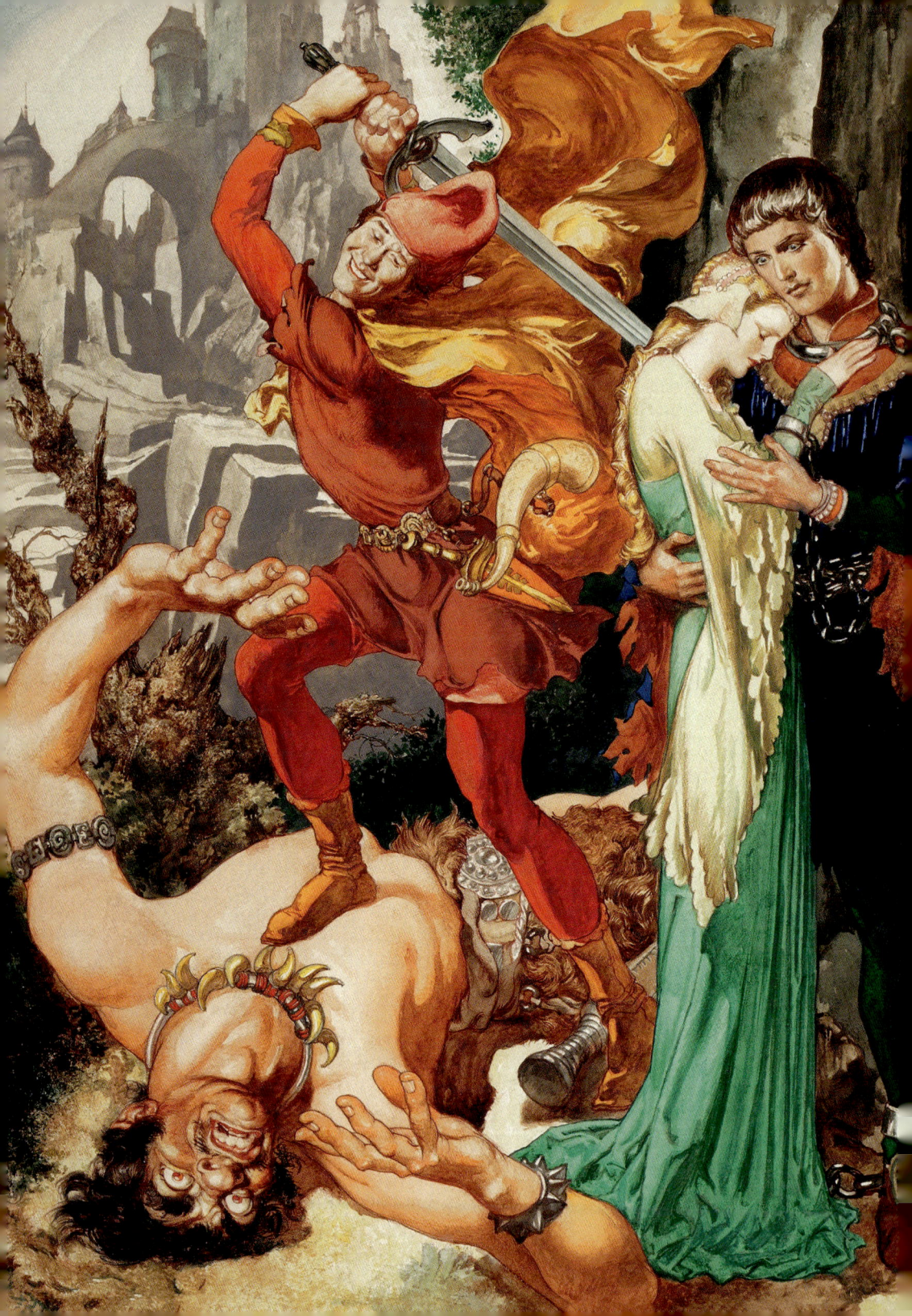

LES ORIGINES DU FANTASY ART

PAR DIAN HANSON

On entend souvent citer Jérôme Bosch ou Maxfield Parrish comme le premier artiste « fantastique », mais les pionniers les plus directs du fantasy art sont un groupe d'illustrateurs de livres pour enfants de la fin du XIXe siècle et du début du XXe. Au milieu du XIXe, la littérature enfantine se détacha des contes moraux souvent austères pour raconter des histoires plus divertissantes et fantaisistes.

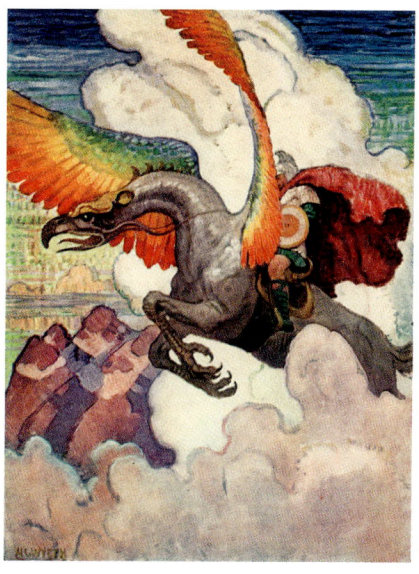

Les Aventures d'Alice au pays des merveilles ouvrirent la voie en 1865, encourageant les auteurs à donner des contes populaires traditionnellement lugubres une interprétation plus légère, ludique et féerique. La période qui s'étend de 1880 à 1914, date à laquelle le secteur de l'édition fut grandement ralenti par la Première Guerre mondiale, est aujourd'hui reconnue comme l'Âge d'or de la littérature jeunesse : Les Aventures de Pinocchio furent publiées en 1883, Le Magicien d'Oz de L. Frank Baum en 1900, Pierre Lapin de Beatrix Potter en 1902, Les Dieux de Pegana de Lord Dunsany en 1905,
Peter Pan dans les jardins de Kensington de J.M. Barrie en 1906, Le Vent dans les saules de Kenneth Grahame en 1908, puis le plus robuste Tarzan, seigneur de la jungle d'Edgar Rice Burroughs entra en scène en 1912, inaugurant la veine des contes fantastiques plus adultes.

Les livres pour enfants arboraient généralement des compositions peintes en couverture pour se distinguer sur les étagères des libraires, mais Pierre Lapin fut le premier à proposer des illustrations tout le long de l'histoire, ce qui accrut son succès. Les maisons d'édition se hâtèrent alors de produire des éditions illustrécs des classiques de la littérature enfantine et c'est ainsi qu'une

Opposite: Vilmos András Pogány, known as Willy, was an Austro-Hungarian artist who specialized in fairy-tale illustration, working mainly in pastels. Unnamed fairy-tale illustration, mixed media on board, circa 1915, 60.9 x 47 cm (24 x 18.5 inches). Courtesy of Heritage Auctions.

Above: Newell Convers Wyeth, known as N. C., was one of America's greatest illustrators and the most conflicted. He railed against the shallowness of commercial art while prospering from the proceeds. His illustrations sold calendars, cigarettes, cereal, and Coca-Cola, but also many classics of youth literature, including *King Arthur, Treasure Island*, and *Robinson Crusoe*. This was for Bulfinch's *Legends of Charlemagne*, released in 1924.

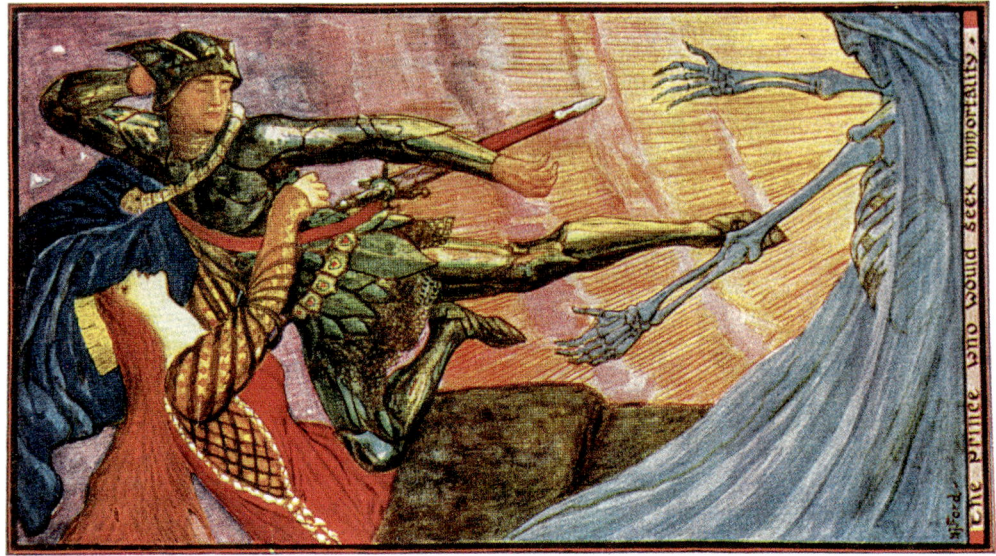

nouvelle catégorie d'artistes apparut, prompte à satisfaire cette demande. Les plus appréciés avaient conservé une imagination d'enfant, qui imprégnait souvent tous les domaines de leur vie.

Walter Crane, un des pionniers du genre, illustra son premier « recueil jouet » de contes de fées – un livret de six pages vendu six pence en Angleterre – en 1865. En 1888, il collabora avec Oscar Wilde sur *Le Prince heureux et autres contes (Happy Prince and Other Stories)* et en 1891, il illustra *La Plaine étincelante (The Story of the Glittering Plain)*, le célèbre roman fantastico-merveilleux de William Morris. Il militait parallèlement au sein du mouvement socialiste alors naissant et s'aliéna une partie de ses fans américains en assistant à des meetings anarchistes.

Les compositions que Henry Justice (H.J.) Ford imagina pour les contes de fées d'Andrew Lang (*The Blue Fairy Book*, *The Red Fairy Book*, etc.), publiés entre 1889 et 1910, donnèrent corps aux tropes du genre – dragons, griffons et invincibles héros – mais Ford fit les frais de la censure quand, âgé de 61 ans, il épousa une veuve de guerre de 26 ans.

On se souvient surtout de Maxfield Parrish pour son travail publicitaire, mais aussi pour ses nombreuses illustrations de livres destinés aux enfants et la composition qu'il peignit en 1901 pour la nouvelle « The Reluctant Dragon », intégrée l'année suivante au recueil *Dream Days*, qui fit du dragon un ingrédient essentiel du fantasy art.

William Wallace (W.W.) Denslow se fit un nom en collaborant avec L. Frank Baum sur *Le Magicien d'Oz*, *Father Goose: His Book* et *Dot and Tot of Merryland*. Les deux hommes se fâchèrent pour une histoire de droits d'auteur, mais Denslow tira suffisamment d'argent de leur partenariat

Above: Henry Justice Ford was one more master of England's Golden Age of Children's Literature. His specialty was fairy tales, specifically for a series collectively known as *Andrew Lang's Fairy Books*.

Opposite: René Bull was an English cartoonist, illustrator, photographer, and adventurer who took up book illustration in 1905. His most famous work was *The Arabian Nights*. This painting, titled *The Snake Charmer,* is pen and watercolor on paper, 22.2 x 31.7 cm (8.75 x 12.5 inches). Courtesy of Heritage Auctions.

MASTERPIECES OF FANTASY ART

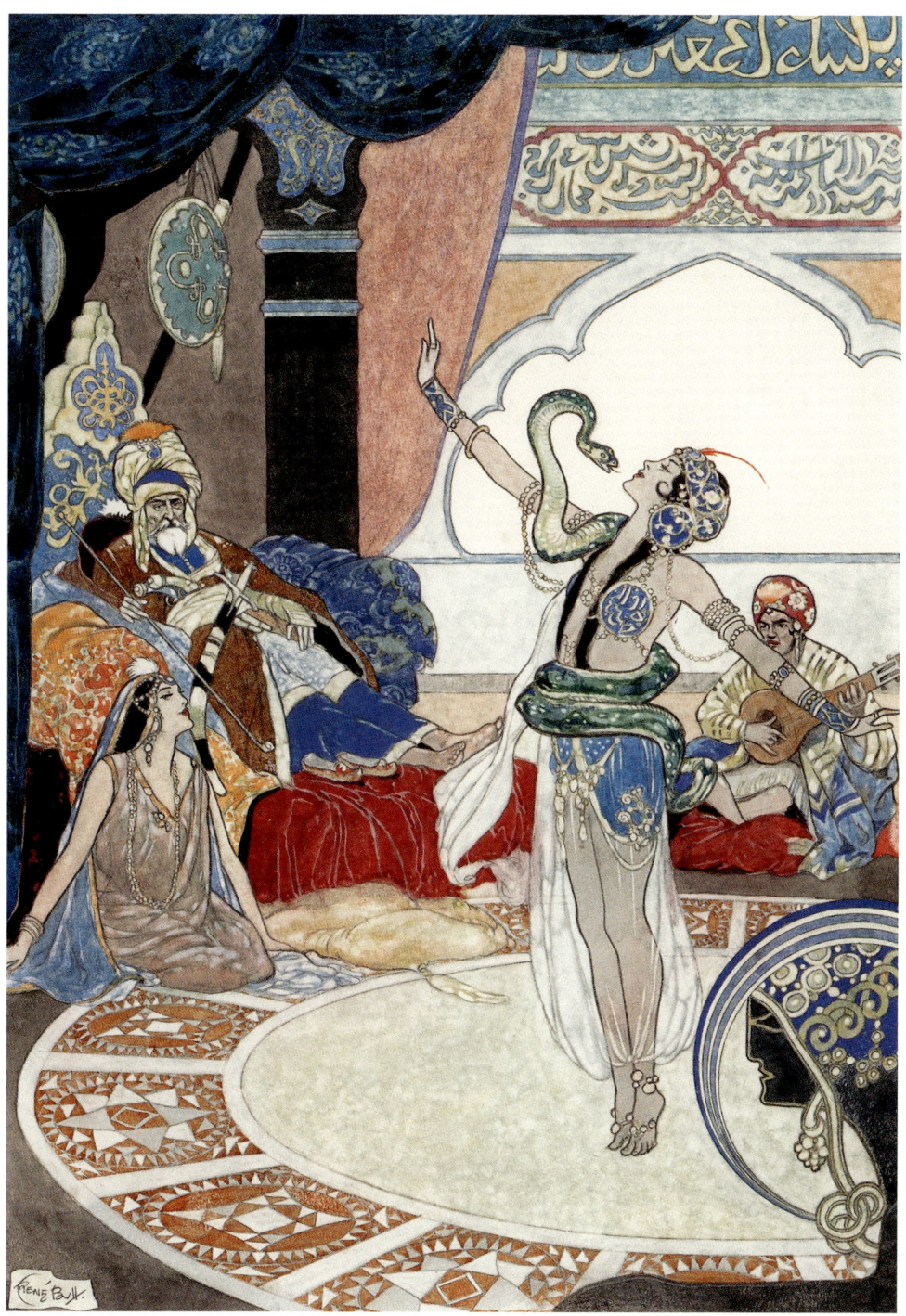

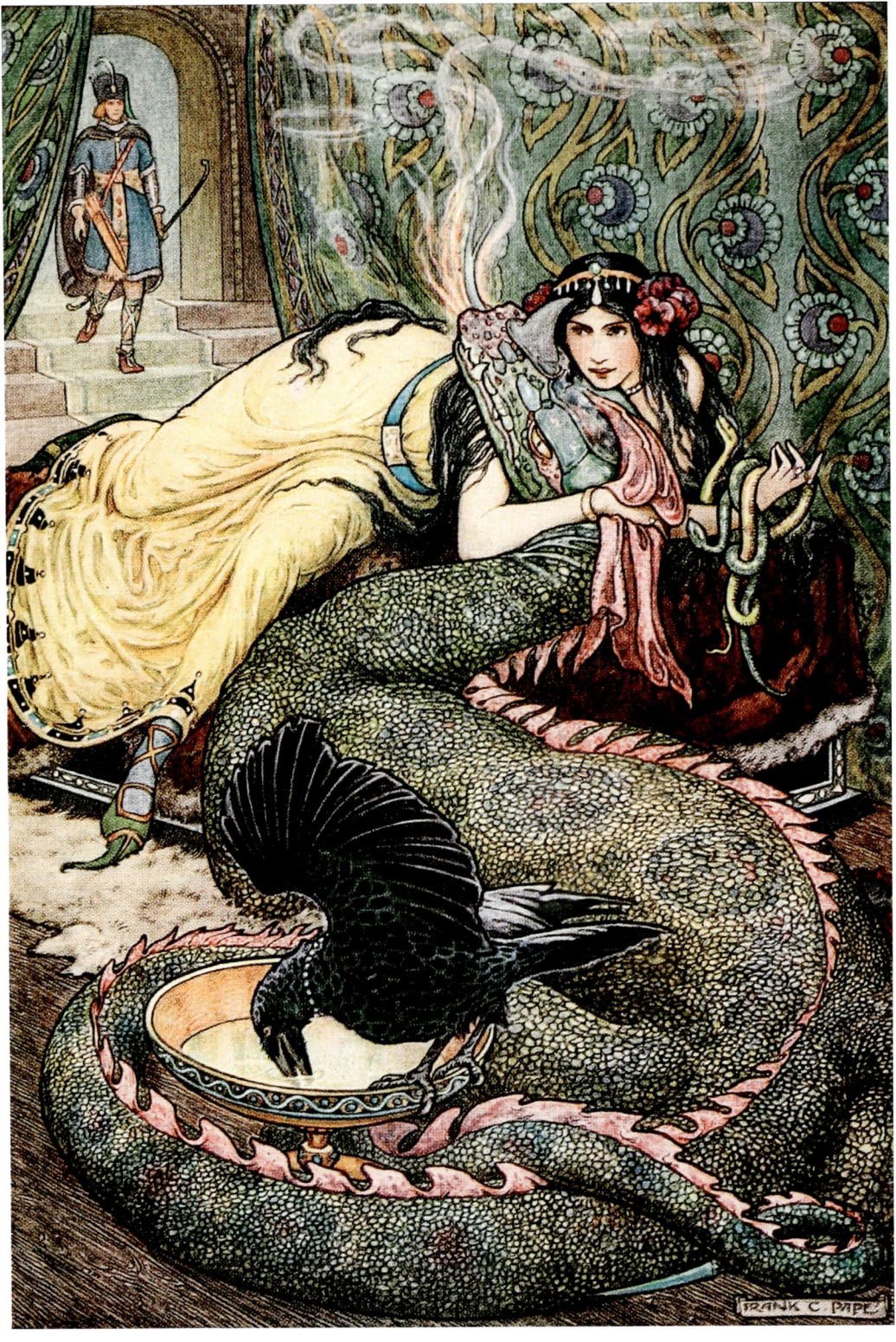

FRANK C. PAPE

pour s'offrir Bluck's Island, aux Bermudes, où il prit sa retraite et s'autoproclama roi Denslow I. Il n'y eut pas de reine Denslow. W.W. divorça de ses trois épouses successives.

John R. Neill reprit l'illustration de la série de L. Frank Baum après la rupture entre ce dernier et Denslow, pour devenir un spécialiste renommé du pays d'Oz. Dans un registre plus controversé, il illustra aussi la réédition de *Little Black Sambo* en 1908.

Les illustrations qu'Arthur Rackham réalisa au tournant du XXe siècle pour *Les Voyages de Gulliver*, *Rip Van Winkle*, *Alice au pays des merveilles*, *Peter Pan* et les *Contes de fées des frères Grimm* sont d'une noirceur assez glaçante comparées aux autres livres alors proposés aux enfants, souvent réalisées au crayon, à l'encre et en nébuleux lavis sombres pour conserver aux contes leur part inquiétante. Il fut un père dévoué pour sa fille unique, qui apparaît souvent dans ses dessins.

Sidney Sime trima cinq années dans les mines de charbon du nord de l'Angleterre avant de pouvoir se payer une école d'art et d'être secouru, puis lancé, par l'auteur Edward Plunkett, 18e baron de Dunsany, le célèbre Lord Dunsany qui a imaginé le monde de Pegana avant même l'invention de la fiction fantastique. Sime illustra *Les Dieux de Pegana* en 1905, puis toutes les œuvres de Dunsany jusqu'en 1922.

Newell Convers (N.C.) Wyeth fut, parmi les illustrateurs américains de livres pour enfants, celui qui eut le plus de succès : à eux seuls, ses tableaux pour *L'Île au Trésor* de 1911 lui rapportèrent suffisamment pour qu'il s'offre une maison et un atelier. Suivirent d'autres classiques de la littérature enfantine : entre 1913 et 1921, il illustra *Enlevé ! (Kidnapped)*, *Robin des Bois*, *Le Dernier des Mohicans*, *Robinson Crusoé* et *Rip Van Winkle*. Il affirmait n'avoir que mépris pour les commandes publicitaires qui l'avaient rendu riche et ne se consacrait plus qu'à l'art « noble » quand son petit-fils et lui furent tués par un train en 1945.

William (Willy) Pogány grandit dans une famille de fermiers austro-hongrois, parmi le bétail. Il travailla dur pour entrer à l'école d'art à Budapest puis à Paris et se trouvait à Londres lorsque sortit le *Rip Van Winkle* de Rackham en 1906. Le succès du livre fit croître la demande d'illustrations féeriques et Pogány se glissa dans la brèche. Il mit en images *The Welsh Fairy Book*, puis *La Complainte du vieux marin (The Rime of the Ancient Mariner)*, *Tannhauser*, *Parsifal* et *Lohengrin*, ce qui lui permit d'immigrer en Amérique en 1914. Il se retrouva employé dans l'industrie du cinéma, où la « fantaisie » était plus débridée encore que dans les contes de fées.

Harry Clarke se rendit célèbre en tant qu'artiste verrier, vitrailliste dans la veine Art nouveau, mais il illustra aussi *Les Contes de Hans Christian Andersen* en 1916, puis les *Tales of Mystery and Imagination* d'Edgar Allan Poe in 1919. Comme Poe il mourut prématurément, de la tuberculose.

James (J.) Allen St. John et Clinton Pettee sont tous deux connus pour avoir illustré les œuvres d'Edgar Rice Burroughs, en particulier *Tarzan*. À 43 ans, St. John était déjà un artiste et illustrateur de renom quand il fut sollicité pour la publication du *Retour de Tarzan* en 1915. Il signa ensuite la couverture des 32 romans suivants de Burroughs. Pettee était un illustrateur de *pulps* moins aguerri, mais eut l'honneur de peindre le premier portrait connu de Tarzan, pour le numéro d'octobre 1912 du magazine *The All-Story*, aujourd'hui considéré comme l'objet de collection le plus précieux de la culture *pulp* – certains exemplaires en bon état se sont vendus 60 000 $. Que Tarzan y soit pour quelque chose ou pas, les deux artistes ont vécu une existence sans histoires.

Opposite: An illustration by Frank C. Papé for
"The Story of Nikitich and Marina," from *The Russian
Story Book*, released in 1916.

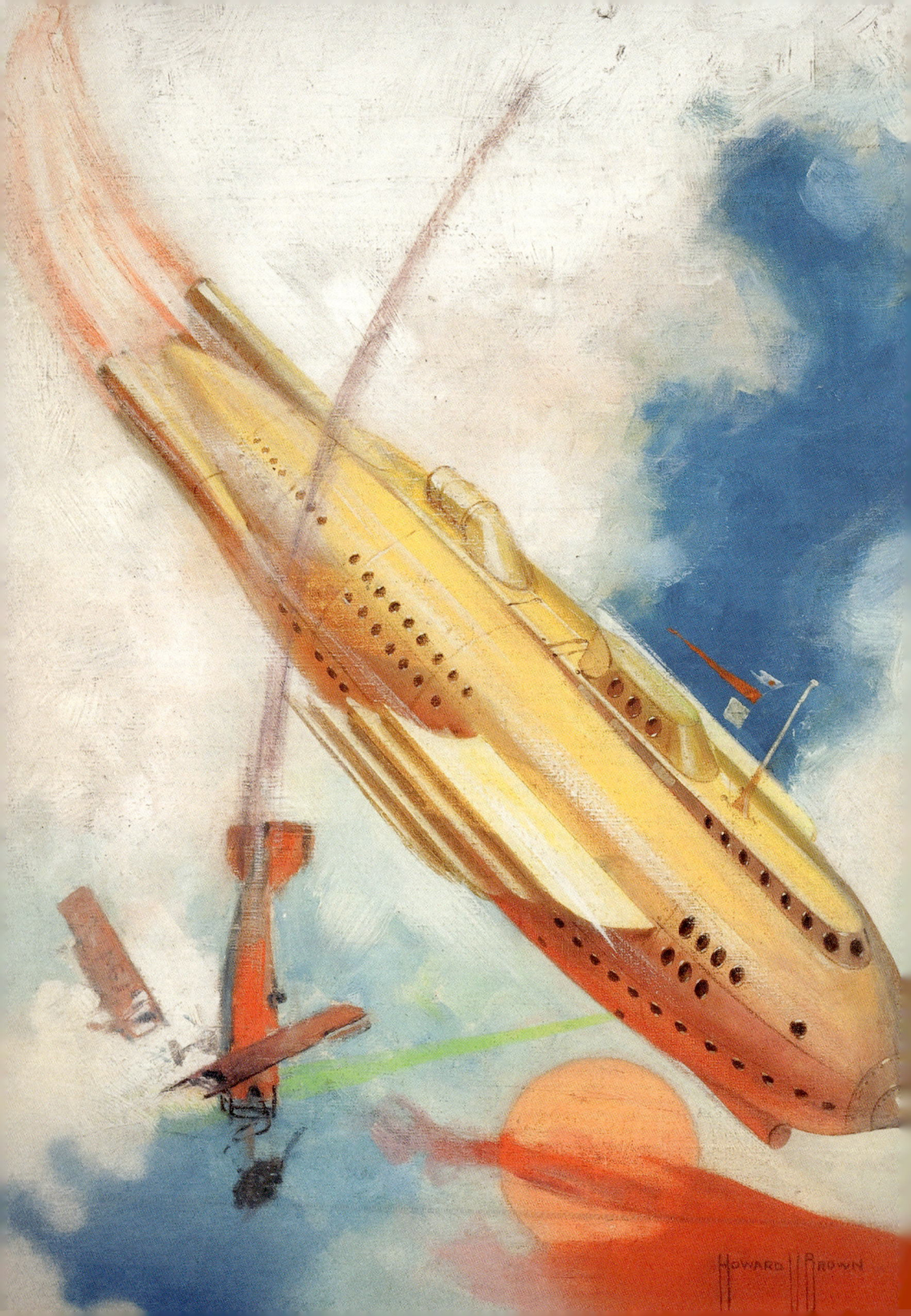

FANTASY OR SCI-FI?

BY DIAN HANSON

Some argue there is no appreciable difference between science fiction and fantasy art. At first glance they seem so similar: bright primary colors, exciting action, fearless heroes, and improbable scenarios. One, however, turns on possibility; the other, the impossible.

The origins of fantasy art and writing go back to fairy tales, to dream worlds that can never be, while sci-fi is based on the highly speculative extrapolation of known science. There is something grown up and concrete about sci-fi, while fantasy taps our childlike yearning and imagination. A spaceship, no matter how silly, is sci-fi; a winged horse is fantasy.

Weird Tales introduced fantasy fiction — and fantasy art — to the American newsstand in 1923. Here H.P. Lovecraft spun his Cthulhu Mythos, Robert E. Howard introduced Conan's savage world, and Robert Bloch published his first stories, straight out of high school. The magazine's covers, by J. Allen St. John, C.C. Senf, Hugh Rankin, and most famously by Margaret Brundage, mixed beautiful nude women with demons and fanciful beasts.

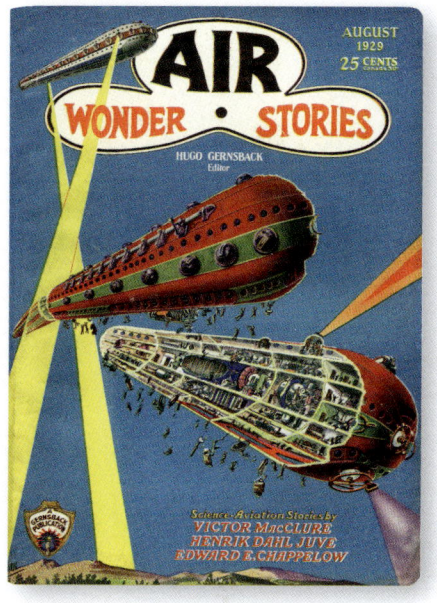

Hugo Gernsback's *Amazing Stories*, launched in 1926, codified sci-fi with the invented word "scientifiction" for stories of space travel to alien worlds, something the immigrant from Luxembourg thought would surely happen in the near future. *Science Wonder Stories* and *Air Wonder Stories*, both becoming simply *Wonder Stories*, followed in 1929, with the same rockets and scientific gadgetry, imaginatively portrayed on covers by Frank R. Paul.

All of these magazines quickly built strong followings, and many bought and enjoyed them equally. Which doesn't change the fact that travel by rocket and a ride on a dragon are two very different things.

Opposite: An easy test for determining if an illustration is fantasy or science fiction is the presence or absence of rocket ships. When Howard V. Brown made his huge spacecraft the centerpiece of his cover for the December 1930 issue of *The Popular Magazine* he defined it as sci-fi.

Oil on canvas, 47 x 63.5 cm (18.5 x 25 inches). Courtesy of Heritage Auctions.

Above: Air Wonder Stories, August 1929.

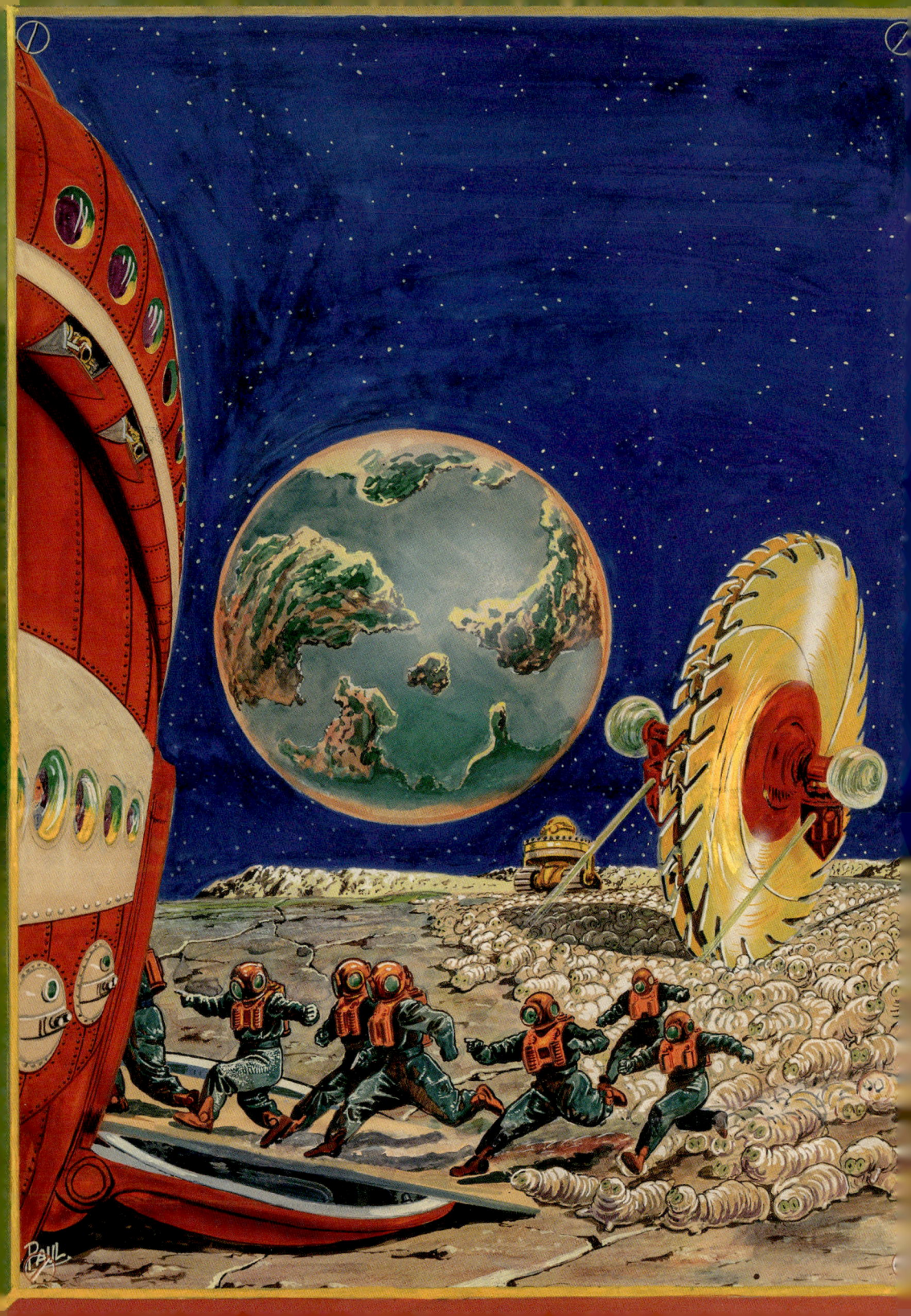

FANTASY ODER SCIENCE-FICTION?

VON DIAN HANSON

Manche meinen, es gebe keinen nennenswerten Unterschied zwischen Science-Fiction und Fantasykunst. Auf den
ersten Blick erscheinen sie einander so ähnlich: leuchtende
Primärfarben, aufregende Action, furchtlose Helden und
unwahrscheinliche Szenarien. Die eine jedoch basiert auf
Möglichem, die andere auf dem Unmöglichen.

Die Ursprünge von Fantasykunst und -literatur gehen
auf Märchen zurück, auf Traumwelten, die es nie geben
wird, während Science-Fiction auf einer hochspekulativen
Extrapolation bekannter wissenschaftlicher Erkenntnisse
beruht. Science-Fiction hat etwas Erwachsenes und Kon-
kretes, während Fantasy an unsere kindlichen Sehnsüchte
und Fantasien anknüpft. Ein Raumschiff, egal, wie absurd
es aussehen mag, ist Science-Fiction; ein geflügeltes Pferd
ist Fantasy.

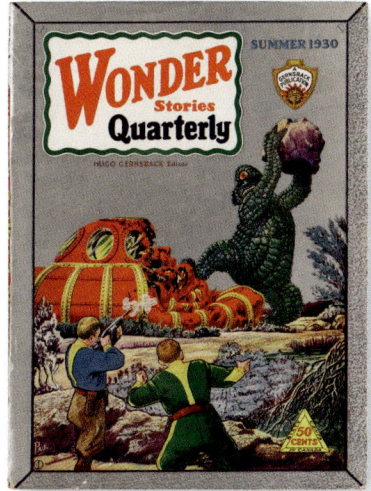

Weird Tales brachte Fantasyliteratur – und Fantasykunst –
1923 an die amerikanischen Kioske. Hier spann H. P. Love-
craft seinen Cthulhu-Mythos, stellte Robert E. Howard Conans wilde Welt vor und veröffentlichte
Robert Bloch, frisch von der Highschool, seine ersten Geschichten. Auf den Titelbildern der Zeitschriften, gestaltet von J. Allen St. John, C. C. Senf, Hugh Rankin und, am berühmtesten, Margaret
Brundage, prangten schöne nackte Frauen zusammen mit Dämonen und fantastischen Tieren.

Hugo Gernsbacks 1926 auf den Markt gebrachte *Amazing Stories* schrieben Science-Fiction
mit dem erfundenen Wort „scientifiction" für Geschichten von Raumfahrten zu außerirdischen
Welten fest, etwas, das der Immigrant aus Luxemburg in naher Zukunft für sicher möglich hielt.
Science Wonder Stories und *Air Wonder Stories*, die schlicht zu *Wonder Stories* verschmolzen, folgten
1929 mit den gleichen Raketen und wissenschaftlichen Geräten, die Frank R. Paul fantasievoll auf
den Titelseiten darstellte. All diese Zeitschriften bauten sich bald schon eine Anhängerschaft auf,
viele kauften die Hefte und vergnügten sich damit. Das ändert jedoch nichts an der Tatsache, dass
ein Flug mit einer Rakete und ein Ritt auf einem Drachen zwei völlig verschiedene Dinge sind.

Opposite: Frank R. Paul was the master of science fiction
cover art, combining bright primary colors with imaginative spacecraft and interstellar threat. *The Vanguard
to Neptune* for *Wonder Stories Quarterly*, Spring 1932,
mixed media on board, 42 x 57 cm (16.5 x 22.5 inches).
Courtesy of Heritage Auctions.

Above: With this Summer 1930 issue of *Wonder Stories*,
Air Wonder Stories and *Science Wonder Stories* became
one. Frank R. Paul provided the cover.

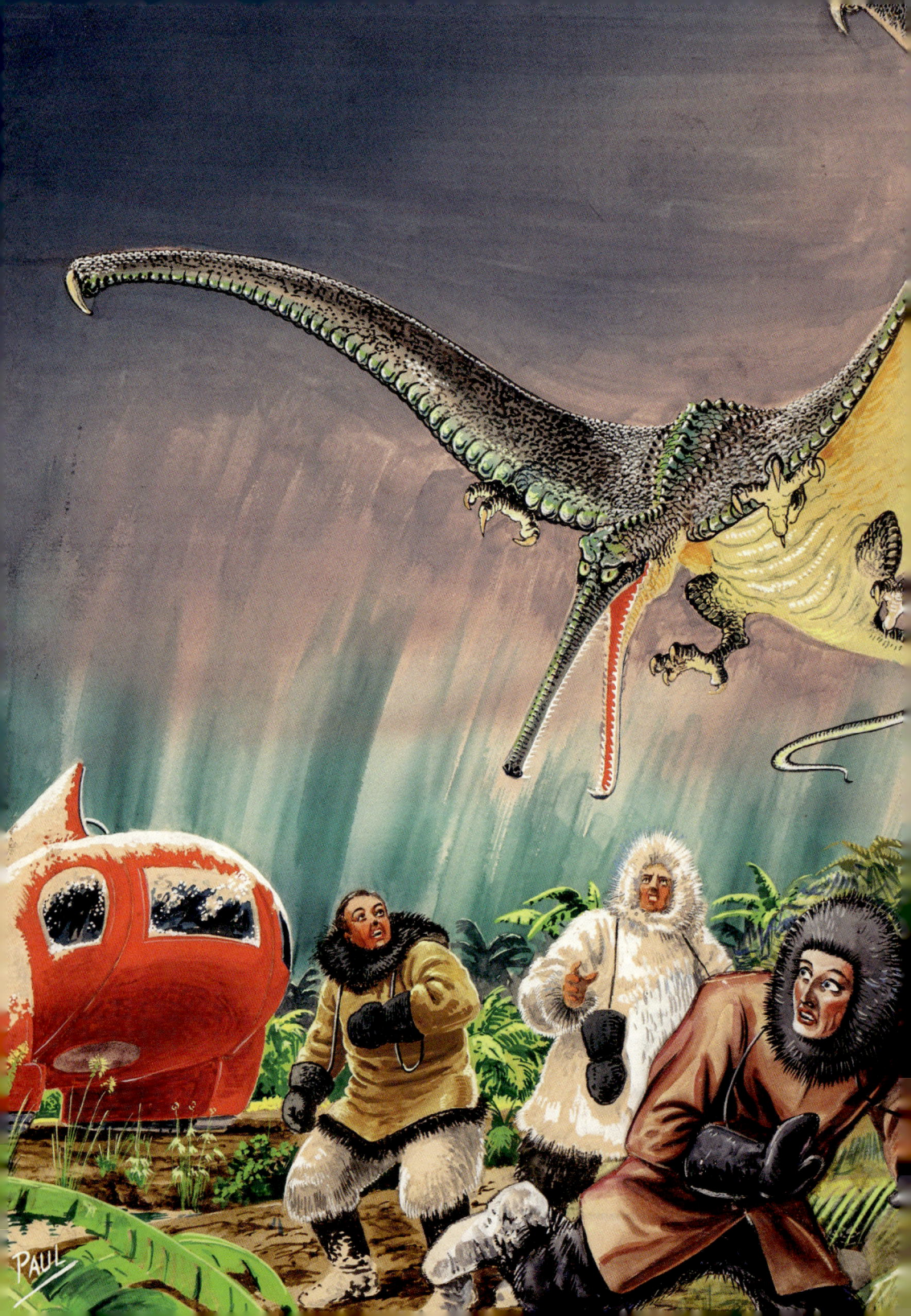

FANTASY OU SCIENCE-FICTION ?

PAR DIAN HANSON

Certains affirment qu'il n'existe pas de différence notable entre la science-fiction et le fantasy art. Il est vrai qu'au premier regard, ils semblent très similaires : des couleurs primaires éclatantes, de l'action qui fouette les sangs, des héros intrépides et des intrigues improbables. Pourtant l'un carbure au possible et l'autre à l'impossible.

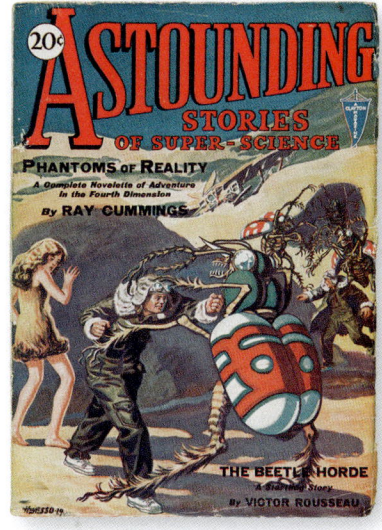

L'art et l'écriture de fantasy puisent leur origine dans les contes de fées, des mondes rêvés qui ne seront jamais réels, tandis que la science-fiction s'élabore à partir d'une exploration hautement spéculative de la science connue. La science-fiction a quelque chose d'adulte, de concret, alors que la fantasy se nourrit des aspirations et de l'imaginaire de l'enfance. Un vaisseau spatial, aussi improbable soit-il, c'est de la science-fiction ; un cheval ailé, c'est de la fantasy.

Weird Tales a lancé la fiction fantasy – et par ricochet le fantasy art – sur le marché américain en 1923. Dans ses pages, H.P. Lovecraft développe son Mythe de Cthulhu, Robert E. Howard présente le monde barbare de Conan

et Robert Bloch publie ses premières histoires, à peine sorti du lycée. Les couvertures du magazine, signées J. Allen St. John, C.C. Senf, Hugh Rankin et surtout Margaret Brundage, mêlent femmes nues sublimes, démons et bêtes chimériques.

Le magazine *Amazing Stories* lancé par Hugo Gernsback en 1926 codifie la science-fiction en inventant le terme « scientifiction » pour qualifier les histoires de voyage spatial vers des mondes extraterrestres, dont cet immigré du Luxembourg pensait qu'ils auraient lieu dans un avenir proche. *Science Wonder Stories* et *Air Wonder Stories*, condensés sous le titre *Wonder Stories*, suivent en 1929, avec en couverture les mêmes fusées et les mêmes gadgets scientifiques, imaginés par le très créatif Frank R. Paul.

Toutes ces revues ont rapidement acquis un lectorat fidèle, qui prenait plaisir à les acheter et les lire. Il n'empêche qu'un voyage en fusée et une balade à dos de dragon sont deux choses très différentes.

Opposite: Paul's covers concentrated on the downside of space travel, with explorers regularly beset by terrifying monsters and machines. His spacecraft eschewed aerodynamic design for a blunt-nosed bullet effect, often, as here, painted red. *The Blue Tropics* for the April 1940 cover of *Fantastic Adventures* magazine, gouache and

watercolor on board, 31.7 x 42 cm (12.5 x 16.5 inches). Courtesy of Heritage Auctions.

Above: Astounding Stories of Super-Science launched with this issue in January 1930 as a direct competitor to *Amazing Stories*. Cover painting by Hans Wesso.

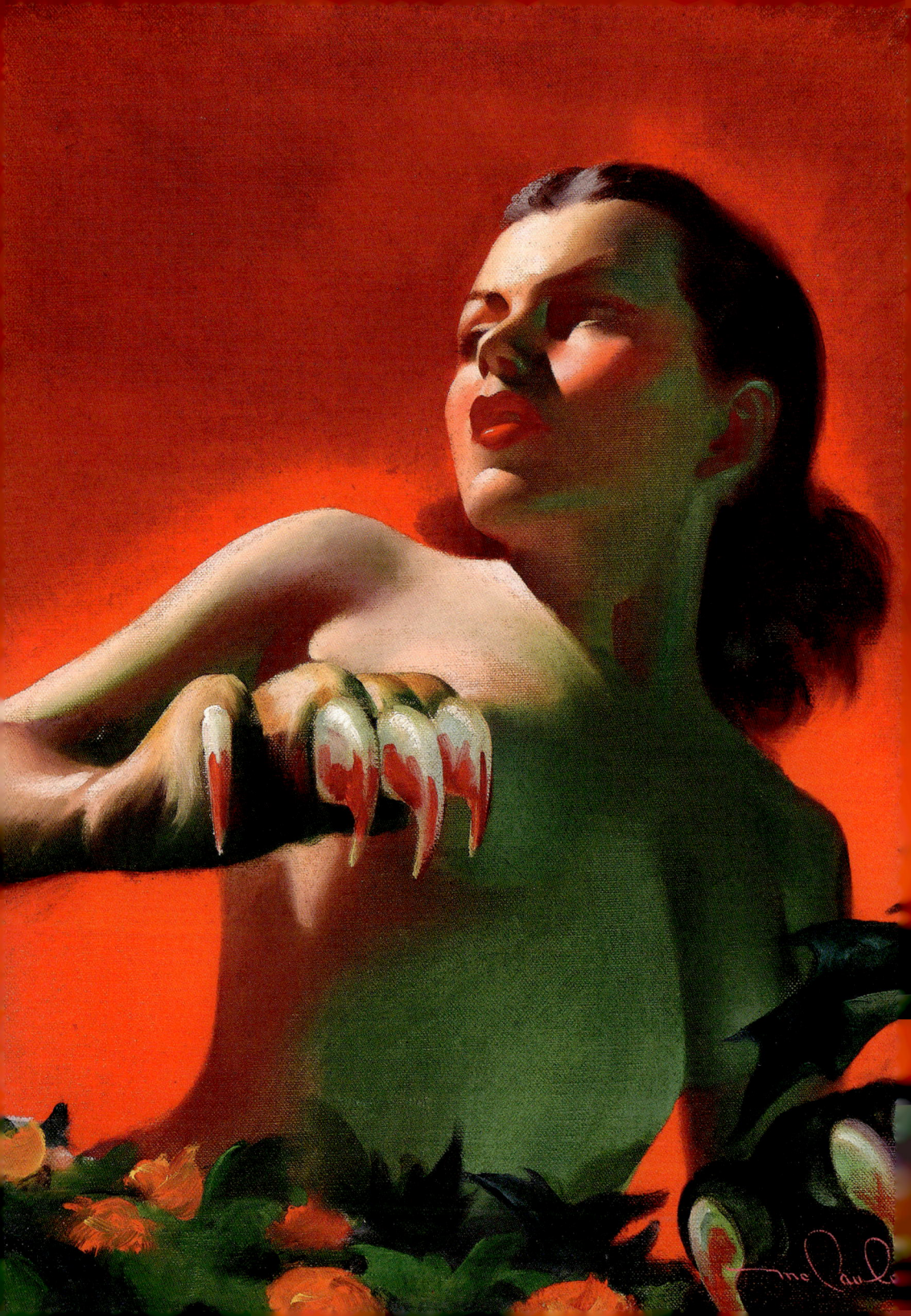

NEW WORLD, NEW WAVE

BY DIAN HANSON

World War II remade the world, including magazine publishing. Wartime paper shortages raised the price of printing, a cost that major magazines could absorb but that pulps dependent on newsstand sales—especially newsstand sales to young men—couldn't. One by one the fantasy pulps that proliferated during the Depression years died off. When men came home from war they found only *Weird Tales*, *Startling Stories*, *Thrilling Wonder Stories*, *Amazing Stories*, *Fantastic Adventures*, *Famous Fantastic Mysteries*, and *Planet Stories* left, and even these had subtly changed. Politics and propaganda competed with true fantasy writing in the early '40s. The September 1944 issue of *Amazing Stories* bannered "Every Story in This Issue by a Soldier," with a cover illustration of a marine in dress blues defending a WAC from a bald satyr. *Weird Tales'* July 1941 cover, featuring a fabulous illustration by Hannes Bok for the novelette "The Robot God," by Ray Cummings, also headlined a story titled "I Killed Hitler." Even outside the pulps fantasy writers often referenced the war. Tolkien denied that politics played a part in his *Rings* trilogy, but C.S. Lewis's *The Chronicles of Narnia* is set in wartime with a classic battle between good and evil characters representing England and Germany.

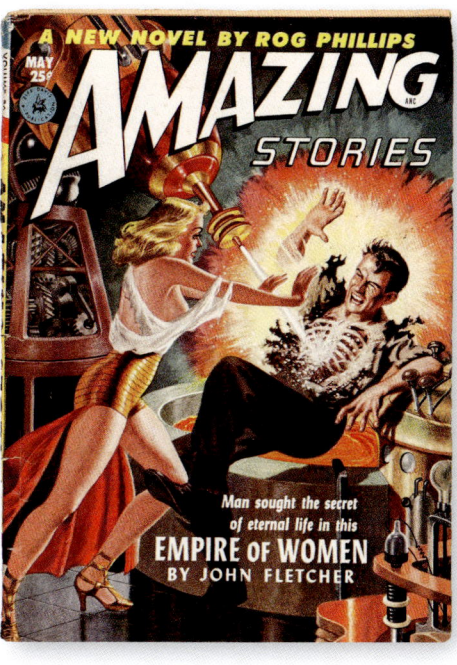

The most notable visual changes in postwar pulps were the pin-up-inspired covers. Pin-ups were huge in the war, supposedly to boost morale among fighting men, and subsequently spread into all media, from calendars to advertising to the alluring vixens on fantasy pulps. The women

Opposite: Harold McCauley was a staff artist for the publishing house Ziff-Davis from 1946, illustrating covers for their many pulp titles, but became most associated with the provocative fantasy magazines *Imagination* and *Imaginative Tales*. His covers always incorporated pin-up elements, and in the 1950s he moved into pin-up calendar work, and then into illustrating the sex magazine *Rogue*. This stunning cover, titled *Tiger Woman of Shadow Valley*, appeared on *Amazing Stories*, October 1949. Oil on canvas, 45.7 x 61 cm (18 x 24 inches).

Above: After an adventuresome life that included capture by the Germans in WWI and rescue moments before his execution, Lawrence Sterne Stevens turned to fantasy pulp illustration in 1948, at age 64. This *Amazing Stories* cover is dated May 1952.

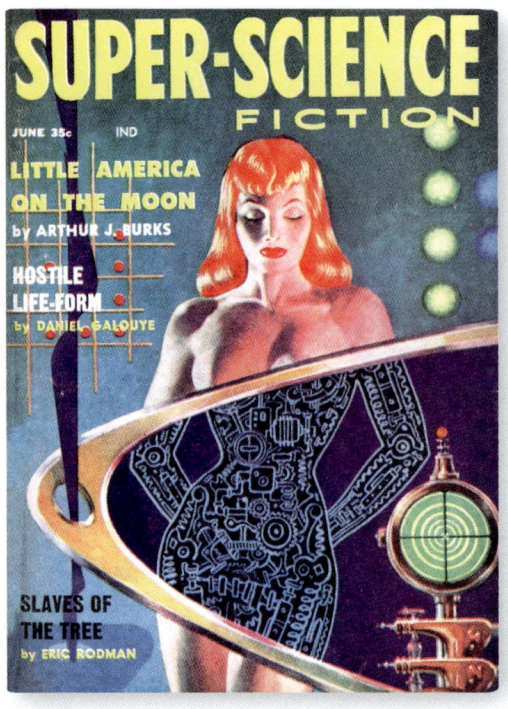

became bustier, their costumes more fetish-istically sexy in the hands of artists Edmund Emshwiller, Virgil Finlay, Norman Saunders, and especially Harold McCauley, official cover artist for *Imaginative Tales*, launched by pulp publishing house Ziff-Davis in 1954.

By far the biggest postwar event in fantasy publishing, however, was the launch of EC Comics' new line in 1950. Imagine being a 25-year-old college student when your father suddenly dies and leaves you a comic book company. This was the reality of William Maxwell "Bill" Gaines, who immediately quit college and turned his father's Educational and Entertaining Comics Company into the infamous EC Comics, home to *Weird Fantasy* and *Weird Science*, as well as *Tales From the Crypt*, *The Haunt of Fear*, *The Vault of Horror*, *Shock SuspenStories*, and *MAD* magazine. Here in four glorious years—before the American government accused Gaines of inciting juvenile delinquency, before rival publishers formed the Comics Code Authority to destroy his most popular titles—the fantasy art careers of Wally Wood, Roy Krenkel, Al Williamson, and the great Frank Frazetta were launched.

EC heralded a new direction in fantasy art, where the art overpowered the words, dominating every page instead of just the cover. When *Creepy*, *Eerie*, and *Vampirella* debuted in the 1960s, and *Métal Hurlant* and *Heavy Metal* followed in the 1970s, they all owed their existence to the creative audacity of Bill Gaines and EC Comics.

Fantasy art would never take a backseat again.

Above: Super-Science Fiction, June 1958, with one of the greatest Kelly Freas covers ever; a masterpiece of fantasy modernism,

Opposite: The Summer 1955 issue of *Planet Stories* with a mid-century modern cover by Kelly Freas.

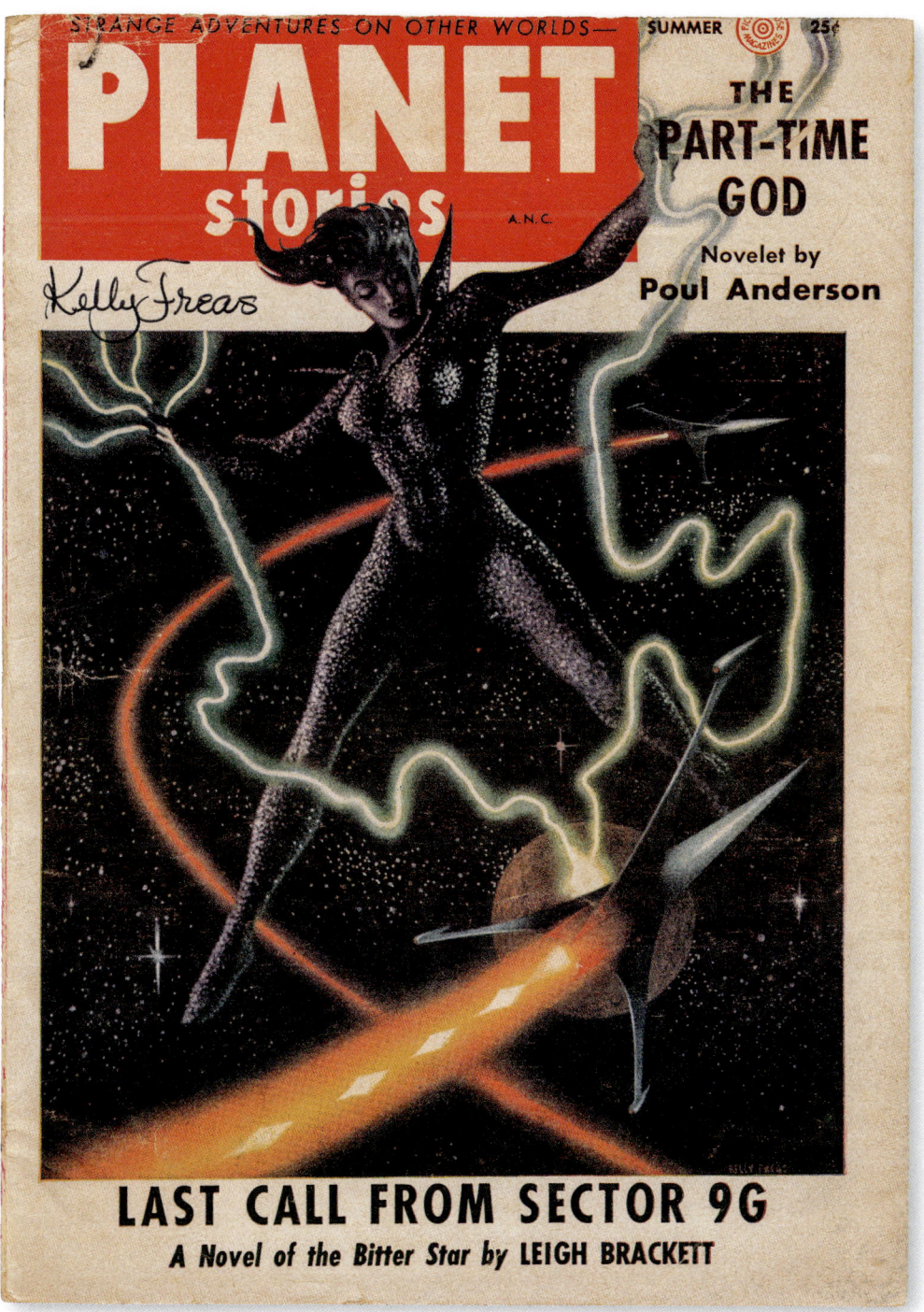

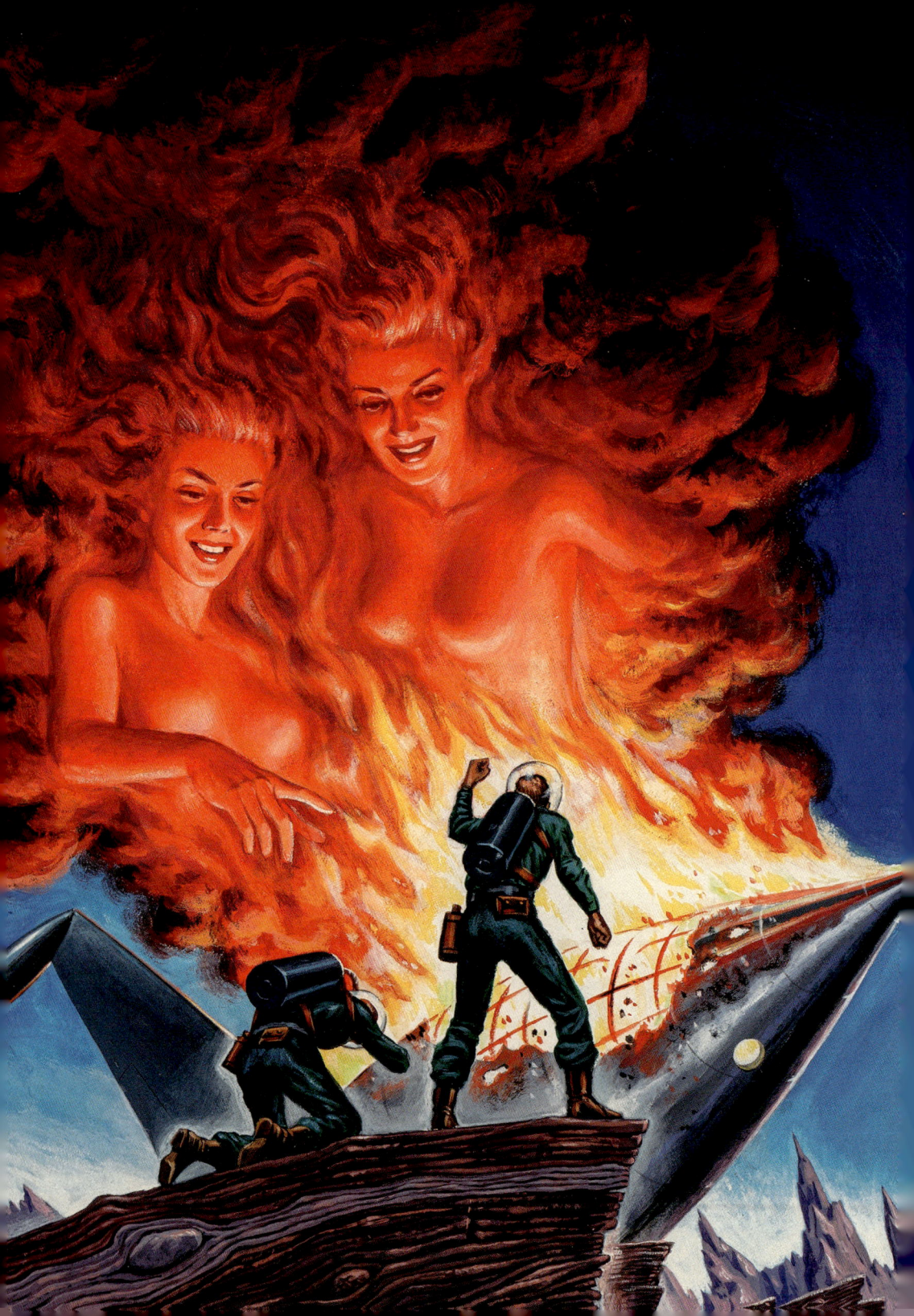

NEUE WELT, NEUE WELLE

VON DIAN HANSON

Der Zweite Weltkrieg gestaltete die Welt um und veränderte auch das Verlegen von Zeitschriften. Die Papierknappheit der Kriegsjahre erhöhte die Preise für Druckwerke; Kosten, die größere Zeitschriften verkraften konnten, Pulps jedoch, die von den Verkäufen an Zeitungskiosken – vor allem von Verkäufen an junge Männer – abhängig waren, schafften das nicht. So musste von den während der Depression sich so zahlreich vermehrenden Fantasy-Pulps ein Titel nach dem anderen sein Erscheinen einstellen. Als die Männer aus dem Krieg zurückkamen, mussten sie feststellen, dass nur noch *Weird Tales, Startling Stories, Thrilling Wonder Stories, Amazing Stories, Fantastic Adventures, Famous Fantastic Mysteries* und *Planet Stories* übrig geblieben waren, und auch diese Hefte waren leicht verändert. Während der frühen 1940er-Jahre konkurrierten Politik und Propaganda mit den eigentlichen Fantasygeschichten. Aufmacher der *Amazing-Stories*-Ausgabe vom September 1944 war die

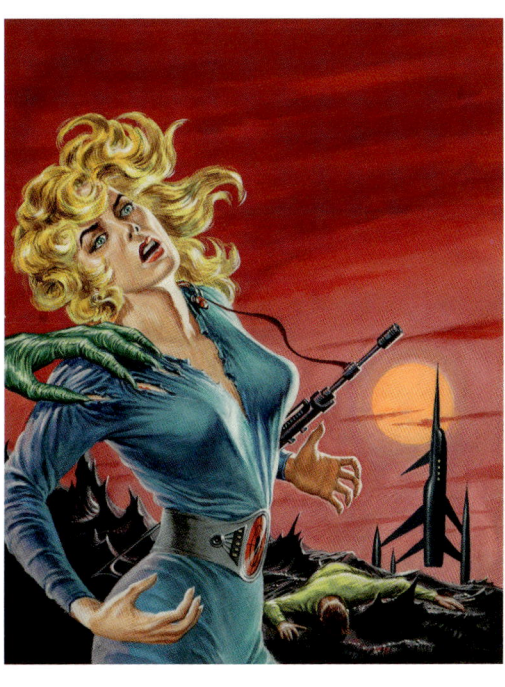

Schlagzeile „Every Story in this Issue by a Soldier", und das Titelbild zeigte einen Marinesoldaten in seiner schicken blauen Uniform, der ein Mitglied des Frauenkorps gegen einen kahlköpfigen Satyr verteidigt. Auch auf dem Cover der *Weird Tales* vom Juli 1941, das mit einer großartigen Illustration von Hannes Bok für den Kurzroman *The Robot God* von Ray Cummings aufwartete, wurde eine Geschichte mit dem Titel „I killed Hitler" hervorgehoben. Selbst außerhalb der Pulps nahmen Fantasyautoren oft Bezug auf den Krieg. Tolkien bestritt, dass in seiner *Herr-der-Ringe*-Trilogie Politik eine Rolle spielte, doch *The Chronicles of Narnia* von C. S. Lewis spielt

Opposite: Somehow *Startling Stories,* Summer 1954, got away with these bare, albeit nipple-free, breasts by Ed Emshwiller titled *The Spiral of the Ages.* Oil on board, 36.8 x 47 cm (14.5 x 18.5 inches). Courtesy of Heritage Auctions.

Above: Desire Woman, by Edmund Emshwiller, for the cover of *Super-Science Fiction,* June 1957. Acrylic on board, 1957, 36.8 x 27.3 cm (14.5 x 10.75 inches).

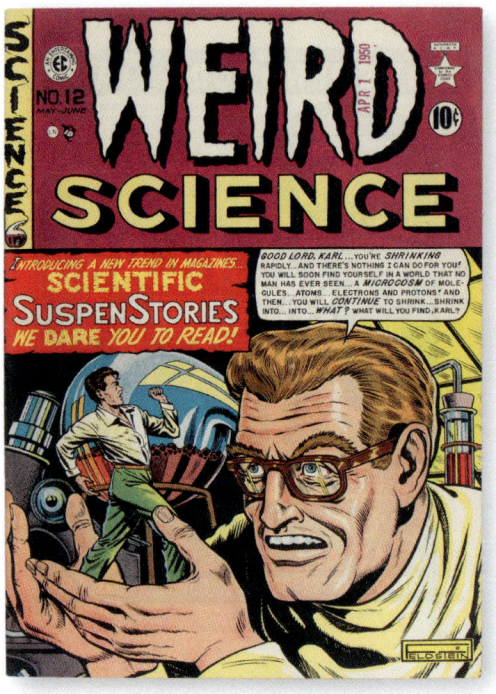

zu Kriegszeiten, und es gibt eine klassische Schlacht zwischen den Guten und den Bösen, die England und Deutschland repräsentieren.

Die bemerkenswerteste optische Veränderung bei den Pulps der Nachkriegszeit waren die mit Pin-ups belebten Cover. In den Kriegsjahren waren Pin-ups eine Riesensache, angeblich sollten sie die Moral der kämpfenden Truppe aufrechterhalten und machten sich dann in sämtlichen Medien breit. Unter den Händen von Künstlern wie Edmund Emshwiller, Virgil Finlay, Norman Saunders und vor allem Harold McCauley, dem offiziellen Covergestalter für die 1954 vom Pulp-Verlag Ziff-Davis auf den Markt gebrachten *Imaginative Tales*, wurden die Frauen immer vollbusiger, und ihre Kleidung gestaltete sich auf immer fetischistischere Weise sexy.

Das in dieser Zeit bei Weitem größte Ereignis in der Welt der Fantasykunst war allerdings der Start der neuen Programmreihe von EC Comics im Jahre 1950. Man stelle sich vor, ein 25-jähriger Collegestudent zu sein, und plötzlich stirbt der Vater und hinterlässt einen Comicverlag. Das erlebte William Maxwell „Bill" Gaines, der sofort das College sausen ließ und den Verlag Educational and Entertaining Comics in die berüchtigten EC Comics verwandelte, die *Weird Fantasy* und *Weird Science* wie auch *Tales from the Crypt*, *The Haunt of Fear*, *The Vault of Horror*, *Shock SuspenStories* und die Zeitschrift *MAD* herausbrachten. Hier begannen im Laufe von vier Jahren – bevor die amerikanische Regierung Gaines anklagte, der Jugendkriminalität Vorschub zu leisten, und konkurrierende Verleger die Comics Code Authority gründeten, um den erfolgreichsten Titeln den Garaus zu machen – die Fantasykunstkarrieren von Wally Wood, Roy Krenkel, Al Williamson und des großen Frank Frazetta.

EC läutete eine neue Richtung in der Fantasykunst ein, in der die Kunst die Texte dominierte. Als in den 1960er-Jahren *Creepy*, *Eerie* und *Vampirella* debütierten und in den 1970er-Jahren *Métal Hurlant* und *Heavy Metal* folgten, hatten all diese Publikationen ihre Existenz dem schöpferischen Wagemut von Bill Gaines und EC Comics zu verdanken.

Fantasykunst würde nie wieder eine untergeordnete Rolle spielen.

Above: Weird Science No. 12 was actually the first issue of the iconic EC Comics title, as publisher Bill Gaines found it easier to transfer the contracts from a previous title to the new magazine and continue the old numbering. Cover by Al Feldstein, 1950. Artwork is copyrighted material owned by William M. Gaines, Agent, Inc. All Rights Reserved

Opposite: A Sound of Thunder by Kelly Freas for the cover of Planet Stories, January 1954, to illustrate a Ray Bradbury story.

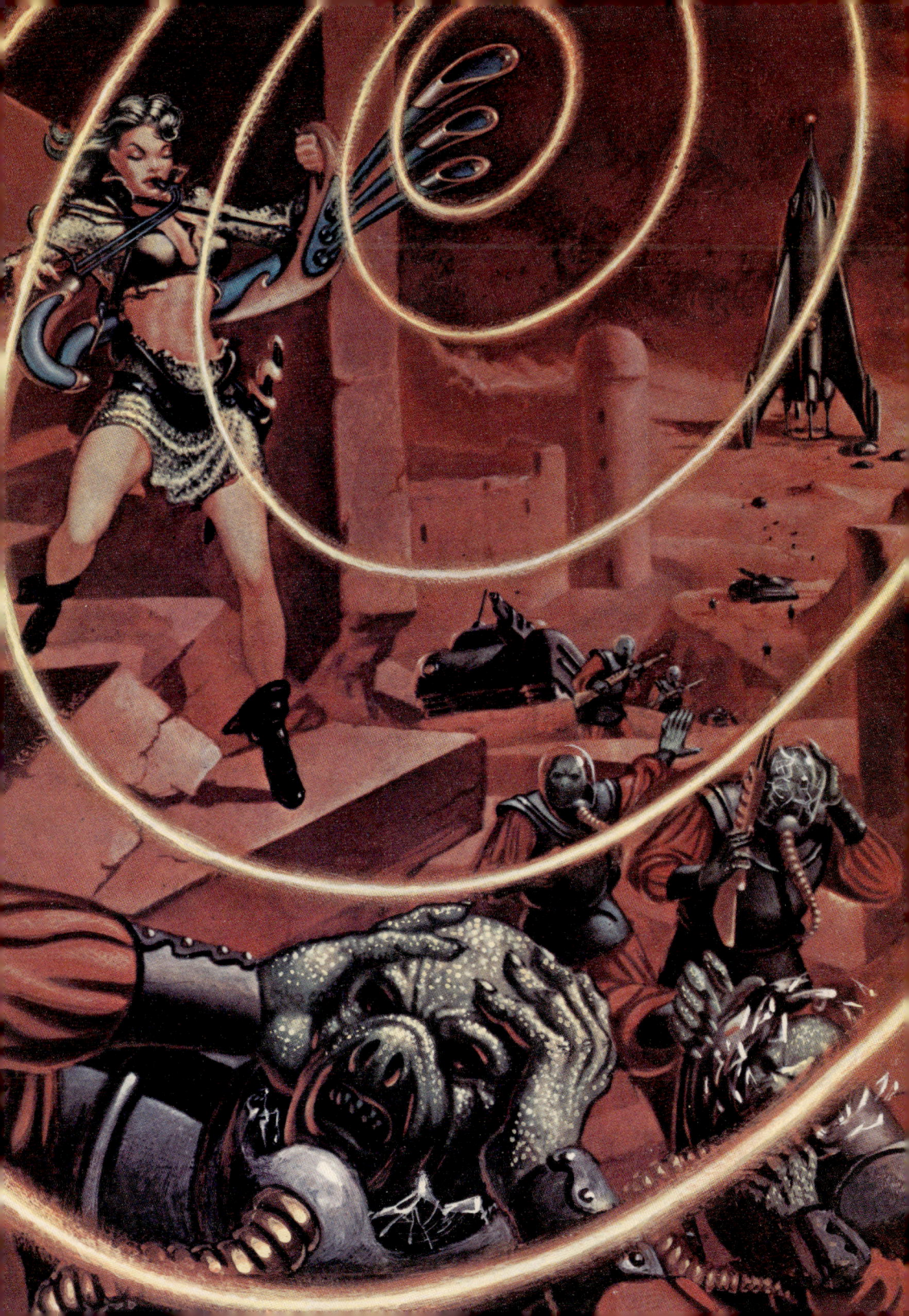

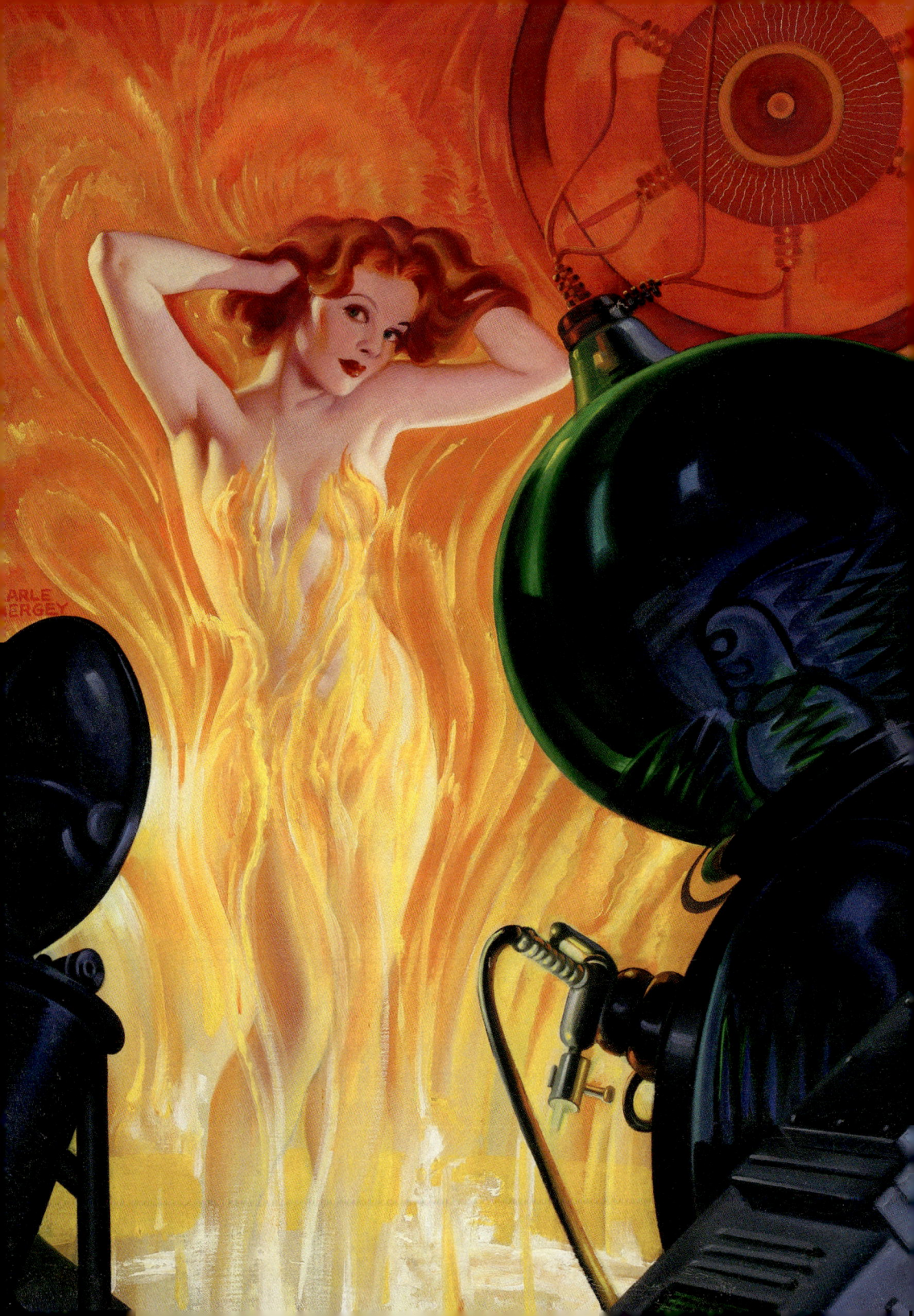

NOUVEAU MONDE, NOUVELLE VAGUE

PAR DIAN HANSON

La Seconde Guerre mondiale a remodelé le monde et la presse magazine avec lui. Les pénuries de papier ont fait grimper les coûts d'impression pendant la guerre et si les grands magazines ont pu absorber cette hausse, ce n'est pas le cas des *pulps*, qui dépendent des ventes en kiosques, en particulier auprès des jeunes hommes. Un par un, les *pulps* de fantasy qui avaient proliféré pendant la Dépression disparaissent. Quand les hommes reviennent du front, ils ne retrouvent que *Weird Tales*, *Startling Stories*, *Thrilling Wonder Stories*, *Amazing Stories*, *Fantastic Adventures*, *Famous Fantastic Mysteries* et *Planet Stories* et même ces titres-là ont opéré un changement subtil. Au début des années 1940, la politique et la propagande jouent des coudes avec l'imaginaire. L'*Amazing Stories* de septembre 1944 arbore le slogan « Chaque histoire de ce numéro est signée d'un soldat » en travers de sa une, où un Marine en uniforme bleu protège une femme soldat contre un satyre chauve. Le *Weird Tales* de juillet 1941 met à l'honneur l'histoire courte « The Robot God » de Ray Cummings avec une fabuleuse illustration de Hannes Bok et annonce une histoire intitulée « J'ai tué Hitler ». En dehors des *pulps* aussi les auteurs font souvent référence à la guerre. Tolkien a toujours nié l'aspect politique de sa trilogie de l'Anneau, mais *Les Chroniques de Narnia* de C.S. Lewis se déroulent en temps de guerre et narrent l'affrontement classique entre des bons et mauvais qui représentent l'Angleterre et l'Allemagne.

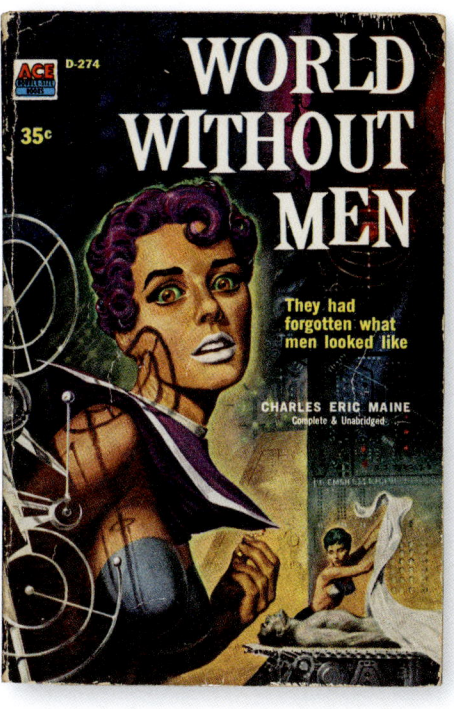

Opposite: Earle Bergey was one of the most diversified and prolific pulp cover artists. In the 1930s he was a leading pin-up artist, but also illustrated fitness, romance, and detective titles. In the 1940s he added fantasy covers, generally incorporating his skill with pin-up, to the delight of readers. This is titled *The Cybernetic Brains*, for *Startling Stories*, September 1950. Oil on canvas, 45.7 x 68.5 cm (18 x 27 inches). Courtesy of Heritage Auctions.

Above: World Without Men, by Charles Eric Maine, was published in 1958 when scientists around the world were racing to perfect a human birth control pill. The novel posits a future when men have been completely eliminated after women lose all morality from access to a birth control drug, and the effort by a few women to re-create the male sex. Okay, so the book's not much, but the cover by Ed Emshwiller is great.

Parmi les changements qui sautent aux yeux dans les *pulps* de l'après-guerre, il y a l'arrivée des pin-up en couverture. Immensément populaires pendant le conflit, conçues officiellement pour remonter le moral des troupes, elles envahissent tous les médias et supports, des calendriers à la publicité, en passant par les *pulps* fantasy, où elles se font plus vénéneuses. Les femmes prennent de la poitrine et leurs costumes oscillent entre fétichisme et sensualité sous le pinceau d'artistes comme Edmund Emshwiller, Virgil Finlay, Norman Saunders et surtout Harold McCauley, l'illustrateur attitré des unes d'*Imaginative Tales*, lancé par la maison d'édition de *pulps* Ziff Davis en 1954.

L'événement le plus marquant de l'après-guerre est cependant, et de loin, la sortie de la nouvelle collection d'EC Comics, en 1950. Imaginez plutôt : vous êtes un étudiant de 25 ans, votre père meurt soudainement et vous héritez d'une maison d'édition de bandes dessinées. C'est ce qui est arrivé à William Maxwell « Bill » Gaines. Il lâche immédiatement l'université pour transformer l'Educational & Entertaining Comics Company de son père en EC Comics, qui édite *Weird Fantasy* et *Weird Science*, mais aussi *Les Contes de la crypte*, *The Haunt of Fear*, *The Vault of Horror*, *Shock SuspenStories* et le magazine *MAD*. Pendant une parenthèse enchantée de quatre ans – avant que les autorités américaines accusent Gaines d'inciter la jeunesse à la délinquance et que des éditeurs rivaux fondent la Comics Code Authority pour détruire ses titres les plus populaires – la maison a lancé la carrière de grands artistes fantasy, parmi lesquels Wally Wood, Roy Krenkel, Al Williamson et le grand Frank Frazetta.

EC a propulsé le fantasy art dans une nouvelle dimension, où l'art l'emporte sur les mots et domine chaque page et plus seulement la couverture. *Creepy*, *Eerie* et *Vampirella* font leur apparition dans les années 1960, *Métal Hurlant* et *Heavy Metal* suivent dans les années 1970, et tous doivent leur existence à l'audace créative de Bill Gaines et d'EC Comics.

Le fantasy art ne se contentera plus jamais du second plan.

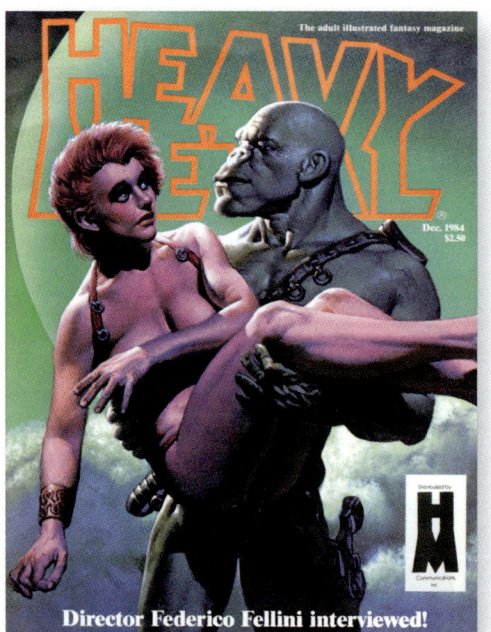

Left: Heavy Metal magazine, December 1984, with cover art by Richard Corben.

Opposite: The Positronic Man by Stephen Youll, for the novel of the same title by Isaac Asimov and Robert Silverberg. Oil on masonite, 1994, 81 x 50 cm (32 x 19.5 inches).

Following left: Kelly Freas began his fantasy/sci-fi illustration career with a cover for *Weird Tales* in 1950. This poster is from a cover he painted for *Planet Stories*, May 1954.

Following right: A partially inked fantasy illustration by Bernie Wrightson from the late 1970s. Graphite and ink on paper, 58.4 x 44.4 cm (23 x 17.5 inches). Courtesy of Heritage Auctions.

MASTERPIECES OF FANTASY ART

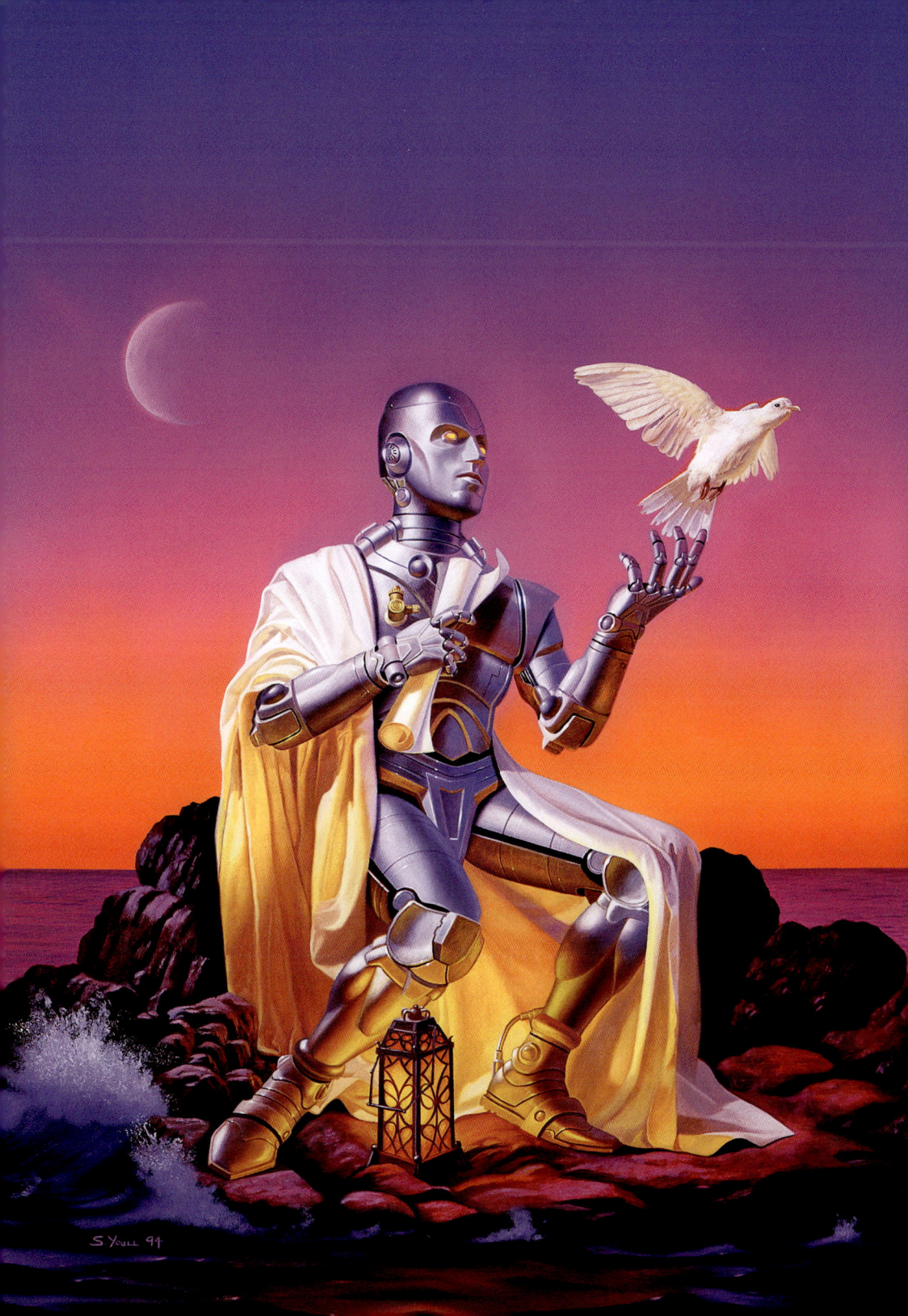

S Youll 94

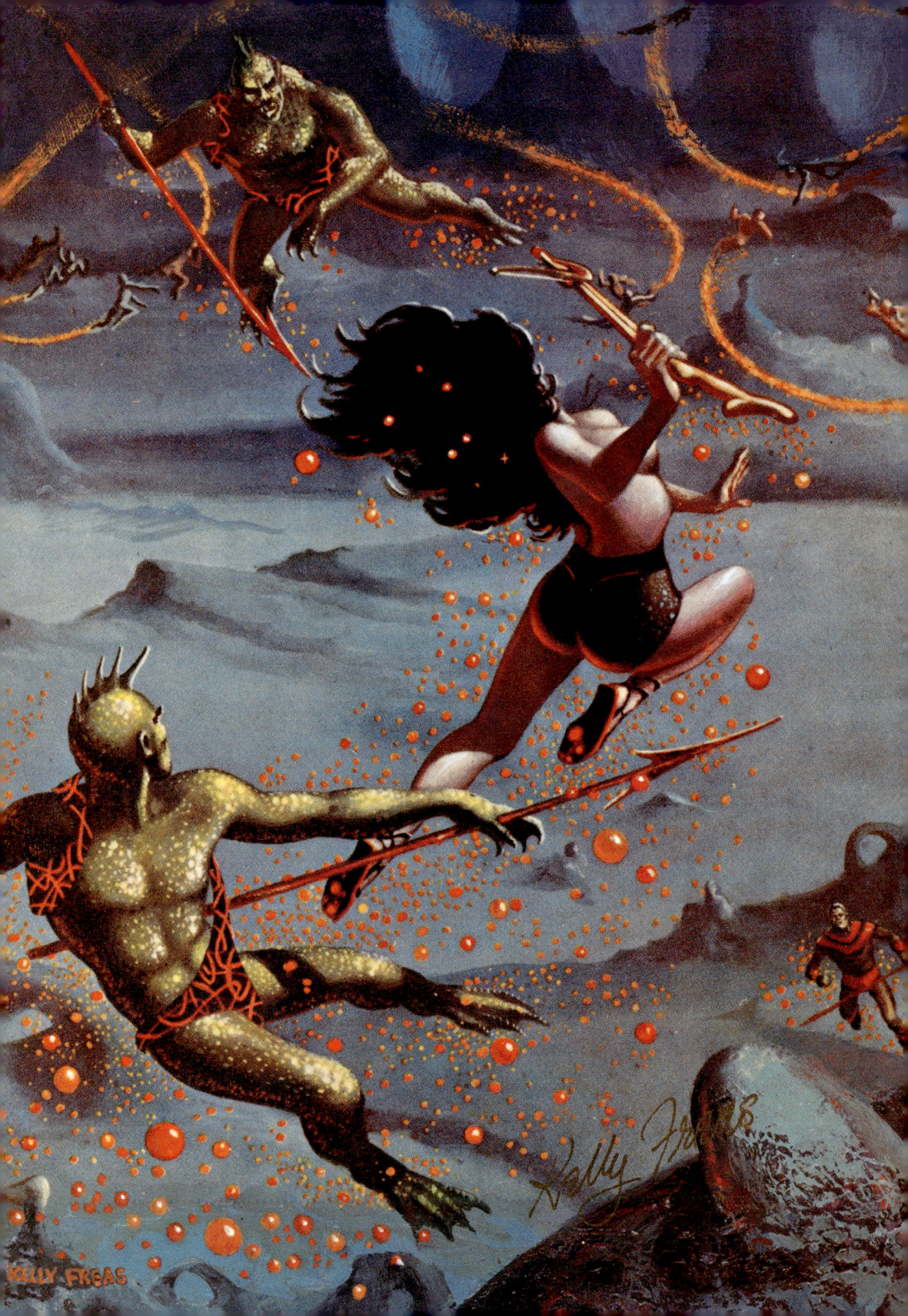

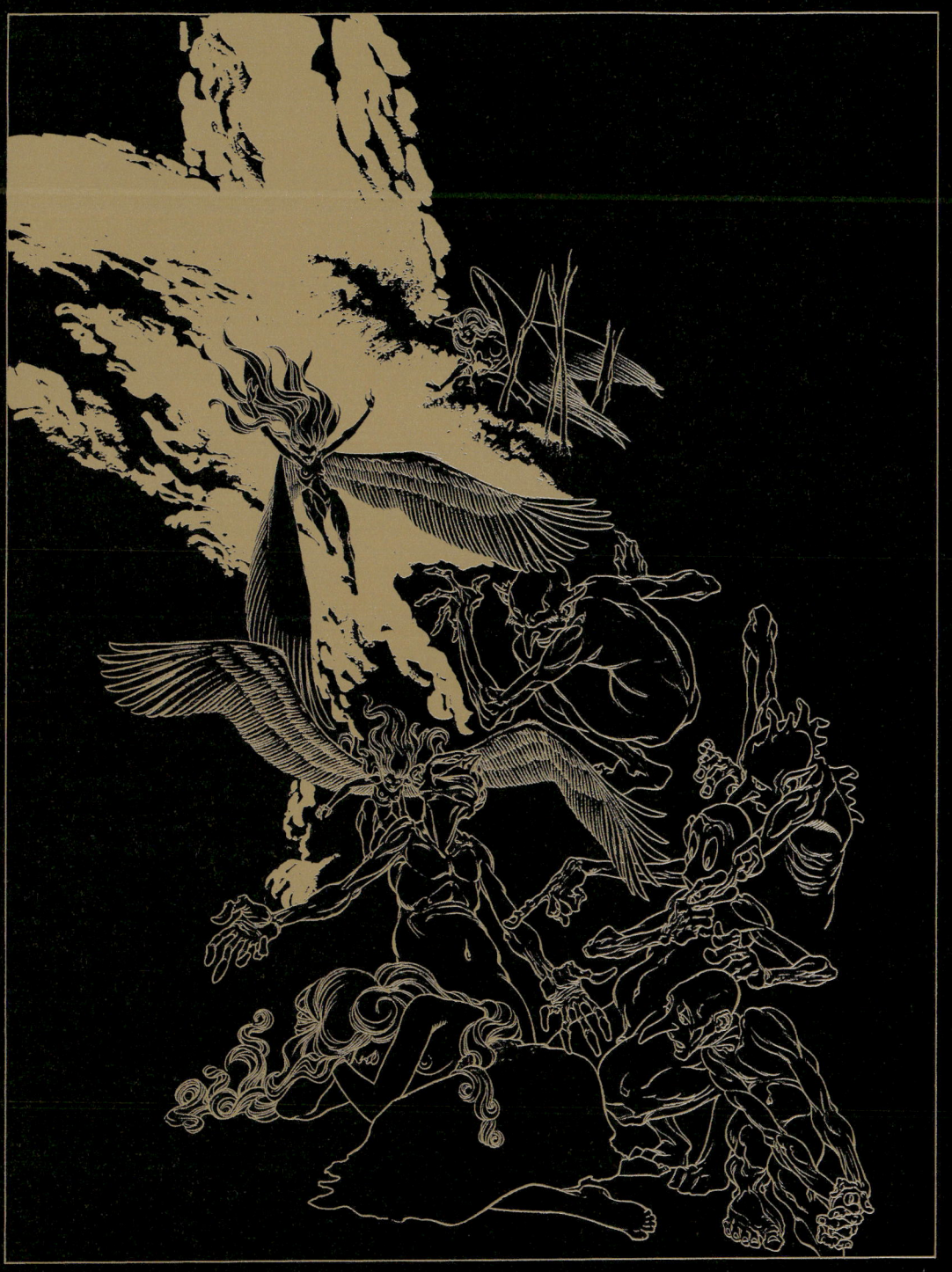

Julie Bell

Julie

1958–

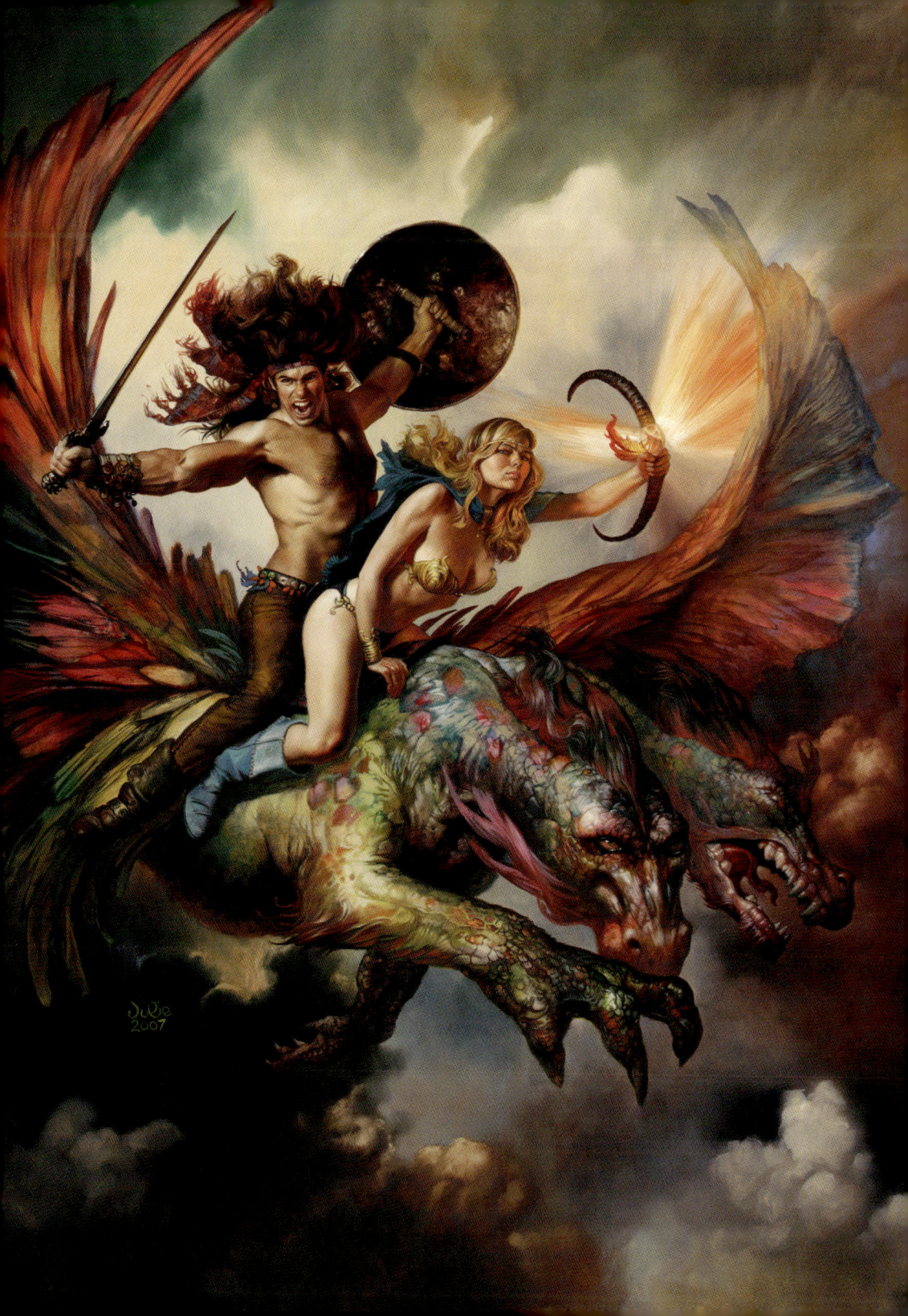

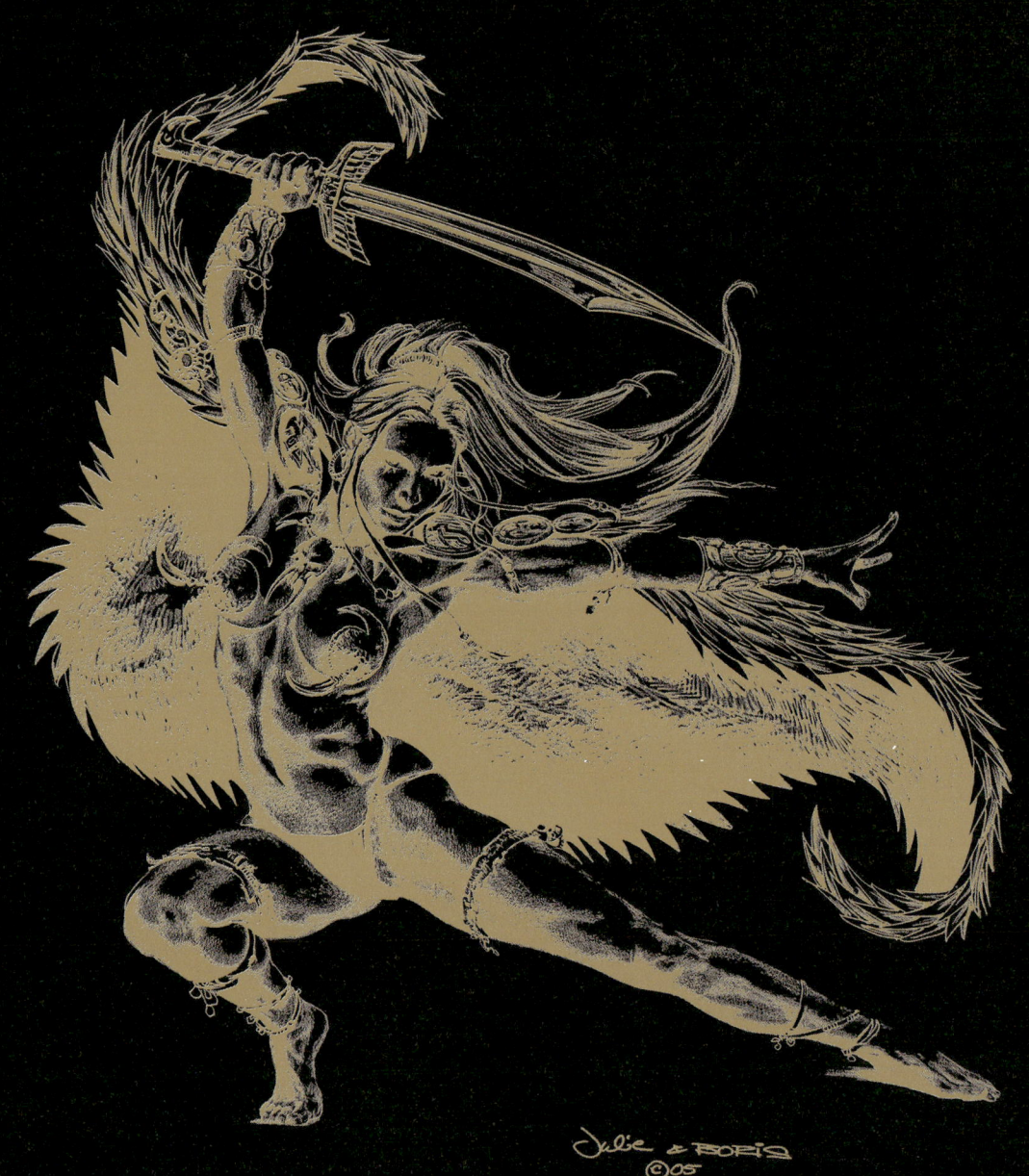

JULIE BELL
THE VISIONARY

"When I feel this particular...
obsession about an idea or an image,
that's when I know I want to paint it."

Julie Bell wants it to be clear: she is not just Mrs. Boris Vallejo. "Boris is a huge pillar of the fantasy art world; he casts an enormous shadow," she says. "We work together in the same studio every day and I love that togetherness, but for years I was in that shadow and am finally coming into my own light. There are now people who learn about Boris through me. That makes me kind of happy."

It's true that Bell's first paintings bore a striking resemblance to her husband's, but that was intentional. While she had taken many, many drawing classes over the years she'd been discouraged from painting until, as an award-winning bodybuilder, she was asked to model for Vallejo, and he took over her art education.

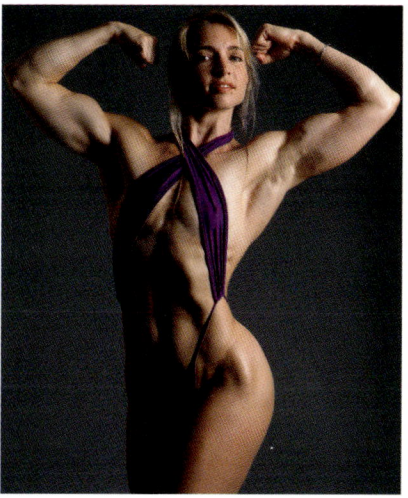

"I always wanted to do something with art, but didn't know how to get involved in it," she says. While living in Texas with her first husband, a college professor, and raising two small children, she studied art books in the library. "I'd see books that had illustration styles I liked, and I'd write letters to the publisher with pictures of my artwork. I had no idea." The young family moved around, following her husband's teaching jobs. In the early '80s they landed in Ohio, where one day her husband brought home a set of weights.

"I used to climb trees a lot when I was a kid, and was proud that I could do chin-ups [from the branches]. There was a chin-up bar included in the weight set and I jumped up and did a few. My husband was amazed. I started lifting the weights."

Before she even set foot in a gym she began placing in local bodybuilding contests. "I couldn't really train my legs properly at home, though," she says, "so I went to the gym." There, for the first time since her marriage, she made friends of her own. It sounds like a small thing, but during Bell's chaotic childhood friends were hard to have and hold.

Previous right: Victory Flight, a personal piece that helped Bell refine her unique dragon technique. Oil on board, 2007, 68.5 x 50.8 cm (27 x 20 inches).

Opposite: Warrior Woman drawing by Bell and Vallejo, 2005. Courtesy of Heritage Auctions.

Above: In 1989 Bell was at the top of her bodybuilding game and winner of the Natural Eastern Classic. Boris Vallejo met her at the contest after-party and immediately asked her to model. Photo by Boris Vallejo.

Bell was born in 1958 in Beaumont, Texas, where her father was a successful architect. Her mother was artistically talented, but mentally ill and alcoholic. When her parents divorced in 1970 her mother took her three daughters to live in Atlanta with an alcoholic stepfather, but even before that, life was challenging.

"[My mother] was taking me to bars and really crazy places, and at 10 or 11 years old I'd be taking the wheel, driving the car, trying to keep her awake. I learned to be hypervigilant, looking out for my younger sisters." She found comfort in *Archie* comics and the wholesome teenage world represented there, especially after the divorce, when her fractious stepfather was starting fights and losing jobs, forcing the family to move, and the girls to change schools, multiple times a year. "I read *Archie* comics to this day," she laughs, "for a few minutes at the end of the day. It takes my brain away from everything." She also developed a serious crush on Mighty Mouse, imagining the upright rodent as her future husband.

For artistic inspiration she turned to *MAD* magazine, drawing her own TV show parodies. She occasionally had friends who joined her in this, but friends lasted only until the next move, so her most reliable support came from teachers. She got hooked on art classes, beginning at age 15, and continued with them after returning to Texas for college and kept at it in every college where her husband taught.

The weightlifting was arguably another art project for Bell. She always loved life drawing classes, saying, "There's so much happening there: the shapes and the architecture and the flow of the whole thing." Now she was the architect, designing and creating a new body from the ground up. She entered more contests, placing 13th in the Miss USA contest after winning at county and state levels. She still drew, but only for herself.

Then in 1989 she entered and won the Natural Eastern Classic, sponsored by Bob Bonham of the Strong & Shapely Gym in East Rutherford, NJ. Bob threw a party for the contestants, and invited his friend Boris Vallejo. Boris asked Julie to pose for him that very day.

"I didn't know I would be nude, but I wasn't real worried about it because I had studied life drawing for years and years," says Bell. "It was very professional," but also love at first sight. "Boris and I both had marriages that were somewhat dysfunctional. We had decided to accept it, but when we met we both felt, 'Life doesn't have to be that way. We can have the kind of relationship we had dreamt of.'" They were married in 1994.

Part of that dream was that both were artists. Bell brought photos of her work the first day she posed, and Vallejo provided gentle criticism. He offered to let her watch him paint and she asked to learn his style. "He just made me feel like I could do it," she said. She made her first commercial sale to *Heavy Metal* in 1990, her first cover appearing on the January 1992 issue.

Boris, meanwhile, was painting Julie. His first portrait was titled *Alpnu*, showing a lean, muscular goddess with a challenging stare. From this point on his women tended to a leaner, more frank muscularity, inspired by his new muse.

Julie did become adept at the Vallejo style, so much so that people found it hard to tell who'd done what. She published three books of her work (*The Julie Bell Portfolio*, 1994; *Hard Curves*, 1997; and *Soft as Steel*, 1999) before Running Press got the idea to print collaborative collections of both artists. "They thought it would be a good hook, and there was more material for a book," she says. Nine volumes have appeared to date, as well as yearly calendars. There was also a Vallejo-style poster for *Aqua Teen Hunger Force Colon Movie*, 2007; and album covers for Meatloaf's *Bat Out of Hell III: The Monster Is Loose*, 2006; and *Hang Cool Teddy Bear*, 2010.

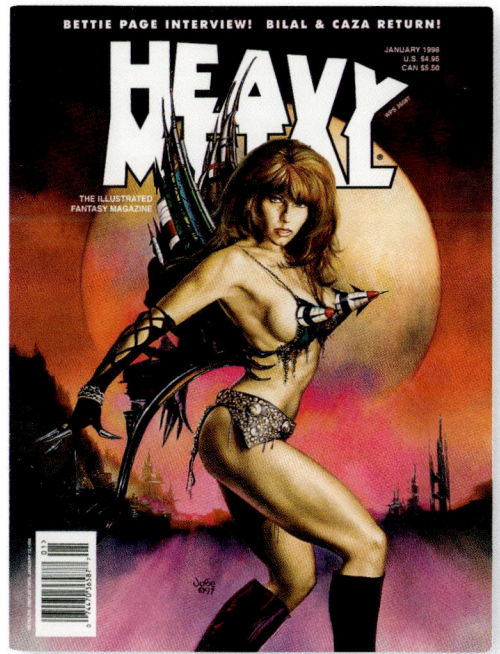

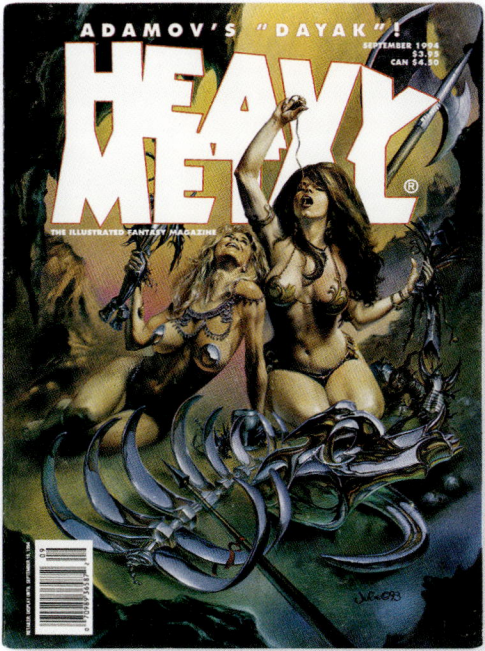

The world didn't really need two Vallejos, though; Julie had to forge her own style. "It started with dragons," she says. "I was extremely frustrated that my dragons didn't look like Boris's dragons. I came to realize that painting fantasy creatures comes from much deeper in your own creative well. Boris finally said, 'Do your own damn dragons!'" She created a more stylized creature, in tones of pink, purple, red, and orange, that's become a signature palette. Her lifelong love of art nouveau further influenced her emerging style; then she found animal art.

"I've read that the children of alcoholics personify animals as if they're getting real feeling from them," she says. "I rediscovered my love in painting them when doing a series of wolf covers for Tor Books." Now she sells her fantasy art—she prefers the term *visionary realism*—through Rehs Contemporary Gallery in New York, and her animal art through Legacy Galleries and Martin Gallery. Julie still collaborates with Boris on fantasy art projects, but is moving more towards fine art. "I love being able to paint what I want to paint and have people buy that and appreciate it," says Julie. "Boris sees me waking up every day exhilarated, can't wait to run into the studio and paint what I want, and he's just a little bit jealous."

Above: Bell's first commercial sale was a cover for *Heavy Metal* magazine in 1990. Four more covers followed, including these, from January 1998 and September 1994.

Following spread: Pegasus Befriends the Muses, published in the 2020 *Boris Vallejo and Julie Bell Fantasy Calendar,* oil on wooden panel, 2019, 121.9 x 152.4 cm (48 x 60 inches).

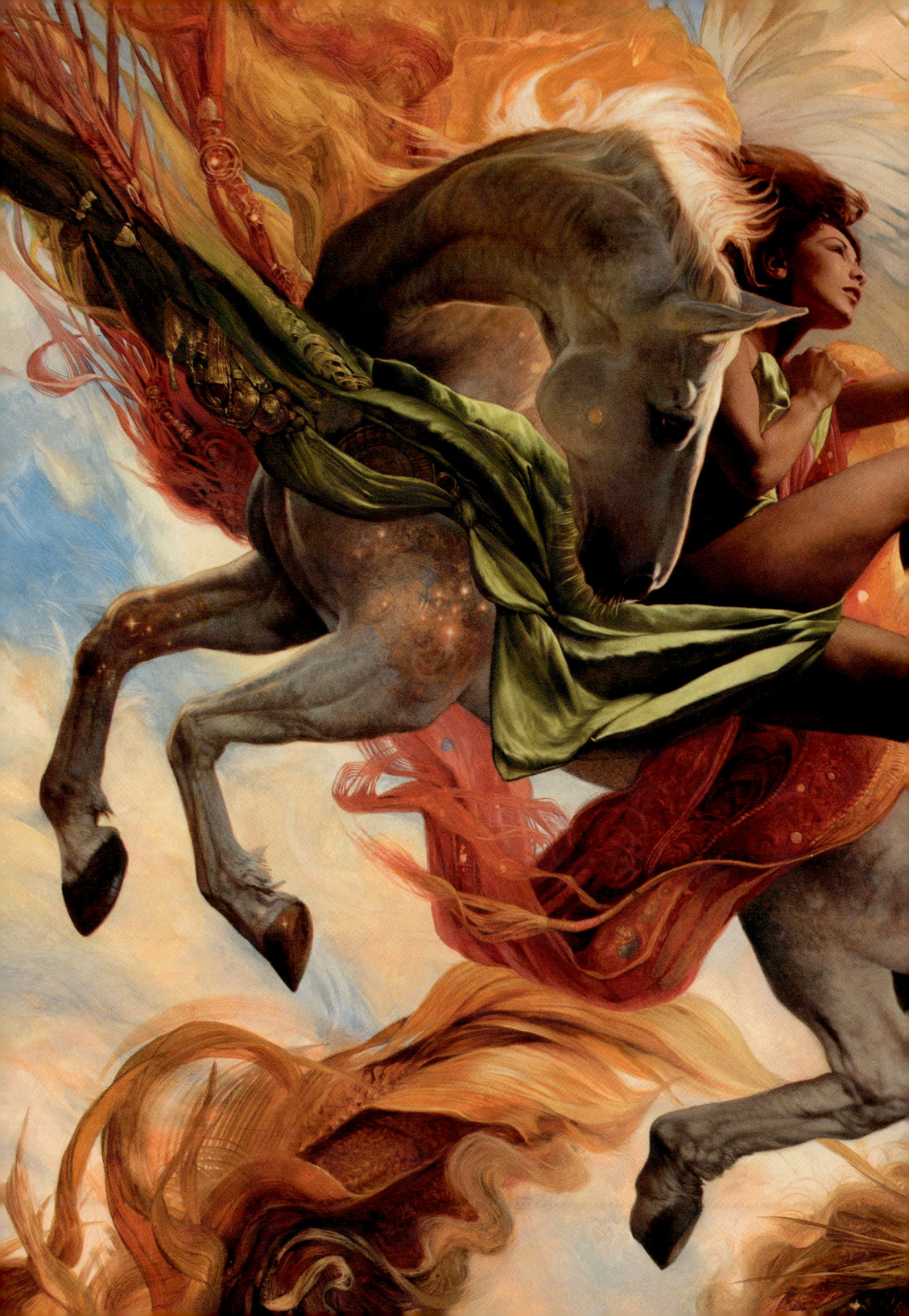

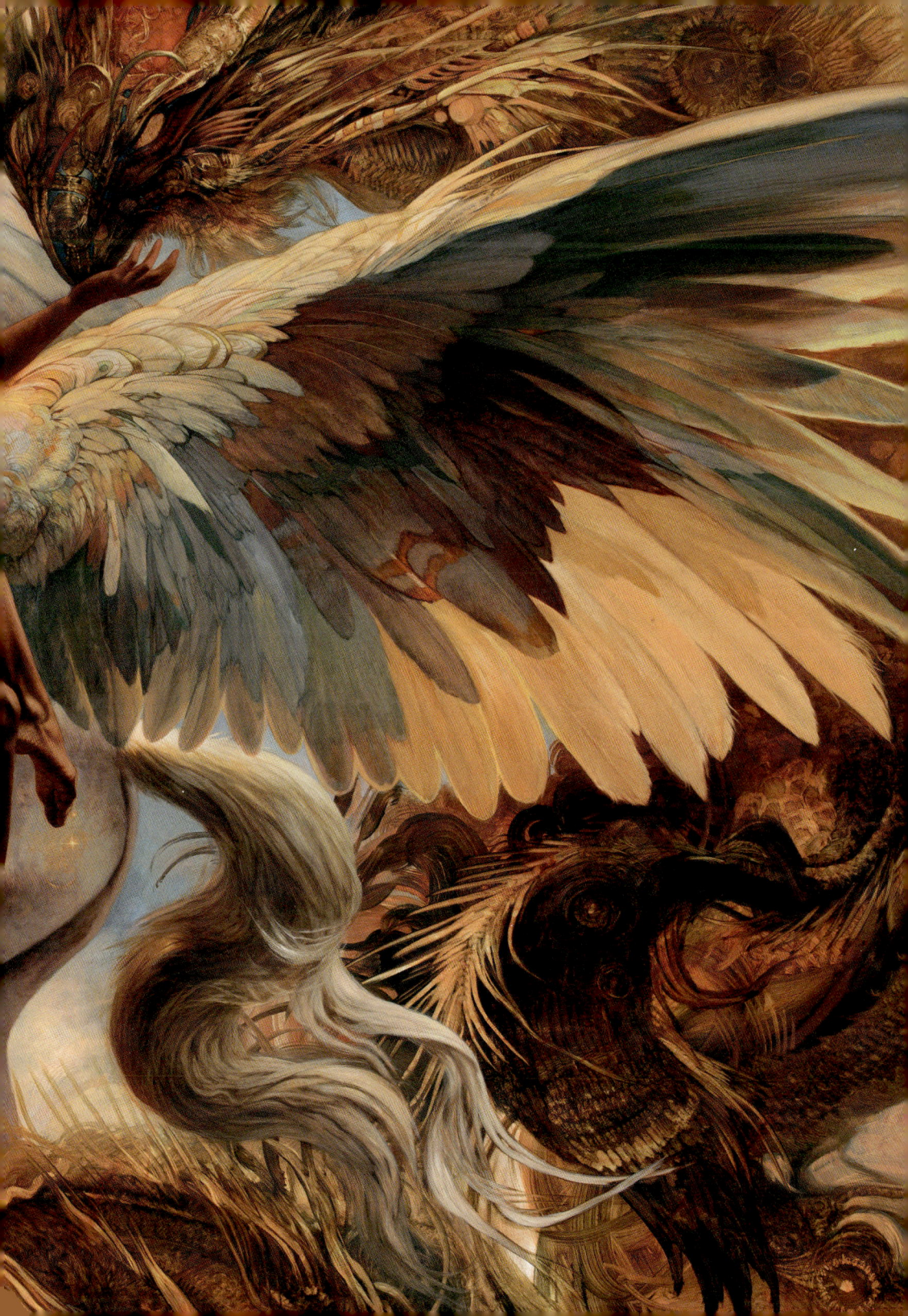

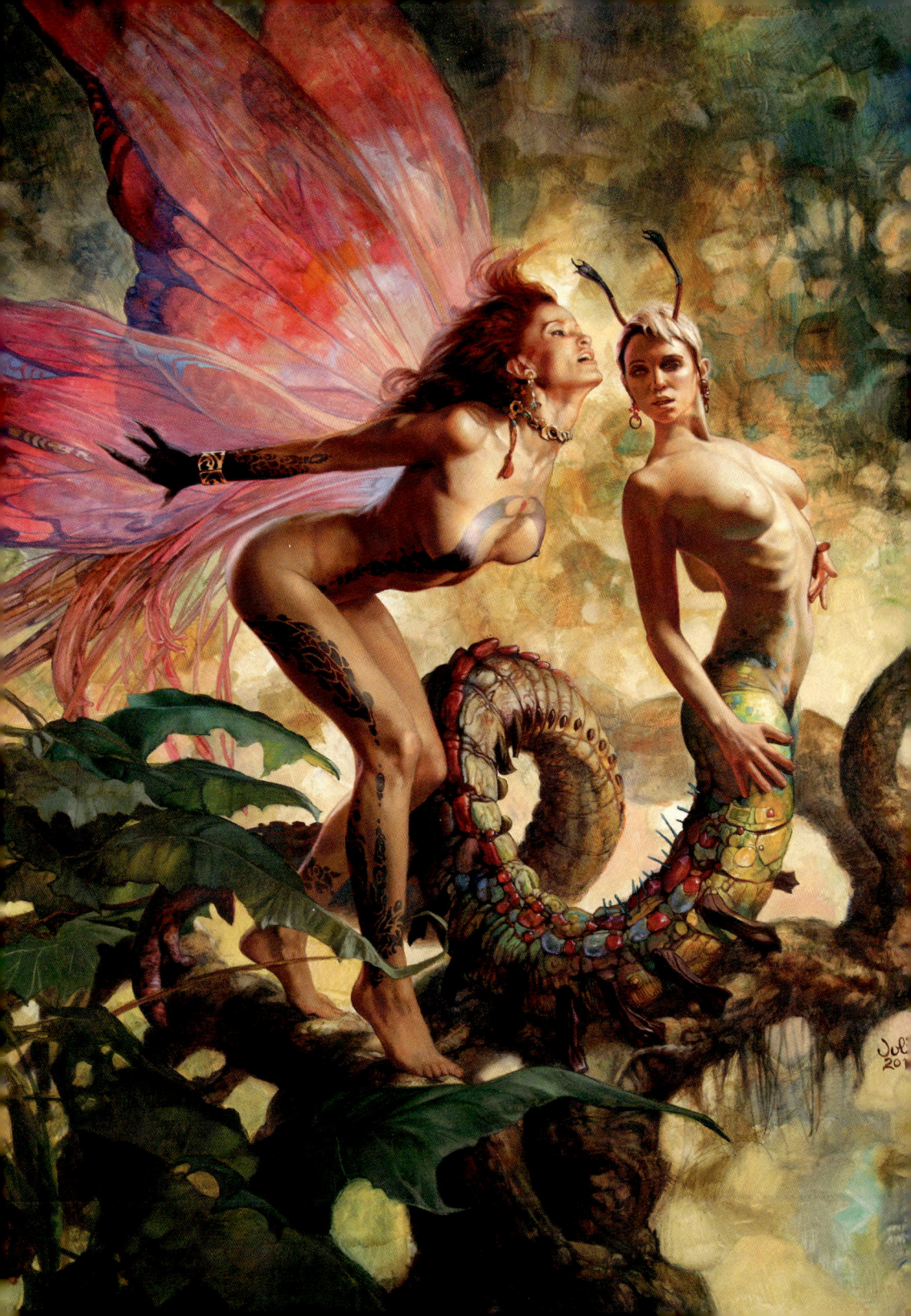

JULIE BELL
DIE VISIONÄRIN

„Sobald ich diese ganz besondere . . .
fixe Ideef für einen Einfall oder ein Bild
erspüre, weiß ich, dass ich das malen will."

Julie Bell legt Wert auf die Feststellung: Sie ist nicht
bloß Mrs Boris Vallejo. „Boris ist ein riesiger Pfeiler
in der Welt der Fantasykunst; er wirft einen enormen
Schatten", sagt sie. „Wir arbeiten jeden Tag im gleichen
Atelier zusammen, und ich liebe diese Gemeinsamkeit,
doch jahrelang war ich in diesem Schatten und komme
endlich in mein eigenes Licht. Mittlerweile gibt es Leute,
die über mich von Boris und seinem Werk erfahren. Das
macht mich in gewisser Weise glücklich."

Es stimmt, dass Bells erste Gemälde eine verblüffende
Ähnlichkeit mit denen ihres Mannes aufwiesen, aber
das war beabsichtigt. Während sie im Laufe der Jahre
viele, viele Zeichenkurse absolviert hatte, fand sie die
Malerei entmutigend, bis Vallejo sie als preisgekrönte
Bodybuilderin bat, für ihn als Modell zu arbeiten, und er
ihre Kunstausbildung übernahm.

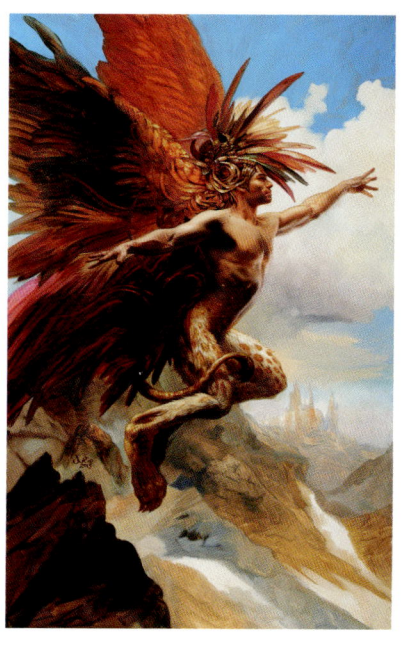

„Ich wollte schon immer etwas mit Kunst machen,
doch ich wusste nicht, wie ich dabei mitmischen
könnte", sagt sie. Als sie mit ihrem ersten Mann, einem
Collegeprofessor, in Texas lebte und zwei Kinder groß-
zog, vertiefte sie sich in der Bibliothek in Kunstbücher.
„Da entdeckte ich Bücher mit Illustrationsstilen, die ich mochte, also schrieb ich Briefe an die
Verlage mit Bildern von meinen Kunstwerken. Ich hatte keine Ahnung." Die junge Familie zog,
je nachdem, wo ihr Mann Lehraufträge erhielt, immer wieder um. In den frühen 1980er-Jahren
landeten sie in Ohio, und dort brachte ihr Mann eines Tages einen Satz Gewichte mit nach Hause.

„Als Kind bin ich oft auf Bäume geklettert und war stolz darauf, dass ich [an Ästen] Klimmzüge machen konnte. Zu dem Satz Gewichte gehörte auch eine Stange für Klimmzüge. Ich sprang
auf und machte ein paar. Mein Mann war verblüfft. Dann fing ich an, die Gewichte zu stemmen."

Noch bevor sie überhaupt einen Fuß in ein Fitnessstudio setzte, fing sie an, bei örtlichen
Bodybuilding-Wettbewerben mitzumachen. „Meine Beine konnte ich zu Hause allerdings nicht
so richtig trainieren", sagt sie, „deshalb besuchte ich dann ein Fitnessstudio." Dort fand sie zum
ersten Mal seit ihrer Heirat auch eigene Freunde. Das hört sich nach einer Kleinigkeit an, doch

*Opposite: Seeing Her Future, for the 2011 Boris Vallejo
and Julie Bell Fantasy Calendar,* oil on wooden panel,
2010, 61 x 45.7 cm (24 x 18 inches).

*Above: Liberation, published in the 2014 Boris Vallejo
and Julie Bell Fantasy Calendar,* oil on board, 2013,
68.5 x 45.7 cm (27 x 18 inches).

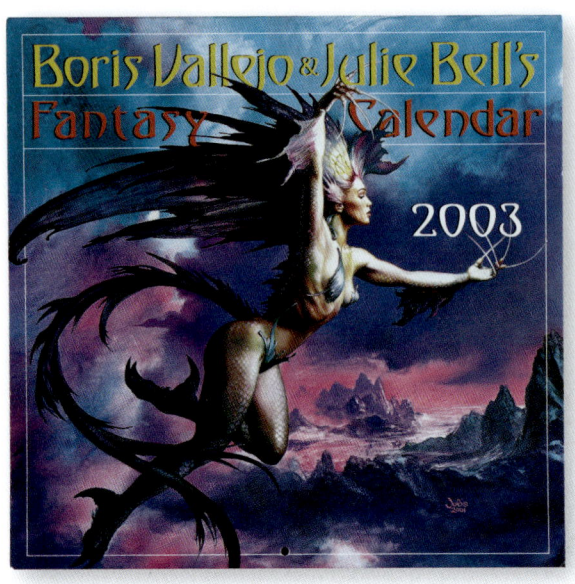

während Bells chaotischer Kindheit konnte sie nur schwer Freunde finden und halten.

Bell wurde 1958 in Beaumont, Texas geboren, wo ihr Vater als erfolgreicher Architekt arbeitete. Ihre Mutter war künstlerisch begabt, doch psychisch krank und Alkoholikerin. Als sich ihre Eltern 1970 scheiden ließen, nahm die Mutter ihre drei Töchter mit nach Atlanta, wo sie mit einem trunksüchtigen Stiefvater zusammenleben mussten. Doch auch schon zuvor hatte das Leben einiges an Herausforderungen geboten.

„[Meine Mutter] nahm mich mit in Bars und zu echt verrückten Orten, und mit zehn oder elf musste ich das Steuer übernehmen, den Wagen fahren und dabei versuchen, sie wach zu halten. Ich lernte, äußerst wachsam zu sein und auf meine jüngeren Schwestern aufzupassen." Trost fand sie mit *Archie*-Comics und in der heilen Teenagerwelt, die in diesen Heften dargestellt war, vor allem nach der Scheidung, als ihr zänkischer Stiefvater Schlägereien anfing und Jobs verlor, was die Familie mehrfach im Jahr dazu zwang umzuziehen, und die Mädchen immer wieder die Schule wechseln mussten. „*Archie*-Comics lese ich bis heute", lacht sie, „ein paar Minuten lang, am Ende des Tages. Das macht mir den Kopf frei von allem." Sie entwickelte auch eine ernsthafte Schwärmerei für Mighty Mouse und stellte sich das wackere Nagetier als ihren künftigen Ehemann vor.

Was die künstlerische Inspiration betraf, wandte sie sich der Zeitschrift *MAD* zu und zeichnete ihre eigenen Parodien zu Fernsehshows. Gelegentlich hatte sie auch Freunde, die dabei mitmachten, doch die Freundschaften hielten nur bis zum nächsten Umzug. Die zuverlässigste Unterstützung erhielt sie also von Lehrern. Ab ihrem 15. Lebensjahr begeisterte sie sich für Kunstunterricht, setzte den Besuch solcher Klassen nach der Rückkehr nach Texas am College fort und behielt das an jedem College, an dem ihr Mann unterrichtete, bei. Das Gewichtheben war für Bell wohl ein weiteres Kunstprojekt. Den Unterricht im Aktzeichnen mochte sie immer und sagte: „Da passiert so viel: die Formen und die Architektur und der Fluss des Ganzen." Jetzt war sie die Architektin, die von Grund auf einen neuen Körper entwarf und schuf. Sie nahm an weiteren Wettbewerben teil und belegte, nachdem sie auf Bezirks- und Staatsebene gewonnen hatte, im Miss-USA-Wettbewerb Platz 13. Sie zeichnete immer noch, aber nur für sich selbst. Dann, 1989, nahm sie am Natural Eastern Classic teil und gewann. Gesponsert wurde der Wettbewerb von Bob Bonham vom Strong & Shapely Gym in East Rutherford, N. J. Bob veranstaltete eine Party für die Teilnehmer und lud seinen Freund Boris Vallejo ein. An ebenjenem Tag bat Boris Julie, für ihn zu posieren.

Above: Vallejo and Bell have produced an annual *Boris Vallejo & Julie Bell Fantasy Calendar* since 2001, showcasing work by both artists, 2003 has a cover by Bell.

Opposite: From Bell's Franklin Mint Temptation Rides sculpture series of demonesses on motorcycles: *Passion Burns.*

„Ich wusste nicht, dass es ein Nacktposieren sein sollte, aber damit hatte ich eigentlich keine Probleme, denn viele Jahre lang hatte ich Aktzeichnen studiert", sagt Bell. „Es war sehr professionell", aber auch Liebe auf den ersten Blick. „Boris und ich führten beide Ehen, die ziemlich zerrüttet waren. Wir hatten entschieden, das zu akzeptieren, doch als wir einander begegneten, spürten wir beide: ‚So muss das Leben nicht sein. Wir können jene Art von Beziehung haben, von der wir geträumt haben.'" 1994 heirateten sie.

Zu diesem Traum gehörte, dass sie beide Künstler waren. Am ersten Tag, an dem sie posierte, brachte Bell Fotos von ihren Werken mit, und Vallejo beurteilte sie mit wohlmeinender Kritik. Er bot ihr an, ihm beim Malen zuzuschauen, und sie bat ihn, seinen Stil erlernen zu dürfen. „Er gab mir einfach das Gefühl, dass ich das schaffen könnte", sagte sie. Ihr erster kommerzieller Verkauf ging 1990 an *Heavy Metal*, ihr erstes Cover erschien auf der Ausgabe vom Januar 1992.

Währenddessen malte Boris Julie. Sein erstes Porträt hatte den Titel *Alpnu* und zeigte eine schlanke, muskulöse Göttin mit einem herausfordernden Blick. Von diesem Zeitpunkt an gestaltete er, inspiriert von seiner neuen Muse, Frauen mit schlankerem, aber offen muskulösem Körperbau.

Julie war bald im Vallejo-Stil geübt, so sehr, dass es den Leuten schwerfiel zu sagen, wer welches Bild gemalt hatte. Sie veröffentlichte drei Bücher mit ihren Werken (*The Julie Bell Portfolio*, 1994; *Hard Curves*, 1997, und *Soft as Steel*, 1999), bis Running Press die Idee hatte, Bücher zu drucken, die Werke beider Künstler vereinten. „Sie meinten, das wäre eine gute Masche, und es kam mehr Material für ein Buch zusammen", sagt sie. Bis heute sind neun Bände erschienen, dazu jährliche Kalender. Es gab auch ein Plakat im Vallejo-Stil für *Aqua Teen Hunger Force Colon Movie*, 2007, und Albumcover für Meatloafs *Bat Out of Hell III: The Monster is Loose*, 2006, und *Hang Cool Teddy Bear*, 2010. Die Welt brauchte allerdings nicht unbedingt zwei Vallejos; Julie musste ihren eigenen Stil herausbilden. „Ich fing an, Drachen zu malen", sagt sie. „Ich war überaus frustriert, dass meine Drachen nicht so aussahen wie Boris' Drachen. Mir wurde klar, dass das Malen von Fantasygeschöpfen sich aus Quellen der Kreativität speiste, die viel tiefer in einem selbst verborgen sind. Schließlich meinte Boris: ‚Mal deine eigenen verdammten Drachen!'" Sie schuf eine deutlicher stilisierte Kreatur in pinken, violetten, roten und orangefarbenen Tönen, die zu ihrer charakteristischen Palette wurden. Zudem beeinflusste ihre lebenslange Liebe zum Art nouveau ihren sich entwickelnden Stil; dann entdeckte sie die Tiermalerei. „Ich habe gelesen, dass Kinder von Alkoholikern Tiere so personifizieren, als würden sie ihnen Gefühle entgegenbringen", sagt sie. „Als ich für Tor Books eine Reihe von Buchtiteln mit Wölfen malte, habe ich meine Liebe zur Tiermalerei neu entdeckt." Heute verkauft sie ihre Fantasykunst – sie bevorzugt die Bezeichnung „*visionärer Realismus*" – über die Rehs Contemporary Gallery in New York und ihre Tiermalerei über Legacy Galleries und die Martin Gallery. Noch immer arbeitet Julie für Fantasykunstprojekte mit Boris zusammen, doch sie wendet sich mehr dem Verkauf von bildender Kunst zu. „Es gefällt mir, wenn ich das malen kann, worauf ich Lust habe, und es Leute gibt, die diese Sachen kaufen und mögen", sagt Julie. „Boris sieht, wie ich jeden Tag beschwingt aufwache und es kaum erwarten kann, ins Atelier zu laufen und das zu malen, was ich malen will. Ein bisschen eifersüchtig ist er schon."

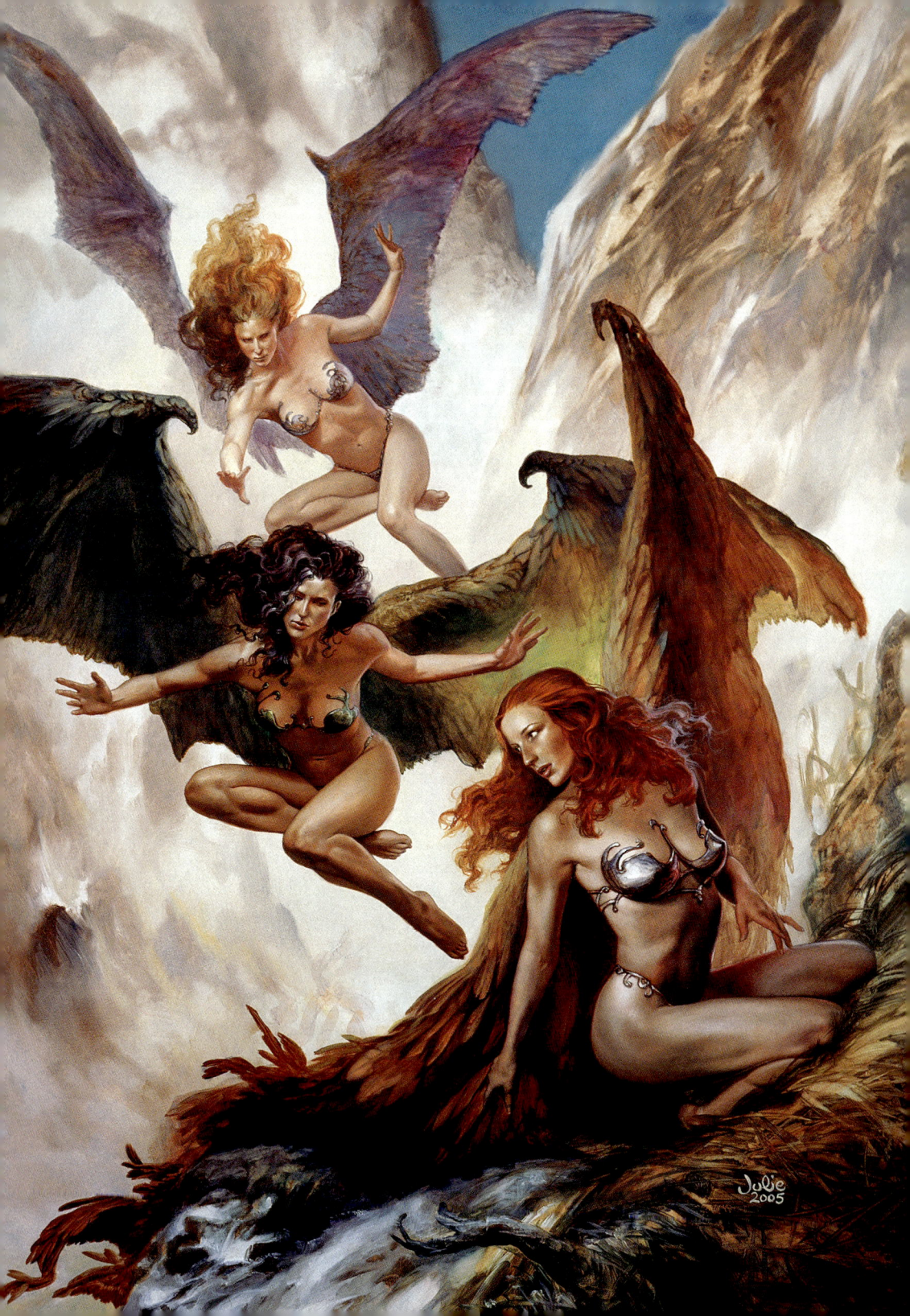

JULIE BELL
LA VISIONNAIRE

« Quand je ressens cette… obsession particulière pour une idée ou une image, je sais qu'il faut que la peigne. »

Julie Bell veut que ce soit clair : elle n'est pas que Mme Boris Vallejo. « Boris est un énorme pilier dans le monde du fantasy art ; il projette une ombre immense, explique-t-elle. Nous travaillons dans le même atelier chaque jour et j'adore que nous soyons ensemble, mais j'ai passé des années dans cette ombre et je sors enfin dans la lumière, ma lumière. Il y a maintenant des gens qui découvrent Boris par moi. Cela me fait un certain plaisir. »

Il est vrai que les premières toiles de Bell présentent une ressemblance frappante avec celles de son mari, mais elle est intentionnelle. Elle a suivi pléthore de cours de dessin au fil des années, mais s'est découragée de la peinture. Devenue culturiste et primée, elle accepte de poser pour Vallejo, qui prend en main son éducation artistique.

« J'ai toujours voulu faire de l'art, mais je ne savais pas comment entrer dans le milieu », raconte-t-elle. Alors qu'elle vit au Texas avec son premier mari professeur d'université et qu'elle élève leurs deux jeunes enfants, elle étudie des livres d'art à la bibliothèque. « Je voyais des livres dont les illustrations me plaisaient et j'écrivais des lettres aux éditeurs avec des photos de mon travail. Je n'avais aucune idée de ce qu'il fallait faire. » La petite famille déménage souvent, au gré des mutations de monsieur. Au début des années 1980 elle atterrit dans l'Ohio et un jour le mari rapporte à la maison un jeu de poids.

« Je grimpais beaucoup aux arbres quand j'étais enfant et j'étais fière de savoir faire des tractions accrochée aux branches. Le jeu incluait une barre de tractions, je me suis levée d'un bond et j'en ai fait quelques-unes. Mon mari était impressionné. J'ai commencé à lever de la fonte. »

Sans avoir mis les pieds dans une salle de sport, elle commence à se classer dans les concours locaux de bodybuilding. « Je ne pouvais pas muscler correctement mes jambes à la maison, raconte-t-elle, alors je suis allée à la salle. » Là, pour la première fois depuis son mariage, elle se fait des amis de son côté. Cela peut sembler peu de chose, mais dans l'enfance chaotique de Bell, les amis étaient rares, et éphémères.

Opposite: Cruel Fate, for the 2006 Boris Vallejo and Julie Bell Fantasy Calendar, oil on board, 2005, 71.1 x 45.7 cm (28 x 18 inches).

Above: He Waits for Her, for the 2006 Boris Vallejo and Julie Bell Fantasy Calendar, oil on board, 2005, 66 x 45.7 cm (26 x 18 inches).

Bell naît en 1958 à Beaumont (Texas), où son père est un architecte à succès. Sa mère est douée pour les arts, mais elle est alcoolique et souffre de troubles mentaux. Quand ses parents divorcent, en 1970, sa mère prend ses trois filles avec elle et elles s'installent à Atlanta avec un beau-père alcoolique lui aussi, mais la vie était déjà difficile avant cela.

« [Ma mère] m'emmenait dans des bars et dans d'autres endroits vraiment dingues et à 10-11 ans je prenais le volant, je conduisais la voiture, j'essayais de la maintenir éveillée. J'ai appris à être hyper vigilante, à m'occuper de mes sœurs plus jeunes. » Elle trouve du réconfort dans les bandes dessinées d'*Archie* et le monde adolescent salutaire qui y est représenté, en particulier après le divorce, quand son beau-père, hargneux, enchaîne les bagarres et les licenciements, obligeant la famille à déménager et les filles à changer d'école, plusieurs fois par an. « Je lis encore les BD d'*Archie*, confie-t-elle en riant. Quelques minutes en fin de journée. Cela libère mon cerveau de tout. » Elle tombe aussi très amoureuse de Super-Souris *(Mighty Mouse)*, qu'elle fantasme en futur époux.

Pour l'inspiration artistique, elle jette son dévolu sur le magazine *MAD* et dessine ses propres parodies d'émissions de télé. Il arrive que des amis se joignent à elle, mais les amis ne durent que jusqu'au déménagement suivant, si bien que son soutien le plus fiable lui vient des professeurs. Elle devient accro aux cours d'art, qu'elle commence à fréquenter à 15 ans, et les poursuit à son retour au Texas, quand elle entre à l'université, puis sur chaque campus où enseigne son mari.

D'un certain point de vue, la musculation est aussi un projet artistique pour Bell. Elle a toujours adoré les cours de modèle vivant : « Il s'y passe tellement de choses : les formes, l'architecture, la fluidité de l'ensemble. » Elle devient l'architecte, elle conçoit et façonne un nouveau corps à partir de rien. Elle s'inscrit à davantage de concours, se classe 13e à celui de Miss USA après l'avoir emporté au niveau du comté et de l'État. Elle dessine toujours, mais pour elle-même.

En 1989, elle gagne la Natural Eastern Classic, sponsorisée par Bob Bonham de la salle de gym Strong & Shapely Gym d'East Rutherford (New Jersey). Bob organise une fête pour les participants au concours et invite son ami Boris Vallejo. Le même jour, Boris demande à Julie de poser pour lui.

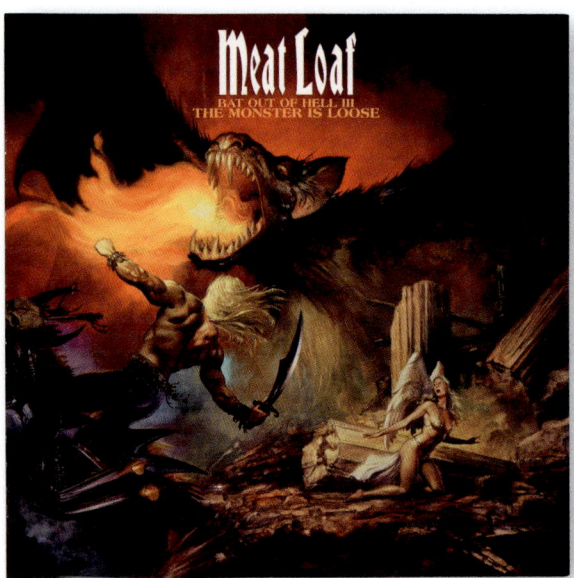

« Je ne savais pas que je serais nue, mais cela ne m'a pas vraiment inquiétée parce que je pratiquais le dessin sur modèle vivant depuis des années, explique Bell. C'était très professionnel », mais c'est aussi un coup de foudre. « Boris et moi étions tous les deux dans des mariages qui ne fonctionnaient pas. Nous en avions pris notre parti, mais quand nous nous sommes rencontrés nous nous sommes tous les deux dit : "Rien ne nous oblige à vivre comme ça ? Nous pouvons avoir le genre de relation dont nous rêvions." » Ils se marieront en 1994.

Ce rêve se nourrit notamment du fait qu'ils sont tous deux des artistes. Bell a apporté des photos de son travail le premier jour où elle est venue poser pour Vallejo, qui lui a prodigué des critiques constructives. Il lui propose de le regarder peindre et elle demande à apprendre son style. « Il m'a simplement fait sentir que j'en étais capable », raconte-t-elle. Elle conclut sa première vente en 1990, avec *Heavy Metal* et signe sa première couverture pour le numéro de janvier 1992.

Boris, lui, peint Julie. Son premier portrait d'elle, intitulé *Alpnu*, montre une déesse fine et tout en muscles avec un regard plein de défi. À partir de là ses personnages féminins tendront vers une musculature plus allongée, mieux dessinée, inspirée par sa nouvelle muse.

Julie est effectivement devenue une adepte du style Vallejo, au point que les gens avaient du mal à savoir qui avait

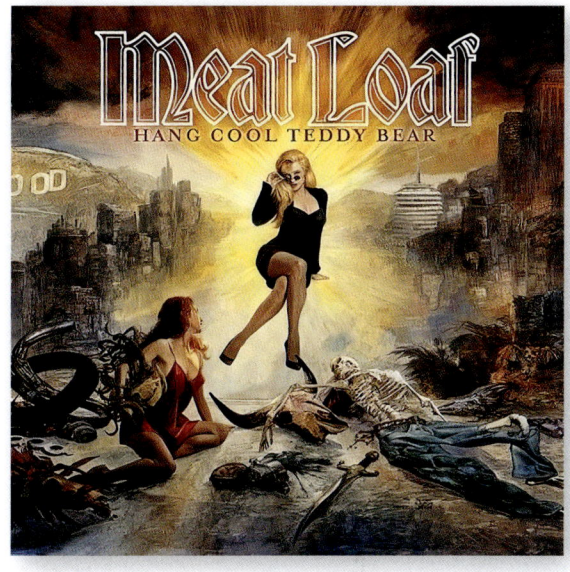

peint quoi. Elle a publié trois ouvrages sur son travail personnel (*The Julie Bell Portfolio*, 1994 ; *Hard Curves*, 1997 et *Soft as Steel*, 1999) avant que Running Press ait l'idée d'éditer une série d'œuvres signées des deux artistes. « Ils pensaient que ce serait accrocheur et cela faisait une matière plus riche pour les livres », dit-elle. Neuf tomes sont sortis à ce jour, ainsi que des calendriers chaque année. Ils ont aussi collaboré sur une affiche parodique de Vallejo pour *Aqua Teen Hunger Force Colon Movie* en 2007 et sur les pochettes des albums de Meatloaf *Bat Out of Hell III : The Monster Is Loose* (2006) et *Hang Cool Teddy Bear* (2010).

Cependant le monde n'avait pas besoin de deux Vallejo. Julie a dû forger son propre style. « J'ai commencé par les dragons, raconte-t-elle. J'étais extrêmement frustrée que mes dragons ne ressemblent pas à ceux de Boris. Je me suis rendu compte que peindre des créatures fantastiques suppose de puiser au plus profond de votre propre créativité. Boris a fini par me dire : "Tu n'as qu'à faire tes dragons à toi !" » Elle imagine alors une créature plus stylisée, dans des tons roses, violets, rouges et orange, qui deviennent sa palette signature. Son amour indéfectible pour l'Art nouveau influence encore ce style qui émerge, jusqu'à ce qu'elle découvre l'art animalier.

« J'ai lu que les enfants d'alcooliques personnifient les animaux comme s'ils ressentaient de leur part de vrais sentiments, explique-t-elle. J'ai redécouvert combien j'aimais les peindre en réalisant une série de couvertures avec des loups pour Tor Books. » Elle vend aujourd'hui son fantasy art – elle préfère le terme de *réalisme visionnaire* – par l'intermédiaire de la Rehs Contemporary Gallery de New York et ses œuvres animalières aux Legacy Galleries et à la Martin Gallery. Julie collabore toujours avec Boris sur divers projets de fantasy art, mais se rapproche de l'art « noble ». « J'adore pouvoir peindre ce que je veux, puis que des gens l'achètent et l'apprécient, dit Julie. Boris me voit galvanisée dès le réveil, impatiente de courir à l'atelier pour peindre ce que j'ai envie de peindre, et il est un tout petit peu jaloux. »

Opposite: Meat Loaf commissioned Bell for the cover of his *Bat Out of Hell III: The Monster Is Loose*, 2006.

Above: Hang Cool Teddy Bear was the 10th album by Meat Loaf, released in 2010, with this Julie Bell cover.

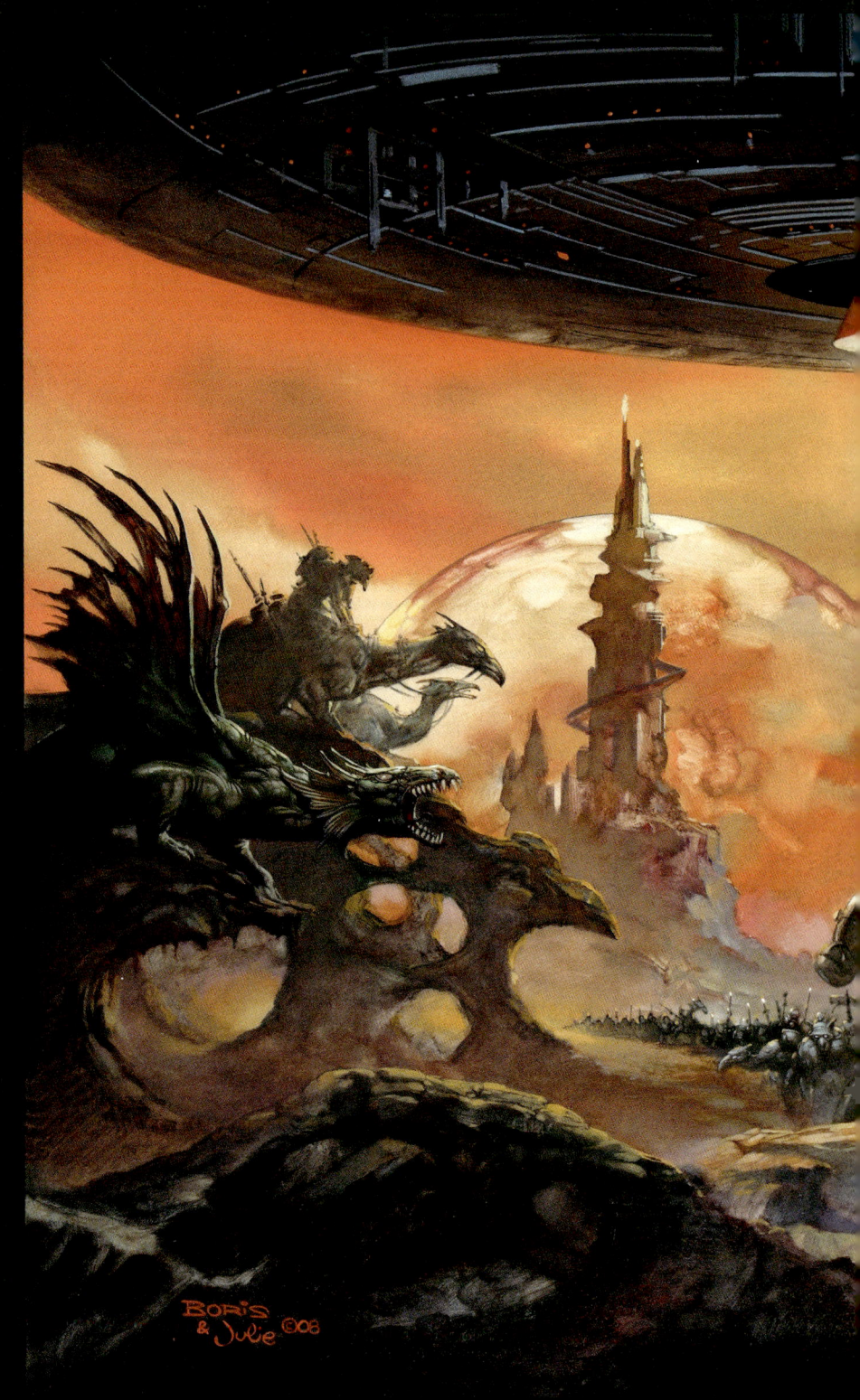

BORIS
& Julie ©08

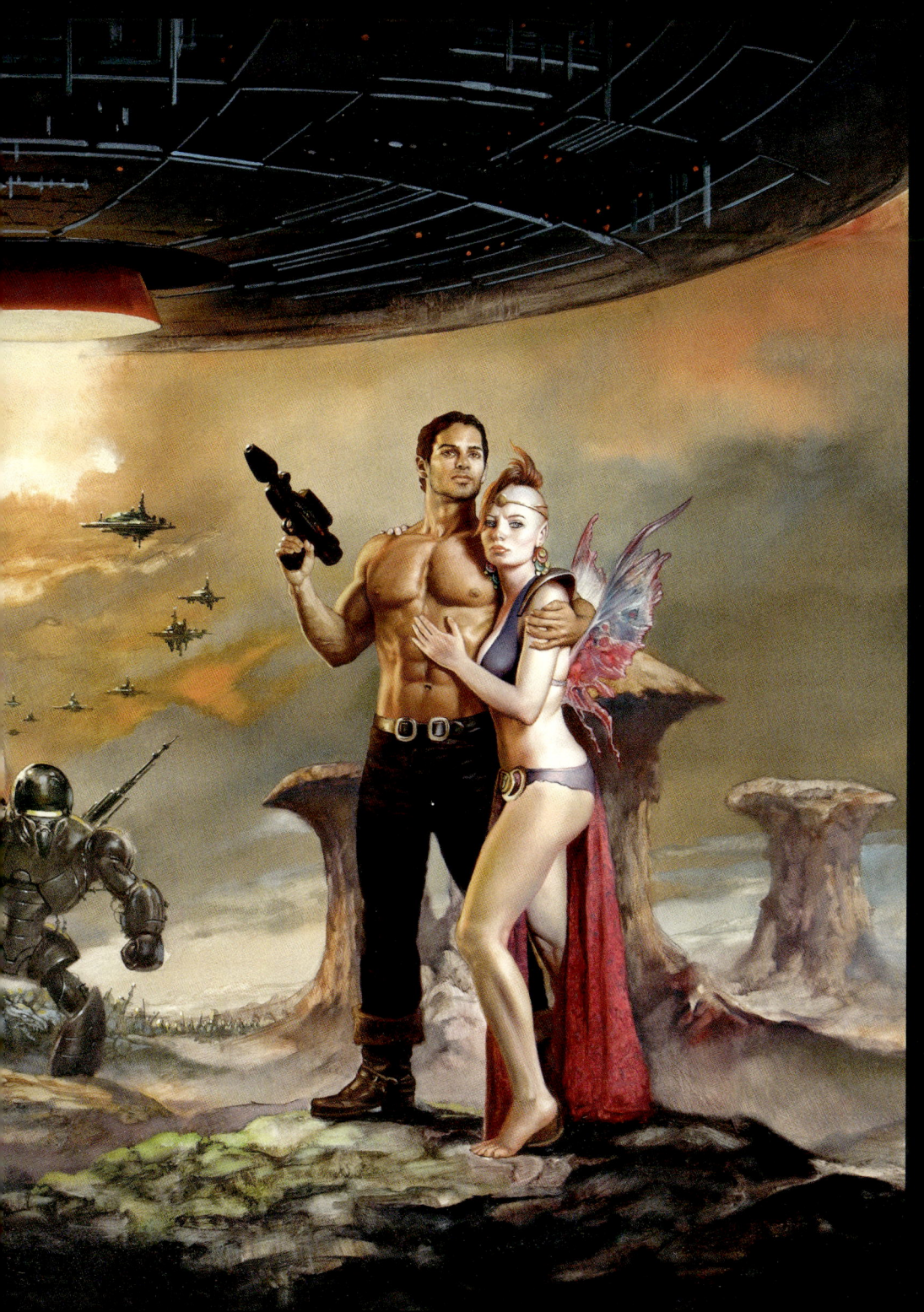

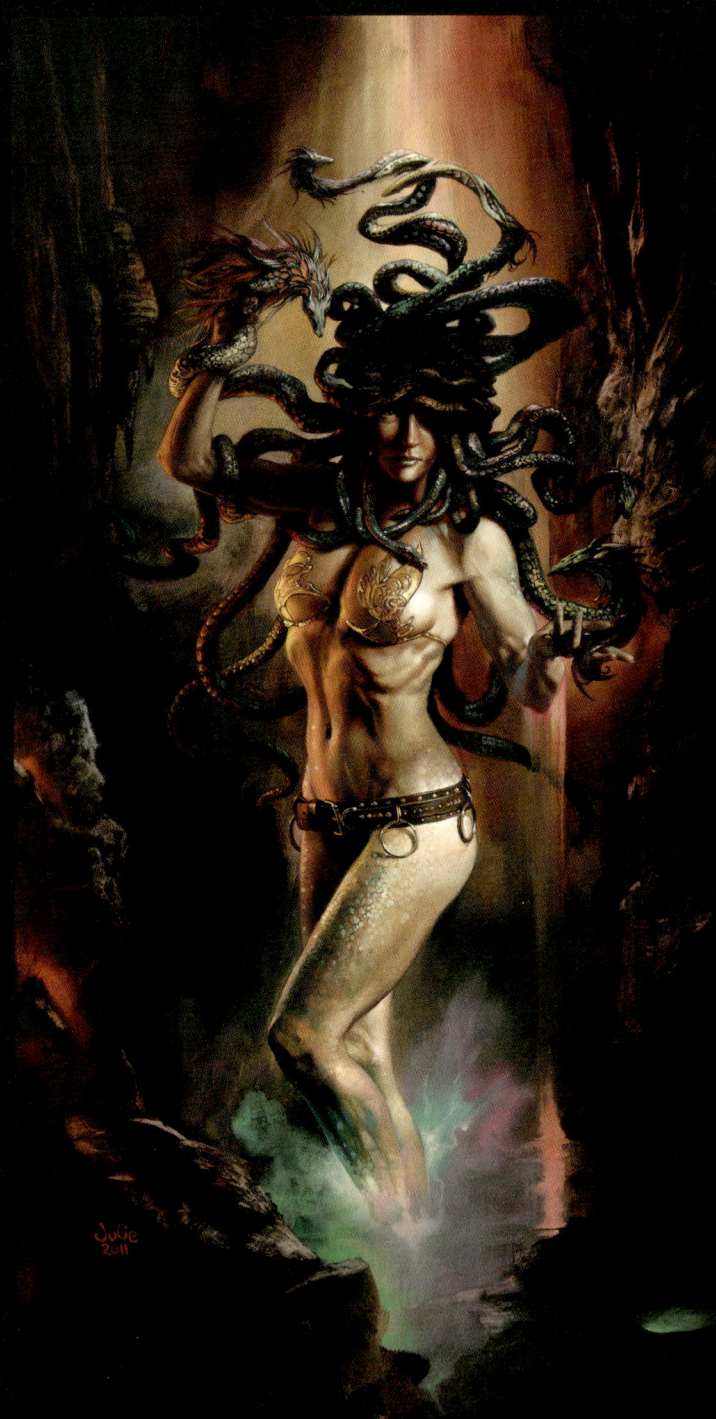

Previous spread: Galactic Love, by Julie Bell and Boris Vallejo, oil on board, 2003.

Left: Medusa, for the 2012 *Boris Vallejo and Julie Bell Fantasy Calendar*, oil on board, 2011, 71.1 x 35.5 cm (28 x 14 inches).

Opposite: The Huntress, for *Heavy Metal* magazine, reused for *Julie Bell Trading Cards* from Cardz. Oil on board, 1996, 68.5 x 43.1 cm (27 x 17 inches).

Following left: Anyea, for the 2010 *Boris Vallejo and Julie Bell Fantasy Calendar*, oil on board, 2009, 71.1 x 50.8 cm (28 x 20 inches).

Following right: Warrior Assault, for the 2011 *Boris Vallejo and Julie Bell Fantasy Calendar*, 2010, oil on board, 2010, 71.1 x 50.8 cm (28 x 20 inches).

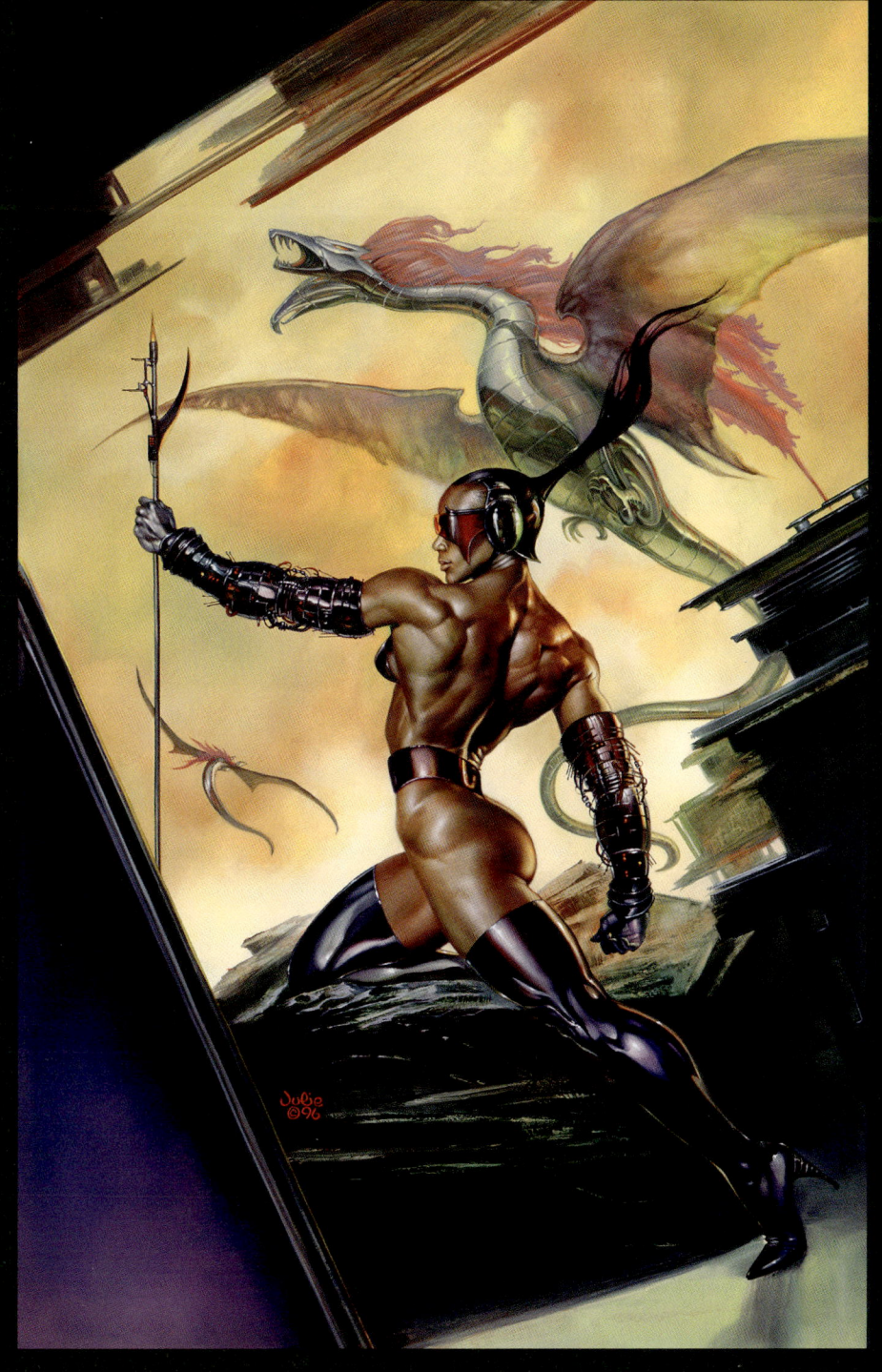

JULIE BELL

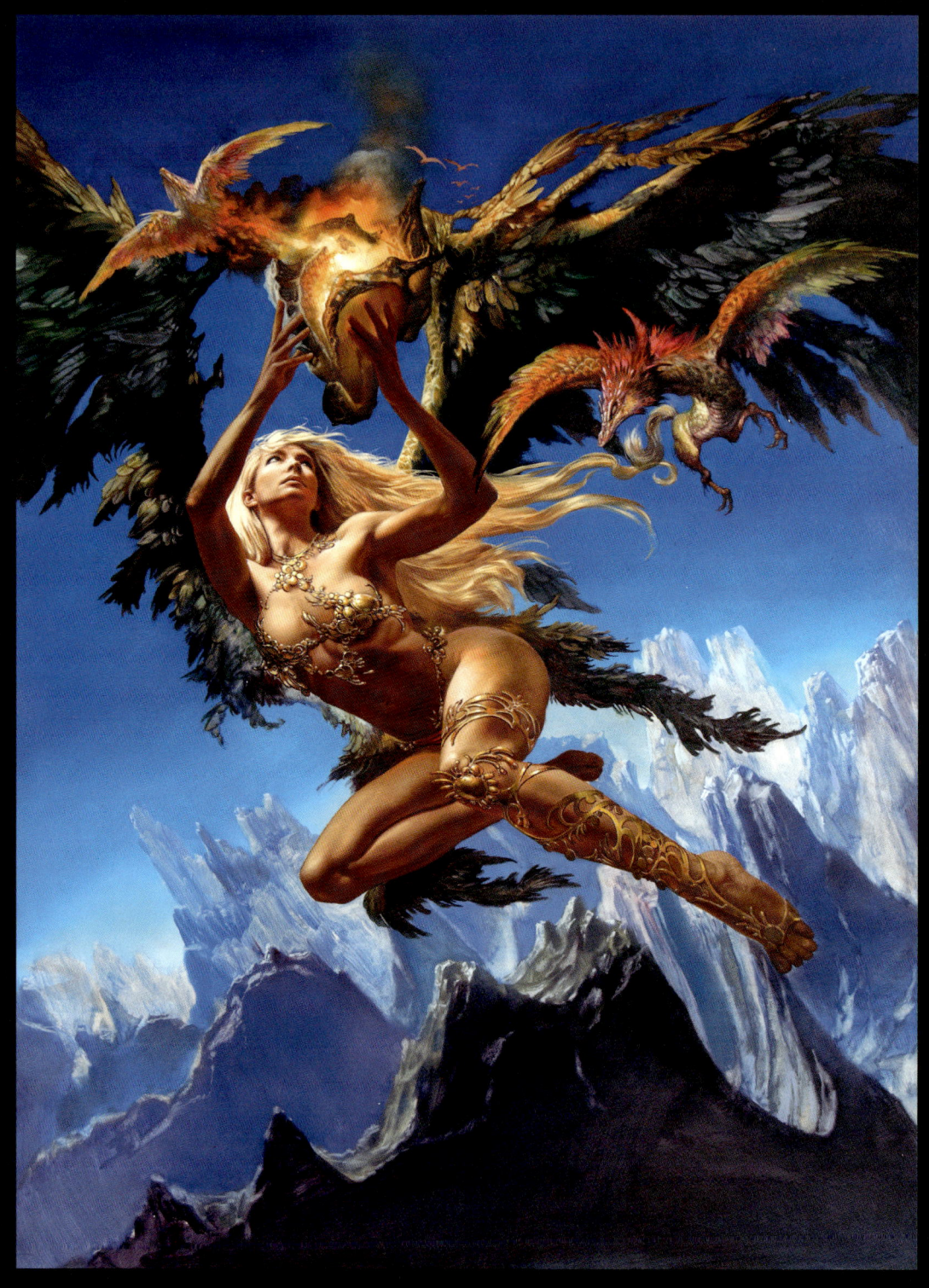

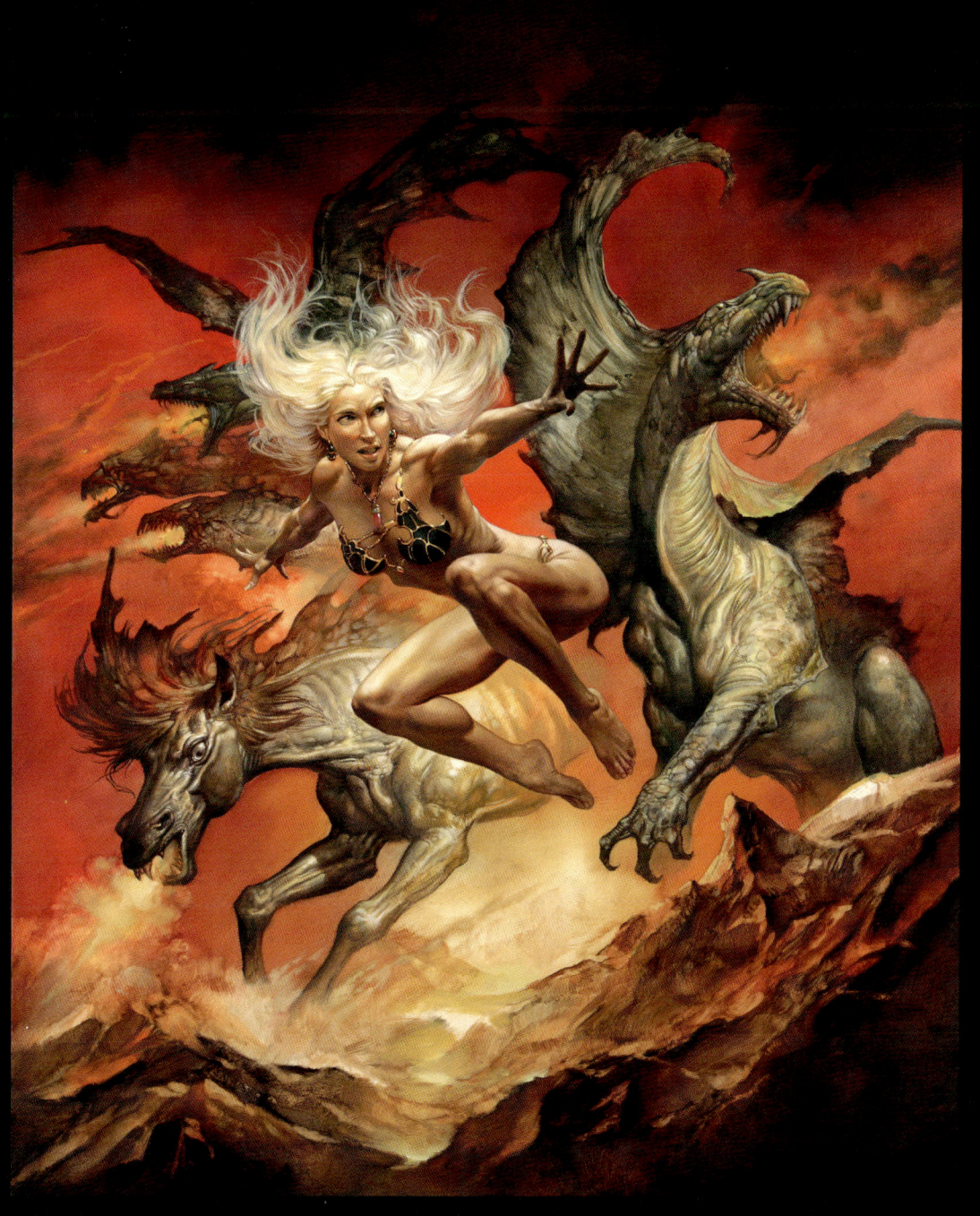

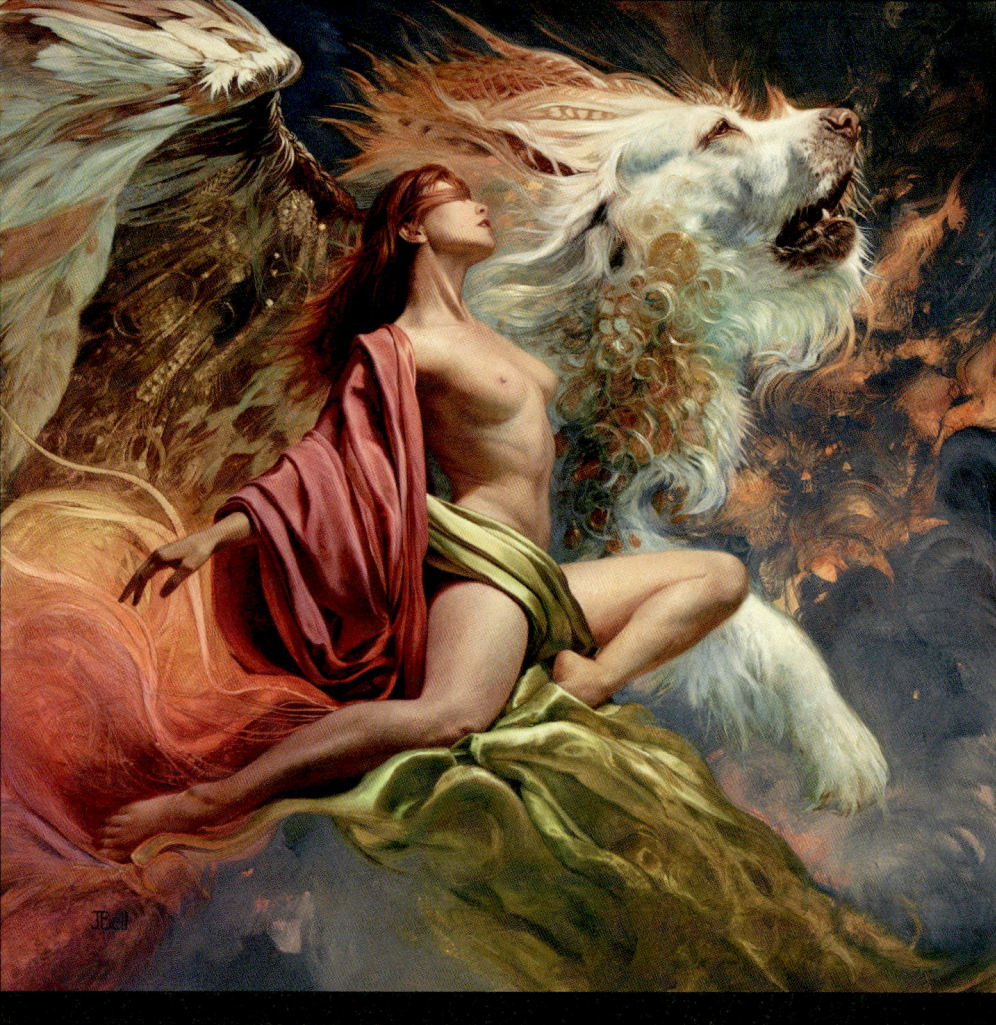

Above: Unfolding Rainbow, for the *2019 Boris Vallejo and Julie Bell Fantasy Calendar*, and featured in the 2018 film *Mandy*. Oil on board, 2018, 76.2 x 76.2 cm (30 x 30 inches).

Opposite: The Changeling, for the *2010 Boris Vallejo and Julie Bell Fantasy Calendar*, oil on wooden panel, 2009, 61 x 45.7 cm (24 x 18 inches).

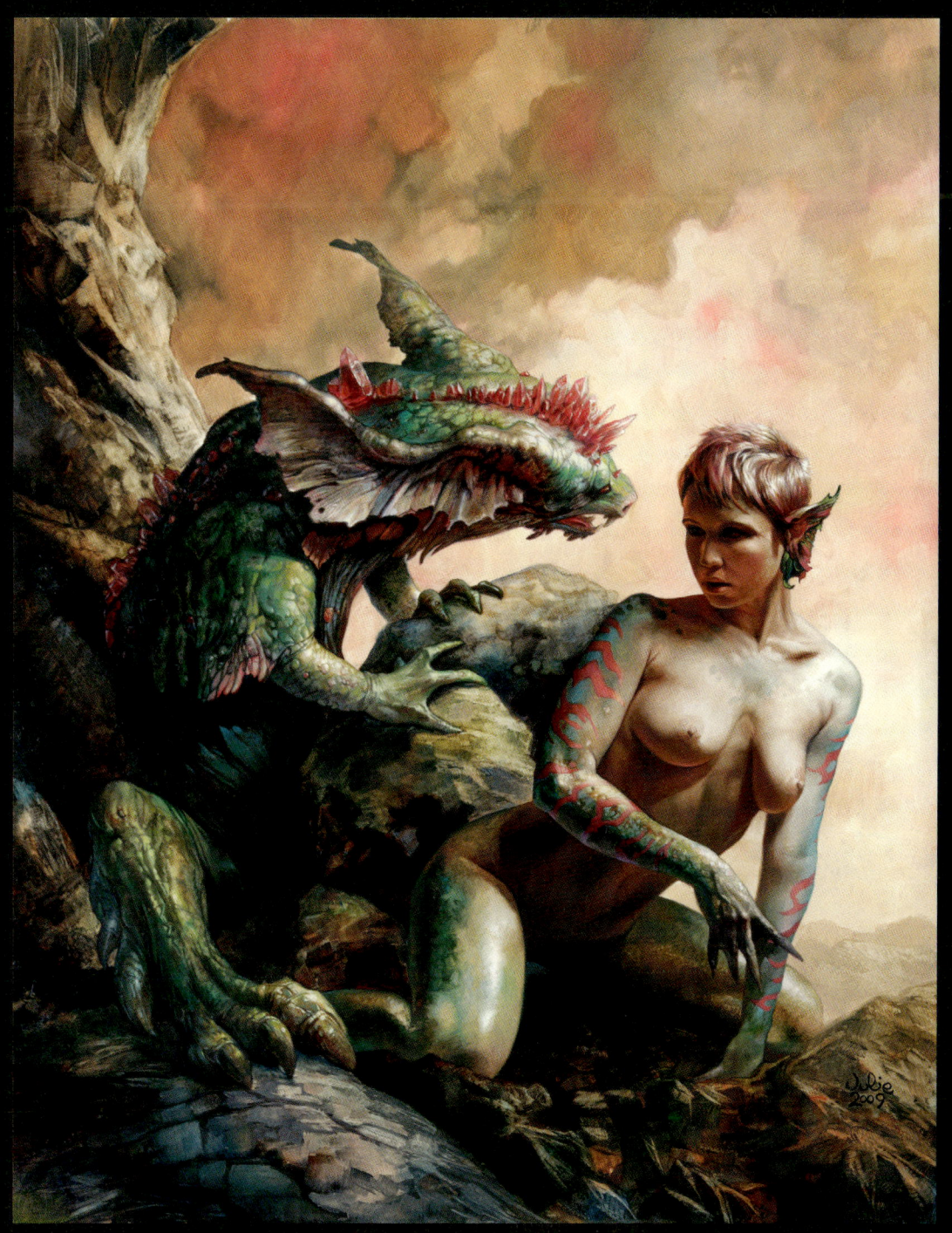

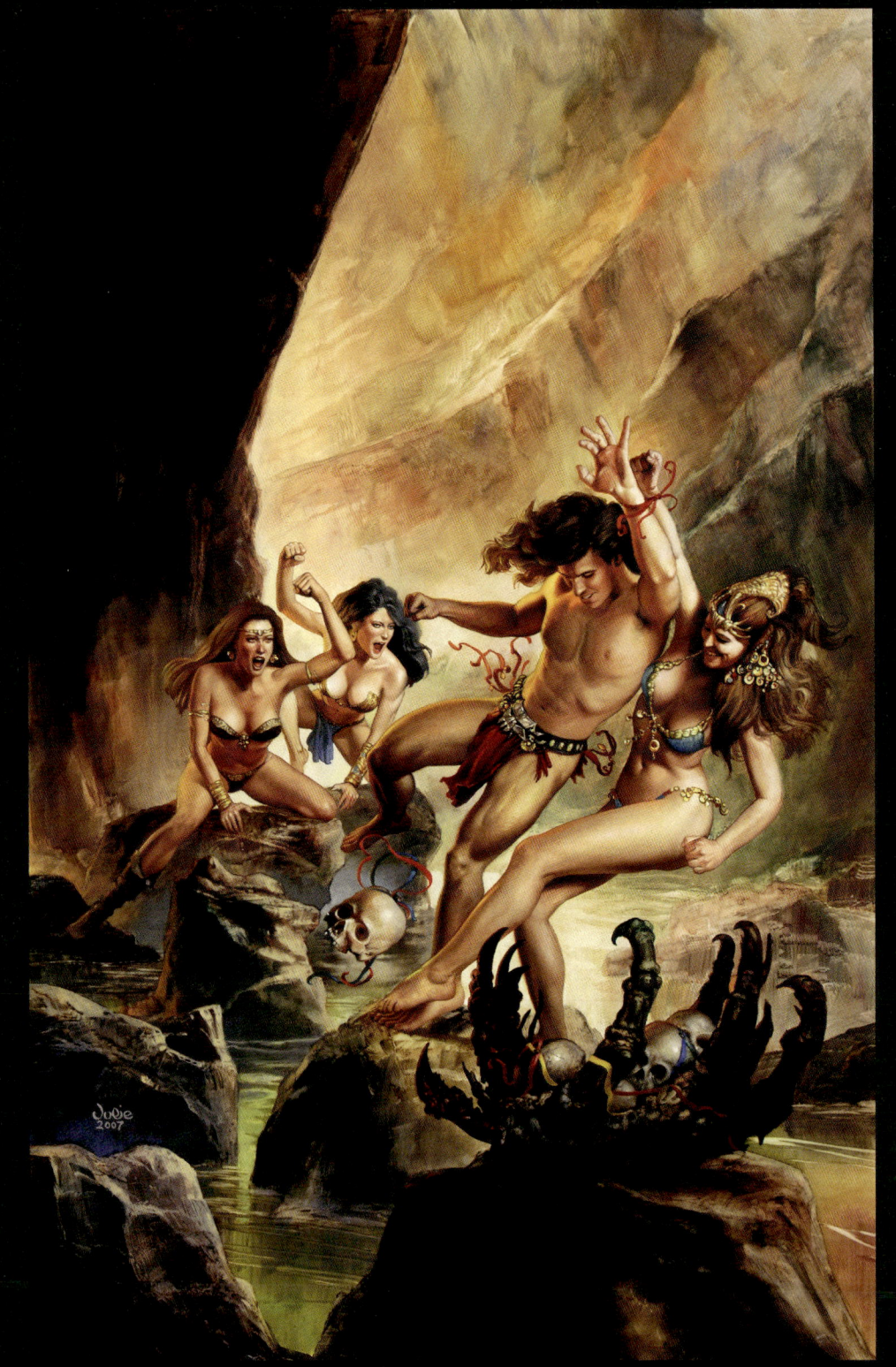

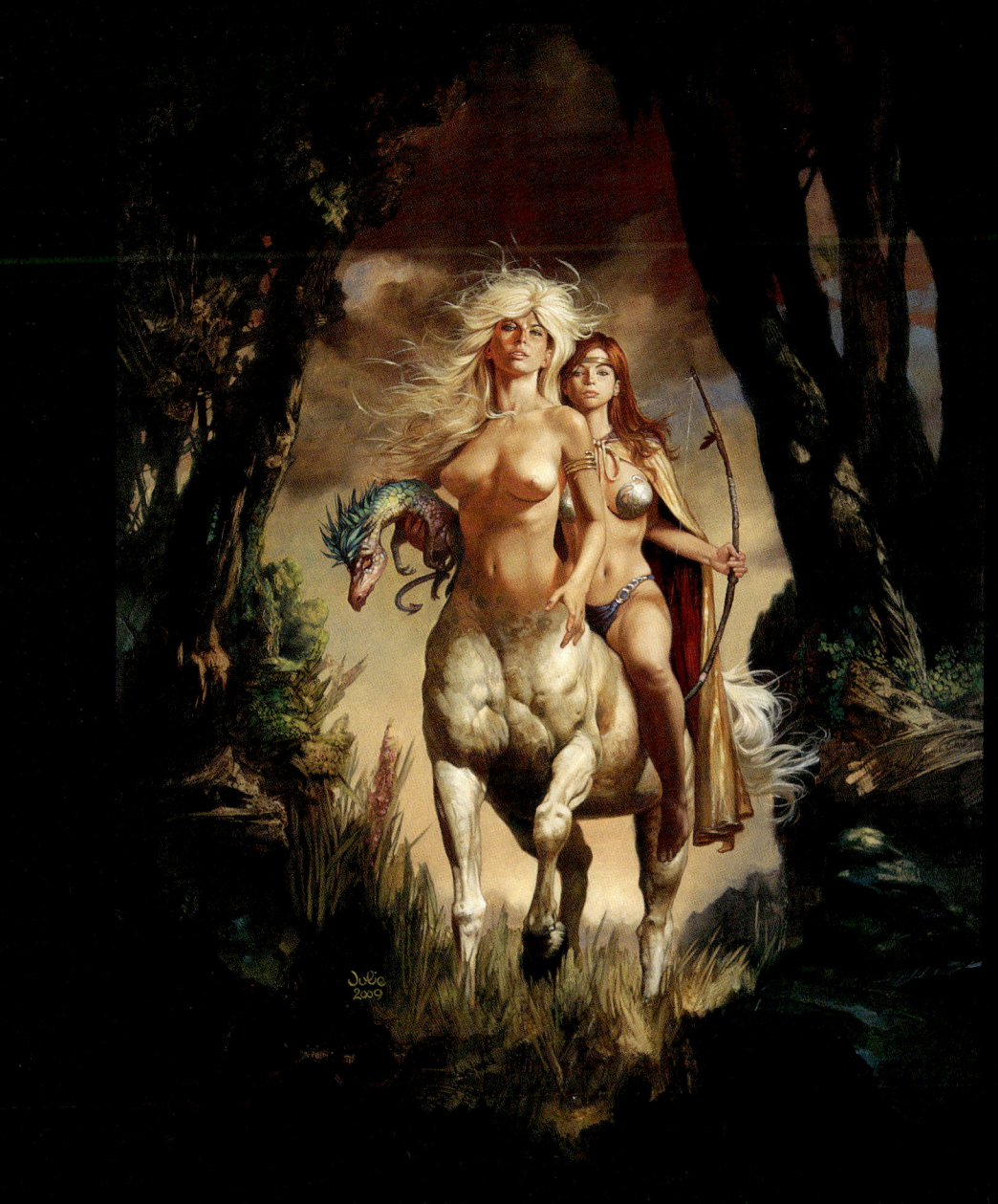

Opposite: The Game, for the *2008 Boris Vallejo and Julie Bell Fantasy Calendar*, oil on board, 2007, 68.5 x 43.1 cm (27 x 17 inches).

Above: Blood Sisters, for the *2001 Boris Vallejo and Julie Bell Fantasy Calendar*, oil on board, 2000, 61 x 45.7 cm (24 x 18 inches).

JULIE BELL

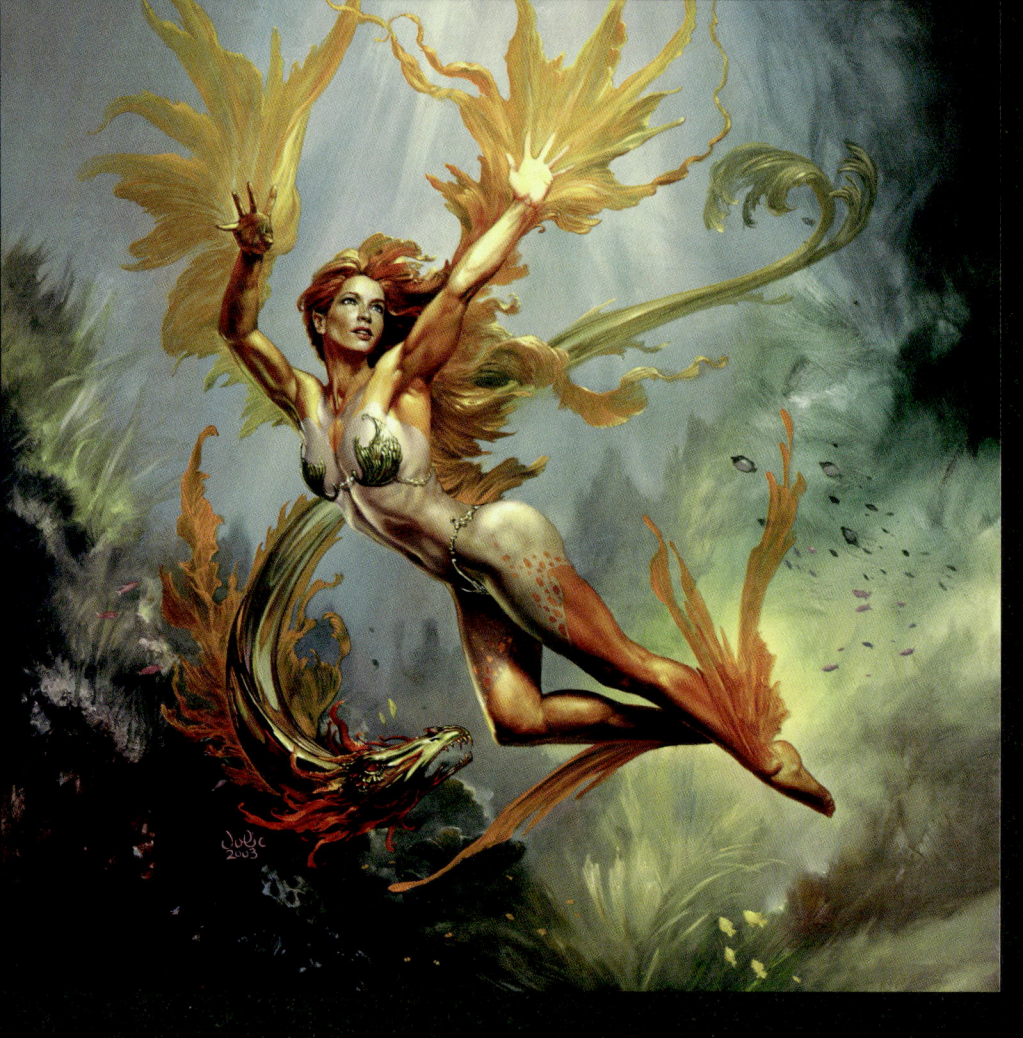

Above: Flame Fish, for the *Julie Bell Trading Cards* by Cardz, and used in the *2004 Boris Vallejo and Julie Bell Fantasy Calendar,* oil on board, 2003.

Opposite: The Day They Left, used in the *2012 Boris Vallejo and Julie Bell Fantasy Calendar,* oil on board, 2011, 43.1 x 43.1 cm (17 x 17 inches).

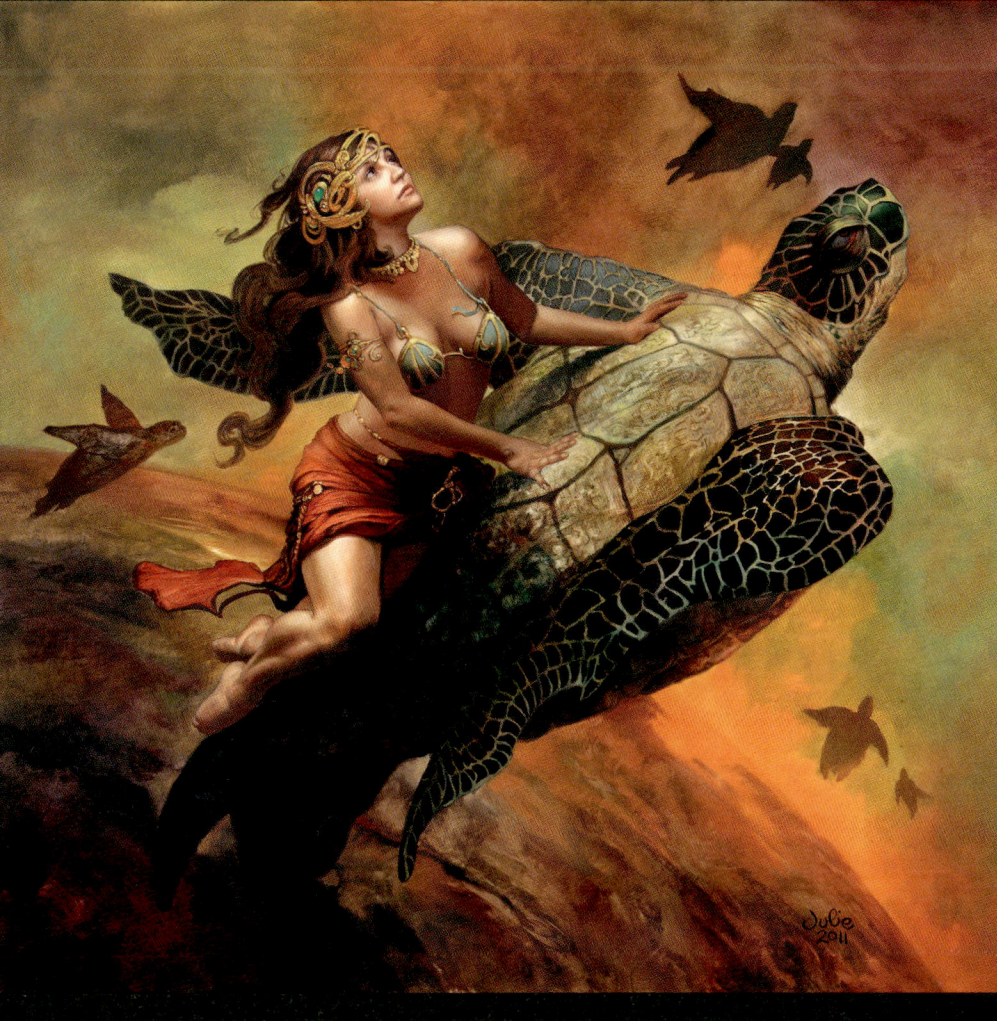

Following left: Adolphus and Valerio, for the 2009 Boris Vallejo and Julie Bell Fantasy Calendar, oil on board, 2008, 71.1 x 43.1 cm (28 x 17 inches).

Following right: From the Mist, for the 2012 Boris Vallejo and Julie Bell Fantasy Calendar, oil on board, 2011, 61 x 45.7 cm (24 x 18 inches).

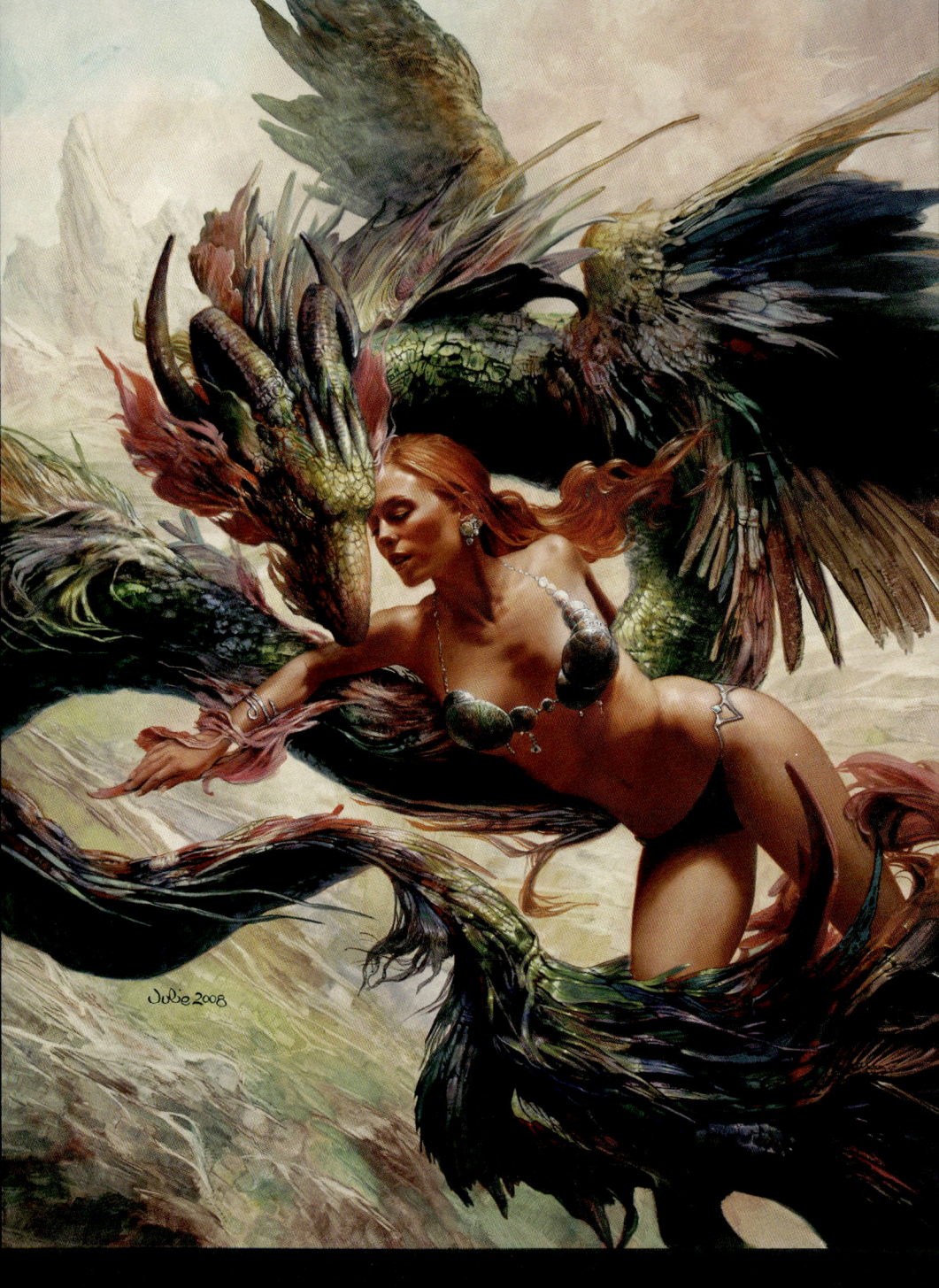

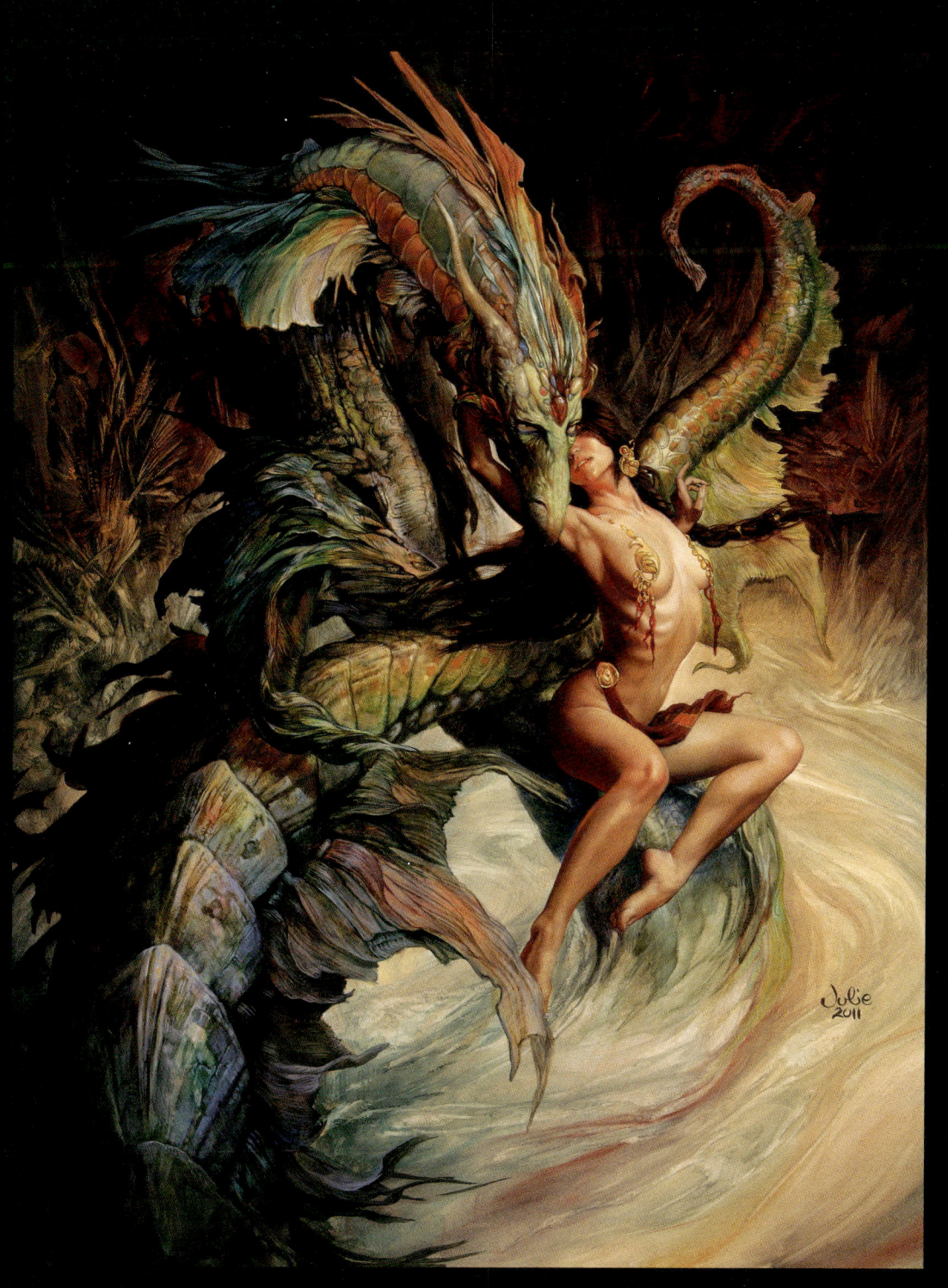

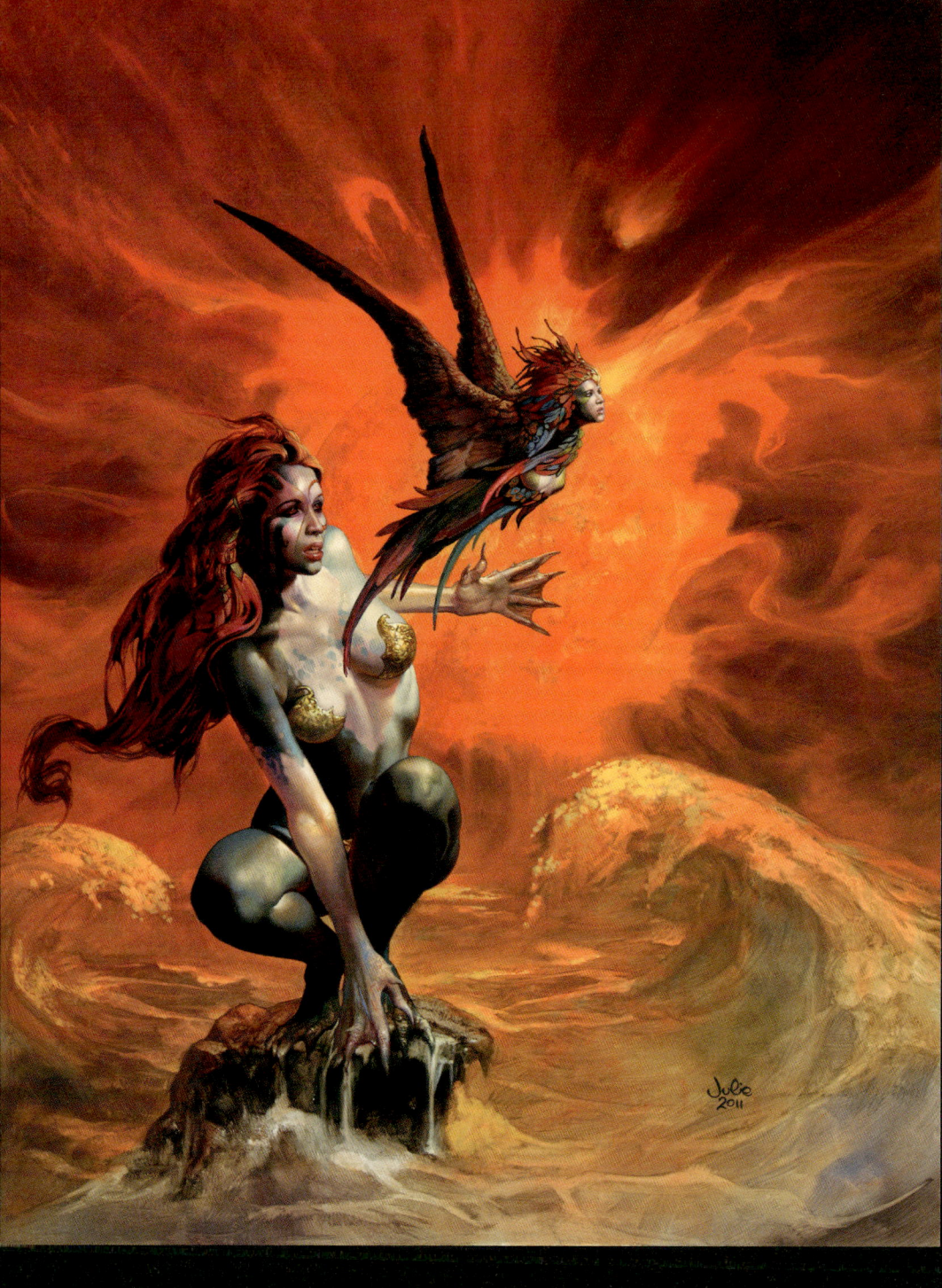

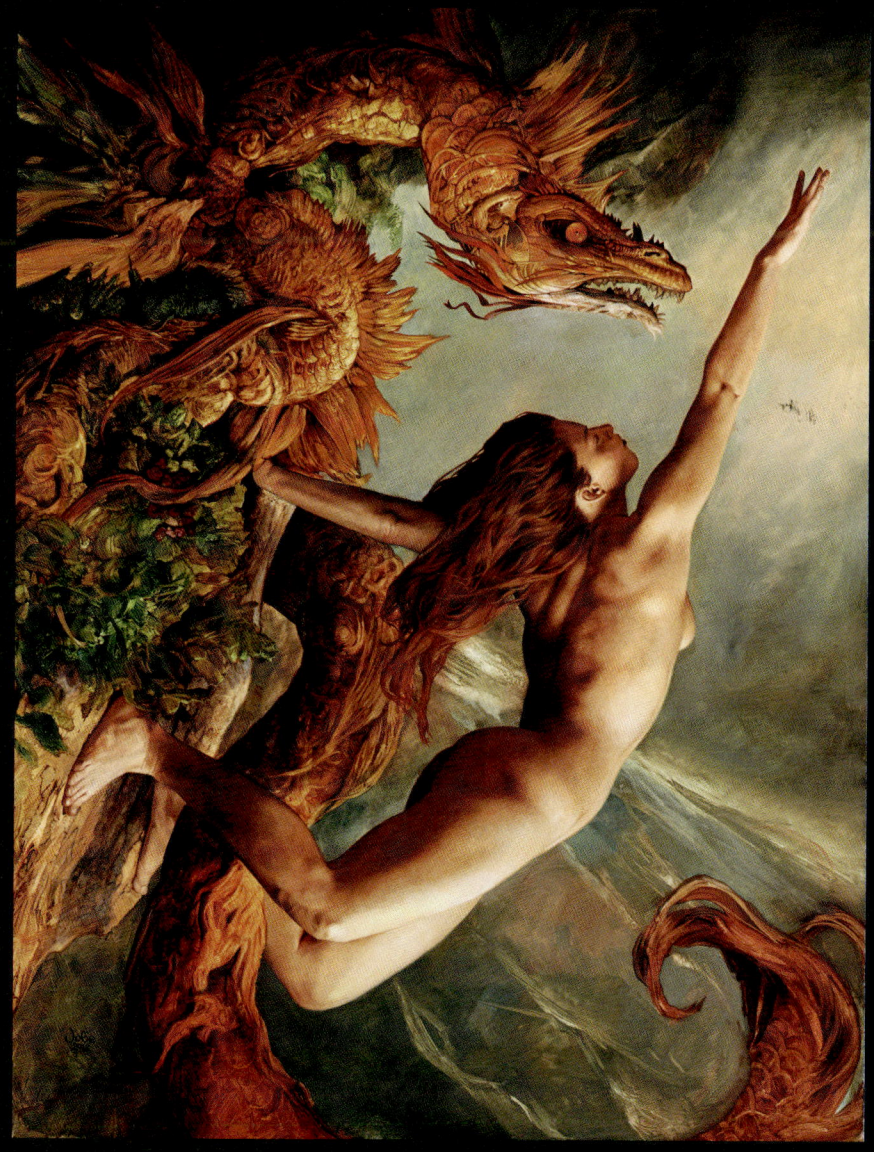

Opposite: Little Sister, used in the *2012 Boris Vallejo and Julie Bell Fantasy Calendar*, oil on board, 2011, 58.4 x 45.7 cm (23 x 18 inches).

Above: Leap, for the *2013 Boris Vallejo and Julie Bell Fantasy Calendar*; also took first place for Imaginative Realism at the Art Renewal Center International Salon 2012. Oil on board, 2012, 101.6 x 76.2 cm (40 x 30 inches).

Following left: End of the Day, for the *2004 Boris Vallejo and Julie Bell Fantasy Calendar*, oil on board, 2003, 71.1 x 43.1 cm (28 x 17 inches).

Following right: Sketch by Julie Bell, pen and gouache on paper, 1998, 36.6 x 24.1 cm (14.4 x 9.5 inches). Courtesy of Heritage Auctions.

JULIE BELL

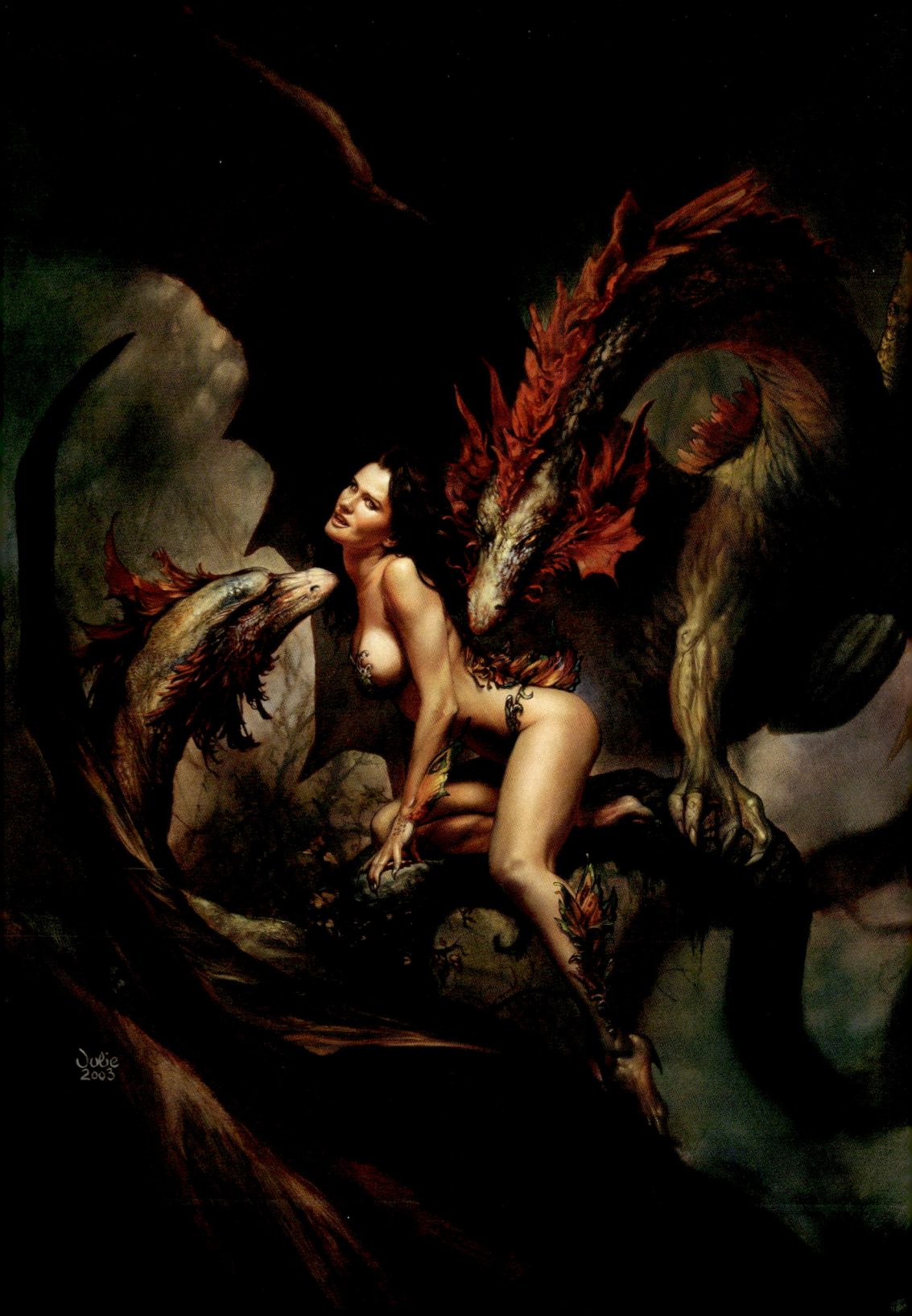

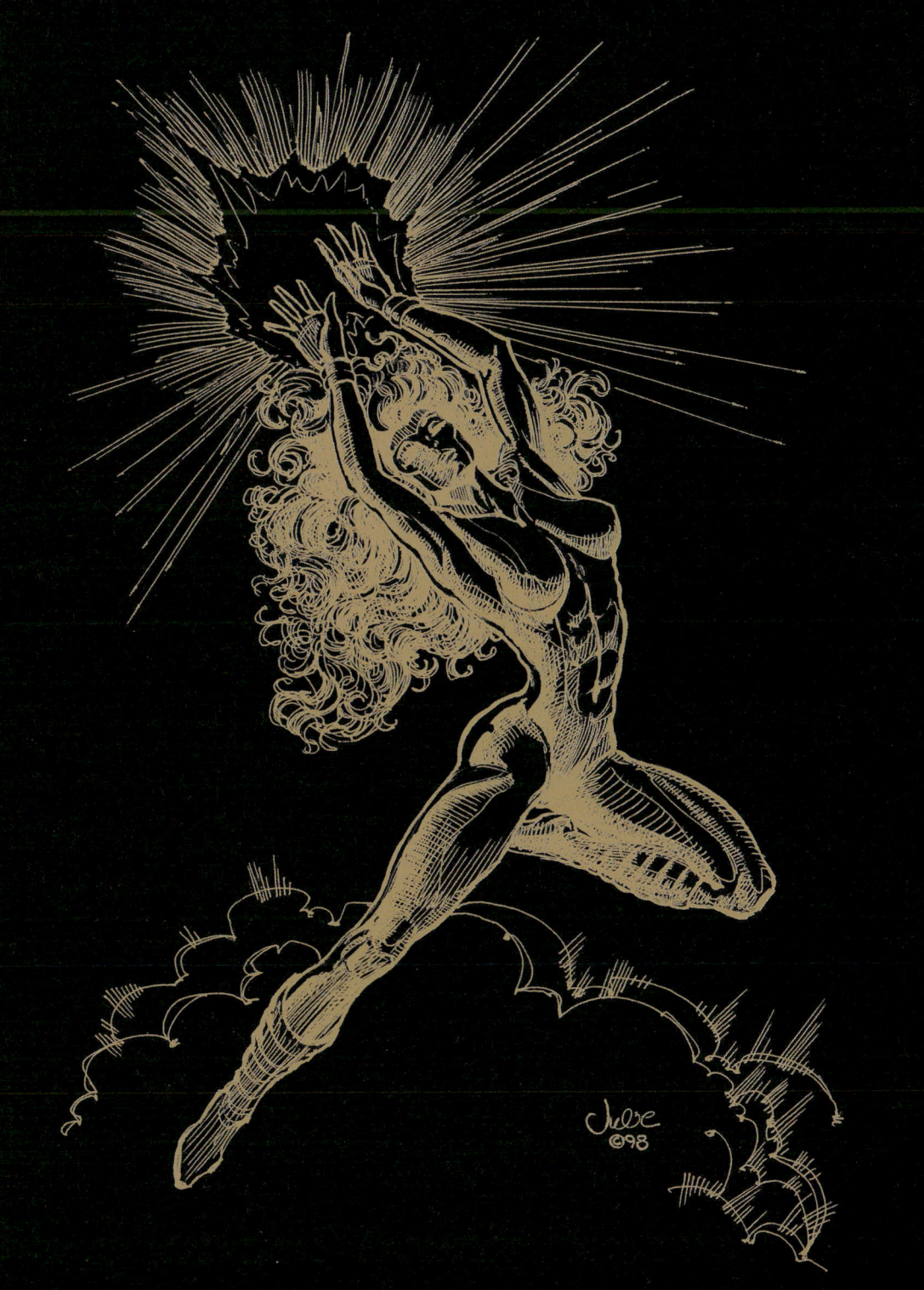

Philippe Druillet

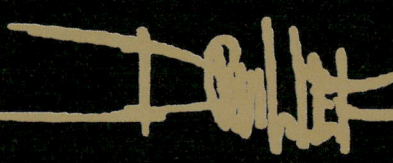

1944-

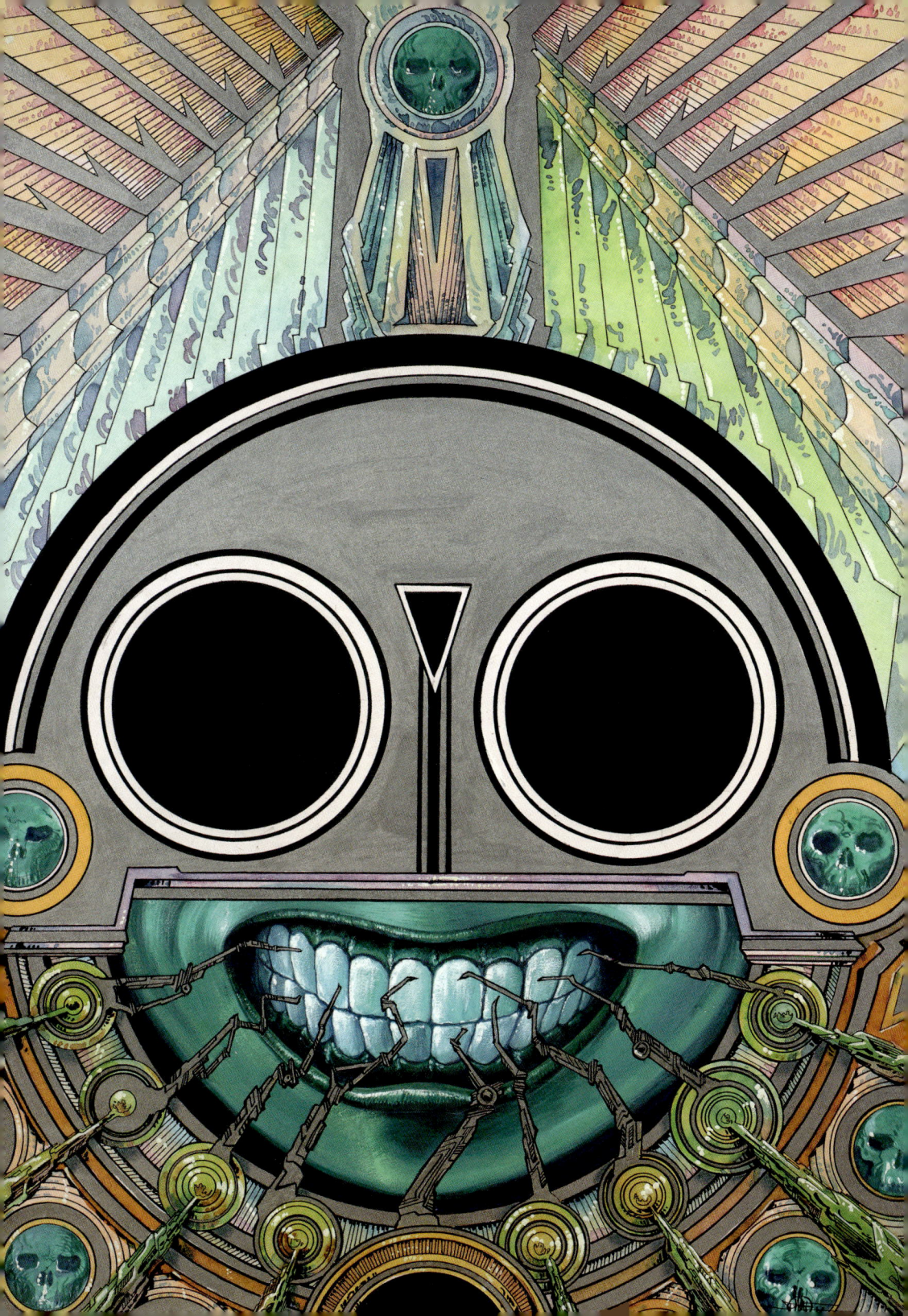

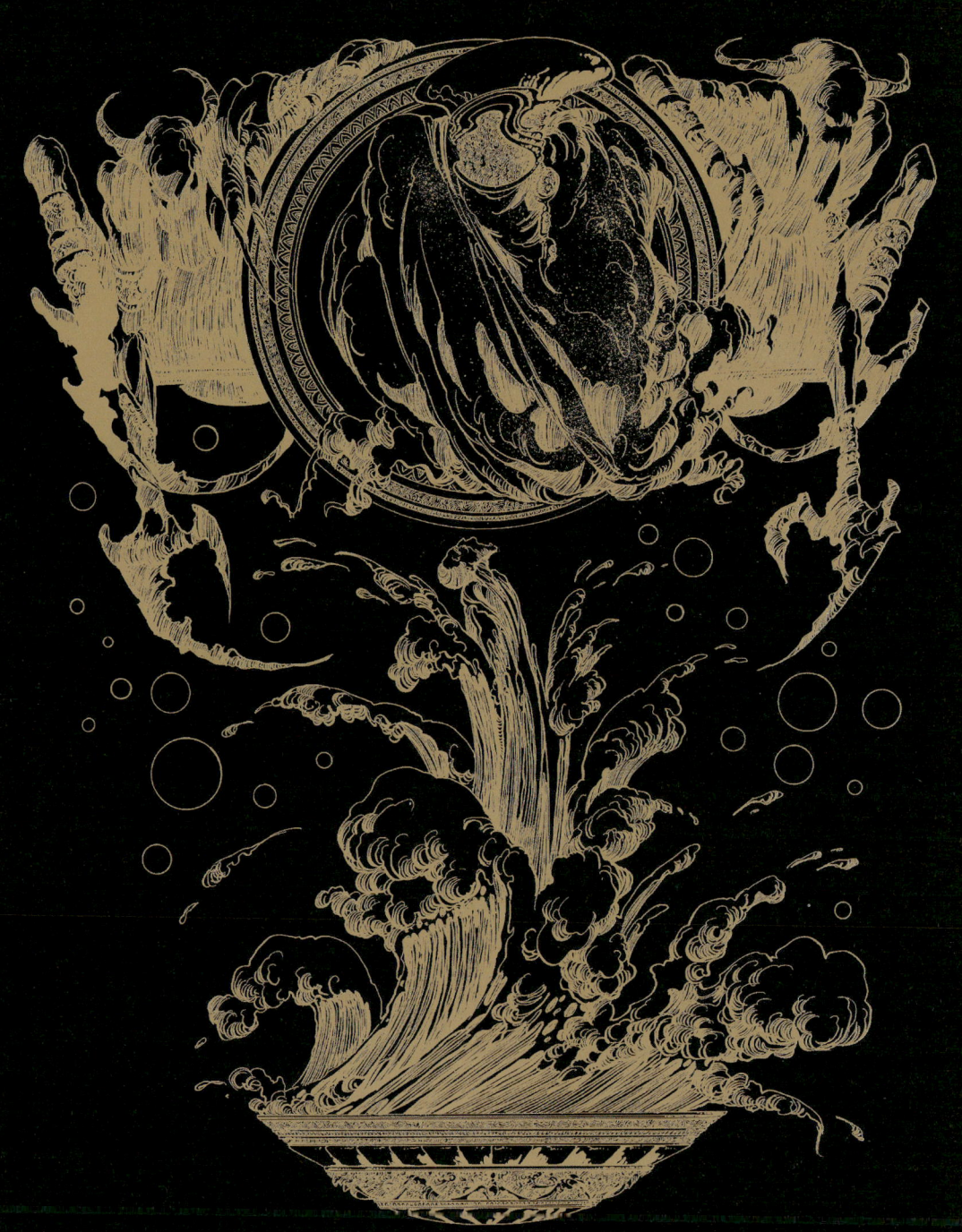

PHILIPPE DRUILLET
SPACE ARCHITECT

BY ZAK SMITH

Most influential illustrators have something to solidify their work in the mainstream mind: Frazetta is that guy who did the Conan covers, Giger has the *Alien*, Syd Mead has *Blade Runner*, McQuarrie has *Star Wars*, Mœbius has the *Fifth Element*. Philippe Druillet, though, has proven unsummarizable, at least to the English-speaking world. While his contemporaries could be tranched into "fantasy" or "science fiction" when Hollywood needed them to be, Druillet is always both. His art called as much on the forgotten as on the not-yet-invented, and although his claw marks are everywhere in contemporary visual culture, Druillet's vision — chaotic, misanthropic, imposingly ornate, unbelievably damaged — resists translation.

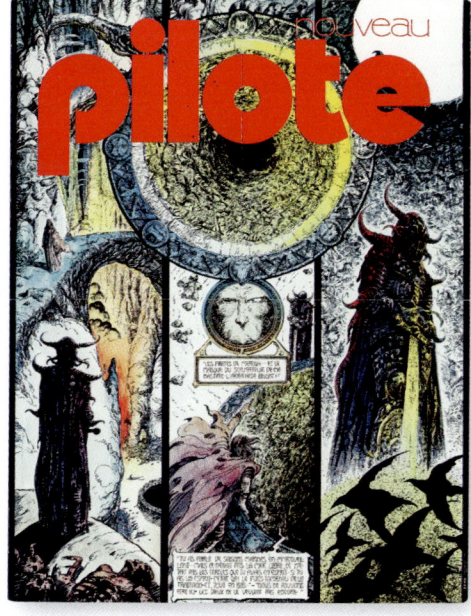

Mœbius, Druillet's longtime friend, rival, and neighbor, once apologized for the toothlessness of one of his own stories, saying, "To draw truly good monsters without drawing upon the darker zones of your psyche is always difficult, and clearly I did not carry these inside me. Philippe's nightmares are true. They reach something within us all."

He was born in the city of Toulouse on June 28, 1944, to Fascist parents about to flee it, and named after Philippe Henriot, a collaborator known as the "French Goebbels." The first doctor to examine the child was arch-nihilist author and brutal anti-Semite Louis-Ferdinand Céline. The family lived in Spain until Druillet's father died in 1952.

Previous right: Illustration for *Métal Hurlant,* oil and gouache on board by Philippe Druillet, 1978.

Opposite: Interior illustration for *Druillet — Lovecraft: Démons et Merveilles,* from Éditions Opta/André Sauret, 1976. Ink on paper by Philippe Druillet, 1975, 59.9 x 40 cm (23.6 x 15.75 inches).

Above: A 1973 poster for the "new" *Pilote,* the leading French comic magazine, published between 1959 and 1989, with art from Philippe Druillet's *Yragael* saga. The magazine appealed to an adolescent readership and went into decline when Druillet, Mœbius, writer Jean-Pierre Dionnet, and accounts manager Bernard Farkas founded *Métal Hurlant,* with more blatantly adult content.

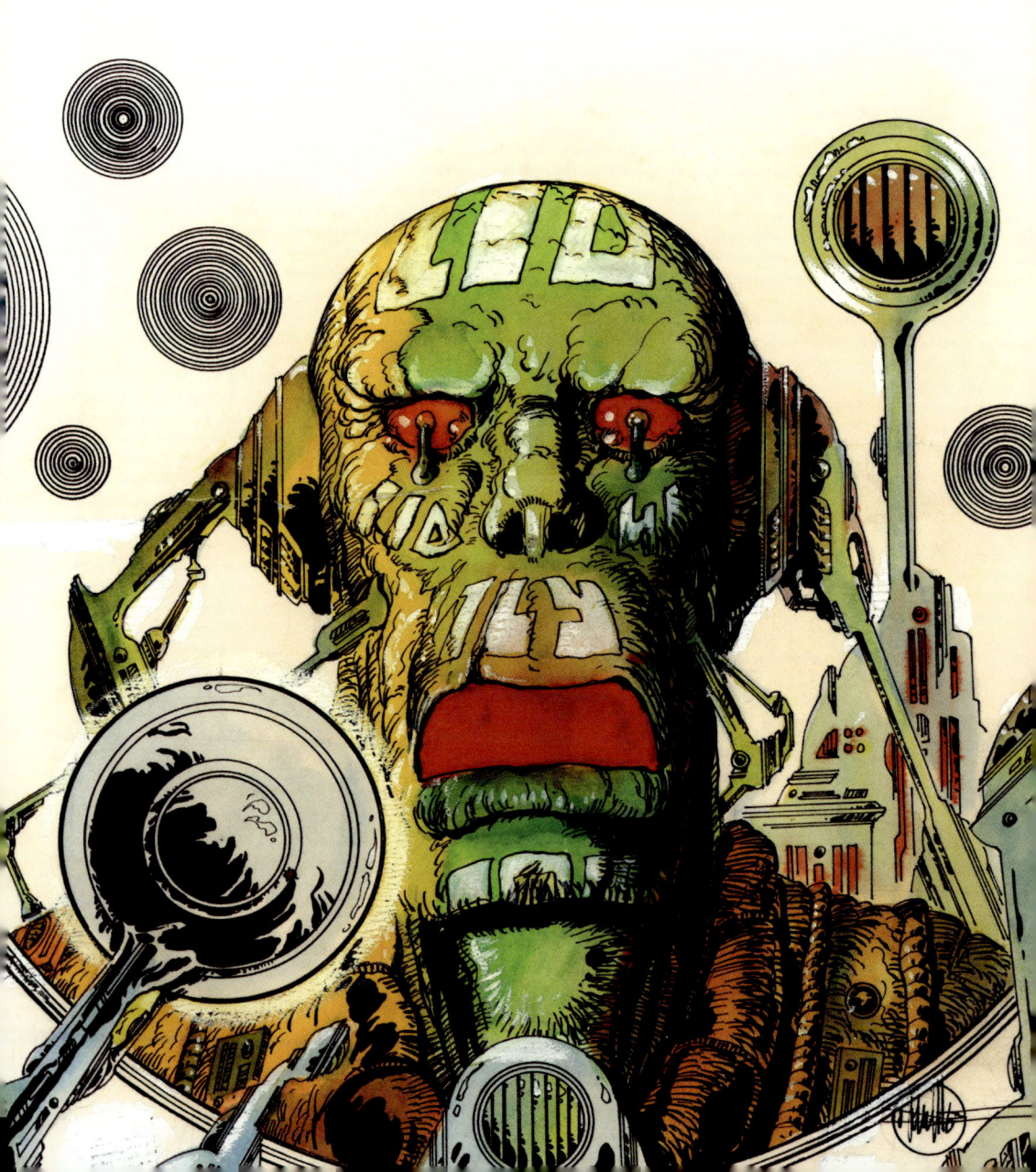

The young Druillet felt as alienated from his own parents as from the Spanish locals: "Only one positive point of these years in Spain, one day I find myself in front of the Sagrada Família, the basilica of Gaudí, in Barcelona. And here I stand in front of this deluge of forms, these high triangles, these friezes in the form of feminine sexes."

Back in France, the creative child discovered Gustave Doré, Gustave Moreau, and subtler inspiration: "In the summer, we returned to our family home in Gers. There, I am fascinated by the old reaper-binders that I discover in a shed. All these claws, these toothed wheels, these transmissions, this metal! Without knowing it, our eye stores images and our imagination seeks a key. My spaceships were born indirectly from old rusty tractors in Gers. And then there were incredible starry skies, summer! Superimpose an agricultural machine and these galaxies, and you have my graphic universe."

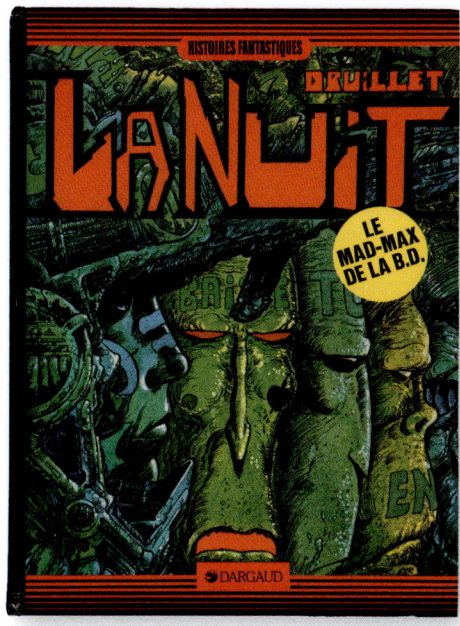

After a few years as a photographer (learning important things about how shadows fall across surfaces) and French correspondent for *Famous Monsters of Filmland* (learning important things about monsters), Druillet met his first wife, Nicole, and began to draw in earnest, producing his first Lone Sloane comic, "Le Mystère des Abîmes"—a space opera gargoyled with the wings and spires that would come to dominate his style. More projects quickly followed and Druillet took each as an opportunity to experiment: dark, almost funerary images for Conan novels; posters for the films of cult director Jean Rollin, their lesbian vampires as symmetrical and constructed as their neo-arte-nouveau borders (even Giger could make a conventionally attractive woman when he wanted, but the only part of a human Druillet's inhuman art sympathized with was the mouth, and only when it was screaming); moody covers for *Fiction* and *Galaxie* spiked with demonic architecture and decor.

In 1969, Druillet began working with *Pilote*, the seminal French comic magazine that published classics like Asterix and Blueberry—Saturday nights at Druillet's home became a kind of salon for the cutting edge of French comics' artists and writers.

By the dawn of the '70s it had all begun to gel; *Sloane: The Six Voyages*, *Urm le Fou*, and *Delirius* used sprawling, often panel-less pages to drop readers into a vortex of nightmarish symmetries, baroque detail, expressionistically costumed bodies, staggering scale, primitive gods, and psychedelic color. You would be wrong to blame any of this on LSD: "…it's the only drug I've never taken. Otherwise, I took everything in the world—including unknown things."

Opposite: Druillet cover art of *Vuzz* for *Phenix*, December 1973, a 64-page French magazine of *bande dessinée*, strip comics created for the French/Belgian market. It later appeared as a *Métal Hurlant* cover. Gouache on board, 50.8 x 43.1 cm (20 x 17 inches).

Above: La Nuit (*The Night*) is regarded as Druillet's darkest, most nihilistic, book. Described as a "post-atomic rock opera," it is dedicated to his wife Nicole, who died from cancer in 1975. In *La Nuit*, published 1976, drug-addicted bikers fight to the death.

"I have no trust in the human being. Only in my friends, and the people I love. I've spent my life telling that in my works: the end of societies. I don't give a hundred years to the human species. We are in a period of transitions and, sadly, in history, these have never passed without blood being shed."

Druillet—along with Mœbius and writer Jean-Pierre Dionnet—formed *Métal Hurlant* magazine in 1974 to showcase the new breed of comics artists. The sensibility was surreal, darkly deadpan, avant-garde, cinematic, exotic, subversive, a little sleazy, and far more lavish than anything the underground had ever produced before. "It was a period of madness," said Druillet. "There were permanently about 40 people in my house, the drugs were circulating, they invented a new way of drawing, without the slightest limit." At one point he and Dionnet purportedly broke into another magazine's offices to steal their subscriber list. Druillet's excesses were legendary.

Nicole's death by cancer the following year sent Druillet deep into depression, addiction, and work. While he managed to produce the classic *La Nuit*—a tale in poison red and toxic green of a dying Earth ravaged by mad bikers (and a precursor to *Mad Max*)—he couldn't manage to pull himself together enough to work with any of the directors knocking on his door. (He did manage to do some—barely used—work on William Friedkin's *Sorcerer*, a psychological thriller ironically eclipsed by the explicitly Druillet-inspired *Star Wars* the same year).

In 1979, Druillet remarried and—though still pursued by depression and addiction—his resumé in the following decades became, like many of his contemporaries', impressive and strange in a way that reflected how *Métal Hurlant* had helped carve out a wider space in European culture for comics and the artists who made them. Druillet created editioned prints, had gallery shows, created sets and storyboards for a science-fiction adaptation of a Wagner opera, worked on short films, created sculptures and furniture and jewelry, designed lighters and perfume bottles, made frescos, produced logos and advertising campaigns, wrote an autobiography (*Delirium*, Editions Les Arènes, 2014), won numberless awards, and represented French comics at a French-Japanese cultural summit. Having already illustrated Umberto Eco, Michael Moorcock, and H.P. Lovecraft, Druillet began, in 1981, to draw his most ambitious literary adaptation to date, a version of Gustave Flaubert's *Salammbô*—a science-fantasy version, naturally. Throughout its three volumes Druillet is as decadent and innovative as ever, with a new fluidity of rendering and color reminiscent of contemporary American comics. Even more surprising than this, Druillet then adapted his adaptation into a video game that—at least visually—did it justice (*Salammbô: Battle for Carthage*, Cryo Interactive, 2003).

It is in that new medium that Druillet's influence on our visual world can be most firmly, if belatedly, felt—it took decades but finally a technology exists that can find a new way to interpret the dizzying and intricate three-dimensionality of his alien hellscapes—in dozens of games by creators raised on *Métal Hurlant* and what *Métal Hurlant* inspired. Few gamers now are unfamiliar with cities of batwing and bone or with the squared and howling mouths set in slit-eyed barbaric slab-sided green orc heads tracing their lineage back from '00s *Warcraft* to '90s *Warhammer* to '80s *2000AD* comics born from careful study of the rigid Technicolor mouthfuls of anguish and defiance in Druillet's most distinctive faces.

Opposite: For *Chaos*, Druillet's final Lone Sloane graphic novel, released in 2000. Sloane, who was destroyed in *Salammbô* Vol. 3, is resurrected by a mysterious heroine. Acrylic on paper, 90.1 x 64.5 cm (33.5 x 25.4 inches).

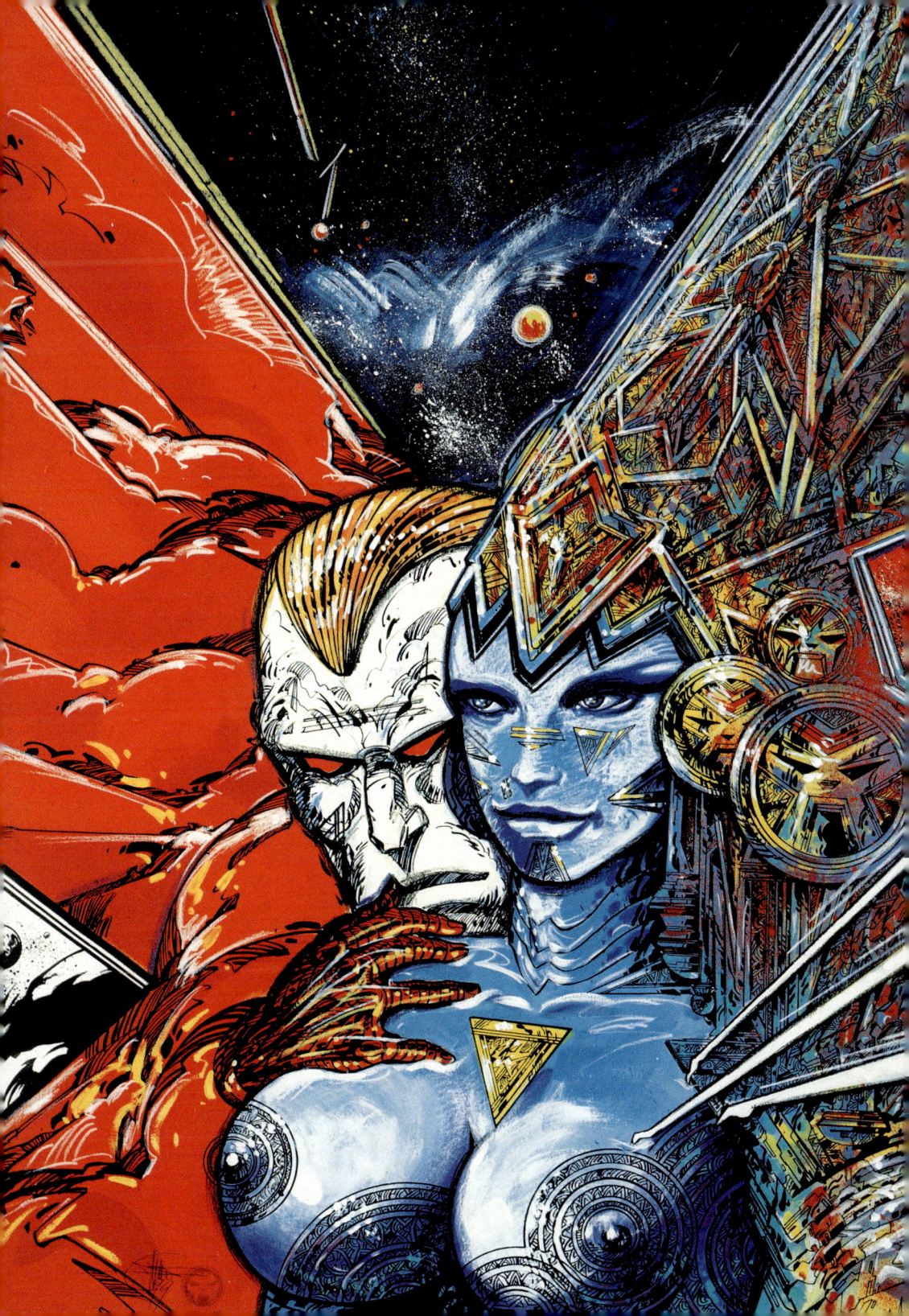

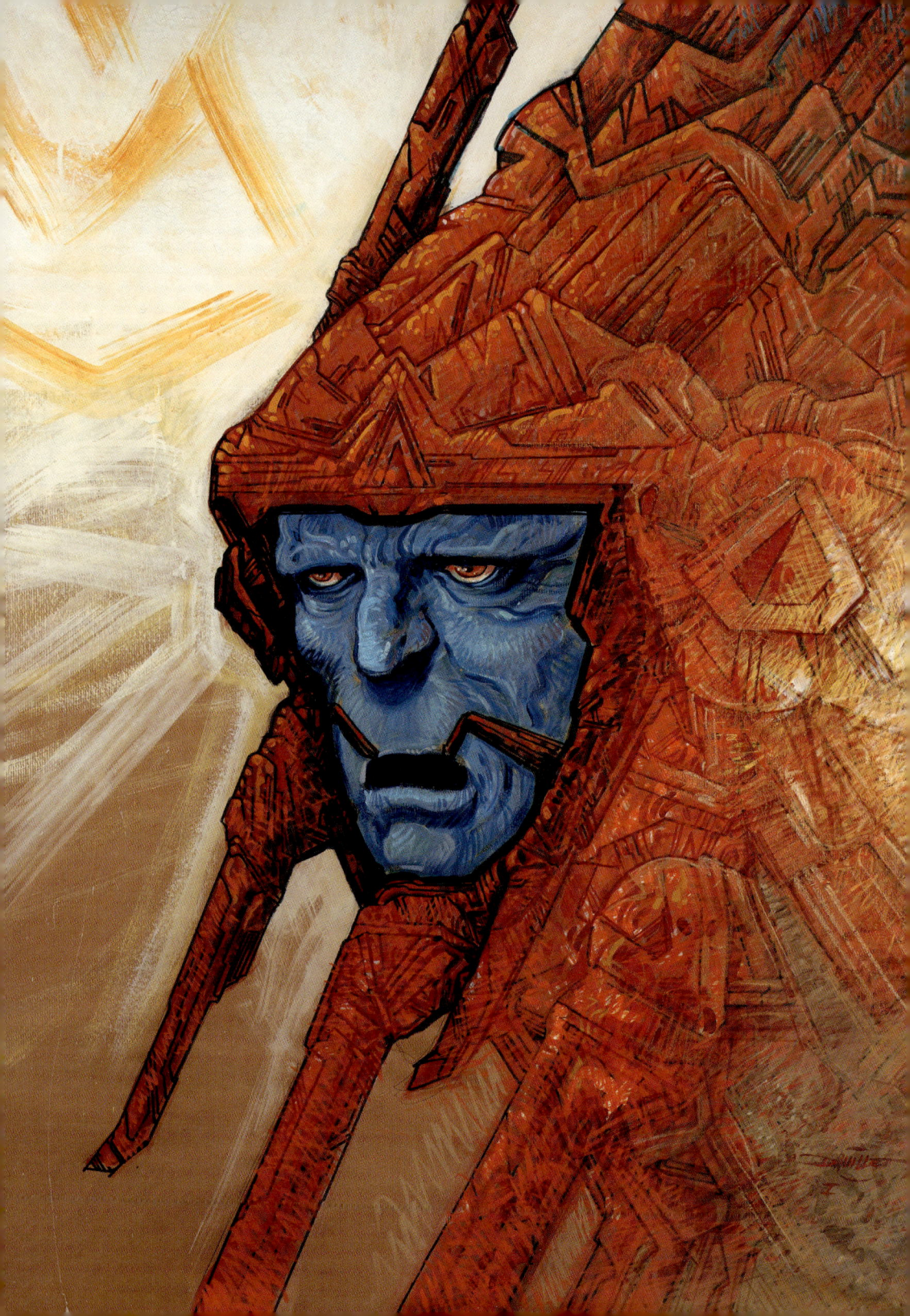

PHILIPPE DRUILLET
ARCHITEKT DES RAUMES

VON ZAK SMITH

Die meisten einflussreichen Illustratoren bieten in ihren Arbeiten etwas, das sie im Geiste des Mainstreams verfestigt: Frazetta ist der, der die Conan-Cover schuf, Giger wird mit Aliens verbunden, Syd Mead mit *Blade Runner*, McQuarrie mit *Star Wars*, Mœbius mit *The Fifth Element*. Philippe Druillet jedoch hat sich als nicht so einfach klassifizierbar erwiesen, zumindest für die englischsprachige Welt. Während seine Zeitgenossen, wenn es Hollywood nötig erschien, unter „Fantasy" oder „Science-Fiction" eingeordnet werden konnten, gehört Druillet stets beiden an – seine Kunst bezog sich ebenso sehr auf das Vergessene wie auf das Noch-nicht-Erfundene, und obwohl seine Kratzspuren überall in der zeitgenössischen visuellen Kunst präsent sind, widersteht Druillets – chaotische, misanthropische, eindrucksvoll verzierte, unglaublich lädierte – Vision einer Übertragung.

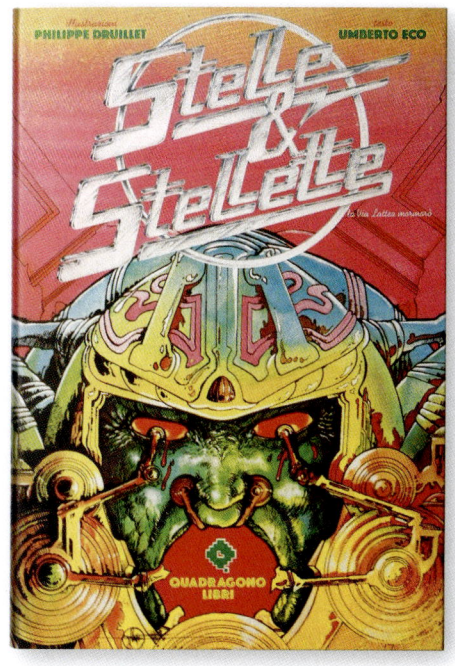

Mœbius, Druillets langjähriger Freund, Rivale und Nachbar, entschuldigte sich einst für die Zahnlosigkeit einer seiner eigenen Geschichten und sagte: „Richtig gute Monster zu zeichnen, ohne dabei aus den dunkleren Zonen der eigenen Psyche zu schöpfen, ist immer schwierig, und solche gehörten offensichtlich nicht zu meinem Innersten. Philippes Albträume sind wahr. Sie rühren an etwas, das in uns allen steckt."

Druillet wurde am 28. Juni 1944 in Toulouse als Sohn faschistischer Eltern geboren, die kurz davor waren, der Stadt zu entfliehen, und erhielt seinen Namen nach Philippe Henriot, einem Kollaborateur, der als der „französische Goebbels" bekannt war. Der erste Arzt, der das Kind untersuchte, war der erznihilistische Autor und knallharte Antisemit Louis-Ferdinand Céline. Bis zum Tode von Druillets Vater 1952 lebte die Familie in Spanien.

Opposite: Masque No. 1, for the series *Masques*, 1987. Gouache on craft paper mounted on frame, 114.8 x 80 cm (45.2 x 31.5 inches).

Above: Stelle & Stellette, 1976, is a graphic novel written by Umberto Eco and illustrated by Druillet, his first Italian release.

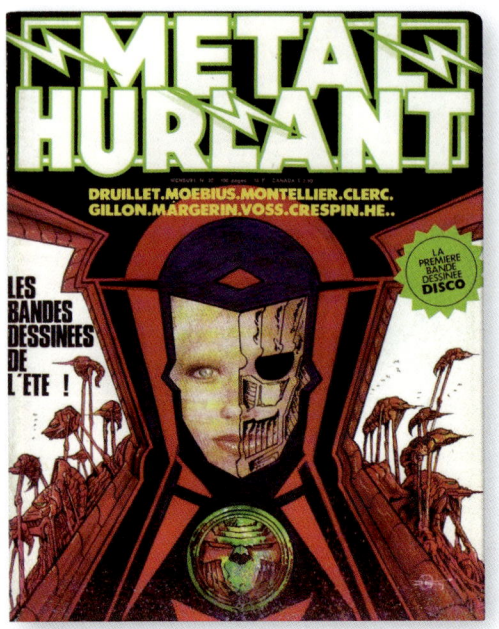

Der junge Druillet fühlte sich von seinen Eltern wie auch von den Menschen seiner spanischen Umgebung entfremdet: „Um wenigstens einen positiven Aspekt jener Jahre in Spanien zu nennen: Eines Tages stand ich vor der Sagrada Familia, der von Gaudí entworfenen Basilika in Barcelona. Und da stehe ich nun vor dieser Sintflut von Formen, diesen hohen Dreiecken, diesen Friesen in Form weiblicher Geschlechtsteile."

Zurück in Frankreich, entdeckte das kreative Kind Gustave Doré, Gustave Moreau und feinere Inspirationen: „Im Sommer kehrten wir zum Heim unserer Familie im Département Gers zurück. Dort faszinierten mich die alten Mähbinder, die ich in einem Schuppen entdeckte. All diese Zangen, diese Zahnräder, diese Getriebe, dieses Metall! Ohne die Dinge zu kennen, speichert unser Auge Bilder ab, und unsere Fantasie sucht einen Schlüssel. Meine Raumschiffe wurden indirekt von alten, rostigen Traktoren im Gers in die Welt gesetzt. Und dann – Sommer! – gab es diesen unglaublichen sternenübersäten Himmel. Legen Sie eine landwirtschaftliche Maschine und diese Galaxien übereinander, und Sie haben mein zeichnerisches Universum."

Nach ein paar Jahren als Fotograf (in denen er wichtige Dinge darüber, wie Schatten auf Oberflächen fallen, lernte) und als französischer Korrespondent für *Famous Monsters of Filmland* (was ihn wichtige Dinge über Monster lehrte) lernte Druillet seine erste Frau Nicole kennen und fing richtig an zu zeichnen. Er produzierte seinen ersten Lone-Sloane-Comic, *Le Mystère des Abîmes*, eine mit jenen Flügeln und Spitzen ausgestattete Weltalloper, die seinen Stil künftig dominieren sollte. Bald schon folgten weitere Projekte, und Druillet nutzte jedes als eine Gelegenheit zum Experimentieren: düstere, fast begräbnishafte Bilder für Conan-Geschichten, Poster für Filme des Kultregisseurs Jean Rollin – seine lesbischen Vampire sind so symmetrisch und konstruiert wie seine Neo-Art-nouveau-Ränder (selbst Giger konnte, wenn er wollte, eine im herkömmlichen Sinne attraktive Frau zustande bringen, doch der einzige Aspekt eines Menschen, mit dem Druillets entmenschlichte Kunst sympathisierte, war der Mund, und das auch nur dann, wenn er schrie) –, düstere, mit dämonischer Architektur und entsprechendem Dekor gespickte Cover für *Fiction* und *Galaxie*.

1969 begann Druillet seine Zusammenarbeit mit *Pilote*, der bahnbrechenden französischen Comiczeitschrift, die Klassiker wie Asterix und Blueberry veröffentlichte – und die Samstagabende im Hause Druillet entwickelten sich zu einer Art Salon für die Besten unter den französischen Comiczeichnern und -autoren.

Above: As one of the founders of *Métal Hurlant*, Druillet produced many covers, this for the August 1978 issue.

Opposite: Petite femme de la nuit, ink and gouache on board, 1978, 63 x 48 cm (24.8 x 18.9 inches).

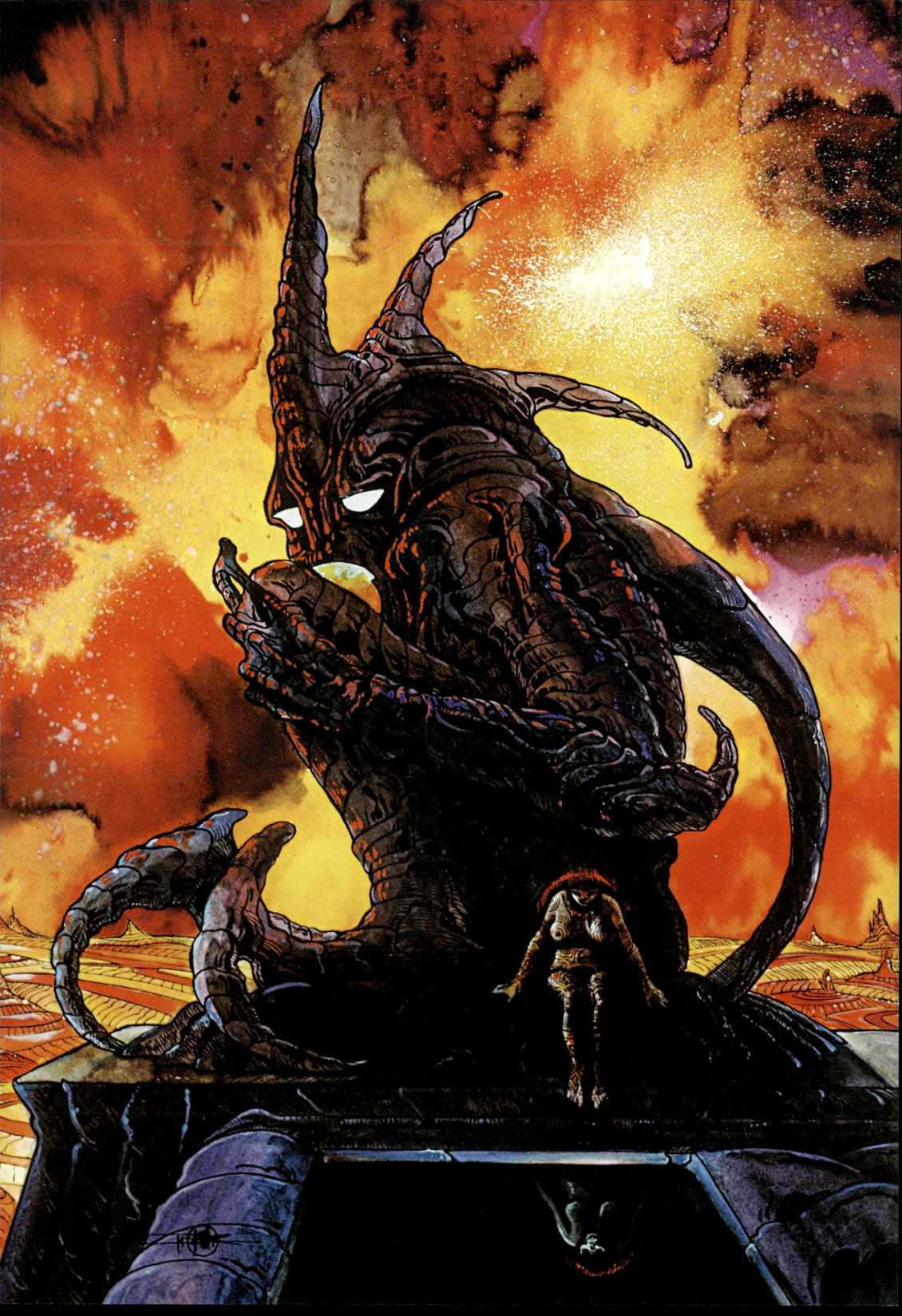

„Ich habe kein Vertrauen in die Menschen. Nur in meine Freunde und in die Leute, die ich mag. Ich habe mein Leben damit verbracht, dies in meinen Werken kundzutun: das Ende der Gesellschaften. Ich gebe der Spezies Mensch keine hundert Jahre mehr. Wir leben in einer Periode des Wandels, und diese endeten – traurigerweise – nie ohne Blutvergießen."

Mit Beginn der 1970er-Jahre hatte alles angefangen, Form anzunehmen: *Sloane: The Six Voyages*, *Urm le Fou* und *Delirius* nutzten ausladende, oft ohne Einzelbilder gestaltete Seiten, um die Leser in einen Strudel beklemmender Symmetrien, barocker Details, expressionistisch kostümierter Gestalten, überwältigender Ausmaße, primitiver Götter und psychedelischer Farbe zu stürzen. Man läge falsch, irgendetwas davon LSD zuzuschreiben: „… das ist die einzige Droge, die ich nie genommen habe. Ansonsten hab ich alles konsumiert, was die Welt zu bieten hat – einschließlich unbekannter Substanzen."

Druillet gründete 1974 – gemeinsam mit Mœbius und dem Autor Jean-Pierre Dionnet – die Zeitschrift *Métal Hurlant*, um die neue Spezies von Comickünstlern zu präsentieren. Die Sensibilität war surreal, auf düstere Weise emotionslos, avantgardistisch, filmisch, exotisch, subversiv, ein wenig anrüchig und sehr viel verschwenderischer als alles, was der Underground zuvor je hervorgebracht hatte. „Es war eine Periode der Tollheit", sagte Druillet. „In meinem Haus trieben sich ständig um die 40 Leute herum, Drogen wurden herumgereicht, und sie erfanden eine neue Art des Zeichnens ohne auch nur den Hauch einer Begrenzung." Einmal brachen er und Dionnet angeblich in die Büros einer anderen Zeitschrift ein, um deren Abonnentenliste zu klauen. Druillets Exzesse waren legendär.

Im Jahr darauf starb Nicole an Krebs, und ihr Tod ließ Druillet tief in Depressionen, Sucht und Arbeit versinken. Er schaffte es zwar, den Klassiker *La Nuit* zu produzieren – eine Geschichte in giftigem Rot und toxischem Grün einer sterbenden Erde, die von durchgeknallten Bikern verwüstet wurde (und ein Vorläufer von *Mad Max*) –, jedoch nicht, sich so weit zusammenzureißen, um mit irgendeinem der Regisseure arbeiten zu können, die bei ihm anklopften. (Er schaffte es, ein paar – kaum benutzte – Arbeiten zu William Friedkins *Sorcerer* fertigzustellen, einem psychologischen Thriller, der ironischerweise im gleichen Jahr vom explizit Druillet-inspirierten *Star Wars* in den Schatten gestellt wurde).

1979 heiratete Druillet wieder, und seine Vita gestaltete sich – obgleich er nach wie vor mit Depressionen und seiner Sucht zu kämpfen hatte – während der nächsten Jahrzehnte wie die vieler seiner Zeitgenossen beeindruckend und außergewöhnlich auf eine Art und Weise, die widerspiegelte, wie *Métal Hurlant* geholfen hatte, in der europäischen Kultur für Comics und die Künstler, die sie schufen, mehr Raum zu erkämpfen. Druillet schuf Auflagendrucke, hatte Galerieausstellungen, gestaltete Sets und Storyboards für eine Science-Fiction-Adaption einer Wagner-Oper, arbeitete an Kurzfilmen, entwarf Skulpturen, Möbel und Schmuck, Feuerzeuge und Parfumflakons, malte Fresken, produzierte

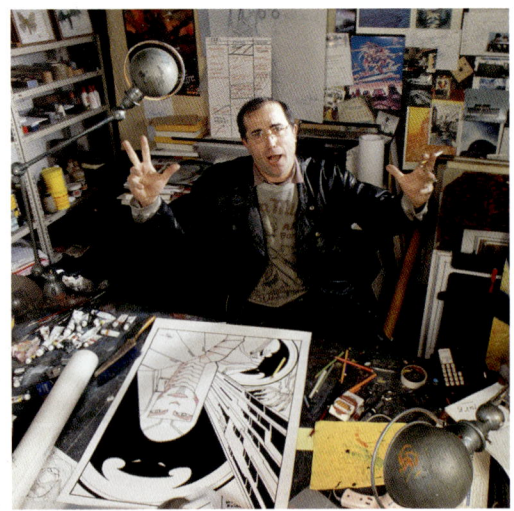

Logos und Werbekampagnen, schrieb eine Autobiografie (*Delirium*, Éditions Les Arènes, 2014), gewann zahllose Preise und repräsentierte bei einem französisch-japanischen Kulturgipfel den französischen Comic. Nachdem er bereits Umberto Eco, Michael Moorcock und H. P. Lovecraft illustriert hatte, begann Druillet 1981, seine bis dahin anspruchsvollste literarische Adaptation zu zeichnen, eine – natürlich – Science-Fantasy-Version von Gustave Flauberts *Salambo*. Bei allen drei Bänden dieses Werks ist Druillet durchgängig so dekadent und innovativ wie seit jeher und zeigt in der Wiedergabe und in der Farbgestaltung eine neue Fluidität, die an zeitgenössische amerikanische Comics erinnert. Danach übernahm Druillet – was noch überraschender war – seine Adaptation für ein Videospiel, das dem, zumindest in visueller Hinsicht, gerecht wurde (*Salammbô: Battle for Carthage*, Cryo Interactive, 2003).

In ebendiesem neuen Medium kann Druillets Einfluss am deutlichsten, wenn auch im Nachhinein, erspürt werden – es dauerte zwar Jahrzehnte,

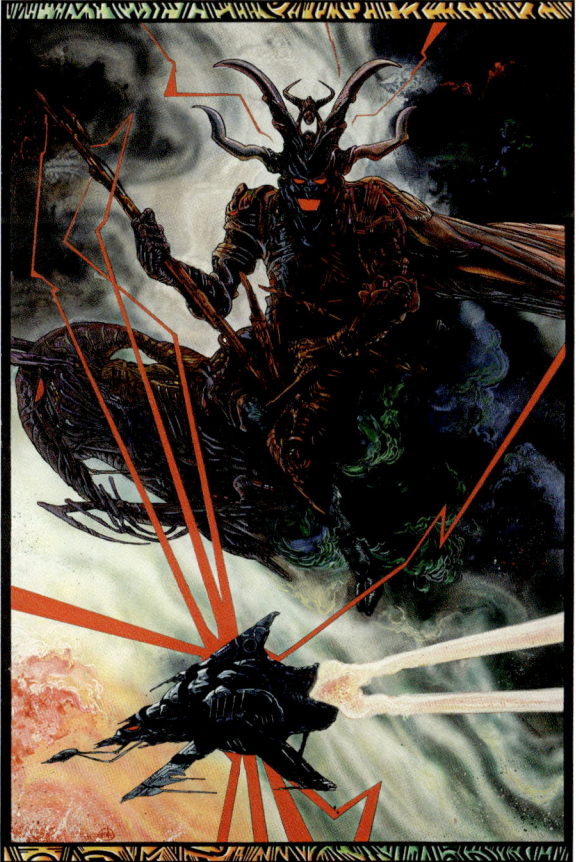

doch endlich gibt es eine Technologie, die eine neue Möglichkeit finden kann, die schwindelerregende und komplizierte Dreidimensionalität seiner fremdartigen höllischen Landschaften zu interpretieren: in Dutzenden von Künstlern gestalteten Spielen, die mit *Métal Hurlant* groß geworden sind und von dieser Zeitschrift inspiriert wurden. Wenige Spieler sind heute mit Fledermaus- und Knochenstädten nicht vertraut oder mit den quadratischen und heulenden Mäulern, die in schlitzäugigen, barbarischen, von Schwarten begrenzten grünen Ork-Köpfen klaffen und deren Ursprung sich über die *Warcraft*-Comics der 00er- und die *Warhammer*-Comics der 90er-Jahre bis zu den *2000-AD*-Comics der 1980er-Jahre zurückverfolgen lässt, die ihre Entstehung dem sorgfältigen Studium der von Pein und Trotz geprägten Mäuler in den charakteristischsten Gesichtern zu verdanken haben, die Druillet gezeichnet hatte.

Opposite: Philippe Druillet in his cluttered studio, 1988. Photo by Sergio Gaudenti/Sygma via Getty Images.

Above: A page from *Salammbô*, Vol. 1, Druillet's 1981 retelling of Gustave Flaubert's story of sex and the First Punic War, starring Lone Sloane. Gouache on board, 95 x 69.8 cm (37.4 x 27.5 inches).

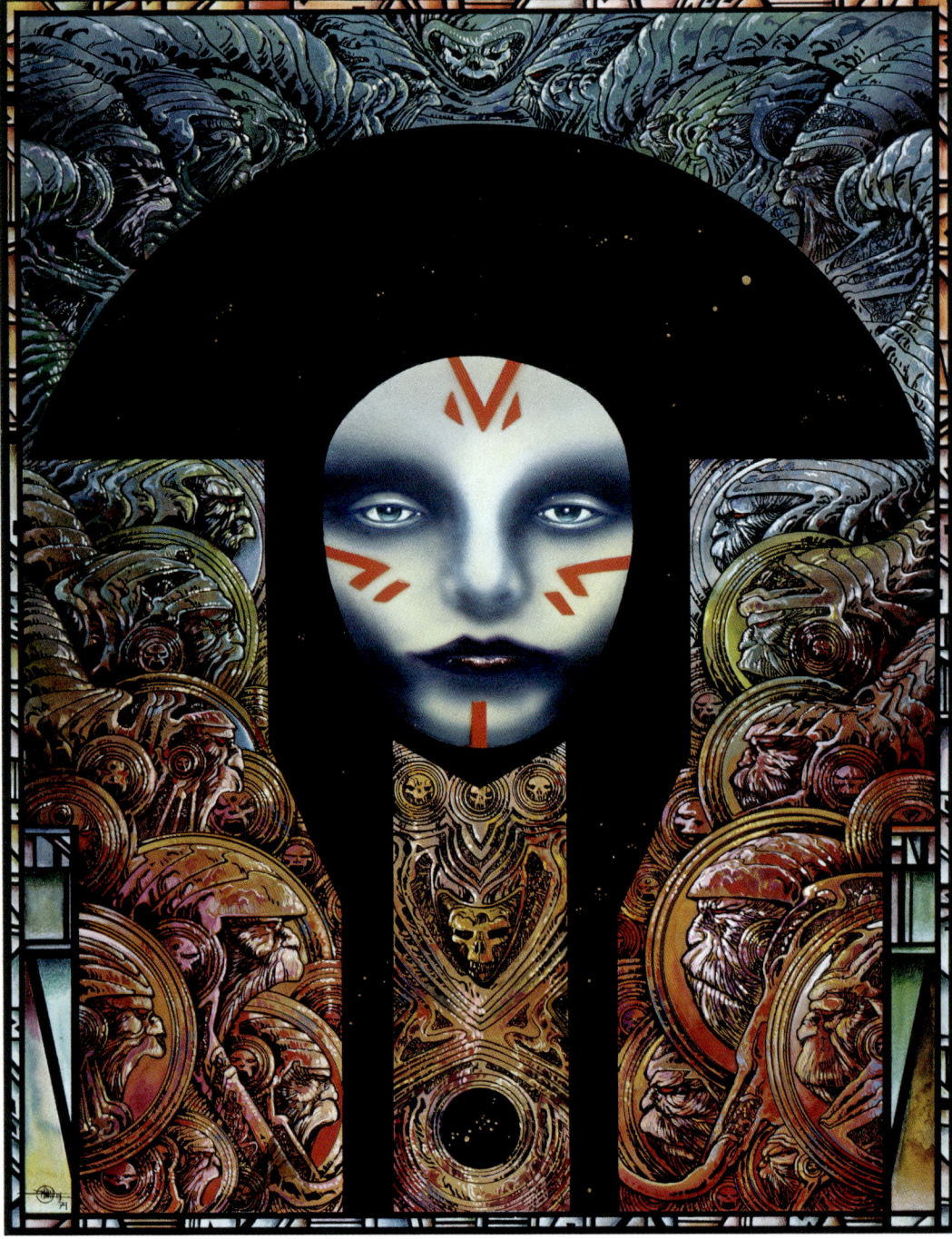

PHILIPPE DRUILLET
L'ARCHITECTE DE L'ESPACE

PAR ZAK SMITH

La plupart des grands noms de l'illustration ont quelque chose qui les ancre dans l'esprit du grand public : Frazetta est le gars des couvertures de Conan, Giger a l'Alien, Syd Mead a *Blade Runner*, McQuarrie a *Star Wars*, Mœbius a *Le Cinquième Élément*. Philippe Druillet, lui, échappe à toute synthèse, en tout cas aux yeux du monde anglophone. Alors que ses contemporains se classaient tantôt dans la fantasy, tantôt dans la science-fiction selon les besoins de Hollywood, Druillet a toujours pratiqué les deux genres – son art fait autant appel aux temps oubliés qu'à ceux qui restent à inventer – et même s'il a laissé son empreinte griffue dans toute la culture visuelle contemporaine, la vision de Druillet – chaotique, misanthrope, ornementée à l'extrême, incroyablement abîmée – résiste à la traduction.

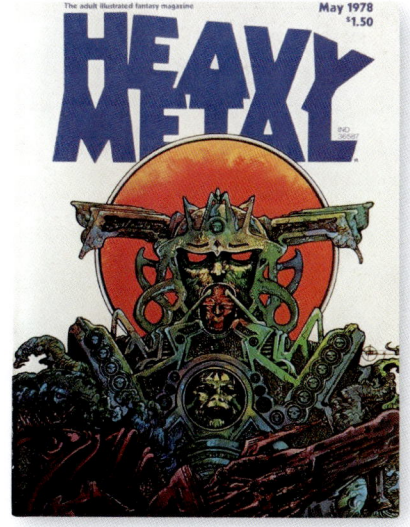

Mœbius, l'ami de longue date, le rival et le voisin de Druillet, s'est un jour excusé du manque de mordant d'une de ses propres histoires en ces termes : « Il est toujours difficile de dessiner des monstres vraiment bons sans puiser dans les zones les plus sombres de votre psyché et il est clair que je n'avais pas cela en moi. Les cauchemars de Philippe sont vrais. Ils touchent à quelque chose que nous avons tous en nous. »

Il est né à Toulouse le 28 juin 1944 de parents fascistes qui s'apprêtaient à fuir la France et l'ont baptisé ainsi en hommage à Philippe Henriot, collaborateur surnommé « le Goebbels français ». Le premier médecin à examiner l'enfant est l'écrivain anarcho-nihiliste et férocement antisémite Louis-Ferdinand Céline. La famille vit en Espagne jusqu'à la mort du père de Druillet, en 1952.

Le jeune Druillet se sent en décalage avec ses parents autant qu'avec la population locale : « Seul point positif de ces années en Espagne : un jour, je me retrouve devant la Sagrada Família, la basilique de Gaudí, à Barcelone. Et là, je reste en arrêt devant ce déluge de formes, ces hauts triangles, ces frises en forme de sexes féminins. »

Opposite: A portrait from Salammbô, *Vol. 1, 1981. Instead of Carthage, Druillet's* Salammbô *is set in outer space. Gouache on board, 60 x 50 cm (23.6 x 19.7 inches).*

Above: Heavy Metal *was just a year old and still entirely relying on content translated from its French parent magazine when Druillet created this cover for the May 1978 issue.*

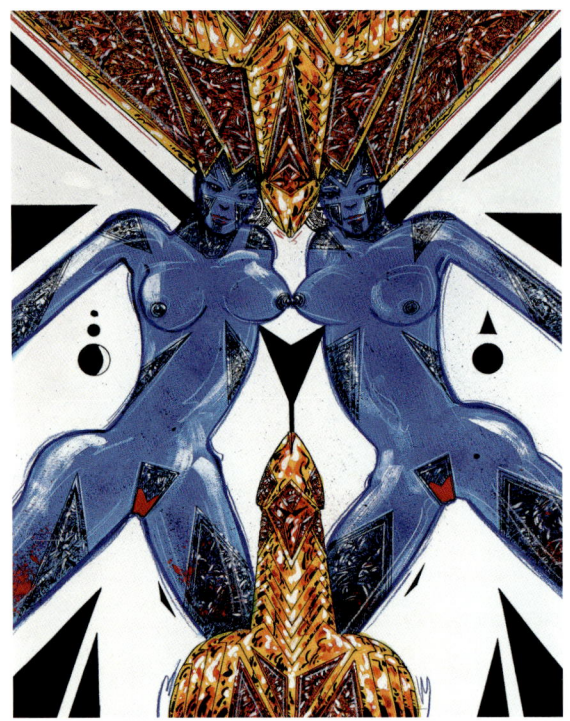

De retour en France, l'enfant créatif découvre Gustave Doré, Gustave Moreau et des sources d'inspiration plus inattendues : « L'été, nous retournions dans le fief familial du Gers. Là, je suis fasciné par les vieilles moissonneuses-lieuses que je découvre dans un hangar. Toutes ces griffes, ces roues dentées, ces transmissions, ce métal ! Sans le savoir, notre œil stocke des images et notre imaginaire cherche une clé. Mes vaisseaux spatiaux sont nés indirectement de vieux tracteurs rouillés du Gers. Et puis, il y avait des ciels étoilés incroyables, l'été ! Superposez une machine agricole et ces galaxies, et vous avez mon univers graphique. »

Après quelques années comme photographe (métier qui lui apprend des choses importantes sur la façon dont les ombres jouent sur les surfaces) et correspondant en France de *Famous Monsters of Filmland* (qui lui apprend des choses importantes sur les monstres), Druillet rencontre sa première épouse, Nicole, et commence à dessiner sérieusement. Il produit sa première bande dessinée de Lone Sloane, « Le Mystère des Abîmes » – un space opera déformé d'ailes et de flèches qui domineront son style. Les projets s'enchaînent et Druillet aborde chacune de ses missions comme une nouvelle expérience – des images sombres, presque macabres pour les romans de Conan, des vampires lesbiennes aussi construites et symétriques que leurs bordures néo-Art nouveau sur ses affiches pour les films du réalisateur culte Jean Rollin (même Giger savait dessiner une femme d'une beauté conventionnelle quand il voulait, mais la seule partie du corps humain avec laquelle l'art inhumain de Druillet accepte de se compromettre est la bouche, à condition qu'elle hurle), des couvertures maussades que viennent fouetter une architecture et des décors démoniaques pour *Fiction* et *Galaxie*.

En 1969, Druillet entame sa collaboration avec *Pilote*, le légendaire magazine de bande dessinée français qui publie des classiques comme *Astérix* et *Blueberry* – et les samedis soirs se tient chez Druillet un genre de salon où se retrouvent les artistes et auteurs avant-gardistes de la BD française.

À l'aube des années 1970, tout commence à prendre forme : *Sloane, Les Six Voyages*, *Urm le Fou* et *Delirius* emploient des pages entières, souvent sans cases, pour précipiter les lecteurs dans un vortex de symétries cauchemardesques, de détails baroques, de corps dissimulés sous des costumes

Above: Thirty years after adapting Flaubert's *Salammbô* as a space opera starring his Lone Sloane character, Druillet returned to the subject to paint 42 nude female portraits inspired by the priestess Salammbô. They were published in an edition of 350 by Éditions Glénat in 2010. Acrylic on board, each 64.7 x 44.9 cm (25.5 x 17.7 inches).

Opposite: An exquisitely colored portrait of Salammbô, the beautiful priestess and eponymous title character of Druillet's 1981 graphic novel, Vol. 1. Ink and watercolor on board, 95 x 69.8 cm (37.4 x 27.5 inches).

MASTERPIECES OF FANTASY ART

expressionnistes, d'échelles sidérantes, de dieux primitifs et de couleurs psychédéliques. On aurait tort d'attribuer tout ou partie de cela au LSD : « … C'est la seule drogue que j'aie jamais prise. Autrement j'ai pris tout ce qui existe au monde – y compris des trucs inconnus. »

Druillet monte le magazine *Métal Hurlant* avec Mœbius et l'auteur Jean-Pierre Dionnet en 1974 pour diffuser le travail d'une nouvelle race de dessinateurs de BD. La sensibilité du titre est surréaliste, sombrement caustique, avant-gardiste, cinématographique, exotique, subversive, un peu glauque et bien plus somptueuse que tout ce que l'underground a produit jusqu'alors. « C'était une période de folie, raconte Druillet. Il y avait en permanence une quarantaine de personnes chez moi, la drogue circulait, on inventait une nouvelle manière de dessiner, sans la moindre limite. » À un moment, Dionnet et lui se seraient introduits dans les bureaux d'un autre magazine pour voler sa liste d'abonnés. Les excès de Druillet sont légendaires.

La mort de Nicole, emportée par le cancer l'année suivante, plonge Druillet dans la dépression, l'addiction et le travail. Il parvient à produire le classique *La Nuit* – un conte rouge poison et vert toxique sur une planète moribonde ravagée par des motards fous (précurseur de *Mad Max*) – mais il est incapable de se ressaisir suffisamment pour travailler avec aucun des réalisateurs qui viennent frapper à sa porte. (Il réalise bien quelques croquis – à peine utilisés – pour *Le Convoi de la peur*, un thriller psychologique de William Friedkin qui, belle ironie, est éclipsé par un film où les références à Druillet sont explicites, *Star Wars*, sorti la même année.)

En 1979, Druillet se remarie et, bien que toujours taraudé par la dépression et l'addiction, au cours des décennies suivantes son curriculum s'étoffe, comme celui de nombre de ses contemporains, et se pare d'une étrangeté qui reflète combien *Métal Hurlant* a participé à défricher un espace plus vaste pour la bande dessinée et ses auteurs dans la culture européenne. Druillet réalise des tirages en édition limitée, expose dans les galeries, crée décors et story-boards pour l'adaptation en science-fiction

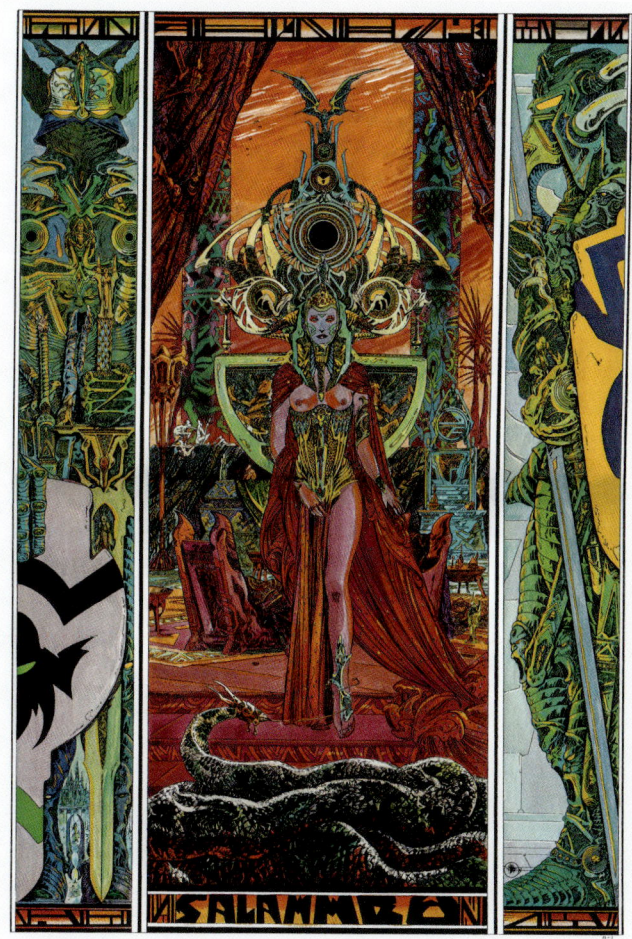

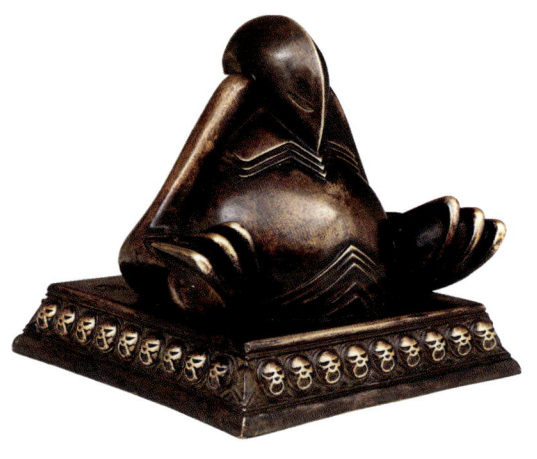

d'un opéra de Wagner, collabore à des courts métrages, façonne sculptures, mobilier et bijoux, conçoit des briquets et des flacons de parfum, peint des fresques, produit des logos et des campagnes de pub, écrit une autobiographie (*Delirium*, Éditions Les Arènes, 2014), remporte d'innombrables prix et représente la BD française lors d'un sommet culturel franco-japonais. Après avoir illustré Umberto Eco, Michael Moorcock et H.P. Lovecraft, en 1981 Druillet s'attaque à son adaptation littéraire la plus ambitieuse, une version *science fantasy* (bien entendu) du *Salammbô* de Gustave Flaubert, en trois volumes. Druillet s'y montre plus décadent et novateur que jamais, mais doué d'une nouvelle fluidité dans le trait et la couleur qui rappelle les comics américains contemporains. Plus surprenant encore, Druillet a ensuite réadapté son adaptation en un jeu vidéo qui, visuellement du moins, lui rend justice (*Salammbô: Battle for Carthage*, Cryo Interactive, 2003).

C'est dans ce nouveau domaine que l'influence de Druillet sur notre univers visuel, bien que tardive, est la plus flagrante ; il a fallu des dizaines d'années pour qu'existe enfin une technologie apte à forger une nouvelle interprétation de la tridimensionnalité complexe, vertigineuse, de ses paysages infernaux. Des dizaines de jeux relèvent ce défi, conçus par les enfants de *Métal Hurlant*. Rares sont les gamers actuels qui ne connaissent pas les villes faites d'os et d'ailes de chauve-souris, les bouches anguleuses et béantes qui fendent la face émaciée barbare d'orques verts aux yeux mi-clos. On les retrouve dans le Warcraft des années 2000, le Warhammer des années 1990 et les comics *2000AD* des années 1980, tous nés de l'étude attentive des visages les plus emblématiques de Druillet, un tissu d'angoisses et de menace en Technicolor.

Above: In 1982 Druillet added decorative arts to his resumé, founding Space Art Creations, blending fantasy and sculpture. The 1984 sculpture *Le Dieu Noir* (*The Black God*) was produced in black and bronze, in an edition of eight, 20 x 20 x 20 cm (7.8 x 7.8 x 7.8 inches)

Opposite: The cover art for *Lone Sloane Gail*, Druillet's 1978 graphic novel, in which his lonely adventurer is jailed on a distant planet. Ink and gouache on board, 84.8 x 64.5 cm (33.4 x 25.4 inches).

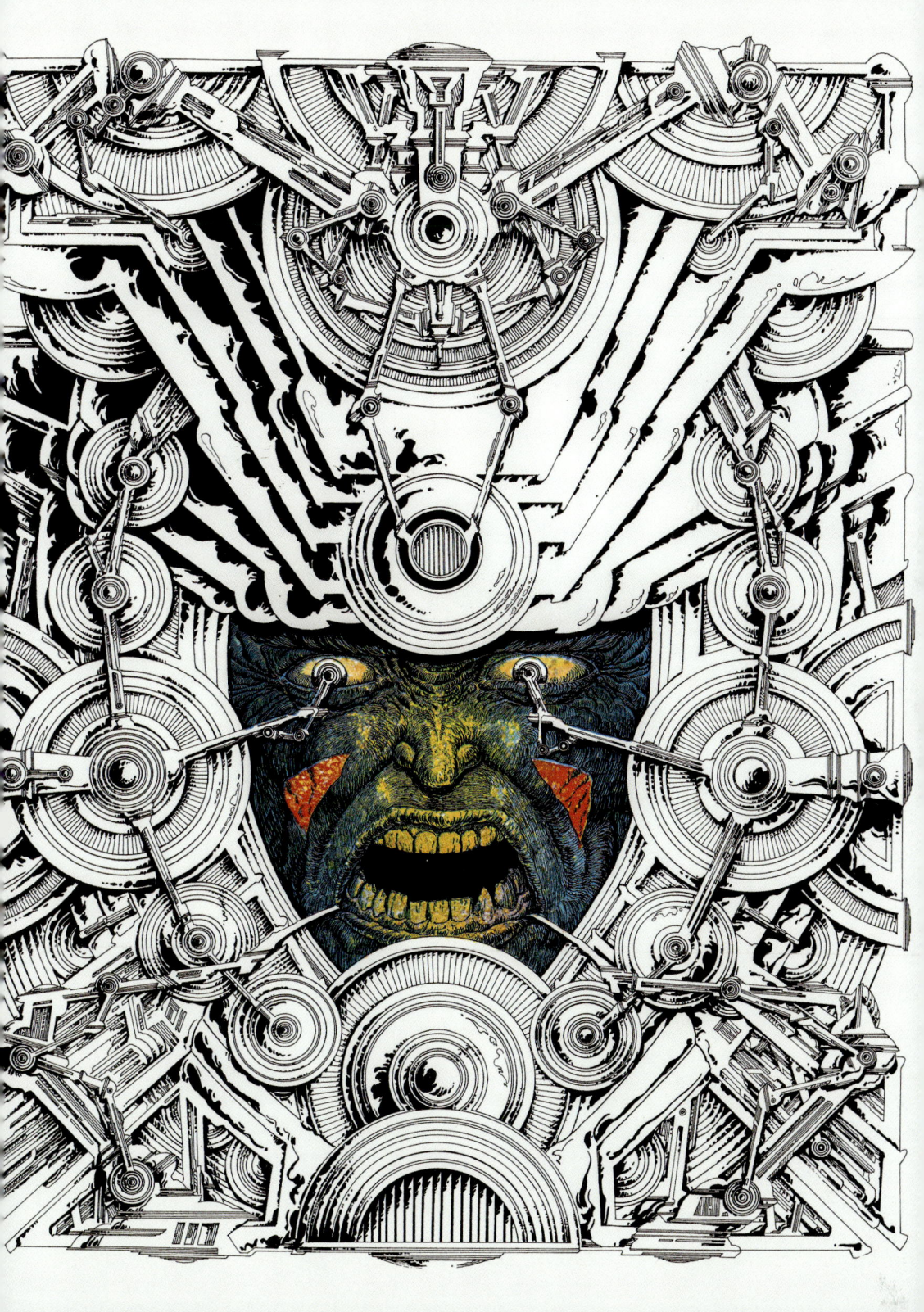

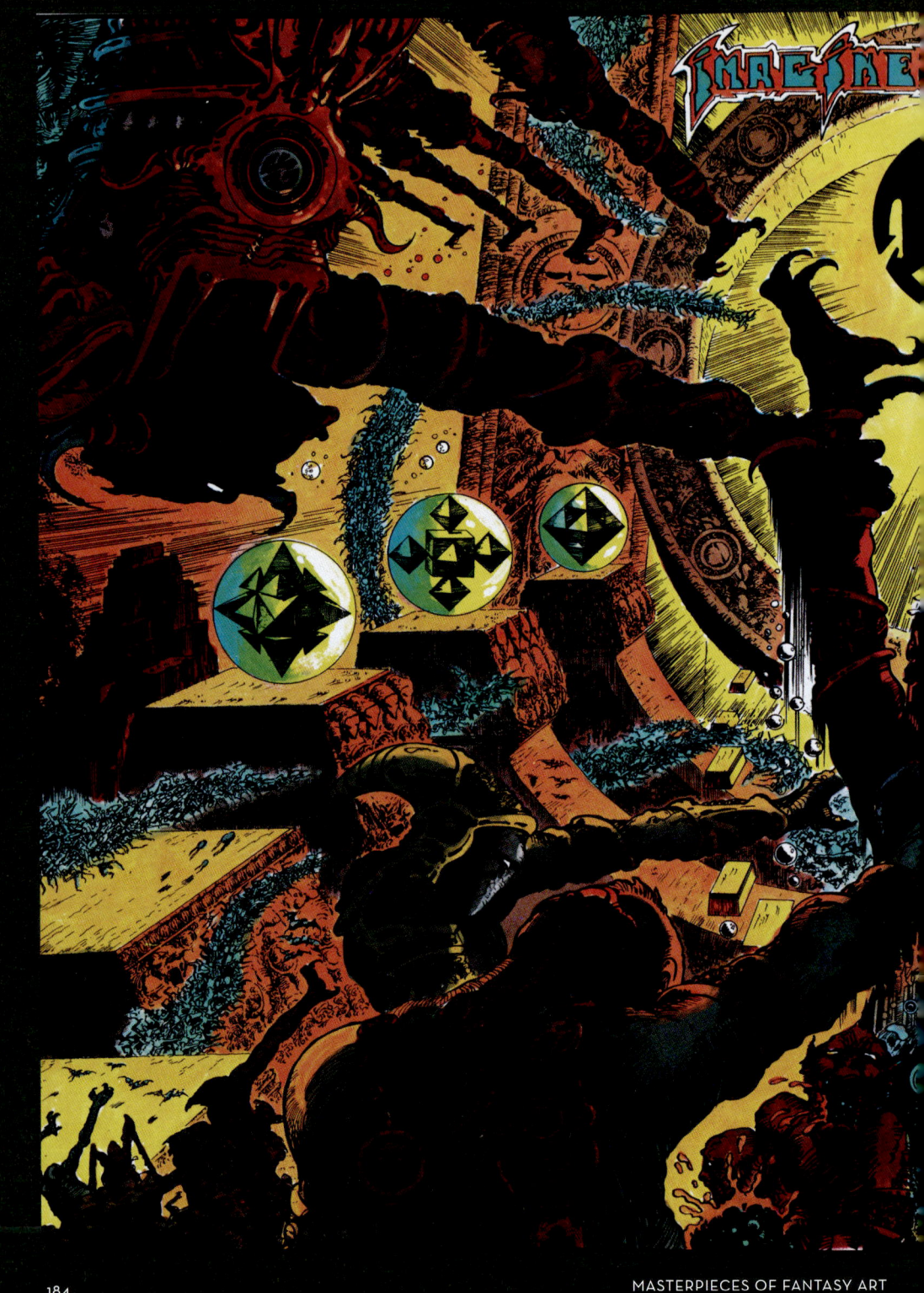

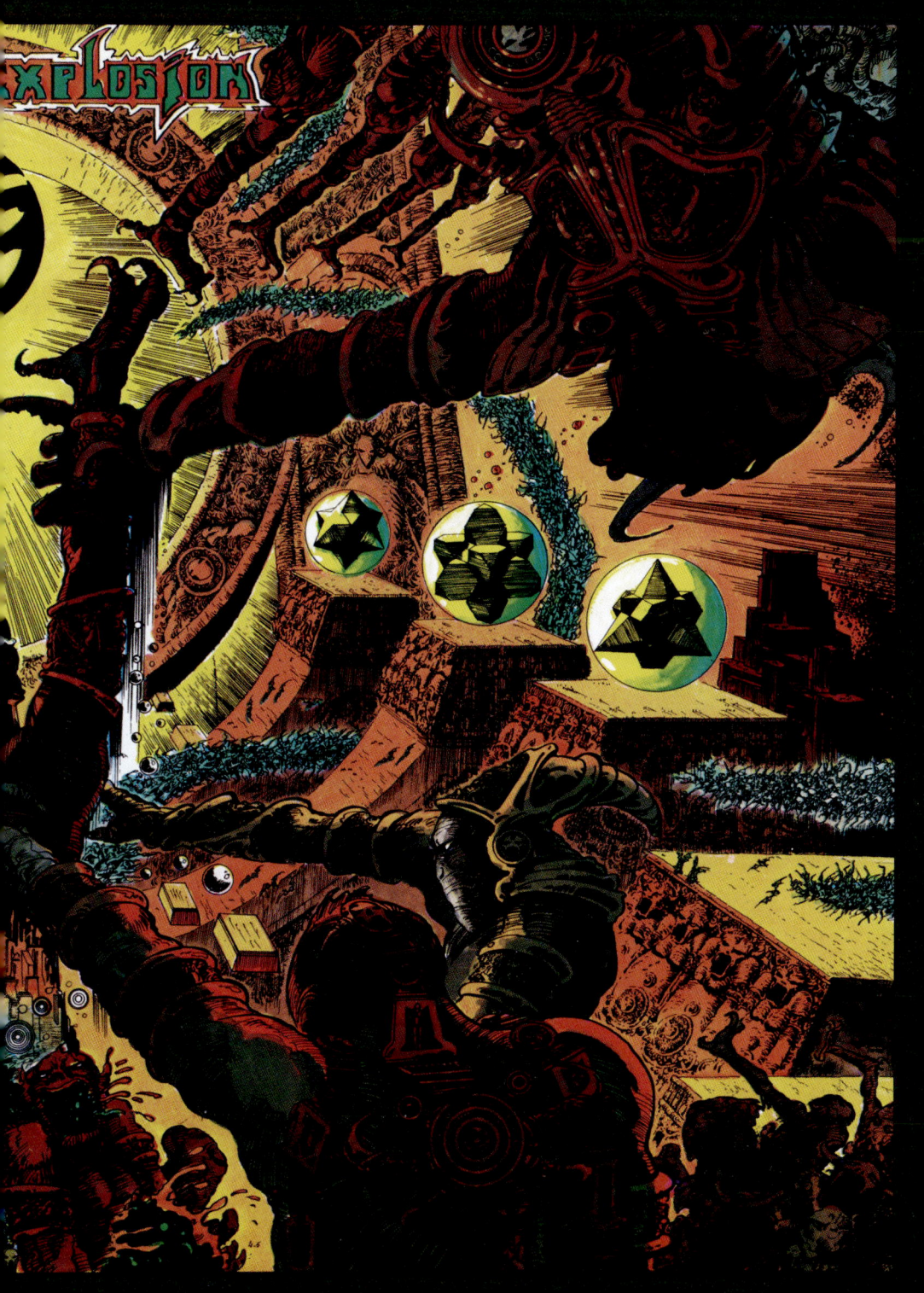

EXPLOSION

PHILIPPE DRUILLET

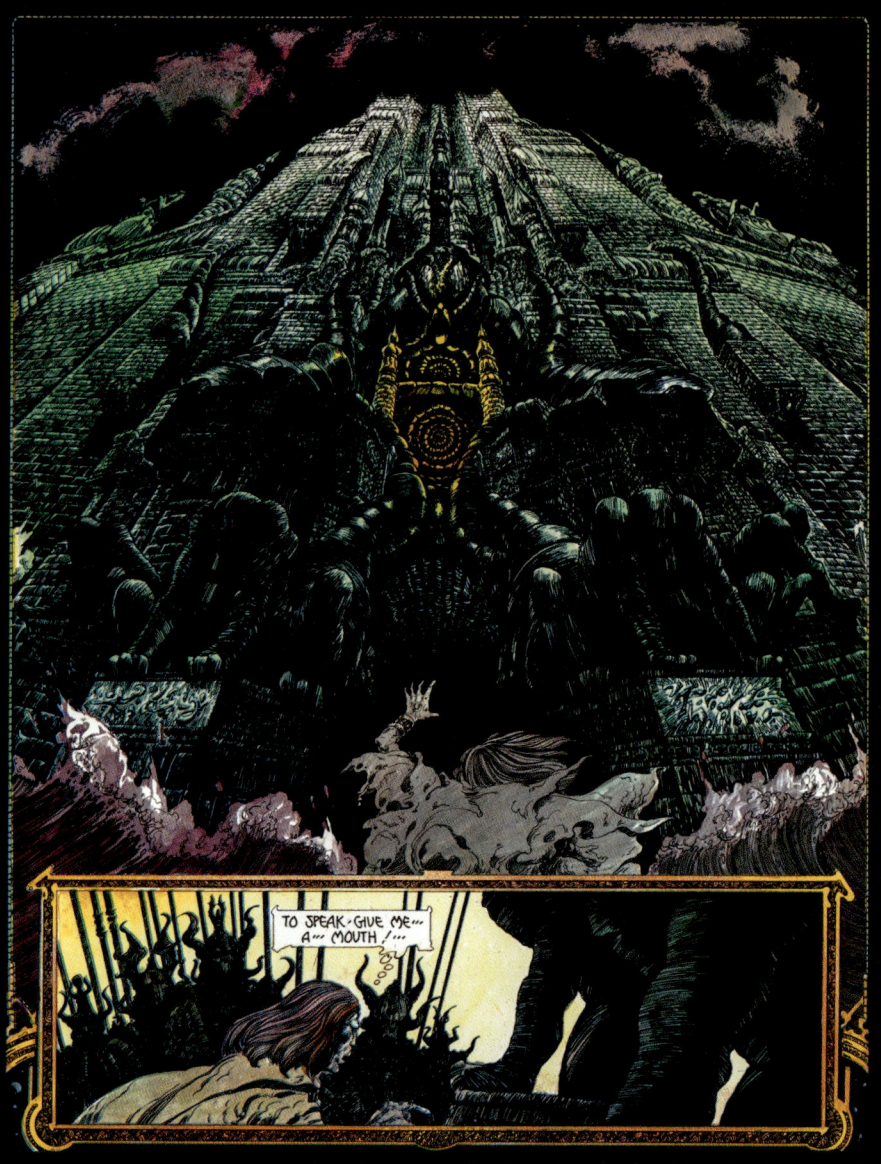

Above: This early painting was originally the opening page of *Les Isles du Vent Sauvage* (*The Isles of the Wild Wind*) a Lone Sloane story, repurposed in 1970 as a record album cover for the band Grail. Ink on paper with enhanced color for printing, 84.8 x 64.5 cm (33.4 x 25.4 inches).

Opposite: Illustration for *Yragael*, 1973. Ink on paper with enhanced color for printing, 99.8 x 69.8 cm (39.3 x 27.5 inches).

Previous spread: A spread from *Yragael*, a 1973 graphic novel, written by Michel Demuth, inspired by Michael Moorcock's *Elric le Nécromancien*. Ink and enhanced color on paper print, 69.8 x 160 cm (27.5 x 63 inches).

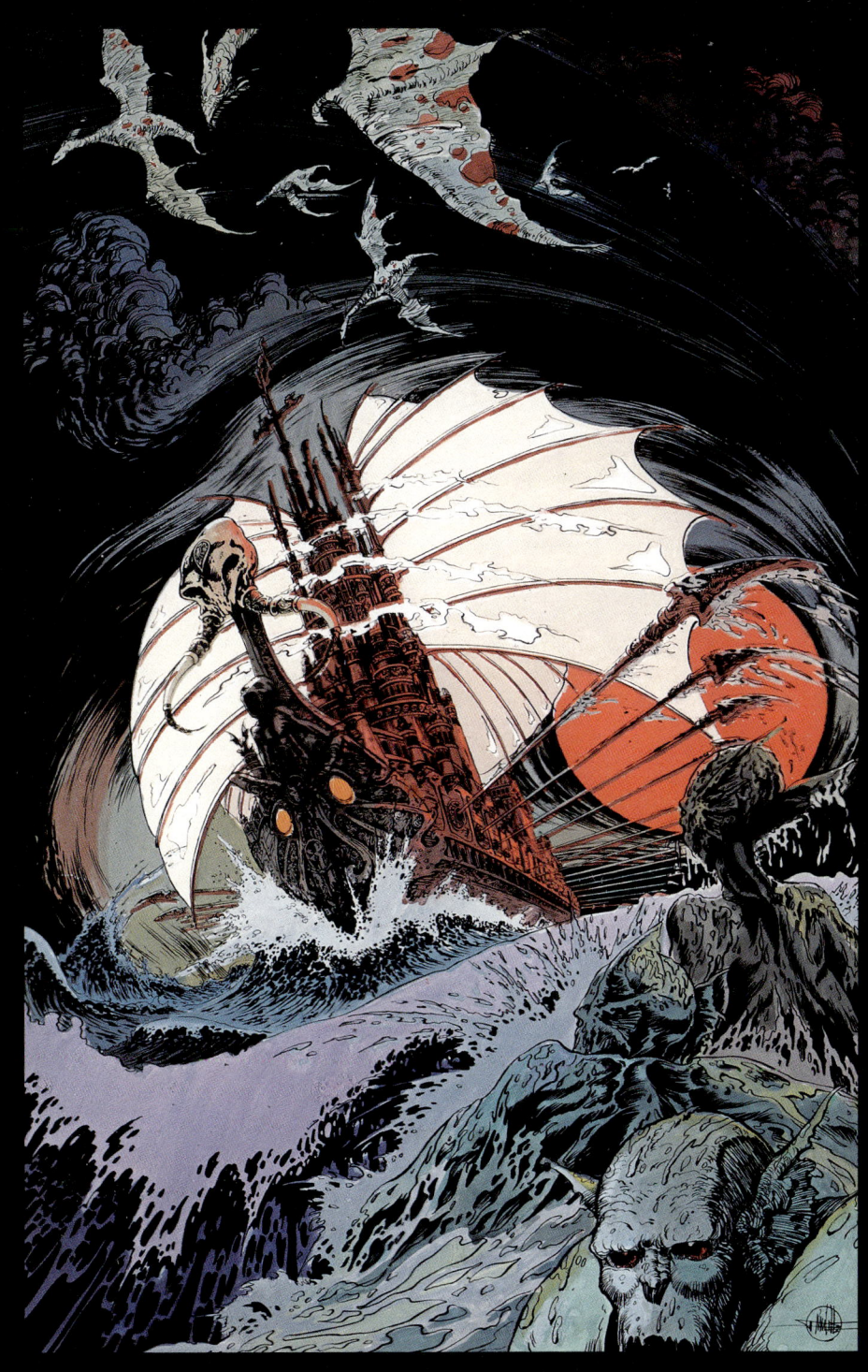

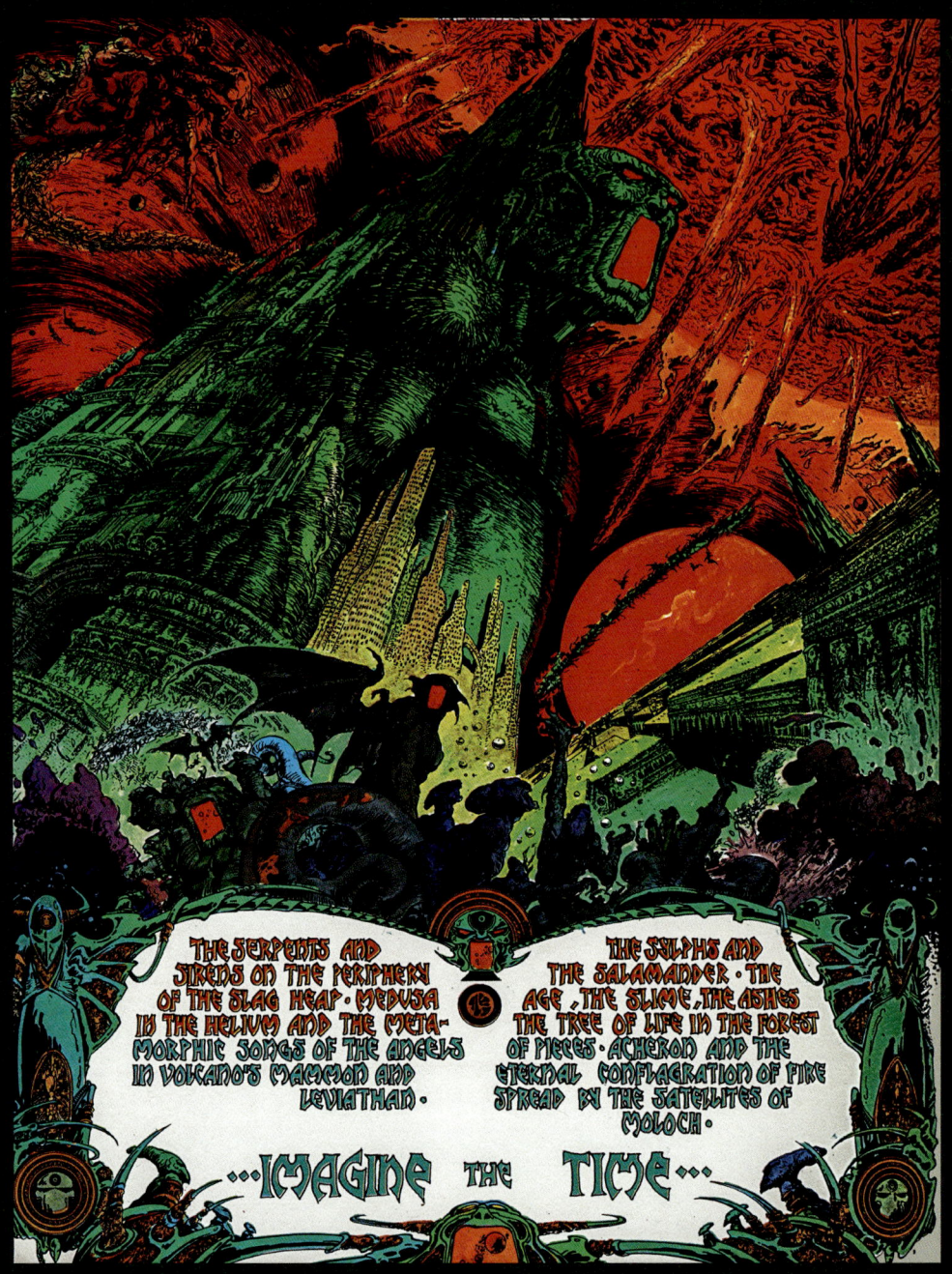

Above and opposite: Illustrations for *Yragael*, 1973.
Ink on paper with enhanced color for printing,
99.8 x 69.8 cm (39.3 x 27.5 inches).

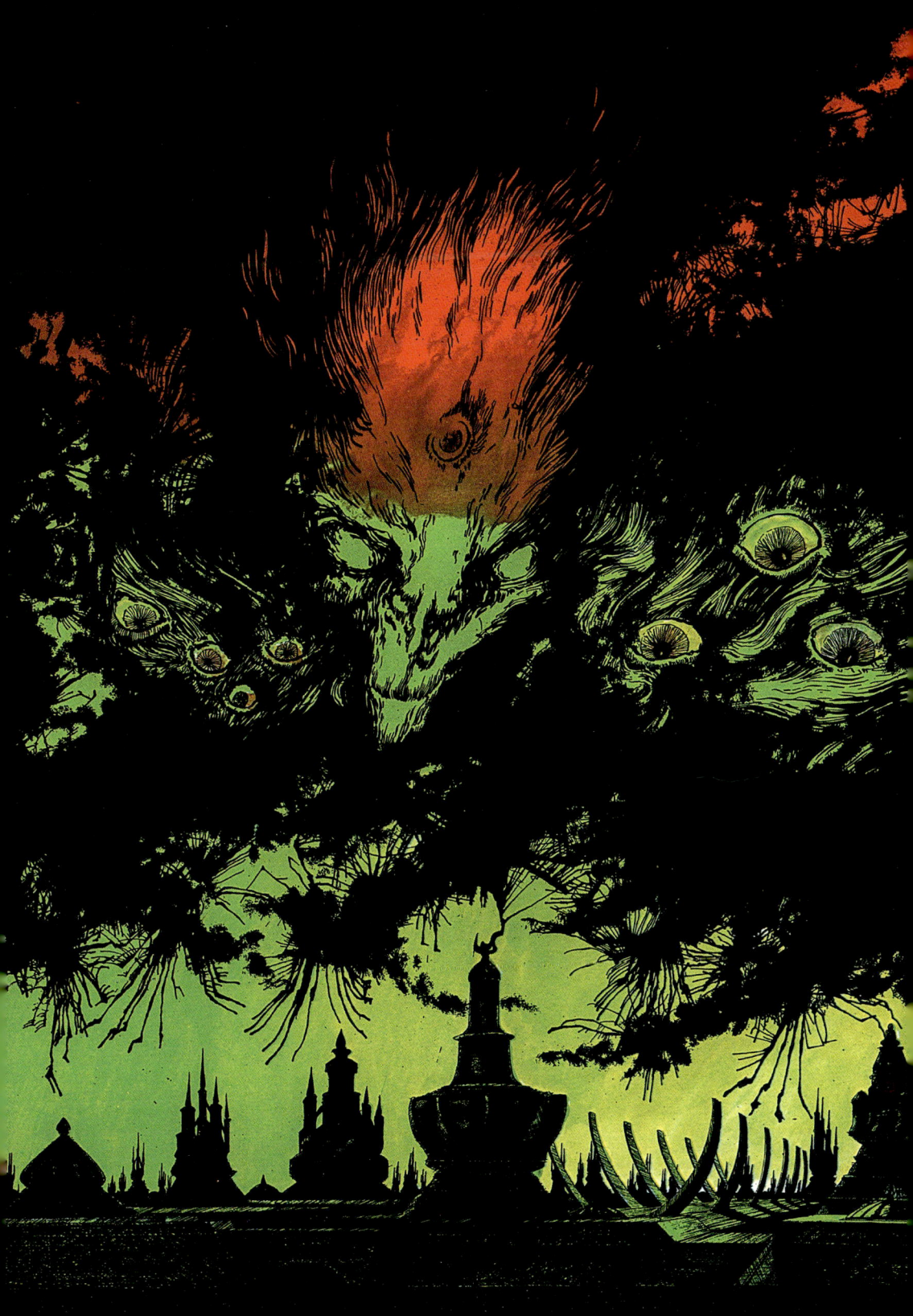

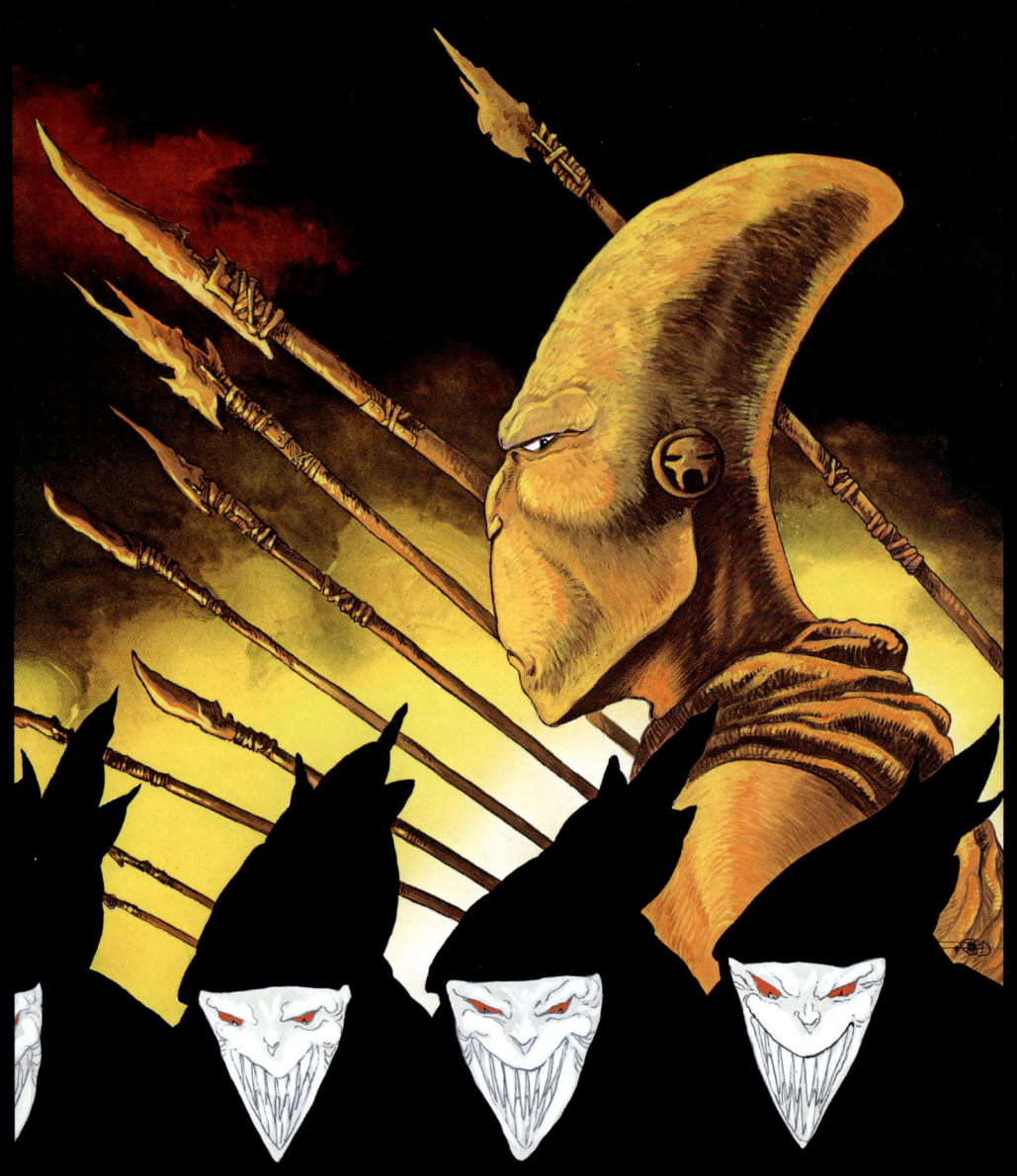

Above: A dynamic image of Drullet's singular character Vuzz, for the 1982 cover of *La-bas, Vuzz Epilogue,* from Humanoïdes Associés. Gouache on board, 65 x 50 cm (25.6 x 19.7 inches).

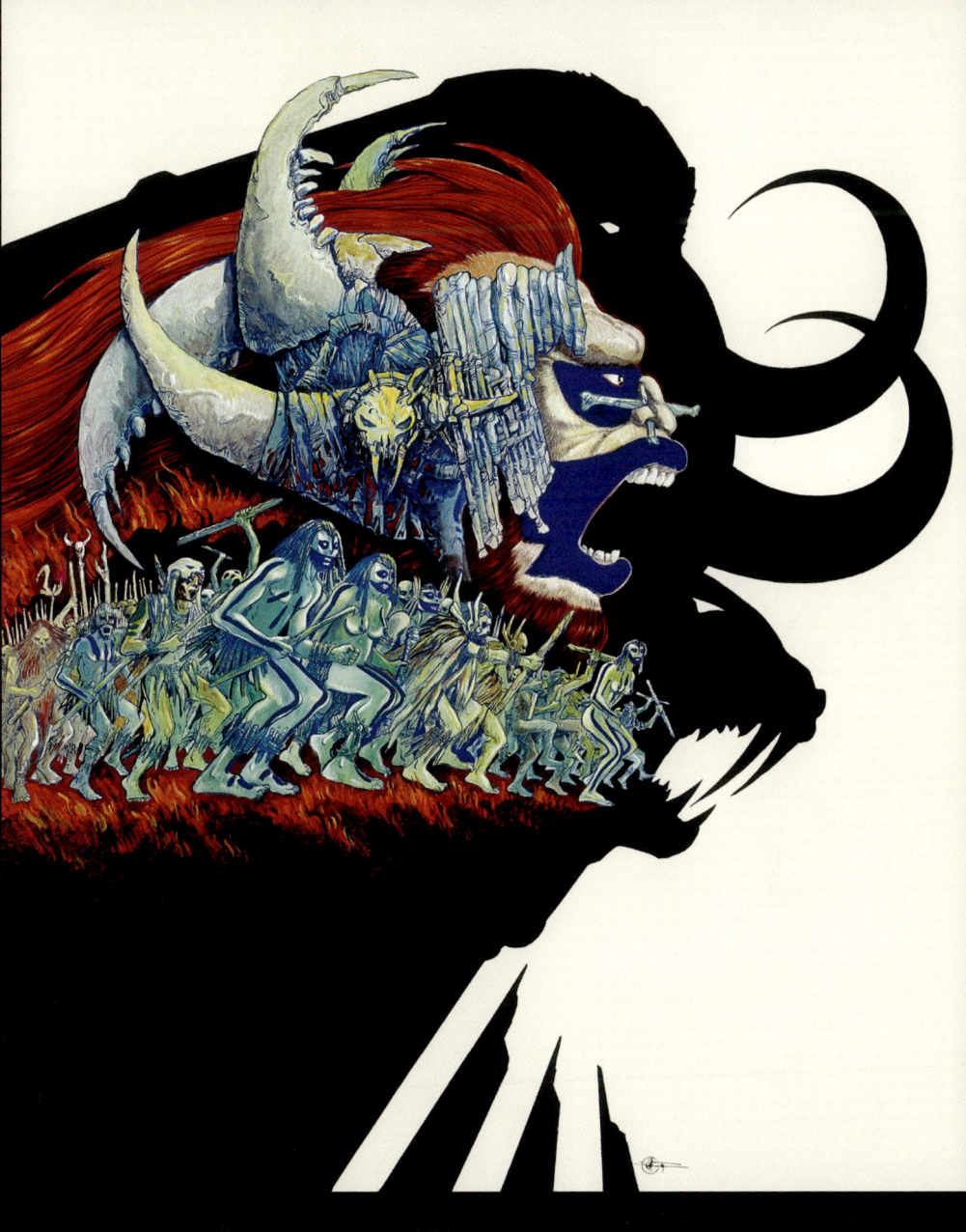

Above: Quest For Fire, movie poster art for the 1982
French release of the film by Jean-Jacques Annaud.

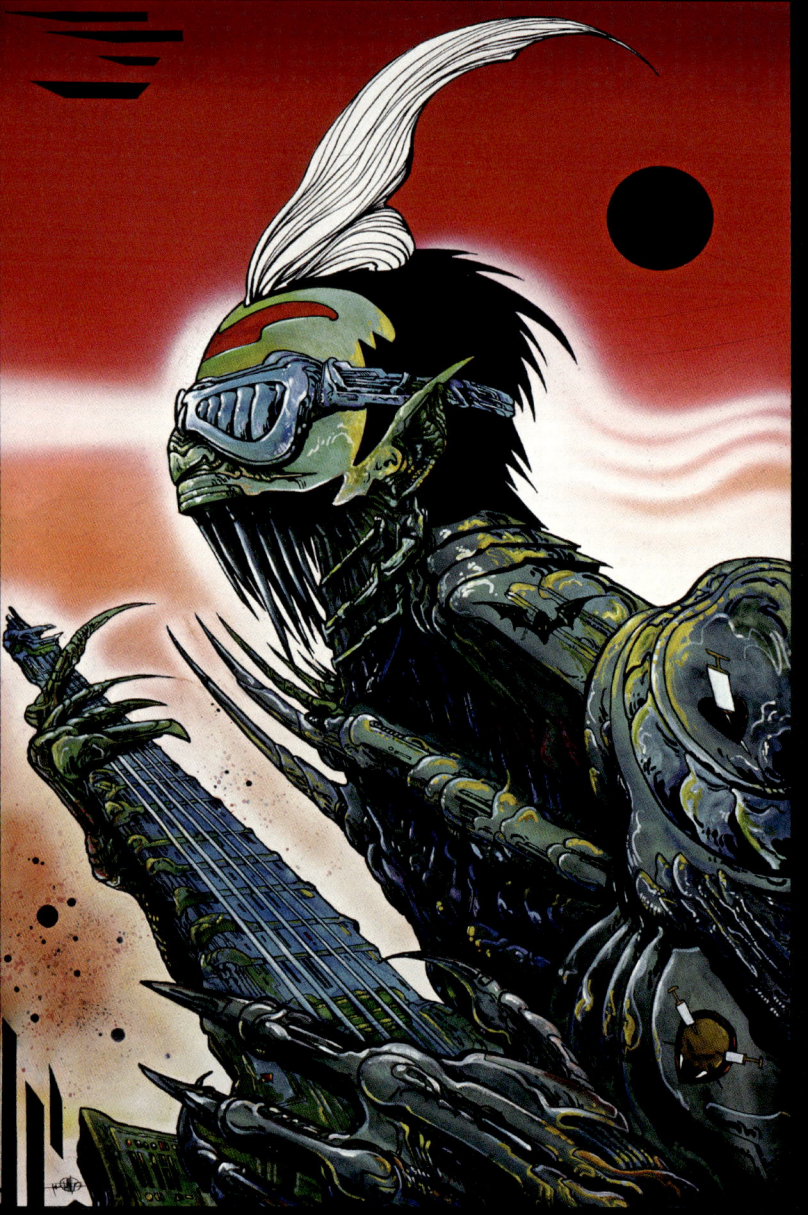

Above: Illustration for a poster advertising the 1980 release of the Cramps album *Songs the Lord Taught Us,* in the French market. 116.8 x 80 cm (46 x 31.5 inches).

Opposite: A monumental cover painting for the 1993 hardback graphic novel *Yragael.* Acrylic on canvas, 256.5 x 160 cm (101 x 63 inches).

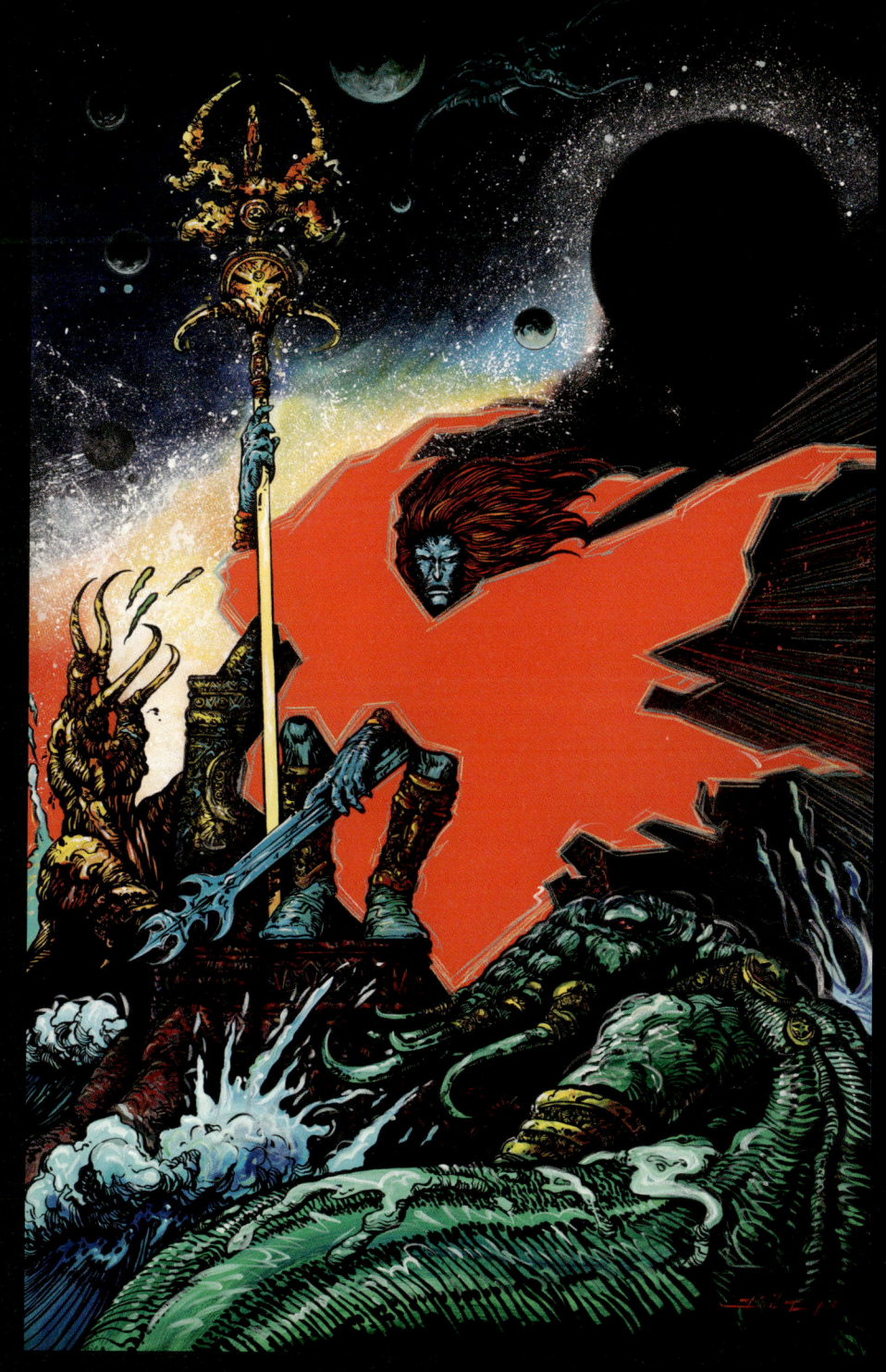

PHILIPPE DRUILLET

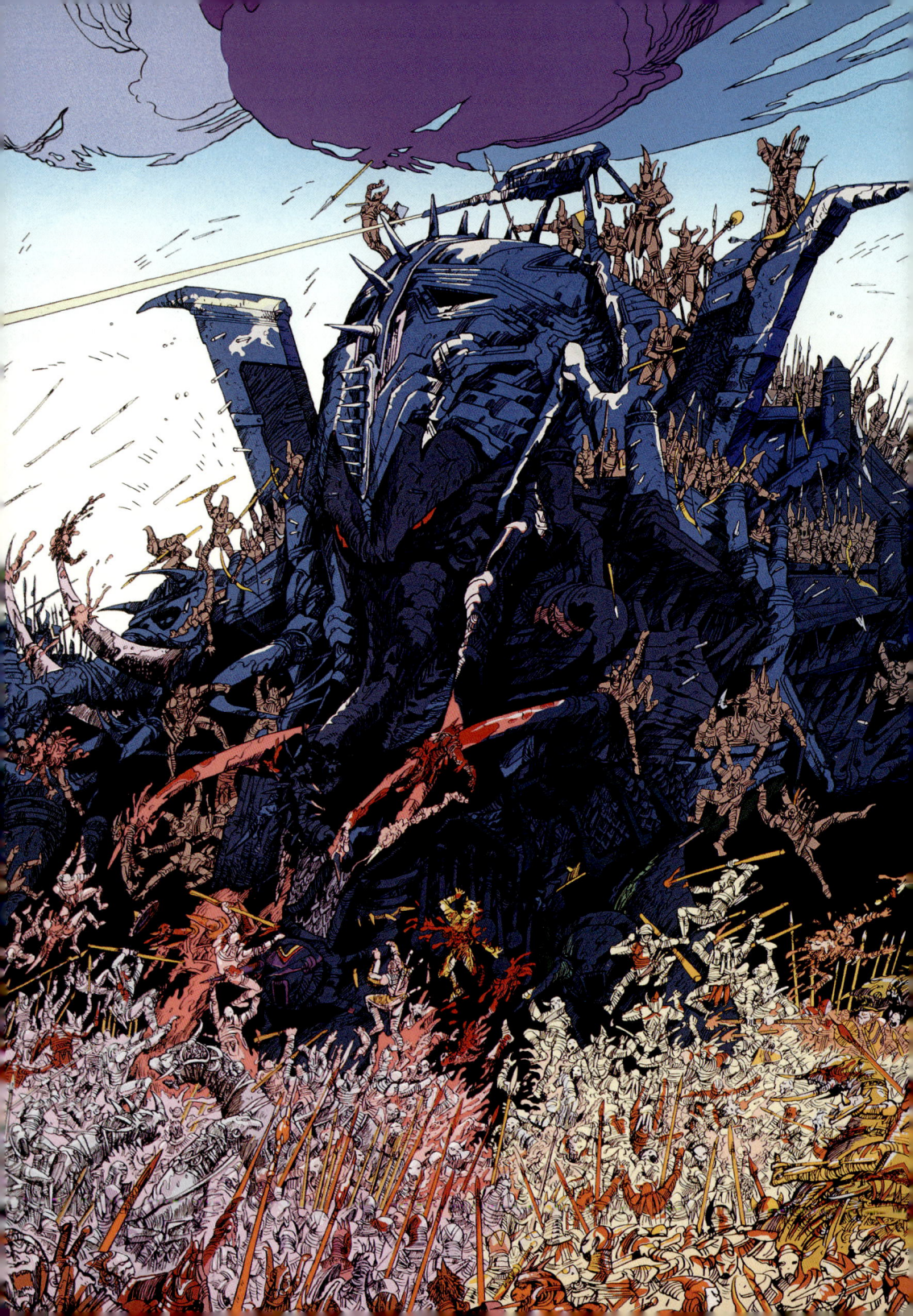

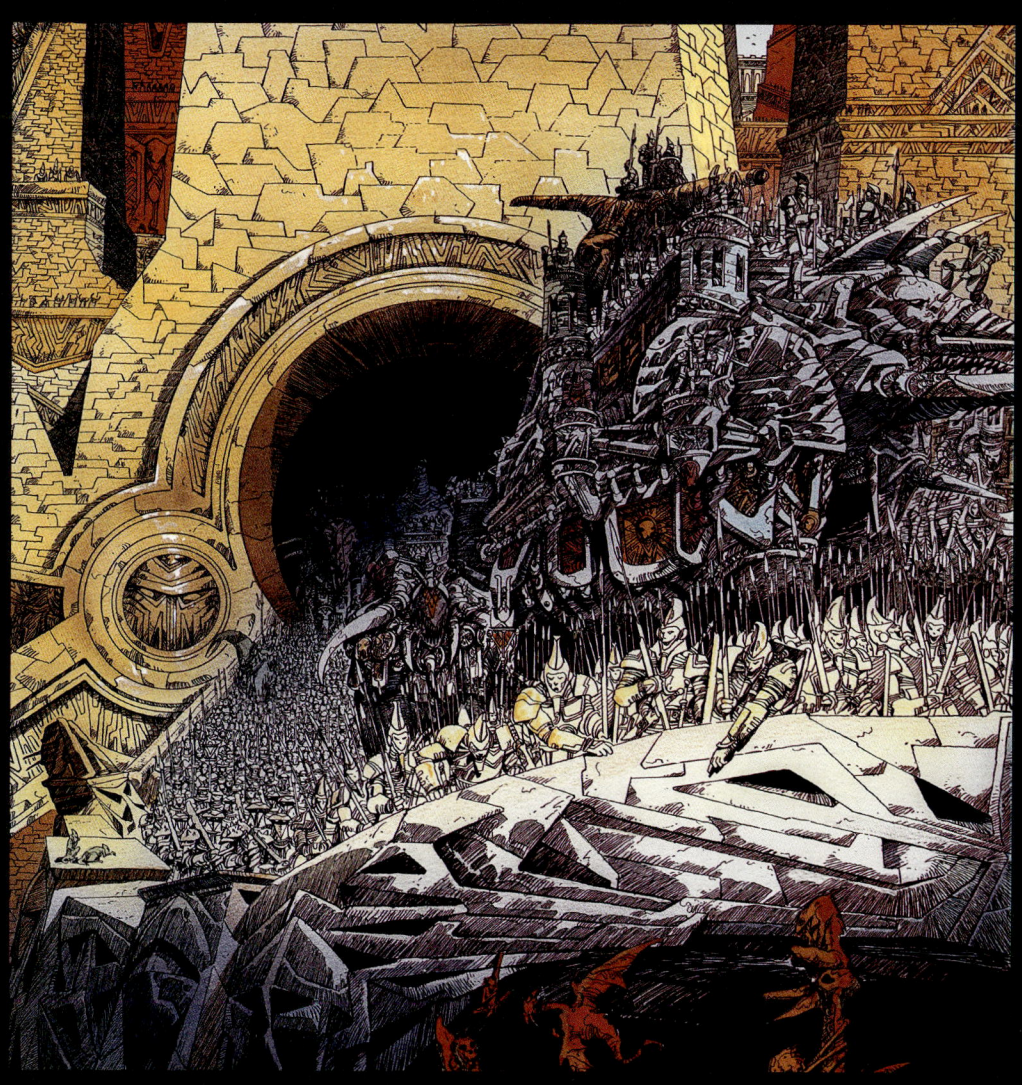

Opposite: Illustration for *Salammbô 3: Matho,* published in 1986 by Éditions Dargaud. Ink and acrylic on board, 85 x 63.5 cm (41.3 x 27.5 inches).

Above: An illustration for the book *Chaos,* 2001, featuring the return of Lone Sloane after more than two decades. Ink on paper, with enhanced color for printing, 104.9 x 69.8 cm (33.5 x 25 inches.)

PHILIPPE DRUILLET

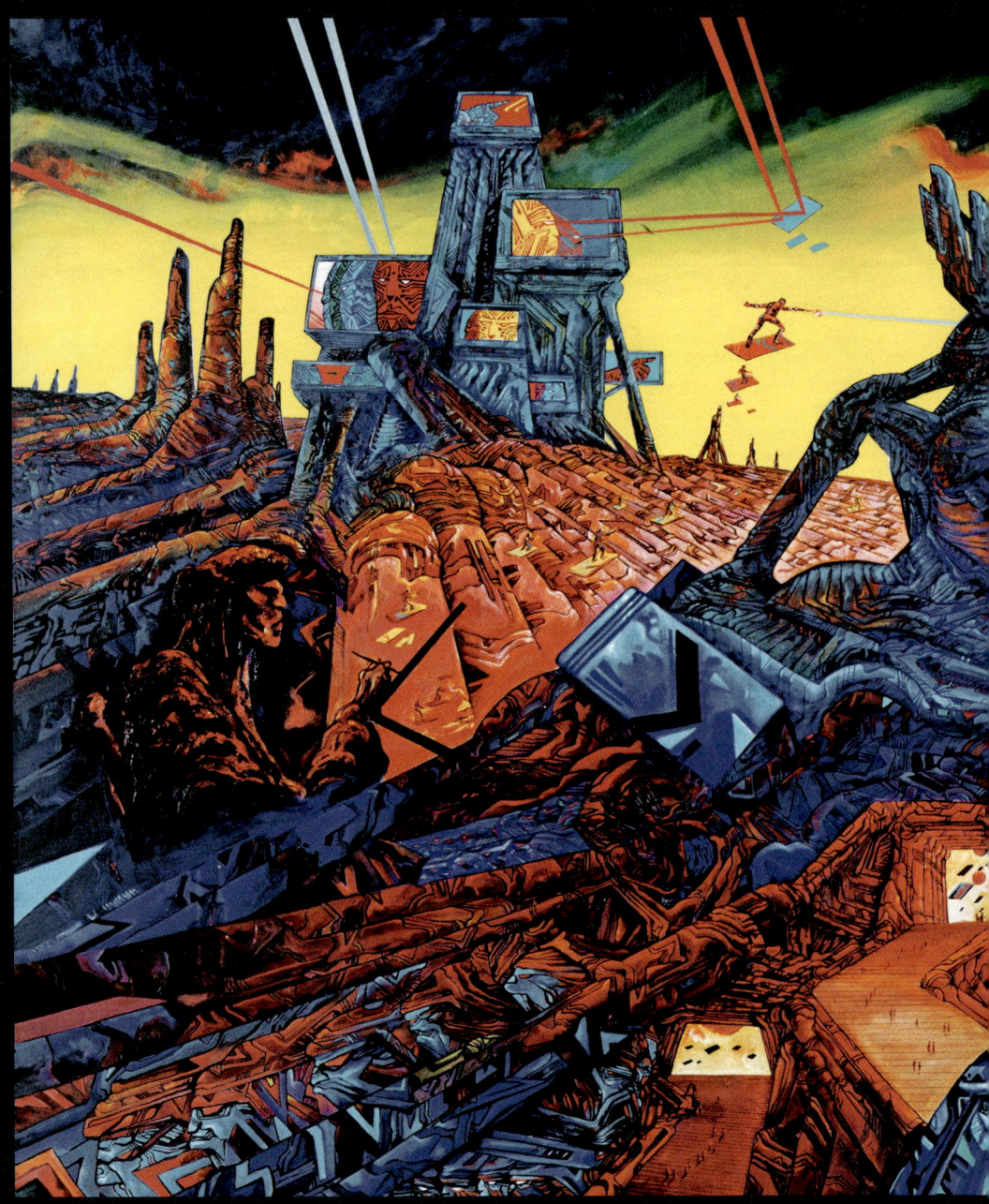

Above: Angouleme, France, hosts a yearly festival celebrating *bande dessinée*. In 1985 the theme was new technologies, for which Druillet created this spectacular mural in oil on canvas, 180 x 300 cm (70.85 x 118 inches).

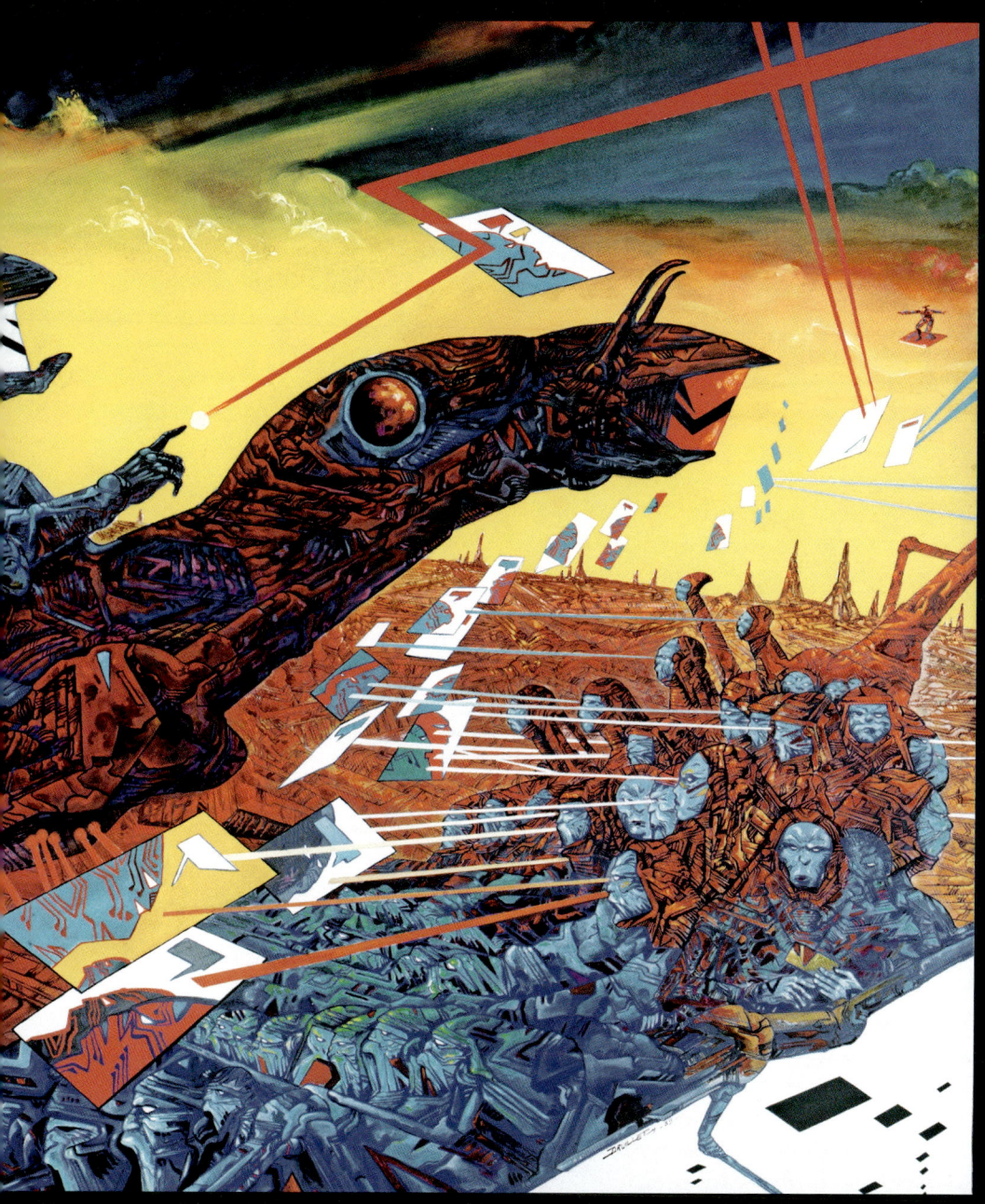

Following left: This painting appeared on the February 1980 issue of *Métal Hurlant* with the serialization of Druillet's *Salammbô*. Ink, gouache, and Ecoline watercolor on board, 64.8 x 50 cm (25.5 x 19.7 inches).

Following right: Druillet self-portrait, circa 1975.

PHILIPPE DRUILLET

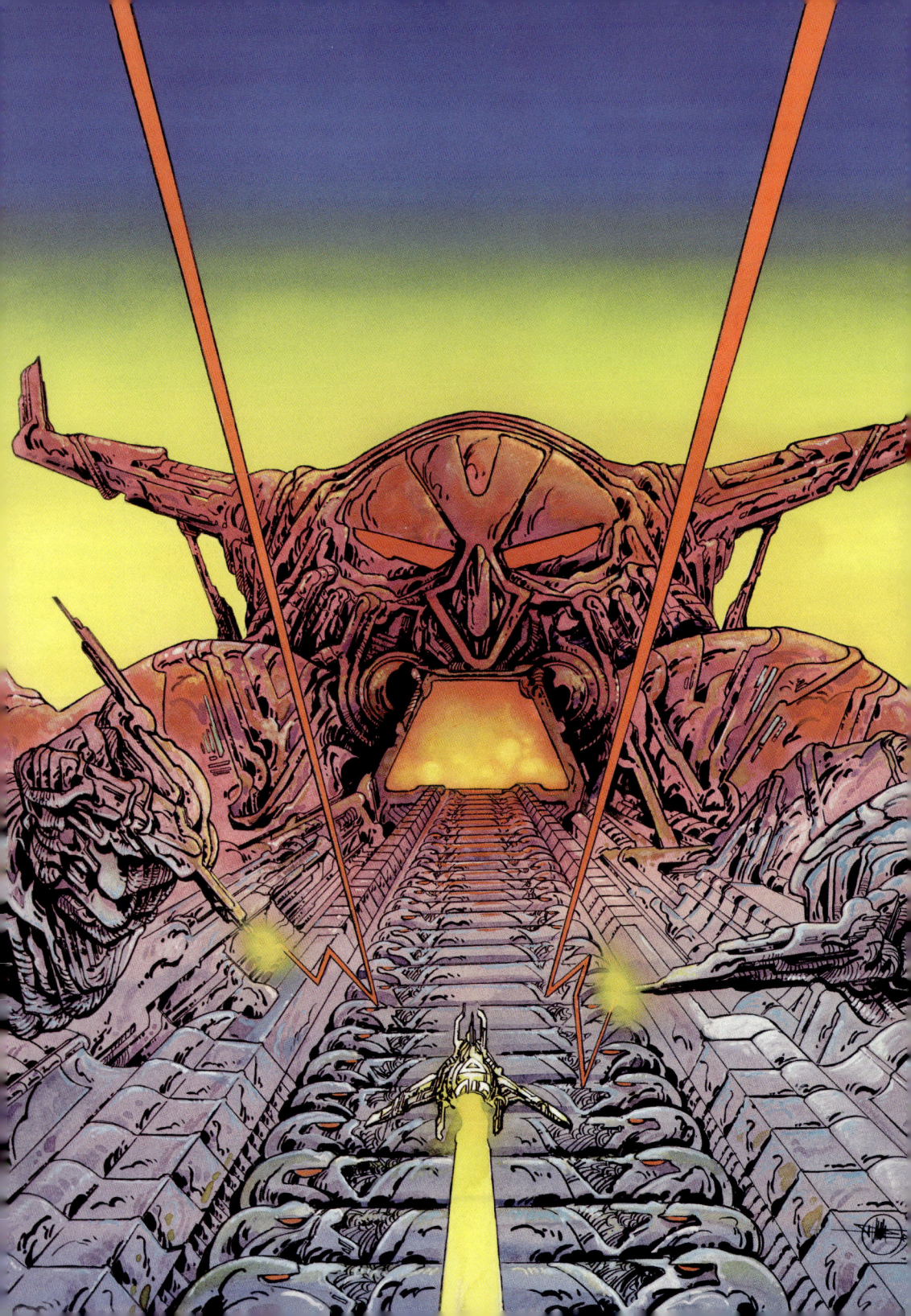

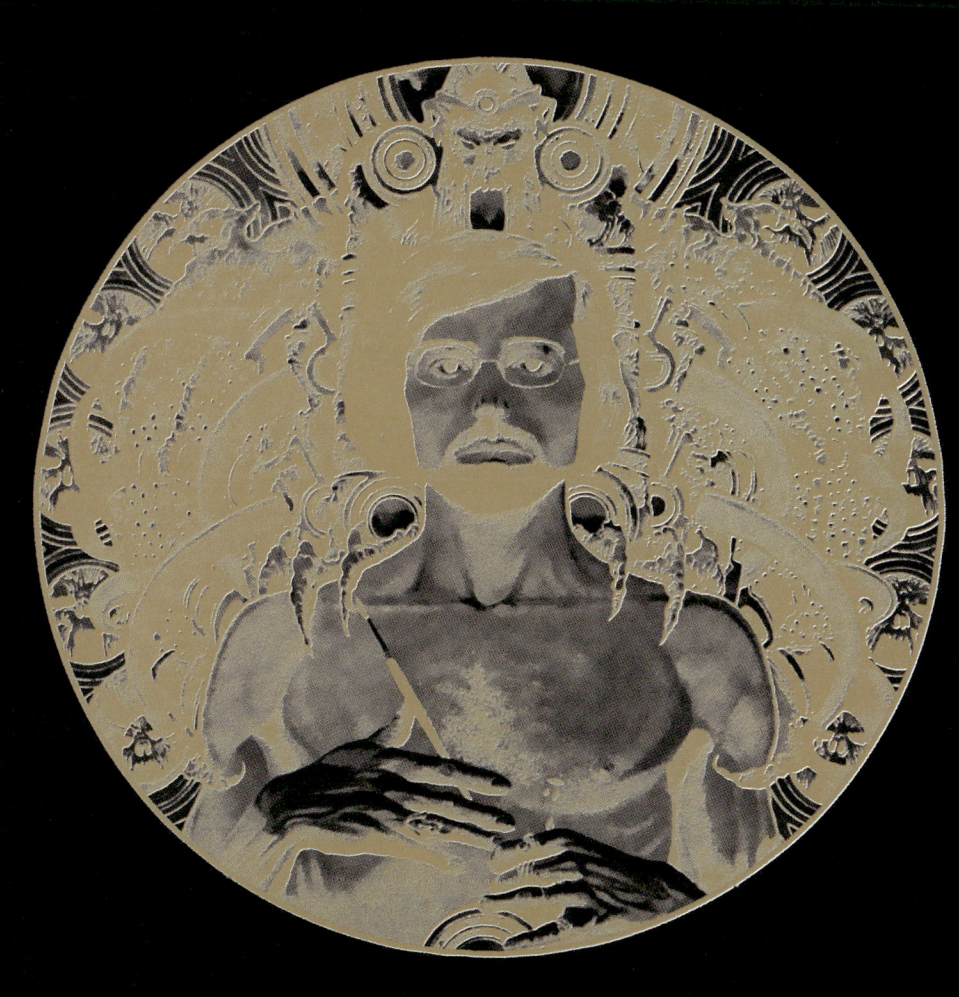

Frank Frazetta

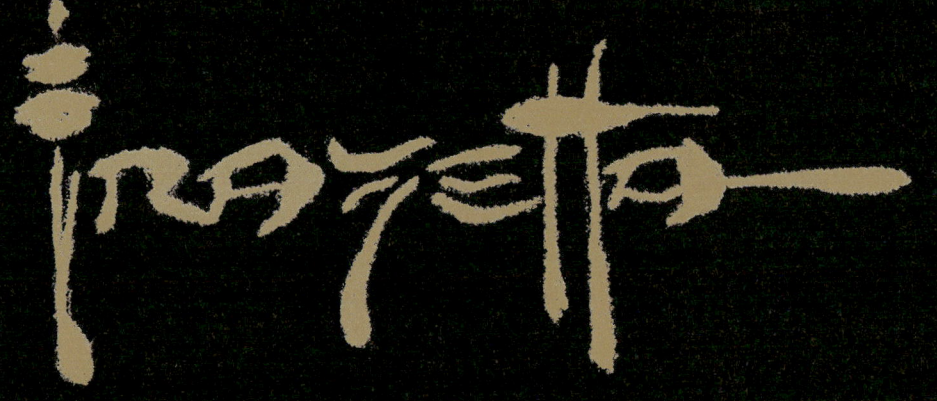

1928–2010

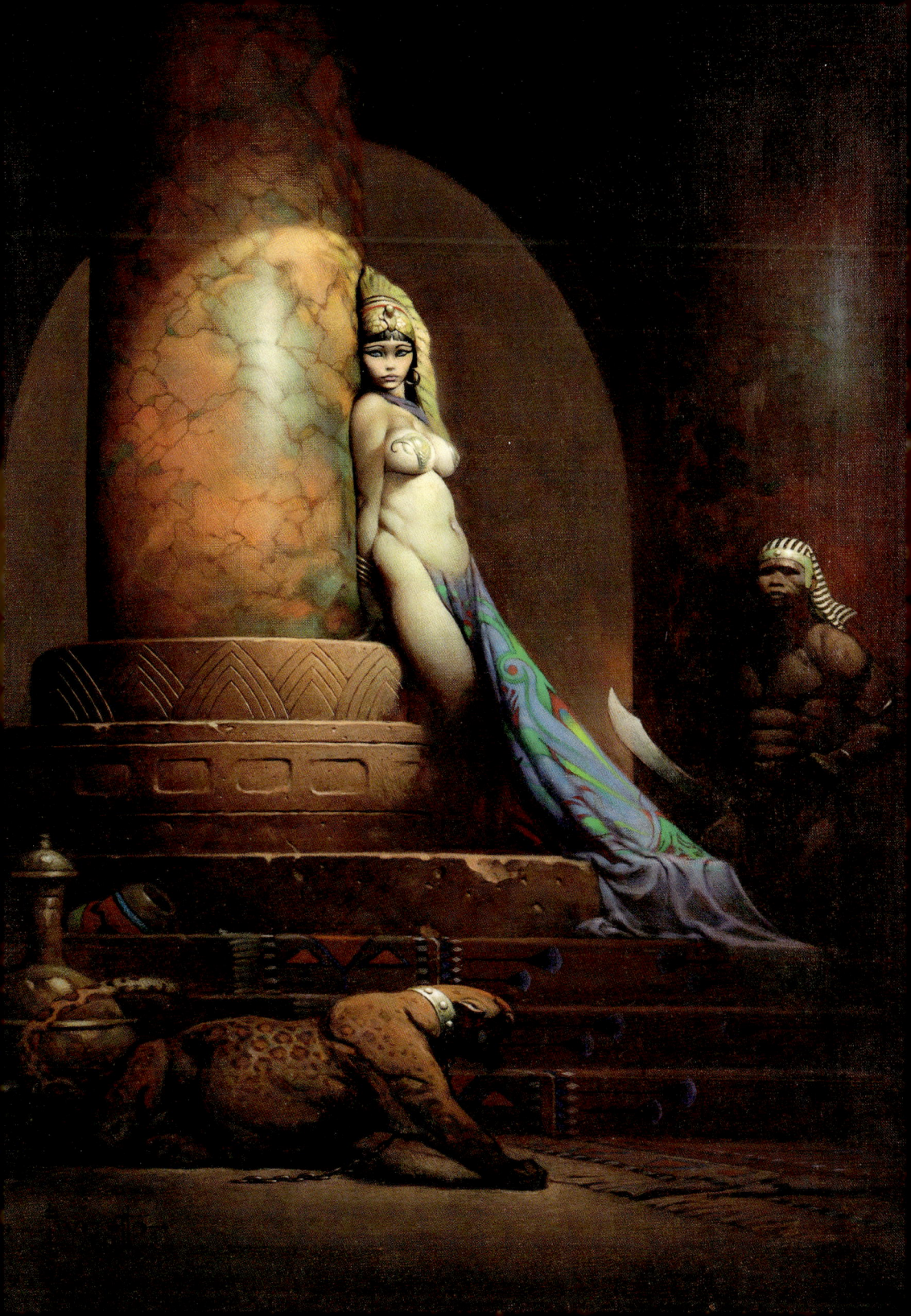

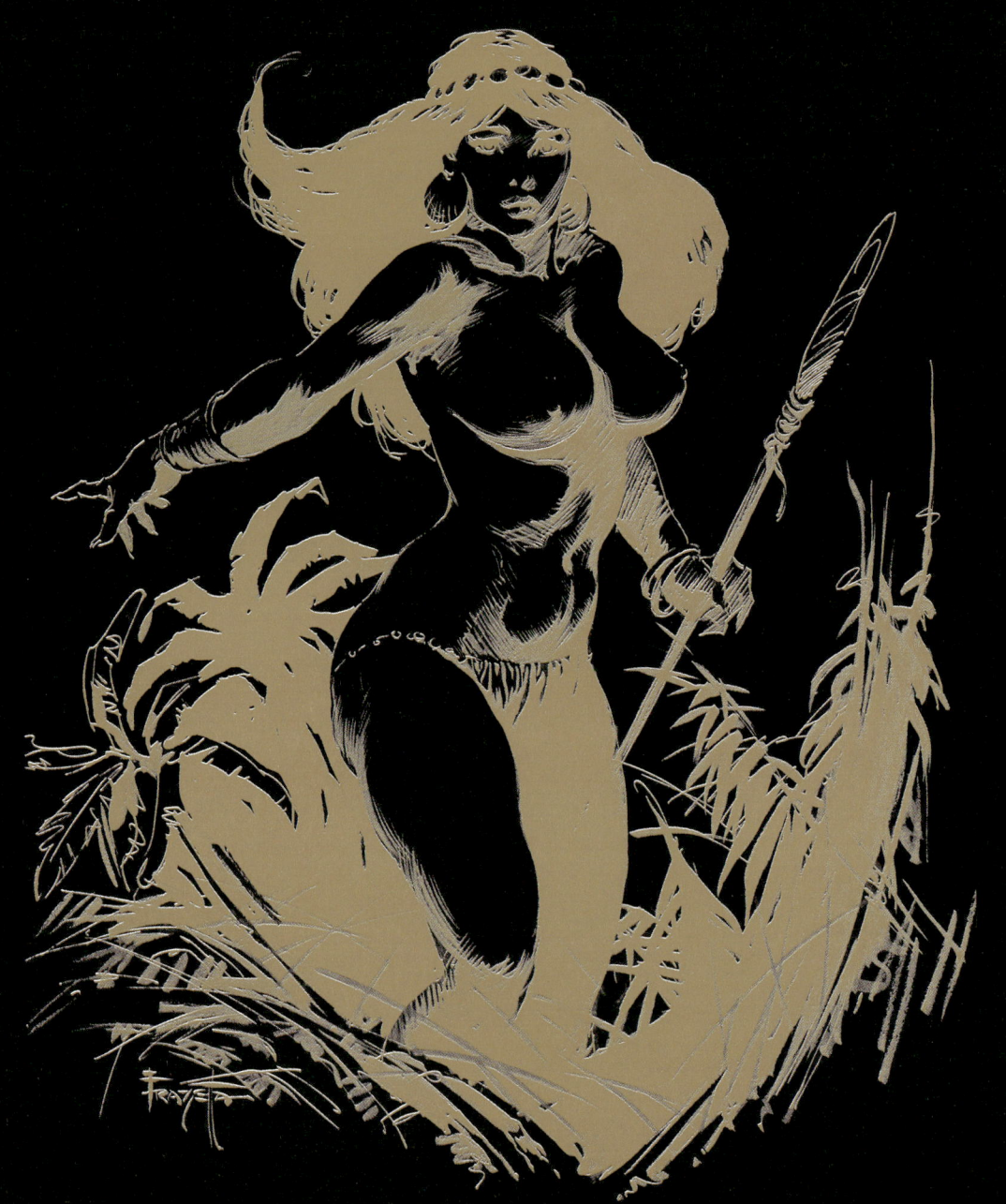

FRANK FRAZETTA
THE GOD

*"When it came to my art
I went my own way and did
not follow the trends."*

He was born Frank Frazzetta in Brooklyn in 1928, and soon dropped a "z" from his name for aesthetic appeal. His talent came naturally, nudged along by a grandmother who rewarded him with pennies for each finished piece. At age eight he was enrolled in the Brooklyn Academy of Fine Arts, a small school with a big name, at a cost of $8 a month, a considerable sum mid-Depression. The sole instructor, Michele Falanga, aged 69 in 1936, doted on his youngest pupil and Frazetta loyally attended classes until age 15, even after Falanga died and it "became more like a club," according to Frazetta, with students teaching each other. When the school closed he found work with Bernard Baily Studio, where artist John Giunta befriended him and helped develop his unlikely superhero Snowman for a *Tally-Ho Comics* one-shot (December 1944). Work for *Treasure Comics* followed, and in 1947 he took over "Looie Lazybones," a "Li'l Abner" knock-off, for Standard Comics. He later credited Standard's art director Ralph Mayo with teaching him anatomy, or rather, with handing him an anatomy book, which he copied in its entirety in one night, much improving the look of Looie and his hillbilly squeeze Clarabelle.

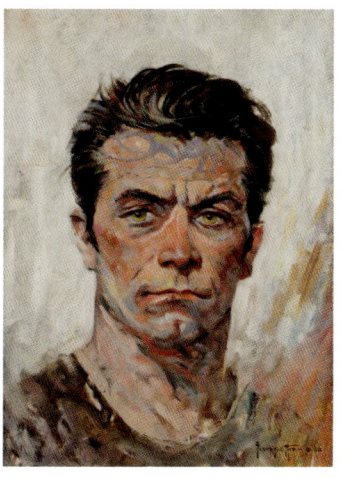

By 1948 Frazetta, just 20, was a fully established artist, drawing Western, mystery, historical, and fantasy comics for Famous Funnies, Heroic Comics, EC Comics, National Comics, Avon Comics, and others. Whether he found time to finish high school is unclear. Also hazy is his claim that the New York Giants scouted him in—take your pick—the 1940s, '50s, or early '60s. The most probable version has him noticed in 1947 and offered a spot on their Texas farm team, which he turned down because (a) he had a girlfriend, and (b) it would require him to leave Brooklyn. Being handsome, athletic, and charismatic—he bragged that he never went a day without sex—both the girlfriend and offer make sense, as does a Brooklyn boy's distaste for Texas. He

Previous right: Egyptian Queen, for the cover of *Eerie* No. 23, September 1969, brought $5.4 million at auction in 2019, setting world records for illustration and comic art. Frazetta repainted the Queen's face after it was printed on the *Eerie* cover, for a substantially different look. Oil on canvas, 64.7 x 50.1 cm (25.5 x 19.75 inches). Courtesy of Heritage Auctions.

Opposite: A pen and ink drawing by Frazetta from the mid-1960s. 26.6 x 21.5 cm (10.5 x 8.5 inches). Courtesy of Heritage Auctions.

Above: This self-portrait from 1962 shows off Frazetta's movie star looks as well as his impeccable technique. The original now hangs in director Robert Rodriguez's Frazetta museum. Oil on board.

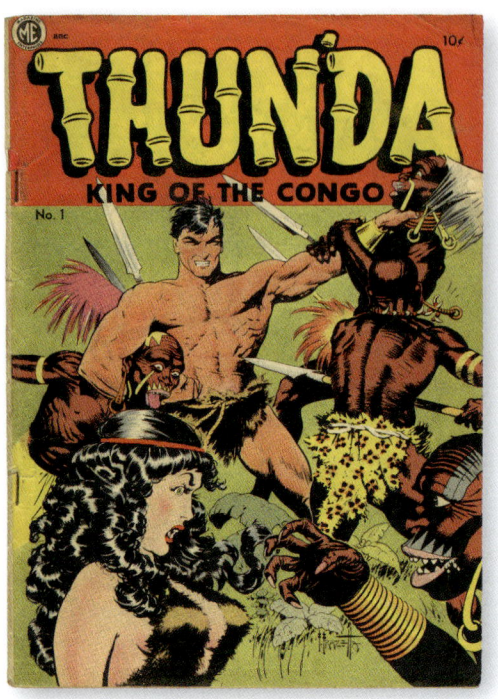

also pointed out, years later, that minor league baseball was just long bus rides for low pay.

His playboy days ended in 1952 when Frazetta met 17-year-old Eleanor "Ellie" Kelly. The two married in 1956 and produced four children: Alfonso (known as Frank Jr.) William, Heidi, and Holly. In 1954 he took a full-time job with Al Capp to ghost "Li'l Abner," and with a fast-growing family he stuck with it until 1962, when Capp reduced his salary. Frazetta quit and faced hardship. Publishers rejected his "Sweet Adeline" comic strip, and when he tried to return to comic books he was told his work was "old style." He painted nudes for several men's magazines (all but three paintings now lost) and illustrations for Midwood Books' line of adult paperbacks. Finally, in late 1962, his friend Roy Krenkel found him a job with Ace Books, doing covers and spot illustrations for a series of Edgar Rice Burroughs novels—mostly Tarzan. He perfected his fantasy style at Ace, and immediately picked up similar work for Lancer Books, Canaveral Press, and Fawcett Publications.

Comics, too, came calling when Warren Publishing launched the horror title *Creepy*, inspired by EC Comics, in 1964, followed by *Blazing Combat* (1965), *Eerie* (1966), and *Vampirella* (1969). Frazetta did 32 memorable covers for the four magazines, including the defining first cover for *Vampirella*. He also got work from *MAD*, and it was a 1964 portrait of Ringo Starr, for a Breck shampoo parody, that won his first film poster commission, for *What's New Pussycat?*, in 1965. Thirteen posters followed in the next five years, leading to album covers for film soundtracks and front and back covers for Herman's Hermits' fourth album.

And then came Conan. Up until that time all of Frazetta's work was done "for hire," which allowed publishers to keep his originals. This changed in 1966 when Lancer commissioned covers for the first comprehensive paperback series of Conan. Frazetta agreed only on condition he retain the rights to his originals, then created eight stunning career-making covers, beginning with *Conan the Adventurer* in 1966, and ending with *Conan the Buccaneer* in 1971. His Conan became *the* Conan—primitive, heavily muscled, and darkly brooding—serving as inspiration for Dino De Laurentiis's *Conan the Barbarian*, and the casting of champion bodybuilder Arnold Schwarzenegger in the title role. Frazetta increased the value of, and collectors' yearning for, the Conan paintings by refusing to sell any of the eight.

All that '60s work allowed Frazetta to purchase a ramshackle farmhouse on 67 acres in Pennsylvania's Pocono Mountains in 1971. The book and magazine cover commissions, including

Above: Thun'da, from 1952, is the only comic book drawn entirely by Frazetta, who was just 24 at the time, but already an established artist.

Opposite: Black Panther, used as the cover of the Edgar Rice Burroughs novel *The Land of Hidden Men*, Ace Books, 1978. Oil on board, 1972.

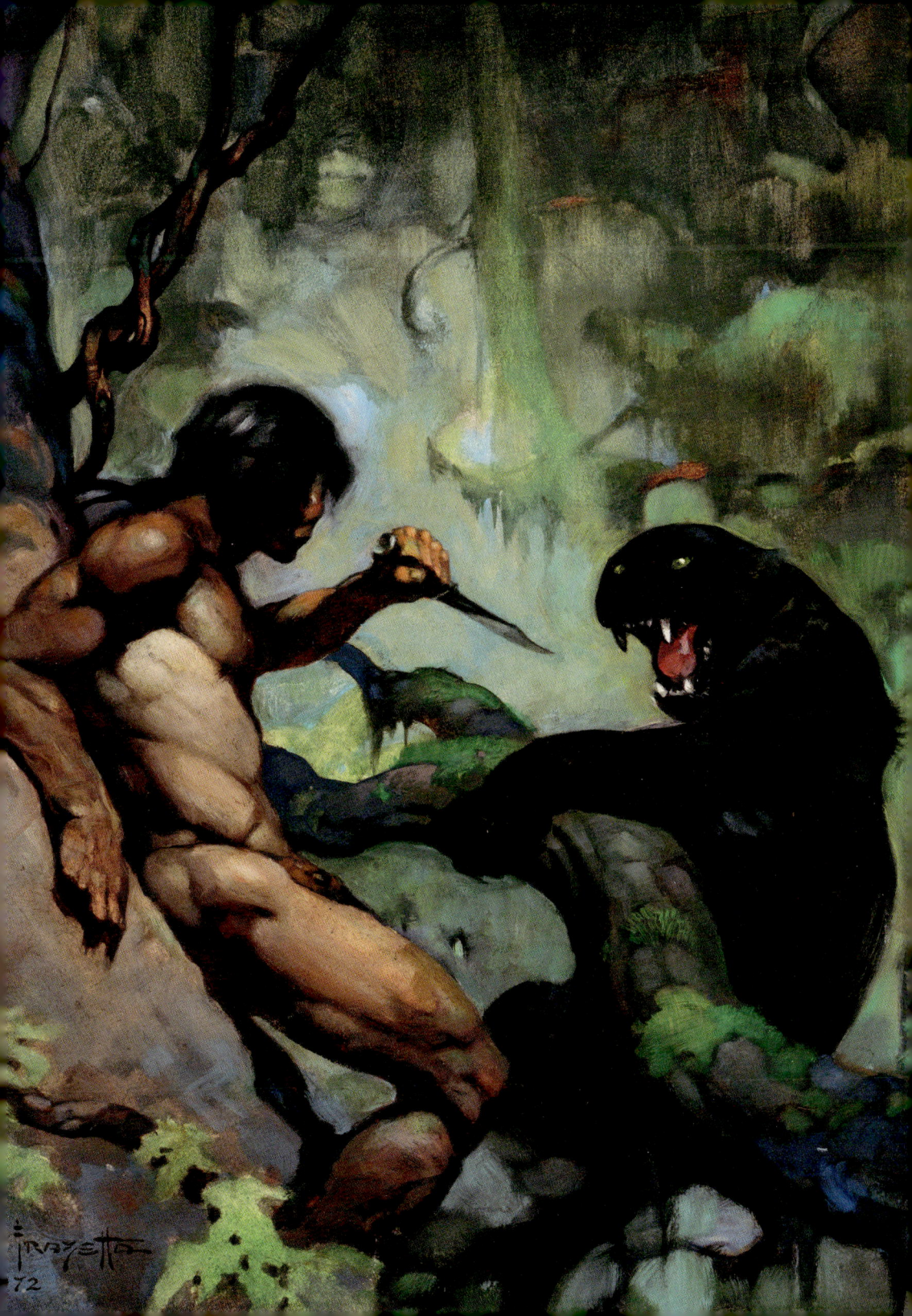

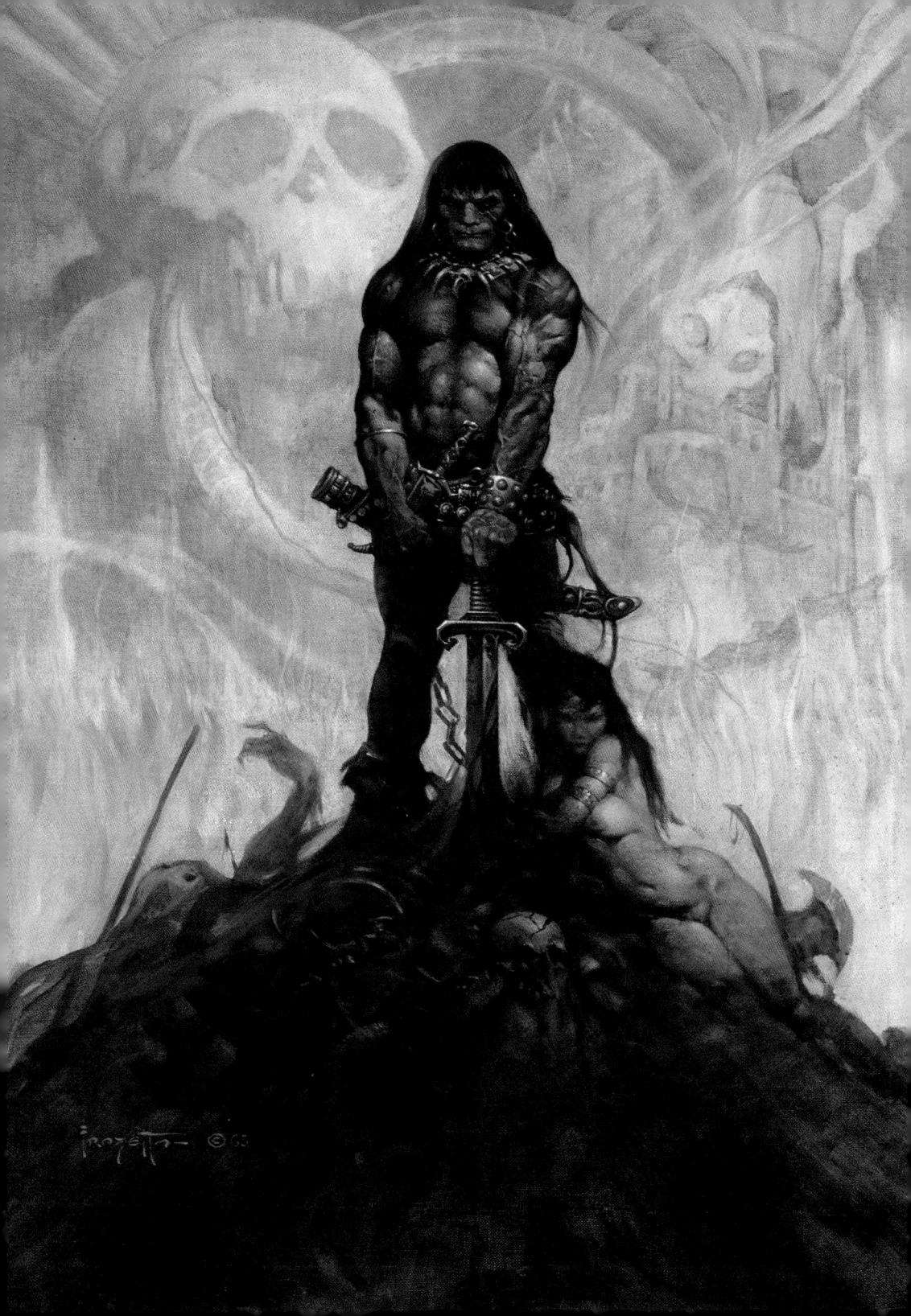

several for *National Lampoon*, kept
coming; he did eight more movie
posters, album covers for Molly
Hatchet and Nazareth, and the first
three of many monographs. He
worked so fast he could complete a
painting in a single night, meaning he
could earn a week's wage in a matter
of hours and spend the rest of his time
fixing the house, clearing the fields, or
playing ball with his kids.

In 1982 director Ralph Bakshi
convinced Frazetta to partner on *Fire
and Ice*, a film based on his art. Though
panned at the time, the 1983 film is
now such a cult favorite that director
Robert Rodriguez—a Frazetta friend
and fan—is remaking it in live action.

In 1986 Frazetta opened a gallery
in East Stroudsburg, Pennsylvania,
called Frazetta's Fantasy Corner, where
Ellie sold his monographs and signed
prints. The book cover and magazine
commissions had mostly ended, but

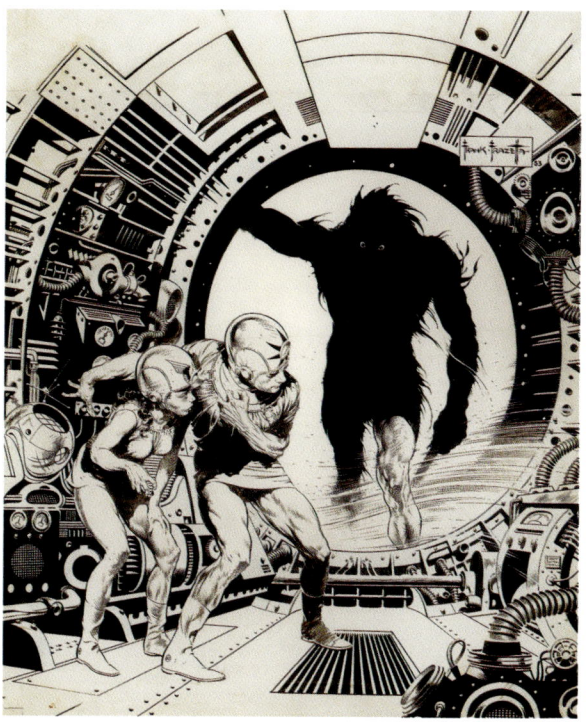

the demand for original paintings was high, and kept going up into the '90s, as Frazetta's health
faltered. It took years to diagnose hyperthyroidism, which led to the first of many strokes in 1995.
When the strokes numbed his right hand, he taught himself to paint with his left and soldiered on.

In 2001 Frank designed and built the Frazetta Art Museum next to his home. The fortunate
visitor found the great artist himself holding court, while Ellie sold books, prints, and T-shirts. She
always handled the business side, so it was understandable that her death in July 2009 left a void in
every sphere of Frank's life and in the lives of his children. The museum closed and chaos ensued,
exaggerated and falsified by an exuberant press. The troubles were soon settled, but Frank, who
had decamped to Florida following Ellie's death, never returned to their home of 38 years. He
died less than a year later, on May 10, 2010.

Two months after Frazetta's death, Kirk Hammett of Metallica paid the family $1 million for
Conan the Adventurer, finally breaking up the eight Conan paintings, but most other iconic works
have stayed in the family, and in 2015 the Frazetta Art Museum reopened, under the direction of
Frank Jr. It's pretty great, if you ever find yourself in eastern Pennsylvania.

Opposite: This iconic painting was originally created for
the cover of Lancer Books' *Conan the Adventurer* in 1966,
reprinted on Sphere Books' edition in 1973, and on the
Ace edition in 1977. Dino De Laurentiis then chose it as
the advance poster for *Conan the Barbarian*, starring
Arnold Schwarzenegger, in 1980.

Above: Buck Rogers in the original cover art for *Famous
Funnies* No. 213, 1953. Frazetta had already mastered his
art form at age 25, after 10 years of daily drawing. Ink on
paper, 71.1 x 63.5 cm (28 x 25 inches). Courtesy of Heritage
Auctions.

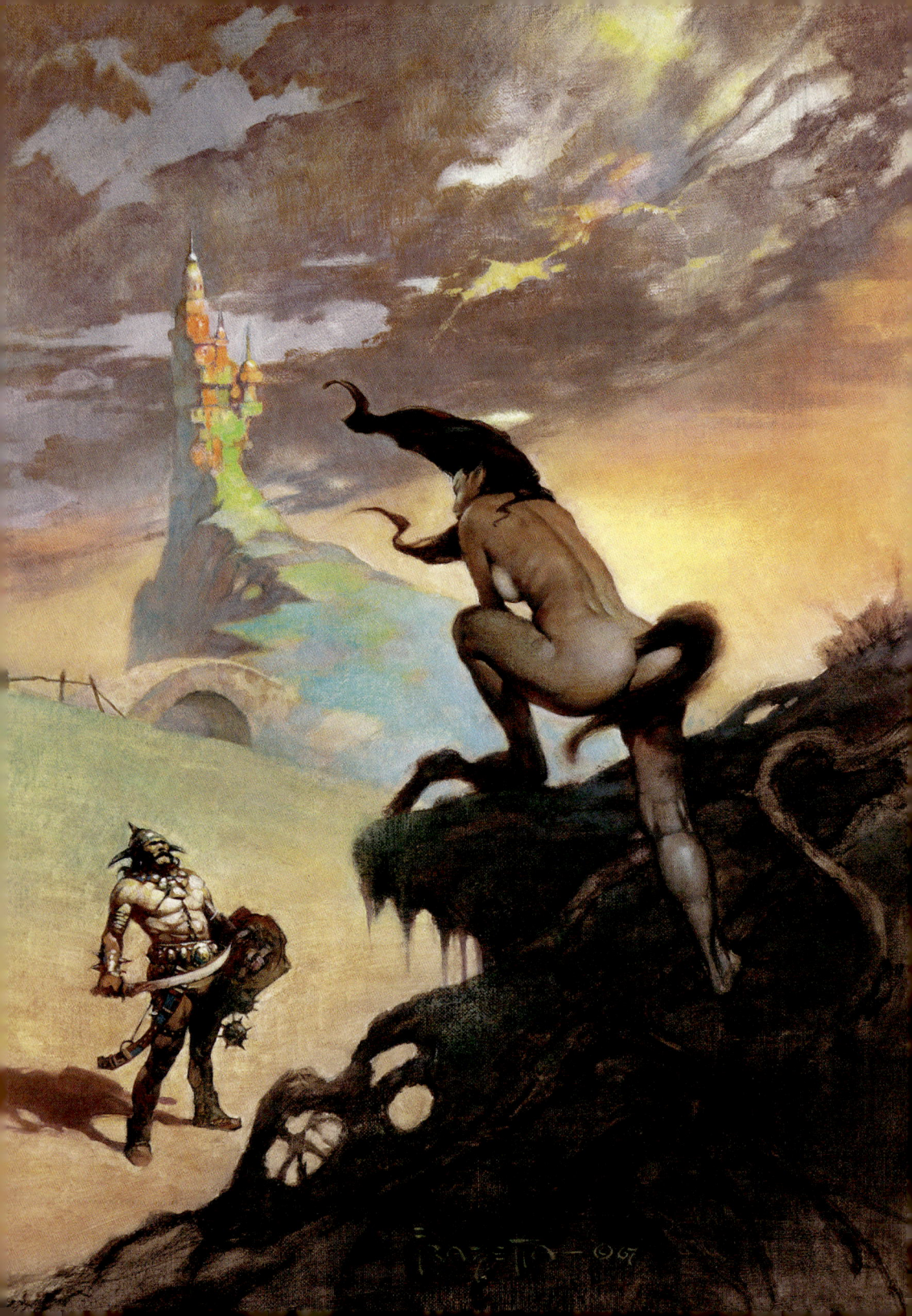

FRANK FRAZETTA
DER GOTT

„Wenn es auf meine Kunst ankam, ging ich meinen eigenen Weg und folgte keinen Trends."

1928 wurde er als Frank Frazzetta in Brooklyn geboren und strich aus ästhetischen Gründen schon bald ein „z" aus seinem Namen. Sein Talent entwickelte sich, ermutigt von einer Großmutter, die ihn für jedes vollendete Blatt mit ein paar Pennys belohnte, wie selbstverständlich. Bereits im Alter von acht Jahren war er für eine Monatsgebühr von acht Dollar – in Zeiten der Depression ein erklecklicher Betrag – an der Brooklyn Academy of Fine Arts eingeschrieben. Der einzige Lehrer, Michele Falanga, der 1936 69 Jahre alt war, hatte einen Narren an seinem jüngsten Schüler gefressen, und Frazetta wohnte bis zu seinem 15. Lebensjahr ergeben dem Unterricht bei, auch nachdem Falanga gestorben war und die Klasse, wie Frazetta meinte, „eher eine Art Klub wurde", in dem sich die Studenten gegenseitig etwas beibrachten. Als die Schule geschlossen wurde, fand er Arbeit im Bernard Baily Studio, wo sich der Künstler John Giunta mit ihm anfreundete und ihm half, seinen merkwürdigen Superhelden Snowman für eine einmalige Comicausgabe von *Tally-Ho* (Dezember 1944) auszuarbeiten. Es folgten Arbeiten für *Treasure Comics*, und 1947 übernahm er für Standard Comics „Looie Lazybones", ein „Li'l Abner"-Imitat. Später schrieb er dem Artdirector von Standard, Ralph Mayo, das Verdienst zu, ihm Anatomie beigebracht zu haben, oder besser gesagt, ihm ein Anatomiebuch in die Hand gedrückt zu haben, das er in einer Nacht komplett kopierte, was dazu führte, dass sich das Aussehen von Looie und seiner Hinterwäldlertusse Clarabelle deutlich verbesserte.

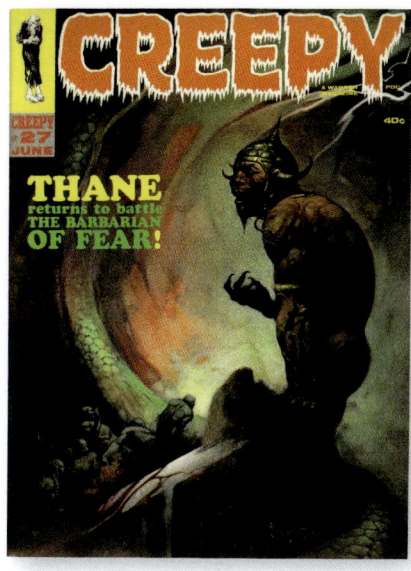

Um 1948, mit gerade 20, war Frazetta ein voll etablierter Künstler und zeichnete Western, Mystery, historische und Fantasycomics für Famous Funnies, Heroic Comics, EC Comics, National Comics, Avon Comics und andere. Ob er die Zeit fand, die Highschool abzuschließen, ist unklar. Auch etwas vage ist seine Behauptung, die New York Giants hätten ihn in den 1940er-, 1950er- oder in den frühen 1960er-Jahren – man suche es sich aus – gescoutet. Die wahrscheinlichste

Opposite: Pony Tail, for the cover of L. Sprague de Camp's 1967 Paperback Library edition of *The Tritonian Ring.* Oil on board, 50.8 x 40.6 cm (20 x 16 inches). Courtesy of Heritage Auctions.

Above: Creepy No. 27, June 1969, with a Frazetta barbarian cover. He produced 32 covers for Warren Publishing's *Creepy, Eerie,* and *Vampirella* magazines.

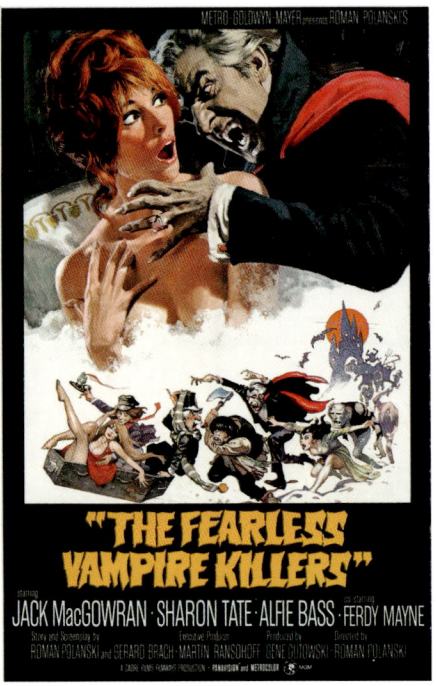

Version besagt, dass er 1947 wohl auffiel und man ihm einen Platz im Team ihrer Texas-Farm anbot, was er jedoch ablehnte, weil er a) eine Freundin hatte und das b) bedeutet hätte, dass er Brooklyn hätte verlassen müssen. Da er gut aussehend, athletisch und charismatisch war – er prahlte damit, dass es bei ihm keinen Tag ohne Sex gebe –, machen sowohl die Freundin wie auch das Angebot Sinn, genau wie die Abneigung eines Burschen aus Brooklyn gegen Texas. Jahre später führte er zudem an, Baseball in einer unteren Liga bedeute bloß lange Busfahrten für wenig Geld.

Seine Zeiten als Playboy waren 1952 zu Ende, als Frazetta die 17-jährige Eleanor „Ellie" Kelly kennenlernte. Die beiden heirateten 1956 und bekamen vier Kinder: Alfonso, bekannt als Frank Junior, William, Heidi und Holly. 1954 nahm er einen Ganztagsjob bei Al Capp an, dem er für *Li'l Abner* zuarbeiten sollte. Da er eine schnell wachsende Familie ernähren musste, blieb er bis 1962 dabei, als Capp seinen Lohn kürzte. Frazetta ging und geriet in Not. Verleger lehnten seinen Comicstrip *Sweet Adeline* ab, und als er versuchte, wieder in der Comicbranche unterzukommen, erklärte man ihm, seine Arbeiten seien „alte Schule". Für verschiedene Herrenmagazine malte er Akte (bis auf drei Bilder sind sie heute alle verloren) und Illustrationen für Midwood Books' Reihe von Taschenbüchern für Erwachsene. Schließlich, Ende 1962, fand sein Freund Roy Krenkel bei Ace Books einen Job für ihn: Er gestaltete Cover und einzelne Illustrationen für eine Reihe von Edgar-Rice-Burroughs-Romanen – meistens Tarzan. Bei Ace Books perfektionierte er seinen Fantasystil und begann sofort damit, ähnliche Arbeiten für Lancer Books, Canaveral Press und Fawcett Publications anzunehmen.

Als Warren Publishing 1964 den von EC Comics inspirierten Horrortitel *Creepy* lancierte, dem *Blazing Combat* (1965), *Eerie* (1966) und *Vampirella* (1969) folgten, bekam er auch Aufträge für Comics. Für diese vier Zeitschriften schuf Frazetta 32 denkwürdige Cover, darunter das erste und prägende Titelbild für *Vampirella*. Auch von MAD erhielt er Aufträge, und so brachte ihm ein Porträt von Ringo Starr, das er für eine parodistische Anzeige für Breck-Shampoo zeichnete, 1965 seinen ersten Auftrag zum Entwurf eines Filmplakats für *What's New Pussycat?* ein. In den nächsten fünf Jahren folgten dreizehn weitere Plakate, und schließlich wurde er engagiert, Albumcover für Filmmusiken und die Vorder- und die Rückseite für das vierte Album der Herman's Hermits zu entwerfen.

Und dann kam Conan. Bis zu diesem Zeitpunkt waren alle Werke von Frazetta als Auftragsarbeiten entstanden, was bedeutete, dass die Originalbilder bei den Verlegern blieben. Dies änderte sich 1966, als Lancer Coverentwürfe für die erste umfassende Taschenbuchreihe zu Conan zu

Above: The Finnish movie poster for Roman Polanski's 1967 comedy *The Fearless Vampire Killers*, with art by Frazetta. 60.9 x 40.6 cm (24 x 16 inches).

Opposite: Full Moon with Demons, oil on board, undated.

MASTERPIECES OF FANTASY ART

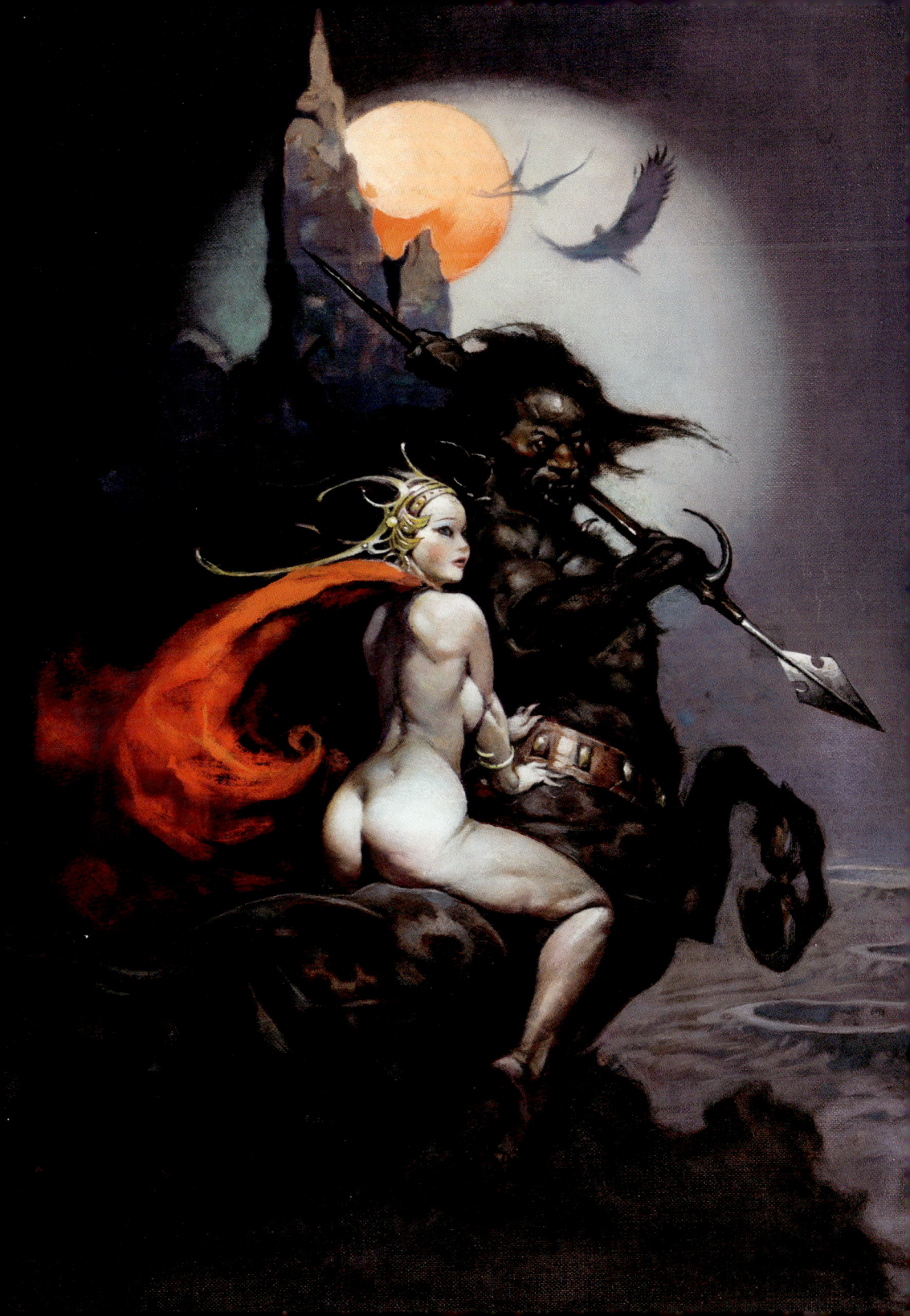

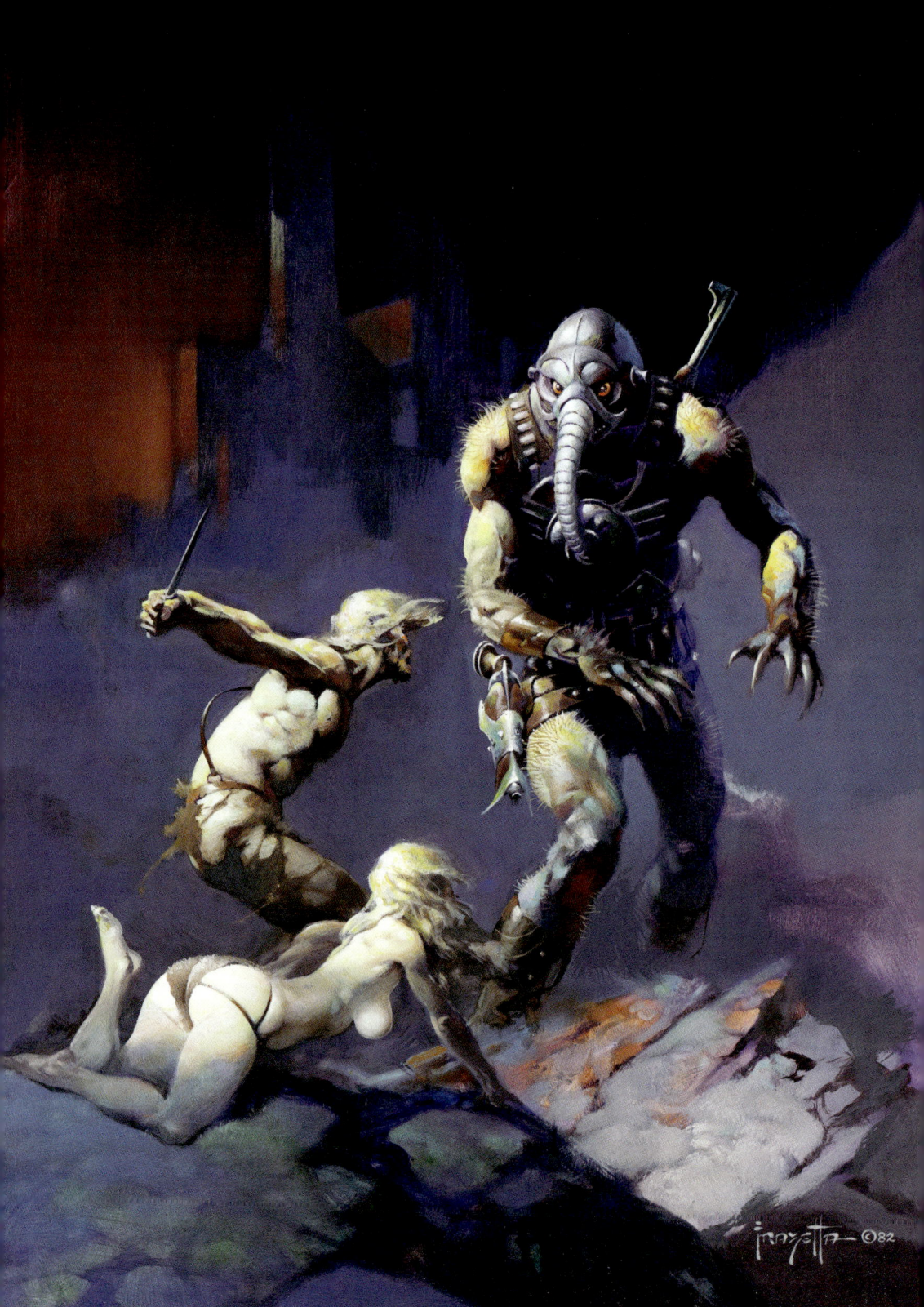

vergeben hatte. Frazetta stimmte nur unter der Bedingung zu, dass die Rechte an den Original-
bildern bei ihm verblieben, und schuf daraufhin acht fantastische, karrierefördernde Cover, zuerst,
1966, zu *Conan the Adventurer* und als Letztes, 1971, das zu *Conan the Buccaneer*. Sein Conan wurde
zu *dem* Conan – unzivilisiert, muskelbepackt und düster grübelnd –, der Dino De Laurentiis als
Inspiration für den Film *Conan der Barbar* diente und als Vorlage für das Casting des Bodybuilder-
Champions Arnold Schwarzenegger für die Titelrolle. Frazetta steigerte den Wert seiner Conan-
Gemälde – und das Verlangen von Sammlern –, indem er es ablehnte, auch nur eines der acht
Gemälde zu verkaufen.

All diese Aufträge der 1960er-Jahre ermöglichten Frazetta 1971 den Kauf eines maroden Bau-
ernhauses auf einem Grundstück von 67 Morgen Land in den Pocono Mountains, Pennsylvania.
Weitere Aufträge für Titelbilder von Büchern und Zeitschriften, darunter einige für *National
Lampoon*, kamen; er schuf acht weitere Filmplakate, Albumcover für Molly Hatchet und Nazareth
und die Titelbilder der ersten drei von vielen Monografien. Er arbeitete so schnell, dass er ein
Gemälde während einer einzigen Nacht vollenden konnte, was bedeutete, dass er innerhalb von
Stunden einen Wochenlohn verdiente, und verbrachte dann den Rest seiner Zeit damit, das Haus
zu reparieren, die Felder zu bearbeiten, oder beim Ballspielen mit seinen Kindern.

1982 überzeugte der Regisseur Ralph Bakshi Frazetta, gemeinsam mit ihm an *Feuer und Eis*
zu arbeiten, einem Trickfilm auf der Grundlage von Frazettas Kunst. Auch wenn er damals ein
Misserfolg war – der Film von 1983 hat mittlerweile einen solchen Kultstatus erlangt, dass der Regisseur Robert Rodriguez (ein Frazetta-Freund und -Fan) an einem Remake als Realfilm arbeitet.

1986 eröffnete Frazetta in East Stroudsburg, Pennsylvania eine Galerie mit dem Namen
Frazetta's Fantasy Corner, in der Ellie seine Monografien und signierte Drucke verkaufte. Aufträge
für Buch- und Zeitschriftencover kamen immer seltener, doch die Nachfrage nach seinen
Originalwerken war hoch und steigerte sich noch bis in die 1990er-Jahre, als Frazettas Gesundheit
schwächelte. Es dauerte Jahre, bis eine Schilddrüsenüberfunktion diagnostiziert wurde, die 1995
zum ersten von vielen Schlaganfällen führte. Als die Schlaganfälle seine rechte Hand gefühllos
gemacht hatten, brachte er sich das Malen mit der Linken bei und arbeitete unermüdlich weiter.

2001 entwarf Frank das Frazetta Art Museum und baute es neben seinem Haus auf. Manche
Besucher hatten das Glück und erlebten den großen Künstler persönlich, wie er Hof hielt,
während Ellie Bücher, Drucke und T-Shirts verkaufte. Sie hatte sich stets um das Geschäftliche
gekümmert, und so war es verständlich, dass ihr Tod im Juli 2009 in jedem Bereich von Franks Leben und in dem ihrer Kinder eine Leere hinterließ. Das Museum wurde geschlossen, und Chaos
brach aus, das von einer nicht zu bändigenden Presse übertrieben und verfälscht dargestellt wurde.
Die Probleme waren bald gelöst, aber Frank, der nach Ellies Tod nach Florida übersiedelte, kehrte
nie wieder in das 38 Jahre lang gemeinsam bewohnte Haus zurück. Er starb, weniger als ein Jahr
später, am 10. Mai 2010.

Zwei Monate nach Frazettas Tod zahlte Kirk Hammett von Metallica der Familie für *Conan the
Adventurer* eine Million Dollar und erwarb damit eines der acht bis dahin unverkäuflichen Conan-
Gemälde. Die meisten anderen ikonischen Werke jedoch sind im Besitz der Familie geblieben, und
2015 wurde das Frazetta Art Museum unter der Leitung von Frank Junior wiedereröffnet. Es ist
wirklich sehenswert – falls Sie jemals in Ost-Pennsylvania sein sollten …

Opposite: Cover painting for the 21st-century edition of
L. Ron Hubbard's 1982 novel *Battlefield Earth*, "a Saga of
the Year 3000." Oil on board.

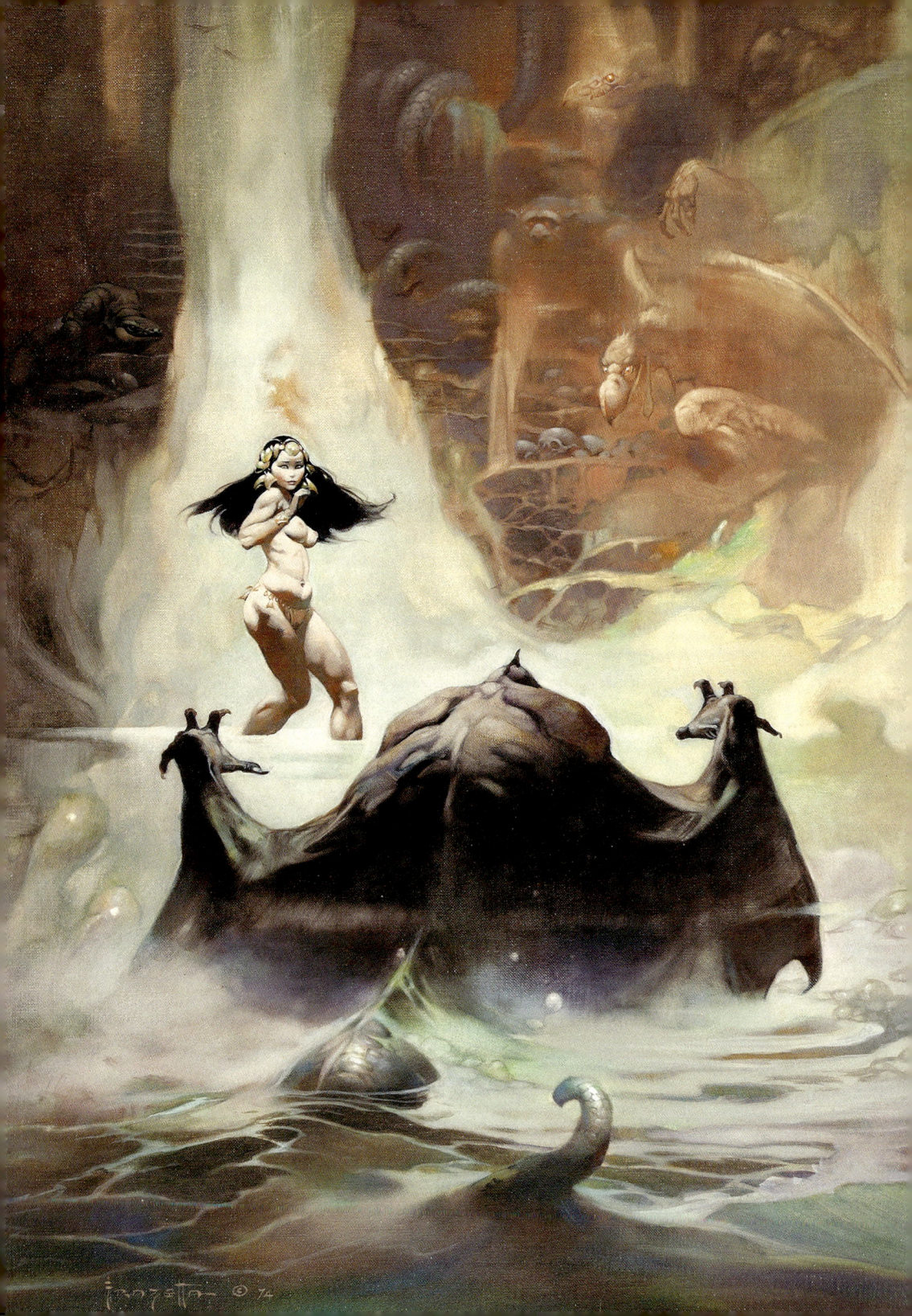

FRANK FRAZETTA
LE DIEU

« En matière d'art, j'ai suivi ma propre
voie et je ne me suis jamais conformé
à la tendance. »

Né Frank Frazzetta à Brooklyn en 1928, il ne tarde pas
à effacer un « z » de son patronyme par souci esthétique.
Son talent est inné, nourri par une grand-mère qui le récompense de quelques pièces pour chaque dessin achevé.
À 8 ans, il est accepté à la Brooklyn Academy of Fine Arts,
un établissement modeste, malgré son nom ronflant et son
tarif de 8 $ par mois, une somme considérable en pleine
Dépression. Leur seul enseignant, Michele Falanga, âgé de
69 ans en 1936, adore son plus jeune élève et Frazetta suit
fidèlement ses cours jusqu'à ses 15 ans ; il continue même
à fréquenter l'école après la mort de Falanga, alors qu'elle
est « devenue un genre de club », selon Frazetta, où les
élèves apprennent les uns des autres. Lorsque l'école ferme
ses portes, il trouve une place au studio Bernard Baily,
où l'artiste John Giunta le prend sous son aile et l'aide
à élaborer son improbable superhéros *Snowman* pour un
hors-série de Tally-Ho Comics (décembre 1944). Il travaille ensuite pour Treasure Comics et en 1947 il reprend
Looie Lazybones, une contrefaçon de *Li'l Abner* publiée chez Standard Comics. Il remerciera plus
tard le directeur artistique de Standard Ralph Mayo de lui avoir enseigné l'anatomie, ou plutôt de
lui avoir tendu un manuel d'anatomie, qu'il a recopié entièrement en une nuit, ce qui a grandement
profité à l'allure de Looie et de son acolyte péquenaude Clarabelle.

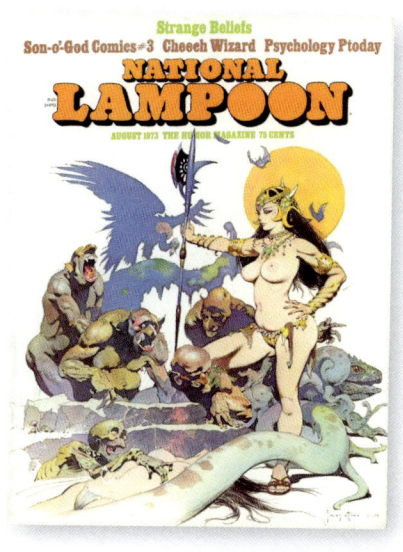

En 1948, Frazetta, tout juste âgé de 20 ans, est un artiste établi, qui signe des bandes dessinées
de western, de mystère, historiques et fantasy pour Famous Funnies, Heroic Comics, EC Comics,
National Comics, Avon Comics et d'autres. On ignore s'il a trouvé le temps de terminer le lycée.
Une autre zone d'ombre entoure sa soi-disant sélection par les New York Giants dans les années –
barrez les mentions inutiles – 1940, 1950 ou 1960. La version la plus probable est qu'il aurait été
remarqué en 1947 et qu'ils lui auraient proposé d'intégrer leur centre de formation au Texas, offre
qu'il aurait déclinée parce que 1) il avait une petite amie et 2) il aurait fallu qu'il quitte Brooklyn.
Beau gosse, athlétique et charismatique comme il était – il se vantait de ne pas passer une journée
sans sexe –, l'histoire de la petite amie est très crédible, tout autant que la répugnance d'un gosse de

Opposite: At the Earth's Core, for the 1974 Ace Books'
edition of the Edgar Rice Burroughs novel about Dian
the Beautiful. Oil on canvas board, 74.9 x 54.6 cm
(29.5 x 21.5 inches).

Above: Frazetta produced three covers for
National Lampoon: April 1971, June 1972,
and this, the most provocative, for August 1973.

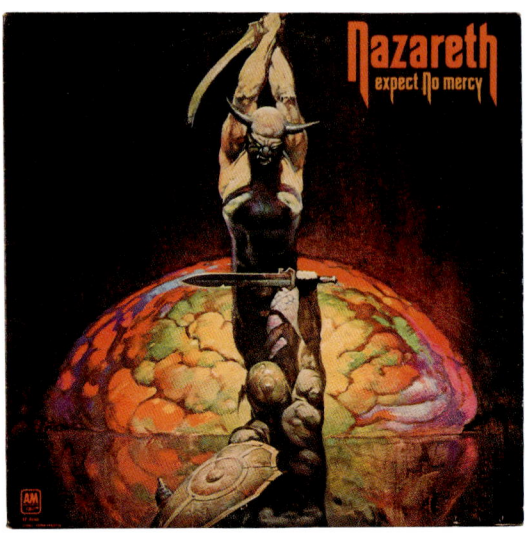

Brooklyn pour le Texas. Il a aussi souligné, des années plus tard, que la ligue mineure de baseball se résumait à des trajets interminables en car pour une paye ridicule.

Frazetta met un terme à sa carrière de playboy en 1952, quand il rencontre Eleanor « Ellie » Kelly, alors âgée de 17 ans. Ils se marient en 1956 et font quatre enfants : Alfonso, appelé Frank Junior, William, Heidi et Holly. En 1954, il travaille à plein temps avec Al Capp sur *Li'l Abner* et, sa famille s'agrandissant, il garde cet emploi stable jusqu'en 1962, quand Capp réduit son salaire. Frazetta démissionne et traverse une période de vaches maigres. Les éditeurs refusent sa BD *Sweet Adeline* et quand il tente de revenir aux comics il s'entend dire que son style est trop « vieux jeu ». Il peint des nus pour plusieurs magazines masculins (seulement trois de ces œuvres nous sont parvenues) et des illustrations pour la collection de livres de poche pour adultes de Midwood Books. Fin 1962, son ami Roy Krenkel lui trouve enfin du travail chez Ace Books, pour réaliser des couvertures et des illustrations spot sur une série de romans d'Edgar Rice Burroughs – principalement des histoires de Tarzan. Chez Ace, il parfait son style fantasy et décroche aussitôt des commandes pour Lancer Books, Canaveral Press et Fawcett Publications.

Le secteur des comics aussi reprend contact quand Warren Publishing lance son magazine d'horreur *Creepy* inspiré d'EC Comics en 1964 et que sortent ensuite *Blazing Combat* (1965), *Eerie* (1966) et *Vampirella* (1969). Frazetta réalise 32 couvertures mémorables pour ces quatre titres, notamment la couverture mythique du premier numéro de *Vampirella*. Il collabore aussi avec *MAD* et c'est un portrait de Ringo Starr qu'il brosse en 1964 dans une parodie de pub pour le shampooing Breck qui lui vaut sa première demande d'affiche de film, pour *Quoi de neuf, Pussycat ?* (*What's New Pussycat ?* en 1965). Il en signe treize autres en cinq ans, puis conçoit des visuels pour des pochettes de bandes originales et celle du quatrième album de Herman's Hermits.

C'est alors que Conan entre en scène. Jusqu'alors Frazetta travaillait « à la commande » ce qui dans le droit américain permettait aux éditeurs de conserver ses originaux. Tout change en 1966 quand Lancer lui confie les couvertures de la première collection complète des aventures de Conan en format poche. Frazetta accepte à la condition expresse de conserver les droits sur ses originaux ; il crée ensuite huit œuvres sensationnelles, de la trempe de celles qui font une carrière, entre celle pour *Conan l'Aventurier* (*Conan the Adventurer*, 1966) et sa dernière pour *Conan le Boucanier* (*Conan the Buccaneer*, 1971). Son Conan est devenu *le* Conan – primitif, musculeux et ténébreux – qui inspirera Dino De Laurentiis pour son film *Conan le Barbare* et le choix du champion de culturisme Arnold Schwarzenegger pour le rôle titre. Frazetta fait grimper la valeur de ses couvertures pour Conan – et attise la convoitise des collectionneurs – en refusant de vendre aucune des huit.

Above: Nazareth licensed the art created for *Eerie* No. 8, March 1967, for its 1977 *Expect No Mercy* album cover.

Opposite: The Silver Warrior, for the cover of Michael Moorcock's 1977 Random House paperback novel. Oil on board, 1976.

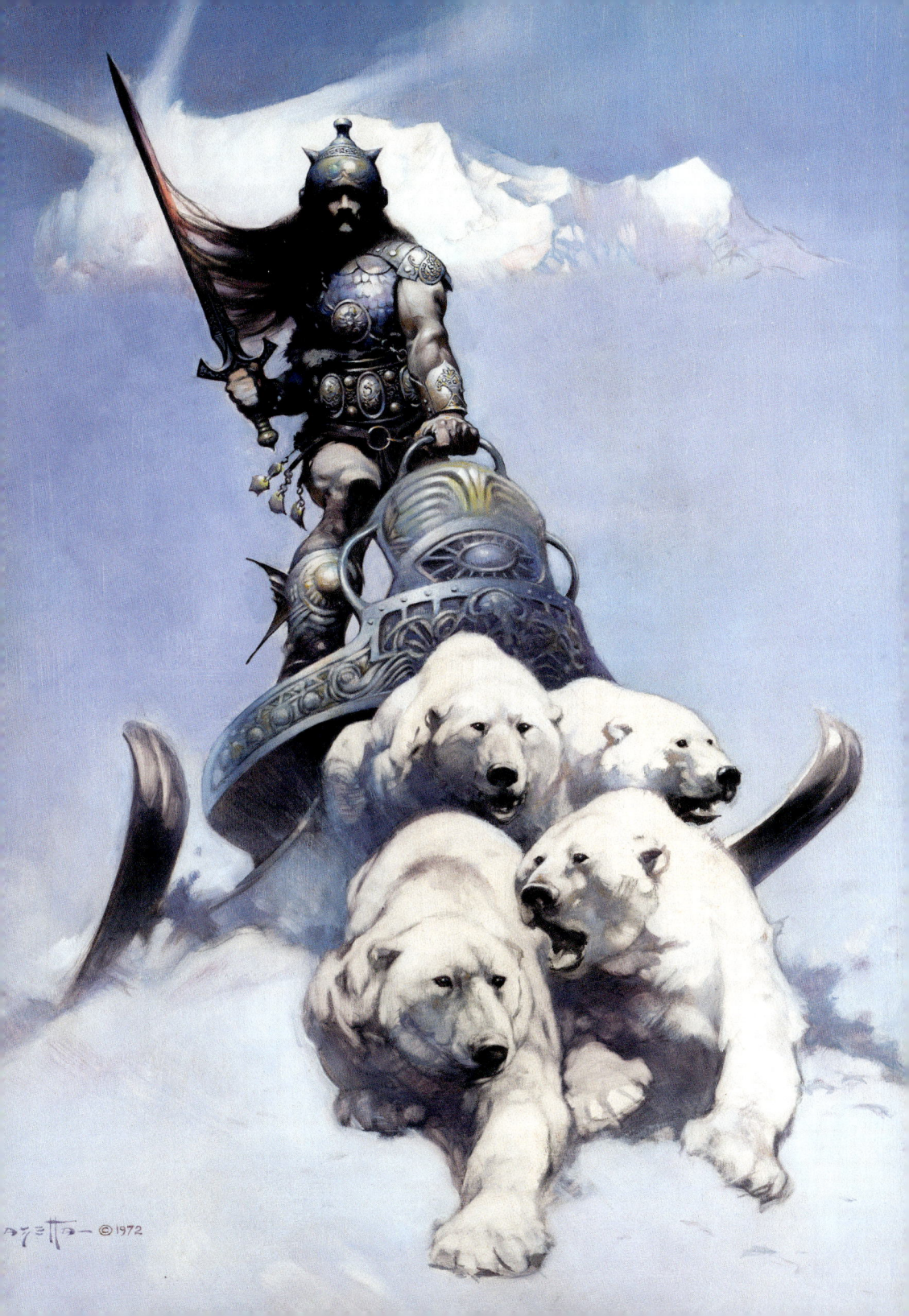

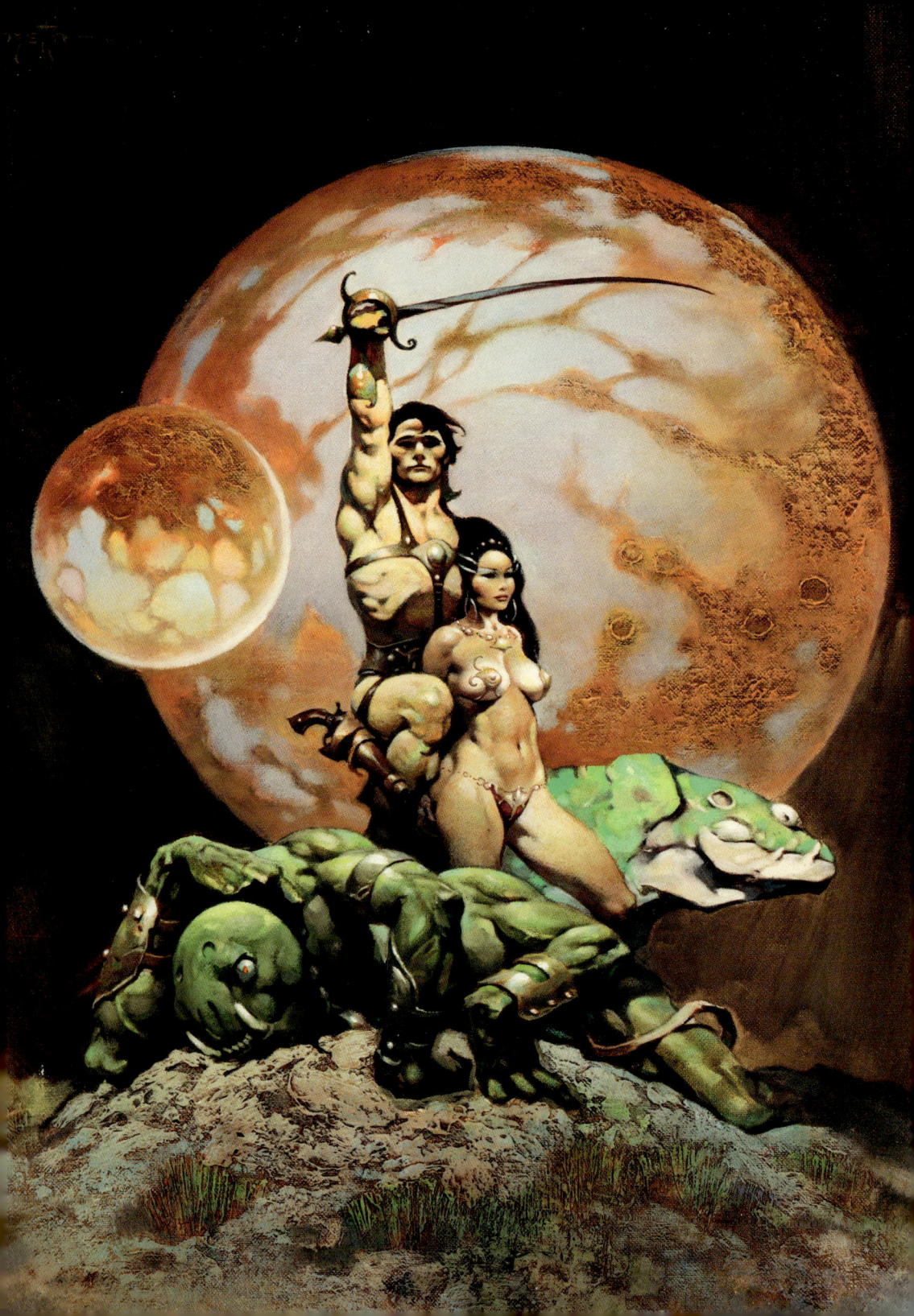

Grâce au beau travail abattu dans les années 1960, Frazetta acquiert une ferme délabrée sur 35 hectares de terrain dans les Poconos, en Pennsylvanie, en 1971. Les commandes continuent à tomber pour des couvertures de livres et de magazines, notamment plusieurs pour *National Lampoon* ; il réalise huit autres affiches de films, des pochettes de disque pour Molly Hatchet et Nazareth, et publie ses trois premières monographies. Il travaille si vite qu'il peut terminer une toile en une seule nuit, ce qui signifie qu'il peut gagner une semaine de salaire en quelques heures et passer le reste de son temps à rénover la maison, nettoyer le terrain ou jouer au ballon avec ses enfants.

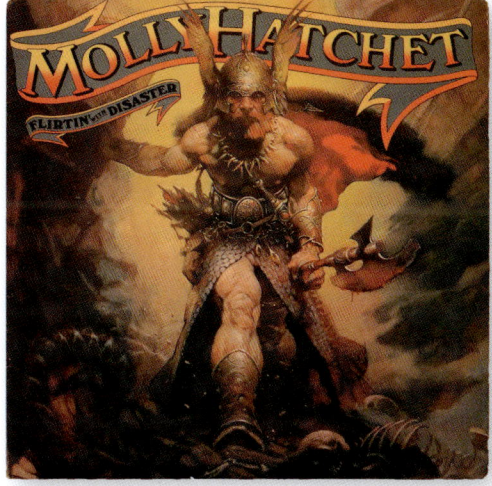

En 1982, le réalisateur Ralph Bakshi convainc Frazetta de s'associer à lui sur le long-métrage animé *Tygra, la glace et le feu (Fire and Ice)*. Descendu en flammes à sa sortie en 1983, il est devenu tellement culte que le réalisateur Robert Rodriguez – ami et fan de Frazetta – a décidé d'en faire un film.

En 1986, Frazetta ouvre sa galerie à East Stroudsburg, en Pennsylvanie, Frazetta's Fantasy Corner, où Ellie vend ses monographies et des tirages dédicacés. Les commandes des éditeurs et magazines se tarissent, mais la demande d'œuvres originales est forte et continue de croître au début des années 1990, tandis que la santé de Frazetta vacille. Avec des années de retard, les médecins lui diagnostiquent une hyperthyroïdie, qui provoque la première d'une longue série d'attaques en 1995. Quand ces attaques engourdissent sa main droite, il apprend à peindre de la gauche et poursuit sa route vaillamment.

En 2001, Frank conçoit et fait bâtir le Frazetta Art Museum à côté de sa maison. L'heureux visiteur y rencontre le grand artiste en personne, qui tient salon tandis qu'Ellie vend livres, tirages et T-shirts. C'est elle qui s'est toujours occupée de l'aspect financier, si bien que sa mort en 2009 laisse un vide immense dans toutes les sphères de la vie de Frank et de leurs enfants. Le musée ferme et le chaos s'installe, exagéré et falsifié par une presse délirante. Les problèmes sont bientôt réglés, mais Frank, qui a décampé en Floride à la mort d'Ellie, ne reviendra jamais dans ce qui a été leur foyer pendant 38 ans. Il meurt moins d'un an plus tard, le 10 mai 2010.

Deux mois après la mort de Frazetta, Kirk Hammett de Metallica payait un million de dollars pour l'original de *Conan l'Aventurier*, brisant finalement le lien d'exclusivité entre ces huit couvertures mythiques, mais la plupart des autres œuvres majeures du maître sont restées dans le giron familial et en 2015 le Frazetta Art Museum a rouvert ses portes, sous la direction de Frank Junior. C'est un endroit plutôt génial, si vous passez un jour dans l'est de la Pennsylvanie.

Opposite: Princess of Mars, for the cover of Doubleday's 1970 hardback edition of the Edgar Rice Burroughs classic. Oil on board.

Above: Molly Hatchet produced three albums featuring glorious Frazetta artwork. The first was *Molly Hatchet,* 1978, with *Death Dealer,* followed by this, *Flirtin' With Disaster,* in '79, with the painting *Dark Kingdom,* and finally *Beatin' the Odds,* with *Conan the Conquerer,* in 1980.

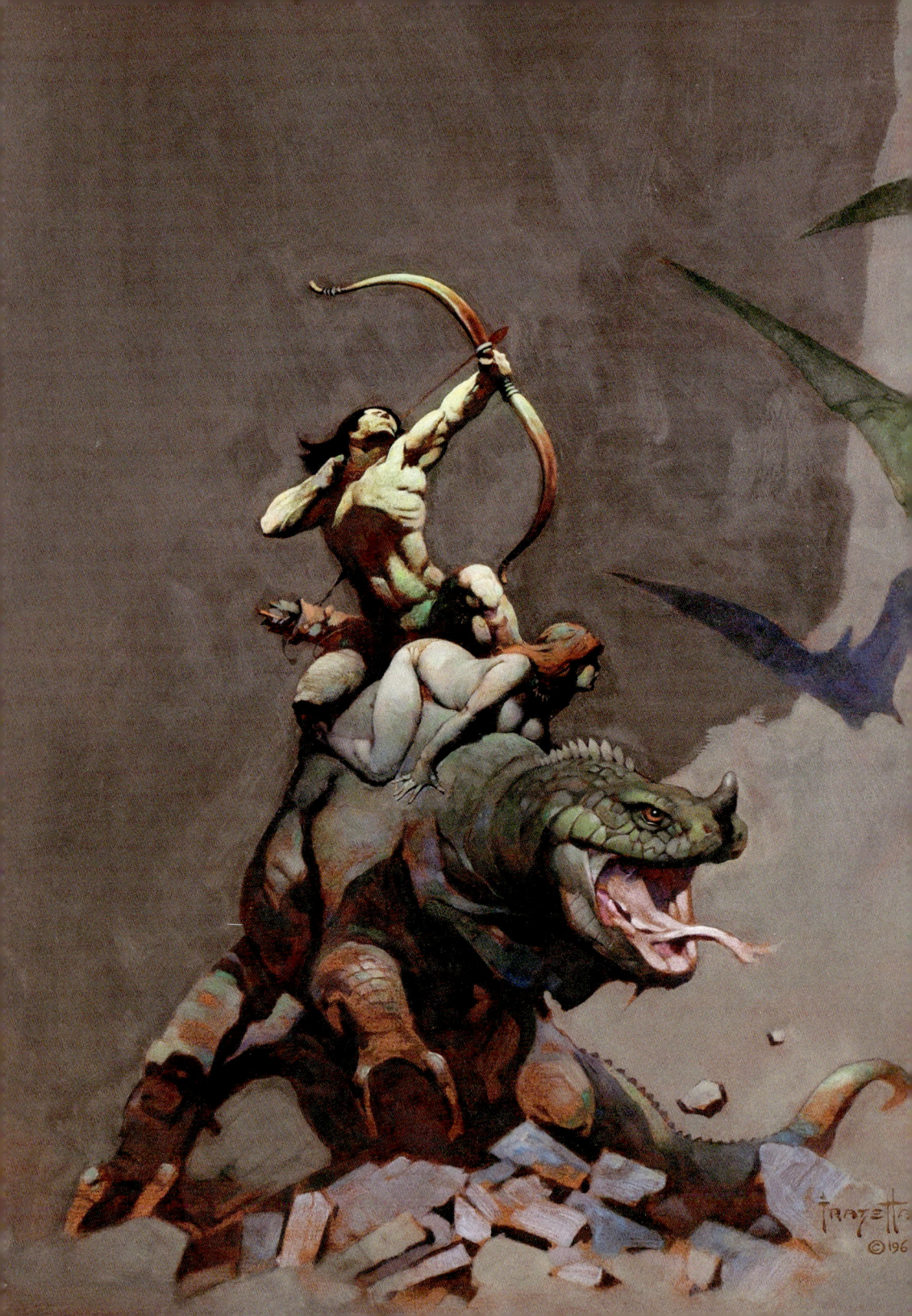

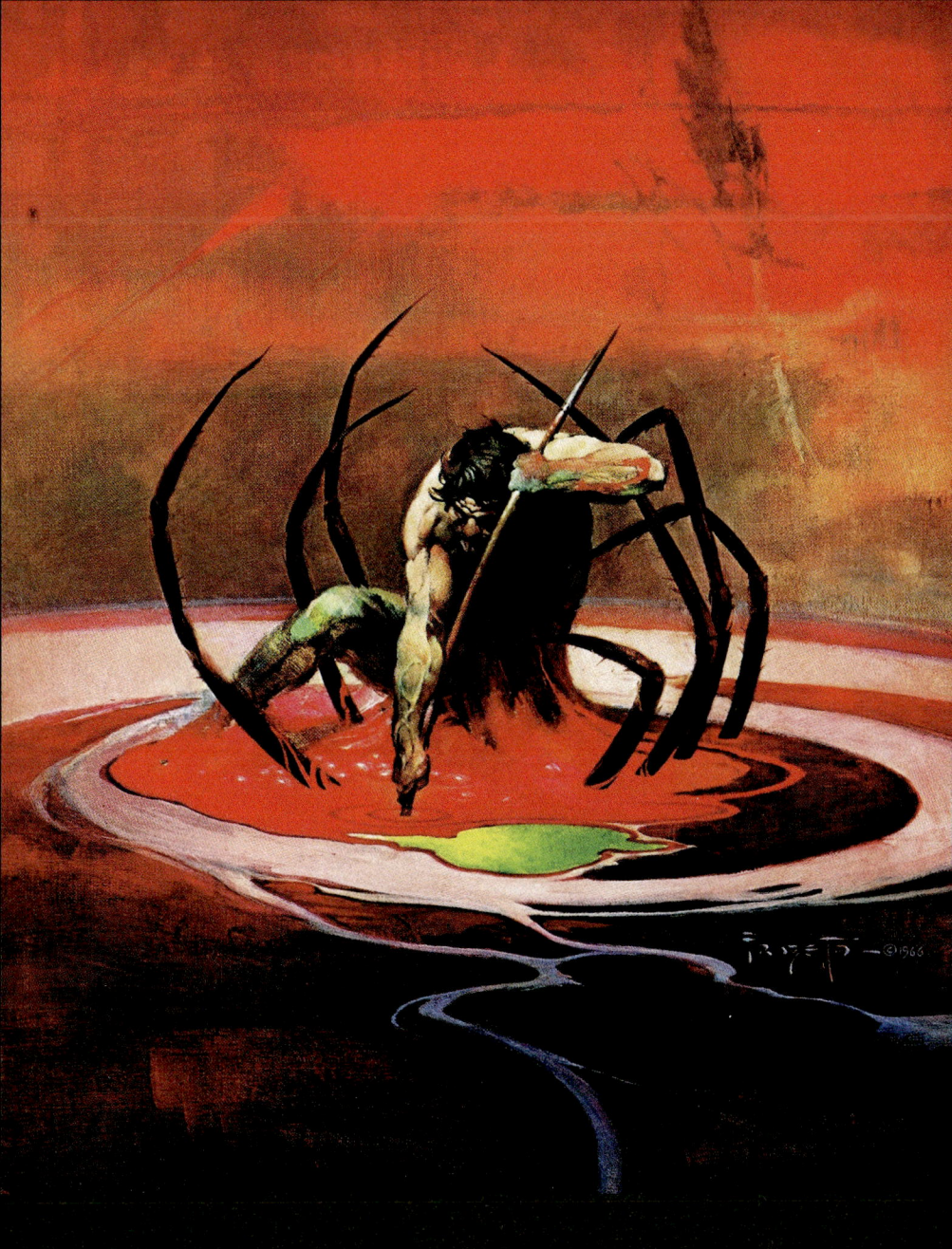

Opposite: Jongor Fights Back, for the 1967 Popular Library edition of Robert Moore Williams's novel. Frazetta painted covers for three Jongor novels, with this perhaps the best. Oil on Masonite, 60.3 x 39.3 cm (23.75 x 15.5 inches).

Above: Spiderman, for the cover of the Warner Books edition of Bob Shaw's *Night Walk*. Oil on board, 1966.

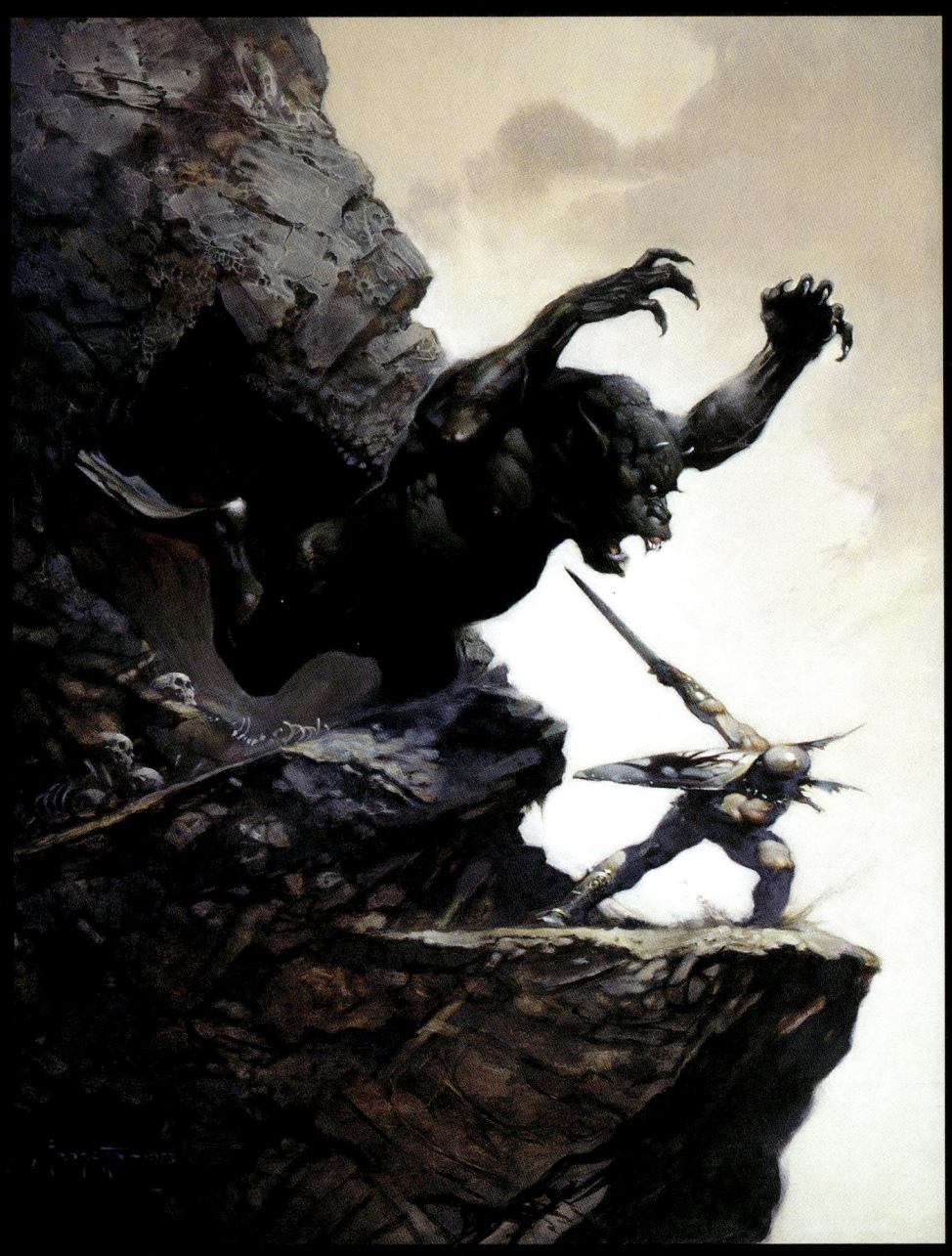

Above: The Cave Demon, for the cover of
Death Angel's Shadow, part of Karl Edward
Wagner's *Kane* series, in 1978. Oil on board.

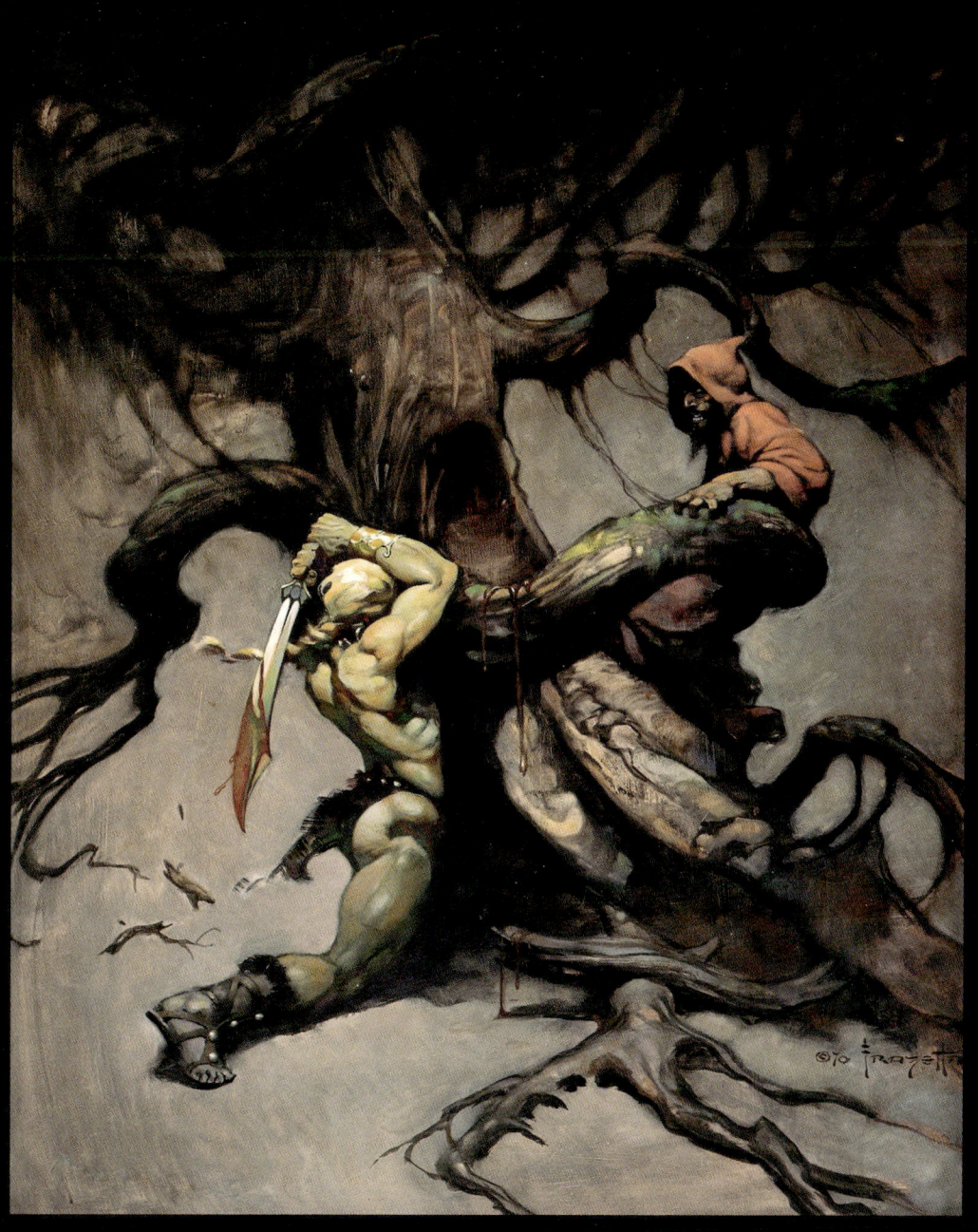

Above: Tree of Death, used on the cover of
Flashing Swords! No. 2, 1973. Oil on board, 1970,
49.5 x 40 cm (19.5 x 15.75 inches).

FRANK FRAZETTA

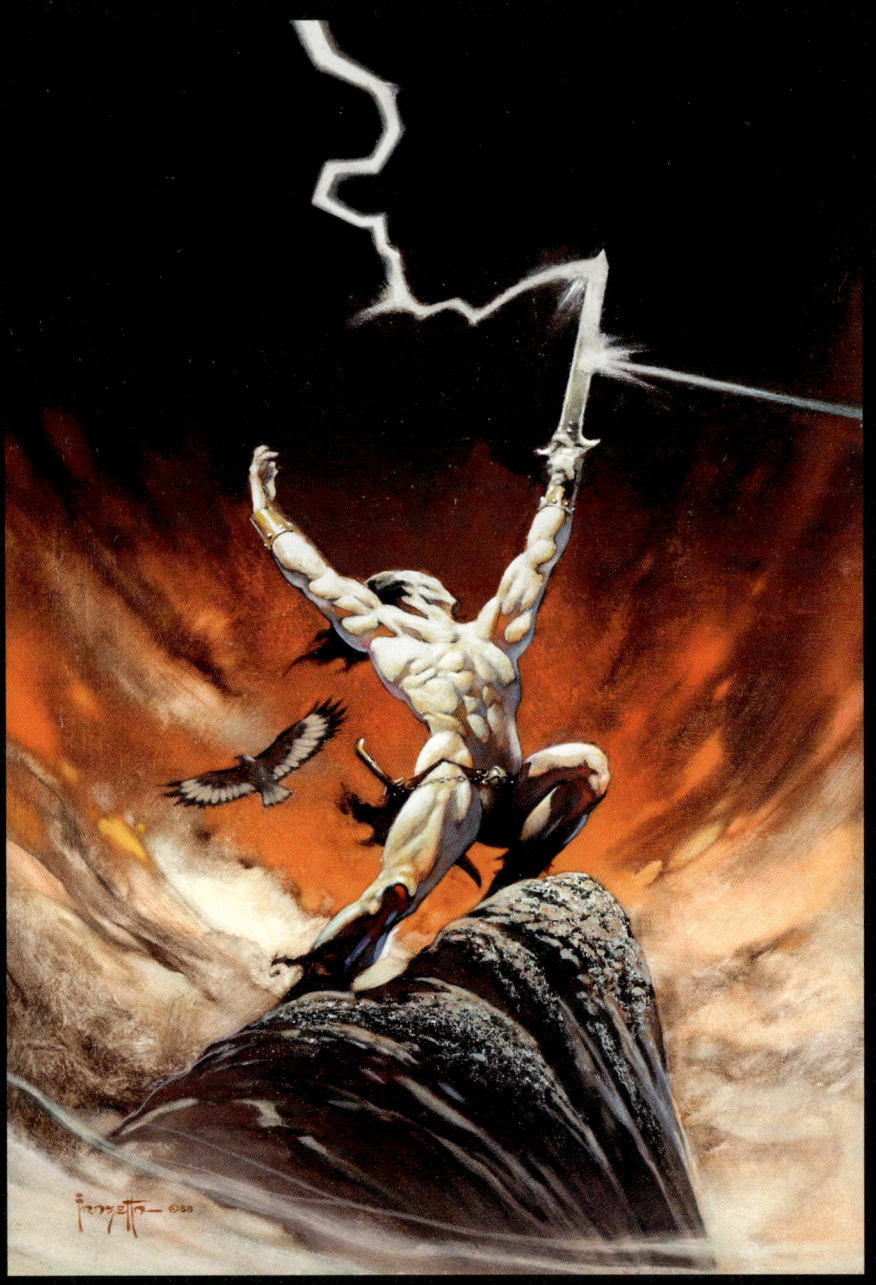

Above: The Tempest, for a computer ad campaign,
oil on Masonite, 1988, 61 x 41.9 cm (24 x 16.5 inches).

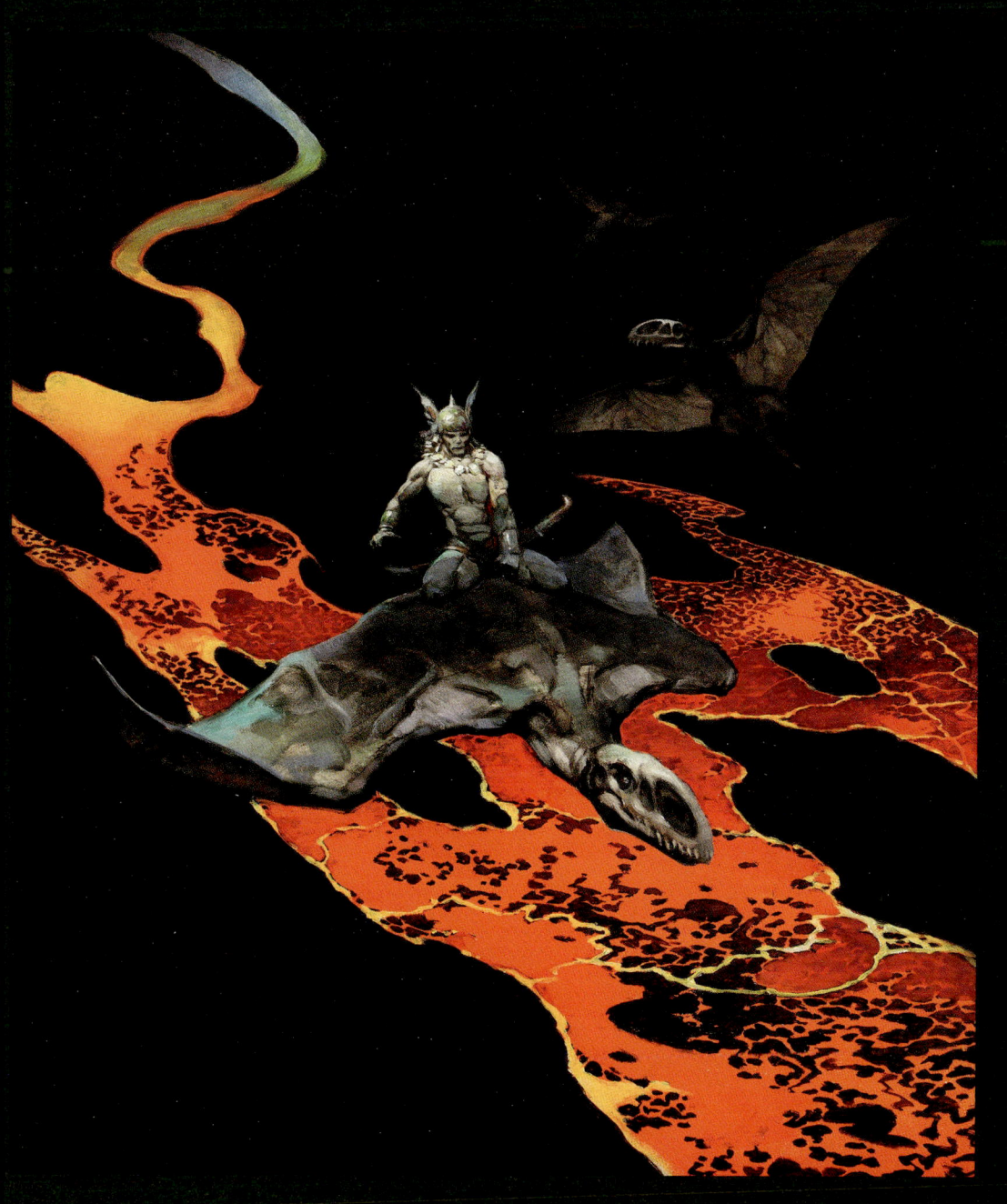

Above: Thor's Flight, for the cover of Lin Carter's
Thongor in the City of Magicians, 1968. Oil on
canvas board, 60.9 x 50.8 cm (24 x 20 inches).
Courtesy of Heritage Auctions.

FRANK FRAZETTA

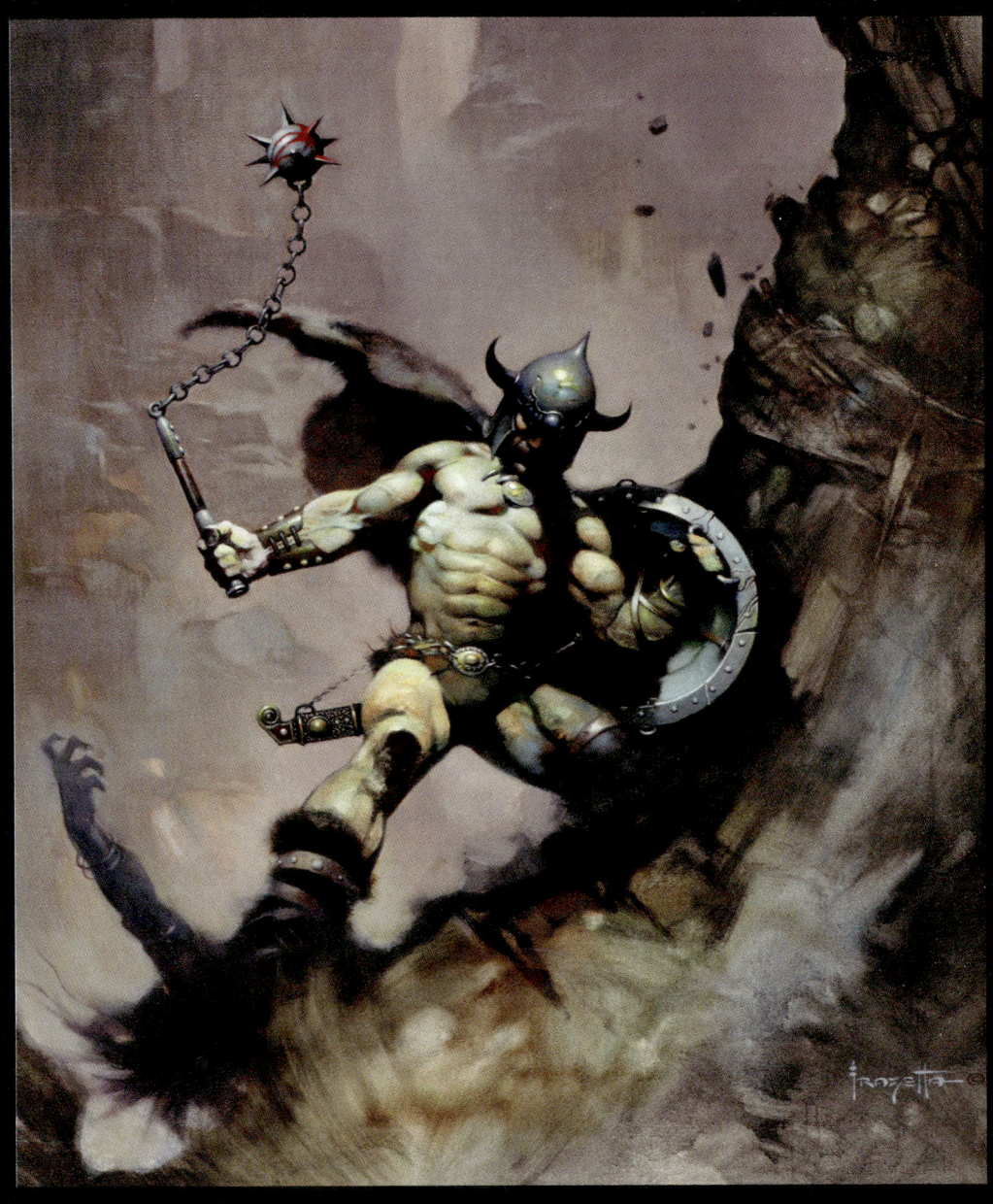

Above: Warrior with Ball and Chain, for the anthology
Flashing Swords! No. 1, from Dell Books, 1973.
Oil on board, 58.4 x 48.2 cm (23 x 19 inches). Courtesy
of Heritage Auctions.

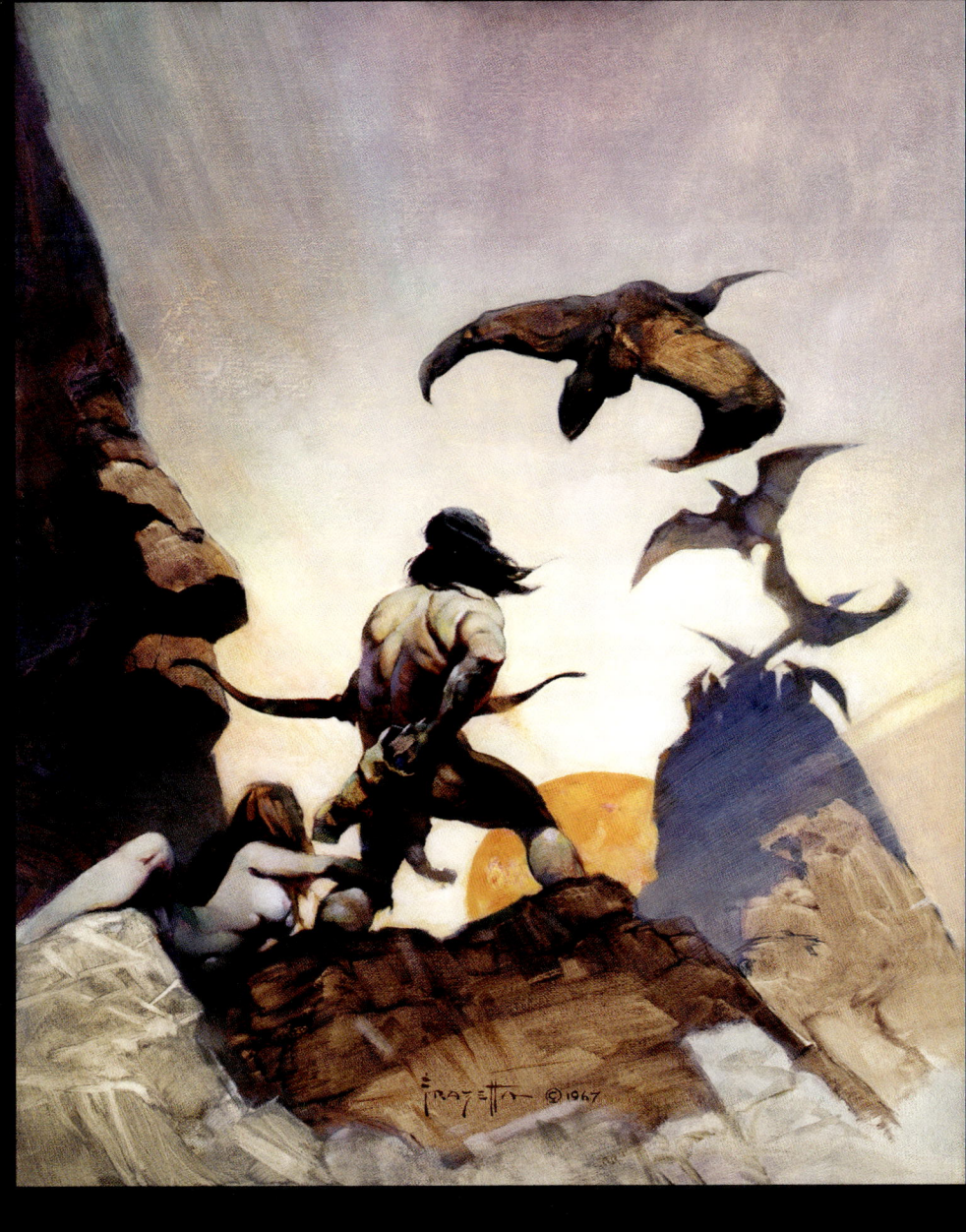

Above: Jongor Fights Back, for the cover of Robert
Moore Williams's novel of the same name. Oil on
Masonite, 1967, 60.3 x 39.3 cm (23.75 x 15.5 inches).

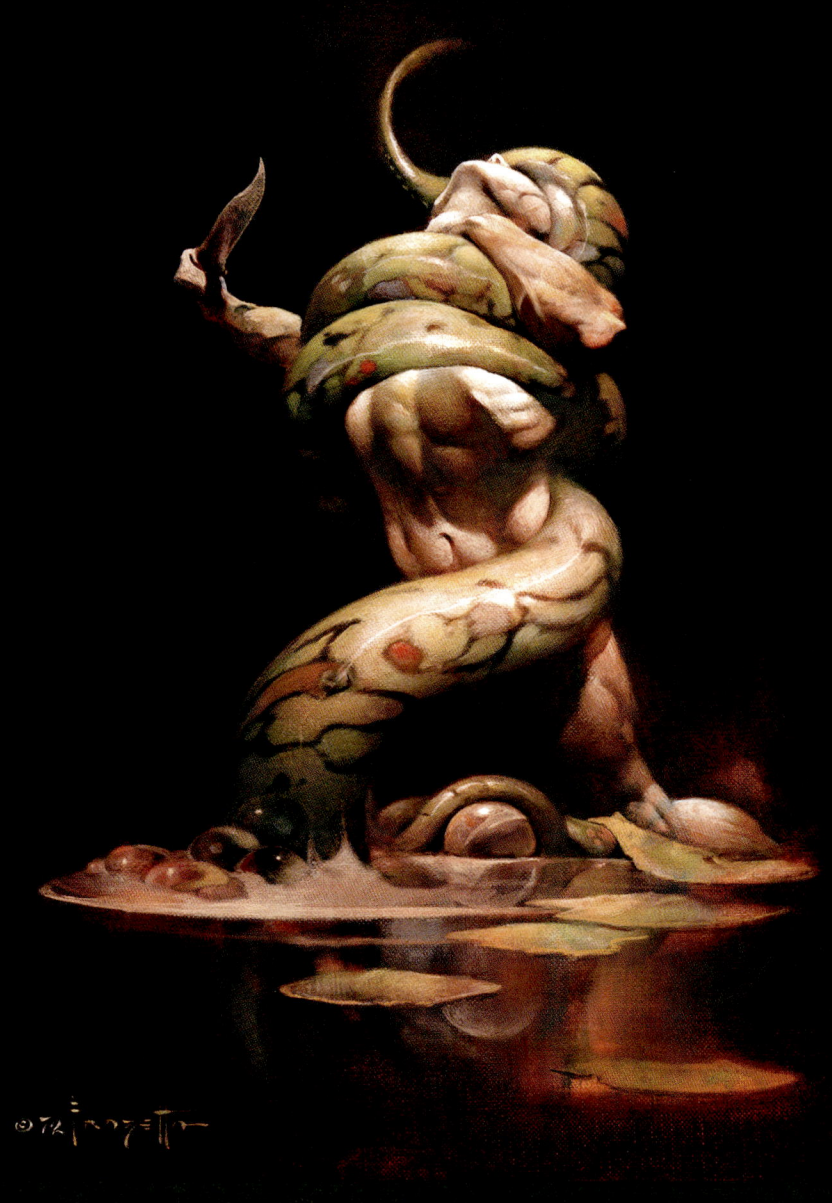

Above: The Serpent, for the cover of Andrew Offutt's 1973 Dell paperback, *Ardor on Aros.* Oil on board.

Opposite: Bloodstone, for the cover of Karl Edward Wagner's 1976 novel, oil on board, 47 x 30.4 cm (18.5 x 12 inches).

MASTERPIECES OF FANTASY ART

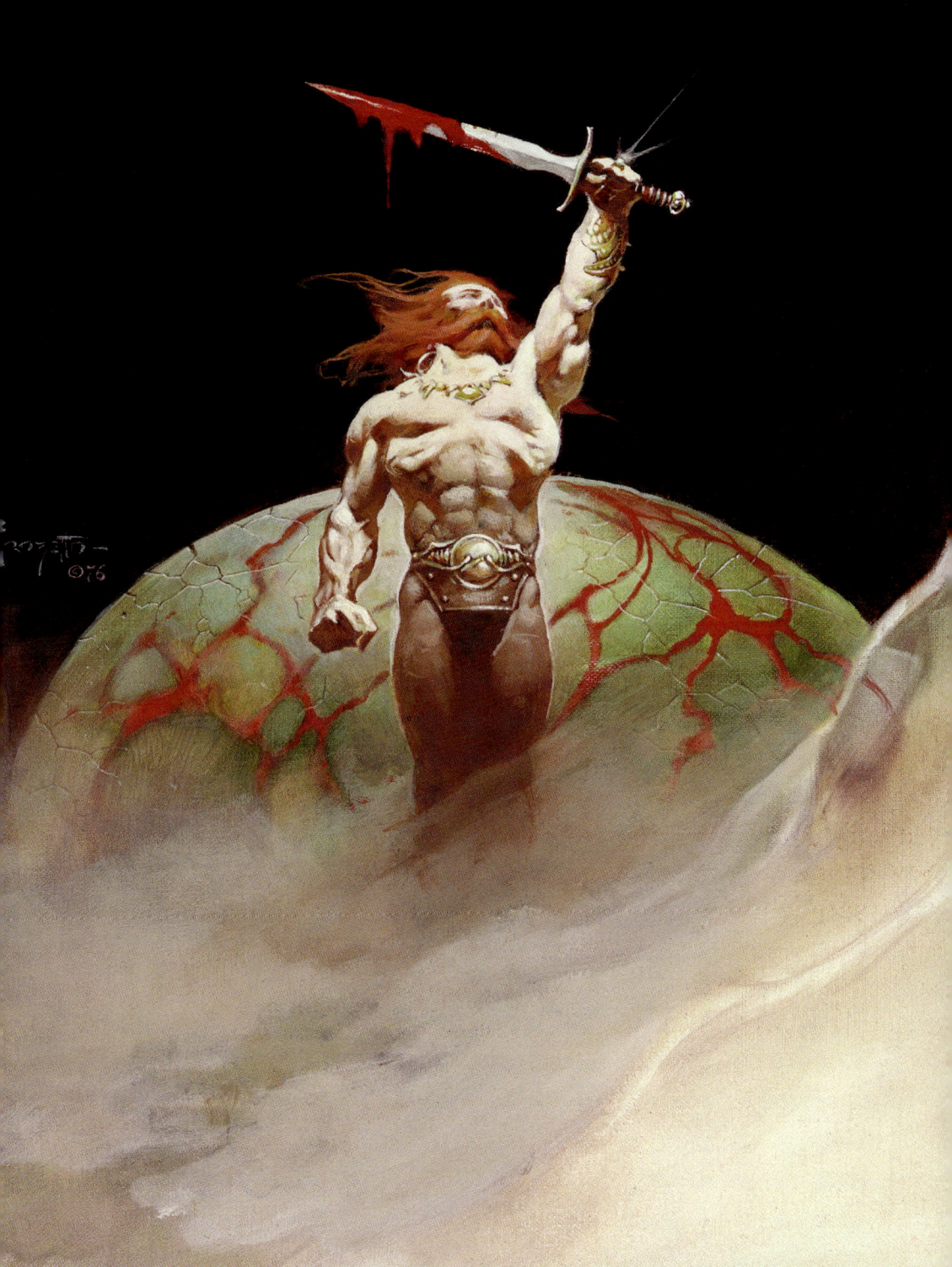

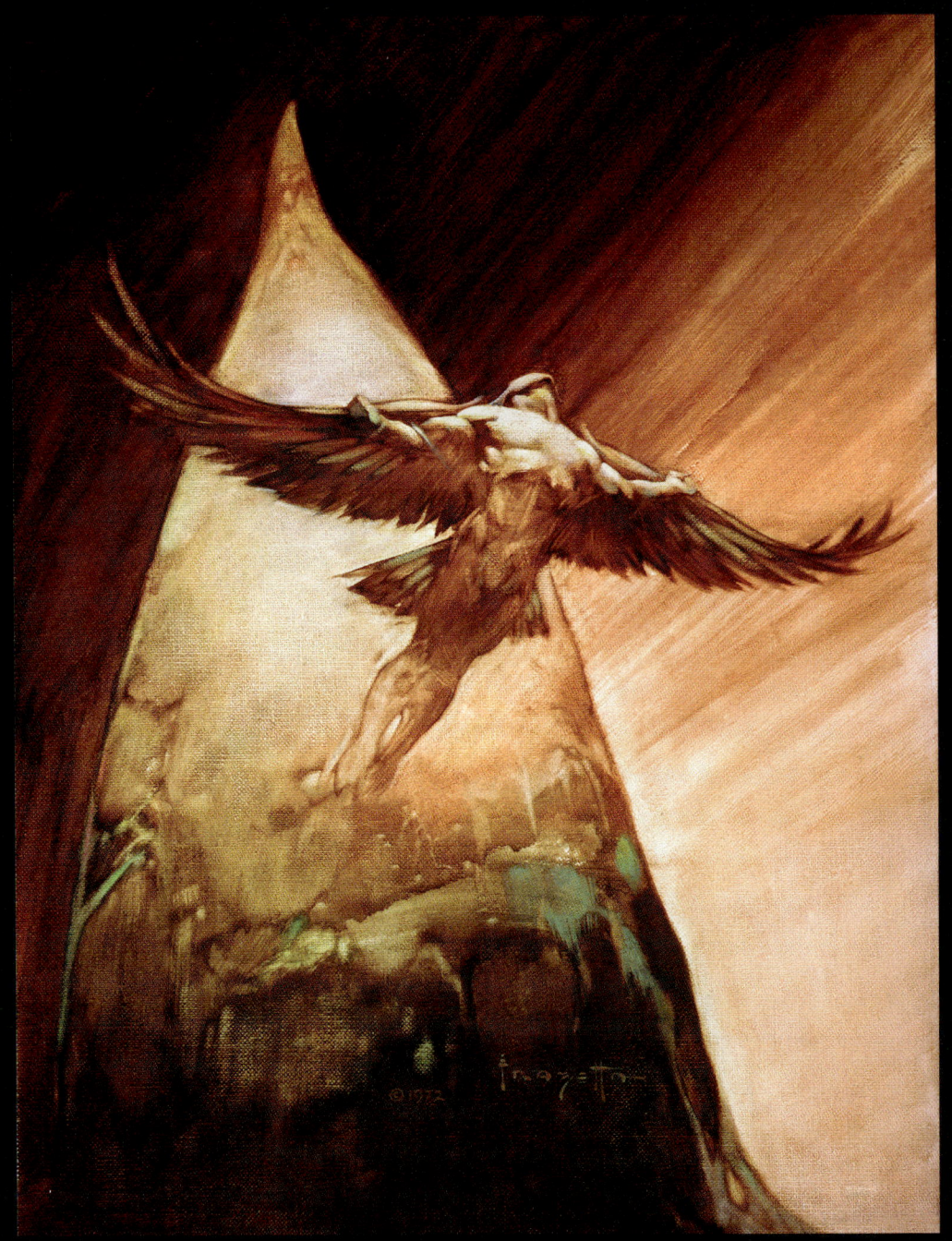

Above: The Flight of Icarus, also known as *Birdman*. Oil on board, 1972.

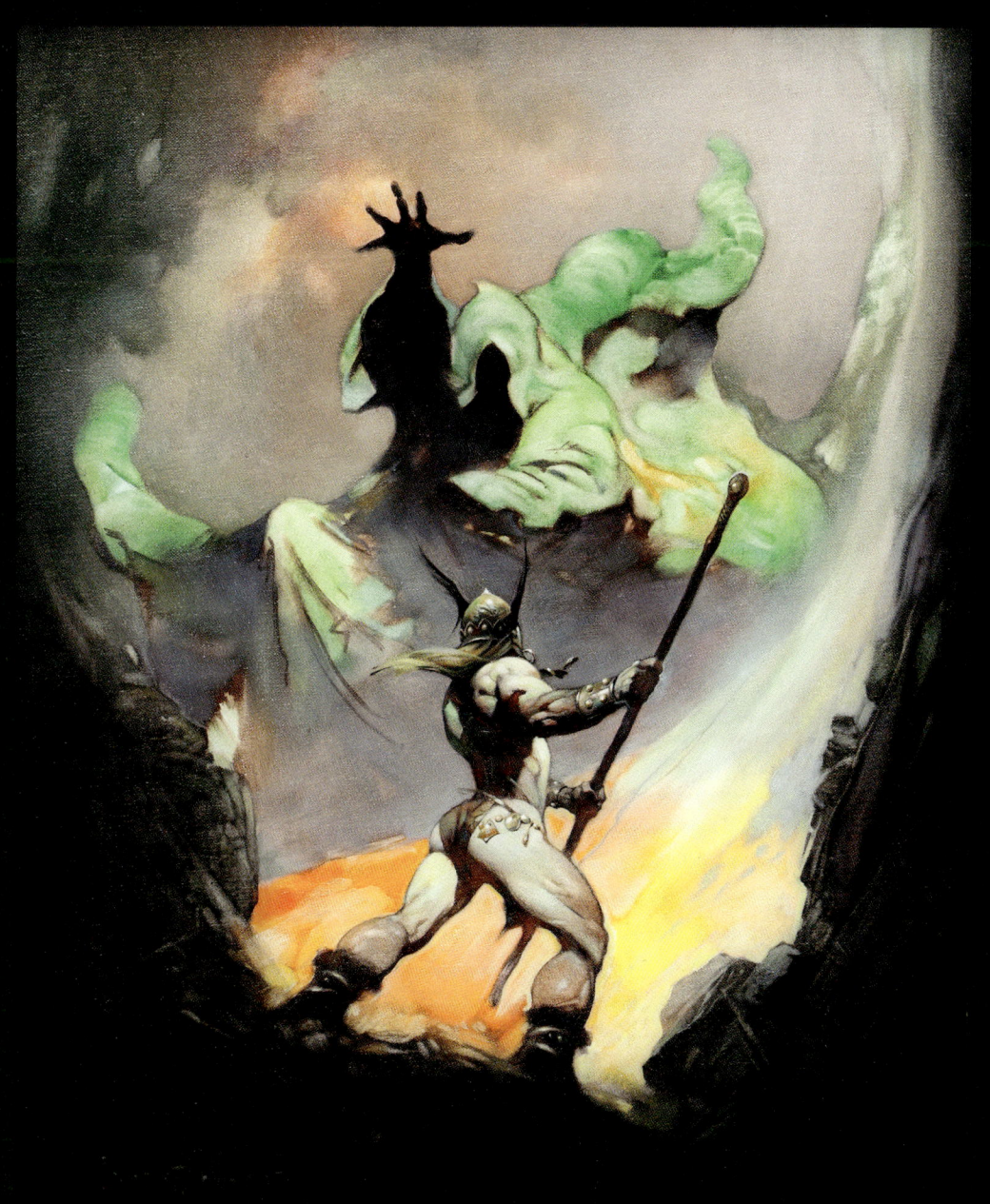

Above: The Norseman, for the cover of
Flashing Swords! No. 1, oil on board, 1972,
59.6 x 44.4 cm (23.5 x 17.5 inches).

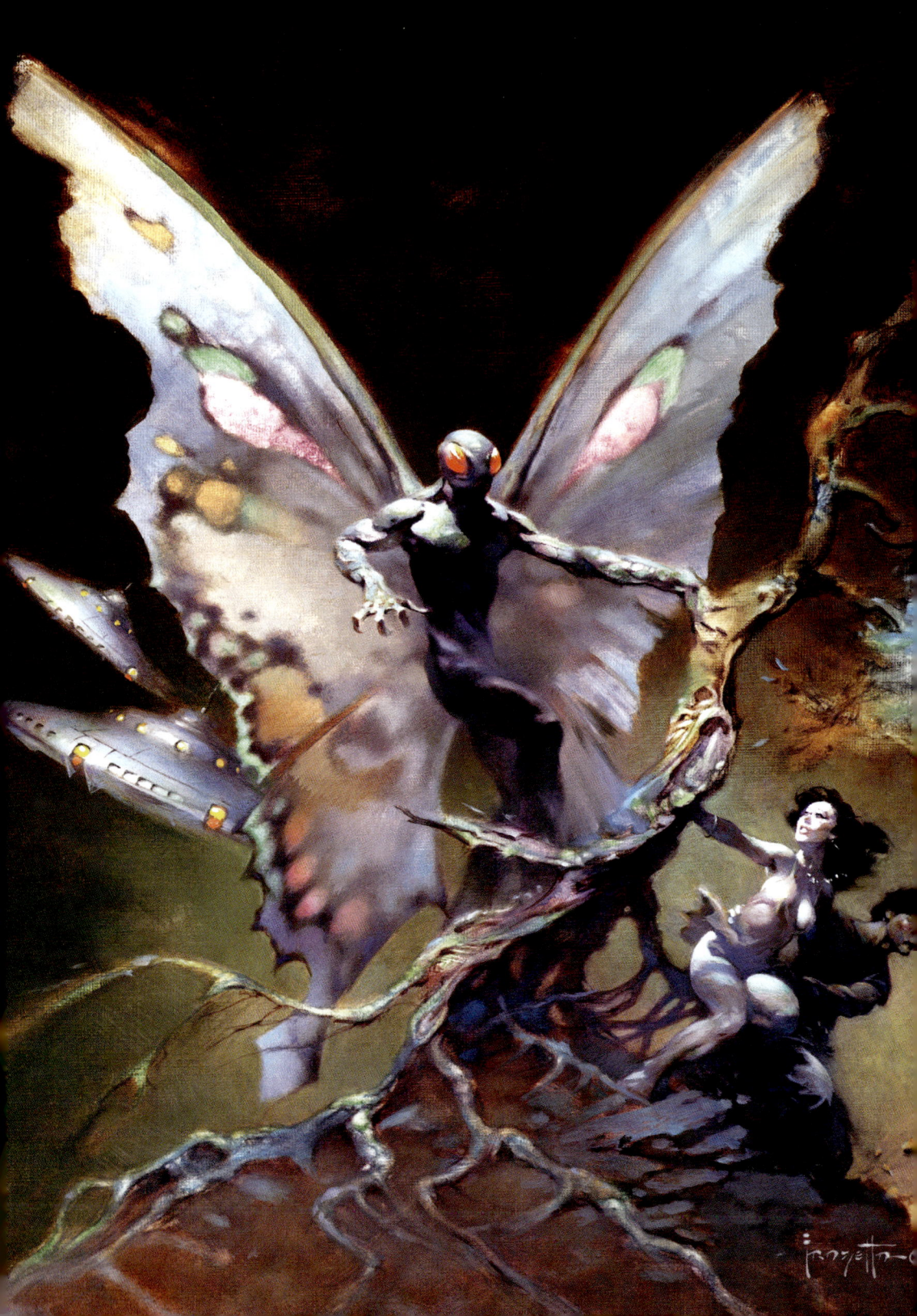

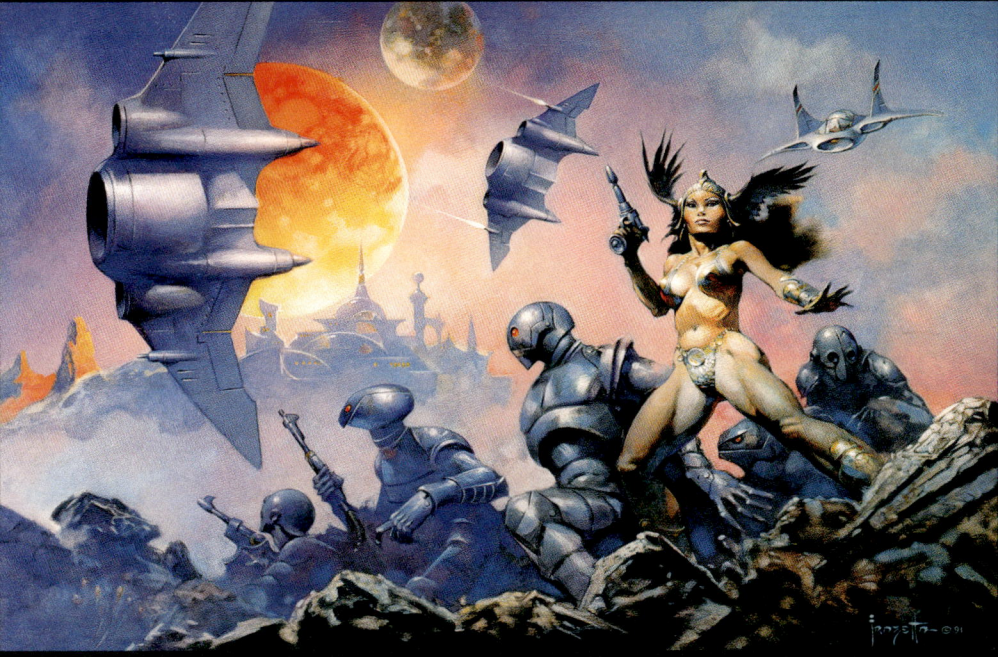

Opposite: The Mothman, for the May 1980 cover of *High Times* magazine, to illustrate a story titled "Beware of the Mothman." It later appeared on the cover of John Keel's *The Mothman Prophesies,* 1991. Oil on board.

Above: Dawn Attack, for the wraparound cover of the 1991 paperback *L. Ron Hubbard Presents Writers of the Future* No. 7, a compilation of winners of the annual Writers of the Future competition established by Hubbard in 1985. Oil on board.

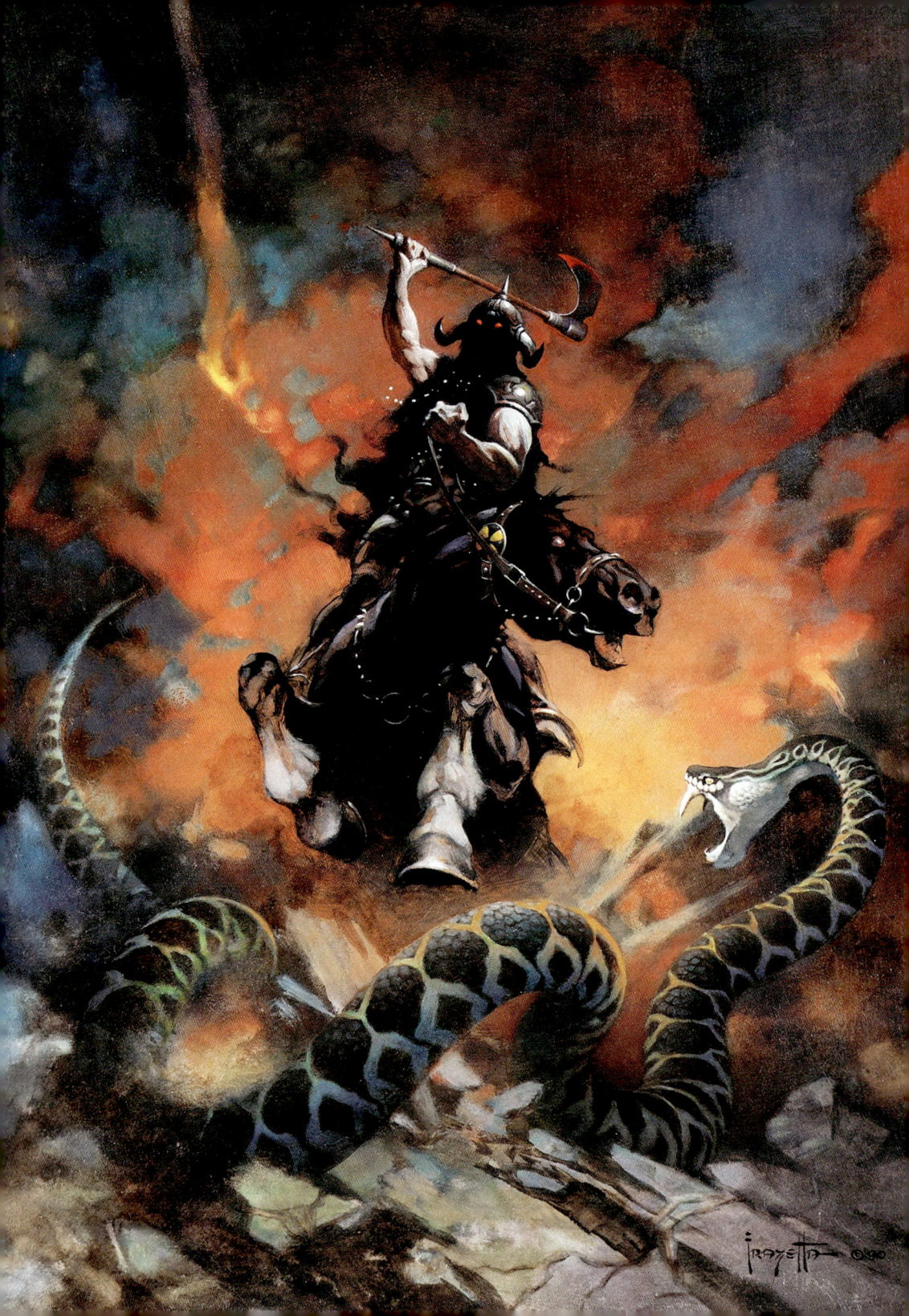

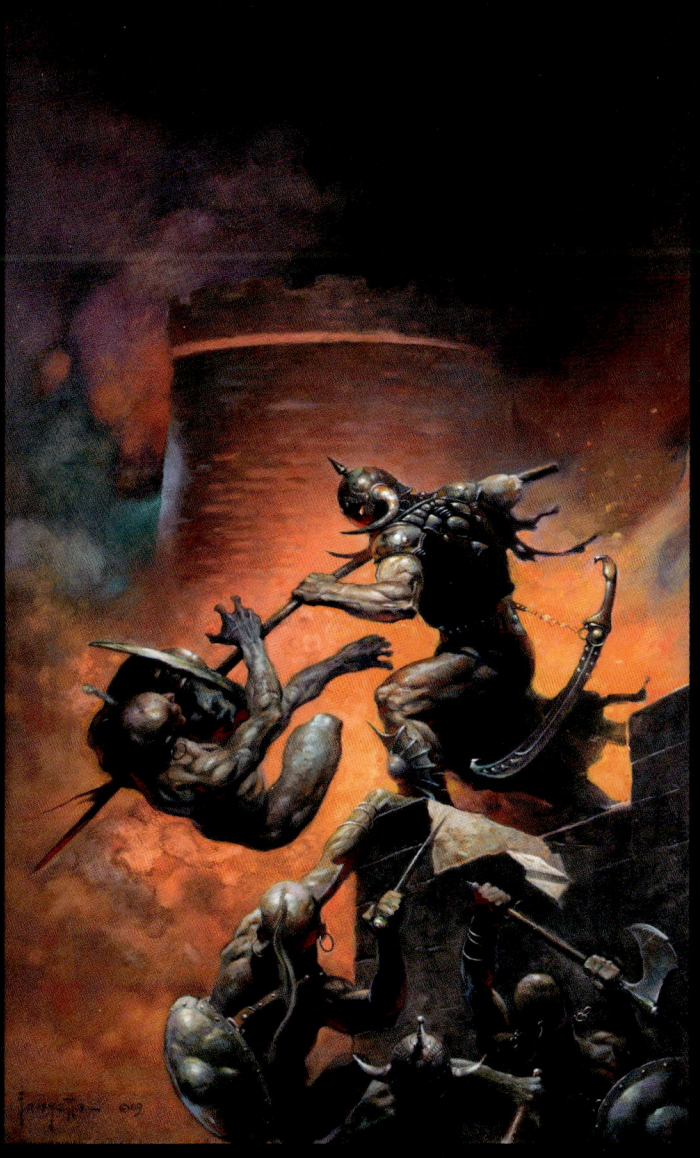

Opposite: Death Dealer No. 6, the last of Frazetta's *Death Dealer* paintings, was used on the cover of the *Death Dealer No. 6* comic, 2007. Oil on Masonite, 1996, 76.2 x 45.7 cm (30 x 18 inches). Courtesy of Heritage Auctions.

Above: Death Dealer No. 5, for the cover of Jim Silke's *Death Dealer Plague of Knives* novel, 1990, and on Yngwie Malmsteen's 2001 *War To End All Wars* album. Oil on board.

Following left: The Swamp Demon, for John Jakes's *Witch of the Dark Gate*, 1972, and repurposed by Joshua Ortega, Josh Medors, and Jay Fotos in 2008 for *Swamp Demon*, a one-shot comic book. Oil on board.

Following right: A self-portrait for the story "Came the Dawn," scheduled for EC Comics' *Shock Illustrated* No. 4, 1956. The issue was never published.

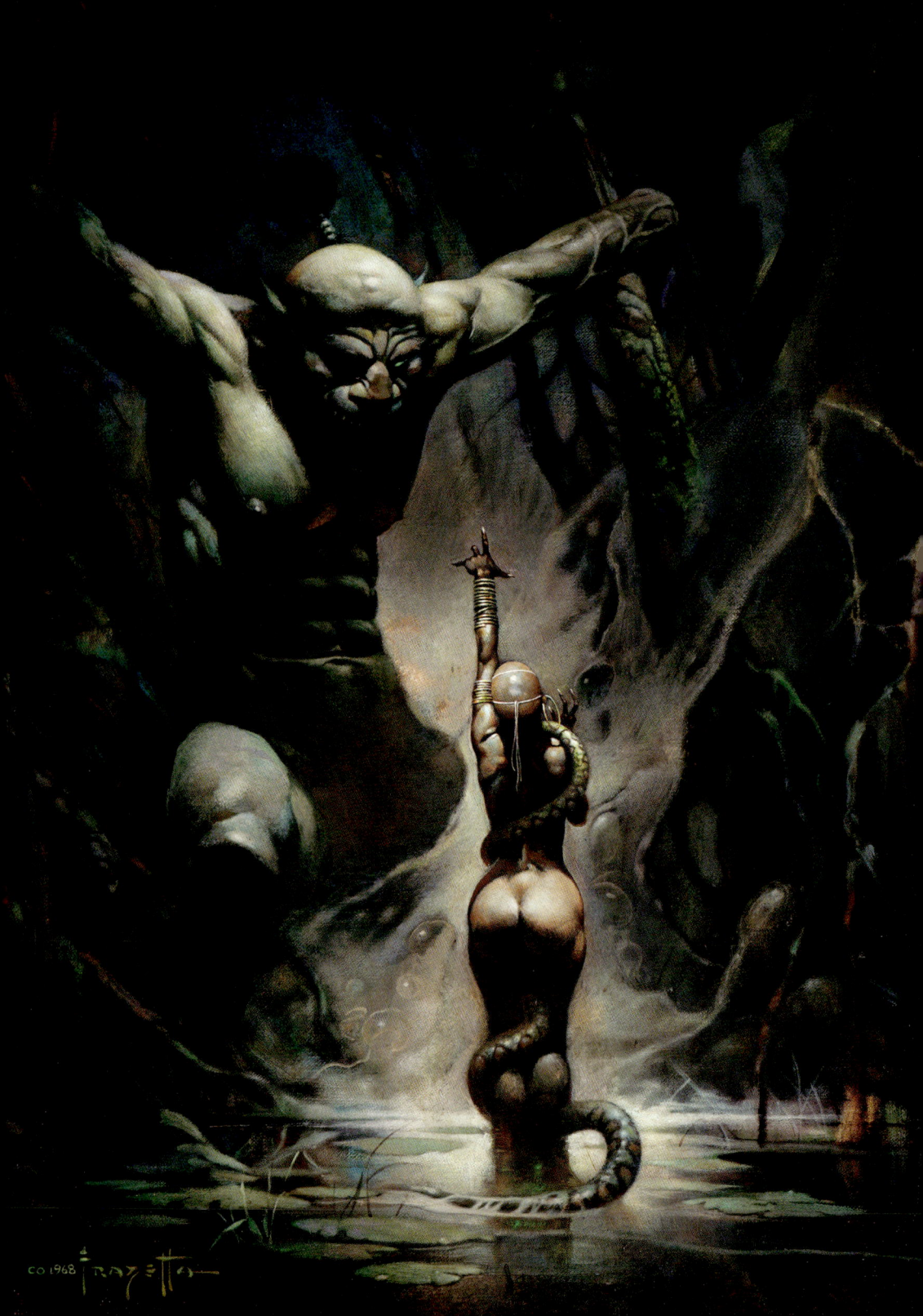

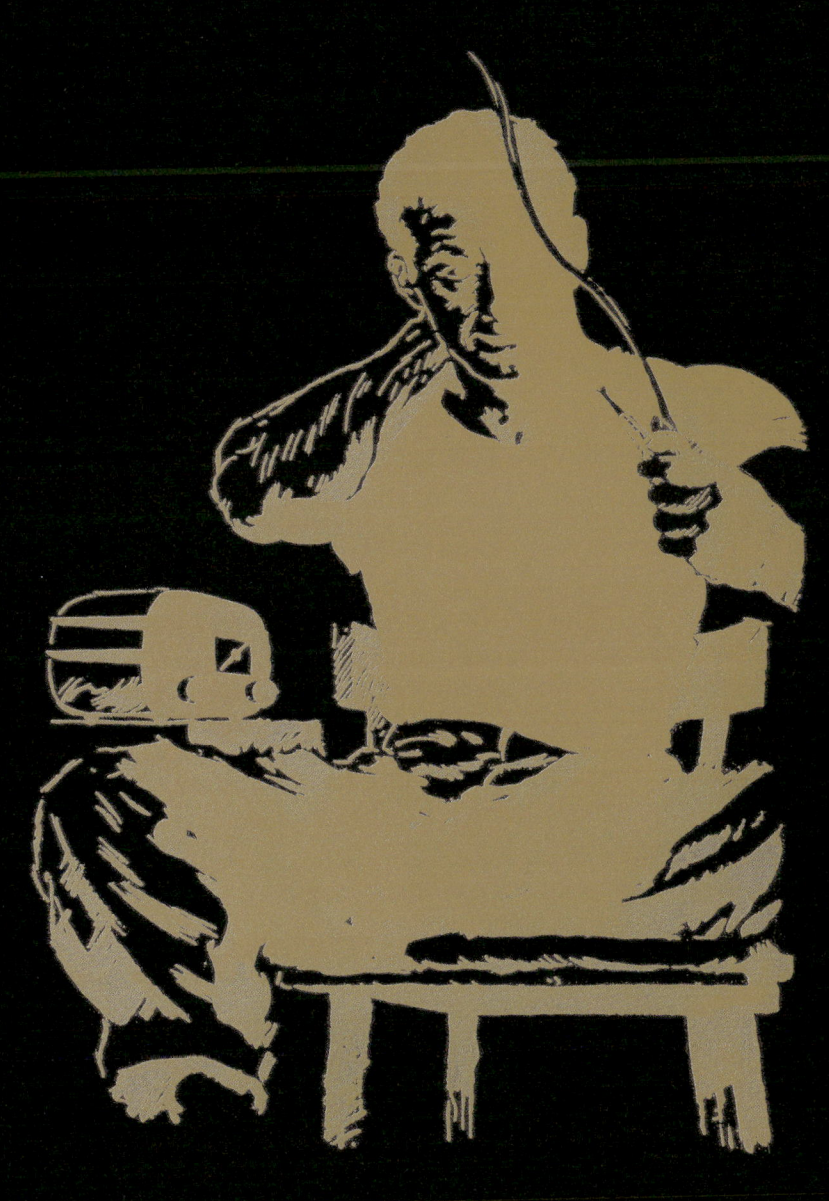

H. R. Giger

HR GIGER

1940-2014

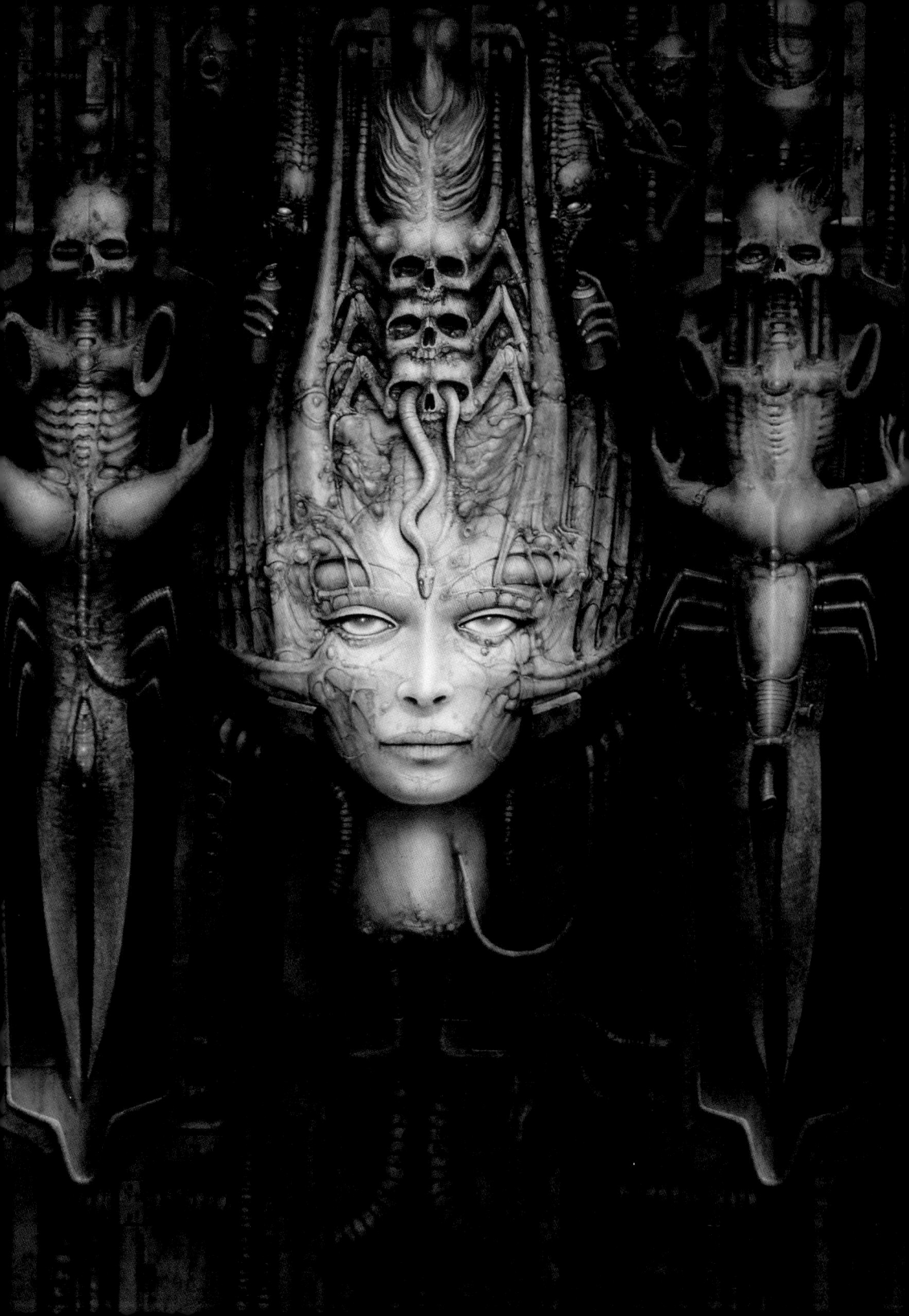

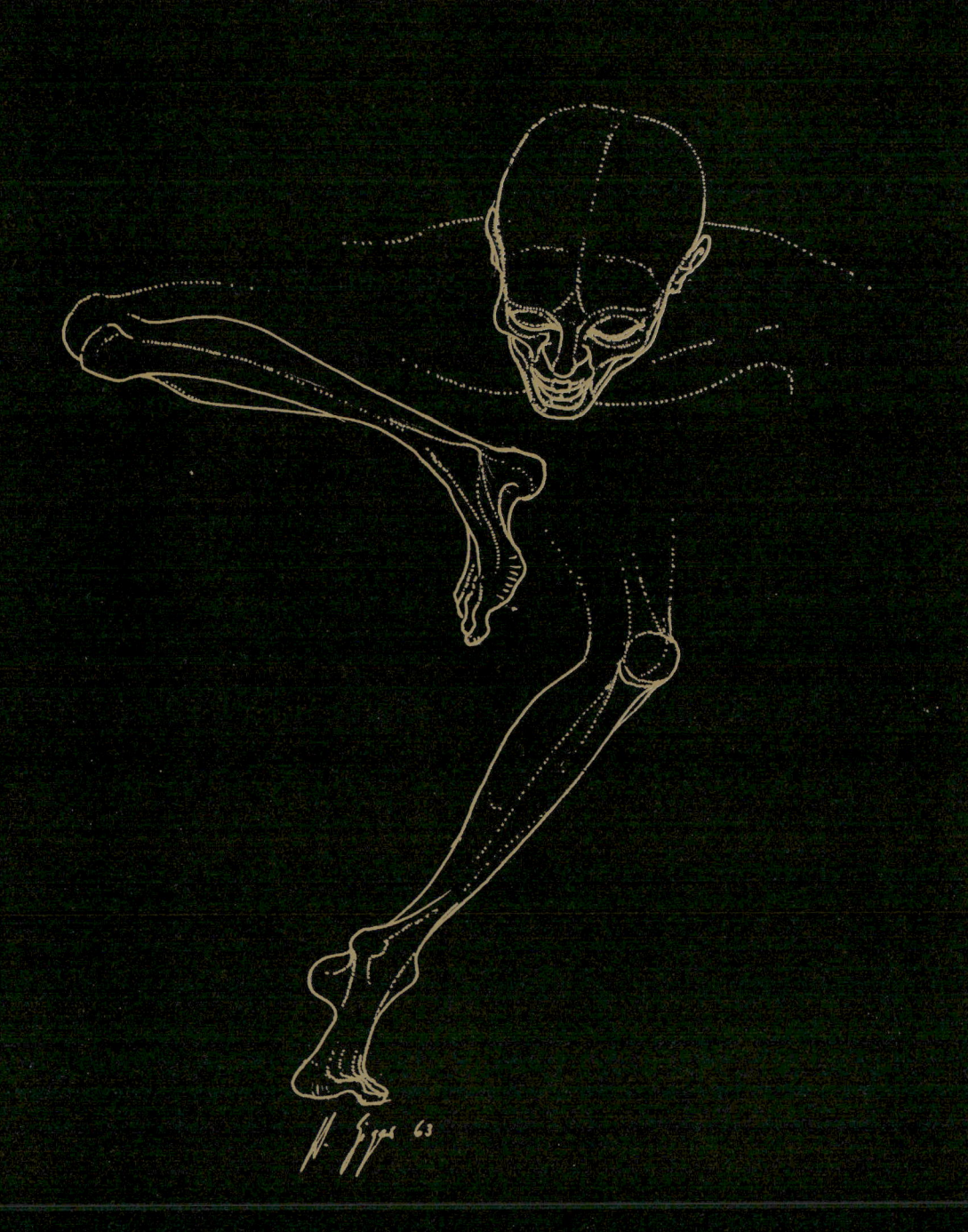

H.R. GIGER
THE BIOMECHANIC

"Sometimes people only see horrible, terrible things in my paintings, [but] there is hope and a kind of beauty in there somewhere, if you look for it."

Hansruedi Giger was born in Chur, Graubünden, Switzerland, in 1940. It was a dangerous time, even in a neutral country, though Hansruedi was too young to understand much but a persistent and pervasive anxiety. The fear infected him and soon attached to shadows, crawling things, and to the dark crooked passageway beside the building housing his father's pharmacy and the family apartment above it. In 1946 the drug company Ciba-Geigy sent his father the odd gift of a human skull; Dad gave it to six-year-old Hansruedi, who attached a string and pulled it along the street as a plaything. A few years later he built a ghost train, a homemade house of horrors full of crude monsters and skeletons in the above-mentioned passageway, and charged neighborhood children to ride it. Like most great artists he also began drawing at an early age; and as with most, his mother supported him and his father did not. Undeterred, Hansruedi became adept at illustrating sexual fantasies, winning friends in the schoolyard while his grades plummeted. After serving time in the military, in 1962

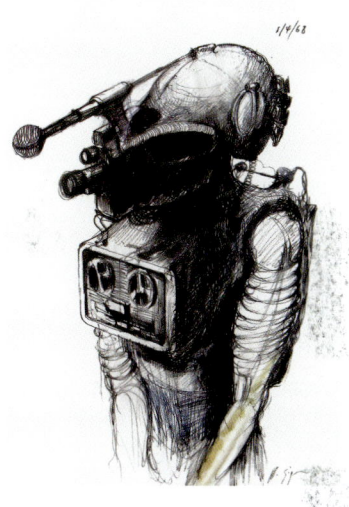

Hansruedi did manage to get into Zurich's School of Applied Arts, where he studied architecture and industrial design to appease his dad. While he was at it he perfected his drawing and learned to paint. After graduation, in 1965, he briefly designed office furniture for Knoll International, but by '68 his father's worst fears had come to pass: his son was a confirmed artist and experimental filmmaker, living in squalor with a promiscuous actress. To be fair, Giger was promiscuous as well, though his love for Li Tobler was all consuming. Their chaotic nine years together were his most creative, and Li is the central feature of his most famous work, *Li II*, created in 1974. Her suicide in 1975—with his gun, on his studio floor—left him "with a great emptiness."

Giger's original technique involved scrubbing pigment through a sieve onto paper, scraping away patches of unwanted ink with a razor blade and filling in detail with a Rapidograph pen. His discovery of the airbrush, in 1972, was a great step forward. Not that his self-punishing technique

Previous right: Li II, 1974, acrylic on paper laid on wood, 200 x 140 cm (78.7 x 55 inches).

Opposite: Untitled sketch, ink on paper, 1963, 27.4 x 19 cm (10.8 x 7.5 inches).

Above: A concept sketch of *Humanoid*, for the film *Swiss Made 2069*. Felt pen and India ink on paper, 1968, 45.2 x 33 cm (17.8 x 13 inches).

held him back. From 1961 he produced covers for the underground magazines *Clou*, *Schöngeist*, and *Fallbeil*. During his years with Tobler he created posters and album cover art for the bands Floh de Cologne and The Shiver, and in 1968 published the *Biomechanoids* portfolio, his prescient vision of flesh fused with technology. He sold prints and posters and mounted regular exhibitions.

Around the time he took up the airbrush — or spray gun, as he called it — he received a small inheritance from an uncle, with which he acquired a house in suburban Zurich. He immediately set about covering the walls with biomechanoid paintings. Much of the work came directly from his nightmares, paralyzing dreams that left him gasping for breath. His third wife, Carmen, said, in the film *Dark Star: H.R. Giger's World*, "He doesn't stop. Either he loses his fear or he draws until he gets it right." But it wasn't all fear. Giger was also obsessed with sexual imagery: sex, birth, and death, beginning and end. Li hated the house, but it was there she chose to end her life, and there, the same year, that Giger's fame was born.

It happened like this: A friend visited Salvador Dalí in Spain, bringing along Giger's poster catalog. Alejandro Jodorowsky arrived around the same time, hoping to convince Dalí to appear in his film *Dune*; Dalí showed him Giger's work. Two months later Jodorowsky asked Giger to make production designs for the doomed film and, straight from his childhood terrors, Giger created shit-spewing Harkonnen Castle. Jodorowsky's *Dune* proved unfilmable — estimates put production costs at $20 million, unheard of at the time — but Giger's drawings were included in *Necronomicon*, his startling 1977 monograph, along with some phallic-domed monsters he called *Necronom IV* and *V*.

The book fell into the hands of Ridley Scott as he was plotting his film *Alien*.

The next chapter is well documented. Scott was blown away and contacted Giger. Giger

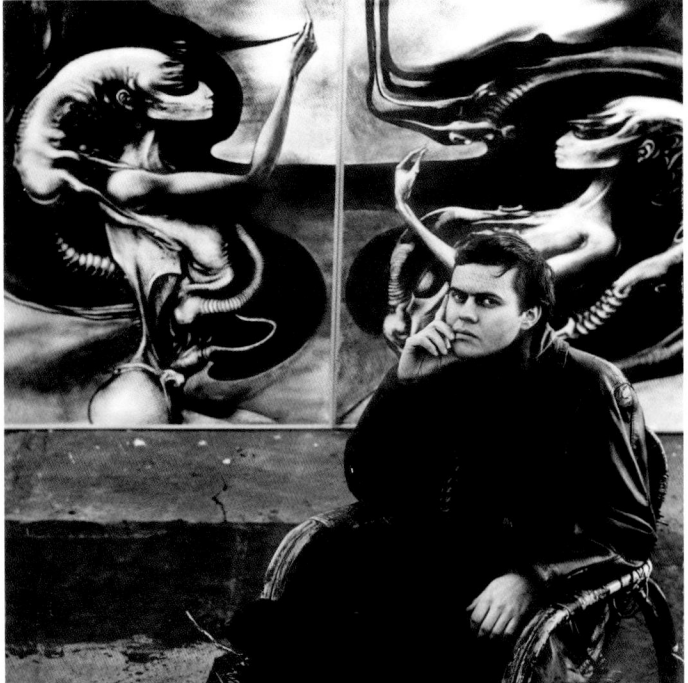

produced the critical conceptual designs of the alien in every life stage, from egg (altered several times, as Giger's original model, according to Scott, looked like "some great fanny," Brit slang for vagina), to face-hugger, to chest-bursting infant and on to the terrifying adult. Giger's designs defined the film, winning him an Oscar for Best Visual Effects in 1980, and the film would define him for the rest of his life.

Unfortunately, Giger was never allowed to shape a film so completely again. His creature was reused in the *Alien* sequels, but new designs were rejected; most of his concepts for *Poltergeist*

II were cut from the film; his radical redesign of the Batmobile for *Batman Forever* didn't go into production, and his villain for *Killer Condom* was, well, just a condom with teeth. He was more successful with 1995's *Species*, for which he designed sexy, deadly protagonist Sil, with a spiked back made from a lion's spine, and with *Prometheus*, Ridley Scott's 2012 fifth installment in the *Alien* franchise, which developed Giger's unused concepts from the first film.

The art world was never pleased with Giger's Hollywood success. His response was to embrace the commercial world, doing album covers for Emerson, Lake and Palmer and Blondie, but also for metal bands like Magma, Triptykon, and Celtic Frost, whose frontman, Tom Gabriel Fischer, served as Giger's personal assistant at the end of his life. There were Giger books, posters, and T-shirts, but also sculptures, furniture, watches, a mic stand for Jonathan Davis of Korn, even absinthe and, to drink it, three Giger bars, though the first, opened in Tokyo in the late '80s, didn't please him and soon closed. That misstart led him to build his own in Chur, in 1992, and another in his museum in 2003.

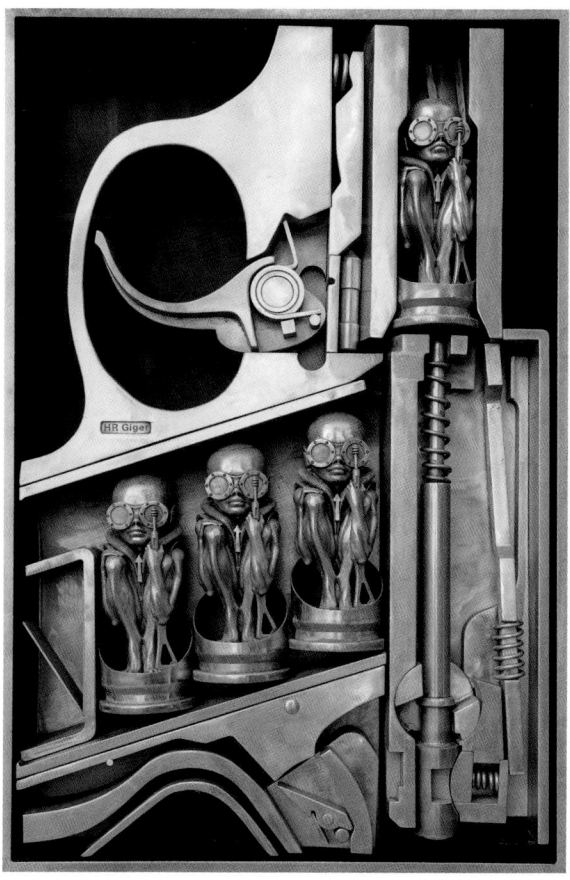

The Museum HR Giger opened in the medieval Château St. Germain in 1998, in the walled city of Gruyéres, to house the artist's most iconic works. Wonderful as it is, it never eclipsed his home in Zurich, where he lived for 44 years, as the true archive. There, the rare wall space not covered in art was painted black, with the shutters always closed, creating a dark, jumbled womb of creativity. Books filled a bathtub; early sketches interleaved with old magazines; the yard was overgrown, its sculptures twining with tree branches until wood and metal melded into botanical biomechanoids. And threading through it all, the ghost train. "He feels at home in places we run from in fear," explains curator Andreas Hirsch, in *Dark Star*.

Giger died May 12, 2014, shortly after making *Dark Star*. The cause is listed as complications from a fall, but it's clear in the film that he's already suffered a stroke or other medical misfortune. He's survived by his wife, Carmen Maria Scheifele Giger; by ex-wife Mia Bonzanigo; and by Müggi III, last of a series of identical Siamese cats.

Opposite: Hansruedi Giger in front of his diptych *Alpha (Zwei Frauen)*, 1967.

Above: Birth Machine, 1999, aluminum, 200 x 140 x 25 cm (78.7 x 55.1 x 9.8 inches). Photo by Matthias Belz.

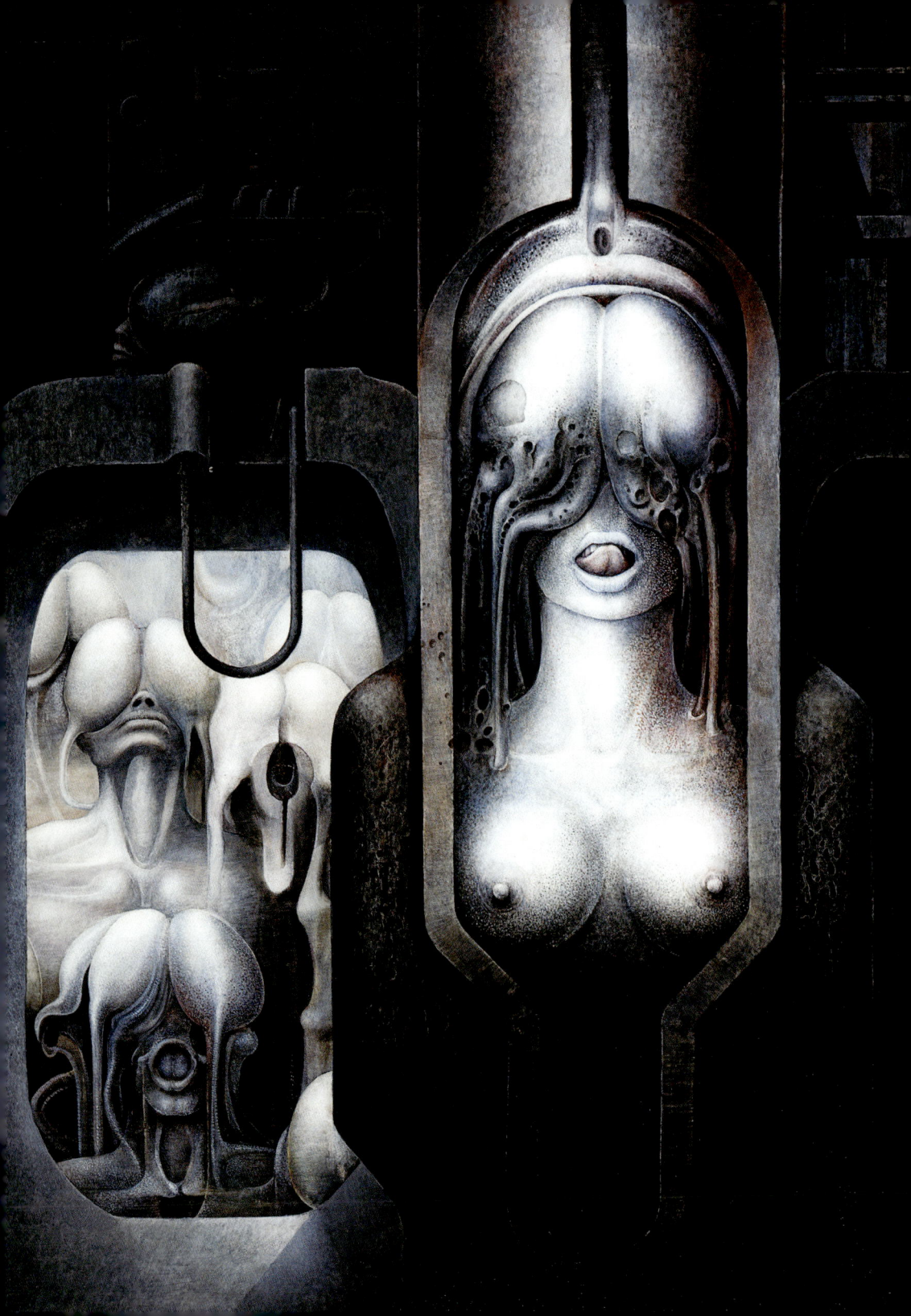

H.R. GIGER
DER BIOMECHANIKER

„Die Leute sehen in meinen Gemälden manchmal nur grässliche, fürchterliche Dinge, doch wenn man genauer hinschaut, finden sich in ihnen auch Hoffnung und eine gewisse Schönheit."

Hans Rudolf Giger, in seiner Jugend „Ruedi" und als Erwachsener „Hansruedi" genannt, wurde 1940 in Chur, Graubünden, Schweiz, geboren. Es war eine gefährliche Zeit, selbst in einem neutralen Land, doch Ruedi war zu jung und verspürte nur eine beständige und allgegenwärtige Furcht. Diese Furcht steckte ihn an und verband sich bald mit Schatten, mit allem, was krabbelte, und dem dunklen, gewundenen Durchgang neben dem Gebäude, in dem die Apotheke seines Vaters war und im Stockwerk darüber die Wohnung der Familie. 1946 schickte der Arzneimittelhersteller Ciba-Geigy seinem Vater das seltsame Geschenk eines menschlichen Schädels; der Vater gab ihn dem sechsjährigen Ruedi, der den Schädel an eine Schnur knüpfte und ihn auf der Straße wie ein Spielzeug hinter sich herzog. Ein paar Jahre später baute er im erwähnten Durchgang eine Geisterbahn, ein selbst konzipiertes Haus des Schreckens voller primitiver Monster und Skelette, und und ließ die Kinder aus der Nachbarschaft für die Fahrt mit der Geisterbahn bezahlen. Auch er fing, wie die meisten

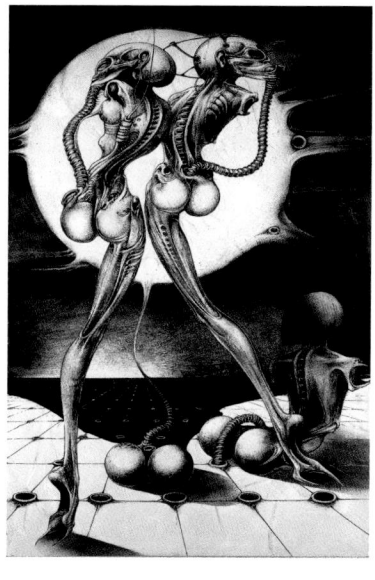

großen Künstler, schon in jungen Jahren an zu zeichnen; und wie in den meisten Fällen fand er dafür die Unterstützung seiner Mutter, die des Vaters jedoch nicht. Ruedi ließ sich nicht beirren und illustrierte mit Geschick sexuelle Fantasien, was ihm auf dem Schulhof Freunde brachte, doch seine Zensuren wurden immer schlechter. 1962, nach seinem Militärdienst, schaffte es Ruedi, an der Zürcher Hochschule für Angewandte Kunst angenommen zu werden, wo er, um seinen Vater zufriedenzustellen, Architektur und Industriedesign studierte. Während dieses Studiums perfektionierte er seine Zeichenkünste und lernte zu malen. Nach seinem Studienabschluss 1965 entwarf er kurzzeitig Büromöbel für Knoll International, doch um 1968 waren die schlimmsten Befürchtungen seines Vaters eingetreten: Sein Sohn war nun tatsächlich als Künstler und experimenteller Filmemacher aktiv und lebte mit einer promisken Schauspielerin in erbärmlichen Verhältnissen. Fairerweise muss gesagt werden, dass Giger genauso promisk war, seine Liebe zu Li Tobler jedoch war überwältigend. Die chaotischen neun Jahre, die sie gemeinsam verbrachten, waren Gigers kre-

Opposite: Phallelujah, 1968-69, oil on wood, 100 x 74 cm (39.4 x 29.1 inches).

Above: Atomic Children, 1967-68, India ink on paper laid on wood, 170 x 108 cm (66.9 x 42.5 inches).

ativste Zeit, und Li ist das zentrale Motiv seines berühmtesten Werks, *Li II*, das er 1974 schuf. Ihr Selbstmord 1975 – mit seiner Waffe in seinem Atelier – ließ ihn „mit einer großen Leere" zurück.

Zu Gigers typischen Techniken gehörte das Scheuern von Pigmenten durch ein Sieb auf Papier, mit einer Rasierklinge kratzte er unerwünschte Partien von Tusche weg, und Details zeichnete er mit einem Röntgenstift ein. Als er 1972 die Airbrushtechnik für sich entdeckte, war dies ein großer Schritt vorwärts.

Die strapaziöse Technik, mit der er sich herumquälte, bremste ihn jedoch nicht. Von 1961 an gestaltete er Cover für die Undergroundzeitschriften *Clou*, *Schöngeist* und *Fallbeil*. Während seiner Jahre mit Tobler schuf er Plakate und gestaltete Albumcover für die Bands Floh de Cologne und The Shiver, und 1968 veröffentlichte er das Portfolio *Biomechanoiden*, seine vorausschauende Vision von mit Technik durchwachsenen Körpern. Er verkaufte Drucke und Plakate und zeigte seine Arbeiten regelmäßig in Ausstellungen.

Ungefähr zur selben Zeit, als er sich die Airbrushtechnik zu eigen machte – „Spritzpistole", wie Giger sie nannte –, wurde ihm von einem Onkel ein bescheidenes Erbe zuteil, von dem er sich ein Haus in einem Zürcher Vorort kaufte. Sofort machte er sich daran, die Wände mit biomechanoiden Malereien zu bedecken. Viele dieser Arbeiten entsprangen direkt seinen Albträumen, lähmenden Träumen, die ihn nach Luft ringen ließen. Seine Frau Carmen erklärte im Film *Dark Star: H.R. Giger's World*: „Er hält nicht inne. Entweder er verliert seine Angst, oder er zeichnet, bis er alles hinbekommt." Doch es war nicht alles Angst. Giger war auch von sexuellen Bilderwelten besessen: Sex, Geburt und Tod, Anfang und Ende. Li hasste das Haus, aber sie entschied sich, dort ihrem Leben ein Ende zu setzen, und dort wurde, im gleichen Jahr, auch Gigers Ruhm geboren.

Dies trug sich folgendermaßen zu: Ein Freund besuchte Salvador Dalí in Spanien und brachte ihm den Katalog von Gigers Plakaten mit. Ungefähr zur selben Zeit traf Alejandro Jodorowsky ein und hoffte, Dalí zu überzeugen, in seinem Film *Dune* aufzutreten. Dalí zeigte ihm Gigers Werke. Zwei Monate später bat Jodorowsky Giger, Szenenbilder für den zum Scheitern verurteilten Film zu entwerfen. Direkt auf seine Kindheitsängste zurückgreifend, schuf Giger das Scheiße speiende Harkonnen-Schloss. Jodorowskys *Dune* erwies sich als unrealisierbar – die Produktionskosten wurden auf 20 Millionen Dollar geschätzt, damals eine ungeheure Summe –, doch Gigers Zeichnungen wurden, zusammen mit einigen phallusbewehrten Monstern, die er „Necronom IV" und „Necronom V" nannte, in *Necronomicon* aufgenommen, seine aufsehenerregende, 1977 erschienene Monografie.

Das Buch fiel in die Hände von Ridley Scott, der damals gerade seinen Film *Alien* plante. Das nächste Kapitel ist gut dokumentiert. Scott war hingerissen und kontaktierte Giger. Giger produzierte die entscheidenden konzeptionellen Entwürfe des Aliens in allen Lebensphasen, vom Ei (das mehrmals verändert wurde, da Gigers Modell laut Scott wie „eine prima Möse" aussah) über den „Gesichtsklammerer" und das dann aus dem Brustkorb platzende Kleinwesen bis zum entsetzlichen ausgewachsenen Geschöpf. Gigers Entwürfe prägten den Film, brachten ihm 1980 einen Oscar für die Besten visuellen Effekte ein, und und der Film sollte ihn für den Rest seines Lebens definieren.

Unglücklicherweise war es Giger nie wieder vergönnt, einen Film noch einmal so stark zu prägen. In den *Alien*-Fortsetzungen wurde seine Kreatur wieder eingesetzt, neue Entwürfe wurden jedoch abgelehnt; die meisten seiner Entwürfe für *Poltergeist II* wurden aus dem Film herausgeschnitten; sein radikaler Neuentwurf des Batmobils für *Batman Forever* wurde gar nicht erst produziert, und sein Bösewicht für *Kondom des Grauens* war halt bloß ein Kondom mit Zähnen. Mehr Erfolg hatte er 1995 mit dem Film *Species*, für den er die sexy und todbringende

Protagonistin Sil mit ihrem stacheligen, aus der Wirbelsäule eines Löwen gefertigten Rücken gestaltete, und mit *Prometheus*, Ridley Scotts fünfter Folge in der *Alien*-Reihe, die Gigers für den ersten Film nicht benutzten Entwürfe verwendete.

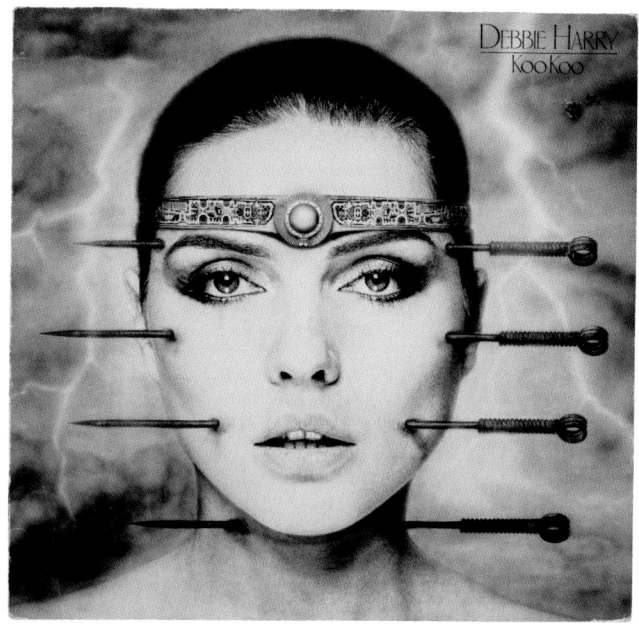

Gigers Erfolg in Hollywood war der Kunstwelt nie ganz geheuer. Seine Reaktion bestand darin, dass er sich nun erst recht dem Kommerziellen zuwandte und Albumcover für Emerson, Lake and Palmer und für Blondie gestaltete, aber auch für nur lokal bekannte Metalbands wie Magma, Triptykon und Celtic Frost, deren Leadsänger Tom Gabriel Fischer Giger in dessen letzten Lebensjahren als persönlicher Assistent diente. Es gab Giger-Bücher, -Plakate, -T-Shirts, aber auch Skulpturen, Möbel, Uhren, einen Mikrofonständer für Jonathan Davis von Korn, sogar einen Absinth und – damit er auch getrunken werden konnte – drei Giger-Bars, deren erste, Ende der 1980er-Jahre in Tokio eröffnete Bar Giger jedoch nicht gefiel und bald wieder schloss. Dieser Fehlstart führte dazu, dass er 1992 seine eigene in Chur einrichtete und 2003 eine weitere in seinem Museum.

Das Museum HR Giger wurde 1998 im mittelalterlichen Château St. Germain im von einer Stadtmauer umgebenen schweizerischen Greyerz eröffnet und beherbergt die ikonischsten Werke des Künstlers. So wunderbar das Museum auch ist, hat es Gigers Haus in Zürich, wo er 44 Jahre lang lebte, als das wahre Giger-Archiv nie in den Schatten gestellt. Die wenigen nicht von Kunst geschmückten Wände in diesem Haus wurden schwarz gestrichen und die Fensterläden stets verschlossen gehalten, um auf diese Weise einen dunklen, ungeordneten Schoß der Kreativität zu schaffen. Eine Badewanne war voller Bücher; frühe Zeichnungen ragten zwischen alten Zeitschriften hervor; der Garten war verwildert, und seine Skulpturen waren von den Ästen der Bäume so umschlungen, dass Holz und Metall zu botanischen Biomechanoiden verschmolzen. Und durch das Ganze zog sich die Geisterbahn. „Er fühlt sich an Orten zu Hause, von denen unsereiner aus Furcht wegläuft", erklärt der Kurator Andreas Hirsch in *Dark Star*.

Giger starb am 12. Mai 2014, kurz nachdem *Dark Star* fertiggestellt war. Als Todesursache wurden Komplikationen nach einem Sturz genannt, doch im Film wird deutlich, dass Giger bereits an den Folgen eines Schlaganfalls oder anderen medizinischen Problemen litt. Überlebt haben ihn seine Frau Carmen Maria Scheifele Giger, seine Ex-Frau Mia Bonzanigo und Müggi III, die letzte einer ganzen Reihe identischer Siamkatzen.

Above: Debbie Harry commissioned Giger to introduce her solo career with the cover for *KooKoo*, 1981, and hired him to direct her music videos for "Backfired" and "Now I Know You Know."

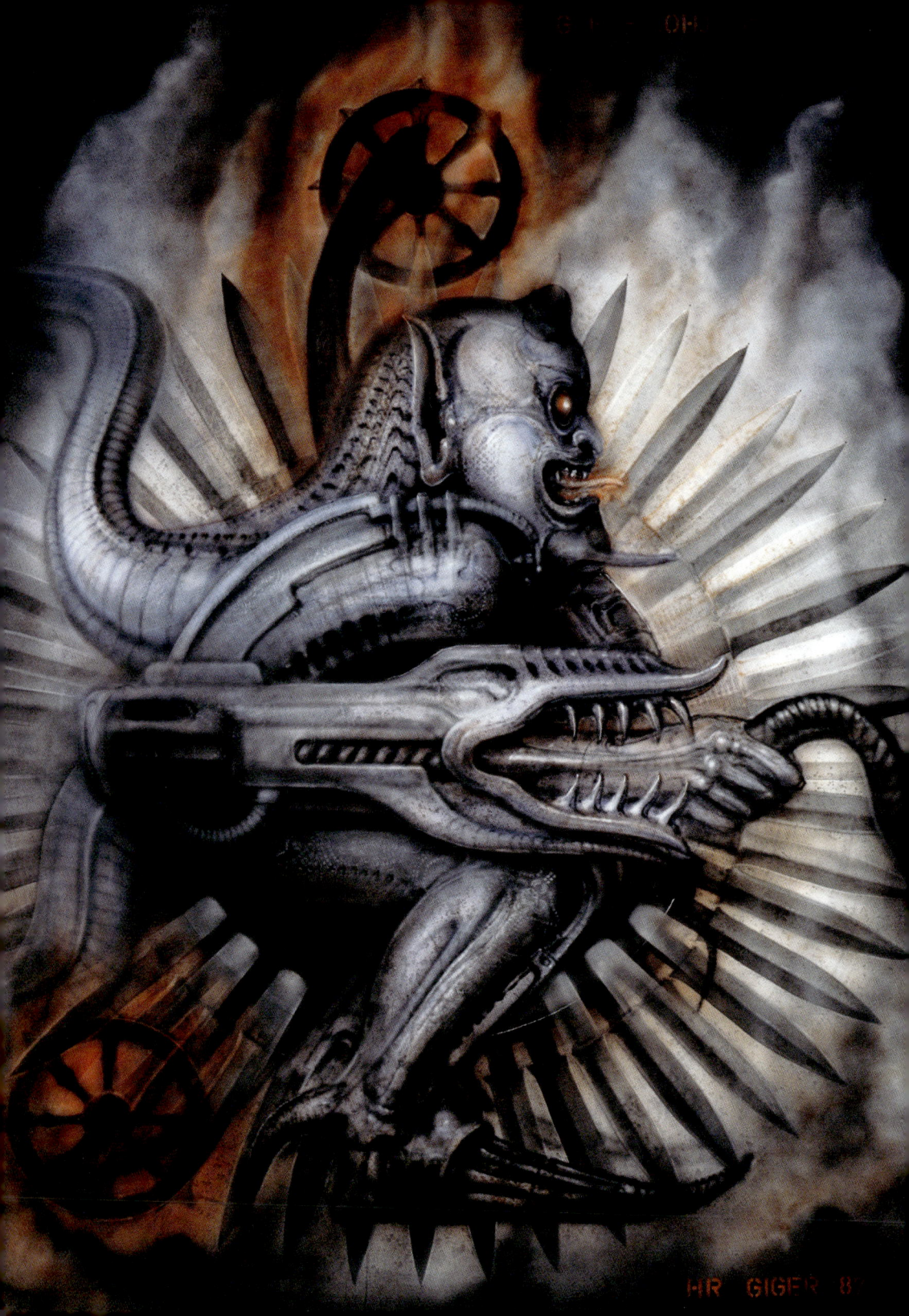

HR GIGER 8

H.R. GIGER
LE BIOMÉCANIQUE

« Parfois les gens ne voient dans mes peintures que des choses horribles, terribles, [mais] il y a de l'espoir et un genre de beauté quelque part là-dedans, si vous regardez bien. »

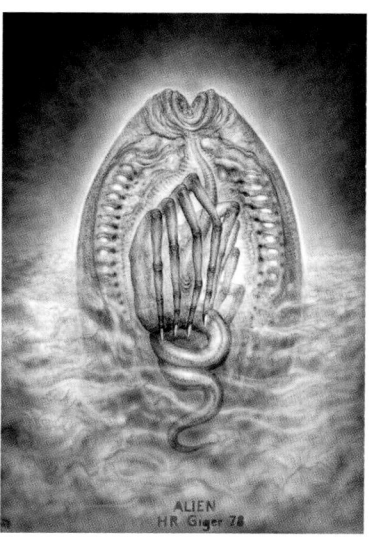

Hans Rudolf Giger, surnommé Ruedi dans son enfance et Hansruedi une fois adulte, est né à Coire, dans le canton suisse des Grisons, en 1940. L'époque est dangereuse, même dans un pays neutre. Ruedi est trop jeune pour comprendre cette angoisse invasive et persistante, mais la peur l'infecte et s'accroche très tôt aux ombres, aux créatures rampantes et à la ruelle sombre qui se tord derrière le bâtiment où il vit avec sa famille, au-dessus de la pharmacie de son père. En 1946, l'entreprise pharmaceutique Ciba-Geigy envoie comme étrange cadeau commercial à son père un crâne humain ; le papa l'offre au petit Ruedi, qui lui attache une ficelle et le promène dans les rues comme un jouet. Quelques années plus tard, il construit un train fantôme, une maison des horreurs remplie de monstres hideux et de squelettes qu'il installe dans la fameuse ruelle et pour lesquels il fait payer les enfants du quartier. Comme la plupart des grands artistes, il commence aussi à dessiner très jeune, et comme souvent, sa mère le soutient mais son père pas du tout. Déterminé, Ruedi s'adonne, avec talent, à la représentation de fantasmes sexuels et gagne des points auprès des copains dans la cour de récréation tandis qu'il en perd en classe. Après un passage dans l'armée, en 1962 Ruedi réussit à intégrer l'École des Arts appliqués de Zurich, où il étudie l'architecture et le design industriel pour rassurer son père. Il peaufine aussi son coup de crayon et apprend à peindre. Il obtient son diplôme en 1965, il dessine un temps des meubles de bureau pour Knoll International, mais en 1968 les pires craintes du père se confirment : son fils est déjà un artiste et un réalisateur expérimental confirmé, qui vit dans la crasse avec une actrice aux mœurs légères. Soyons justes, les mœurs de Giger sont tout aussi légères, bien qu'il éprouve pour Li Tobler une passion dévorante. Les neuf années que dure leur liaison chaotique sont les plus créatives de l'artiste et Li est le personnage central de son œuvre la

Opposite: Goho Dohji, created for the movie *Teito monogatari* (Tokyo: The Last Megalopolis), 1987, acrylic on paper, 140 x 100 cm (55.1 x 39.3 inches).

Above: Dan O'Bannon, screenwriter of *Alien*, became acquainted with Giger's work when he served as special effects supervisor for the doomed *Dune* project. It was he who put Giger's *Necronomicon* into Ridley Scott's hands, and he who hired Giger with his own money to conceptualize the alien egg case, seen here, and the facehugger, to convince Scott to use his vision for the film. Concept drawing for alien egg case designed for the film *Alien*, acrylic on paper, 100 x 70 cm (39.4 x 27.6 inches).

plus célèbre, *Li II*, réalisée en 1974. Son suicide en 1975, avec son arme à lui, dans son atelier, lui laisse « un grand vide ».

La technique originale de Giger consiste à frotter le pigment sur le papier à travers un crible, à gratter les taches d'encre indésirables à la lame de rasoir et à dessiner les détails au stylo technique Rapidograph. Il franchit un pas en avant crucial en 1972 lorsqu'il découvre l'aérographe.

Cette technique laborieuse, voire masochiste, ne le retient pas, bien au contraire. À partir de 1961, il produit des illustrations de une pour les magazines underground *Clou*, *Schöngeist* et *Fallbeil*. Au cours de ses années auprès de Li Tobler, il conçoit des affiches et des pochettes de disques pour les groupes Floh de Cologne et The Shiver et en 1968 il publie le portfolio *Biomécanoïdes*, vision presciente d'une fusion entre chair et technologie. Il vend des affiches et monte régulièrement des expositions.

À peu près au moment où il commence à utiliser l'aérographe – qu'il appelle « pistolet à peinture » –, il reçoit un petit héritage d'un oncle, qu'il emploie pour acheter une maison dans la banlieue de Zurich. Il entreprend immédiatement de couvrir les murs de compositions biomécaniques. La plupart de ces œuvres viennent de ses cauchemars, des terreurs nocturnes paralysantes qui le laissent exsangue depuis l'enfance. Sa femme Carmen racontera dans le documentaire *Dark Star: H.R. Giger's World* : « Il ne s'arrête jamais. Soit il distance sa peur, soit il dessine jusqu'à la saisir avec justesse. » Mais il n'y a pas que la peur. Giger est aussi obsédé par l'imagerie sexuelle : le sexe, la naissance et la mort, le début et la fin. Li déteste la maison. C'est pourtant là qu'elle choisit de mettre fin à ses jours et que, la même année, naît la renommée de Giger. Voici comment :

Salvador Dalí reçoit en Espagne un ami qui lui apporte un catalogue des affiches de Giger. Alejandro Jodorowsky arrive à peu près au même moment, espérant convaincre le maître de participer à son film *Dune* ; Dalí lui montre le travail de Giger. Deux mois plus tard, Jodorowsky demande des croquis à Giger pour la production de ce film qui ne se fera pas et Giger puise dans les terreurs de ses jeunes années pour créer le château des Harkonnen. Le *Dune* de Jodorowsky se révèle irréalisable, avec un budget estimé à 20 millions de dollars, une somme inédite à l'époque, mais les dessins de Giger pour le projet figurent dans *Necronomicon*, sa saisissante monographie de 1977, aux côtés des monstres phalliques qu'il baptise Necronom IV et V.

Le livre tombe entre les mains de Ridley Scott, alors en plein travail préparatoire de son film *Alien*. Le chapitre suivant de sa carrière est bien connu. Scott est impressionné et contacte aussitôt Giger. Giger produit les dessins conceptuels déterminants de l'alien aux différentes étapes de sa vie, de l'œuf (modifié plusieurs fois parce que le modèle original de Giger ressemblait, d'après Scott, à « une énorme chatte »), au face-hugger, puis au nouveau-né éventreur, le chest-burster, et à la terrifiante forme adulte. Les créations de Giger définissent le film et lui valent l'Oscar des meilleurs effets spéciaux en 1980, mais c'est aussi par ce film que l'artiste a été défini le reste de sa vie.

Giger n'aura malheureusement jamais l'opportunité de façonner à nouveau si complètement un film. Sa créature est réutilisée dans les épisodes ultérieurs de la saga, mais ses nouveaux croquis sont refusés ; la plupart de ses idées pour *Poltergeist II* sont coupées au montage, sa réinvention radicale de la Batmobile pour *Batman Forever* ne passe pas l'étape du tournage et son personnage de méchant, *Killer Condom*, n'est, disons-le, qu'une capote avec des dents. Il a plus de succès en 1995 avec *La Mutante (Species)*, film pour lequel il imagine la sexuelle et mortifère Sil, dont des vertèbres de lion percent le dos, puis en 2012 avec le *Prometheus* de Ridley Scott, cinquième opus de la franchise *Alien*, pour lequel il peut enfin développer les idées qui n'ont pas été employées dans le premier film.

Le monde de l'art a toujours vu d'un mauvais œil le succès hollywoodien de Giger. En guise de riposte, il se tourne vers la création publicitaire, signe des pochettes d'album pour Emerson,

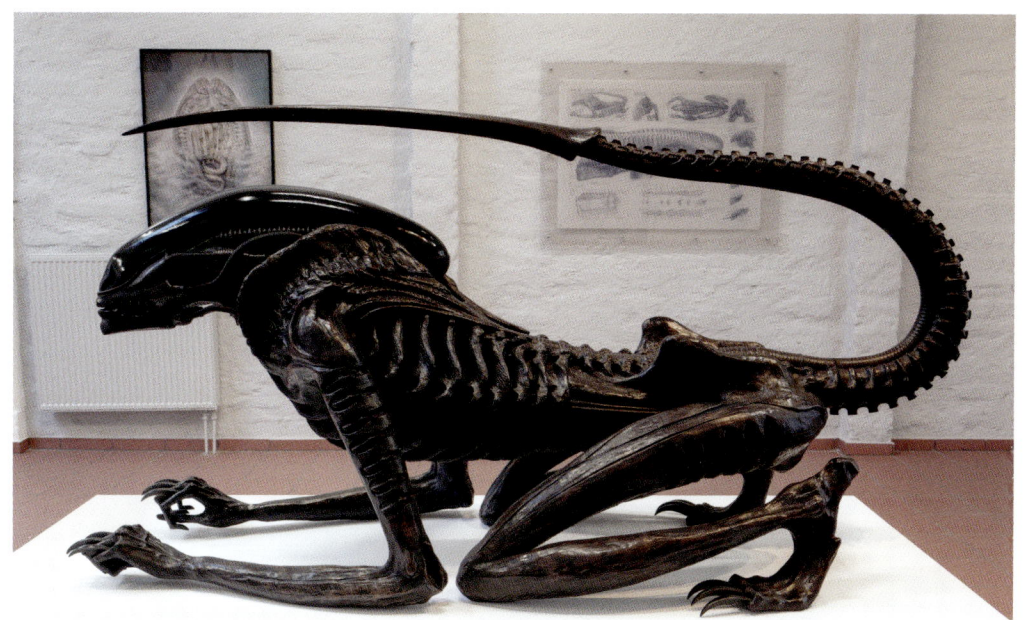

Lake & Palmer et Blondie, mais aussi pour des groupes de métal comme Magma, Triptykon et Celtic Frost, dont le leader, Tom Gabriel Fischer, sera l'assistant personnel de Giger à la fin de sa vie. Des livres, des affiches et des T-shirts Giger sont édités, ainsi que des sculptures, des meubles, des montres, un pied de micro pour Jonathan Davis de Korn, et même de l'absinthe, et pour la boire trois bars Giger – le premier, ouvert à Tokyo à la fin des années 1980, ne lui plaît pas et ferme rapidement. Ce faux départ le conduit à construire son propre bar à Coire, en 1992, puis un autre au sein de son musée en 2003.

Le musée HR Giger, ouvert en 1998 au château médiéval Saint-Germain, dans la cité fortifiée de Gruyères, accueille les œuvres les plus célèbres de l'artiste. Aussi merveilleux qu'il soit, il n'éclipsera jamais la valeur documentaire de sa maison de Zurich, qu'il habita pendant 44 ans. Sur ses murs, les rares espaces sans dessins sont peints en noir et les volets restent fermés en permanence pour créer un giron encombré, obscur, propice à sa créativité. La baignoire est remplie de livres, d'anciens croquis dépassent de piles de vieux magazines, le jardin est en friche, ses sculptures s'enlacent aux branches des arbres jusqu'à ce que le bois et le métal forment des biomécanoïdes botaniques. Le train fantôme parcourt cet univers. « Il se sent chez lui dans des endroits que nous fuyons en courant », explique le conservateur Andreas Hirsch dans *Dark Star*.

Giger meurt le 12 mai 2014, peu après avoir fait *Dark Star*. Il aurait succombé aux suites d'une chute, mais dans le film il est évident qu'il a déjà subi une attaque ou connu un autre grave problème de santé. Il laisse derrière lui sa femme, Carmen Maria Scheifele Giger, son ex-femme Mia Bonzanigo et Müggi III, dernier d'une lignée de chats siamois identiques.

Above: Giger's sculpture *Alien III/Necronom*, 2005, polyester and metal, with paint, 110 x 86.8 x 220 cm (43.3 x 34.2 x 86.6 inches), created first in 1990 as concept art for the film *Alien III*, then displayed in Giger's garden until 2005, when he reworked the design into this completed artwork. Photo by Matthias Belz.

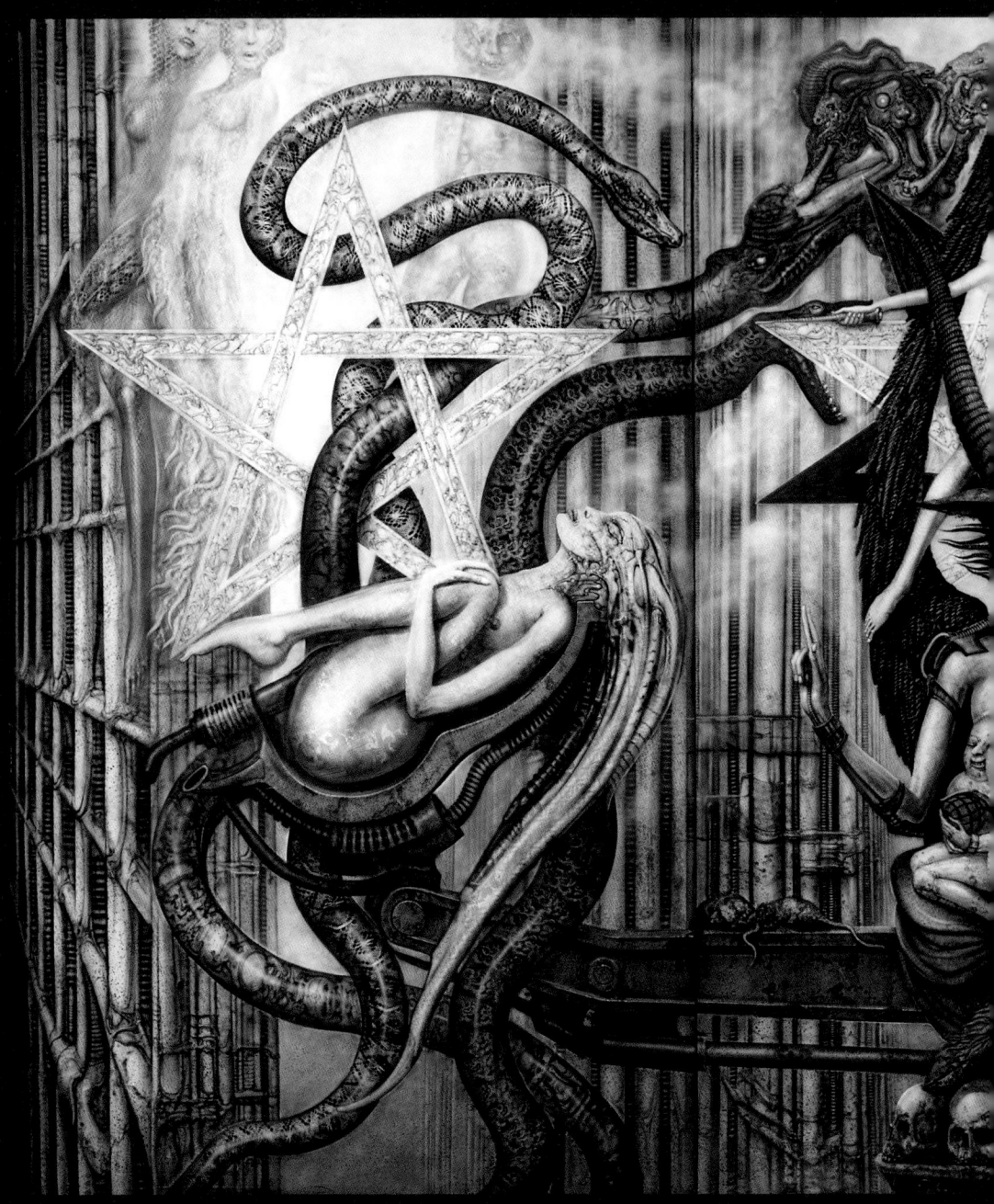

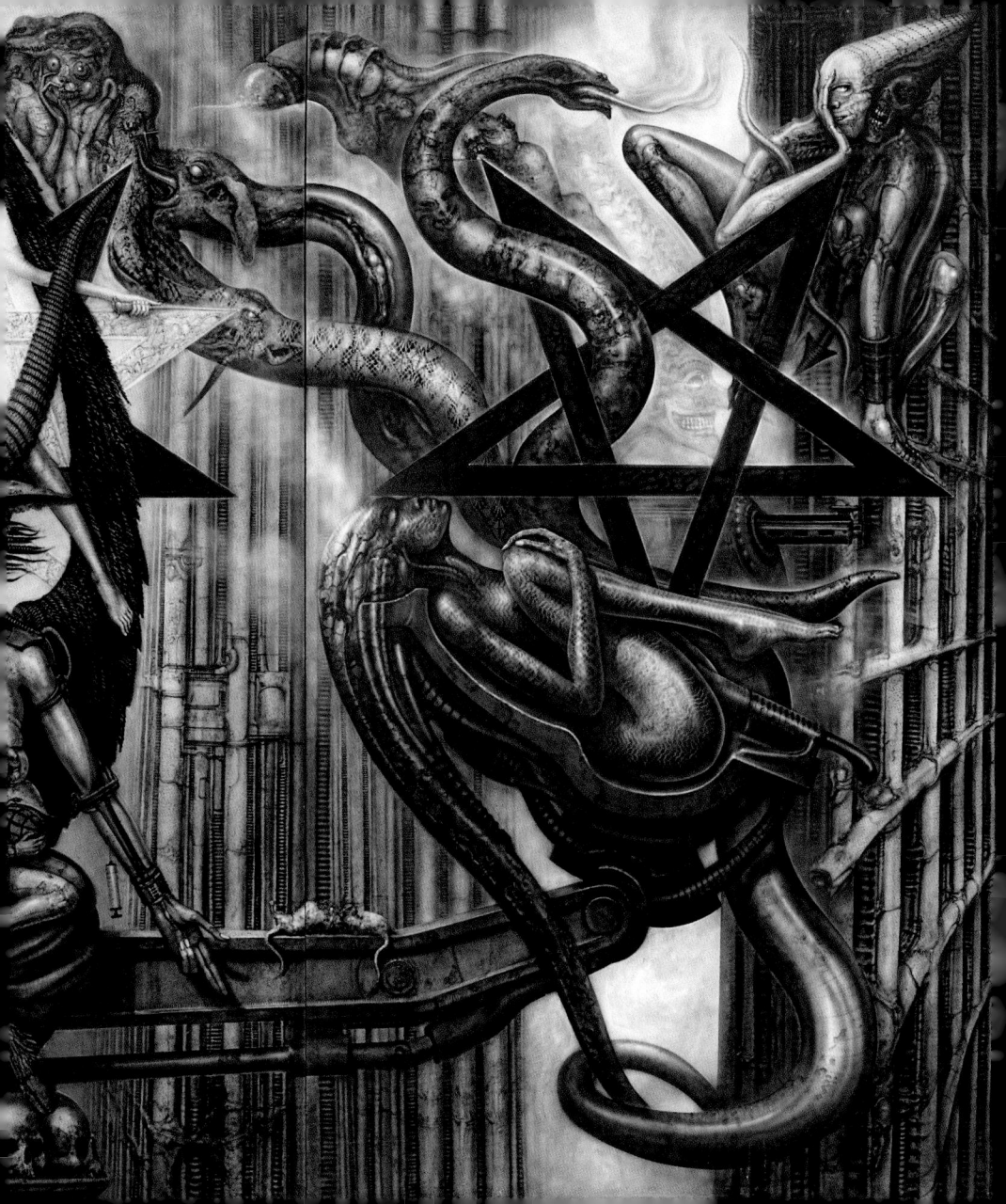

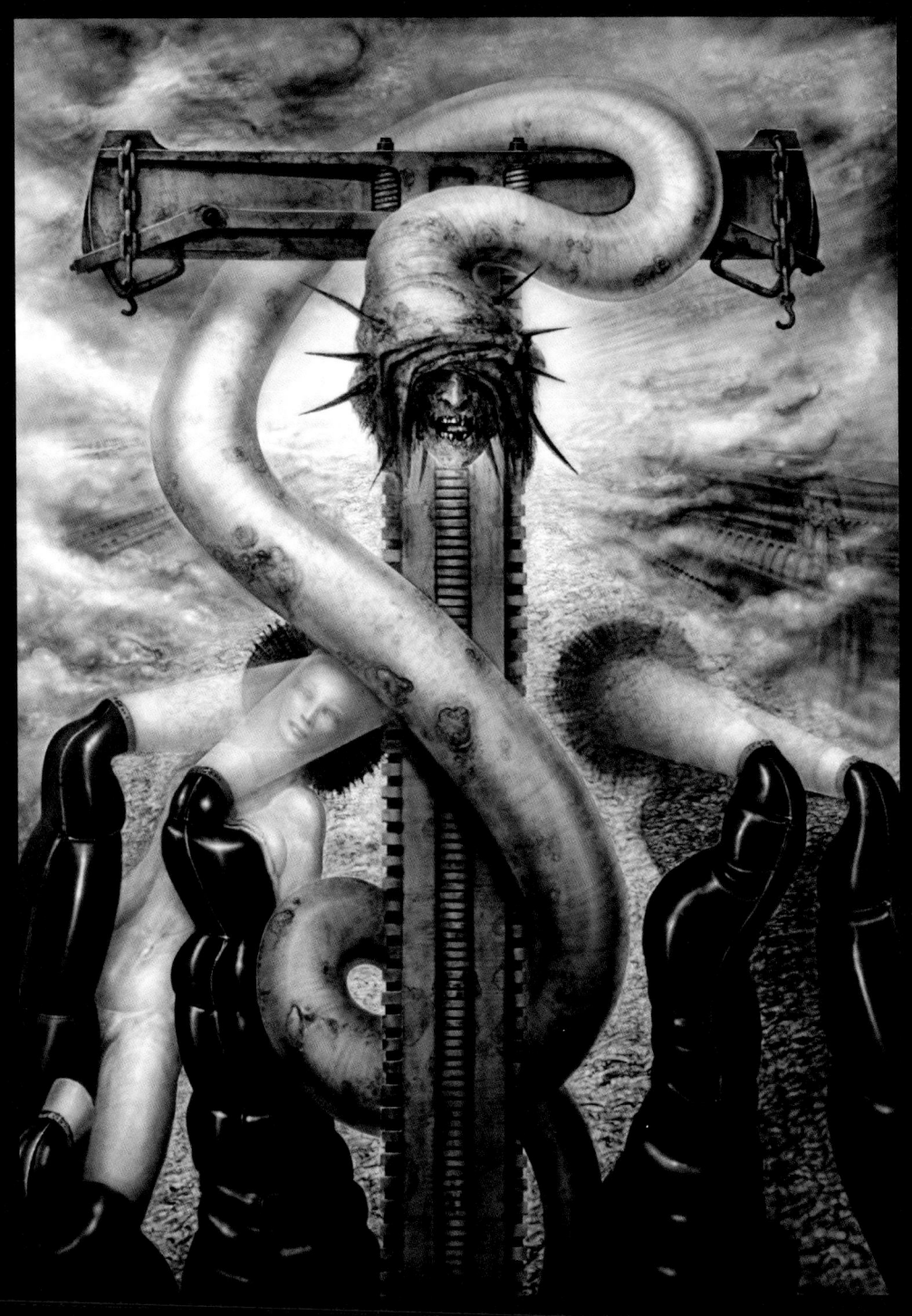

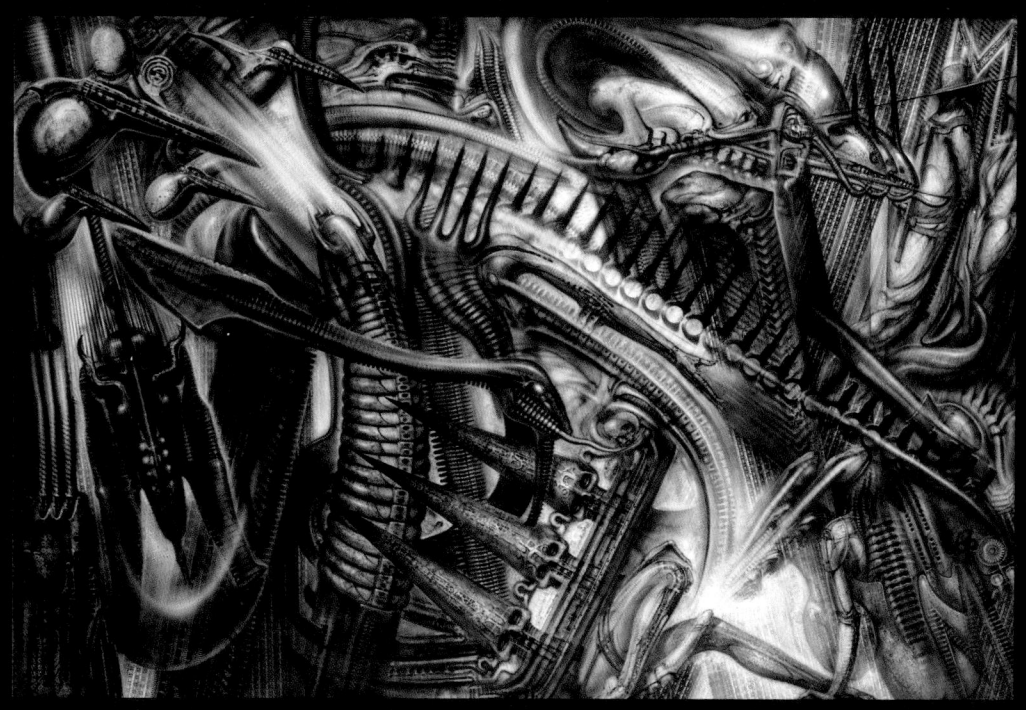

Previous spread: The Spell IV, for the cover of *Necronomicon*, 1977. Acrylic on paper laid on wood, 240 x 420 cm (95.5 x 165.4 inches).

Opposite: Chidher Grün, 1975, acrylic on paper laid on wood, 200 x 140 cm (78.7 x 55 inches).

Above: New York City (A City Looking for a Murderer), 1981, acrylic and ink on paper, 140 x 200 cm (55 x 78.7 inches).

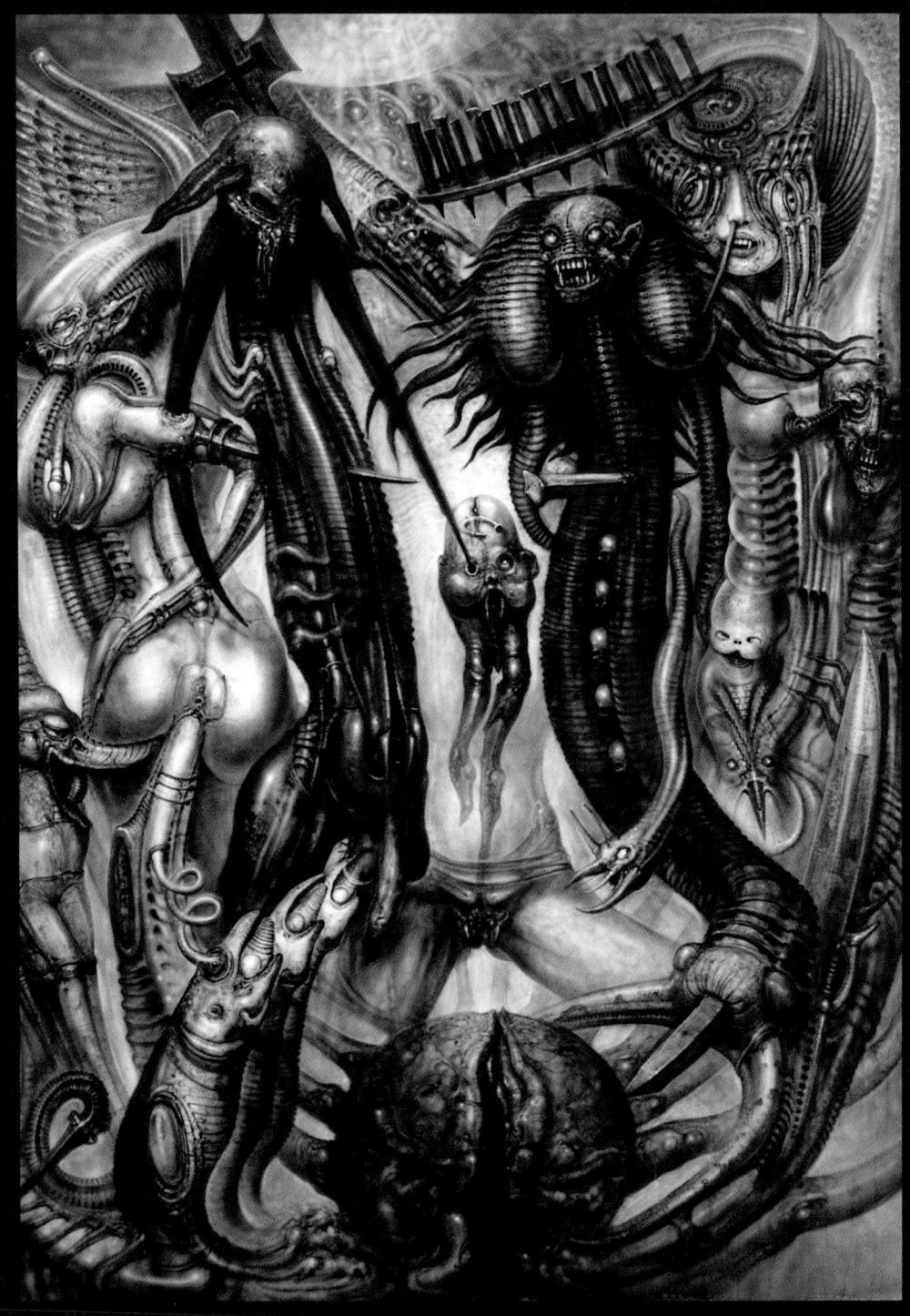

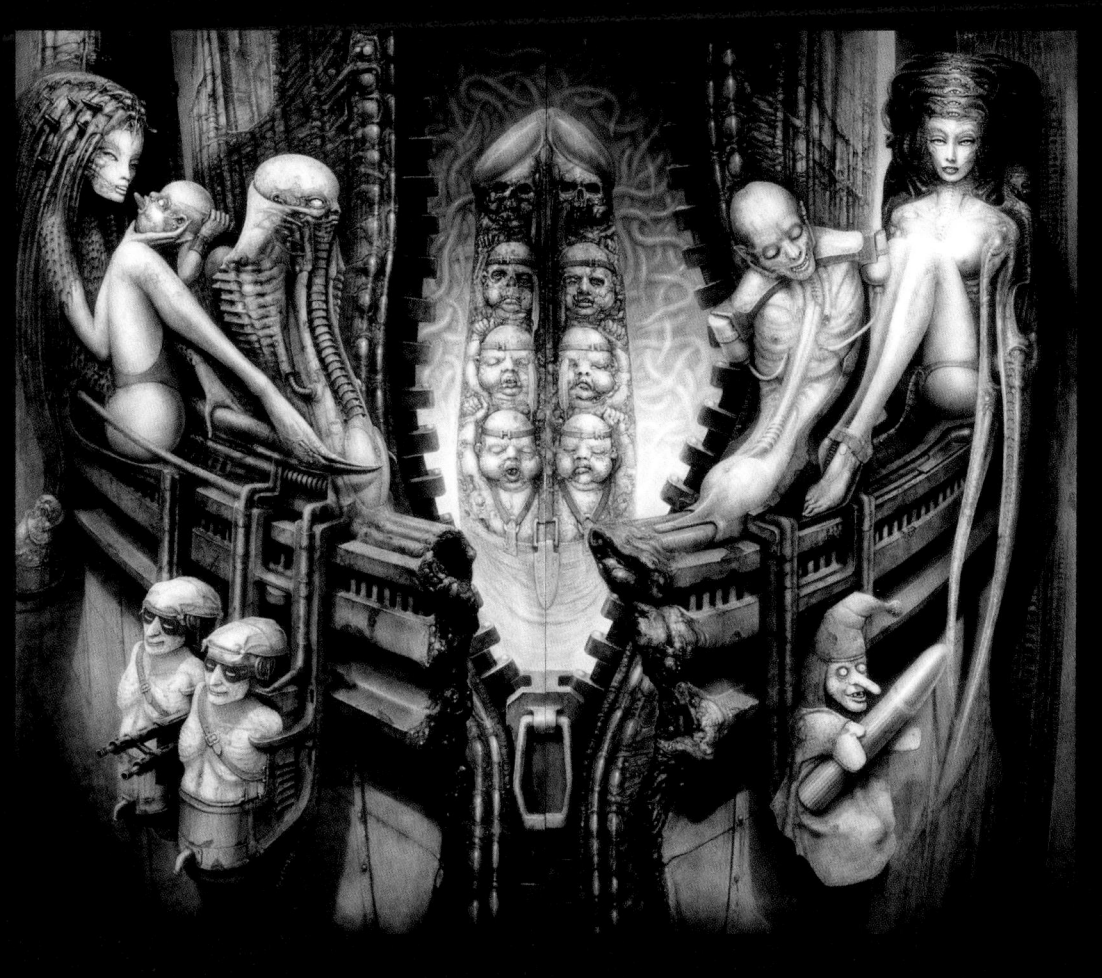

Opposite: Vlad Tepes, 1978, acrylic on paper
laid on wood, 200 x 140 cm (78.7 x 55 inches).

Above: Passagen-Tempel (Leben), acrylic on paper
laid on wood, 1974, 240 x 280 cm (94.5 x 110.2 inches).

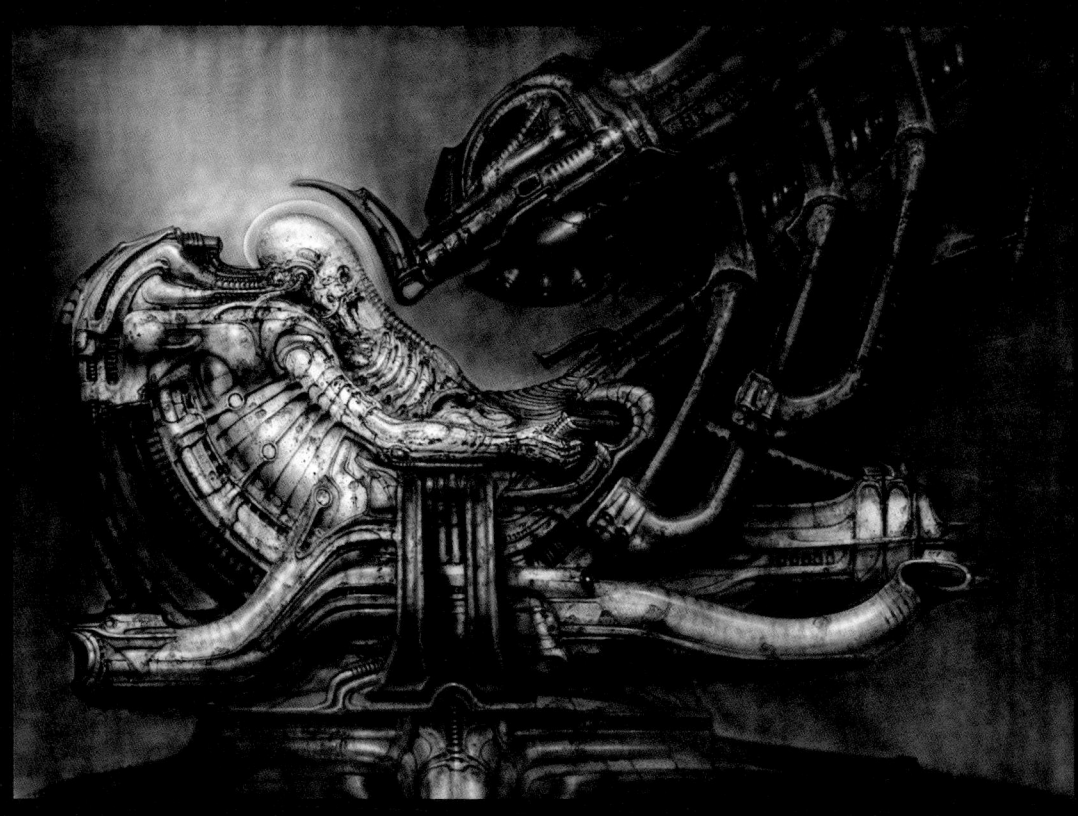

Above: Necronom V, acrylic on paper laid on wood, 1976, 100 x 150 cm (39.4 x 59 inches).

Opposite: Mordor VI, 1975, acrylic on paper laid on wood, 100 x 70 cm (39.4 x 27.6 inches).

Following spread: Necronom V, acrylic on paper on wood, 1976, 100 x 150 cm (39.4 x 59 inches).

MASTERPIECES OF FANTASY ART

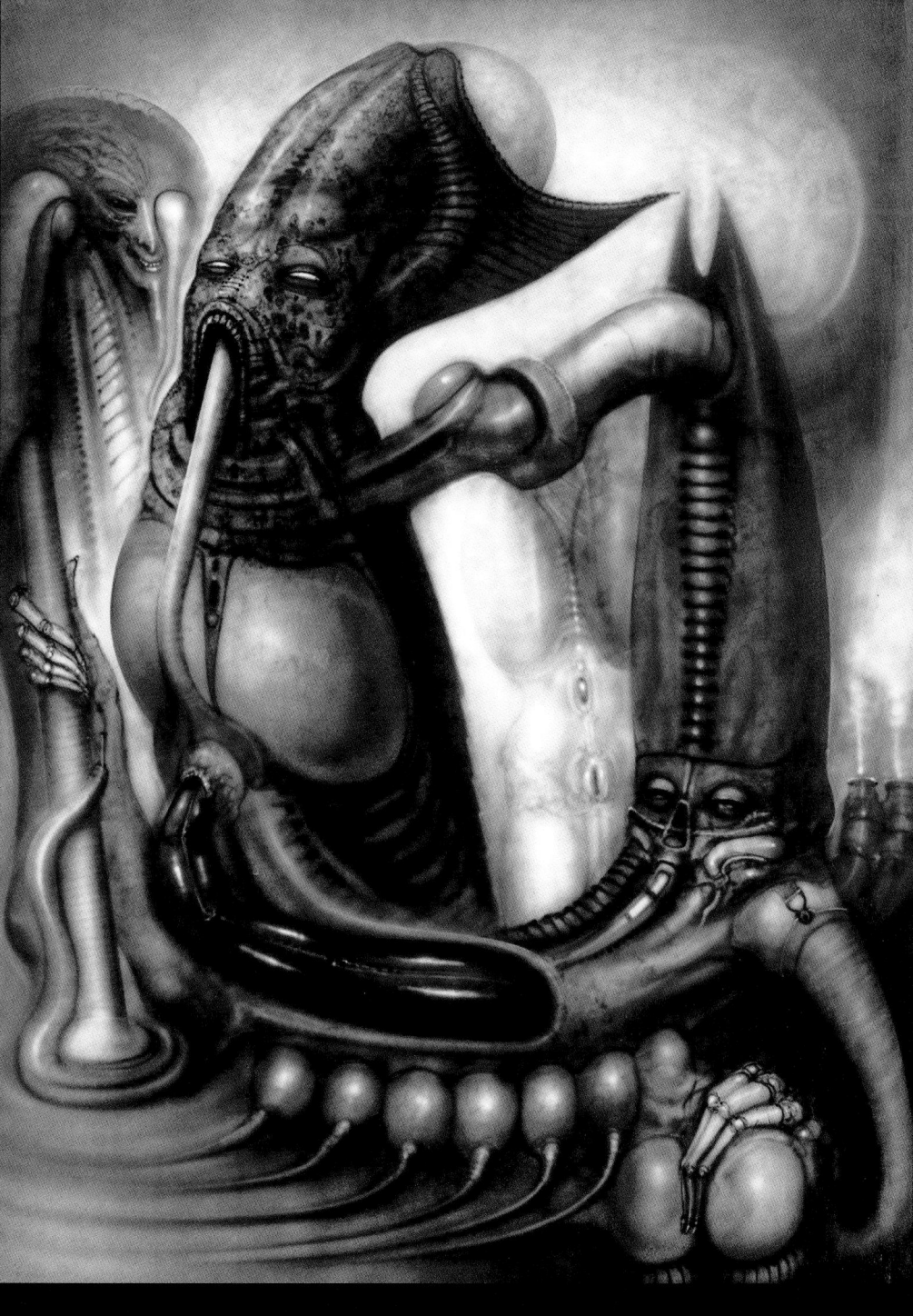

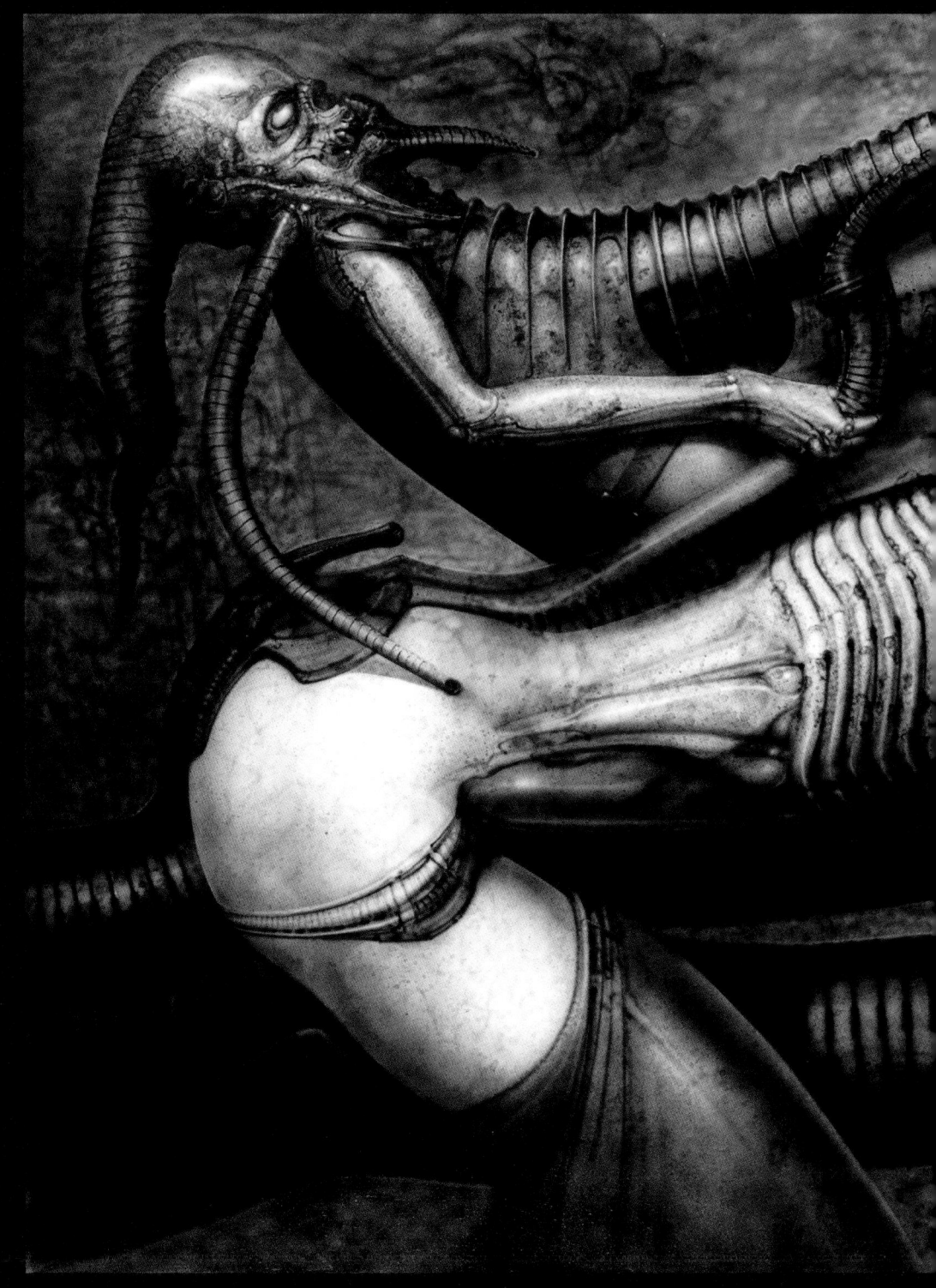

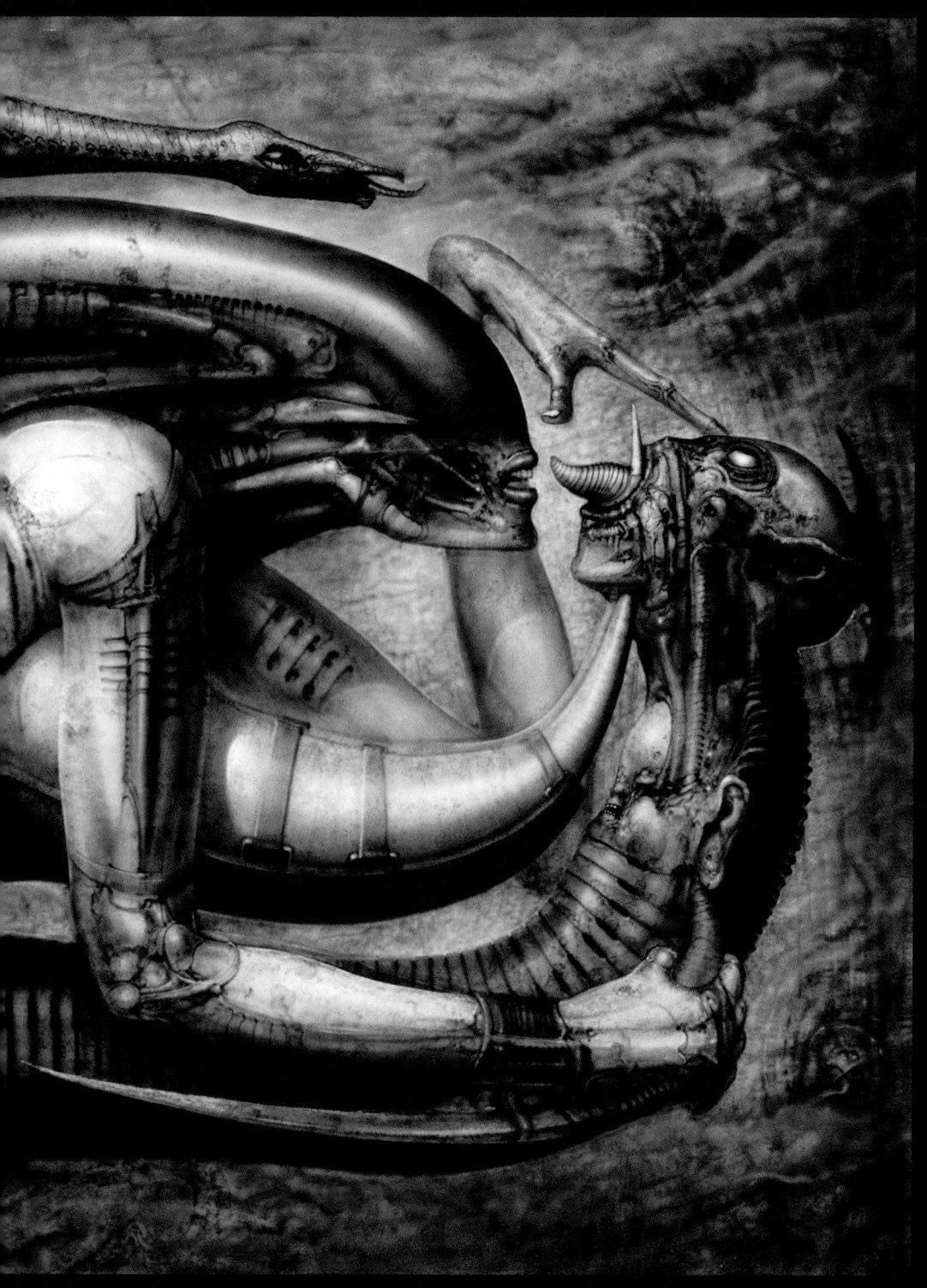

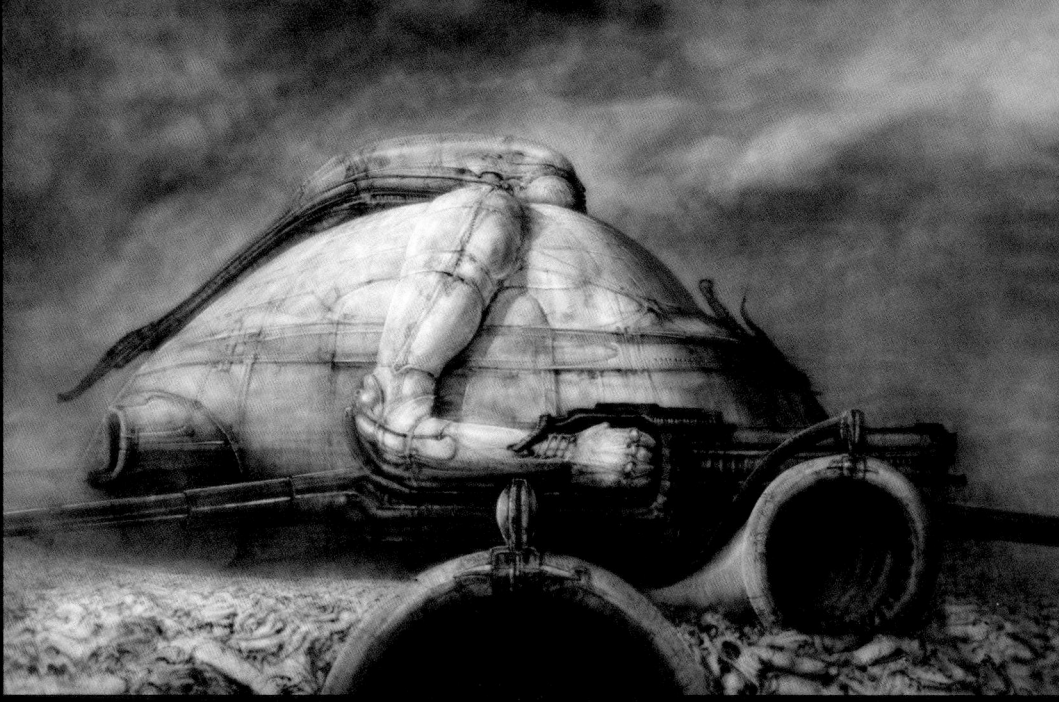

Above: One of the greatest movies never made was Alejandro Jodorowsky's *Dune*. In the 1970s Jodorowsky assembled the greatest artists and actors of the era in an attempt to bring Frank Herbert's fantasy epic to the screen. Salvador Dalí was to play Emperor Shaddam Corrino IV, and Orson Welles Baron Harkonnen, with Pink Floyd signed for the musical score. The storyboards were done by Mœbius, and concept art by Giger. In the end, no studio would take on the cost, but these beautiful drawings remain. Here, Giger's vision for Castle Harkonnen. 1975, acrylic on paper, 70 x 100 cm (39.4 x 27.6 inches).

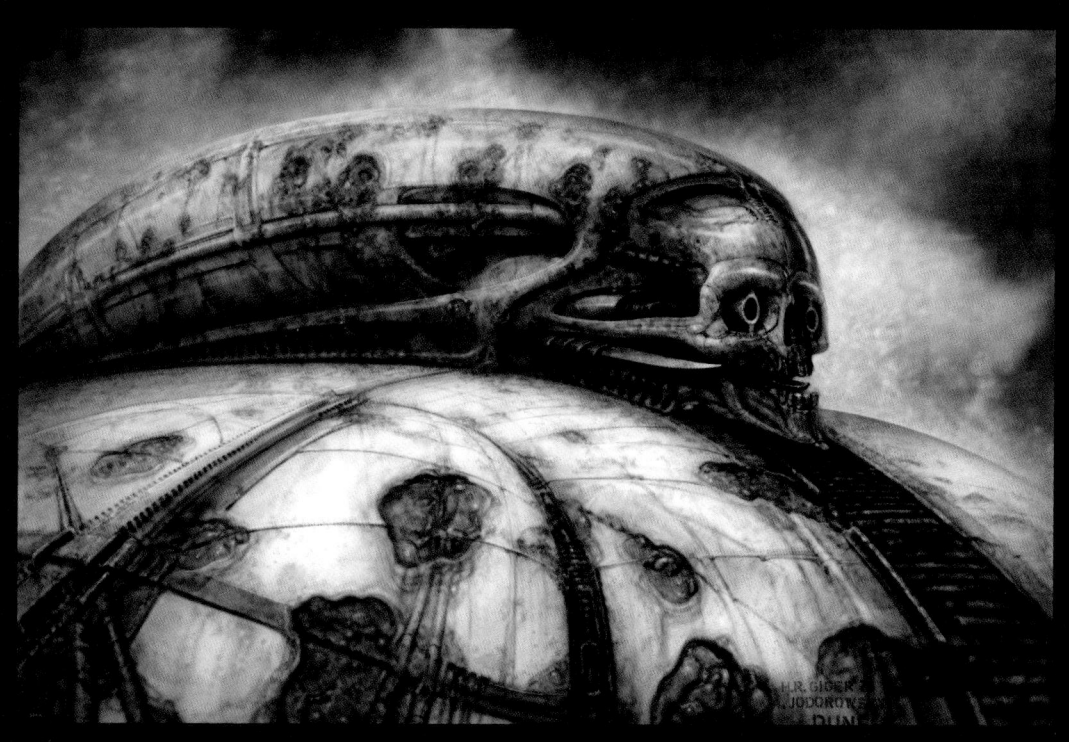

Above: Chris Foss, the third concept artist contributing to *Dune*, along with Mœbius and Giger, said that Giger's concept was so completely unique that every film since has copied it. Detail of the head atop the Harkonnen castle train, with face retracted to show the skull beneath. 1976, acrylic on paper, 70 x 100 cm (39.4 x 27.6 inches).

H.R. GIGER

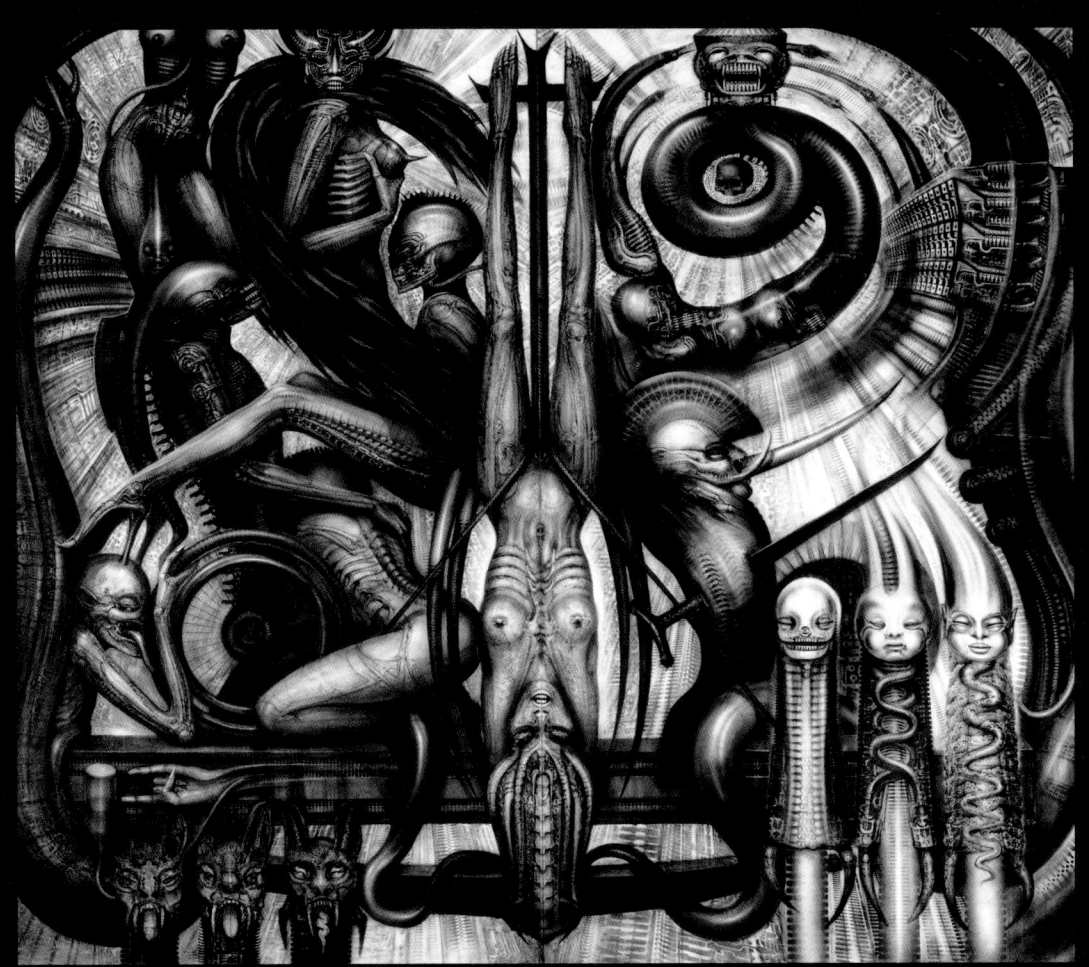

Above: *Chinese Evolution*, 1981–84, acrylic on paper
laid on wood, 240 x 280 cm (94.5 x 110.2 inches).

Opposite: *Todgebärmaschine II (Death Birth Machine II)*,
1977, acrylic on paper laid on wood, 200 x 140 cm
(78.7 x 55.1 inches).

MASTERPIECES OF FANTASY ART

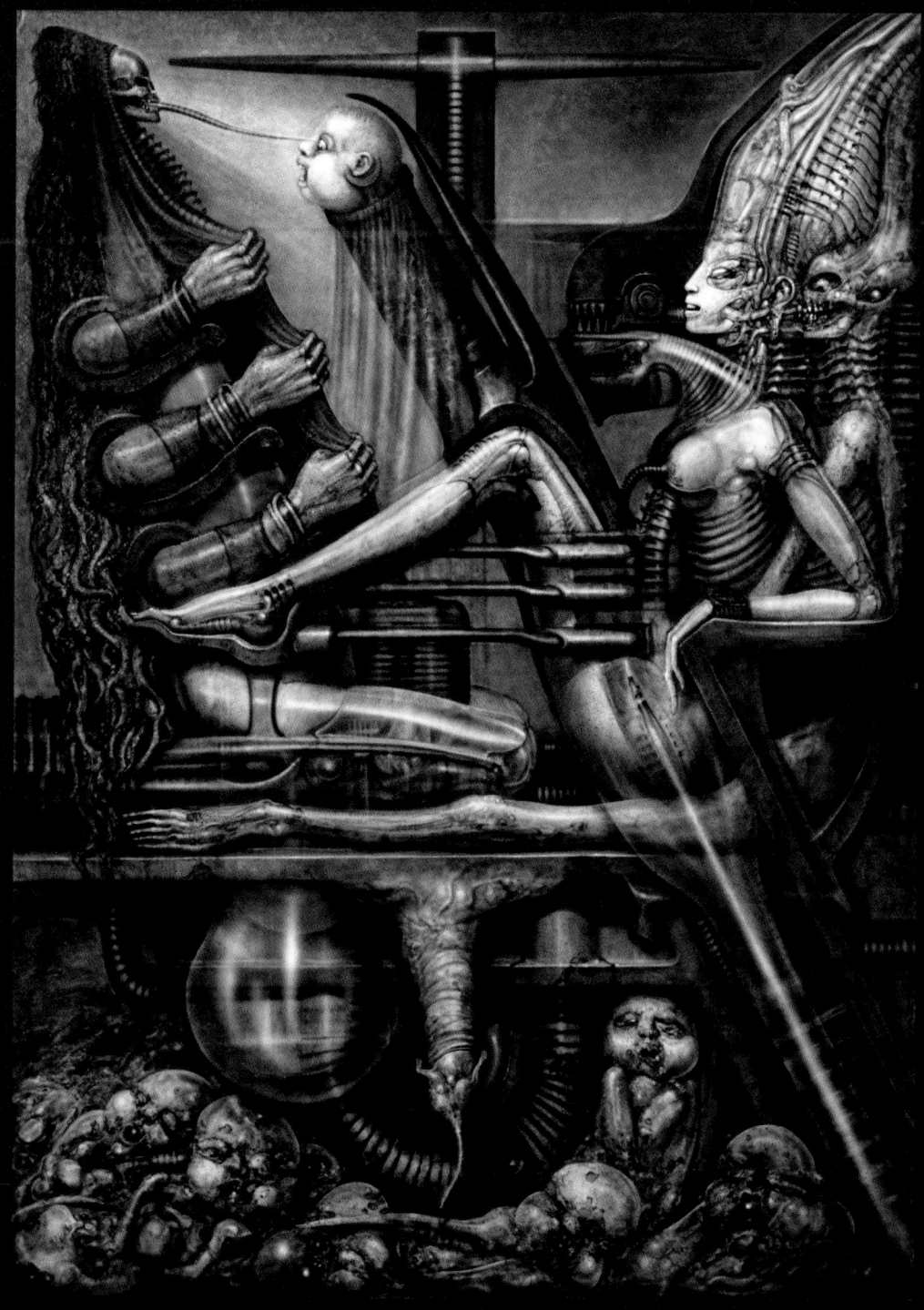

H.R. GIGER

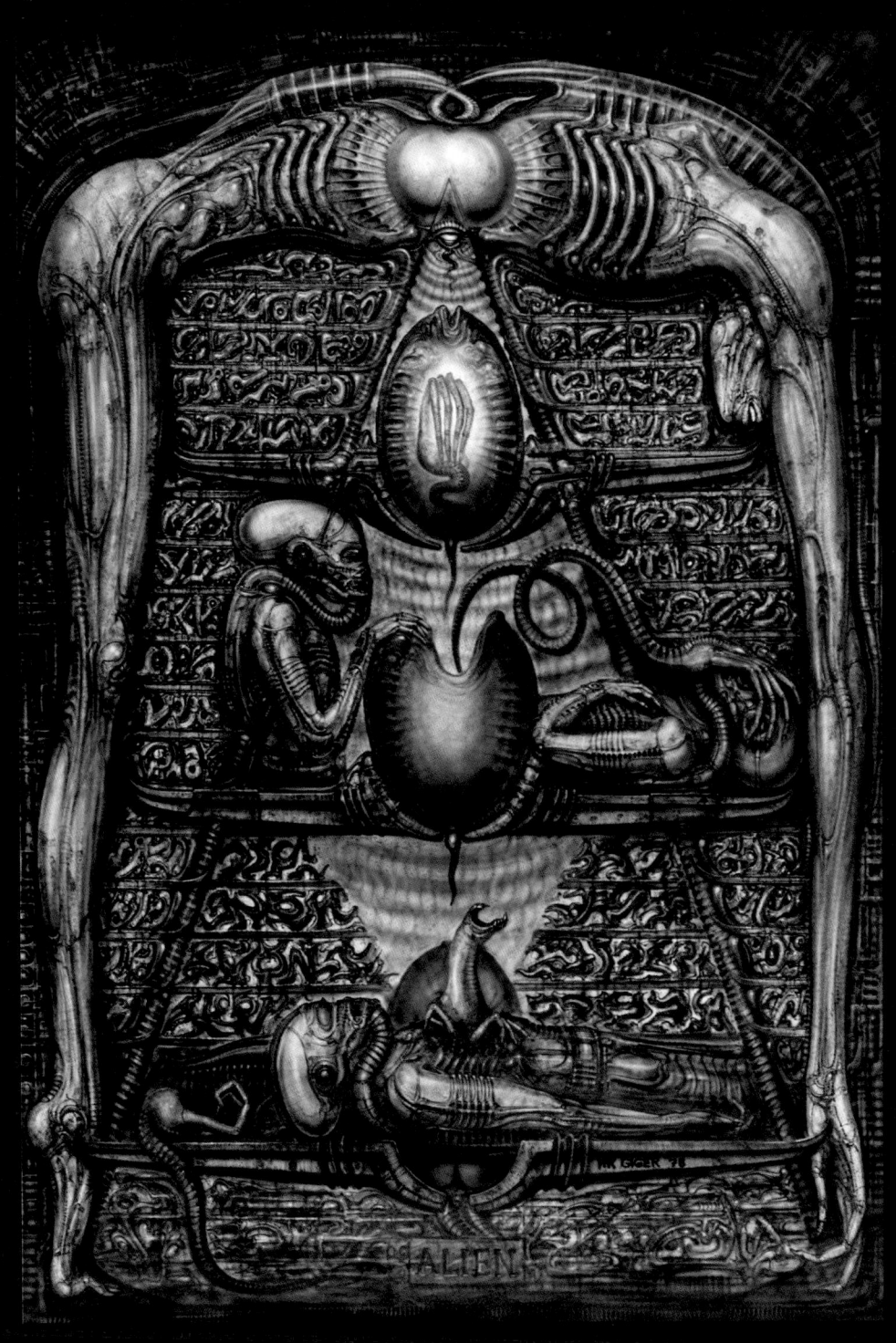

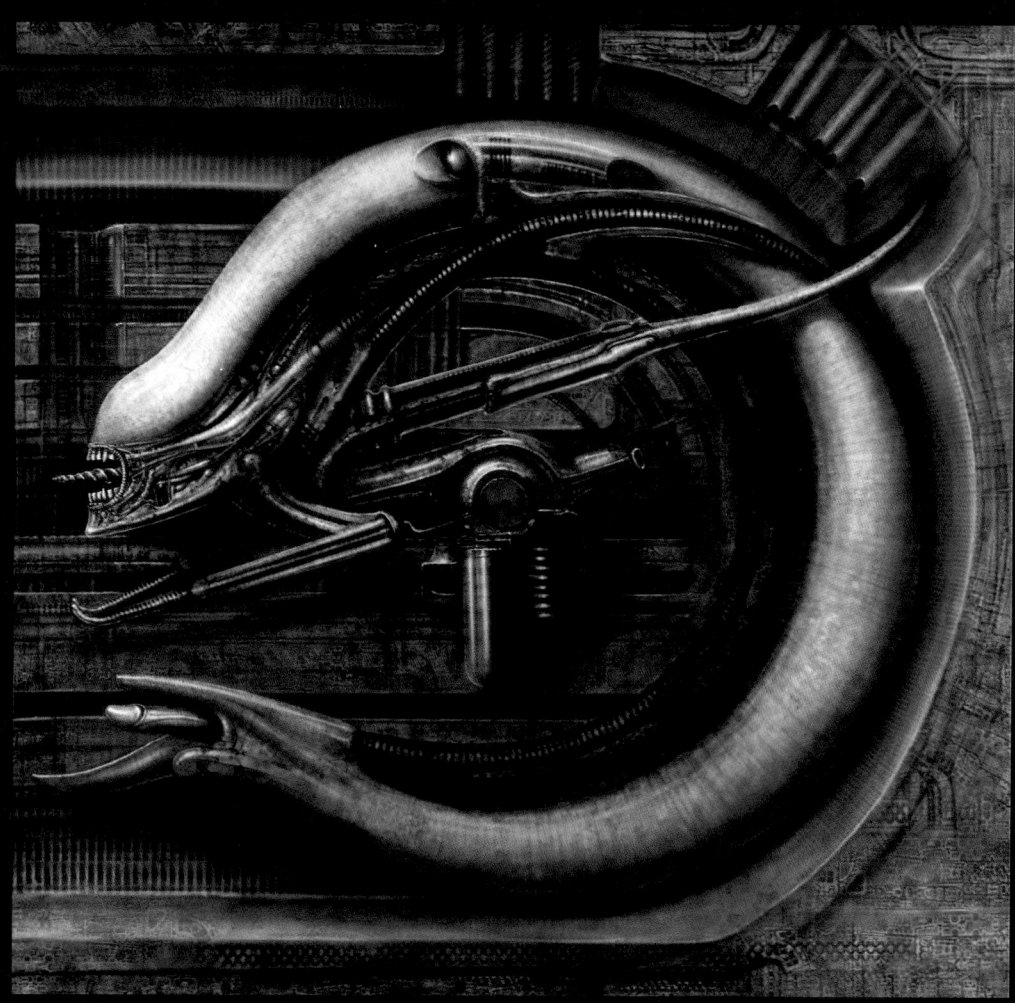

Opposite: Hieroglyphs, concept painting for an early version of the script for the film *Alien*, in which the alien eggs were kept in an ornate temple, adorned by these hieroglyphics detailing their life cycle. 1978, acrylic on paper, 200 x 140 cm (78.7 x 55 inches).

Above: *Alien Monster V*, 1979, acrylic on paper laid on wood, 140 x 140 cm (55.1 x 55.1 inches).

Following spread: *Li I*, 1974, acrylic and India ink on photo, 70 x 97 cm (27.6 x 38.2 inches).

Page 270: *Biomechanoid*, 1976, acrylic on paper laid on wood, 100 x 70 cm (39.4 x 27.6 inches).

Page 271: *Kopf I*, 1966, ink on paper laid on wood, 42 x 60 cm (16.5 x 23.6 inches).

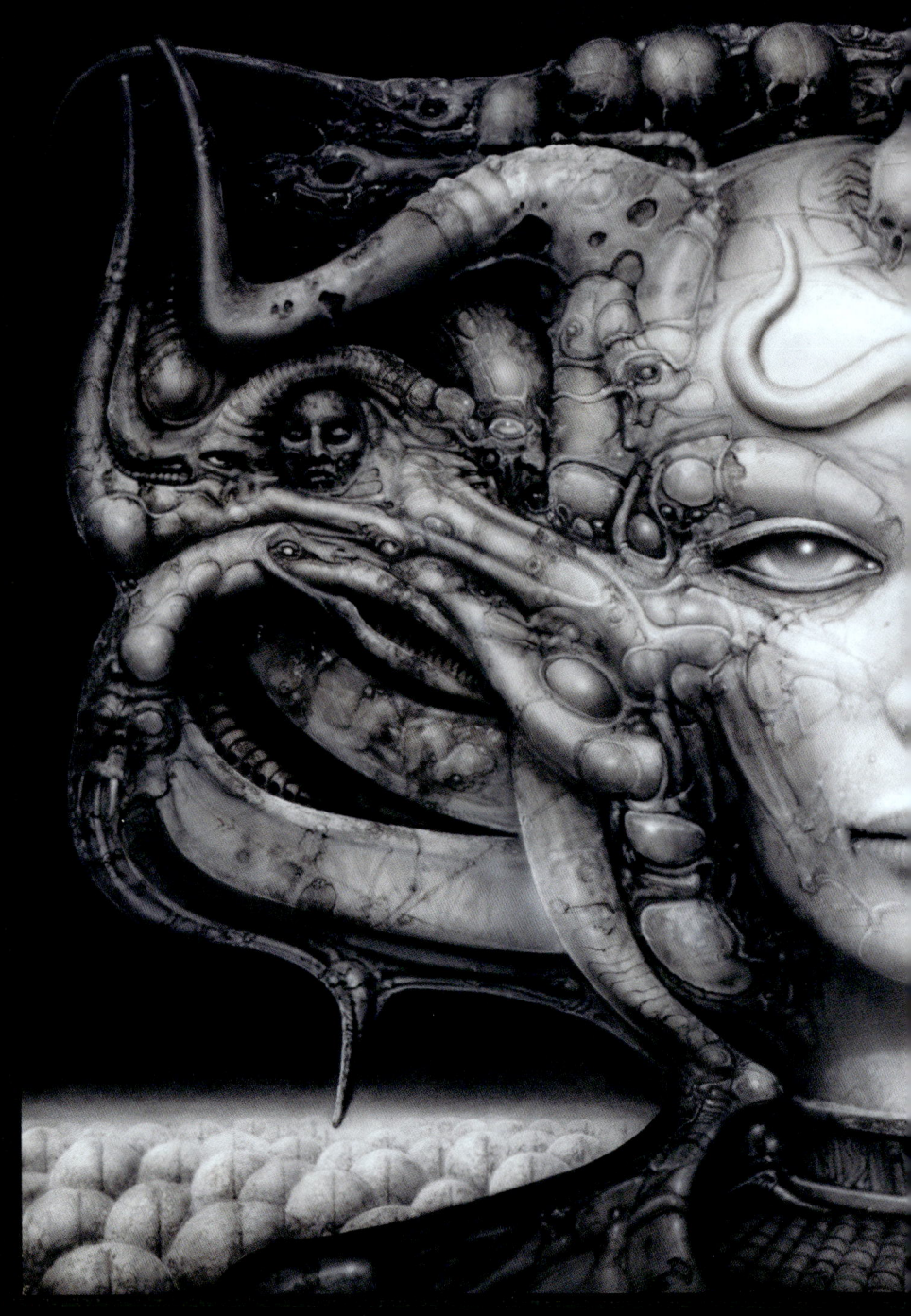

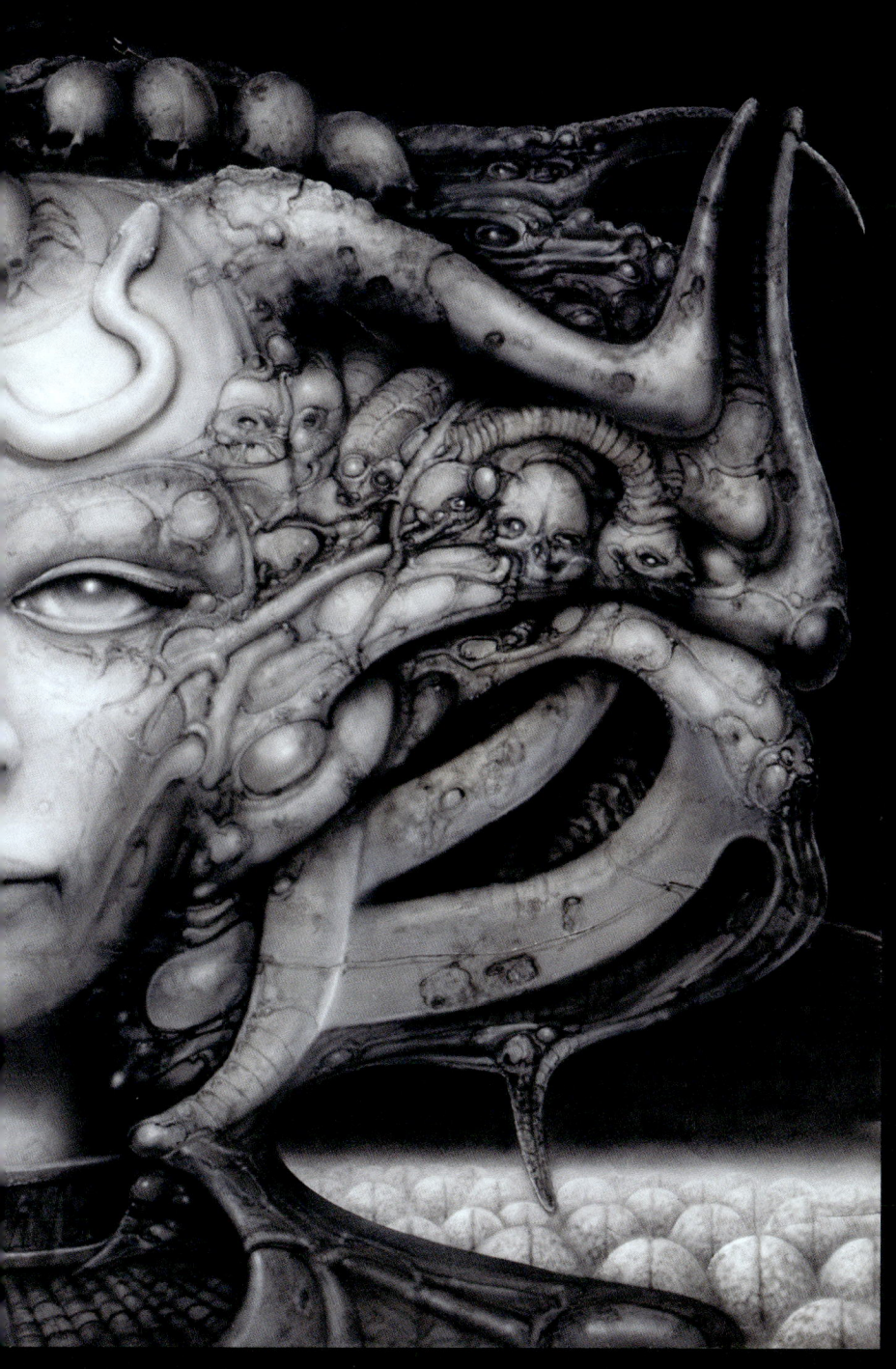

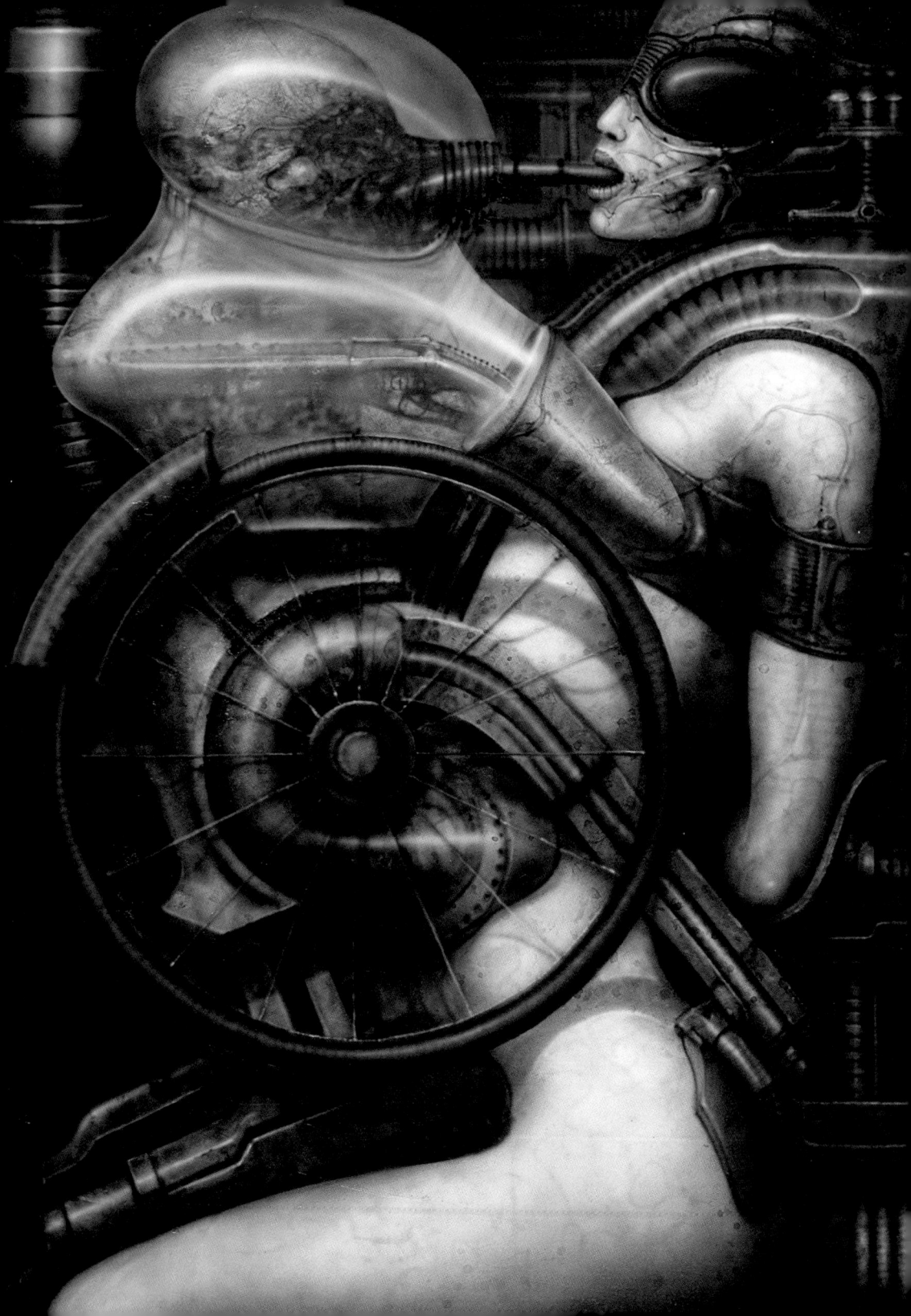

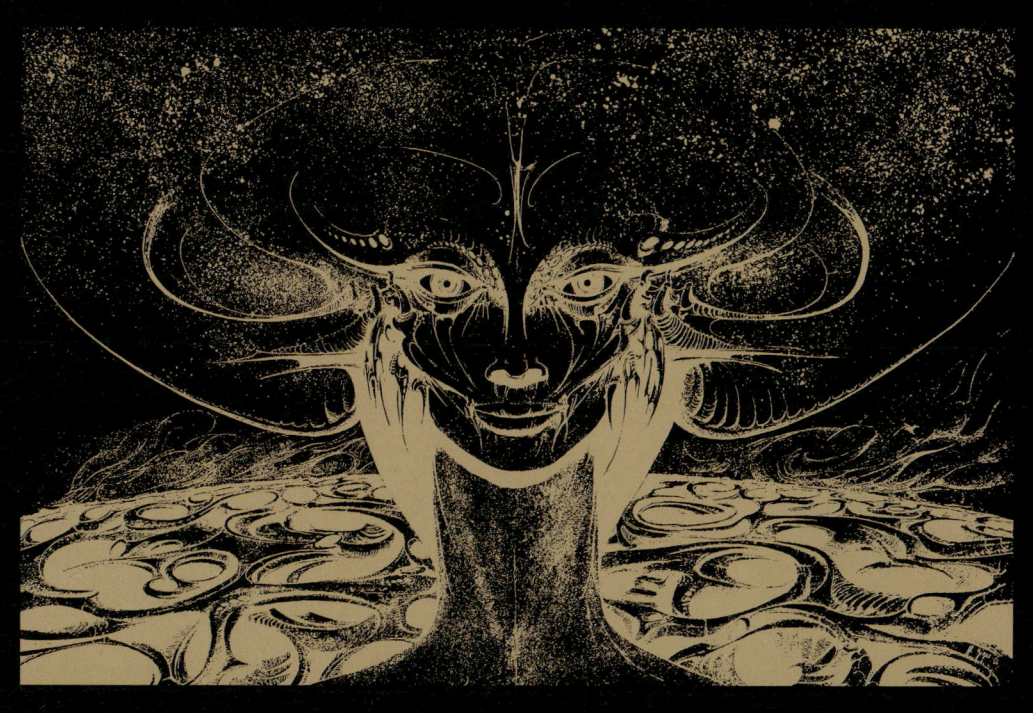

The Brothers Hildebrandt

1939—2024
1939—2006

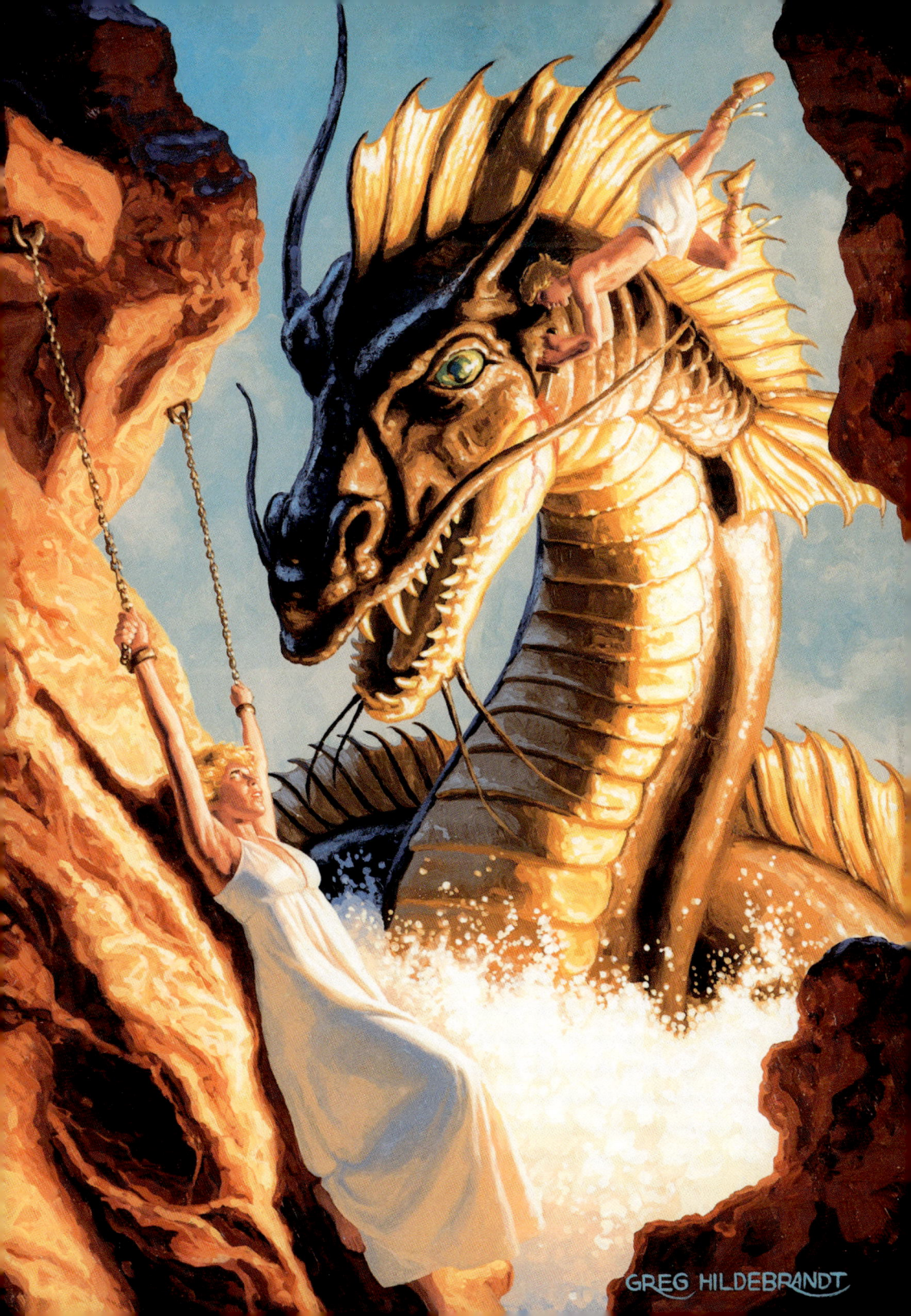
GREG HILDEBRANDT

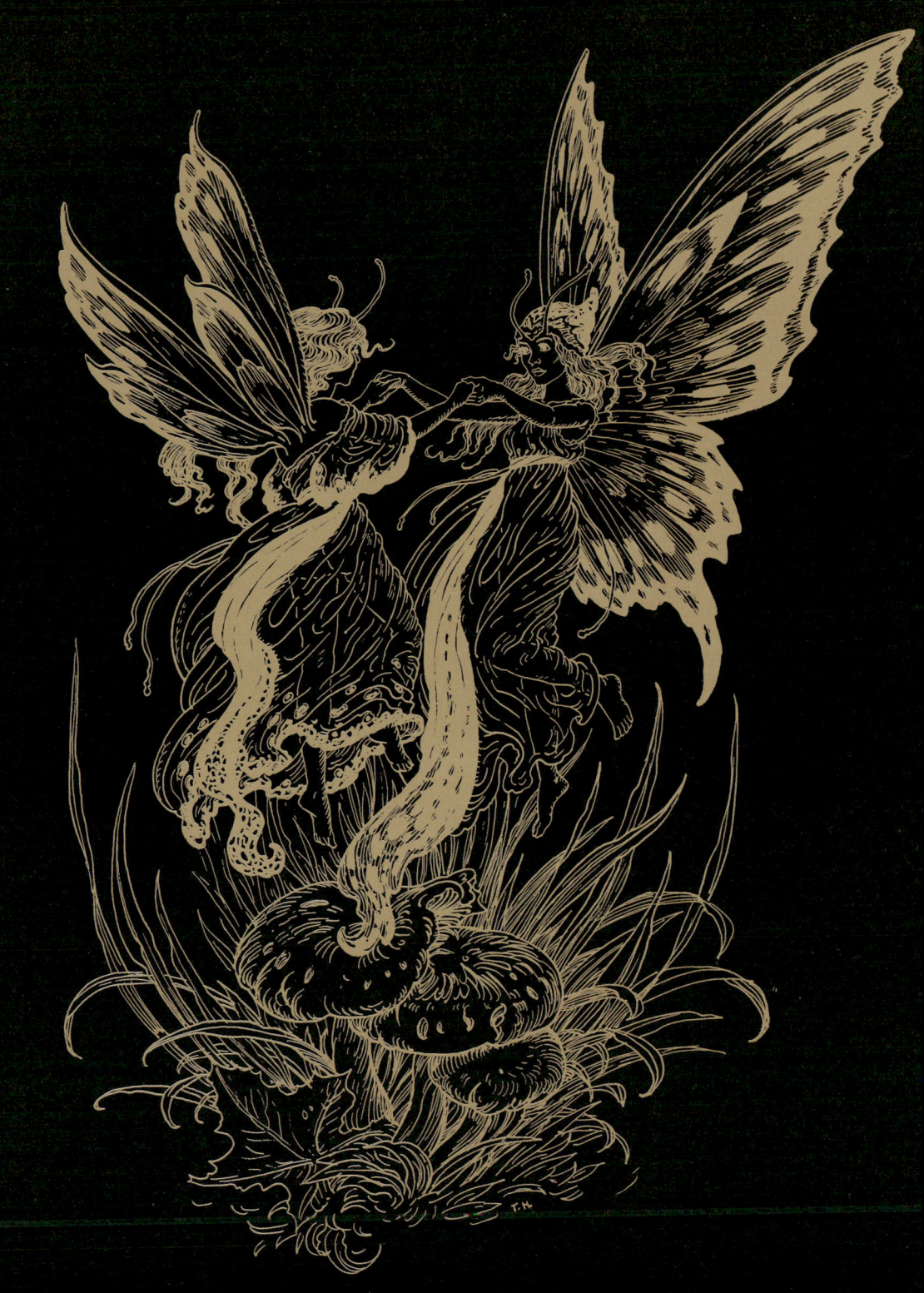

THE BROTHERS HILDEBRANDT
MASTERS OF LIGHT

"Being nice is a choice
I make every day."
— Greg Hildebrandt

Like Darth Vader, some artists embrace the dark side; identical twins Tim and Greg Hildebrandt, who famously painted an original *Star Wars* poster, preferred the light. For instance, in 1963, as the pill ushered in the sexual revolution, Frank Sinatra renounced the Church in *Playboy*, and Cary Grant experimented with LSD, the 24-year-old Hildebrandts were busy illustrating Christ's last week on Earth. And why not? The straight and narrow path led the Detroit-born brothers right where they wanted to go.

In 1939, when the Brothers Hildebrandt, as they came to be called, were born, Motor City was a good place to live and work. The automotive industry recovered faster than most from the Great Depression, and strong unions made the city a model of middle-class success. Greg and Tim's dad worked at General Motors, and both parents supported their interest in art. "As a kid it was *great*," Tim told *Starlog* magazine in 1982. " ...there we were, these two people, with equal talent, interested in *exactly* the same things." Their parents let them cover the walls of their bedroom with drawings they copied from the Sunday comics: Burne Hogarth's *Tarzan* and Hal Foster's *Prince Valiant*, as well as anything by Disney, and anything colorful. Greg later joked they were so obsessed with color they ate a box of crayons at age two.

They were equally obsessed with filmmaking, inspired by Detroit's ornate old theaters as much as by the movies shown there. They'd often smuggle in their 8 mm Kodak Brownie movie camera, pirating *War of the Worlds* at age 14 to study George Pal's technique, then building elaborate min-iature cities to stage their own global apocalypse. After high school they took a six-month course at Meinzingers Art School, because they'd read somewhere it was required to work at Disney. Disney was always the goal, but instead Dad got them jobs at the Jam Handy Organization, where the 18-year-olds learned animation making auto industry training films. It wasn't *Bambi*, but it was good practice for when Bishop Fulton Sheen called.

The Hildebrandts' years with the charismatic Bishop, star of the 1950s TV show *Life Is Worth Living*, started with that Christ project. The artwork was sent to a Franciscan publishing house in New Jersey, whose owner showed it to Sheen, who invited the brothers to his New York office. Sheen was charmed by the young twins and hired them to travel across Africa and South America, filming scenes of poverty. For the next six years they made what Greg called "contrast movies," intercutting their Third World footage with scenes of well-fed American teenagers to raise money for hunger relief. What they experienced in those years left the brothers with a deep affection for Sheen, and a lifelong social conscience.

Previous right: Perseus and Andromeda, for Greg Hildebrandt's Favorite Fairy Tales, 1984. Acrylic on board, 1983, 57.1 x 39.3 cm (22.5 x 15.5 inches). Courtesy of Heritage Auctions.

Opposite: Interior illustration for The Rita and Tim Hildebrandt Fantasy Cookbook, ink on paper by Tim Hildebrandt, circa 1982, 34.2 x 23.5 cm (13.5 x 9.25 inches). Courtesy of Heritage Auctions.

When Sheen resigned his post in 1969 the brothers turned to illustrating children's books for Holt, Rinehart and Winston, Random House, and Western Publishing, makers of the popular Little Golden Books. Something of those years always stayed with them, a pastel, kid-friendly quality rare in fantasy art. This inviting warmth impressed the editors at Ballantine Books, who chose them to illustrate the 1976 J.R.R. Tolkien calendar, christened them the Brothers Hildebrandt, and launched their fantasy art career.

The Tolkien canvases are huge, measuring four to six feet wide. One brother painted the left side, and one painted the right, with a single palette placed between them. There was little discussion; they'd worked in tandem all their lives.

The 1976 calendar won the brothers a strong fan following; they were signed to do two more, with the 1977 selling more than 1,000,000 copies—a first for any calendar. This led to collaboration with author Jerry Nichols to create their own fantasy novel, *Urshurak*. While working on the book in 1977 they were asked to create a sci-fi movie poster—fast. The film was set to premiere in two weeks, but the director hated his poster. The brothers completed a huge painting in 36 hours—36 hours of frantic, nonstop work, sleeping in four-hour shifts—but still, they painted the iconic *Star Wars* poster in just 36 hours. They were paid $4,000, which was pretty good back in 1977, but as Greg says, the real windfall was "$1,000,000 worth of publicity." *The Biography of J.R.R. Tolkien* and *The Complete Guide to Middle Earth* quickly followed, along with illustrations for *The Sword of Shannara*, a novel with a strong Tolkien influence. They completed *Urshurak* in 1979, and in 1980 produced two stunning posters for *Clash of the Titans*, one based, at the studio's insistence, on their *Star Wars* poster.

Then, in 1981, the Brothers Hildebrandt stunned the fantasy art world by dissolving their partnership. Both said the real surprise was that they hadn't done it sooner, while admitting it was terrifying. They were raised as one, had worked as one; each had to know if he was actually an artist, or just half an artist.

Tim and Greg didn't see or speak to each other for 10 years. Tim painted calendars for Dungeons & Dragons' *Realms of Wonder* and *Dragonriders of Pern*, collaborated with his wife Rita on *The Fantasy Cookbook*, created the poster for *The Secret of NIMH*, and produced the low-budget horror film *The Deadly Spawn*, shot largely in his barn. Greg returned to children's books, illustrating *A Christmas Carol*, *Pinocchio*, *Peter Pan*, *The Wizard of Oz*, and *Alice in Wonderland*, as well as production concepts for the film *Krull*. Both did magazine covers and advertising commissions.

In 1993 the brothers reunited, now confident in their separate, unique talents. They took over Milt Caniff's *Terry and the Pirates* comic strip and collaborated on 158 paintings for Marvel. They never returned to exclusive collaboration, though, and in 1999 Greg entered a new phase with no connection to his brother: his American Beauties pin-ups. He's completed more than 100 to date, and devotes most of his time to updating this classic art form.

Tim published an instructional guide to his painting technique in 2000, and in 2001 the brothers delighted fans with *Greg and Tim Hildebrandt: The Tolkien Years*. In 2004, in addition to his pin-ups, Greg became the official artist for Trans-Siberian Orchestra after discovering the band's producer Paul O'Neill was a big fan.

Tim Hildebrandt died in 2006, at age 67. "I don't even have a sense that Tim is dead," Greg told *Filmfax* in 2015. "I talk to him. I dream about him." In 2017 Paul O'Neill died at age 61, putting future Trans-Siberian projects in doubt. Greg took that one hard too, but he kept on going, doing what he loved, buoyed by his wife and agent Jean Scrocco. Greg passed away on October 31, 2024, at the age of 85.

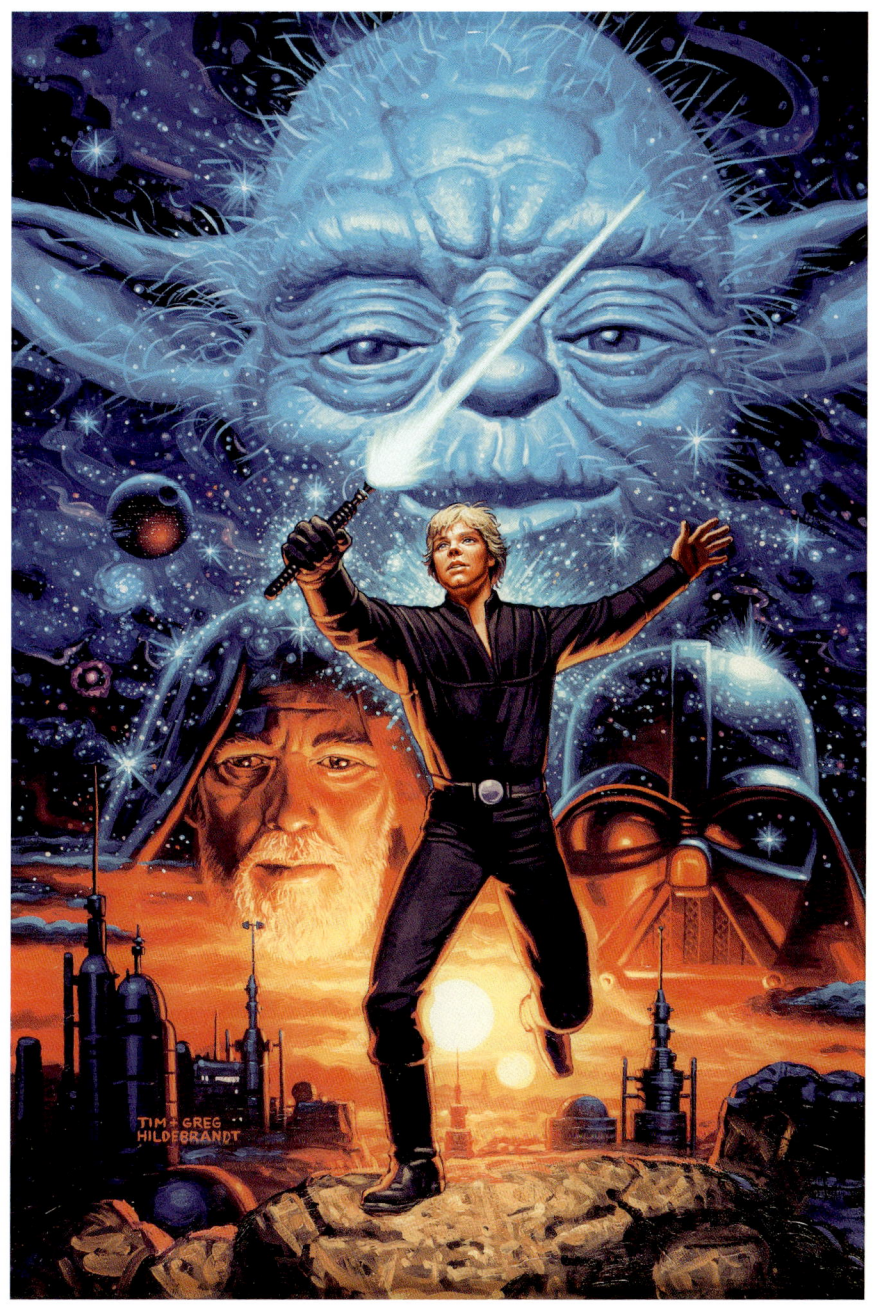

Above: The Four Jedi, for *Star Wars Galaxy Series 3* trading cards, promo card P6. Image was also used as the cover of *Star Wars Galaxy* magazine No. 5. Oil on board by the Brothers Hildebrandt, 1995, 83.8 x 54.6 cm (33 x 21.5 inches). Courtesy of Heritage Auctions.

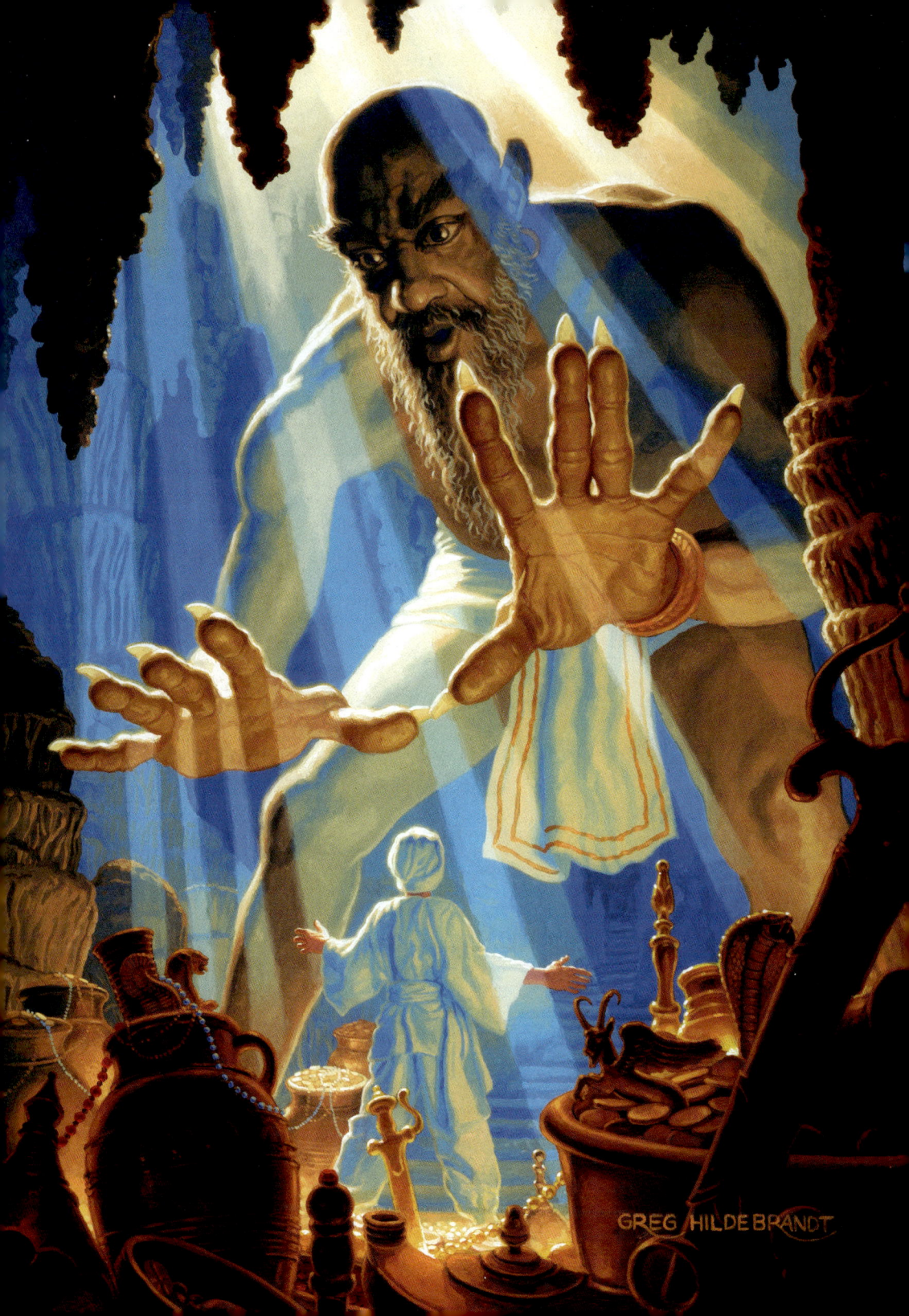

GREG HILDEBRANDT

GEBRÜDER HILDEBRANDT
MEISTER DES LICHTS

„Nett zu sein ist eine Entscheidung,
die ich jeden Tag treffe."
— Greg Hildebrandt

Manche Künstler machen sich, wie Darth Vader, die dunkle Seite zu eigen. Die eineiigen Zwillinge Tim und Greg Hildebrandt, die bekanntlich das Originalplakat für *Star Wars* malten, bevorzugten das Helle. Zum Beispiel 1963 – als die Pille die sexuelle Revolution einleitete, Frank Sinatra sich im *Playboy* von der Kirche abwandte und Cary Grant mit LSD experimentierte –, da illustrierten die 24-jährigen Hildebrandts eifrig Christi letzte Woche auf Erden. Und warum nicht? Der direkte und enge Pfad führte die in Detroit geborenen Brüder genau da hin, wo sie hinwollten.

1939, als die Gebrüder Hildebrandt, wie sie später genannt wurden, auf die Welt kamen, war Motor City Detroit ein guter Ort zum Leben und Arbeiten. Die Automobilindustrie erholte sich von den Jahren der Großen Depression schneller als die meisten anderen, und starke Gewerkschaften sorgten dafür, dass die Stadt zu einem Modell für den Erfolg der Mittelklasse wurde. Gregs und Tims Vater arbeitete bei General Motors, und beide Elternteile förderten das Interesse der Kinder an Kunst. „Für ein Kind war das *großartig*", erzählte Tim 1982 der Zeitschrift *Starlog*, „… da waren wir also, wir beiden, mit dem gleichen Talent und *genau* an den gleichen Sachen interessiert." Ihre Eltern duldeten es, dass sie die Wände ihres Schlafzimmers mit Zeichnungen bedeckten, die sie aus den Comics der Sonntagsausgaben der Zeitung kopierten: Burne Hogarths *Tarzan* und Hal Fosters *Prince Valiant*, aber auch alles Mögliche von Disney, überhaupt alles, was schön bunt war. Greg scherzte später, sie seien so besessen von Farben gewesen, dass sie im Alter von zwei Jahren eine Schachtel Farbstifte aufgefuttert hätten.

Auch vom Filmemachen waren sie ganz besessen. Die verschnörkelten alten Kinos von Detroit inspirierten sie ebenso wie die Filme, die dort gezeigt wurden. Oft schmuggelten sie ihre Kodak-Brownie-8-mm-Filmkamera in den Saal und raubkopierten, da waren sie 14, *War of the Worlds*, um George Pals Technik zu studieren, und bauten hinterher ausgefeilte Ministädte, um ihre eigene globale Apokalypse zu inszenieren. Nach der Highschool belegten sie einen sechs Monate dauernden Kurs an Meinzingers Art School, weil sie irgendwo gelesen hatten, der werde vorausgesetzt, wenn man bei Disney arbeiten wolle. Disney war immer schon das Ziel, doch stattdessen beschaffte ihnen der Vater Jobs bei der Jam Handy Organization, wo die 18-Jährigen Animation beim Produzieren von Lehrfilmen für die Autoindustrie erlernten. *Bambi* war es zwar nicht, doch es war eine gute Übung, bis sich Bischof Fulton Sheen meldete.

Mit dem erwähnten Christus-Projekt begannen die Jahre der Hildebrandts mit dem charismatischen Bischof, Star der Fernsehshow *Life Is Worth Living*. Die Bilder waren an einen

Opposite: *Aladdin*, for Greg Hildebrandt's *Favorite Fairy Tales*. Acrylic on board by Greg Hildebrandt, 1984, 66 x 45.7 cm (26 x 18 inches).

Franziskaner-Verlag in New Jersey geschickt worden, dessen Eigentümer sie Sheen zeigte, und der lud die Brüder ein, ihn in seinem New Yorker Büro zu besuchen. Sheen war von den jungen Zwillingen entzückt und engagierte sie für Reisen durch Afrika und Südamerika, wo sie Szenen der Armut filmen sollten. Während der nächsten sechs Jahre taten sie also das, was Greg „Kontrastfilme" nannte, und schnitten ihr Filmmaterial aus der Dritten Welt mit Szenen wohlgenährter amerikanischer Teenager zusammen, um damit Geld für die Hungerhilfe zu sammeln. Ihre Erlebnisse jener Jahre sorgten dafür, dass die Brüder für Sheen eine tiefe Zuneigung hegten und sich während ihres ganzen Lebens einer gesellschaftlichen Verantwortung bewusst waren.

Als Sheen 1969 von seinem Posten zurücktrat, wandten sich die Brüder der Illustration von Kinderbüchern für Random House, Holt, Rinehart und Winston and Western Publishing zu, den Machern der populären Little Golden Books. Eines ist ihnen aus jenen Jahren geblieben – eine pastellene, kinderfreundliche Qualität, die in der Fantasykunst selten ist. Diese einladende Wärme beeindruckte die Herausgeber bei Ballantine Books, die die beiden erwählten, den J.R.R.-Tolkien-Kalender für 1976 zu illustrieren, sie „Gebrüder Hildebrandt" tauften und damit ihre Karriere in der Fantasykunst anstießen. Die Tolkien-Leinwände sind mit einer Breite von rund 122 bis 183 cm ziemlich groß. Einer der Brüder malte die linke Hälfte, der andere die rechte – zusammen mit nur einer Palette, die sie zwischen sich platziert hatten. Besprochen werden musste nicht viel; ihr Leben lang hatten sie als Tandem gearbeitet.

Mit dem Kalender für 1976 gewannen die Brüder eine starke Fangemeinde; sie erhielten einen Vertrag für zwei weitere, und vom Kalender für 1977 wurden mehr als eine Million Exemplare verkauft – ein Novum für einen Kalender überhaupt. Dies führte zu einer Zusammenarbeit mit dem Autor Jerry Nichols, mit dem sie ihren eigenen Fantasyroman, *Urshurak*, produzierten. 1977, noch während sie an diesem Buch arbeiteten, wurden sie gefragt, ob sie – auf die Schnelle – ein Science-Fiction-Filmplakat gestalten könnten. Die Premiere des Films sollte bereits zwei Wochen später sein, doch der Regisseur hasste das vorgesehene Plakat. Innerhalb von 36 Stunden vollendeten die Brüder ein großes Gemälde – 36 Stunden fieberhafter Arbeit im Nonstop-Modus. Geschlafen wurde nur in Vier-Stunden-Schichten, aber – innerhalb von 36 Stunden malten sie das ikonische Plakatmotiv für *Star Wars*. Sie erhielten dafür ein Honorar von 4.000 Dollar, was für 1977 eine ziemlich gute Bezahlung war, doch wie Greg meint: Der eigentliche warme Regen war die „Werbung, die eine Million Dollar wert war". Gleich darauf folgten Arbeiten für *The Biography of J. R. R. Tolkien* und *The Complete Guide to Middle Earth*, dazu Illustrationen für *The Sword of Shannara*, einen Roman mit starkem Tolkien-Einfluss. 1979 vollendeten sie *Urshurak,* und 1980 produzierten sie zwei fantastische Plakate für *Clash of the Titans*, von dem eines auf Drängen des Studios auf ihrem *Star-Wars*-Poster basierte.

Dann jedoch, 1981, überraschten die Gebrüder Hildebrandt die Welt der Fantasykunst mit der Ankündigung, ihre Arbeitsgemeinschaft aufzulösen. Beide sagten, die eigentliche Überraschung sei der Umstand, dass sie diese Trennung nicht schon früher vollzogen hätten, während sie aber gleichzeitig einräumten, dass es furchterregend sei. Sie waren wie eine einzige Person aufgezogen worden, hatten wie eine Einheit zusammengearbeitet; beide wollten sie nun endlich wissen, ob sie jeder ein Künstler oder nur halbe Künstler waren.

Zehn Jahre lang sahen sich Tim und Greg nicht mehr und sprachen auch nicht miteinander. Tim malte Kalender für Dungeons & Dragons, *Realms of Wonder* und *Dragonriders of Pern*, erarbeitete gemeinsam mit seiner Frau Rita *The Fantasy Cookbook*; er schuf das Plakat für *The Secret of NIMH* und produzierte den Low-Budget-Horrorfilm *The Deadly Spawn*, der im Wesentlichen in seiner Scheune gedreht wurde. Greg wandte sich wieder Kinderbüchern zu und illustrierte

A Christmas Carol, Pinocchio, Peter Pan, The Wizard of Oz und *Alice in Wonderland*, zudem gestaltete er Produktionsentwürfe für den Film *Krull*. Beide Hildebrandts schufen Cover für Zeitschriften und arbeiteten an Werbeaufträgen.

1993 taten sich die Brüder wieder zusammen, denn nun waren sie sich ihres jeweils eigenständigen, einmaligen Talents sicher. Sie übernahmen die Gestaltung von Milt Caniffs Comicstrip „Terry and the Pirates" und erarbeiteten gemeinsam 158 Gemälde für Marvel. Sie kehrten jedoch nie wieder zu ihrer früheren, ausschließlich gemeinsamen Produktionsweise zurück, und 1999 begann Greg eine neue Phase seiner Arbeit, die nichts mit seinem Bruder zu tun hatte: seine Pin-ups amerikanischer Schönheiten. Bis heute hat er davon mehr als 100 vollendet und widmet den größten Teil seiner Zeit einer Aktualisierung dieser klassischen Kunstform.

Tim veröffentlichte 2000 ein Lehrbuch zu seiner Maltechnik,

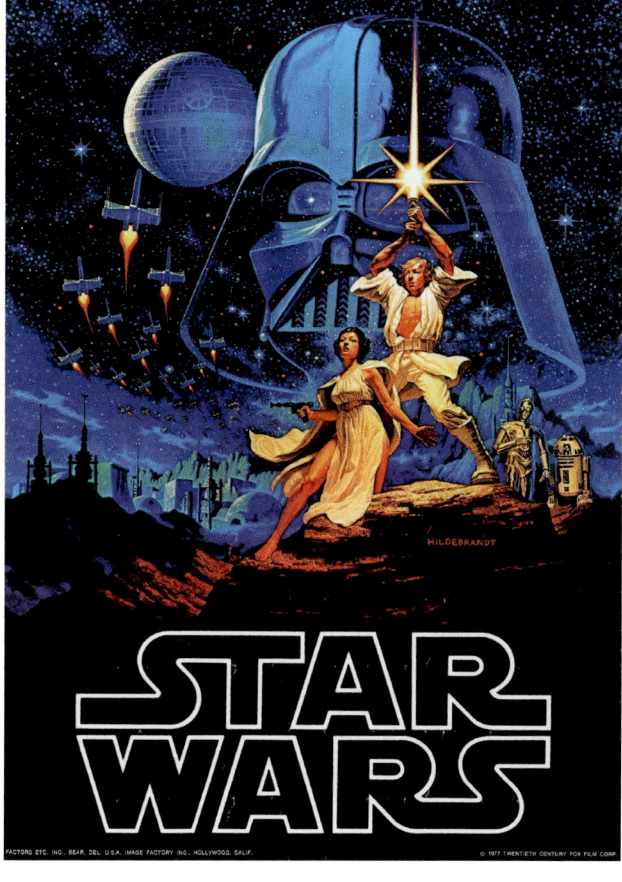

und 2001 erfreuten die Brüder ihre Fans mit *Greg and Tim Hildebrandt: The Tolkien Years*. 2004 wurde Greg, nachdem er festgestellt hatte, dass Paul O'Neill, Produzent der Band, ein großer Fan war, neben seiner Arbeit an den Pin-ups offizieller Künstler des Trans-Siberian Orchestra.

Tim Hildebrandt starb 2006 im Alter von 67 Jahren. „Ich habe nicht einmal das Gefühl, dass Tim tot ist", erklärte Greg 2015 gegenüber *Filmfax*. „Ich rede mit ihm. Ich träume von ihm." 2017 starb Paul O'Neill mit 61 Jahren, damit herrscht Ungewissheit über künftige Projekte des Trans-Siberian Orchestra. Auch das war für Greg ein schwerer Schlag, doch er machte, ermutigt von seiner Frau und Agentin Jean Scrocco, weiter und arbeitete an allem, was er mochte. Greg ist am 31. Oktober 2024 im Alter von 85 Jahren verstorben.

Above: The commission to paint this *Star Wars* poster, with a punishing 36-hour deadline, made the Hildebrandts $4,000 in 1977, and gave them $1,000,000 worth of publicity. Bathrobes and bedsheets served as their clothing reference. 104 x 68.5 cm (41 x 27 inches).

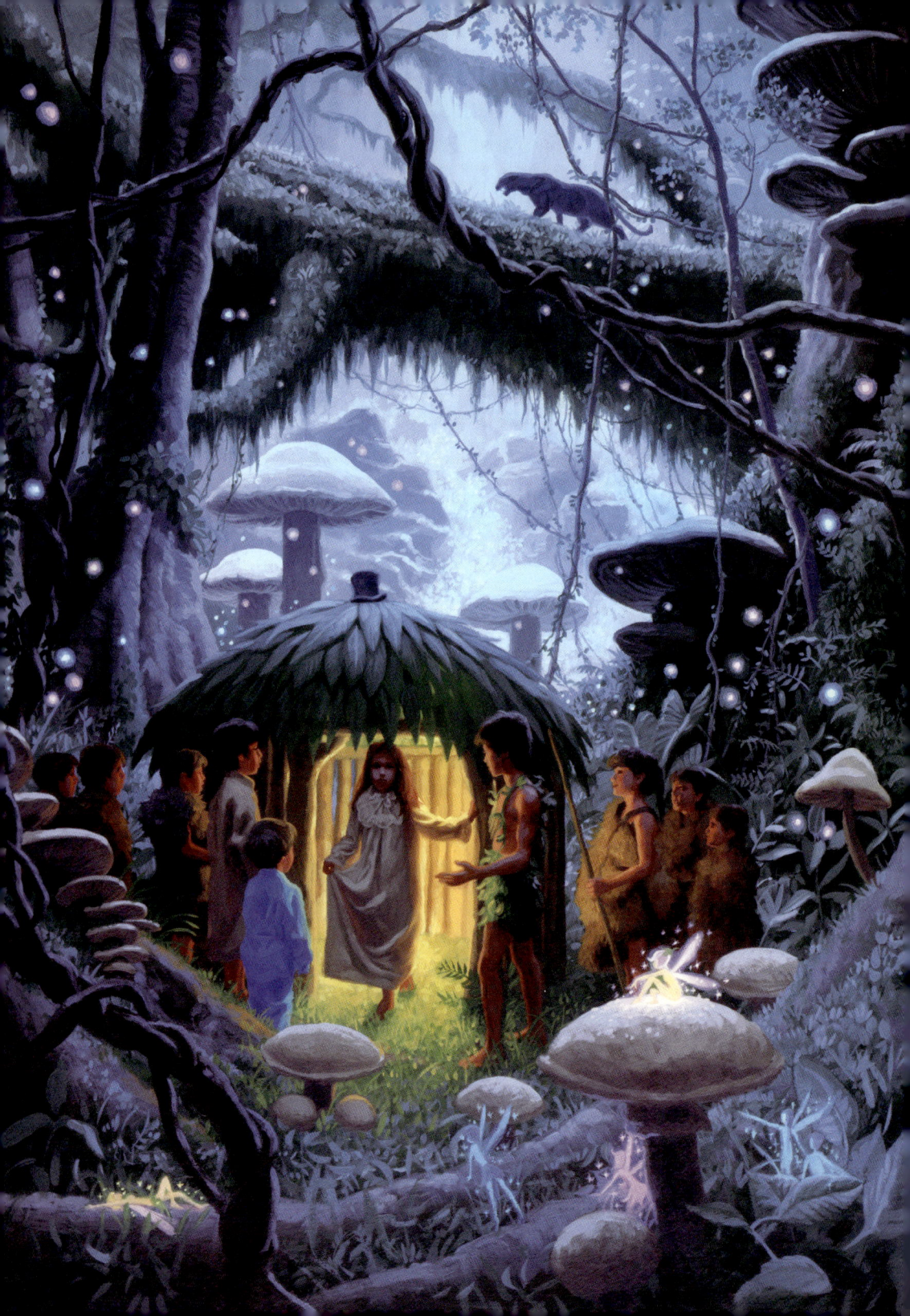

LES FRÈRES HILDEBRANDT
LES MAÎTRES DE LA LUMIÈRE

*« Être gentil, c'est un choix
que je fais chaque jour. »
— Greg Hildebrandt*

À la manière de Dark Vador, certains artistes se vouent au côté obscur. Les vrais jumeaux Tim et Greg Hildebrandt, notamment célèbres pour avoir peint l'affiche originale de *Star Wars*, préféraient la lumière. Jugez plutôt : en 1963, alors que la pilule inaugure la révolution sexuelle, que Frank Sinatra annonce tourner le dos à l'Église dans *Playboy* et que Cary Grant s'essaie au LSD, les Hildebrandt, âgés de 24 ans, sont occupés à illustrer la dernière semaine du Christ sur la Terre. Pourquoi pas ? Ce chemin étroit et rectiligne mena les deux natifs de Détroit précisément là où ils voulaient aller.

En 1939, à la naissance de ceux qu'on appellera bientôt Brothers Hildebrandt, il fait bon vivre et travailler à Motor City. L'industrie automobile se remet de la Grande Dépression plus vite que beaucoup d'autres et les puissants syndicats du secteur ont fait de la ville un modèle de réussite pour classes moyennes. Le père de Greg et Tim est employé chez General Motors et leurs deux parents encouragent leur goût pour l'art. « Pour des gosses, c'était génial, racontait Tim dans le magazine *Starlog* en 1982. Nous étions deux, de talent égal, tous les deux intéressés *exactement* par les mêmes choses. » Leurs parents les laissent couvrir leurs murs de dessins recopiés dans les bandes dessinées du dimanche, le *Tarzan* de Burne Hogarth et le *Prince Vaillant* de Hal Foster, ainsi que de personnages Disney, tout ce qui a de la couleur. Greg racontera en plaisantant que leur obsession partagée pour la couleur était telle qu'ils ont mangé toute une boîte de pastels à deux ans.

Ils sont tout aussi obsédés par le cinéma, tant par les salles de Détroit aux airs de vieux théâtres que par les films qui y sont projetés. Ils apportent en douce leur petite caméra Kodak Brownie 8 mm et piratent notamment *La Guerre des mondes (War of the Worlds)* à 14 ans pour étudier la technique de George Pal, puis construisent des maquettes urbaines compliquées où ils mettent en scène leur propre apocalypse miniature. Après le lycée, ils suivent pendant six mois les cours de l'école d'art Meinzingers, parce qu'ils ont lu quelque part que l'établissement est la voie royale pour travailler chez Disney. Disney est leur objectif depuis toujours, mais papa les fait engager à la Jam Handy Organization, où les jumeaux de 18 ans apprennent l'animation en réalisant des films pour la formation des ouvriers de l'industrie automobile. Ce n'est pas *Bambi*, mais c'est un bon entraînement et ils sont prêts quand Fulton Sheen les appelle.

Les années que les frères Hildebrandt passeront aux côtés du charismatique évêque Sheen, vedette de l'émission télévisée des années 1950 *Life Is Worth Living*, démarrent avec ce projet sur le Christ. Les illustrations sont envoyées à une maison d'édition franciscaine du New Jersey. L'éditeur les montre à Sheen, qui donne rendez-vous aux deux frères à son bureau de New York. Sheen

Opposite: Wendy's House in the Woods, for Peter Pan, 1987. Acrylic on board by Greg Hildebrandt, 1986, 53.3 x 40.6 cm (21 x 16 inches).

est séduit par les jeunes jumeaux et les charge de sillonner l'Afrique et l'Amérique du Sud pour filmer la misère. Pendant six ans, ils réalisent ce que Greg appelle des « films à contraste », où ils intercalent leurs images du tiers-monde avec des scènes dans lesquelles des adolescents américains bien nourris font des collectes pour les populations qui meurent de faim. De cette expérience naîtront chez eux une affection profonde pour Sheen et une conscience sociale qui durera toute leur vie.

Quand Sheen démissionne, en 1969, les jumeaux se tournent vers l'illustration de livres pour enfants et collaborent avec Holt, Rinehart and Winston, Random House et Western Publishing, qui édite la collection populaire des Little Golden Books. Ils garderont quelque chose de ces années, une facette pastel et ludique rare dans le fantasy art. Cette douceur chaleureuse et engageante impressionne les éditeurs de Ballantine Books, qui les choisissent pour illustrer un calendrier J.R.R. Tolkien de l'année 1976, les baptisent Brothers Hildebrandt et lancent leur carrière dans le fantasy art. Les toiles sur Tolkien sont immenses – entre 1,20 et 1,80 mètre de large. Un frère peint le côté gauche tandis que l'autre peint le droit, avec une palette commune placée entre eux. Ils parlent peu ; ils ont travaillé en tandem toute leur vie.

Grâce au calendrier de 1976, les jumeaux conquièrent des fans nombreux et fidèles ; ils signent pour deux de plus et celui de 1977 se vend à plus d'un million d'exemplaires – une première pour un calendrier. Ces contrats les amènent à collaborer avec l'auteur Jerry Nichols pour créer leur propre roman fantastique, *Urshurak*. En 1977, alors qu'ils travaillent à leur livre, on leur demande de concevoir l'affiche d'un film de science-fiction… vite ! L'avant-première du film doit avoir lieu deux semaines plus tard, mais le réalisateur a détesté l'affiche prévue. Les deux frères achèvent une immense toile en 36 heures – 36 heures de travail frénétique, ininterrompu, au cours desquelles ils dorment par tranches de quatre heures, mais toujours est-il qu'ils peignent l'illustre première affiche officielle de *Star Wars* en seulement 36 heures. Ils sont payés 4 000 $, ce qui est une jolie somme en 1977, mais comme le dit Greg, le vrai pactole était « le million de dollars de recettes publicitaires ». La biographie de Tolkien *(The Biography of J.R.R. Tolkien)* et le guide complet de la Terre du Milieu *(The Complete Guide to Middle Earth)* ne tardent pas à suivre, ainsi que des

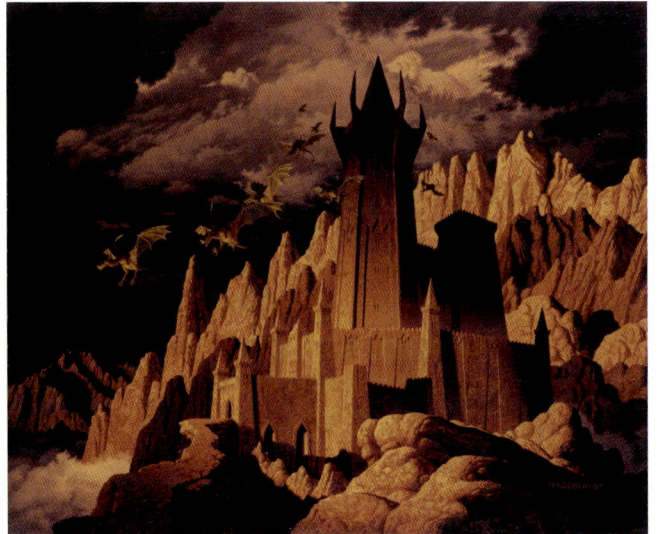

illustrations pour *L'Épée de Shannara (The Sword of Shannara)*, un roman fortement inspiré de Tolkien. Ils terminent *Urshurak* en 1979 et en 1980 ils produisent deux affiches saisissantes pour *Le Choc des Titans (Clash of the Titans)*, dont une prend pour base, à la demande insistante du studio, leur affiche de *Star Wars*.

En 1981, les frères Hildebrandt stupéfient le monde du fantasy art en annonçant la fin de leur partenariat. Les deux hommes expliquent que le plus étonnant est qu'ils ne se soient pas séparés plus tôt, tout en admettant que c'est terrifiant.

Ils ont été élevés comme un seul homme, ils ont toujours travaillé comme un seul homme ; chacun d'eux a besoin de savoir s'il est un artiste à part entière, ou juste la moitié d'un artiste.

Tim et Greg passent dix ans sans se voir ni se parler. Tim peint les calendriers *Realms of Wonder* et *Dragonriders of Pern* pour la série Donjons et Dragons, publie en collaboration avec sa femme Rita le livre de recettes *The Fantasy Cookbook,* crée l'affiche de *Brisby et le Secret de NIMH (The Secret of NIMH)* et produit le film d'horreur à petit budget *The Deadly Spawn*, principalement tourné dans sa grange. Greg revient aux livres pour enfants ; il illustre *Un chant de Noël, Pinocchio, Peter Pan, Le Magicien d'Oz* et *Alice au pays des merveilles* et réalise des croquis pour la production du film *Krull*. Tous deux signent également diverses couvertures de magazines et commandes publicitaires.

En 1993, les frères se retrouvent, rassurés sur l'authenticité et l'unicité de leur talent. Ils reprennent la bande dessinée de Milt Caniff *Terry et les Pirates* et réalisent ensemble 158 œuvres pour Marvel. Ils ne se sont cependant promis aucune exclusivité et en 1999 Greg entame une nouvelle phase de sa carrière sans lien avec son frère : ses pin-up *American Beauties*. Il en a peint plus de 100 à ce jour et consacre la majeure partie de son temps à mettre ce classique de l'art américain au goût du jour.

Tim a publié un manuel d'apprentissage de sa technique picturale en 2000 et en 2001 les jumeaux ont comblé leurs fans avec la sortie de *Greg and Tim Hildebrandt: The Tolkien Years*. En 2004, en plus de ses pin-up, Greg est devenu l'artiste officiel de l'orchestre transsibérien après avoir découvert que son producteur, Paul O'Neill, était un grand admirateur de son travail.

Tim Hildebrandt est mort en 2006, à 67 ans. « Je n'ai même pas l'impression que Tim est mort, confiait Greg à *Filmfax* en 2015. Je lui parle. Je rêve de lui. » En 2017, Paul O'Neill est mort à son tour, à 61 ans, ce qui a remis en question de futurs projets transsibériens. Un autre coup dur pour Greg, mais il a continué à faire ce qu'il aimait, encouragé par sa femme et agent Jean Scrocco. Greg est décédé le 31 octobre 2024, à l'âge de 85 ans.

Opposite: The Dark Tower, image for December in the *1978 J.R.R. Tolkien Calendar*. Acrylic on board by the Brothers Hildebrandt, 1977, 76.2 x 106.6 cm (30 x 42 inches).

Above: The artwork for 1981's *Clash of the Titans* movie poster was one of the last commissions taken by the Brothers Hildebrandt before their creative split. 104 x 68.5 cm (41 x 27 inches).

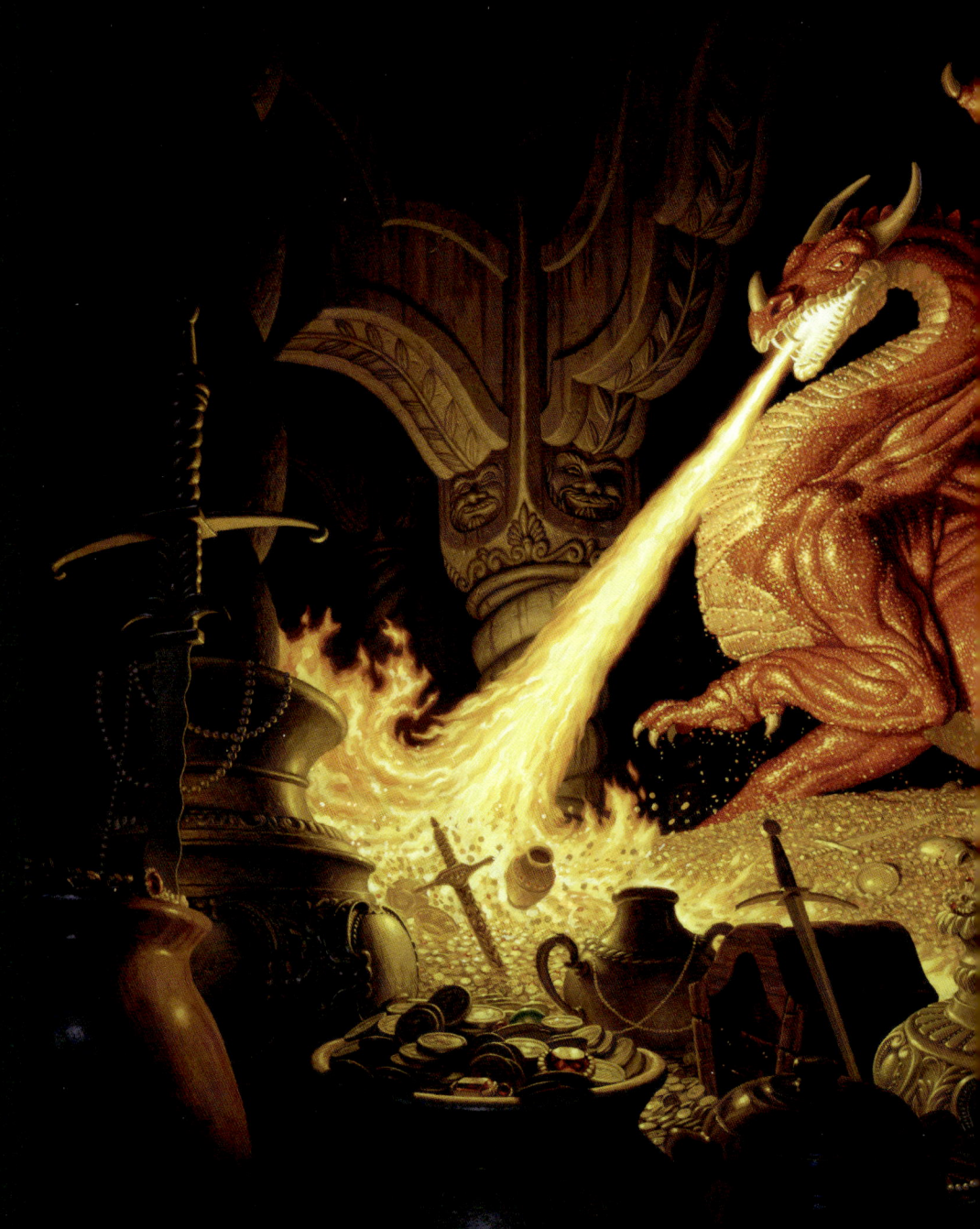

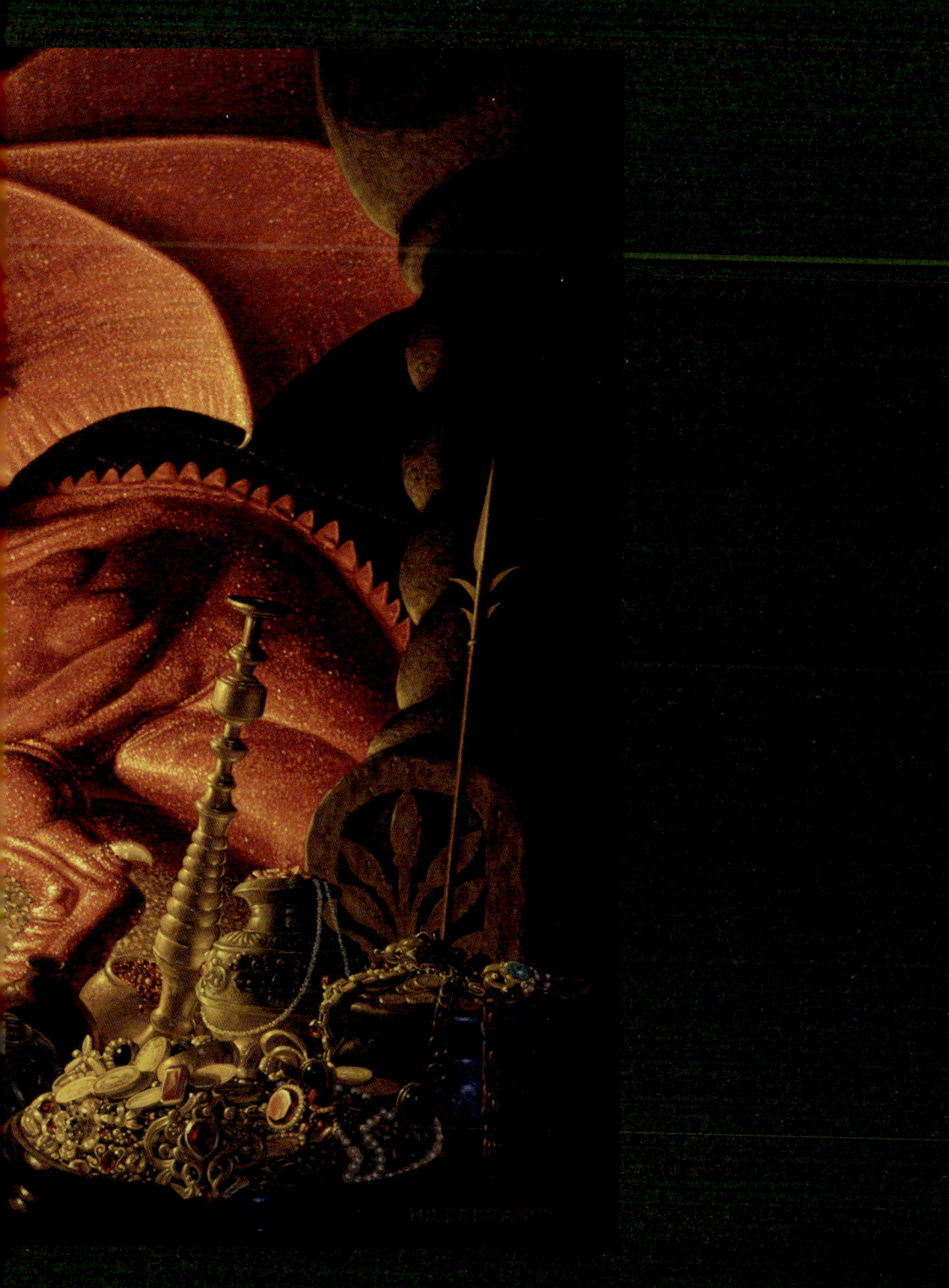

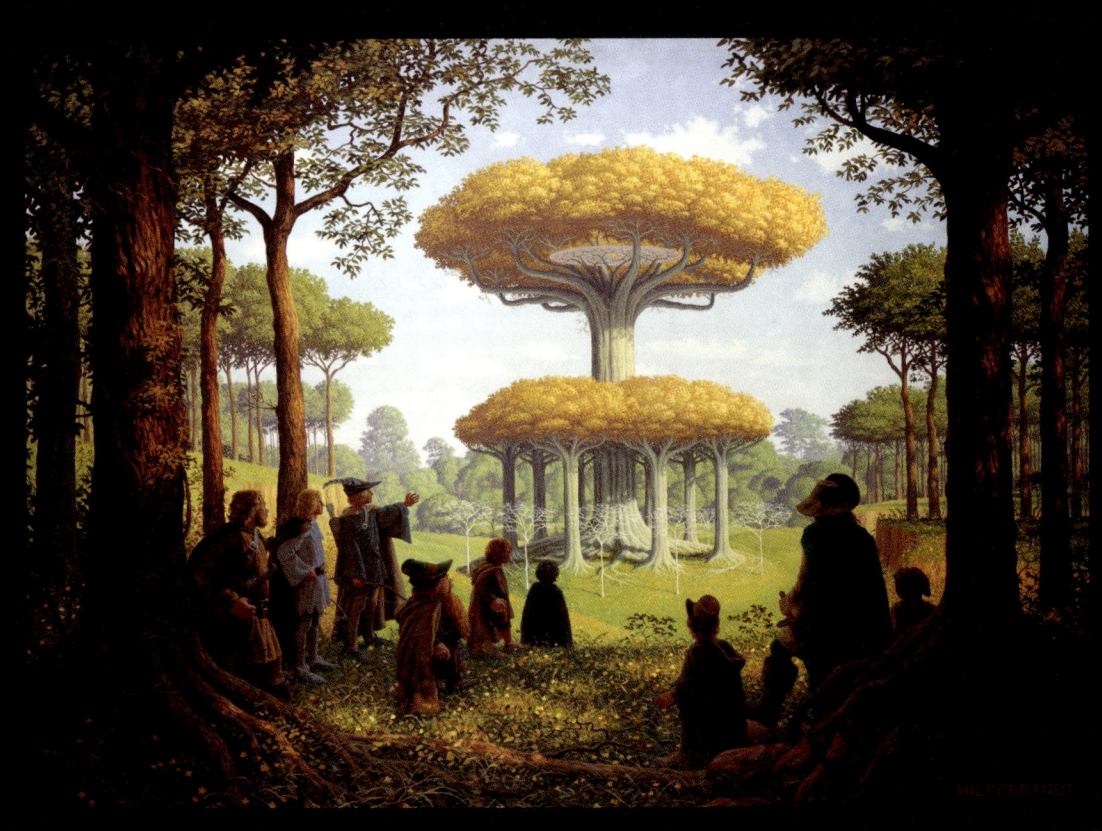

Previous spread: Smaug's Lair, image for January
in the *1977 J.R.R. Tolkien Calendar*. Acrylic on board
by the Brothers Hildebrandt, 1976, 122 x 122 cm
(48 x 48 inches).

Above: Lothlorien, the Elven Forest, image for May
in the *1977 J.R.R. Tolkien Calendar*. Acrylic on board
by the Brothers Hildebrandt, 1976, 106.6 x 121.9 cm
(36 x 42 inches).

MASTERPIECES OF FANTASY ART

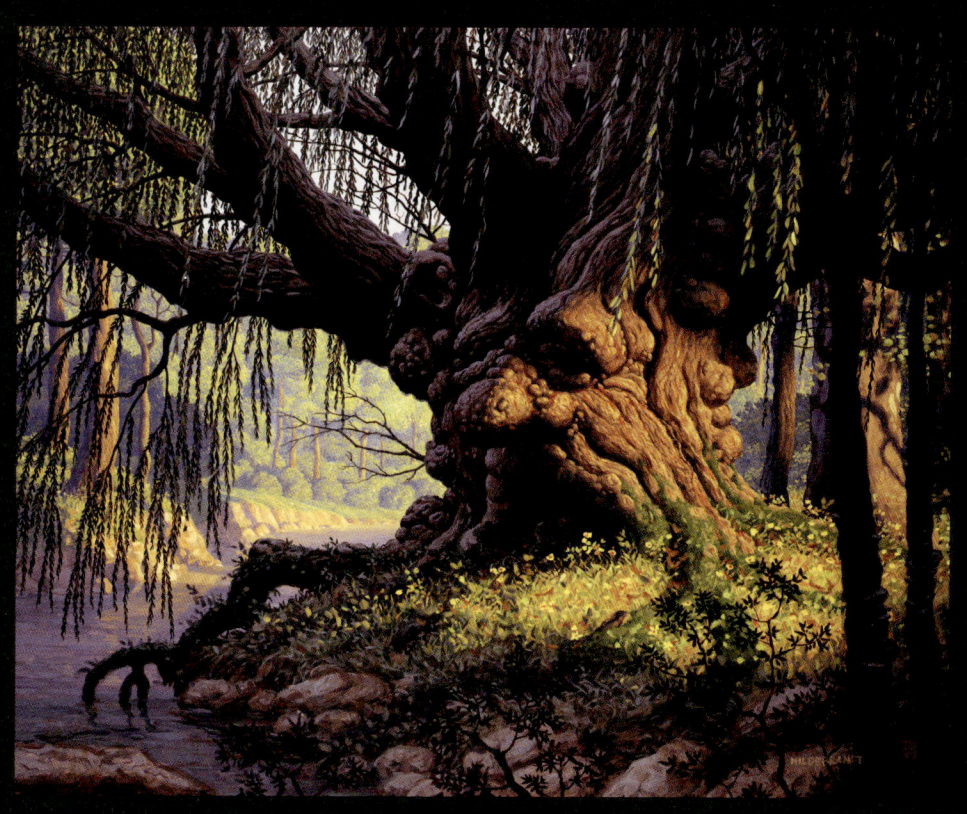

Above: Old Man Willow, image for February
in the *1978 J.R.R. Tolkien Calendar*. Acrylic
on board by the Brothers Hildebrandt, 1977,
91.4 x 106.6 cm (42 x 48 inches).

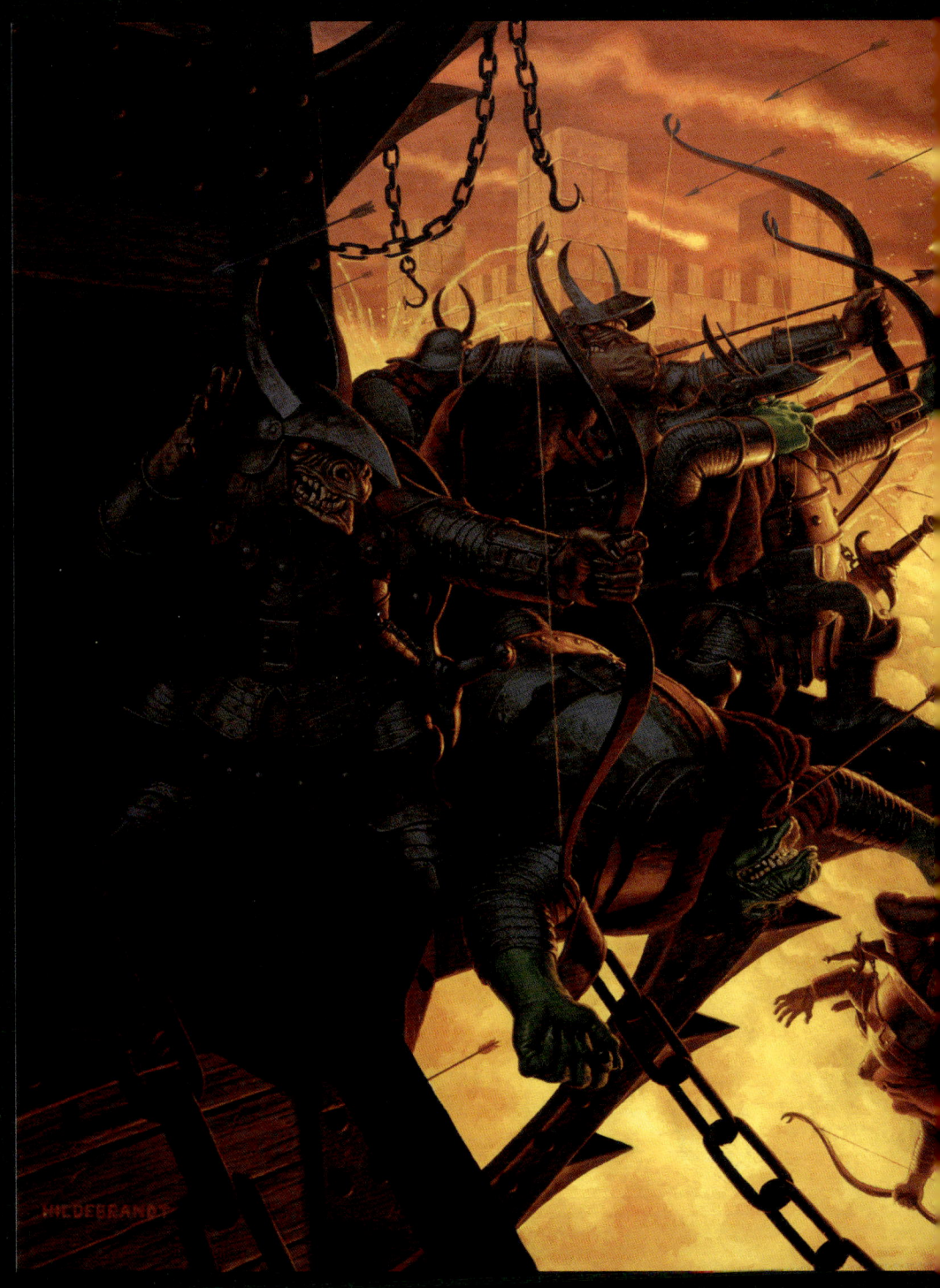

HILDEBRANDT

MASTERPIECES OF FANTASY ART

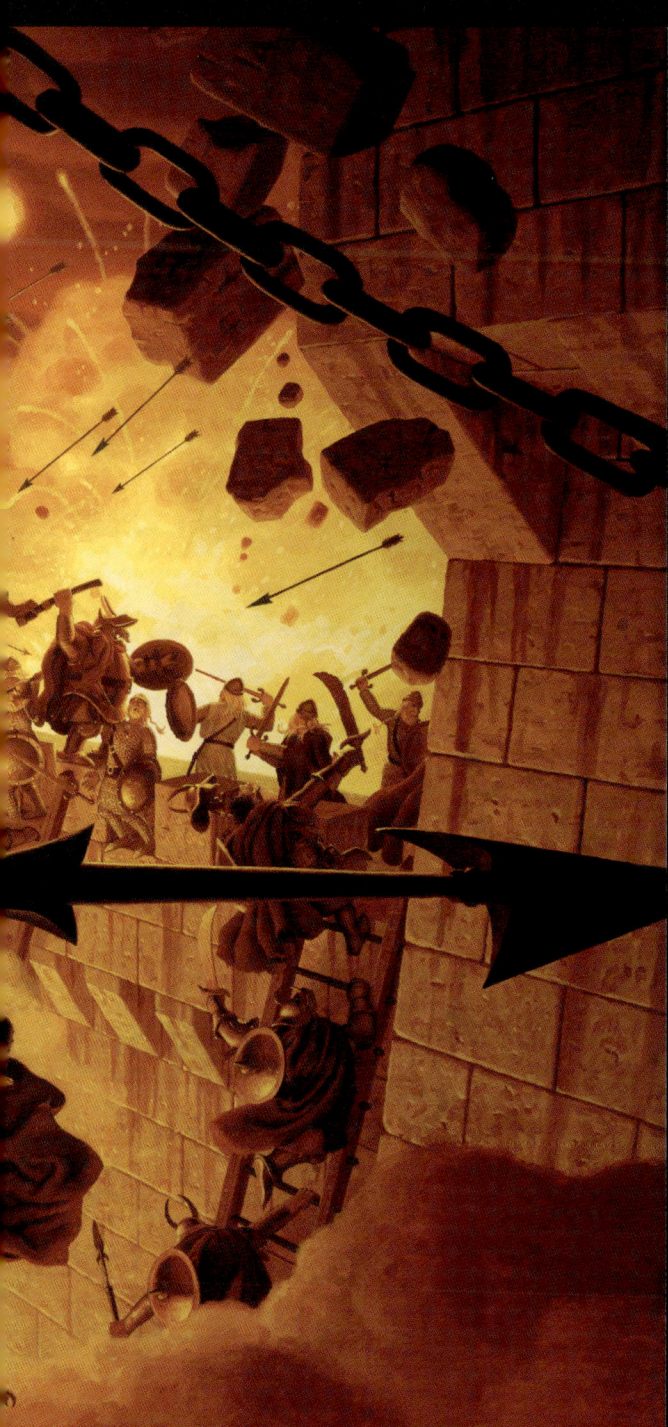

Left: The Siege of Minas Tirith, image for September in the *1977 J.R.R. Tolkien Calendar*. Acrylic on board by the Brothers Hildebrandt, 1976, 122 x 122 cm (48 x 48 inches).

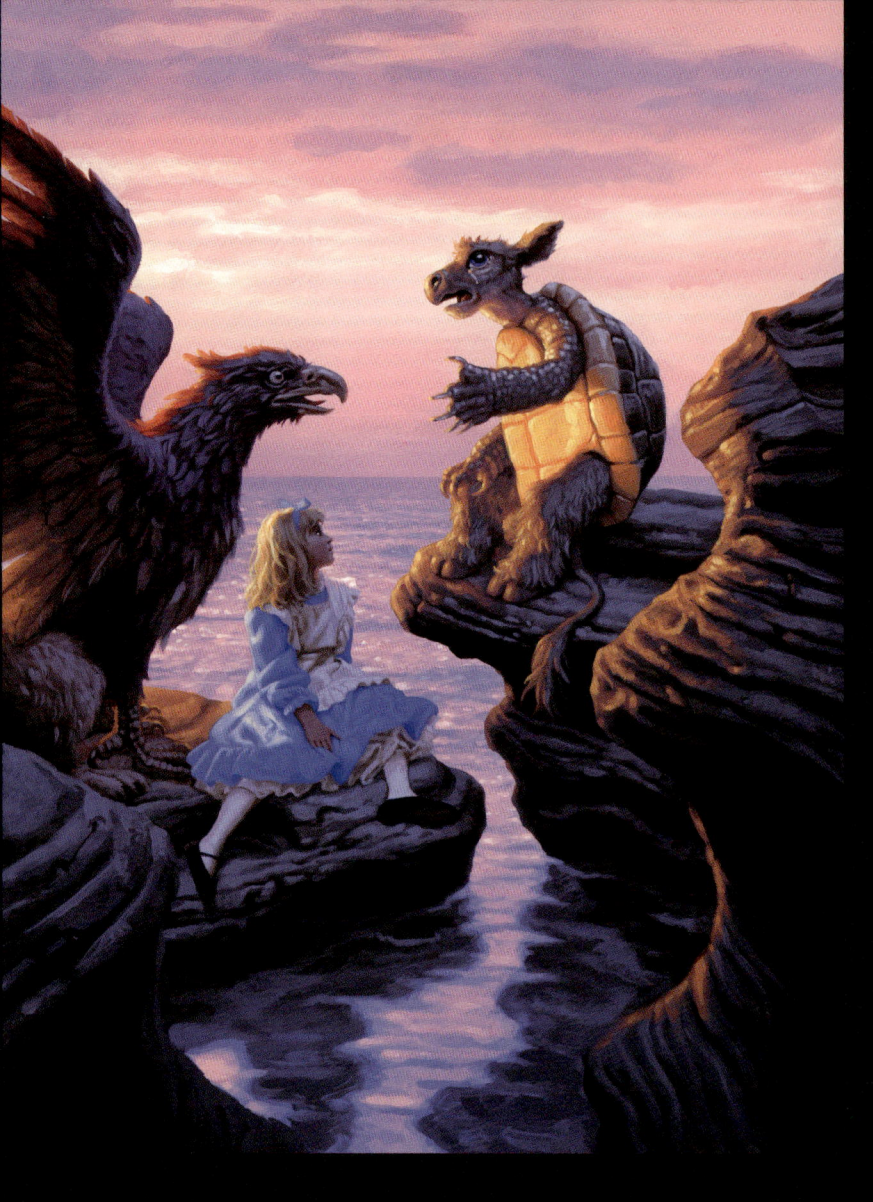

Above: The Mock Turtle, for the 1990 edition of *Alice in Wonderland*. Acrylic on board by Greg Hildebrandt, 1989, 53.3 x 40.6 cm (21 x 16 inches).

Opposite: Whale in a Waistcoat, for the 1988 edition of *Davy and the Goblin*. Acrylic on board by Greg Hildebrandt, 1987, 53.3 x 40.6 cm (21 x 16 inches).

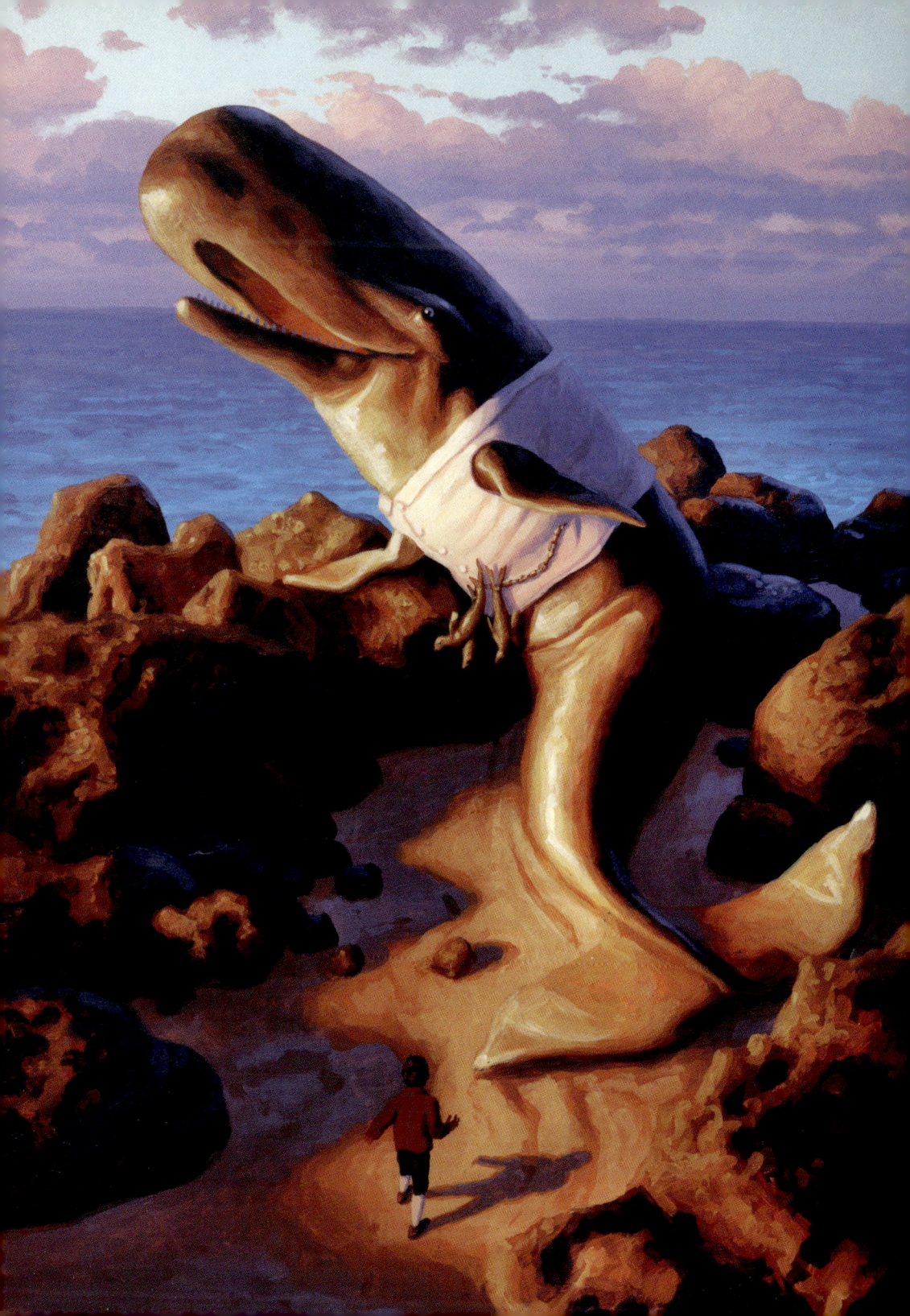

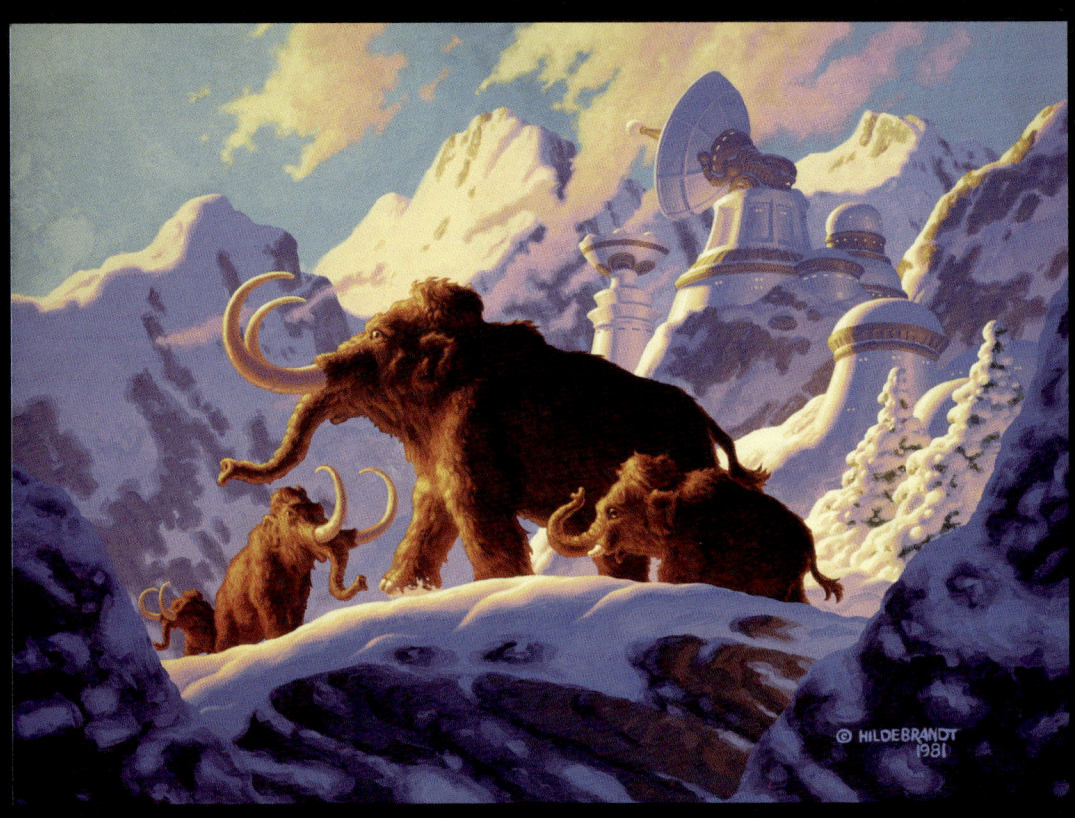

Above: Mastodons, for *The Brothers Hildebrandt 1982 Atlantis Calendar*, 1981, acrylic on board.

Opposite: *Pixie in Flight*, acrylic on Masonite by the Brothers Hildebrandt, undated, 91.4 x 68.2 cm (36 x 27 inches).

Following left: *Mad Science*, No. 73 in the *American Beauties* series. Acrylic on board by Greg Hildebrandt, who modeled for the scientist, 2012.

Following right: *Test Tube Baby*, mixed media on board by Greg Hildebrandt, undated, 76.2 x 50.8 cm (30 x 20 inches). Courtesy of Heritage Auctions.

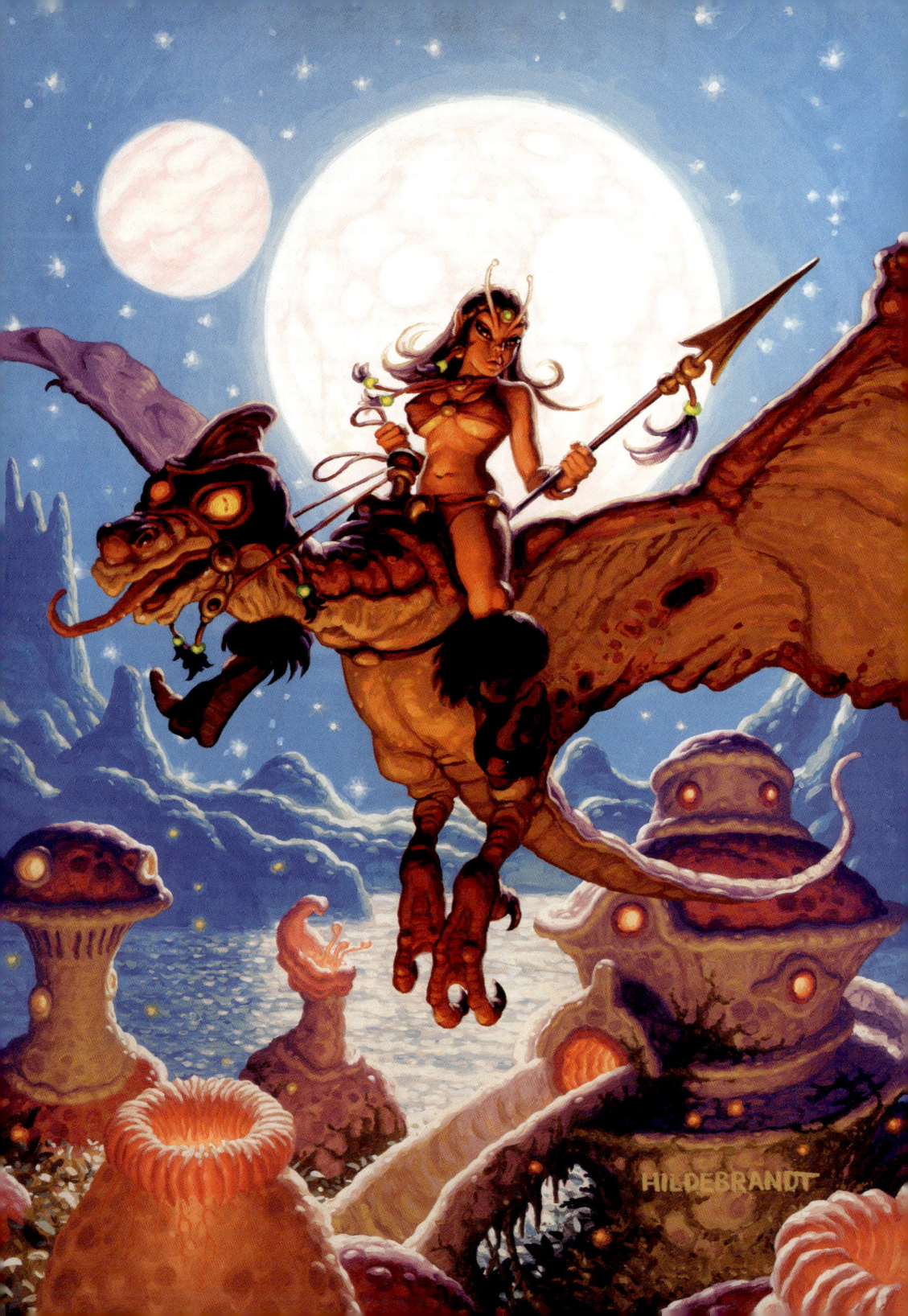

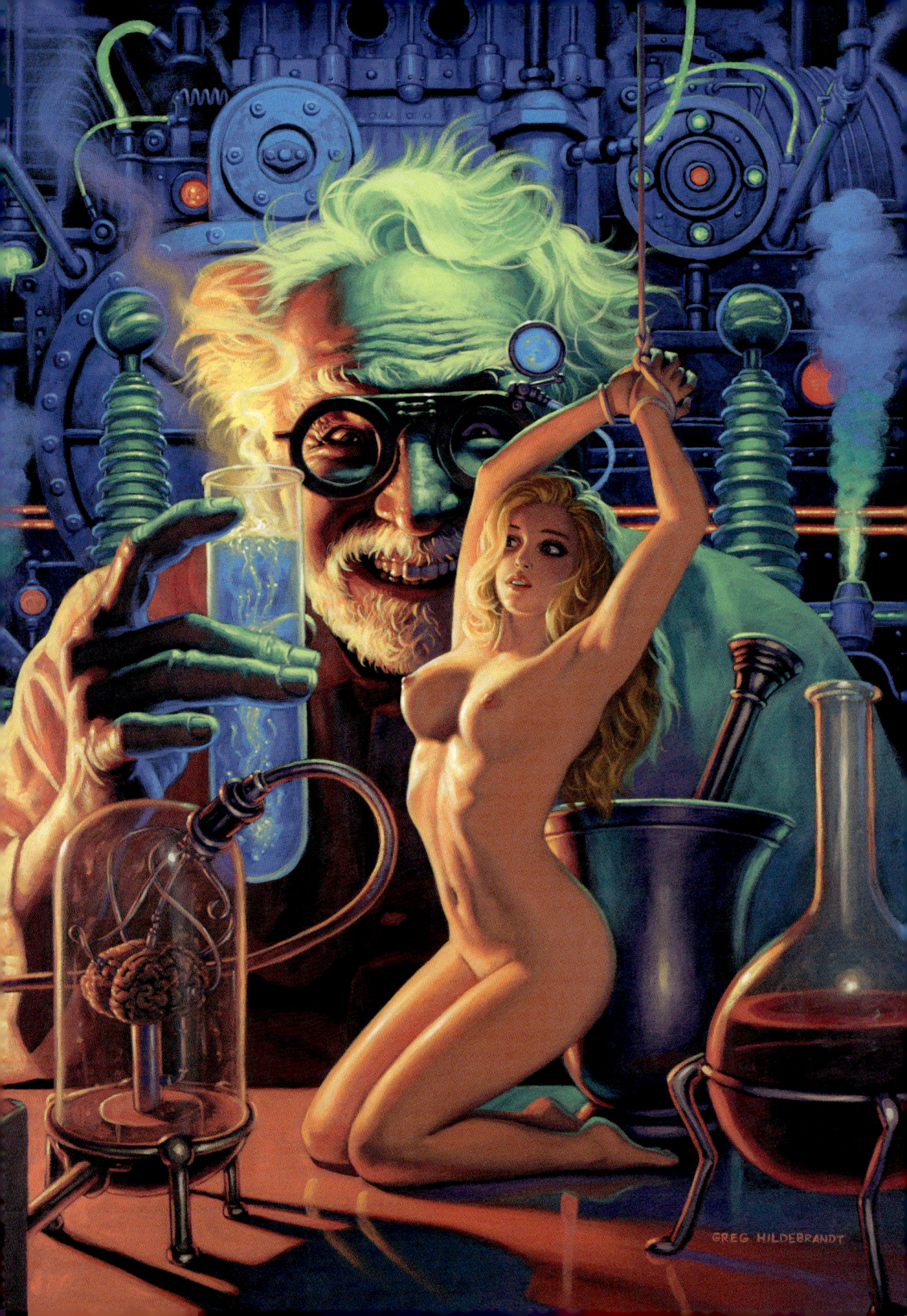

GREG HILDEBRANDT

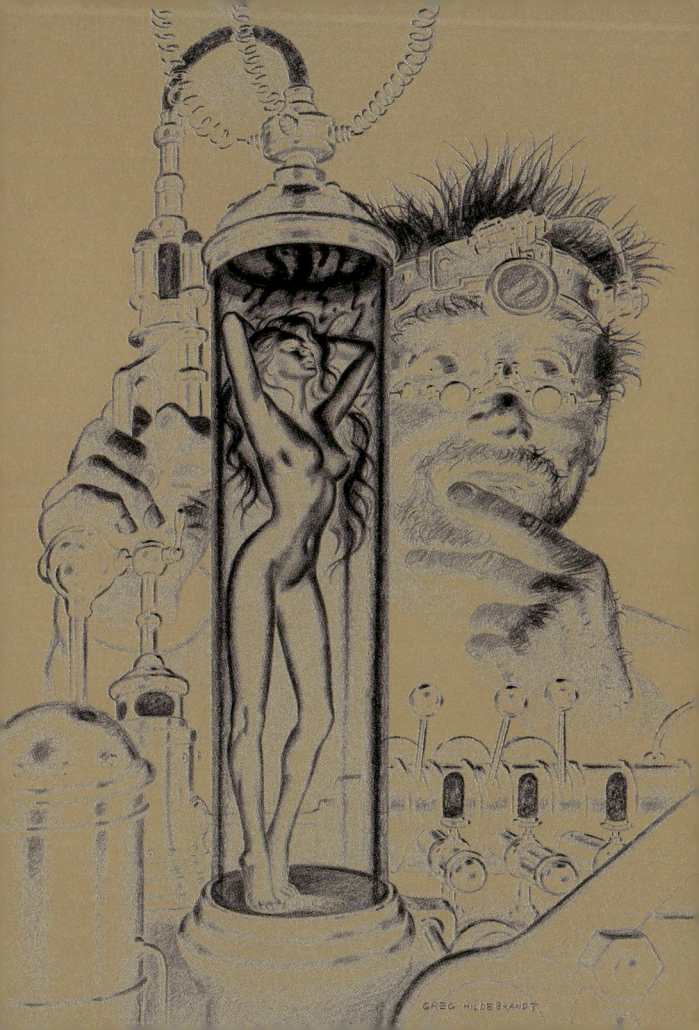

Jeffrey Catherine Jones

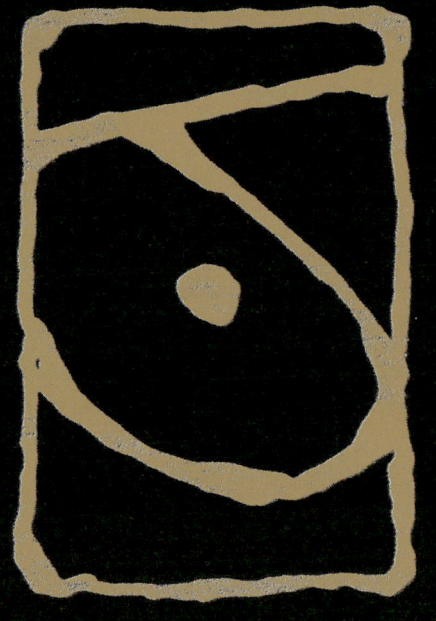

1944-2011

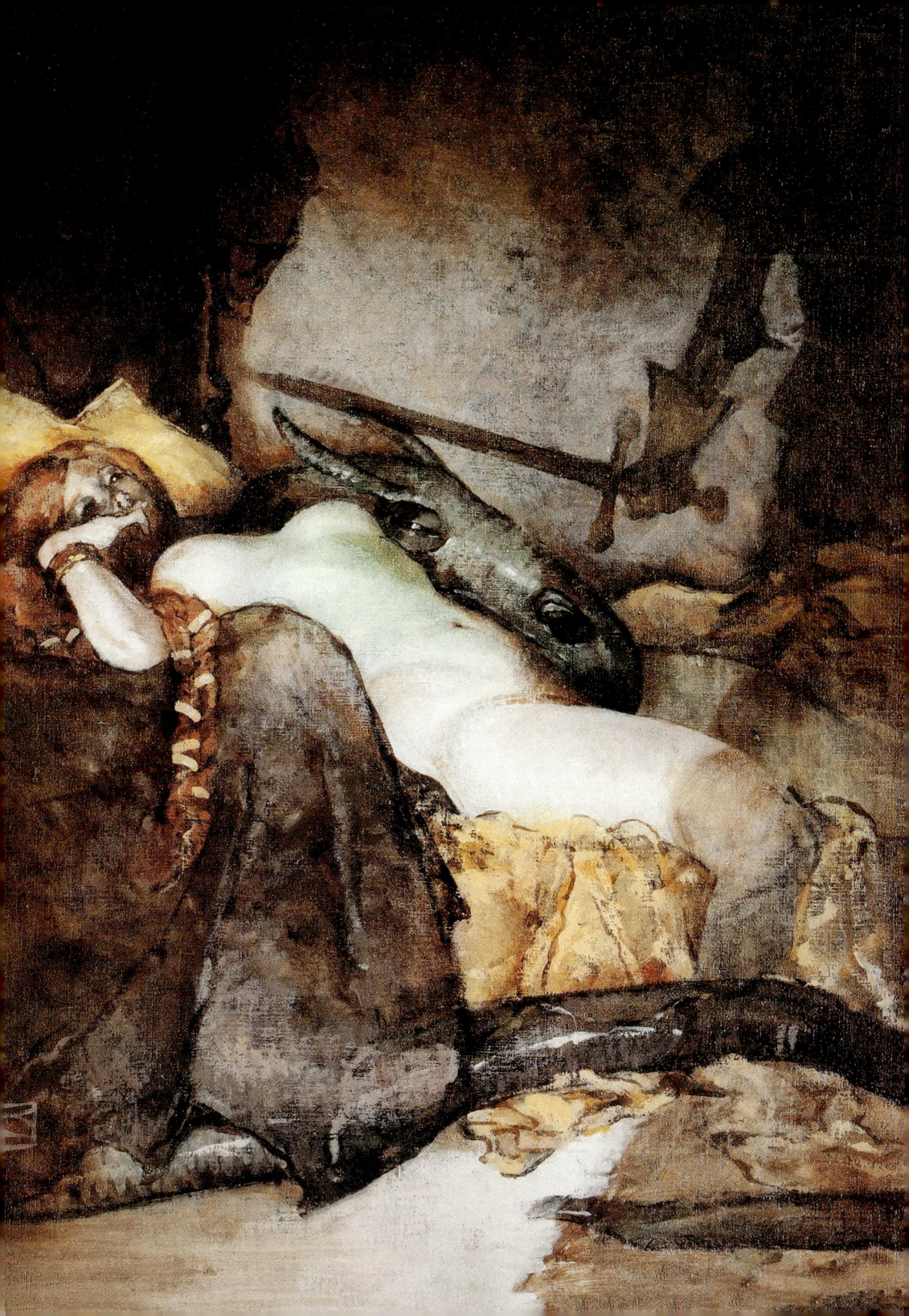

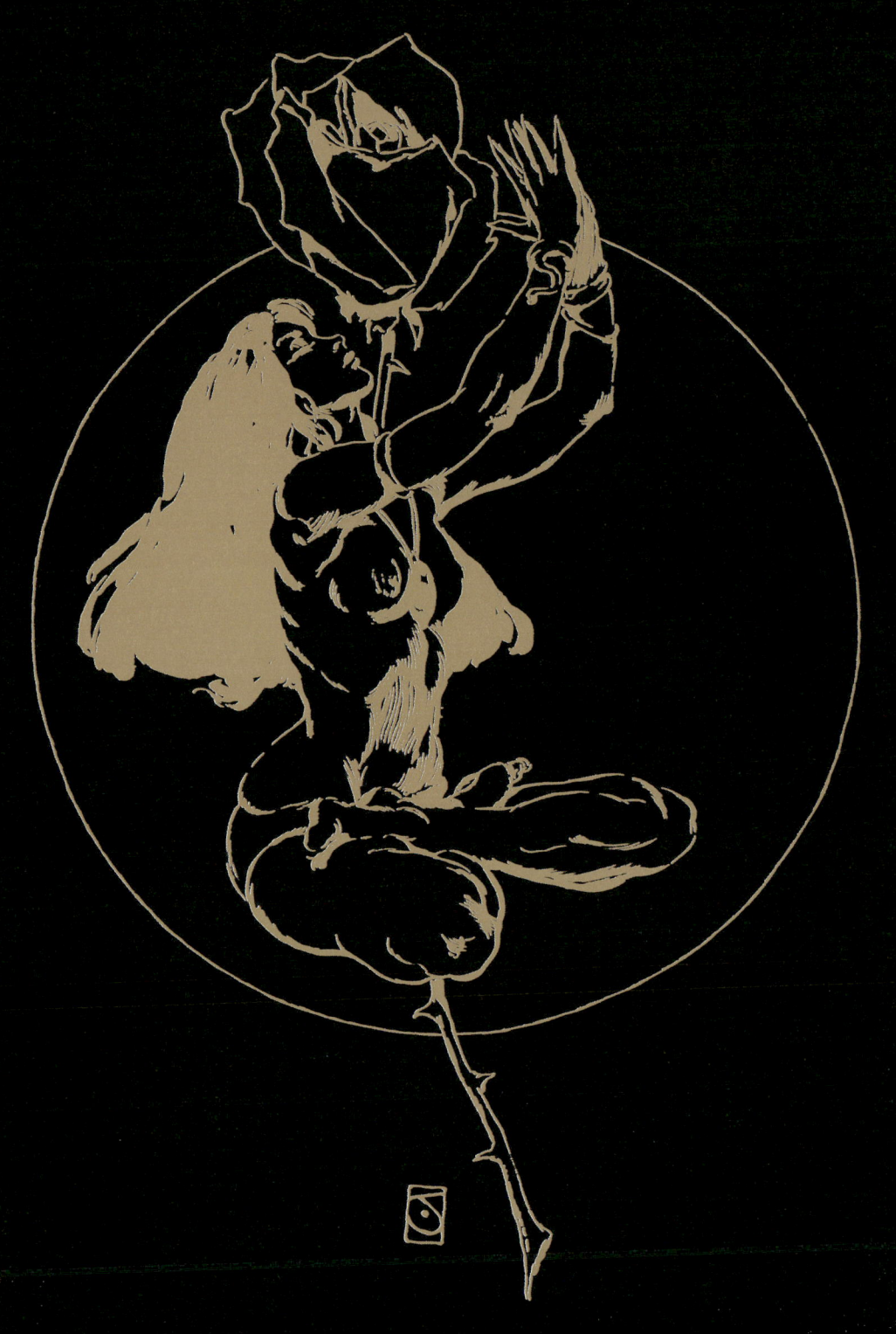

JEFFREY CATHERINE JONES
TORTURED GENIUS

Jeffrey Durwood Jones was born in Atlanta, Georgia, in 1944, and spent his first years in his grandparents' grand, crumbling estate, surrounded by feisty old Southern belles. His father was a career military officer; Jones first met him at age three and immediately realized, as he later wrote, "I would always be defenseless against him." Jones understood that he'd never be the man his father wanted him to be, but couldn't admit until 1998 that he didn't want to be a man at all. It was then, at age 55, that the artist Jeff Jones became Jeffrey Catherine Jones.

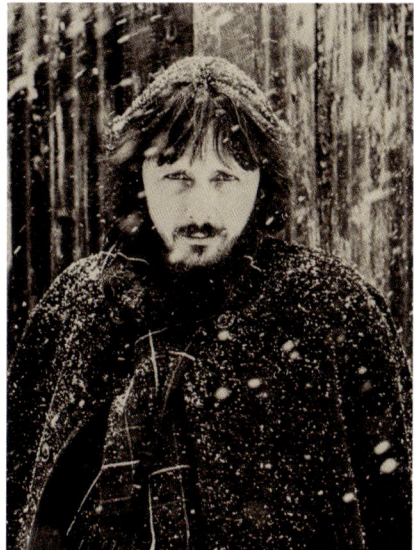

Long before that he was a 21-year-old student submitting his John Carter knock-off, titled *John Garter*, to the Edgar Rice Burroughs fanzine *ERB-dom*, and, after getting his degree in geology from Georgia State College, a young husband moving his pregnant wife to New York so he could pursue his dream of an art career.

When Jones and wife, Louise, arrived in February 1967, New York City was ground zero of a publishing boom; he quickly found work to support the family—daughter Julianna was born in July—drawing for King Comics, Gold Key, and Charlton. He created covers and interiors for the sci-fi and horror magazines *Creepy, Eerie, Vampirella, Amazing Stories, Fantastic Stories, Boris Karloff's Tales of Mystery*, and *Weird Tales of the Macabre*. In 1969 Jones, Bernie Wrightson, and Mike Kaluta even, briefly, created their own *Creepy* knock-off, titled *Web of Horror*. After they completed three issues the publishers mysteriously disappeared, along with their paychecks.

Jones also painted paperback covers, beginning with *Red Shadows*, a collection of Robert E. Howard short stories, released in 1968. Frank Frazetta was then king of the fantasy book cover,

Previous right: Dragon Slayer (aka Indiscretion), circa 1980, by Jeffrey Jones, released as a lithographic print in 1992 by Glimmer Graphics. Courtesy of Heritage Auctions.

Opposite: Meditating Woman with a Rose, for *A Jeffrey Jones Portfolio*, from Middle Earth Publishers, 1973. Ink on paper, 30.4 x 27.9 cm (12 x 11 inches). Courtesy of Heritage Auctions.

Above: In 1978 the partners in the Studio: Bernie Wrightson, Michael Kaluta, Barry Windsor-Smith, and Jeffrey Jones, sponsored their own comic art convention and produced a beautiful souvenir program featuring this photo of Jeff. Copyright Sean Smith.

"I'm all alone. It's something between me and the paper or canvas, and until I leave that place I need that solitude."

but his prices had gone up and he was making the outrageous demand—in the publishers' opinion—to keep his original art. Ace Books sought a more amenable Frazetta, and found him in Jones, who was particularly good at the fleshy females Frazetta fans loved. And like Frazetta, Jones was prolific. Though no one could match Frazetta's painting-in-a-night, Jones often did one a week between 1968 and 1977, creating hundreds of covers for Ace, Berkley, Belmont, Pyramid, Centaur Press, and others. Some called him a Frazetta clone—among them Frazetta himself—but Frank later softened, saying Jones was "the greatest living painter."

And Jones was, in fact, developing a style distinctly his own, first published in adult magazines. In 1972 he provided illustrations for *Esquire* and *Gallery*, and seven months of two-page comics in *Swank*. Then his one-page *Idyl* strip debuted in *National Lampoon*, and no one called him a clone again.

Done in black and white, pen and ink, *Idyl* starred a never named, always naked, impossibly voluptuous, often pregnant and/or tattooed heroine and her equally sexy friends. The strip ran every issue until 1975. A year later Jones left his studio in Woodstock, where he'd lived since 1971, and returned to New York City to join Bernie Wrightson, Barry Windsor-Smith, and Michael Kaluta to lease a large loft in New York's Chelsea neighborhood. They called it the Studio. It was a union, of sorts, established to bolster the artists' desire to get better pay and better treatment from their mutual publishers, while providing each other the kind of creative encouragement publishers wouldn't or couldn't give.

Jones's marriage was over by then; Louise was working for Warren, publisher of *Creepy* et al, and dating comic artist Walt Simonson, leaving Jeff time to consider his life and its purpose. He came to the conclusion that "illustration is immoral," saying, "I wanted to be published so badly that in the beginning I took on a lot of work that I hated…I was losing my joy." As a result, he was also losing jobs. When he moved into the Studio in 1976 he decided to do only work that

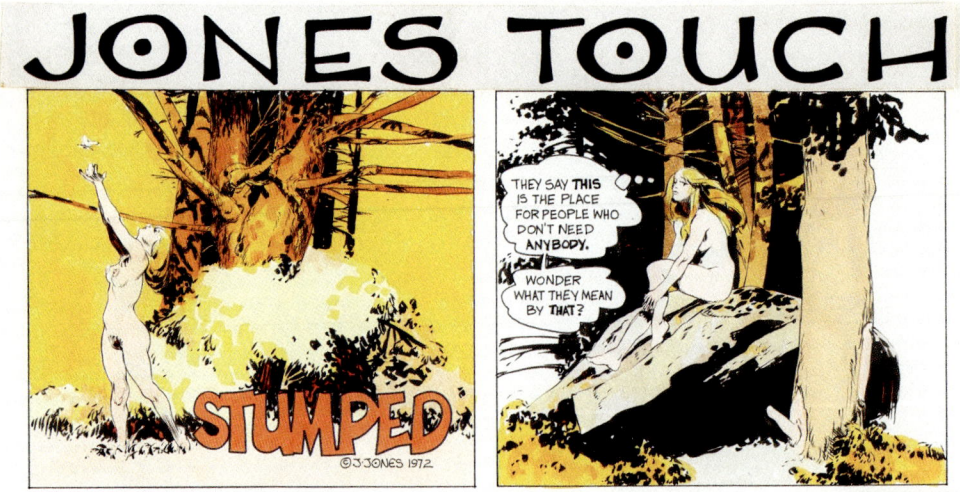

he loved, including his post-*Idyl* strip *I'm Age*, which ran in *Heavy Metal* from 1981 to 1987; private commissions, signed posters, and prints; *The Studio*, a book on the four artists who shared the loft (Dragon's Dream, 1979); the limited-edition portfolio *The Drawings of Jeffrey Jones* (Cygnus, 1982); and the books *Age of Innocence: The Romantic Art of Jeffrey Jones* (Underwood, 1994), *The Art of Jeffrey Jones* (Underwood, 2002), and *Jeffrey Jones: A Life in Art* (IDW, 2011).

Though these later books list Jones's birth name, he had officially, if not legally, transitioned to Jeffrey Catherine Jones in 1998, at the same time marrying second wife Maryellen McMurray. Jones had never felt comfortable in his male body: when he shared his Woodstock studio with Vaughn Bode in

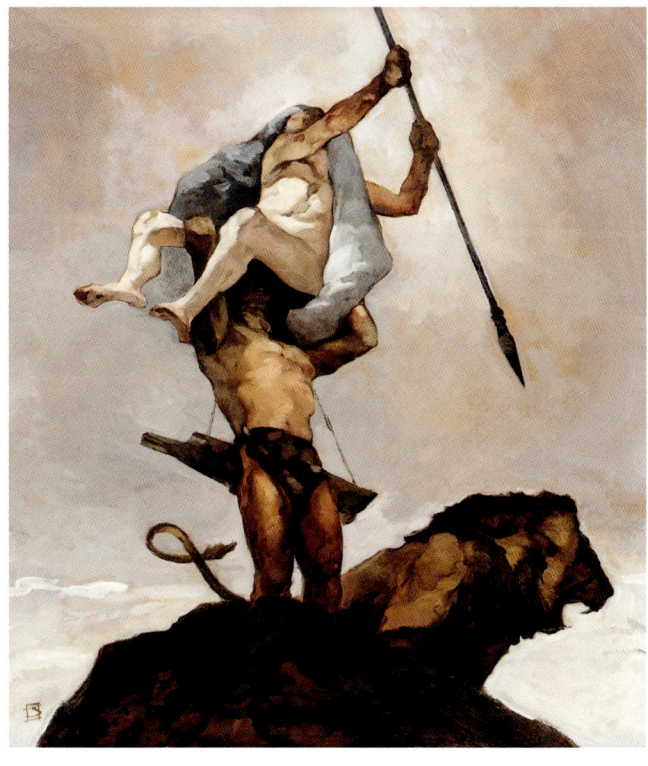

1971, the two enjoyed cross-dressing and experimented with female hormones. He became accomplished with wigs and makeup and gave many of the women he painted his own feminized face. Jeffrey believed transition would end the internal turmoil, but the pain continued and in 2002 she suffered a severe breakdown, resulting in a long hospitalization. Jones lost her home and studio, but was eventually nursed back to health by her daughter and a few close friends. In 2006 Jeff confessed to longtime friend Arnie Fenner that, "I still think like a man and desire women like a man does. I thought it would make me less depressed and I was wrong…the only thing I can do at this point is accept things as they are."

In 2004 she returned to painting, mostly landscapes of the Catskill Mountains near her Kingston, New York, apartment. In her final years she suffered from emphysema, bronchitis, and heart disease, which led to her death on May 19, 2011. A documentary titled *Better Things: The Life & Choices of Jeffrey Catherine Jones*, on which Jones collaborated, was released in 2012, followed by the book *Jeffrey Jones: The Definitive Reference* (Vanguard, 2013).

Opposite: At the same time Jones was doing *Idyl* he was providing a more frankly sexual strip titled *Jones Touch* to *Swank*, what was euphemistically known as a "men's sophisticate" magazine. This strip, "Stumped," was for the April 1972 issue. Detail, watercolor and ink over pencil on board, 57.1 x 40.64 cm (22.5 x 16 inches). Courtesy of Heritage Auctions.

Above: Untitled, undated painting. Oil on canvas, 64.7 x 54.6 cm (25.5 x 21.5 inches). Courtesy of Heritage Auctions.

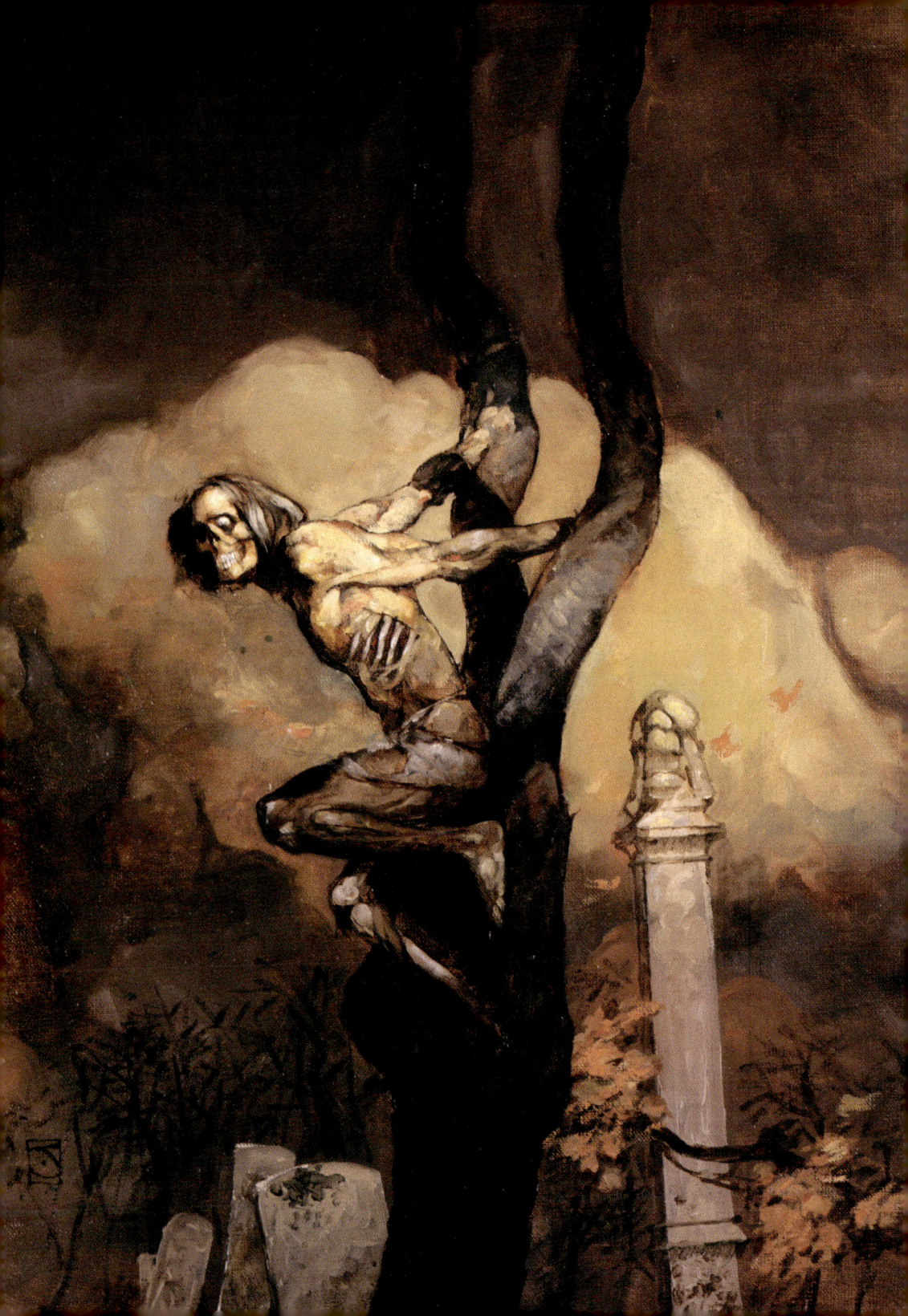

JEFFREY CATHERINE JONES
DAS GEQUÄLTE GENIE

Jeffrey Durwood Jones wurde 1944 in Atlanta, Georgia geboren und verbrachte seine ersten fünf Jahre, umgeben von temperamentvollen, alten Südstaatenschönheiten, auf dem zerfallenden herrschaftlichen Anwesen seiner Großeltern. Sein Vater war Berufsoffizier bei der Armee; im Alter von drei Jahren lernte Jones ihn zum ersten Mal kennen und bemerkte, wie er später schrieb, sofort, dass er „ihm gegenüber stets wehrlos wäre". Jones begriff, dass er nie der Mann sein könnte, den sein Vater erwartete, doch erst 1998 konnte er eingestehen, dass er überhaupt kein Mann sein wollte. Zu diesem Zeitpunkt, im Alter von 55 Jahren, wurde aus dem Künstler Jeff Jones die Künstlerin Jeffrey Catherine Jones.

Viele Jahre zuvor, als 21-jähriger Student, schickte er sein John-Carter-Imitat mit dem Titel *John Garter* an das Edgar-Rice-Burroughs-Fanmagazin *ERB-dom*, und nachdem er am Georgia State College seinen Abschluss in Geologie gemacht hatte, zog der junge Ehemann mit seiner schwangeren Frau nach New York, damit er seinen Traum von einer Karriere in der Kunst weiterverfolgen konnte.

Als Jones und seine Frau Louise im Februar 1967 in New York City eintrafen, stand der Stadt ein verlegerischer Boom bevor; schnell fand er Arbeit, um seine Familie ernähren zu können – Tochter Julianna wurde im Juli geboren –, und so zeichnete er für King Comics, Gold Key und Charlton. Er gestaltete Cover und Innenseiten für Science-Fiction- und Horrorzeitschriften wie *Creepy*, *Eerie*, *Vampirella*, *Amazing Stories*, *Fantastic Stories*, *Boris Karloff's Tales of Mystery* und *Weird Tales of the Macabre*. 1969 schufen Jones, Bernie Wrightson und Mike Kaluta sogar für kurze Zeit unter dem Titel *Web of Horror* ihr eigenes *Creepy*-Imitat. Nachdem sie drei Hefte vollendet hatten, verschwanden die Verleger unerklärlicherweise mitsamt ihren Gehaltsschecks.

Jones malte auch Cover für Taschenbücher, zuerst für *Red Shadows*, einen 1968 erschienenen Sammelband mit Kurzgeschichten von Robert E. Howard. Frank Frazetta war zu jener Zeit der König der Fantasybuchcover, doch seine Preise waren gestiegen, und er stellte die – nach Ansicht der Verleger – unerhörte Forderung, seine Originale behalten zu können. Ace Books suchte nach einem umgänglicheren Frazetta und fand ihn in Jones, der besonders gut die üppigen Frauen malen konnte, die Frazetta-Fans so sehr mochten. Und wie Frazetta war Jones produktiv. Obgleich niemand wie Frazetta ein Gemälde in nur einer Nacht fertigstellen konnte, schaffte Jones in den Jahren von 1968 bis 1977 oft eines pro Woche und schuf Hunderte von Covermotiven für Ace, Berkley, Belmont, Pyramid, Centaur Press und andere. Manche – darunter auch Frazetta selbst – nannten ihn einen Frazetta-Klon, doch relativierte Frank dies später, indem er Jones als „den größten lebenden Maler" bezeichnete.

Opposite: At Night (aka *Want Eyes*), for the cover
of *Creepy* No. 120, August 1980. Oil on canvas, 1975.

„Ich bin ganz allein. Da spielt sich etwas zwischen mir und dem Papier oder der Leinwand ab, und bis ich diesen Platz verlasse, brauche ich diese Einsamkeit."

Tatsächlich entwickelte Jones einen ganz persönlichen Stil, der zuerst in Zeitschriften für Erwachsene zu sehen war. 1972 lieferte er Illustrationen für *Esquire* und *Gallery,* und sieben Monate lang veröffentlichte er in *Swanks* Comics von zwei Seiten Länge. Dann debütierte sein Strip von einer Seite, *Idyl,* im *National Lampoon,* und fortan bezeichnete ihn niemand mehr als einen Klon.

Hauptfiguren von *Idyl,* mit Feder und Tusche in Schwarz-Weiß ausgeführt, waren eine nie namentlich bezeichnete, stets nackte und unglaublich verlockende, oft schwangere und/oder tätowierte Heldin und ihre Freundinnen, die genauso sexy aussahen. Bis 1975 erschien der Strip in jeder Ausgabe. Ein Jahr später gab Jones sein Atelier in Woodstock auf, wo er seit 1971 gelebt hatte, und kehrte nach New York City zurück, um sich Bernie Wrightson, Barry Windsor-Smith und Michael Kaluta anzuschließen, die ein weitläufiges Loft im New Yorker Stadtteil Chelsea anmieteten. Sie nannten es *The Studio.* Es war eine Art Zusammenschluss, der den Künstlern helfen sollte, von ihren jeweiligen Verlegern besser bezahlt und besser behandelt zu werden, und in dem die Künstler gleichzeitig einander die kreative Ermutigung geben wollten, die ihnen die Verleger nicht geben würden oder konnten.

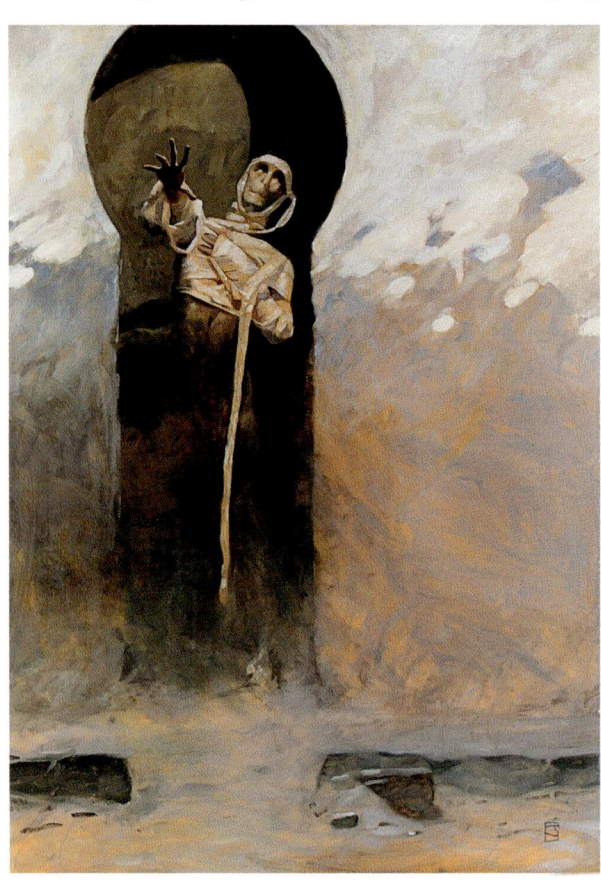

Jones' Ehe war damals beendet; Louise arbeitete für Warren, den Verlag unter anderem von *Creepy,* und war mit dem Comickünstler Walt Simonson zusammen. So blieb Jeff genug Zeit, über sein Leben und seine Zielsetzungen nachzudenken. Er kam zu dem Schluss, dass „Illustration unmoralisch" sei, und sagte: „Ich war so begierig darauf, veröffentlicht zu werden, dass ich anfangs eine Menge an Arbeit annahm, die ich hasste ... Ich verlor meine Lust daran." Daraufhin verlor er auch Aufträge. Als er 1976 in The Studio zog, beschloss er, nur noch Sachen zu machen, die er mochte, darunter seinen *Idyl*-Folgestrip „I'm Age", der von 1981 bis 1987 in *Heavy Metal* erschien; er arbeitete an privaten Aufträgen, signierte Plakate und Drucke; *The Studio,* ein Buch über die vier Künstler, die sich das Loft teilten, wurde veröffentlicht (Dragon's Dream, 1979); *The Drawings of Jeffrey Jones* (Cygnus, 1982), ein Portfolio mit limitierter Auflage und die Bücher *Age of Innocence: The Romantic Art of Jeffrey Jones* (Underwood, 1994), *The Art of Jeffrey Jones* (Underwood, 2002) und *Jeffrey Jones: A Life in Art* (IDW, 2011).

Obwohl diese späteren Bücher Jones' Geburtsnamen anführten, war er 1998 offiziell, wenn auch rechtlich nicht zu Jeffrey Catherine Jones übergegangen und hatte zur gleichen Zeit seine zweite Frau Maryellen McMurray geheiratet. In seinem männlichen Körper hatte sich Jones nie wohlgefühlt: Als er sich sein Atelier in Woodstock 1971 mit Vaughn Bode teilte, amüsierten sich die beiden mit Crossdressing und experimentierten mit weiblichen Hormonen. Er kam immer besser mit Perücken und Make-up zurecht, und vielen Frauen, die er malte, verlieh er sein eigenes feminisiertes Gesicht. Jeffrey glaubte, seine Umwandlung würde den inneren Aufruhr beenden, doch er quälte sich weiter, und 2002 erlitt er einen schweren Zusammenbruch, dem ein langer Krankenhausaufenthalt folgte.

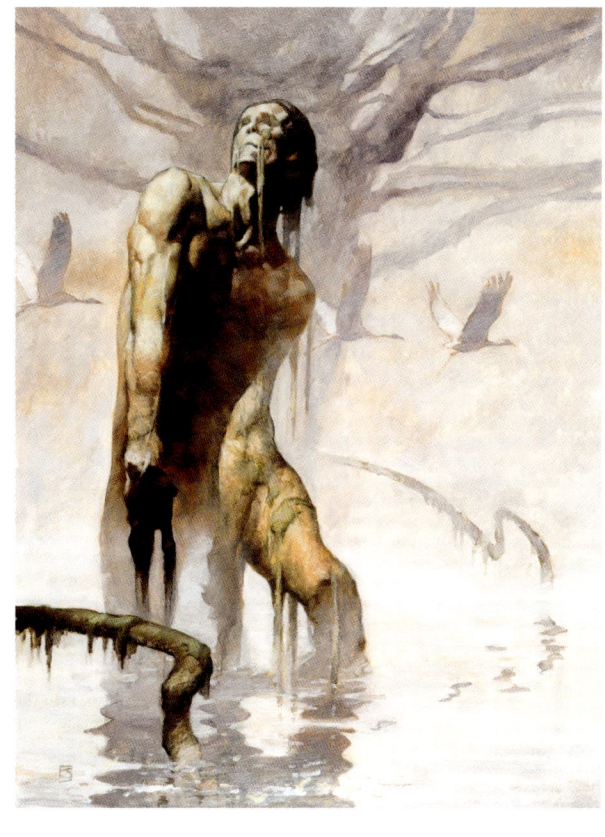

Jones verlor ihre Wohnung und das Atelier, wurde jedoch von ihrer Tochter und ein paar engen Freunden gesund gepflegt. 2006 gestand Jeff gegenüber seinem langjährigen Freund Arnie Fenner ein, dass „ich noch immer denke wie ein Mann und Frauen begehre wie ein Mann. Ich dachte, es würde mich weniger depressiv machen, und lag damit falsch … das Einzige, was ich zu diesem Zeitpunkt tun kann, ist, die Dinge so zu akzeptieren, wie sie sind."

2004 kehrte sie zur Malerei zurück und schuf zumeist Landschaftsbilder der Catskill Mountains, die in der Nähe ihrer Wohnung in Kingston, New York lagen. In ihren letzten Jahren litt sie an einem Emphysem, an Bronchitis und an einer Herzerkrankung, an der sie am 19. Mai 2011 starb. Eine Dokumentation mit dem Titel *Better Things: The Life & Choices of Jeffrey Catherine Jones*, an der Jones mitgearbeitet hatte, wurde 2012 veröffentlicht, und danach erschien noch das Buch *Jeffrey Jones: The Definitive Reference* (Vanguard, 2013).

Opposite: The Mummy, usage unknown, is a simplified version of Jones's 1974 *Mummy* produced as a jigsaw puzzle. Oil on canvas, circa 1995, 91.4 x 63.5 cm (36 x 25 inches). Courtesy of Heritage Auctions.

Above: The Monster Man, the October plate for the *1998 Edgar Rice Burroughs Calendar.* Oil on canvas, 1997, 91.4 x 66.4 cm (36 x 26 inches). Courtesy of Heritage Auctions.

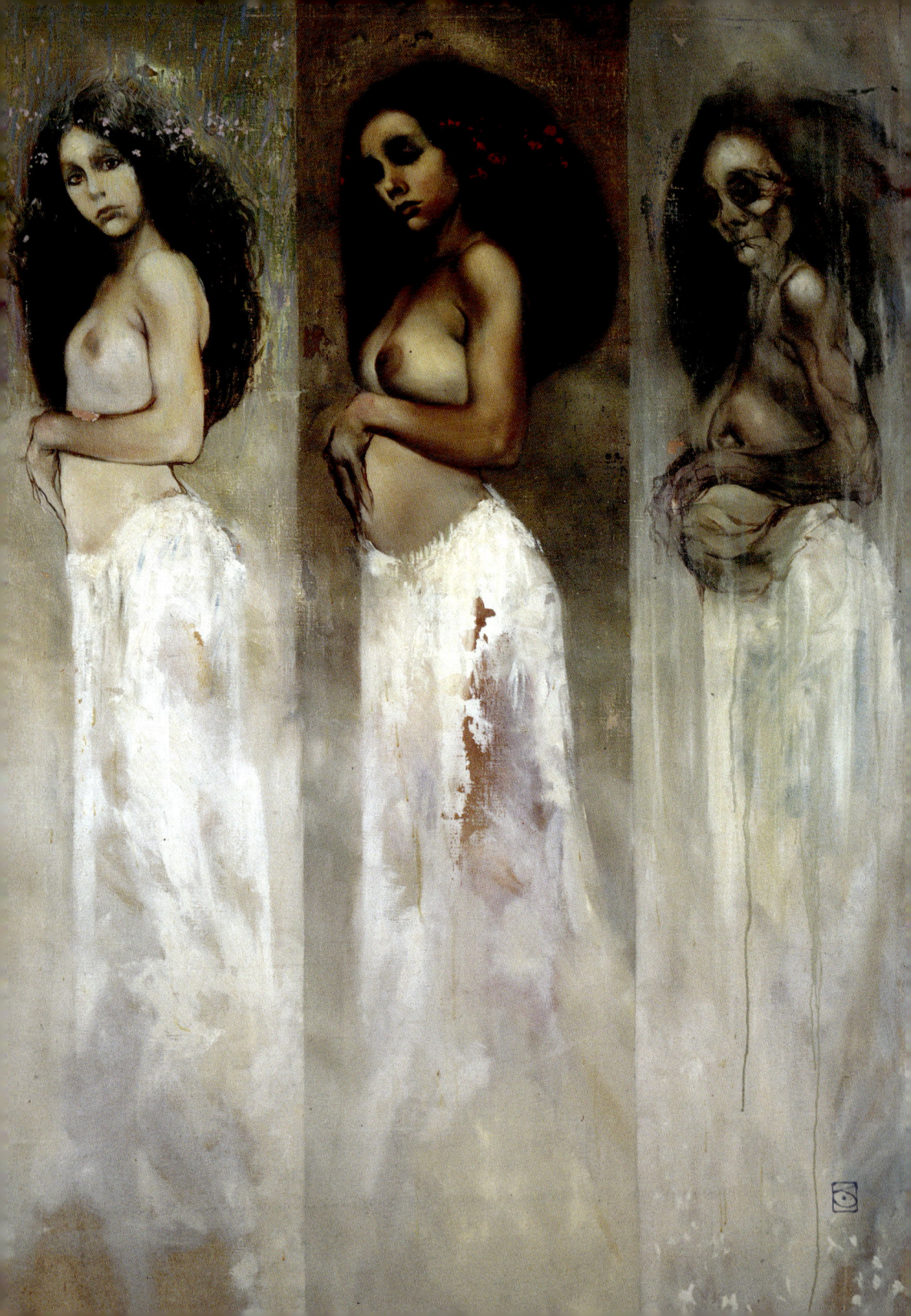

JEFFREY CATHERINE JONES
LE GÉNIE TORTURÉ

Jeffrey Durwood Jones naît à Atlanta (Georgie) en 1944 et passe ses premières années sur le domaine aussi majestueux que décrépi de ses grands-parents, entouré de belles du Sud âgées mais fougueuses. Son père est officier de carrière ; Jones ne le rencontre qu'à trois ans et comprend aussitôt, comme il l'écrira plus tard, qu'il sera « toujours sans défense face à lui ». Jones se rend compte qu'il ne sera jamais l'homme que son père aurait voulu qu'il soit, mais il ne s'avouera qu'en 1998 qu'elle ne sera pas un homme du tout. C'est ainsi qu'à 55 ans l'artiste Jeff Jones est devenu Jeffrey Catherine Jones.

Bien avant cela, étudiant de 21 ans, Jones propose sa parodie de John Carter, intitulée *John Garter*, au fanzine de Edgar Rice Burroughs *ERB-dom*. Une fois diplômé en géologie du Georgia State College, il embarque sa jeune épouse enceinte à New York pour y réaliser ses rêves de carrière artistique.

À l'arrivée de Jones et de sa femme Louise, en février 1967, New York connaît les premières heures d'une explosion de l'édition ; il ne tarde pas à trouver du travail pour faire vivre sa famille – sa fille Julianna naît en juillet – et dessine pour King Comics, Gold Key et Charlton. Il conçoit des couvertures et des pages intérieures pour les magazines de science-fiction et d'horreur *Creepy*, *Eerie*, *Vampirella*, *Amazing Stories*, *Fantastic Stories*, *Boris Karloff's Tales of Mystery* et *Weird Tales of the Macabre*. En 1969, Jones, Bernie Wrightson et Mike Kaluta publient même, brièvement, leur propre version de *Creepy*, intitulée *Web of Horror*. Après trois numéros, les responsables de publication disparaissent, avec leur paye.

Jones peint aussi des couvertures de livres de poche et commence par illustrer la collection de nouvelles de Robert E. Howard *Red Shadows*, sortie en 1968. Frank Frazetta règne alors en maître sur les couvertures de livres fantasy, mais ses tarifs ont flambé et il a l'audace – du point de vue des éditeurs – de vouloir conserver ses œuvres originales. Ace Books recherche un Frazetta mieux disposé et le trouve en Jones, qui excelle particulièrement dans le domaine fétiche des fans de Frazetta, les femelles charnues. Et comme Frazetta, Jones est prolifique. Si personne n'égale la rapidité de Frazetta, qui peint ses toiles en une nuit, Jones en réalise souvent une par semaine entre 1968 et 1977 ; des centaines de couvertures pour Ace, Berkley, Belmont, Pyramid, Centaur Press et d'autres. Certains le surnomment le clone de Frazetta, notamment le maestro lui-même, mais Frank s'est ensuite adouci, qualifiant Jones de « plus grand peintre vivant ».

De fait, Jones développe aussi un style éminemment personnel, qui paraît d'abord dans des magazines pour adultes. En 1972, il signe des illustrations pour *Esquire* et *Gallery* et, pendant sept mois, deux pages de bande dessinée dans *Swank*. Son comic-strip d'une page « Idyl » fait ensuite

Opposite: Three Ages of Woman. As with many of his paintings of women, this appears to be his own face, though he predicted his own old age incorrectly. Oil on canvas, 1970.

« Je suis tout seul. C'est entre moi et le papier ou la toile et jusqu'à ce que je quitte cet endroit j'ai besoin de solitude. »

ses débuts dans *National Lampoon* et plus personne ne le traitera de clone.

Réalisée en noir et blanc, au stylo et à l'encre, la série « Idyl » met en scène une héroïne sans nom, toujours nue, invraisemblablement voluptueuse, souvent enceinte et/ou tatouée, et ses amis tout aussi sexy. Le strip est présent dans tous les numéros jusqu'en 1975. Un an plus tard, Jones quitte son studio de Woodstock, où il vit depuis 1971, et retourne à New York City pour partager avec Bernie Wrightson, Barry Windsor-Smith et Michael Kaluta un immense loft dans le quartier de Chelsea. Ils baptisent l'endroit The Studio. C'est un genre de syndicat, créé pour aider les artistes à obtenir d'être mieux payés et mieux traités par leurs divers clients/éditeurs, tout en procurant à chacun les encouragements créatifs que ces mêmes clients n'étaient pas disposés à ou capables de leur offrir.

Le mariage de Jones est fini. Louise travaille pour Warren, qui publie *Creepy* (etc.), et sort avec le dessinateur de comics Walt Simonson, ce qui laisse le loisir à Jeff de réfléchir à sa vie et à ses ambitions. Il parvient à la conclusion que « l'illustration est immorale » : « J'avais tellement envie d'être publié qu'au début j'ai accepté plein de commandes que j'ai détestées, dira-t-il. Je perdais ma joie. » Par ricochet, il perd aussi des clients. Lorsqu'il s'installe dans les locaux du Studio, en 1976, il décide de n'y faire que ce qu'il aime, notamment sa bande dessinée post-« Idyl » « I'm Age », publiée dans *Heavy Metal* entre 1981 et 1987, des commandes privées, des affiches et tirages dédicacés ; *The Studio*, un livre sur les quatre artistes qui partagent le loft (Dragon's Dream, 1979), le portfolio en édition limitée *The Drawings of Jeffrey Jones* (Cygnus, 1982), ainsi que les livres *Age of Innocence : The Romantic Art of Jeffrey Jones* (Underwood, 1994), *The Art of Jeffrey Jones* (Underwood, 2002) et *Jeffrey Jones : A Life in Art* (IDW, 2011).

Bien que ces ouvrages récents arborent le nom de naissance de Jones, il a officiellement, sinon légalement, effectué sa transition pour devenir Jeffrey Catherine Jones en 1998, à l'époque où il a épousé sa seconde femme, Maryellen McMurray. Jones ne s'est jamais senti à l'aise dans son corps d'homme ; à l'époque où il partageait son atelier de Woodstock avec Vaughn Bode, en 1971, ils aimaient s'habiller en femmes et avaient testé les hormones féminines. Jones parachève son apparence avec des perruques et du maquillage et donne son visage ainsi féminisé à nombre de ses personnages. Jeffrey pensait que la transition apaiserait ses tourments intérieurs, mais la douleur persiste et en 2002 elle tombe dans une grave dépression et passe un long moment à l'hôpital. Jones perd son domicile et son atelier mais elle se remet sur pied, grâce au soutien de sa fille et de quelques proches. En 2006, Jeff confie à son vieil ami Arnie Fenner : « Je pense encore comme un homme et je désire les femmes comme un homme. Je pensais que je serais moins déprimée, mais j'avais tort… Tout ce que je peux faire, au point où j'en suis, c'est accepter les choses comme elles sont. »

En 2004, elle recommence à peindre, principalement des paysages des Catskills, près de son appartement de Kingston, dans l'État de New York. Les dernières années de sa vie, elle souffre d'emphysème, de bronchites et d'affections cardiaques, qui conduisent à son décès, le 19 mai 2011. Un documentaire intitulé *Better Things : The Life & Choices of Jeffrey Catherine Jones*, auquel Jones a participé, sort en 2012, suivi du livre *Jeffrey Jones : The Definitive Reference* (Vanguard, 2013).

Opposite: Ceremony (aka *The Veil*), released as a limited-edition print titled Crescent. Oil on canvas, 1970.

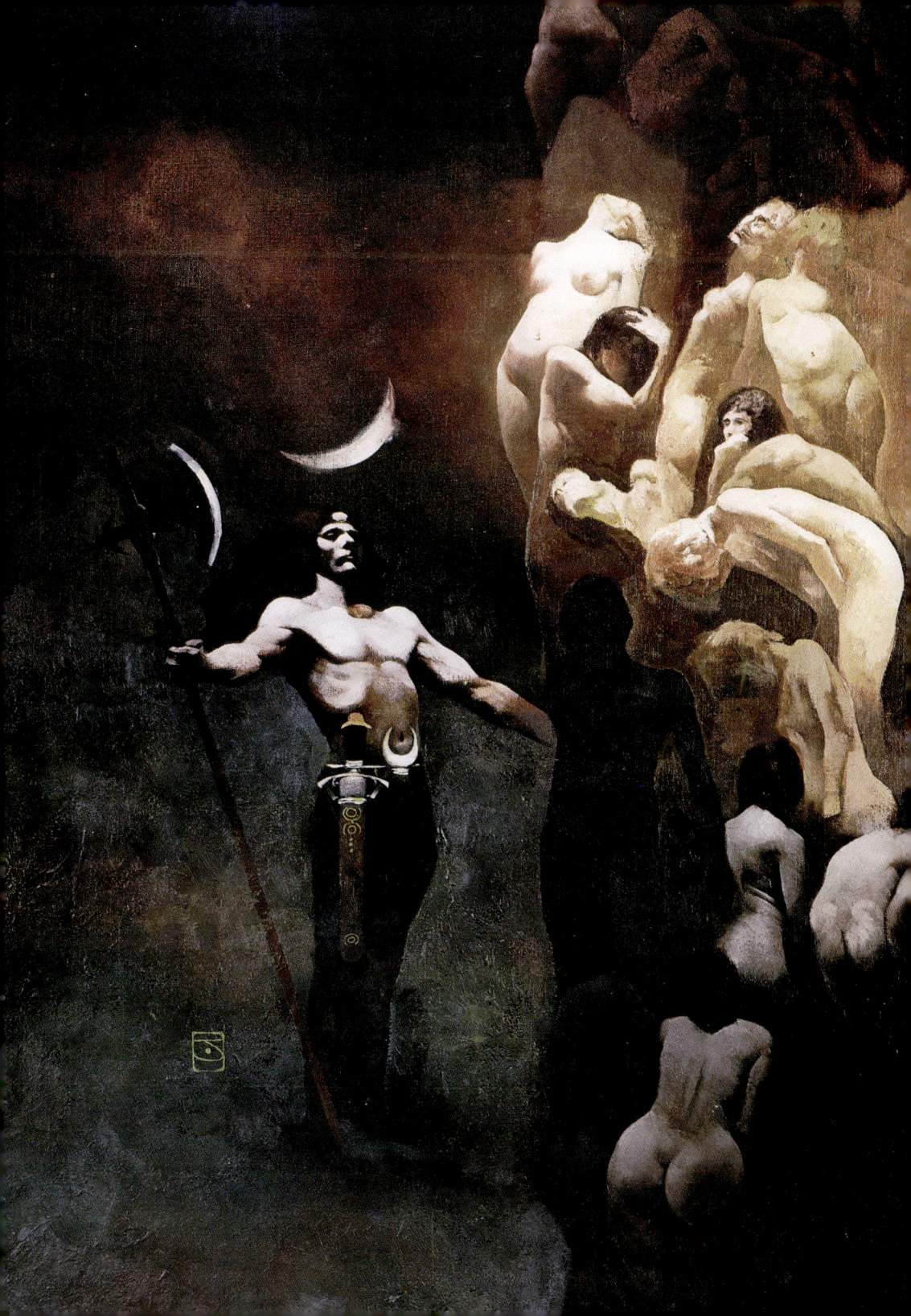

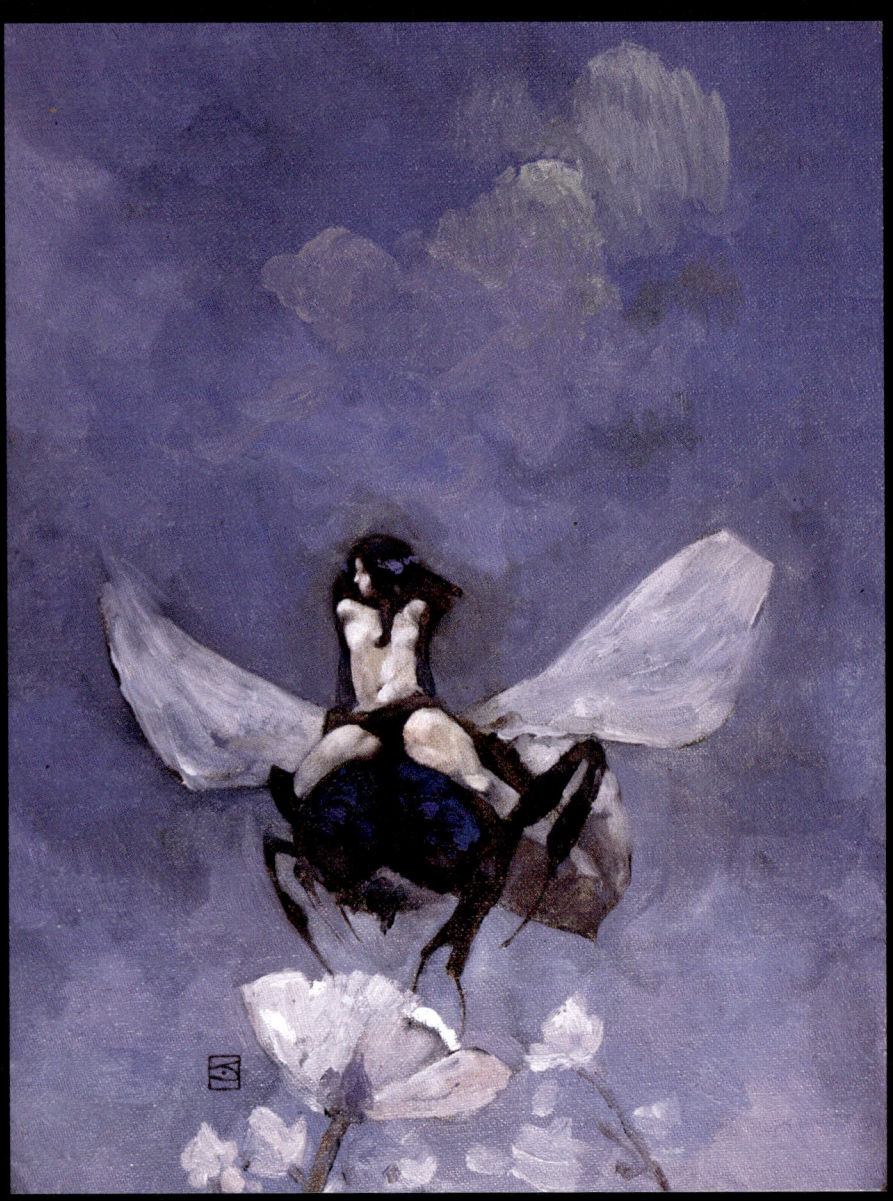

Above: *Bumblebee in Blue*, for the cover of *Fantastic Science Fiction and Fantasy Stories*, September 1974. Oil on canvas, 1974.

Opposite: Dark of the Woods, for the cover of the 1970 Dean R. Koontz novel from Ace Books. Mixed media on paper, circa 1969, 55.8 x 30.4 cm (22 x 12 inches). Courtesy of Heritage Auctions.

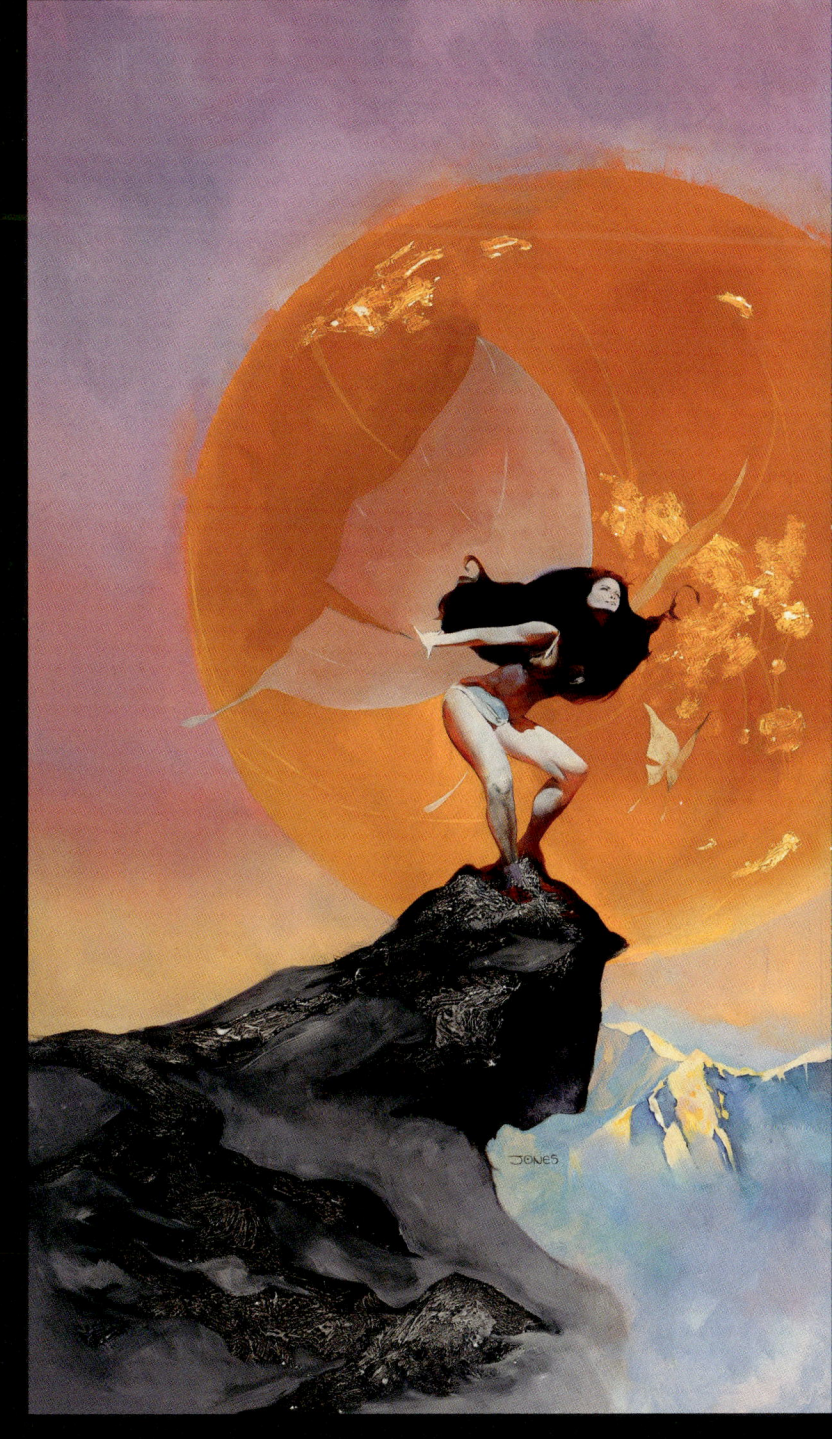

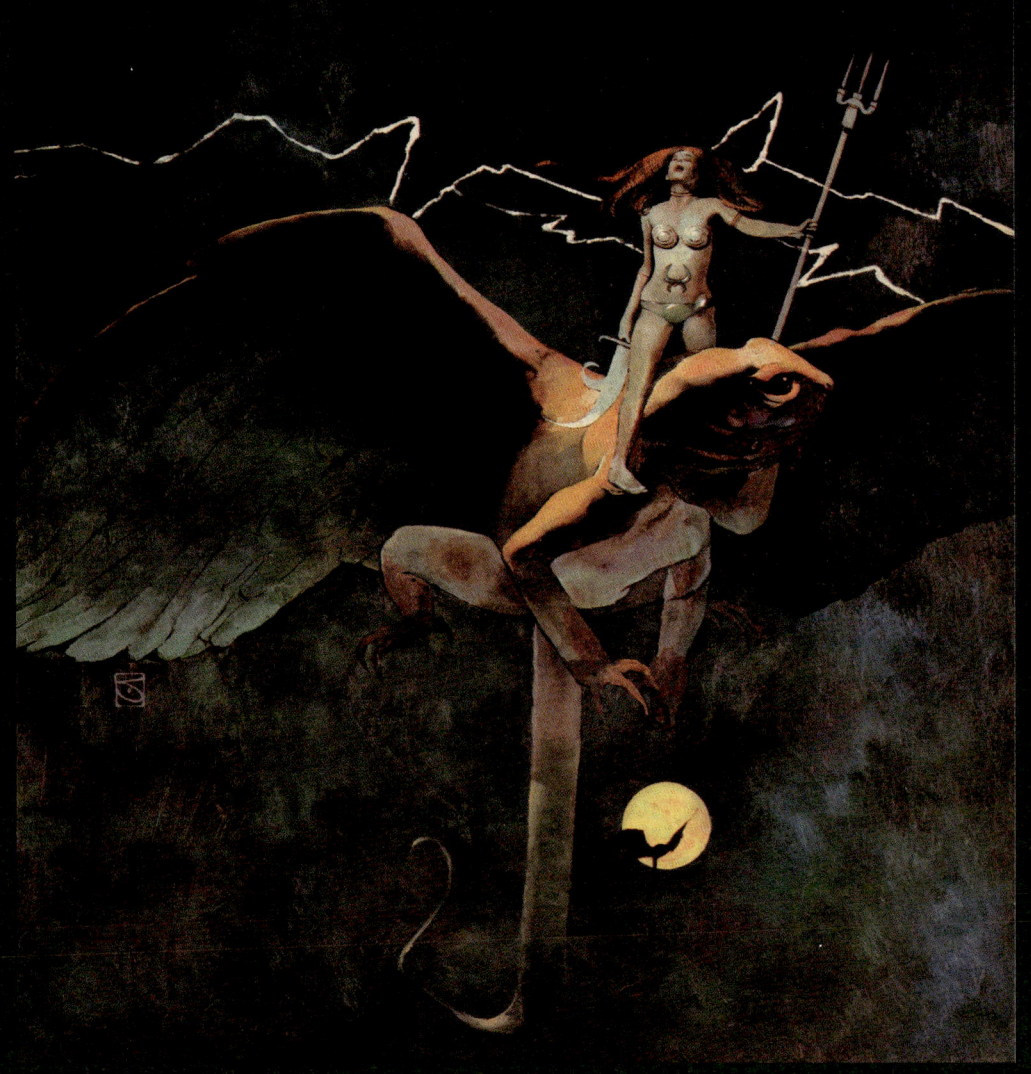

Above: The Rider, for the cover of *Nightmare* magazine
No. 6, December 1971. *Nightmare* was yet another
competitor for Warren's *Creepy* and *Eerie* fantasy/horror
comics. Oil on canvas, 1971.

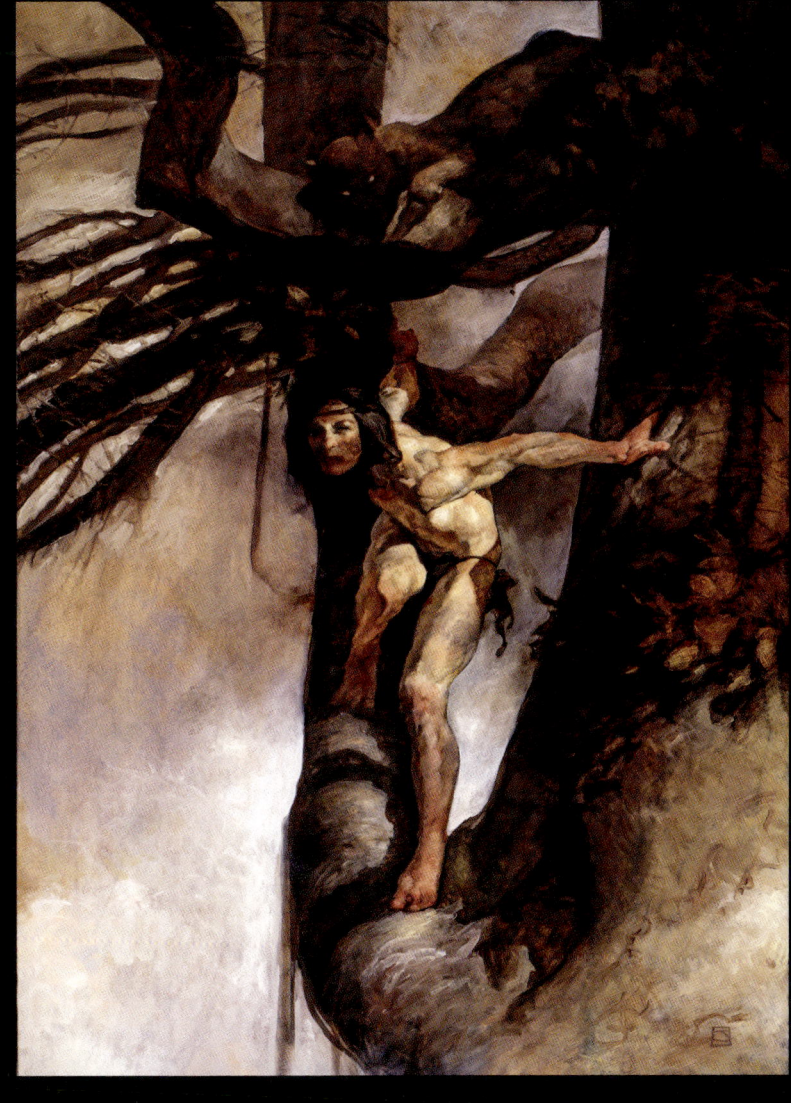

Above: Tarzan of the Apes, 1995, used in *The Art of Jeffrey Jones*, Series II trading cards, and as the January image in the *1998 Edgar Rice Burroughs Calendar*. Oil on canvas.

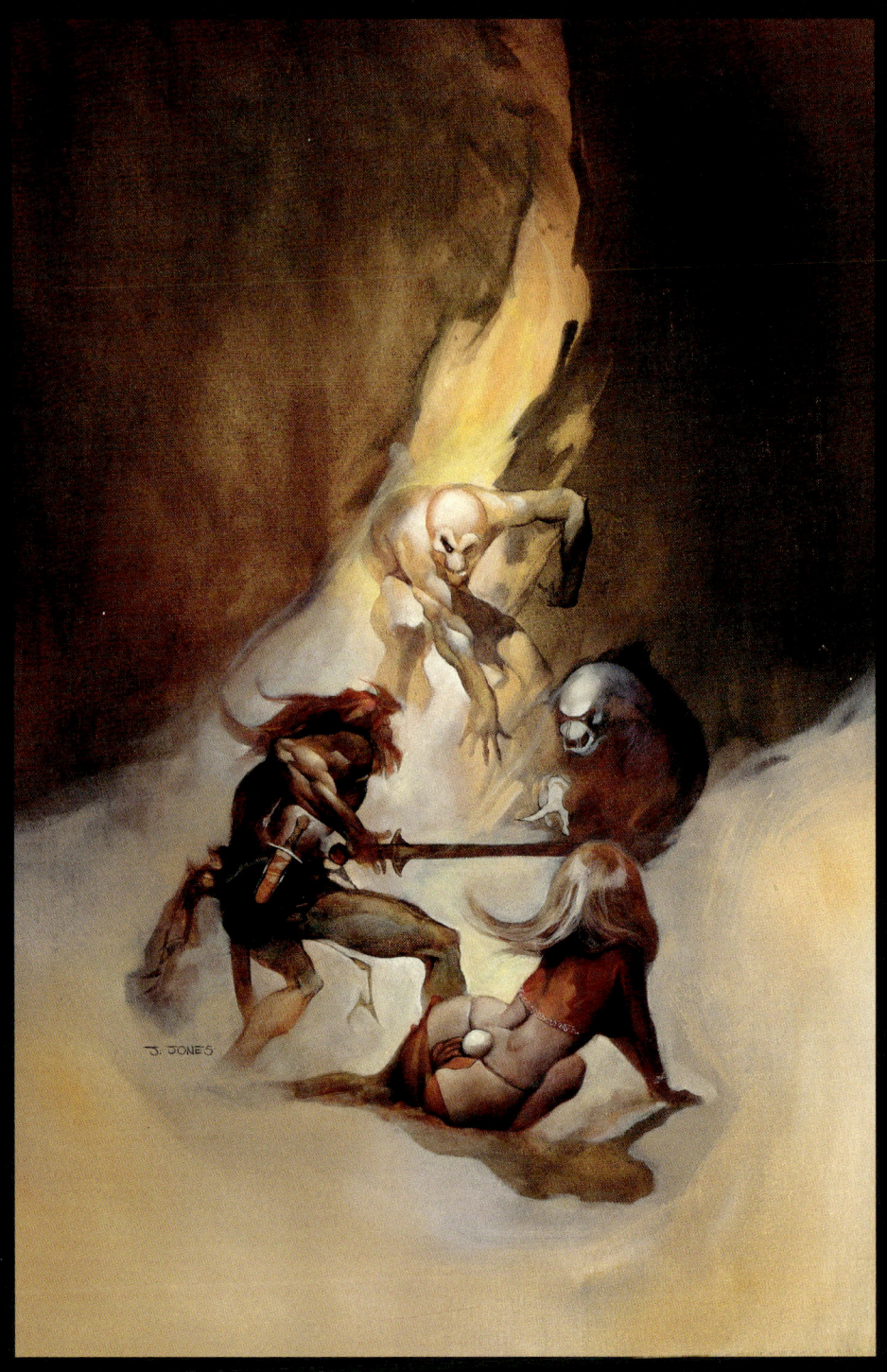

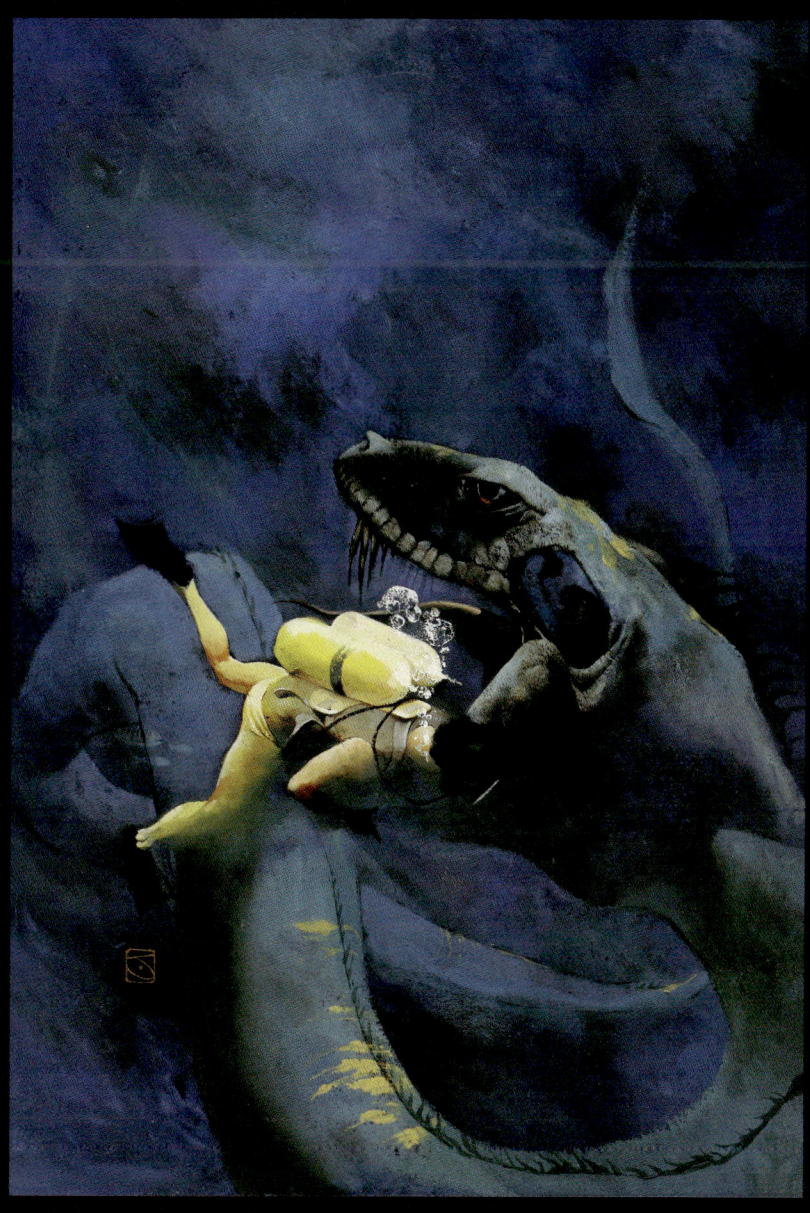

Opposite: Flame Winds, for the cover of Norvell W. Page's 1969 Berkley Books novel. Oil on canvas board, 71.1 x 45.2 cm (28 x 18 inches).

Above: Sea Siege, for the cover of Andre Norton's 1971 Ace Books novel. Oil on Masonite, 76.2 x 50.8 cm (30 x 20 inches).

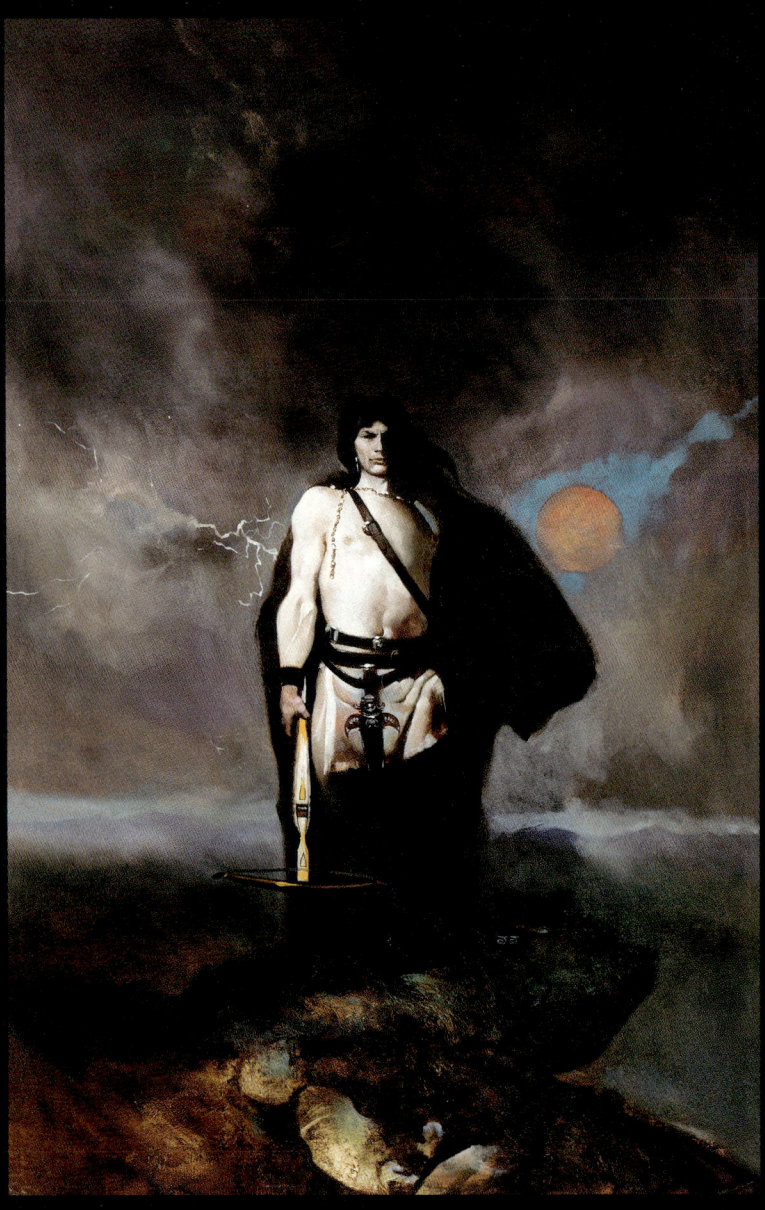

Above: Kothar: Barbarian Swordsman, for the 1969 novel by Gardner Fox. Oil on board, 91.4 x 55.8 cm (36 x 22 inches). Courtesy of Heritage Auctions.

Opposite: Messenger of Zhuvastou, for the 1973 novel by Andrew J. Offutt. Oil on canvas, 76.2 x 45.7 cm (30 x 18 inches). Courtesy of Heritage Auctions.

MASTERPIECES OF FANTASY ART

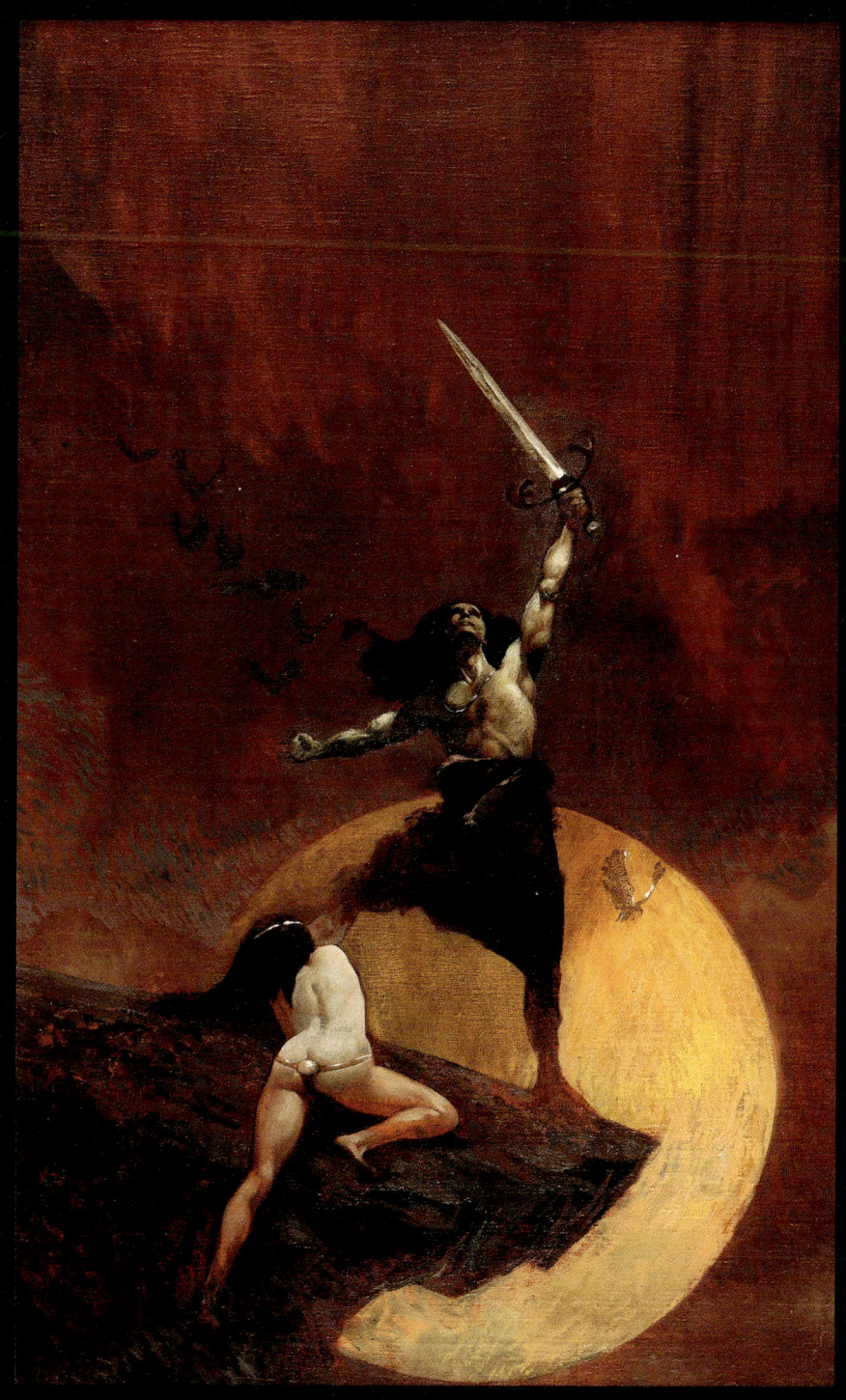

JEFFREY CATHERINE JONES

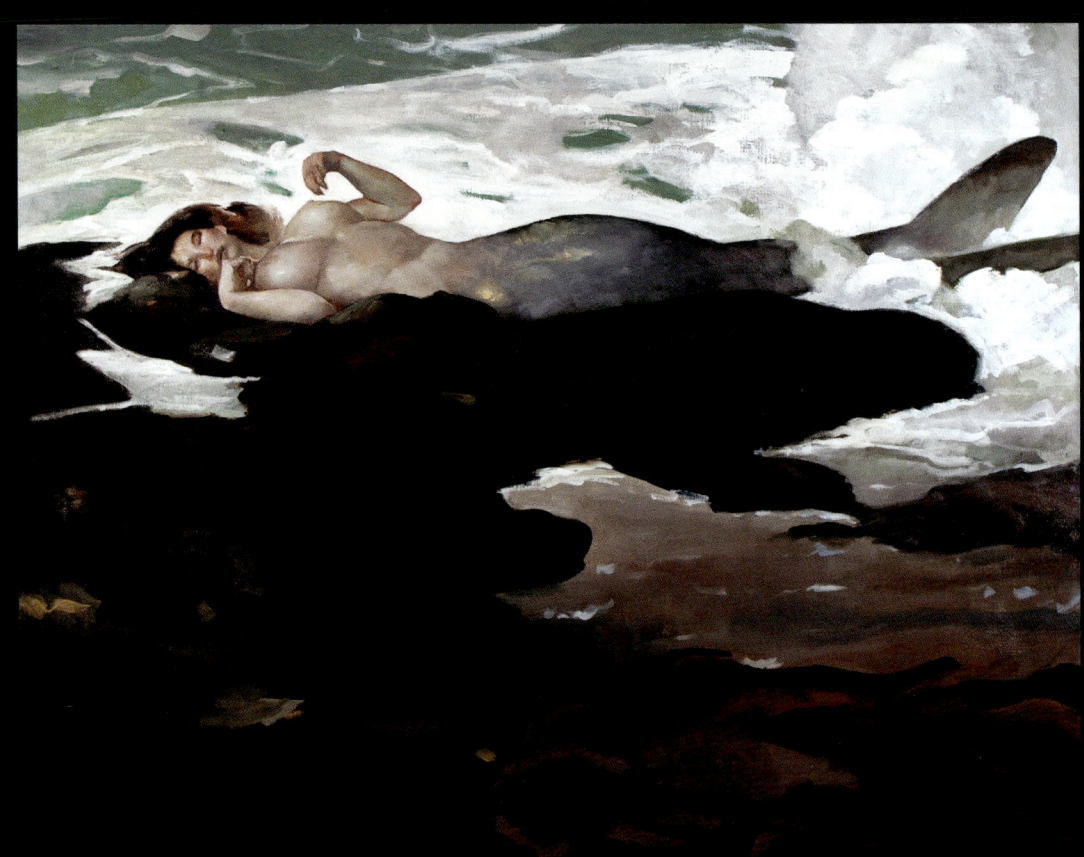

Above: One of Jones's finer mermaids, usage unknown, oil on canvas, 1998, 121.9 x 152.4 cm (48 x 60 inches). Courtesy of Heritage Auctions.

Opposite: Tarzan and the Golden Lion, oil on canvas, 2001, 187.9 x 127 cm (74 x 50 inches). Courtesy of Heritage Auctions.

Following left: Viking Charge, oil on canvas, 1996, 90.1 x 64.7 cm (35.5 x 25.5 inches). Courtesy of Heritage Auctions.

Following right: On All Fours, nude sketch, ink on paper, circa 1975, 17.7 x 22.8 cm (7 x 9 inches).

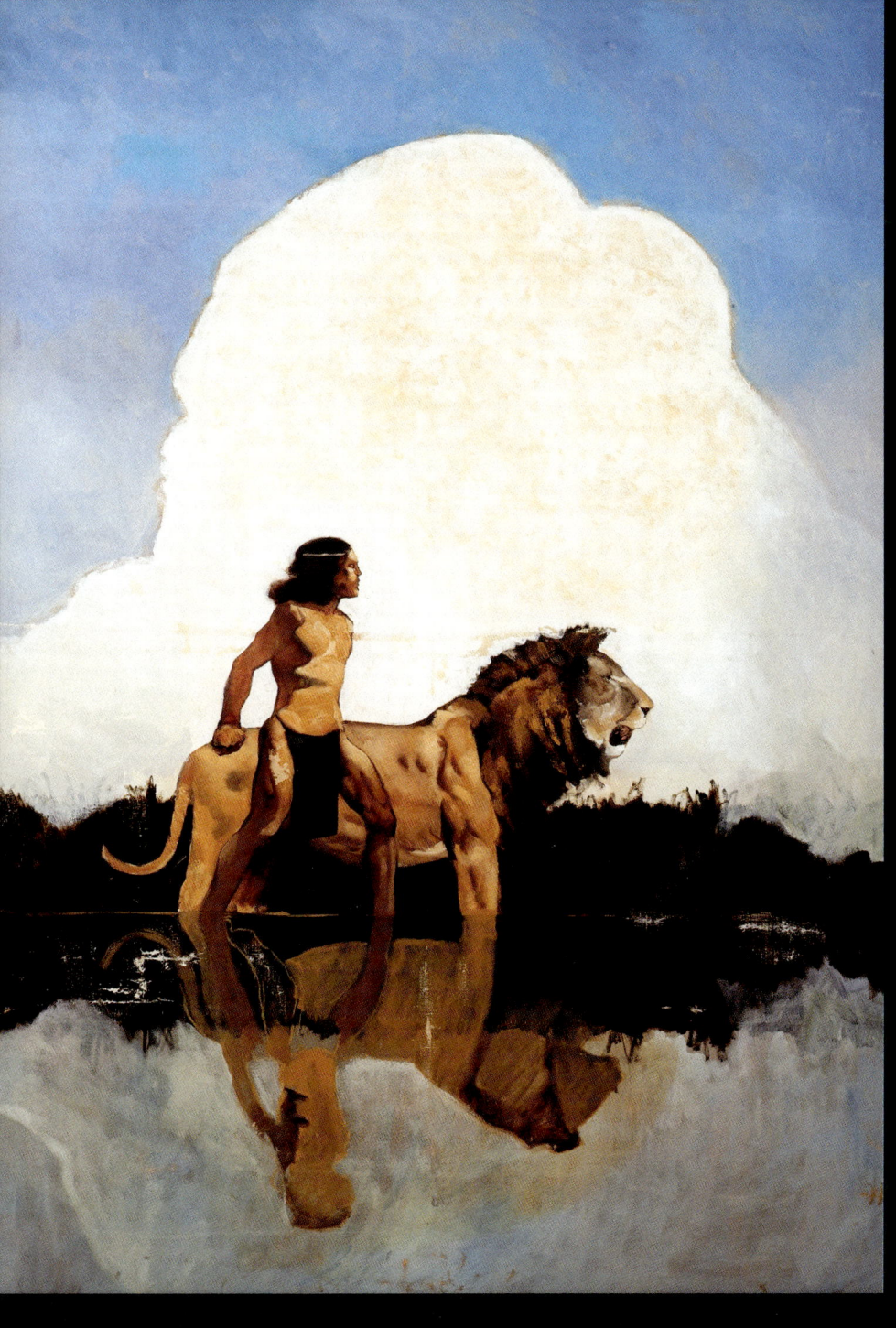

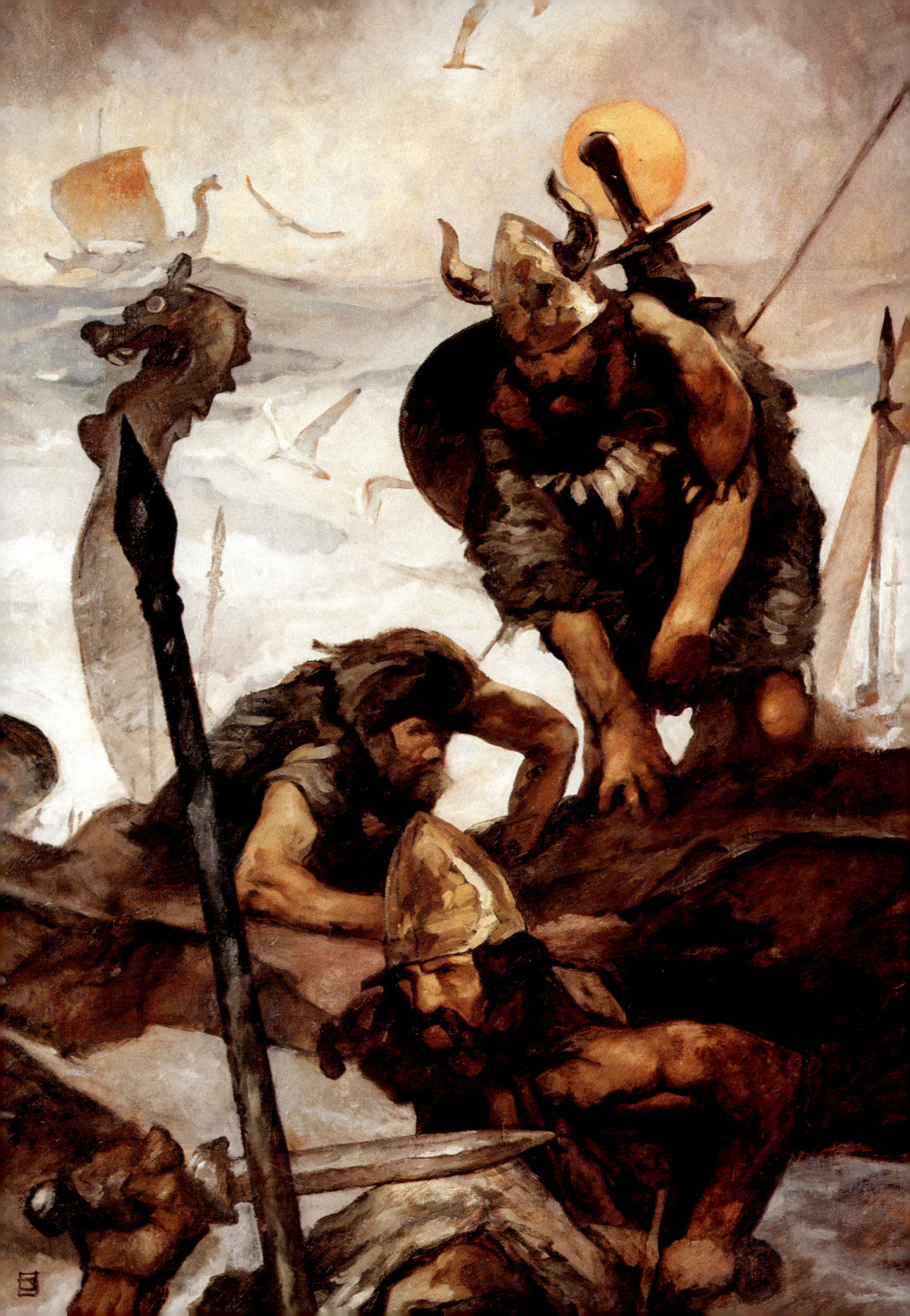

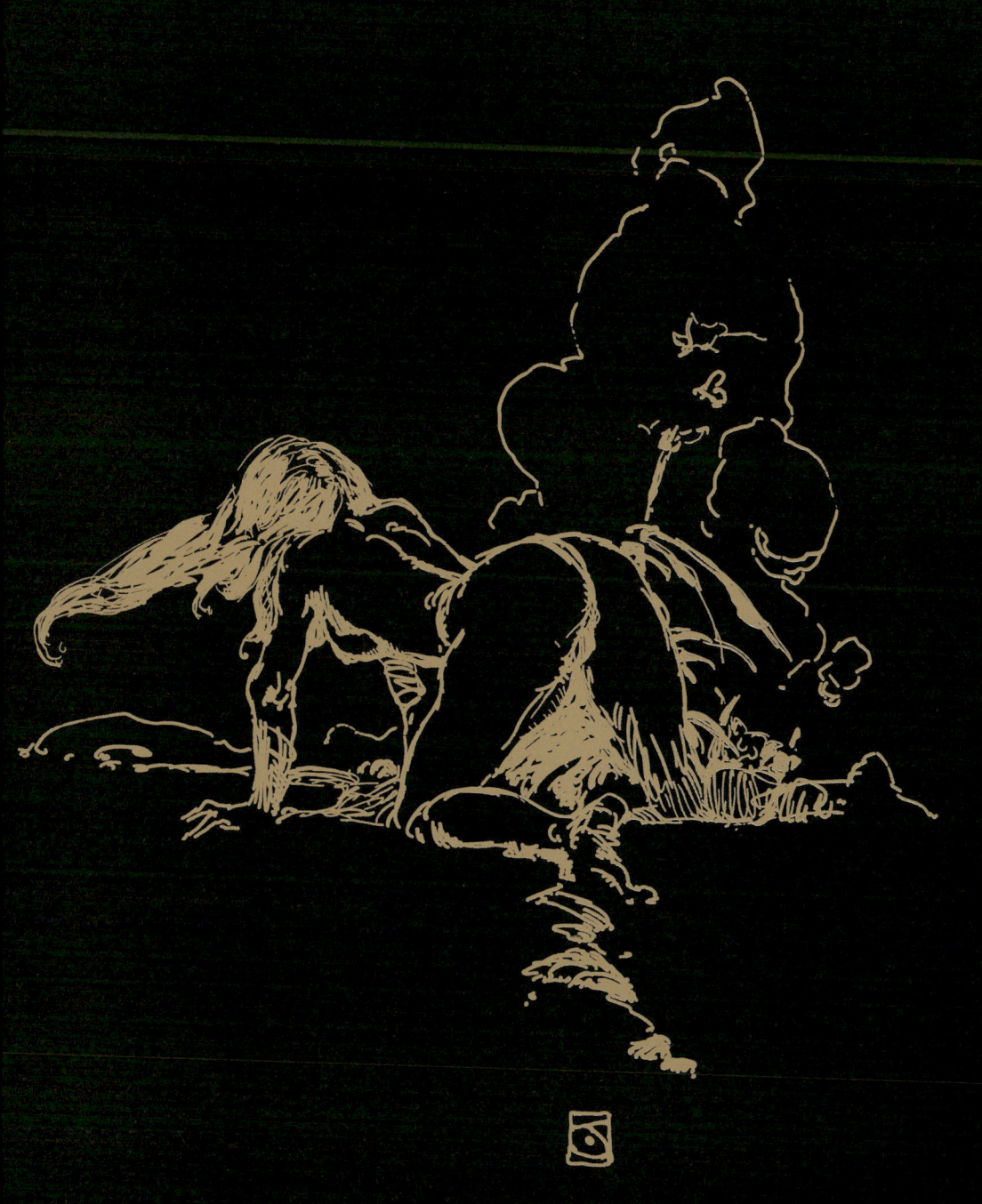

Rodney Matthews

1945-

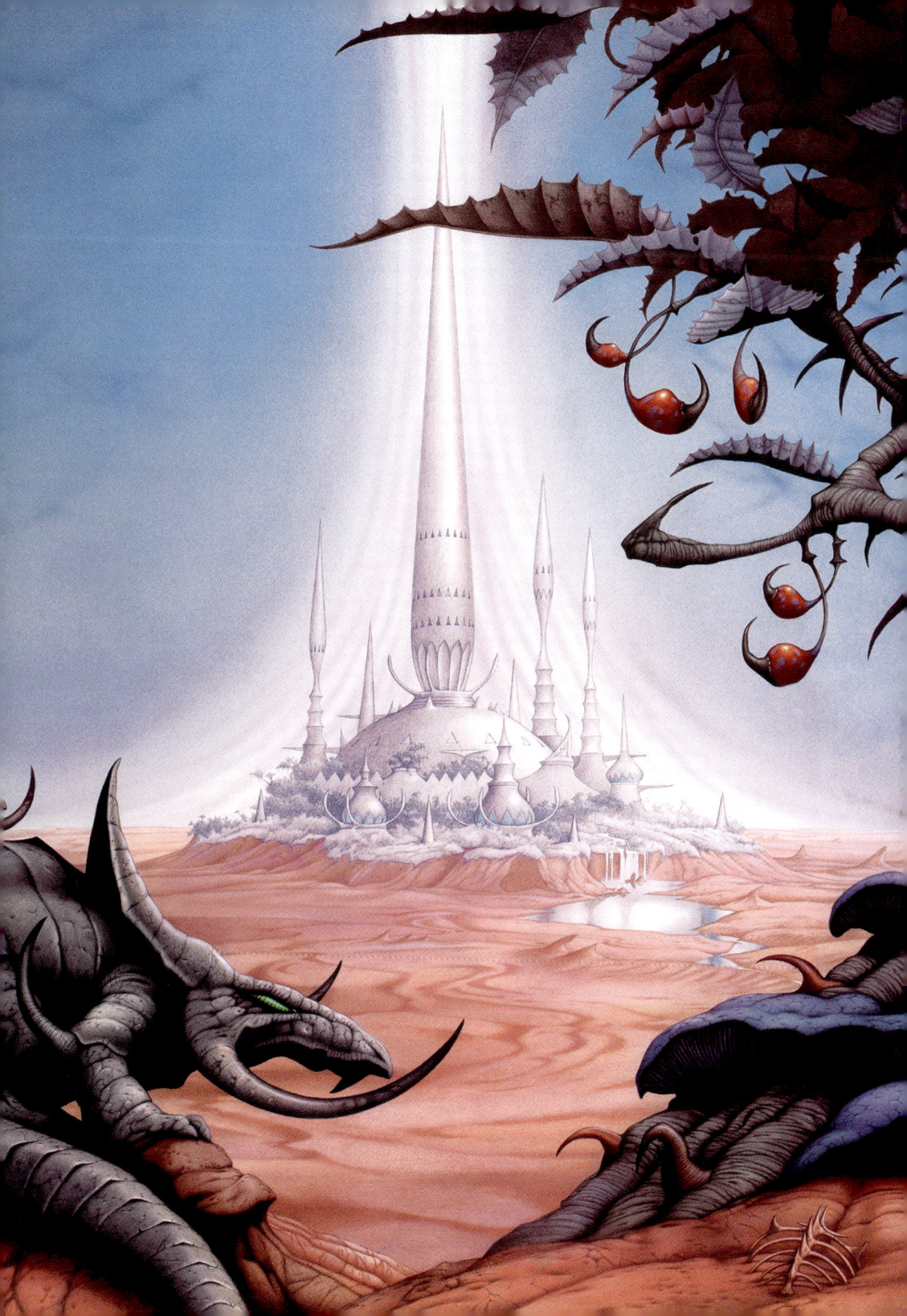

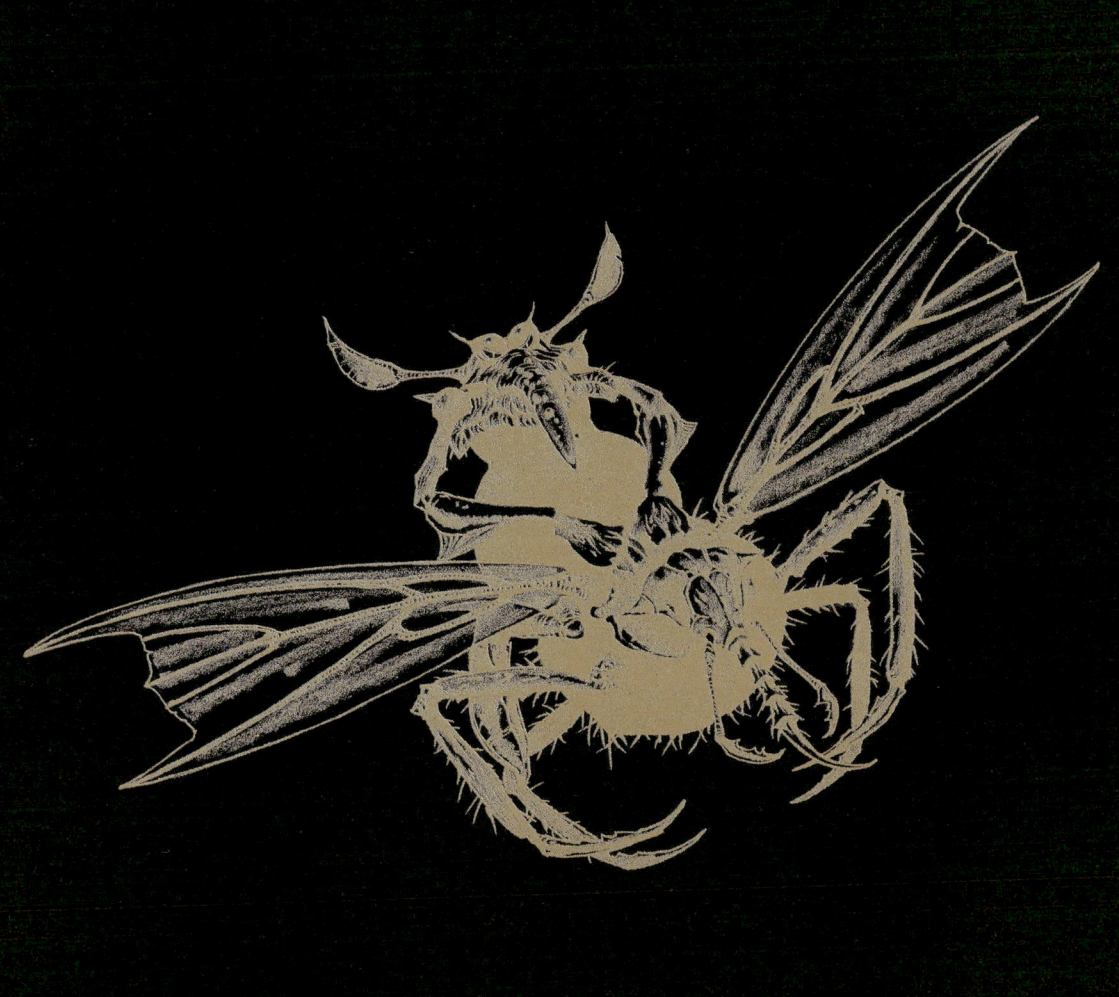

RODNEY MATTHEWS
THE ROCK STAR

BY ZAK SMITH

"I do like graceful shapes. But in nature you have things like beautiful flowers, like roses, that smell nice but when you get close you often find yourself with a thorn in your thumb."

The fantasists of the 1970s represent the midpoint of a great transformation then taking place in the world of illustration—the surrealistic images the acid culture used to show itself to itself were increasingly repurposed to serve the graphic arts' more traditional masters: merchants selling luxury goods and good parents looking for things to read to their children.

The art of Rodney Matthews, the least expressionistic of prog-rock artists, sits poised quite comfortably at this midpoint—imagined but palpable, made alien but not alienating. His work bears none of the chaos, asymmetry, digression, fixation, abstraction, or obscurity of hallucination. Matthews simply puts you on his knee, looks out the window at something—a mantis, a moth, a sailing ship—and tells you a story about it. The exaggerations of shape and color are no more than the rhymes and emphasis of a father by the fire in mid-yarn. The curves across his surfaces aren't the coiled art nouveau lines of his early rival Roger

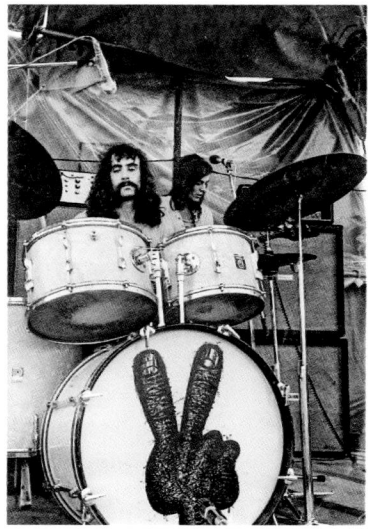

Dean, but rather match the size and arc of Matthews's hands' rotation on his wrist as he builds up scenery piece by piece.

Each image exists only to serve the place it depicts: a curtain opened on a dramatic moment in a vivid world Matthews has carefully catalogued—an occupiable snow globe of discrete objects and specific creatures, glowing shapes, horizons defined by insectile architecture, arabesque anatomies, orchids, and fungi—and wouldn't dream of telling you how to feel about it. The images are smooth and concrete; the objects never surrender their sense of volume to moody lighting. The outlines are hard, the technique is layered, seamless, refusing to ever devolve back into blobs of pooled paint or streaks of clotted ink, as if translated directly from the storyteller's mind.

When darkness comes into Rodney Matthews's landscapes it comes not as brutality, ferocity, or psychosis but as adventure. His metaphor for evil is the thorn shape, and evil in his world is like a thorn; dangerous, yes, but no more than an obstacle: static, simple, an essential part of the

Previous right: Chase the Dragon, for the cover of Magnum's 1982 record album. Ink on paper, 1980, 39.8 x 39.8 cm (15.7 x 15.7 inches).

Opposite: Fly Rider, for the personal project *Oddney's*

Otherland, pencil on paper, 2003, 29.8 x 41.9 cm (11.75 x 16.5 inches). Courtesy of Heritage Auctions.

Above: Rodney playing drums with his second band, Squidd, at the second Glastonbury Festival, 1971.

beauty it is attached to and—above all—natural. Evil isn't a force or a condition, it's just another character.

Like his art, Matthews's life has been punctuated with minor eruptions of picturesque violence. Born in Paulton, England, in 1945, he says, "I made my own catapults with metal and adjustable grips…and sometimes kids got hurt, and we might have swapped battles that got out of hand. Cuts and different things. Then there were the gashes I received in my dad's workshop. Always bleeding somewhere in the house." He also equipped his friends with bespoke armor and watched a squirrel bite his father in the head.

Not all of these incidents were consequence-free: one of his homemade guns blew up in his face, causing a slanting distortion to the vision in his left eye that may have contributed to his signature style. Matthews credits brushes with death later in life ("I used to drive far too fast drunkenly in my Lotus and had various situations where I should have been killed, like spinning at speed and the thing should have rolled. But it didn't. It stuck to the road. I got blown up by the IRA in my office in Park Street. And escaped without a scratch.") for leading to his eventual conversion to Christianity; a series of near-amputations in the wood shop led to his engineer father recommending that he should draw for a living instead.

He did—after a childhood carrying snakes and toads in his pockets around the Somerset countryside, Matthews went to West of England College of Art and soon got a job at an ad agency. He was powerfully influenced by the close observation of Arthur Rackham's sinewy branches; by the symmetry, detail, and vivid color of Edmund Dulac; and by Walt Disney—whose inventions he first encountered when his father drew a Disney menagerie along the wallpaper in his room.

His father also had a pair of drum kits in the attic, which sparked Matthews's lifelong love of music, and his early career involved as much drumming as drawing. Matthews soon became a fixture of the emerging prog scene, rubbing shoulders with musicians from Cream, Yes, and King Crimson. His artistic style fit—and formed alongside—the new music: inventive, esoteric, positioned at a remove from mundane life, but its theatrical presentation and thorny edge also made it attractive to early metal bands like Scorpions and Diamond Head.

Ad work gave Matthews versatility and a work ethic, but the assignments bored him—he finally quit when asked to dream up a way to sell a plastic toilet—and he formed a graphics company with fellow artist/musician Terry Brace. In 1969, an underground-comix-influenced sleeve for Thin Lizzy's *New Day*, finished between assignments at the agency, kicked off a 40-year career in album cover illustration. In 1974—just as his band Squidd was breaking up and his painting style was coming into its own—an opportunity from Peter Ledeboer at the seminal and wildly successful Big O poster company paved the way for even greener pastures.

Fantasy writer Michael Moorcock, creator of drug-fueled antihero Elric, intermittent member of space-rock pioneers Hawkwind, and all-around '70s science-fantasy Johnny Appleseed, helped Matthews break into book cover illustration. Their collaboration on a series of posters based on Moorcock's Eternal Champion characters included some of Matthews's most absorbing detail work. Matthews's book cover commissions often followed traditional pulp compositions—one or two figures posed against an exotic landscape—but rendered everything as organic, blacklit, and bent.

Later, the contradictions in Matthews's work—inviting and warm, but at its most distinctive when least optimistic—found a counterpart in the Christian thrash scene: "In the mid-'80s I did an interview with *Kerrang!* which caught the eye of Dave Williams, manager of a band called Seventh Angel. In 1989 he approached me to talk about sleeve artwork. I checked out the band

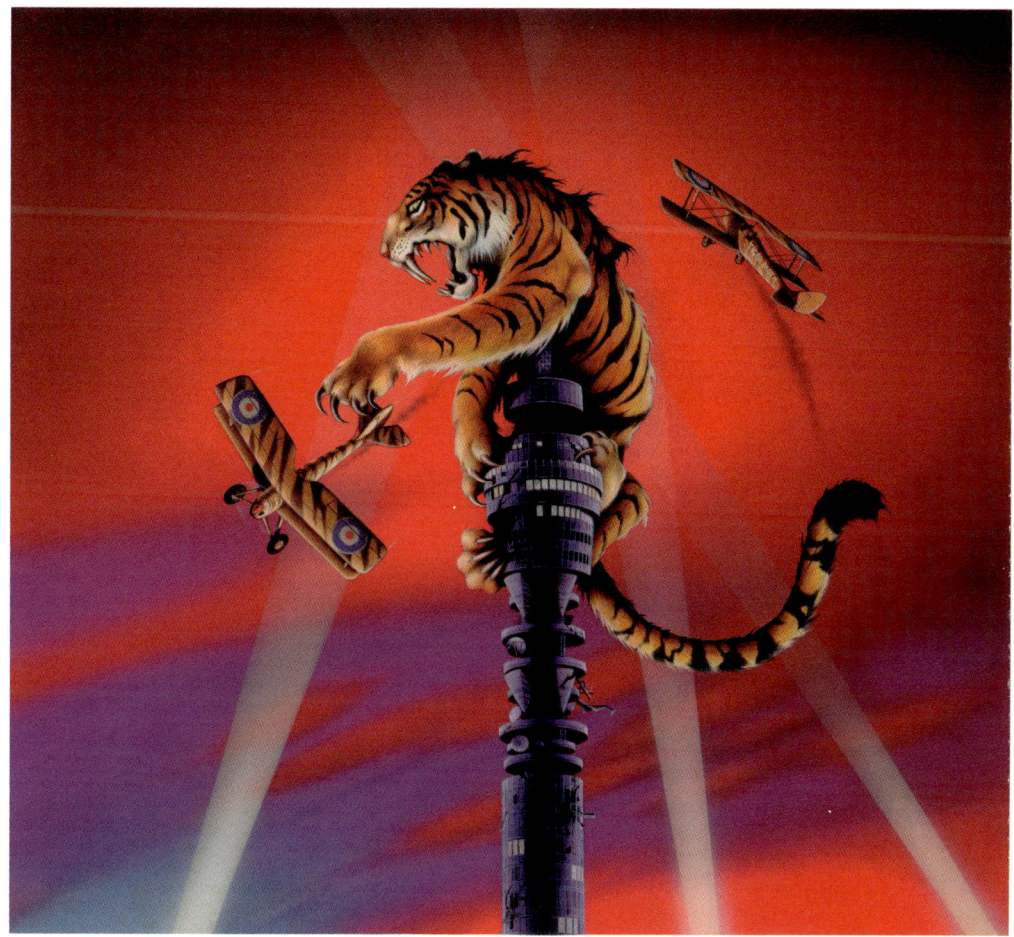

for authenticity (as is my custom) and yes, they really were Christians, but like myself at the time, loud and hairy!"

Likewise, the Technicolor clarity of his work eased his transition to conceptual design, including video games for Sony's Psygnosis Limited starting in the late '90s, the children's television series *Lavender Castle* in 1998 and *The Magic Roundabout* film in 2005. "I've always had a pretty good idea of what my creatures, warriors, and you-name-them look like at the reverse or over the horizon," he explained.

But then Matthews's long career has been all about hybridizing the expanded realities of psychedelia with the otherworlds of classic British fantasy—where everything is twice as big, cheerfully inexplicable, and seen from behind a hedge. No one more effectively cast dreamscapes as play sets.

Above: Crazy Nights, for the Tygers of Pan Tang's 1981 album cover. Matthews's original design had the "tyger" battling bankers wearing dunce caps in flying saucers. Ink on paper, 1981, 32 x 32 cm (12.6 x 12.6 inches).

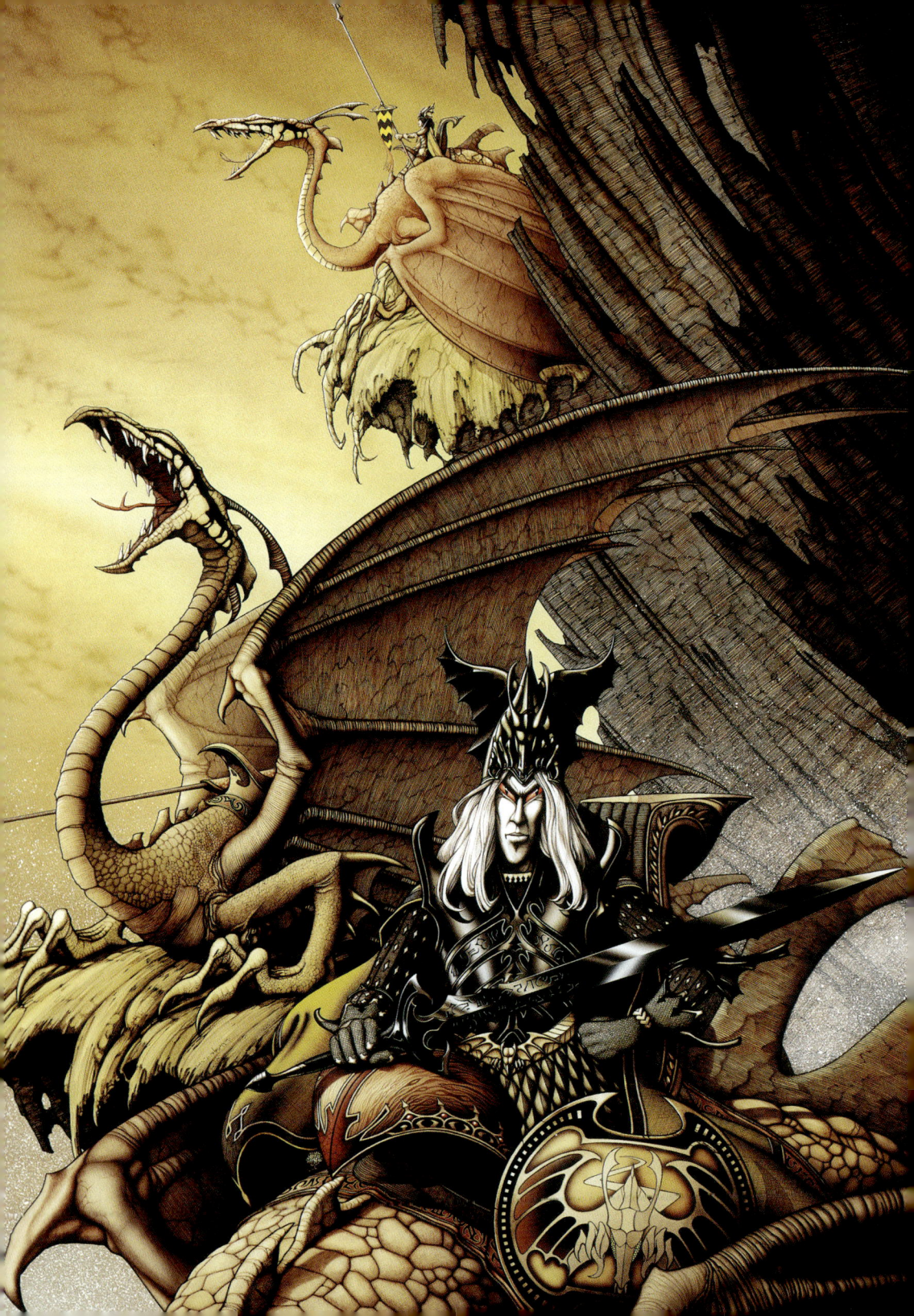

RODNEY MATTHEWS
DER ROCKSTAR

VON ZAK SMITH

„Ich mag ansprechende Formen. Doch in der Natur gibt es Dinge wie schöne Blumen, Rosen zum Beispiel, die zwar angenehm duften, aber kommt man ihnen nahe, hat man plötzlich einen Dorn im Daumen."

Die Fantasykünstler der 1970er-Jahre repräsentieren die Wende, die sich damals in der Welt der Illustration vollzog. Die surrealistischen Bilder der Acid-Kultur wurden zunehmend einer neuen Verwendung zugeführt – sie sollten den traditionelleren Meistern der bildenden Künste dienen: Händlern, die Luxusgüter verkauften, und wohlmeinenden Eltern, die nach Dingen Ausschau hielten, die sie ihren Kindern vorlesen konnten.

Die Kunst von Rodney Matthews, des am wenigsten expressionistischen der Prog-Rock-Künstler, hockt ganz angenehm ausbalanciert an dieser Wende – imaginiert, doch fühlbar, fremdartig gemacht, aber nicht befremdend. Sein Werk weist nichts von jenem Chaos, von Asymmetrie, Abschweifung, Fixiertheit, Abstraktion oder von Undeutlichkeit einer Halluzination auf. Matthews setzt den Betrachter einfach auf sein Knie, schaut aus dem Fenster, betrachtet etwas – eine Gottesanbeterin, eine Motte, ein Segelschiff – und erzählt ihm dazu eine Geschichte. Die Übertreibungen von Form und Farbe entsprechen nur den Versen und dem Nachdruck, den ein Vater am Lagerfeuer dem Höhepunkt seines Erzählens verleiht. Die kurvigen Linien, die er über seine Oberflächen zieht, sind nicht die gewundenen Jugendstillinien seines frühen Rivalen Roger Dean, sie entsprechen vielmehr der Größe und dem Bogen, den Matthews beschreibt, während er die Szenerie aufbaut.

Jedes Bild existiert nur, um dem Ort, den es darstellt, dienlich zu sein: ein Vorhang, der sich zu einem dramatischen Moment in einer anschaulichen Welt öffnet, die Matthews sorgsam katalogisiert hat – eine besetzbare Schneekugel aus diskreten Objekten und spezifischen Kreaturen, leuchtenden Formen, Horizonten, die durch eine insektenähnliche Architektur, araboskenhafte Anatomien, Orchideen und Pilze definiert sind –, und er würde nicht einmal im Traum daran denken, dem Betrachter zu sagen, was er davon halten solle. Die Bilder sind glatt und fest umrissen; die Objekte geben ihren Sinn für Volumen nie einer Lichtstimmung preis. Die Umrisse sind hart, die Technik ist die einer Schichtung, nahtlos, und verweigert sich einer Rückverwandlung in Kleckse angesammelter Farbe oder Streifen aus geronnener Tinte, als sei alles direkt aus dem Kopf des Geschichtenerzählers übersetzt.

Bricht Dunkelheit über Rodney Matthews' Landschaften herein, dann nicht als etwas Grausames, Wildes oder als psychotische Störung, sondern als Abenteuer. Seine Metapher für das Böse ist die Kontur eines Stachels, und in seiner Welt ist das Böse wie ein Stachel; gefährlich, ja, aber nicht gefährlicher als ein Hindernis: statisch, einfach, ein wesentlicher Teil der Schönheit, mit der es verbunden ist, und – vor allem – etwas ganz Natürliches. Das Böse ist keine Macht oder ein Zustand, es ist bloß eine andere Gestalt.

Opposite: The Dragon Lord, one of 12 paintings inspired by Michael Moorcock's *The Eternal Champion* trilogy and commissioned for posters by the British company Big O.

In 2011 it was licensed by Roxxcalibur for the cover of their *Lords of the NWOBHM* album. Ink and gouache on paper, 1976, 100 x 69.8 cm (39.4 x 27.5 inches).

Wie seine Kunst wurde Matthews' Leben durch kleine Ausbrüche pittoresker Gewalt unterbrochen. Der 1945 in Paulton, England, Geborene erzählt: „Ich habe meine eigenen Katapulte aus Metall und mit verstellbaren Griffen gebastelt … und manchmal wurden Kinder verletzt, und wir haben uns Schlachten geliefert, die vielleicht gelegentlich außer Kontrolle gerieten. Es gab Schnittverletzungen und alles Mögliche. Dann zog ich mir auch noch Wunden in der Werkstatt meines Vaters zu. Immer blutete jemand im Haus." Er stattete seine Freunde auch mit maßgeschneiderten Rüstungen aus und sah, wie sein Vater von einem Eichhörnchen in den Kopf gebissen wurde.

Nicht alle dieser Zwischenfälle blieben ohne Konsequenzen: Eine seiner selbstgebauten Schusswaffen explodierte ihm ins Gesicht, was zu einer Verzerrung der Sehkraft seines linken Auges führte, die vielleicht etwas mit seinem typischen Stil zu tun hat. Später in seinem Leben bezog sich Matthews auf Begegnungen mit dem Tod („Früher fuhr ich mit meinem Lotus viel zu schnell und angetrunken und erlebte verschiedene Situationen, die für mich tödlich hätten ausgehen können. Die Räder drehten zum Beispiel mal bei hoher Geschwindigkeit durch, und die Karre hätte sich eigentlich überschlagen müssen. Aber das passierte nicht. Sie blieb fest auf der Straße. Einmal versuchte die IRA, mich in meinem Büro in der Park Street in die Luft zu sprengen. Aber ich kam ohne einen Kratzer davon"), die schließlich zu seiner Bekehrung zum Christentum führten; eine Reihe von Fastamputationen in der Holzhandlung führten dazu, dass ihm sein Ingenieur-Vater dazu riet, seinen Lebensunterhalt besser mit Zeichnen zu verdienen.

Was er auch tat – nach einer Kindheit, während der er in der ländlichen Gegend von Somerset Schlangen und Kröten in seinen Taschen mit sich herumtrug, besuchte Matthews das West of England College of Art und bekam binnen kurzer Zeit einen Job in einer Werbeagentur. Stark beeinflusst wurde er durch die genaue Betrachtung der kräftigen Astwerke von Arthur Rackham; von der Symmetrie, den Details und den lebhaften Farben eines Edmund Dulac und von Walt Disney – dessen Schöpfungen ihm zum ersten Mal begegneten, als ihm sein Vater eine Disney-Menagerie auf die Tapete seines Zimmers zeichnete.

Auf dem Dachboden hatte sein Vater auch ein Schlagzeug, das Matthews' lebenslange Leidenschaft für Musik entfachte, und in den frühen Jahren seiner Karriere beschäftigte er sich mit Schlagzeugspiel genauso oft wie mit Zeichnen. Bald schon gehörte Matthews fest zur aufkommenden Prog-Rock-Szene und hatte Umgang mit Musikern von Cream, Yes und King Crimson. Sein künstlerischer Stil passte zu dieser neuen Musik und bildete sich parallel zu ihr heraus: einfallsreich, esoterisch, abgekehrt vom profanen Leben, doch die theatralische Darbietung und das Dornig-Kantige seiner Kunst machten sie auch für frühe Metalbands wie die Scorpions und Diamond Head attraktiv.

Die Arbeit für die Werbeagentur verschaffte Matthews Flexibilität und förderte seine Arbeitsmoral, doch die Aufträge langweilten ihn – er schmiss den Job schließlich, als man ihn bat, sich Gedanken über den Verkauf einer Plastiktoilette zu machen –, und so gründete er gemeinsam mit seinem Künstler- und Musikerkollegen Terry Brace ein Grafikbüro. 1969 wurde dann eine zwischen den Aufträgen für die Agentur fertiggestellte und von Underground-Comix beeinflusste Plattenhülle für Thin Lizzys *New Day* zum Initial einer 40 Jahre währenden Karriere als Albumcoverillustrator. 1974 – gerade als sich seine Band Squidd auflöste und sich sein Malstil zu einem unverkennbar eigenen entwickelt hatte – bereitete eine Gelegenheit, die ihm Peter Ledeboer von der einflussreichen und ausgesprochen erfolgreichen Plakatfirma Big O bot, den Weg zu noch saftigeren Gründen.

Der Fantasyautor Michael Moorcock, Schöpfer des drogenberauschten Antihelden Elric, zeitweiliges Mitglied der Space-Rock-Pioniere Hawkwind und an der in den 1970er-Jahren

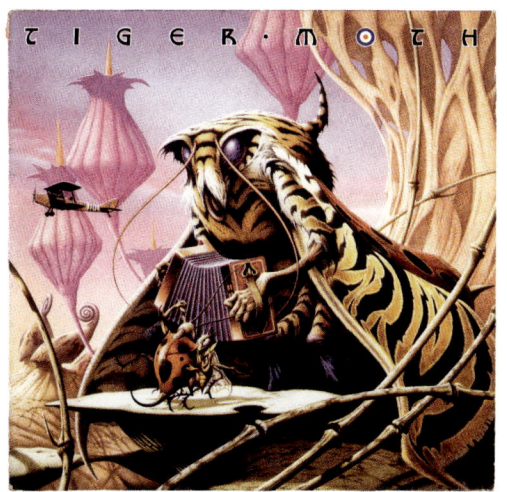
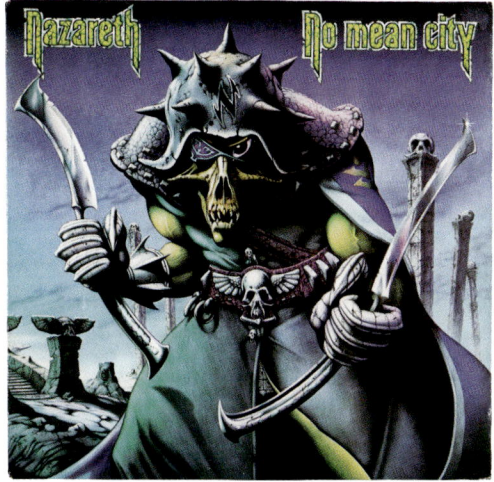

allgegenwärtigen Science-Fantasy Johnny Appleseed beteiligt, half Matthews beim Einstieg in die Gestaltung von Buchtiteln. Bei ihrer Zusammenarbeit für eine Serie von Postern, die sich auf die Figuren von Moorcocks *Eternal Champion* beziehen, entstanden auch einige von Matthews' fesselndsten, bis ins Detail ausgearbeiteten Werken. Bei seinen Aufträgen für Buchcover hielt Matthews sich meist an traditionelle Pulp-Kompositionen – eine oder zwei Figuren stehen vor dem Hintergrund einer exotischen Landschaft –, doch alles ist organisch, in Schwarzlicht getaucht und gebogen dargestellt.

Später fanden die Widersprüche in Matthews' Werk – einladend und warm, doch am unverwechselbarsten, wenn es am wenigsten Optimismus ausstrahlte – ein Gegenüber in der christlichen Trash-Szene: „Mitte der 1980er-Jahre gab ich der Zeitschrift *Kerrang!* ein Interview, auf das Dave Williams, Manager der Band Seventh Angel, aufmerksam wurde. 1989 sprach er mich an, um mit mir über die künstlerische Gestaltung einer Plattenhülle zu reden. Ich überprüfte (wie es meine Gewohnheit ist) die Band auf ihre Authentizität, und ja, sie waren tatsächlich Christen, aber wie ich zu jener Zeit laut und langhaarig!"

Desgleichen erleichterte die Technicolor-Klarheit seines Werks seine Übernahme in die konzeptionelle Gestaltung zum Beispiel von ab den späten 1990er-Jahren entwickelten Videospielen der von Sony übernommenen Psygnosis Limited, für die Kinderfernsehserie *Lavender Castle* 1998 und den Film *The Magic Roundabout* 2005. „Ich hatte immer eine ziemlich genaue Vorstellung davon, wie meine Kreaturen, Krieger und was weiß ich auf ihrer Kehrseite oder hinter dem Horizont aussehen", erklärte er.

Doch letztendlich ging es in Matthews' langer Karriere darum, die erweiterten Realitäten des Psychedelischen mit der Anderwelt der klassischen britischen Fantasy zu verbinden – wo alles doppelt so groß, auf fröhliche Weise unerklärlich und von hinter einer Hecke aus betrachtet ist. Niemand hat Traumlandschaften als Spielesets effektiver gestaltet.

Above left: Tiger Moth's debut album, 1984, with Matthews's cover art. The artist says this is his favorite cover, being a fan of all variety of insects.

Above right: Nazareth's *No Mean City* album, 1979, with cover art by Matthews.

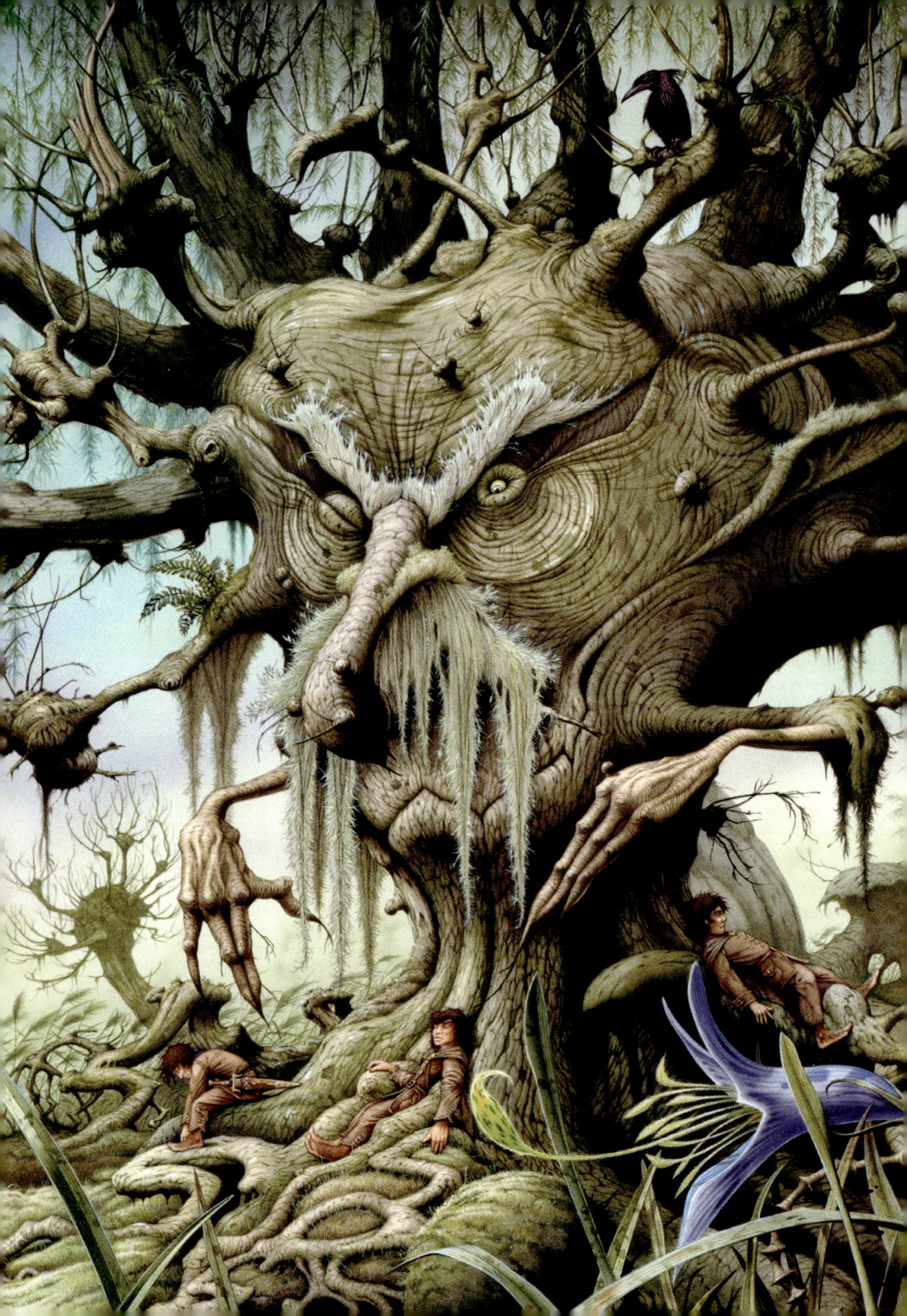

RODNEY MATTHEWS
LA ROCK-STAR

PAR ZAK SMITH

« J'aime les formes gracieuses. Mais dans la nature il existe par exemple des fleurs magnifiques, comme les roses ; elles sentent bon mais si vous vous rapprochez, vous vous retrouvez souvent avec une épine dans le pouce. »

Les artistes fantasy des années 1970 représentent un point médian de l'ample transformation que vit alors le monde de l'illustration – les images surréalistes qui se diffusaient dans l'entre-soi d'une culture sous acide sont alors recyclées pour satisfaire les mécènes plus conventionnels des arts graphiques : les marchands de produits de luxe et les bons parents en quête de saines lectures pour leurs enfants.

L'art de Rodney Matthews, le moins expressionniste des artistes de la scène rock progressive, se tient en équilibre à ce carrefour éphémère, à l'aise – imaginé mais palpable, étranger sans être inquiétant. Le chaos, l'asymétrie, l'abstraction, la noirceur, les digressions et fixations de l'hallucination sont absents de son travail. Matthews vous installe sur ses genoux, regarde quelque chose par la fenêtre – une mante religieuse, une mite, un bateau à voiles – et il vous raconte une histoire. Les formes et les couleurs exagérées ne sont que les rimes et l'emphase d'un *pater familias* assis au coin du feu. Les volutes à sa surface ne sont pas les lignes aux relents d'Art nouveau de son rival Roger Dean, mais plutôt l'empreinte du geste, de l'arc ample que tracent la main et le poignet, agiles, à mesure que Matthews élabore son décor.

Chaque image n'existe que pour servir le lieu qu'elle dépeint : un rideau s'ouvre sur une scène dramatique dans un monde vibrionnant dont Matthews a dressé un catalogue précis – une boule à neige habitée par des objets discrets et des créatures particulières, des formes luisantes, des horizons que dessinent une architecture d'insectes, des anatomies en arabesque, des orchidées et des champignons – et dont il se garde bien de vous dire ce qu'il doit vous inspirer. Les images sont lisses et concrètes ; les objets ne laissent jamais l'éclairage tronquer l'intégrité de leur volume. Les contours sont nets, la technique, elle, fonctionne par strates que rien ne laisse deviner, ni taches de peinture humide, ni traînées d'encre coagulée, comme si l'image était transcrite directement de l'esprit du conteur au papier.

Quand l'obscurité déteint sur les paysages de Rodney Matthews, elle n'est pas de l'ordre de la brutalité, de la férocité ou de la psychose, mais de l'aventure. La forme de l'épine est sa métaphore du mal, car dans son monde le mal est comme une épine – dangereuse, oui, mais pas plus qu'un obstacle : elle est statique, simple, elle fait partie intégrante de la beauté qu'elle protège et, surtout, elle est naturelle. Le mal n'est pas une force ou un état, c'est juste un autre personnage.

Comme son art, la vie de Matthews est ponctuée par les éruptions bénignes d'une violence pittoresque. Né à Paulton, en Angleterre, en 1945, il raconte : « Je fabriquais mes propres catapultes avec du métal et des poignées réglables… et il arrivait que des gosses soient blessés, quand nos

Opposite: Old Man Willow, another classic image from *Lord of the Rings.* Ink on paper, 2000, 56.9 x 40.9 cm (22.4 x 16.1 inches).

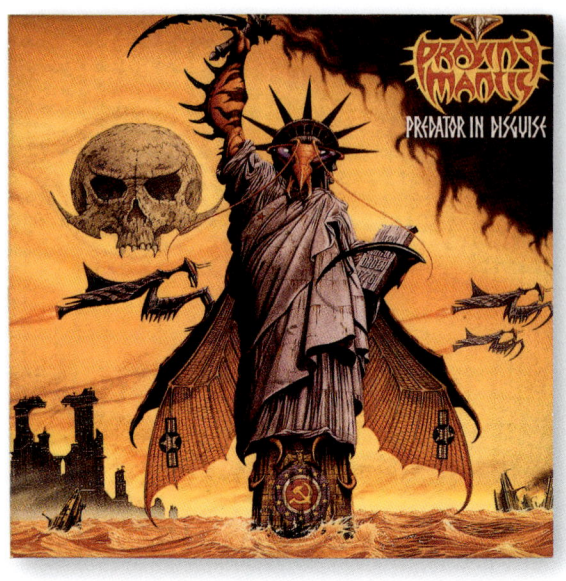

bagarres dégénéraient un peu trop. Des coupures, ce genre de choses. Et puis il y avait les entailles que je me faisais à l'atelier de mon père. Toujours quelque chose qui saignait, à la maison. » Il équipe aussi ses amis d'armures personnalisées et voit un écureuil mordre son père à la tête.

Ces incidents n'ont pas tous été sans conséquence : une de ses armes bricolées lui a explosé à la figure, endommageant sa vue de l'œil gauche d'une façon qui a pu influer sur son style. Matthews raconte avoir plusieurs fois frôlé la mort (« Je conduisais ma Lotus beaucoup trop vite en état d'ivresse et j'ai vécu plusieurs situations dont je n'aurais pas dû sortir vivant, comme déraper à pleine vitesse et ne pas faire de tonneaux alors que c'est ce qui aurait dû arriver. La voiture a collé à la route. L'IRA a essayé de me faire sauter dans mon bureau de Park Street. Et je m'en suis sorti sans une égratignure. ») et justifie ainsi sa conversion tardive au christianisme. C'est parce qu'il a failli se trancher des membres à l'atelier de menuiserie de son père ingénieur que celui-ci lui conseille de plutôt dessiner pour gagner sa vie.

C'est ce qu'il a fait. Après une enfance passée à se balader dans la campagne du Somerset avec des serpents et des crapauds dans ses poches, Matthews entre au West of England College of Art et décroche bientôt un petit boulot dans une agence de pub. Il est profondément marqué par l'observation méticuleuse des branches tendineuses d'Arthur Rackham, par la symétrie, les détails et les couleurs vives d'Edmund Dulac et par Walt Disney – dont il a découvert les créations quand son père a dessiné toute une ménagerie Disney sur le papier peint de sa chambre d'enfant.

Son père garde aussi un ensemble de batterie au grenier, qui déclenche chez Matthews une passion pour la musique ; ses débuts professionnels sont d'ailleurs autant une affaire de batterie que de dessin. Matthews devient une figure de la scène rock progressive émergente et côtoie les musiciens de Cream, Yes et King Crimson. Son style artistique colle avec – et se développe en même temps que – cette nouvelle musique : inventive, ésotérique, à des années-lumière de la banalité quotidienne, mais sa représentation scénique et son penchant « épineux » séduit aussi des groupes de métal pionniers comme Scorpions et Diamond Head.

Grâce à la publicité, Matthews gagne en polyvalence et acquiert une éthique professionnelle, mais les commandes l'ennuient. Il jette l'éponge quand on lui demande d'imaginer un moyen poétique pour vendre des toilettes en plastique et monte une société de graphisme avec son ami artiste et musicien Terry Brace. En 1969, la pochette influencée par les *comix* underground qu'il dessine pour l'album *New Day* de Thin Lizzy entre deux missions pour l'agence de pub lance

Above: Praying Mantis' *Predator In Disguise* album, 1991, with cover art by Matthews. The artist took heat for portraying the U.S. as a sinister power.

Opposite: Time on Our Side, commissioned in 2016 for the first of three Rolling Stones compilation records, all from live performances. Ink on paper, 2016, 31 x 60.9 cm (12.2 x 24 inches).

MASTERPIECES OF FANTASY ART

une carrière de quarante ans dans l'illustration de pochettes de disques. En 1974, alors que son groupe Squidd se sépare et que son style pictural arrive à maturité, Peter Ledeboer lui donne sa chance chez le créateur d'affiches Big O, un précurseur qui connaît alors un énorme succès, et de nouveaux horizons s'ouvrent devant lui.

L'auteur fantasy Michael Moorcock, créateur d'Elric l'antihéros drogué jusqu'aux yeux, membre intermittent du groupe pionnier du space rock Hawkwind et prolifique héraut de la science-fantasy dans les années 1970, aide Matthews à percer dans l'illustration de couvertures de livres. Leur collaboration sur une série d'affiches imaginées à partir des personnages de Champions éternels de Moorcock a généré certaines des œuvres les plus méticuleuses et captivantes de Matthews. Les illustrations qu'il réalise sur commande pour les maisons d'édition se calquent souvent sur la composition des *pulps* traditionnels – un ou deux personnages placés dans un paysage exotique – mais tout y est organique, distordu, presque phosphorescent.

Plus tard, les contradictions inhérentes au travail de Matthews – accueillant et chaleureux, mais caractérisé au mieux lorsqu'il est le moins optimiste – trouvent un équivalent sur la scène trash chrétienne : « Au milieu des années 1980, j'ai fait une interview pour le magazine *Kerrang !* qui a été remarquée par Dave Williams, le manager d'un groupe qui s'appelait Seventh Angel. En 1989, il m'a contacté pour parler illustration de jaquettes. J'ai vérifié le pedigree de ces gars (comme je le fais toujours) et oui, ils étaient de vrais chrétiens, mais comme moi à l'époque, bruyants et chevelus ! »

De la même façon, la résolution Technicolor de son travail facilite son passage au design conceptuel, notamment sur des jeux vidéo pour la société Psygnosis, rachetée par Sony, à partir de la fin des années 1990, sur la série d'animation pour enfants « Lavender Castle » en 1998 et sur le film *Pollux – Le Manège enchanté* en 2005. « J'ai toujours eu une idée assez précise de ce à quoi ressemblent mes créatures, mes guerriers et ce que vous voudrez d'autre à l'intérieur, de l'autre côté de l'horizon », expliquait-il.

Rien de plus logique finalement, puisque Matthews a consacré sa longue carrière à croiser les réalités dilatées de l'expérience psychédélique avec les autres mondes de la fantasy britannique classique – où tout est deux fois plus grand, gaiement inexplicable et vu à couvert d'une haie. Personne n'a mieux transformé les paysages oniriques en terrains de jeu.

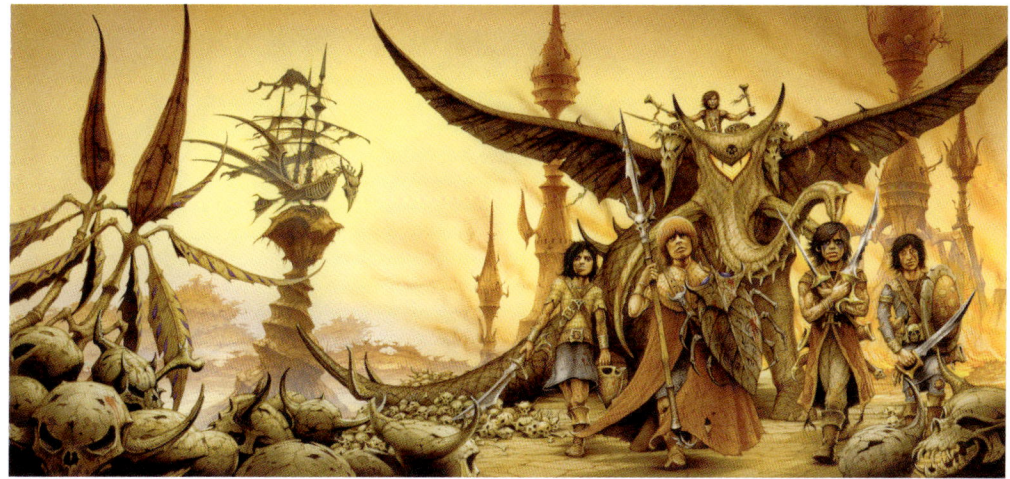

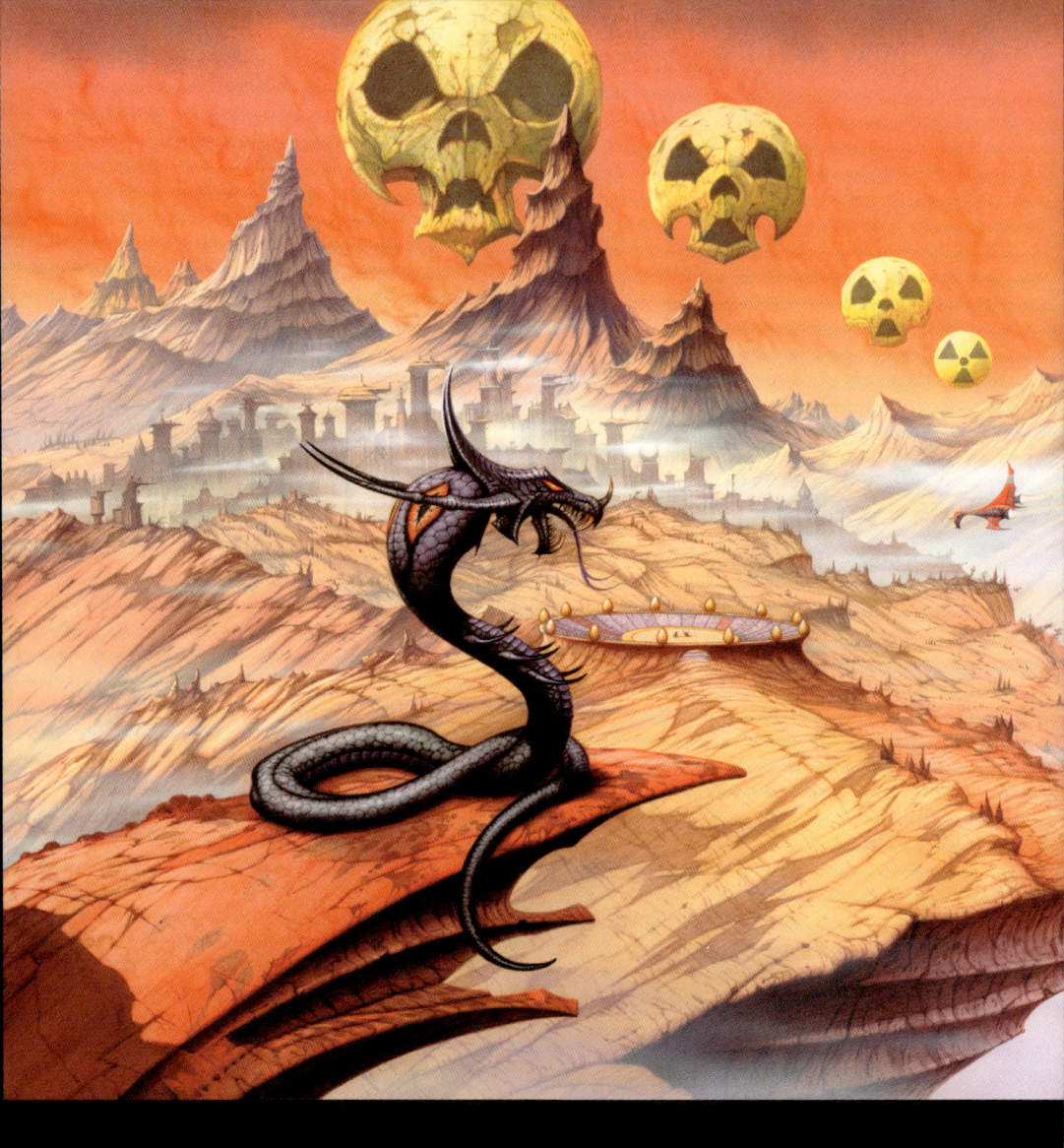

Above: Arena, for the wraparound cover of Asia's sixth studio album, 1996. The scene represents good versus evil, the skulls incorporating the symbol for nuclear power. Ink on paper, 1995, 49.7 x 99.8 cm

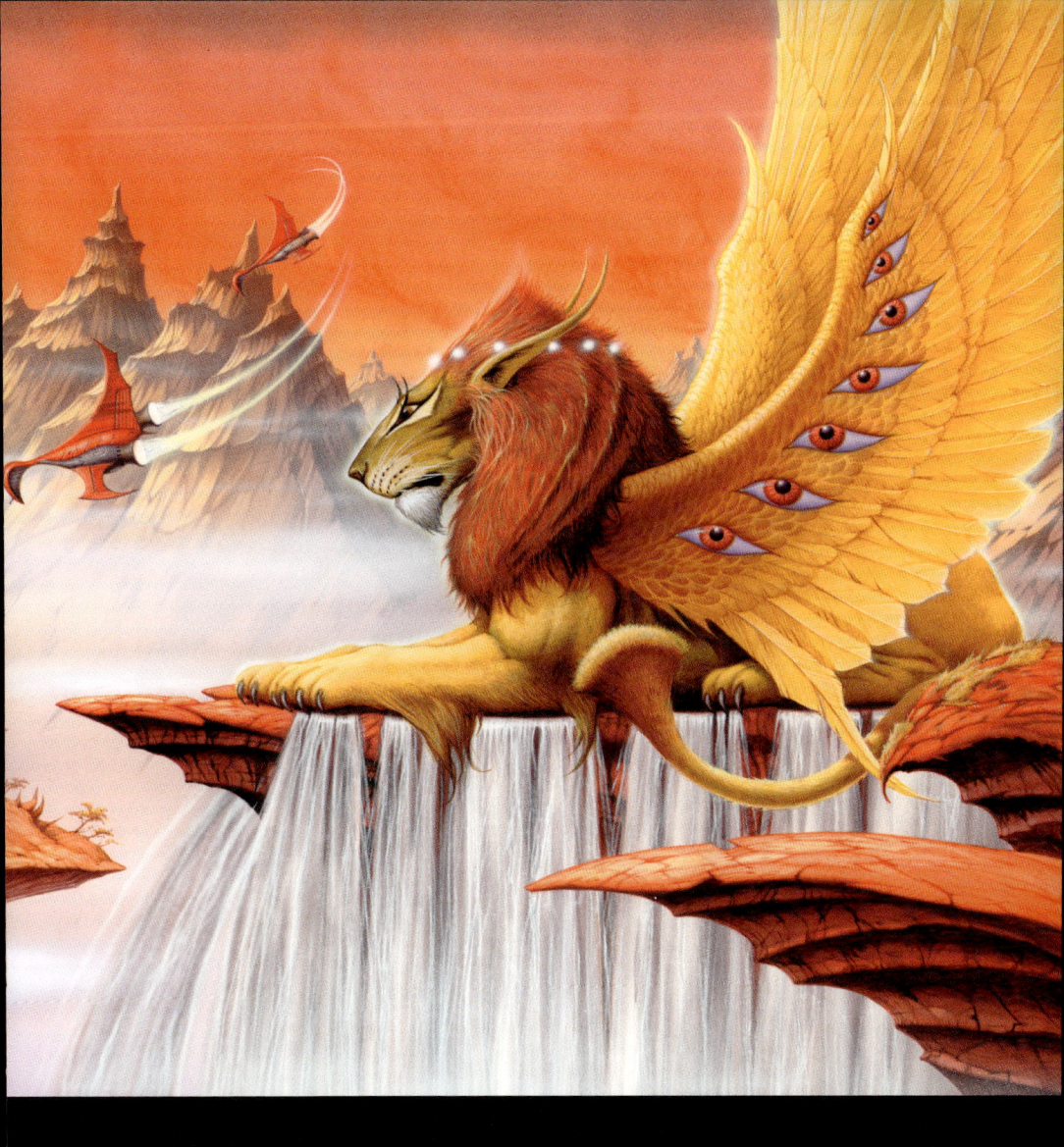

Following spread: Mirador, originally created for a poster released by the Pace Minerva company, 1981, and licensed that same year for a Magnum album of the same name. Ink on paper, 1981, 59.9 x 99.8 cm (23.6 x 39.3 inches).

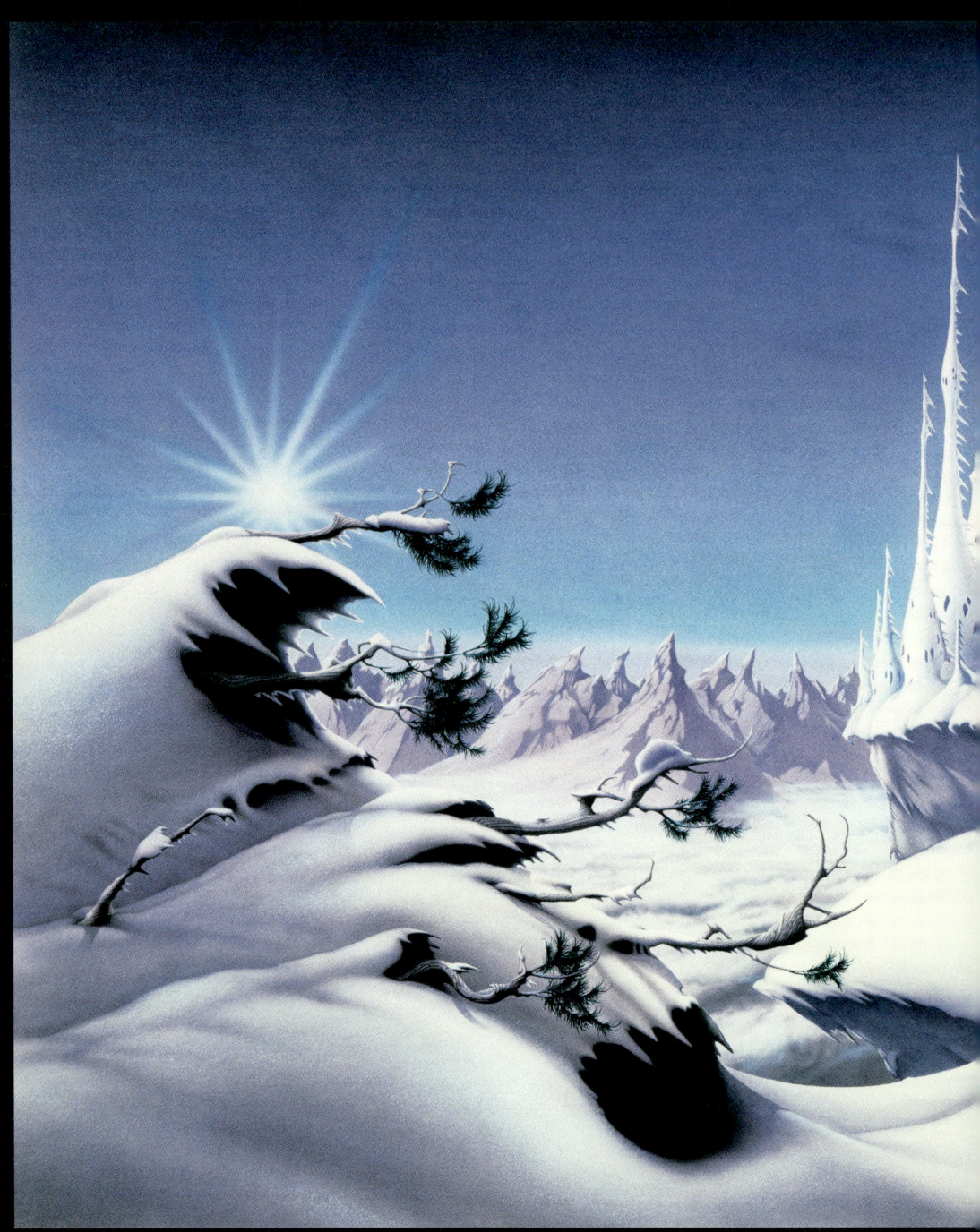

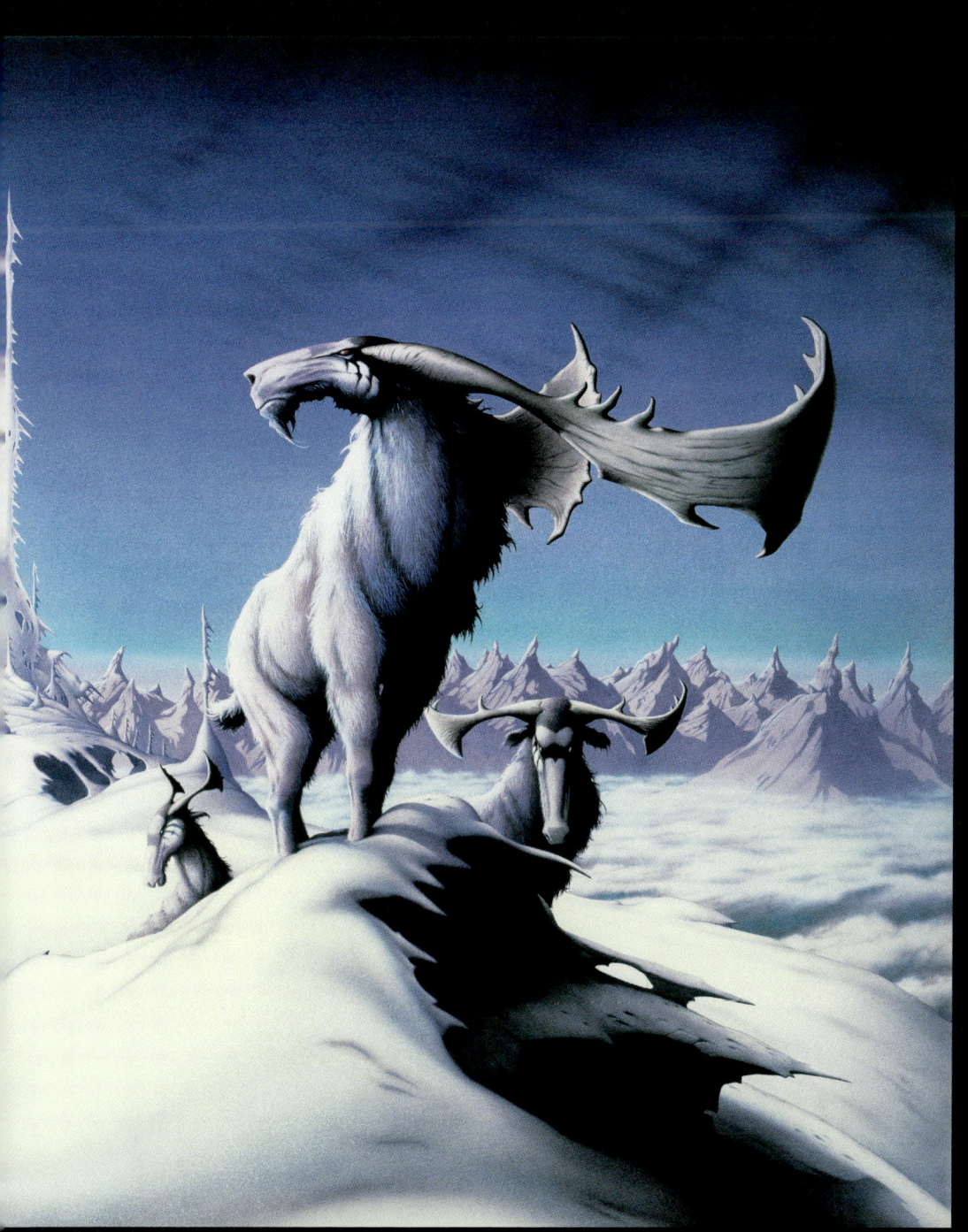

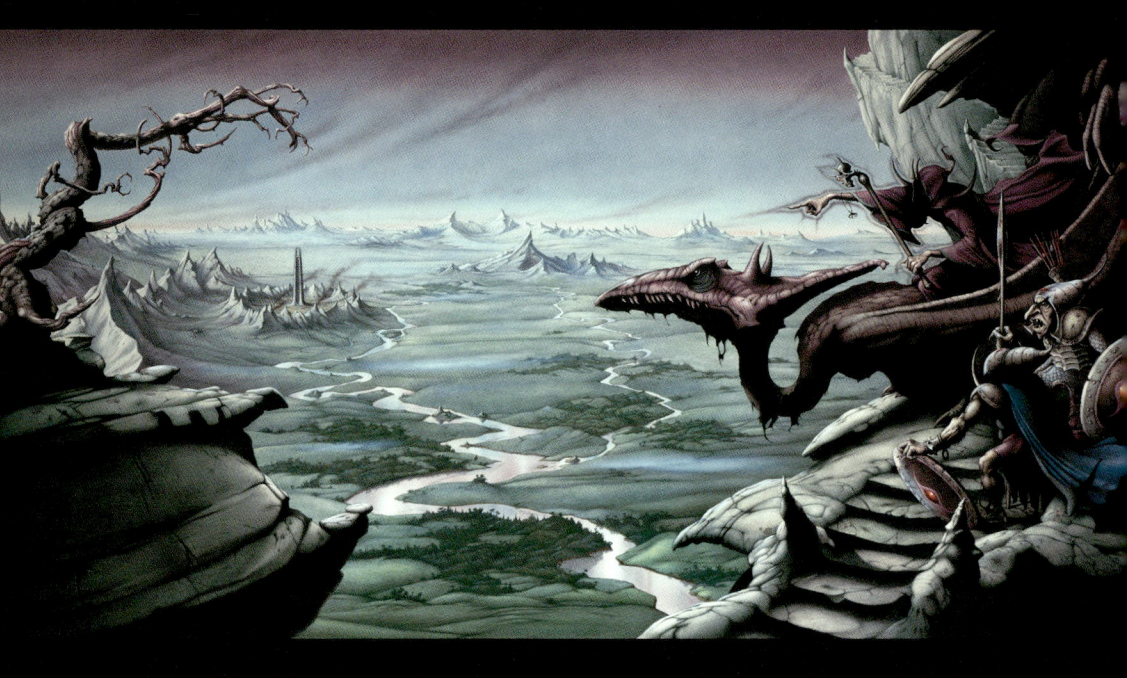

Above: A View Over Isengard, wraparound cover for the 1977 rerelease of Bo Hansson's 1970 album *Music Inspired by the Lord of the Rings*. Ink on paper, 49.7 x 99.8 cm (19.6 x 39.3 inches).

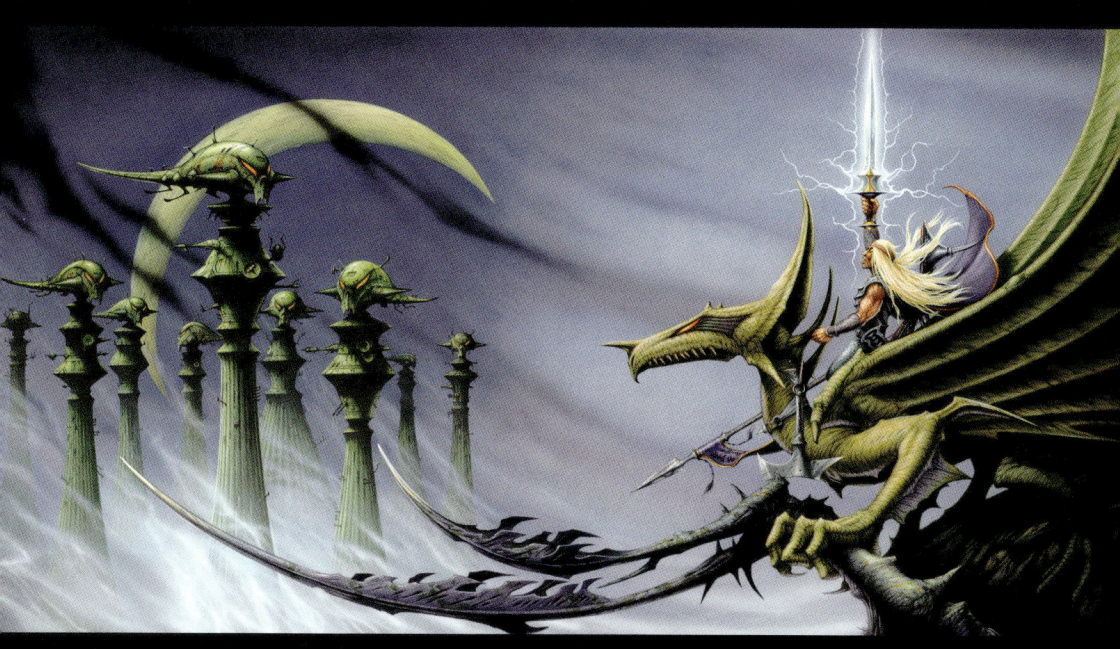

Above: Immortal, for the wraparound cover of former Magnum front man Bob Catley's 2008 album. Ink on paper, 2008, 33.7 x 68.8 cm (13.3 x 27.1 inches).

Following spread: The Thief, a private commission of Smaug from *The Hobbit*. It was licensed by Roxxcalibur for their 2015 album *Gems of the NWOBHM*. Ink on paper, 2014, 40.9 x 56.9 cm (16.1 x 22.4 inches).

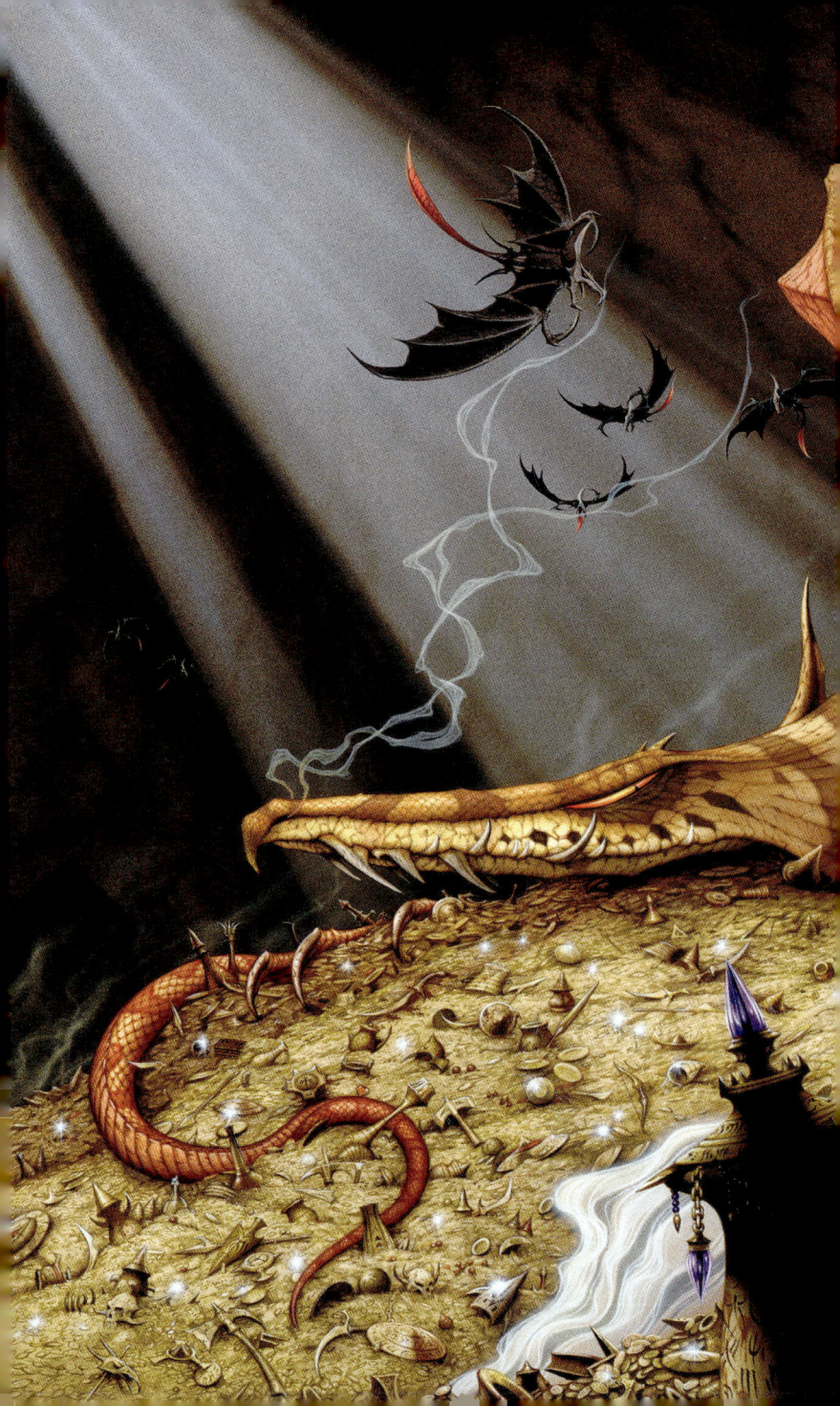

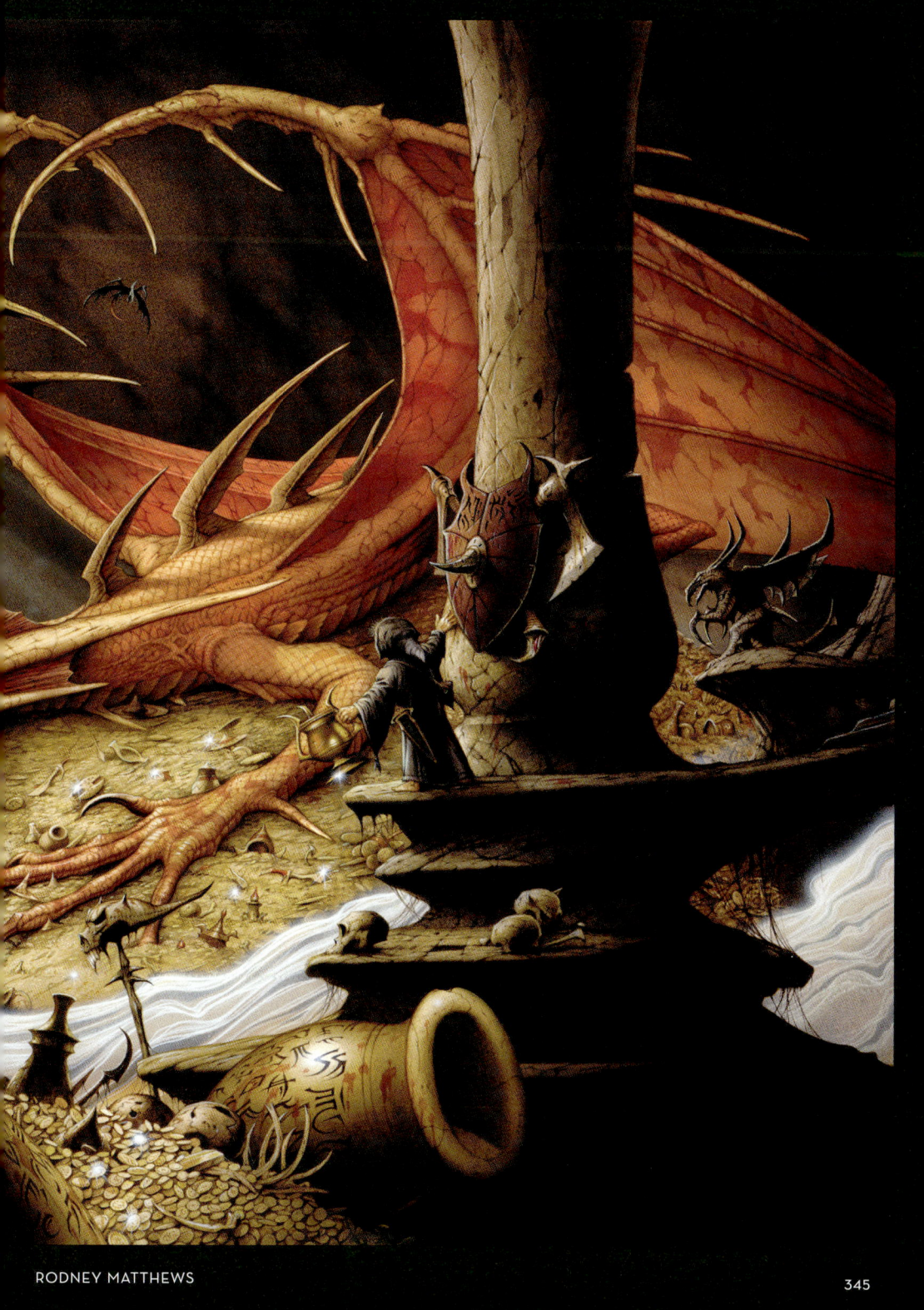

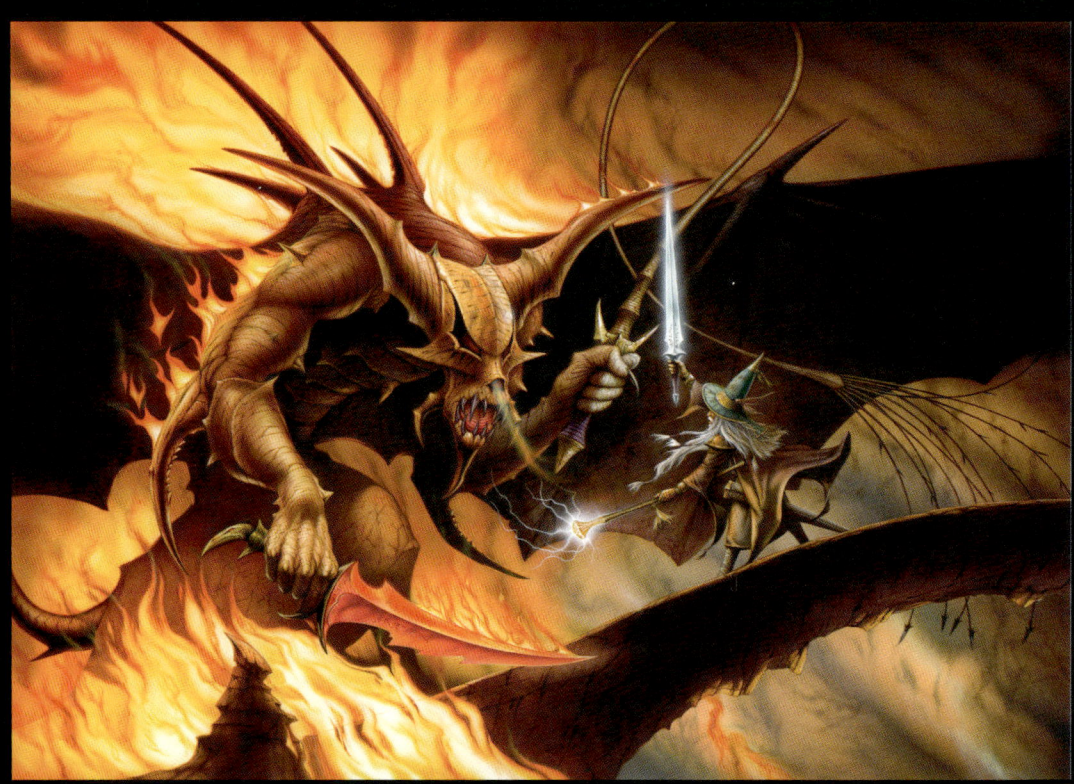

Above: You Shall Not Pass!, in which Gandalf battles the Balrog, a classic *Lord of the Rings* theme. Ink on paper, 2010, 40.9 x 56.9 cm (16.1 x 22.4 inches).

Opposite: The Gate to the Wonderland, a private commission inspired by Matthews's song "Stargate," written in the early 1970s for his band Squidd. Ink on paper, 2007, 47 x 60.9 cm (18.5 x 24 inches).

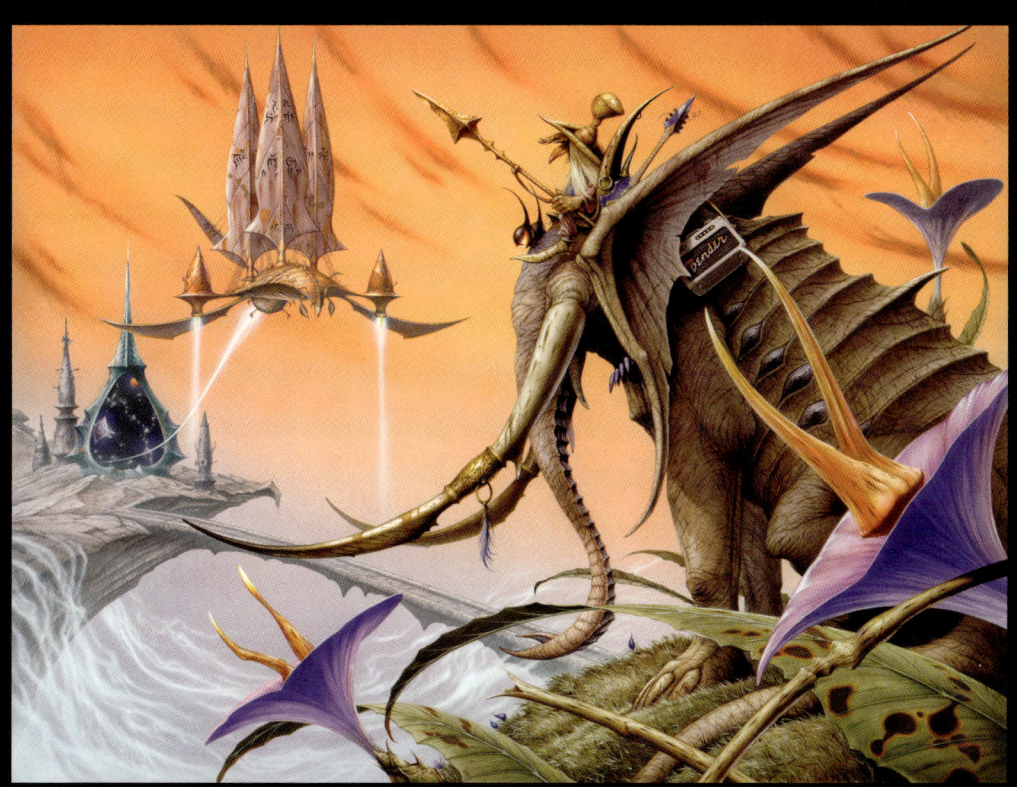

Following spread: The Heavy Metal Hero, featured on the cover of Diamond Head's 1987 compilation album *Am I Evil?* Ink on paper, 1985, 69.8 x 99.8 cm (27.5 x 39.3 inches).

Page 350: Stop the Slaughter, inspired by Matthews's concern for the environment and endangered species. Ink on paper, 1981, 99.8 x 69.8 cm (39.3 x 27.5 inches).

Page 351: Desert Warrior, pencil on vellum, 2001, 38.1 x 37.4 cm (15 x 14.75 inches). Courtesy of Heritage Auctions.

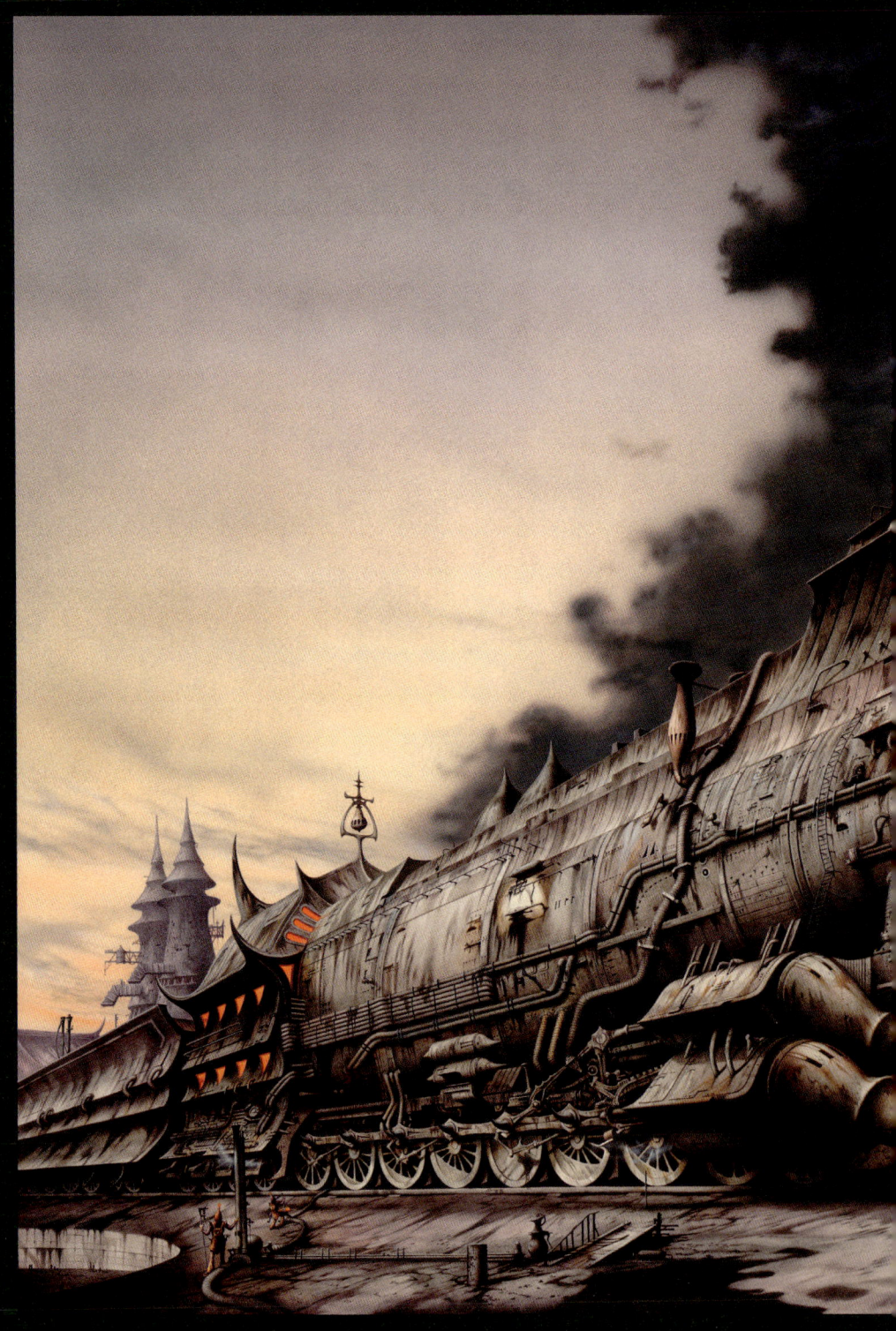

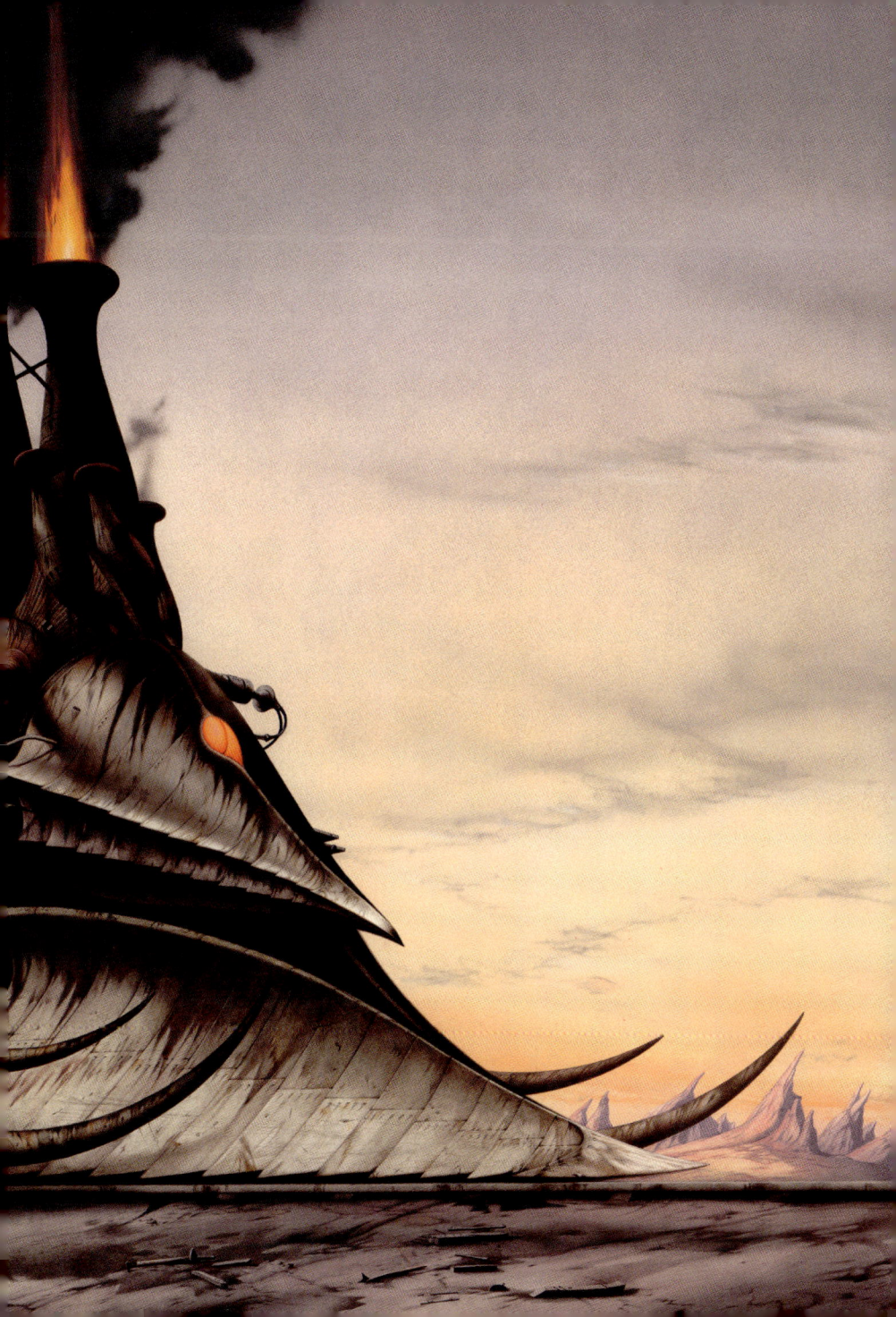

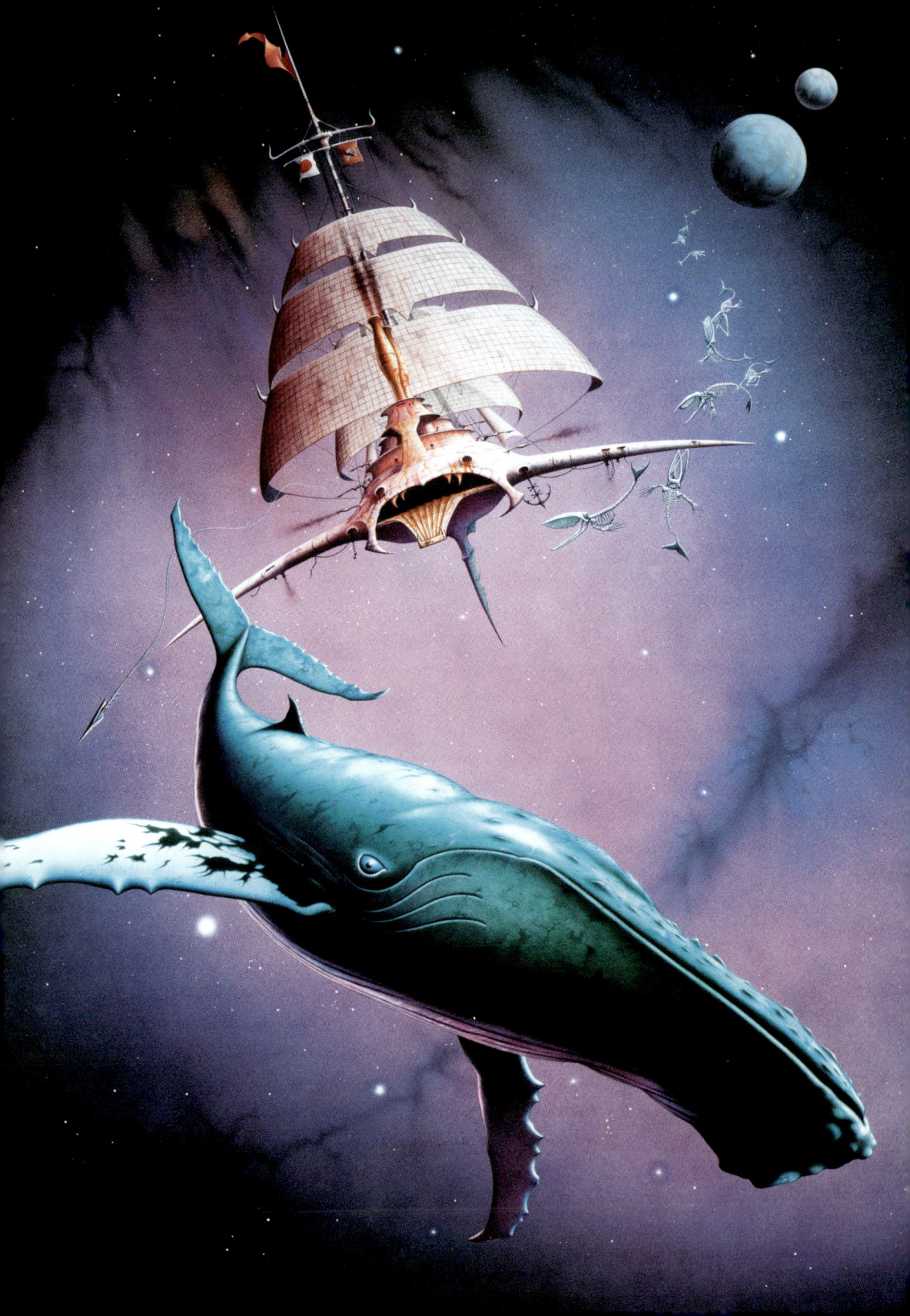

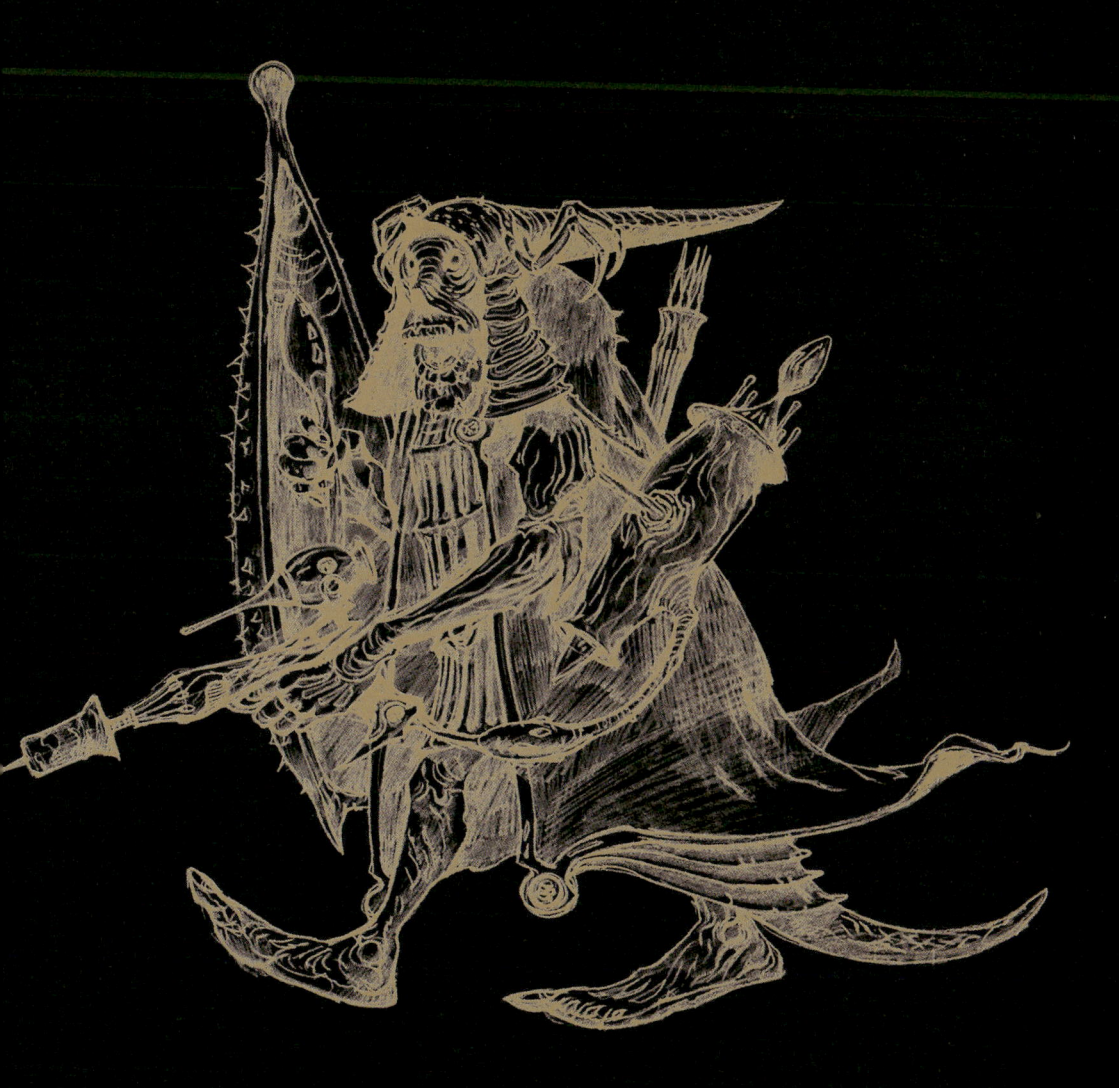

Moebius

MŒBIUS

1938-2012

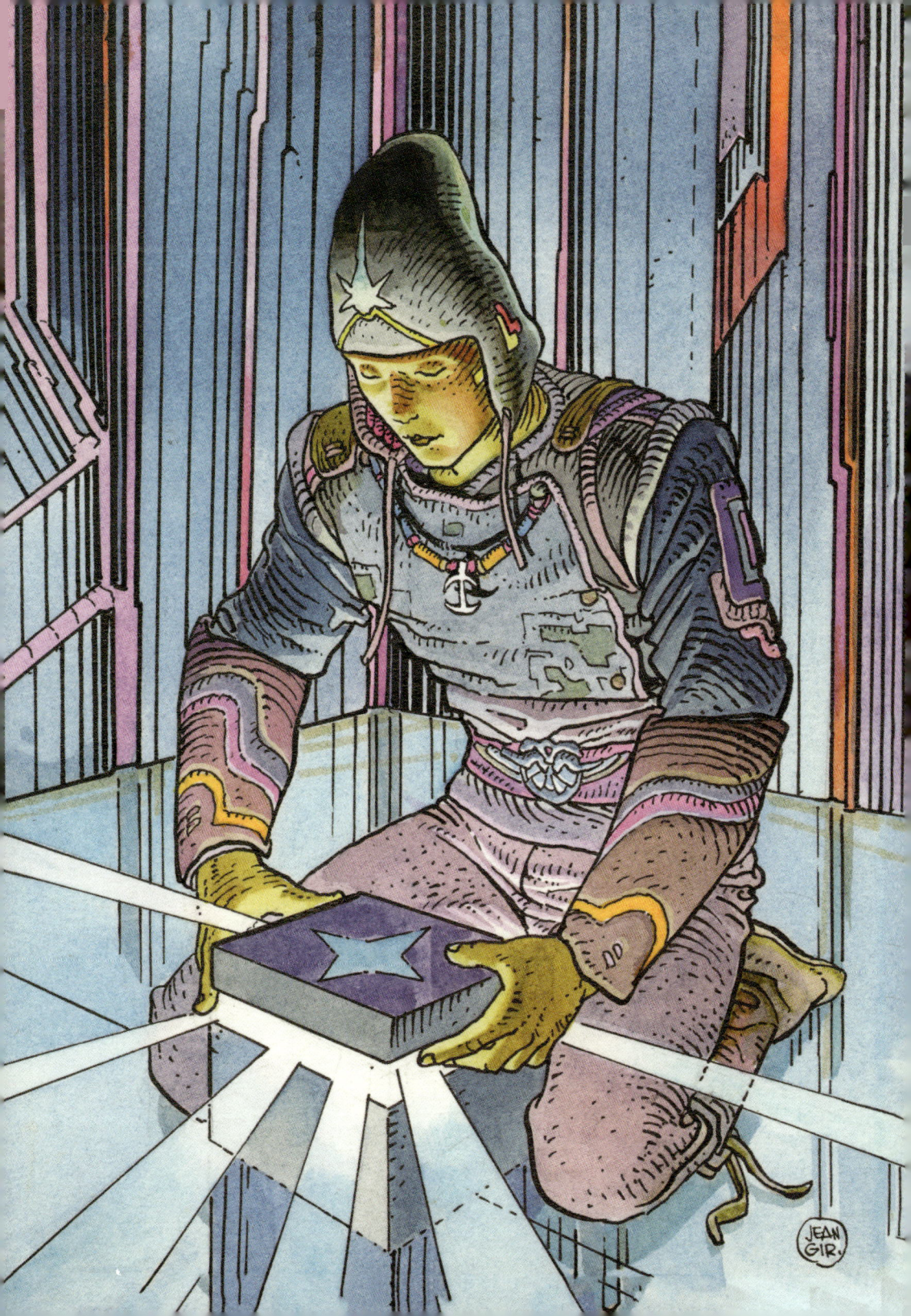

CHER BENEDIKT!

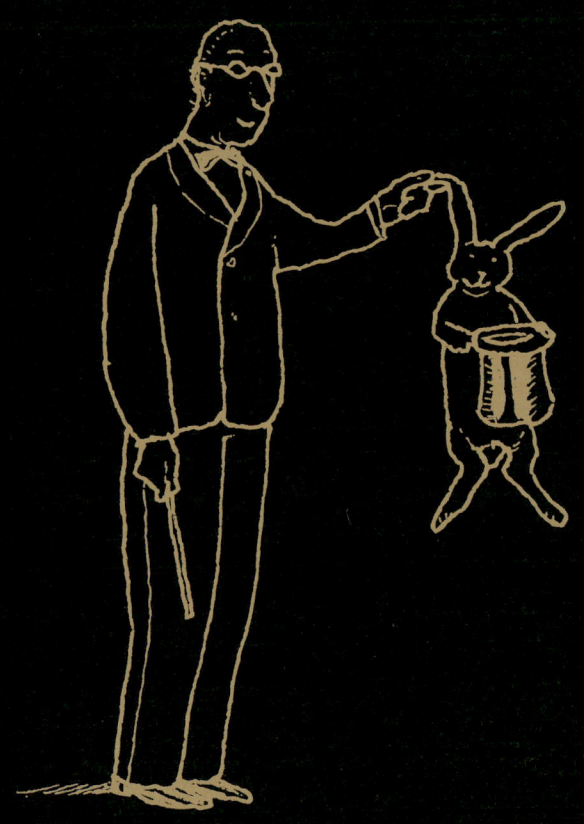

MERCI POUR CES CINQ CENT
QUARANTE ANNÉES DE MAGIE!

MŒBIUS

MŒBIUS
PSYCHEDELIC SURREALIST

"The comics were not only stories to enjoy; for me they were drawings that possessed me."

Jean Henri Gaston Giraud, aka Mœbius, was born in the Parisian suburb of Nogent-sur-Marne in 1938 and, following his parents' separation in 1941, was raised by his grandparents in nearby Fontenay-sous-Bois. He was a child of the war, with all that entails, and at war's end he sought escape in *bandes dessinées*—Franco-Belgian comics—and in the local cinema's low-budget American cowboy films. At age 16 Giraud enrolled at the École Supérieure des Arts Appliqués—High School of Applied Arts—where he learned classical drawing, and his teachers tried to squash his enthusiasm for Western comics. In 1956, in the middle of his third year, he sold his first Western comic, titled *Frank et Jérémie*, to *Far West* magazine, enabling him to leave school for an extended visit with his mother, then living in Mexico. He returned six months later, transformed by the people he'd met, the desert landscape, and the Mexican light, just like that in the Western films.

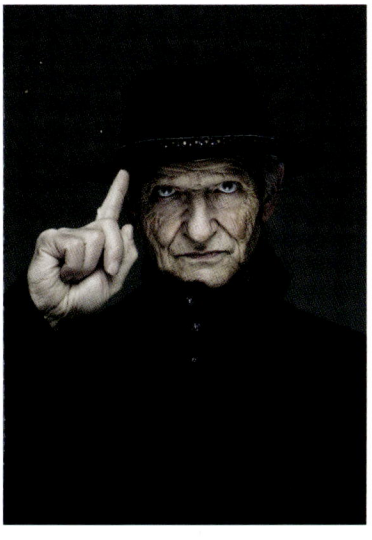

Now 19, Giraud returned to France determined to be a children's cartoonist. He found steady work for historical, Western, and Catholic magazines, including *Fripounet et Marisette*, *Coeurs Vaillants*, and *Ames Vaillantes*. This early work was inspired by the insanity of André Franquin's *Spirou et Fantasio*, by Maurice "Morris" De Bevere's *Lucky Luke*, and especially by the work of Western artist Joseph "Jijé" Gillian, who took him on as an assistant in 1961.

In 1963 Giraud met Jean-Michel Charlier, writer and managing editor of *Pilote* magazine, who had been looking for a competent Western artist since visiting Edwards Air Force Base in the Mojave Desert of California earlier that year. The rugged landscape moved him the way Mexico had moved Giraud, and he returned with the concept for a Western strip with an unlikely hero. Charlier approached Jijé. Jijé suggested Giraud.

Giraud said he named his character by glancing down at a *National Geographic* magazine open on his desk, where he saw a letter to the editor signed "Blueberry." The contrast of this soft name for a

Previous right: Starwatcher Opens a Box of Light, for the cover of *PFL*, published by Moebius's publishing house Éditions Aedena, 1986. Black and colored inks, 14.5 x 10.5 cm (5.7 x 4.1 inches).

Opposite: Sketch by Mœbius for publisher Benedikt Taschen.

Above: Jean Giraud, aka Mœbius, at the yearly *bande dessinée* festival in Angouleme, France, 2011. Photo by Nicolas Guérin. Contour/Getty Images.

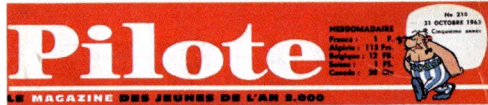

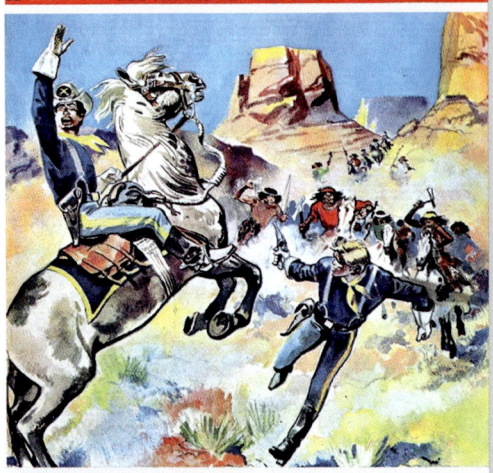

rough loner fighting racial injustice in the Old West appealed to him, and to Charlier. Giraud, who also loved new wave French cinema, gave Blueberry the rugged face of actor Jean-Paul Belmondo. When the strip debuted in *Pilote* as *Fort Navajo* in October 1963 it was an immediate success that blossomed into a series of 48- to 64-page graphic novels, though Blueberry evolved considerably through his astounding 42-year run. When Giraud—who signed his panels Gir—saw Sergio Leone's *A Fistful of Dollars* in 1964, Blueberry adopted Clint Eastwood's cigars; when he saw *The Wild Bunch* in 1969, Blueberry became more ruthless; when the sexual revolution hit France, Blueberry got a girlfriend, Chihuahua Pearl, all of which helped maintain his relevance and popularity.

Still, there was more to Giraud than Blueberry, and in 1974 he resurrected a character invented the same year Blueberry was born: his alter-ego Mœbius, originally created for a series of fantasy strips published in *Hara-Kiri* magazine (precursor to *Charlie Hebdo*) between May 1963 and November '65. Along with aspiring screenwriter Jean-Pierre Dionnet, artist Philippe Druillet, and financier Bernard Farkas, Mœbius formed the publishing house Les Humanoïdes Associés and released the first issue of *Métal Hurlant* (*Howling Metal*) magazine, dated January 1975. It was an entirely new kind of *bande dessinée* featuring surreal fantasy strips and adult storylines for the psychedelic generation.

Giraud had been introduced to marijuana during that trip to Mexico in 1956—not for fun, he said, but as a tool for creation. He used it intermittently for the rest of his life, always in small quantities, and only to fuel his artistic imagination, most vividly represented by his 70-page wordless masterpiece *40 Days Dans le Désert B*, 1999.

Mœbius's best-known creations are the futuristic warrior Arzach, mounted on his mutant pterodactyl, star of wordless panel stories featured in the first four issues of *Métal Hurlant*; *Le Garage Hermétique (The Airtight Garage)*, serialized in issues 6 through 41; and *L'Incal (The Incal)*, a graphic novel written by Alejandro Jodorowsky and published in many installments between 1981 and '88. Arzach would return in several forms throughout Mœbius's career, as the inspiration for Taarna in the film *Heavy Metal* (1981); as the gentle Starwatcher; and as Arzak the Surveyor in a trilogy left incomplete upon his death. *The Airtight Garage* was published in the U.S. by Marvel in 1987 and by Titan Books in the U.K. in 1989. *L'Incal* grew from *The Long Tomorrow*, written with Dan O'Bannon, whom Mœbius met while working with Jodorowsky on his doomed *Dune* adaptation in 1975. Mœbius also designed costumes for Ridley Scott's *Alien* (1979),

Above: Jean Giraud's Blueberry character first appeared in the story *Fort-Navajo*, published in the October 31, 1963 issue of *Pilote* magazine.

Opposite: Le monde d'Edena, published as a companion volume to Mœbius's series of graphic novels inspired by a 1983 ad campaign he created for the car manufacturer Citroën. 2010 © Mœbius Production.

created storyboards and design for *Tron* (1982), and concept art for *The Abyss* (1989) and *The Fifth Element* (1997).

In 1979 Mœbius teamed with director René Laloux to make the animated feature film *Les Maîtres du Temps*, released in 1982. "Incredibly cheap — it was more than independent," he told Geoff Boucher of the *Los Angeles Times*, but, like the Ralph Bakshi/Frank Frazetta film *Fire and Ice*, it has since developed a cult following.

Most Americans discovered Mœbius through *Heavy Metal* magazine, introduced in 1977 as a straightforward translation of *Métal Hurlant* before it expanded to include American artists. This new audience brought about some unexpected commissions, such as *The Silver Surfer: Parable* miniseries for Marvel comics (1988–89) and album covers for two Jimi Hendrix compilations.

Through all this Mœbius success Giraud continued drawing Blueberry. When Charlier, the strip's writer, died in 1989 Giraud took over the text as well as the art and created five 48-page *Mister Blueberry* graphic novels. He tried twice to kill off the character, but both attempts met with such outrage he had to resurrect him, before finally laying him to rest in 2005.

Between 2000 and 2010 Mœbius devoted most of his time to the six-volume *Inside Mœbius*, a 700-page fantasy starring Mœbius in his late prime, encountering his younger self, his dog, Blueberry, Arzach (renamed Arzak), Malvina, Stel, Atan, and other creations from his long career. Additional monographs include *The Art of Mœbius* (1989), *Arzach* (1996), *The Long Tomorrow* (2013), *The Incal* trilogy (2014–16), and *The World of Edena* (2016).

Giraud lived with Claudine Conin from 1967 to 1987, and with Isabelle Champeval from 1988 until his death on March 10, 2012. His first marriage produced two children, Héléne (1970) and Julien (1973), while Raphaël (1989) and Nausicaa (1995) came from the second. Isabelle Giraud continues as curator and publisher of her late husband's works through their collaborative company Mœbius Production, ensuring the conservation of his art, reputation, and influence to the present day.

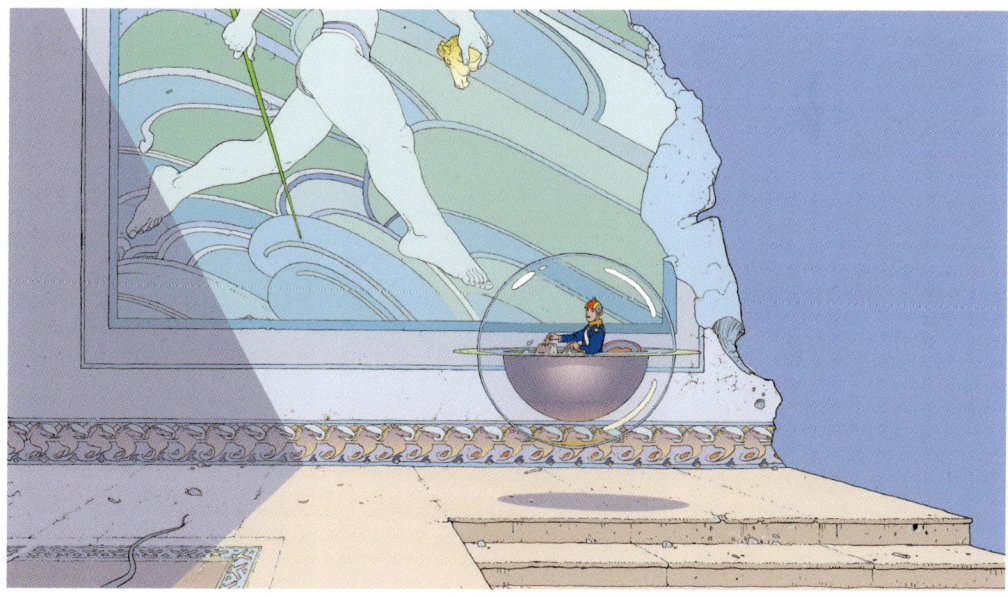

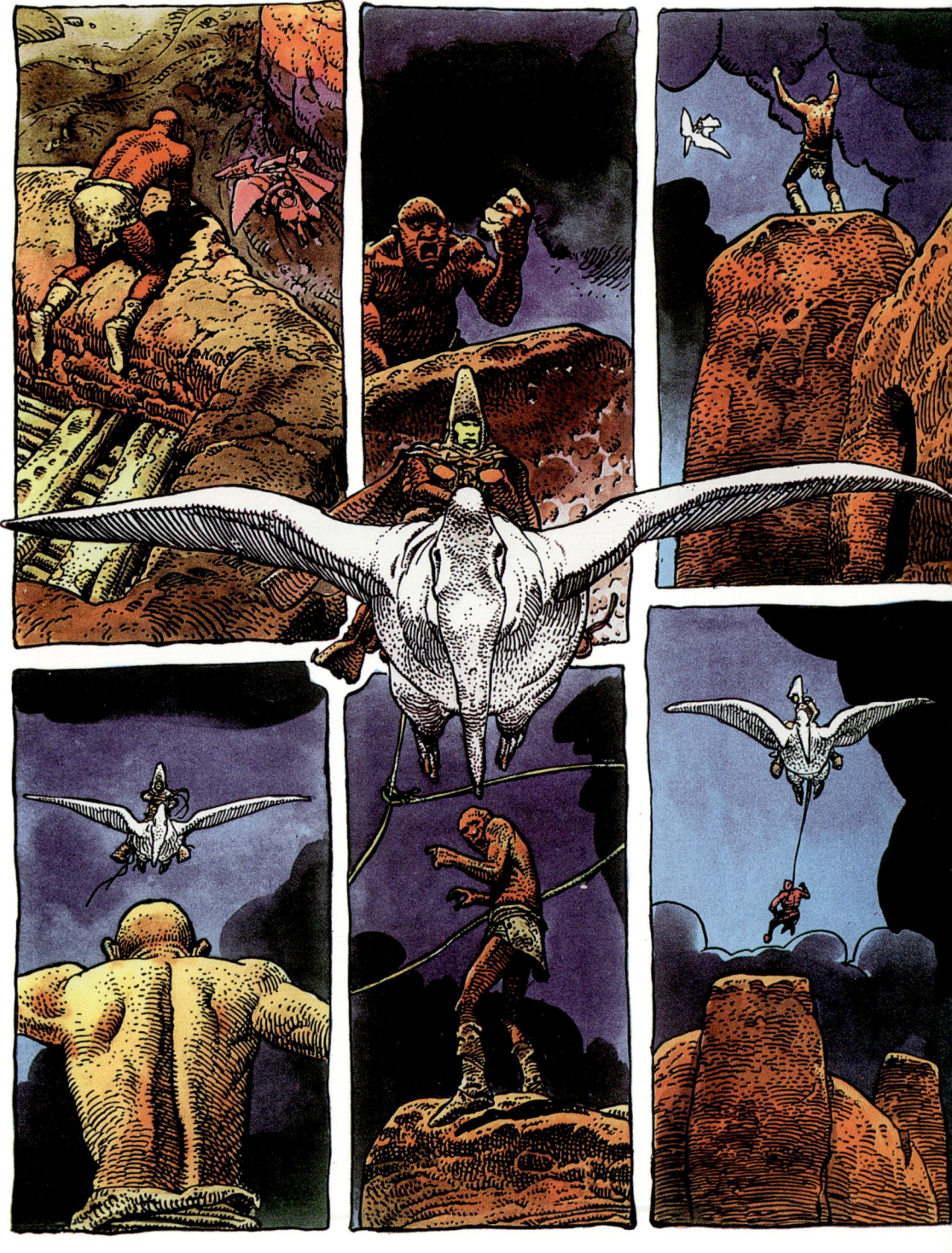

MŒBIUS
PSYCHEDELISCHER SURREALIST

„Comics waren nicht nur Geschichten,
an denen man sich erfreuen konnte; für mich
waren es Zeichnungen, von denen ich ganz
besessen war."

Jean Henri Gaston Girard, aka Mœbius, wurde 1938 im Pariser Vorort Nogent-sur-Marne geboren und wuchs nach der Trennung seiner Eltern 1941 bei seinen Großeltern im nahe gelegenen Fontenay-sous-Bois auf. Er war ein Kind des Krieges, mit allem, was das mit sich brachte, und nach dem Ende des Krieges flüchtete er sich in die Welt der *bandes dessinées* – französisch-belgischer Comics – und in die amerikanischer Low-Budget-Cowboyfilme, die im örtlichen Kino liefen. Mit 16 schrieb Giraud sich an der École Supérieure des Arts Appliqués ein, der Hochschule für Angewandte Künste, an der er klassisches Zeichnen lernte, doch die dortigen Lehrer versuchten, seinen Enthusiasmus für Westerncomics zu ersticken. 1956, mitten in seinem dritten Studienjahr, verkaufte er seinen ersten Westerncomic mit dem Titel *Frank et Jérémie* an die Zeitschrift *Far West*, was es ihm ermöglichte, die Schule für einen längeren Aufenthalt bei seiner Mutter, die damals in Mexiko lebte, zu verlassen. Sechs Monate später kehrte er zurück und war verändert – durch die Menschen, die er kennengelernt hatte, die Wüstenszenerien des Landes, genau wie in den Westernfilmen, und das mexikanische Licht.

Bei seiner Rückkehr nach Frankreich war der mittlerweile 19-jährige Giraud entschlossen, als Cartoonist für Kinder zu arbeiten. Er bekam regelmäßige Aufträge für historische, Western- und katholische Zeitschriften, darunter *Fripounet et Marisette*, *Cœurs Vaillants* und *Ames Vaillantes*. Diese frühen Arbeiten waren inspiriert von den Verrücktheiten von André Franquins *Spirou et Fantasio*, von Maurice „Morris" De Beveres *Lucky Luke* und insbesondere von den Arbeiten des Western-künstlers Joseph „Jijé" Gillian, der ihn 1961 als seinen Assistenten aufnahm.

1963 lernte Giraud Jean-Michel Charlier kennen, Autor und leitender Redakteur der Zeit-schrift *Pilote*, der auf der Suche nach einem kompetenten Westernkünstler war, seit er Anfang des Jahres die Edwards Air Force Base in der kalifornischen Mojave-Wüste besucht hatte. Die schroffe Landschaft brachte ihn auf den gleichen Weg, auf den Mexiko Giraud gelenkt hatte, und so kehrte er mit einem Konzept für einen Westernstrip mit einem merkwürdigen Helden zurück. Charlier sprach Jijé an, und Jijé schlug Giraud vor.

Giraud sagte, er habe den Namen seiner Figur gefunden, als er auf eine Ausgabe der Zeitschrift *National Geographic* blickte, die offen auf seinem Schreibtisch lag, und er einen Brief an den Her-ausgeber entdeckte, der mit „Blueberry" unterschrieben war. Der Kontrast dieses sanften Namens zu seiner Figur eines ruppigen Einzelgängers, der im alten Westen gegen rassistische Ungerechtig-keiten ankämpfte, gefiel ihm und Charlier. Giraud, der auch das französische *Nouvelle-Vague*-Kino

Opposite: A page from the original *Arzach* comic, printed in *Métal Hurlant* in 1976, and reprinted in the 1977 *Heavy Metal Presents Arzach*. © 2023 Humanoids, Inc. Los Angeles.

Following right: Le Secret de la Pyramide (*The Secret of the Pyramid*), unpublished, ink and colored ink on paper, 36 x 51 cm (14.1 x 20 inches). 2008 © Mœbius Production.

mochte, verlieh Blueberry die markanten Gesichtszüge des Schauspielers Jean-Paul Belmondo. Als der Strip unter dem Titel *Fort Navajo* im Oktober 1963 in der Zeitschrift *Pilote* debütierte, erwies er sich als ein Senkrechtstarter, der sich zu einer Serie von 48- bis 64-seitigen Comicgeschichten auswuchs, wobei sich Blueberry während der erstaunlichen Laufzeit von 42 Jahren erheblich entwickelte. Als Giraud – der seine Zeichnungen mit „Gir" signierte – 1964 Sergio Leones *Für eine Handvoll Dollar* sah, übernahm Blueberry Clint Eastwoods Zigarillos; als er 1969 *The Wild Bunch – Sie kannten kein Gesetz* gesehen hatte, wurde Blueberry unbarmherziger; als die sexuelle Revolution Frankreich veränderte, bekam auch Blueberry mit Chihuahua Pearl eine Freundin. All diese Aspekte trugen dazu bei, dass die Figur so lange bedeutsam und populär blieb.

Gleichwohl gab es für Giraud noch mehr als Blueberry, und 1974 ließ er eine Persönlichkeit auferstehen, die er im gleichen Jahr erfunden hatte, in dem Blueberry geboren wurde: sein Alter Ego Mœbius, das er ursprünglich für eine Reihe von Fantasystrips geschaffen hatte, die zwischen Mai 1963 und November 1965 in der Zeitschrift *Hara-Kiri* (der Vorgängerin von *Charlie Hebdo*) veröffentlicht wurden.

Gemeinsam mit dem ehrgeizigen Drehbuchautor Jean-Pierre Dionnet, dem Künstler Philippe Druillet und dem Finanzier Bernard Farkas gründete Mœbius den Verlag Les Humanoïdes Associés und gab im Januar 1975 die erste Ausgabe von *Métal Hurlant* (Schreiendes Metall) heraus. Dabei handelte es sich um eine völlig neue Art von *bandes dessinées*, die surreale Fantasystrips und Geschichten für Erwachsene der psychedelischen Generation erzählten.

Während jener Reise 1956 nach Mexiko hatte Giraud zum ersten Mal Marihuana konsumiert – nicht zum Vergnügen, wie er sagte, sondern als ein Hilfsmittel zur Förderung der Kreativität. Er nutzte den Stoff zeitweise noch sein ganzes Leben lang, stets in kleinen Mengen und nur als Anregung für seine künstlerische Phantasie, die sein 70-seitiges wortloses Meisterwerk *40 Days Dans le Désert „B"*, 1999, am lebhaftesten repräsentiert.

Mœbius bekannteste Schöpfungen sind der mit mutierenden Flugfingern gerüstete futuristische Krieger Arzach, Star von Bildgeschichten ohne Worte, die in den ersten vier Ausgaben von *Métal Hurlant* erschienen; *Le Garage Hermétique (Die Luftdichte Garage / The Airtight Garage)*, eine Fortsetzungsgeschichte, die in den Ausgaben 6 bis 41 veröffentlicht wurde, und *L'Incal (The Incal)*, ein von Alejandro Jodorowsky verfasster Bilderroman, der zwischen 1981 und 1988 in vielen Folgen publiziert wurde. Arzach kehrte im Laufe von Mœbius' Karriere immer wieder in verschiedenen Formen zurück, als Inspiration für Taarna im Film *Heavy Metal* (1981), als der liebenswürdige Starwatcher und als Arzach the Surveyor in einer Trilogie, die bis zu Mœbius' Tod unvollendet blieb; *The Airtight Garage* wurde in den USA 1987 von Marvel herausgebracht und 1989 von Titan Books in Großbritannien; *L'Incal* erwuchs aus dem mit Dan O'Bannon geschriebenen *The Long Tomorrow*, den Mœbius kennenlernte, als er 1975 mit Jodorowsky an dessen gescheiterter *Dune*-Adaption arbeitete. Mœbius entwarf auch Kostüme für Ridley Scotts *Alien* (1979), schuf Storyboards und Gestaltungen für *Tron* (1982) und Concept-Art für *The Abyss* (1989) und *The Fifth Element* (1997).

1979 tat sich Mœbius mit dem Regisseur René Laloux zusammen, um den 1982 erschienenen Animationsfilm *Les Maîtres du Temps* zu erarbeiten. „Unglaublich billig – es war mehr als nur independent", erklärte er Geoff Boucher von der *Los Angeles Times*. Aber wie der Ralph-Bakshi-Frank Frazetta-Film *Fire and Ice* hat das Werk im Laufe der Zeit eine eingeschworene Fangemeinde gewonnen.

Die meisten Amerikaner entdeckten Mœbius durch die Zeitschrift *Heavy Metal*, die 1977 als direkte Übersetzung von *Métal Hurlant* auf den Markt kam, bevor sie, erweitert um amerikanische

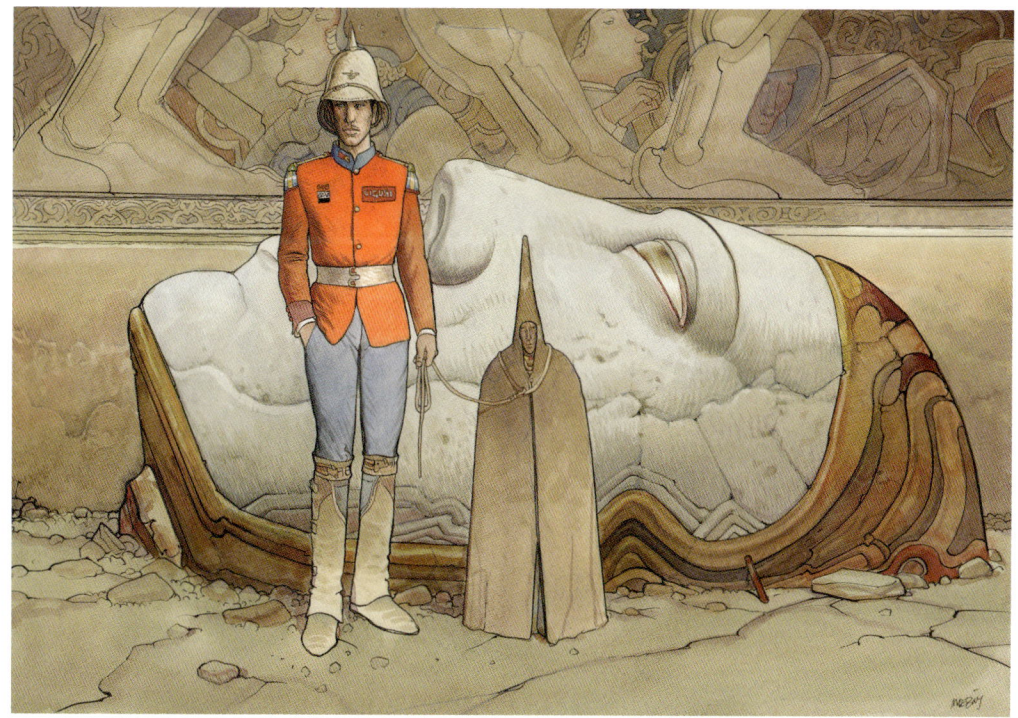

Künstler, expandierte. Dieses neue Publikum sorgte für einige unerwartete Aufträge wie zum Beispiel die Miniserie *The Silver Surfer: Parable* für Marvel Comics (1988/89) und Albumcover für zwei Jimi-Hendrix-Sammelwerke.

Bei all diesem Erfolg als Mœbius zeichnete Giraud weiterhin Blueberry-Geschichten. Als Charlier, der Autor der Strips, 1989 starb, übernahm Giraud neben der Gestaltung der Bilder auch die Abfassung der Texte und schuf fünf 48-seitige *Mister-Blueberry*-Bildergeschichten. Zweimal versuchte er, die Figur sterben zu lassen, doch beide Versuche trafen auf so viel Entrüstung, dass er sie wiederauferstehen lassen musste, bevor er sie 2005 schließlich zu Grabe tragen konnte.

Die meiste Zeit zwischen 2000 und 2010 widmete sich Mœbius dem sechsbändigen *Inside Mœbius*, einer 700-seitigen Fantasygeschichte, in der Mœbius in der Blüte seiner späten Jahre auftrat, der seinem jüngeren Ich begegnet, dazu sein Hund Blueberry, Arzach (nun Arzak genannt), Malvina, Stel, Atan und andere Geschöpfe, die er während seiner langen Karriere erfand. Als weitere Monografien müssen *The Art of Mœbius* (1989), *Arzach* (1996) und *The Long Tomorrow* (2013), *The Incal*-Trilogie (2014–2016) und *The World of Edena* (2016) genannt werden.

Giraud lebte von 1967 bis 1987 mit Claudine Conin zusammen und von 1988 bis zu seinem Tod am 10. März 2012 mit Isabelle Champeval. Aus seiner ersten Ehe hatte er zwei Kinder, Hélène (1970) und Julien (1973), während Raphaël (1989) und Nausicaa (1995) aus der zweiten Ehe stammen. Isabelle Giraud kümmert sich über ihre gemeinsame Firma Mœbius Production weiter als Kuratorin und Verlegerin um die Werke ihres verstorbenen Mannes, um die Gewährleistung der Erhaltung seiner Kunst, seines Rufs und seines Einflusses bis in die Gegenwart.

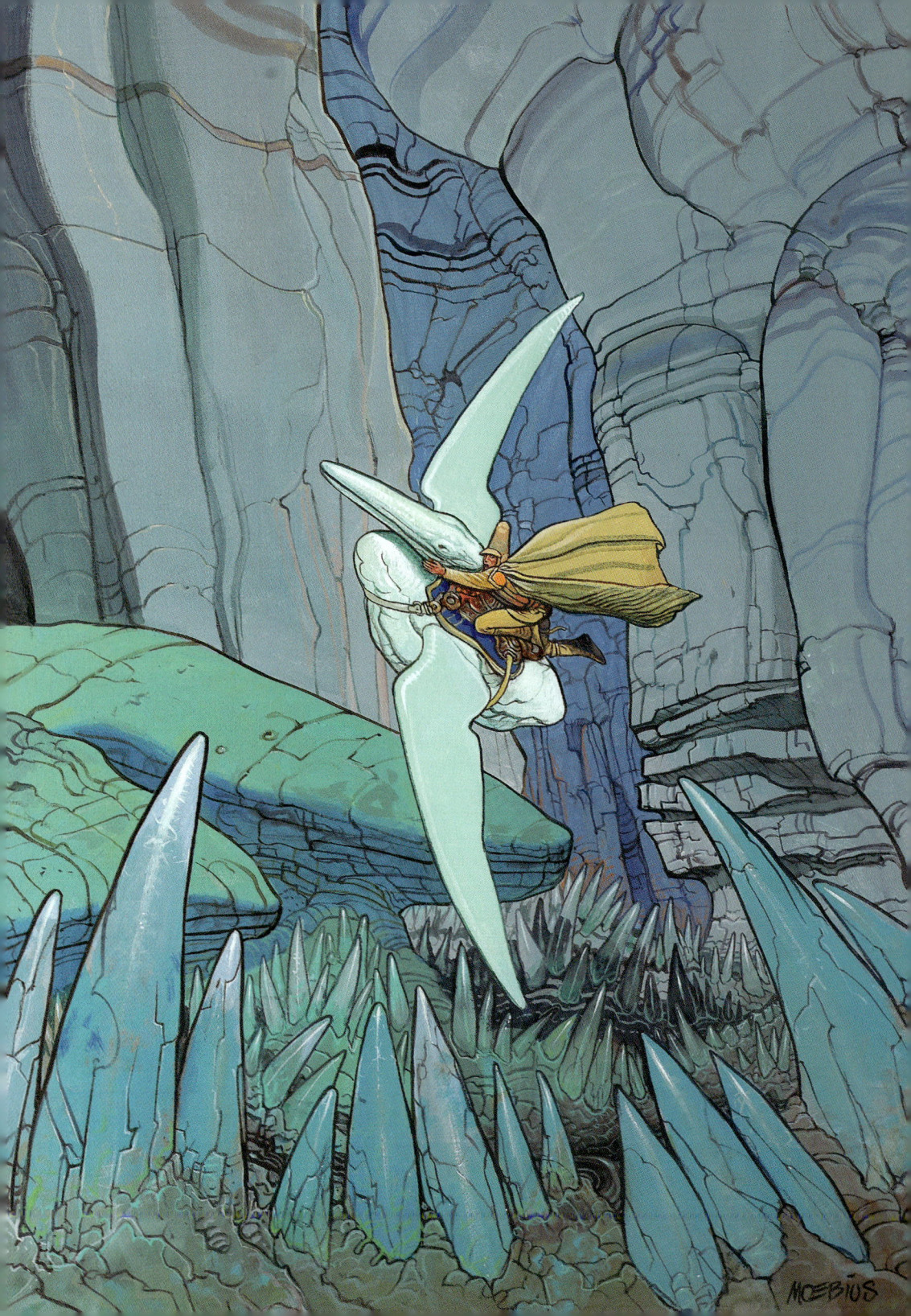

MŒBIUS
LE SURRÉALISTE PSYCHÉDÉLIQUE

« À mes yeux, les bandes dessinées n'étaient pas que des histoires pour divertir ; c'étaient des dessins qui me possédaient. »

Jean Henri Gaston Giraud, alias Mœbius, est né en banlieue parisienne, à Nogent-sur-Marne, en 1938. Ses parents se séparent très tôt quand il a trois ans. Il est élevé par ses grands-parents dans la commune voisine de Fontenay-sous-Bois. Enfant de la guerre et de l'après-guerre, il s'évade de ce contexte lourd grâce aux bandes dessinées et aux westerns américains de série B qu'il va voir au cinéma de quartier. À l'âge de 16 ans, il rentre à l'École supérieure des arts appliqués de Paris, où il apprend le dessin classique. Ses professeurs remettent parfois en question son enthousiasme pour les histoires de cowboys et d'indiens. En 1956, au milieu de sa 3ᵉ année, il quitte la France pour les vacances et part rejoindre sa mère au Mexique. Pour financer son départ, il avait déjà vendu au magazine *Far-West* sa première bande dessinée western, intitulée *Frank et Jérémie*. Il ne reviendra que six mois plus tard, au printemps 1957, transformé. Les personnes qu'il a rencontrées, les paysages désertiques, les lumières du Mexique semblables à ceux des westerns, façonneront la voie qu'il empruntera désormais. Il a 19 ans, et revient avec la ferme idée de devenir dessinateur de littérature enfantine. Il produit régulièrement toutes sortes d'histoires et d'illustrations, comiques, historiques ou westerns pour les revues catholiques, tels *Fripounet et Marisette*, *Cœurs vaillants* et *Âmes vaillantes*. Il est fasciné par le trait nerveux de Franquin, dessinateur de *Spirou*, de Morris dans *Lucky Luke*, et par le spécialiste du western Joseph Gillain, alias « Jijé », qui le prend comme assistant en 1961.

En 1963, Jean-Michel Charlier, auteur et co-créateur du magazine *Pilote*, cherche justement un artiste western compétent depuis qu'il a visité la base aérienne d'Edwards dans le désert Mojave. La beauté brute des paysages l'émeut comme le Mexique a touché Jean Giraud et lui inspire une idée de bande dessinée western menée par un héros atypique. Il en parle à Jijé qui le met en contact avec Jean Giraud : l'histoire s'intitulera *Fort Navajo*.

Lorsqu'il commence ce projet, Jean Giraud choisit de dessiner le personnage principal sous le nom de Blueberry, à la faveur d'un numéro du magazine *National Geographic* ouvert sur le bureau. Ce héros pourvu d'un fort caractère pourfend l'injustice raciale dans le Grand Ouest. Jean Giraud, pétri de culture cinématographique, amoureux de la Nouvelle Vague, s'inspire du visage buriné de l'acteur Jean-Paul Belmondo. En octobre 1963, quand le premier épisode paraît dans *Pilote* sous le titre *Fort Navajo*, le succès est immédiat ; cette parution sera à l'origine d'une collection d'albums de BD de 48 à 64 pages ; 42 années de parutions au cours desquelles Blueberry évolue considérablement. Quand Jean Giraud, qui signe alors ses planches « Gir », voit *Pour une poignée de dollars* de Sergio Leone, en 1964, Blueberry adopte le cigare de Clint Eastwood ; quand il voit *La Horde sauvage* en 1969, Blueberry devient plus cinglant ; quand la révolution sexuelle s'empare

Opposite: Arzak, L'Arpenteur, cover artwork for the 1977 monograph Arzak the Surveyor. 2008 © Mœbius Production.

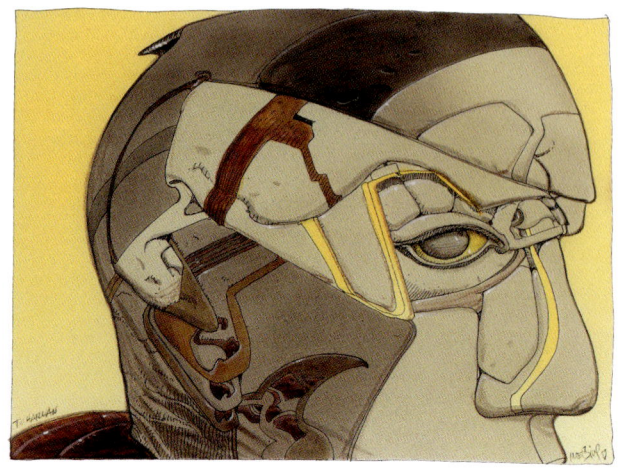

de la France, Blueberry rencontre Chihuahua Pearl. Cette aptitude à la transformation participe à maintenir la pertinence et le niveau de popularité de la série.

Cependant l'œuvre de Jean Giraud ne s'arrête pas aux westerns réalistes du style de Blueberry. Le dessinateur a créé son alter ego sous le pseudonyme de « Mœbius » inventé à l'origine pour créer une série d'histoires fantastiques ou humoristiques publiées dans le magazine *Hara-Kiri* (précurseur de *Charlie Hebdo*) en 1963–1965 (de mai 1963 à novembre 1965). En décembre 1974, Mœbius fonde la maison d'édition Les Humanoïdes associés, avec Jean-Pierre Dionnet jeune scénariste, le dessinateur Philippe Druillet, et le financier Bernard Farkas. Ils créent ensemble la revue emblématique *Métal Hurlant* qui sort en janvier 1975. Ils inaugurent un tout nouveau genre de BD, composé d'histoires fantastiques, surréalistes ou de science-fiction et destiné aux adultes et aux adolescents de la génération psychédélique.

Il expérimente de dessiner tout en ayant consommé de l'herbe, découverte qu'il tient de son passage au Mexique en 1956. Il en sera consommateur toute sa vie par intermittence, alternant coupure et reprise et refusant toute consommation addictive ou simplement récréative, rappelant souvent qu'il fume de très petites quantités. Cette pratique sera l'objet de son livre *40 jours dans le désert B (1999)*, où il est question de « se désherber ».

Ses créations les plus célèbres sont le guerrier futuriste Arzach, monté sur son ptérodactyle mutant, héros d'une série d'histoires sans texte, ce qui est révolutionnaire en bande dessinée, publiées dans les quatre premiers numéros de *Métal Hurlant* ; *Le Garage hermétique*, publié en feuilleton de courtes pages dans les numéros 6 à 41 ; *L'Incal*, une histoire en 6 albums, en collaboration avec le scénariste Alejandro Jodorowsky, publiée entre 1981 et 1988. Arzach a inspiré Taarna, une guerrière chevauchant un oiseau, dans le film *Métal hurlant* (1981). Il reprendra tout au long de sa carrière son personnage d'Arzach sous diverses formes et orthographes comme Starwatcher ou Arzak l'Arpenteur interrompu par son décès (scénario achevé et dessins en cours). *Le Garage hermétique (The Airtight Garage)* est publié aux États-Unis par Marvel en 1987 et par Titan Books au Royaume-Uni en 1989 ; *The Long Tomorrow* écrit avec Dan O'Bannon rencontré à l'occasion du projet avorté de *Dune* au cinéma. Cette bande dessinée réalisée en 1976 deviendra par la suite la base graphique de Mœbius pour *L'Incal*.

Mœbius a créé aussi des costumes pour *Alien* de Ridley Scott (1979), des story-boards et des dessins préparatoires pour *Tron* (1982) et des concepts artistiques pour *Abyss* (1989) et pour *Le Cinquième Élément* (1997).

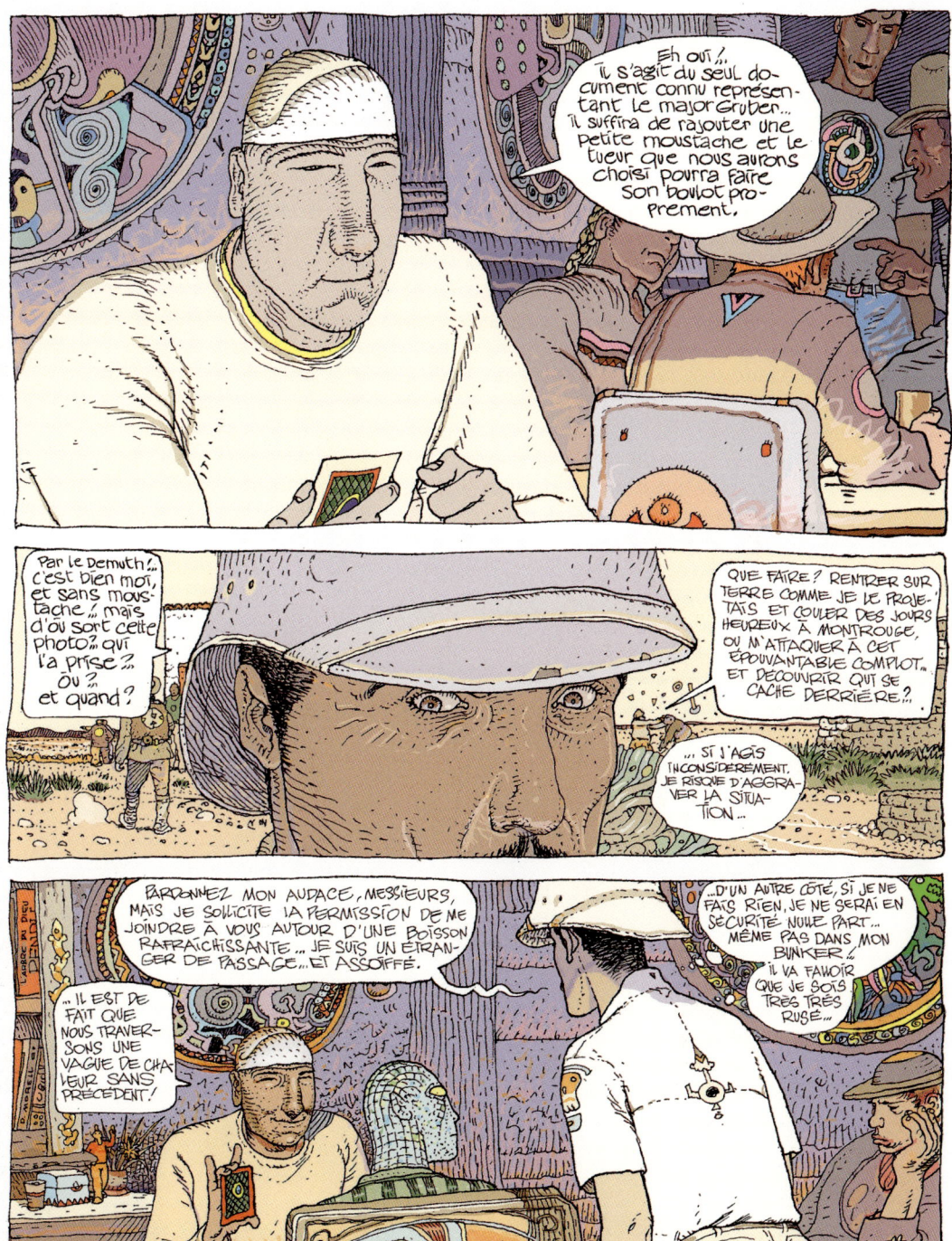

En 1979, avec René Laloux il réalise son propre film d'animation qui sort en 1982, *Les Maîtres du Temps*. Au départ c'était un 56 min programmé pour la télé, qui, projeté ensuite comme film en salle, est devenu un film culte. La majorité du public américain a découvert Mœbius dans le magazine *Heavy Metal* lancé sur le marché en 1977 comme une simple traduction de *Métal Hurlant* avant d'intégrer des artistes américains. La diffusion américaine de son œuvre a déclenché des commandes inattendues, comme celle de l'adaptation du comic *Silver Surfer : Parabole* pour Marvel (1988/89).

Tandis que Mœbius surfe sur le succès, Jean Giraud continue à dessiner *Blueberry*. Quand son scénariste Jean-Michel Charlier meurt, en 1989 au milieu d'un scénario inachevé, il prend en charge l'écriture du scénario et produira la série *Mister Blueberry* prenant la forme de cinq albums de bandes dessinées.

Entre 2000 et 2010, Mœbius consacre une partie de son temps, en sus des commandes principales, à écrire une autobiographie dessinée en six tomes intitulée *Inside Mœbius*, 700 pages de la vie fantasmée d'un Mœbius dans la fleur de l'âge qui dialogue avec ses propres doubles aux différents âges de la vie, et interfère avec ses créatures que sont ses personnages en quête de leur auteur : Blueberry, Arzach, Malvina, Stel et Atan et d'autres figures de sa longue carrière.

Jean Giraud a vécu avec Claudine Conin de 1967 à 1987 puis avec Isabelle Champeval de 1988 à sa disparition, le 10 mars 2012. Deux enfants sont nés de son premier mariage, Hélène (1970) et Julien (1973), et deux enfants de son second mariage, Raphaël (1989) et Nausicaa (1995). Isabelle Giraud est aujourd'hui éditrice et commissaire d'expositions des œuvres de son époux. La société familiale Mœbius Production qu'ils avaient fondée ensemble veille toujours à ce jour à la conservation et au rayonnement de l'œuvre de l'artiste.

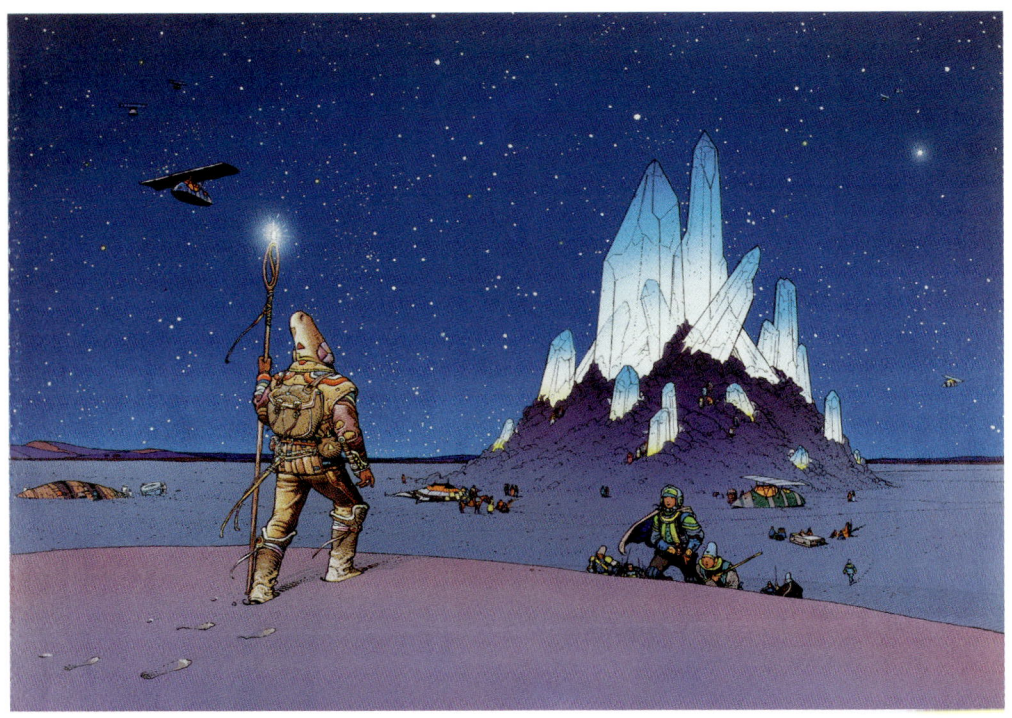

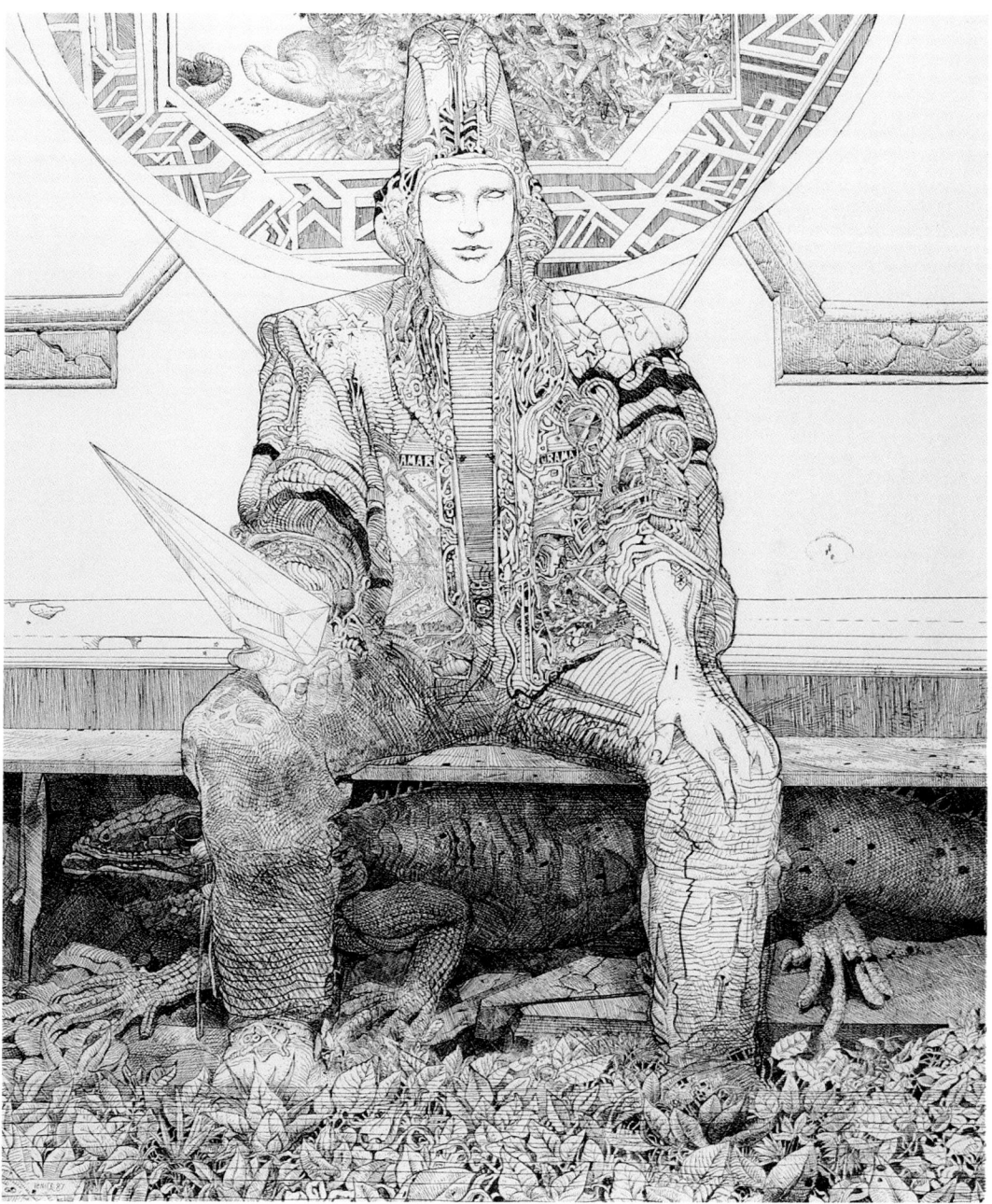

Opposite: The Crystal Major, from the book *Starwatcher*, Éditions Aedena, 1986. © Mœbius Production.

Above: Rama Starwatcher au Lézard, highly detailed engraving of Mœbius's *Starwatcher*, 1987, released in a numbered edition of 120. Lithograph, 2015, 43.1 x 35.5 cm (17 x 14 inches). 2015 © Mœbius Production.

MŒBIUS LE SURRÉALISTE PSYCHÉDÉLIQUE

Opposite: The first cover for *Métal Hurlant* magazine,
December 1974. Jean Giraud was co-founder of the
magazine, and adopted the name Mœbius for all his
work in the new title. Ink, watercolor, and graphite on
board, 1974, 47 x 44.70 cm (18.5 x 17.8 inches).
© 2023 Humanoids, Inc. Los Angeles.

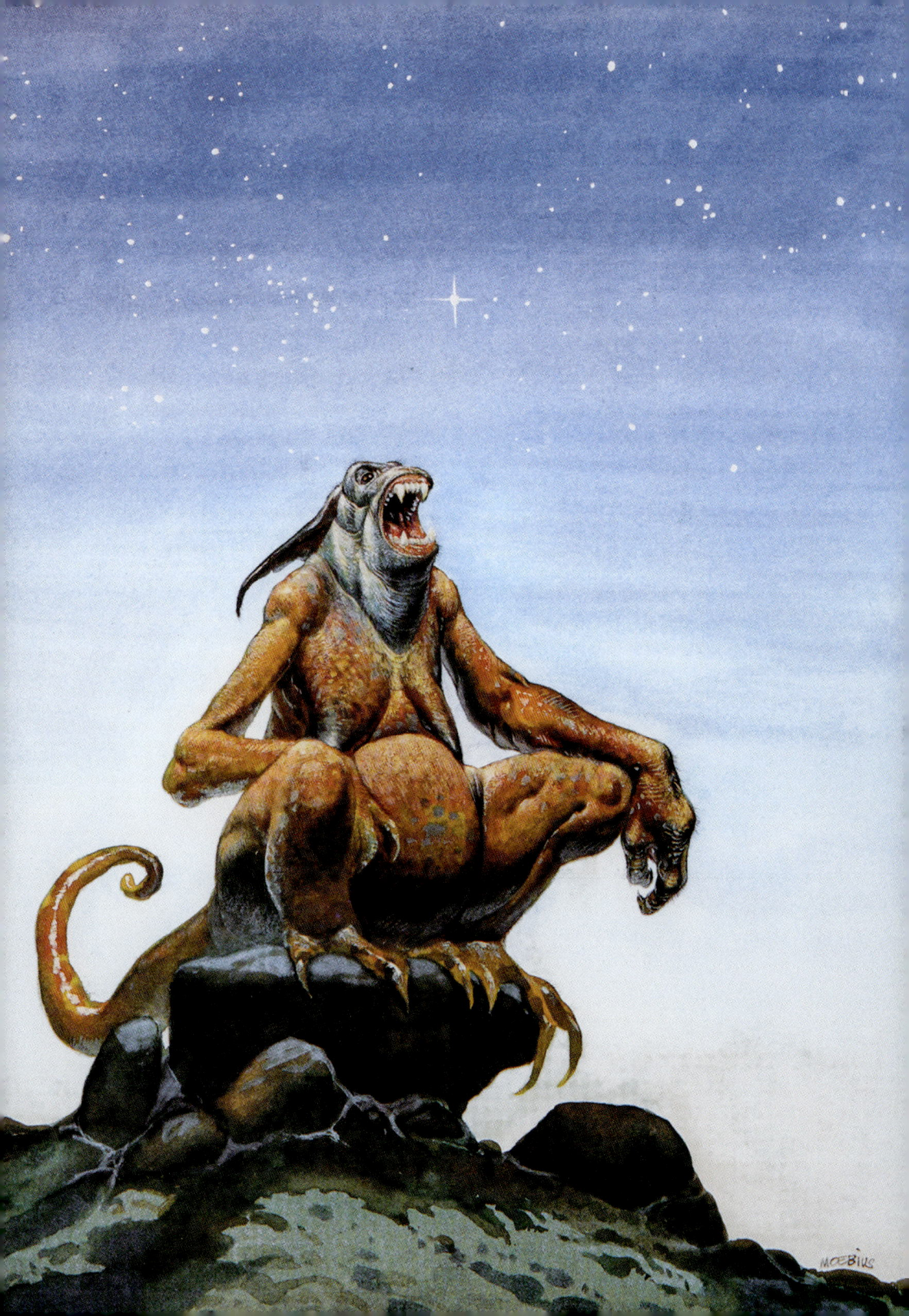

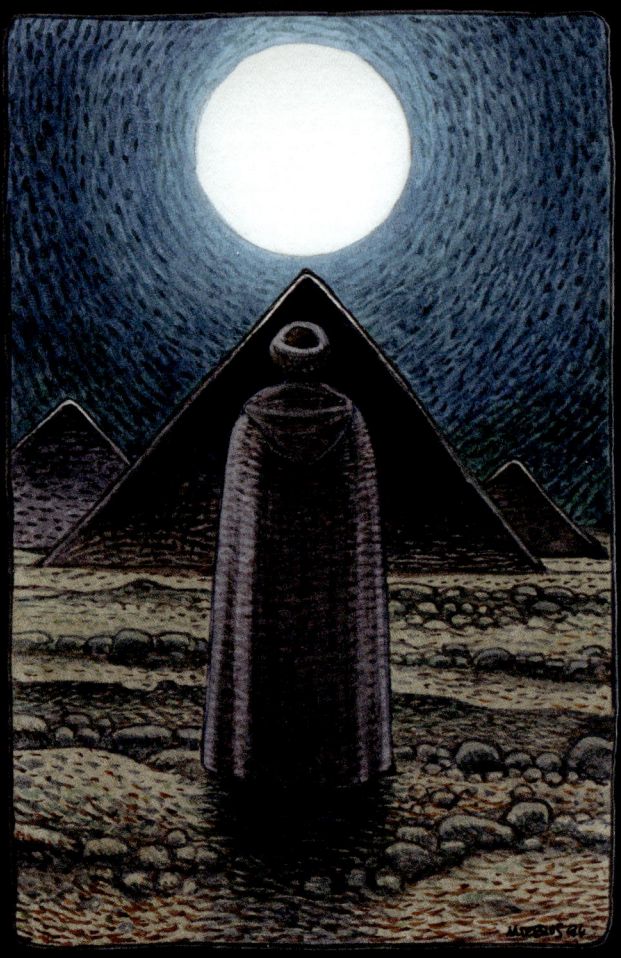

Above: L'Alchimiste, one of 35 illustrations Mœbius created for Paulo Coelho's 1998 *The Illustrated Alchemist: A Fable About Following Your Dreams.* 1995 © Mœbius Production.

Opposite: Ballade, plate No. 6 from a short story appearing in the book *L'Homme est-il bon?* (*Is Man Good?*), published by Les Humanoïdes Associés. Black and colored inks on paper, 1977, 35.5 x 27.8 cm (13.9 x 10.9 inches). © 2023 Humanoids, Inc. Los Angeles.

Following spread: Major Dragoon appeared as the wraparound cover for *Mœbius Comics* No. 6, 1996, and was reproduced as a lithographic print on paper in 2000, 50 x 70 cm (20 x 28 inches). 1994 © Mœbius Production.

MASTERPIECES OF FANTASY ART

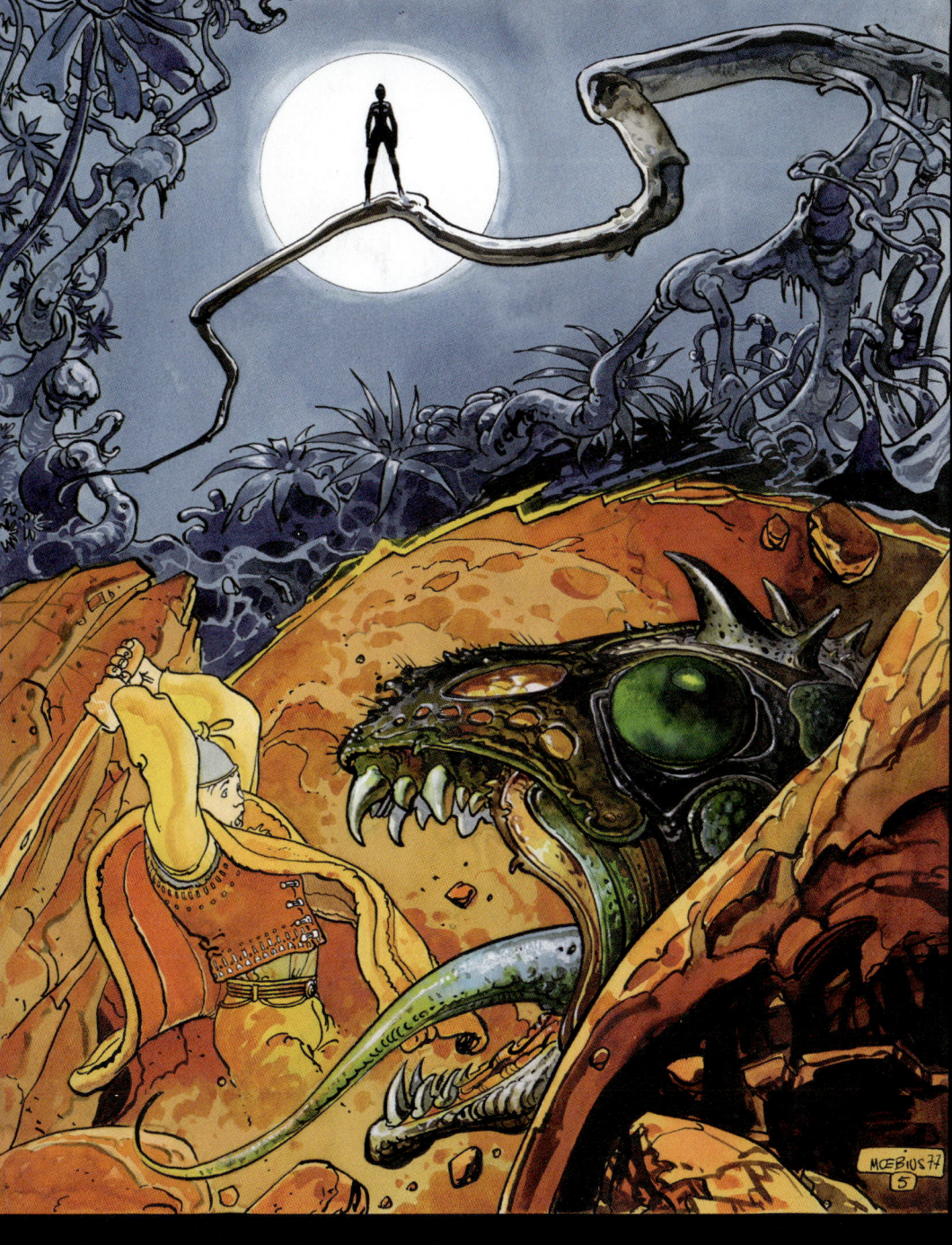

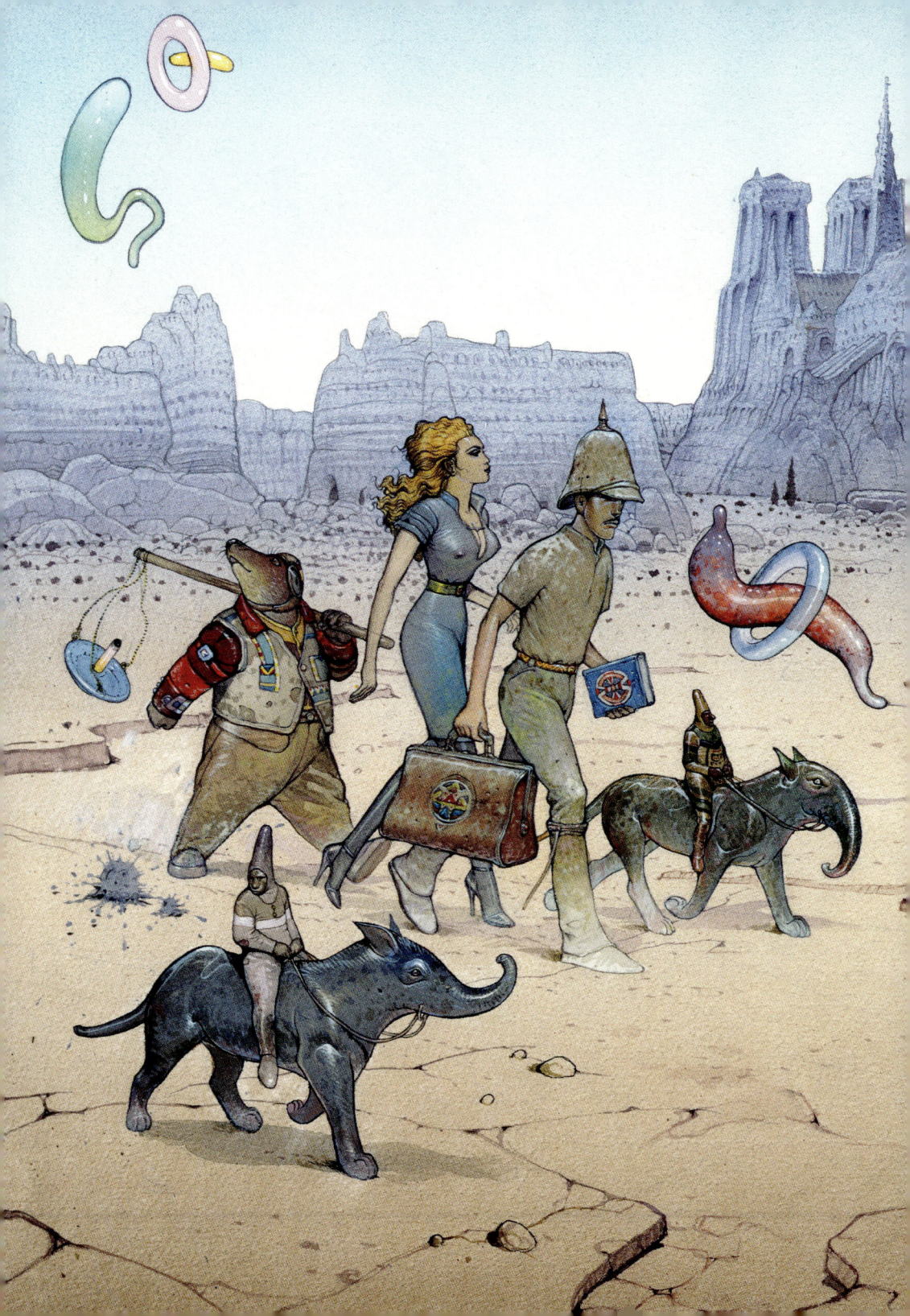

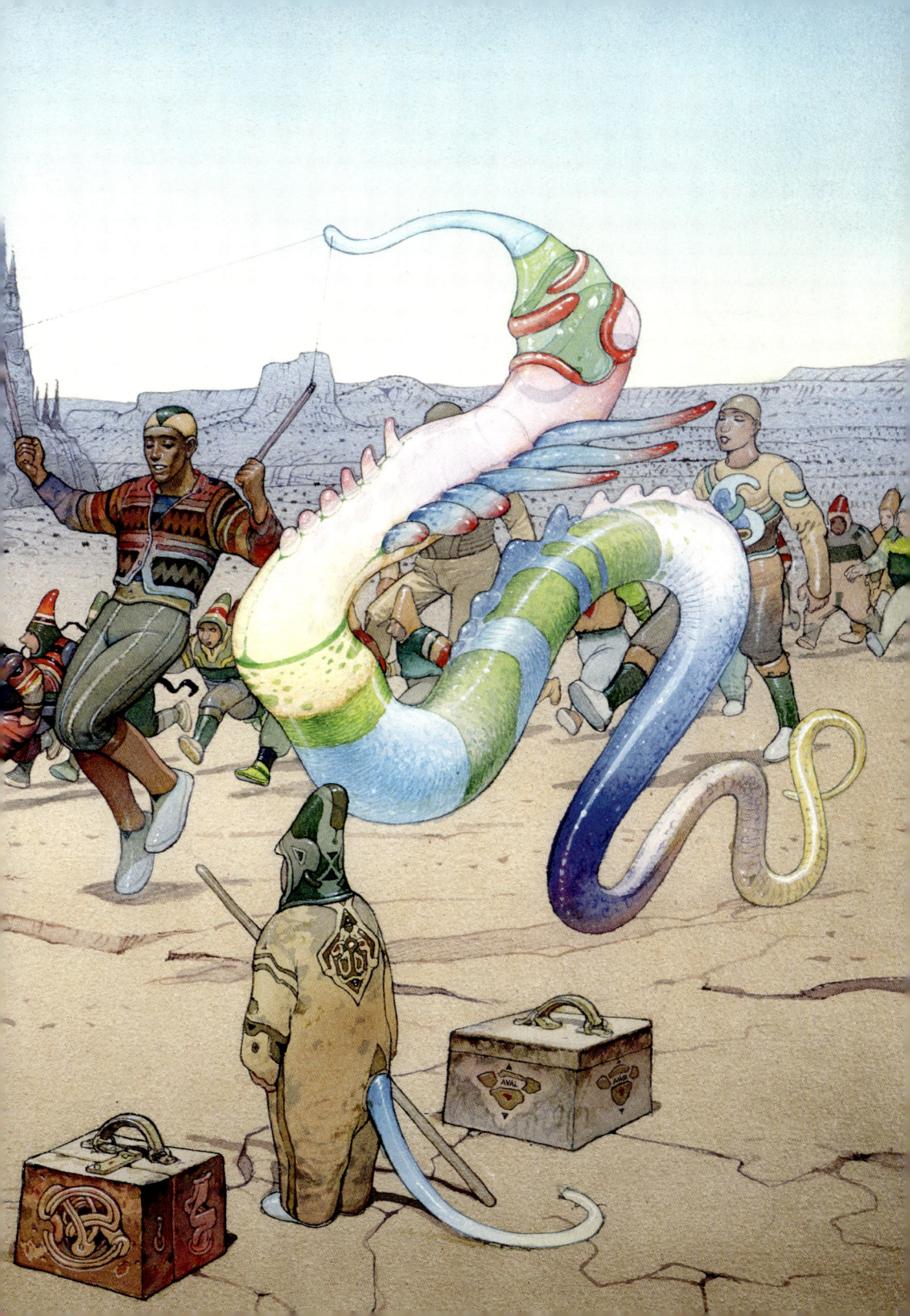

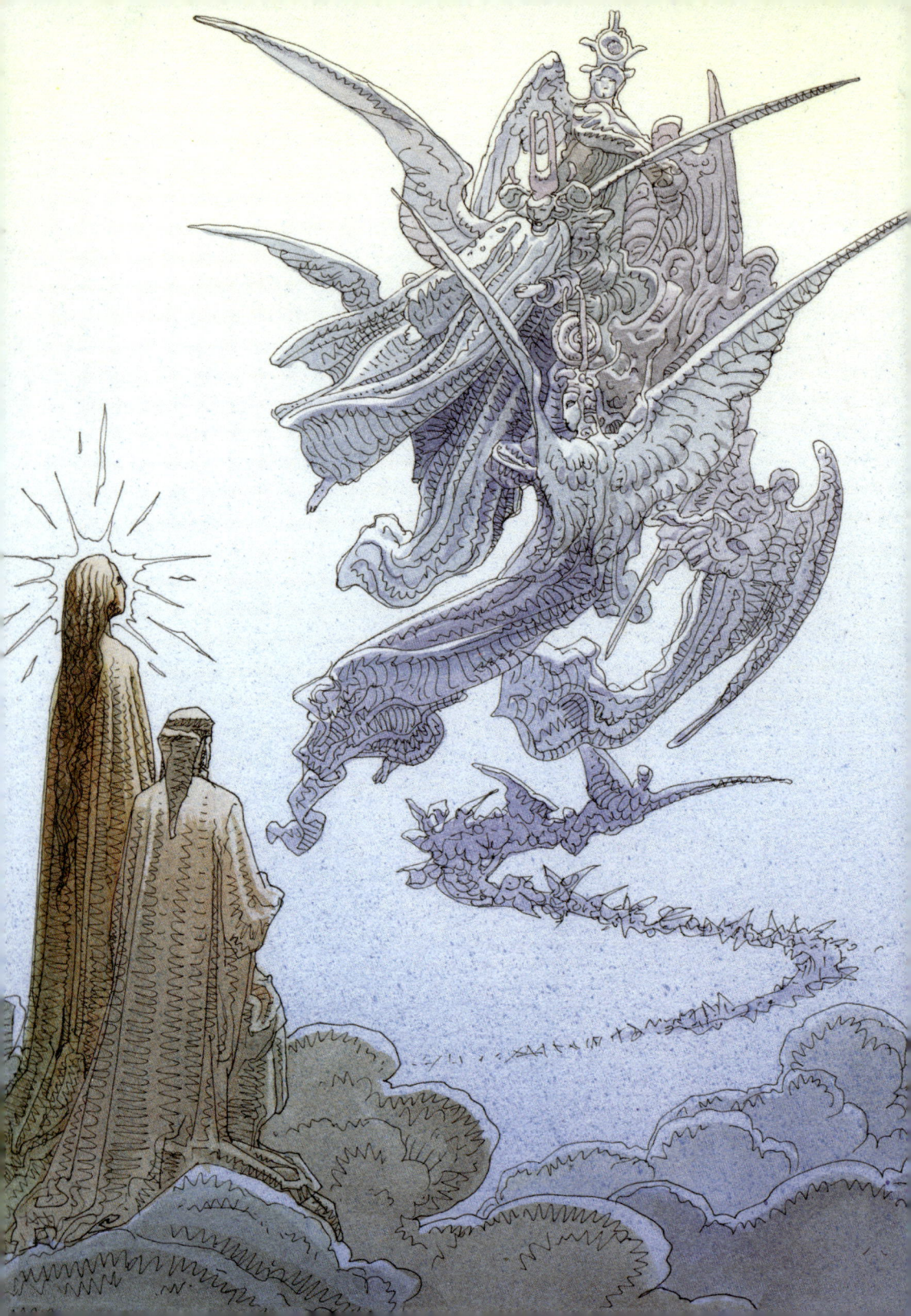

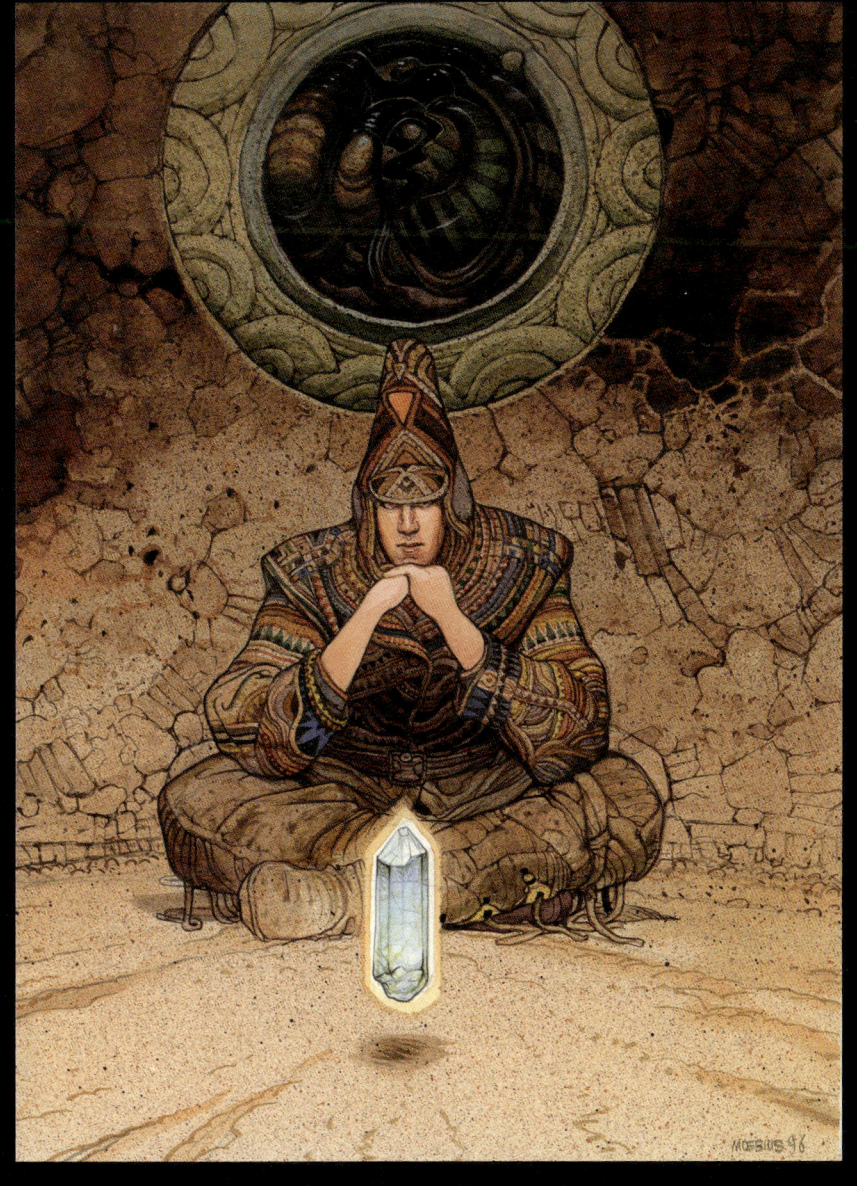

Opposite: Hommage à Gustave Doré. In 1999, Nuages Gallery in Milan published three illustrated editions of Dante Alighieri's *La Divina Commedia* (*The Divine Comedy*): *Inferno*, *Purgatorio*, and *Paradiso*, each illustrated by a different artist. Mœbius got *Paradiso*, including this image of Dante encountering a heavenly host. 1999 © Mœbius Production.

Above: Building the Crystal, for *The Crystal Saga* in the portfolio *Edena*. Ink, pastel, and watercolor on paper, 1986, 32 x 24 cm (12.7 x 9.5 inches).

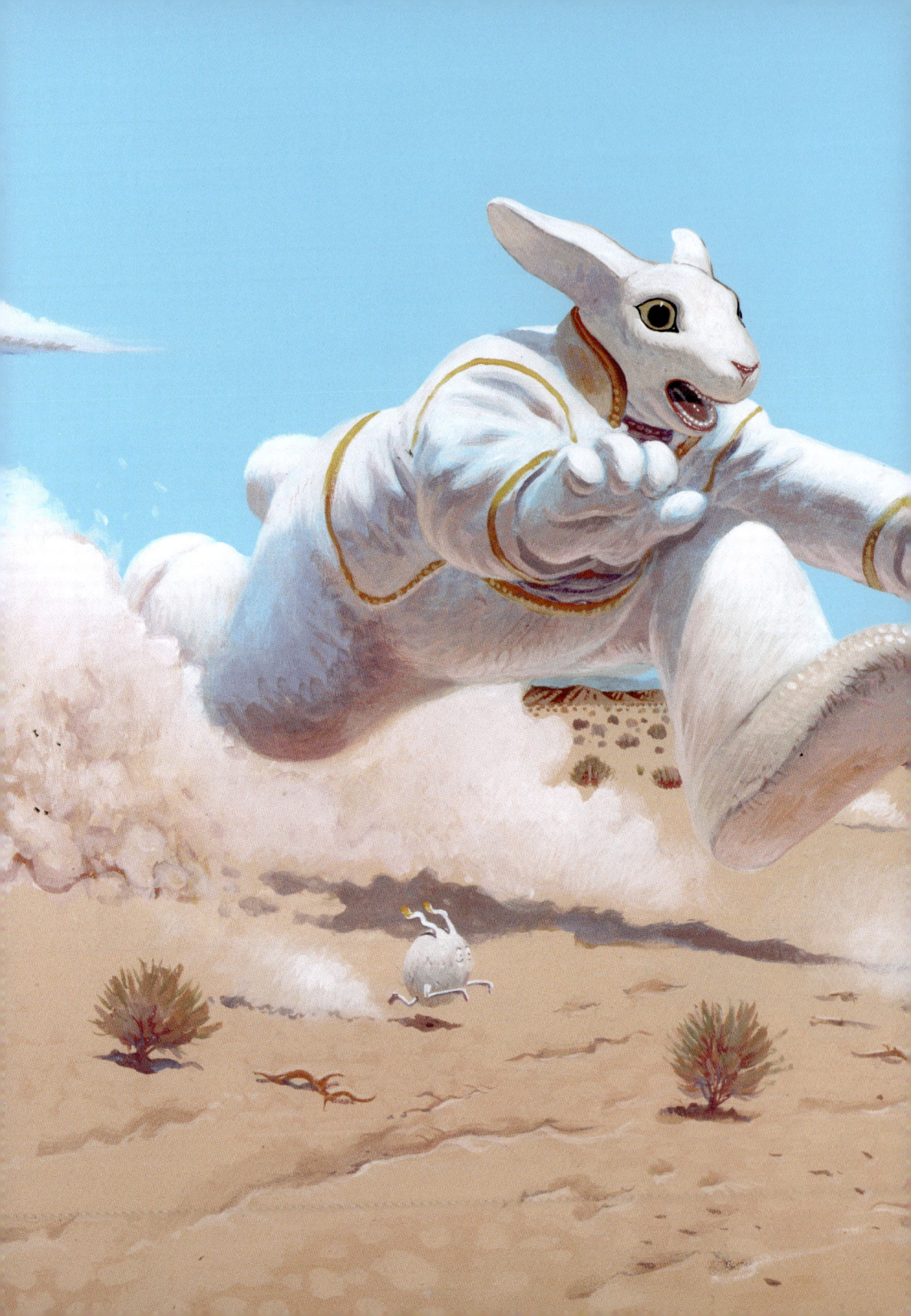

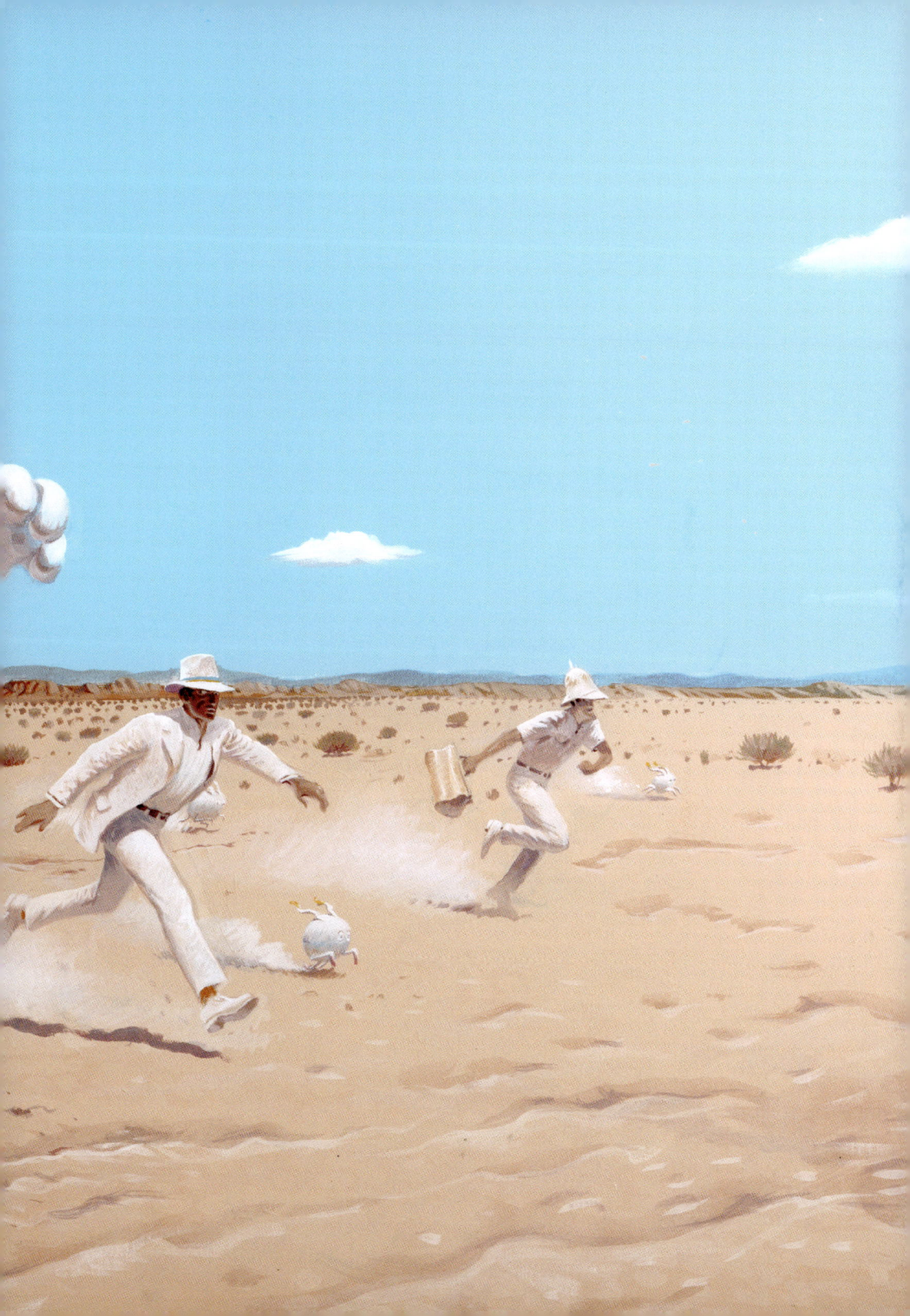

Previous spread: La Chasse au Major
(*The Major's Hunt*), Acrylic on canvas,
89 x 130 cm (35 x 51 inches).
2009 © Mœbius Production.

Right: La Course, acrylic on canvas
board, 65 x 54 cm (25.6 x 21.3 inches).
2008 © Mœbius Production.

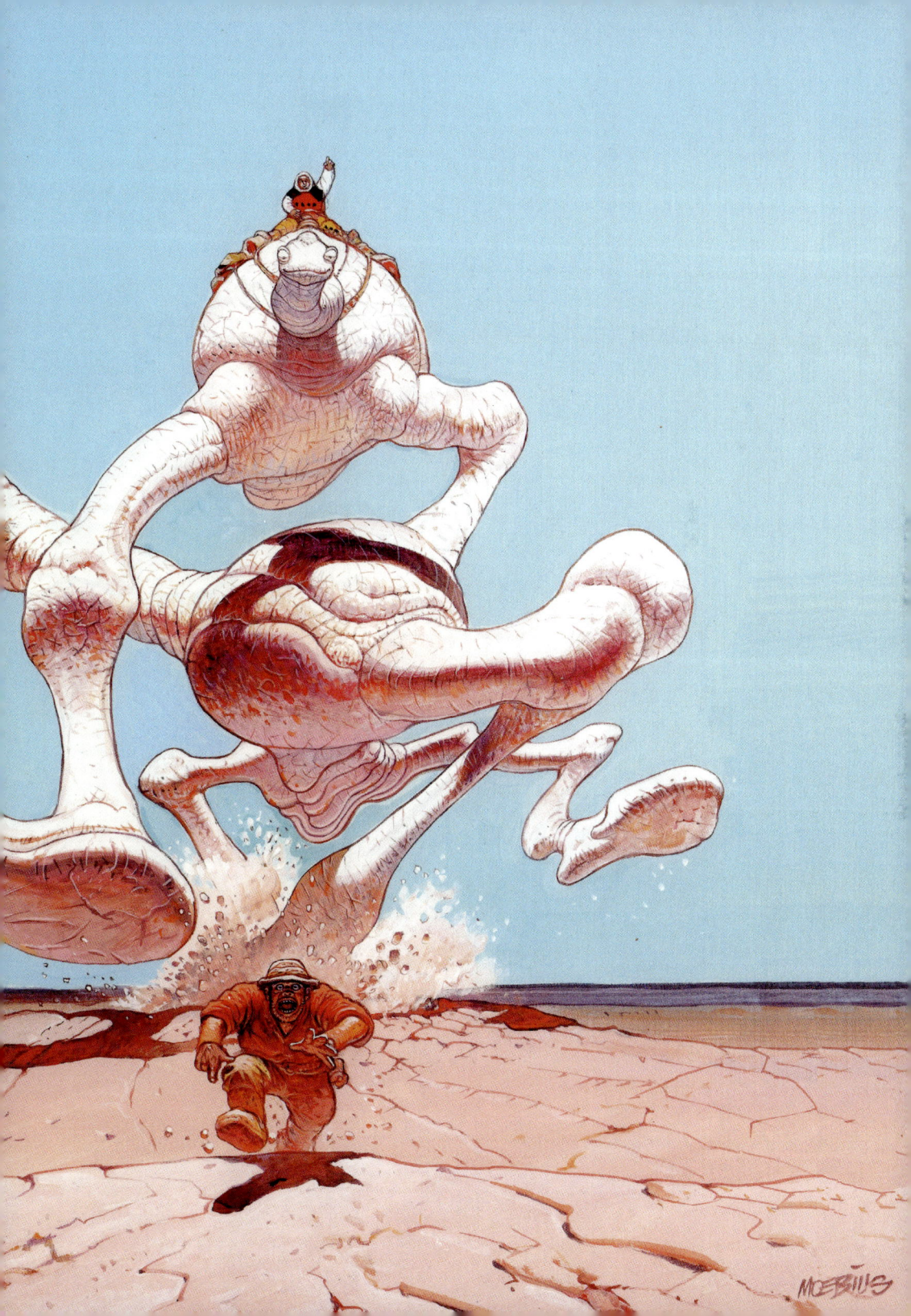

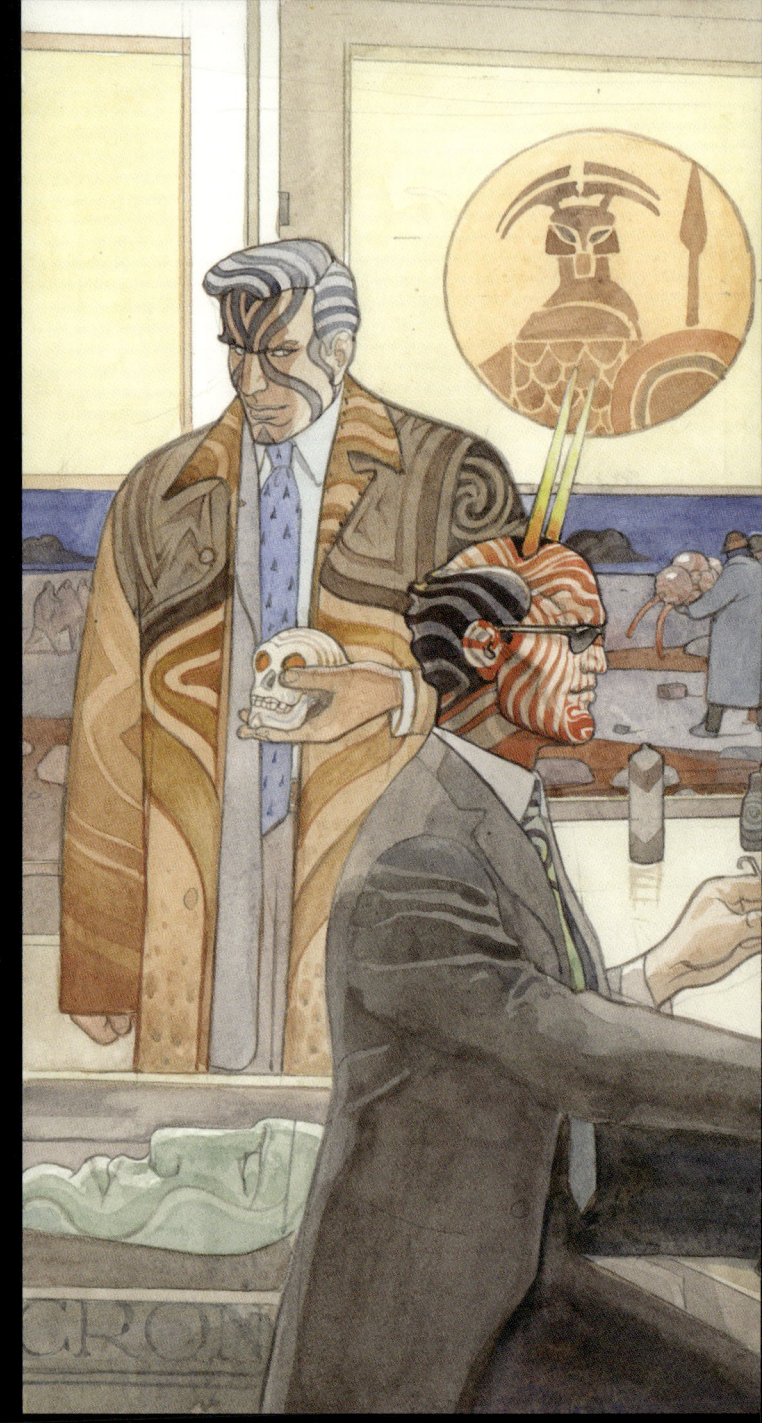

Right: Zeus, Poséidon et Hadès, unpublished, ink and colored ink on paper, 31 x 41 cm (12.2 x 16.1 inches). 2005 © Mœbius Production.

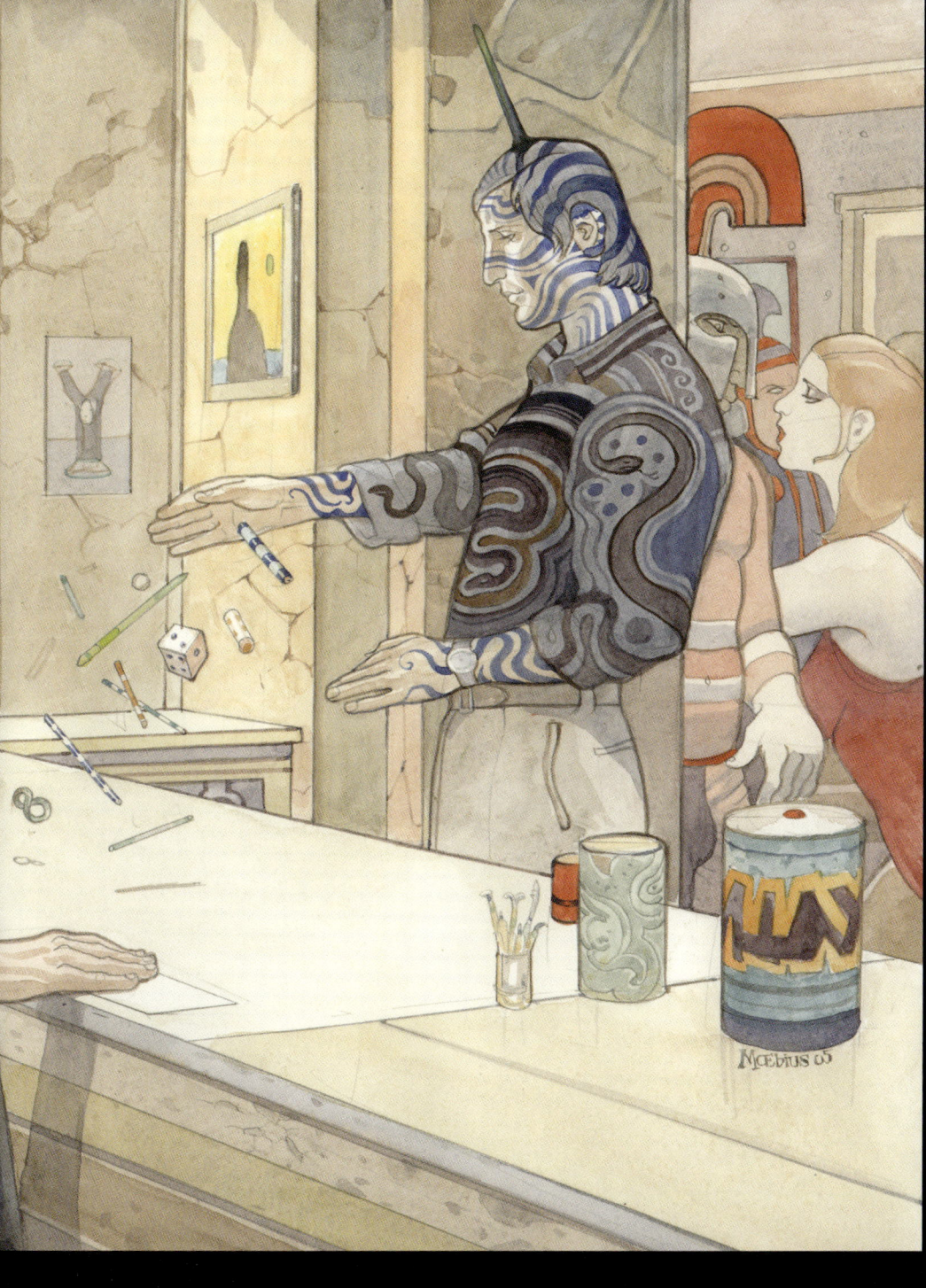

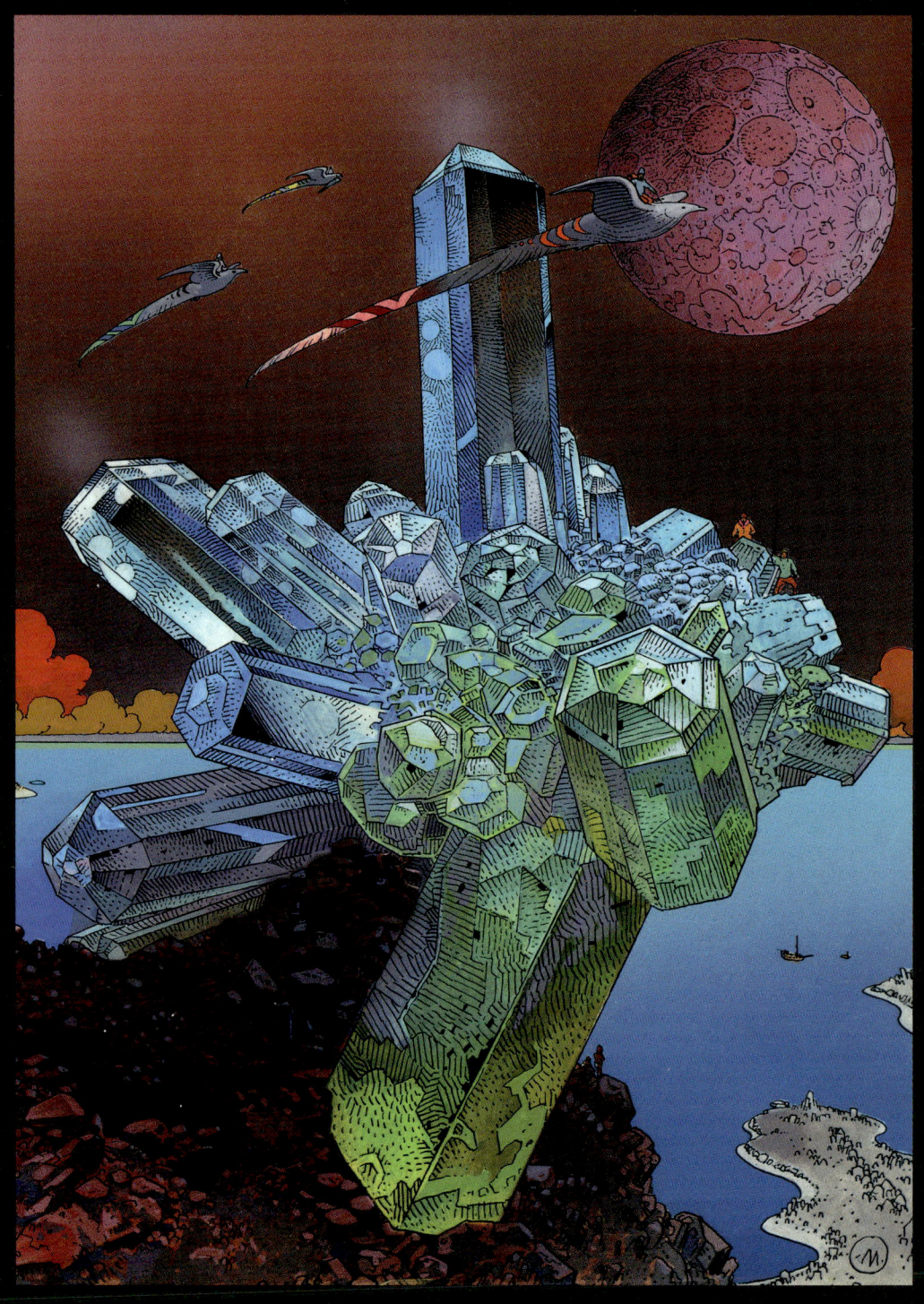

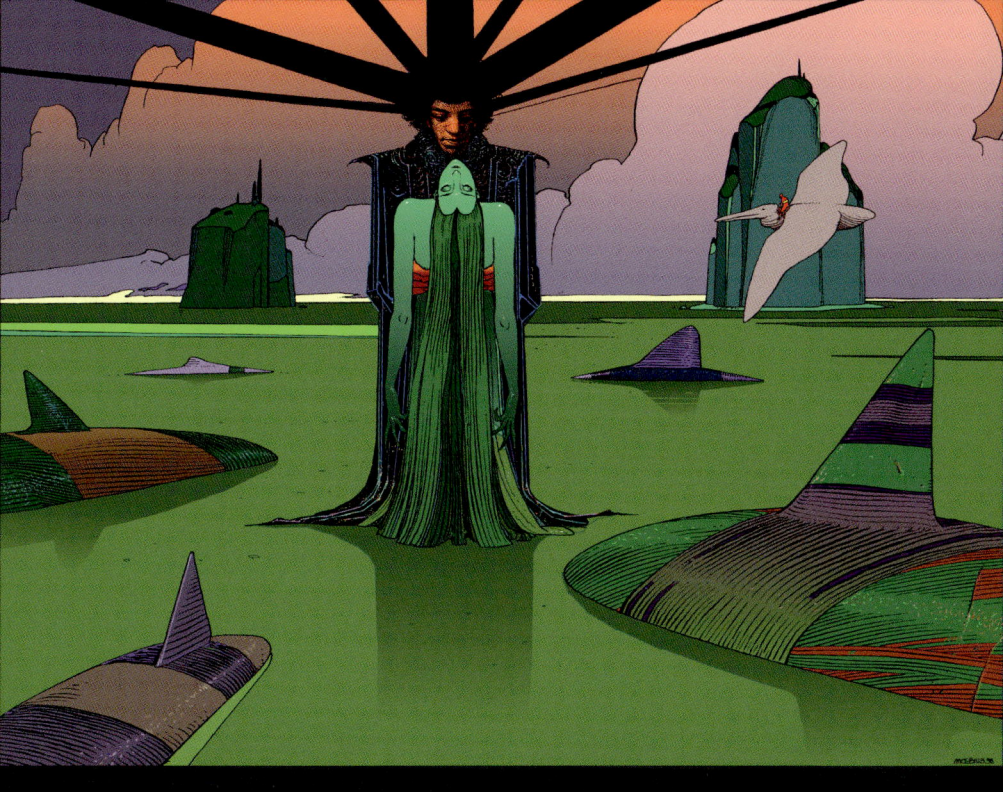

Opposite: *Cap Blue Cristal*, India ink and colored ink on paper. 1983 © Mœbius Production.

Above: *Hendrix, le lac*, for *Jimi Hendrix Emotions Électriques*, a collaborative book between writer Jean-Noel Coghe and Mœbius. 1998 © Mœbius Production.

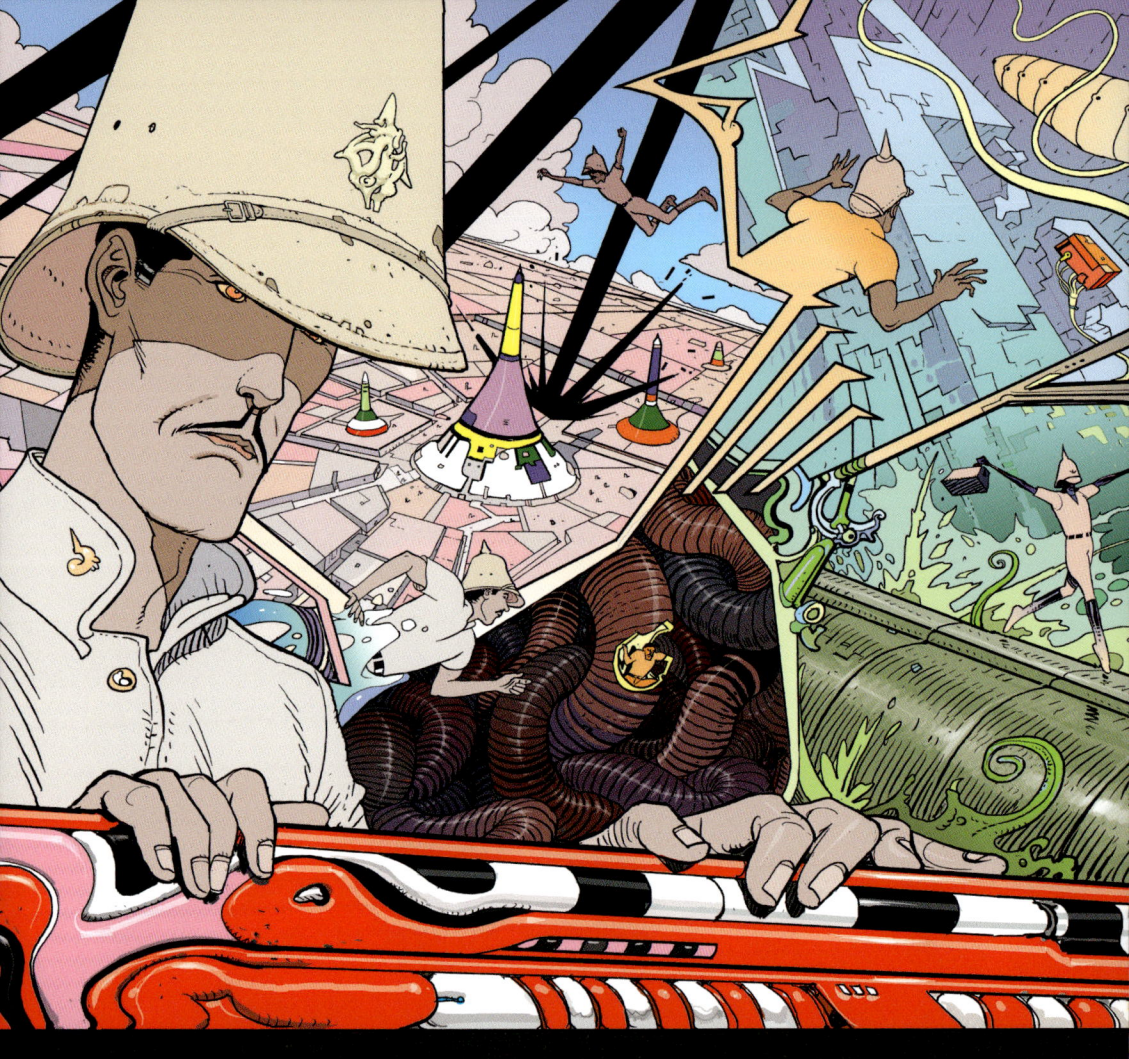

Above: La Fresque du Major, a massive fresco portraying
the adventures of Major Grubert, created for public
display in Poitiers, France. 2007 © Mœbius Production.

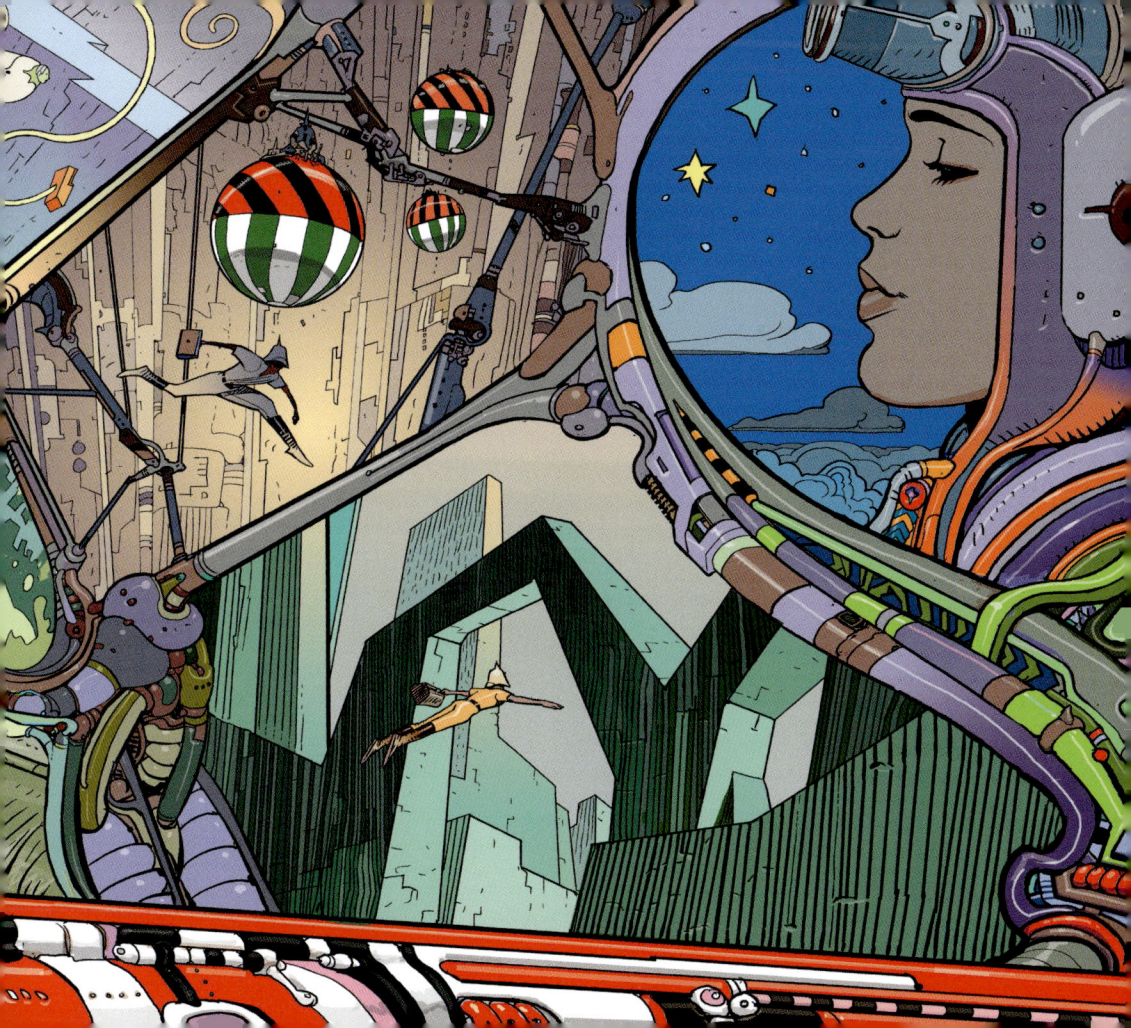

Opposite: From *Inside Mœbius, tome 6,* 2004.
© Mœbius Production.

Following left: Arzak, le rocher, 1995
© Mœbius Production.

Following right: Starwatcher with Butterflies,
ink on paper, 25 x 19 cm (9.8 x 7.4 inches).
© Mœbius Production.

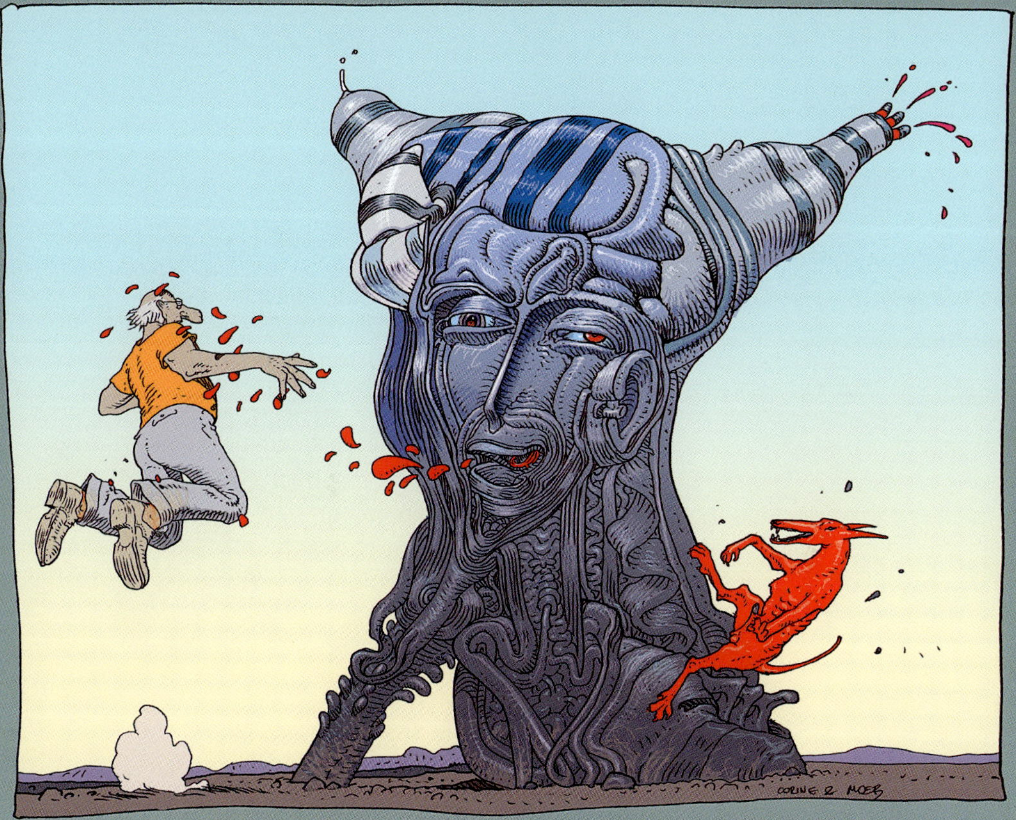

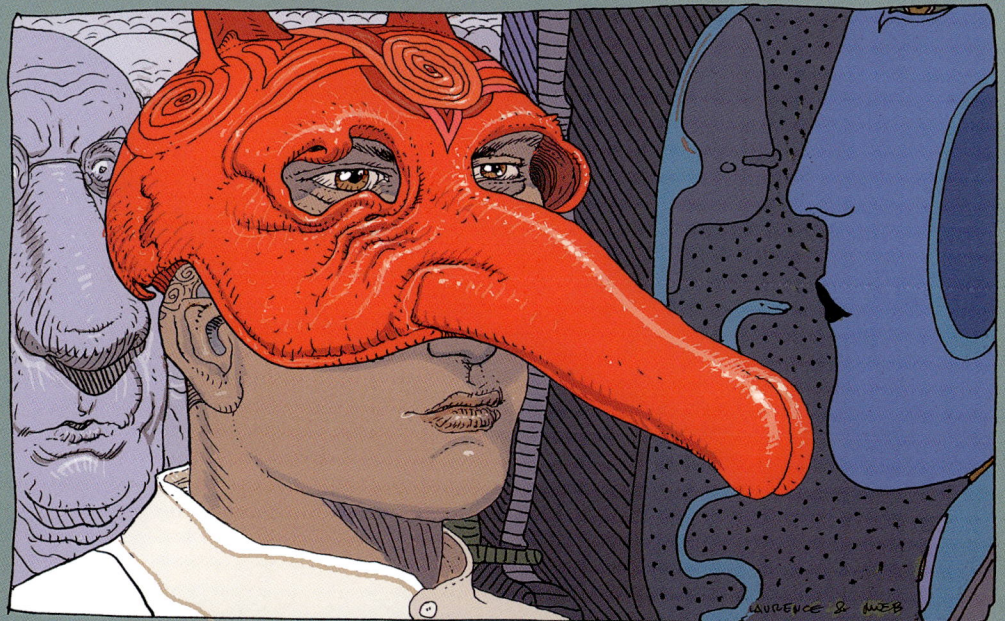

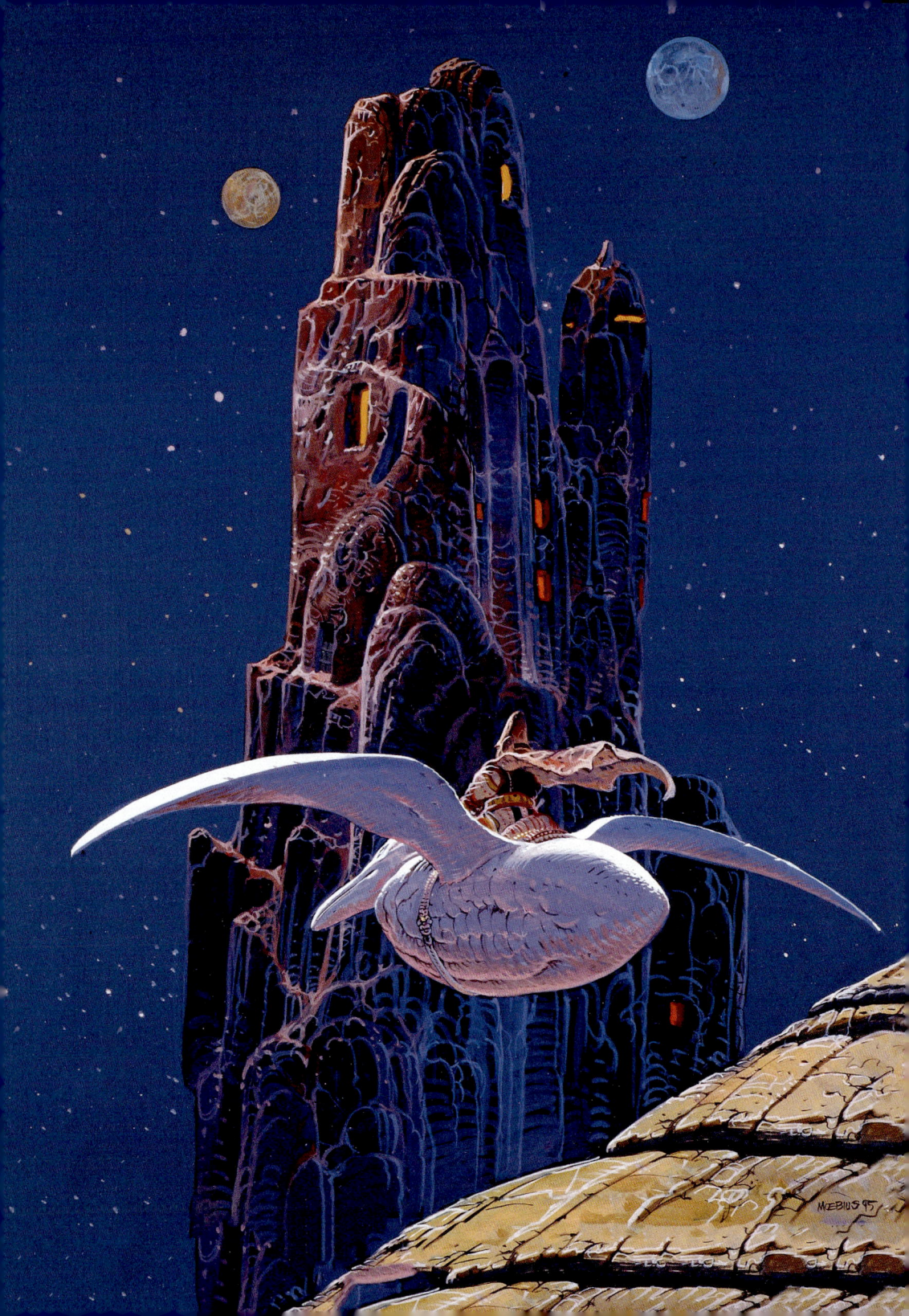

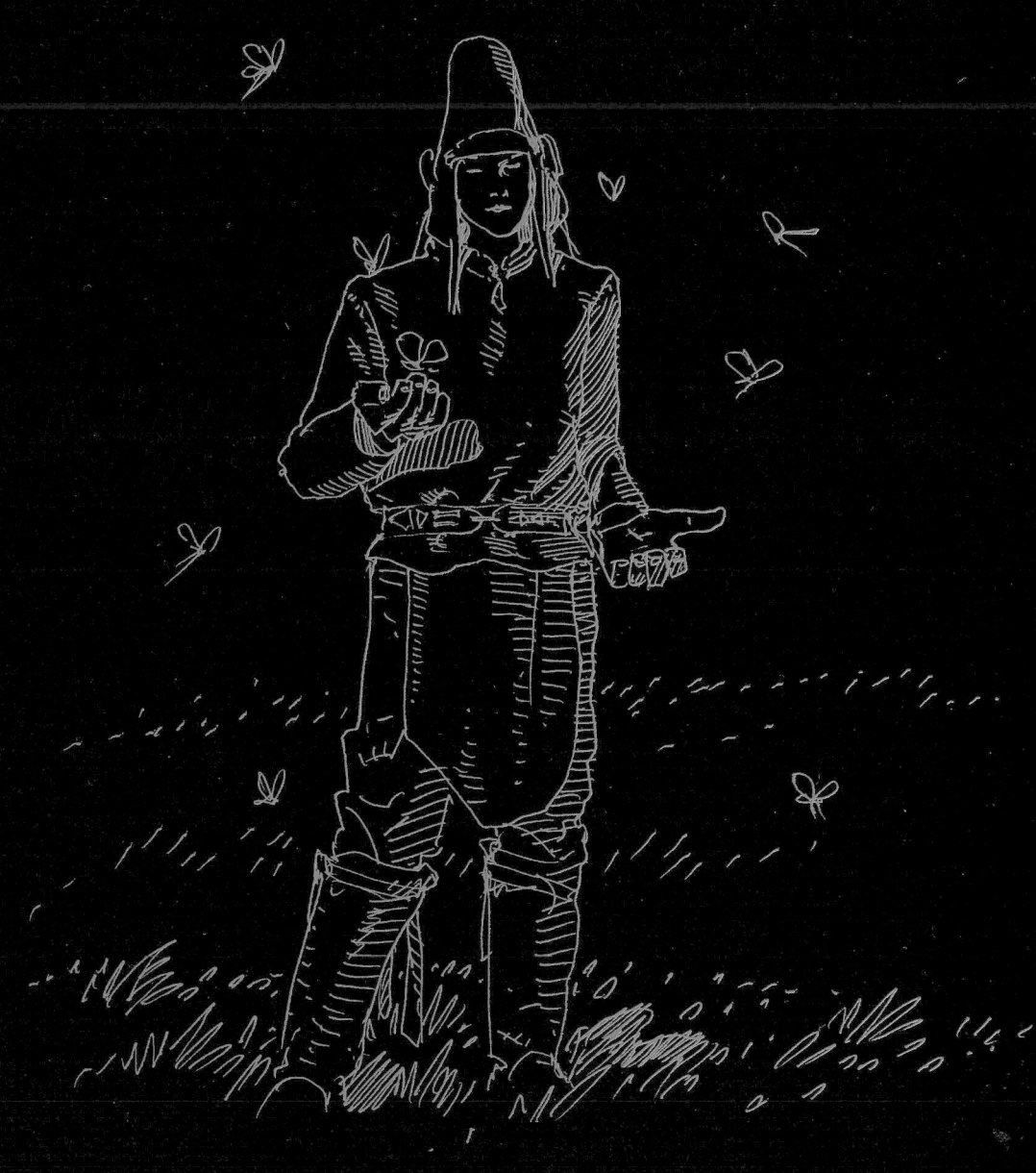

Rowena Morrill

Rowena

1944-2021

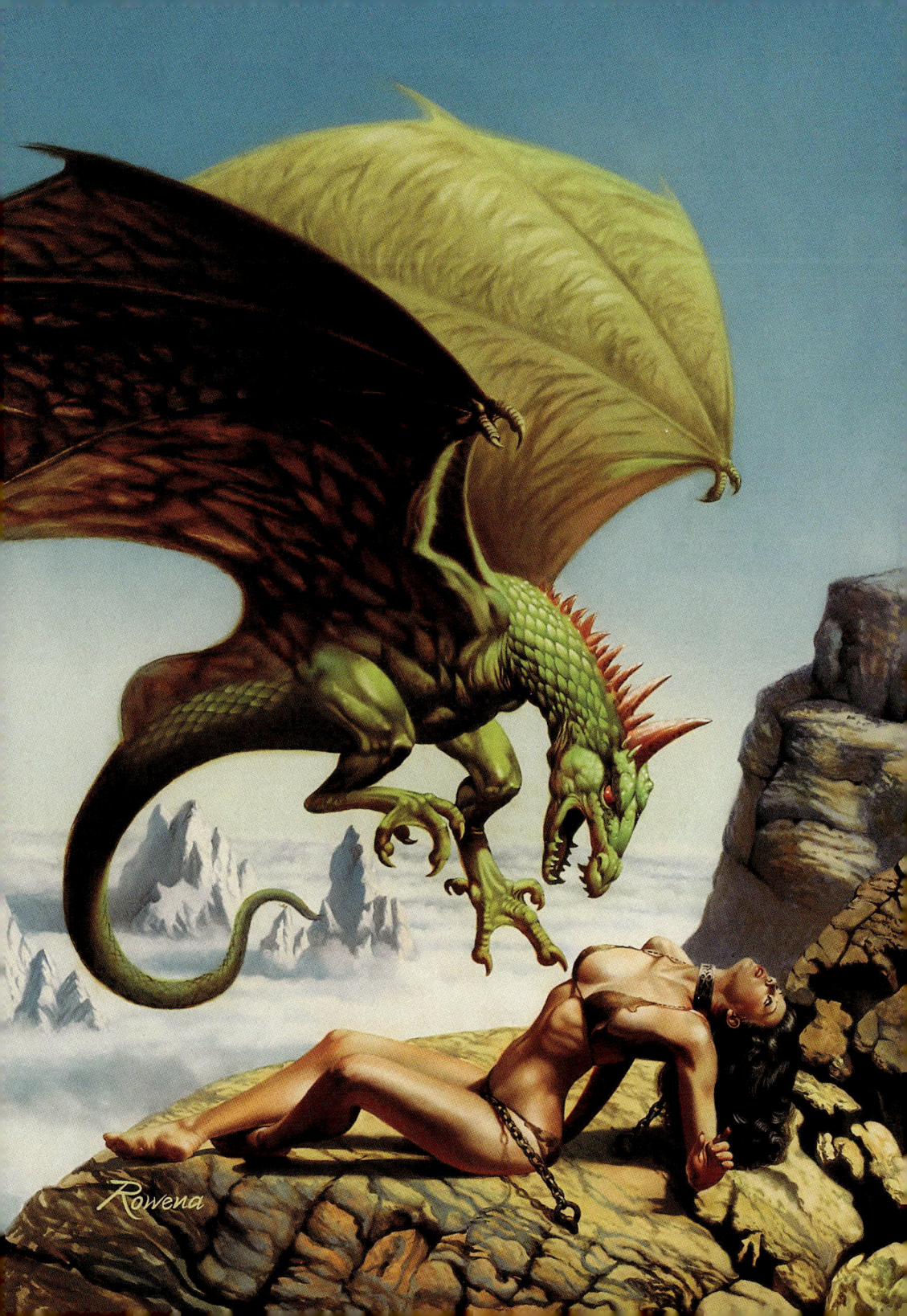

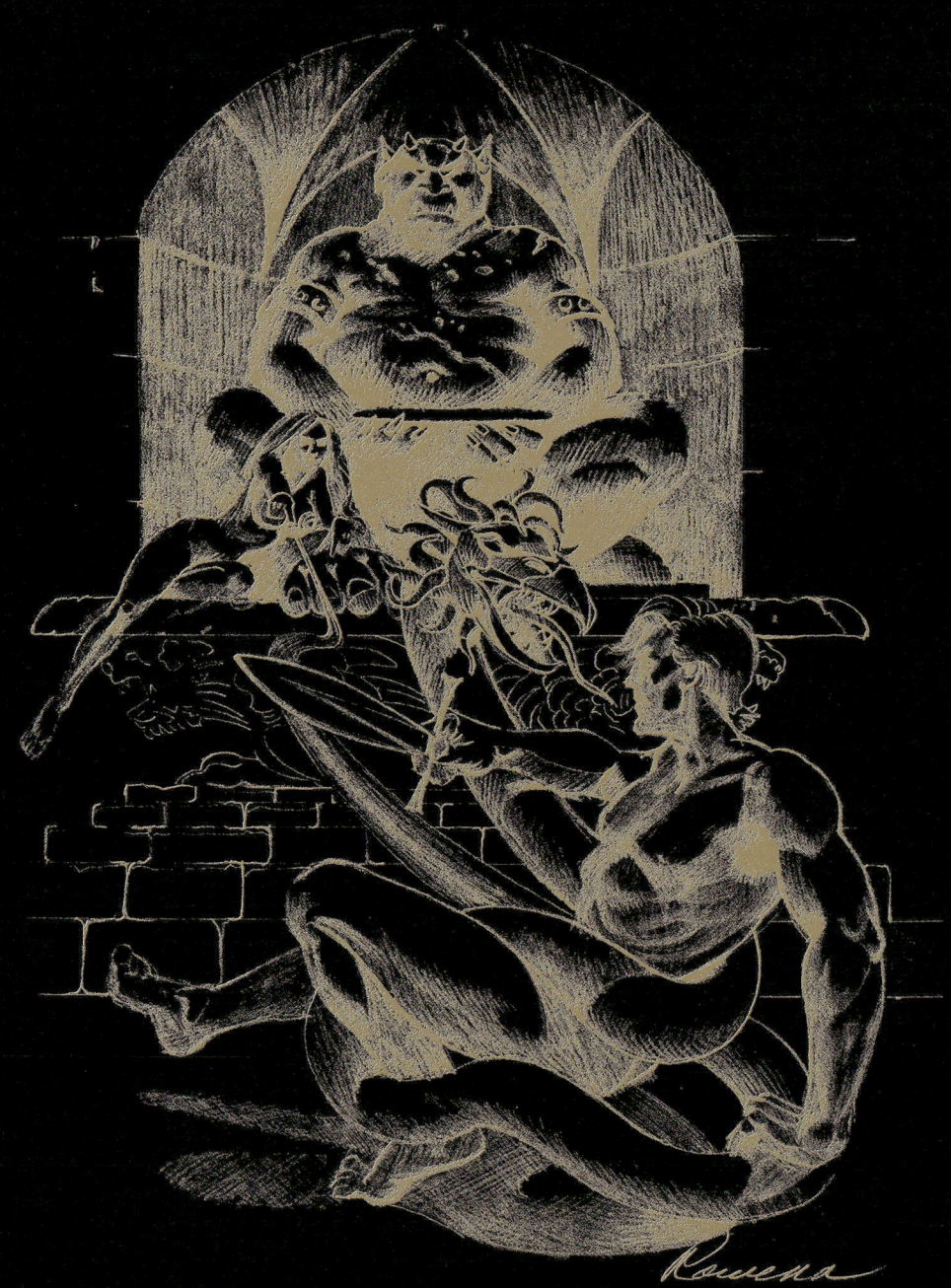

ROWENA MORRILL
THE PIONEER

> "I think the male/female dynamic of fantasy art is great. That's what people love to see."

Rowena Morrill is a rarity among fantasy artists: a talented female interloper in a largely male domain. When she first presented her portfolio at Ace Books in the mid-'60s they gave her a romance novel to illustrate, "something with a nurse." She found the subject uninspiring, but fortunately Ace took a second look at her samples and, seeing she was adept at human figures, offered her a fantasy book illustration. A career was born.

"I called up Ace because it started with 'A' and was first in the phone book," she laughs. This was typical of Morrill's approach to life: take the simple, spontaneous route. That call to Ace came with her move from Philadelphia to New York City after flunking out of Temple University's Tyler School of Art. She'd been trying for a master's degree in order to teach art — not because she wanted to teach, but because she saw it as an easy career path. But then she only studied art in the first place because it seemed easy, after majoring in music for the same reason. This cavalier attitude was probably the result of her rootless childhood.

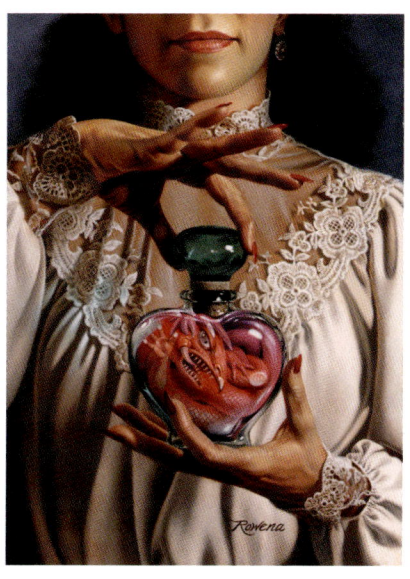

Rowena Morrill was born in Mississippi — in a town she forgot — in 1944. She left that first home at the age of just six weeks: her father was a military chaplain and they moved often, though unlike most Army brats she loved the vagabond life. "I couldn't wait to get to the next place. We moved to Japan when I was five. We had three servants and they taught me to make origami and draw things." The family returned to the States when she was nine, then moved on to Italy at 13, where she was introduced to classical art, though she still took no personal interest. She finished high school in the U.S., studied piano at the University of Puget Sound, south of Seattle, and married immediately after receiving her degree. It being the early 1960s, she became a housewife for a minute or so, soon growing bored and leaving her husband to attend art school.

Previous right: King Dragon, for the cover of the 1980 Andrew Offutt novel. The artwork stirred controversy when *The New York Daily News* reported it was found in Saddam Hussein's townhouse during the fall of Baghdad; it turned out to be a copy. Oil on canvas, 63.5 x 38.1 cm (25 x 15 inches).

Opposite: Lady of the Snow Mist preliminary cover sketch for Andrew Offutt's 1980 novel *Shadows Out of Hell.* Pencil on paper, 1979, 29.2 x 17.7 cm (11.5 x 7 inches). Courtesy of Heritage Auctions.

Above: Forbidden Fragrance, oil on canvas, 1998.

From there, on to New York, center of publishing, where she conveniently had a sister she could impose on. With a phone book she flipped open to "P" to call the first listing under "Publishers." In those halcyon days you could just walk in and get an assignment, and once the nurse cover was out of the way she got a fantasy novel titled *Isobel*, for which she painted a nude woman kneeling before the devil.

They didn't try to foist any more romance covers on her.

Morrill had found her niche and spent the next 30 years painting hundreds of paperback covers for writers such as Theodore Sturgeon, H.P. Lovecraft, Anne McCaffrey, and Philip K. Dick, and illustrations for magazines including *Playboy*, *Heavy Metal*, and Bob Guccione's wonderful *Omni*. She lived on New York's cushy Upper West Side, married twice more and produced a son. As much as she loved her life and career, she never could embrace the fantasy fiction she illustrated.

"I thought they were truly dreadful, even the Lovecraft books. I would skim quickly to find a concept." The concepts generally involved a sexy woman, often with Morrill's face. "I just liked my face. I posed for myself and would have someone photograph me." The rest of the time she used a photo studio in Manhattan frequented by other illustrators: Robert Osonitsch Limited. Osonitsch, still in business, provides sets, costumes, models, and photographic services for artists' reference. "I loved him. He'd come up with everything but the dragon."

But then each fantasy artist must find his or her own inner dragon. Morrill used photos of various reptiles, trying to create an anatomically plausible beast. Her approach to creating other

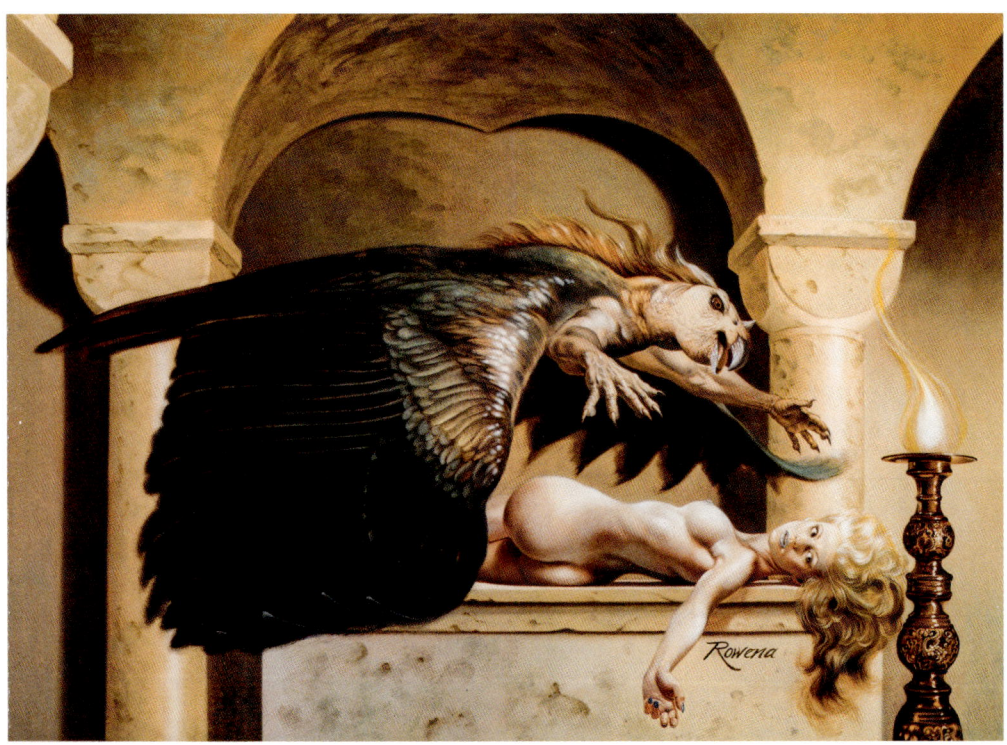

fantasy creatures was the same: sample extant animals and assemble the parts in a way that worked aesthetically and mechanically. Oils were her medium, preferred for their fluidity. She considered herself a slow painter, capable of only one canvas a week, and needed paints she could "smear around," that wouldn't dry too quickly.

Though Morrill tired of painting and essentially retired in the late '90s, her name resurfaced in 2003 with the fall of Saddam Hussein. It was initially reported that two of her paintings, *Shadows Out of Hell*, of a platinum-tressed hero rescuing an equally blonde nude female, and *King Dragon*, showing a chained woman menaced by a flying lizard, were found hanging in one of Hussein's homes. As it turned out, the artworks

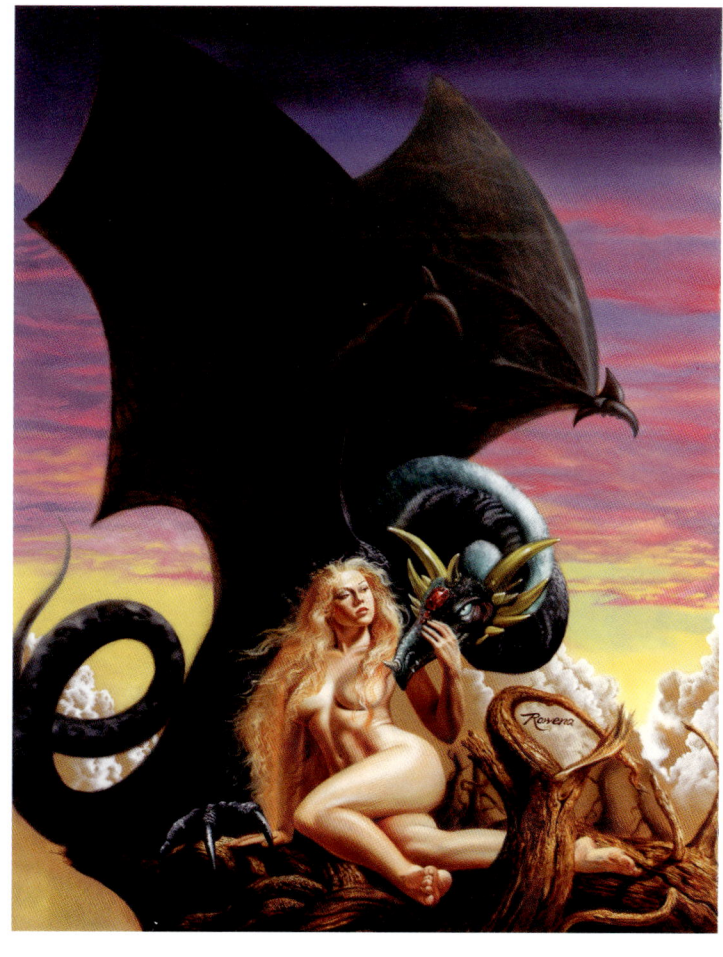

were huge prints Hussein had commissioned or acquired. That same year it was revealed that several Morrill works had been copied and distributed in propaganda tracts by the Children of God sex cult. Morrill enjoyed the fuss from a distance, snug in her upstate New York home, where she spent her last days playing with her Saint Bernard dog and exploring the Internet. She died in 2021 at the age of seventy-six.

"I've had a great career and a great life; I always just painted what I thought was exciting and fun and colorful. I pleased myself, and how many can look back on life and say that?"

Opposite: Bird God, for the cover of Roger Zelazny's 1981 novel *Madwand.* Oil on board, 1989.

Above: Girl with Black Dragon, for the cover of the July 1989 issue of *Heavy Metal.* Oil on canvas, 1989.

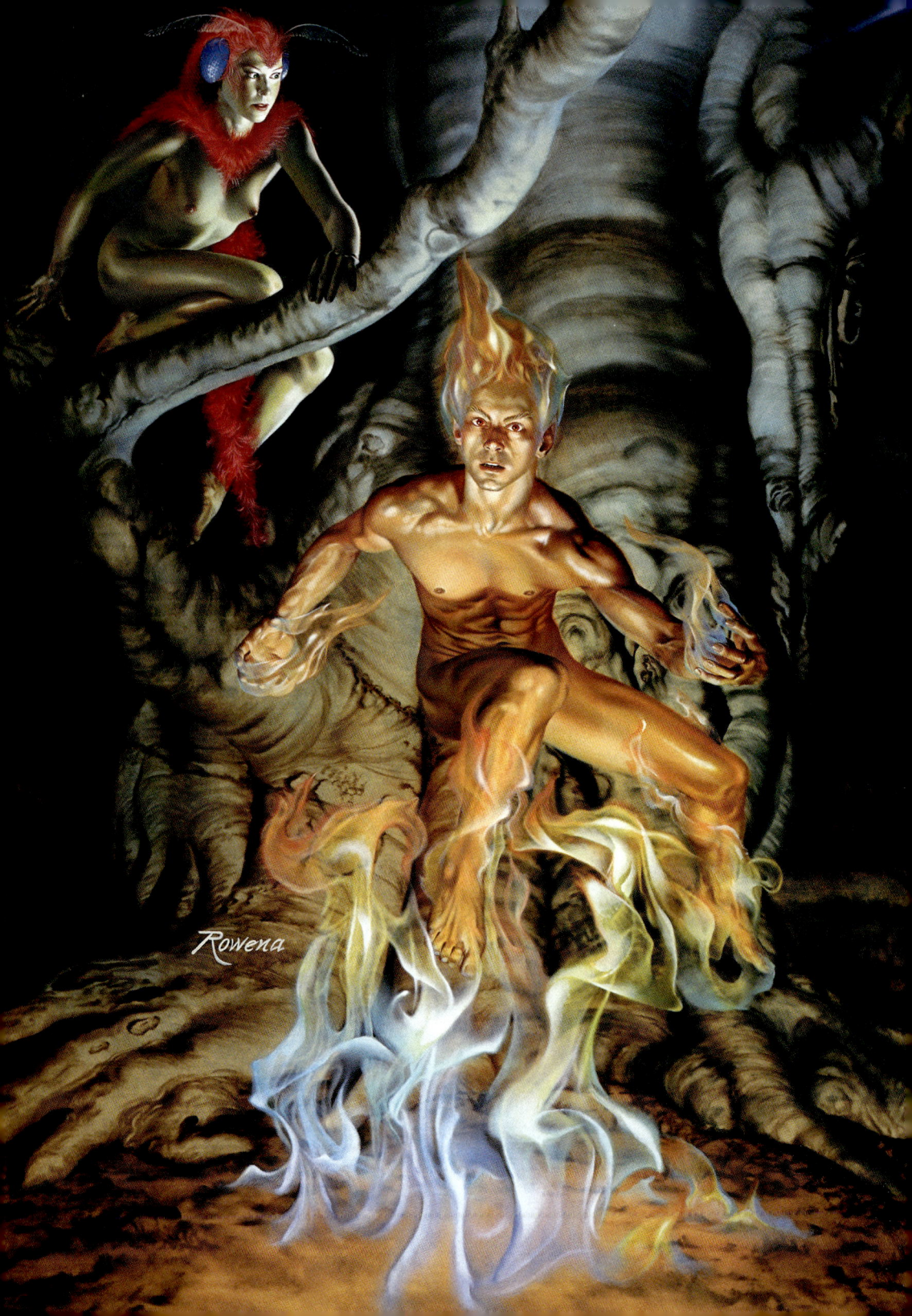

ROWENA MORRILL
DIE PIONIERIN

*„Ich finde, die Dynamik von männlich/
weiblich in der Fantasykunst ist großartig.
So etwas sehen die Leute gerne."*

Unter Fantasykünstlern ist Rowena Morrill ein Unikum:
ein begabter weiblicher Eindringling in eine weitgehend
männliche Domäne. Als sie ihr Portfolio Mitte der 1960er-
Jahre zum ersten Mal bei Ace Books präsentierte, beauftragte man sie mit der Illustration eines Liebesromans –
„irgendwas mit einer Krankenschwester". Das Thema fand
sie wenig reizvoll, aber glücklicherweise schaute man sich
bei Ace ihre Probearbeiten noch ein zweites Mal an und
stellte fest, dass sie sehr gut in der Darstellung menschlicher
Figuren war, und so bot man ihr die Illustration eines
Fantasybuchs an. Das war der Beginn einer Karriere.

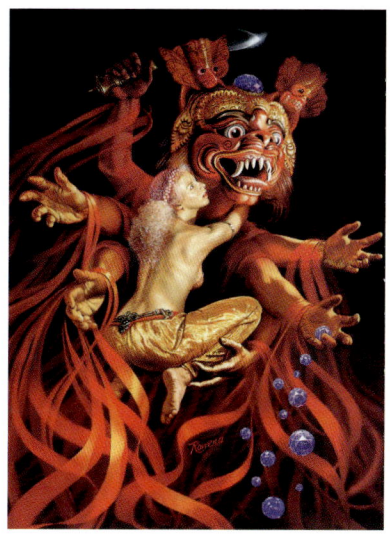

„Ich rief zuerst bei Ace an, weil der Name mit A
beginnt und im Telefonbuch ganz vorne stand", sagt sie
lachend. Das war typisch für Morrills Vorgehensweise im
Leben: instinktiv den unkompliziertesten Weg nehmen.
Den Anruf bei Ace machte sie, nachdem sie von der
Temple University's Tyler School of Art geflogen war,
gleich nach ihrem Umzug von Philadelphia nach New
York City. Sie hatte versucht, als Abschluss ihren Master zu machen, um später Kunst zu unterrichten – nicht weil sie gerne unterrichten wollte, sondern weil sie das, nachdem sie aus dem
gleichen Grund Musik als Hauptfach studiert hatte, als einen leichten beruflichen Weg sah. Diese
nachlässige Einstellung war vermutlich Folge ihrer Kindheit ohne Wurzeln.

Rowena Morrill wurde 1944 in Mississippi geboren, in einer Stadt, die sie seither vergessen
hat. Dieses erste Zuhause verließ sie, als sie gerade erst sechs Wochen alt war: Ihr Vater war ein
Militärpfarrer, und oft zogen sie um, doch anders als die meisten Armeegören mochte sie dieses
Vagabundenleben. „Ich konnte es gar nicht erwarten, an den nächsten Ort zu kommen. Als ich
fünf war, zogen wir nach Japan. Wir hatten drei Bedienstete, und sie brachten mir das Falten
von Origamis und das Zeichnen von Dingen bei." Als sie neun war, kehrte die Familie in die
Vereinigten Staaten zurück, als sie dreizehn war, zog sie nach Italien, wo sie klassische Kunst
kennenlernte, aber noch immer keinerlei persönliches Interesse daran zeigte. Sie schloss dann die
Highschool in den USA ab, studierte Piano an der University of Puget Sound, südlich von Seattle,

Opposite: Night Demon and Fire Girl, used as the
cover of *The Art of Rowena* portfolio, 1983, oil on board,
81.2 x 60.9 cm (32 x 24 inches).

Above: Crimson Demon, for *The Art of Rowena,* 2000.

Following right: Waterfall, oil on board, 1992,
69.8 x 48.9 cm (27.5 x 19.25 inches).

und sofort nachdem sie ihren Abschluss hatte, heiratete sie. Es waren die frühen 1960er-Jahre, und für ungefähr eine Minute wurde sie Hausfrau, doch das wurde ihr bald zunehmend langweilig, so verließ sie ihren Mann, um die Kunstschule zu besuchen.

Von da aus ging es weiter nach New York, dem Zentrum des Verlagswesens, wo sie praktischerweise eine Schwester hatte, der sie zur Last fallen konnte. In einem Telefonbuch blätterte sie bis zum Buchstaben „P", um beim ersten Verlag anzurufen, der unter „Publishers" aufgeführt war. Zu jenen glücklichen Zeiten konnte man einfach irgendwo hereinspazieren und einen Auftrag ergattern. Als das Krankenschwesterncover abgehakt war, übergab man ihr einen Fantasyroman mit dem Titel *Isobel*, für den sie eine nackte Frau malte, die vor dem Teufel kniete.

Danach versuchte niemand mehr, ihr Cover für Liebesromane anzudrehen.

Morrill hatte ihre Nische gefunden und verbrachte die nächsten 30 Jahre damit, Hunderte von Taschenbuchcovers für Schriftsteller wie Theodore Sturgeon, H. P. Lovecraft, Anne McCaffey und Philip K. Dick und Illustrationen für Zeitschriften wie den *Playboy*, *Heavy Metal* und Bob Gucciones wunderbares *Omni* zu malen. Sie wohnte in der angenehmen Upper West Side von New York, heiratete noch zweimal und brachte einen Sohn zur Welt. Sosehr sie ihr Leben und ihren Beruf auch mochte – mit den Fantasygeschichten, die sie illustrierte, konnte sie eigentlich nie etwas anfangen.

„Ich fand sie wirklich schrecklich, selbst die Bücher von Lovecraft. Ich überflog sie schnell, um einen Entwurf zu finden." Die Entwürfe bezogen in der Regel eine sexy Frau ein, die oft Morrills Gesicht hatte. „Ich mochte mein Gesicht einfach. Ich posierte für mich selbst und organisierte mir dann jemanden, der mich fotografierte." Ansonsten nutzte sie ein Fotostudio in Manhattan, das auch andere Illustratoren frequentierten: Robert Osonitsch Limited. Osonitsch, noch immer im Geschäft, bietet Sets an, Kostüme, Models und fotografische Dienstleistungen für Bedürfnisse von Künstlern. „Ich mochte ihn. Er ließ sich alles Mögliche einfallen, nur keine Drachen."

Letztendlich muss jedoch jeder Fantasykünstler seinen oder ihren eigenen inneren Drachen finden. Morrill benutzte Fotos verschiedener Reptilien und versuchte so ein anatomisch glaubwürdiges Tier zu schaffen. Die gleiche Herangehensweise wählte sie auch beim Entwerfen anderer Fantasykreaturen: Sie nahm sich Muster existierender Tiere vor und fügte Teile ihrer Körper so zusammen, dass es ästhetisch und mechanisch funktionierte.

Ihr Medium waren Ölfarben, die sie wegen ihrer flüssigen Konsistenz bevorzugte. Sie betrachtet sich selbst als eine langsame Malerin, die pro Woche nur eine Leinwand zustande brachte und Farben brauchte, mit denen sie „herumschmieren" konnte und die nicht so schnell trockneten.

Obgleich Morrill der Malerei überdrüssig und Ende der 1990er-Jahre eigentlich im Ruhestand war, kam ihr Name 2003 mit dem Sturz Saddam Husseins noch einmal auf. Zunächst wurde berichtet, zwei ihrer Gemälde, *Shadows Out of Hell*, das einen Helden mit Platinlocken zeigte, der eine blond gelockte Nackte rettete, und *King Dragon*, auf dem eine angekettete Frau zu sehen war, die von einer fliegenden Echse bedroht wurde, seien an den Wänden eines von Husseins Häusern entdeckt worden. Wie sich herausstellte, waren die Werke großformatige Kunstdrucke, die Hussein in Auftrag gegeben oder erworben hatte. Im gleichen Jahr stellte sich heraus, dass verschiedene Werke von Morrill kopiert und über Propagandatraktate für den Sexkult der Children of God (Kinder Gottes) verteilt wurden. Morrill genoss das ganze Theater aus der Ferne, gemütlich in ihrem Zuhause in Upstate New York, wo sie ihre letzten Tage damit verbrachte, mit ihrem Bernhardinerhund zu spielen und das Internet zu erkunden. Sie verstarb 2021 im Alter von 76 Jahren.

„Ich hatte einen tollen Beruf und ein großartiges Leben; ich malte immer nur das, was ich für spannend, amüsant und farbenprächtig hielt. Ich erfreute mich meines Daseins – und wie viele können auf ihr Leben zurückschauen und so etwas sagen?"

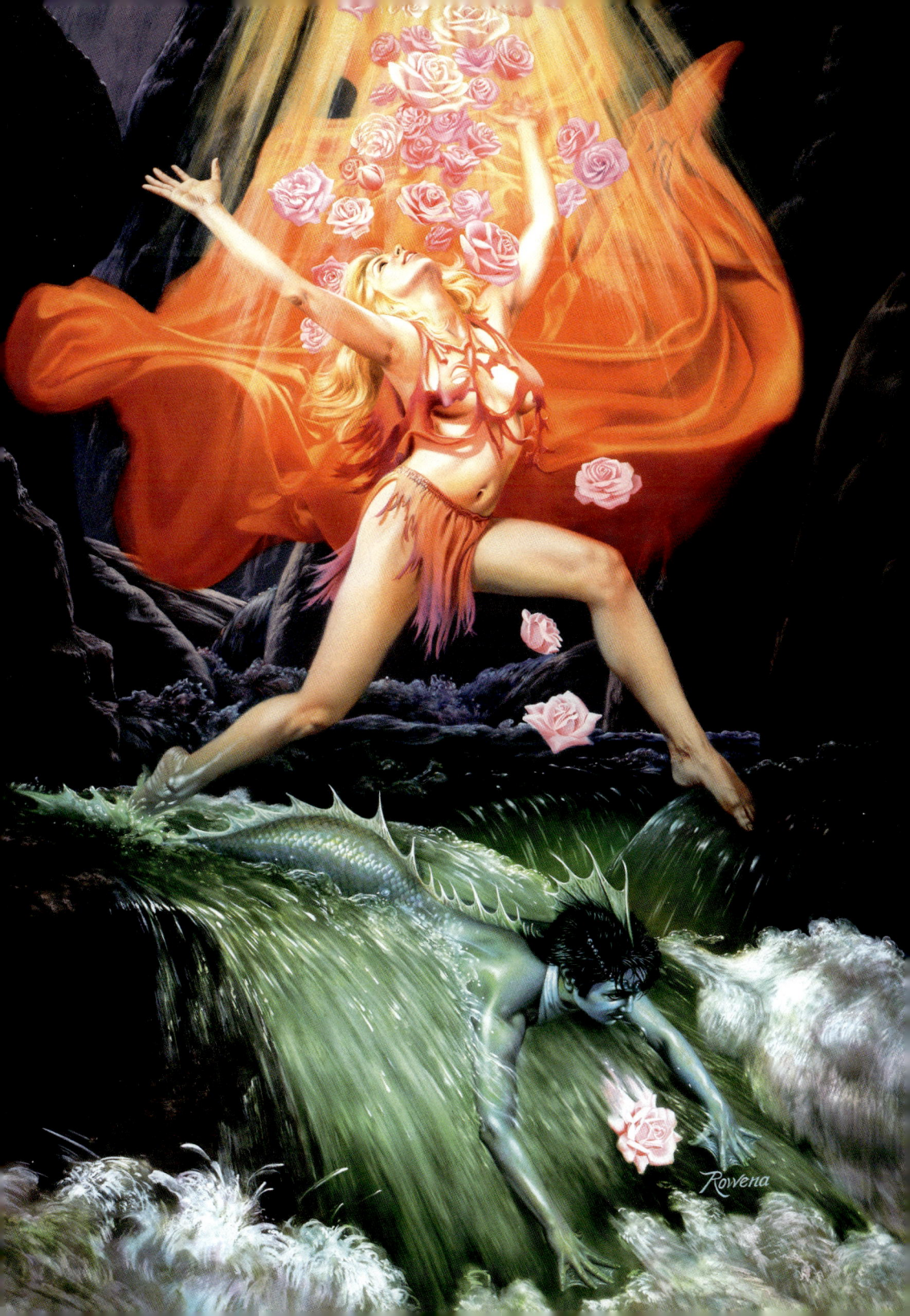

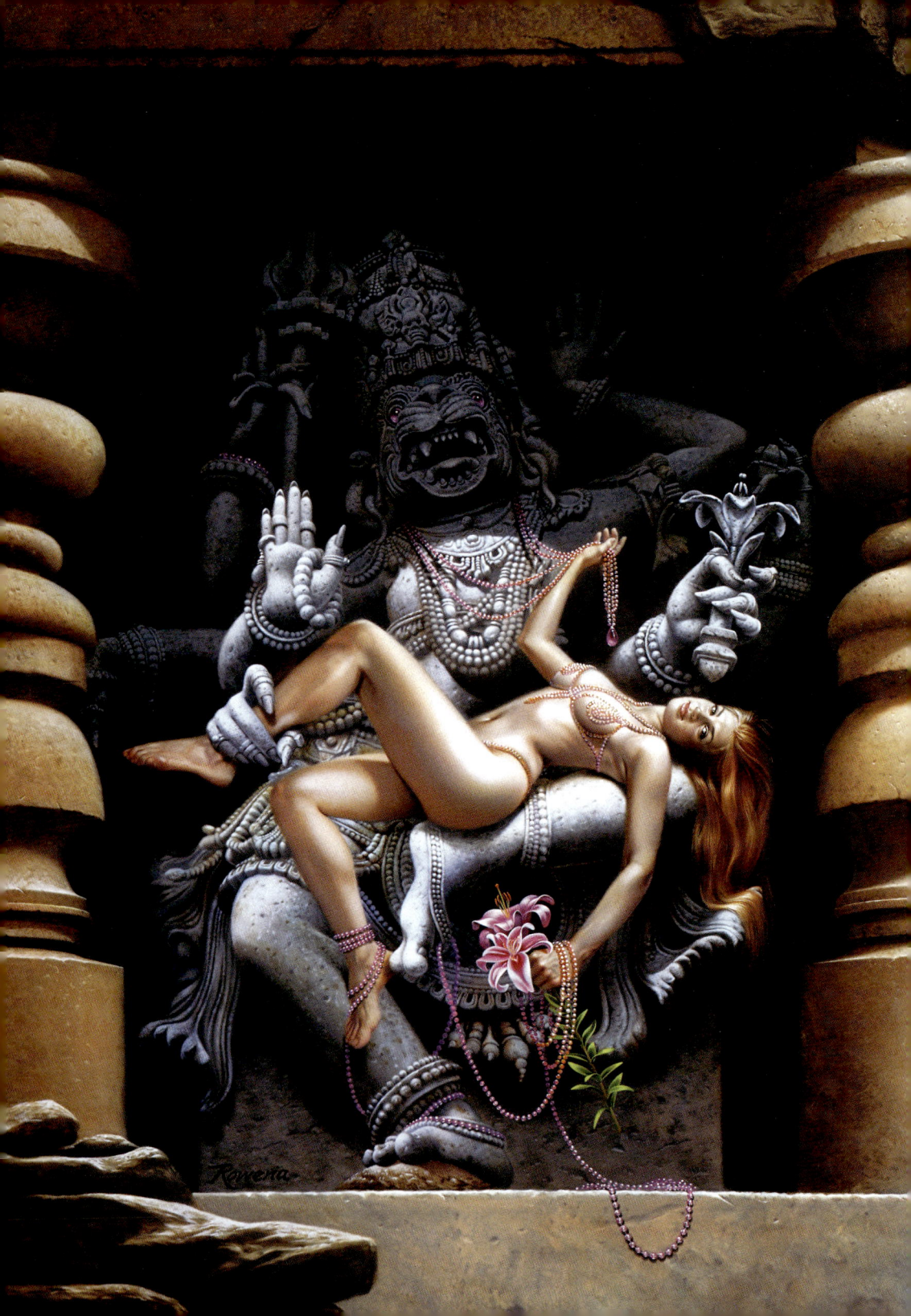

ROWENA MORRILL
LA PIONNIÈRE

« Je trouve que la dynamique homme/
femme du fantasy art est géniale.
C'est ce que les gens adorent voir. »

Rowena Morrill est une rareté parmi les artistes de
fantasy : une femme talentueuse dans un milieu masculin.
Quand elle présente pour la première fois son portfolio
à Ace Books au milieu des années 1960, ils lui confient
l'illustration d'un roman à l'eau de rose, « un truc avec une
infirmière ». Elle n'est pas du tout inspirée par le sujet, mais
heureusement Ace regarde de plus près les échantillons
de son travail et, constatant son goût pour les silhouettes
humaines, lui propose d'illustrer un livre fantasy. Sa carrière
est lancée.

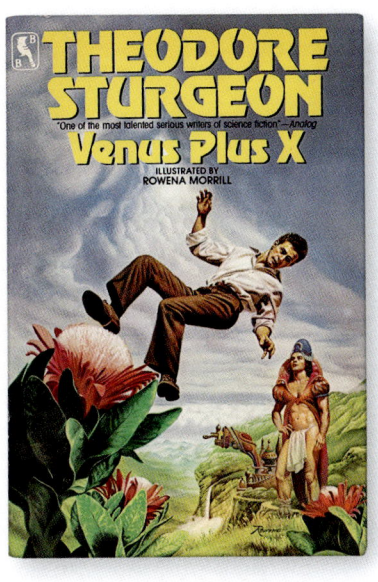

« J'ai téléphoné à Ace parce qu'ils étaient les premiers
dans l'annuaire », raconte-t-elle en riant. L'anecdote est
typique de la façon dont Morrill aborde la vie : aller au
plus simple, au plus spontané. Cet appel à Ace coïncide
avec son déménagement de Philadelphie à New York
City après qu'elle a été recalée par la Tyler School of Art
de la Temple University. Elle voulait passer une maîtrise
afin d'enseigner l'art, non par passion pour la pédagogie,
mais parce qu'elle se disait que ce serait une carrière
facile. Elle a d'ailleurs commencé le dessin parce que cela semblait facile, après des études de
musique entreprises pour la même raison. Cette attitude je-m'en-foutiste résulte sans doute de son
enfance chaotique.

Rowena Morrill naît dans le Mississippi, dans une ville dont elle a oublié le nom, en 1944.
Elle quitte ce premier foyer à tout juste six semaines : son père est aumônier dans l'armée et la
famille déménage très souvent ; contrairement à beaucoup d'enfants de militaires, elle aime cette
vie nomade. « J'étais impatiente d'arriver dans l'endroit suivant. Nous avons vécu au Japon quand
j'avais cinq ans. J'avais trois domestiques, qui m'ont appris l'origami et le dessin. » La famille
retourne aux États-Unis quand elle a neuf ans, puis part pour l'Italie quand elle en a 13. Elle y
découvre l'art classique, bien qu'elle ne s'y intéresse pas particulièrement. Elle termine le lycée aux
États-Unis, étudie le piano à l'université de Puget Sound, au sud de Seattle, et se marie dès qu'elle
a obtenu son diplôme. Nous sommes au milieu des années 1960, elle devient femme au foyer,
l'espace d'une minute ou deux, s'ennuie ferme et quitte son époux pour entrer à l'école d'art.

Opposite: Stone Demon, for the cover
of *The Art of Rowena*, acrylic on board, 2000.

Above: Venus Plus X, the 1984 trade paperback by
Theodore Sturgeon, illustrated by Morrill.

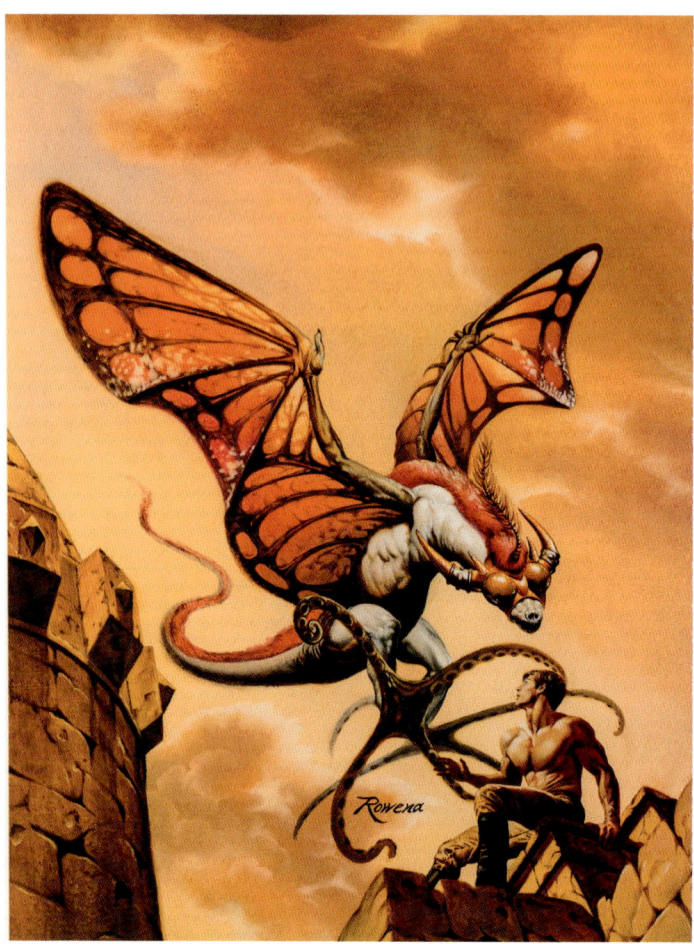

Elle débarque à New York, capitale de l'édition, où la chance veut qu'elle ait une sœur à laquelle elle peut s'imposer, et qui dispose d'un annuaire. Elle l'ouvre à P comme « Publishers ». En cette époque bénie, il suffisait d'entrer quelque part pour se voir confier une commande, et une fois l'histoire de l'infirmière écartée, elle décroche un roman fantasy intitulé *Isobel*, pour lequel elle peint une femme nue agenouillée devant le diable.

Ils n'essaieront plus de lui fourguer de l'eau de rose.

Morrill a trouvé sa niche et passe les 30 années suivantes à peindre des centaines de couvertures de livres de poche pour des auteurs comme Theodore Sturgeon, H.P. Lovecraft, Anne McCaffrey et Philip K. Dick, ainsi que des illustrations pour divers magazines dont *Playboy*, *Heavy Metal* et le merveilleux *Omni* de Bob Guccione. Elle vit dans le très chic Upper West Side de Manhattan, s'est mariée deux fois de plus et a eu un fils. Elle a eu beau aimer sa vie et sa carrière, elle n'a jamais été conquise par la fiction fantasy qu'elle illustrait.

« Je trouvais ces livres vraiment atroces, même ceux de Lovecraft. Je les feuilletais rapidement pour trouver une idée. » L'idée implique en général une femme sexy, souvent dotée du visage de Morrill. « J'aimais mon visage. Je posais pour moi-même et je demandais à quelqu'un de me photographier. » Le reste du temps, elle utilise un studio photo new-yorkais fréquenté par d'autres illustrateurs, Robert Osonitsch Limited. Osonitsch, toujours aux affaires, fournit aux artistes en quête de références des décors, des costumes, des mannequins et des services photographiques. « Je l'adorais. Il avait tout, à part le dragon. »

Après tout, chaque artiste fantasy ne doit-il pas trouver son propre dragon intérieur ? Morrill utilise des photos de divers reptiles et tente de créer une bête anatomiquement plausible. Elle adopte la même approche pour créer ses autres créatures fantasy : prendre des morceaux d'animaux existants et les assembler de façon à ce qu'ils fonctionnent ensemble en termes esthétiques et mécaniques.

Elle travaille de préférence l'huile, dont elle apprécie la fluidité. Elle se considère comme une peintre lente, incapable de réaliser plus d'une toile par semaine, et explique avoir besoin d'une peinture qu'elle puisse « barbouiller », qui ne sèche pas trop vite.

Morrill s'est lassée de peindre et a pris sa retraite à la fin des années 1990, mais son nom a refait surface en 2003, à la chute de Saddam Hussein. Les médias ont dans un premier temps rapporté que deux de ses toiles – *Shadows Out of Hell*, qui montre un héros aux tresses blondes sauvant une femme nue tout aussi blonde, et *King Dragon*, où une femme enchaînée est menacée par un lézard volant – ont été retrouvées exposées dans une des propriétés du dictateur. Il s'est avéré qu'il s'agissait de reproductions en très grand format commandées ou acquises par Hussein. La même année, il était révélé que plusieurs œuvres de Morrill avaient été copiées et distribuées sur des tracts de propagande émis par la secte pédophile des Enfants de Dieu. Morrill savoure le tapage à l'abri de son luxueux home new-yorkais, où elle a passé ses derniers journées à jouer avec son Saint-Bernard et à explorer Internet. Elle est décédée 2021, à l'age de soixante-seize.

« J'ai eu une belle carrière et une belle vie ; je me suis toujours contentée de peindre ce que je trouvais excitant, amusant, vivant. Je me suis fait plaisir, et combien de gens peuvent faire ce constat ? »

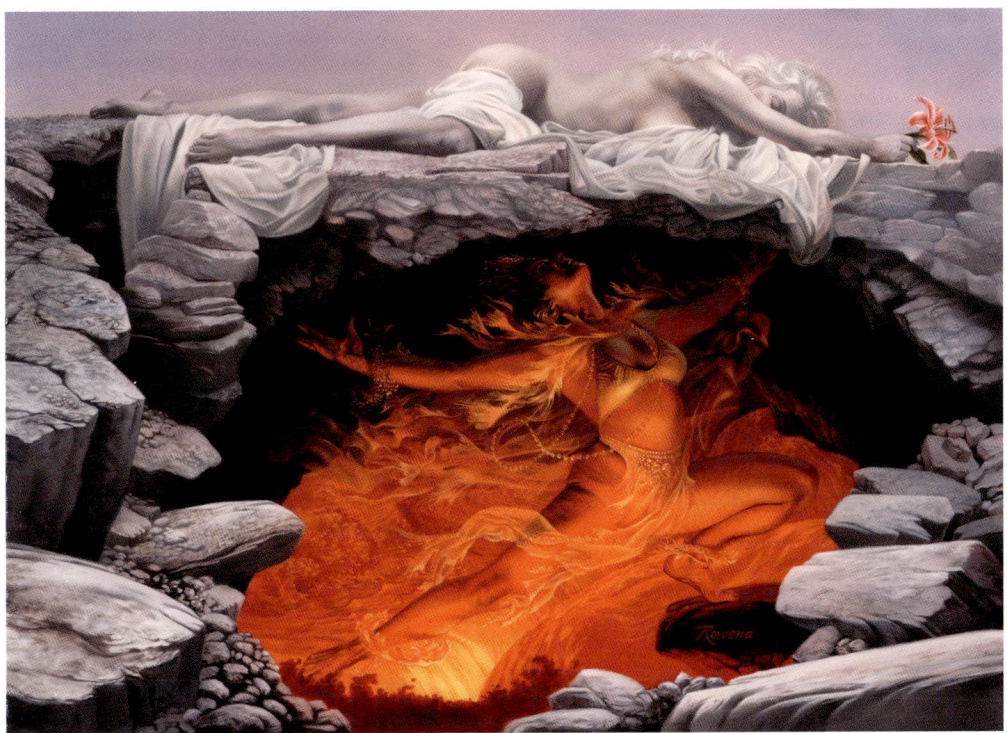

Opposite: The Wrong Place to Sit, for the cover of Clark Ashton Smith's 1981 novel *The City of the Singing Flame.* Oil on board, 1980.

Above: The Lava Pit, oil on canvas, undated.

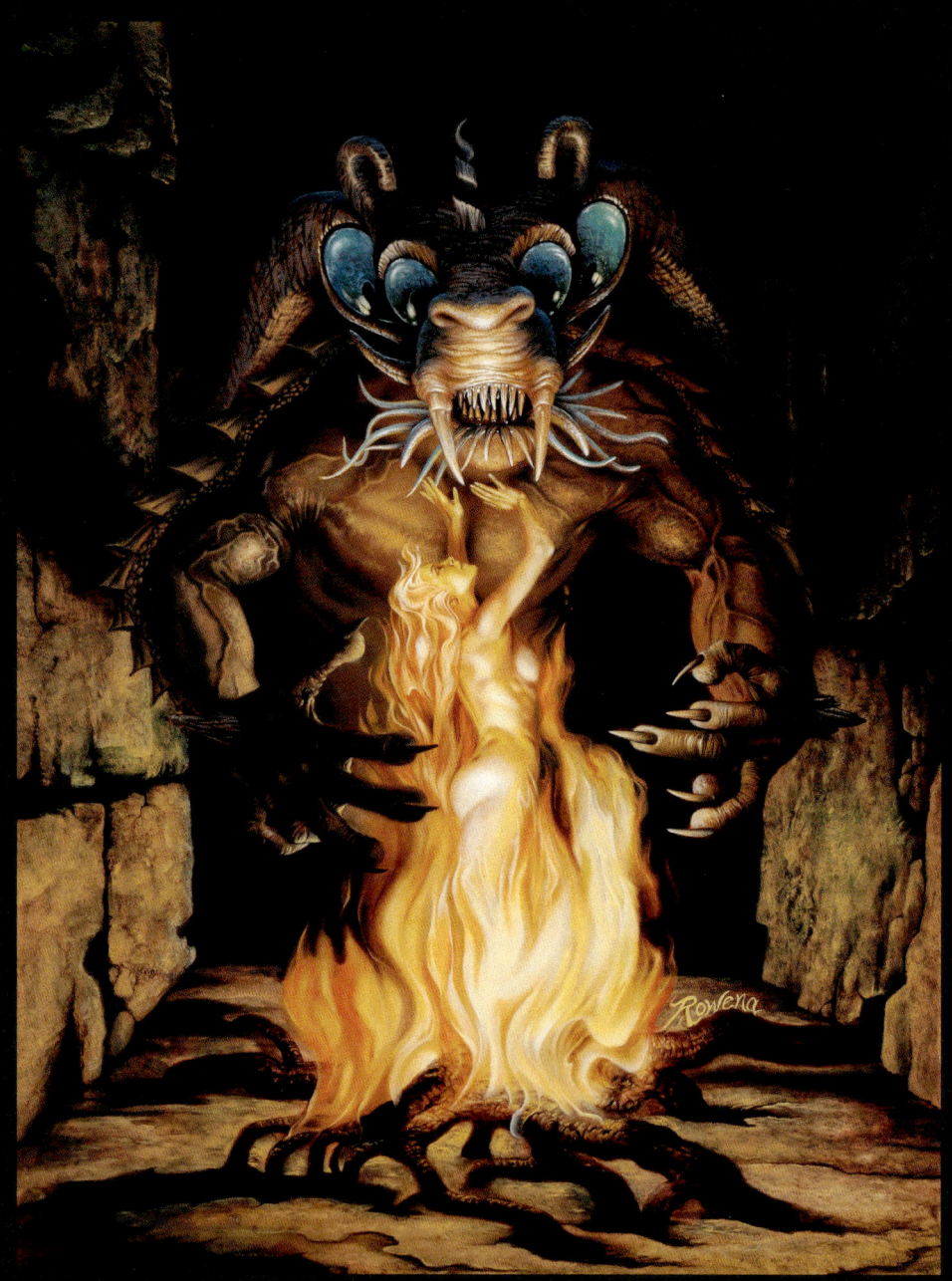

Above: Fiery Vision, commissioned as the display box artwork for *Rowena Fantasy Art Trading Cards*, a 90-card set. Oil on board, 1993, 58.4 x 43.1 cm (23 x 17 inches).

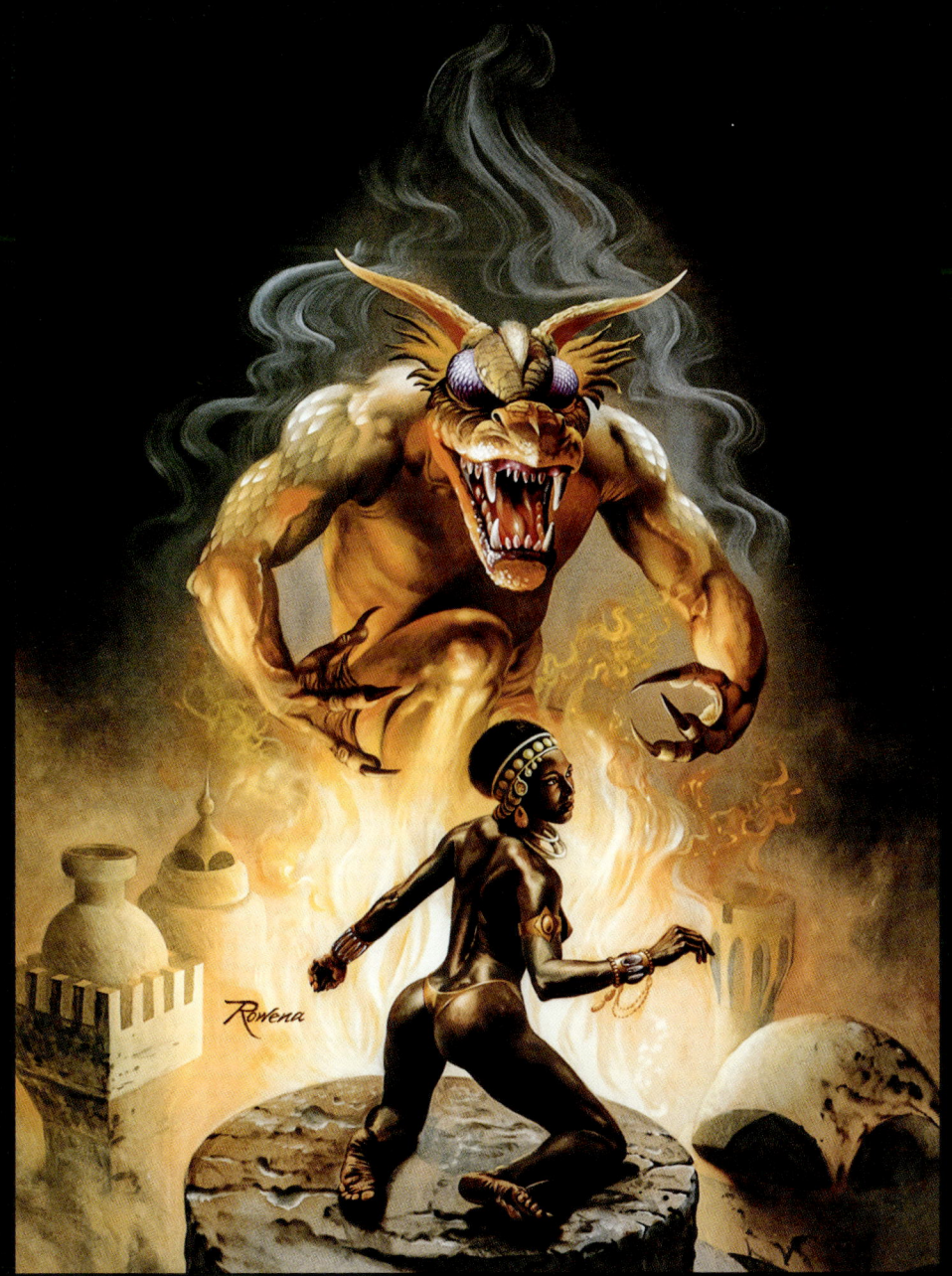

Above: Golem, for the cover of Alfred Bester's 1989 novel *Golem 100*. The published version added panties to the golem's intended victim. The uncensored version appeared as the cover of Morrill's 1985 French monograph *Imagine*. Oil on board.

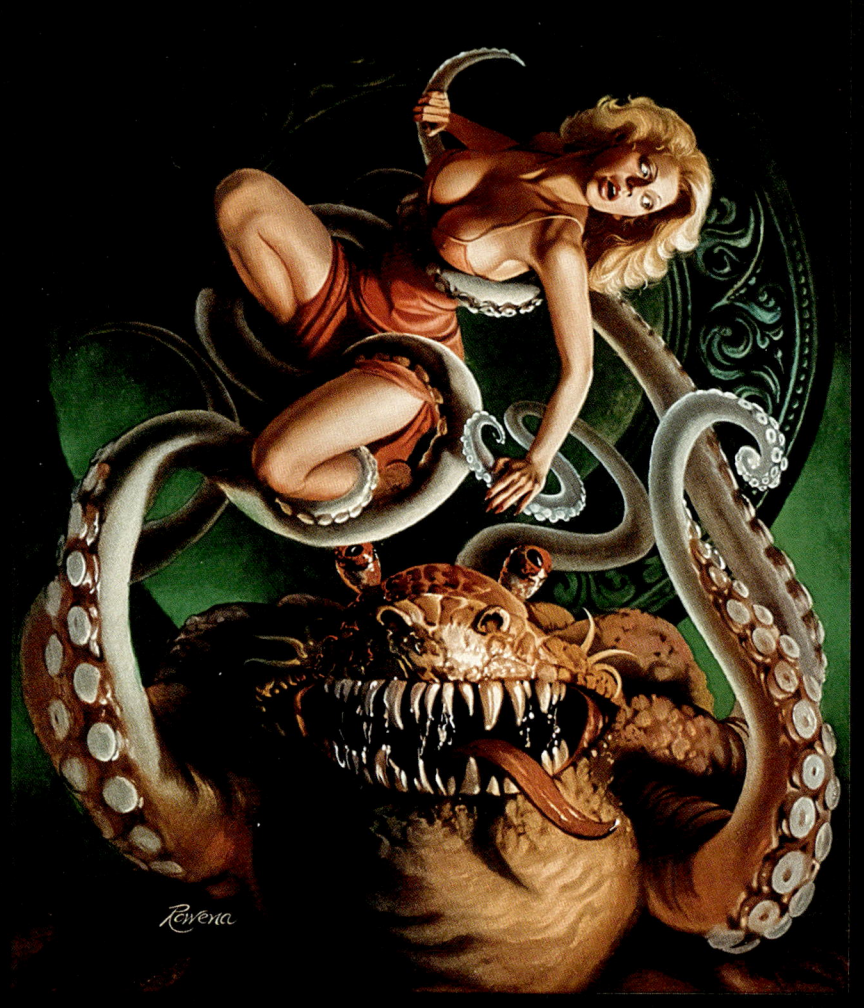

Above: *Entwined and Entangled*, for the cover of the 1978 paperback *Unknown Five*, a compilation of stories by Alfred Bester, Theodore Sturgeon, Isaac Asimov, Cleve Cartmill, and Jane Rice from the 1940s fantasy magazine, *Unknown*. Oil on board, 1977.

Opposite: *The Imps from Under the Rocks*, for *The Fantastic Art of Rowena*, oil on board, 1983.

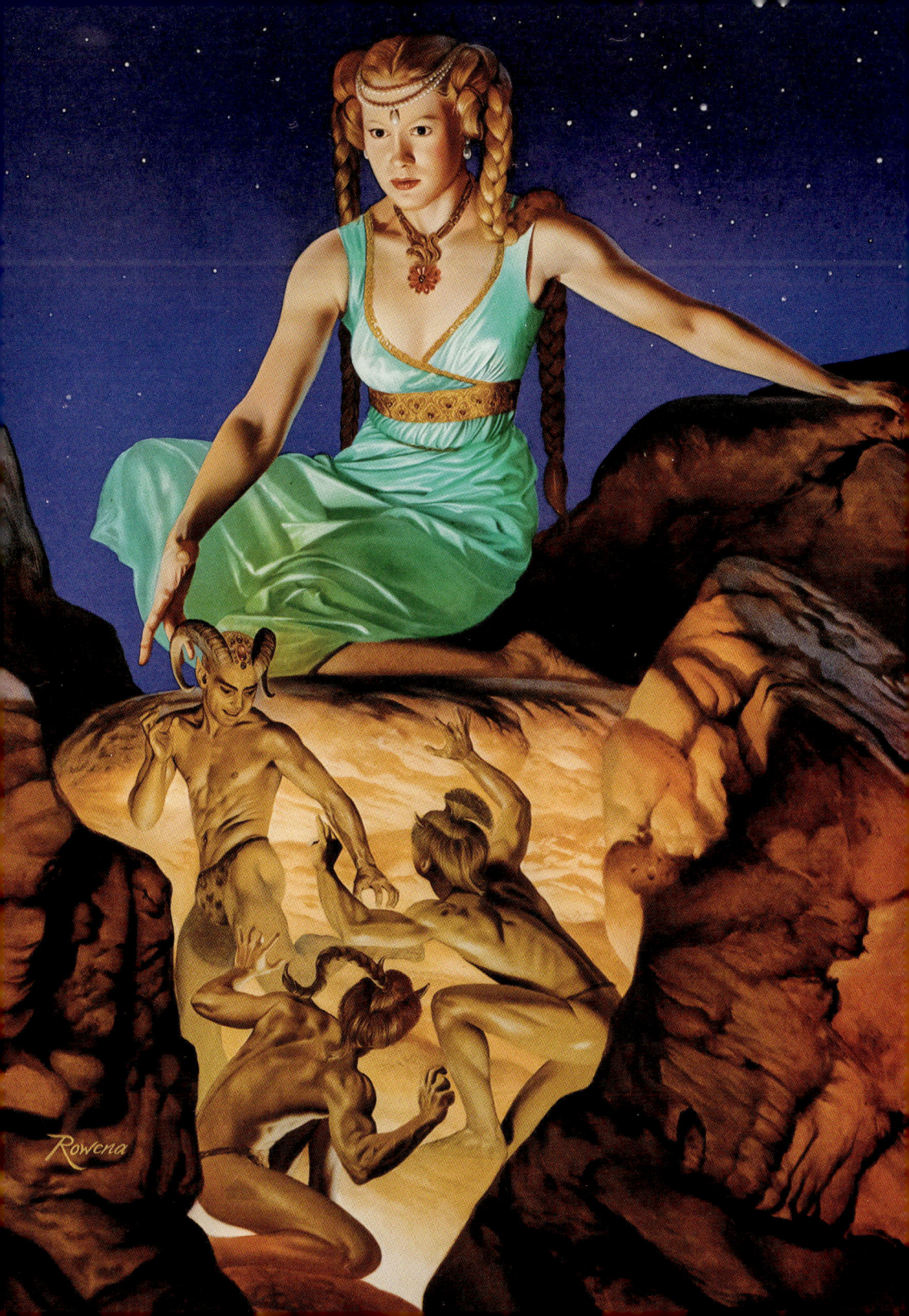

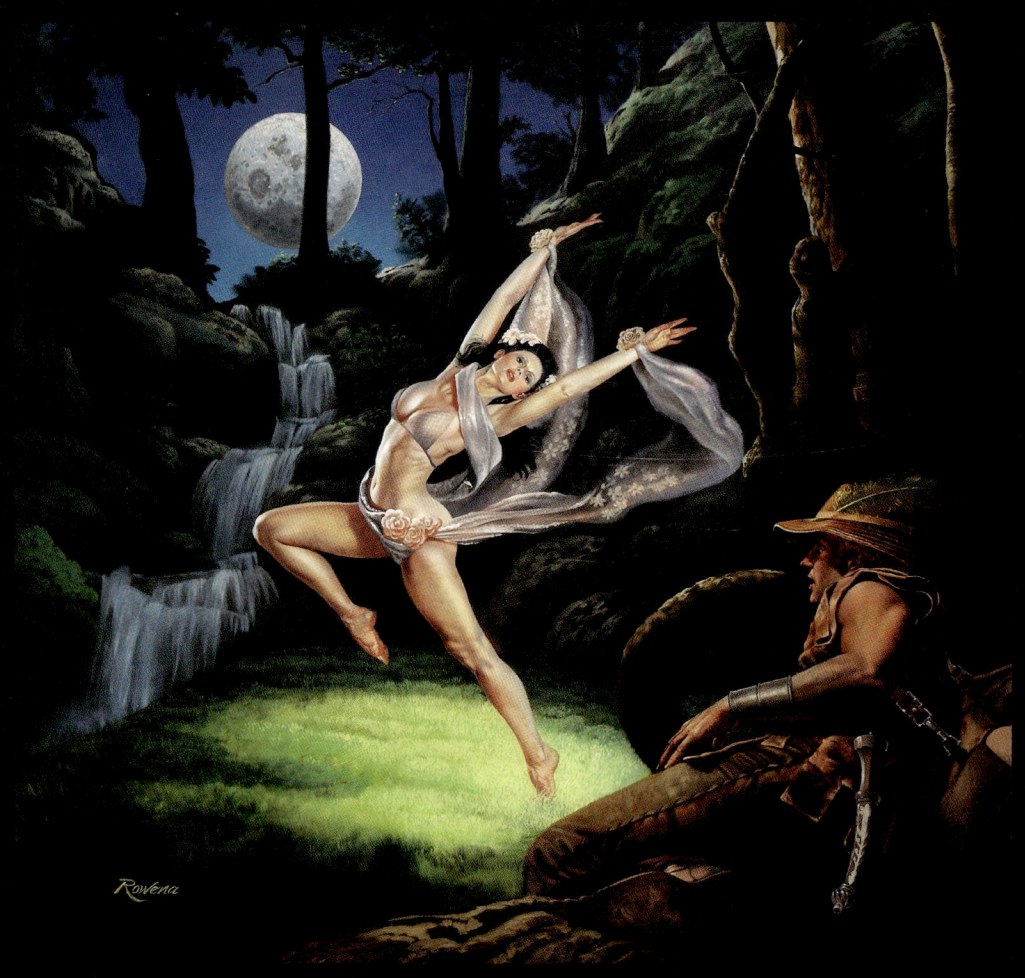

Above: Beren and Luthien, image for February in the *1981 J.R.R. Tolkien Calendar*, from Ballantine Books. Oil on board, 1980, 60.9 x 63.5 cm (24 x 25 inches). Courtesy of Heritage Auctions.

Opposite: Martin Bear & Friends, for the cover of the 1998 children's fantasy book by Thomas Hauser. Acrylic on board, 1997, 60.9 x 47 cm (24 x 18.5 inches). Courtesy of Heritage Auctions.

Following left: Flame Goddess, cover art for *The Fantastic Art of Rowena Morrill*. Oil on board, 1983, 66 x 39.4 cm (26 x 15.5 inches). Courtesy of Heritage Auctions.

Following right: Carried Away, preliminary sketch for the cover of Jack Williamson's 1980 novel *Three From the Legion*. Pencil on board, 36.8 x 22.2 cm (14.5 x 8.75 inches). Courtesy of Heritage Auctions.

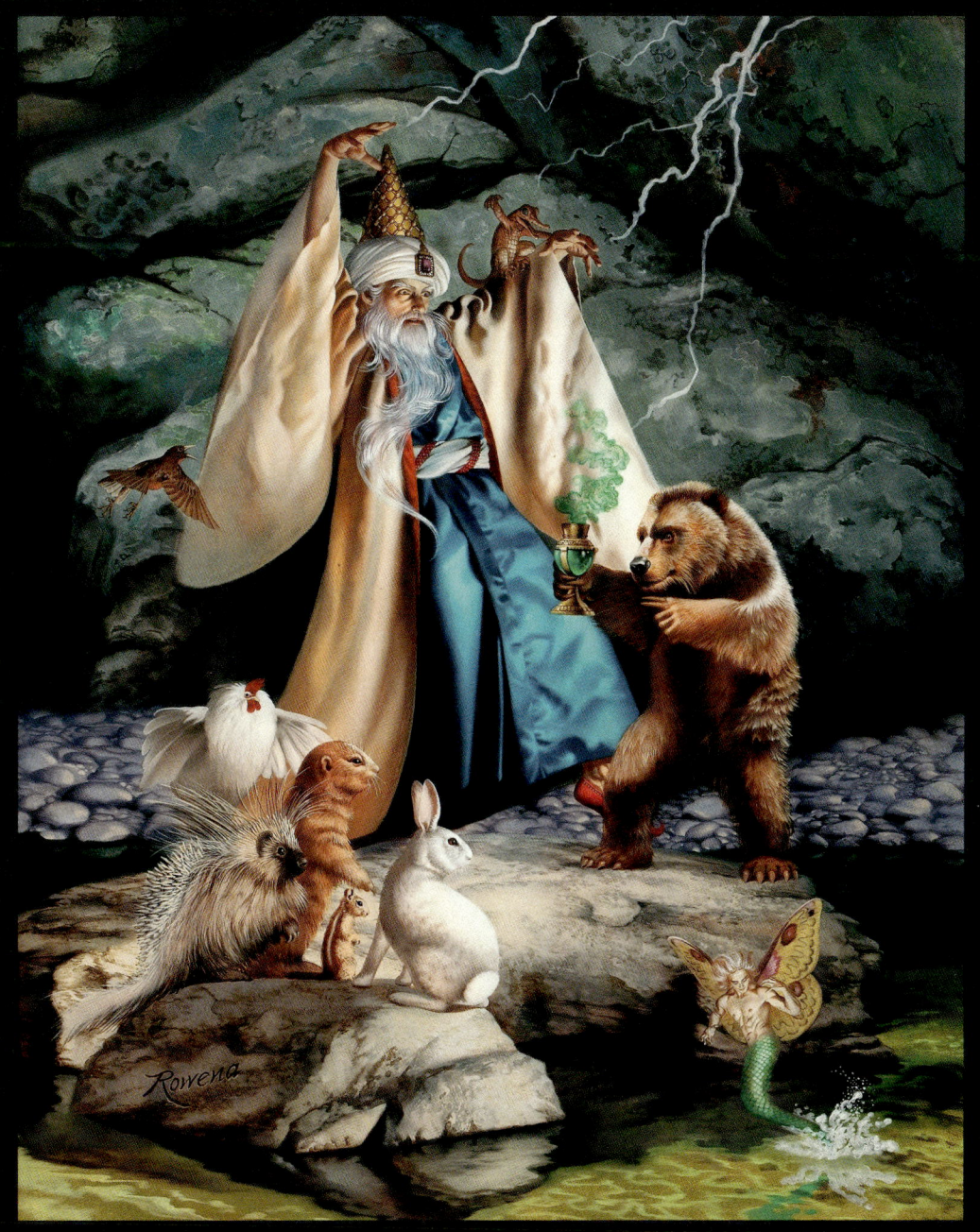

ROWENA MORRILL

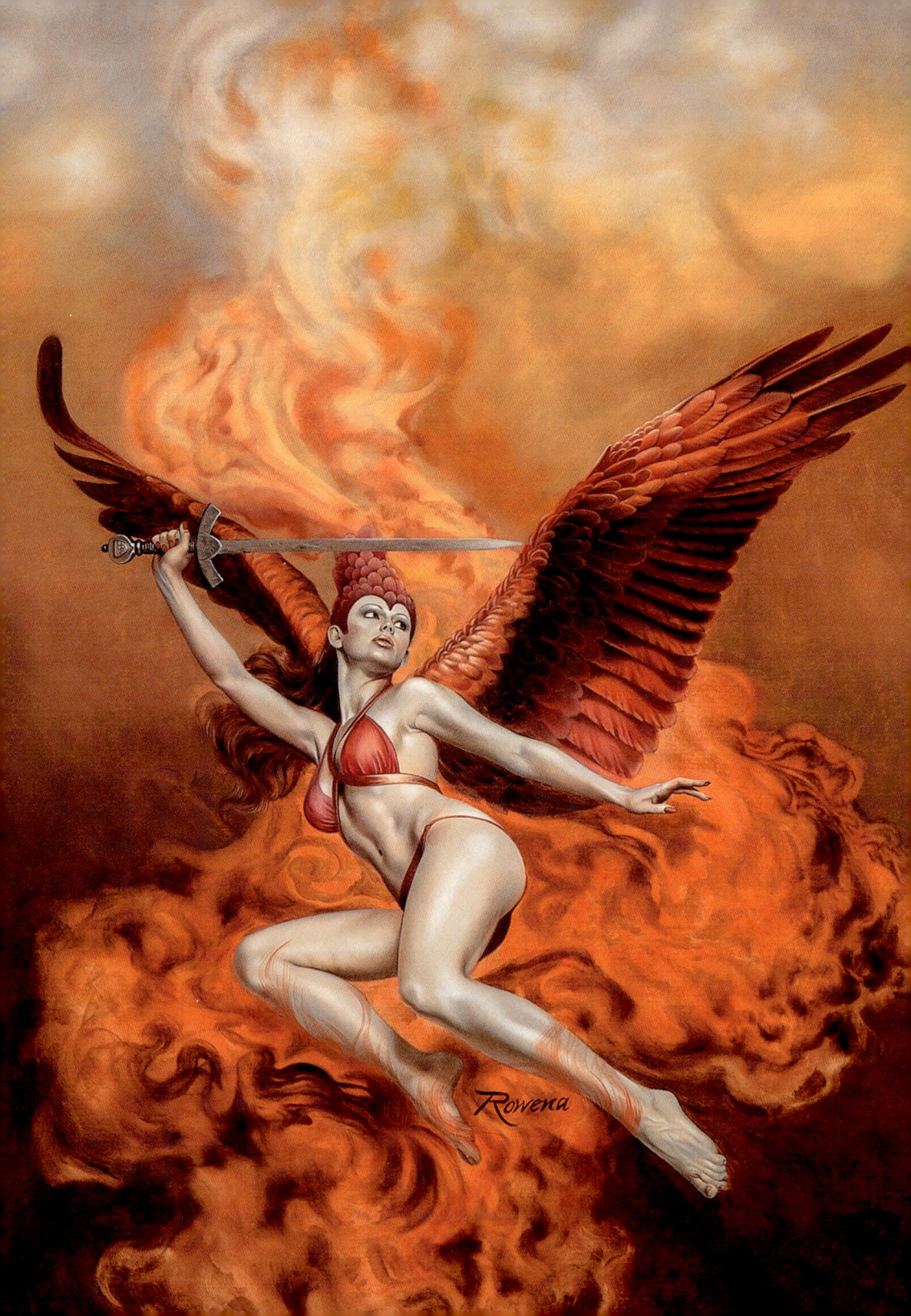

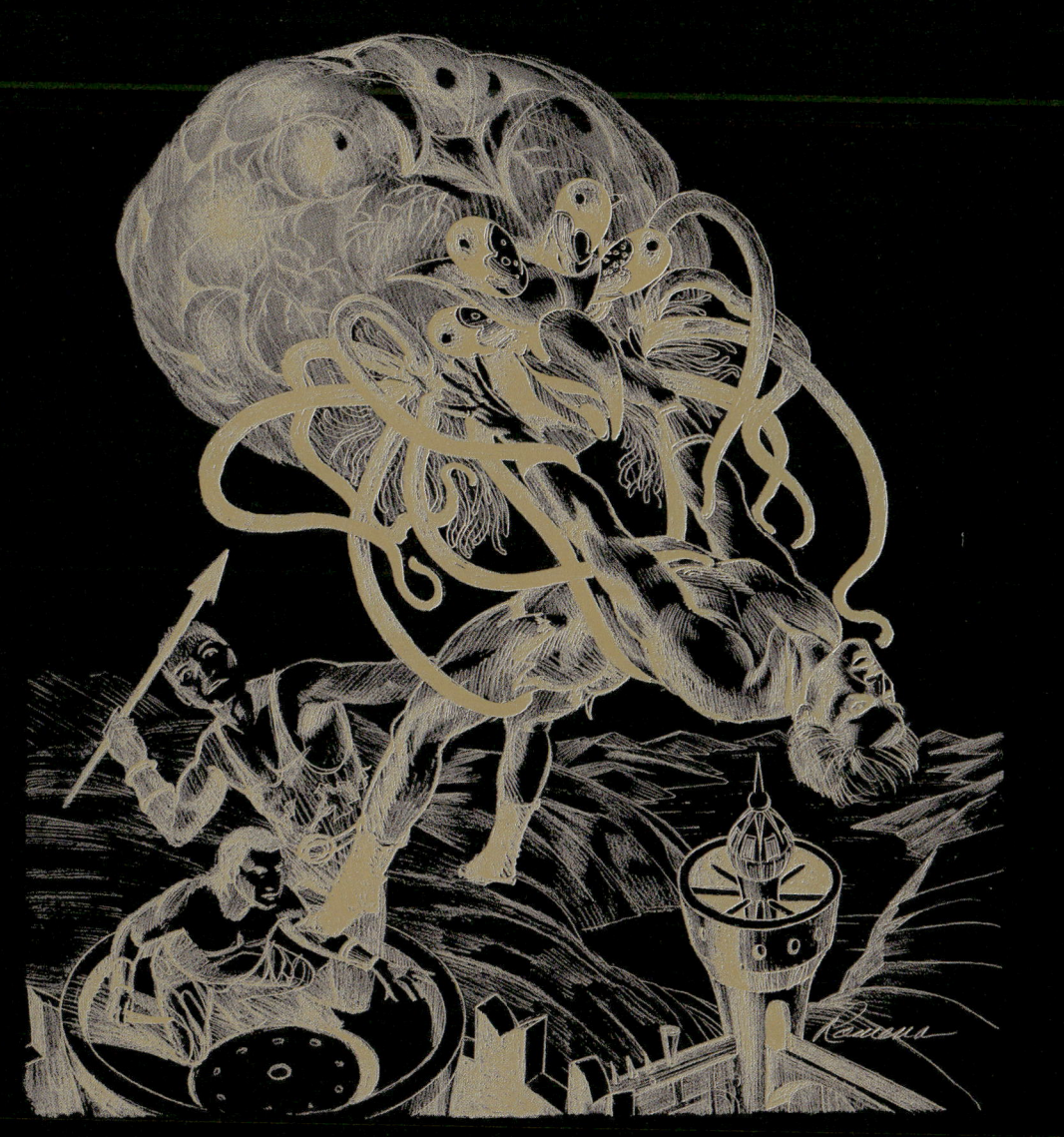

SANJULIAN

Sanjulian

1941-

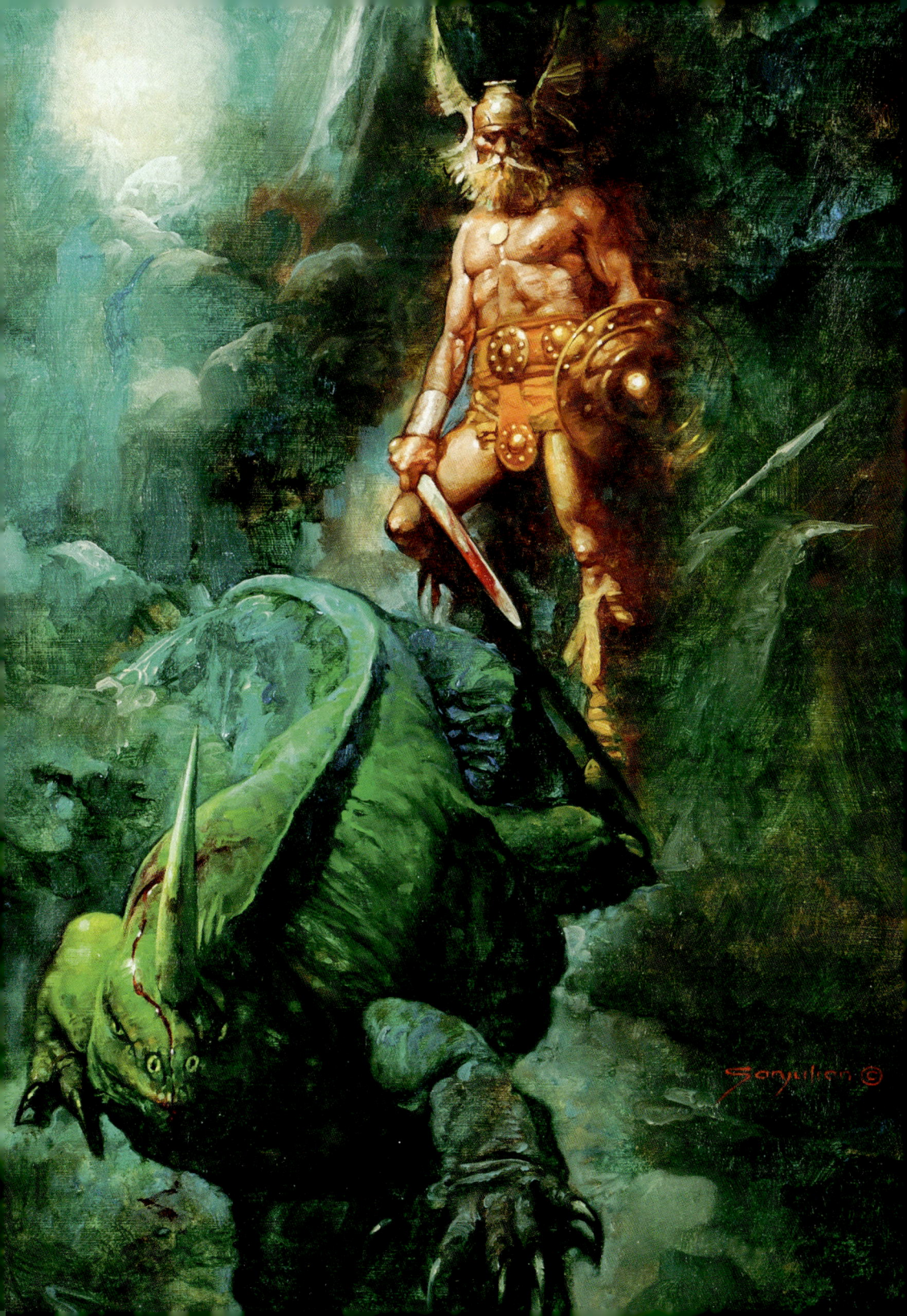

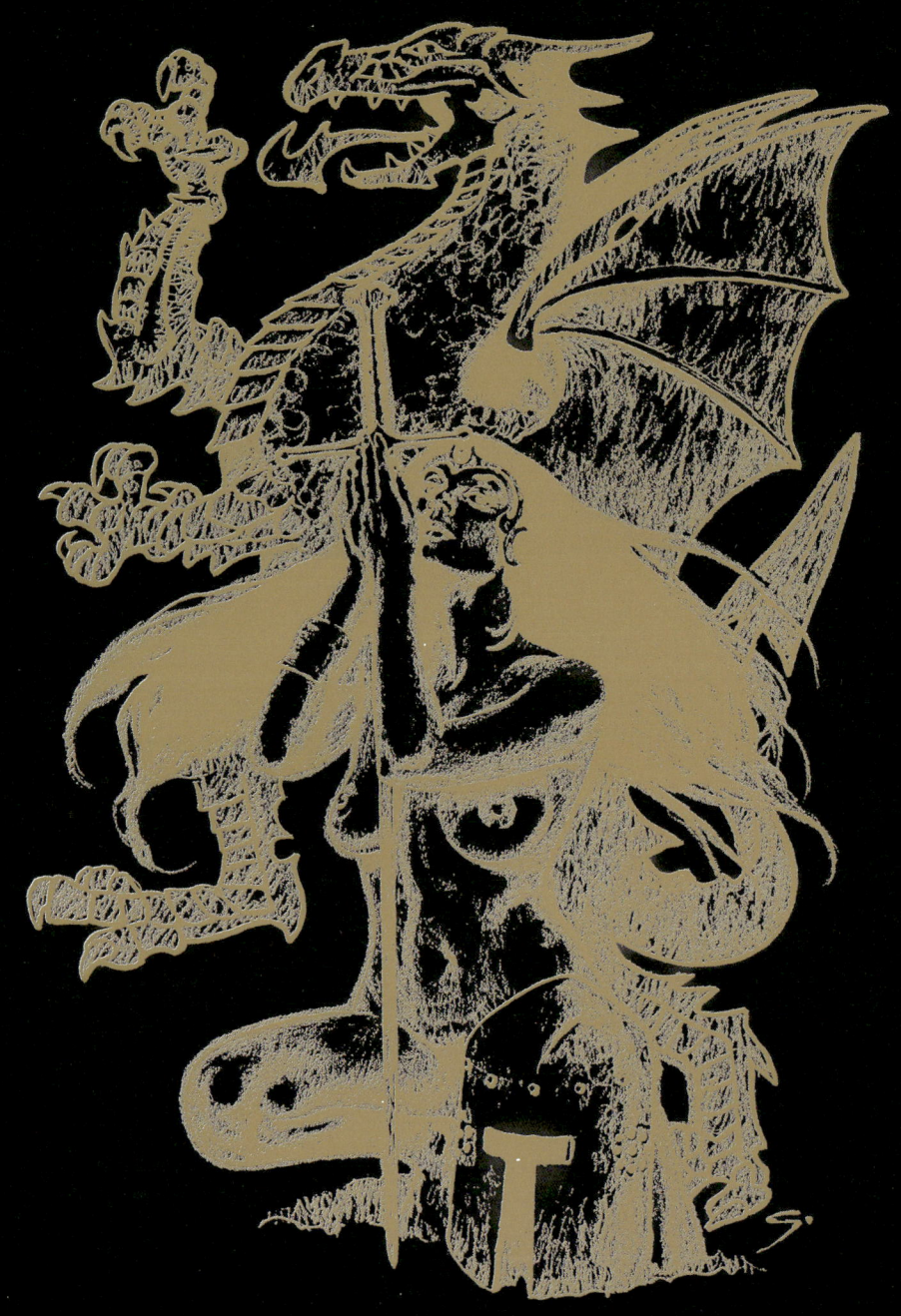

SANJULIAN
THE CLASSICIST

"I spontaneously drew everything I saw; art was always my true vocation."

In 1971 dapper, handsome Josep Toutain, owner of Selecciones Ilustradas artists' agency in Barcelona, Spain, dropped unannounced into the offices of Warren Publishing in New York. Jim Warren remembers it was 4:00 in the afternoon and he had a date at 4:30, but when Toutain opened his portfolio and began showing his artists' work to the publisher of *Creepy*, *Eerie*, and *Vampirella* magazines Warren forgot all about the girl, caring only for the exquisite art before him.

"I'm looking at page after page of this incredible art, in a style that was best described as 'European,'" Warren told Jon B. Cook in a 1999 interview. "The company entered a new phase and a new level. It was the era of the Barcelona artists."

One of the artists presented to Warren that day was Manuel Pérez-Sanjulian Clemente, and he immediately received work on the Warren magazines, starting with the enviable assignment of revamping *Vampirella*. There'd been 11 previous covers for the title, done by Frank Frazetta, Bill Hughes, Vaughn Bode, Ken Kelly, Jeff Jones, and others, with just as many visions of the character.

Sanjulian created a sophisticated, contemporary vixen with a commanding gaze, essentially rebranding Vampirella for all future artists. He would do 22 covers in total, beginning with numbers 12 through 16, his very first fantasy work. Prior to Toutain's visit to Warren, Selecciones Ilustradas represented the artist for comics and book cover work in Europe, starting in 1961, while he was still a student at the Reial Acadèmia Catalana de Belles Arts de Sant Jordi in Barcelona.

Sanjulian, as he has been known throughout his career, was born in Barcelona in 1941, two years after the Spanish Civil War ended and in the midst of World War II. His father was a Navy man in the war and a merchant marine commander after, so Sanjulian assumed he would go to sea in the family tradition. At the same time he was drawing constantly, inspired by his favorite book, *Treasure Island*, and by the African adventure stories of H. Rider Haggard (*King Solomon's Mines*, etc.), though never with any sense that this could lead to a career. Only after enrolling in Barcelona's nautical school at age 18 did he realize he could never be happy as a sailor. His parents were disappointed but would not stand in the way of his determination and clear talent. They allowed him to switch over to the Royal Academy, where he completed a four-year course in drawing and painting.

Ten years of illustration commissions followed, mostly for clients in England and Scandinavia. Like Mœbius, he was fascinated with cowboys and the American West, so these cover commissions were his favorites. When Toutain proposed approaching the American market he quickly worked up samples, hoping for more in this genre, not realizing that Americans were turning away from

Previous right: Valley of the Dragons, oil on canvas, undated, 52 x 39.3 cm (20.5 x 15.5 inches). Courtesy of Heritage Auctions.

Opposite: Lady Warrior with Dragon, pencil on paper, undated, 36.1 x 27.9 cm (14.25 x 11 inches).

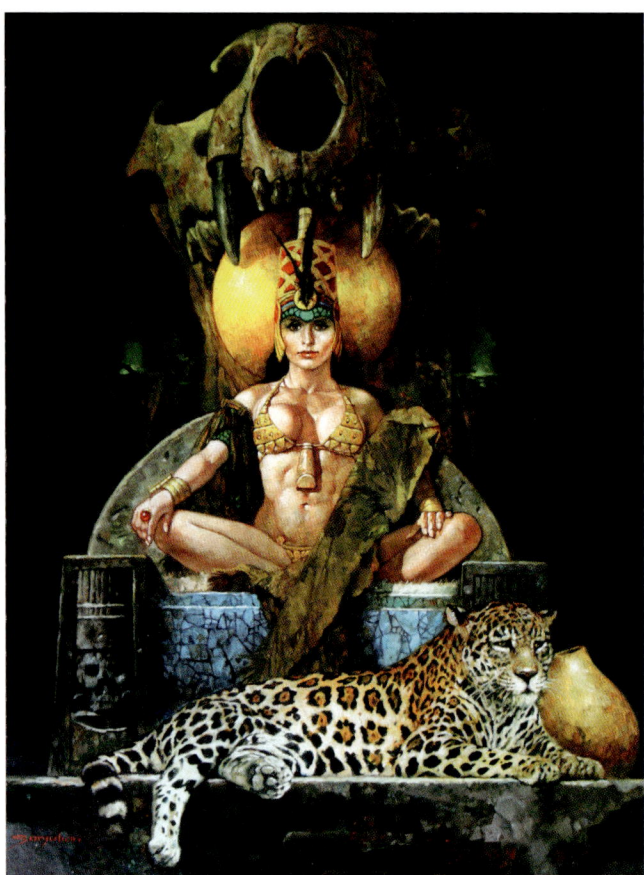

the old West by 1970. His work with Warren firmly fixed him as a fantasy artist, and after a few years the paperback cover market also opened up. He'd become infatuated with Conan—"I knew I could present a fantastic result; it attracted me immediately"—and he finally got his chance in 1978 with *Conan and the Sorcerer* for Ace Books, followed by *The Blade of Conan* (1979), *The Treasure of Tranicos* (1980), *Conan the Mercenary* (1981), and *The Flame Knife* (1981). More than 50 covers for fantasy subjects followed, from DAW, Dell, and Bantam, as well as Ace. And in Spain the American paychecks went far, so far that Sanjulian was able to buy a home on the southern coast, surrounded by gardens for "maximum tranquility and my beloved sea always close," a sea he loved even more when he didn't have to ply it as a sailor. He married and raised two sons, and continues to paint in oils, as he always has, but is also embracing computer illustration. "It is the means of current expression and is the future, so I see no problem in using it effectively."

His newer works are not limited to fantasy—he especially enjoys historical themes—but he admits that fantasy "will always have a preferential place," as the art form that made his name, launched his career, bought his home, raised his sons and, maybe most important, saved him from the briny deep.

Above: Priestess with Jaguar, oil on board.

Opposite: Ghita of Alizarr, reproduced as card No. 6 in *The Sanjulian Collection* trading cards. Oil on board, circa 1985, 47 x 34.9 cm (18.5 x 13.75 inches.). Courtesy of Heritage Auctions.

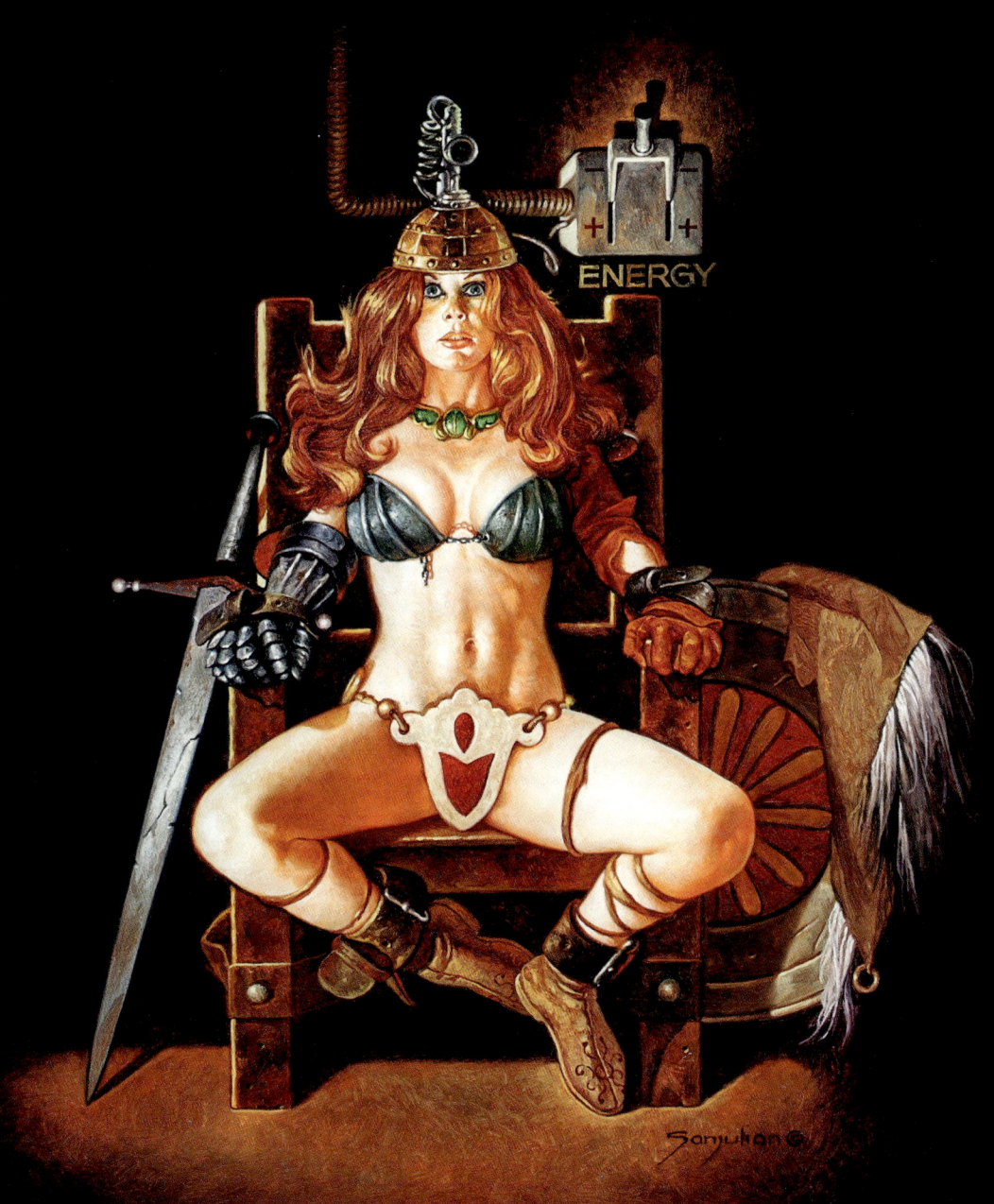

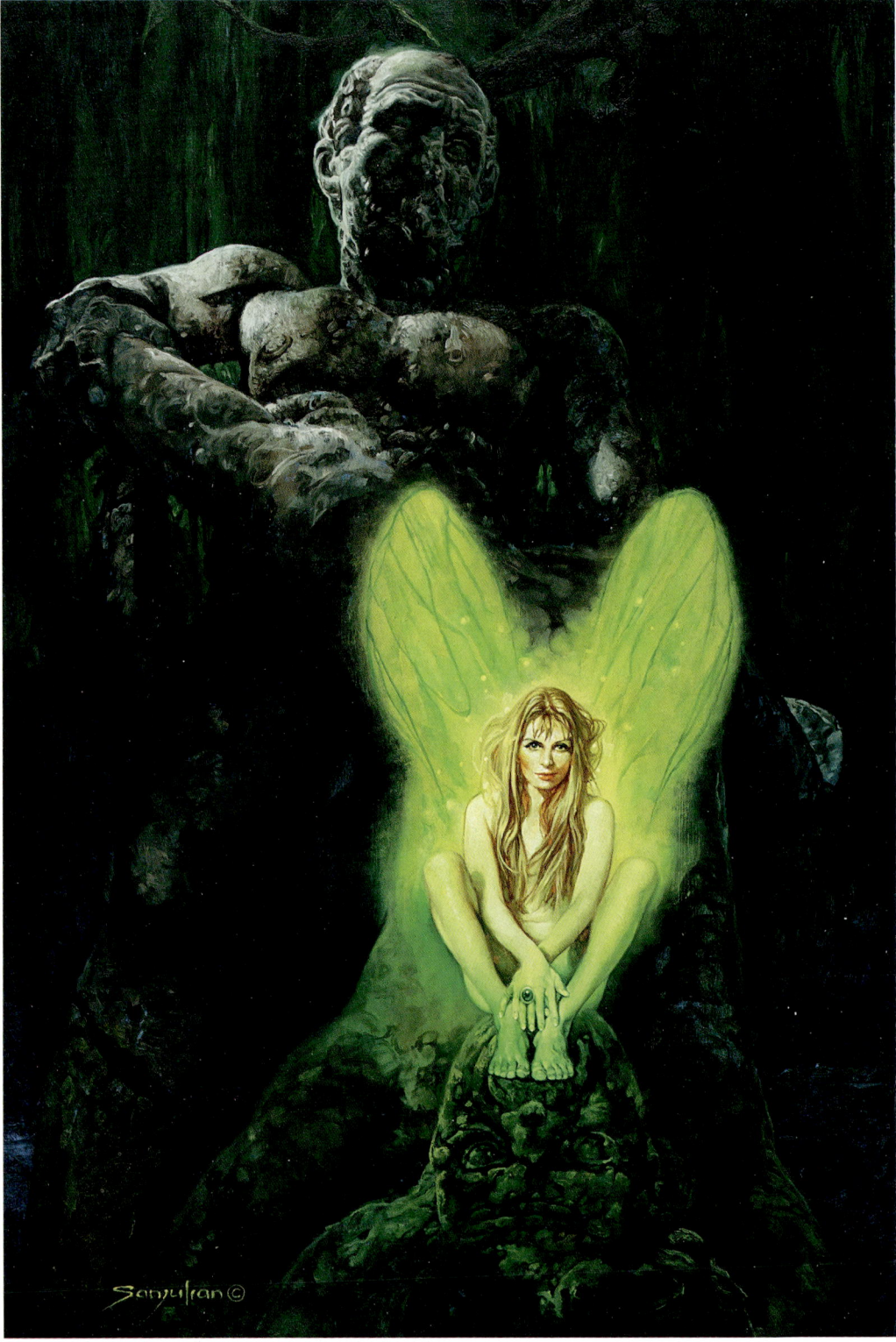

SANJULIAN
DER KLASSIZIST

„Spontan habe ich alles gezeichnet, was ich sah; Kunst war schon immer meine wahre Berufung."

1971 schneite ein eleganter, gut aussehender Josep Toutain, Betreiber der Künstleragentur Selecciones Ilustradas in Barcelona, Spanien, unangekündigt in die Büros von Warren Publishing, New York herein. Jim Warren erinnert sich noch, dass es vier Uhr nachmittags war und er um 16.30 Uhr eigentlich ein Rendezvous hatte, doch als Toutain sein Portfolio öffnete und dem Verleger der Zeitschriften *Creepy*, *Eerie* und *Vampirella* die Arbeiten seiner Künstler zu zeigen begann, vergaß Warren das Mädel und hatte nur noch Augen für die exquisite Kunst, die da vor ihm lag.

„Ich schaute mir Seite für Seite dieser unglaublichen Kunst an, die in einem Stil gehalten war, den man am besten als ‚europäisch' bezeichnen könnte", erklärte Warren 1999 Jon B. Cook in einem Interview. „Der Verlag trat nun eine neue Phase ein und erreichte auch ein anderes Niveau. Es war die Ära der Barcelona-Künstler."

Einer der Künstler, dessen Werke Warren an jenem Tag zu sehen bekam, war Manuel Pérez-Sanjulian Clemente, und sofort bekam er Aufträge für die Zeitschriften von Warren, und als Erstes erhielt er die beneidenswerte Aufgabe, *Vampirella* aufzupolieren. Zuvor gab es elf Cover für diesen Titel, gestaltet von Künstlern wie Frank Frazetta, Bill Hughes, Vaughn Bode, Ken Kelly, Jeff Jones und anderen, und damit auch ebenso viele verschiedene Vorstellungen der Figur. Sanjulian schuf das Bild eines raffinierten, zeitgenössischen verführerischen Weibs mit gebieterischem Blick und verlieh damit der Figur eine Prägung, die auch für alle künftigen Künstler verbindlich war. Insgesamt sollte Sanjulian 22 Cover gestalten, beginnend mit den Ausgaben 12 bis 16, seiner allerersten Fantasyarbeit. Vor Toutains Besuch bei Warren vertrat Selecciones Ilustradas den Künstler und verschaffte ihm in Europa bereits seit 1961, als Sanjulian noch an der Königlichen Akademie der Künste San George in Barcelona studierte, Aufträge für Comics und Buchcover.

Sanjulian – unter diesem Namen war er während seiner gesamten Karriere bekannt – wurde 1941, zwei Jahre nach dem Ende des spanischen Bürgerkriegs und mitten in den Wirren des Zweiten Weltkriegs, in Barcelona geboren. Sein Vater war während des Krieges bei der Marine und danach Kapitän bei der Handelsmarine, und so ging Sanjulian davon aus, dass auch er – der Familientradition folgend – zur See fahren würde. Gleichzeitig war er, inspiriert von seinem Lieblingsbuch *Die Schatzinsel* und durch die afrikanischen Abenteuergeschichten von H. Rider Haggard (*King Solomon's Mines* usw.), ständig am Zeichnen, doch kam er nie auf die Idee, dass dies eine berufliche Zukunft für ihn sein könnte. Erst nachdem er sich mit 18 an der Seefahrtsschule in Barcelona eingeschrieben hatte, stellte er fest, dass er als Seemann wohl nie glücklich werden könnte. Seine Eltern reagierten enttäuscht, stellten sich seiner Bestimmung und seinem erkennbaren Talent jedoch nicht in den Weg. Sie erlaubten es ihm, an die Königliche Akademie zu wechseln, wo er eine vierjährige Ausbildung in Zeichnen und Malen absolvierte.

Opposite: Fairy and Golem, oil on canvas, undated, 49.5 x 33 cm (19.5 x 13 inches). Courtesy of Heritage Auctions.

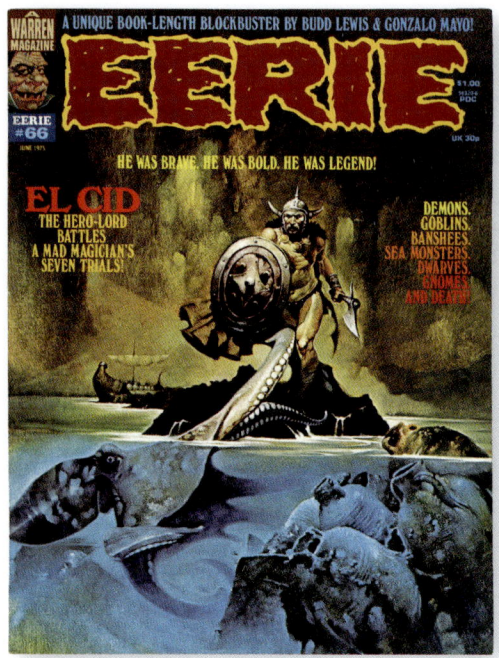

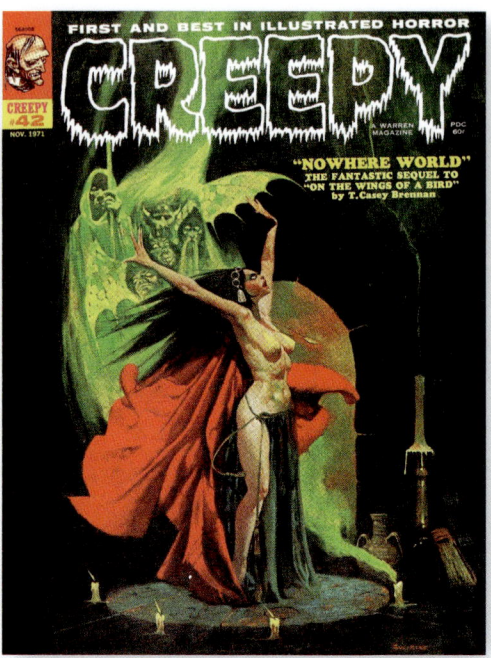

Es folgten zehn Jahre mit Aufträgen für Illustrationen, meist für Kunden in England und in Skandinavien. Wie Mœbius faszinierten ihn Cowboys und der amerikanische Westen, entsprechend waren ihm Coveraufträge mit dieser Thematik am liebsten. Als Toutain vorschlug, den amerikanischen Markt anzugehen, arbeitete er schnell Proben aus und hoffte auf mehr in diesem Genre, ohne zu merken, dass sich die Amerikaner seit 1970 vom alten Westen abwandten. Seine Zusammenarbeit mit Warren legte ihn nachdrücklich als Fantasykünstler fest, und nach ein paar Jahren eröffneten sich ihm auch Möglichkeiten auf dem Markt für Taschenbuchcover. In Conan war er ganz vernarrt – „Ich wusste, dass ich ein fantastisches Ergebnis vorlegen könnte; das Thema zog mich sofort an" –, und schließlich bekam er 1978 mit *Conan and the Sorcerer* für Ace Books seine Chance. Dem folgten *The Blade of Conan* (1979), *The Treasure of Tranicos* (1980), *Conan the Mercenary* (1981) und *The Flame Knife* (1981). In den Jahren danach schuf er, im Auftrag von DAW, Dell und Bantam wie auch für Ace, noch mehr als 50 Cover zu Fantasy-Themen. Und in Spanien kam Sanjulian mit den amerikanischen Honorarschecks ziemlich weit, so weit, dass er sich an der Südküste ein von Gärten umgebenes Haus kaufen konnte, das ihm „maximale Ruhe und mein geliebtes Meer immer ganz nah" bot, ein Meer, das er umso mehr liebte, als er nicht gezwungen war, es als Seemann zu befahren. Er heiratete, zog zwei Söhne groß und malt – wie schon seit jeher – weiterhin in Öl, beschäftigt sich aber auch mit Computerillustrationen. „Das ist heutzutage und in Zukunft das Ausdrucksmittel, ich sehe also kein Problem darin, es auch entsprechend einzusetzen."

Seine neueren Arbeiten sind nicht auf Fantasy beschränkt – vor allem mit historischen Themen beschäftigt er sich gerne –, doch er räumt ein, dass Fantasy als die Kunstform, mit der er bekannt wurde, die seine Karriere beförderte, ihm den Hauskauf und die Ernährung seiner Söhne ermöglichte, für ihn „stets an erster Stelle stehen wird". Noch wichtiger vielleicht: Sie hat ihn vor den Tiefen des Meeres bewahrt.

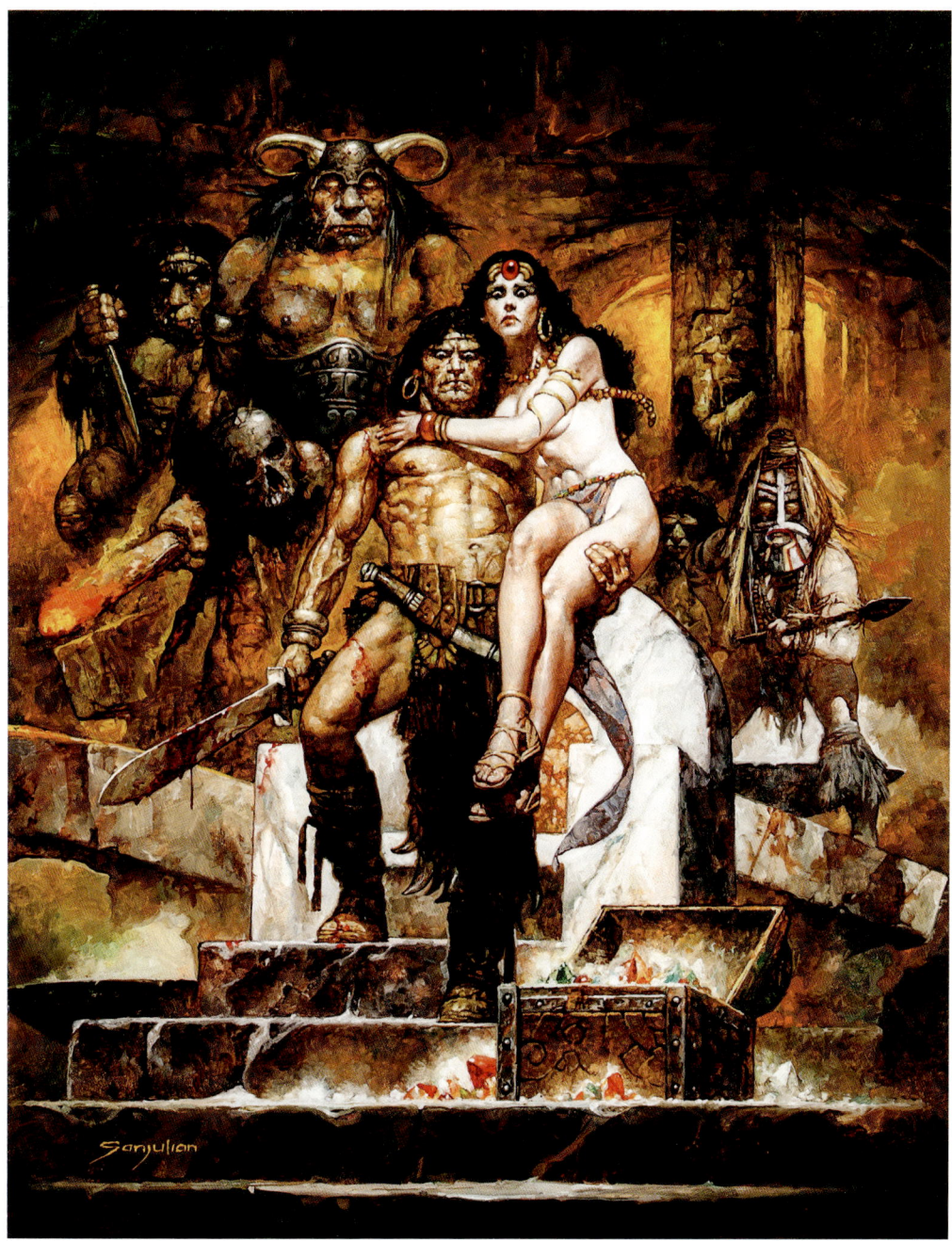

Opposite: Eerie No. 66, 1975, and *Creepy* No. 42, 1971, both with Sanjulian covers.

Above: The Jewels of Gwahlur, illustrating a short story in the Conan saga. Oil on canvas, undated, 69.8 x 54.6 cm (27.5 x 21.5 inches). Courtesy of Heritage Auctions.

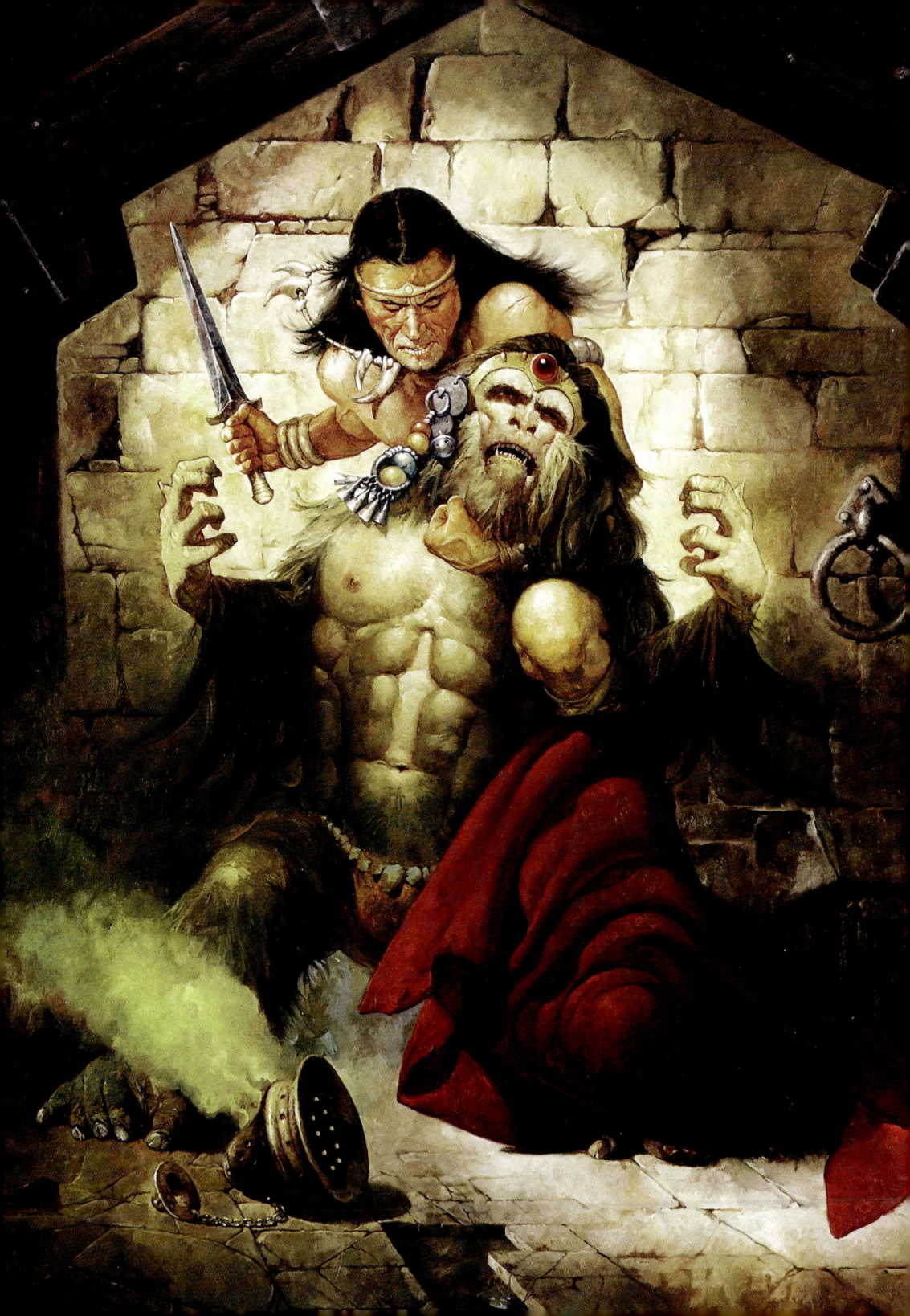

SANJULIAN
LE CLASSICISTE

« Spontanément, je dessinais tout ce que je voyais ; l'art a toujours été ma vraie vocation. »

En 1971, le jeune et fringant Josep Toutain, gérant de l'agence d'artistes Selecciones Ilustradas à Barcelone, en Espagne, débarque sans être annoncé dans les bureaux new-yorkais de Warren Publishing. Jim Warren se souvient encore qu'il était 16 heures et qu'il avait un rendez-vous galant à 16 h 30. Pourtant, quand Toutain ouvre son portfolio et commence à présenter le travail des artistes dont il s'occupe à l'éditeur des magazines *Creepy*, *Eerie* et *Vampirella*, Warren oublie la donzelle tant il est happé par les œuvres superbes qu'il a devant lui.

« Page après page, j'admire des œuvres incroyables, dans un style que je qualifierai "d'européen", expliquait Warren à Jon B. Cook dans une interview de 1999. La maison entrait dans une nouvelle phase et atteignait un nouveau niveau. C'était l'ère des artistes barcelonais. »

Un des artistes présentés à Warren est Manuel Pérez-Sanjulian Clemente, qui se voit immédiatement confier du travail pour les magazines Warren ; sa première mission, fort enviée, consiste à repenser *Vampirella*. Onze couvertures ont déjà été réalisées pour le titre, notamment par Frank Frazetta, Bill Hughes, Vaughn Bode, Ken Kelly et Jeff Jones, qui ont exprimé autant de visions du personnage. Sanjulian imagine une diablesse sophistiquée, contemporaine, impérieuse, qui donne le ton de Vampirella à ses futurs interprètes. Il signera 22 couvertures en tout, à commencer par les numéros 12 à 16, son tout premier travail dans le domaine de la fantasy. Avant la visite de Toutain à Warren, Selecciones Ilustradas représentait l'artiste pour des bandes dessinées et des illustrations de jaquettes en Europe depuis 1961, alors qu'il était encore étudiant à l'Académie royale des Beaux-Arts de San George à Barcelone.

Sanjulian, nom sous lequel il a fait carrière, naît à Barcelone en 1941, deux ans après la fin de la guerre civile et en pleine Seconde Guerre mondiale. Son père sert dans la Marine pendant la guerre puis devient capitaine de la marine marchande, si bien que Sanjulian part du principe qu'il suivra la tradition familiale et sillonnera les mers. Il dessine déjà en permanence, inspiré par son livre préféré, *L'Île au trésor*, et par les aventures africaines de H. Rider Haggard (*Les Mines du roi Salomon*, etc.), sans pour autant se dire qu'il pourrait en faire son métier. Ce n'est qu'après s'être inscrit au centre nautique de Barcelone, à 18 ans, qu'il comprend que la vie de marin ne le rendra pas heureux. Ses parents sont déçus, mais ne se mettent pas en travers de son chemin et de son talent évident. Ils l'autorisent à s'inscrire à la Royal Academy, où il étudie pendant quatre ans le dessin et la peinture.

Dix années d'illustrations sur commande suivent, le plus souvent pour des clients anglais ou scandinaves. Comme Mœbius, il est fasciné par les cowboys et le Grand Ouest américain, et ce sont donc les commandes qu'il préfère. Quand Toutain propose de démarcher les éditeurs

Opposite: Rogues in the House, depicting Conan battling Thak the Apeman, for *The Sword's Edge*, 2010.

Oil on canvas, undated, 124.4 x 91.4 cm (49 x 36 inches). Courtesy of Heritage Auctions.

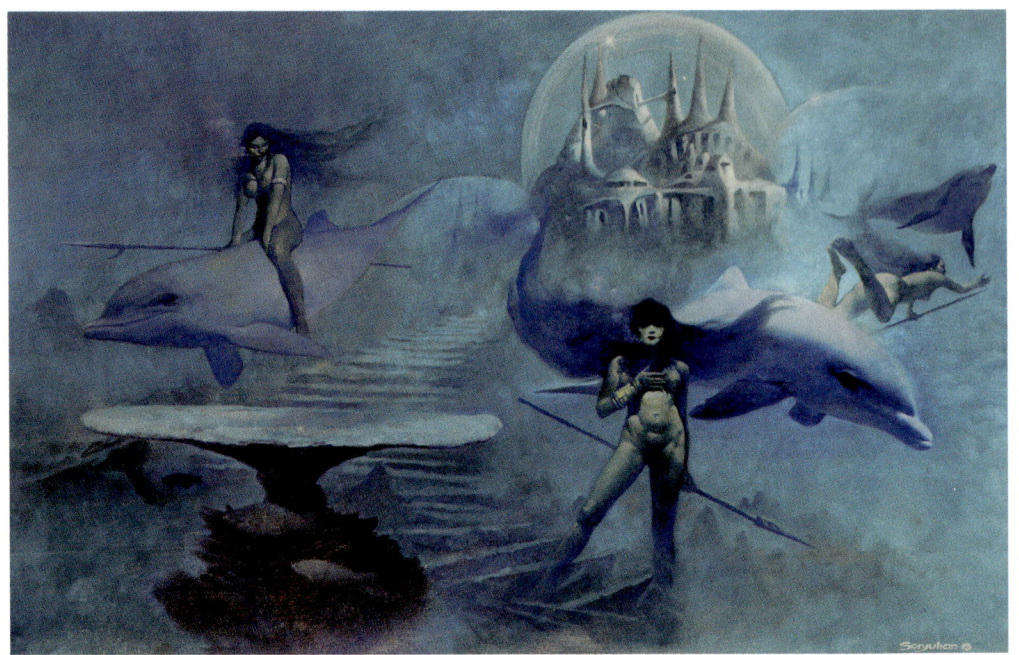

américains, il rassemble rapidement des échantillons de son travail dans l'espoir de décrocher davantage de missions dans ce genre, sans se rendre compte qu'en 1970 les Américains tournent le dos au Far West. Sa collaboration avec Warren l'établit en tant qu'artiste fantasy, et au bout de quelques années le marché des couvertures de livres commence aussi à s'ouvrir à lui. Il se prend de passion pour Conan – « Je savais que je parviendrais à un résultat fantastique, j'ai tout de suite été attiré » – et sa chance finit par se présenter en 1978 avec *Conan and the Sorcerer* pour Ace Books, puis *The Blade of Conan* (1979), *The Treasure of Tranicos* (1980), *Conan the Mercenary* (1981) et *The Flame Knife* (1981). Il signera ensuite une cinquantaine de projets fantasy, pour DAW, Dell & Bantam, ou Ace. En Espagne, une paye en dollars mène loin, si loin que Sanjulian peut s'offrir une maison sur la côte septentrionale, perdue dans la végétation pour jouir « d'une tranquillité maximale et de la mer que j'aime tant toujours proche ». Car il aime la mer, tant qu'il ne la parcourt pas en marin. Il s'est marié, a élevé deux fils et continue à peindre à l'huile, comme il l'a toujours fait, mais il s'essaie aussi à l'illustration par ordinateur. « C'est le moyen d'expression actuel et c'est l'avenir, alors je ne vois aucun problème à l'utiliser de façon efficace. »

Ses œuvres plus récentes ne se limitent pas à la fantasy – il apprécie particulièrement les thèmes historiques – mais il admet que la fantasy « aura toujours une place de choix » dans son cœur, comme la forme artistique grâce à laquelle il s'est fait un nom, une carrière, une vie confortable pour lui et ses enfants et – peut-être surtout – grâce à laquelle il a évité les profondeurs saumâtres.

Above: Under the Sea, for a wraparound cover for *Heavy Metal*, February 1983. Acrylic on canvas, 1982, 42.5 x 64.1 cm (16.75 x 25.25 inches). Courtesy of Heritage Auctions.

Opposite: Red Nails, for *The Sword's Edge*, 2010, oil on canvas, undated, 121.9 x 91.4 cm (48 x 36 inches). Courtesy of Heritage Auctions.

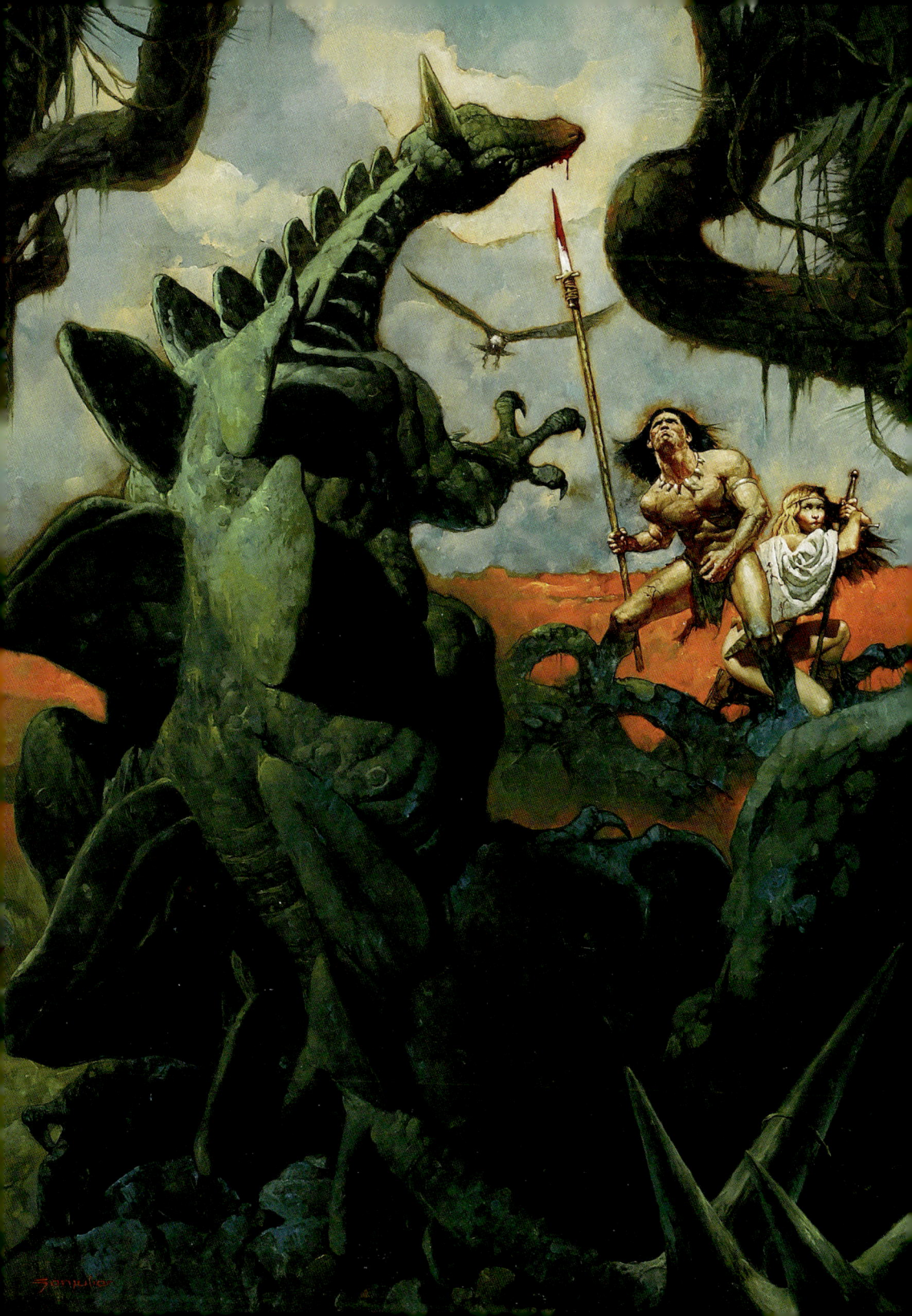

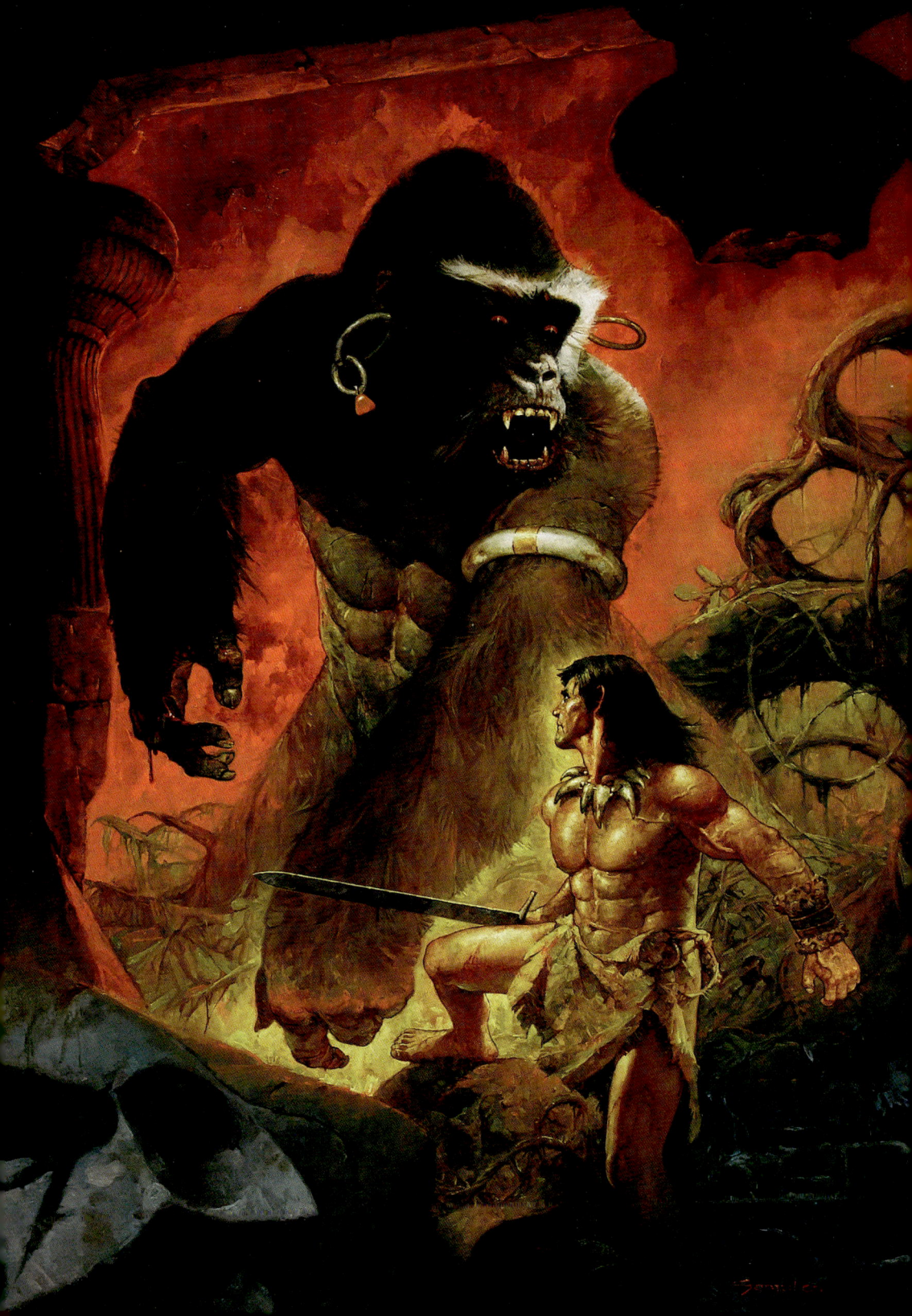

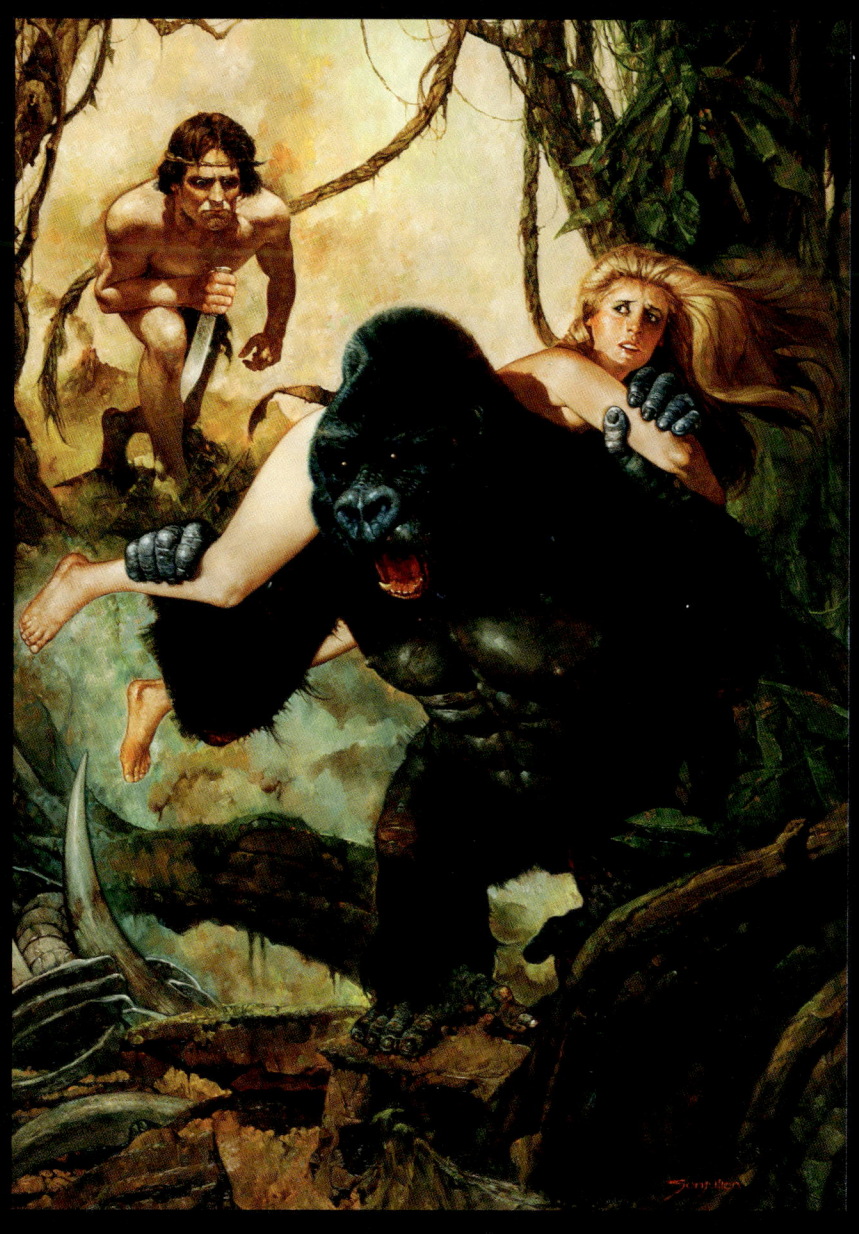

Opposite: Shadows in the Moonlight, for *The Sword's Edge*, 2010, oil on canvas, undated, 121.9 x 91.4 cm (48 x 36 inches). Courtesy of Heritage Auctions.

Above: Tarzan Saves Jane from Kerchak, oil on canvas, undated, 122 x 86.3 cm (48 x 34 inches).

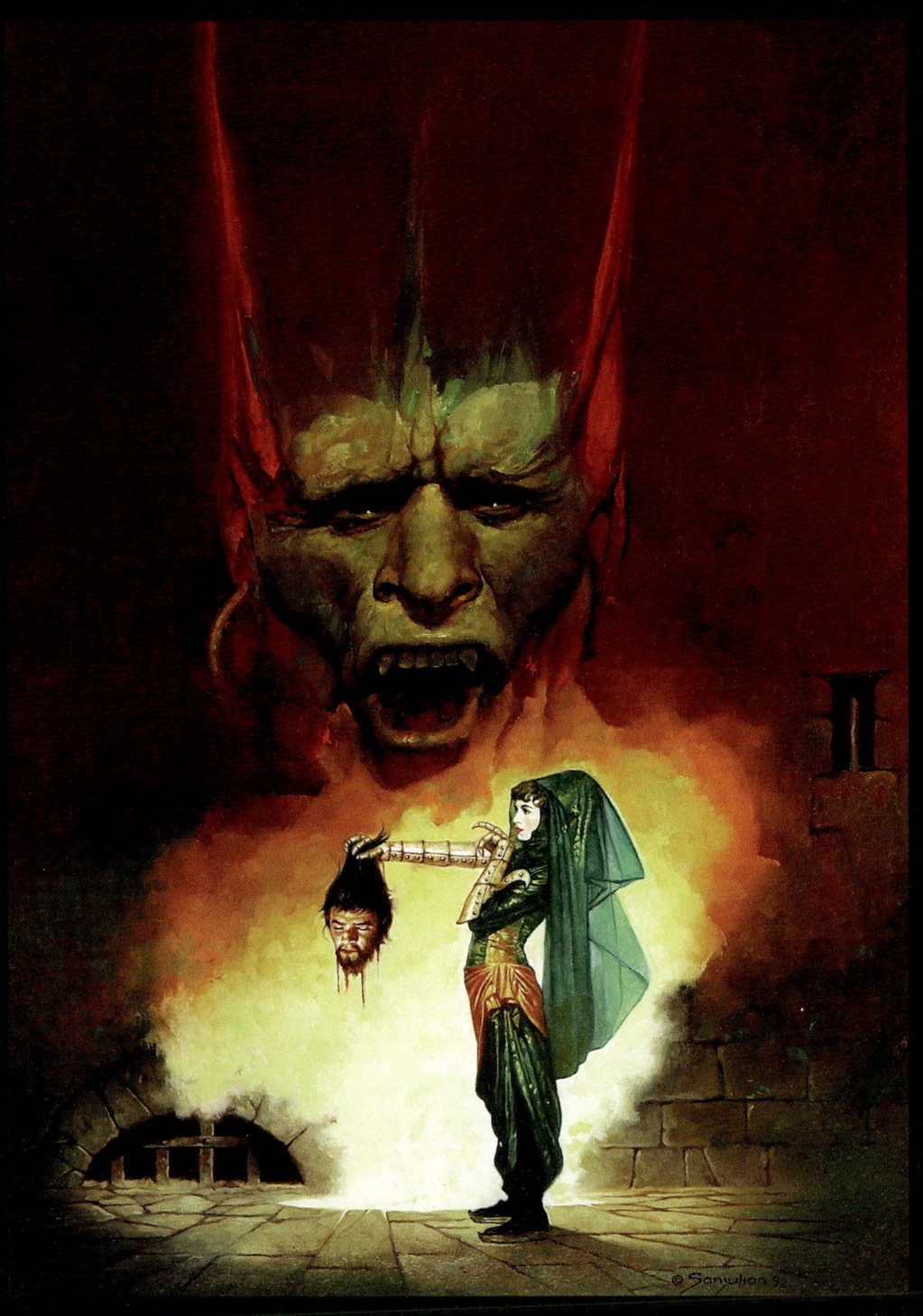

MASTERPIECES OF FANTASY ART

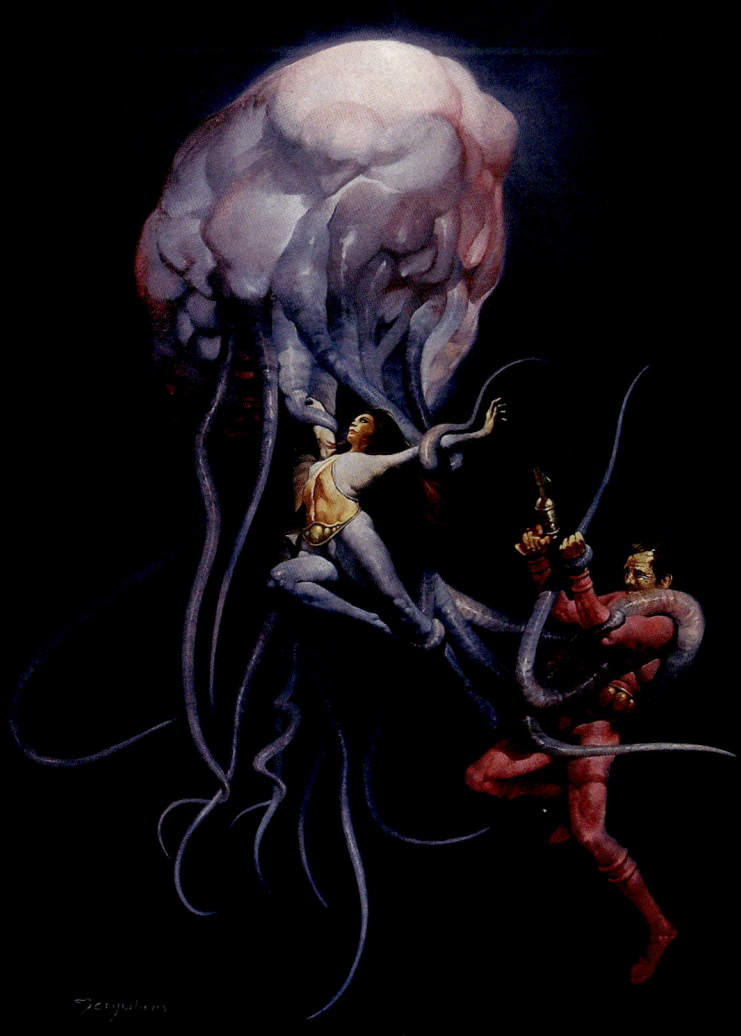

Opposite: *El Pozo* (*The Well*), oil on canvas, 1992, 41.9 x 30.4 cm (16.5 x 12 inches). Courtesy of Heritage Auctions.

Above: *Buck Blaster and Thelma Starburst,* for the cover of *Eerie* No. 76, August 1976, oil on canvas, 60.9 x 47 cm (24 x 18.5 inches). Courtesy of Heritage Auctions.

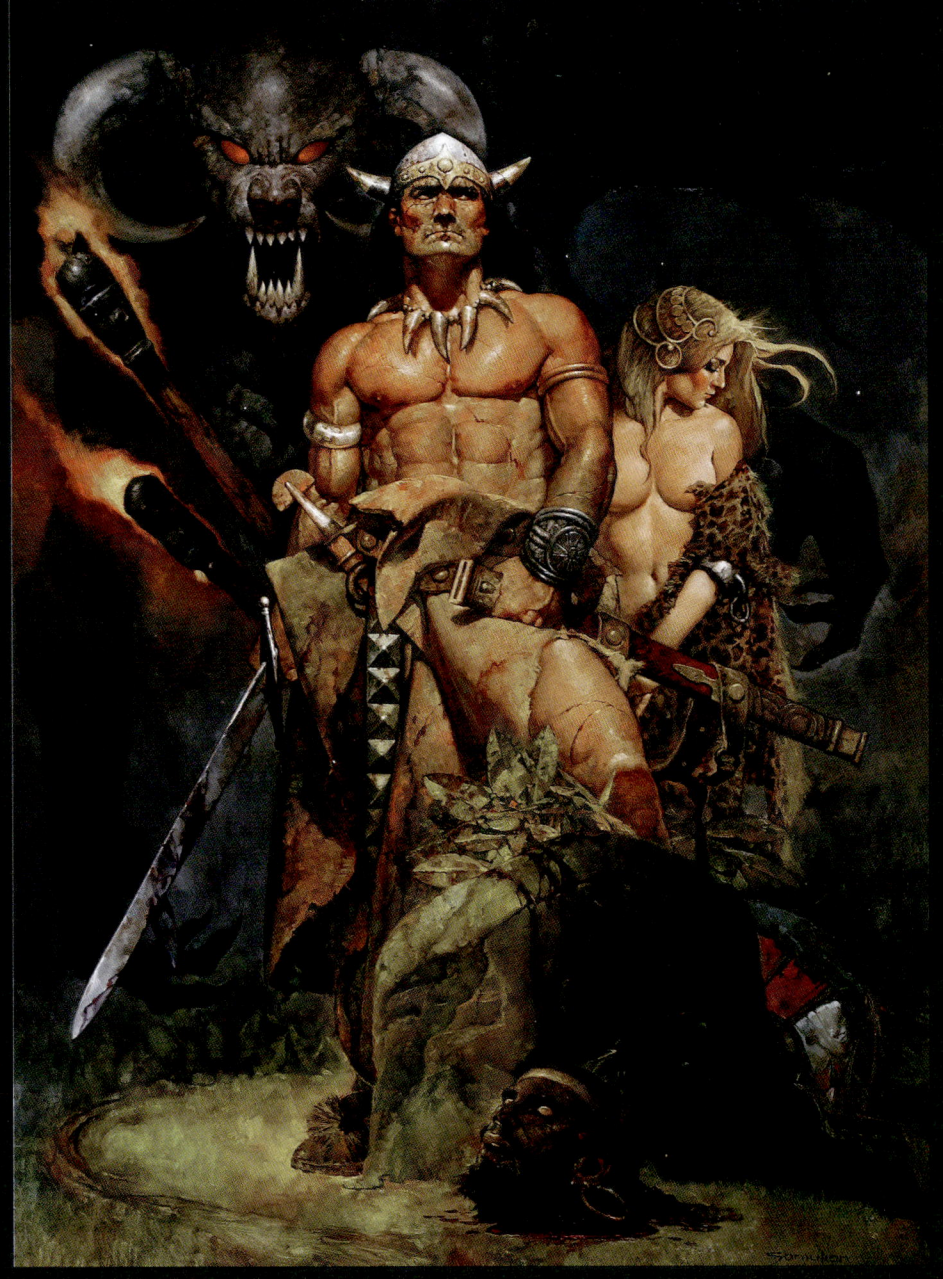

Above: The Vale of Lost Women, for *The Sword's Edge,* 2010, oil on canvas, undated, 121.9 x 91.4 cm (48 x 36 inches). Courtesy of Heritage Auctions.

MASTERPIECES OF FANTASY ART

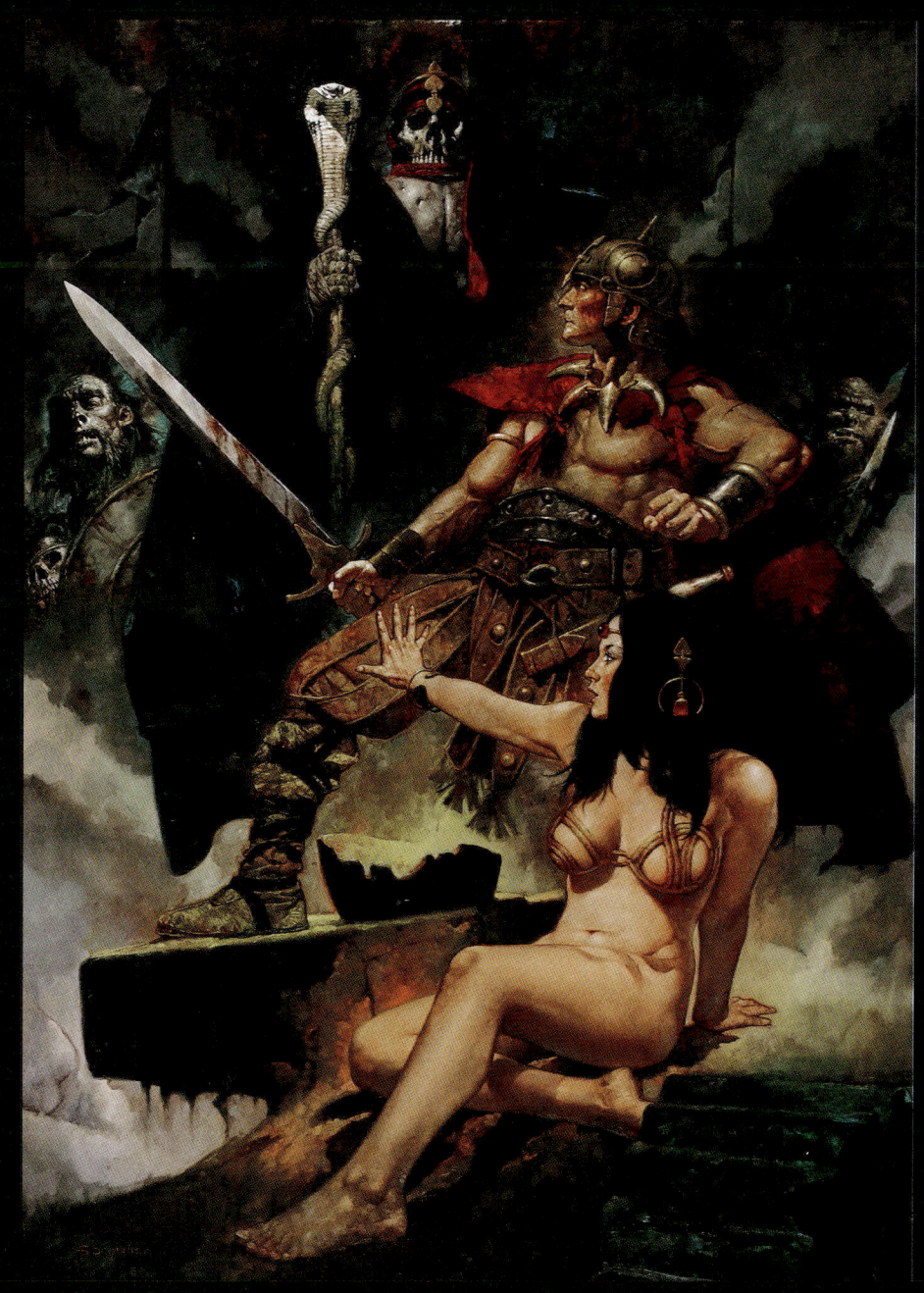

Above: Black Colossus, for *The Sword's Edge*, 2010,
oil on canvas, undated, 121.9 x 91.4 cm (48 x 36 inches).
Courtesy of Heritage Auctions.

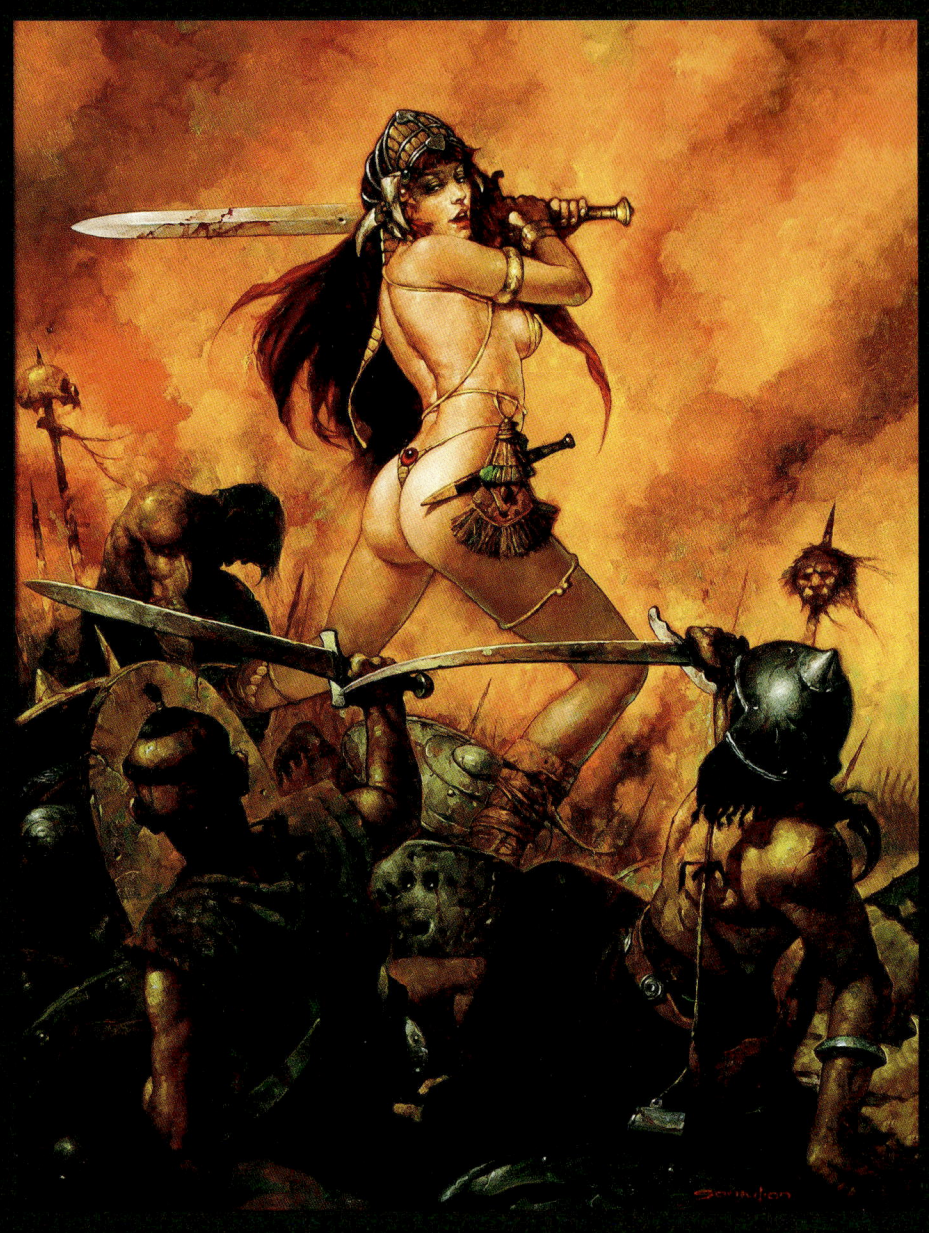

Above: Private commission. Oil on canvas, 2007,
83.8 x 68.5 cm (33 x 27 inches).

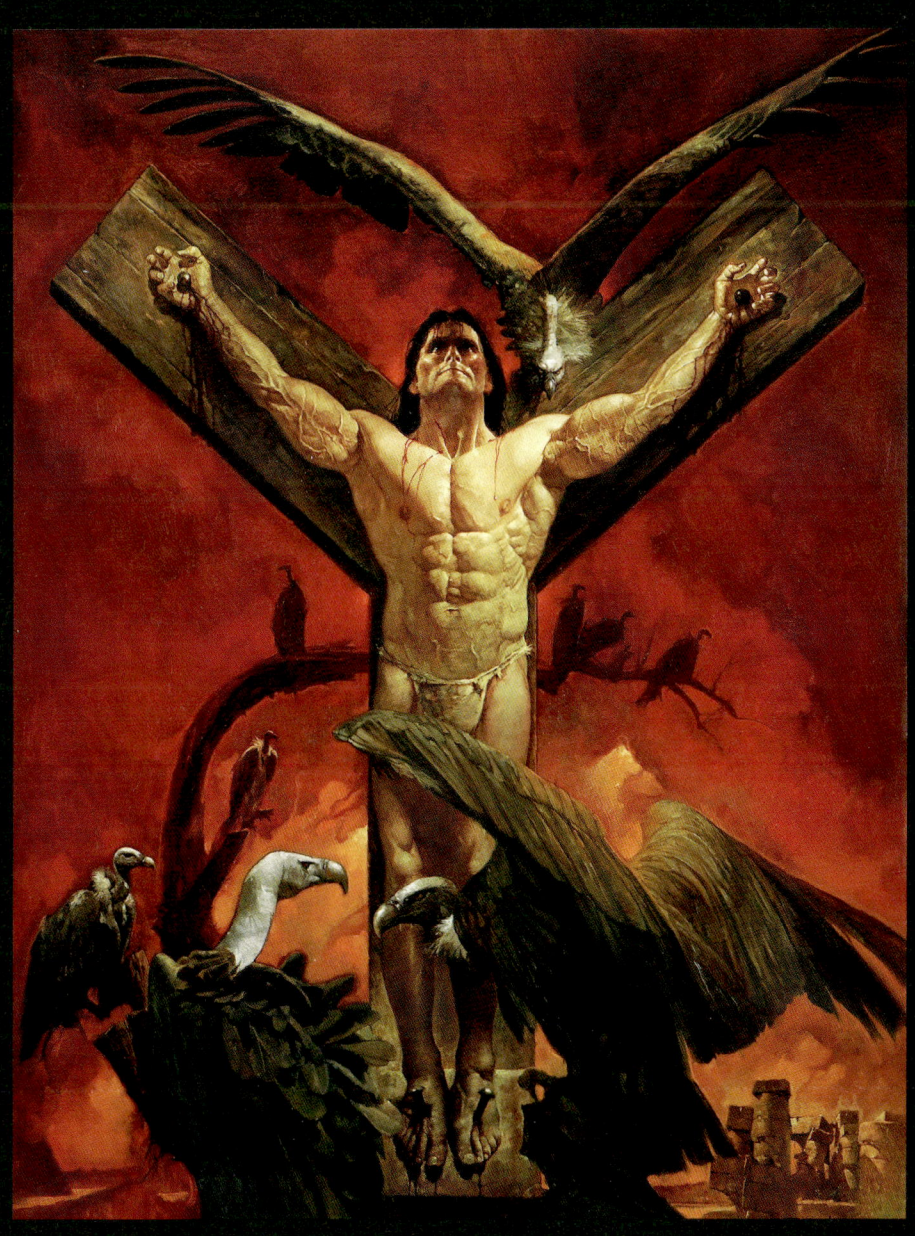

Above: A Witch Shall Be Born, for *The Sword's Edge,* 2010,
oil on canvas, undated, 121.9 x 91.4 cm (48 x 36 inches).
Courtesy of Heritage Auctions.

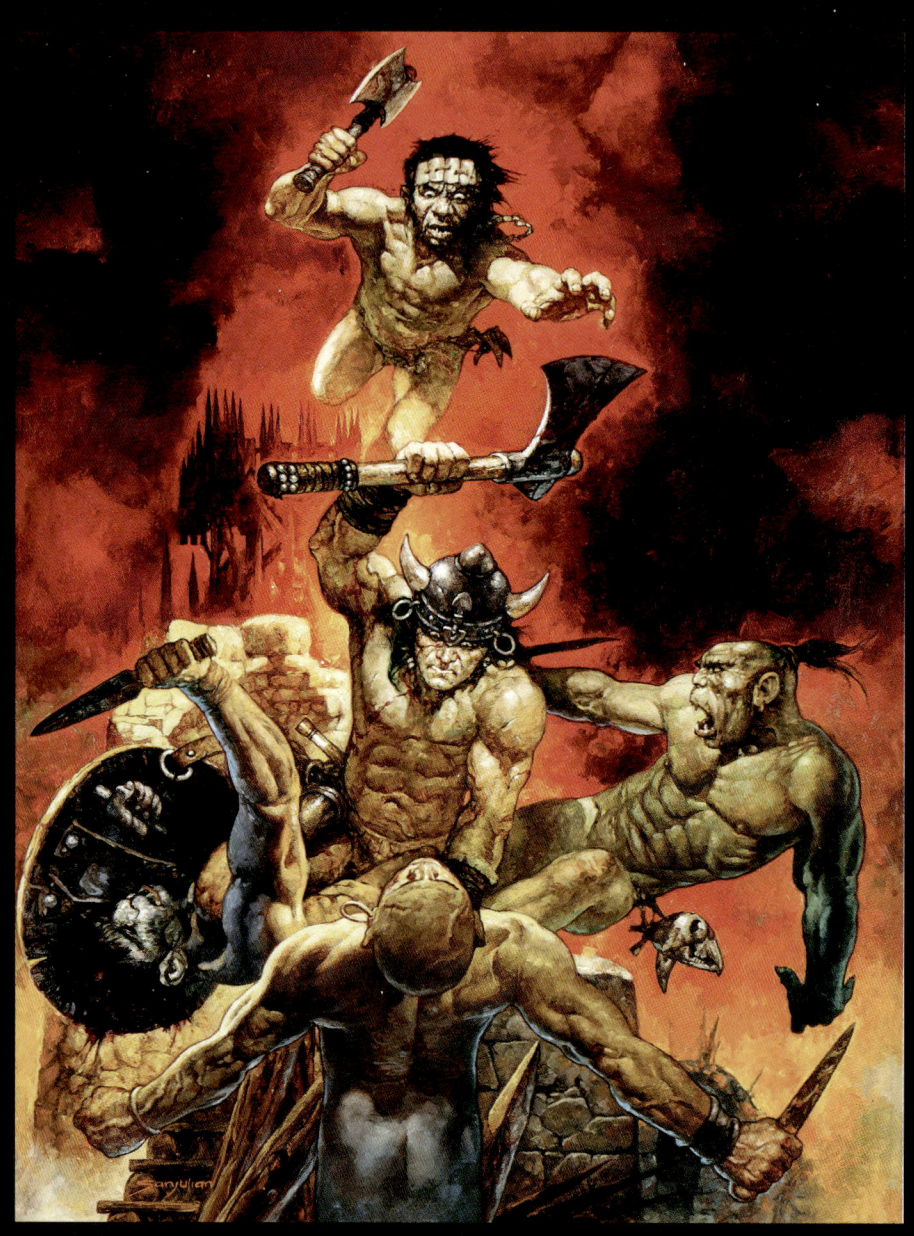

Above: Conan: The Black Stranger, oil on canvas,
undated, 72.3 x 53.3 cm (28.5 x 21 inches).

MASTERPIECES OF FANTASY ART

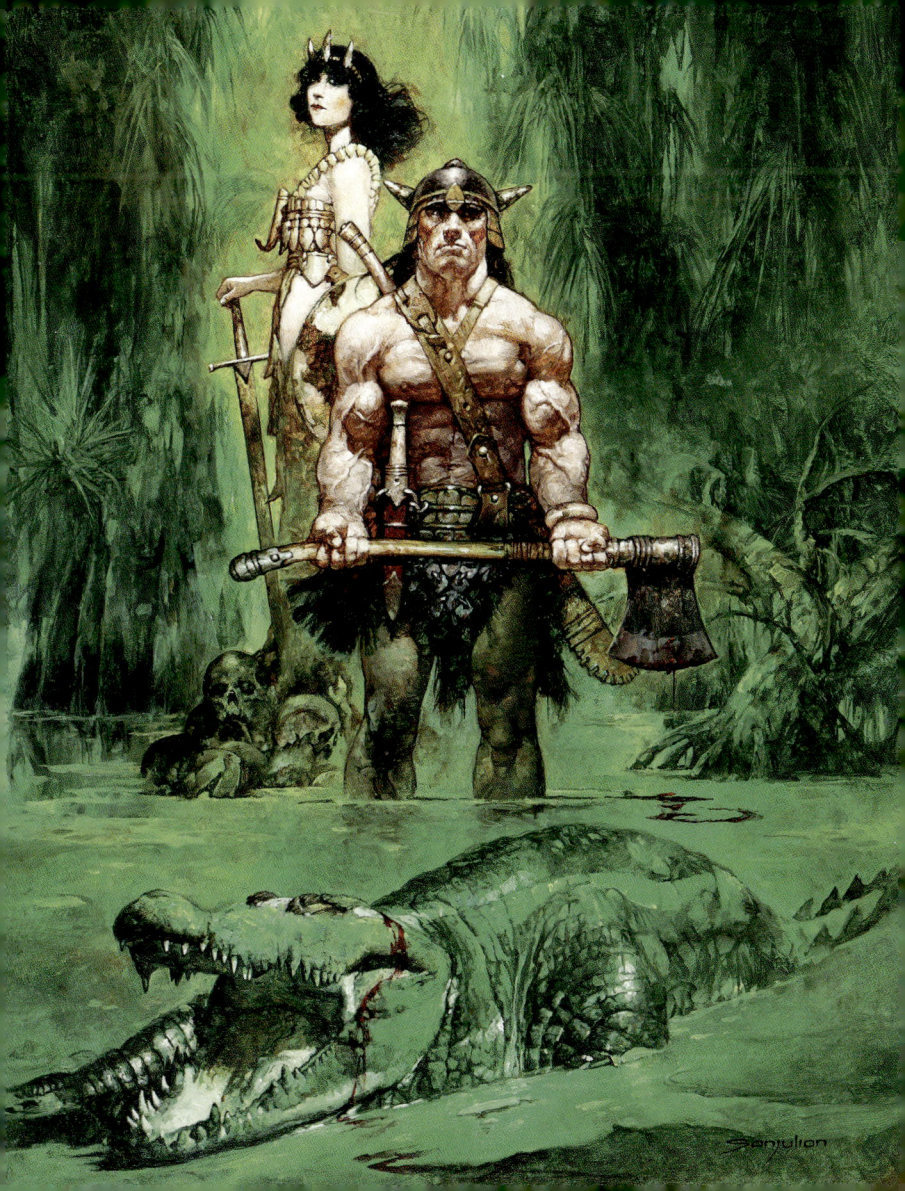

Sanjulian

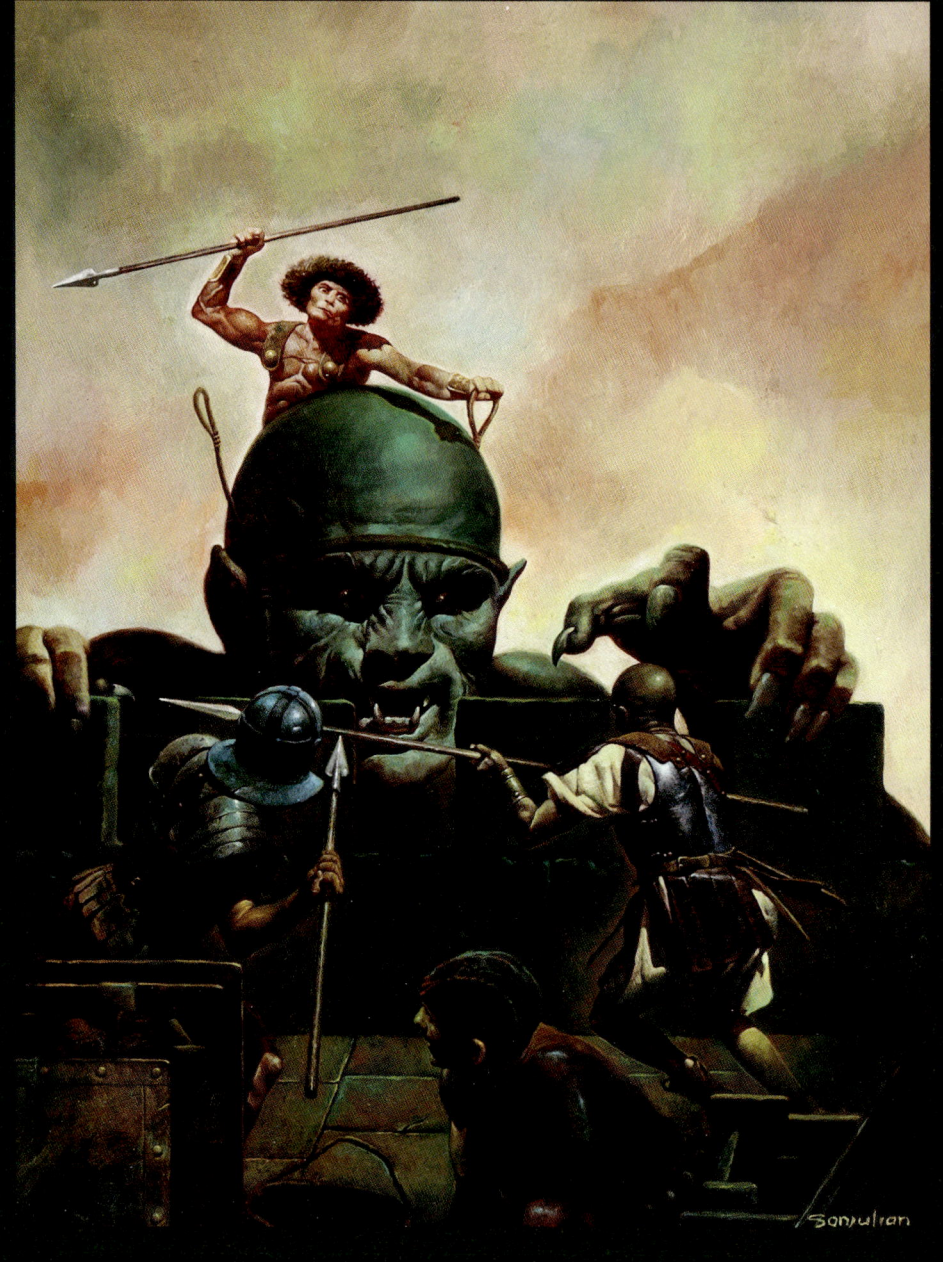

Above: Cover painting for *Eerie* No. 102,
oil on art paper, 1979, 35.5 x 26.6 cm (14 x 10.5 inches).
Courtesy of Heritage Auctions.

Opposite: Back cover painting for *Sanjulian Master Visionary,* oil on canvas, 2000, 57.1 x 35.5 cm (22.5 x 14 inches).

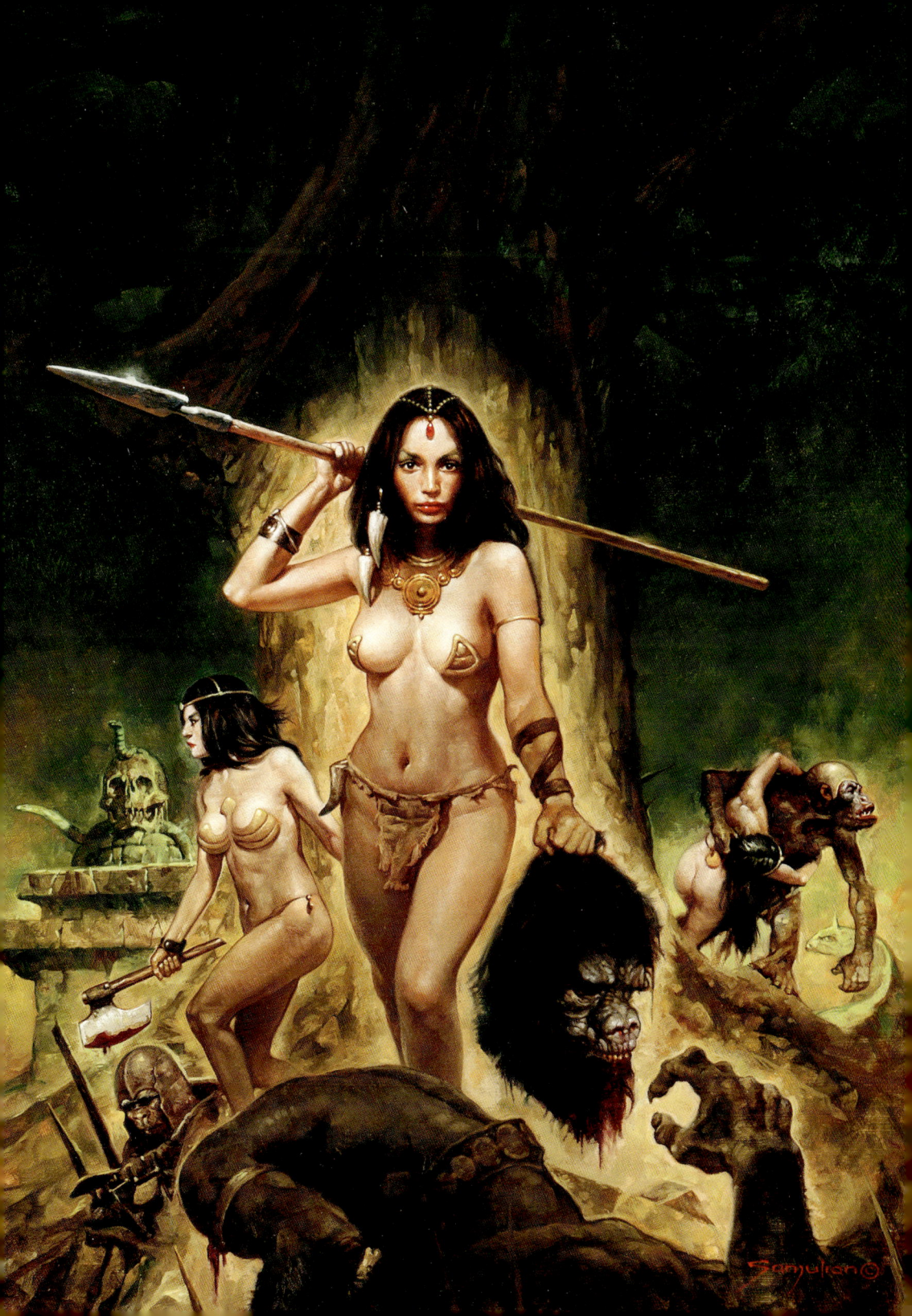

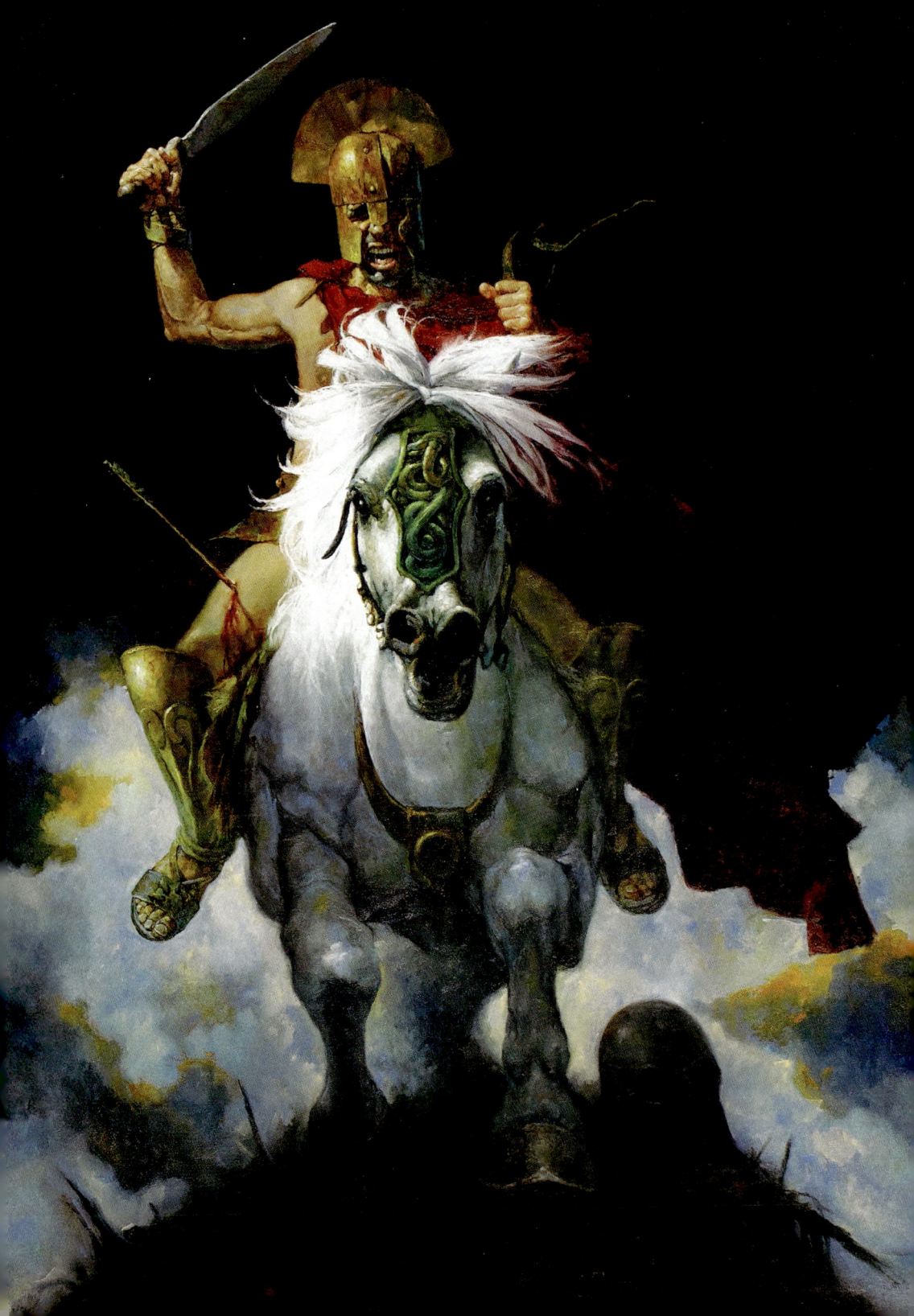

Boris Vallejo

Boris

1941-

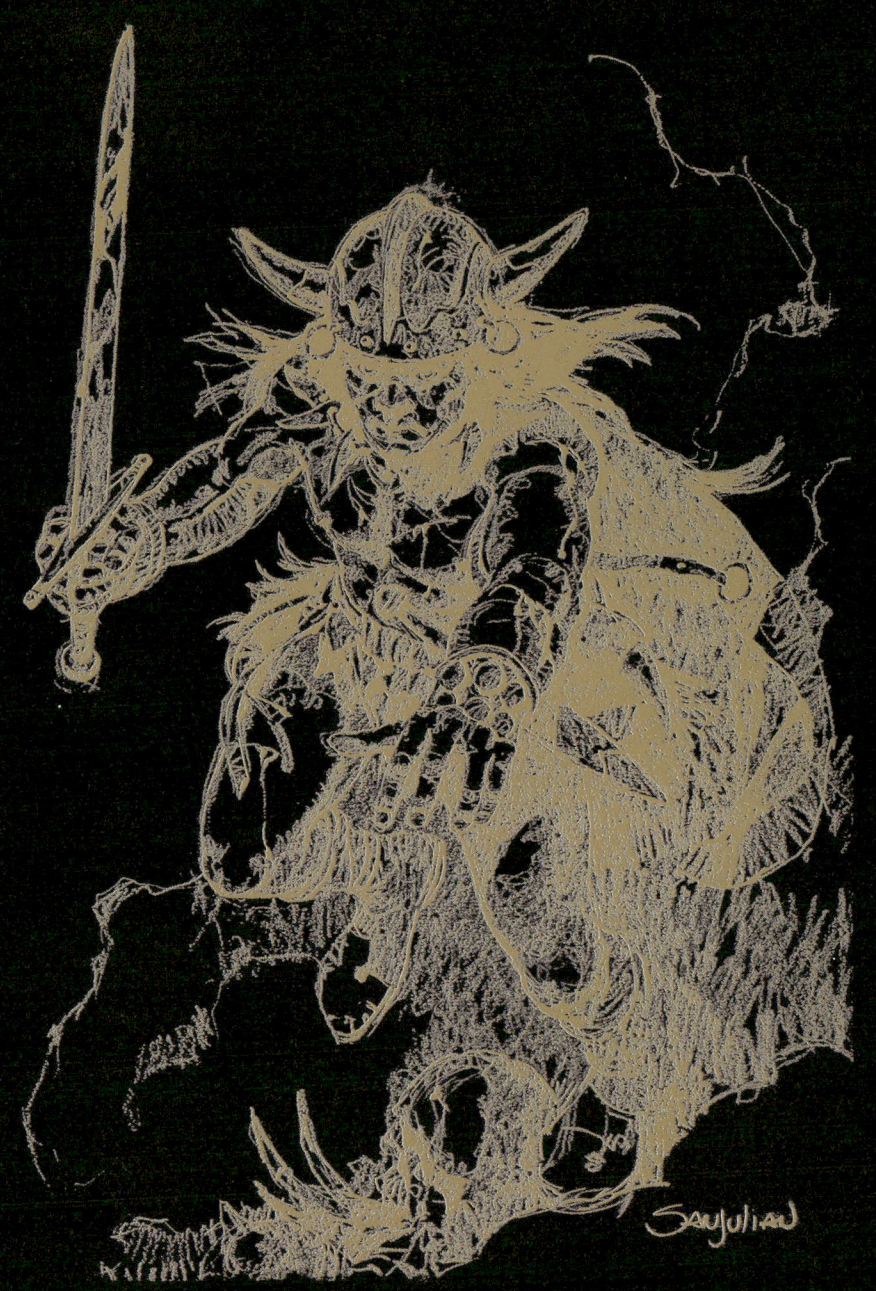

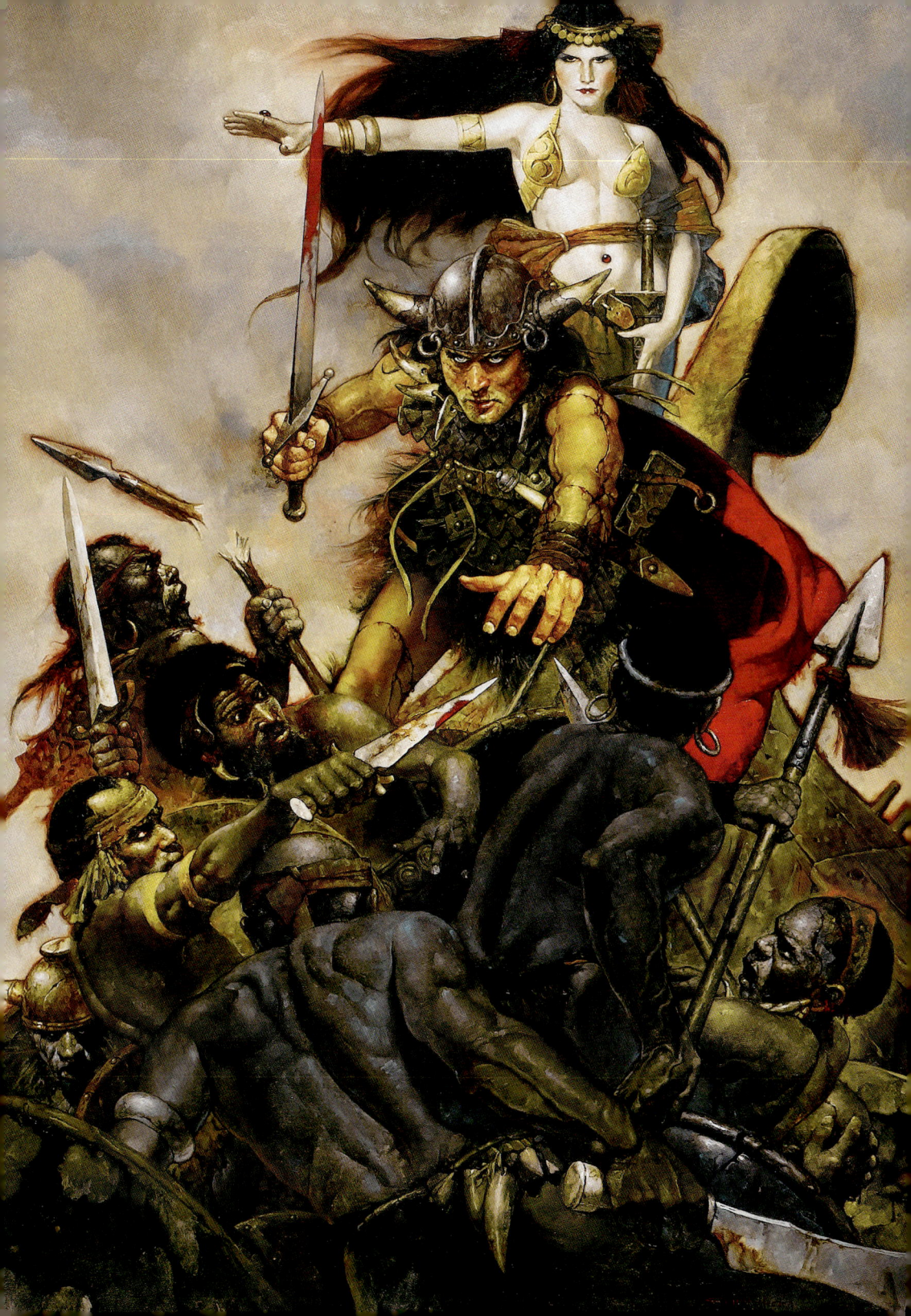

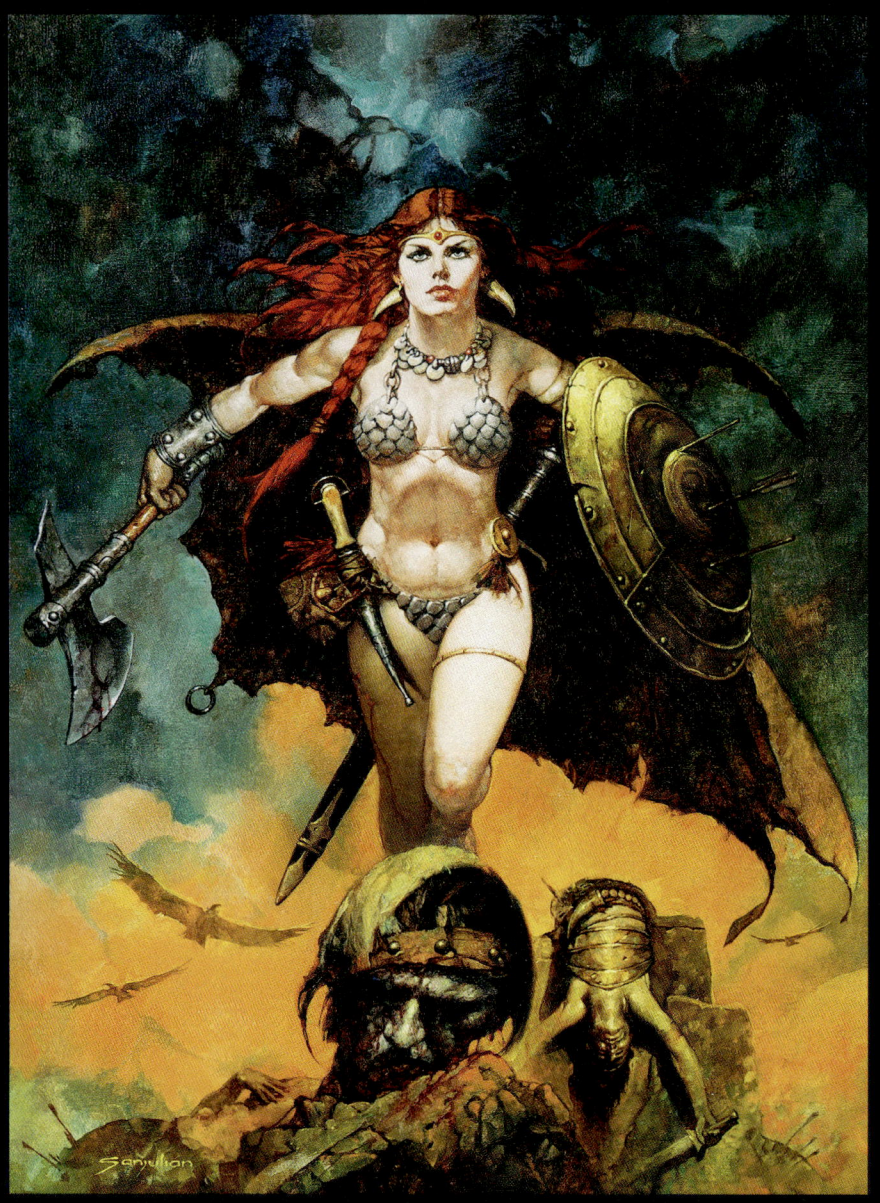

Opposite: Roman Centurian, oil on canvas, undated, 137.1 x 104.1 cm (54 x 41 inches). Courtesy of Heritage Auctions.

Above: Female warrior, for *The Sword's Edge*, 2010, oil on canvas, undated, 60.9 x 44.4 cm (24 x 17.5 inches).

Following left: Queen of the Black Coast, for *The Sword's Edge*, 2010, oil on canvas, undated, 121.9 x 91.4 cm (48 x 36 inches). Courtesy of Heritage Auctions.

Following right: Detail sketch for *Queen of the Black Coast*, blue pencil over graphite on board, undated, 40.6 x 28.5 cm (16 x 11.25 inches).

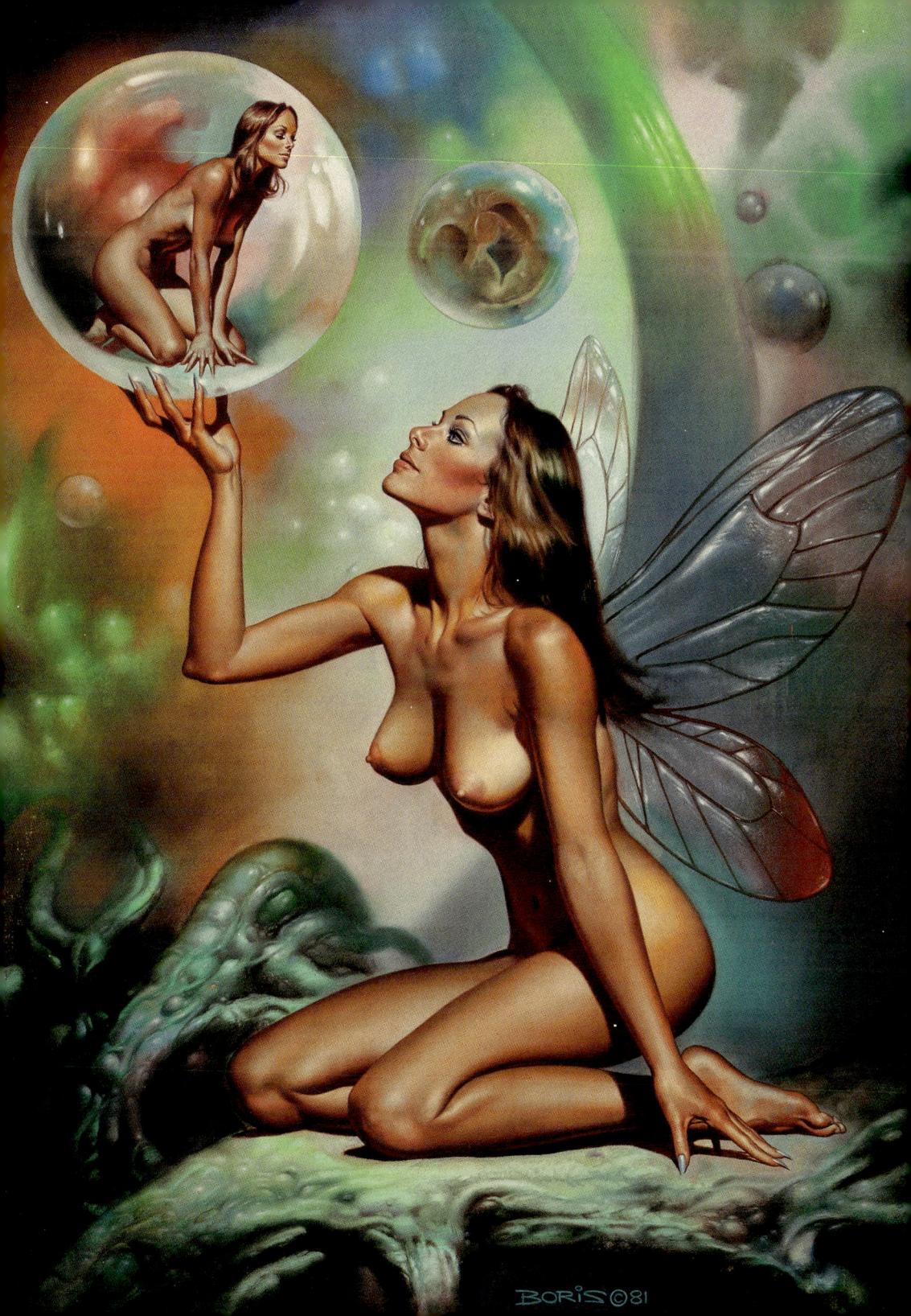

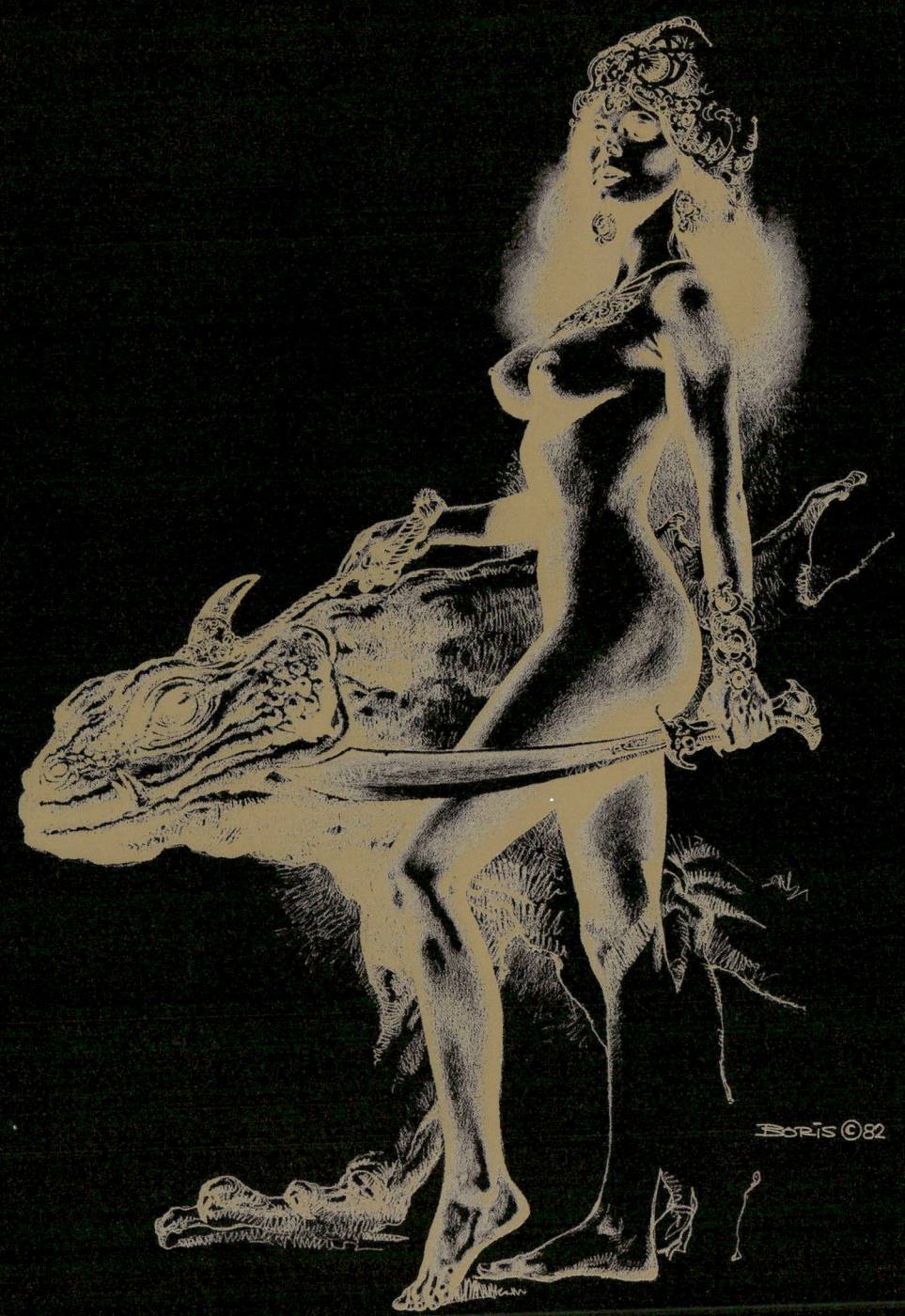

BORIS VALLEJO
MASTER OF MUSCLE

"We all are attracted to bodies, otherwise we wouldn't exist!"

BY ZAK SMITH

No matter the alleged subject—fantasy, science fiction, erotica, comics, or even the occasional comedy commission—Boris Vallejo's real subject is always the body. These bodies do a thousand things in his work: wield weapons, embrace demons, stand dazzled or defiant before creatures, leap at dinosaurs, recline against rocks and trees, ride flying dragons and unicorns past richly colored planets and clouds, stand near wolves, caress beasts, twist, wrestle, emerge from massive eggs and flowers, sprout and curl beneath black leather or butterfly wings, and crawl their way across landscapes and each other—but they remain indelibly bodies. Perfectly lit, heroically posed, intrepid, stoic. The villains are operatic and noble, the monsters ripped from a classical anatomy textbook, and, on his trading cards, the superheroes are less wearing outfits than head-to-toe tattoos.

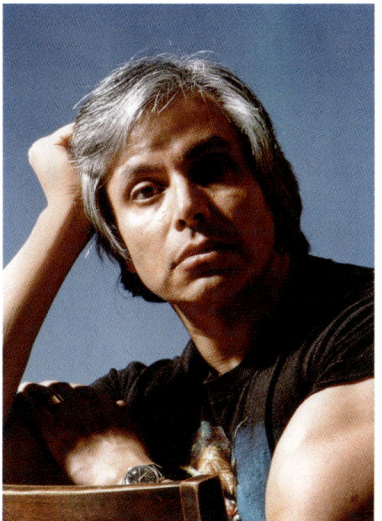

Vallejo was hailed early on as "the next Frazetta," but the art of the two painters of manly men differed in ways that paralleled the different kinds of manly men they were. Frazetta, who almost played major league baseball, was willing to foreshorten, distort or obscure the body, to throw a leg, an arm, or even a face into shadow for the sake of getting the action right, whereas Vallejo, a lifelong bodybuilder, animates each image from the center outward with a meticulously rendered and perfectly lit body—exposed ("Costumes bored me and I don't enjoy doing period clothes"), posed clearly in frozen time, and enthusiastically loved—like an eight-minute guitar solo in the middle of a nine-minute song.

Though associated with heavy metal covers, Vallejo has a traditionalist streak. Born in 1941, the son of a prominent lawyer in Lima, Peru, he grew up loving classical music and playing the violin—when not drawing on the kitchen walls or reading about half-naked heroes.

"I have always been interested in science fiction and fantasy. One of my first idols was Tarzan. I read all the Tarzan books. I used to do these drawings of Tarzan going around with the apes and

Previous right: First Love, for Vallejo's book *Mirage,* 1982. Oil on board, 1981, 73.6 x 48.2 cm (29 x 19 inches).

Opposite: Searchers, for *Mirage* book, 1982. Pencil on paper, 1982, 50.8 x 38.1 cm (20 x 15 inches).

Above: Boris Vallejo, circa 1975.

fighting savage animals and so on. Subsequently I discovered the work of Chesley Bonestell, as well as J. Allen St. John, who was the classic illustrator for Tarzan."

The year 1957 was momentous for the 16-year-old Vallejo—he found his first illustration job, first wife, and first bodybuilding magazine. After a two-year detour into medical school—which left him with an even greater passion for, and knowledge of, anatomy —Vallejo spent five years on scholarship at Peru's Escuela Nacional Superior Autónoma de Bellas Artes. In 1964 he arrived in New York—knowing no English and carrying little more than his violin, $80, and some samples of his work. With the help of some fellow Peruvians, Vallejo got a job at an agency, drawing whatever needed to be drawn: advertisements, greeting cards, pictures of pots and pans.

As more interesting work began to roll in, including his first and only interior comic book work—a war story for Marvel in 1966—and covers for Warren and Marvel magazines like *Eerie*, *Dracula Lives!*, *Tales of the Zombie*, and, of course, *Savage Sword of Conan*, Vallejo's style began to develop. In 1975 he shifted from magazines to book covers, including an entire series featuring his childhood hero Tarzan. Gorgeously plausible monsters, academic poses, and clustered detail made Vallejo's work stand out among fields of colored haze and crowds of hunched muscle that defined the sword-and-sorcery genre at the time. The chauvinistic slave world of John Norman's controversial *Gor* novels was arguably better served than it deserved by Vallejo's talent for richly rendering human (and reptilian) flesh—complete with tan lines and all the gradations of tone revealed when Vallejo aimed his studio lights at his bodybuilding models.

"Students ask us what colors we use for skin tones," (the "we" here includes Vallejo's second wife, Julie Bell) "and really there is no such thing. When we paint skin tones we practically use the whole palette we have available. Normally I have on my palette anywhere between 18 to 24 colors."

The poster for the (ironically nudity-free) rerelease of *Barbarella* in 1977 garnered him yet more attention, and the 1978 monograph *The Fantastic Art of Boris Vallejo* established him as a leading light in the field, and—though an admirer of Michelangelo, Rubens, and Velasquez—he led the charge across the bridge from the stylized and "painterly" palettes and finish of late pulp illustration into the full-spectrum gloss of '80s mainstream fantasy. Much of his most arresting work during this period is among his most atypical (*The Nebulon Horror*, 1980; *The Girl Who Owned a City*, 1977), erotic (*Siren Song*, 1979) or both (*Soap*, 1981).

In the '80s, Vallejo began publishing a new calendar each year, illustrated his first wife, writer Doris Vallejo's, books, and had commissions rolling in from every direction: Roger Corman had him paint his actors in costume for the posters of adventure-exploitation films like *Barbarian Queen*, while for *National Lampoon* he ironically referenced his own style by painting Chevy Chase striking mock-heroic poses for the *Vacation* and *European Vacation* posters. His textures became smoother and his figures became ever more oiled and athletic. In interviews Vallejo always emphasizes how organic the art-making process has seemed to him: "Styles evolve naturally as you go along. To me, painting comes so naturally I don't really think about it intellectually."

In 1989, as he so often had before, Vallejo invited a fellow bodybuilder to model at his studio. He painted her as an Etruscan goddess of the underworld, holding an axe, with her hair coiling purple across a gold bikini. She was a painter, too. They fell in love. Marrying in 1994, Boris Vallejo

Opposite: Gryphon Keeper appeared in *The Fabulous Women of Boris Vallejo and Julie Bell*, 2006. Oil on board, 1989, 101.6 x 82.5 cm (40 x 32.5 inches).

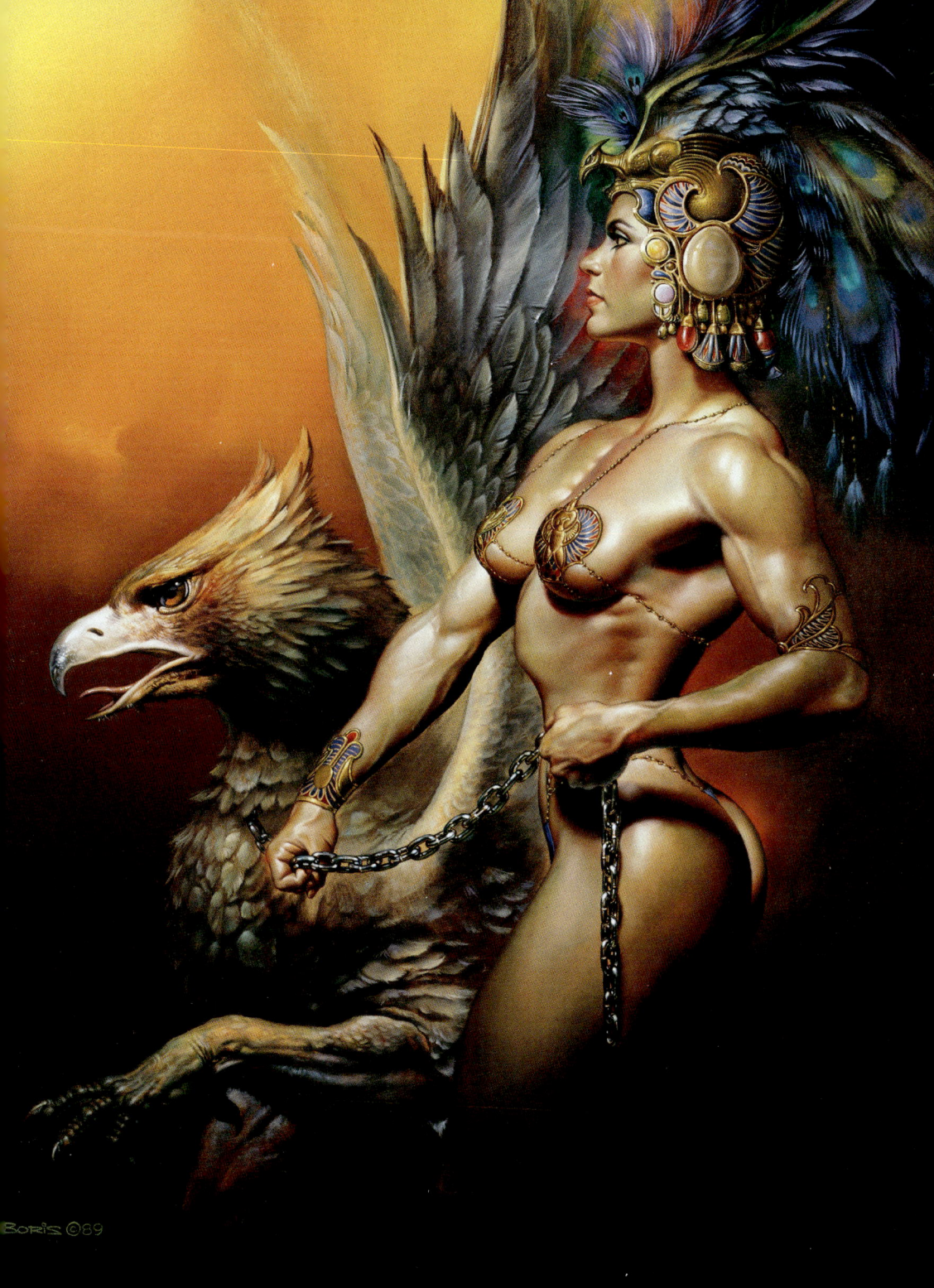

and Julie Bell became known as the "First Couple of Fantasy Art," sharing a studio and often collaborating, including on a 2018 album cover for Andrew W.K.

Having worked for 50 years and produced everything from video game boxes (*Star Control, Golden Axe II, Phantasy Star IV, Ecco the Dolphin*) to a photo-monograph of butts (*Hindsight: Boris Vallejo — His Photographic Art*, 1998) Vallejo's influence is immeasurable. He not only works like a machine, "It's no effort for me — I know exactly not only when it's finished but I know before it's finished. I can say, 'OK, it's gonna be another day, two, maybe five hours' — whatever it is — to the point that it's finished," but machines want to work like him: the digital painting programs now used by game and film concept artists are full of filters and tools designed precisely to imitate the gleaming highlights, blue shadows, observed-but-idealized curves, distant floating backgrounds and smooth-but-specific textures found only on the canvases of the eminent Boris.

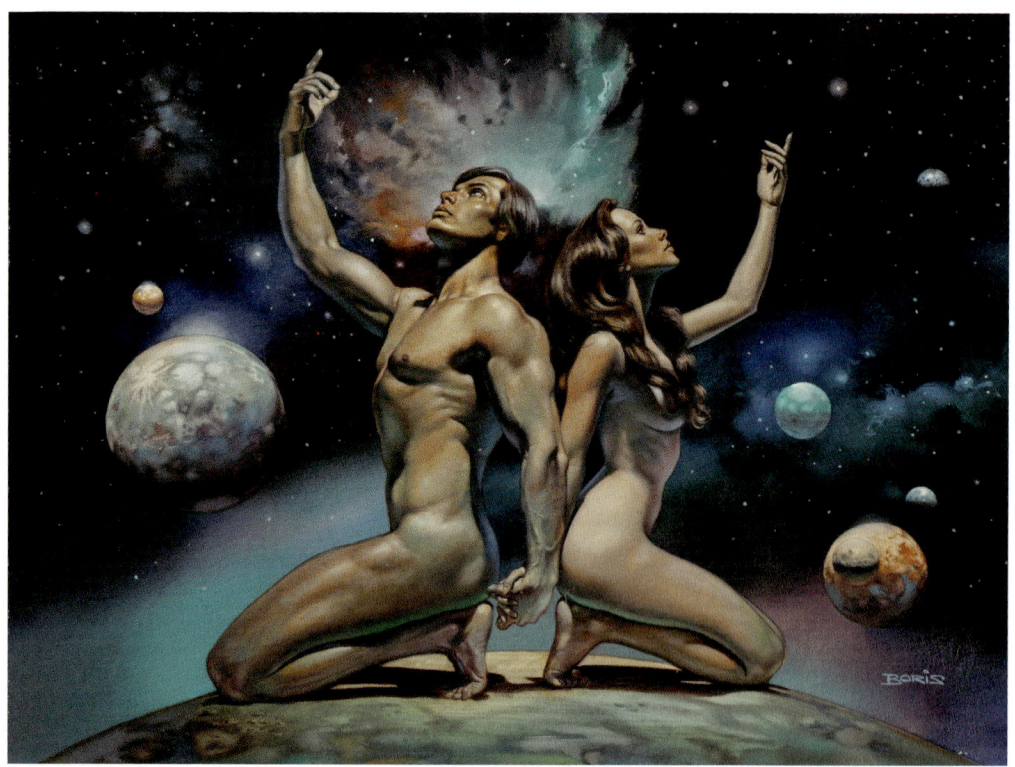

Above: Reaching for the Stars, for the July 1978 cover of *Future Life* magazine. Oil on board, 1978, 58.4 x 45.7 cm (23 x 18 inches). Courtesy of Heritage Auctions.

Opposite: The Lavalite World, for the cover of Philip José Farmer's 1977 Ace Books novel. Acrylic on board, 1977, 63.5 x 40.6 cm (25 x 16 inches).

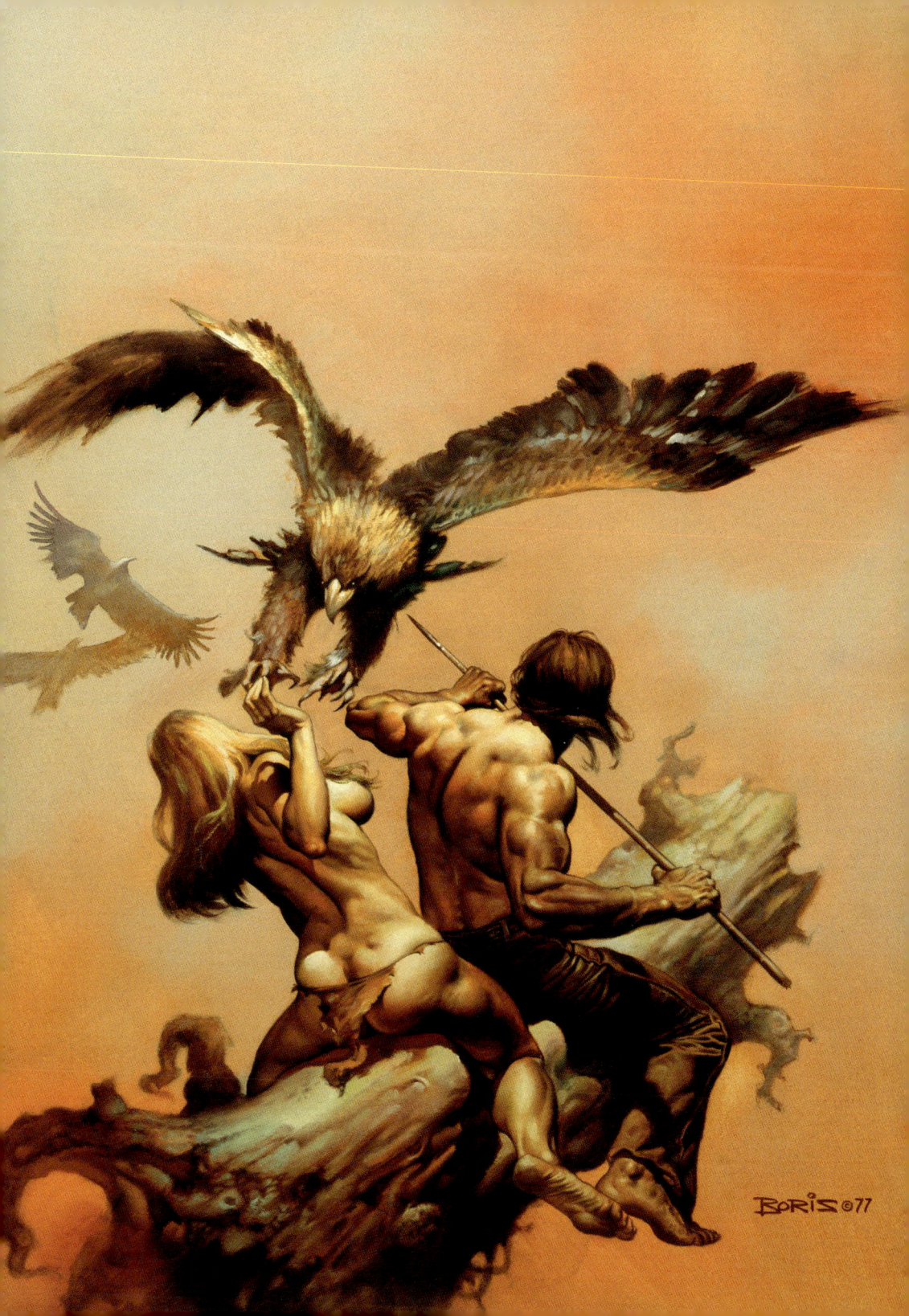

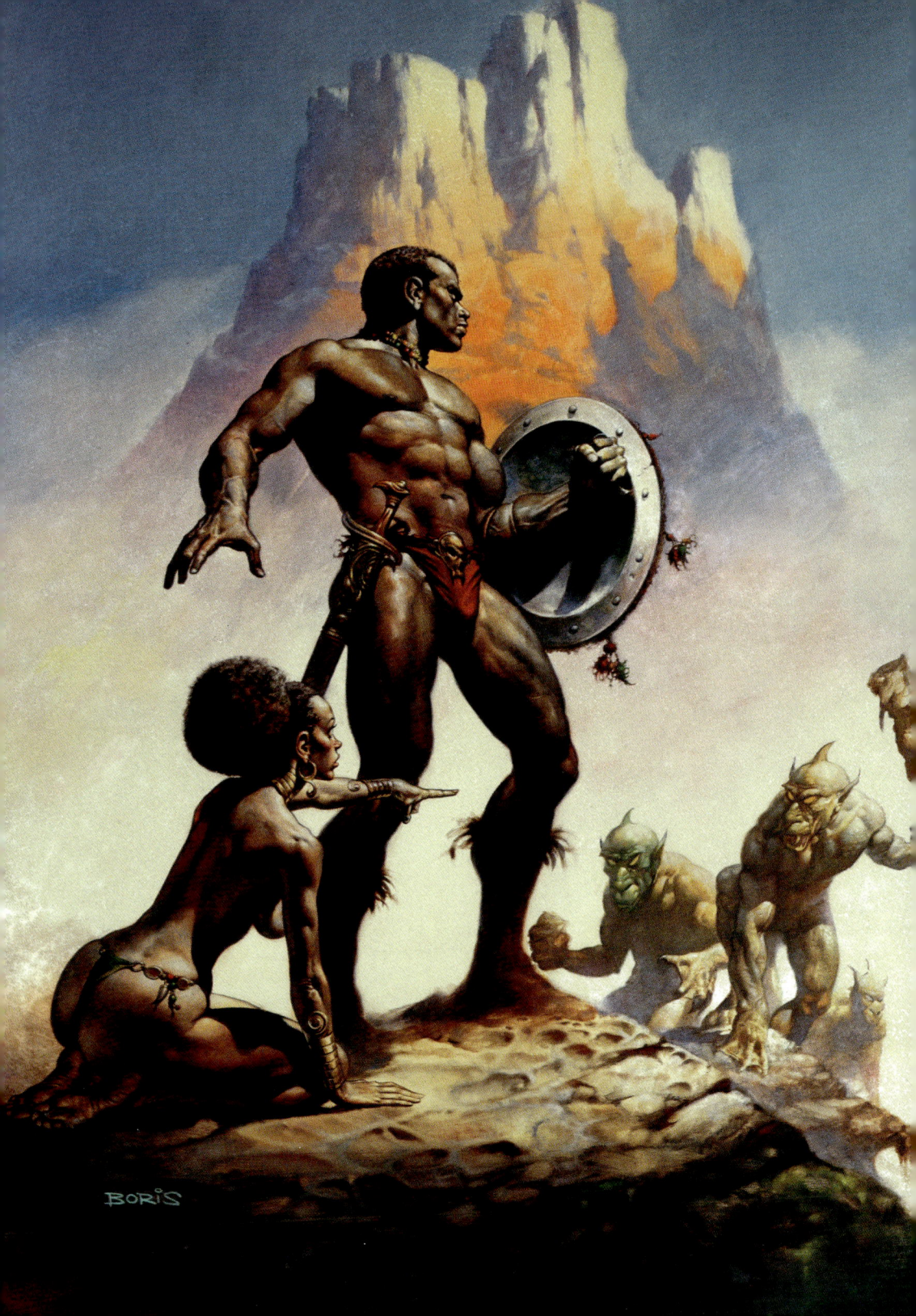

BORIS VALLEJO
MEISTER DER MUSKULATUR

VON ZAK SMITH

„Wir alle fühlen uns von Körpern angezogen, sonst würden wir nicht existieren!"

Ganz gleich, um welches vermeintliche Thema es geht – Fantasy, Science-Fiction, Erotika, Comics oder auch um einen der gelegentlichen Comedyaufträge –, Boris Vallejos eigentliches Thema ist immer der Körper. Diese Körper machen in seinen Werken tausend Dinge: schwingen Waffen, umarmen Dämonen, stehen verwirrt oder herausfordernd vor Kreaturen, stürzen sich auf Dinosaurier, lehnen sich an Felsen und Bäume, reiten auf fliegenden Drachen und Einhörnern über prachtvoll farbige Planeten und Wolken hinweg, stehen neben Wölfen, streicheln Tiere, winden, ringen oder schälen sich aus gewaltigen Eiern und Blumen heraus, wachsen und schlängeln sich unter schwarzem Leder oder Schmetterlingsflügeln hervor und suchen ihren Weg kriechend über Landschaften und übereinander – doch sie bleiben unauslöschlich Körper. In perfektem Licht, heroischen Posen, unerschrocken, stoisch. Die Bösewichte haben etwas

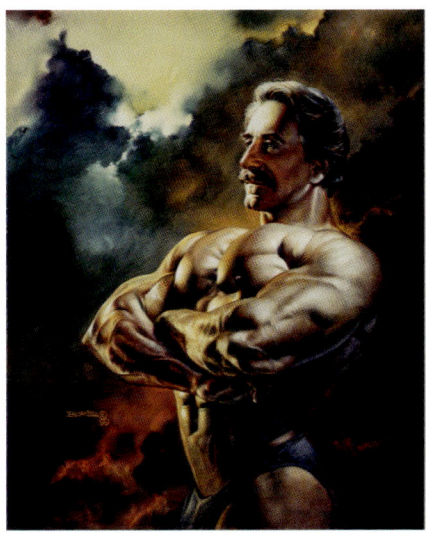

Opernhaftes und Nobles, die Monster sind wie aus einem klassischen Anatomielehrbuch geschnitten, und die Superhelden auf seinen Tauschkarten sind weniger mit Kleidung ausgestattet als von Kopf bis Fuß tätowiert.

Vallejo wurde schon früh als „der nächste Frazetta" gefeiert, doch die Kunst der beiden Maler mannhafter Männer unterschied sich in einer Art und Weise, die den unterschiedlichen mannhaften Männern, die sie waren, entsprach. Frank Frazetta, der beinahe Baseball in der Major League gespielt hätte, war bereit, Körper perspektivisch zu verkürzen, sie verzerrt oder verdeckt darzustellen, ein Bein, einen Arm oder sogar ein Gesicht zu verschatten, sofern dadurch die Handlung besser verdeutlicht wurde, wohingegen Vallejo, zeitlebens Bodybuilder, jedes Bild von seinem Mittelpunkt nach außen mit einem akribisch wiedergegebenen und perfekt ausgeleuchteten Körper belebt: entblößt („Gewänder langweilten mich, und historische Kleidung zu malen

Opposite: Nubian Warrior, mixed media on board, 1978, 71.7 x 51.4 cm (28.25 x 20.25 inches).

Above: Joe Weider, a founding father of American bodybuilding through his many magazines, including

Your Physique, Mr. America, Muscle Power, Flex, and *Muscle & Fitness*, commissioned Vallejo to paint his portrait, which now hangs in the Joe & Betty Weider Museum of Physical Culture at the University of Texas, Austin.

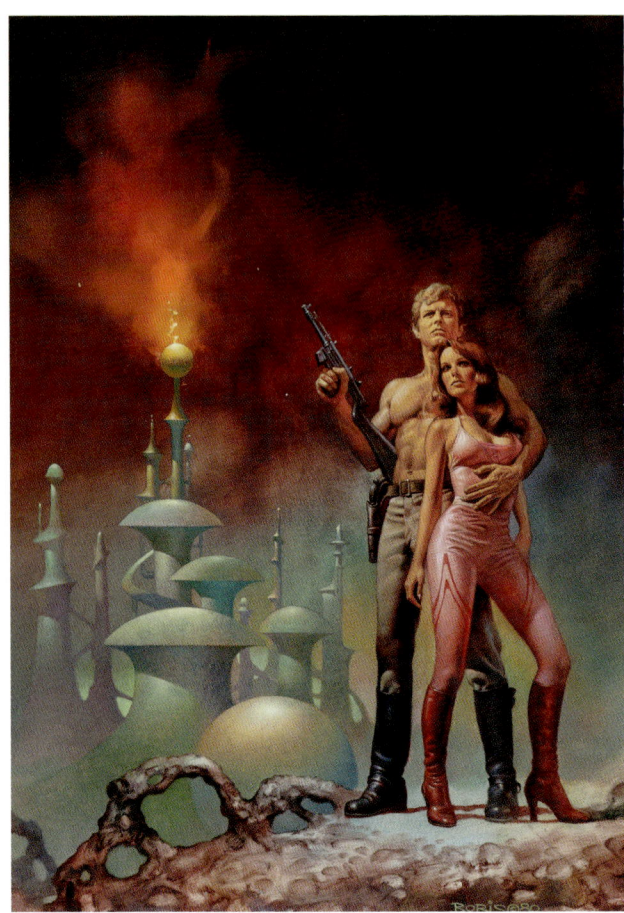

macht mir keinen Spaß"), offen-
sichtlich in einem eingefrorenem
Moment dargestellt und begeistert
geliebt – wie ein achtminütiges
Gitarrensolo in der Mitte eines
Neun-Minuten-Songs.

Obgleich man ihn mit Heavy-
Metal-Albumcovers verbindet,
hat Vallejo eine traditionalistische
Ader: Der 1941 geborene Sohn
eines prominenten Anwalts in
Lima, Peru, wuchs mit einer
Liebe zu klassischer Musik auf und
spielte Violine – wenn er nicht
gerade auf die Wände der Küche
zeichnete oder etwas über halb
nackte Helden las.

„Science-Fiction und Fantasy
haben mich schon immer interessiert. Tarzan war eines meiner
ersten Idole. Ich habe alle Tarzan-
Bücher gelesen. Ich fertigte immer
Zeichnungen von Tarzan an, wie
er mit den Affen herumläuft und
gegen wilde Tiere kämpft und so
weiter. Danach entdeckte ich das
Werk von Chesney Bonestell wie
auch J. Allen St. John, der der klassische Illustrator für Tarzan war."

1957 war für den 16-jährigen
Vallejo ein bedeutsames Jahr – er fand seinen ersten Job als Illustrator, begegnete seiner ersten Frau
und entdeckte zum ersten Mal eine Bodybuildingzeitschrift. Nach einem zweijährigen Abstecher
an die medizinische Hochschule – der ihm eine noch größere Leidenschaft für und Kenntnis der
Anatomie vermittelte – verbrachte Vallejo fünf Jahre als Stipendiat an der Escuela Nacional Superior Autónoma de Bellas Artes von Peru. 1964 kam er nach New York – ohne Englischkenntnisse
und mit nur wenig mehr im Gepäck als seiner Violine, achtzig Dollar und ein paar Proben seiner
Arbeiten. Dank der Unterstützung einiger peruanischer Landsleute bekam Vallejo einen Job in
einer Agentur und zeichnete, was auch immer benötigt wurde: Anzeigen, Grußkarten, Bilder von
Töpfen und Pfannen.

*Above: Flash Gordon, for the cover of the 1980 Ace
Tempo Novel edition of Flash Gordon Book One:
Massacre in the 22nd Century. Oil on board, 1980,
59.6 x 40.6 cm (23.5 x 16 inches). Courtesy of Heritage
Auctions.*

*Opposite: Mimir, for Boris Vallejo's 1992 Mythology
Calendar. This giant god of Norse mythology's name
translates to "the wise one." He combined knowledge with
great strength, holding the entire Kjolen mountain range
on his shoulders, as portrayed here. Oil on paper, 1991,
91.4 x 50.8 cm (36 x 20 inches).*

MASTERPIECES OF FANTASY ART

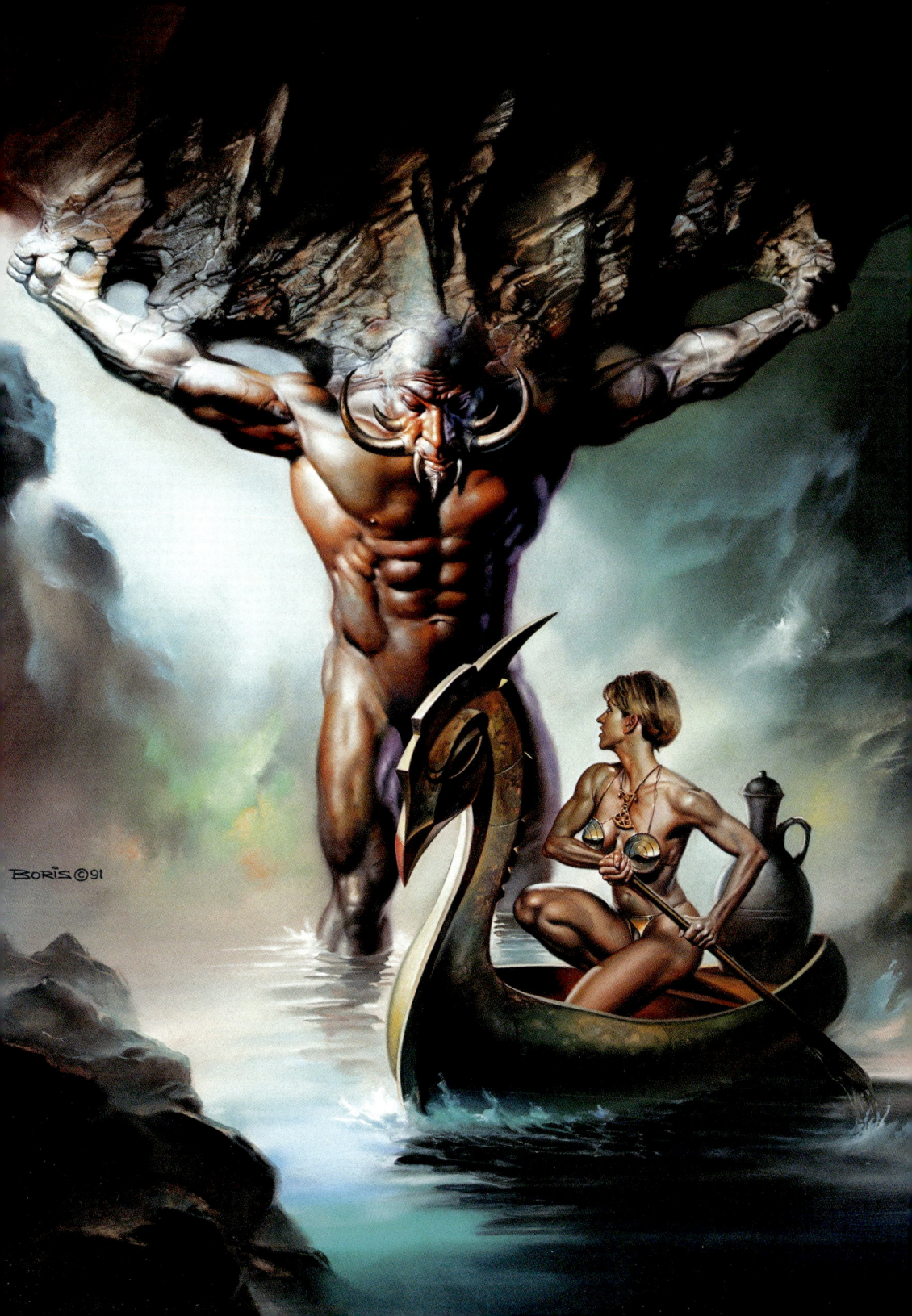

Als Aufträge für interessantere Dinge eintrudelten, darunter sein erster und einziger Auftrag für die Innenseiten eines Comics – eine Kriegsgeschichte für Marvel, 1966 – und Cover für Zeitschriften von Warren und Marvel wie *Eerie*, *Dracula Lives!*, *Tales of the Zombie* und, natürlich, *Savage Sword of Conan*, begann sich Vallejos Stil herauszubilden. 1975 wechselte er von Zeitschriftencovers zu Titelbildern für Bücher, darunter eine komplette Reihe zu Tarzan, dem Helden seiner Kindheit. Prächtige überzeugende Monster, akademische Posen und Detailreichtum sorgten dafür, dass Vallejos Arbeiten aus Feldern bunten Nebels und Pulks gebeugter Muskeln, die das Genre von Schwertkampf und Magie damals kennzeichneten, herausragten. Die chauvinistische Sklavenwelt der kontroversen *Gor*-Romane von John Norman hat von Vallejos Talent für eine detailreiche Darstellung von Menschenfleisch (und dem von Reptilien) – samt Bräunungsstreifen und all den Abstufungen von Farbtönen, die sich zeigten, wenn Vallejo die Scheinwerfer seines Ateliers auf seine Bodybuildingmodelle ausrichtete – wohl mehr profitiert, als sie verdiente.

„Studenten fragen uns, welche Farben wir für Hauttöne benutzen" (in das „wir" ist hier Julie Bell eingeschlossen, Vallejos zweite Frau), „doch da gibt's keine speziellen Farben. Wenn wir Hauttöne malen, nutzen wir praktisch die gesamte Palette, die uns zur Verfügung steht. Normalerweise habe ich auf meiner Palette zwischen 18 und 24 Farben parat."

Das Poster für die (ironischerweise ohne Nacktheit auskommende) Neuveröffentlichung von *Barbarella* im Jahre 1977 brachte ihm sogar mehr Aufmerksamkeit ein, und die 1978 veröffentlichte Monografie *The Fantastic Art of Boris Vallejo* festigte seine Stellung als herausragender Persönlichkeit auf seinem Gebiet, und – obgleich ein Bewunderer von Michelangelo, Rubens und Velázquez – er schaffte es auch, diese Position aus der Welt der stilisierten und „malerischen" Paletten und Ausführungen von Illustrationen der späten Pulp-Ära in die in ihrer ganzen Bandbreite glänzende Welt der Mainstream-Fantasy der 1980er-Jahre hinüberzuretten. Viele seiner faszinierendsten Werke aus dieser Periode gehören zu seinen untypischsten (*The Nebulon Horror*, 1980; *The Girl Who Owned A City*, 1977), erotischsten (*Siren Song*, 1979) Arbeiten, oder sie vereinen beide Aspekte (*Soap*, 1981).

In den 1980er-Jahren begann Vallejo damit, jedes Jahr einen neuen Kalender zu veröffentlichen; er illustrierte Bücher, die seine erste Frau, die Schriftstellerin Doris Vallejo, verfasst hatte; und von überallher kamen Aufträge: Roger Corman beauftragte ihn, seine Schauspieler für die Plakate von Abenteuer-Exploitationfilmen wie *Barbarian Queen* in Kostümen zu malen, während Vallejo für *National Lampoon* ironisch auf seinen eigenen Stil Bezug nahm, indem er Chevy Chase für *Vacation*- und *European-Vacation*-Plakate pseudoheroische Posen einnehmen ließ und ihn so malte. Seine malerischen Strukturen wurden glatter, und seine Figuren wirkten immer deutlicher eingeölt und noch athletischer.

In Interviews hebt Vallejo stets hervor, wie organisch der künstlerische Prozess des Gestaltens für ihn zu sein schien: „Stile entwickeln sich, während man voranschreitet, ganz von alleine. Das Malen fällt mir ausgesprochen leicht, ich denke darüber wirklich nicht groß nach."

1989 lud Vallejo, wie er das zuvor schon so oft getan hatte, eine Bodybuilderkollegin als Modell in sein Atelier ein. Er malte sie als eine etruskische Gottheit der Unterwelt. Sie hielt dabei eine Axt in der Hand, und ihre purpurfarbenen Haare ringelten sich über einen goldenen Bikini. Auch sie war eine Malerin. Sie verliebten sich. 1994 heirateten Boris Vallejo und Julie Bell und wurden als das „Erste Paar der Fantasykunst" bekannt. Sie teilen sich ein Atelier und arbeiten oft zusammen wie zum Beispiel 2018, als sie für Andrew W. K. gemeinsam ein Albumcover gestalteten.

In den 50 Jahren, die er nun aktiv ist, hat Vallejo von Schachteln für Videospiele (*Star Control, Golden Axe II, Phantasy Star IV, Ecco the Dolphin*) bis zu einer Fotomonografie von Hinterteilen

(*Hindsight: Boris Vallejo – His Photographic Art*, 1998) alles Mögliche produziert, und sein Einfluss ist gewaltig. Er arbeitet nicht nur wie eine Maschine – „Anstrengend ist das für mich nicht, ich weiß nicht nur genau, wann etwas fertig ist, ich kann auch einschätzen, wie lange es dazu noch braucht. Ich kann sagen: Okay, noch ein Tag, noch zwei, vielleicht fünf Stunden, dann habe ich es, was auch immer es ist, so weit, dass es fertig ist" –, Maschinen wollen arbeiten wie er: Die Programme für digitale Malerei, die heute von künstlerischen Gestaltern von Spielen und Filmen benutzt werden, sind mit solchen Filtern und Tools ausgestattet, dass sie die schimmernden Schlaglichter, blauen Schatten, beobachteten, aber idealisierten Rundungen, die fernen schwebenden Hintergründe und die sanften, jedoch ganz besonderen Strukturen imitieren, wie man sie nur auf den Leinwänden des vorzüglichen Boris findet.

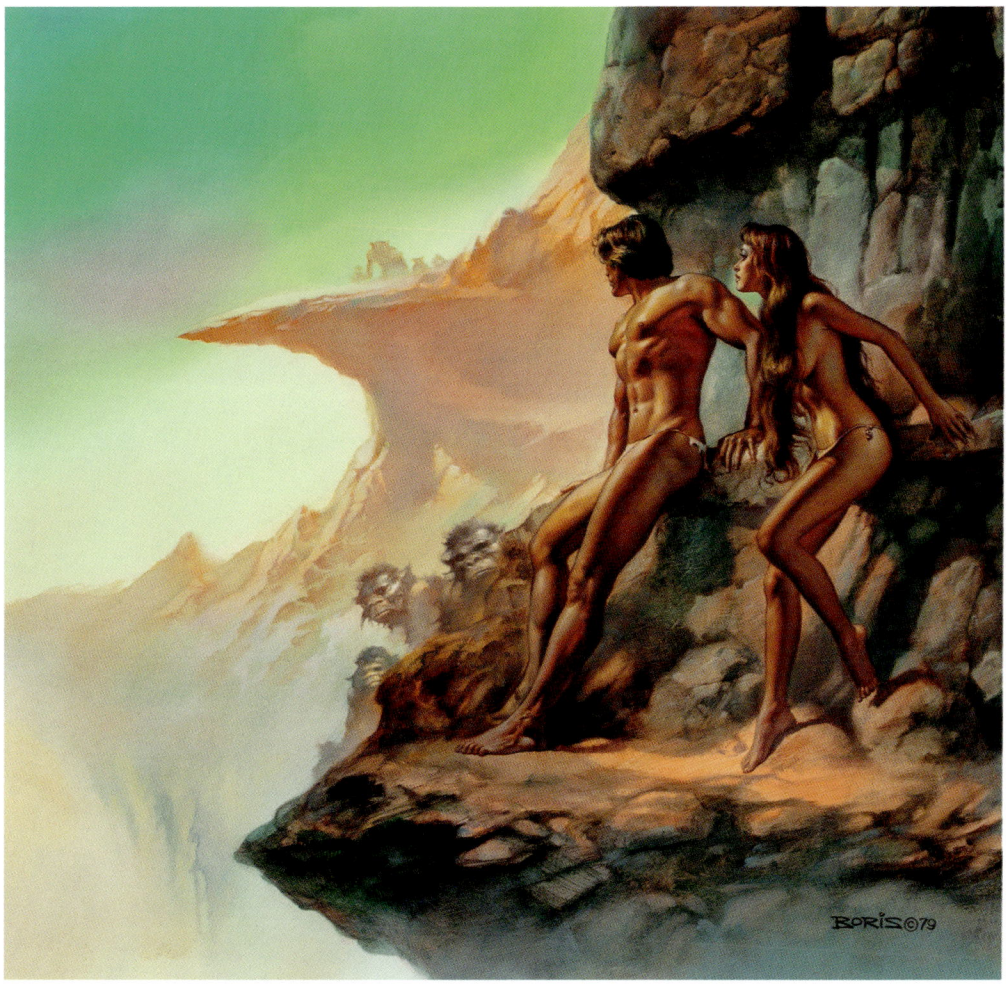

Above: The Makers of Universes, for the cover of Philip José Farmer's 1979 novel *The World of Tiers.*

Oil on board, 1979, 48.9 x 43.8 cm (19.25 x 17.25 inches). Courtesy of Heritage Auctions.

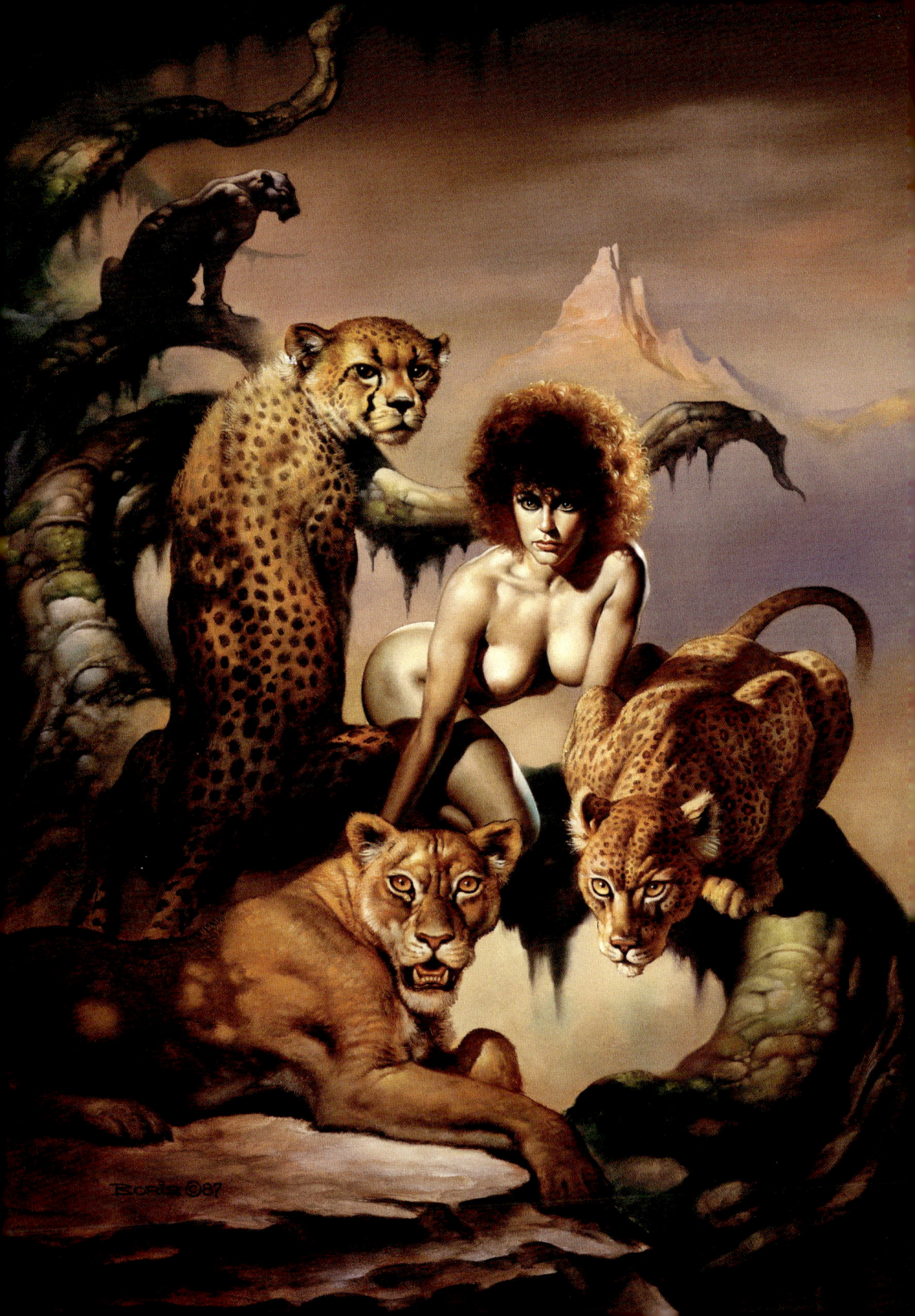

BORIS VALLEJO
LE MAÎTRE DU MUSCLE

« Nous sommes tous attirés par les corps, sinon nous n'existerions pas ! »

PAR ZAK SMITH

Quel que soit le thème apparent – fantasy, science-fiction, érotisme, comics, voire comique pour quelques commandes –, le vrai sujet de Boris Vallejo est toujours le corps. Dans son œuvre, les corps font des milliers de choses : ils brandissent des armes, enlacent des démons, se figent ou se tendent, conquérants, face à diverses créatures, ils bondissent sur des dinosaures, s'adossent à la roche et aux arbres, chevauchent des dragons volants et des licornes à travers les nuages, parmi des planètes au million de couleurs, ils se flanquent de loups et d'autres bêtes qu'ils caressent, ils se tordent, luttent, émergent d'énormes œufs ou de fleurs géantes, poussent et se lovent sous le cuir noir ou des ailes de papillon, ils rampent à la surface des paysages, les uns à travers les autres – mais ils demeurent, indéniablement, des corps. Un éclairage parfait, des poses héroïques, intrépides, stoïques. Les méchants sont nobles comme des personnages d'opéra, les monstres tout droit sortis d'un précis d'anatomie classique et, sur ses cartes à échanger, les superhéros semblent moins costumés que tatoués de la tête aux pieds.

Vallejo a très vite été surnommé « le prochain Frazetta », mais les hommes virils qu'ont créés ces deux peintres sont aussi différents que les hommes virils qu'ils étaient. Frank Frazetta, grand joueur de baseball qui a failli jouer en première ligue, n'hésitait pas à mettre en perspective, déformer ou dissimuler le corps, à laisser dans l'ombre une jambe, un bras ou même un visage pour que l'action soit plus juste, tandis que Vallejo, culturiste passionné, composait chaque tableau à partir du centre, où se dressait invariablement un corps dessiné et éclairé à la perfection – nu ou presque (« Les costumes m'ennuient et je n'aime pas faire les tenues d'époque »), figé dans le temps, aimé avec enthousiasme – comme un solo de guitare de huit minutes au milieu d'une chanson de neuf minutes.

Bien qu'il soit associé aux pochettes d'albums de heavy metal, Vallejo a une facette plus traditionaliste : né en 1941, fils d'un éminent avocat de Lima, au Pérou, il grandit dans l'amour de la musique classique et joue du violon, quand il ne dessine pas sur les murs de la cuisine ou abandonne ses lectures sur des héros demi-nus.

« Je me suis toujours intéressé à la science-fiction et à la fantasy. Une de mes premières idoles a été Tarzan. J'ai lu tous les livres de Tarzan. Je dessinais tout le temps Tarzan qui se baladait avec ses singes et combattait des bêtes sauvages, etc. Ensuite j'ai découvert les œuvres de Chesley Bonestell, puis J. Allen St. John, l'illustrateur du Tarzan classique. »

L'année 1957 marque un jalon important pour le jeune Vallejo, âgé de 16 ans – il décroche son premier travail d'illustration, rencontre sa première femme et ouvre son premier magazine de culturisme. Après deux années à l'école de médecine – qui ne font qu'attiser sa passion pour

Opposite: Mistress of the Cats, for a calendar. Oil over acrylic on board, 1987, 69.2 x 45.7 cm (27.25 x 18 inches).

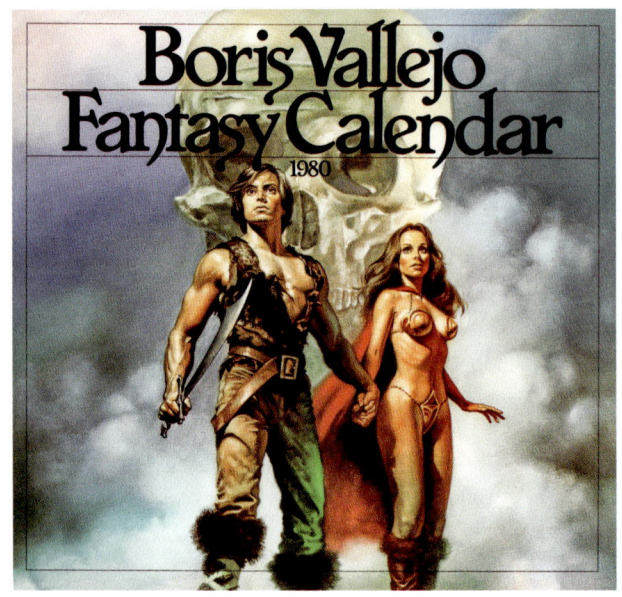

l'anatomie et enrichir ses connaissances sur le sujet –, Vallejo passe cinq ans à l'École nationale des beaux-arts péruvienne. En 1964, il débarque à New York ; il ne parle pas un mot d'anglais et voyage avec sur lui à peine plus que son violon, 80 $ et quelques échantillons de son travail. Grâce à des compatriotes péruviens, Vallejo est embauché dans une agence où il dessine tout ce qui doit l'être : publicités, cartes de vœux, poêles et casseroles…

Il reçoit bientôt des commandes plus intéressantes, notamment pour sa seule bande dessinée destinée au marché américain – une histoire de guerre pour Marvel en 1966 – et signe la couverture de divers titres Warren et Marvel comme *Eerie*, *Dracula Lives!*, *Tales of the Zombie* et, bien sûr, *Savage Sword of Conan*. Le style de Vallejo prend de l'ampleur. En 1975, il abandonne les magazines pour les couvertures de livres, notamment toute une collection consacrée au héros de son enfance, Tarzan. Avec ses monstres magnifiques mais plausibles, ses poses académiques et la myriade de détails qui émaillent ses œuvres, Vallejo se démarque des nappes de brume colorée et des bataillons de Messieurs Muscles qui caractérisent alors l'*heroic fantasy*. L'univers sado-maso machiste des *Chroniques de Gor*, la saga controversée de John Norman, ne méritait sans doute pas d'être si bien servi par Vallejo, particulièrement doué pour représenter la chair humaine (et reptilienne) – avec les marques de bronzage et tous les dégradés chromatiques qui se révélaient lorsque le maître pointait ses projecteurs sur ses modèles bodybuilders.

« Les étudiants nous demandent quelles couleurs nous utilisons pour la peau [ce "nous" inclut sa seconde épouse Julie Bell], mais ce n'est pas comme ça que cela se passe. Quand nous peignons la peau, nous utilisons quasiment toute la palette à notre disposition. En général, j'ai entre 18 et 24 couleurs sur ma palette. »

L'affiche pour la deuxième sortie en salles de *Barbarella* (sans nudité… belle ironie !), en 1977, attire un peu plus l'attention sur lui et la monographie *The Fantastic Art of Boris Vallejo* publiée en 1978 l'établit comme une figure majeure du genre. C'est ainsi que cet admirateur de Michel-Ange, Rubens et Vélasquez mène la charge des artistes qui désertent la rive picturale stylisée et léchée des *pulps* tardifs pour explorer l'imagerie grand public des années 1980 dans tout son spectre et son lustre. La plupart de ses œuvres les plus captivantes sont alors parmi ses plus atypiques (*The Nebulon Horror*, 1980 ; *The Girl Who Owned A City*, 1977), érotiques (*Siren Song*, 1979), ou les deux (*Soap*, 1981).

Above: The first *Boris Vallejo Fantasy Calendar*, 1980.

Opposite: *Siren Song*, used as the cover of Gianni Pilo's *Cthulhu's Dream*, 1986. Oil on board, 1979, 71.1 x 47.6 cm (28 x 18.75 inches).

MASTERPIECES OF FANTASY ART

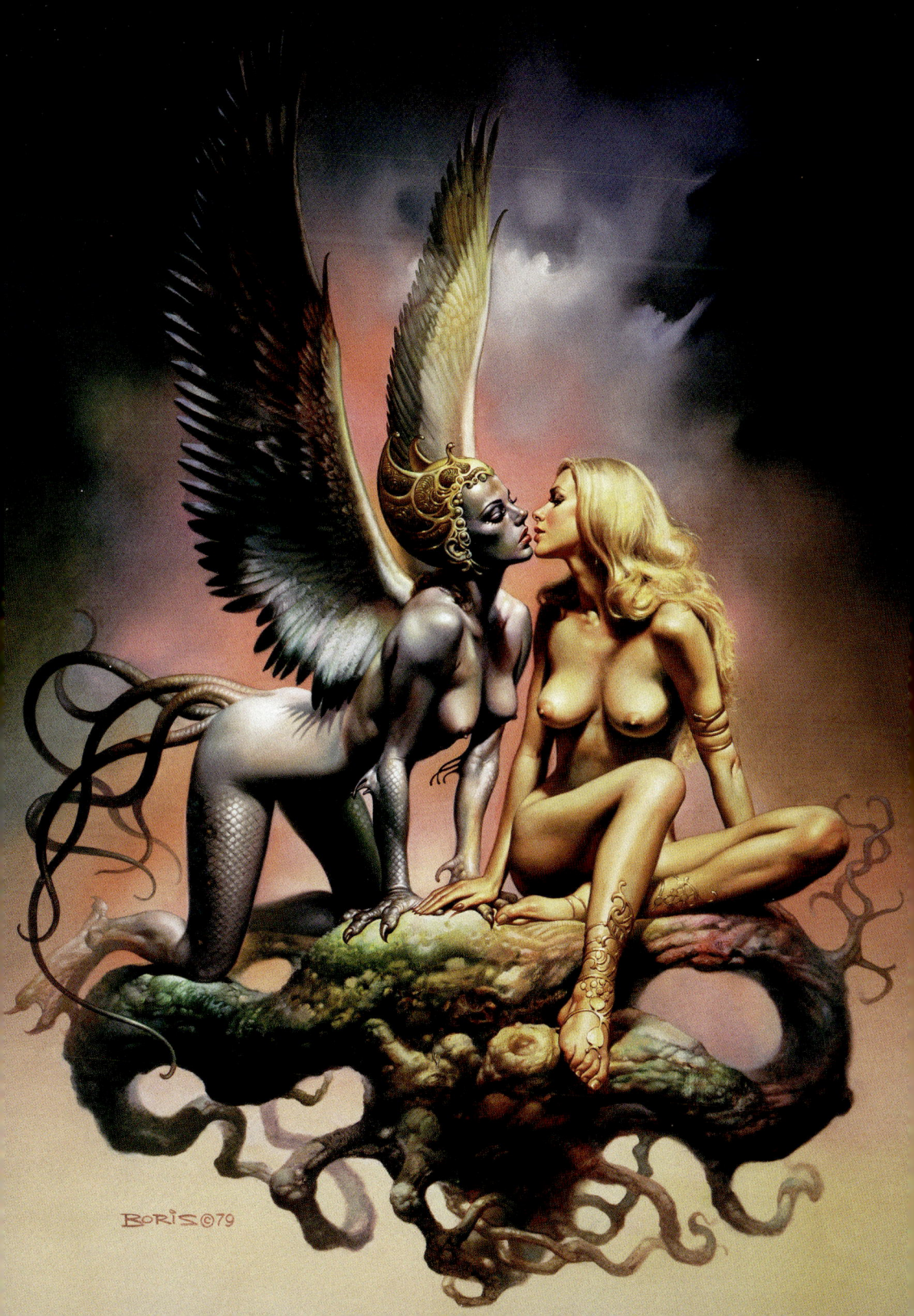

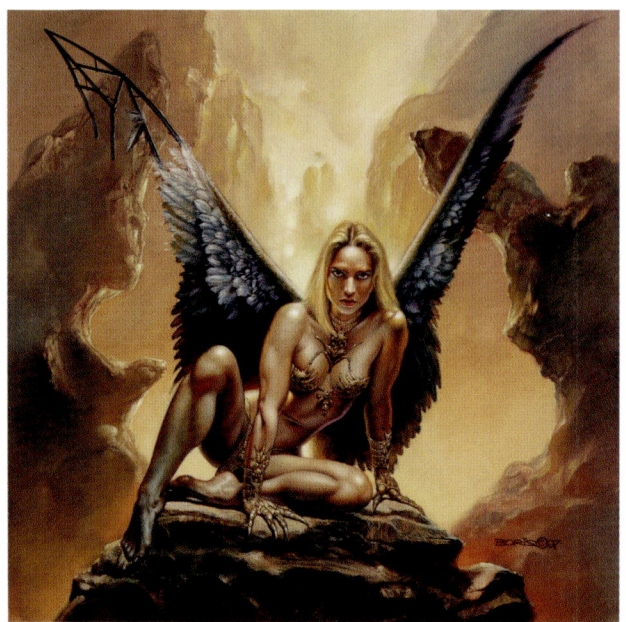

Dans les années 1980, Vallejo commence à publier un calendrier chaque année, il illustre des livres avec sa première femme, l'auteure Doris Vallejo, et reçoit des commandes de toutes parts : Roger Corman lui fait peindre ses acteurs en costumes pour les affiches de films d'aventure (et d'exploitation) comme *Barbarian Queen* et il adresse un clin d'œil ironique à son propre style pour la série tirée du *National Lampoon* en représentant Chevy Chase surjouant une pose de héros sur les affiches de *Bonjour les vacances 1 (Vacation)* et 2 *(European Vacation)*. La texture de ses œuvres s'affine et ses personnages sont toujours plus athlétiques et huilés.

Dans ses interviews, Vallejo insiste sur la manière foncièrement organique avec laquelle il a toujours abordé sa pratique artistique : « Le style évolue naturellement à mesure que vous progressez. Peindre me vient si naturellement que je n'y réfléchis pas vraiment intellectuellement. »

En 1989, comme il le faisait souvent, Vallejo invite une camarade culturiste à poser pour lui dans son atelier. Il la peint en déesse étrusque des Enfers, brandissant une hache, sa chevelure violette tombant en torsades sur un bikini doré. Elle aussi est peintre. Boris Vallejo et Julie Bell tombent amoureux, ils se marient en 1994 et deviennent « le couple phare du fantasy art » ; ils font atelier commun et collaborent souvent, notamment pour une pochette d'album d'Andrew W.K. en 2018.

Après 50 ans d'une carrière jalonnée de productions très diverses, du coffret de jeu vidéo (*Star Control, Golden Axe II, Phantasy Star IV, Ecco the Dolphin*) à une monographie de ses photos de fesses (*Hindsight: Boris Vallejo – His Photographic Art*, 1998), l'influence de Vallejo est incommensurable. Non seulement il travaille comme une machine – « Cela ne me demande pas d'efforts, je sais quand c'est terminé, je le sais même avant que ce soit terminé. Je peux dire : "OK, il va me falloir encore un jour, deux jours ou cinq heures, selon les cas, et ce sera fini." » – mais les machines veulent travailler comme lui : les programmes de peinture numérique qu'utilisent aujourd'hui les illustrateurs dans le cinéma et l'industrie du jeu regorgent de filtres et d'outils conçus précisément pour imiter les rehauts rutilants, les ombres bleues, les courbes étudiées mais idéalisées, les arrière-plans lointains et flottants et les textures lustrées mais toujours diverses qui ne s'observent que dans les toiles de l'éminent Boris.

Above: Broken Wing, used in the *1998 Boris Vallejo and Julie Bell Fantasy Calendar*, oil on board, 1997, 43.1 x 43.1 cm (17 x 17 inches).

Opposite: Jeannie's Kitten, a collaborative effort by Vallejo and Julie Bell, commissioned for the 2013 IlluXCon "the cutting edge of contemporary realist art," held in their home city, Allentown, Pennsylvania. Oil on board, 2013, 64.1 x 45.7 cm (25.25 x 18 inches).

MASTERPIECES OF FANTASY ART

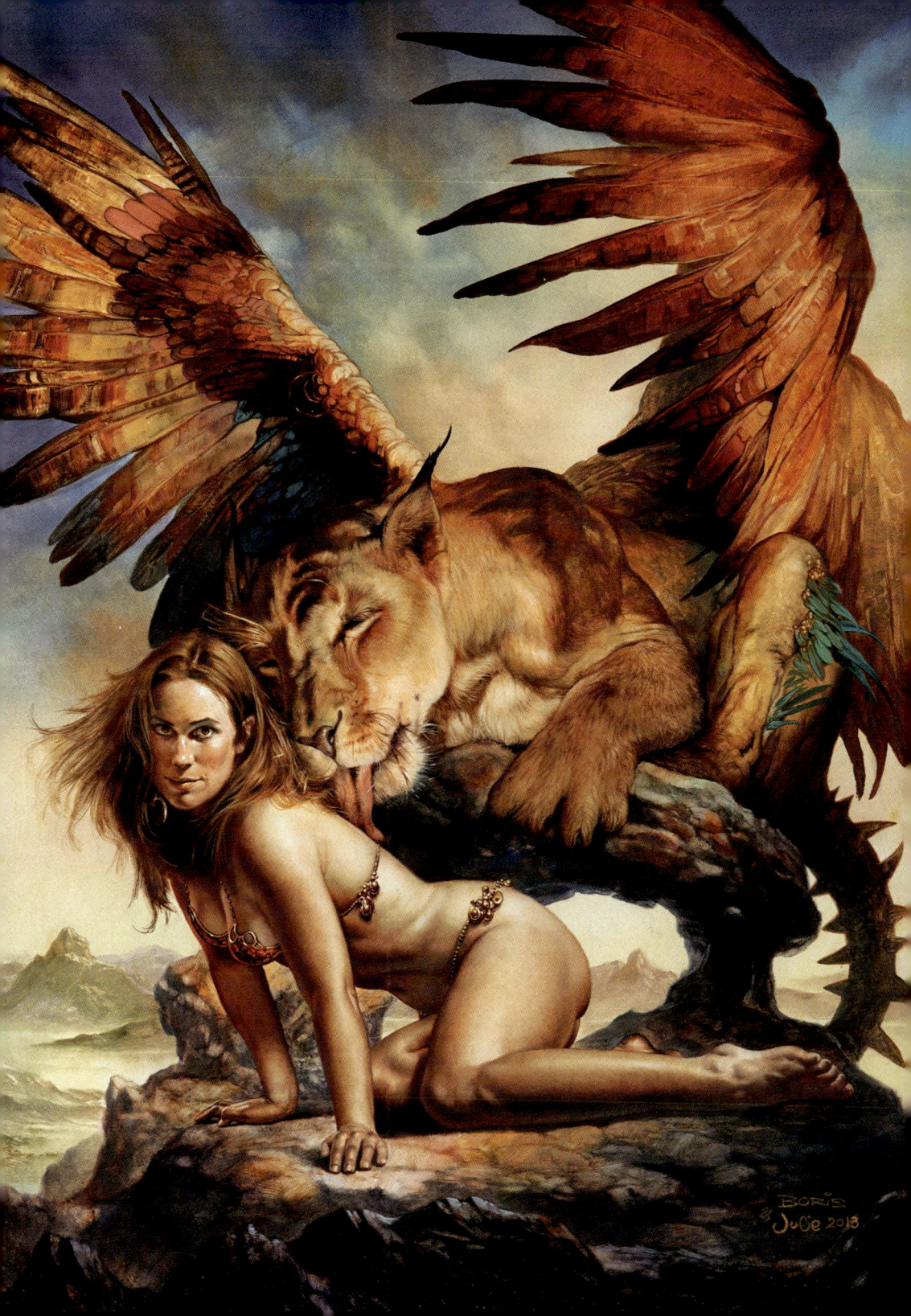

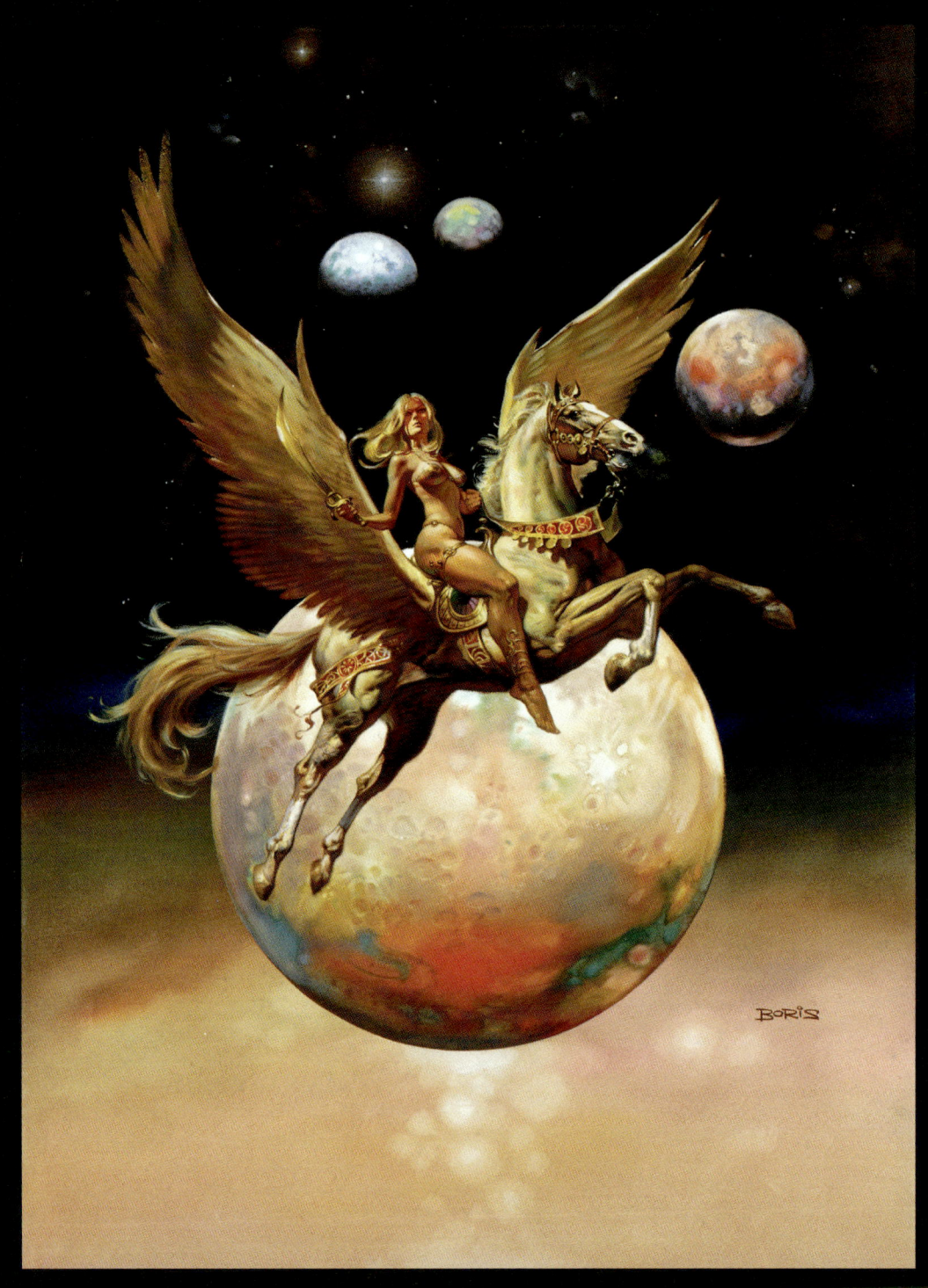

MASTERPIECES OF FANTASY ART

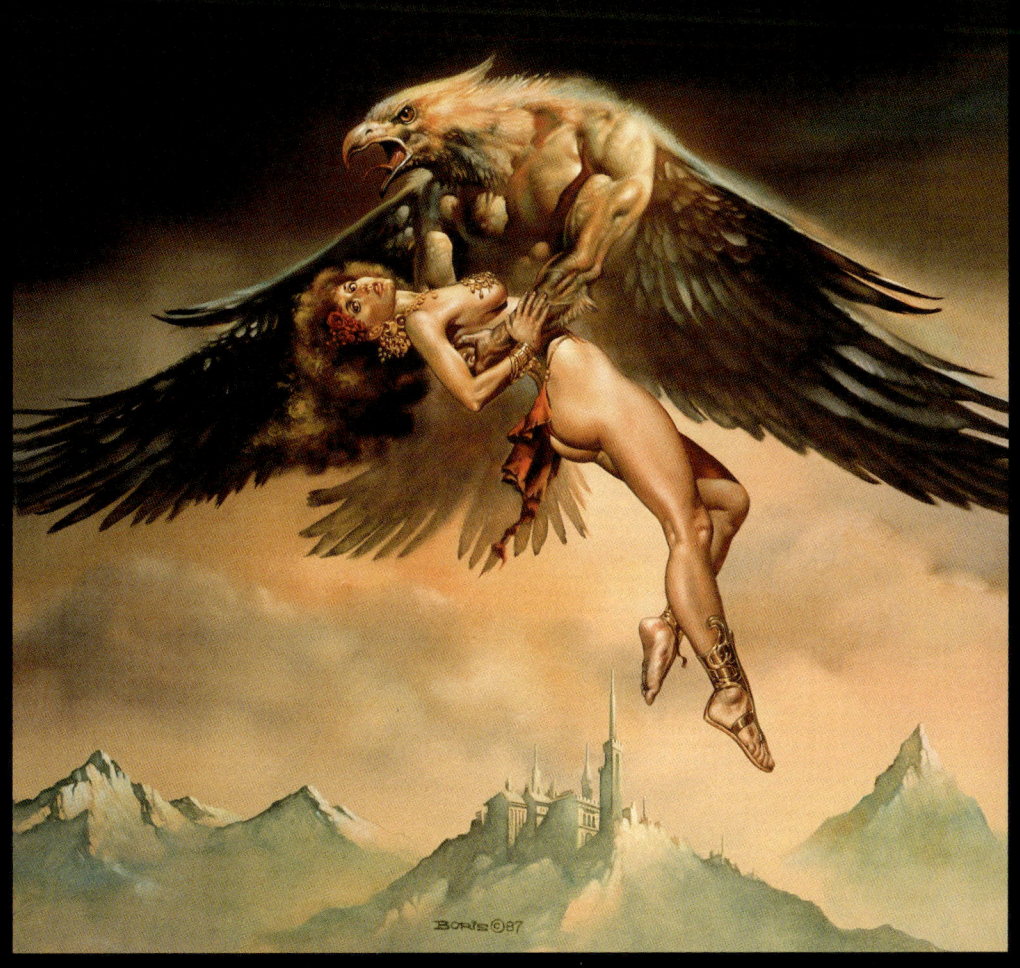

Opposite: Golden Wings, for a set of book plates, oil on board, 1977.

Above: Thiassi Abducting Idunn, for *Boris Vallejo's 1989 Mythology Calendar*. Oil on board, 1987, 49.5 x 53.3 cm (19.5 x 21 inches).

BORIS VALLEJO

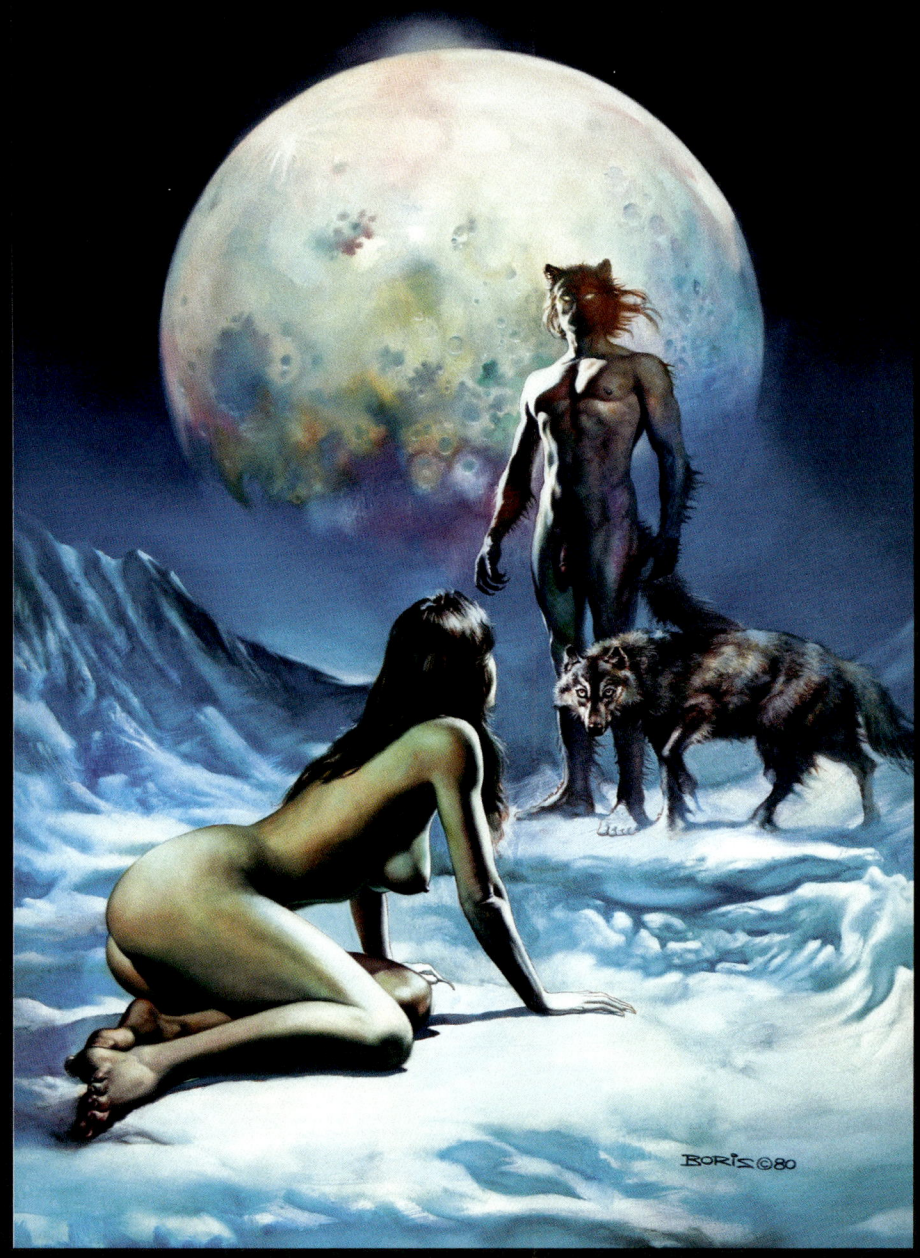

Above: Spoor, aka *Wolfman*, featured in the 1982 book
Mirage. Oil on board, 1980, 99 x 74.9 cm (39 x 29.5 inches).
Courtesy of Heritage Auctions.

MASTERPIECES OF FANTASY ART

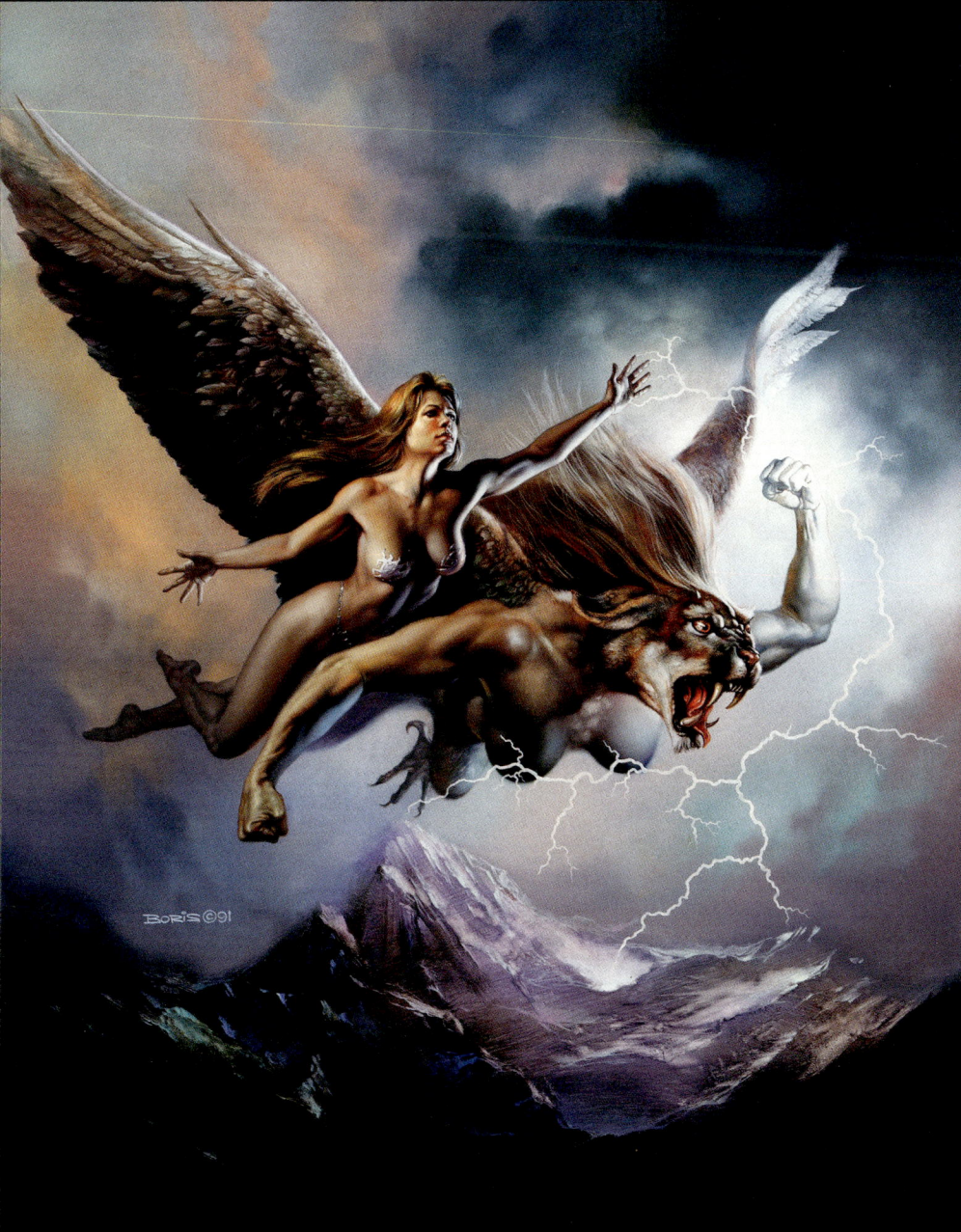

Above: Ilmarinen, Goddess of the Storm, for Boris Vallejo's 1993 Mythology Calendar. Oil on paper, 1991, 76.2 x 61 cm (30 x 24 inches).

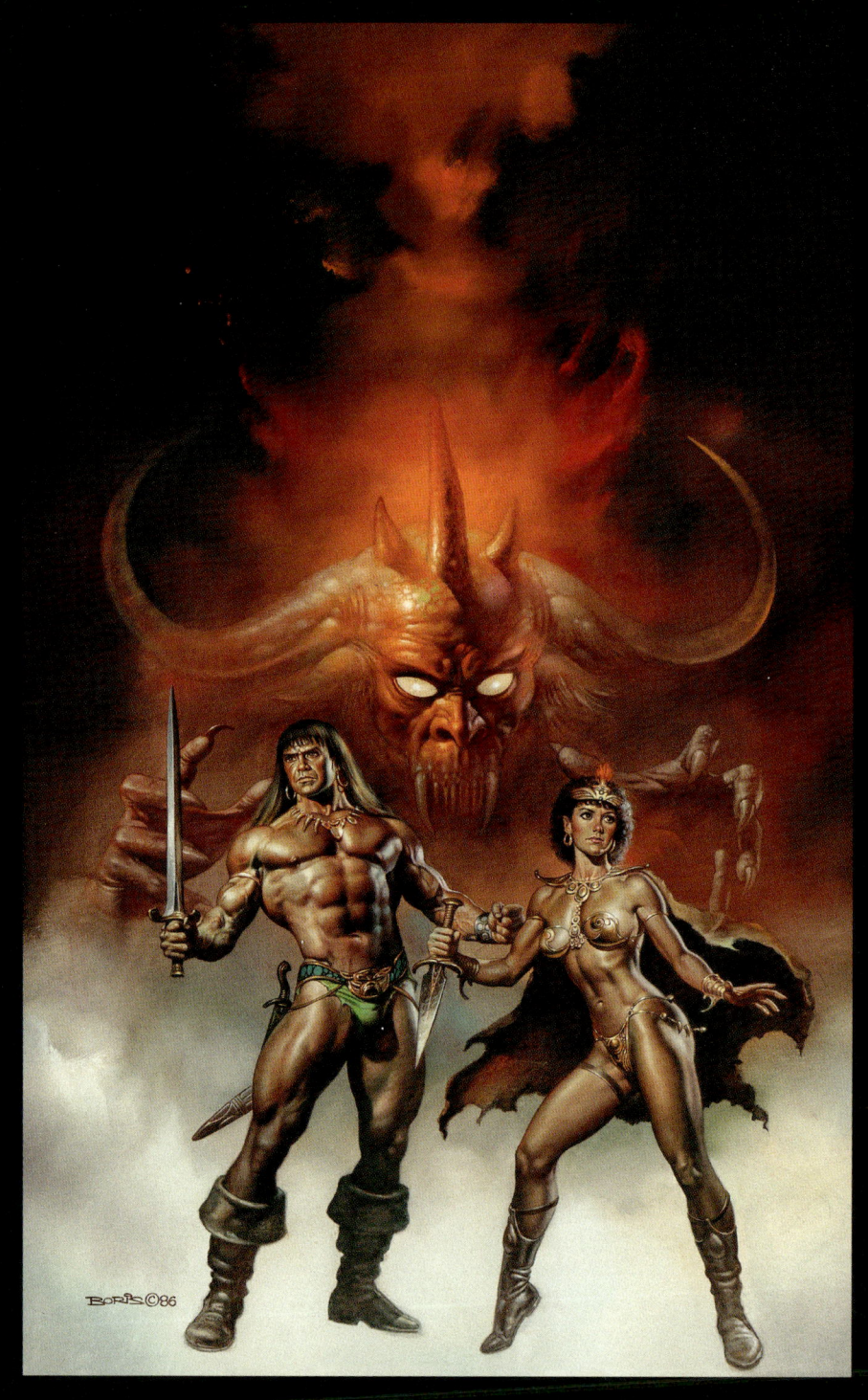

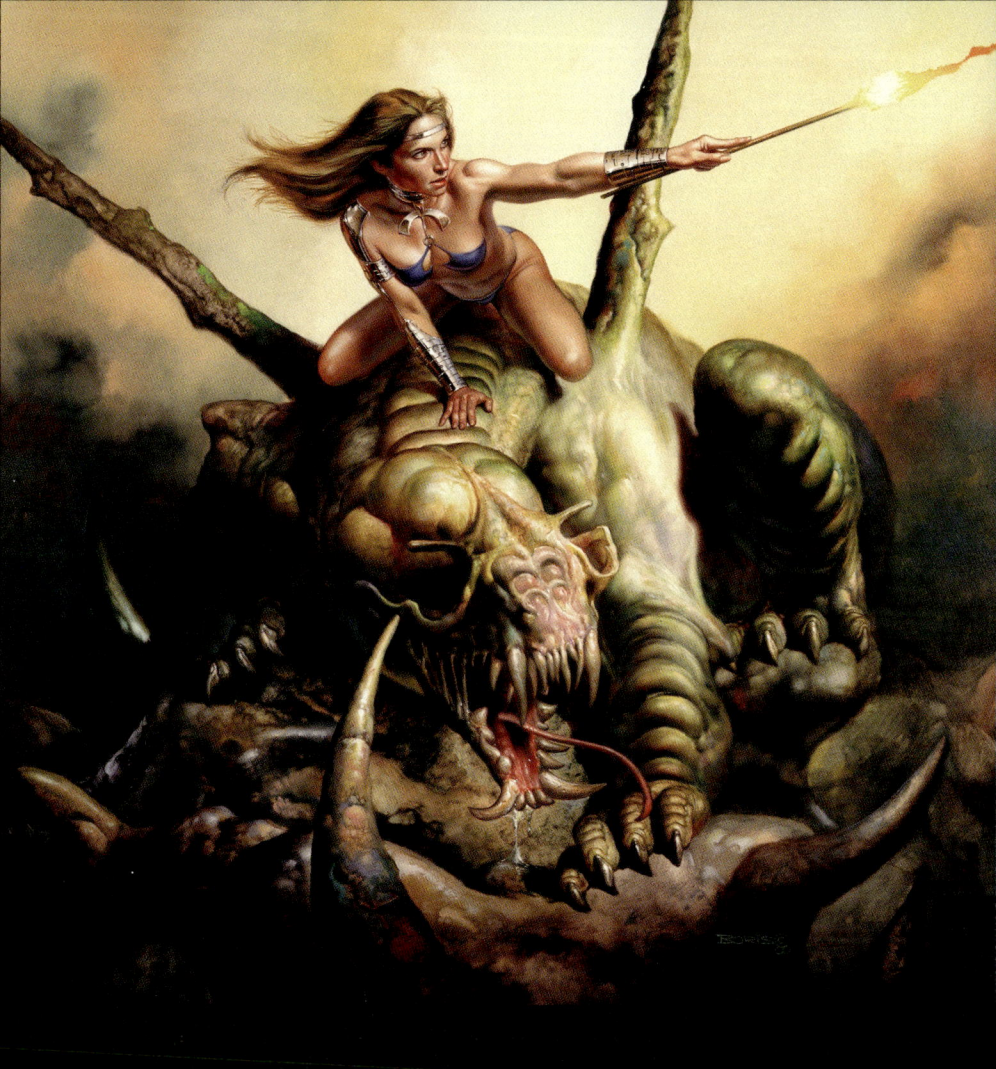

Opposite: Conan the Fearless, for the cover of Steve Parry's 1986 novel. Acrylic on board, 1986, 74.9 x 50.8 cm (29.5 x 20 inches). Courtesy of Heritage Auctions.

Above: The Road Ahead, used in the 2001 *Boris Vallejo and Julie Bell Fantasy Calendar*, oil on board, 2000, 66 x 66 cm (26 x 26 inches).

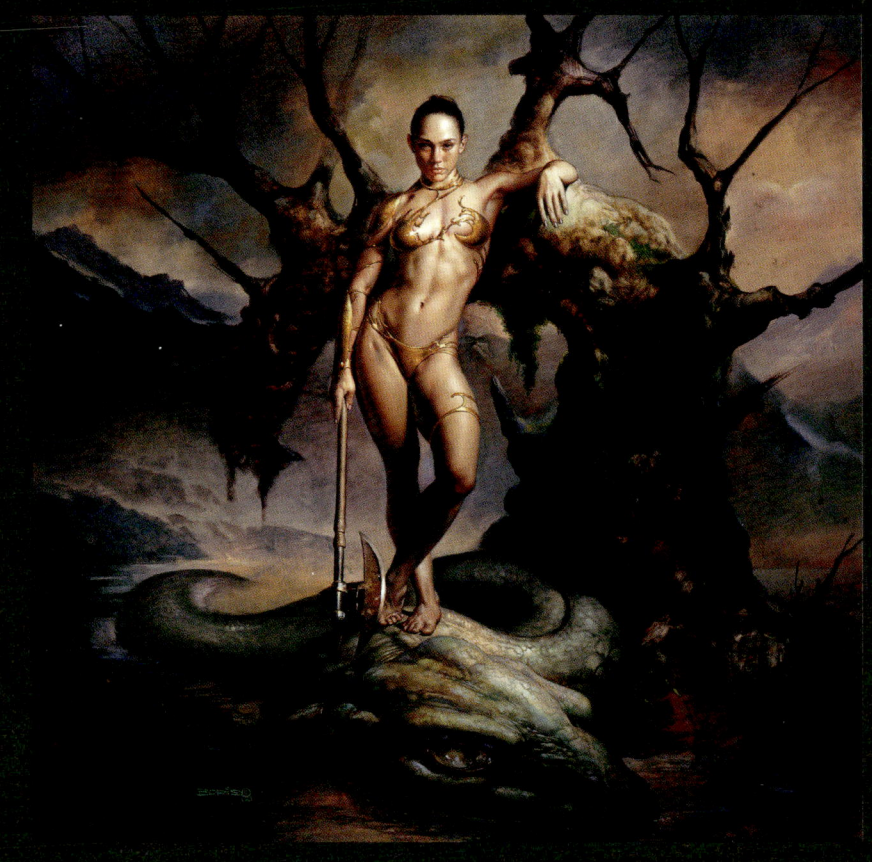

Above: In Victory, for the cover of *Heavy Metal*, March 2003. It later appeared on the cover of *Fantasy Art Essentials*, 2012. Oil on board, 2002, 68.5 x 68.5 cm (27 x 27 inches). Courtesy of Heritage Auctions.

Opposite: Sphinx, oil on board, 1984, 69 x 53.8 cm (27.2 x 21.2 inches). Courtesy of Heritage Auctions.

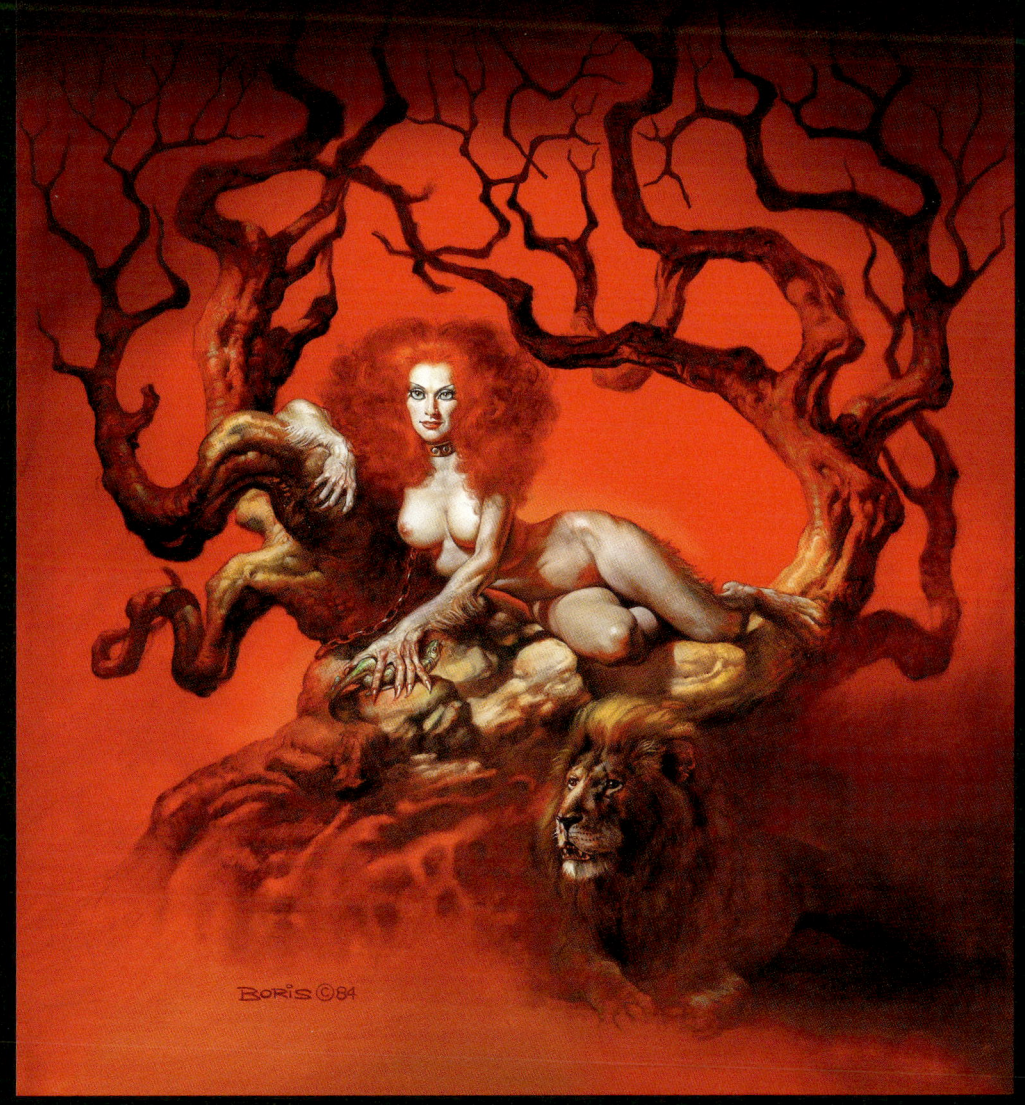

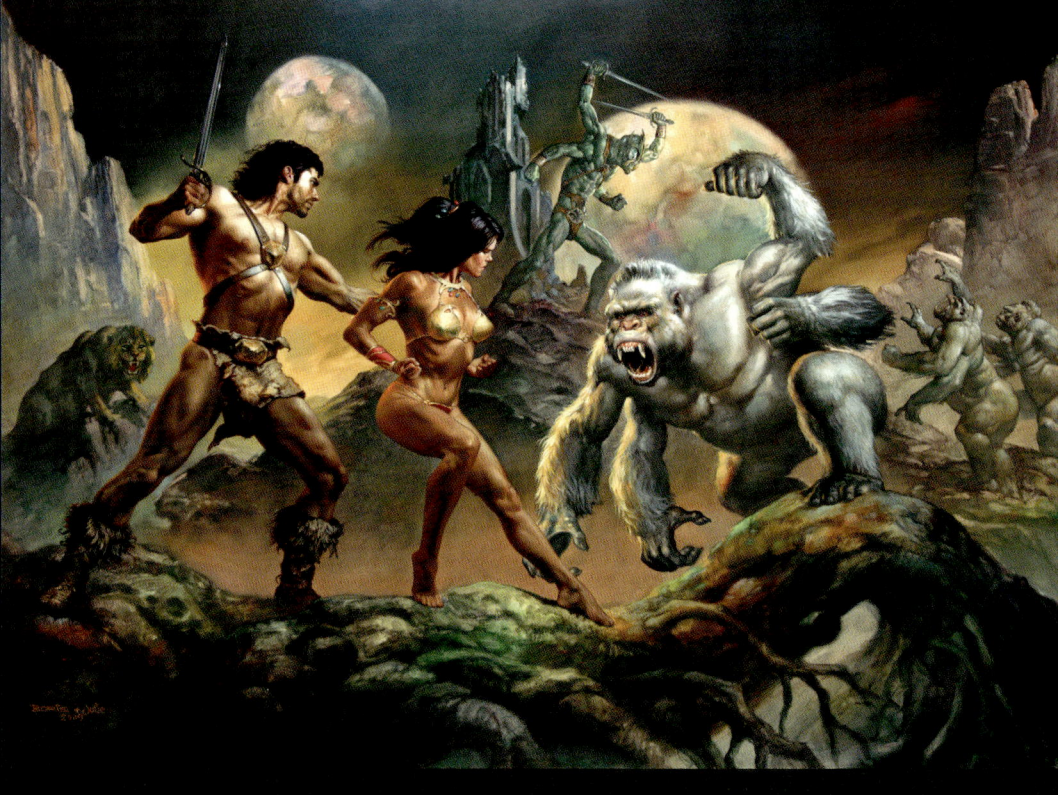

Above: John Carter of Mars with Friends, private commission by Vallejo and Julie Bell, oil on board, 2009, 101.6 x 76.2 cm (40 x 30 inches).

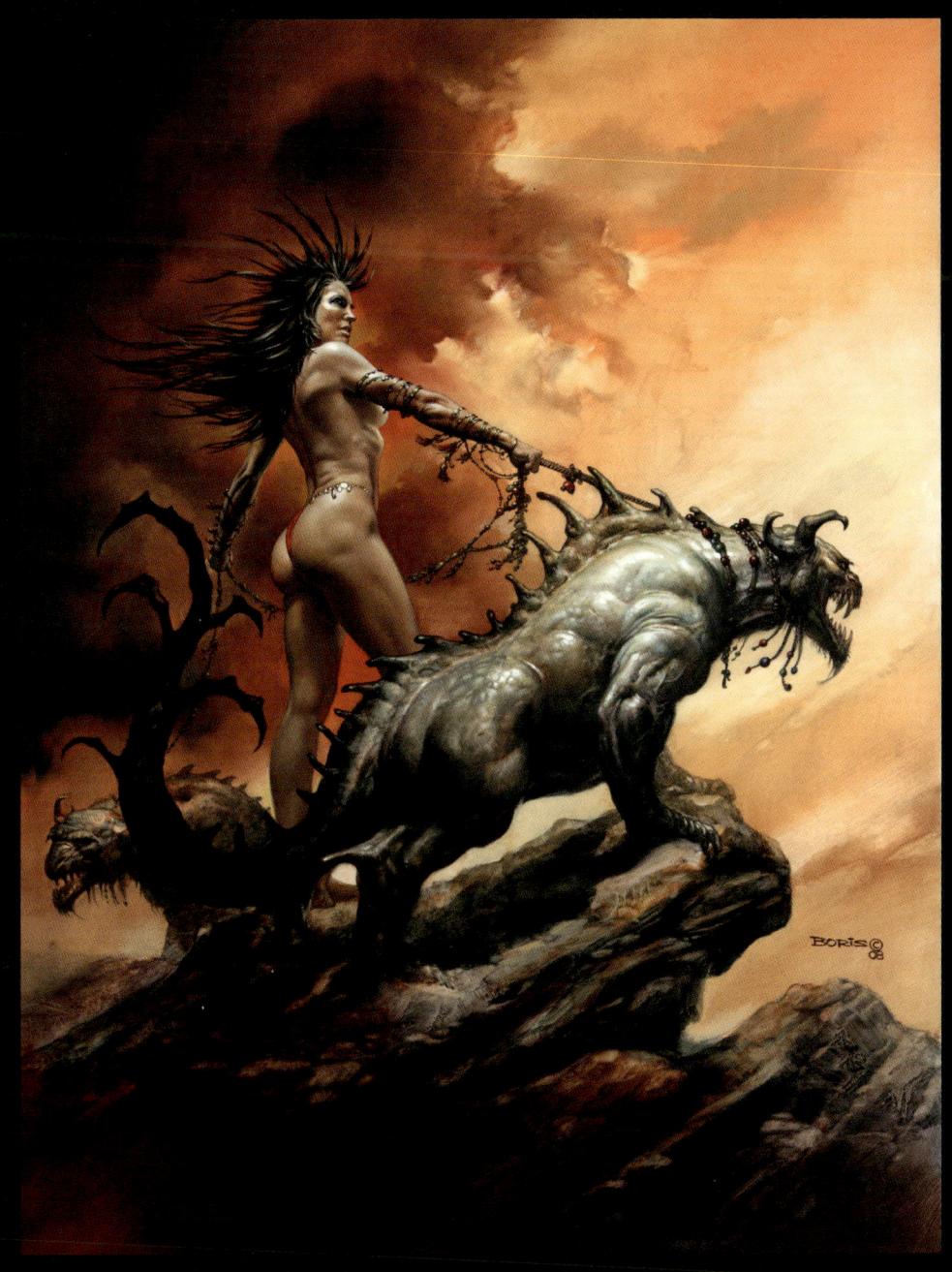

Above: Tales of Fausseah, for the *2009 Boris Vallejo and Julie Bell Fantasy Calendar,* oil on board, 2008, 71.1 x 45.7 cm (28 x 18 inches).

BORIS VALLEJO

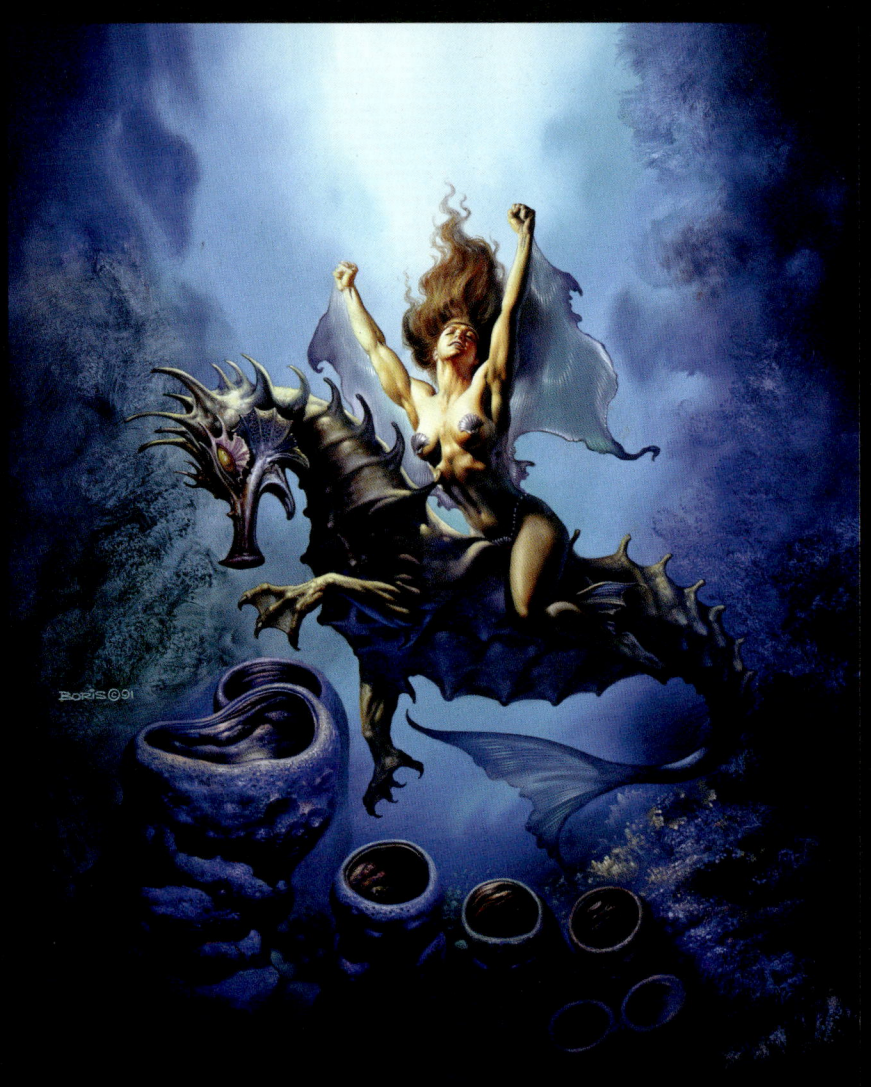

Above: Hippocampus, featured on the cover of
The Fabulous Women of Boris Vallejo and Julie Bell, 1991.
Oil on board, 1991, 68.5 x 53.3 cm (27 x 21 inches).

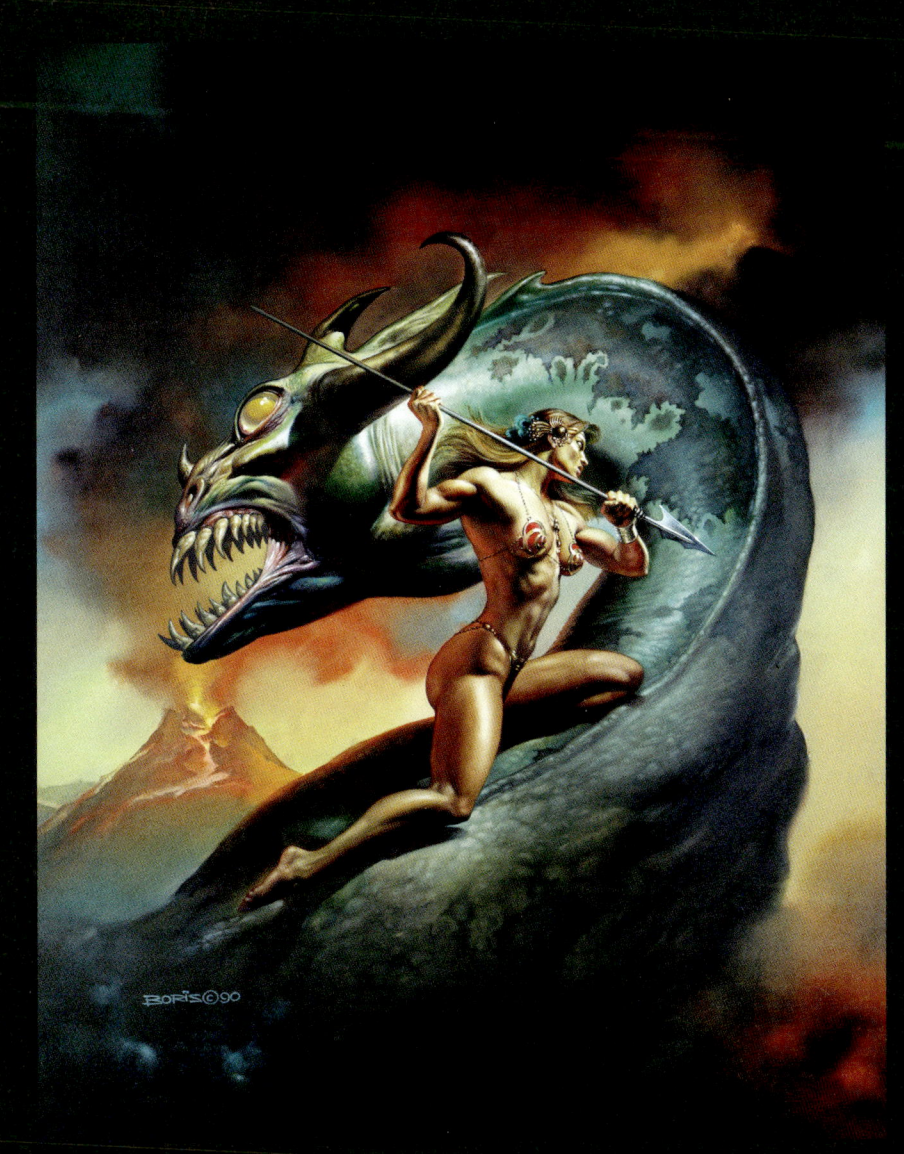

Above: The Basilisk, cover for *Boris Vallejo's 1992 Mythology Calendar*. Oil on board, 1990, 66 x 50.8 cm (26 x 20 inches).

BORIS VALLEJO

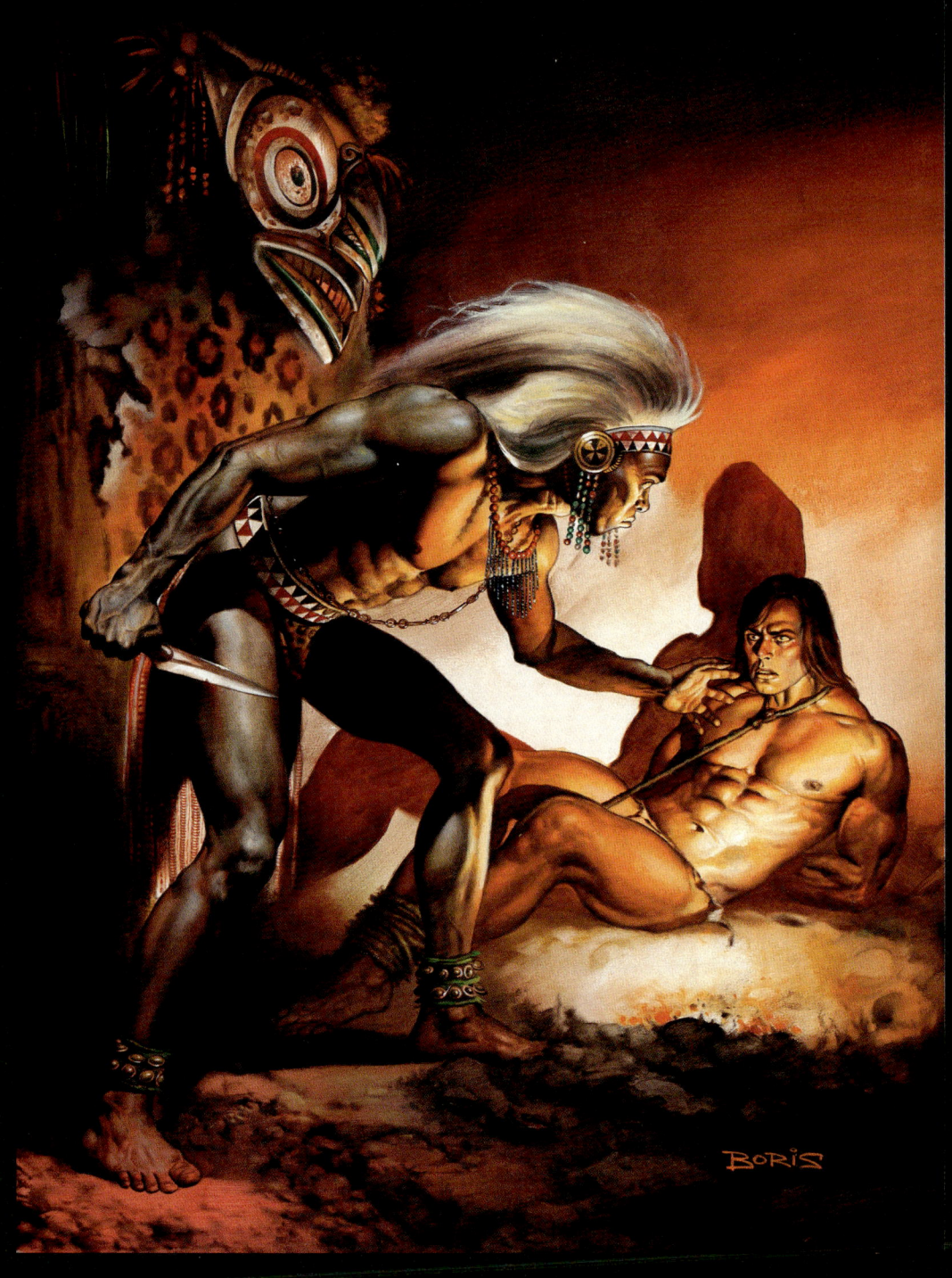

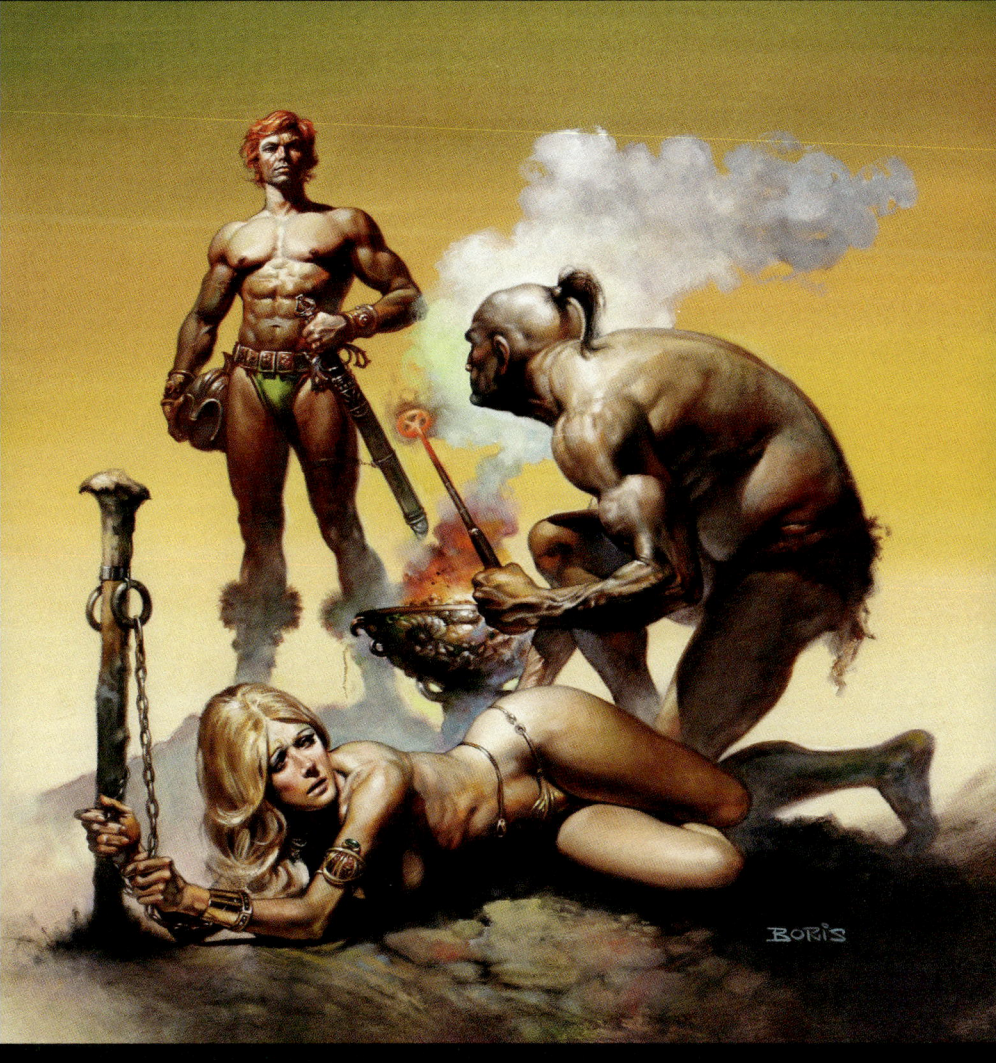

Opposite: Tarzan's Quest, for the cover of Ballantine Books' 1977 edition of the Burroughs classic. Oil on board, 1976, 60.9 x 45.7 cm (24 x 18 inches). Courtesy of Heritage Auctions.

Above: Outlaw of Gor, for the cover of John Norman's 1976 novel *Outlaw of Gor, in the Chronicles of Counter-Earth No. 2.* Oil on board, 1975, 47 x 44.4 cm (18.5 x 17.5 inches). Courtesy of Heritage Auctions.

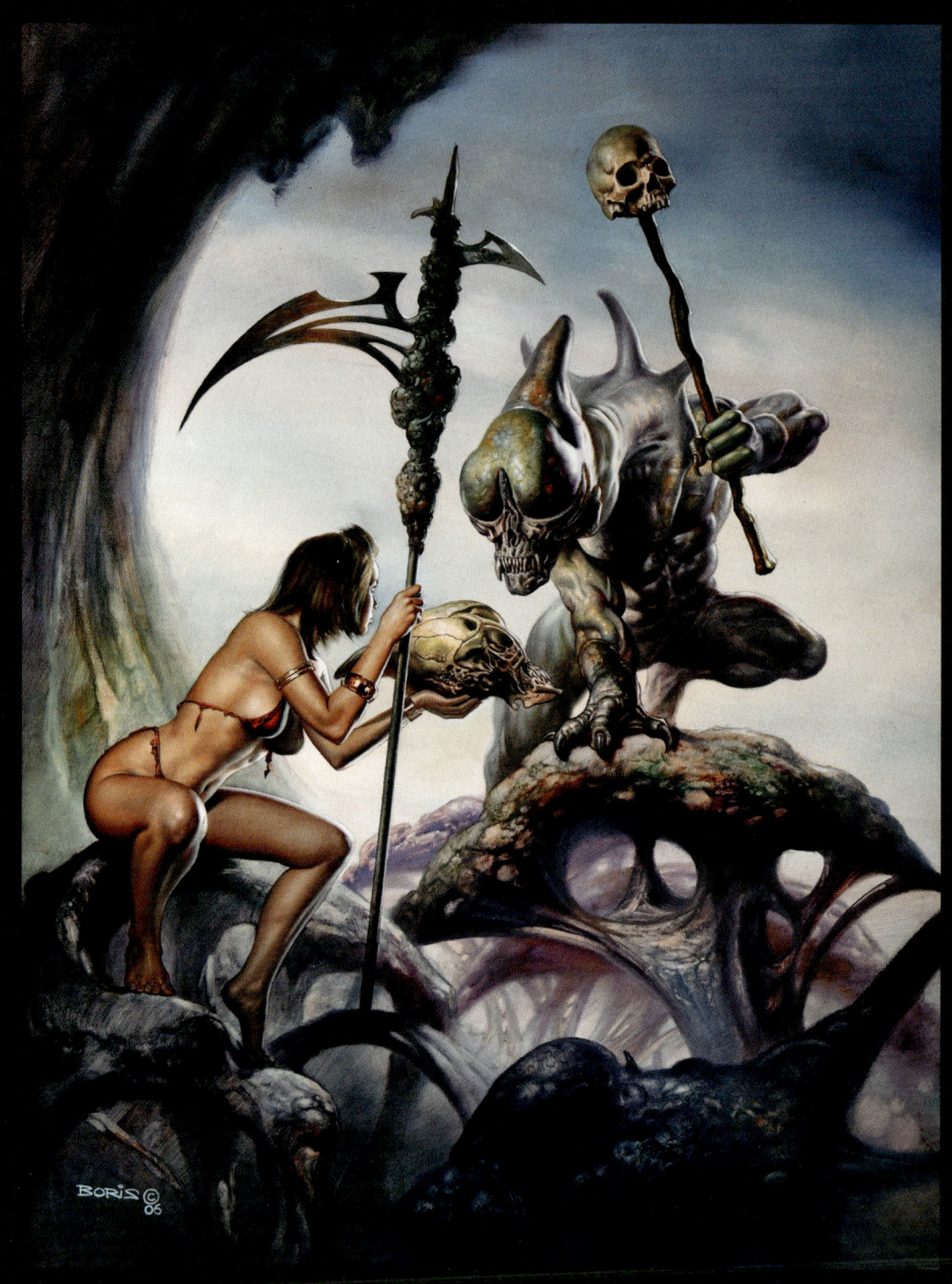

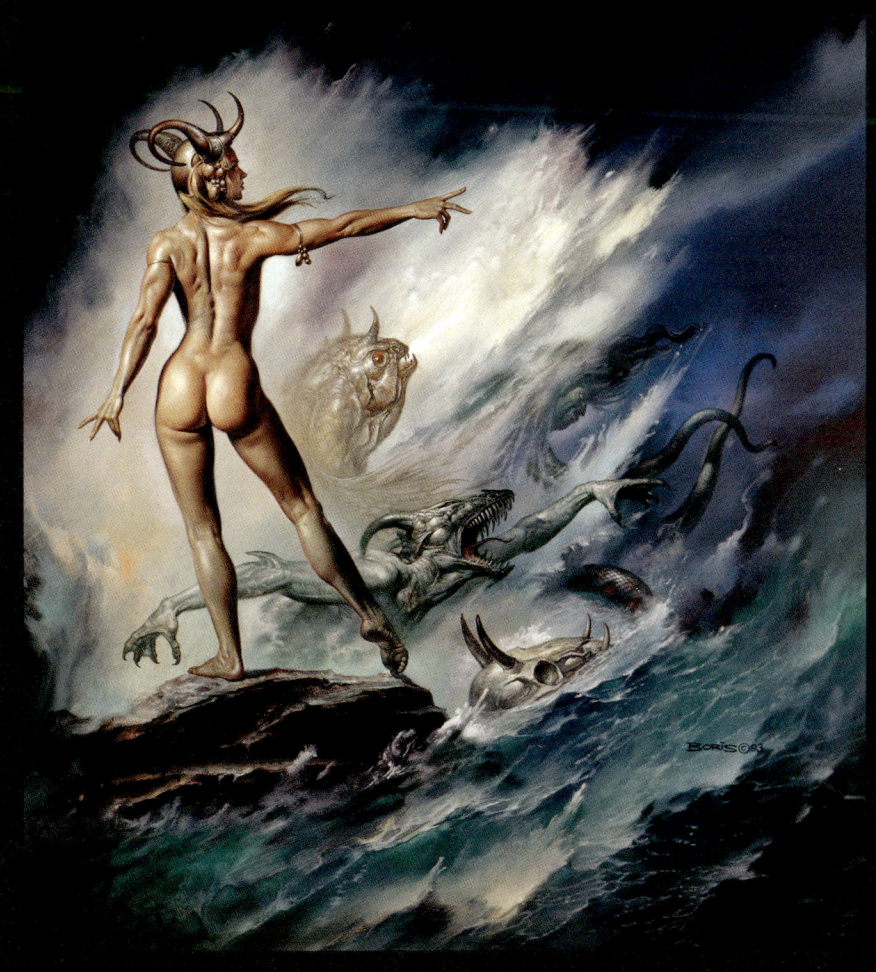

Opposite: Trading, for the *2007 Boris Vallejo and Julie Bell Fantasy Calendar*, oil on board, 2006, 71.1 x 61 cm (28 x 24 inches).

Above: Sea Creatures, for the *1994 Boris Vallejo and Julie Bell Fantasy Calendar*, oil on board, 1993, 71.1 x 61 cm (28 x 24 inches).

Following left: Alpnu, The One, was the first painting Boris completed of Julie Bell. It was included in the *1991 Boris Trading Cards*. Oil on board, 1989, 86.3 x 71.1 cm (34 x 28 inches).

Following right: Self-portrait, ink on paper, 1977.

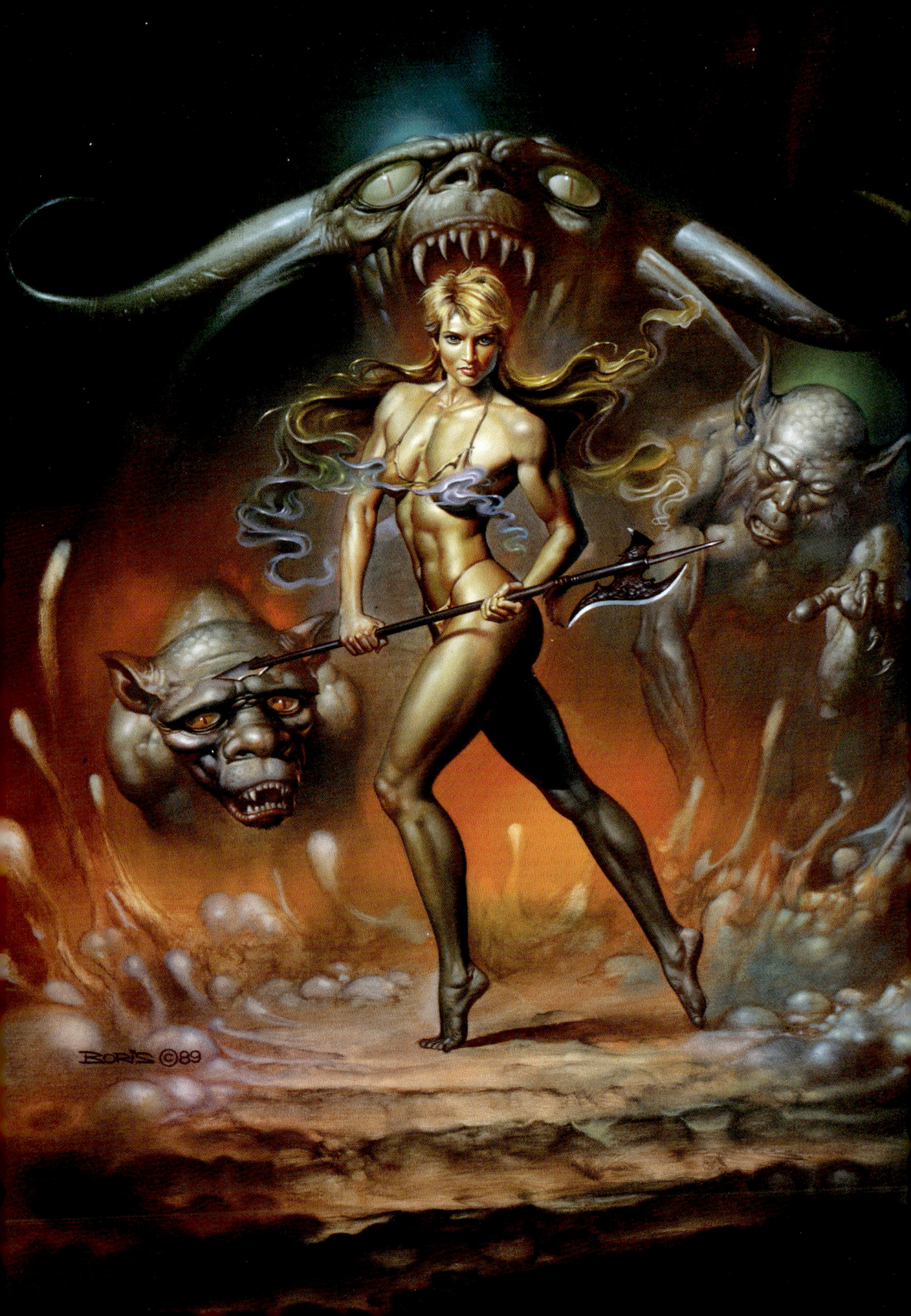

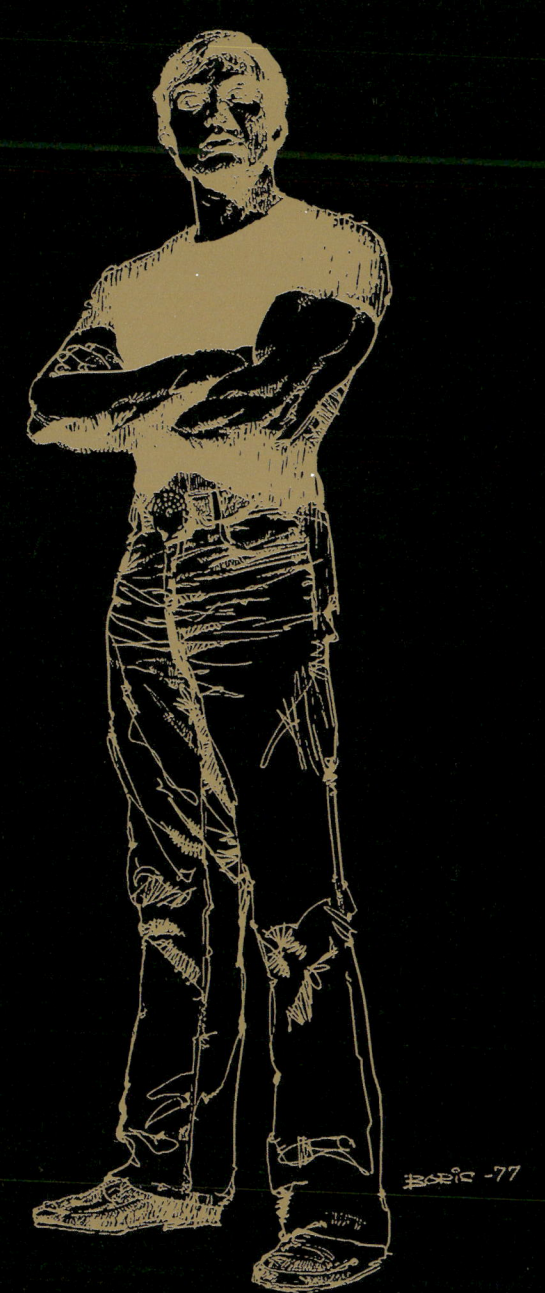

Michael Whelan

1950-

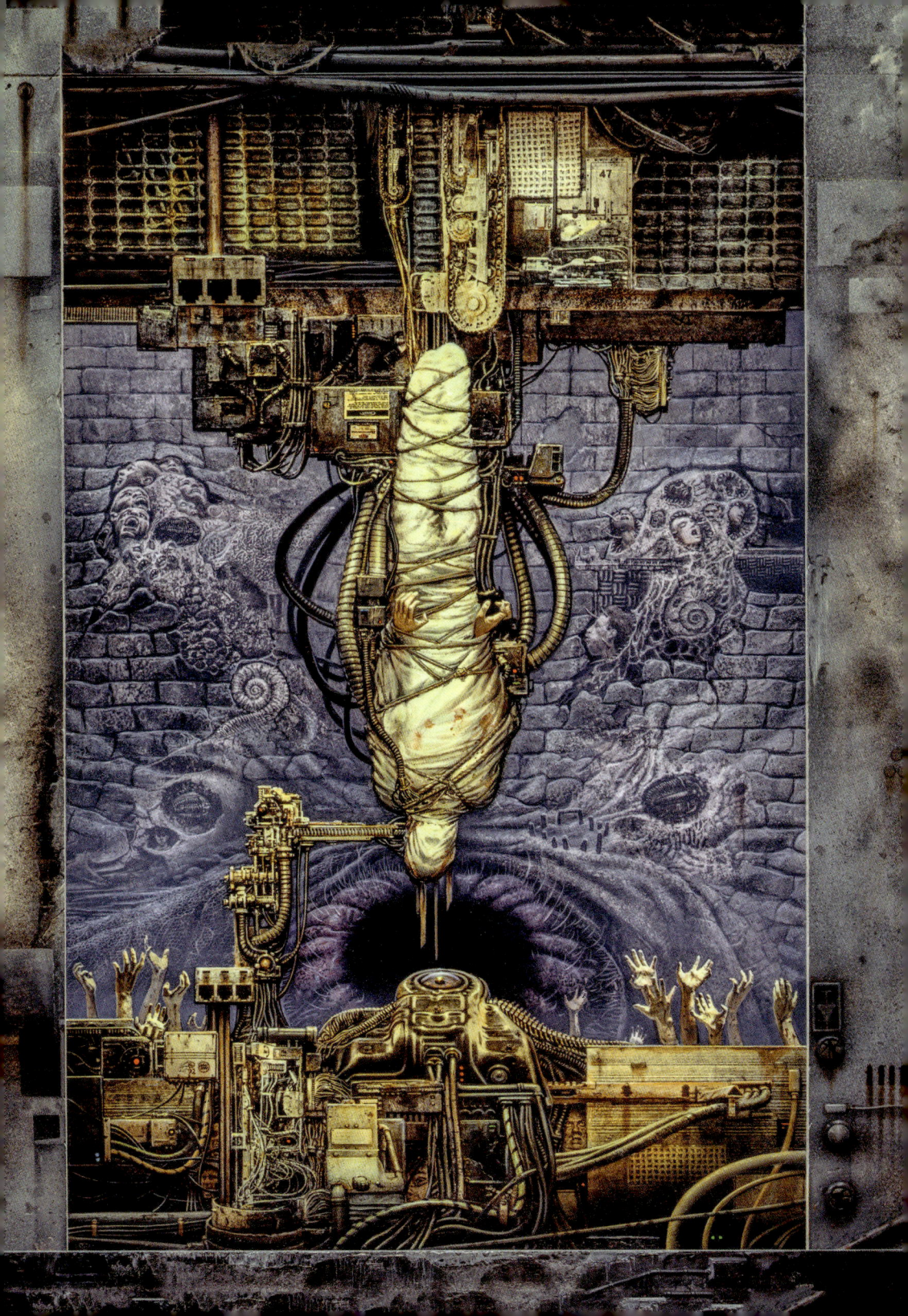

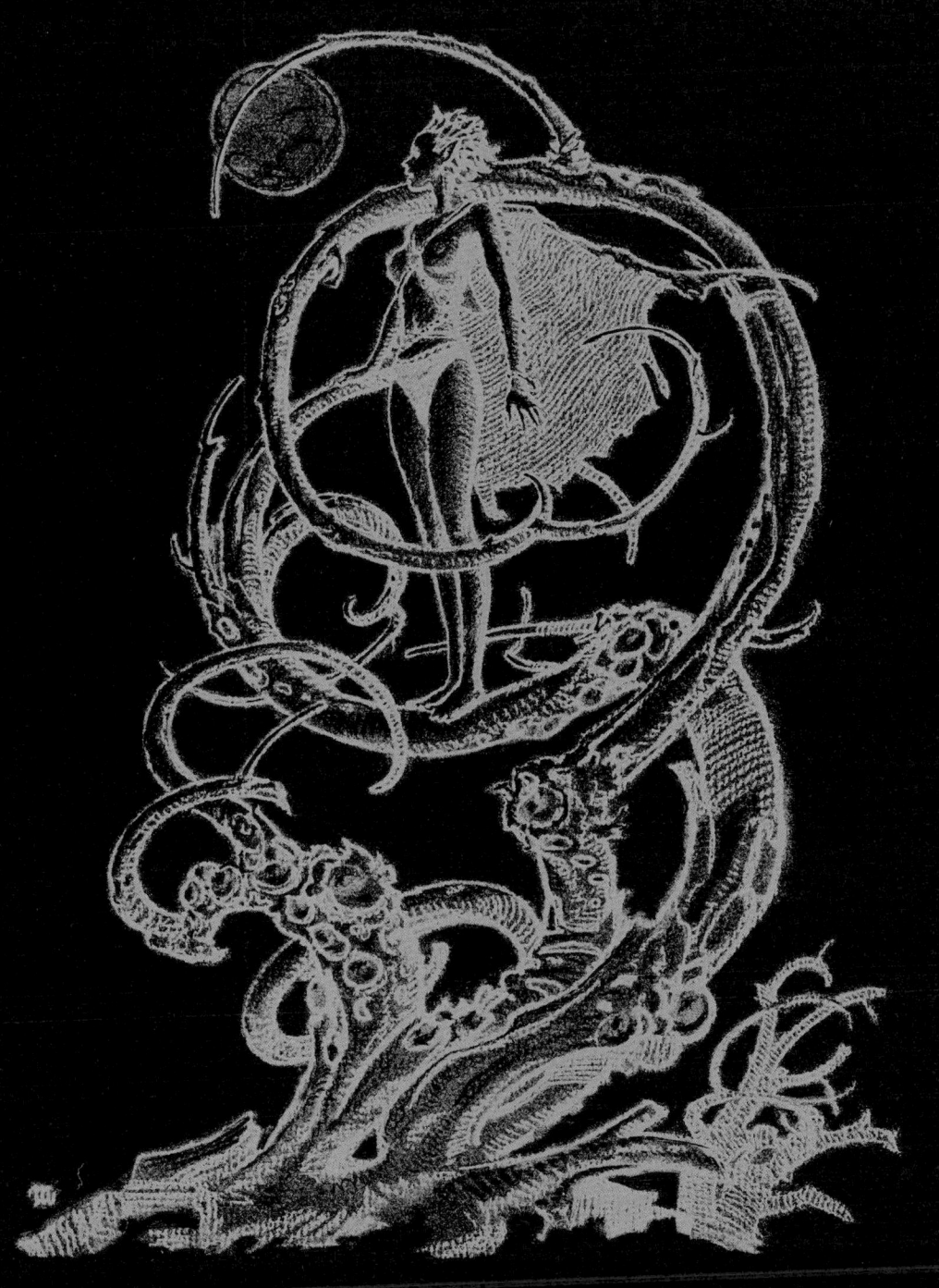

MICHAEL WHELAN
THE REALIST

"A morning doesn't happen where I don't wake up thinking, 'I'm going to have to do some real work today.'"

Oh, what a lucky man is Mr. Michael Whelan. At just 14 he was invited into an adult life-drawing class at the Rocky Mountain School of Art; at 23 he placed drawings in the Comic-Con art show and sold every one; at 24 he made his first sale to Marvel, was asked by Harlan Ellison to illustrate one of his stories, got cover work at Ace Books through the admiration of comics legend Neal Adams and was already doing cover work for DAW Books. All of this culminating, at age 25, with a fully established career. He would never need to show his portfolio again. On top of that, he's a handsome man, a happily married man, a man of wealth and fame. And yet.

Whelan was born in 1950 in Southern California to a restless family. They moved often, with Whelan never completing a year in the same school. "I always felt like the odd person out in every neighborhood that I moved into." He often had paper routes, and riding through the dark streets of yet another new neighborhood he'd ruminate on good and evil, heroes and villains. "When I was 10 I read a story by Richard Matson called 'The Distributor,' about a guy who moves into a neighborhood and sets about destroying it, doing horrible things at night that set neighbor against neighbor until the street is in chaos. I thought, 'I could be that person if I was evil.'"

Seeing the extent of human vulnerability led him, at age 13, to create a character based on the Fantastic Four and their enemies Super-Skrull and the Vanisher, a super-duper-hero who combined all the qualities, good and bad, of these six: basically, an utterly invincible power for good, with certain amoral tendencies. "If he needed money he could pop into a bank and grab some, but I saw him more as a person trying to correct the evils that conventional human society couldn't address."

Whelan found art to be therapeutic from an early age, and a way to make friends quickly in each new school. He perfected his skills copying Marvel comics, and then found "I could sit in the corner of a schoolroom and do a drawing of a monster or a superhero and draw people to me. I'd give away a drawing of an alien and make a new friend."

By age 14 his family was in Denver, and he had moved on to copying Michelangelo. When he showed these works to the life-drawing instructor at Rocky Mountain College of Art and Design he was immediately admitted, though 20 years younger than his fellow students. He remembers the first five minutes being "a little bit of a shock," as he confronted nudity for the first time.

Central though art was to Whelan's young life, his parents pushed for a traditional career, leading to two years lost in pre-med studies. He became adept at drawing muscle and bone but realized he didn't have the stomach for medicine and switched to an art major, ending relations with his parents when he enrolled at Los Angeles' prestigious Art Center College of Design.

Previous right: Cacophony, for the cover of Sepultura's 1993 record album *Chaos A.D.* Mixed media, 1992, 60.9 x 60.9 cm (24 x 24 inches).

Opposite: Untitled, pastels on toned paper, undated, 30.5 x 22.9 cm (12 x 9 inches).

Mom and Dad needn't have worried their son would starve in some garret. By his second year of school, in 1974, he discovered San Diego Comic-Con, entered some fantasy scenes in the amateur art show and sold everything. Flush with confidence, he sent slides of his work to DAW Books in New York and received a positive response. At the same time he entered work in the 32nd World Science Fiction Convention art show in Washington, D.C., and took first place in the professional class, picking up German agent Thomas Schlück for European assignments.

At this point it occurred to Whelan that, rather than more schooling, he needed a new address. He packed all his belongings in his VW Beetle and headed to New York, where he quickly made his first professional sale to Marvel Comics, with covers for barbarian heroes *Ka-Zar* and *Kull*, followed by cover art for *The Enchantress of World's End*, his first assignment for DAW. In April of 1975 he attended LunaCon, where he met the notoriously mercurial Harlan Ellison, who became "an incredibly positive influence on my career." That show also yielded the connection to Neal Adams, another valuable mentor, who connected him to Ace Books.

His career was set. The next year he'd meet his future wife and business partner, Audrey, followed in 1980 by the birth of their daughter Alexa—and his first Hugo Award. A fruitful collaboration with Stephen King began with a cover for *Firestarter*, leading to assignments for the *Dark Tower* series, followed by a portrait of the Jackson brothers for Michael Jackson's *Victory* album; Whelan was described by Jackson in *People* magazine as a "modern-day Maxfield Parrish."

And so it went through the '80s, with gallery shows and increasingly sweet cover assignments with commensurate profits. The acclaim and Hugo Awards piled up, until 1988. "I was trying to express ideas I had about philosophy, the world, in my illustration work, and it was often impossible to do." He became blocked. "I started doing paintings just for myself and hanging them in my house." He struggled with the sexual dynamics of fantasy art—the strong male, the clinging female—and with global patterns of human aggression. "I felt that every time I was coming into my studio I was trying to climb over this wall of negative feelings I had erected. I was constantly painting pictures of huge concrete walls or barriers that I was trying to get past to look at places of beauty or positivity." He worried about his two children—son Adrian was born in 1988—his rootless childhood driving him to be the best father he could be. As usual, he sought self-improvement through art. "My artwork has absolutely been my psychiatrist. There are times when I'm able to achieve genuine catharsis, to flush a negative feeling out of my system. It works for me and also for the person who buys the painting."

And so, today, Whelan paints more and more for himself, only taking on illustration jobs he loves. He's an inductee of Paul Allen's Science Fiction Museum and Hall of Fame and frequent guest at fantasy conventions. At the time of this writing he is working on a series of paintings inspired by dreams of stars falling to Earth. "They're about the collapse of ideals I had when I was younger, about faith in the progress of humanity. A lot of those hopes and dreams for where we're going as a species have crashed to Earth and I want to get this out of my system." He says this with no sense of despair, and the next minute laughs and admits, "I'm a lucky guy. I still can't believe I've gotten away with doing this for a living but, you know, as long as I can get away with it, I will."

Opposite: In a World of Her Own, a personal work inspired by a quote from Stanley Kubrick: "However vast the darkness, we must supply our own light." Acrylic on canvas, 2016, 121.9 x 91.4 cm (48 x 36 inches).

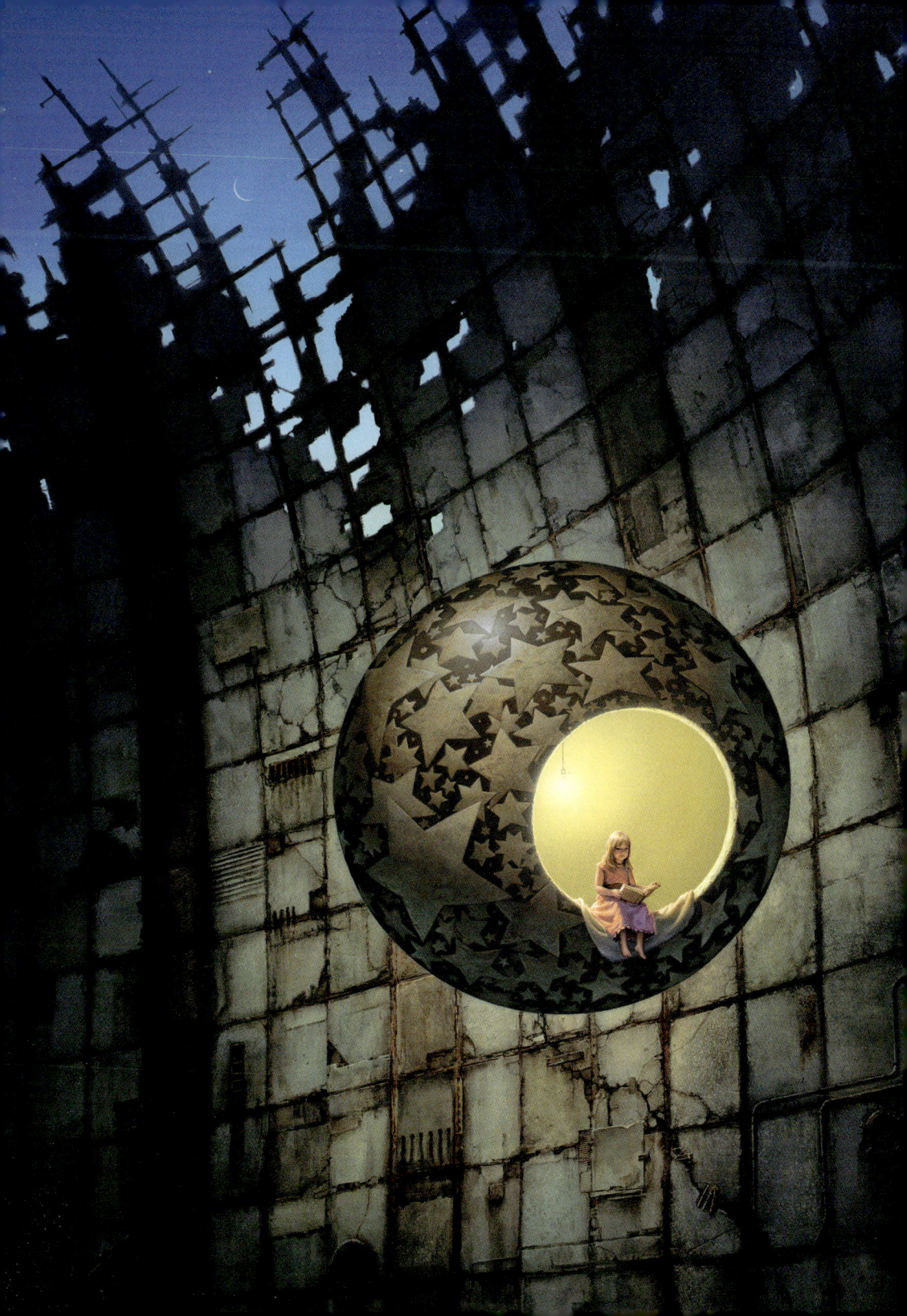

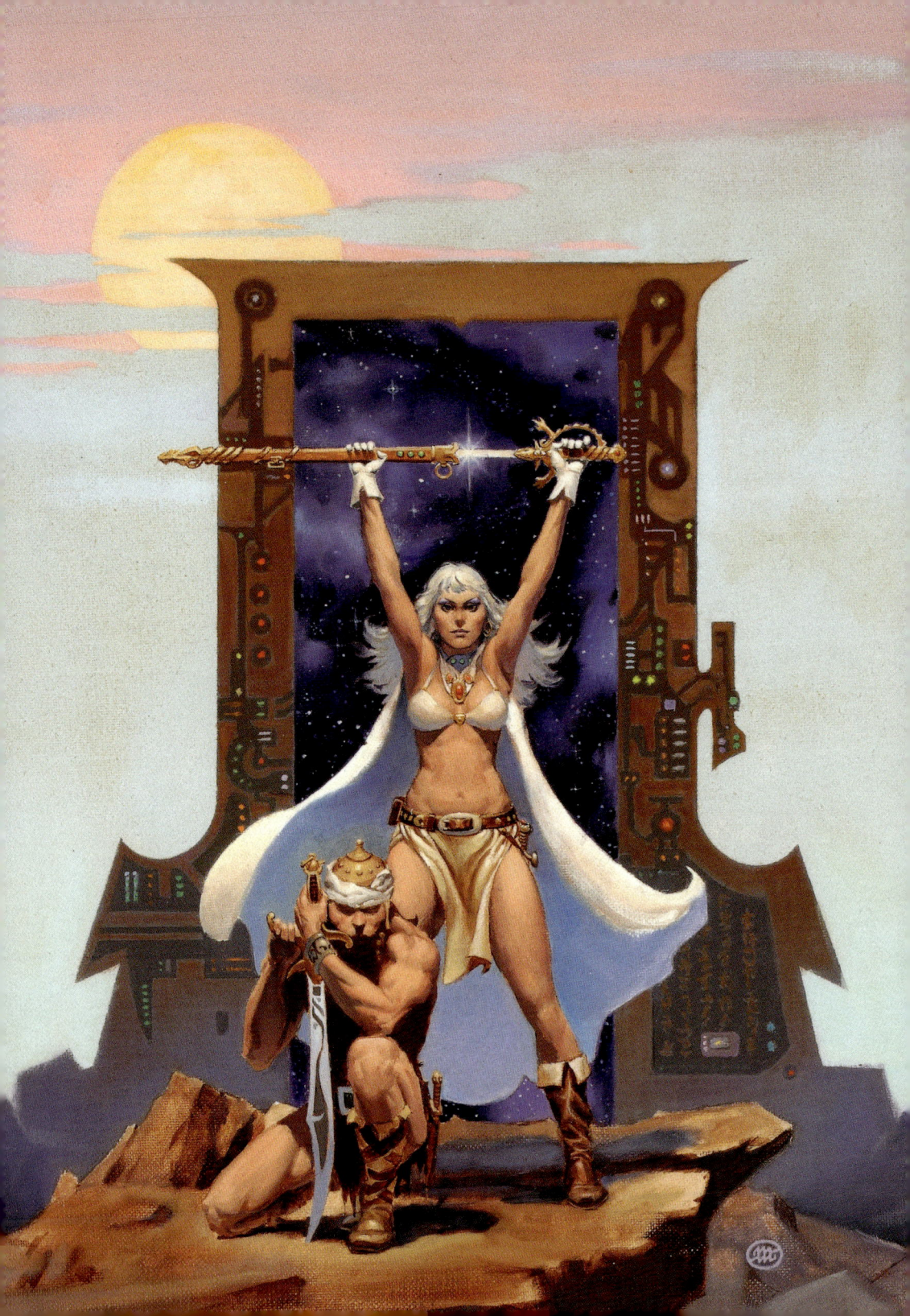

MICHAEL WHELAN
DER REALIST

„Es gibt keinen Morgen, an dem ich nicht aufwache und denke: ‚Heute werde ich ordentlich zu tun haben.'"

Oh, was für ein glücklicher Mensch ist Mr Michael Whelan. Mit gerade mal 14 wurde er an der Rocky Mountain School of Art eingeladen, am Unterricht einer Erwachsenenklasse für Aktzeichnen teilzunehmen; mit 23 brachte er Zeichnungen bei der Kunstschau der Comic-Con unter und verkaufte alle; mit 24 gelang ihm sein erster Verkauf an Marvel, wurde er von Harlan Ellison gebeten, eine seiner Geschichten zu illustrieren, bekam er dank der Bewunderung der Comiclegende Neal Adams von Ace Books Aufträge zur Gestaltung von Covers, und er entwarf bereits Cover für DAW Books. All dies gipfelte in einer abgesicherten Karriere, da war er erst 25. Nie wieder hatte er es nötig, sein Portfolio vorzulegen. Damit nicht genug, ist er zudem ein gut aussehender, glücklich verheirateter Mann, der es zu Wohlstand und Ruhm gebracht hat. Und doch.

Whelan wurde 1950 in Südkalifornien als Kind einer rastlosen Familie geboren. Häufig zogen sie um, und Whelan konnte niemals ein Jahr an der gleichen Schule abschließen. „In jedem Viertel, in das ich zog, fühlte ich mich immer als der Sonderling." Oft trug er Zeitungen aus, und wenn er sich dann durch die dunklen Straßen eines wieder mal neuen Viertels bewegte, grübelte er über das Gute und das Böse nach, über Helden und Schurken. „Als ich zehn war, las ich eine Geschichte von Richard Matson. Sie hieß *The Distributor (Der Lieferant)* und handelte von einem Kerl, der in eine Gegend zieht und anfängt, sie zu zerstören, indem er nachts fürchterliche Dinge tut, die einen Nachbarn gegen den anderen aufbringt, bis die ganze Straße in einem Chaos versinkt. Ich dachte: ‚Wäre ich bösartig, könnte ich dieses Wesen sein.'"

Als er das Ausmaß menschlicher Verwundbarkeit erkannte, schuf er mit 13 Jahren eine Figur, die auf den Fantastischen Vier und ihren Feinden Super-Skrull und The Vanisher basiert, einen tollen Superhelden, der alle Eigenschaften dieser sechs, die guten wie die schlechten, in sich vereinte: im Grunde eine Figur mit absolut unbesiegbarer Stärke und gewissen unmoralischen Tendenzen. „Brauchte er Geld, konnte er mal schnell in eine Bank huschen und sich welches greifen, doch ich sah ihn eher als ein Wesen, das versuchte, die Übel zu beheben, die die normale menschliche Gesellschaft nicht angehen konnte."

Schon in jungen Jahren stellte Whelan fest, dass Kunst eine therapeutische Wirkung hatte und ihm Möglichkeiten bot, in jeder Schule schnell Freunde zu finden. Er perfektionierte seine Fertigkeiten beim Kopieren von Marvel-Comics und merkte: „Ich konnte in der Ecke eines Klassenraums sitzen und ein Monster oder einen Superhelden zeichnen, und das lockte Leute zu mir.

Opposite: One of Whelan's first book cover commissions was for C.J. Cherryh's *Gate of Ivrel*, 1976. He was struggling with the conventions of fantasy art at the time: the damsel in distress clinging to the muscular hero, and decided to flip the scenario and place the woman in the power position. To his surprise, the publishers went for it. Acrylic on board, 1975, 45.7 x 43.1 cm (18 x 17 inches).

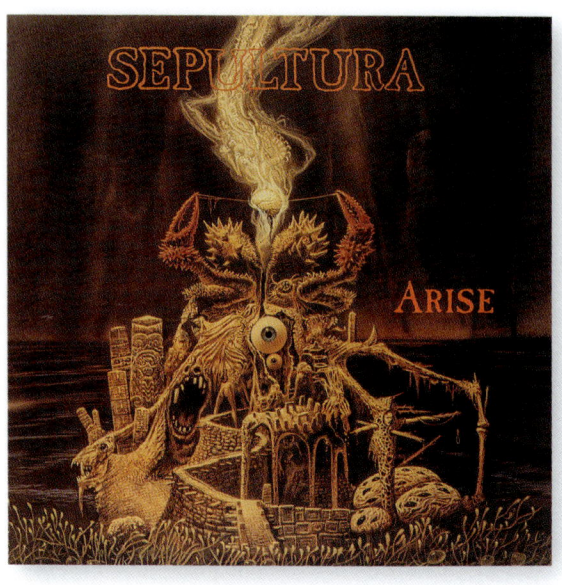

Ich verschenkte dann eine Zeichnung eines Aliens, und schon hatte ich einen neuen Freund gefunden."

Als er 14 war, lebte seine Familie in Denver, und er kopierte mittlerweile Michelangelo. Als er diese Zeichnungen dem Lehrer für Aktzeichnen am Rocky Mountain College of Art and Design zeigte, wurde er, obwohl 20 Jahre jünger als seine Mitstudenten, sofort in dessen Klasse aufgenommen. Die ersten fünf Minuten fand er, wie er sich erinnert, „etwas schockierend", denn zum ersten Mal wurde er mit Nacktheit konfrontiert.

Auch wenn Kunst in Whelans jungen Jahren sein Lebensmittelpunkt war, drängten ihn seine Eltern doch, einen traditionellen Karriereweg einzuschlagen. So verlor er zwei Jahre mit vorbereitenden Medizinstudien. Nun war er zwar im Zeichnen von Muskeln und Knochen versiert, stellte jedoch fest, dass er nicht den Mumm für Medizin hatte, und wechselte ins Hauptfach Kunst. Als er sich am angesehenen Art Center College of Design in Los Angeles einschrieb, gab es einen Bruch in der Beziehung zu seinen Eltern.

Doch Mama und Papa hätten sich keine Sorgen machen müssen, ihr Sohn könnte nun in einer Dachstube verhungern. 1974, in seinem zweiten Jahr am Art Center, entdeckte er die San Diego Comic-Con, reichte bei der Kunstschau für Amateure ein paar Fantasyszenen ein und verkaufte jedes Blatt. So mit Selbstvertrauen gesegnet, schickte er Dias von seinen Arbeiten an DAW Books in New York und erhielt eine positive Antwort. Zur gleichen Zeit reichte er bei der Kunstschau der 32. World Science Fiction Convention in Washington, D. C. Arbeiten ein und kam auf den ersten Platz. Dabei machte er zudem die Bekanntschaft des deutschen Agenten Thomas Schlück, der sich um Aufträge aus Europa kümmerte.

Unter diesen Umständen war es für Whelan wichtiger, eine neue Adresse zu haben, als sich weiter der Ausbildung zu widmen. Er packte seine gesamte Habe in seinen VW Käfer und machte sich auf nach New York, wo ihm schon kurz darauf sein erster professioneller Verkauf an Marvel Comics gelang: Es waren Cover für *Ka-Zar* und *Kull*, Hefte mit Barbarengeschichten, und gleich darauf gestaltete er das Cover für *The Enchantress of World's End*, sein erster Auftrag für DAW. Im April 1975 nahm er an der LunaCon teil, wo er dem bekanntermaßen sehr lebhaften Harlan Ellison begegnete, der „einen unglaublich positiven Einfluss auf meine Karriere" hatte. Bei dieser Schau ergab sich auch der Kontakt zu Neal Adams, einem weiteren hilfreichen Mentor, der ihn mit Ace Books zusammenbrachte.

Seine Karriere war gesichert. Im Jahr darauf würde er seine künftige Frau und Geschäftspartnerin Audrey kennenlernen. 1980 kam dann ihre Tochter Alexa auf die Welt – und er erhielt seinen ersten Hugo. Mit einem Cover für *Firestarter* begann eine fruchtbare Zusammenarbeit mit Stephen King, die zu Aufträgen für die *Dark-Tower*-Serie führte, denen für Michael Jacksons Album *Victory* ein Porträt der Jackson-Brüder folgte; Jackson beschrieb Whelan im *People-*

Magazin als einen „Maxfield Parrish unserer Tage".

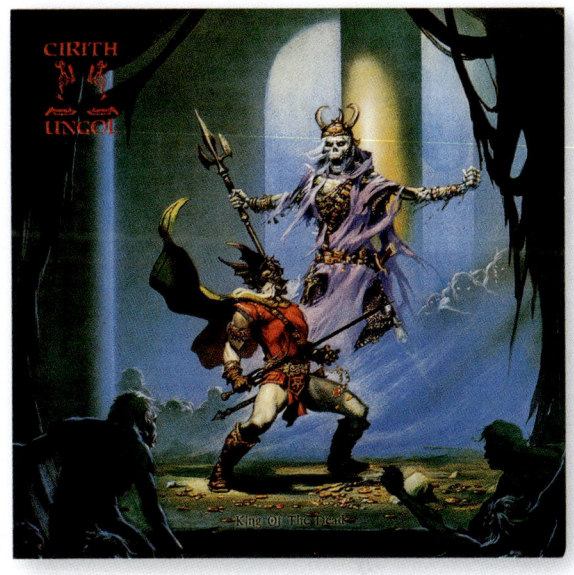

Und so ging es in den 1980er-Jahren weiter, mit Galerieausstellungen und zunehmend coolen Coveraufträgen, die entsprechenden Profit einbrachten. Bis 1988 wuchs die Anerkennung, die Hugo-Preise häuften sich an. „Ich versuchte in meinen Illustrationen Vorstellungen Ausdruck zu verleihen, die ich von Philosophie und von der Welt hatte, und oft war mir das unmöglich." Er begann, unter Blockaden zu leiden. „Ich fing an, nur für mich selbst Gemälde zu schaffen und sie in meinem Haus aufzuhängen." Er rang mit dem sexuellen Kräftespiel in der Fantasykunst – den starken Männerfiguren, den anschmiegsamen Frauen – und mit allgemeinen Strukturen menschlicher Aggression. „Ich hatte das Gefühl, dass ich jedes Mal, wenn ich in mein Atelier kam, versuchte, über diese Mauer negativer Empfindungen, die ich errichtet hatte, hinwegzukommen. Ständig malte ich Bilder mit hohen Betonmauern oder Hindernissen, die ich zu überwinden versuchte, um einen Blick auf Schönes oder Positives zu erhaschen." Er kümmerte sich um seine beiden Kinder – 1988 wurde Sohn Adrian geboren –, denn seine von Entwurzelung geprägte Kindheit spornte ihn dazu an, ihnen der bestmögliche Vater zu sein. Wie immer suchte er nach Selbstvervollkommnung durch die Kunst. „Meine künstlerische Arbeit diente mir regelrecht als Psychiater. Manchmal, wenn ich es zu einer echten Katharsis schaffe, gelingt es mir, ein negatives Gefühl aus meinem Innern zu spülen. Das ist gut für mich und auch für denjenigen, der das Gemälde kauft."

Und so malt Whelan heute mehr und mehr für sich selbst und nimmt nur Aufträge für Illustrationen an, die er mag. Er wurde in Paul Allens Science Fiction Museum und in die Hall of Fame aufgenommen und ist häufiger Gast bei Fantasykongressen. Als dieser Text entstand, arbeitete er gerade an einer Serie von Gemälden, die von Träumen von Sternen, die auf die Erde fallen, inspiriert sind. „Dabei geht es um den Kollaps der Ideale, die ich hatte, als ich jünger war, um den Glauben an den Fortschritt der Menschheit. Eine Menge jener Hoffnungen und Träume, denen wir als Spezies nachjagen, sind auf die Erde gestürzt, und ich will das aus meinen Gedanken und Gefühlen verbannen." Er sagt das ohne eine Spur von Resignation. Eine Minute später lacht er und gesteht ein: „Ich bin ein glücklicher Bursche. Ich kann es noch immer nicht glauben, dass ich es geschafft habe, mir damit meinen Lebensunterhalt zu verdienen. Und solange es noch geht, mach ich damit weiter."

Opposite: Arise, 1991, from the Brazilian metal band Sepultura, with Whelan's 1990 cover painting.

Above: The heavy metal band Cirith Ungol's 1984 *King of the Dead* album, with Whelan's *Bane of the Black Sword*, 1979, cover art.

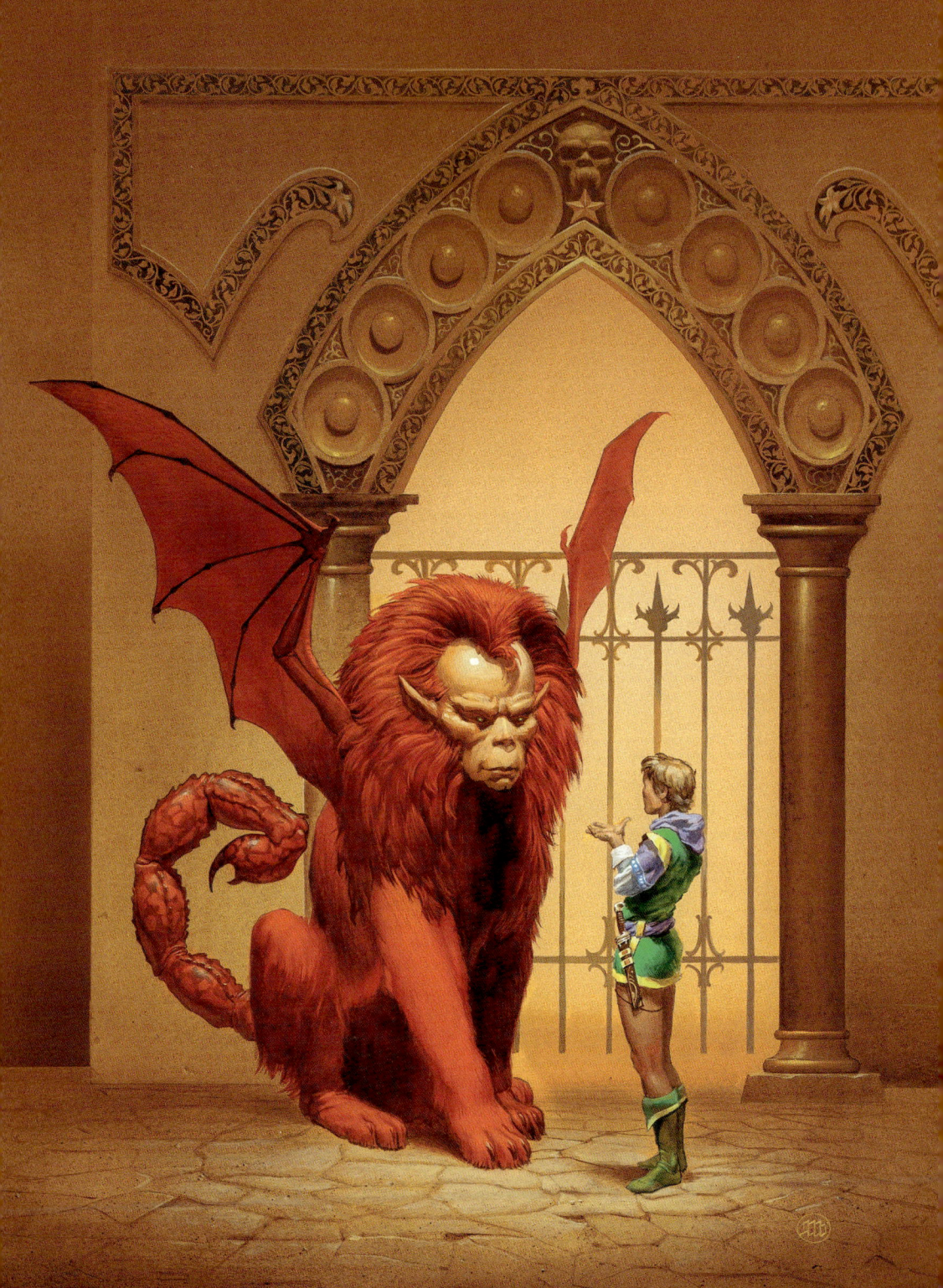

MICHAEL WHELAN
LE RÉALISTE

« Pas un matin ne passe sans que je me
réveille en pensant : il va falloir que
j'abatte un sérieux boulot aujourd'hui. »

Oh, que voilà un heureux homme ! À tout juste 14 ans,
M. Michael Whelan est invité à participer au cours
pour adultes de modèle vivant à l'école d'art de Rocky
Mountain ; à 23, il place des dessins à l'exposition du
Comic-Con et les vend tous ; à 24, il signe sa première pige
pour Marvel, Harlan Ellison lui demande d'illustrer une
de ses histoires, il réalise des couvertures pour Ace Books
grâce à l'admiration que lui porte la légende des comics
Neal Adams et en réalise d'autres pour DAW Books. Son
ascension est fulgurante et à 25 ans, sa carrière est établie.
Il n'aura plus jamais besoin de montrer son portfolio. Pour
couronner le tout, il est aussi bel homme, heureux en
ménage, et auréolé par la gloire et la fortune. Et pourtant.

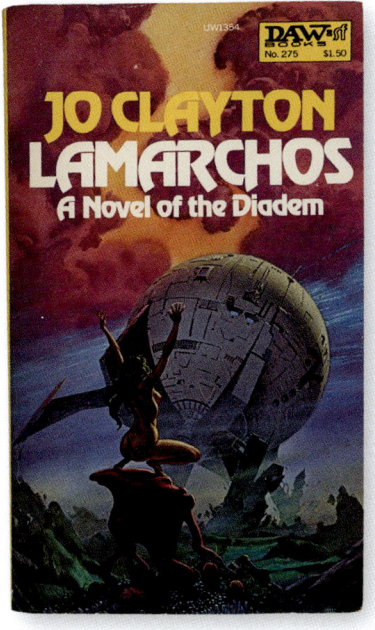

Whelan est né en 1950 en Californie du Sud dans une
famille tourmentée. Ils déménagent souvent, au point que
Whelan ne termine jamais l'année dans l'école où il l'a
commencée. « Dans tous les quartiers où j'arrivais, j'avais
la sensation d'être un intrus », raconte-t-il. Il livre souvent
les journaux et tandis qu'il parcourt les rues sombres de
ces lieux toujours nouveaux il rumine sur le bien et le
mal, les héros et les méchants. « Quand j'avais 10 ans, j'ai lu
une histoire de Richard Matheson intitulée "The Distributor" à propos d'un gars qui arrive dans
un quartier et entreprend de le mettre à feu et à sang ; la nuit, il se livre à d'horribles méfaits qui
montent les voisins les uns contre les autres, jusqu'à ce que la rue plonge dans le chaos. Je me suis
dit : je pourrais être ce gars si j'étais une mauvaise personne. »

Témoin précoce de la vulnérabilité humaine dans son ampleur, à 13 ans il crée un personnage
inspiré des Quatre Fantastiques et de leurs ennemis Super-Skrull et Le Fantôme, un hyper-
superhéros qui combine toutes les qualités et vices des six susnommés : en gros, une force totale-
ment imparable dans le camp du bien, avec une légère tendance à l'immoralité. « S'il avait besoin
d'argent, il entrait dans une banque et en prenait, mais je le voyais davantage comme un redresseur

Opposite: A Spell for Chameleon, for the cover of Piers
Anthony's 1978 novel. Acrylic on board, 1977, 57.7 × 43.1 cm
(22.75 × 17 inches). Courtesy of Heritage Auctions.

Above: Novel from DAW Books, with a cover by Whelan;
Lamarchos, Jo Clayton, 1978.

de torts qui essaie de régler les problèmes face auxquels la société humaine conventionnelle est impuissante. »

Whelan éprouve très tôt les vertus thérapeutiques de l'art. Il parfait son coup de crayon en copiant les comics Marvel et découvre que c'est aussi un bon moyen de se faire des amis rapidement : « Je pouvais me caler au fond de la classe, dessiner un monstre ou un superhéros et attirer l'attention des autres. Un dessin d'extraterrestre donné et j'avais un nouvel ami. »

Quand il a 14 ans, sa famille est à Denver et il est passé aux copies de Michel-Ange. Quand il montre son travail au professeur de modèle vivant du College of Art and Design de Rocky Mountain, il est aussitôt admis dans l'établissement, malgré sa vingtaine d'années de moins que les autres étudiants. Il se souvient que les cinq premières minutes « ont été un peu un choc » ; c'est la première fois qu'il est face à la nudité.

Malgré l'importance de l'art dans la jeune vie de Whelan, ses parents le poussent vers une carrière traditionnelle et il perd deux années en classes préparatoires à l'école de médecine. Il aiguise son goût pour le dessin des muscles et des os mais comprend qu'il n'a pas le cœur assez accroché pour la médecine. Ses parents coupent les ponts quand il s'inscrit au prestigieux Art Center College of Design de Los Angeles.

Maman et papa n'auraient pas dû craindre de voir leur fils mourir de faim dans le caniveau. Dès sa deuxième année d'études, en 1974, il découvre le Comic-Con de San Diego, présente quelques scènes fantasy à l'exposition amateur et vend tout. Il se sent assez confiant pour envoyer des diapos de son travail à DAW Books, à New York, et reçoit une réponse positive. Au même moment, il place des œuvres à l'exposition de la 32ᵉ World Science Fiction Convention à Washington, remporte le premier prix dans la catégorie professionnels et se fait remarquer par l'agent allemand Thomas Schlück, qui va le représenter en Europe.

Arrivé là, Whelan se rend compte qu'il a moins besoin de formation que d'une nouvelle adresse. Il charge tout ce qu'il possède dans sa Coccinelle VW et part pour New York, où il conclut vite sa première vente avec Marvel ; il signe des couvertures pour les titres « barbares » *Ka-Zar* et *Kull*, puis pour *The Enchantress of World's End*, sa première collaboration avec DAW. En avril 1975, il se rend au LunaCon, où il rencontre le lunatique Harlan Ellison, qui exerce dès lors « une influence extrêmement positive sur [sa] carrière ». Cette exposition le met aussi en rapport avec Neal Adams, autre mentor de valeur, qui l'introduit chez Ace Books.

Sa carrière est lancée. L'année suivante il rencontre sa future femme et partenaire en affaires, Audrey, et leur fille Alexa naît en 1980 – alors qu'il reçoit son premier Hugo Award. Il entame une collaboration fructueuse avec Stephen King en réalisant la jaquette de *Firestarter*, ce qui lui permet de décrocher des missions pour la série *Dark Tower*, puis de peindre un portrait des frères Jackson pour l'album *Victory* de Michael Jackson. Dans un entretien avec le magazine *People* Jackson qualifie Whelan de « Maxfield Parrish des temps modernes ».

Les années 1980 s'écoulent ainsi, entre expositions dans diverses galeries et couvertures de plus en plus intéressantes et lucratives. Les louanges et les Hugo Awards s'accumulent, jusqu'en 1988. « J'essayais d'exprimer des idées que j'avais sur la philosophie, le monde, dans mon travail d'illustration et c'était souvent impossible. » Il se retrouve bloqué. « Je me suis mis à peindre seulement pour moi et à exposer mes tableaux dans ma maison. » Il se débat avec les dynamiques sexuelles (genrées) du fantasy art – le mâle puissant, une femelle cramponnée à ses muscles – et plus généralement avec les motifs récurrents de l'agression humaine. « J'avais la sensation qu'à chaque fois que j'entrais dans mon atelier j'essayais de gravir cette muraille de sentiments négatifs que j'avais érigée. Je ne peignais que des murs en béton et des barrières immenses que j'essayais de franchir pour

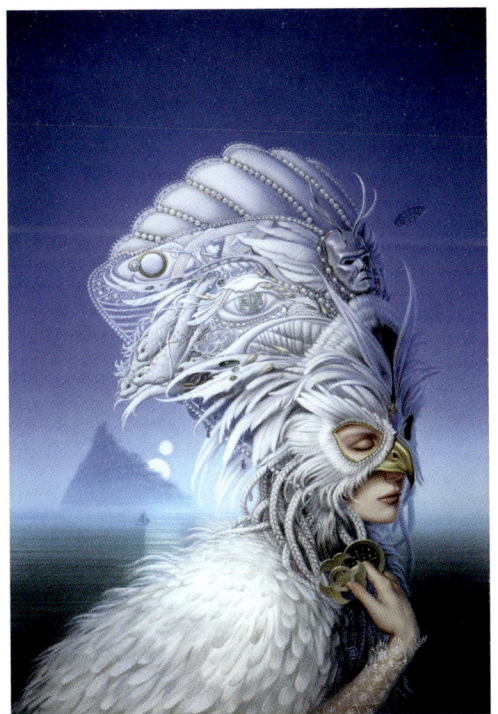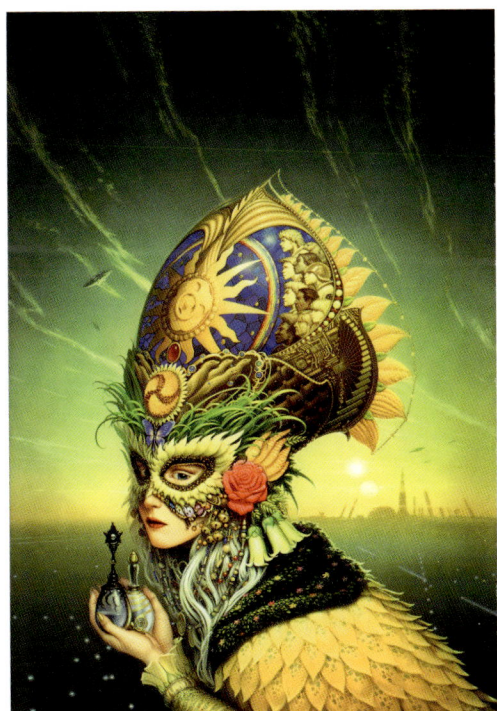

voir des lieux où règneraient la beauté et l'optimisme. » Il s'inquiète pour ses deux enfants – son fils Adrian est né en 1988 –, son passé d'enfant déraciné le pousse à être le meilleur père possible. Comme toujours, il cherche à surmonter les obstacles par l'art. « Mon travail m'a servi de théra-peute, c'est évident. Il m'arrive d'atteindre la véritable catharsis, de réussir à purger mon système de toute négativité. Cela fonctionne pour moi et pour la personne qui achète la toile. »

C'est ainsi qu'aujourd'hui Whelan peint de plus en plus pour lui-même et n'accepte que les commandes qui le séduisent. Il est inscrit au Science Fiction Museum & Hall of Fame de Paul Allen et fréquente encore assidûment les conventions fantasy. À l'heure où nous écrivons, il travaille à une série de toiles inspirées par des rêves d'étoiles tombant sur la Terre. « Elles évoquent l'effondrement des idéaux que j'avais étant jeune, la foi dans le progrès humain. Une grande part de ces espoirs et de ces rêves sur notre avenir en tant qu'espèce ont volé en éclats et je veux sortir cela de mon système. » Il dit cela sans désespoir, puis éclate de rire la minute d'après, pour avouer : « Je suis un gars chanceux. Je n'arrive toujours pas à croire que j'ai réussi à gagner ma vie en faisant cela, mais bon, vous savez, tant que ça marche, je continue ! »

Above left: The Snow Queen, for the cover of the 1989 edition of Joan D. Vinge's novel. Acrylic on panel, 1988, 91.4 x 60.9 cm (36 x 24 inches).

Above right: The Summer Queen, for the cover of Joan D. Vinge's 2003 sequel to *The Snow Queen.* Acrylic on panel, 1990, 91.4 x 60.9 cm (36 x 24 inches).

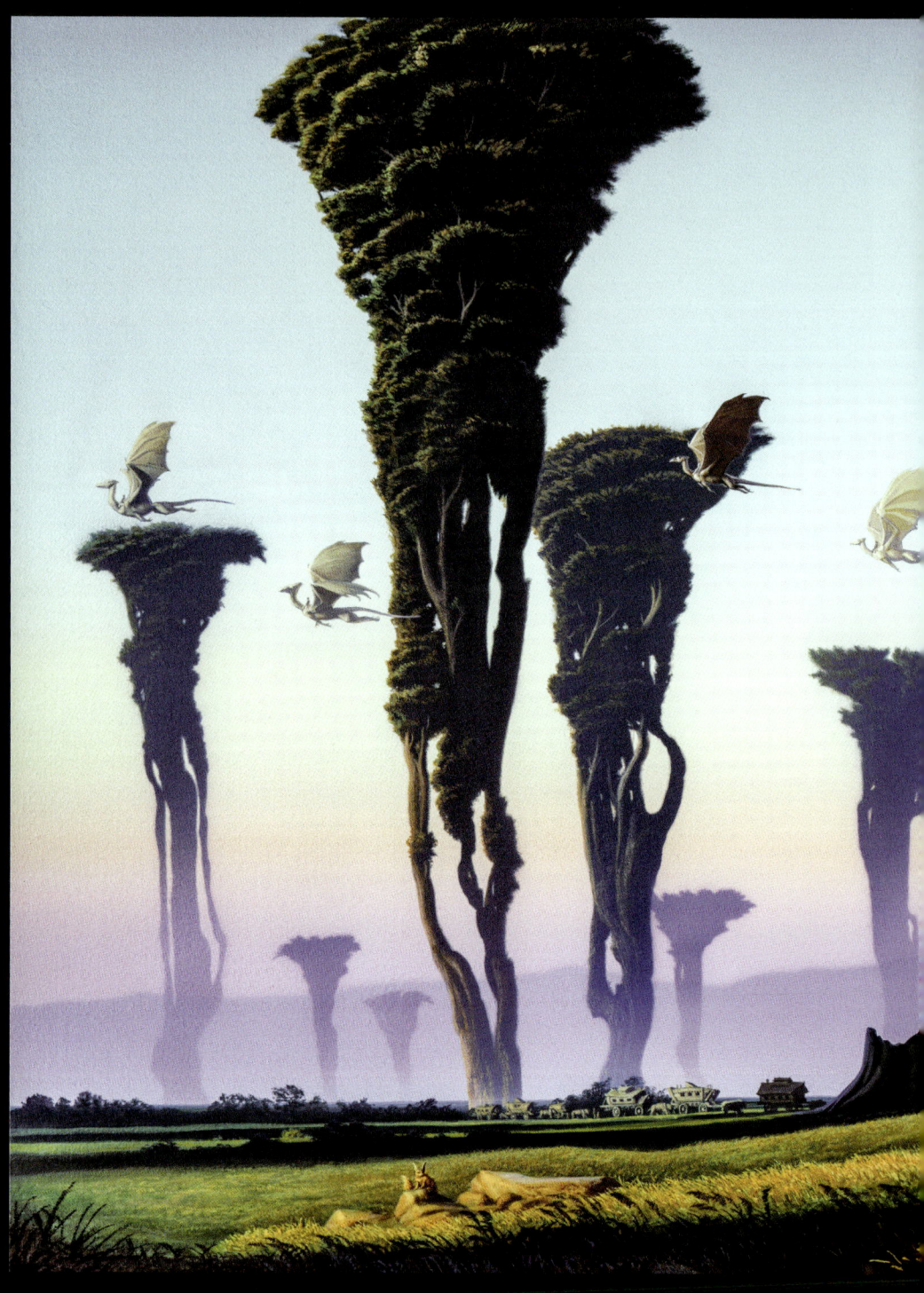

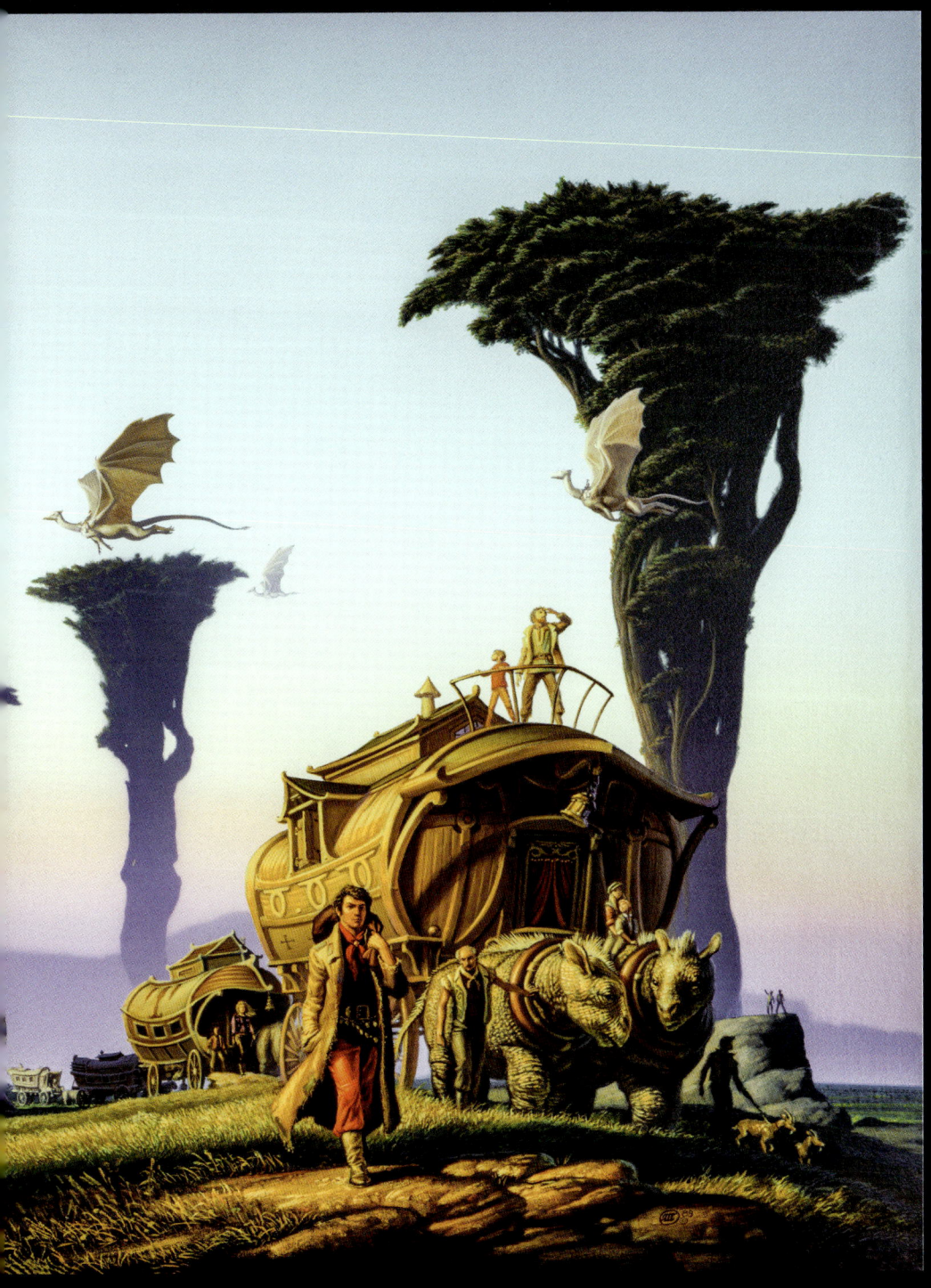

MICHAEL WHELAN

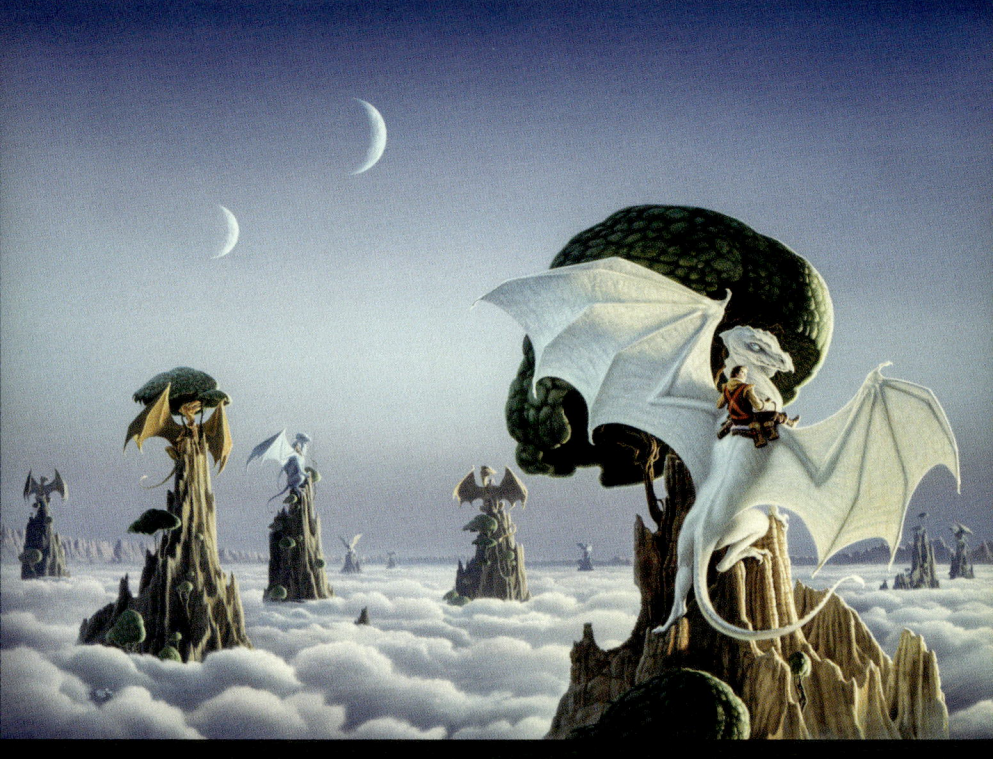

Previous spread: Renegades of Pern, for the cover of Anne McCaffrey's 1989 novel. Acrylic on board, 1988, 50.8 x 76.2 cm (20 x 30 inches).

Above: Weyrworld for the cover of Anne McCaffrey's 1992 novel, *All The Weyrs of Pern*. Acrylic on board, 1990, 68.5 x 91.4 cm (27 x 36 inches).

Opposite: L'Echelle, acrylic on board, 1984.

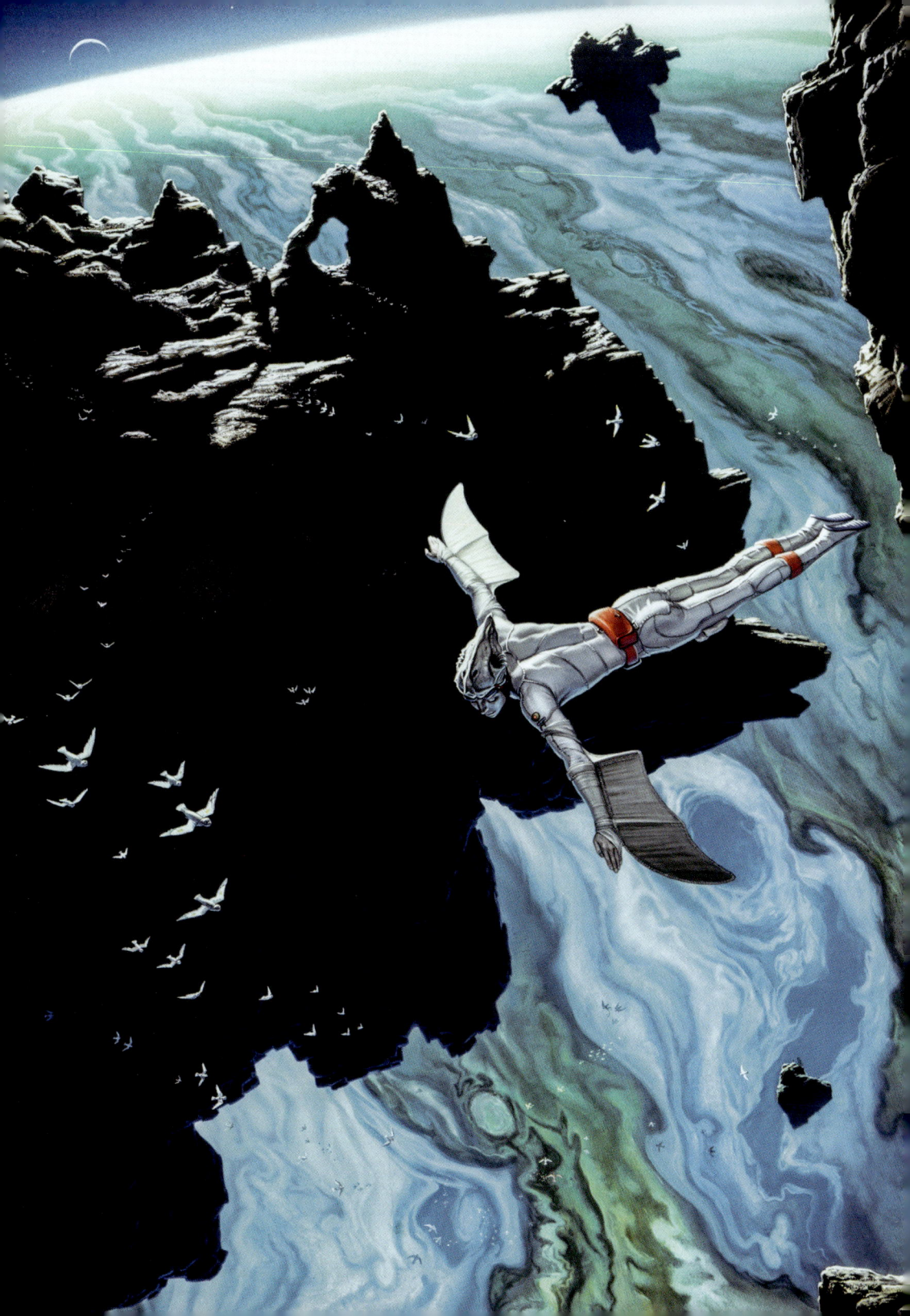

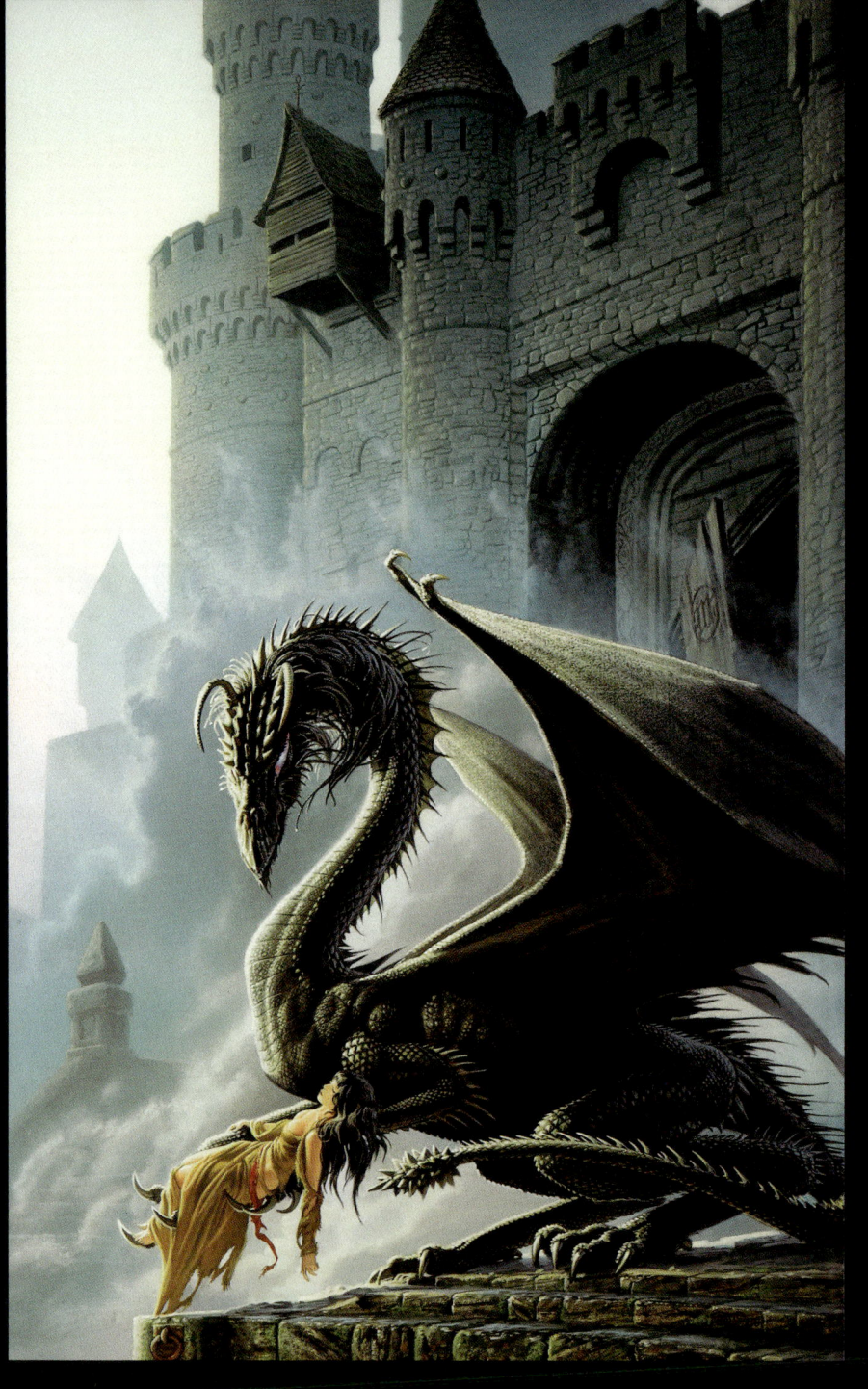

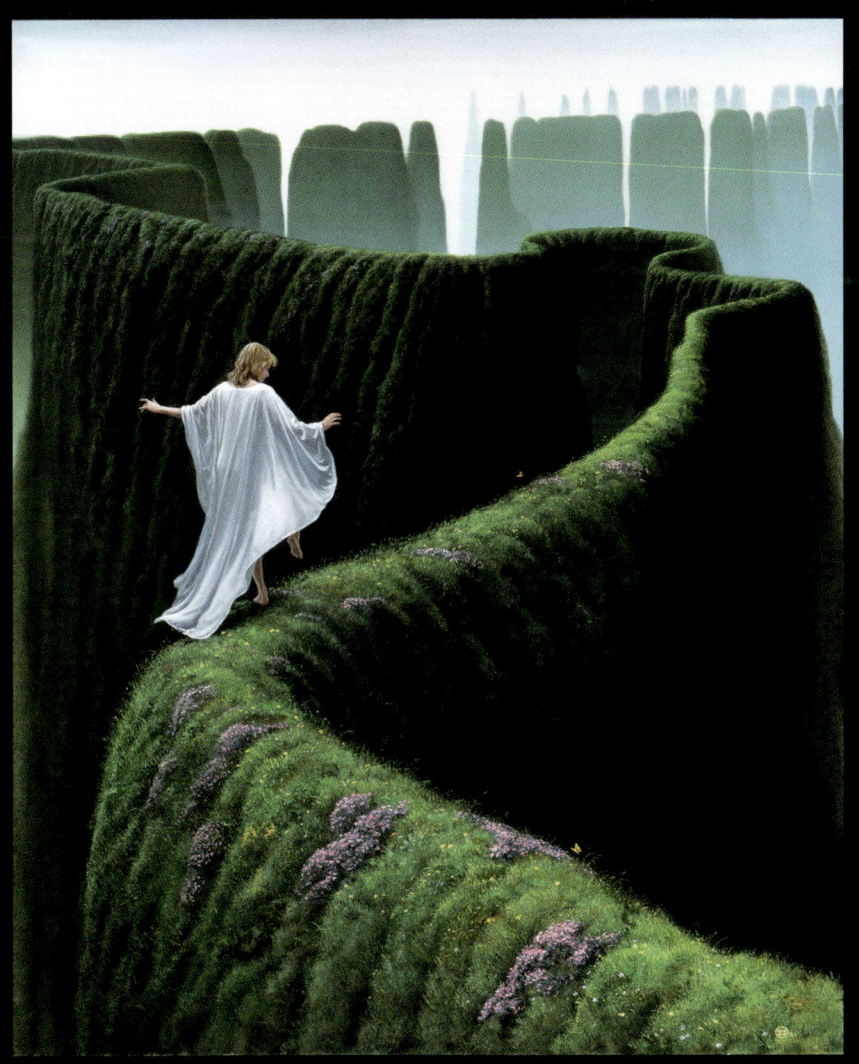

Opposite: Dragonsbane, for the cover of Barbara Hambly's 1985 Del Rey Books novel. Acrylic on board, 1985, 83.8 x 53.3 cm (33 x 21 inches).

Above: Edgedancer is one of Whelan's personal works. Acrylic on gessoboard, 2002, 71.1 x 55.8 cm (28 x 22 inches).

Following spread: The Way of Kings, for the wraparound cover of Brandon Sanderson's 2010 novel. Acrylic on board, 2010, 60.9 x 101.6 cm (24 x 40 inches).

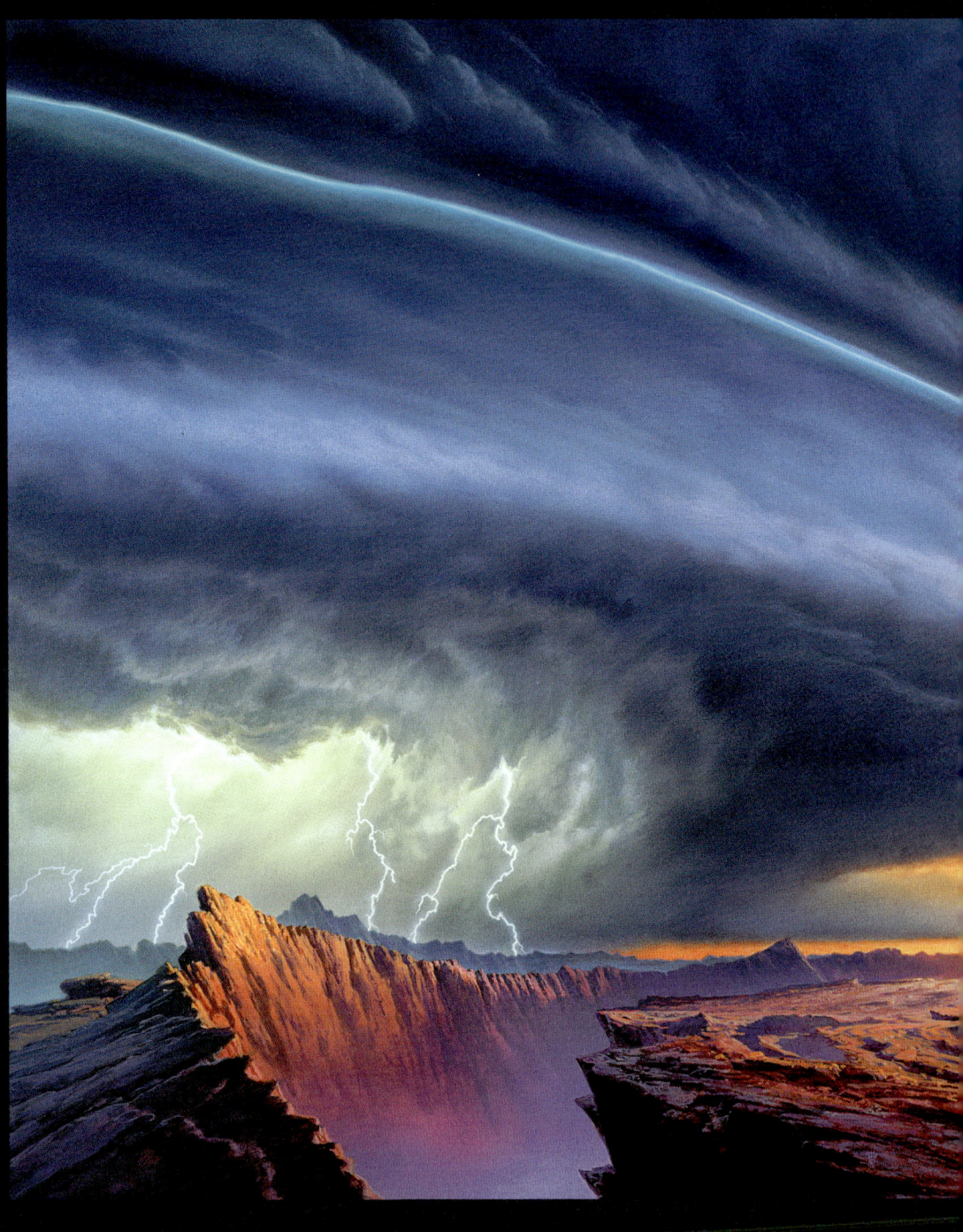

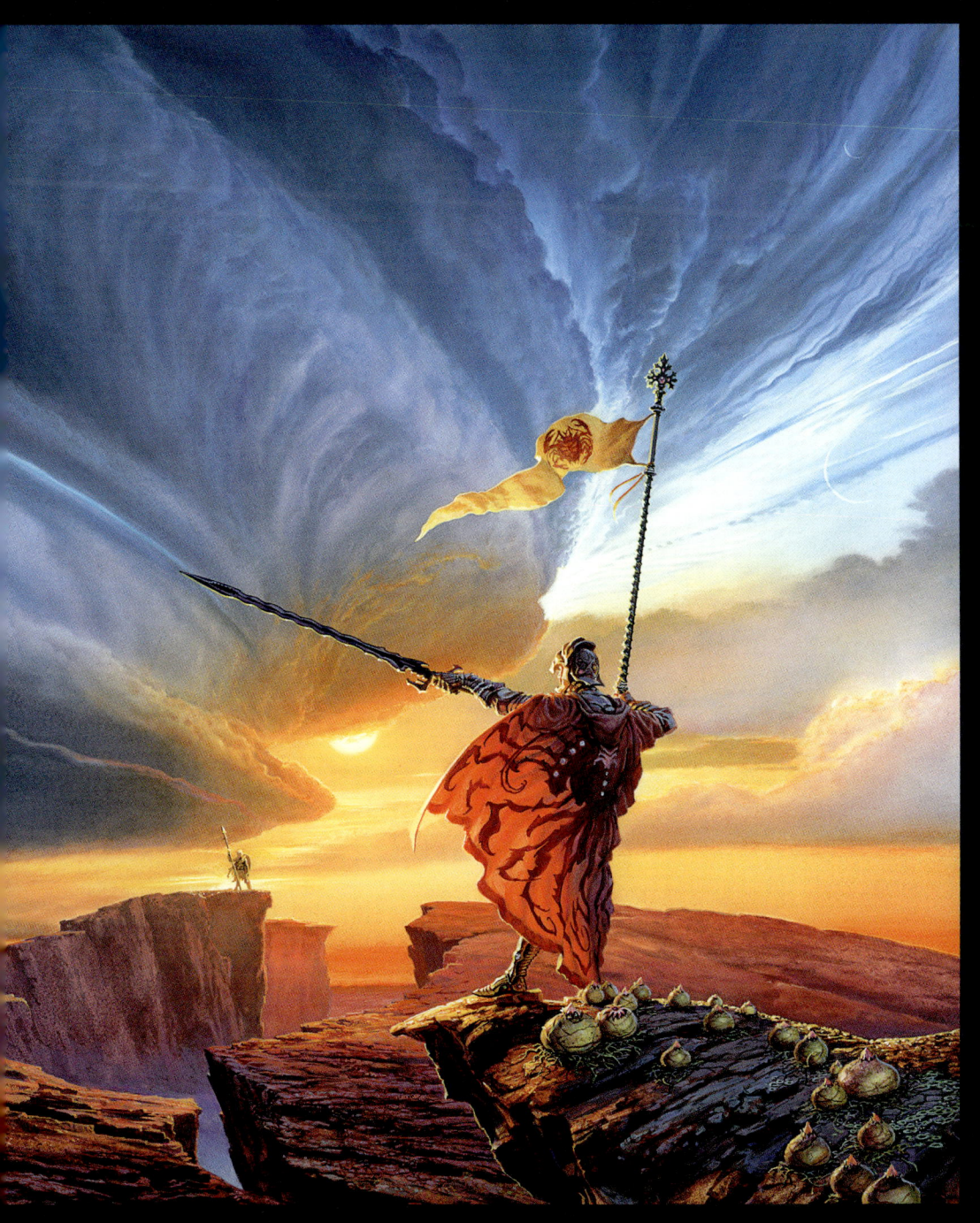

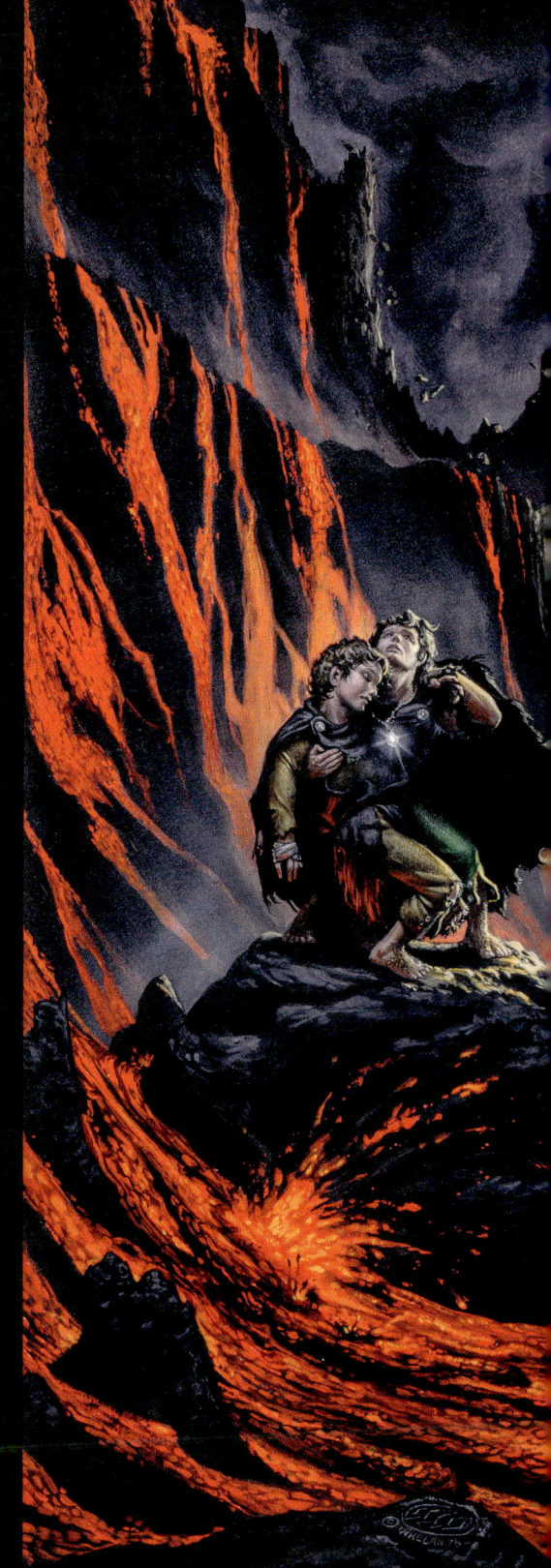

Right: The Eagles Are Coming, aka *At the End of All Things*, for the *1980 J.R.R. Tolkien Calendar*, acrylic on board, 1978, 71.1 x 68.6 cm (28 x 27 inches).

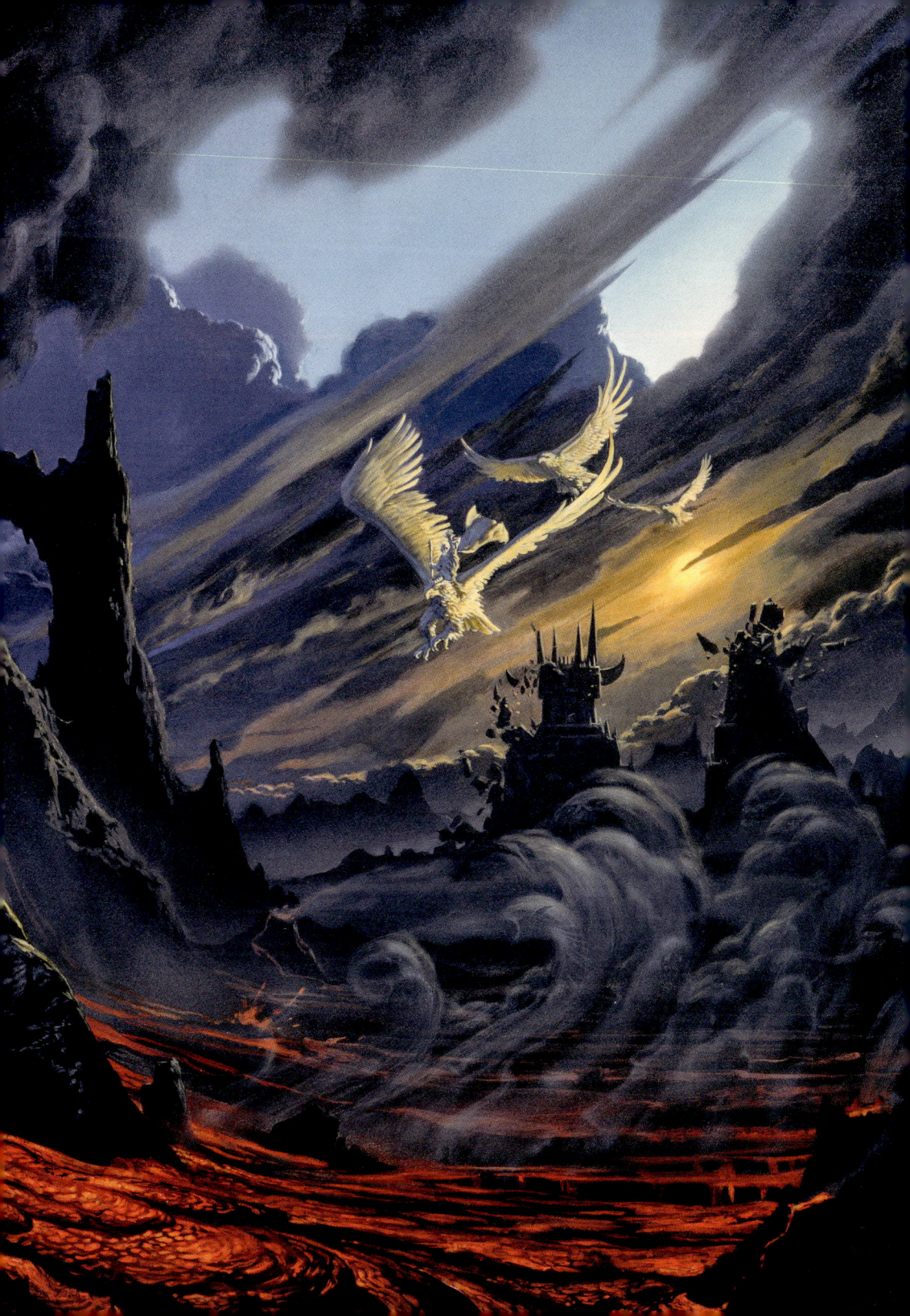

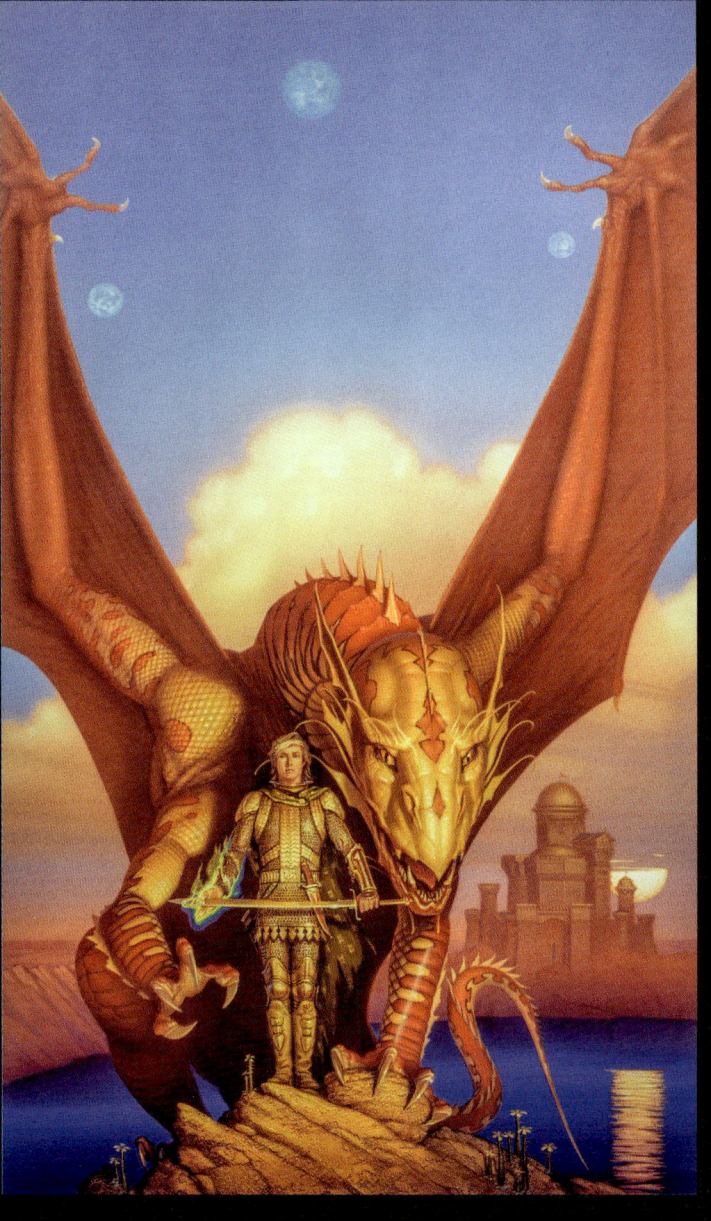

Above: Dragon Lord, for the cover of *Skybowl*, 1993,
by Melanie Rawn. Acrylic on board, 1991, 81.2 x 50.8 cm
(32 x 20 inches).

Opposite: Rising, a personal vision. Acrylic on board, 2007,
91.4 x 60.9 cm (36 x 24 inches).

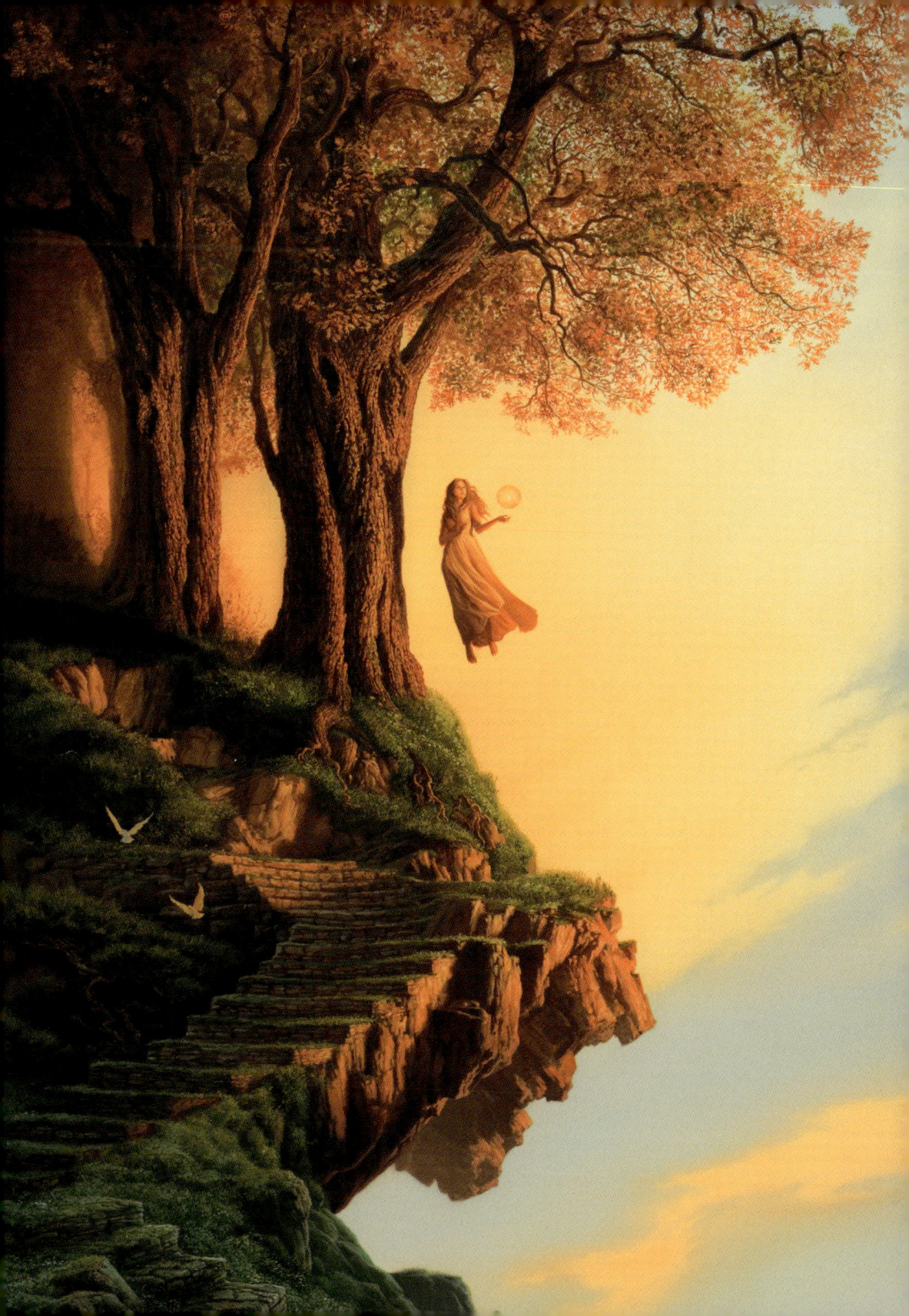

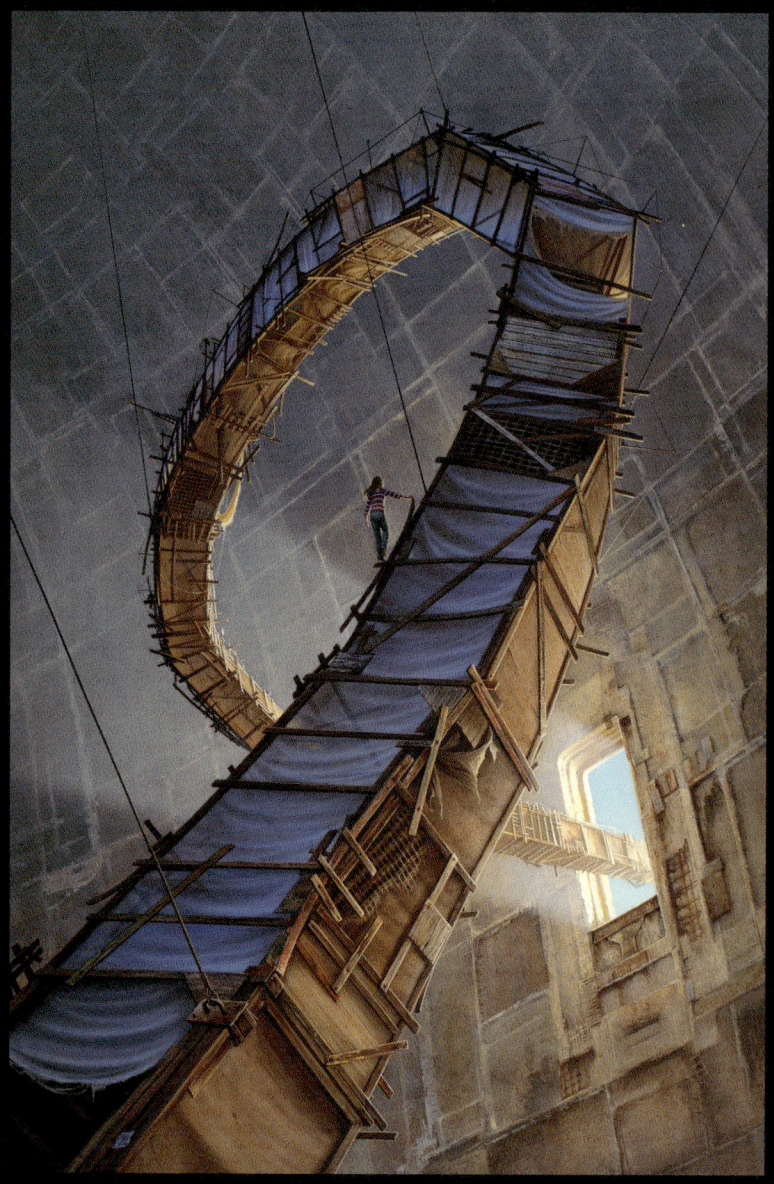

Above: Lumen 9, from the *Lumen Series*, in which figures overcome great obstacles seeking the light. Acrylic on canvas, 2013, 137.1 x 91.4 cm (54 x 36 inches).

Opposite: Lumen 5.1, from the *Lumen Series*, with the light forming an eye, looking outward and inward. Acrylic on canvas, 1999, 76.2 x 50.8 cm (30 x 20 inches).

Following left: Empire of Dreams, a personal work licensed for the cover of *Eclipse 1*, a 2007 anthology of fantasy and science fiction compiled by Jonathan Strahan. Acrylic on gessoboard, 2005, 71.1 x 55.8 cm (28 x 22 inches).

Following right: Self-portrait, graphite on paper.

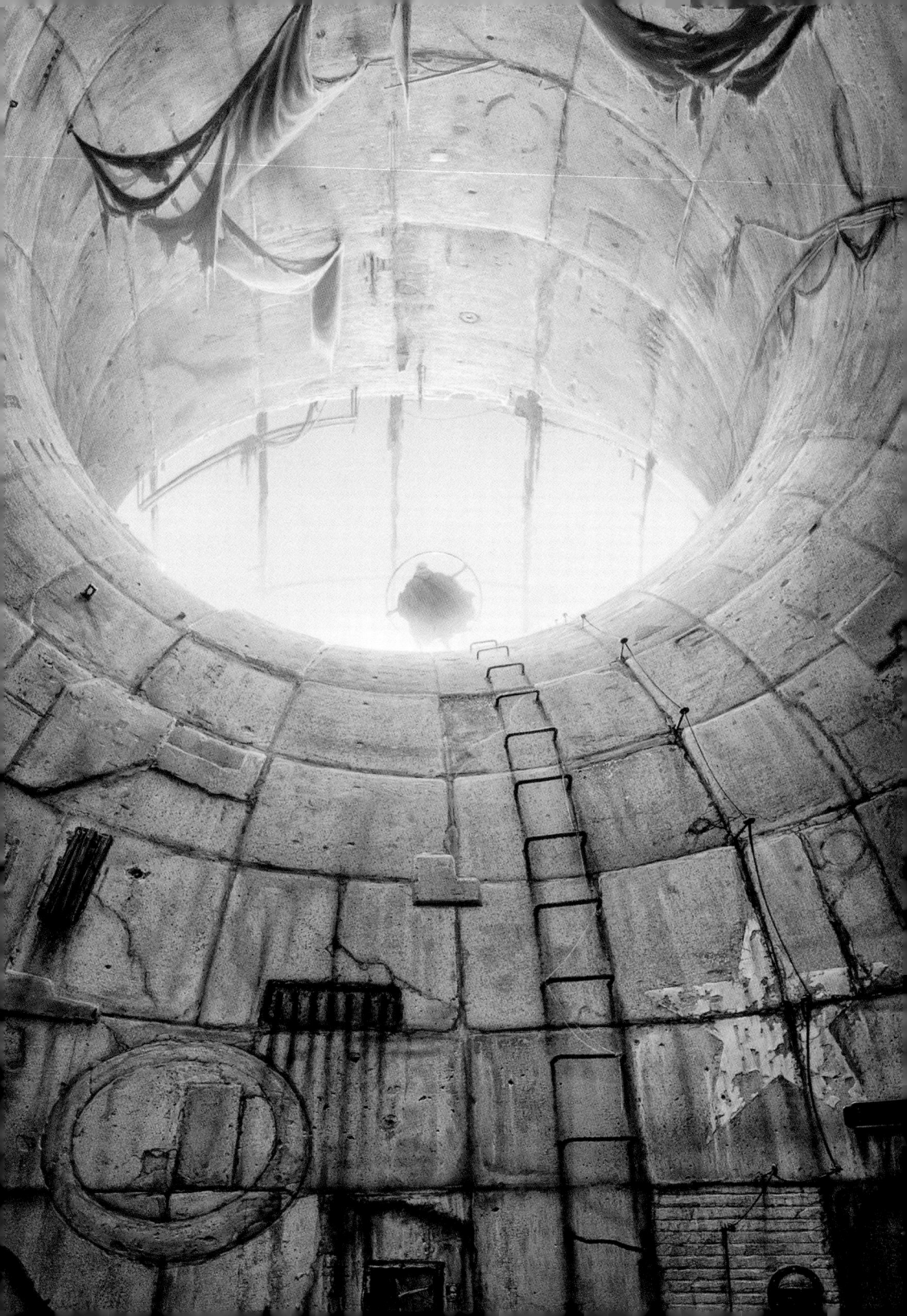

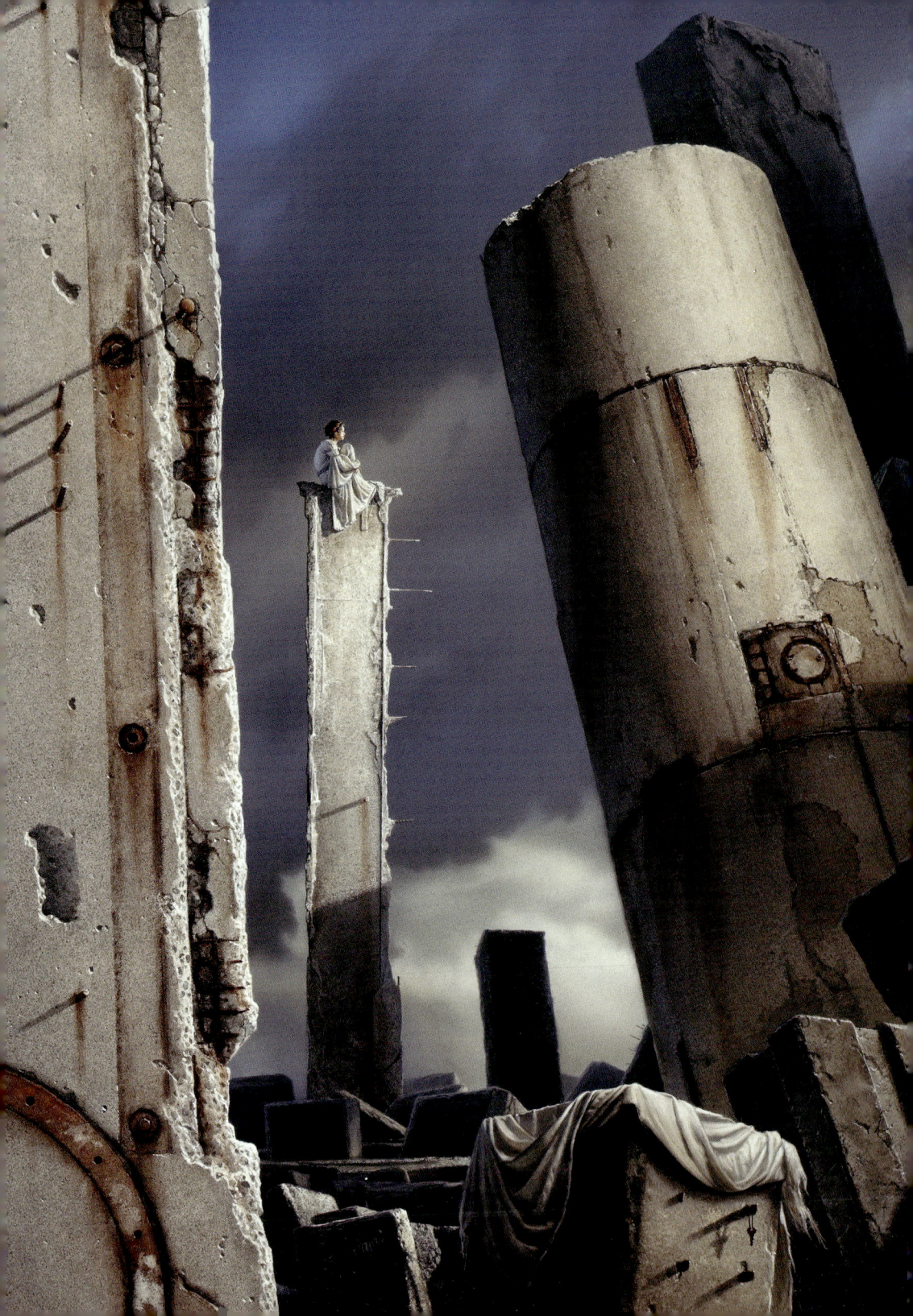

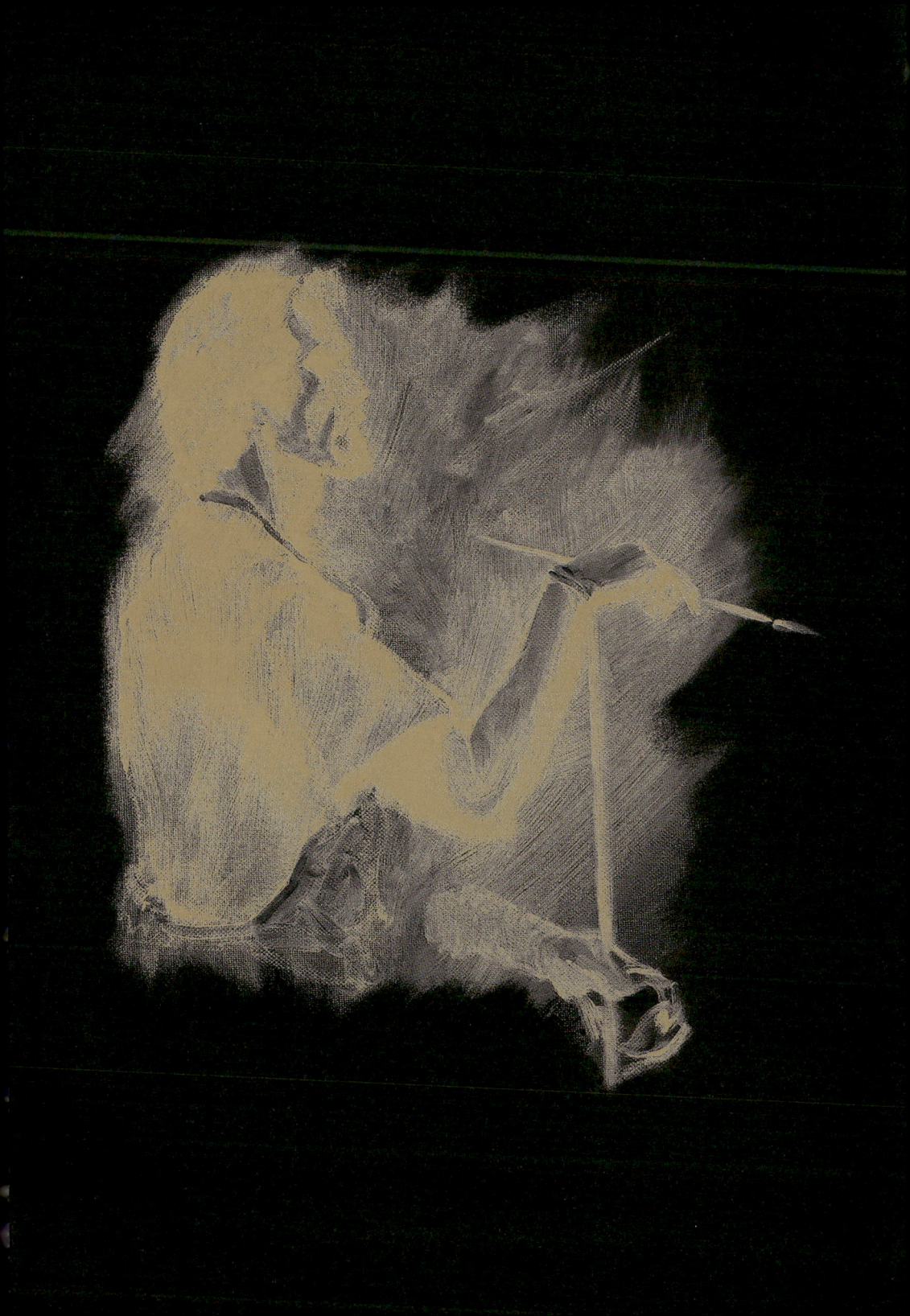

IT REQUIRED THE COLLABORATIVE EFFORTS of many talented people to bring you this book. All are appreciated, but the following went above and beyond: Daniela Asmuth, Josh Baker, Julie Bell, Matthias Belz, Laura Brodian Freas Beraha, Edward Binkley, Simon Bisley, Jean-Pierre Dionnet, Victor Druillet, Jeff Easley, H. R. Giger Estate, Isabelle Giraud, Heritage Auctions, Patrick Hill, Jascha Kempe, Kathrin Murr, Jean Scrocco, Benedikt Taschen, Sara Frazetta Taylor, Saveria De Valence of Artcurial, Boris Vallejo, and Wizards of the Coast.

Opposite: Barbarian Queen film poster original art, oil on board by Boris Vallejo, 1985.

Following page: Life-sized *Vampirella* portrait by Enric Torres-Prat, a re-creation of his famous 1972 poster image for *Vampirella* magazine. Oil on canvas, 58.4 x 189 cm (23 x 74.5 inches). ®&© 2020 Dynamite. All rights reserved.

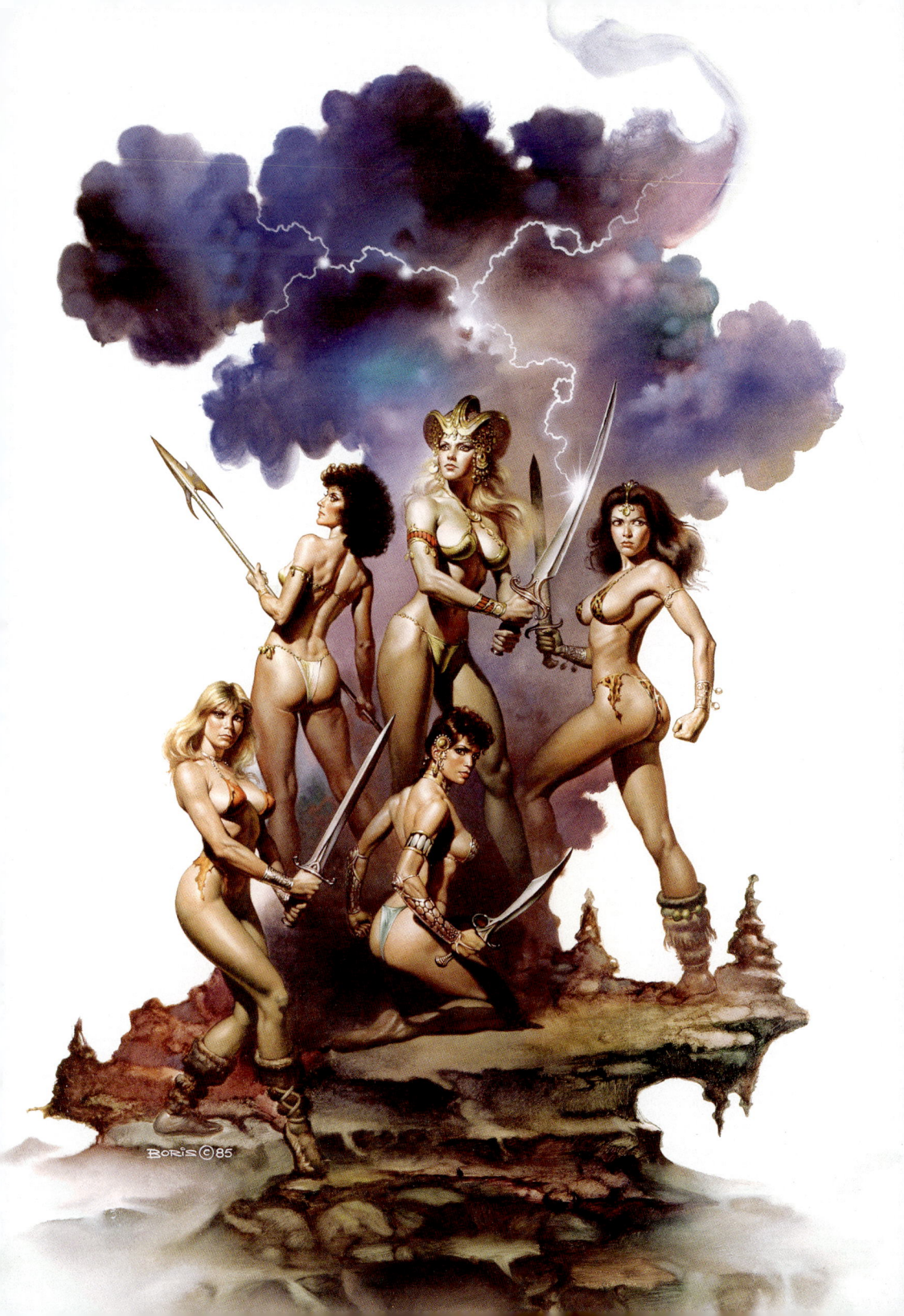

BORIS ©85

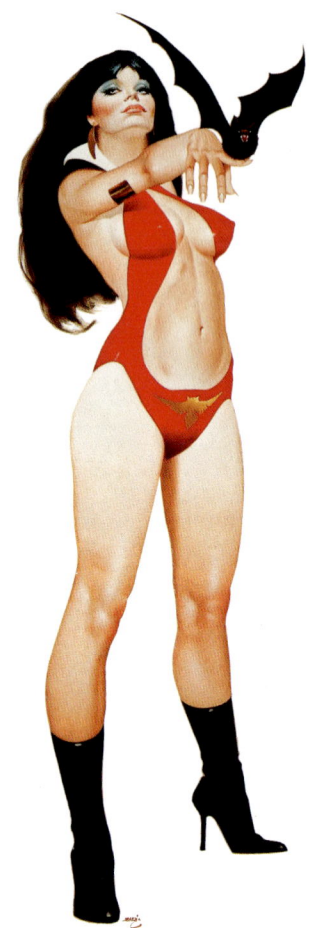

© 2026 TASCHEN GmbH
Hohenzollernring 53, D-50672 Köln, Germany
www.taschen.com

Original edition © 2020 TASCHEN GmbH
German translation by Egbert Baqué, Berlin
French translation by Alice Pétillot, Bordeaux

Printed in Bosnia-Herzegovina
ISBN 978-3-8365-9362-5